This password provides access to documents
and other resources available on the Student Site for
Worlds Together, Worlds Apart, Concise Edition:
www.wwnorton.com/college/history/worlds-together-concise/

WORL-CONC

AP* EDITION

WORLDS TOGETHER, WORLDS APART

Elizabeth Pollard | Clifford Rosenberg | Robert Tignor | Alan Karras

with Jeremy Adelman, Stephen Aron, Peter Brown, Benjamin Elman, Stephen Kotkin, Xinru Liu, Susanne Marchand, Holly Pittman, Gyan Prakash, Brent Shaw, Michael Tsin

W. W. Norton & Company • New York • London

W. W. NORTON & COMPANY has been independent since its founding in 1923, when William Warder Norton and Mary D. Herter Norton first published lectures delivered at the People's Institute, the adult education division of New York City's Cooper Union. The firm soon expanded its program beyond the Institute, publishing books by celebrated academics from America and abroad. By midcentury, the two major pillars of Norton's publishing program—trade books and college texts—were firmly established. In the 1950s, the Norton family transferred control of the company to its employees, and today—with a staff of four hundred and a comparable number of trade, college, and professional titles published each year—W. W. Norton & Company stands as the largest and oldest publishing house owned wholly by its employees.

Printed in the United States of America
First Edition

Director of High School Publishing: Jenna Barry
Editor: Jon Durbin
Associate Editor: Justin Cahill
Editorial Assistants: Penelope Lin, Aimee Lam
Developmental Editors: Ann Shin, Sara Wise
Project Editor: Diane Cipollone
Copy Editor: Nancy Green
Production Manager: Andy Ensor
Managing Editor, College: Marian Johnson
Managing Editor, College Digital Media: Kim Yi
Media Editor: Lisa Moore
Media Editorial Assistant: Chris Hillyer
Marketing Manager, History: Sarah England
Photo Editor: Nelson Colón
Permissions Manager: Megan Jackson
College Permissions Specialist: Bethany Salminen
Design Director: Jillian Burr
Composition: Cenveo® Publisher Services
Manufacturing: R.R. Donnelley-Kendallville

Permission to use copyrighted material is included on page C-1.

Library of Congress Cataloging-in-Publication Data

Names: Pollard, Elizabeth (Elizabeth Ann), author.
Title: Worlds together, worlds apart / Elizabeth Pollard . . . [and fourteen others].
Description: AP edition. | New York : W.W. Norton & Company, [2016] | Includes bibliographical references and index.
Identifiers: LCCN 2015050868 | **ISBN 9780393265705** (hardcover)
Subjects: LCSH: World history—Textbooks. | World history—Examinations—Study guides. | Advanced placement programs (Education)—Examinations—Study guides
Classification: LCC D21 .T53 2016 | DDC 909—dc23 LC record available at http://lccn.loc.gov/2015050868

W. W. Norton & Company, Inc., 500 Fifth Avenue, New York, NY 10110-0017
wwnorton.com

W. W. Norton & Company Ltd., Castle House, 75/76 Wells Street, London W1T 3QT

1 2 3 4 5 6 7 8 9 0

Contents in Brief

Contents

Chapter 2

RIVERS, CITIES, AND FIRST STATES, 3500–2000 BCE 47

Chapter 3

NOMADS, TERRITORIAL STATES, AND MICROSOCIETIES, 2000–1200 BCE 87

Chapter 4

FIRST EMPIRES AND COMMON CULTURES IN AFRO-EURASIA, 1250–325 BCE 125

Chapter 7

HAN DYNASTY CHINA AND IMPERIAL ROME, 300 BCE–300 CE 243

Chapter 8

THE RISE OF UNIVERSAL RELIGIONS, 300–600 CE 281

Chapter 10

BECOMING "THE WORLD," 1000–1300 CE 361

Chapter 11

CRISES AND RECOVERY IN AFRO-EURASIA, 1300–1500 403

Chapter 17

NATIONS AND EMPIRES, 1850–1914 637

Chapter 18

AN UNSETTLED WORLD, 1890–1914 667

Chapter 20

THE THREE-WORLD ORDER, 1940–1975 757

Chapter 21

GLOBALIZATION, 1970–2000 801

99%
JOBS NOT CUTS

Current Trends in World History

Analyzing Global Developments

Going to the Source

CHAPTER 9

CHAPTER 10

CHAPTER 11

CHAPTER 12

CHAPTER 13

CHAPTER 14

CHAPTER 15

CHAPTER 16

CHAPTER 17

CHAPTER 18

CHAPTER 19

CHAPTER 20

CHAPTER 21

Maps

Preface

Worlds Together, Worlds Apart has long set the standard for instructors who want to teach a globally integrated world history survey course. As the dynamic field of world history has evolved, so too has *Worlds Together, Worlds Apart*. Building on the successes of the full text, new AP* author Alan Karras (University of California, Berkeley) along with co-authors Elizabeth Pollard (San Diego State University) and Clifford Rosenberg (City College of New York) and original author Robert Tignor (Princeton University) have created a World History textbook specifically designed for the new AP* World History curriculum. Written with clear accessible prose and explanations, the AP* Edition offers a coherent urvey of the field built around world history stories of significance. It also provides the pedagogical support that students need to help them prepare for the AP* World History exam. This globally integrated, chronological approach makes it possible for students to readily make connections and comparisons across time and place, and makes the teaching of the Advanced Placement World History course more manageable for instructors. Some of the major stories presented in the chapters of the AP* edition are the spread of humans across the planet, the first global agricultural revolution, the creation of empires, the building of the Silk Roads, the spread of the Black Death across Afro-Eurasia, the impact of New World silver on global trade, alternative ways to organize societies during the rise of nineteenth-century capitalism, and the rise of the nation-state.

HIGHLIGHTS OF THE AP* EDITION

The AP* Edition provides students with features that are designed to encourage critical thinking and to help them develop historical thinking skills. Chief among these is the **Going to the Source** feature, which gathers at the end of each chapter a collection of primary source documents. It invites students to compare five to seven documents on one of the themes discussed in the chapter. The Questions for Analysis and Long Essay Question that appear at the end of each set of documents were developed with the historical thinking skills in mind. Many of them address the higher level, more challenging skills, such as historical argumentation, interpretation, and synthesis. Flags in the margin alert students and instructors to the primary targeted skill for each question. Instructors should note that while only one skill is targeted in each question, multiple skills may be required to produce the most compelling answers.

Designed to be easy for students to read and to help them develop the skills they need to succeed on the AP* World History exam, this text features a suite of pedagogical and media tools built around **Core Objectives**, which are designed to guide students' reading and to aid them and their instructor in assessing their understanding of the material and concepts. Each of the book's 21 chapters begins with the innovative **Before You Read This Chapter** pedagogy, which highlights the **Global Storylines** and Core Objectives that students need to comprehend while reading the chapter. **Comparison Flags** appear in the margins throughout the chapter to remind students of the Core Objectives while they read and to help them begin to make comparisons and connections on their own. The **After You Read This Chapter** pedagogy includes **Tracing the Global Storylines**, which shows the impact of the chapter's main storyline on each region of the world. The **Thinking About Global Connections** questions highlight major themes that unify the book's global approach, and **Study Questions** place the chapter's **Key Terms** into a historical context.

Within the narrative of each chapter appear two unique features that also encourage critical thinking and the development of historical thinking skills. The **Analyzing Global Developments** feature engages students with real historical data, much of it the result of recent scholarship, and the **Current Trends in World History** feature, which presents new research trends, demonstrates how historical research remains relevant to the world today.

MAJOR THEMES

The primary organizing framework of *Worlds Together, Worlds Apart AP* Edition*—one that runs through the chapters and connects the different parts of the volume—is the theme of **interconnection and divergence**. While describing movements that facilitated global connectedness, this book also shows how different regions developed their own ways of handling or resisting connections and change.

Themes highlight the importance of trade and culture exchange through the recurring efforts of people at **crossing borders—religious, political, and cultural—that brought the world together**. Merchants and educated men and women traded goods and ideas. Whole communities, in addition to select groups, moved to safer or more promising environments. This transregional crossing of ideas, goods, and peoples produced **transformations and conflicts**—a second important theme. The movement of ideas, peoples, products, and germs over long distances upset the balance of power across the world and within individual societies. Such movements changed the relationship of different population groups with other peoples and areas of the world and led over time to dramatic shifts in the ascendancy of regions. **Changes in power arrangements** within and between regions explain which parts of the world and regional groups benefited from integration and which resisted it. Finally, we highlight **the important roles that gender and the environment play in shaping the evolution of societies**. These themes (trade and cultural exchange, transformation and conflict, gender and the environment, and alterations in the balance of power) weave themselves through every chapter of this work and echo themes that students will encounter on the AP* exam. While we highlight major themes throughout, we tell the stories of the people caught in these currents of exchange, conflict, and changing power relations, paying particular attention to the role that gender and the environment play in shaping the evolution of societies.

AP* RESOURCES FOR STUDENTS AND INSTRUCTORS

The AP* Edition's compelling and unique focus on world history stories, themes, and Core Objectives is further reinforced in our support materials for students and instructors. Author Alan Karras has brought together a tremendous media and supplements team including Sharon Cohen, Ryba Epstein, Shane Carter, Wendy Eagan, Suzanne Litrel, Theresa Quindlen, and Sally West. Together, this team has ensured that the AP* Edition of *Worlds Together, Worlds Apart* is supported by an array of print and digital media with tools teachers need to meet course goals—in the classroom and online—and activities for students to develop core skills in reading comprehension, writing, and analysis, and to better understand the geography and contexts in a world history course.

FOR INSTRUCTORS

AP* Instructor's Manual (Sharon Cohen, Springbrook High School)

Written by a master teacher, the Instructor's Manual for has everything AP* teachers need to prepare lectures and classroom activities: lecture ideas, classroom activities, and guidance on how each chapter fits in to the key concept outline. It also highlights "sticky spots" where students often have trouble with challenging concepts. Our Popular Fallacy section provides an exercise that helps to dispel common misconceptions students may have about the material in each chapter.

AP* Test Bank (Ryba Epstein, Shane Carter, Suzanne Litrel)

Organized to correspond to the six periods in the AP World History curriculum framework, this robust test bank includes short-answer, long-essay, and document-based multiple-choice questions for each period, as well as a DBQ section. It also features traditional multiple-choice organized to correspond to the chapters in *Worlds Together, Worlds Apart* and to test the application of the key concepts in the AP* curriculum framework. All Norton test banks are available with ExamView Test Generator software, allowing instructors to easily create, administer, and manage assessments.

Norton Coursepacks

Free Norton Coursepacks (downloadable in Blackboard, WebCT, D2L, and Moodle; additional formats can be provided upon request), include: Guided Reading Exercises, keyed to each chapter's Core Objectives, which instill the three-step Note-Summarize-Assess pedagogy. Each chapter has one exercise built around passages from the text. Review Quizzes include targeted feedback that highlights Core Objective, page reference, and difficulty. *Chrono-Quizzes* end each chapter quiz with a matching question. Online Reader provides over 100 primary-source documents and images. Map

Resources include *iMaps*, where students can peel back each layer to highlight the information they want to see, *StoryMaps* where complex maps are broken into five annotated slides that focus on the *story* behind the *geography*. *World History Tours*, powered by Google Earth are dynamic, interactive primary sources that trace global developments over time. *Map Worksheets* provide each map without labels for offline relabeling and quizzing. Key Term Flash Cards allow students to self-study historical vocabulary.

Classroom Presentation Tools

- **Lecture PowerPoints and Art PowerPoints** feature photographs and maps from the book, retouched for in-class presentation.
- ***Story Maps*** break complex maps into a sequence of five annotated screens that focus on the story behind the geography. Ten maps include such topics as The Silk Road, The Spread of the Black Death, and Population Growth and the Economy.

FOR STUDENTS

INQUIZITIVE

Quizzing to Learn

InQuizitive, Norton's new adaptive quizzing platform, uses interactive questions and guided feedback to motivate students to read and understand the text. Varied question types—featuring images, maps, and sources—prompt critical and analytical thinking on each of the chapter's Core Objectives. Robust grading functionality helps instructors track their students' progress on learning outcomes. Each question is keyed to the AP* course outcomes, including the relevant Historical Thinking Skills and geographic area.

Historical Thinking Skills Workbook

John Irish and Barbara Ozuna, both experienced history teachers, have teamed up to develop this workbook to focus on the historical thinking skills that high school students in the AP* World History course must master in order to perform well on the exam. Nine types of graphic organizers help students hone the skills essential for success in the course, including cause and effect, chronological reasoning, comparison, contextualization, continuity and change over time, periodization, and historical argument.

Student Site

This free site offers students access to additional primary source documents and images, Office Hour videos with the authors, and iMaps. It is ideal for teachers interested in granting students access to additional material without creating or administering online assignments.

Norton Ebooks

Norton Ebooks lets students access the entire book and much more: they can search, highlight, and take notes with ease, as well as collaborate and share their notes with instructors and classmates. Ebooks can be viewed on any device and any platform—laptop, tablet, phone, even a public computer—and will stay synced between devices.

CORRELATION WITH THE CURRENT AP* WORLD HISTORY COURSE FRAMEWORK

PERIOD 1: Technological and Environmental Transformations, to c. 600 B.C.E.	Chapters 1–5
Key Concept 1.1: Big Geography and the Peopling of the Earth	
I: Archeological evidence indicates that during the Paleolithic era, hunting-foraging bands of humans gradually migrated from their origin in East Africa to Eurasia, Australia, and the Americas, adapting their technology and cultures to new climate regions.	
A. Humans developed increasingly diverse and sophisticated tools—including multiple uses of fire—as they adapted to new environments.	• "Tool-Use By Homo Habilis," Ch. 1, pp. 11–12 • "Use of Fire," Ch. 1, p. 13

B. People lived in small groups that structured social, economic, and political activity. These bands exchanged people, ideas, and goods.	• "*Homo Sapiens*: The First Modern Humans," Ch. 1, pp. 14–18 • "The Life of Early Homo Sapiens," Ch. 1, pp. 19–22
Key Concept 1.2: The Neolithic Revolution and Early Agricultural Societies	
I: Beginning about 10,000 years ago, the Neolithic Revolution led to the development of more complex economic and social systems.	
A. Possibly as a response to climatic change, permanent agricultural villages emerged first in the lands of the eastern Mediterranean. Agriculture emerged independently in Mesopotamia, the Nile River Valley, Sub-Saharan Africa, the Indus River Valley, the Yellow River or Huang He Valley, Papua New Guinea, Mesoamerica, and the Andes.	• "Agricultural Innovation: Afro-Eurasia and the Americas," Ch. 1, pp. 27–31 • "Borrowing Agricultural Ideas: Europe," Ch. 1, pp. 31–33
B. People in each region domesticated locally available plants and animals.	• "Agricultural Revolution: Food Production and Social Change, Intro," Ch. 1, p. 22 • "Agricultural Innovation: Afro-Eurasia and the Americas," Ch. 1, pp. 27–31
C. Pastoralism developed in Afro-Eurasian grasslands, negatively affecting the environment when lands were overgrazed.	• "Transhumant Herders and Nomadic Pastoralists," Ch. 1, pp. 23, 26 • "Pastoral Nomadic Communities," Ch. 2, p. 49
D. Agricultural communities had to work cooperatively to clear land and create the water control systems needed for crop production, drastically affecting environmental diversity.	• "Life in Villages," Ch. 1, pp. 33–34 • "Tapping the Waters," Ch. 2, p. 53 • "Climate Change at the End of the Third Millennium BCE in Egypt, Mesopotamia, and the Indus Valley," Ch. 2, pp. 66–67
II: Agriculture and pastoralism began to transform human societies.	
A. Pastoralism and agriculture led to more reliable and abundant food supplies, which increased the population and led to specialization of labor, including new classes of artisans and warriors, and the development of elites.	• "Life in Villages," Ch. 1, pp. 33–34 • "Early Cities Along River Basins," Ch. 2, pp. 48–49 • "The Indus River Valley: A Parallel Culture," Ch. 2, pp. 65–70
B. Technological innovations led to improvements in agricultural production, trade, and transportation.	• "East Asia: Water and Rice," Ch. 1, pp. 27–28 • "Life in Villages," Ch. 1, pp. 33–34 • "Early Cities Along River Basins," Ch. 2, pp. 48–49 • "Nomadic Movement and the Emergence of Territorial States," Ch. 3, pp. 88–92 • "New Technologies," Ch. 4, pp. 127–130
C. Patriarchal forms of social organization developed in both pastoralist and agrarian societies.	• "Revolutions in Social Organization," Ch. 1, pp. 33–35 • "Royal Power, Families, and Social Hierarchy," Ch. 2, pp. 55–56

Key Concept 1.3: The Development and Interactions of Early Agricultural, Pastoral, and Urban Societies	
I: Core and foundational civilizations developed in a variety of geographical and environmental settings where agriculture flourished.	
Core and foundational civilizations include: • Mesopotamia in the Tigris and Euphrates River Valleys • Egypt in the Nile River Valley • Mohenjo-Daro and Harappa in the Indus River Valley • Shang in the Yellow River or Huang He Valley • Olmecs in Mesoamerica • Chavín in Andean South America	• "Between the Tigris and Euphrates Rivers: Mesopotamia," Ch. 2, pp. 52-58 • "'The Gift of the Nile': Egypt," Ch. 2, pp. 58-65 • "The Indus River Valley: A Parallel Culture," Ch. 2, pp. 65-70 • "The Yellow and Yangzi River Basins: East Asia," Ch. 2, pp. 70-73 • "The Chavín in the Andes," Ch. 5, pp. 184-185 • "The Olmecs in Mesoamerica," Ch. 5, pp. 185-187
II: The first states emerged within core civilizations in Mesopotamia and the Nile River Valley.	
A. States were powerful new systems of rule that mobilized surplus labor and resources over large areas. Rulers of early states often claimed divine connections to power. Rulers also often enjoyed military support.	• "Nomadic Movement and the Emergence of Territorial States," Ch. 3, pp. 88-92 • "Society and Ritual Practice," Ch. 3, pp. 107-108 • "Mandate of Heaven," Ch. 4, pp. 150-151
B. As states grew and competed for land and resources, the more favorably situated—including the Hittites, who had access to iron—had greater access to resources, produced more surplus food, and experienced growing populations, enabling them to undertake territorial expansion and conquer surrounding states.	• "Hyksos Invaders," Ch. 3, pp. 95-97 • "The Old and New Hittite Kingdoms (1800-1200 BCE)," Ch. 3, p. 100
C. Pastoralists were often the developers and disseminators of new weapons and modes of transportation that transformed warfare in agrarian civilizations.	• "Transhumant Herders and Nomadic Pastoralists," Ch. 1, pp. 23-26 • "Nomadic Movement and the Emergence of Territorial States," Ch. 3, pp. 88-92 • "Hyksos Invaders," Ch. 3, pp. 95-97 • "State Formation," Ch. 3, pp. 103-107 • "Mycenaean Culture," Ch. 3, pp. 113-114 • "New Technologies," Ch. 4, pp. 127-130
III: Culture played a significant role in unifying states through laws, language, literature, religion, myths, and monumental art.	
A. Early civilizations developed monumental architecture and urban planning.	• "Rivers, Cities, and First States, Introduction" Ch. 2, pp. 47-48 • "Tapping the Waters," Ch. 2, p. 53 • "The World's First Cities," Ch. 2, pp. 53-54 • "Gods and Temples," Ch. 2, pp. 54-55 • "Pharaohs, Pyramids, and Cosmic Order," Ch. 2, pp. 60-61 • "Harappan City Life and Writing," Ch. 2, pp. 67-69 • "Religion and Rule," Ch. 3, p. 94 • "Public Works and Imperial Identity," Ch. 4, pp. 137-138 • "Cities as Sacred Centers," Ch. 5, pp. 186-187

B. Systems of record keeping arose independently in all early civilizations and subsequently spread.	• "First Writing and Early Texts," Ch. 2, p. 56 • "Writing and Scribes," Ch. 2, pp. 63–65 • "The Development of Writing," Ch. 2, p. 64 • "Harappan City Life and Writing," Ch. 2, pp. 67–69 • "Sumerian Origins of Writing," Ch. 2, p. 80 • "Shang Writing," Ch. 3, pp. 108–109 • "The Phoenicians," Ch. 4, pp. 142, 143
C. States developed legal codes that reflected existing hierarchies and facilitated the rule of governments over people.	• "Nomadic Movement and the Emergence of Territorial States," Ch. 3, pp. 88–92 • "Mesopotamian Kingship," Ch. 3, pp. 88–92 • "Legal Authority in Expanding Territorial States," Ch. 3, pp. 118–123.
D. New religious beliefs that developed in this period—including the Vedic religion, Hebrew monotheism, and Zoroastrianism—continued to have strong influences in later periods.	• "Nomads and the Indus River Valley," Ch. 3, pp. 101–103 • "Zoroastrianism, Ideology, and Social Structure," Ch. 4, pp. 136–137 • "The Israelites," Ch. 4, pp. 142–143 • "Vedic Culture Settles Down," Ch. 4, p. 144
E. Trade expanded throughout this period from local to regional to interregional with civilizations exchanging goods, cultural ideas, and technology.	• "Religion and Trade in Middle Kingdom Egypt (2055–1650 BCE)," Ch. 3, pp. 94–95 • "Trade and the Rise of a Private Economy," Ch. 3, pp. 99–100 • "Nubia: Kush and Meroe," Ch. 5, pp. 188–190
F. Social hierarchies, including patriarchy, intensified as states expanded and cities multiplied.	• "Royal Power, Families, and Social Hierarchy," Ch. 2, pp. 55–56 • "Society and Ritual Practice," Ch. 3, pp. 107–108 • "Social and Economic Controls," Ch. 4, p. 151
PERIOD 2: Organization and Reorganization of Human Societies, c. 600 B.C.E. to c. 600 C.E.	Chapters 5–8
Key Concept 2.1: The Development and Codification of Religious and Cultural Traditions	
I: Codifications and further developments of existing religious traditions provided a bond among people and an ethical code to live by.	
A. The association of monotheism with Judaism further developed with the codification of the Hebrew Scriptures, which also reflected the influence of Mesopotamian cultural and legal traditions. The Assyrian, Babylonian, and Roman empires conquered various Jewish states at different points in time. These conquests contributed to the growth of Jewish diasporic communities around the Mediterranean and Middle East.	• "The Israelites," Ch. 4, pp. 142–143 • "Hellenistic Adaptation and Resistance," Ch. 6, pp. 211–212 • "Sasanian Persia," Ch. 8, p. 293 • "Religious Conflict in Imperial Borderlands," Ch. 8, pp. 294–295

B. The core beliefs outlined in the Sanskrit scriptures formed the basis of the Vedic religions—later known as Hinduism. These beliefs included the importance of multiple manifestations of Brahma and teachings about reincarnation, and they contributed to the development of the social and political roles of a caste system.	• "Brahmans, Their Challengers, and New Beliefs," Ch. 5, pp. 174–176 • "The Hindu Transformation," Ch. 8, pp. 296–298 • "Culture and Ideology Instead of an Empire," Ch. 8, pp. 298–299
II: New belief systems and cultural traditions emerged and spread, often asserting universal truths.	
A. The core beliefs about desire, suffering, and the search for enlightenment preached by the historic Buddha and collected by his followers in sutras and other scriptures were, in part, a reaction to the Vedic beliefs and rituals dominant in South Asia. Buddhism changed over time as it spread throughout Asia—first through the support of the Mauryan Emperor Ashoka, and then through the efforts of missionaries and merchants, and the establishment of educational institutions to promote Buddhism's core teachings.	• "Buddha and Buddhism," Ch. 5, pp. 175–176 • "Prophets and the Founding Texts: Comparing Confucius and the Buddha," Ch. 5, pp. 176–177 • "The Regime of Aśoka," Ch. 6, pp. 214–216 • "The Transformation of the Buddha," Ch. 8, p. 298 • "Buddhism in China," Ch. 8, pp. 301–302
B. Confucianism's core beliefs and writings originated in the writings and lessons of Confucius. They were elaborated by key disciples who sought to promote social harmony by outlining proper rituals and social relationships for all people in China, including rulers.	• "Worlds Turned Inside Out, Intro," Ch. 5, pp. 163, 164 • "Innovations in Thought," Ch. 5, pp. 168–169 • "Prophets and the Founding Texts: Comparing Confucius and the Buddha," Ch. 5, pp. 176–177 • "Axial Age Thinkers and Their Ideas," Ch. 5, pp. 182–183
C. In major Daoist writings, the core belief of balance between humans and nature assumed that the Chinese political system would be altered indirectly. Daoism also influenced the development of Chinese culture.	• "Innovations in Thought," Ch. 5, pp. 168–169 • "Political and Religious Change in East Asia," Ch. 8, pp. 299–302
D. Christianity, based on core beliefs about the teachings and divinity of Jesus of Nazareth as recorded by his disciples, drew on Judaism and Roman and Hellenistic influences. Despite initial Roman imperial hostility, Christianity spread through the efforts of missionaries and merchants through many parts of Afro-Eurasia, and eventually gained Roman imperial support by the time of Emperor Constantine.	• "The Rise of Christianity," Ch. 7, pp. 264–265 • "The Appeal of Christianity," Ch. 8, pp. 282–288 • "One God, Two Communities: Comparing the Structures of Christianity and Judaism, 600 CE," Ch. 8, p. 288 • "Continuity of Rome in the East: Byzantium," Ch. 8, pp. 290–291 • "Religious Conflict in Imperial Borderlands," Ch. 8, pp. 294–295
E. The core ideas in Greco-Roman philosophy and science emphasized logic, empirical observation, and the nature of political power and hierarchy.	• "The Mediterranean World," Ch. 5, pp. 176–184

F. Art and architecture reflected the values of religions and belief systems.	• "New Cities and a Changing Economy," Ch. 5, pp. 173–174 • "Naturalistic Science and Realistic Art," Ch. 5, p. 181 • "New Images of Buddha in Literature and Art," Ch. 6, p. 219 • "The Appeal of Christianity," Ch. 8, pp. 282–287 • "The Hindu Transformation," Ch. 8, pp. 296–298

III: Belief systems generally reinforced existing social structures while also offering new roles and status to some men and women. For example, Confucianism emphasized filial piety, and some Buddhists and Christians practiced a monastic life.

- "Innovations in Thought," Ch. 5, pp. 168–169
- "Buddha and Buddhism," Ch. 5, pp. 175–176
- "India as a Spiritual Crossroads," Ch. 6, p. 218
- "The Rise of Christianity," Ch. 7, pp. 264–265
- "The Appeal of Christianity," Ch. 8, pp. 282–288
- "Buddhism in China," Ch. 8, pp. 301–302
- "Christianity in Western Europe," Ch. 9, pp. 347–348

IV: Other religious and cultural traditions, including shamanism, animism, and ancestor veneration persisted.

"Cities as Sacred Centers," Ch. 5, pp. 186–187

"Globalizing Empires: The Han Dynasty and Imperial Rome," Ch. 7, p. 254

Key Concept 2.2: The Development of States and Empires

I: The number and size of key states and empires grew dramatically as rulers imposed political unity on areas where previously there had been competing states.

Key states and empires include *[Note: Students should know the location and names of the key empires and states.]*: • Southwest Asia: Persian empires • East Asia: Qin and Han empires • South Asia: Mauryan and Gupta empires • Mediterranean region: Phoenicia and its colonies, Greek city-states and colonies, and Hellenistic and Roman empires • Mesoamerica: Teotihuacan, Maya city-states • Andean South America: Moche • North America: from Chaco to Cahokia	• "The Phoenicians," Ch. 4, p. 142 • "The Mediterranean World," Ch. 5, pp. 176–184 • "Alexander and the Emergence of a Hellenistic World," Ch. 6, pp. 204–212 • "Chandragupta and the Mauryan Empire," Ch. 6, pp. 213–216 • "The Han Dynasty (206 BCE–220 CE)," Ch. 7, pp. 245–255 • "The Qin Dynasty," Ch. 7, pp. 245–247 • "The Roman Empire," Ch. 7, pp. 255–267 • "The Parthians," Ch. 7, pp. 266–267 • "Sasanian Persia," Ch. 8, p. 293 • "Mesoamericans," Ch. 8, pp. 305–309 • "Andean States of South America," Ch. 10, pp. 384–385 • "Cahokians in North America," Ch. 10, pp. 386–387

II: Empires and states developed new techniques of imperial administration based, in part, on the success of earlier political forms.	
A. In order to organize their subjects, in many regions the rulers created administrative institutions, including centralized governments as well as elaborate legal systems and bureaucracies.	• "Zoroastrianism, Ideology, and Social Structure," Ch. 4, pp. 136–137 • "The Early Zhou Empire in East Asia (1045–771 BCE)," Ch. 4, pp. 147–152 • "The Qin Dynasty (221–207 BCE): A Crucial Forerunner," Ch. 7, pp. 245–247 • "Han Power and Administration," Ch. 7, pp. 248–249 • "Emperors, Authoritarian Rule, and Administration," Ch. 7, pp. 260–261
B. Imperial governments promoted trade and projected military power over larger areas using a variety of techniques, including: issuing currencies; diplomacy; developing supply lines; building fortifications, defensive walls, and roads; and drawing new groups of military officers and soldiers from the location populations or conquered populations.	• "Economic Innovations," Ch. 5, pp. 179–180 • "Plantation Slavery and Money-Based Economies," Ch. 6, pp. 210–212 • "China and the Silk Economy," Ch. 6, pp. 225–226 • "The Qin Dynasty (221–207 BCE): A Crucial Forerunner," Ch. 7, pp. 245–247 • "Military Expansion and the Silk Roads," Ch. 7, pp. 252–253 • "Military Manpower and the War Ethos," Ch. 7, p. 259 • "Political Institutions and Internal Conflict," Ch. 7, pp. 259–260 • "Emperors, Authoritarian Rule, and Administration," Ch. 7, pp. 260–261 • "Town and City Life," Ch. 7, p. 262 • "Economy and New Scales of Production," Ch. 7, pp. 263–264
III: Unique social and economic dimensions developed in imperial societies in Afro-Eurasia and the Americas.	
A. Imperial cities served as centers of trade, public performance of religious rituals, and political administration for states and empires.	• "The Integration of a Multicultural Persian Empire," Ch. 4, pp. 135–136 • "Formation of New City-States," Ch. 5, pp. 177–179 • "Cosmopolitan Cities," Ch. 6, pp. 208–209 • "Hellenistic Adaptation and Resistance," Ch. 6, pp. 211–212 • "Commerce on the Red Sea and Indian Ocean," Ch. 6, pp. 227–230 • "Town and City Life," Ch. 7, p. 262 • "The Appeal of Christianity," Ch. 8, pp. 282–283 • "Continuity of Rome in the East: Byzantium," Ch. 8, pp. 290–291 • "Teotihuacan," Ch. 8, pp. 305–306
B. The social structures of empires displayed hierarchies that included cultivators, laborers, slaves, artisans, merchants, elites, or caste groups.	• "Plantation Slavery and Money-Based Economies," Ch. 6, pp. 210–212 • "Social Hierarchy," Ch. 7, pp. 250–251 • "Social and Gender Relations," Ch. 7, p. 263 • "Culture and Ideology Instead of an Empire," Ch. 8, pp. 298–299

C. Imperial societies relied on a range of methods to maintain the production of food and provide rewards for the loyalty of the elites.	• "Dynastic Institutions and Control of the Land," Ch. 4, pp. 148–150 • "Plantation Slavery and Money-Based Economies," Ch. 6, pp. 210–212 • "The Qin Dynasty (221–207 BCE): A Crucial Forerunner," Ch. 7, pp. 245–247 • "The Eastern Han Dynasty," Ch. 7, pp. 254–255 • "Political Institutions and Internal Conflict," Ch. 7, pp. 259–260 • "Economy and New Scales of Production," Ch. 7, pp. 263–264
D. Patriarchy continued to shape gender and family relations in all imperial societies of this period.	• "Domestic Life," Ch. 7, p. 250 • "Social and Gender Relations," Ch. 7, p. 263
IV: The Roman, Han, Persian, Mauryan, and Gupta empires encountered political, cultural, and administrative difficulties that they could not manage, which eventually led to their decline, collapse, and transformation into successor empires or states.	
A. Through excessive mobilization of resources, imperial governments generated social tensions and created economic difficulties by concentrating too much wealth in the hands of elites.	• "The Persian Empire," Ch. 4, pp. 134–138 • "Plantation Slavery and Money-Based Economies," Ch. 6, pp. 210–212 • "Social Upheaval and Natural Disaster," Ch. 7, pp. 253–254 • "Economy and New Scales of Production," Ch. 7, pp. 263–264
B. Security issues along their frontiers, including the threat of invasions, challenged imperial authority.	• "Chandragupta and the Mauryan Empire," Ch. 6, pp. 213–216 • "Military Expansion and the Silk Road," Ch. 7, pp. 252–253 • "Empires, Allies, and Frontiers," Ch. 7, pp. 268–269 • "The 'Fall' of Rome in the West," Ch. 8, pp. 288–290
Key Concept 2.3: Emergence of Interregional Networks of Communication and Exchange	
I: Land and water routes became the basis for interregional trade, communication, and exchange networks in the Eastern Hemisphere.	
A. Many factors, including the climate and location of the routes, the typical trade goods, and the ethnicity of people involved, shaped the distinctive features of a variety of trade routes, including Eurasian Silk Roads, Trans-Saharan caravan routes, Indian Ocean sea lanes, and Mediterranean sea lanes.	• "Formation of New City-States," Ch. 5, pp. 177–179 • "Economic Innovations," Ch. 5, pp. 179–180 • "India as a Spiritual Crossroads," Ch. 6, p. 218 • "The Formation of the Silk Roads," Ch. 6, pp. 220–230
II: New technologies facilitated long-distance communication and exchange.	
A. New technologies permitted the use of domesticated pack animals to transport goods across longer routes.	• "New Technologies," Ch. 4, pp. 127, 130 • "The Chavín in the Andes," Ch. 5, pp. 184–185 • "Sasanian Persia," Ch. 8, p. 293

B. Innovations in maritime technologies, as well as advanced knowledge of the monsoon winds, stimulated exchanges along maritime routes from East Africa to East Asia.	• "India as a Spiritual Crossroads," Ch. 6, p. 218 • "Development of Maritime Trade," Ch. 10, pp. 362-365
III: Alongside the trade in goods, the exchange of people, technology, religious and cultural beliefs, food crops, domesticated animals, and disease pathogens developed across extensive networks of communication and exchange.	
A. The spread of crops, including rice and cotton from South Asia to the Middle East, encouraged changes in farming and irrigation techniques.	• "Public Works and Imperial Identity," Ch. 4, pp. 137-138
B. The spread of disease pathogens diminished urban populations and contributed to the decline of some empires.	• "Town and City Life," Ch. 7, p. 262
C. Religious and cultural traditions—including Christianity, Hinduism, and Buddhism—were transformed as they spread.	• "Continuity of Rome in the East: Byzantium," Ch. 8, pp. 290-291 • "The Hindu Transformation," Ch. 8, pp. 296-298 • "The Transformation of the Buddha," Ch. 8, p. 298 • "Changing Daoist Traditions," Ch. 8, p. 300 • "Buddhism in China," Ch. 8, pp. 301-302
PERIOD 3: Regional and Interregional Interactions, c. 600 C.E. to c. 1450	Chapters 8-12
Key Concept 3.1: Expansion and Intensification of Communication and Exchange Networks	
I: Improved transportation technologies and commercial practices led to an increased volume of trade, and expanded the geographical range of existing and newly active trade networks.	
A. Existing trade routes—including the Silk Road, the Mediterranean Sea, the Trans-Saharan, and the Indian Ocean basin—flourished, and promoted the growth of powerful new trading cities.	• "Trade in Sub-Saharan Africa," Ch. 9, pp. 329-330 • "Development of Maritime Trade," Ch. 10, pp. 362-365 • "Political Divisions," Ch. 10, pp. 365-366 • "Economic and Political Developments," Ch. 10, pp. 372-373 • "Trade Between East Africa and the Indian Ocean," Ch. 10, p. 384 • "Cahokians in North America," Ch. 10, pp. 386-388 • "Mongols in China," Ch. 10, pp. 392-393 • "The Catholic Church, State Building, and Economic Recovery," Ch. 11, pp. 416-420 • "Political Consolidation and Trade in the Iberian Peninsula," Ch. 11, pp. 420-422 • "Trade and Exploration Under The Ming," Ch.11, pp. 428-430 • "European Exploration and Expansion," Ch. 12, pp. 444-446 • "Aztec Society," Ch. 12, pp. 449-450
B. Communication and exchange networks developed in the Americas.	• "The Americas," Ch. 10, pp. 384-388

C. The growth of interregional trade in luxury goods was encouraged by significant innovations in previously existing transportation and commercial technologies, including the caravanserai, use of the compass, astrolabe, and larger ship designs in sea travel; and new forms of credit and monetization.	• "Islam and the Silk Trade: Adapting Religion to Opulence," Ch. 12, pp. 344-345 • "The Old Trade and the New," Ch. 12, pp. 442-445 • "Silver, Sugar, and Slaves," Ch. 12, pp. 457-458 • "Asian Relations with Europe," Ch. 12, pp. 464-466
D. Commercial growth was also facilitated by state practices; including the Inca road system; trading organizations, including the Hanseatic League; and state-sponsored commercial infrastructures, including the Grand Canal in China.	• "An Economic Revolution," Ch. 9, pp. 337-339 • "Economic and Political Developments," Ch. 10, pp. 372-373 • "The Revival of Asian Economies," Ch. 12, pp. 442-443
E. The expansion of empires—including China, the Byzantine Empire, the Caliphates, and the Mongols—facilitated Afro-Eurasian trade and communication as new peoples were drawn into their conquerors' economies and trade networks.	• "Continuity of Rome in the East: Byzantium," Ch. 8, pp. 290-291 • "The Abbasid Revolution," Ch. 9, pp. 326-327 • "Islam in a Wider World," Ch. 9, pp. 328-330 • "Territorial Expansion Under the Tang Dynasty," Ch. 9, pp. 333-334 • "Tang Interactions with Korea and Japan," Ch. 9, pp. 342-345 • "Song China: Insiders versus Outsiders," Ch. 10, pp. 372-376 • "The Mongol Transformation of Afro-Eurasia," Ch. 10, pp. 388-393 • "The Islamic Heartland," Ch. 11, pp. 411-416 • "Ming China," Ch. 11, pp. 424-430
II: The movement of peoples caused environmental and linguistic effects.	
A. The expansion and intensification of long-distance trade routes often depended on environmental knowledge and technological adaptations to it.	• "Vikings and Christendom," Ch. 9, pp. 348-350 • "What Was Islam," Ch. 10, pp. 367-368 • "Who Were the Mongols?" Ch. 10, p. 388
B. Some migrations had a significant environmental impact, including: • The migration of Bantu-speaking peoples who facilitated transmission of iron technologies and agricultural techniques in Sub-Saharan Africa • The maritime migrations of the Polynesian peoples who cultivated transplanted foods and domesticated animals as they moved to new islands	• "Bantus of Sub-Saharan Africa," Ch. 8, pp. 302-305

C. Some migrations and commercial contacts led to the diffusion of languages throughout a new region or the emergence of new languages.	• "Bantus of Sub-Saharan Africa," Ch. 8, pp. 302–305 • "What Was Islam," Ch. 10, pp. 367–368
III: Cross-cultural exchanges were fostered by the intensification of existing, or the creation of new, networks of trade and communication.	
A. Islam, based on the revelations of the prophet Muhammad, developed in the Arabian peninsula. The beliefs and practices of Islam reflected interactions among Jews, Christians, and Zoroastrians with the local Arabian peoples. Muslim rule expanded to many parts of Afro-Eurasia due to military expansion, and Islam subsequently expanded through the activities of merchants and missionaries.	• "The Origins and Spread of Islam," Ch. 9, pp. 322–333 • "The Islamic World in a Time of Political Fragmentation," Ch. 10, pp. 365–368 • "The Islamic Heartland," Ch. 11, pp. 411–416
B. In key places along important trade routes, merchants set up diasporic communities where they introduced their own cultural traditions into the indigenous culture.	• "Sasanian Persia," Ch. 8, p. 293 • "The Sogdians As Lords of the Silk Roads," Ch. 8, pp. 293–294 • "Development of Maritime Trade," Ch. 10, pp. 362–365 • "The Old Trade and the New," Ch. 12, pp. 442–443
C. As exchange networks intensified, an increased number of travelers within Afro-Eurasia wrote about their travels. Their writings illustrate both the extent and the limitations of intercultural knowledge and understanding.	• "Buddhism in China," Ch. 8, pp. 301–302 • "Mongols in China," Ch. 10, pp. 392–393 • "Traveling Around the Mongol World," Ch. 10, pp. 396–401
D. Increased cross-cultural interactions resulted in the diffusion of literary, artistic, and cultural traditions, as well as scientific and technological innovations.	• "Religious Change and Empire in Western Africa-Eurasia," Ch. 8, pp. 282–291 • "Buddhism on the Silk Roads," Ch. 8, pp. 294–296 • "Buddhism in China," Ch. 8, pp. 301–302 • "The Origins and Spread of Islam," Ch. 9, pp. 322–333 • "Confucian Administrators," Ch. 9, p. 335 • "The Blossoming of Abbasid Culture," Ch. 9, p. 328 • "India as a Cultural Mosaic," Ch. 10, pp. 368–372 • "Song China: Insiders versus Outsiders," Ch. 10, pp. 372–377 • "Toltecs in Mesoamerica," Ch. 10, p. 386 • "The Renaissance," Ch. 11, pp. 422–424 • "The Reformation," Ch. 12, pp. 458–460
IV: There was continued diffusion of crops and pathogens, including epidemic diseases like the bubonic plague, throughout the Eastern Hemisphere along the trade routes.	
• "Bantu Migrations," Ch. 8, pp. 303–304 • "The Black Death," Ch. 11, pp. 404–409	

Key Concept 3.2: Continuity and Innovation of State Forms and Their Interactions	
I: Empires collapsed and were reconstituted; in some regions new state forms emerged.	
A. Following the collapse of empires, most reconstituted governments, including the Byzantine Empire and the Chinese dynasties—Sui, Tang, and Song—combined traditional sources of power and legitimacy with innovations better suited to their specific local context.	• "The Tang State," Ch. 9, pp. 333-345 • "Song China: Insiders versus Outsiders," Ch. 10, pp. 372-377 • "Rebuilding States," Ch. 11, pp. 409-411 • "The Tools of Empire Building," Ch. 11, pp. 413-414 • "The Catholic Church, State Building, and Economic Recovery," Ch. 11, pp. 416-420 • "Restoring Order," Ch. 11, p. 424 • "Centralization Under The Ming," Ch. 11, pp. 425-427
B. In some places, new forms of governance emerged including those developed in various Islamic states, the Mongol Khanates, city-states, and decentralized government (feudalism) in Europe and Japan.	• "Mesoamericans," Ch. 8, pp. 305-309 • "The Origins and Spread of Islam," Ch. 9, pp. 322-333 • "India as a Cultural Mosaic," Ch. 10, pp. 368-372 • "The Empire of Mali," Ch. 10, pp. 382-384 • "The Ottoman Empire," Ch. 11, pp. 412-416 • "Political Consolidation and Trade in the Iberian Peninsula," Ch. 11, pp. 420-422
C. Some states synthesized local with foreign traditions.	• "The Abbasid Revolution," Ch. 9, pp. 326-328 • "Tang Interactions with Korea and Japan," Ch. 9, pp. 342-345 • "The Tools of Empire Building," Ch. 11, pp. 413-414
D. In the Americas, as in Afro-Eurasia, state systems expanded in scope and reach; networks of city-states flourished in the Maya region and, at the end of this period, imperial systems were created by the Mexican ("Aztecs") and Inca.	• "Mesoamericans," Ch. 8, pp. 305-309 • "Aztec Society," Ch. 12, pp. 449-450 • "The Incas," Ch. 12, pp. 451-452
II: Interregional contacts and conflicts between states and empires encouraged significant technological and cultural transfers, including transfers between Tang China and the Abbasids, transfers across the Mongol empires, transfers during the Crusades, and transfers during Chinese maritime activity led by Ming Admiral Zheng He.	
• "New Empires and Common Cultures, Intro" Ch. 9, pp. 321-322 • "The Blossoming of Abbasid Culture," Ch. 9, p. 328 • "Tang Interactions with Korea and Japan," Ch. 9, pp. 342-345 • "Relations with the Islamic World," Ch. 10, pp. 379-381 • "The Mongol Transformation of Afro-Eurasia," Ch. 10, pp. 388-393 • "Trade and Exploration Under the Ming," Ch. 11, pp. 428-430	

Key Concept 3.3: Increased Economic Productive Capacity and Its Consequences	
I: Innovations stimulated agricultural and industrial production in many regions.	
A. Agricultural production increased significantly due to technological innovations.	• "Territorial Expansion Under the Tang Dynasty," Ch. 9, pp. 333-334 • "Economic and Political Developments," Ch. 10, pp. 372-373 • "Andean States of South America," Ch. 10, pp. 384-385 • "Aztec Society," Ch. 12, pp. 449-450 • "The Incas," Ch. 12, pp. 451-452
B. Demand for foreign luxury goods increased in Afro-Eurasia. Chinese, Persian, and Indian artisans and merchants expanded their production of textiles and porcelains for export; industrial production of iron and steel expanded in China.	• "Economic and Political Developments," Ch. 10, pp. 372-373 • "The Old Trade and the New," Ch. 12, pp. 442-445
II: The fate of cities varied greatly, with periods of significant decline, and with periods of increased urbanization buoyed by rising productivity and expanding trade networks.	
A. Multiple factors contributed to the decline of urban areas in this period, including invasions, disease, and the decline of agricultural productivity.	• "The Fall of Tang China," Ch. 9, p. 345 • "Vikings and Christendom," Ch. 9, pp. 348-350 • "Conquest and Empire," Ch. 10, pp. 388-393 • "The Black Death, Ch. 11, pp. 404-409 • "Ming China," Ch. 11, pp. 424-430
B. Multiple factors contributed to urban revival, including: the end of invasions; the availability of safe and reliable transport; the rise of commerce and warmer temperatures between 800 and 1300; increased agricultural productivity and subsequent rising population; and greater availability of labor.	• "Song China: Insiders versus Outsiders," Ch. 10, pp. 372-376 • "The Americas," Ch. 10, pp. 384-388 • "Rebuilding States," Ch. 11, pp. 409-411 • "The Ottoman Empire," Ch. 11, pp. 412-416 • "The Catholic Church, State Building, and Economic Recovery," Ch. 11, pp. 416-422 • "Ming China," Ch. 11, pp. 424-430
III: Despite significant continuities in social structures and in methods of production, there were also some important changes in labor management and in the effect of religious conversion on gender relations and family life.	
A. The diversification of labor organization that began with settled agriculture continued in this period. Forms of labor organization included free peasant agriculture, nomadic pastoralism, craft production and guild organization, various forms of coerced and unfree labor, government-imposed labor taxes, and military obligations.	• "An Economic Revolution," Ch. 9, pp. 337-339 • "Charlemagne's Fledgling Empire," Ch. 9, pp. 345-347 • "Christianity in Western Europe," Ch. 9, pp. 347-348 • "Trade Between East Africa and the Indian Ocean," p. 384 • "The Iberian Empires in the Americas," Ch. 12, pp. 454-458

B. As in the previous period, social structures were shaped largely by class and caste hierarchies. Patriarchy persisted; however, in some areas, women exercised more power and influence, most notably among the Mongols and in West Africa, Japan, and Southeast Asia.	• "Gender in Early Islam," Ch. 9, pp. 327-328 • "Organizing the Tang Empire," Ch. 9, pp. 334-336 • "Charlemagne's Fledgling Empire," Ch. 9, pp. 345-347 • "Christianity in Western Europe," Ch. 10, pp. 349-350 • "India as a Cultural Mosaic," Ch. 10, pp. 368-372 • "Economic and Political Developments," Ch. 10, pp. 372-373 • "China's Neighbors: Nomads, Japan, and Southeast Asia," Ch. 10, pp. 373-376 • "Christian Europe," Ch. 10, pp. 377-381 • "West Africa and the Mande-Speaking Peoples," Ch. 10, p. 382 • "Who Were the Mongols?" Ch. 10, p. 388
C. New forms of coerced labor appeared, including serfdom in Europe and Japan and the elaboration of the *mit'a* in the Inca Empire. Free peasants resisted attempts to raise dues and taxes by staging revolts. The demand for slaves for both military and domestic purposes increased, particularly in central Eurasia, parts of Africa, and the eastern Mediterranean.	• "Continuity of Rome in the East: Byzantium," Ch. 8, pp. 290-291 • "Silver, Sugar, and Slaves," Ch. 12, p. 457
D. The diffusion of Buddhism, Christianity, Islam, and Neoconfucianism often led to significant changes in gender relations and family structure.	• "Gender in Early Islam," Ch. 9, pp. 327-328
PERIOD 4: Global Interactions, c. 1450 to c. 1750	Chapters 11-14
Key Concept 4.1: Globalizing Networks of Communication and Exchange	
I: In the context of the new global circulation of goods, there was an intensification of all existing regional patterns of trade that brought prosperity and economic disruption to the merchants and governments in the trading regions of the Indian Ocean, Mediterranean, Sahara, and overland Eurasia.	
• "Economic and Political Effects of Global Commerce," Ch. 13, pp. 408-481 • "The Qing Dynasty Asserts Control," Ch. 13, pp. 500-502	
II: European technological developments in cartography and navigation built on previous knowledge developed in the classical, Islamic, and Asian worlds, and included the production of new tools, innovations in ship designs, and an improved understanding of global wind and currents patterns—all of which made transoceanic travel and trade possible.	
• "European Exploration and Expansion," Ch. 12, pp. 444-445 • "Technology and Cartography," Ch. 14, pp. 532-533	
III: [illegible]able new transoceanic maritime reconnaissance occurred in this period.	
[illegible] development of maritime technology [illegible] ills led to increased travel to and [illegible] and resulted in the construc- [illegible] empire.	• "Trade and Exploration Under The Ming," Ch, 11, pp. 428-430

B. Spanish sponsorship of the first Columbian and subsequent voyages across the Atlantic and Pacific dramatically increased European interest in transoceanic travel and trade.	• "First Encounters," Ch. 12, pp. 445-448
C. Northern Atlantic crossings for fishing and settlements continued and spurred European searches for multiple routes to Asia.	• "First Encounters," Ch. 12, pp. 445-448
IV: The new global circulation of goods was facilitated by royal chartered European monopoly companies that took silver from Spanish colonies in the Americas to purchase Asian goods for the Atlantic markets. Regional markets continued to flourish in Afro-Eurasia by using established commercial practices and new transoceanic shipping services developed by European merchants.	
A. European merchants' role in Asian trade was characterized mostly by transporting goods from one Asian country to another market in Asia or the Indian Ocean region.	• "Asian Relations with Europe," Ch. 12, pp. 464-466 • "The Dutch in Southeast Asia," Ch. 13, pp. 495-496
B. Commercialization and the creation of a global economy were intimately connected to new global circulation of silver from the Americas.	• "Silver, Sugar, and Slaves," Ch. 12, pp. 457-458 • "Economic and Political Effects of Global Commerce," Ch. 13, pp. 480-484 • "The Ottoman Empire," Ch. 13, pp. 496-498 • "Administrative and Economic Problems," Ch. 13, pp. 499-500
C. Influenced by mercantilism, joint-stock companies were new methods used by European rulers to control their domestic and colonial economies and by European merchants to compete against one another in global trade.	• "Extracting Wealth: Mercantilism," Ch. 13, pp. 481-484 • "The Dutch in Southeast Asia," Ch. 13, pp. 495-496
D. The Atlantic system involved the movement of goods, wealth, and free and unfree laborers, and the mixing of African, American, and European cultures and peoples.	• "Silver, Sugar, and Slaves," Ch. 12, pp. 457-458 • "The Slave Trade and Africa," Ch. 13, pp. 488-495 • "The Atlantic Trade in Slaves from Africa (1501-1900)," Ch. 13, p. 492
V: The new connections between the Eastern and Western hemispheres resulted in the Columbian Exchange.	
A. European colonization of the Americas led to the spread of diseases—including smallpox, measles, and influenza—that were endemic in the Eastern Hemisphere among Amerindian populations, and the unintentional transfer of vermin, including mosquitoes and rats.	• "Cortés and Conquest," Ch. 12, pp. 450-451 • "The Columbian Exchange," Ch. 12, pp. 452-454 • "The European Conquest of the Americas and Amerindian Mortality," Ch. 12, p. 453
B. American foods became staple crops in various parts of Europe, Asia, and Africa. Cash crops were grown primarily on plantations with coerced labor and were exported mostly to Europe and the Middle East in this period.	• "The Columbian Exchange," Ch. 12, pp. 452-454 • "Corn and the Rise of Slave-Supplying Kingdoms in West Africa," Ch. 12, pp. 476-477 • "Exchanges and Expansions in North America," Ch. 13, pp. 484-486 • "The Plantation Complex in the Caribbean," Ch. 13, pp. 487-488

C. Afro-Eurasian fruit trees, grains, sugar, and domesticated animals were brought by Europeans to the Americas, while other foods were brought by African slaves.	• "The Columbian Exchange," Ch. 12, pp. 452–454
D. Populations in Afro-Eurasia benefited nutritionally from the increased diversity of American food crops.	• "Corn and the Rise of Slave-Supplying Kingdoms in West Africa," Ch. 12, pp. 454–455
E. European colonization and the introduction of European agriculture and settlements practices in the Americas often affected the physical environment through deforestation and soil depletion.	• "The Columbian Exchange," Ch. 12, pp. 452–454 • "Expanding Mainland Colonies," Ch. 13, pp. 484–487 • "The Plantation Complex in the Caribbean," Ch. 13, pp. 487–488
VI: The increase in interactions between newly connected hemispheres and intensification of connections within hemispheres expanded the spread and reform of existing religions and created syncretic belief systems and practices.	
• "Political Divisions," Ch. 10, pp. 365–367 • "The Spread of Sufism," Ch. 10, p. 367 • "The Reformation," Ch. 12, pp. 458–460 • "Religious Warfare in Europe," Ch. 12, pp. 461–462 • "Religion and Chinese Influence," Ch. 14, p. 534 • "Spiritual Encounters," Ch. 14, pp. 543–544	
VII: As merchants' profits increased and governments collected more taxes, funding for the visual and performing arts, even for popular audiences, increased along with an expansion of literacy.	
Key Concept 4.2: New Forms of Social Organization and Modes of Production	
I: Beginning in the 14th century, there was a decrease in mean temperatures, often referred to as the Little Ice Age, around the world that lasted until the 19th century, contributing to changes in agricultural practices and the contraction of settlement in parts of the Northern Hemisphere.	
"The Black Death," Ch. 11, pp. 404–405	
II: Traditional peasant agriculture increased and changed, plantations expanded, and demand for labor increased. These changes both fed and responded to growing global demand for raw materials and finished products.	
A. Peasant labor intensified in many regions.	• "Trade and Exploration Under the Ming," Ch. 11, p. 428 • "The Mughal Empire," Ch. 13, pp. 498–499 • "Imperial Expansion and Migration," Ch. 13, pp. 506–508 • "Western European Economies," Ch. 13, p. 509
B. Slavery in Africa continued both the traditional incorporation of slaves into households and the export of slaves to the Mediterranean and the Indian Ocean.	• "Silver, Sugar, and Slaves," Ch. 12, pp. 457–458 • "Capturing and Shipping Slaves," Ch. 13, pp. 488–493
C. The growth of the plantation economy increased the demand for slaves in the Americas.	• "Silver, Sugar, and Slaves," Ch. 12, pp. 457–458

D. Colonial economies in the Americas depended on a range of coerced labor.	• "First Conquests," Ch. 12, pp. 448–454 • "The Iberian Empires in the Americas," Ch. 12, pp. 454–457 • "Silver, Sugar, and Slaves," Ch. 12, pp. 457–458
III: As social and political elites changed, they also restructured ethnic, racial, and gender hierarchies.	
A. Both imperial conquests and widening global economic opportunities contributed to the formation of new political and economic elites.	• "Diversity and Control," Ch. 11, pp. 415–416 • "First Conquests," Ch. 12, pp. 448–454 • "The Iberian Empires in the Americas," Ch. 12, pp. 454–457 • "Silver, Sugar, and Slaves," Ch. 12, pp. 447–458 • "Africa's New Slave-Supplying States," Ch. 13, pp. 493–495 • "The Ottoman Empire," Ch. 13, pp. 496–498 • "The Qing Dynasty Asserts Control," Ch. 13, pp. 500–502
B. The power of existing political and economic elites fluctuated as they confronted new challenges to their ability to affect the policies of the increasingly powerful monarchs and leaders.	• "The Mughal Empire," Ch. 13, pp. 498–499 • "Unification of Japan," Ch. 13, pp. 503–505 • "Challenges to Authority and Tradition," Ch. 14, p. 539
C. Some notable gender and family restructuring occurred, including demographic changes in Africa that resulted from the slave trades.	• "Africa's New Slave-Supplying States," Ch. 13, pp. 493–495 • "The Thirty Years' War," Ch. 13, pp. 508–509

Key Concept 4.3: State Consolidation and Imperial Expansion	
I: Rulers used a variety of methods to legitimize and consolidate their power.	
A. Rulers continued to use religious ideas, art, and monumental architecture to legitimize their rule.	• "Aztec Society," Ch. 12, pp. 449–450 • "Dynastic Monarchies," Ch. 13, pp. 509–510 • "Science and the Arts," Ch. 14, pp. 525–526 • "Safavid Culture, Shiite State," Ch. 14, p. 527 • "Architecture and the Arts," Ch. 14, p. 527 • "Religion, Architecture, and the Arts," Ch. 14, pp. 527–528 • "The Political Uses of Space," Ch. 14, pp. 530–531 • "The Asante, Oyo, and Benin Cultural Traditions," Ch. 14, pp. 535–536
B. States treated different ethnic and religious groups in ways that utilized their economic contributions while limiting their ability to challenge the authority of the state.	• "The Qing Dynasty Asserts Control," Ch. 13, pp. 500–502 • "The Ottoman Cultural Synthesis," Ch. 14, pp. 525–526 • "Universal Laws and Religious Tolerance," Ch. 14, p. 539 • "The Enlightenment and the Origins of Racial Thought," Ch. 14, p. 542 • "Intermarriage and Cultural Mixing," Ch. 14, p. 544

C. Recruitment and use of bureaucratic elites, as well as the development of military professionals, became more common among rulers who wanted to maintain centralized control over their populations and resources.	• "Diversity and Control," Ch. 11, pp. 415-416 • "Building a Bureaucracy," Ch. 11, p. 426 • "Unification of Japan," Ch. 13, pp. 503-505
D. Rulers used tribute collection and tax farming to generate revenue for territorial expansion.	• "Aztec Society," Ch. 12, pp. 449-450 • "The Incas," Ch. 12, pp. 451-452 • "The Iberian Empires in the Americas," Ch. 12, pp. 454-458 • "Absolutist Government and Serfdom," Ch. 13, p. 506
II: Imperial expansion relied on the increased use of gunpowder, cannons, and armed trade to establish large empires in both hemispheres.	
A. Europeans established new trading-post empires in Africa and Asia, which proved profitable for the rulers and merchants involved in new global trade networks, but these empires also affected the power of the states in interior West and Central Africa.	• "Africa's New Slave-Supplying States," Ch. 13, pp. 493-495
B. Land empires—including the Manchu, Mughal, Ottoman, and Russian—expanded dramatically in size.	• "Mughal India and Commerce," Ch. 12, pp. 462-464 • "The Ottoman Empire," Ch. 13, pp. 496-498 • "The Mughal Empire," Ch. 13, pp. 498-499 • "The Qin Dynasty Asserts Control," Ch. 13, pp. 500-502 • "Muscovy Becomes the Russian Empire," Ch. 13, p. 506
C. European states established new maritime empires in the Americas, including the Portuguese, Spanish, Dutch, French, and British.	• "The Atlantic World," Ch. 12, pp. 445-458
III: Competition over trade routes, state rivalries, and local resistance all provided significant challenges to state consolidation and expansion.	
• "The Ottoman Empire," Ch. 13, pp. 496-498 • "Transformations in the Islamic Heartland," Ch. 13, p. 496 • "The Mughal Empire," Ch. 13, pp. 498-499 • "The Thirty Years' War," Ch. 13, pp. 508-509	
PERIOD 5: Industrialization and Global Integration, c. 1750 to c. 1900	Chapters 15-18

Key Concept 5.1: Industrialization and Global Capitalism	
I: Industrialization fundamentally changed how goods were produced.	
A. A variety of factors led to the rise of industrial production, including: • Europe's location on the Atlantic Ocean • The geographical distribution of coal, iron, and timber • European demographic changes • Urbanization • Improved agricultural productivity • Legal protection of private property • An abundance of rivers and canals • Access to foreign resources • The accumulation of capital	• "The Industrial Revolution," Ch. 15, pp. 576–579
B. The development of machines, including steam engines and the internal combustion engine, made it possible to exploit vast new resources of energy stored in fossil fuels, specifically coal and oil. The fossil fuels revolution greatly increased the energy available to human societies.	• "The Industrial Revolution," Ch. 15, pp. 576–579
C. The development of the factory system concentrated labor in a single location and led to an increasing degree of specialization of labor.	• "Integration of the World Economy," Ch. 17, pp. 648–649
D. As the new methods of industrial production became more common in parts of northwestern Europe, they spread to other parts of Europe and the United States, Russia, and Japan.	• "New Technologies, Materials, and Business Practices," Ch. 17, pp. 647–648
E. The "second industrial revolution" led to new methods in the production of steel, chemicals, electricity and precision machinery during the second half of the nineteenth century.	• "Industry, Science, and Technology," Ch. 17, pp. 647–649
II: New patterns of global trade and production developed and further integrated the global economy as industrialists sought raw materials and new markets for the increasing amount and array of goods produced in their factories.	
A. The need for raw materials for the factories and increased food supplies for the growing population in urban centers led to the growth of export economies around the world that specialized in mass producing natural resources. The profits from these raw materials were used to purchase finished goods.	• "The Industrial Revolution," Ch. 15, pp. 576–579 • "Brazilian Expansion and Economic Development," Ch. 17, pp. 643–644 • "New Trade with Africa," Ch. 15, p. 574

B. The rapid development of steam-powered industrial production in European countries and the U.S. contributed to these regions' increase in their share of global manufacturing. While Middle Eastern and Asian countries continued to produce manufactured goods, these regions' share in global manufacturing declined.	• "New Technologies, Materials, and Business Practices," Ch. 17, pp. 647-648 • "Effects in India," Ch. 15, pp. 584-585
C. The global economy of the 19th century expanded dramatically from the previous period due to increased exchanges of raw materials and finished goods in most parts of the world. Some commodities gave merchants and companies based in Europe and the U.S. a distinct economic advantage.	• "Global Expansionism and an Age of Imperialism," Ch. 17, pp. 649-659 • "The Opium War and the 'Opening' of China," Ch. 15, pp. 586-588 • "Reforms in Egypt," Ch. 15, p. 582 • "Economic Reordering," Ch.15, pp. 574-581 • "New Trade with Africa," Ch. 15, p. 574 • "Colonial Administrations in Africa," Ch.17, pp. 655-656
D. The need for specialized and limited metals for industrial production, as well as the global demand for gold, silver and diamonds as forms of wealth, led to the development of extensive mining centers.	• "Women's Status in Colonies," Ch. 18, p. 691
III: To facilitate investments at all levels of industrial production, financiers developed and expanded various financial institutions.	
A. The ideological inspiration for economic changes lies in the development of capitalism and classical liberalism associated with Adam Smith and John Stuart Mill.	• "Socialists and Communists," Ch. 16, p. 614
B. The global nature of trade and production contributed to the proliferation of large-scale transnational businesses that relied on various financial instruments.	• "Economic and Industrial Development," Ch. 17, pp. 641-642 • "Integration of the World Economy," Ch. 17, pp. 648-649 • "Global Expansion and an Age of Imperialism," Ch. 17, pp. 649-659
IV: There were major developments in transportation and communication, including railroads, steamships, telegraphs, and canals.	
• "Industrial Revolution," Ch. 15, pp. 576-579 • "Economic and Industrial Development," Ch. 17, pp. 641-642 • "Movements of Labor and Technology," Ch. 17, p. 648 • "India and the Imperial Model," Ch. 17, pp. 650-651	
V: The development and spread of global capitalism led to a variety of responses.	
A. In industrialized states, many workers organized themselves to improve working conditions, limit hours, and gain higher wages, while others opposed industrialists' treatment of workers by promoting alternative visions of society, including Marxism.	• "Working and Living," Ch. 15, pp. 579-581 • "Restoration and Resistance," Ch. 16, p. 612 • "Fourier and Utopian Socialism," Ch. 16, pp. 614-615 • "Marxism," Ch. 16, pp. 615-616 • "Strikes and Revolts," Ch. 18, pp. 691-692

B. In Qing China and the Ottoman Empire, some members of the government resisted economic change and attempted to maintain preindustrial forms of economic production, while other members of the Qing and Ottoman governments led reforms in imperial policies.	• "Reforming Egypt and the Ottoman Empire," Ch. 15, pp. 581-583 • "Persistence of the Qing Empire," Ch. 15, pp. 585-588 • "China Under Pressure," Ch.17, pp. 664-665
C. In a small number of states, governments promoted their own state-sponsored visions of industrialization.	• "Reforms in Egypt," Ch. 15, p. 582 • "Japan's Transformation and Expansion," Ch. 17, pp. 659-662 • "Russian Transformation and Expansion," Ch. 17, pp. 662-664
D. In response to criticisms of industrial global capitalism, some governments mitigated the negative effects of industrial capitalism by promoting various types of reforms.	• "Reforms in Egypt," Ch. 15, p. 582 • "Building Nationalism," Ch. 17, p. 639 • "Irish Nationalism in Great Britain," Ch. 17, p. 647
VI: The ways in which people organized themselves into societies also underwent significant transformations in industrialized states due to the fundamental restructuring of the global economy.	
A. New social classes, including the middle class and the industrial working class, developed.	• "Economic Reordering," Ch. 15, pp. 574-576
B. Family dynamics, gender roles, and demographics changed in response to industrialization.	• "The Industrial Revolution," Ch. 15, pp. 576-579
C. Rapid urbanization that accompanied global capitalism often led to unsanitary conditions.	• "Urban Life and Work Routines," Ch. 15, p. 579
Key Concept 5.2: Imperialism and Nation-State Formation	
I: Industrializing powers established transoceanic empires.	
A. States with existing colonies strengthened their control over those colonies.	• "India and the Imperial Model," Ch. 17, pp. 650-651 • "Colonizing Africa," Ch. 17, pp. 651-656 • "Africa's Newest Hunters and Gatherers: Greed, Environmental Degradation, and Resistance," Ch.17, pp. 654-655
B. European states, as well as the Americans and the Japanese, established empires throughout Asia and the Pacific, while Spanish and Portuguese influence declined.	• "Revolutions in Spanish and Portuguese America," Ch .15, pp. 569-573 • "Colonial Reordering in India," Ch. 15, pp. 583-585 • "India and the Imperial Model," Ch. 17, pp. 650-651 • "The American Empire," Ch. 17, pp. 656-658 • "Japan's Transformation," Ch. 17, pp. 659-662 • "Russian Transformation and Expansion," Ch. 17, pp. 662-664 • "China Under Pressure," Ch. 17, pp. 664-665
C. Many European states used both warfare and diplomacy to establish empires in Africa.	• "Change and Trade in Africa," Ch. 15, pp. 573-574 • "Islamic Revitalization," Ch. 16, pp. 603-607 • "Colonizing Africa," Ch. 17, pp. 651-656 • "Africa's Newest Hunters and Gatherers: Greed, Environmental Degradation, and Resistance," Ch. 17, pp. 654-655

D. In some parts of their empires, Europeans established settler colonies.	• "India and the Imperial Model," Ch. 17, pp. 650–651 • "Colonizing Africa," Ch. 17, pp. 651–656
E. In other parts of the world, industrialized states practiced economic imperialism.	• "The East India Company's Monopoly," Ch. 15, pp. 583–584 • "The Opium War and the 'Opening' of China," Ch. 15, pp. 586–588 • "The Caste War of the Yucatan," Ch. 16, pp. 620–622 • "The American Empire," Ch. 17, pp. 656–658
II: Imperialism influenced state formation and contraction around the world.	
A. The expansion of U.S. and European influence over Tokugawa Japan led to the emergence of Meiji Japan.	• "Japan's Transformation and Expansion," Ch. 17, pp. 659–662
B. The United States and Russia emulated European transoceanic imperialism by expanding their land borders and conquering neighboring territories.	• "The American Empire," Ch. 17, pp. 656–658 • "Russian Transformation and Expansion," Ch. 17, pp. 662–663
C. Anti-imperial resistance took various forms including direct resistance within empires and the creation of new states on the peripheries.	• "Islamic Revitalization," Ch.16, pp. 603–607 • "Charismatic Military Men in Non-Islamic Africa," Ch. 16, pp. 607–608 • "Native American Prophets," Ch. 16, pp. 617–620 • "The Caste War of the Yucatan," Ch. 16, pp. 620–622 • "The Rebellion of 1857 in India," Ch. 16, pp. 622–626 • "African Resistance," Ch. 17, pp. 654–655
III: New racial ideologies, especially social Darwinism, facilitated and justified imperialism.	
• "Charles Darwin and Natural Selection," Ch. 17, pp. 648–649	
Key Concept 5.3: Nationalism, Revolution, and Reform	
I: The rise and diffusion of Enlightenment thought that questioned established traditions in all areas of life often preceded the revolutions and rebellions against existing governments.	
A. Enlightenment philosophers applied new ways of understanding the natural world to human relationships, encouraging observation and inference in all spheres of life; they also critiqued the role that religion played in public life, insisting on the importance of reason as opposed to revelation. Other Enlightenment philosophers developed new political ideas about the individual, natural rights, and the social contract.	• "Revolutionary Transformations and New Languages of Freedom," Ch. 15, pp. 560–561 • "Political Reorderings," Ch.15, pp. 561–573 • "Asserting Independence from Britain," Ch. 15, pp. 561–564

B. The ideas of Enlightenment philosophers, as reflected in revolutionary documents—including the American Declaration of Independence, the French Declaration of the Rights of Man and Citizen, and Bolivar's Jamaica Letter—influenced resistance to existing political authority.	• "The North American War of Independence, 1776–1783," Ch. 15, pp. 561–565 • "The French Revolution," Ch. 15, pp. 565–567 • "Revolution in Saint-Dominguez (Haiti)," Ch. 15, p. 569 • "Revolutions in Spanish and Portuguese America," Ch. 15, pp. 569–573
C. Enlightenment ideas influenced many people to challenge existing notions of social relations, which contributed to the expansion of rights as seen in expanded suffrage, the abolition of slavery, and the end of serfdom.	• "Abolition of Slave Trade," Ch. 15, pp. 573–574 • "Revamping the Russian Monarchy," Ch. 15, p. 581
II: Beginning in the 18th century, peoples around the world developed a new sense of commonality based on language, religion, social customs and territory. These newly imagined national communities linked this identity with the borders of the state, while governments used this idea to unite diverse populations.	
• "Canada," Ch. 17, p. 642 • "Latin America," Ch. 17, pp. 642–644 • "Consolidation of Nation-States in Europe," Ch. 17, pp. 644–647	
III: Increasing discontent with imperial rule propelled reformist and revolutionary movements.	
A. Subjects challenged centralized imperial governments.	• "The Rebellion," Ch. 16, pp. 609–611 • "Native American Prophets," Ch. 16, pp. 617–620 • "The Caste War of the Yucatan," Ch. 16, pp. 620–622 • "The Rebellion of 1857 in India," Ch. 16, pp. 622–626
B. American colonial subjects led a series of rebellions—including the American Revolution, the Haitian Revolution, and the Latin American independence movements—that facilitated the emergence of independent states in the United States, Haiti, and mainland Latin America. French subjects rebelled against their monarchy.	• "The North American War of Independence, 1776–1783," Ch. 15, pp. 561–565 • "The French Revolution, 1789–1799," Ch. 15, pp. 565–567 • "Revolution in Saint-Dominguez (Haiti)," Ch. 15, p. 569 • Revolutions in Spanish and Portuguese America," Ch. 15, pp. 569–573
C. Slave resistance challenged existing authorities in the Americas.	• "Abolition of the Slave Trade," Ch. 15, pp. 573–574
D. Increasing questions about political authority and growing nationalism contributed to anticolonial movements.	• "Insurgencies Against Colonizing and Centralizing States," Ch. 16, pp. 612–626 • "The Rebellion of 1857 in India," Ch. 16, pp. 622–626 • "The Boxer Uprising in China," Ch. 18, pp. 685–688
E. Some of the rebellions were influenced by diverse religious ideas.	• "Alternative Visions of the Nineteenth Century, Introduction," Ch. 16, pp. 601–602 • "Prophecy and Revitalization in the Islamic World and Africa," Ch. 16, pp. 602–608 • "Prophecy and Rebellion in China," Ch. 16, pp. 609–611

IV: The global spread of European political and social thought and the increasing number of rebellions stimulated new transnational ideologies and solidarities.	
A. Discontent with monarchist and imperial rule encouraged the development of political ideologies, including liberalism, socialism, and communism.	• "Restoration and Resistance," Ch. 16, p. 612 • "Nationalism," Ch. 16, pp. 612–614 • "Socialists and Communists," Ch. 16, p. 614 • "Fourier and Utopian Socialism," Ch. 16, pp. 614–615 • "Marxism," Ch. 16, pp. 615–616
B. Demands for women's suffrage and an emergent feminism challenged political and gender hierarchies.	• "Revolutionary Transformations," Ch. 15, pp. 566–567 • "On the Rights of Women," Ch. 15, p. 592 • "Fourier and Utopian Socialism," Ch. 16, pp. 614–615 • "Women's Issues in the West," Ch. 18, pp. 690–691 • "Women's Status in Colonies," Ch. 18, p. 691
Key Concept 5.4: Global Migration	
I: Migration in many cases was influenced by changes in demography in both industrialized and unindustrialized societies that presented challenges to existing patterns of living.	
A. Changes in food production and improved medical conditions contributed to a significant global rise in population in both urban and rural areas.	• "Urban Life and Work Routines," Ch. 15, p. 579
B. Because of the nature of the new modes of transportation, both internal and external migrants increasingly relocated to cities. This pattern contributed to the significant global urbanization of the 19th century. The new methods of transportation also allowed for many migrants to return, periodically or permanently, to their home societies.	• "The Industrial Revolution," Ch. 15, pp. 576–579 • "Economic and Industrial Development," Ch. 17, pp. 641–642 • "Brazil's 'Exclusive' Nation-State," Ch. 17, p. 643
II: Migrants relocated for a variety of reasons.	
A. Many individuals chose freely to relocate, often in search of work.	• "Social Protest and Emigration," Ch. 15, pp. 579–581 • "Brazil's 'Exclusive' Nation-State," Ch. 17, p. 643 • "Movements of Labor and Technology," Ch. 17, p. 648
B. The new global capitalist economy continued to rely on coerced and semicoerced labor migration, including slavery, Chinese and Indian indentured servitude, and convict labor.	• "New Trade with Africa," Ch. 15, p. 574 • "Brazil's 'Exclusive' Nation-State," Ch. 17, p. 643
III: The large-scale nature of migration, especially in the 19th century, produced a variety of consequences and reactions to the increasingly diverse societies on the part of migrants and the existing populations.	
A. Due to the physical nature of the labor in demand, migrants tended to be male, leaving women to take on new roles in the home society that had been formerly occupied by men.	• "Asserting Independence from Britain," Ch. 15, pp. 561–564 • "Economic Development," Ch. 17, p. 660 • "Women's Issues in the West," Ch. 18, pp. 690–691

B. Migrants often created ethnic enclaves in different parts of the world that helped transplant their culture into new environments and facilitated the development of migrant support networks.	• "Building Unified States," Ch. 17, p. 646 • "Movements of Labor and Technology," Ch. 17, p. 648 • "Defining 'The Nation'," Ch. 17, pp. 644–645
C. Receiving societies did not always embrace immigrants, as seen in the various degrees of ethnic and racial prejudice and the ways states attempted to regulate the increased flow of people across their borders.	• "Regulating the Environment and Immigration," Ch. 18, pp. 667–668
PERIOD 6: Accelerating Global Change and Realignments, c. 1900 to the Present	Chapters 17-Epilogue
Key Concept 6.1: Science and the Environment	
I: Researchers made rapid advances in science that spread throughout the world, assisted by the development of new technology.	
A. New modes of communication and transportation reduced the problem of geographic distance.	• "Movements of Labor and Technology," Ch. 17, p. 648 • "Industrialization and Modern Economy," Ch. 18, pp. 689–690
B. The Green Revolution produced food for the earth's growing population as it spread chemically and genetically enhanced forms of agriculture.	• "Agricultural Production," Ch. 21, pp. 823–825
C. Medical innovations increased the ability of humans to survive and live longer lives.	• "Health," Ch. 18, pp. 821–822
D. Energy technologies including the use of petroleum and nuclear power raised productivity and increased the production of material goods.	• "New Technologies, Materials, and Business Practices," Ch. 17, pp. 647–648
II: During a period of unprecedented global population expansion, humans fundamentally changed their relationship with the environment.	
A. As human activity contributed to deforestation, desertification, and increased consumption of the world's supply of fresh water and clean air, humans competed over these and other resources more intensely than ever before.	• "Natural Resources and the Environment," Ch. 21, pp. 825–826
B. The release of greenhouse gases and other pollutants into the atmosphere contributed to debates about the nature and causes of climate change.	• "Natural Resources and the Environment," Ch. 21, pp. 825–826 • "Health," Ch. 21, pp. 821–822 • "Global Warming," Epilogue, p. 847
III: Disease, scientific innovations, and conflict led to demographic shifts.	
A. Diseases associated with poverty persisted, while other diseases emerged as new epidemics and threats to human survival. In addition, changing lifestyles and increased longevity led to higher incidence of certain diseases.	• "Urban Life," Ch. 18, pp. 679–683 • "Poverty, Disease, Genocide," Epilogue, pp. 862–863

B. More effective forms of birth control gave women greater control over fertility and transformed sexual practices.	• "The Demography of Globalization," Ch. 21, pp. 817–820
C. Improved military technology and new tactics led to increased levels of wartime casualties.	• "Stalemate," Ch. 19, pp. 719–721 • "The Bitter Costs of War," Ch. 20, pp. 759–761 • "Allied Advances and the Atomic Bomb," Ch. 20, p. 763 • "Japan's Efforts to Expand," Ch. 20, p. 761 • "World War II Casualties," Ch. 20, pp. 764–765
Key Concept 6.2: Global Conflicts and Their Consequences	
I: Europe dominated the global political order at the beginning of the 20th century, but both land-based and transoceanic empires gave way to new states by the century's end.	
A. The older land-based Ottoman, Russian, and Qing empires collapsed due to a combination of internal and external factors.	• "The Boxer Uprising in China," Ch. 18, pp. 685–688 • "The Russian Revolution," Ch. 19, pp. 721–723 • "The Fall of the Central Powers," Ch. 19, pp. 723–726
B. Some colonies negotiated their independence.	• "Negotiated Independence in India and Africa," Ch. 20, pp. 770–774
C. Some colonies achieved independence through armed struggle.	• "The Algerian War of Independence," Ch. 20, p. 775 • "Vietnam," Ch. 20, pp. 776–777 • "The Last Holdouts," Ch. 21, p. 806
II: Emerging ideologies of anti-imperialism contributed to the dissolution of empires and the restructuring of states.	
A. Nationalist leaders and parties in Asia and Africa challenged imperial rule.	• "A Modernizing Elite," Ch. 18, p. 702 • "Africa for Africans," Ch. 20, pp. 772–774 • "Vietnam," Ch. 20, pp. 776–777
B. Regional, religious, and ethnic movements challenged both colonial rule and inherited imperial boundaries.	• "A Divided Anticolonial Movement in India," Ch. 19, pp. 742–743 • "Building a Nation," Ch. 17, p. 642 • "Limits to Autonomy," Ch. 20, p. 782
C. Transnational movements sought to unite people across national boundaries.	• "Socialists and Communists," Ch. 16, p. 614 • "The Pan Movements," Ch. 18, pp. 703–704
D. Movements to redistribute land and resources developed within states in Africa, Asia, and Latin America, sometimes advocating communism and socialism.	• "Anticolonial Visions of Modern Life," Ch. 19, p. 739
III: Political changes were accompanied by major demographic and social consequences.	
A. The redrawing of old colonial boundaries led to population resettlements.	• "India," Ch. 20, pp. 770–772 • "Palestine, Israel, and Egypt," Ch. 20, pp. 774–775 • "Internal Divisions, External Rivalries," Epilogue, pp. 855–856

B. The migration of former colonial subjects to imperial metropoles (the former colonizing country, usually in the major cities) maintained cultural and economic ties between the colony and the metropole even after the dissolution of empires.	• "Emigration, Immigration, Internal Migration," Ch. 18, p. 679 • "The Algerian War of Independence," Ch. 20, p. 775
C. The proliferation of conflicts led to various forms of genocide or ethnic violence.	• "Empire and War," Ch. 19, p. 721 • "The Bitter Costs of War," Ch. 20, pp. 759–761 • "Violence," Ch. 21, pp. 827–828
IV: Military conflicts occurred on an unprecedented global scale.	
A. World War I and World War II were the first "total wars." Governments used ideologies, including fascism, nationalism and communism, to mobilize all of their state's resources, including peoples, both in the home countries and the colonies or former colonies, for the purpose of waging war. Governments also used a variety of strategies, including political speeches, art, media, and intensified forms of nationalism, to mobilize these populations.	• "Radio" and "Film and Advertising," Ch. 19, p. 728 • "The Soviet Union and Socialism," Ch. 19, pp. 723–733 • "Italian Fascism," Ch. 19, p. 734 • "Chinese Nationalism," Ch. 19, p. 743 • "Nationalism and the Rise of the Muslim Brotherhood in Egypt," Ch. 19, p. 744
B. The sources of global conflict in the first half of the century varied, and included imperialist expansion by European powers and Japan, competition for resources, and the economic crisis engendered by the Great Depression.	• "The Great War," Ch. 19, pp. 718–719 • "Liberal Democracy Under Pressure," Ch. 19, pp. 730–732 • "Japan's Efforts to Expand," Ch. 20, p. 761
C. The global balance of economic and political power shifted after the end of World War II and rapidly evolved into the Cold War. The United States and the Soviet Union emerged as superpowers, which led to ideological struggles between capitalism and communism throughout the globe.	• "The Beginning of the Cold War," Ch. 20, pp. 763–768
D. The Cold War produced new military alliances, including NATO and the Warsaw Pact, and promoted proxy wars in Latin America, Africa, and Asia.	• "The Beginning of the Cold War," Ch. 20, pp. 763–768 • "Tensions Within the Three Worlds," Ch. 20, pp. 785–788
V: Although conflict dominated much of the 20th century, many individuals and groups—including states—opposed this trend. Some individuals and groups, however, intensified the conflicts.	
A. Groups and individuals challenged the many wars of the century, and some promoted the practice of nonviolence as a way to bring about political change.	• "Imagining an Indian Nation," Ch. 19, p. 740 • "Gandhi and Nonviolent Resistance," Ch. 19, pp. 740–742 • "Southern Africa," Ch. 20, pp. 775–776 • "The United States," Ch. 20, pp. 777–778 • "Mounting Costs," Ch. 21, p. 802

B. Groups and individuals, including the Non-Aligned Movement, opposed and promoted alternatives to the existing economic, political, and social orders.	• "Southern Africa," Ch. 20, pp. 775-776 • "Women's Issues, Civil Rights, and Environmental Concerns," Ch. 20, pp. 785-786 • "Acceptance of and Resistance to Democracy," Ch. 21, pp. 830-831
C. Militaries and militarized states often responded to the proliferation of conflicts in ways that further intensified conflict.	• "Latin American Revolution," Ch. 20, pp. 783-784 • "Three Worlds," Ch. 20, pp. 777-784
D. More movements used violence against civilians to achieve political aims.	• "War on Terror," Epilogue, pp. 844-845 • "Islamic Militancy," Epilogue, p. 845
Key Concept 6.3: New Conceptualizations of Global Economy, Society, and Culture	
I: States responded in a variety of ways to the economic challenges of the 20th century.	
A. In the communist states of the Soviet Union and China governments controlled their national economies.	• "The Soviet Union and Socialism," Ch. 19, pp. 732-733 • "The Maoist Model," Ch. 20, pp. 782-783
B. At the beginning of the 20th century in the United States and parts of Europe, governments played a minimal role in their national economies. With the onset of the Great Depression, governments began to take a more active role in economic life.	• "The American New Deal," Ch. 19, pp. 731-732 • "Italian Fascism," Ch. 19, pp. 734-735
C. In newly independent states after World War II, governments often took on a strong role in guiding economic life to promote development.	• "Palestine, Israel, and Egypt," Ch. 20, pp. 774-775
D. In a trend accelerated by the end of the Cold War, many governments encouraged free market economic policies and promoted economic liberalization in the late 20th century.	• "Finance and Trade," Ch. 21, pp. 807-809 • "Latin American Revolution," Ch. 20, pp. 783-784
II: States, communities, and individuals became increasingly interdependent, a process facilitated by the growth of institutions of global governance.	
A. New international organizations formed to maintain world peace and to facilitate international cooperation.	• "The Peace Settlement and the Impact of the War," Ch. 19, p. 726 • "Supranational Organizations," Ch. 21, pp. 826-827
B. Changing economic institutions and regional trade agreements reflected the spread of principles and practices associated with free market economics throughout the world.	• "Limits to Autonomy," Ch. 20, pp. 781-782 • "Global Finance and Deregulated Markets," Ch. 21, pp. 807-808 • "Supranational Organizations," Ch. 21, pp. 826-827 • "Chronology," Ch. 21, p. 833

C. Movements throughout the world protested the inequality of environmental and economic consequences of global integration.	• "Natural Resources and the Environment," Ch. 21, pp. 825–826
III: People conceptualized society and culture in new ways; rights-based discourses challenged old assumptions about race, class, gender, and religion. In much of the world, access to education, as well as participation in new political and professional roles, became more inclusive in terms of race, class, and gender.	
• "Africa for Africans," Ch. 20, pp. 772–773 • "Women's Issues, Civil Rights, and Environmental Concerns," Ch. 20, pp. 785–786 • "Supranational Organizations," Ch. 21, pp. 826–827 • "Women and Work," Ch. 21, p. 823 • "Education," Ch. 21, p. 822 • "South Africa and Nelson Mandela," Ch. 21, p. 806	
IV: Popular and consumer culture became more global.	
• "New Media," Ch. 21, pp. 814–815 • "Global Culture," Ch. 21, pp. 813–816	

ACKNOWLEDGMENTS

For the AP Edition we have some familiar and new friends at Norton to thank. Chief among them is Jon Durbin, who once again played a major role in bringing this edition to publication. So too did Jenna Barry through her tireless work make the AP edition possible. Ann Shin, our developmental editor, did a remarkable job in helping to address reviewers' comments and streamline the Concise Edition that made this one possible. Sara Wise, the Developmental Editor for the AP edition, brought new levels of creativity to bear as she worked with the AP and ancillary authors. Jillian Burr is responsible for the book's beautiful and effective design. Tacy Quinn and Chris Hillyer have done a masterful job strengthening the media support materials to meet the ever more complex classroom and assessment needs of instructors. Diane Cipollone, our project editor, and Andrew Ensor, our production manager, have done a great job getting the book published on time with a very tight schedule. *Worlds Together, Worlds Apart* has always been incredibly creative and distinctive looking, and the AP Edition covers are even more eye-catching and memorable than the first four editions.

But the AP Edition also relied upon AP teacher expertise. Chief among these has been Sharon Cohen, whose work on the Instructor's Manual has made it an invaluable resource to teachers. Other members of the AP Community, past and present, also helped to inform the way that we approached the new course and exam design by both describing to us how they teach the course, reviewing all of the new content for this edition, and writing ancillaries to match. We would like to thank: Linda Black, Mike Burns, Steve Corso, Wendy Eagan, Ryba Epstein, Charlie Hart, James Harris, Ben Kahrl, Suzanne Littrell, John Maunu, Barbara Ozuna, James Sabathne, Julie Sanders, Erik Vincent, James Wehrli, and Patrick Whelan.

About the Authors

ALAN KARRAS (*Ph.D. University of Pennsylvania*) is the Associate Director of International & Area Studies at the University of California, Berkeley, and has served as chair of the College Board's test development committee for world history and as co-chair of the College Board's commission on AP history course revisions. He studies the eighteenth-century Atlantic world and global interactions more broadly concerning illegal activities like smuggling and corruption.

ELIZABETH POLLARD (*Ph.D. University of Pennsylvania*) is associate professor of history at San Diego State University. Her research expertise focuses on women accused of witchcraft in the Roman world and on the exchange of goods and ideas between the Mediterranean and the Indian Ocean. Her pedagogical interests include the effectiveness of web-based technology and world history in teaching, learning, and writing about ancient history.

CLIFFORD ROSENBERG (*Ph.D. Princeton University*) is associate professor of European history at City College and the Graduate Center, CUNY. He specializes in the history of modern France and its empire and is the author of *Policing Paris: The Origins of Modern Immigration Control Between the Wars*. He is working now on the spread of tuberculosis between France and Algeria since the mid-nineteenth century.

ROBERT TIGNOR (*Ph.D. Yale University*) is professor emeritus and the Rosengarten Professor of Modern and Contemporary History at Princeton University and the three-time chair of the history department. With Gyan Prakash, he introduced Princeton's first course in world history nearly twenty years ago. Professor Tignor has taught graduate and undergraduate courses in African history and world history and written extensively on the history of twentieth-century Egypt, Nigeria, and Kenya. Besides his many research trips to Africa, Professor Tignor has taught at the University of Ibadan in Nigeria and the University of Nairobi in Kenya.

JEREMY ADELMAN (*D.Phil. Oxford University*) is currently the Director of the Council for International Teaching and Research at Princeton University and the Walter S. Carpenter III Professor of Spanish Civilization and Culture. He has written and edited five books, including *Republic of Capital: Buenos Aires and the Legal Transformation of the Atlantic World*, which won the best book prize in Atlantic history from the American Historical Association, and most recently *Sovereignty and Revolution in the Iberian Atlantic*. Professor Adelman is the recent recipient of a Guggenheim Memorial Foundation Fellowship and the Frederick Burkhardt Award from the American Council of Learned Societies.

STEPHEN ARON (*Ph.D. University of California, Berkeley*) is professor of history at the University of California, Los Angeles, and executive director of the Institute for the Study of the American West, Autry National Center. A specialist in frontier and Western American history, Aron is the author of *How the West Was Lost: The Transformation of Kentucky from Daniel Boone to Henry Clay* and *American Confluence: The Missouri Frontier from Borderland to Border State*. He is currently editing the multivolume *Autry History of the American West* and writing a book with the tentative title *Can We All Just Get Along: An Alternative History of the American West*.

PETER BROWN (*Ph.D. Oxford University*) is the Rollins Professor of History at Princeton University. He previously taught at London University and the University of California, Berkeley. He has written on the rise of Christianity and the end of the Roman Empire. His works include *Augustine of Hippo, The World of Late Antiquity, The Cult of the Saints, Body and Society, The Rise of Western Christendom,* and *Poverty and Leadership in the Later Roman Empire*. He is presently working on issues of wealth and poverty in the late Roman and early medieval Christian worlds.

BENJAMIN ELMAN (*Ph.D. University of Pennsylvania*) is professor of East Asian studies and history at Princeton University. He is currently serving as the chair of the Princeton East Asian Studies Department. He taught at the University of California, Los Angeles, for over fifteen years. His teaching and research fields include Chinese intellectual and cultural history, 1000–1900; the history of science in China, 1600–1930; the history of education in late imperial China; and Sino-Japanese cultural history, 1600–1850. He is the author of five books: *From Philosophy to Philology: Intellectual and Social Aspects of Change in Late Imperial China; Classicism, Politics, and Kinship: the Ch'ang-chou School of New Text Confucianism in Late Imperial China; A Cultural History of Civil Examinations in Late Imperial China; On Their Own Terms: Science in China, 1550–1900;* and *A Cultural History of Modern Science in China*. He is the creator of Classical Historiography for Chinese History at www.princeton.edu/~classbib/, a bibliography and teaching website published since 1996.

STEPHEN KOTKIN (*Ph.D. University of California, Berkeley*) is professor of European and Asian history as well as international affairs at Princeton University. He formerly directed Princeton's program in Russian and Eurasian studies (1996–2009). He is the author of *Magnetic Mountain: Stalinism as a Civilization, Uncivil Society: 1989 and the Implosion of the Communist Establishment*, and *Armageddon Averted: The Soviet Collapse, 1970–2000*. He is a coeditor of *Mongolia in the Twentieth Century: Landlocked Cosmopolitan*. Professor Kotkin has twice been a visiting professor in Japan.

XINRU LIU (*Ph.D. University of Pennsylvania*) is associate professor of early Indian history and world history at the College of New Jersey. She is associated with the Institute of World History and the Chinese Academy of Social Sciences. She is the author of *Ancient India and Ancient China, Trade and Religious Exchanges, ad 1–600; Silk and Religion, an Exploration of Material Life and the Thought of People, ad 600–1200; Connections across Eurasia, Transportation, Communication, and Cultural Exchange on the Silk Roads*, coauthored with Lynda Norene Shaffer; and *A Social History of Ancient India* (in Chinese). Professor Liu promotes South Asian studies and world history studies in both the United States and the People's Republic of China.

SUZANNE MARCHAND (*Ph.D. University of Chicago*) is professor of European and intellectual history at Louisiana State University, Baton Rouge. Professor Marchand also spent a number of years teaching at Princeton University. She is the author of *Down from Olympus: Archaeology and Philhellenism in Germany, 1750–1970* and *German Orientalism in the Age of Empire: Religion, Race and Scholarship*.

HOLLY PITTMAN (*Ph.D. Columbia University*) is professor of art history at the University of Pennsylvania, where she teaches art and archaeology of Mesopotamia and the Iranian Plateau. She also serves as curator in the Near East Section of the University of Pennsylvania Museum of Archaeology and Anthropology. Previously she served as a curator in the Ancient Near Eastern Art Department of the Metropolitan Museum of Art. She has written extensively on the art and culture of the Bronze Age in the Middle East and has participated in excavations in Cyprus, Turkey, Syria, Iraq, and Iran, where she currently works. Her research investigates works of art as media through which patterns of thought, cultural development, and historical interactions of ancient cultures of the Near East are reconstructed.

GYAN PRAKASH (*Ph.D. University of Pennsylvania*) is professor of modern Indian history at Princeton University and a member of the Subaltern Studies Editorial Collective. He is the author of *Bonded Histories: Genealogies of Labor Servitude in Colonial India, Another Reason: Science and the Imagination of Modern India*, and *Mumbai Fables*. Professor Prakash edited *After Colonialism: Imperial Histories and Postcolonial Displacements* and *Noir Urbanisms*, coedited *The Space of the Modern City* and *Utopia/Dystopia*, and has written a number of articles on colonialism and history writing. He is currently working on a history of the city of Bombay. With Robert Tignor, he introduced the modern world history course at Princeton University.

BRENT SHAW (*Ph.D. Cambridge University*) is the Andrew Fleming West Professor of Classics at Princeton University, where he is director of the Program in the Ancient World. He was previously at the University of Pennsylvania, where he chaired the Graduate Group in Ancient History. His principal areas of specialization as a Roman historian are Roman family history and demography, sectarian violence and conflict in Late Antiquity, and the regional history of Africa as part of the Roman Empire. He has published *Spartacus and the Slaves Wars*; edited the papers of Sir Moses Finley, *Economy and Society in Ancient Greece*; and published in a variety of books and journals, including the *Journal* *of Roman Studies*, the *American Historical Review*, the *Journal of Early Christian Studies*, and *Past & Present*.

MICHAEL TSIN (*Ph.D. Princeton*) is associate professor of history and international studies at the University of North Carolina at Chapel Hill. He previously taught at the University of Illinois at Chicago, Princeton University, Columbia University, and the University of Florida. Professor Tsin's primary interests include the histories of modern China and colonialism. He is the author of *Nation, Governance, and Modernity in China: Canton, 1900–1927*. He is currently writing a social history of the reconfiguration of Chinese identity in the twentieth century.

AP* EDITION

WORLDS TOGETHER,
WORLDS APART

Before You Read This Chapter

GLOBAL STORYLINES

- Communities, from long ago to today, produce creation narratives in order to make sense of how humans came into being.
- Hominid development across millions of years results in modern humans (*Homo sapiens*) and the traits that make us "human."
- During the period from 200,000 to 12,000 years ago, humans live as hunter-gatherers and achieve major breakthroughs in language and art.
- Global revolution in domesticating crops and animals leads to settled agricultural-based communities, while other communities develop pastoral ways of life.

CORE OBJECTIVES

- **DESCRIBE** various creation narratives traced in this chapter, including the narrative of human evolution, and **EXPLAIN** why they differ.
- **TRACE** the major developments in hominid evolution that resulted in the traits that make *Homo sapiens* "human."
- **DESCRIBE** human ways of life and cultural developments from 200,000 to 12,000 years ago.
- **COMPARE** the ways communities around the world shifted to settled agriculture and **ANALYZE** the significance this shift had for social organization.

CHAPTER

1

Becoming Human

KEY TERMS

australopithecines p. 6
creation narratives p. 4
domestication p. 22
evolution p. 5
hominids p. 5
Homo erectus p. 12
Homo habilis p. 12
Homo sapiens p. 14
hunting and gathering p. 20
pastoralism p. 23
settled agriculture p. 22

In 2003, in a remote corner of the Ethiopian highlands of Africa, a team of evolutionary biologists came upon fossil remains lodged in volcanic rock. Identifying and reassembling these remains took six years, but the researchers eventually reconstructed one of the most revealing sets of human fossils ever found: a nearly complete skeleton of an adult male, and the partial remains of another adult and a juvenile. By establishing the age of the volcanic rock, the team determined that the bones were about 160,000 years old. Although the skeletal remains were not identical to those of modern men and women, they were close enough to form part of the family of modern humans. In short, the bones represented the oldest record of *Homo sapiens*. The fossil finds confirmed what earlier studies had suggested: *Homo sapiens*, or modern humans, originated in a small region of Africa about 200,000 years ago and migrated out of Africa between 100,000 and 50,000 years ago.

Most of the common traits of human beings—the abilities to make tools, engage in family life, use language, and refine cognitive abilities—evolved over many millennia and crystallized around the time *Homo sapiens* migrated out of Africa. Only with the beginning of settled agriculture did significant cultural differences develop between groups of humans, as artifacts such as tools, cooking devices, and storage containers reveal. The differences in humankind's cultures are less than 15,000 or 20,000 years old.

This chapter lays out the origins of humanity from its common source. It shows how many different hominids (represented today by humans, chimpanzees, gorillas, and orangutans) preceded modern humans, and that humans came from only one—very recent—stock of hominid migrants out of Africa. Fanning out across the world, our ancestors adapted to environmental constraints and opportunities. They created languages, families, and clan systems, often innovating to defend themselves against predators. One of the biggest breakthroughs was the domestication of plants and animals and the creation of settled agriculture. With this development, humans could stop following food and begin producing it where they desired.

Creation Narratives

For thousands of years, humans have constructed, out of their values and available evidence, narratives of how the world, and humans, came to be. These **creation narratives** have varied over time and across cultures, depending on a society's values and the evidence available. To understand the origins of modern humans, we must come to terms with scales of time: the billions, millions, and hundreds of thousands of years through which the universe, earth, and life on it, developed into what they are today. Though the hominids that eventually evolved into modern humans lived millions of years ago, our tools for telling the modern creation narrative are relatively new.

COMPARISON

DESCRIBE the various creation narratives, and **EXPLAIN** why they differ.

Only 350 years ago, English clerics claimed on the basis of biblical calculations and Christian tradition that the first day of creation was Sunday, October 23, 4004 BCE. Modern science, however, indicates that the origin of the universe dates back 13.8 billion years, and the hominid separation from African pongids (members of the ape family) began 6 or 7 million years ago. These new discoveries have proved as mind-boggling to Hindus and Muslims as to Christians and Jews—all of whom believed, in different ways, that the universe was not so old and that divine beings had a role in creating it and all life, including the first humans. (See Going to the Source: Creation Narratives.) For millennia, human communities across the globe have constructed narratives that extend back differing lengths of time and suggest various roles for humans and gods in the process of universal creation. For instance, the Judeo-Christian narrative portrays a single God creating a universe out of nothingness, populating it with plants, animals, and humans, in a span of six days. The centuries-old creation story of the Yoruba peoples of West Africa depicts a divine being descending from the heavens in human form and becoming the godlike king Oduduwa, who established the Yoruba kingdom and the rules by which his subjects were to live. The foundational texts of Hinduism, which date to the seventh or sixth century BCE, account that the world is millions, not billions, of years old. Chinese Han dynasty (206 BCE–220 CE) astronomers believed that at the world's beginning the planets were conjoined and that they would merge again at the end of time. The Buddhists' cosmos comprised millions of worlds, each consisting of a mountain encircled by four continents, its seas surrounded by a wall of iron.

Yet even the million-year time frames and multiple planetary systems that ancient Asian thinkers endorsed did not prepare their communities for the idea that humans are related to apes. In all traditional cosmologies, humans came into existence fully formed, at a single moment, as did the other beings that populated the world. Modern discoveries about humanity's origins have challenged these traditions, because no tradition conceived that creatures evolved into new kinds of life, that humans had descended from apes, and that all of humanity originated in a remote corner of Africa.

Hominids to Modern Humans

The modern scientific creation narrative of human evolution would have been unimaginable even just over a century ago, when Charles Darwin was formulating his ideas about human origins. As we will see in this section, scientific discoveries have shown that modern humans evolved from earlier hominids. Through adaptation to their environment, various species of hominids developed new physical characteristics and distinctive skills. Millions of years after the first hominids appeared, the first modern humans—*Homo sapiens*—emerged and spread out across the globe.

EVOLUTIONARY FINDINGS AND RESEARCH METHODS

New insights into the time frame of the universe and human existence have occurred over a long period of time. Geologists made early breakthroughs in the eighteenth century when their research into the layers of the earth's surface revealed a world much older than biblical time implied. Evolutionary biologists, most notably Charles Darwin (1809–1882), concluded that all life had evolved over long periods from simple forms of matter. In the twentieth century astronomers, evolutionary biologists, and archaeologists have developed sophisticated dating techniques to pinpoint the chronology of the universe's creation and the evolution of all forms of life on earth. Their discoveries have radically transformed humanity's understanding of its own history (see **Current Trends in World History: Determining the Age of Fossils and Sediments**). A mere century ago, who would have accepted the idea that the universe came into being 13.7 billion years ago, that the earth appeared about 4.5 billion years ago, and that the earliest life forms began to exist about 3.8 billion years ago?

Yet, modern science suggests that human beings are part of a long evolutionary chain stretching from microscopic bacteria to African apes that appeared about 23 million years ago, and that Africa's "Great Ape" population separated into three distinct groups of **hominids**: one becoming present-day gorillas; the second becoming chimpanzees; and the third group becoming modern humans only after following a long and complicated evolutionary process. Our focus will be on the third group of hominids, who became modern humans. A combination of traits, evolving over several million years, distinguished humans from other hominids, including: (1) lifting the torso and walking on two legs (bipedalism), thereby freeing hands and arms to carry objects and hurl weapons; (2) controlling and then making fire; (3) fashioning and using tools; (4) developing cognitive skills and an enlarged brain and therefore the capacity for language; and (5) acquiring a consciousness of "self." All these traits were in place at least 150,000 years ago.

Two terms central to understanding any discussion of hominid development are evolution and natural selection. **Evolution** is the process by which species of plants and animals change and develop over generations, as certain traits are favored in reproduction. The process of evolution is driven by a mechanism called *natural selection*, in which members of a species with certain randomly occurring traits that are useful for environmental or other reasons survive and reproduce with greater success than those without the traits. Thus, biological evolution (human or otherwise) does not imply progress to higher forms of life, only successful adaptation to environmental surroundings.

EARLY HOMINIDS, ADAPTATION, AND CLIMATE CHANGE

The term *modern humans* refers to members of the *Homo sapiens* subspecies that evolved about 200,000 years ago. Through evolution, *Homo sapiens* developed the traits that make us distinct from the many other species and subspecies of hominids (such as the australopithecines, *Homo habilis,* and *Homo erectus* discussed in this section). "Modern" (and "recent") when applied to humans is relative, especially when compared to the life of the universe (which dates to 13.8 billion years ago) and even to the earliest hominids

Current Trends in World History

Determining the Age of Fossils and Sediments

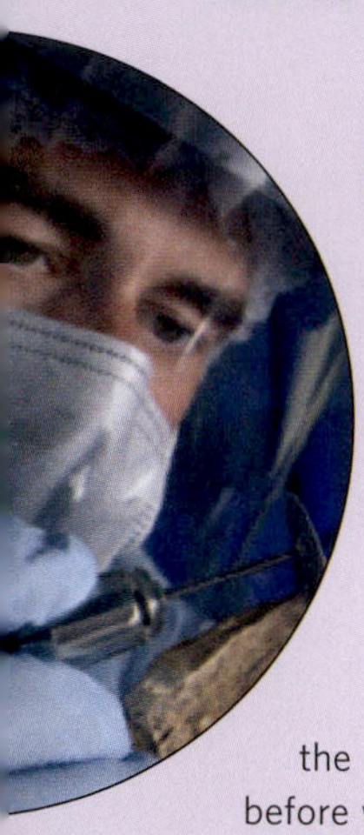

Our knowledge of human origins has been the result of several remarkable scientific breakthroughs. Only recently have scholars been able to date fossil remains and to use biological research to understand the relationships among the world's early peoples.

The first major advance in the study of prehistory (the time before written historical records) occurred in the mid-twentieth century, and it involved the use of *radiocarbon dating*. All living things contain the radiocarbon isotope C^{14}, which plants acquire directly from the atmosphere and animals acquire indirectly when they consume plants or other animals. When these living things die, the C^{14} isotope begins to decay into a stable nonradioactive element, C^{12}. Because the rate of decay is regular and measurable, it is possible to determine the age of fossils that leave organic remains for up to 40,000 years.

A second major dating technique, the *potassium-argon method*, also involves analysis of the changing chemical structure of objects over time. Scientists can calculate the age of nonliving objects by measuring the ratio of potassium to argon in them, since potassium decays into argon. This method allows scientists to calculate the age of objects up to a million years old. It also enables them to date the sediments in which researchers find fossils—as a gauge of the age of the fossils themselves.

DNA (deoxyribonucleic acid) analysis is a third crucial tool for unraveling the beginnings of modern humans. DNA, which determines biological inheritances, exists in two places within the cells of all living organisms—including the human body. *Nuclear DNA* occurs in the nucleus of every cell, where it controls most aspects of physical appearance and makeup. *Mitochondrial DNA* occurs outside the nucleus of cells and is located in mitochondria, structures used in converting the energy from food into a form that cells can use. Nuclear and mitochondrial DNA exists in males and females, but only mitochondrial DNA from females passes to their offspring, as the females' egg cells carry their mitochondria with their DNA to the offspring; sperm cells from males do not donate any DNA to the egg cell at fertilization. By examining mitochondrial DNA, researchers can measure genetic relatedness and variation among living organisms—including human beings. Such analysis has enabled researchers to pinpoint human descent from an original African population to other, genetically related populations that lived approximately 100,000 years ago.

The genetic similarity of modern humans suggests that the population from which all *Homo sapiens* descended originated in Africa about 200,000 years ago. When these humans began to move out of Africa around 100,000 years ago, they spread eastward into Southwest Asia and then throughout the rest of Afro-Eurasia. One group migrated to Australia about 50,000 years ago. Another group moved into the area of Europe about 40,000 years ago. When the scientific journal *Nature* published these findings in 1987, it inspired a groundswell of public interest—and a contentious scientific debate that continues today.

As this chapter demonstrates, the environment, especially climate, played a major role in the appearance of hominids and the eventual dominance of *Homo sapiens*. But how do we know so much about the world's climate going so far back in time? This brings us to the fourth of the scientific breakthroughs, known as marine isotope stages. By exploring the marine

(7 million years ago). This section's discussion demonstrates that as modern humans evolved from earlier hominids, they passed through successive waves of adaptation, innovation, and migration.

Australopithecines In 1924, near Johannesburg, South Africa, a scientist named Raymond Dart discovered the pint-sized skull and bones of a creature that had both ape-like and humanoid features. Dart labeled his bipedal find *Australopithecus africanus*. **Australopithecines** existed not only in southern Africa but in the north as well. In 1974, an archaeological team working at a site in present-day Ethiopia unearthed a relatively intact skeleton of a young adult female australopithecine in the valley of the Awash River. While the technical name for the find became *Australopithecus afarensis*, the researchers who found the skeleton gave it the nickname Lucy, based on the popular Beatles song "Lucy in the Sky with Diamonds."

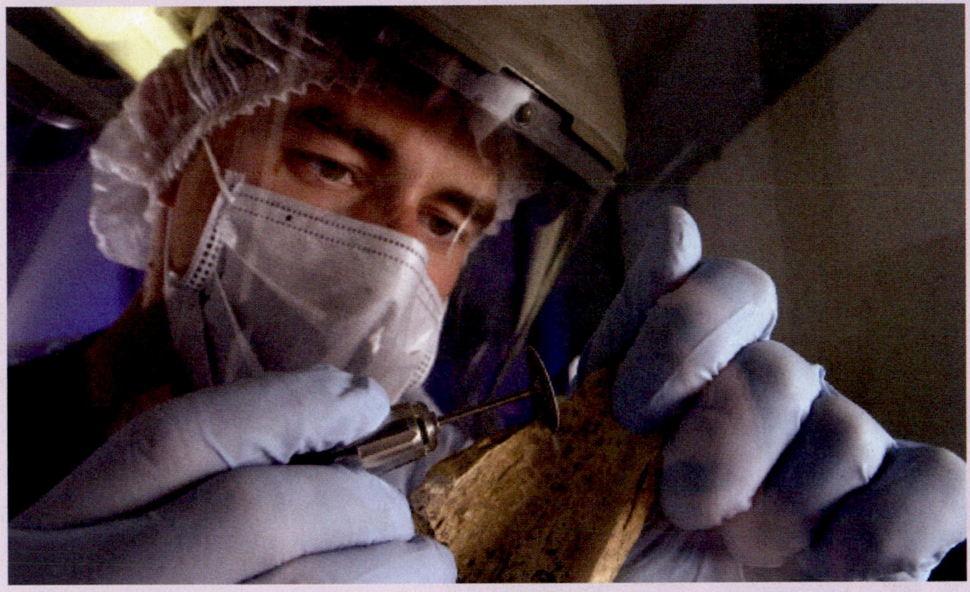

Neanderthal DNA Extraction This sample of fossilized bone from an early hominid will have its genetic material extracted and sequenced.

life, mainly pollen and plankton, deposited in deep seabeds and measuring the levels of oxygen-16 and oxygen-18 isotopes in these life forms, oceanographers and climatologists are able to determine the temperature of the world hundreds of thousands and even millions of years ago and thus to chart the cooling and warming cycles of the earth's climate.

QUESTIONS FOR ANALYSIS

- How has the study of prehistory changed since the mid-twentieth century? What are the consequences?
- How does the study of climate and environment relate to the origins of humans?

Explore Further

Lawrence Barham and Peter Mitchell, *The First Africans: African Archaeology from the Earliest Toolmakers to Most Recent Foragers* (2008).

Graeme Barker, *Agricultural Revolution in Prehistory: Why Did Foragers Become Farmers* (2006).

Lucy was remarkable. She stood a little over three feet tall, she walked upright, her skull contained a brain within the ape size range (i.e., one-third human size), and her jaw and teeth were human-like. Her arms were long, hanging halfway from her hips to her knees—suggesting that she might not have been bipedal at all times and sometimes resorted to arms for locomotion, in the fashion of a modern baboon. Above all, Lucy's skeleton was relatively complete and showed us that hominids were walking around as early as 3 million years ago. (See Table 1.1.) It is important to emphasize that australopithecines were not humans but that they carried the genetic and biological material out of which modern humans would later emerge. These precursors to modern humans had a key trait for evolutionary survival: they were remarkably good adapters. They could deal with dynamic environmental shifts, and they were intelligent.

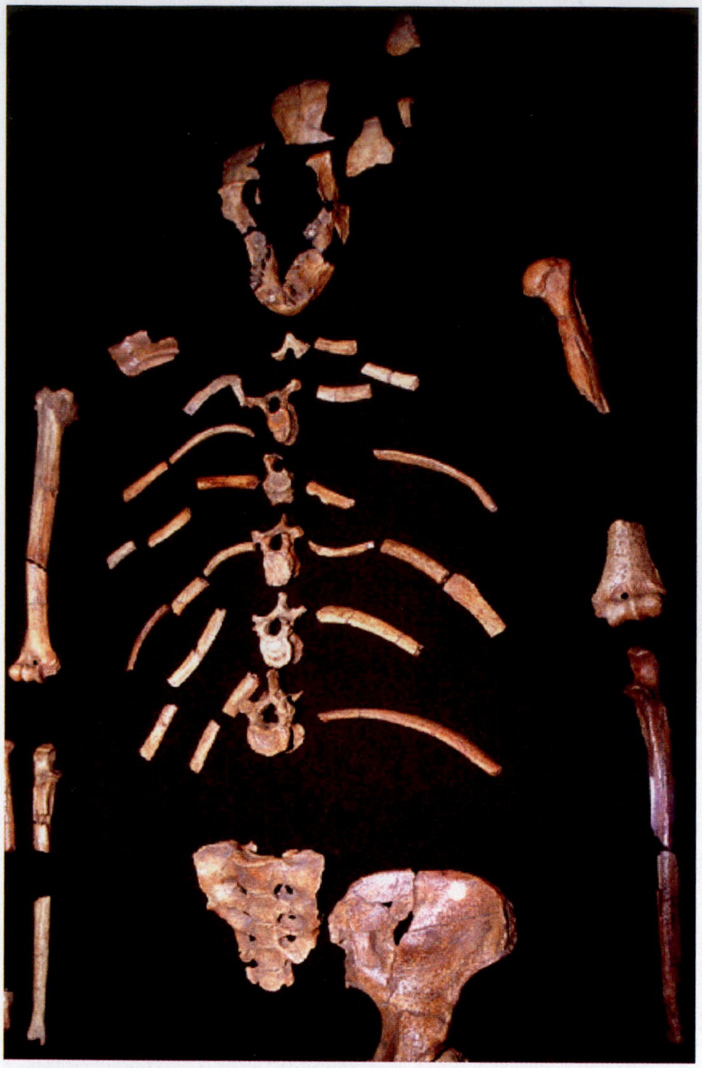

Fossil Bones of Lucy Archaeologist Donald Johanson discovered the fossilized bones of this young female in the Afar region of Ethiopia. Lucy's bones are believed to date from approximately 3.2 million years ago and provide evidence of some of the first hominids to appear in Africa. This find was of great importance because the bones were so fully and completely preserved.

TABLE 1.1 | Human Evolution

SPECIES	TIME
Orrorin tugenensis	6 MILLION YEARS AGO
Australopithecus anamensis	4.2 MILLION YEARS AGO
Australopithecus afarensis (INCLUDING LUCY)	3.4 MILLION YEARS AGO
Australopithecus africanus	3.0 MILLION YEARS AGO
Homo habilis (INCLUDING DEAR BOY)	2.5 MILLION YEARS AGO
Homo erectus and *Homo ergaster* (INCLUDING JAVA AND PEKING MAN)	1.8 MILLION YEARS AGO
Homo heidelbergensis (COMMON ANCESTOR OF *NEANDERTHALS* AND *HOMO SAPIENS*)	600,000 YEARS AGO
Neanderthals	200,000 YEARS AGO
Homo sapiens	200,000 YEARS AGO
Homo sapiens sapiens (MODERN HUMANS)	35,000 YEARS AGO

COMPARISON

TRACE the major developments in hominid evolution that resulted in the traits that make *Homo sapiens* "human."

Adaptation For hominids, like the rest of the plant and animal world, survival required constant adaptation (the ability to alter behavior and to innovate, finding new ways of doing things). During the first millions of years of hominid existence, these slow changes involved primarily physical adaptations to the environment. The places where researchers have found early hominid remains in southern and eastern Africa had environments that changed from being heavily forested and well watered to being arid and desert-like, and then back again. (See Map 1.1.) Hominids had to keep pace with these changing physical environments or else risk extinction. In fact, many of the early hominid groups did die out.

In adapting, early hominids began to distinguish themselves from other mammals that were physically similar to themselves. It was not their hunting prowess that made the hominids stand out, because plenty of other species chased their prey with skill and dexterity. The single trait that gave early hominids a real advantage for survival was bipedalism: they became "two-footed" creatures that stood upright. At some point, the first hominids were able to remain upright and move about, leaving their arms and hands free for other useful tasks, like carrying food over long distances. Once they ventured into open savannas (grassy plains with a few scattered trees), about 1.7 million years ago, hominids had a tremendous advantage. They were the only primates (an order of mammals consisting of man, apes, and monkeys) to move consistently on two legs. Because

MAP 1.1 | Early Hominids

The earliest hominid species evolved in Africa millions of years ago.

- Judging from this map, what were the main geographic features of their environment?
- According to this chapter, how did the changing environment of eastern and southern Africa shape the evolution of these modern human ancestors?

they could move continuously and over great distances, they were able to migrate out of hostile environments and into more hospitable locations.

Environmental Changes The climate in eastern and southern Africa, where hominid development began, was conducive to the development of diverse plant and animal species. When the world entered its fourth great ice age approximately 40 million years ago, the earth's temperatures dropped and its continental ice sheets, polar ice sheets, and mountain glaciers increased. This ice age lasted until 12,000 years ago. Like all ice ages, this fourth ice age had alternating warming and cooling phases that lasted between 40,000 and 100,000 years each. Between 15 and 10 million years ago, the climate in Africa went through one such cooling and drying phase. To the east of Africa's Rift Valley, stretching from South Africa north to the Ethiopian highlands, the cooling and drying forced forests to contract and savannas to spread. It was in this region that some apes left the shelter of the trees, stood up, and learned to walk, to run, and to live in savanna lands—thus becoming the precursors to humans, and distinctive as a new species.

Using two feet for locomotion augmented the means for obtaining food and avoiding predators and improved the chances these creatures had to survive in constantly changing environments. In addition to being bipedal, hominids had opposable thumbs. This trait, shared with other primates, gave hominids great physical dexterity, enhancing their ability to explore and to alter materials found in nature. Manual dexterity and standing upright also enabled them to carry young family members if they needed to relocate, or to throw missiles (such as rocks and sticks) with deadly accuracy to protect themselves or to obtain food.

Hominids used their increased powers of observation and memory, what we call cognitive skills, to gather wild berries and grains and to scavenge the meat and marrow of animals that had died of natural causes or as the prey of predators. All primates are good at these activities, but hominids came to excel at them. Cognitive skills, which also included problem solving and—eventually—language, were destined to become the basis for further developments. Early hominids were highly social. They lived in bands of about twenty-five individuals, trying to survive by hunting small game and gathering wild plants. Not yet a match for large predators, they had to find safe hiding places. They thrived in places where a diverse supply of wild grains and fruits and abundant wildlife ensured a secure, comfortable existence. In such locations, small hunting bands of twenty-five could swell through alliances with others to as many as 500 individuals. Like other primates, hominids communicated through gestures, but they also may have developed a very basic form of spoken language that led (among other things) to the establishment of rudimentary cultural codes such as common rules, customs, and identities.

Early hominids lived in this manner for up to 3 million years, changing their way of life very little except for moving around the African landmass in their never-ending search for more favorable environments. Even so, their survival is surprising. There were not many of them, and they struggled in hostile environments surrounded by a diversity of large mammals, including predators such as lions.

As the environment changed over the millennia, these early hominids gradually changed as well. Over a period of 3 million years, their brains more than doubled in size; their foreheads became more elongated; their jaws became less massive; and they took on a much more human look. Adaptation to environmental changes also created new skills and aptitudes, which expanded the ability to store and analyze information. With larger brains, hominids could form mental maps of their worlds—they could learn, remember what they learned, and convey these lessons to their neighbors and offspring. In this fashion, larger groups of hominids created communities with shared understandings of their environments.

Diversity Recent discoveries in Ethiopia and Kenya suggest that hominids were both older and more diverse than early australopithecine finds had suggested. In southern

Kenya in 2000, researchers excavated bone remains, at least 6 million years old, of a chimpanzee-sized hominid (named *Orrorin tugenensis*) that walked upright on two feet. This discovery indicates that bipedalism must be millions of years older than scientists thought based on Lucy and the earlier *Australopithecus africanus* discovery. Moreover, these hominids' teeth indicate that they were closer to modern humans than to australopithecines. In their arms and hands, though, which show characteristics needed for tree climbing, the *Orrorin* hominids seemed more ape-like than the australopithecines. So *Orrorin* hominids were still somewhat tied to an environment in the trees. Other fossils, found at sites in the Afar depression in Ethiopia (just south of the area where Lucy was found) and in northern Kenya, have revealed additional distinct species of early hominids.

The fact that different kinds of early hominids were living in isolated societies and evolving separately, though in close proximity to one another, in eastern Africa between 4 and 3 million years ago indicates much greater diversity among their populations than scholars previously imagined. The environment in eastern Africa generated a fair number of different hominid populations, a few of which would provide our genetic base, but most of which would not survive in the long run.

TOOL-USE BY *HOMO HABILIS*

One million years after Lucy, the first beings whom we assign to the genus *Homo*, or "true human," appeared. Like early hominids, *Homo habilis* was bipedal, possessing a smooth walk based on upright posture. *Homo habilis* had an even more important advantage over other hominids: brains that were growing larger. Big brains are the site of innovation: learning and storing lessons so that humans could pass those lessons on to later generations, especially in the making of tools and the efficient use of resources (and, we suspect, in defending themselves). Mary and Louis Leakey, who made astonishing fossil discoveries in the 1950s at Olduvai Gorge in present-day north central Tanzania, identified these important traits. The Leakeys' finds included an intact skull that was 1.8 million years old. They nicknamed the creature whose skull they had unearthed Dear Boy.

The Leakeys Louis Leakey and his wife, Mary, were dedicated archaeologists whose work in East Africa established the area as one of the starting points of human development. Mary Leakey was among the most successful archaeologists studying hominids in Africa. Her finds, including the one in this photograph from Laetoli, Tanzania, highlight the activities of early men and women in Africa. The footprints, believed to be those of an *Australopithecus afarensis*, date from 3.7 to 3 million years ago.

Objects discovered with Dear Boy demonstrated that by this time early humans had begun to make tools for butchering animals and, possibly, for hunting and killing smaller animals. The tools were flaked stones with sharpened edges for cutting apart animal flesh and scooping out the marrow from bones. To mimic the slicing teeth of lions, leopards, and other carnivores, these early humans had devised these tools through careful chipping. Dear Boy and his companions had carried usable rocks to distant places where they made their implements with special hammer stones—tools to make tools. Unlike other tool-using animals (for example, chimpanzees), early humans were now intentionally fashioning implements, not simply finding them when needed. More

Olduvai Gorge, Tanzania Olduvai Gorge is arguably the most famous archaeological site containing hominid finds. Mary and Louis Leakey, convinced that early human beings originated in Africa, discovered the fossil remains of *Homo habilis* ("Skillful Man") in this area beginning in 1959. They argued that these findings represent a direct link to *Homo erectus*.

important, they were passing on knowledge of these tools to their offspring and, in the process, gradually improving the tools. The Leakeys, believing that making and using tools represented a new stage in the evolution of human beings, gave Dear Boy and his companions the name ***Homo habilis***, or "Skillful Man." While scholars today may debate whether tool making (rather than walking upright or having a large brain) is the key trait that distinguishes the first humans from earlier hominids, *Homo habilis*'s skills made them the forerunners, though very distant, of modern men and women.

MIGRATIONS OF *HOMO ERECTUS*

By 1 million years ago many of the hominid species that flourished together in Africa had died out. One surviving species, which emerged about 1.8 million years ago, had a large brain capacity and walked truly upright; it therefore gained the name ***Homo erectus***, or "Standing Man." Three important features distinguished *Homo erectus* from their competitors and made them more able to cope with environmental changes: their family dynamics, use of fire, and ability to travel long distances. Discoveries in Asia and Europe show that *Homo erectus* migrated out of Africa in some of the earliest waves of hominid migration around the globe.

Family Dynamics One of the traits that contributed to the survival of *Homo erectus* was the development of extended periods of caring for their young. Although their enlarged brain gave these hominids advantages over the rest of the animal world, it also brought one significant problem: their heads were too large to pass through the females' pelvises at birth. Their pelvises were only big enough to deliver an infant with a cranial capacity that was about a third an adult's size. As a result, offspring required a long period of protection by adults as they matured and their brain size tripled.

This difference from other species also affected family dynamics. For example, the long maturing process gave adult members of hunting and gathering bands time to train their children in those activities. In addition, maturation and brain growth required mothers to spend years breast-feeding and then preparing food for children after their weaning. In order to share the responsibilities of child-rearing, mothers relied on other women (their own mothers, sisters, and friends) and girls (often their own daughters) to help in the nurturing and protecting, a process known as *allomothering* (literally, "other mothering").

Use of Fire *Homo erectus* began to make rudimentary attempts to control their environment by means of fire. It is hard to tell from fossils when humans learned to use fire. The most reliable evidence comes from cave sites less than 250,000 years old, where early humans apparently cooked some of their food, but some have suggested that hominid mastery of fire occurred as early as 500,000 years ago. Fire provided heat, protection, a gathering point for small communities, and a way to cook food. It was also symbolically powerful: here was a source of energy that humans could extinguish and revive at will. The uses of fire had enormous long-term effects on human evolution. Because they were able to boil, steam, and fry wild plants, as well as otherwise undigestible foods (especially raw muscle fiber), early humans could expand their diets. Because cooked foods yield more energy than raw foods and because the brain, while only 2 percent of human body weight, uses between 20 and 25 percent of all the energy that humans take in, cooking was decisive in the evolution of brain size and functioning.

Early Migrations Being bipedal, *Homo erectus* could move with a smooth and rapid gait, so they could cover large distances quickly. They were the world's first long-distance travelers, forming the first mobile human communities. Around 1 or 2 million years ago, *Homo erectus* individuals migrated first into the lands of Southwest Asia. From there, they traveled along the Indian Ocean shoreline, moving into South Asia and Southeast Asia and later northward into what is now China. Their migration was a response in part to the environmental changes that were transforming the world. The Northern Hemisphere experienced thirty major cold phases during this period, marked by glaciers spreading over vast expanses of the northern parts of Eurasia and the Americas. The glaciers formed as a result of intense cold that froze much of the world's oceans, lowering them some

Skulls of Ancestors of *Homo sapiens* Shown here are seven skulls of ancestors of modern-day men and women, arranged to highlight brain growth over time. The skulls represent (left to right): *Adapis*, a lemur-like animal that lived 50 million years ago; *Proconsul*, a primate that lived about 23 million years ago; *Australopithecus africanus*; *Homo habilis*; *Homo erectus*; *Homo sapiens* from the Qafzeh site in Israel, about 90,000 years old; and Cro-Magnon *Homo sapiens sapiens* from France, about 22,000 years old.

325 feet below present-day levels. These lower ocean levels made it possible for the migrants to travel across land bridges into Southeast Asia and from East Asia to Japan, as well as from New Guinea to Australia. The last parts of the Afro-Eurasian landmass to be occupied were in Europe.

Discoveries of the bone remains of "Java Man" and "Peking Man" (named according to the places where archaeologists first unearthed their remains) confirmed early settlements of *Homo erectus* in Southeast and East Asia. The remains of Java Man, found in 1891 on the island of Java, turned out to be those of an early *Homo erectus* that had dispersed into Asia nearly 2 million years ago. Peking Man, found near Beijing in the 1920s, was a cave dweller, toolmaker, and hunter and gatherer who settled in the warmer climate in northern China perhaps 400,000 years ago. Peking Man's brain was larger than that of his Javan cousins, and there is evidence that he controlled fire and cooked meat in addition to hunting large animals. He made tools of vein quartz, quartz crystals, flint, and sandstone. A major innovation was the double-faced axe, a stone instrument whittled down to sharp edges on both sides to serve as a hand axe, a cleaver, a pick, and probably a weapon to hurl against foes or animals. Even so, these early predecessors still lacked the intelligence, language skills, and ability to create culture that would distinguish the first modern humans from their hominid relatives.

HOMO SAPIENS: THE FIRST MODERN HUMANS

Homo sapiens—a bigger-brained, more dexterous, and more agile species of humans that appeared in the highlands of eastern Africa about 200,000 years ago—differed notably from their precursors, including *Homo habilis* and *Homo erectus*. Their distinctive traits, including greater cognitive skills, made *Homo sapiens* the first modern humans and enabled them to spread out from Africa and flourish in even more diverse regions across the globe than *Homo erectus* did.

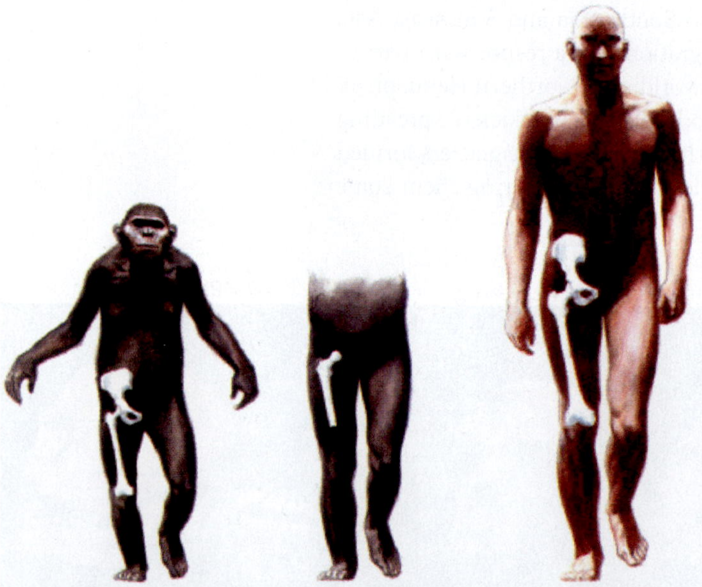

The Physical Evolution of Hominids These three figures show the femur bones of Lucy, *Orrorin tugenensis* (one of the earliest of the hominids, who may have existed as many as 6 million years ago), and *Homo sapiens*. *Homo sapiens* have a larger femur bone and were bigger than Lucy was—a representative of the hominid species *Australopithecus afarensis*—but have the same bone structure.

Large-scale shifts in Africa's climate and environment about 200,000 years ago put huge pressures on all types of mammals, including hominids. In these extremely warm and dry environments, the smaller, quicker, and more adaptable mammals survived. What counted now was no longer large size and brute strength, but the ability to respond quickly, with agility, and with great speed. The eclipse of *Homo erectus* by *Homo sapiens* was not inevitable. After all, *Homo erectus* was already scattered around Africa and Eurasia by the time *Homo sapiens* emerged; in contrast, current thinking suggests that even as late as 100,000 years ago there were only about 10,000 *Homo sapiens* adults living in a small part of the African landmass. But when *Homo sapiens* moved out of Africa and the two species encountered each other in the same places across the globe, *Homo sapiens* individuals were better suited to survive—in part because of their greater cognitive and language skills.

The *Homo sapiens* newcomers followed the trails blazed by earlier migrants when they moved out of Africa sometime between 120,000 and 50,000 years ago. (See Map 1.2.) In many places, they moved into the same areas as their genetic cousins, moving across Southwest Asia and from there into central Asia—but not into the area of Europe. They flourished and reproduced. By 30,000 years ago, the population of *Homo sapiens* had grown to about 300,000. Between 60,000 and 12,000 years ago, these modern humans were surging into areas tens of thousands of miles from the Rift Valley and the Ethiopian highlands of Africa (see **Analyzing Global Developments: The Age of the Universe and Human Evolution**).

In the area of present-day China, *Homo sapiens* were thriving and creating distinct regional cultures. Consider Shandingdong Man, a *Homo sapiens* who dates to about 18,000 years ago. His physical characteristics were closer to those of modern humans, and he had a similar brain size. His stone tools, which included choppers and scrapers for preparing food, were similar to those of the *Homo erectus* Peking Man. His bone needles, however, were the first stitching tools of their kind found in China, and they indicated the making of garments. Some of the needles measured a little over an inch in length and had small holes drilled in them. Shandingdong Man also buried his dead. In fact, a tomb of grave goods includes ornaments suggesting the development of aesthetic tastes and religious beliefs.

Homo sapiens were also migrating into the northeastern fringe of East Asia. In the frigid climate there, they learned to follow herds of large Siberian grazing animals. The bones and dung of mastodons made decent fuel and good building material. Pursuing their prey eastward as the large-tusked herds sought pastures in the steppes (treeless grasslands) and marshes, these groups migrated across the ice to Japan. Archaeologists have discovered a mammoth fossil in the colder north of Japan, for example, and an elephant fossil in the warmer south. Elephants in particular roamed the warmer parts of Inner Eurasia. The hunters and gatherers who moved into Japan gathered wild plants for sustenance, and they dried, smoked, or broiled meat by using fire.

About 16,000 years ago, *Homo sapiens* began edging into the weedy landmass that linked Siberia and North America (which hominids had not populated). This thousand-mile-long land bridge, later called Beringia, must have seemed like an extension of familiar steppe-land terrain. For thousands of years, modern humans poured eastward and southward into North America. The oldest known location of human settlement in the Americas is Broken Mammoth, a 14,000-year-old site in central Alaska. A final migration occurred about 8,000 years ago by boat, since by then the land bridge had disappeared under the sea. (See Table 1.2.)

Using their cognitive abilities to adapt to new environments and to innovate, these migrants, who were the first discoverers of America, began to fill up the landmasses. They found ample prey in the herds of woolly mammoths, caribou, three-ton giant sloths, and 200-pound beavers. But the explorers could also themselves be prey—for they encountered saber-toothed tigers, long-legged eagles, and giant bears that moved faster than horses. The melting of the glaciers about 8,000 years ago and the resulting disappearance of the land bridge eventually cut off the first Americans from their Afro-Eurasian origins. Thereafter, the Americas became a world apart from Afro-Eurasia.

COMPARISON

COMPARE the narrative of human evolution to the creation narratives covered earlier.

Although modern humans evolved from earlier hominids, no straight-line descent tree exists from the first hominids to *Homo sapiens*. Increasingly, scientists view our origins as shaped by a series of progressions and regressions as hominid species adapted or failed to adapt and died out. The remains of now-extinct hominid species, such as *Homo ergaster*, *Homo heidelbergensis*, and *Homo neanderthalis* (see Table 1.1), offer intriguing glimpses of ultimately unsuccessful branches of the complex human evolutionary tree. Spreading into Europe and parts of Southwest Asia along with other hominids, Neanderthals, for example, had big brains, used tools, wore clothes, buried their dead, hunted, lived in rock

ARCTIC OCEAN
NORTH SEA
EUROPE
AFRO - EURASIA
INNER ASIA
by 25,000 BCE
CASPIAN SEA
ARAL SEA
BLACK SEA
CENTRAL ASIA
50-40,000 BCE
MEDITERRANEAN SEA
by 60,000 BCE
SOUTHWEST ASIA
EAST ASIA
100,000 BCE
100,000 BCE
AFRICA
SOUTH ASIA
ARABIAN SEA
Bay of Bengal
SOUTHEAST ASIA
SOUTH CHINA SEA
ATLANTIC OCEAN
INDIAN OCEAN
120,000 BCE
60-50,000 BCE
AUSTRALIA
Spread of Homo erectus before 200,000 years ago
Colonization of Homo sapiens
Area occupied by Homo neanderthalensis
Area occupied by Homo erectus
Coastline at time of glacial maximum
Maximum extent of ice sheets c.16,000 BCE
Land exposed by lower sea level c. 16,000 BCE
0 1000 2000 Miles
0 1000 2000 Kilometers

MAP 1.2 | Early Migrations: Out of Africa

Hominid species began migrating out of Africa hundreds of thousands of years ago, but only *Homo sapiens* went to all major inhabitable regions.

- According to this map, what regions did *Homo sapiens* spread to, and in what order?
- How did geography shape each species' migration patterns?
- Based on your reading of the chapter, why do you think *Homo sapiens* migrated to more distant lands than *Homo erectus* did?

Analyzing Global Developments

The Age of the Universe and Human Evolution

Our universe is nearly 14 billion years old. Our sun, earth, and solar system appeared nearly 4.5 billion years ago, and the earliest life forms on earth appeared 3.8 billion years ago. Hominids, however, only appeared on the scene about 7 million years ago, which represents not even 1 percent of the total time that the earth has existed. They were for a long time confined to the African landmass, learning to walk on two legs there, devising simple tools at first and perfecting their use over time. Africa remained the homeland for many different hominid groups for nearly 5 million years before *Homo erectus* ventured out of the continent, moving into central Asia, East Asia, Southeast Asia, and Europe, though not into the Americas. There were probably other waves of hominid migrations out of Africa, but the most important of the migrations out of Africa occurred between 100,000 and 50,000 years ago when modern humans, *Homo sapiens*, left the continent and, with amazing rapidity, filled up all of the globe's landmasses. (See Map 1.2 to trace the migrations of *Homo erectus* and *Homo sapiens*.)

QUESTIONS FOR ANALYSIS

- Describe how we know the age of the universe. How do we know when and how hominids first appeared and their evolutionary patterns?
- Explain why hominids and *Homo sapiens* are so late in the evolutionary cycle. Why did they prevail over other hominids?
- In your opinion, which of the different families of hominids deserves the designation of the first humans and why?
- Why are scientists disinclined to see a straight-line evolution from the earliest hominids to modern humans?

The Big Bang Moment in the Creation of the Universe	13.8 BILLION YEARS AGO (BYA)	
The Formation of the Sun, Earth, and Solar System	4.5 BYA	
Earliest Life Forms appear	3.8 BYA	
Multicellular Organisms appear	1.5 BYA	
First Hominids appear	7 MILLION YEARS AGO (MYA)	<1% of Earth's Existence
Australopithecus afarensis appears (including Lucy)	3.4 MYA	
Homo habilis appears (including Dear Boy)	2.5 MYA	
Homo erectus appears (including Java and Peking Man)	1.8 MYA	
Homo erectus leave Africa	1.5 MYA	
Neanderthals appear	200,000 YEARS AGO	
Homo sapiens appear	200,000 YEARS AGO	
Homo sapiens leave Africa	100,000 to 50,000 YEARS AGO	
Homo sapiens migrate into Asia	50,000 YEARS AGO	
Homo sapiens migrate into Europe	40–50,000 YEARS AGO	
Homo sapiens migrate into Australia	40,000 YEARS AGO	
Homo sapiens migrate into the Americas	16,000 YEARS AGO	
Homo sapiens sapiens appear (modern humans)	35,000 YEARS AGO	

Sources: Chris Scarre (ed.), *The Human Past: World Prehistory and the Development of Human Societies* (2005); Ian Tattersall, *Masters of the Planet: The Search for Our Human Origins* (2012).

shelters, and even interacted with *Homo sapiens*. Yet when faced with environmental challenges, *Homo sapiens* survived, while Neanderthals died out 38,000 years ago.

Indeed, several species could exist simultaneously, but some were more suited to changing environmental conditions—and thus more likely to survive—than others. Although the examples emphasized in this chapter—*Homo habilis* and *Homo erectus*—were among some of the world's first human-like inhabitants, they probably were not direct ancestors of modern men and women. By 25,000 years ago, DNA analysis reveals, nearly all genetic cousins to *Homo sapiens* had become extinct. *Homo sapiens*, with their physical agility and superior cognitive skills, were ready to populate the world.

TABLE 1.2 | Migrations of *Homo sapiens*

SPECIES	TIME
Homo erectus leave Africa	c. 1.5 MILLION YEARS AGO
Homo sapiens leave Africa	c. 100,000 to 50,000 YEARS AGO
Homo sapiens migrate into Asia	c. 50,000 YEARS AGO
migrate into Europe	c. 50–40,000 YEARS AGO
migrate into Australia	c. 40,000 YEARS AGO
migrate into the Americas	c. 16–11,000 YEARS AGO

The Life of Early *Homo Sapiens*

COMPARISON

DESCRIBE human ways of life and cultural developments from 200,000 to 12,000 years ago.

In the period from 200,000 to around 12,000 years ago, early *Homo sapiens* were similar to other hominids in that they lived by hunting and gathering, but their use of language and new cultural forms represented an evolutionary breakthrough. Earlier hominids could not form large, lasting communities, as they had limited communication skills. While simple commands and hand signals developed over time, complex linguistic expression escaped them. This achievement was one of the last in the evolutionary process of becoming human; it did not occur until between 100,000 and 50,000 years ago. Many scholars view it as the critical ingredient in distinguishing human beings from other animals. It is this skill that made *Homo sapiens* "sapiens," which is to say "wise" or "intelligent"—humans who could create culture.

LANGUAGE

Few things set *Homo sapiens* off from the rest of the animal world more starkly than their use of language. Although the beginnings and development of language are controversial, scholars agree that the cognitive abilities involved in language development marked an evolutionary milestone. Some earlier hominids could express themselves by grunting, but natural language (the use of sounds to make words that convey meaning to others) is unique to modern humans. The development of language required a large brain and complex cognitive organization to create word groups that would convey symbolic meaning. Verbal communication required an ability to think abstractly and to communicate abstractions. Language was a huge breakthrough, because individuals could teach words and ideas to neighbors and offspring. Language thus enhanced the ability to accumulate knowledge that could be transmitted across both space and time.

Biological research has demonstrated that humans can make and process many more primary and distinctive sounds, called phonemes, than other animals can. Whereas a human being can utter fifty phonemes, an ape can form only twelve. Also, humans can process sounds more quickly than other primates can. With fifty phonemes it is possible to create more than 100,000 words; by arranging those words in different sequences and developing rules in language, individuals can express countless subtle and complex meanings. Recent research suggests that use of complex languages occurred about 100,000 years ago and that the nearest approximation to humanity's earliest language existing today belongs to two African peoples, the !Kung of southern Africa and the Hadza

MAP 1.3 | Original Language Family Groups

The use of complex language developed 100,000 years ago among *Homo sapiens* in Africa. As humans dispersed throughout the globe, nineteen language families evolved from which all modern languages originate.

- How many different landmasses did language evolve on? Which landmasses have a greater number of language families and why might that be?
- On the basis of this map, what geographic features kept emerging language families distinct from one another?
- Why do you think separate languages emerged over time?

of Tanzania. These peoples make a clicking sound by dropping the tongue down from the roof of the mouth and exhaling. As humans moved out of Africa and spread around the globe, they expanded their original language into nineteen language families, from which all of the world's languages then evolved. (See Map 1.3.) It was the development of language and the cultural forms discussed later in this section that allowed *Homo sapiens* to engage dynamically with their environments.

HUNTING AND GATHERING

Although these early humans were developing language skills that distinguished them from their hominid relatives, like their predecessors they remained hunters and gatherers until around 12,000 years ago (for almost 95 percent of our existence). As late as 1500 CE, as much as 15 percent of the world's population still lived by **hunting and gathering.** Early *Homo sapiens* hunted animals, fished, and foraged for wild berries, nuts, fruit, and grains, rather than planting crops, vines, or trees. Even today hunting and gathering societies endure, although only in the most marginal locations—often at the edge of deserts. Researchers consider the present-day San peoples of southern Africa as an isolated remnant continuing their traditional hunting-and-gathering modes of life. Modern scholars use the San to reveal how men and women must have lived hundreds of thousands of years ago.

The fact that hominid men and women (going back to *Homo erectus* and *habilis* and beyond) survived as hunters and gatherers for millions of years, that early *Homo sapiens* also lived this way, and that a few contemporary communities still forage for food suggests the powerful attractions of this way of life. Hunters and gatherers could find enough food in about three hours of foraging each day, thus affording time for other pursuits such as relaxation, interaction, and friendly competitions with other members of their bands. Scholars believe that these small bands were relatively egalitarian compared with the more male-dominated societies that arose later. They speculate that men specialized in hunting and women specialized in gathering and childrearing. Scholars also believe that women made a larger contribution and had high status because the dietary staples of the community were cereals and fruits, whose harvesting and preparation were likely women's responsibility.

The San Hunters and Gatherers of Southern Africa The San, who live in the Kalahari Desert in present-day Botswana, continue to follow a hunting and gathering existence that has died out in many parts of the world. Hunting and gathering was the way that most humans lived for millennia.

PAINTINGS, SCULPTURE, AND MUSIC

The ability to draw allowed *Homo sapiens* to understand their environment, to bond among their kin groups (groups related by blood ties), and to articulate important mythologies. Accomplished artwork from this era has been found across Afro-Eurasia. For instance, in a deep cave at Altamira in Spain more than two dozen life-size figures of bison, horses, and wild bulls, all painted in vivid red, black, yellow, and brown, are arranged across the ceiling of the huge chamber. More than 50,000 similarly stunning works of art have been found in caves across Europe and elsewhere. The images on cave walls accumulated over a period of 25,000 years, and they changed little in that time. The subjects are often large game—animals that early humans would have considered powerful symbols. The artists rendered these animals in such a way that the natural contours of the cave wall defined a bulging belly or an eye socket. The remarkably few human images show hunters, naked females, or dancing males. There are also many handprints made by blowing paint around a hand placed on the cave wall, or by dipping hands in paint and then pressing them to the wall. There are even abstract symbols such as circles, wavy lines, and checkerboards; often these appear at places of transition in the caves.

Scholars have rejected an initial theory that these paintings were decorative, for the deep caves were not homes and had no natural light to render the images visible. Perhaps the images helped the early humans to define themselves as separate from other parts of nature. Alternatively, they might have been the work of powerful shamans, individuals believed to hold special powers to understand and control the forces of the cosmos. The subjects and the style of the paintings are similar to images engraved or painted on rocks by some hunter-and-gatherer societies living today, especially the San and the !Kung peoples of southern Africa. In those societies, paintings mark important places of ritual: shamans make them during trances while mediating with the spirit world on behalf of their communities.

Paintings were not the only form of artistic expression for early humans. Archaeologists also have unearthed small sculptures of animals shaped out of bone and stone that are even older than the paintings. Most famous are figurines of rotund, and perhaps pregnant females. Statuettes like the so-called Venus of Willendorf, found in Austria, demonstrate that successful reproduction was a very important theme. Other sculptures represent animals in postures of movement or at rest.

The caves of early men and women also resounded to the strains of music. In 2008 archaeologists working in southwestern Germany discovered a hollowed-out bone flute with five openings that they dated to approximately 35,000 years ago, roughly the same time that humans began to occupy this region. When researchers put the flute to musical tests, they also concluded that the instrument was capable of making harmonic sounds comparable to those of modern-day flutes.

Only *Homo sapiens* had the cognitive abilities to produce the abundant sculptures and drawings of this era, thus leaving a permanent mark on the symbolic landscape of human development. Such visual expressions marked the dawn of human culture and a consciousness of men's and women's place in the world. Symbolic activity of this sort enabled humans to make sense of themselves, nature, and the relationship between humanity and nature. That relationship with nature—which had remained static for hundreds of thousands of years of hunting and gathering—would change with the agricultural revolution.

Agricultural Revolution: Food Production and Social Change

About 12,000 years ago (around 10,000 BCE), a fundamental shift occurred in the way humans produced food for themselves—what some scholars have called an agricultural, or ecological, revolution. Around the same time, a significant warming trend that had begun around 11,000 BCE resulted in a profusion of plants and animals, large numbers of which began to exist closer to humans. In this era of major change, humans established greater control over nature. The transformation consisted of the **domestication** (the bringing under human control) of wild plants and animals. Population pressure was one factor that triggered the move to settled agriculture, as hunting and gathering alone could not sustain the growth in numbers of people. A revolution in agriculture, in turn, led to a vast population expansion because men and women could now produce more calories per unit of land. As various plants and animals were domesticated around the world, people settled in villages and social relationships changed.

Domestication This detail from a wall painting in the Tassili n'Ajjer mountain range in modern Algeria depicts early domestication of cattle and other animals.

THE BEGINNINGS OF SETTLED AGRICULTURE AND PASTORALISM

Learning to control environments through the domestication of plants and animals was a gradual process. Communities shifted from a hunting-and-gathering lifestyle (which requires moving around in search of food) to one based on agriculture (which requires staying in one place until the soil has been exhausted). **Settled agriculture** refers to the application of human labor and tools to a fixed plot of land for more than one growing cycle. Alternatively, some people adopted a lifestyle based on **pastoralism** (the herding of domesticated animals), which complemented settled farming.

Early Domestication of Plants and Animals The formation of settled communities enabled humans to take advantage of favorable regions and to take risks, spurring agricultural innovation. In areas with abundant wild game and edible plants, people began to observe and experiment with the most adaptable plants. For ages, people gathered grains by collecting seeds that fell freely from their stalks. At some point, observant collectors perceived that they could obtain larger harvests if they pulled grain seeds directly from plants. The process of plant domestication probably began when people noticed that certain edible plants retained their nutritious grains longer than others, so they collected these seeds and scattered them across fertile soils. When ripe, these plants produced bigger and more concentrated crops. Plant domestication occurred when the plant retained its ripe, mature seeds, allowing an easy harvest. People used most seeds for food but saved some for planting in the next growing cycle, to ensure a food supply for the next year.

Dogs were the first animals to be domesticated (although in fact they may have adopted humans, rather than the other way around). Around 9000 BCE, in the area of present-day Iraq, dogs did more than comfort humans. They provided an example of how to achieve the domestication of other animals and, with their herding instincts, they helped humans to control other domesticated animals, such as sheep. In the central Zagros Mountains region, where wild sheep and wild goats were abundant, they became the next animal domesticates. Perhaps hunters returned home with young wild sheep, which then reproduced, and their offspring never returned to the wild. The animals accepted their dependence because the humans fed them. Since controlling animal reproduction was more reliable than hunting, domesticated herds became the primary source of protein in the early humans' diet.

When the number of animals under human control and living close to the settlement outstripped the supply of food needed to feed them, community members could move the animals to grassy steppes for grazing. These pastoralists herded domesticated animals, moving them to new pastures on a seasonal basis. Goats, the other main domesticated animal of Southwest Asia, are smarter than sheep but more difficult to control. The pastoralists may have introduced goats into herds of sheep to better control herd movement. Pigs and cattle also came under human control at this time.

Transhumant Herders and Nomadic Pastoralists Pastoralism appeared as a way of life around 5500 BCE, essentially at the same time that full-time farmers appeared (although the beginnings of plant and animal domestication had begun many millennia earlier). Over time, two different types of pastoralists with different relationships to settled populations developed: transhumant herders and nomadic pastoralists. Transhumant herders were closely affiliated with agricultural villages whose inhabitants grew grains, especially wheat and barley, which required large parcels of land. These herders produced both meat and dairy products, as well as wool for textiles, and exchanged these products with the agriculturalists for grain, pottery, and other staples. Extended families might farm and herd at the same time, growing crops on large estates and grazing their herds in the foothills and mountains nearby. They moved their livestock seasonally, pasturing their flocks in higher lands during summer and in valleys in winter. This movement over short distances is called *transhumance* and did not require herders to vacate their primary living locations, which were generally in the mountain valleys.

In contrast with transhumant pastoralism, *nomadic pastoralism* came to flourish especially in the steppe lands north of the agricultural zone of southern Eurasia. This way of

NORTH AMERICA
Eastern Woodlands
3000 BCE
(Squash)
ATLANTIC OCEAN
Gulf of Mexico
Tehuacan Valley
Mesoamerica
8000–4000 BCE
(Maize, Squash)
SAHARA
Sahel
2000 BCE
(Millet, Sorghum)
Niger R.
ALPS
Equator
SOUTH AMERICA
ANDES
Mesotropics
8000–5000 BCE
(Manioc, Squash, Palms, Yams)
PACIFIC OCEAN
Central Andes
8000–5000 BCE
(Llamas, Potatoes, Guinea Pigs)
ANDES MOUNTAINS
Origin of food domestication
Present-day agricultural land
0 1000 2000 Miles
0 1000 2000 Kilometers

MAP 1.4 | The Origins of Food Production

Agricultural production emerged in many regions at different times. The variety of patterns reflected local resources and conditions.

- How many different locations did agricultural production emerge in?
- Are there any common geographic features among these early food-producing areas?
- Based on your reading of the chapter, why do you think agriculture emerged in certain areas and not in others?

life was characterized by horse-riding herders of cattle and other livestock. Because horses provided decisive advantages in transportation and warfare, they gained more value than other domesticated animals. Thus, horses soon became the measure of household wealth and prestige. Unlike the transhumant herders, the nomadic pastoralists often had no fixed home, though they often returned to their traditional locations. They moved across large distances in response to the size and needs of their herds. The northern areas of the Eurasian landmass stretching from present-day Ukraine across Siberia and Mongolia to the Pacific Ocean became the preserve of these horse-riding pastoral peoples in a region unable to support the extensive agriculture necessary for large settled populations. Historians know much less about these horse-riding pastoral nomads than about the agriculturalists and the transhumant herders, as their numbers were small and they left fewer archaeological traces or historical records. Their role in world history, however, is as important as that of the settled societies. In Afro-Eurasia, they domesticated horses and developed weapons and techniques that at certain points in history enabled them to conquer sedentary societies. As we will see in the next section (and later chapters), they also transmitted ideas, products, and people across long distances, maintaining the linkages that connected east and west.

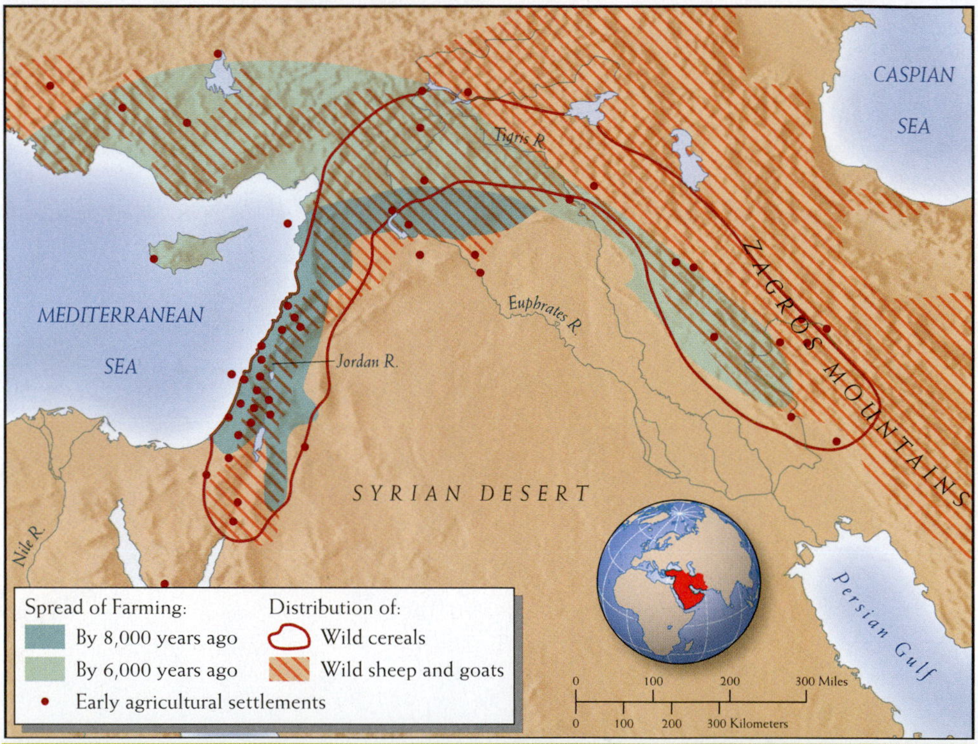

MAP 1.5 | The Birth of Farming in the Fertile Crescent

Agricultural production occurred in the Fertile Crescent starting roughly at 9000 BCE. Though the process was slow, farmers and herders domesticated a variety of plants and animals, which led to the rise of large-scale, permanent settlements.

- What does the map reveal about the environment and natural resources in and around the Fertile Crescent?
- Where do farming and agricultural settlements appear to develop or not? Based on the map, what factors appear to influence the location of agricultural settlements and farming?
- What relationship existed between cereal cultivators and herders of goats and sheep?

AGRICULTURAL INNOVATION: AFRO-EURASIA AND THE AMERICAS

The agricultural revolutions that occurred worldwide between 9000 and 2000 BCE had much in common: climatic change; increased knowledge about plants and animals; and the need for more efficient ways to feed, house, and promote the growth of a larger population. These concerns led peoples in Eurasia, the Americas, and Africa to see the advantages of cultivating plants and domesticating wildlife.

Some communities were independent innovators, developing agricultural techniques based on their specific environments. In Southwest Asia, East Asia, Africa, and the Americas, the distinctive crops and animals that humans first domesticated reflect independent innovation. As we will see in the following section, other communities (such as those in Europe) were borrowers of ideas, which spread through migration and contact with other regions. In all of these populations, the shift to settled agriculture was revolutionary.

COMPARISON

COMPARE the ways communities around the world shifted to settled agriculture.

Southwest Asia: Cereals and Mammals The first agricultural revolution occurred in Southwest Asia in an area bounded by the Mediterranean Sea and the Zagros Mountains, a region known today as the Fertile Crescent because of its rich soils and regular rainfall. Around 9000 BCE, in the southern corridor of the Jordan River valley, humans began to domesticate the wild ancestors of barley and wheat, which were the easiest to adapt to settled agriculture and the easiest to transport. Although the changeover from gathering wild cereals to regular cultivation took several centuries and saw failures as well as successes, by 8000 BCE cultivators were selecting and storing seeds and then sowing them in prepared seedbeds. Moreover, in the valleys of the Zagros Mountains on the eastern side of the Fertile Crescent, similar experimentation was occurring with animals around the same time. Of the six large mammals—goats, sheep, pigs, cattle, camels, and horses—that have been vital for meat, milk, skins, and transportation, humans in Southwest Asia domesticated all except horses. With the presence of so many valuable plants and animals, Southwest Asia led the agricultural revolution and gave rise to many of the world's first major city-states (see Chapter 2).

Large Two-handled Yangshao Pot This pot comes from the village of Yangshao in Henan Province, along the Yellow River in northwest China, where remains were first found in 1921 of a people who lived more than 6,000 years ago. The Yangshao lived in small, rammed-earth fortresses and, without the use of pottery wheels, created fine white, red, and black painted pottery with human faces and animal and geometric designs. This jar dates to the third or second millennium BCE.

East Asia: Water And Rice A revolution in food production also occurred among the coastal dwellers in East Asia although under different circumstances. (See Map 1.6.) As the rising sea level created the Japanese islands, hunters in that area tracked a diminishing supply of large animals, such as giant deer. When big game became extinct, men and women sought other ways to support themselves, and before long they settled down and became cultivators of the soil. In this postglacial period, divergent human cultures flourished in northern and southern Japan. Hunters in the south created primitive pebble and flake tools, whereas those in the north used sharper blades about a third of an inch wide. Production of earthenware pottery—a breakthrough that enabled people to store food more easily—also may have begun in this period in the south. Throughout the

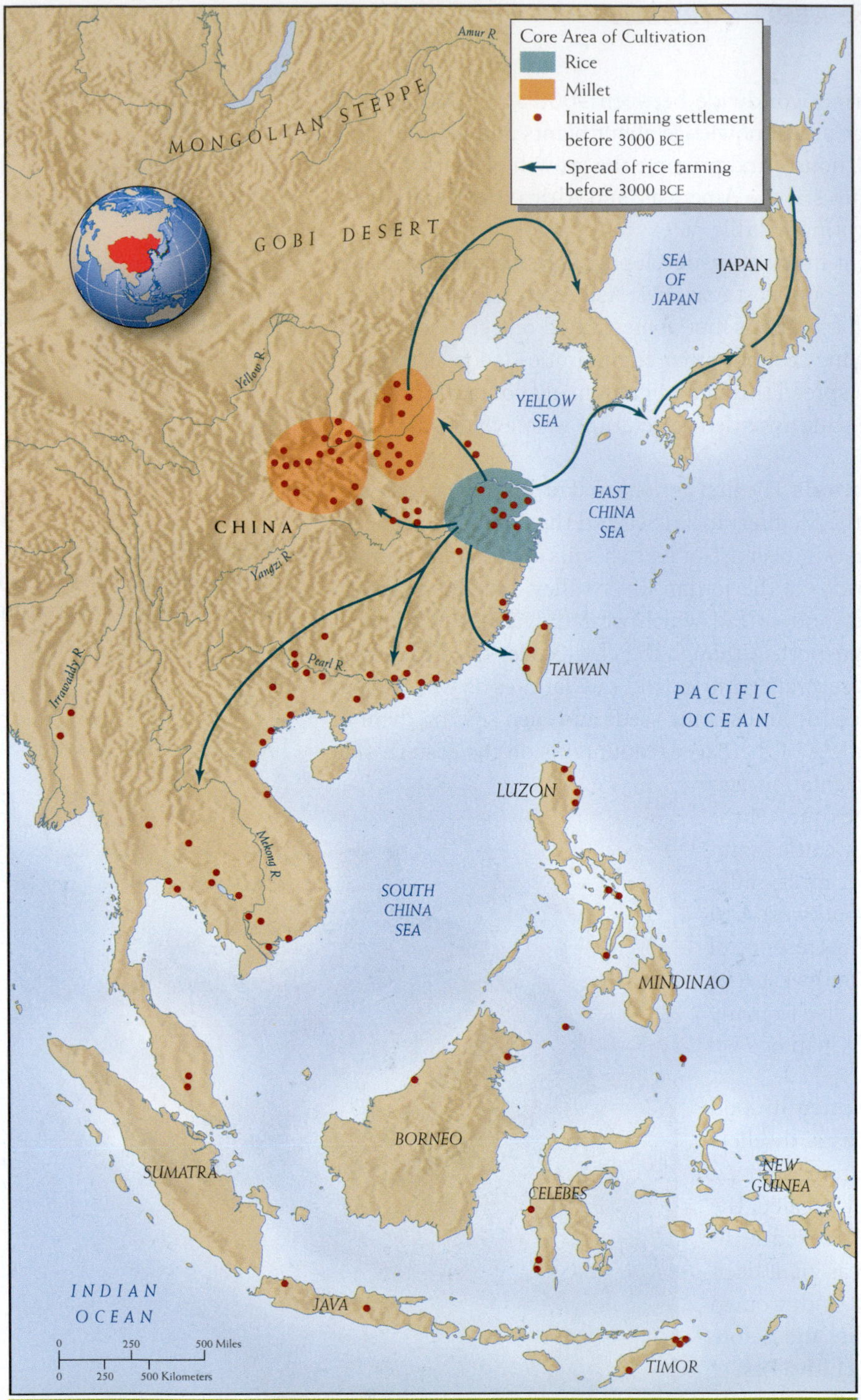

MAP 1.6 | The Spread of Farming in East Asia

Agricultural settlements appeared in East Asia later than they did in the Fertile Crescent.

- According to this map, where did early agricultural settlements appear in East Asia?
- What types of crops and animals were domesticated in East Asia?
- How did the physical features of these regions lend themselves to agricultural production?

rest of East Asia, the spread of lakes, marshes, and rivers created habitats for population concentrations and agricultural cultivation. Two newly formed river basins, along the Yellow River in northern China and the Yangzi River in central China, became densely populated areas that were focal points for intensive agricultural development.

What barley and wheat were for Southwest Asia, rice along the Yangzi and millet along the Yellow River were for East Asia—staples adapted to local environments that humans could domesticate to support a large, sedentary population. Archaeologists have found evidence of rice cultivation in the Yangzi River valley in 6500 BCE, and of millet cultivation in the Yellow River valley in 5500 BCE. Innovations in grain production, including the introduction of a faster-ripening rice from Southeast Asia, spread through internal migration and wider contacts. Ox plows and water buffalo plowshares were prerequisites for large-scale millet planting in the drier north and the rice-cultivated areas of the wetter south. By domesticating plants and animals, the East Asians, like the Southwest Asians, laid the foundations for more populous societies.

Africa: The Race with the Sahara

The evidence of settled agriculture in the various regions of Africa is less clear. Most scholars think that the Sahel area (spanning the African landmass just south of the Sahara Desert) was most likely where hunters and gatherers became settled farmers and herders without borrowing from other regions. In this area, an apparent move to settled agriculture, including the domestication of large herd animals, occurred two millennia before it did along the Mediterranean coast in North Africa. From this innovative heartland, Africans carried their agricultural breakthroughs across the landmass.

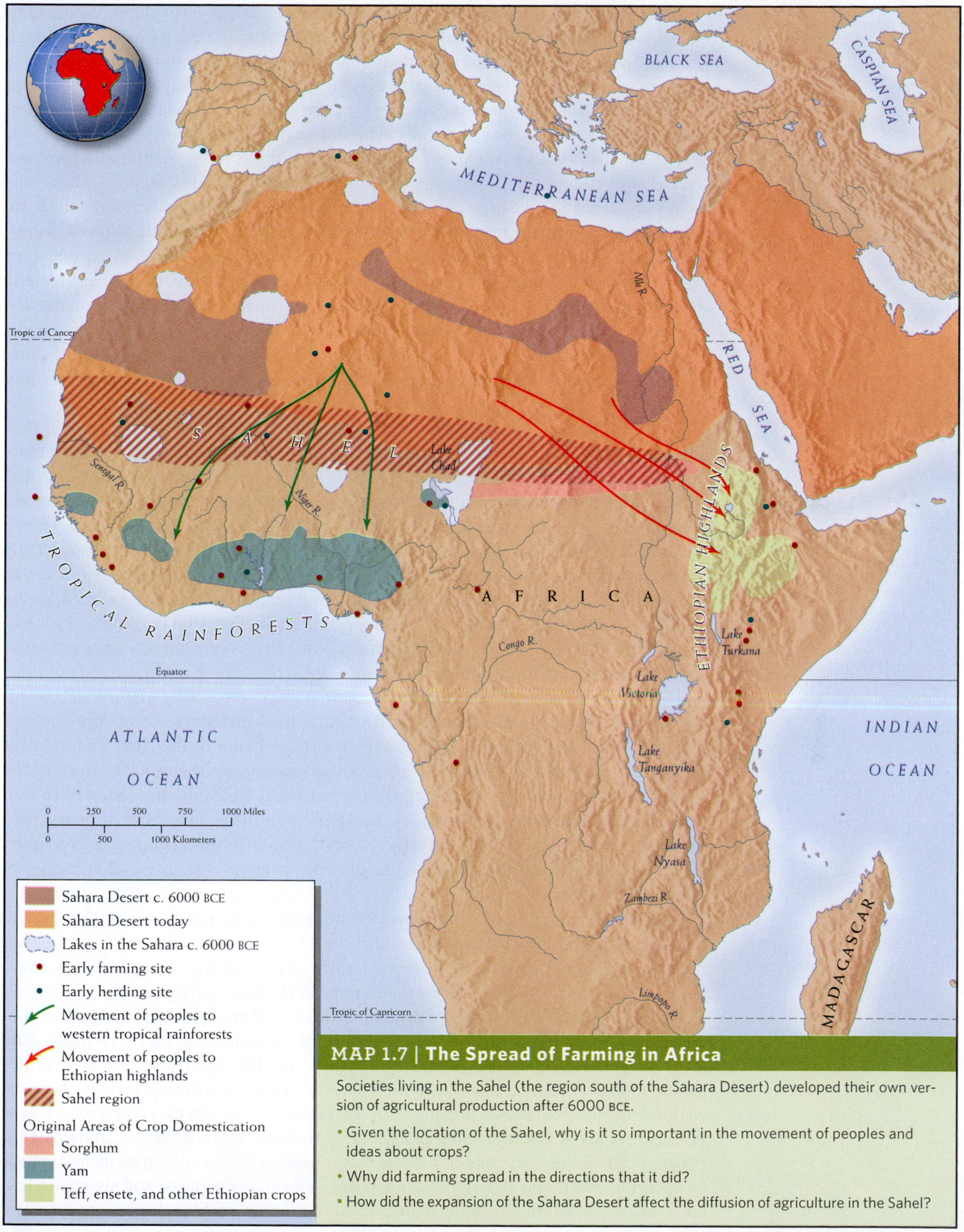

MAP 1.7 | The Spread of Farming in Africa

Societies living in the Sahel (the region south of the Sahara Desert) developed their own version of agricultural production after 6000 BCE.

- Given the location of the Sahel, why is it so important in the movement of peoples and ideas about crops?
- Why did farming spread in the directions that it did?
- How did the expansion of the Sahara Desert affect the diffusion of agriculture in the Sahel?

In the wetter and more temperate locations of the vast Sahel, particularly in mountainous areas and their foothills, villages and towns developed. These regions were lush with grassland vegetation and teeming with animals. Before long, the inhabitants had made sorghum, a cereal grass, their principal food crop. Residents constructed stone dwellings, underground wells, and grain storage areas. In one such population center, fourteen circular houses faced each other to form a main thoroughfare, or a street.

The Sahel was colder and moister in 8000 BCE than it is today. As the world became warmer and the Sahara Desert expanded, around 2000 BCE, this region's inhabitants had to disperse and take their agricultural and herding skills into other parts of Africa. Some went south to the tropical rainforests of West Africa, while others trekked eastward into the Ethiopian highlands. In their new environments, farmers searched for new crops to domesticate. The rainforests of West Africa yielded root crops, particularly the yam and cocoyam, both of which became the principal life-sustaining foodstuffs. The enset plant, similar to the banana, played the same role in the Ethiopian highlands. Thus, the beginnings of agriculture in Africa involved both innovation and diffusion, as Africans applied the techniques that first emerged in the Sahel to new plants and animals.

The Americas: A Slower Transition The shift to settled agriculture occurred more slowly in the Americas. When people crossed Beringia into the Americas, the plants and animals were different enough that early settlers devised ways of living that distinguished them from their ancestors in Afro-Eurasia. When the glaciers melted and water covered the land bridge between East Asia and America, the Americas and their peoples truly became a whole world apart. Early humans in America, called "Clovis people" after an archaeological site near Clovis, New Mexico, used chipped blades and pointed spears to pursue their prey. Although scientists once thought that Clovis communities had wiped out the large Ice Age mammals in the Americas, recent research suggests that climatic change destroyed indigenous plants and trees—the feeding grounds of large prehistoric mammals. This left undernourished mastodons, woolly mammoths, bison, and other mammals vulnerable to human and animal predators. As in Afro-Eurasia, the arrival of a long warming cycle compelled those living in the Americas to adapt to different environments and to create new ways to support themselves. Thus, in the woodland area of the present-day northeastern United States, hunters learned to trap smaller wild animals for food and furs. To supplement the protein from meat and fish, these people also dug for roots and gathered berries. Even as most communities adapted to the settled agricultural economy, they did not abandon basic survival strategies of hunting and gathering.

Food-producing changes in the Americas were different from those in Afro-Eurasia because this area did not undergo the sudden cluster of innovations that revolutionized agriculture in Southwest Asia and elsewhere. Independent innovation occurred more slowly here. Tools ground from stone, rather than chipped implements, appeared in the Tehuacán Valley by 6700 BCE, and evidence of plant domestication there dates back to 5000 BCE. But villages, pottery making, and sustained population growth came later. For many early American inhabitants, the life of hunting, trapping, and fishing went on as it had for millennia. Indeed, researchers have found the remains of ancient shellfishing throughout the coastal Americas from Alaska to Chile on the Pacific Ocean side. On the coast of what is now Peru, people found food by fishing and gathering shellfish from the Pacific. Archaeological remains include the remnants of fishnets, bags, baskets, and textile implements; gourds for carrying water; and stone knives, choppers, scrapers, bone awls, and thorn needles. Some made breakthroughs in the management of fire that enabled them to manufacture pottery; others devised irrigation and water sluices in floodplains. And some even began to send their fish catches inland in return for agricultural produce.

The earliest evidence of plant experimentation in Mesoamerica dates from around 8000 BCE, and the peoples living there continued to domesticate new plants for a long time. Maize, squash, and beans (first found in what is now central Mexico) became dietary staples. The early settlers foraged small seeds of maize, peeled them from ears only a few inches long, and planted them. Maize offered real advantages because it was easy to store over long periods of time, nutritious, and easy to cultivate alongside other plants. Nonetheless, it took 5,000 years for farmers to complete its domestication. Over the years, farmers had to mix and breed different strains of maize for it to evolve from thin spikes of seeds to cobs rich with kernels, with a single plant yielding big, thick ears to feed a growing permanent population. Thus, the agricultural changes afoot in Mesoamerica were slow and late in maturing. The pace was even more gradual in South America, where early settlers clung to their hunting and gathering traditions.

Across the Americas, the settled, agrarian communities found that legumes (beans), grains (maize), and tubers (potatoes) complemented one another in keeping the soil fertile and offering a balanced diet. Unlike the Afro-Eurasians, however, the settlers did not use domesticated animals as an alternative source of protein. In only a few pockets of the Andean highlands is there evidence of the domestication of tiny guinea pigs. Nor did people in the Americas tame animals that could protect villages (as dogs did in Afro-Eurasia) or carry heavy loads over long distances (as cattle and horses did in Afro-Eurasia). Although llamas could haul heavy loads, they were uncooperative and only partially domesticated, and thus mainly useful only for their fur, which was used for clothing.

Head of Mayan Corn God Corn, or maize, was a revered crop in Mesoamerica, where people ritually prayed to their deities for good harvests. Notice the crown made not of precious metals and stones but of corn husks as an example of the cultural emphasis on maize.

Nonetheless, the domestication of plants and animals in the Americas, as well as the presence of villages and clans, suggests significant diversification and refinement of agricultural techniques. At the same time, the centers of such activity were numerous, scattered, and more isolated than those in Afro-Eurasia—and thus more narrowly adapted to local geographical climatic conditions, with little exchange among them. This fragmentation was a distinguishing force in the gradual pace of change in the Americas, and it contributed to their taking a path of development separate from Afro-Eurasia's.

BORROWING AGRICULTURAL IDEAS: EUROPE

In some places, agricultural revolution occurred through the borrowing of ideas from neighboring regions, rather than through innovation. Peoples living at the western fringe of Afro-Eurasia, in Europe, learned the techniques of settled agriculture through contact with other regions. By 6000–5000 BCE, people in parts of Europe close to the

MAP 1.8 | The Spread of Agriculture in Europe

The spread of agricultural production into Europe after 7000 BCE represents geographic diffusion. Europeans borrowed agricultural techniques and technology from other groups, adapting those innovations to their own situations.

- Where did the ideas and techniques originate?
- Through what two pathways did agriculture spread across Europe?
- Did Europe's settled agricultural communities have different features from those that appeared in Southwest Asia, East Asia, and Africa?

societies of Southwest Asia, such as Greece and the Balkans, were abandoning their hunting-and-gathering way of life for an agricultural one. The Franchthi Cave in Greece, for instance, reveals that around 6000 BCE the inhabitants learned how to domesticate animals and plant wheat and barley, having borrowed that innovation from their neighbors in Southwest Asia.

The emergence of agriculture and village life occurred in Europe along two separate paths of borrowing. The first and most rapid trajectory followed the northern rim of the Mediterranean Sea: from what is now Turkey through the islands of the Aegean Sea to mainland Greece, and from there to southern and central Italy and Sicily. Whether the process involved the actual migration of individuals or, rather, the spread of ideas, connections by sea quickened the pace of the transition. Within a relatively short period of time, hunting and gathering gave way to domesticated agriculture and herding.

The second trajectory of borrowing took an overland route: from Anatolia, across northern Greece into the Balkans, then northwestward along the Danube River into the Hungarian plain, and from there farther north and west into the Rhine River valley in modern-day Germany. This route of agricultural development was slower than the Mediterranean route for two reasons. First, domesticated crops, or individuals who knew about them, had to travel by land, as there were few large rivers like the Danube. Second, it was necessary to find new groups of domesticated plants and animals that could flourish in the colder and more forested lands of central Europe, which meant planting crops in the spring and harvesting them in the autumn, rather than the other way around. Cattle rather than sheep became the dominant herd animals.

In Europe, the main cereal crops were wheat and barley (additional plants such as olives came later), and the main herd animals were sheep, goats, and cattle—all of which had been domesticated in Southwest Asia. Hunting, gathering, and fishing still supplemented the new settled agriculture and the herding of domesticated animals.

Thus, across Afro-Eurasia and the Americas, humans changed and were changed by their environments. While herding and gathering remained firmly entrenched as a way of life, certain areas with favorable climates and plants and animals that could be domesticated began to establish settled agricultural communities, which were able to support larger populations than hunting and gathering could sustain.

REVOLUTIONS IN SOCIAL ORGANIZATION

In addition to creating agricultural villages, the domestication of plants and animals brought changes in social organization, notably changes in gender relationships.

COMPARISON

ANALYZE the significance the shift to settled agriculture had for social organization across global regions.

Life in Villages Agricultural villages were established near fields for accessible sowing and cultivating, and near pastures for herding livestock. Villagers collaborated to clear fields, plant crops, and celebrate rituals in which they sang, danced, and sacrificed to nature and the spirit world for fertility, rain, and successful harvests. They also produced stone tools to work the fields, and clay and stone pots or woven baskets to collect and store the crops. The earliest dwelling places of the first settled communities were simple structures: circular pits with stones piled on top to form walls, with a cover stretched above that rested on poles. Social structures were equally simple, being clan-like and based on kinship networks. With time, however, population growth enabled clans to expand. As the use of natural resources intensified, specialized tasks evolved and divisions of labor arose. Some community members procured and prepared food; others built terraces and defended the settlement. Later, residents built walls with stones or mud bricks and clamped them together with wooden fittings. Some villagers became craftworkers, devoting their time to producing pottery, baskets, textiles, or tools, which they could trade to farmers and pastoralists for food. Craft specialization and the buildup of surpluses contributed to social stratification (the emergence of distinct and hierarchically arranged social classes), as some people accumulated more land and wealth while others led the rituals and sacrifices.

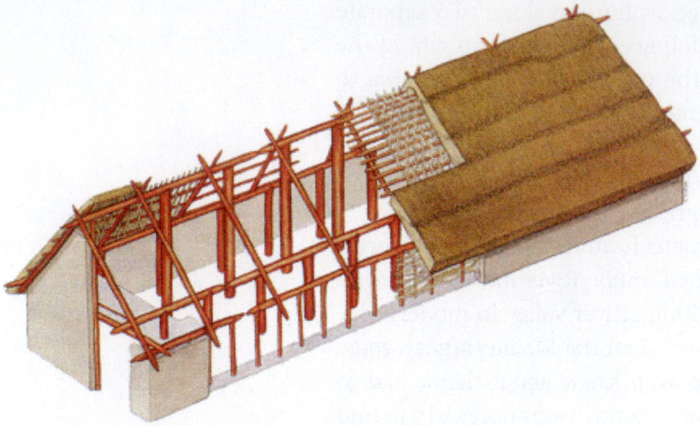

"Long House" The people who opened up the whole of central Europe to agriculture typically lived in communities of six to twelve "long houses." Although large in size (varying between 60 and 120 feet in length), long houses were built on simple principles: a framework of wooden beams and posts with walls made of mud and woven branches beneath a thatched roof. These dwellings probably sheltered large extended family or kinship units that cooperated to provide the hard work needed to carve out pioneer farming settlements along river valleys. This cutaway reconstruction of a long house shows the placement of wall timbers and internal support posts.

Archaeological sites in Southwest Asia have provided evidence of what life was like in some of the earliest villages. At Wadi en-Natuf, for example, located about ten miles from present-day Jerusalem, a group of people known historically as Natufians began to dig sunken pit shelters and to chip stone tools around 12,500 BCE. In the highlands of eastern Anatolia, large settlements clustered around monumental public buildings with impressive stone carvings that reflect a complex social organization. In central Anatolia around 7500 BCE, at the site of Çatal Höyük, a dense honeycomb settlement featured rooms with artwork of a high quality. The walls were covered with paintings, and sculptures of wild bulls, hunters, and pregnant women enlivened many rooms.

After 5500 BCE, people moved into the river valley in Mesopotamia (in present-day Iraq) along the Tigris and Euphrates rivers, and small villages began to appear. They collaborated to build simple irrigation systems to water their fields. Perhaps because of the increased demands for community work to maintain the irrigation systems, the communities in southern Mesopotamia became stratified, with some people having more power than others. We can see from the burial sites and myriad public buildings uncovered by archaeologists that, for the first time, some people had higher status derived from birth rather than through the merits of their work. A class of people who had access to more luxury goods, and who lived in bigger and better houses, now became part of the social organization.

Men, Women, and Evolving Gender Relations Gender roles became more pronounced during the gradual transition to agriculturally based ways of life. For millions of years, biological differences—the fact that females give birth to offspring and lactate to nourish them and that males do not—determined female and male behaviors and attitudes toward each other. One can speak of the emergence of "gender" relations and roles (as opposed to biological differences) only with the appearance of modern humans (*Homo sapiens*). Only when humans began to think in complex symbolic ways and give voice to these perceptions in a spoken language did true gender categories as *man* and *woman* crystallize. At that point, around 150,000 years ago, culture joined biology in governing human interactions.

Hunting This wall painting from Çatal Höyük (in present-day Turkey) depicts humans hunting a bull.

As human communities became larger, more hierarchical, and more powerful, the rough gender egalitarianism of hunting and gathering societies eroded. Although as the primary gatherers women's knowledge of wild plants had contributed to early settled agriculture, they did not necessarily benefit from that transition. Advances in agrarian tools introduced a harsh working life that undermined women's earlier status as farmers. Men, no longer so involved in hunting and gathering, now took on the heavy work of yoking animals to plows. Women took on the backbreaking and repetitive tasks of planting, weeding, harvesting, and grinding the grain into flour. Thus, although agricultural innovations increased productivity, they also increased the drudgery of work, especially for women. Fossil evidence from Abu Hureyra, Syria, reveals damage to the vertebrae, osteoarthritis in the toes, and curved and arched femurs, all suggesting that the work of bending over and kneeling in the fields took its toll on female agriculturalists. The increasing differentiation of the roles of men and women also affected power relations within households and communities. The senior male figure became dominant in these households, and males became dominant over females in leadership positions.

The agricultural revolution marked a greater division among men, and particularly between men and women. Where the agricultural transformation was most widespread, and where population densities began to grow, the social and political differences created inequalities. As these inequalities affected gender relations, patriarchy (the rule of senior males within households) began to spread around the globe.

Conclusion

Over thousands of generations, African hominids evolved from other primates into bipedal, toolmaking, fire-using *Homo erectus*, who migrated far from their native habitats to fill other landmasses. They did so in waves, often in response to worldwide cycles of climatic change. *Homo sapiens*, with bigger brains and consequently greater cognition, emerged in Africa about 200,000 years ago and migrated out of Africa between 100,000 and 50,000 years ago. With greater adaptive skills, they were better prepared to face the elements when a cooling cycle returned, and eventually they became the only surviving branch of the tree of human ancestors. *Homo sapiens* used language and art to engage in abstract, representational thought, and to convey the lessons of experience to their neighbors and descendants. As modern humans stored and shared knowledge, their adaptive abilities increased.

Although modern men and women shared an African heritage, these individuals adapted over many millennia to the environments they encountered as they began to fill the earth's corners and practice hunter-gatherer ways of life. Some settled near lakes and took to fishing, while others roamed the northern steppes hunting large mammals. No matter where they went, their dependence on nature yielded broadly similar social and cultural structures. It took another warming cycle for people ranging from Africa to the Americas to begin putting down their hunting weapons and start domesticating animals and plants.

The changeover to settled agriculture was not uniform worldwide. As communities became more settled, the world's regions began to vary as humans learned to modify nature to fit their needs. The varieties of animals that they could domesticate and the differing climatic conditions and topography that they encountered shaped the ways in which people drifted apart in spite of their common origins. What these settled communities shared, however, was increasing social hierarchy, including an unequal status between men and women.

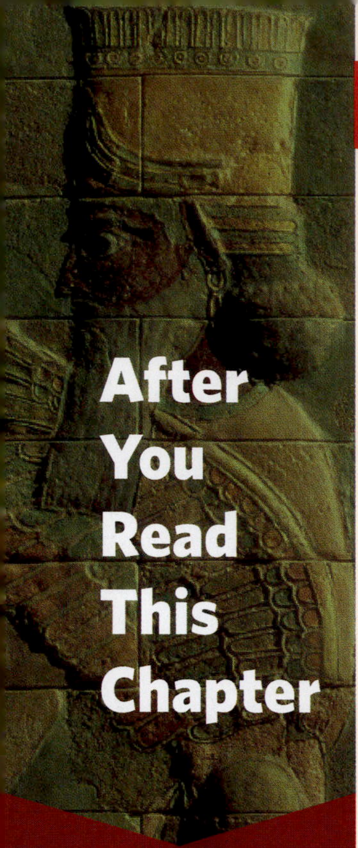

After You Read This Chapter

Go to INQUIZITIVE to see what you've learned—and learn what you've missed—with personalized feedback along the way.

TRACING THE GLOBAL STORYLINES

FOCUS ON: *What Makes Us Human*

- ***Bipedalism:*** Hominids come down from the trees in Africa, become upright, and walk on two legs.
- ***Big brains:*** Ancestors to modern humans make tools and fire and acquire larger brains.
- ***Cognitive skills:*** *Homo sapiens* develop the capacity for language and learn to communicate with one another, develop a sense of self, and produce art.
- ***Village life:*** People domesticate plants and animals, and begin to live in more socially complex communities.

CHRONOLOGY

AFRO-EURASIA

- ◆ ***Australopithecus africanus*** **hominid species appears** 3 mya
- ◆ ***Homo habilis*** **appears** 2.5 mya
- ***Homo erectus*** **appears and migrates** 2.5–1 mya
- **Beginnings of Ice Age Across the Northern Hemisphere** 2.5–1 mya

AFRICA

EUROPE AND THE MEDITERRANEAN

SOUTHWEST AND INNER ASIA

EAST ASIA

THE AMERICAS

**millions of years ago*
***years ago*

5 MYA* — **1 MYA**

THINKING ABOUT GLOBAL CONNECTIONS

- ***Thinking about Exchange Networks and Human Evolution*** Across several million years, the hominid ancestors of humans, especially *Homo erectus*, and then *Homo sapiens*, migrated out of Africa. What role did evolution play in making it possible for our hominid ancestors and then *Homo sapiens* to migrate across the globe?
- ***Thinking about the Environment and Human Evolution*** Climate change and environmental conditions have played a recurring role in the narrative recounted in this chapter. In what specific ways did climate change and the environment help shape the evolution of humans and influence the shift from hunting and gathering to settled agriculture?
- ***Thinking about Changing Gender Relationships and the Agricultural Revolution*** Some scholars have argued that the hunting-and-gathering ways of life for both *Homo erectus* and *Homo sapiens* allowed women—biologically, through their lactation and child-rearing, and calorically, through their dominant role as gatherers—to make a larger and more significant contribution to their communities than their male counterparts. In what ways might the development of settled agriculture usher in a shift, or not, in these gender roles?

STUDY QUESTIONS

1. Why do human communities produce **creation narratives** and what do creation narratives have in common?
2. How do natural selection and adaptation play a role in **evolution**?
3. What are some of the distinctive features of **hominids**, especially **australopithecines**, ***Homo habilis***, and ***Homo erectus***?
4. In what ways are humans, ***Homo sapiens***, different from our hominid ancestors?
5. How did *Homo sapiens* come into being? In what ways did **hunting and gathering** shape the dynamics of early human communities?
6. What do cave art and the so-called Venus figurines suggest about the values of human communities prior to the agricultural revolution?
7. Where, when, and how did the agricultural revolution take place, and what were the results? Describe the process of plant and animal domestication and how that led to **settled agriculture** (via both innovation and borrowing).
8. What is **pastoralism**, and how did varying types of pastoralists (both transhumant herders and nomadic pastoralists) interact with settled agricultural communities?

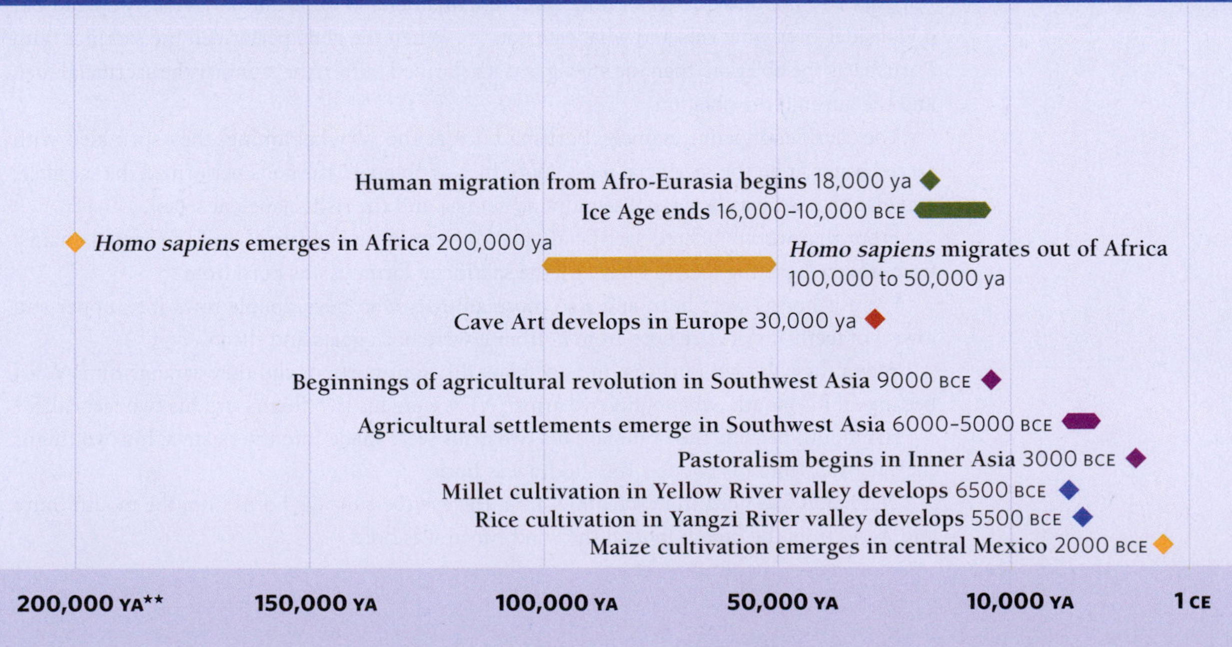
Human migration from Afro-Eurasia begins 18,000 ya
Ice Age ends 16,000–10,000 BCE
Homo sapiens emerges in Africa 200,000 ya
Homo sapiens migrates out of Africa 100,000 to 50,000 ya
Cave Art develops in Europe 30,000 ya
Beginnings of agricultural revolution in Southwest Asia 9000 BCE
Agricultural settlements emerge in Southwest Asia 6000–5000 BCE
Pastoralism begins in Inner Asia 3000 BCE
Millet cultivation in Yellow River valley develops 6500 BCE
Rice cultivation in Yangzi River valley develops 5500 BCE
Maize cultivation emerges in central Mexico 2000 BCE
200,000 YA**
150,000 YA
100,000 YA
50,000 YA
10,000 YA
1 CE

Going to the Source

Creation Narratives

Throughout human history, men and women have tried to explain the origins of humanity and the relationship between human beings, other animals, and the planet on which we all live. Some of these attempts have survived and are presented here. Generally referred to as *creation narratives*, these stories draw upon local circumstances and knowledge in order to explain universal problems and experiences. People in different places around the world, who had no contact with each other, sought to explain things that had no obvious explanation. The documents here represent creation narratives, but there are many others that are not included. All kinds of stories address questions that are fundamental to understanding world history—and to the concept of "worlds apart."

PRIMARY SOURCE 1.1

"The Sacrifice of Purusha" from Rig Veda *(1500 BCE)*

This excerpt from the Hindu religious scripture the *Rig Veda* provides a creation narrative centered on the sacrifice of a primordial being named Purusha, and the results of this sacrifice. It dates to around 1500 BCE, when Vedic peoples migrated into South Asia.

Thousand-headed Purusha, thousand-eyed, thousand-footed—he, having pervaded the earth on all sides, extends ten fingers beyond it.

Purusha alone is all this—whatever has been and whatever is going to be. Further, he is the lord of immortality and also of what grows on account of food.

Such is his greatness; greater, indeed than this is Purusha. All creatures constitute but one-quarter of him, his three-quarters are the immortal in the heaven. With his three-quarters did Purusha rise up; one-quarter of him again remains here. With it did he variously spread out on all sides over what eats and what eats not. . . . When the gods performed the sacrifice with Purusha as the oblation, then the spring was its clarified butter, the summer the sacrificial fuel, and the autumn the oblation.

The sacrificial victim, namely, Purusha born at the very beginning, they sprinkled with sacred water upon the sacrificial grass. With him as oblation, the gods performed the sacrifice, and also the Sādhyas [a class of semidivine beings] and the rishis [ancient seers].

From that wholly offered sacrificial oblation were born the verses and the sacred chants; from it were born the meters [*chandas*]; the sacrificial formula was born from it.

From it horses were born and also those animals who have double rows [i.e., upper and lower] of teeth; cows were born from it, from it were born goats and sheep.

When they divided Purusha, in how many different portions did they arrange him? What became of his mouth, what of his two arms? What were his two thighs and his two feet called?

His mouth became the brāhman; his two arms were made into the rājanya; his two thighs the vaishyas; from his two feet the shūdra was born.

The moon was born from the mind, from the eye the sun was born; from the mouth Indra and Agni, from the breath [*prāna*] the wind [*vāyu*] was born.

From the navel was the atmosphere created, from the head the heaven issued forth; from two feet was born the earth and the quarters (the cardinal directions) from the ear. Thus did they fashion the worlds.

1. **What is being created in this narrative?**
2. **Explain the logic behind the division of Purusha into his multiple parts. Why might this be important to the Vedic peoples?**

PRIMARY SOURCE 1.2

Genesis 1:1–31 from The Bible

Judeo-Christian scripture begins with an account of a singular God bringing order from chaos and forming the world over the course of six days. The narrative is linear but nevertheless explains the creation of the world. Although historians debate about when the Bible was written, they generally believe that several writers compiled it beginning around 1440 BCE when, they think, the Israelites were leaving Egypt.

*

[1]In the beginning God created the heavens and the earth. [2]The earth was without form and
void, and darkness was upon the face of the deep; and the Spirit of God was moving over the
face of the waters. [3]And God said, "Let there be light"; and there was light. [4]And God saw that
the light was good; and God separated the light from the darkness. [5]God called the light Day,
and the darkness he called Night. And there was evening and there was morning, one day. [6]And
God said, "Let there be a firmament in the midst of the waters, and let it separate the waters
from the waters." [7]And God made the firmament and separated the waters which were under
the firmament from the waters which were above the firmament. And it was so. [8]And God
called the firmament Heaven. And there was evening and there was morning, a second day.

[9]And God said, "Let the waters under the heavens be gathered together into one place, and
let the dry land appear." And it was so. [10]God called the dry land Earth, and the waters that
were gathered together he called Seas. And God saw that it was good. [11]And God said, "Let the
earth put forth vegetation, plants yielding seed, and fruit trees bearing fruit in which is their
seed, each according to its kind, upon the earth." And it was so. . . . [13]And there was evening
and there was morning, a third day. [14]And God said, "Let there be lights in the firmament of
the heavens to separate the day from the night; and let them be for signs and for seasons and
for days and years, [15] and let them be lights in the firmament of the heavens to give light upon
the earth." And it was so. . . . [19]And there was evening and there was morning, a fourth day.

[20]And God said, "Let the waters bring forth swarms of living creatures, and let birds fly
above the earth across the firmament of the heavens." . . . [23]And there was evening and there
was morning, a fifth day.

[24]And God said, "Let the earth bring forth living creatures according to their kinds: cattle
and creeping things and beasts of the earth according to their kinds." And it was so. . . .

[26]Then God said, "Let us make man in our image, after our likeness; and let them have
dominion over the fish of the sea, and over the birds of the air, and over the cattle, and over all
the earth, and over every creeping thing that creeps upon the earth." [27]So God created man in
his own image, in the image of God he created him; male and female he created them. [28]And
God blessed them, and God said to them, "Be fruitful and multiply, and fill the earth and subdue it; and have dominion over the fish of the sea and over the birds of the air and over every
living thing that moves upon the earth." . . . [31]And God saw everything that he had made, and
behold, it was very good. And there was evening and there was morning, a sixth day.

1. **What is being created in this narrative?**
2. **How would you explain the order of creation in this narrative and why might that order have mattered at certain times more than others?**

PRIMARY SOURCE 1.3

"The Creation of the Universe" from the Huainanzi *(c. 1100 BCE)*

Yet another understanding of the world's creation is recorded in the *Huainanzi* from second-century BCE Han China. This Confucian text takes the form of dialogues between a prince and court scholars. It reflects Daoist ideas, such as the role of the complementary forces of *yin* and *yang*.

*

Before Heaven and Earth had taken form all was vague and amorphous. Therefore it was called the Great Beginning. The Great Beginning produced emptiness, and emptiness produced the universe. The universe produced material-force, which had limits. That which was clear and light drifted up to become Heaven, while that which was heavy and turbid solidified to become Earth. It was very easy for the pure, fine material to come together but extremely difficult for the heavy, turbid material to solidify. Therefore Heaven was completed first and Earth assumed shape after. The combined essences of Heaven and Earth became the yin and yang; the concentrated essences of the yin and yang became the four seasons; and the scattered essences of the four seasons became the myriad creatures of the world. After a long time the hot Force of the accumulated yang produced fire, and the essence of the fire force became the sun; the cold force of the accumulated yin became water, and the essence of the water force became the moon. The essence of the excess force of the sun and moon became the stars, while Earth received water and soil. [3:1a]

When Heaven and Earth were joined in emptiness and all was unwrought simplicity, then, without having been created, things came into being. This was the Great Oneness. All things issued from this Oneness, but all became different, being divided into various species of fish, birds, and beasts. . . . Therefore while a thing moves it is called living, and when it dies it is said to be exhausted. All are creatures. They are not the uncreated creator of things, for the creator of things is not among things. If we examine the Great Beginning of antiquity we find that man was born out of nothing to assume form as something. Having form, he is governed by things. But he who can return to that from which he was born and become as though formless is called a "true man." The true man is one who has never become separated from the Great Oneness. [14:1a]

1. **According to the *Huainanzi,* what is the Great Oneness?**
2. **Compare this creation narrative to the explanations presented in Primary Sources 1.1 and 1.2. Pay particular attention to the idea of unity and division in each document.**

PRIMARY SOURCE 1.4

Popul Vuh *(date of origin unknown)*

The Mayans of Mesoamerica believed that humans were created by an assembly of divine beings, a story preserved in this excerpt from the *Popul Vuh*, a collection of stories that were passed down in oral tradition and then collated early in the eighteenth century by a Spanish Dominican priest. The story begins with a discussion of human ancestry but ends with a genealogy of the Mayan rulers in Mesoamerica.

*

Here, then, is the beginning of when it was decided to make man, and when what must enter into the flesh of man was sought.

And the Forefathers, the Creators and Makers, who were called Tepeu and Gucumatz said: "The time of dawn has come, let the work be finished, and let those who are to nourish and sustain us appear, the noble sons, the civilized vassals: let man appear, humanity, on the face of the earth." Thus they spoke.

They assembled, came together and held council in the darkness and in the night; then they sought and discussed, and here they reflected and thought. In this way their decisions came clearly to light and they found and discovered what must enter into the flesh of man.

It was just before the sun, the moon, and the stars appeared over the Creators and Makers.

From Paxil, from Cayalá, as they were called, came the yellow ears of corn and the white ears of corn. These are the names of the animals which brought the food: *yac* [the mountain cat], *utiú* [the coyote], *quel* [a small parrot], and *hob* [the crow]. These four animals gave tidings of the yellow ears of corn and the white ears of corn, they told them that they should go to Paxil and they showed them the road to Paxil.

And thus they found the food, and this was what went into the flesh of created man, the made man; this was his blood; of this the blood of man was made. So the corn entered [into the formation of man] by the work of the Forefathers.

●●●

The animals showed them the road. And then grinding the yellow corn and the white corn, Xmucané made nine drinks, and from this food came the strength and the flesh, and with it they created the muscles and the strength of man. This the Forefathers did, Tepeu and Gucumatz, as they were called.

After that they began to talk about the creation and the making of our first mother and father; of yellow corn and of white corn they made their flesh; of corn meal dough they made the arms and the legs of man. Only dough of corn meal went into the flesh of our first fathers, the four men, who were created.

●●●

It is said that they only were made and formed, they had no mother, they had no father. They were only called men. They were not born of woman, nor were they begotten by the Creator nor by the Maker, nor by the Forefathers. Only by a miracle, by means of incantation were they created and made by the Creator, the Maker, the Forefathers, Tepeu and Gucumatz. And as they had the appearance of men, they were men; they talked, conversed, saw and heard, walked, grasped things; they were good and handsome men, and their figure was the figure of a man.

They were endowed with intelligence; they saw and instantly they could see far, they succeeded in seeing, they succeeded in knowing all that there is in the world. When they looked, instantly they saw all around them, and they contemplated in turn the arch of heaven and the round face of the earth.

The things hidden [in the distance] they saw all, without first having to move; at once they saw the world, and so, too, from where they were, they saw it.

Great was their wisdom; their sight reached to the forests, the rocks, the lakes, the seas, the mountains, and the valleys. In truth, they were admirable men, Balam-Quitzé, Balam-Acab, Mahucutah, and Iqui-Balam.

Then the Creator and the Maker asked them: "What do you think of your condition? Do you not see? Do you not hear? Are not your speech and manner of walking good? Look, then! Contemplate the world, look [and see] if the mountains and the valleys appear! Try, then, to see!" they said to [the four first men].

And immediately they [the four first men] began to see all that was in the world. Then they gave thanks to the Creator and the Maker: "We really give you thanks, two and three times!"

1. **Why would the first four men give thanks to the Creator and the Maker?**
2. **How does this creation narrative differ from the others above (Primary Sources 1.1, 1.2, and 1.3)?**

PRIMARY SOURCE 1.5

Yoruba Creation Narrative (date of origin unknown)

The Yoruba people in West Africa developed a creation narrative that explains which gods are associated with aspects of the planet. It also depicts the god Obatala creating and populating the land with palm trees and humans, thus explaining variations in the natural features of the local environment.

*

In the beginning was only the sky above, water and marshland below.

The chief god Olorun ruled the sky, and the goddess Olokun ruled what was below.

Obatala, another god, reflected upon this situation, then went to Olorun for permission to create dry land for all kinds of living creatures to inhabit. He was given permission, so he sought advice from Orunmila, oldest son of Olorun and the god of prophecy.

He was told he would need a gold chain long enough to reach below, a snail's shell filled with sand, a white hen, a black cat, and a palm nut, all of which he was to carry in a bag. All the gods contributed what gold they had, and Orunmila supplied the articles for the bag. When all was ready, Obatala hung the chain from a corner of the sky, placed the bag over his shoulder, and started the downward climb. When he reached the end of the chain he saw he still had some distance to go.

From above he heard Orunmila instruct him to pour the sand from the snail's shell, and to immediately release the white hen.

He did as he was told, whereupon the hen landing on the sand began scratching and scattering it about.

Wherever the sand landed it formed dry land, the bigger piles becoming hills and the smaller piles valleys. Obatala jumped to a hill and named the place Ife. The dry land now extended as far as he could see.

He dug a hole, planted the palm nut, and saw it grow to maturity in a flash. The mature palm tree dropped more palm nuts on the ground, each of which grew immediately to maturity and repeated the process. Obatala settled down with the cat for company.

Many months passed, and he grew bored with his routine.

He decided to create beings like himself to keep him company. He dug into the sand and soon found clay with which to mold figures like himself and started on his task, but he soon grew tired and decided to take a break.

He made wine from a nearby palm tree, and drank bowl after bowl. Not realizing he was drunk, Obatala returned to his task of fashioning the new beings; because of his condition he fashioned many imperfect figures.

Without realizing this, he called out to Olorun to breathe life into his creatures.

The next day he realized what he had done and swore never to drink again, and to take care of those who were deformed, thus becoming Protector of the Deformed.

The new people built huts as Obatala had done and soon Ife prospered and became a city.

When Obatala returned to his home in the sky for a visit, Olokun summoned the great waves of her vast oceans and sent them surging across the land. Wave after wave she unleashed, until much of the land was underwater and many of the people were drowned. Those that had fled to the highest land beseeched the god Eshu who had been visiting, to return to the sky and report what was happening to them. Eshu demanded sacrifice be made to Obatala and himself before he would deliver the message.

The people sacrificed some goats, and Eshu returned to the sky.

When Orunmila heard the news he climbed down the golden chain to the earth, and cast many spells which caused the flood waters to retreat and the dry land reappear.

So ended the great flood

1. **What is the most important thing to be created in this narrative and why?**
2. **Explain the similarities and differences between this creation narrative and the others above.**

PRIMARY SOURCE 1.6

Wall Painting in the Dassili n'Ajjer Mountain Range

This detail from a wall painting in the Tassili n'Ajjer mountain range in North Africa depicts humans interacting with animals.

1. **What are the humans in this painting doing and why?**
2. **Which creation narrative helps explain the activity depicted in the image? How does the narrative you selected explain it?**

Questions for Analysis

Comparison

1. Compare and analyze these creation narratives. Which one do you find to be most compelling and why?

Contextualization

2. How might specific local circumstances have contributed to each of these creation narratives? Do you think these stories are geographically specific?

Long Essay Question

Interpretation

Consider the narrative of human origins presented in this chapter along with the creation narratives in these documents. Explain the relationship between the scientific theory of evolution and these creation narratives.

Before You Read This Chapter

GLOBAL STORYLINES

- Complex societies form around five great river basins.
- Early urbanization brings changes, including new technologies, monumental building, new religions, writing, hierarchical social structures, and specialized labor.
- Long-distance trade connects many of the Afro-Eurasian societies.
- Despite impressive developments in urbanization, most people live in villages or in pastoral nomadic communities.

CORE OBJECTIVES

- **IDENTIFY** the earliest river-basin societies and **ANALYZE** their shared and distinctive characteristics.
- **EXPLAIN** the religious, social, and political developments that accompany early urbanization from 3500 to 2000 BCE.
- **TRACE** and **EVALUATE** the influence of long-distance connections across Afro-Eurasia during this period.
- **COMPARE** early urbanization with the ways of life in small villages and among pastoral nomads.

CHAPTER

2

Rivers, Cities, and First States,

3500–2000 BCE

KEY TERMS

bronze p. 49
city p. 53
city-state p. 54
river basin p. 48
scribes p. 56
social hierarchies p. 54
territorial state p. 58
urban-rural divide p. 49

One of the first urban centers in the world was the ancient city of Uruk. Located in southern Mesopotamia on a branch of the Euphrates River, it was home to more than 10,000 people by the late fourth millennium BCE and boasted many large public structures and temples. One temple had stood there since before 3000 BCE; with plastered mud-brick walls that formed stepped indentations, it perched high above the plain. In another area, administrative buildings and temples adorned with elaborate facades stood in courtyards defined by tall columns. Colored stone cones arranged in elaborate geometric patterns covered parts of these buildings. An epic poem devoted to its later king, Gilgamesh, described Uruk as the "shining city."

Over the years Uruk became an immense commercial and administrative center. A huge wall with seven massive gates surrounded the metropolis, and down the middle ran a canal carrying water from the Euphrates. On one side of the city were gardens, kilns, and textile workshops. On the other was the temple quarter where priests lived, scribes kept records, and lu-gal ("the big man") conferred with the elders. As Uruk grew, many small industries—including potters, metalsmiths, stone bowl makers, and brickmakers—became centralized in response to the increasing sophistication of construction and manufacturing.

Uruk was the first city of its kind in world history. Earlier humans had settled in small communities scattered over the landscape. As some communities gradually became focal points for trade, a few of these hubs grew into cities with large populations and institutions of economic, religious, and political power. Most inhabitants no longer produced their own food, working instead in specialized professions.

Between 3500 and 2000 BCE, a handful of remarkable societies clustered in a few river basins on the Afro-Eurasian landmass. These regions—in Mesopotamia (between the Tigris and Euphrates rivers), in northwest India (on the Indus River), in Egypt (along the Nile), and in China (near the Yangzi and Yellow rivers)—became the heartlands for densely populated settlements with complex cultures. Here the world saw the birth of the first large cities and territorial states. One of these settings (Mesopotamia) brought forth humankind's first writing system, and all laid the foundations for kingdoms radiating out of opulent cities. This chapter describes how each society evolved, and it explores their similarities and differences. It is important to note how exceptional these large cities and territorial states were, and we will see that many smaller societies prevailed elsewhere. The Aegean, Anatolia, western Europe, the Americas, and sub-Saharan Africa offer reminders that most of the world's people dwelt in small communities, far removed culturally from the monumental architecture and accomplishments of the big new states.

Settlement and Pastoralism

COMPARISON

IDENTIFY the earliest river-basin societies and **ANALYZE** their shared characteristics.

Around 3500 BCE, cultural changes, population growth, and technological innovations gave rise to complex societies. Clustered in cities, these larger communities developed new institutions, and individuals took on a wide range of social roles, resulting in new hierarchies based on wealth and gender. At the same time, the number of small villages and pastoral nomadic communities grew.

Water was the key to settlement, since predictable flows of water determined where humans settled. Reliable water supplies allowed communities to sow crops adequate to feed large populations. Abundant rainfall allowed the world's first villages to emerge, but the breakthroughs into big cities occurred in drier zones where large rivers formed beds of rich soils deposited by flooding rivers. With irrigation innovations, soils became arable. Equally important, a worldwide warming cycle expanded growing seasons. The **river basins**—with their fertile soil, irrigation, and available domesticated plants and animals—made possible the agricultural surpluses needed to support city dwellers.

Early Mesopotamian Waterworks From the sixth millennium BCE, irrigation was necessary for successful farming in southern Mesopotamia. By the first millennium BCE, sophisticated feats of engineering allowed the Assyrians to redirect water through constructed aqueducts, like the one illustrated here on a relief from the palace of the Assyrian king Sennacherib at Nineveh.

EARLY CITIES ALONG RIVER BASINS

The material and social advances of the early cities occurred in a remarkably short period—from 3500 to 2000 BCE—in three locations: the basin of the Tigris and Euphrates rivers in central Southwest Asia; the northern parts of the Nile River flowing toward the Mediterranean Sea; and the Indus River basin in northwestern South Asia. About a millennium later a similar process began along the Yellow River and the

Yangzi River in China. (See Map 2.1.) In these regions humans farmed and fed themselves by relying on intensive irrigation agriculture. Gathering in cities inhabited by rulers, administrators, priests, and craftworkers, they changed their methods of organizing communities by worshipping new gods in new ways and by obeying divinely inspired monarchs and elaborate bureaucracies. New technologies appeared, ranging from the wheel for pottery production to metal- and stoneworking for the creation of both luxury objects and utilitarian tools. The technology of writing used the storage of words and meanings to extend human communication and memory.

With cities and new technologies came greater divisions of labor. Dense urban settlement enabled people to specialize in making goods for the consumption of others: weavers made textiles, potters made ceramics, and jewelers made precious ornaments. Soon these goods found additional uses in trade with outlying areas. And as trade expanded over longer distances, raw materials such as wool, metal, timber, and precious stones arrived in the cities. (See Map 2.2.) One of the most coveted metals was copper: easily smelted and shaped (not to mention shiny and alluring), it became the metal of choice for charms, sculptures, and valued commodities. When combined with arsenic or tin, copper hardens and becomes **bronze**, which is useful for tools and weapons. Consequently, this period is often called a Bronze Age, though the term simplifies the breadth of the breakthroughs.

The emergence of cities as population centers created one of history's most durable worldwide distinctions: the **urban-rural divide**. Where cities appeared alongside rivers, people adopted lifestyles based on specialized labor and the mass production of goods. In contrast, most people continued to live in the countryside, where they remained on their lands, cultivating the land or tending livestock, though they exchanged their grains and animal products for goods from the urban centers. The two ways of life were interdependent and both worlds remained linked through family ties, trade, politics, and religion.

PASTORAL NOMADIC COMMUNITIES

Around 3500 BCE, Afro-Eurasia also witnessed the growth and spread of pastoral nomadic communities. The transhumant herder communities that had appeared in Southwest Asia around 5500 BCE (see Chapter 1) continued to be small and their settlements impermanent. They lacked substantial public buildings or infrastructure, but their seasonal moves followed a consistent pattern. Across the vast expanse of Afro-Eurasia's great mountains and its desert barriers, and from its steppe lands ranging across inner and central Eurasia to the Pacific Ocean, these transhumant herders lived alongside settled agrarian people, especially when occupying their lowland pastures. They traded meat and animal products for grains, pottery, and tools produced in the agrarian communities.

In the arid environments of Inner Mongolia and central Asia, transhumant herding and agrarian communities initially followed the same combination of herding animals and cultivating crops that had proved so successful in Southwest Asia. However, because the steppe environment could not support large-scale farming, these communities came to focus on animal breeding and herding. As secondary pursuits they continued to fish, hunt, and farm small plots in their winter pastures. Their economy centered on domesticated cattle, sheep, and horses. As their herds increased, these horse-riding nomads had to move often to new pastures, driving their herds across vast expanses of land. By the second millennium BCE, they had become full-scale nomadic pastoral communities, and they dominated the steppes. In these pastoral nomadic economies of the arid zones of central Eurasia, horses became crucial to survival. These nomadic and transhumant groups played a vital role in connecting cities and spreading ideas throughout Afro-Eurasia.

NORTH AMERICA
ATLANTIC OCEAN
PACIFIC OCEAN
TEHUACAN VALLEY
CHICAMA VALLEY
ANDES MOUNTAINS
SOUTH AMERICA
SAHARA
SAHEL
Desert
Pastoral belt – steppe lands
Tropical rain forest
Agricultural society 3000 BCE
Riverine societies (early cities)
Widespread village culture
0 1000 2000 Miles
0 1000 2000 Kilometers

MAP 2.1 | The World in the Third Millennium BCE

Human societies became increasingly diversified as agricultural, urban, and pastoral nomadic communities expanded.

- In what different regions did pastoralism and river basin societies emerge?
- Considering the geographic features highlighted on this map, why do you think cities appeared in the regions that they did?
- How did geographic and environmental factors promote interaction between nomadic pastoral and sedentary agricultural societies?

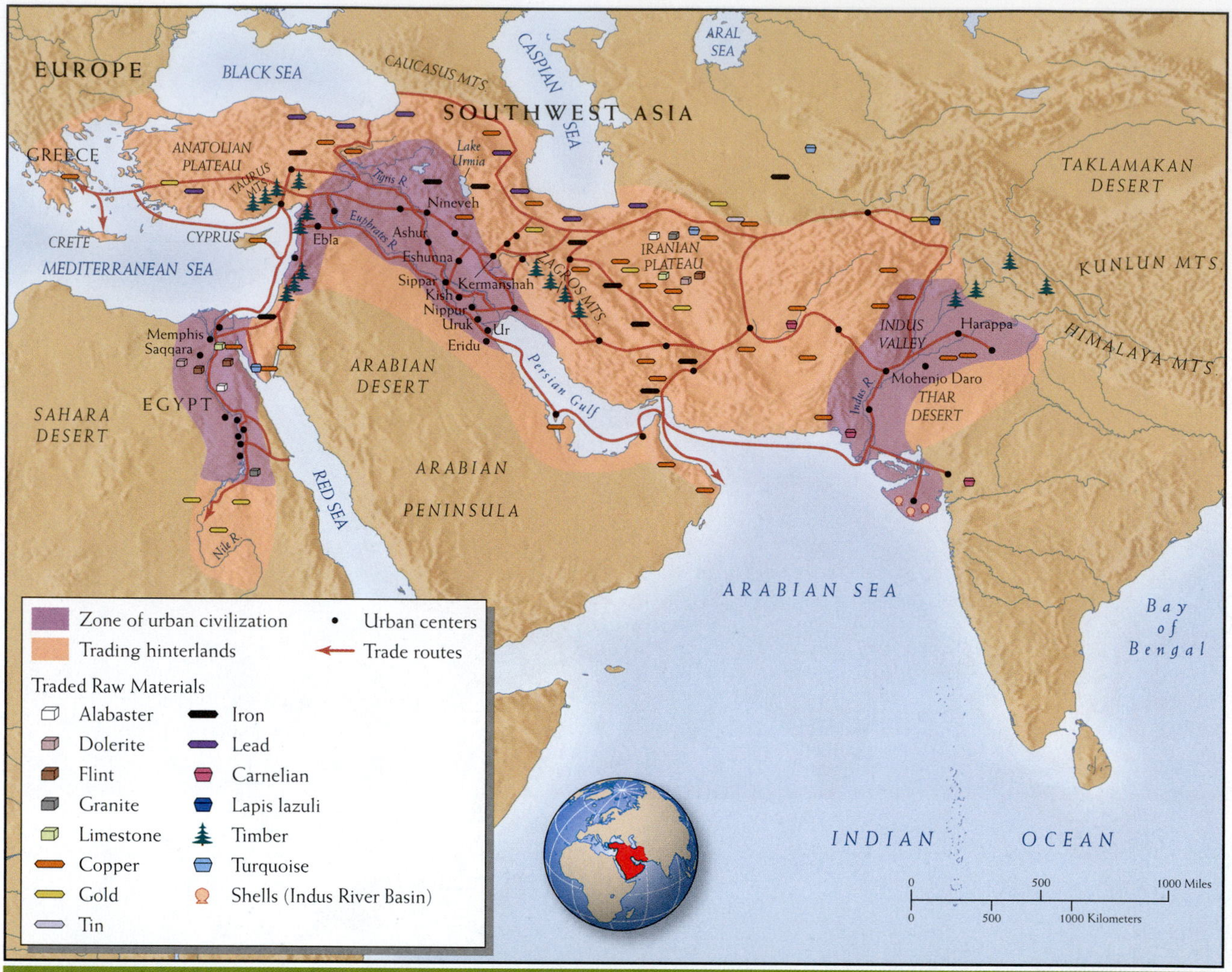

MAP 2.2 | Trade and Exchange in Southwest Asia and the Eastern Mediterranean—Third Millennium BCE

Extensive commercial networks linked the urban cores of Southwest Asia.

- Of the traded raw materials shown on the map, which ones were used for building materials, and which ones for luxury items?
- Why were there more extensive trade connections between Mesopotamians and people to their northwest and east than with Egypt to the west?
- According to the map, in what ways did Mesopotamia become the crossroads of Afro-Eurasia?

Between the Tigris and Euphrates Rivers: Mesopotamia

COMPARISON

EXPLAIN the religious, social, and political developments that accompany early urbanization in the river basin societies from 3500 to 2000 BCE.

The world's first complex society arose in Mesopotamia. Here the river and the first cities changed how people lived. Mesopotamia, whose name is a Greek word meaning "[region] between two rivers," is a landmass including all of modern-day Iraq and parts of Syria and southeastern Turkey. From their headwaters in the mountains to the north and east to their destination in the Persian Gulf, the Tigris and Euphrates rivers are wild and unpredictable. Unpredictable floodwaters could wipe out years of hard work, but when managed properly they could transform the landscape into verdant and productive fields.

Both rivers provided water for irrigation and, although hardly navigable, were important routes for transportation and communication by pack animal and by foot. Mesopotamia's natural advantages—its rich agricultural land and water, combined with easy access to neighboring regions—favored the growth of cities and later territorial states. These cities and states became the sites of important cultural, political, and social innovations.

TAPPING THE WATERS

The first rudimentary advances in irrigation occurred in the foothills of the Zagros Mountains along the banks of the smaller rivers that feed the Tigris. Converting the floodplain of the Euphrates River into a breadbasket, however, required mastering the unpredictable waters. (A floodplain is an area where the river overflows and deposits fertile soil.) Both the Euphrates and the Tigris, unless controlled by waterworks, were unfavorable to cultivators because the annual floods occurred at the height of the growing season, when crops were most vulnerable. Low water levels occurred when crops required abundant irrigation. To prevent the river from overflowing during its flood stage, farmers built levees along the banks and dug ditches and canals to drain away the floodwaters. Engineers devised an irrigation system whereby the Euphrates, the riverbed of which is higher than the Tigris, essentially served as the supply and the Tigris as the drain. Storing and channeling water year after year required constant maintenance and innovation by a corps of engineers.

The Mesopotamians' technological breakthrough was in irrigation, not in agrarian methods. Because the soils were fine, rich, and constantly replenished by the floodwaters' silt, soil tillage was light work. Farmers sowed a combination of wheat, millet, sesame, and barley (the basis for beer, a staple of their diet).

CROSSROADS OF SOUTHWEST ASIA

Though its soil was rich and water was abundant, southern Mesopotamia had few other natural resources apart from the mud, marsh reeds, spindly trees, and low-quality limestone that served as basic building materials. To obtain high-quality, dense wood, stone, metal, and other materials for constructing and embellishing their cities with their temples and palaces, Mesopotamians had to interact with the inhabitants of surrounding regions. In return for textiles, oils, and other commodities, they imported cedar wood from Lebanon, copper and stones from Oman, more copper from Turkey and Iran, and the precious blue gemstone called lapis lazuli, as well as the ever-useful tin, from faraway Afghanistan. Maintaining trading contacts was easy, given Mesopotamia's open boundaries on all sides. The area became a crossroads for the peoples of Southwest Asia, including Sumerians, who concentrated in the south; Hurrians, who lived in the north; and Akkadians, who populated western and central Mesopotamia. Trade and migration contributed to the growth of cities throughout the river basin, beginning with the Sumerian cities of southern Mesopotamia.

THE WORLD'S FIRST CITIES

During the first half of the fourth millennium BCE, a demographic transformation occurred in the Tigris-Euphrates river basin, especially in the southern area called Sumer. The population expanded as a result of the region's agricultural bounty, and many Mesopotamians migrated from country villages to centers that eventually became cities. (A **city** is a large, well-defined urban area with a dense population.) The earliest Sumerian cities—Eridu, Nippur, and Uruk—developed over about 1,000 years, dominating the southern part of the floodplain by 3500 BCE. Buildings of mud brick show successive layers of urban development, as at Eridu, where more than twenty reconstructed temples were piled atop one

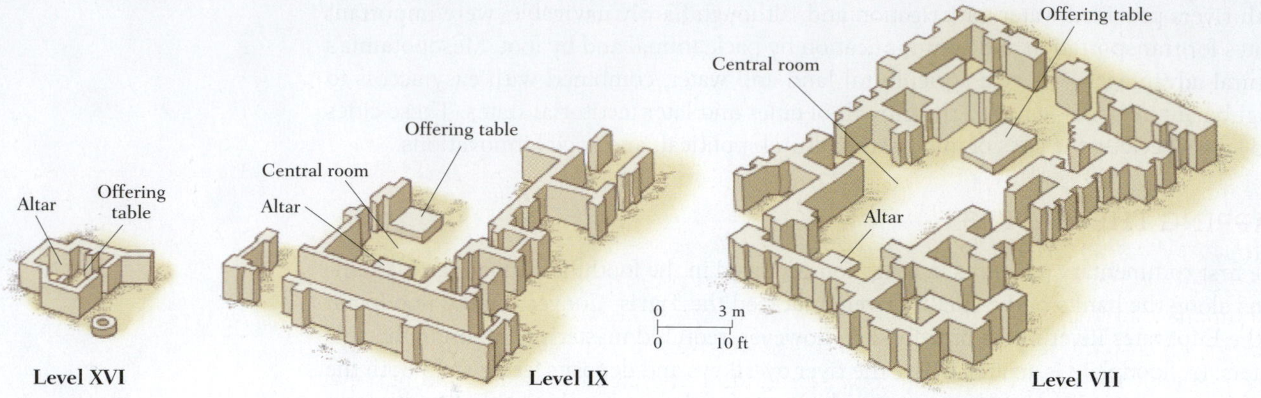

Layout of Eridu Over several millennia, temples of increasing size and complexity were built atop each other at Eridu in southern Iraq. The culmination came with the elaborate structure of level VII.

another across four millennia, resulting in a final temple that rose from a platform like a mountain, visible for miles in all directions.

As the temple grew skyward, the village expanded outward and became a city. From their homes in temples located at the center of cities, the cities' gods broadcast their powers. In return, urbanites provided luxuries, fine clothes, and enhanced lodgings for the gods and their priests. In Sumerian cosmology, created by ruling elites, man existed solely to serve the gods, so the urban landscape reflected this fact: a temple at the core, with goods and services flowing to the center and with divine protection and justice flowing outward.

Some thirty-five cities with religious sanctuaries dotted the southern plain of Mesopotamia. Sumerian ideology glorified a way of life and a territory based on politically equal city-states, each with a guardian deity and sanctuary supported by its inhabitants. (A **city-state** is a political organization based on the authority of a single, large city that controls outlying territories.) Because early Mesopotamian cities served as meeting places for peoples and their deities, they gained status as religious and economic centers. Whether enormous (like Uruk and Nippur) or modest (like Ur and Abu Salabikh), all cities were spiritual, economic, and cultural homes for Mesopotamian subjects.

Simply making a city was therefore not enough: urban design reflected the city's role as a wondrous place to pay homage to the gods and their human intermediary, the king. Within their walls, early cities contained large houses separated by date-palm plantations and extensive sheepfolds. As populations grew, the Mesopotamian cities became denser, houses smaller, and new suburbs spilled out beyond the old walls. The typical layout of Mesopotamian cities reflected a common pattern: a central canal surrounded by neighborhoods of specialized occupational groups. The temple marked the city center, with the palace and other official buildings on the periphery. In separate quarters for craft production, families passed down their trades across generations. In this sense, the landscape of the city mirrored the growing **social hierarchies** (distinctions between the privileged and the less privileged).

GODS AND TEMPLES

The worldview of the Sumerians and, later, the Akkadians included a belief in a group of gods that shaped their political institutions and controlled everything—including the weather, fertility, harvests, and the underworld. As depicted in the *Epic of Gilgamesh* (a second-millennium BCE composition based on oral tales about Gilgamesh, a historical but mythologized king of Uruk), the gods could give but could also take away—with droughts, floods, and death. Gods, and the natural forces they controlled, had to be revered and feared. Faithful subjects imagined their gods as immortal beings whose habits were capricious, contentious, and gloriously work-free.

Each major god of the Sumerian pantheon (an officially recognized group of gods) dwelled in a lavish temple in a particular city that he or she had created, giving rise to each city's character, institutions, and relationships with its urban neighbors. Inside these temples were altars displaying the god's image. Benches lined the walls, with statues of humans standing in perpetual worship of the deity's images. By the end of the third millennium BCE, the temple's platform base had changed to a stepped platform called a *ziggurat*, with the main temple on top. Surrounding the ziggurat were buildings that housed priests, officials, laborers, and servants.

Temples functioned as the god's estate, engaging in all sorts of productive and commercial activities. Temple dependents cultivated cereals, fruits, and vegetables by using extensive irrigation and cared for flocks of livestock. Other temples operated workshops for manufacturing textiles and leather goods, employing craftworkers, metalworkers, masons, and stoneworkers. Enormous labor forces were involved in maintaining this high level of production.

ROYAL POWER, FAMILIES, AND SOCIAL HIERARCHY

Like the temples, royal palaces reflected the power of the ruling elites. Royal palaces appeared around 2500 BCE and served as the official residence of a ruler, his family, and his entourage. As access to palaces and temples over time became limited, gods and kings became inaccessible to all but the most elite. Although located at the edge of cities, palaces were the symbols of permanent secular, military, and administrative authority distinct from the temples' spiritual and economic power.

The Royal Cemetery at Ur shows how Mesopotamian rulers used elaborate burial arrangements to reinforce their religious and socioeconomic hierarchies. Housed in a mud-brick structure, the royal burials held not only the primary remains but also the bodies of more than eighty men and women who had been sacrificed. Huge vats for cooked food, bones of animals, drinking vessels, and musical instruments suggest the lifestyle of those who joined their masters in the graves. Honoring the royal dead by including their followers and possessions in their tombs underscored the social hierarchies—including the vertical ties between humans and gods—that were the cornerstone of these early city-states.

Social hierarchies were an important part of the fabric of Sumerian city-states. Ruling groups secured their privileged access to economic and political resources by erecting systems of bureaucracies, priesthoods, and laws. Priests and bureaucrats served their rulers well, championing rules and norms that legitimized the political leadership. Occupations within the cities were highly specialized, and a list of professions circulated across the land so that everyone could know his or her place in the social order. The king and priest in Sumer were at the top of the list, followed by bureaucrats (scribes and household accountants), supervisors, and craftworkers, such as cooks, jewelers, gardeners, potters, metalsmiths, and traders. The biggest group, which was at the bottom of the hierarchy, comprised workers who were not slaves but who were dependent on their

The Royal Tombs of Ur The Royal Tombs of Ur, excavated in the 1930s, contained thousands of objects in gold, silver, lapis lazuli, and shell that were buried along with elites of the First Dynasty of Ur. Pu-Abi, identified as a queen by the cylinder near her body, was buried in a separate chamber. She was interred in full regalia, including the elaborate headdress shown here.

employers' households. Movement among economic classes was not impossible but, as in many traditional societies, it was rare.

The family and the household provided the bedrock for Sumerian society, and its patriarchal organization, dominated by the senior male, reflected the balance between women and men, children and parents. The family consisted of the husband and wife bound by a contract: she would provide children, preferably male, while he provided support and protection. Monogamy was the norm unless there was no son, in which case a second wife or a slave girl would bear male children to serve as the married couple's offspring. Adoption was another way to gain a male heir. Sons would inherit the family's property in equal shares, while daughters would receive dowries necessary for successful marriage into other families. Some women joined the temple staff as priestesses and gained economic autonomy that included ownership of estates and productive enterprises, although their fathers and brothers remained responsible for their well-being.

FIRST WRITING AND EARLY TEXTS

Mesopotamia was the birthplace of the world's first writing system, inscribed to promote the economic power of the temples and kings. Those who wielded new writing tools were **scribes**; from the very beginning they were near the top of the social ladder, under the big man and the priests. As the writing of texts became more important to the social fabric of cities, and facilitated information sharing across wider spans of distance and time, scribes consolidated their elite status.

Mesopotamians were the world's first record keepers and readers. The precursors to writing appeared in Mesopotamian societies when farming peoples and officials who had been using clay tokens and images carved on stones to seal off storage areas began to use them to convey messages. These images, when combined with numbers drawn on clay tablets, could record the distribution of goods and services.

Around 3200 BCE, someone, probably in Uruk, understood that the marks (most were pictures of objects) could also represent words or sounds. Before long, scribes connected visual symbols with sounds, and sounds with meanings, and they discovered they could record messages by using abstract symbols or signs to denote concepts. Such signs later came to represent syllables, the building blocks of words. By impressing signs into wet clay with the cut end of a reed, scribes pioneered a form of wedge-shaped writing that we call *cuneiform;* it filled tablets with information that was intelligible to anyone who could decipher it, even in faraway locations or in future generations. Developing over 800 years, this Sumerian innovation enhanced the urban elites' ability to trade goods, to control property, and to transmit ideas through literature, historical records, and sacred texts. The result was a profound change in human experience, because representing symbols of spoken language facilitated an extension of communication and memory.

Much of what we know about Mesopotamia rests on our ability to decipher cuneiform script. By around 2400 BCE, texts began to describe the political makeup of southern Mesopotamia, giving details of its history and economy. Adaptable to different languages, cuneiform was borrowed by cities in northern Mesopotamia to write their Semitic language.

City life and literacy gave rise also to written narratives, the stories of a "people" and their origins. "The Temple Hymns," written around 2100 BCE, describe thirty-five divine sanctuaries. The Sumerian King List, known from texts written around 2000 BCE, recounts the reigns of kings by city and dynasty and narrates the long reigns of legendary kings before the so-called Great Flood. A crucial event in Sumerian identity, the Great Flood, found also in Biblical narrative, explained Uruk's demise as the gods' doing. Flooding was the most powerful natural force in the lives of those who lived by rivers, and it helped shape the foundations of Mesopotamian societies.

SPREADING CITIES AND FIRST TERRITORIAL STATES

No single state dominated Mesopotamia in the fourth and third millennia BCE, but the most powerful and influential were the Sumerian city-states (2850–2334 BCE) and their successor, the Akkadian territorial state (2334–2193 BCE). In the north, Hurrians urbanized their rich agricultural zone around 2600 BCE. (See Map 2.3.)

Sumerian city-states, with their expanding populations, soon found themselves competing for agrarian lands, scarce water, and lucrative trade routes. And as pastoralists far and wide learned of the region's bounty, they journeyed in greater numbers to the cities, fueling urbanization and competition. The world's first great conqueror—Sargon the Great (r. 2334–2279 BCE), king of Akkad—emerged from one of these cities. By the end of his reign he had united (by force) the independent Mesopotamian cities south of modern-day Baghdad and brought the era of competitive independent city-states to an end. Sargon's unification of the

MAP 2.3 | The Spread of Cities in Mesopotamia and the Akkadian State, 2600-2200 BCE

Urbanization began in the southern river basin of Mesopotamia and spread northward. Eventually, the region achieved unification under Akkadian power.

- According to this map, what were the natural boundaries of the Mesopotamian cities?
- How did proximity to the Zagros Mountains affect the new urban centers?
- How did the expansion northward reflect the continued influence of geographic and environmental factors on urbanization?

southern cities by alliance, though relatively short-lived, created a **territorial state**. (A territorial state is a form of political organization that holds authority over a large population and landmass; its power extends over multiple cities.) Sargon's dynasty sponsored monumental architecture, artworks, and literary works, which in turn inspired generations of builders, architects, artists, and scribes. And by encouraging contact with distant neighbors, many of whom adopted aspects of Mesopotamian culture, the Akkadian kings increased the geographic reach of Mesopotamian influence. Just under a century after Sargon's death, foreign tribesmen from the Zagros Mountains conquered the capital city of Akkad around 2190 BCE, setting the beginning of a pattern that would fuel epic history writing, namely the struggles between city-state dwellers and those on the margins who lived a simpler way of life. The impressive state created by Sargon was made possible by Mesopotamia's early innovations in irrigation, urban development, and writing. While Mesopotamia led the way in creating city-states, Egypt went a step further, unifying a 600-mile-long landmass under a single ruler.

"The Gift of the Nile": Egypt

In Egypt, complex societies grew on the banks of the Nile River, and by the third millennium BCE their peoples created a distinctive culture and a powerful, prosperous state. The earliest inhabitants along the banks of the Nile were a mixed people. Some had migrated from the eastern and western deserts in Sinai and Libya as these areas grew barren from climate change. Others came from the Mediterranean. Equally important were peoples who trekked northward from Nubia and central Africa. Ancient Egypt was a melting pot where immigrants blended cultural practices and technologies.

Like Mesopotamia, Egypt had densely populated areas whose inhabitants depended on irrigation, built monumental architecture, gave their rulers immense authority, and created a complex social order based in commercial and devotional centers. Yet the ancient Egyptian culture was profoundly shaped by its geography. The environment and the natural boundaries of deserts, river rapids, and sea dominated the country and its inhabitants. Only about 3 percent of Egypt's land area was cultivable, and almost all of that cultivable land was in the Nile Delta—the rich alluvial land lying between the river's two main branches as it flows north of modern-day Cairo into the Mediterranean Sea. This environment shaped Egyptian society's unique culture.

THE NILE RIVER AND ITS FLOODWATERS

Knowing Egypt requires appreciating the pulses of the Nile. The world's longest river, it stretches 4,238 miles from its sources in the highlands of central Africa to its destination in the Mediterranean Sea. Egypt was deeply attached to sub-Saharan Africa; not only did its waters and rich silt deposits come from the African highlands, but much of its original population had migrated into the Nile valley from the west and the south many millennia earlier.

The Upper Nile is a sluggish river that cuts through the Sahara Desert. Rising out of central Africa and Ethiopia, its two main branches—the White and Blue Niles—meet at present-day Khartoum and then scour out a single riverbed 1,500 miles long to the Mediterranean. The annual floods gave the basin regular moisture and enriched the soil. Although the Nile's floodwaters did not fertilize or irrigate fields as broad as those in Mesopotamia, they created green belts flanking the broad waterway. These gave rise to a society whose culture stretched along the navigable river and its carefully preserved banks. Away from the riverbanks, on both sides, lay a desert rich in raw materials but largely uninhabited. (See Map 2.4.) Egypt had no fertile hinterland like the sprawling plains of Mesopotamia. In this way, Egypt was arguably the most river-focused of river-basin cultures.

MAP 2.4 | Old Kingdom Egypt, 2686–2181 BCE

Old Kingdom Egyptian society reflected a strong influence from its unique geographical location.

- What geographical features contributed to Egypt's isolation from the outside world and the people's sense of their unity?
- What natural resource enabled the Egyptians to build the Great Pyramids?
- Based on the map, why do you think it was important to the people and their rulers for Upper and Lower Egypt to be united?

The Nile's predictability as the source of life and abundance shaped the character of the people and their culture. In contrast to the wild and uncertain Euphrates and Tigris rivers, the Nile was gentle, bountiful, and reliable. During the summer, as the Nile swelled, local villagers built earthen walls that divided the floodplain into basins. By trapping the floodwaters, these basins captured the rich silt washing down from the Ethiopian highlands. Annual flooding meant that the land received a new layer of topsoil every year. The light, fertile soils made planting simple. Peasants cast seeds into the alluvial soil and then had their livestock trample them to the proper depth. The never-failing sun, which the Egyptians worshipped, ensured an abundant harvest. In the early spring, when the Nile's waters were at their lowest and no crops were under cultivation, the sun dried out the soil.

The peculiarities of the Nile region distinguished it from Mesopotamia. The Greek historian and geographer Herodotus 2,500 years ago noted that Egypt was the gift of the Nile and that the entire length of its basin was one of the world's most self-contained geographical entities. Bounded on the north by the Mediterranean Sea, on the east and west by deserts, and on the south by waterfalls, Egypt was destined to achieve a common culture. Due to these geographical features, the region was far less open to outsiders than was Mesopotamia, which was situated at a crossroads. Egypt created a common culture by balancing a struggle of opposing forces: the north or Lower Egypt versus the south or Upper Egypt; the red sand versus the black, rich soil; life versus death; heaven versus earth; order versus disorder. For Egypt's rulers the primary task was to bring stability or order, known as *ma'at*, out of these opposites. The Egyptians believed that keeping chaos, personified by the desert and its marauders, at bay through attention to *ma'at* would allow all that was good and right to occur.

THE EGYPTIAN STATE AND DYNASTIES

Once the early Egyptians harnessed the Nile to agriculture, the area changed quickly from being scarcely inhabited to socially complex. A king, called pharaoh and considered semidivine, ensured that the forces of nature, in particular the regular flooding of the Nile, continued without interruption. This task had more to do with appeasing the gods than with running a complex hydraulic system. The king protected his people from chaos-threatening invaders from the eastern desert, as well as from Nubians on the southern borders. In wall carvings, artists portrayed early kings carrying the shepherd's crook and the flail, indicating their responsibility for the welfare of their flocks (the people) and of the land. Under the king an elaborate bureaucracy organized labor and produced public works, sustaining both his vast holdings and general order throughout the realm.

The narrative of ancient Egyptian history follows its thirty-one dynasties, spanning nearly three millennia from 3100 BCE down to its conquest by Alexander the Great in 332 BCE. Since the nineteenth century, scholars have recast the story around three periods of dynastic achievement: the Old Kingdom, the Middle Kingdom, and the New Kingdom. At the end of each era, cultural flourishing suffered a breakdown in central authority, known respectively as the First, Second, and Third Intermediate Periods.

PHARAOHS, PYRAMIDS, AND COSMIC ORDER

The Third Dynasty (2686–2613 BCE) launched the foundational period known as the Old Kingdom, the golden age of ancient Egypt. By the time it began, the basic institutions of the Egyptian state were in place, as were the ideology and ritual life that legitimized the dynastic rulers.

The pharaoh—king as god—presented himself to the population by means of impressive architectural spaces, and the priestly class performed rituals reinforcing his supreme status within the universe's natural order. One of the most important rituals was the Sed festival, which renewed the king's vitality after he had ruled for thirty years and sought to ensure the perpetual presence of water. King Djoser, of the Third Dynasty, celebrated the Sed festival at his tomb complex at Saqqara. This magnificent complex is the world's oldest stone structure, dating to around 2650 BCE. Djoser's architect, Imhotep, designed a step pyramid that ultimately rose some 200 feet above the plain. The whole complex became a stage for state rituals that emphasized the divinity of kingship and the unity of Egypt.

TABLE 2.1 | Dynasties of Ancient Egypt

SPECIES	TIME
Pre-dynastic Period dynasties I and II	3100–2686 BCE
Old Kingdom dynasties III–VI	2686–2181 BCE
First Intermediate Period dynasties VII–X	2181–2055 BCE
Middle Kingdom dynasties XI–XIII	2055–1650 BCE
Second Intermediate Period dynasties XIV–XVII	1650–1550 BCE
New Kingdom dynasties XVIII–XX	1550–1069 BCE
Third Intermediate Period dynasties XXI–XXV	1069–747 BCE
Late Period dynasties XXVI–XXXI	747–332 BCE

Source: Compiled from Ian Shaw and Paul Nicholson, eds., The Dictionary of Ancient Egypt *(1995), pp. 310–11.*

Pharaohs used their royal tombs, and the ritual of death leading to everlasting life, to embody the state's ideology and the principles of the Egyptian cosmos. The pharaoh also employed symbols, throne names, and descriptive titles for himself and his advisers to represent his own power and that of his administrators, the priests, and the landed elite. The Egyptian cosmic order was one of inequality and stark hierarchy, not dissimilar to the hierarchies of Mesopotamia. Established at the time of creation, the universe was the king's responsibility to maintain for eternity.

The step pyramid at Djoser's tomb complex was a precursor to the grand pyramids of the Fourth Dynasty (2613–2494 BCE). These kings erected their monumental structures at Giza, just outside modern-day Cairo and not far from the early royal cemetery site of Saqqara. The pyramid of Khufu, rising 481 feet above ground, is the largest stone structure in the world, and its corners are almost perfectly aligned to due north, west, south, and east. Surrounding these royal tombs at Giza were those of high officials, almost all members of the royal family. The enormous amount of labor involved in building these monuments came from peasant-workers, slaves brought from Nubia, and captured Mediterranean peoples. Through their majesty and complex construction, the Giza pyramids reflect the degree of centralization and the surpluses in Egyptian society at this time.

GODS, PRIESTHOOD, AND MAGICAL POWER

Egyptians understood their world as inhabited by three groups: gods, kings, and the rest of humanity. Official records only showed representations of gods and kings. Yet the people did not confuse their kings with gods—at least during the kings' lifetimes. Mortality was the bar between rulers and deities; after death, kings joined the gods whom they had represented while alive.

As in Mesopotamia, every region in Egypt had its resident god. Some gods, such as Amun (believed to be physically present in Thebes, the political center of Upper Egypt), transcended regional status because of the importance of their hometown. Over the centuries the Egyptian gods evolved, combining often-contradictory aspects into single deities, including: Horus, the hawk god; Osiris, the god of regeneration and the underworld; Isis, who represented the ideals of sisterhood and motherhood; Hathor, the goddess of childbirth and love; Ra, the sun god; and Amun, a creator considered to be the hidden god.

Official religious practices took place in the main temples. The king and his agents offered respect, adoration, and thanks to the gods in their temples. In return, the gods maintained order and nurtured the king and —through him—all humanity. In this contractual relationship, the gods were passive while the kings were active, a difference that reflected their unequal relationship.

The tasks of regulating religious rituals and mediating among gods, kings, and society fell to one specialist class: the priesthood. Creating this class required elaborate rules for selecting and training the priests. Only priests could enter the temples' inner sanctuaries, and the gods' statues only left the temples for great festivals. Thus, priests monopolized communication between spiritual powers and their subjects.

Unofficial religion was also important. Ordinary Egyptians matched their elite rulers in faithfulness to the gods, but their distance from temple life caused them to find different ways to fulfill their religious needs and duties. They visited local shrines, where they prayed, made requests, and left offerings to the gods. Magic had a special importance for commoners, who believed that amulets held extraordinary powers, such as preventing

Egyptian Gods Osiris (*left*) is the dying god who rules over the netherworld. Most frequently he is depicted as a mummy wearing a white crown with plumes and holding the scepter across his chest. The god Horus (*right*), who was also rendered as Ra-Horakhty, is the falcon-headed Egyptian sky god. Horus is the earliest state god of Egypt and is always closely associated with the king. Horus is a member of the nine deities of Heliopolis and is the son of Osiris and Isis.

illness and guaranteeing safe childbirth. To deal with profound questions, commoners looked to omens and divination. Spiritual expression was central to Egyptian culture at all levels, and religion helped shape other cultural achievements, including the development of a written language.

WRITING AND SCRIBES

Egypt, like Mesopotamia, was a scribal culture. By the middle of the third millennium BCE, literacy was well established among small circles of scribes in Egypt and Mesopotamia. The fact that few individuals were literate heightened the scribes' social status. Most high-ranking Egyptians were also trained as scribes working in the king's court, the army, or the priesthood. Some kings and members of the royal family learned to write as well. Although in both cultures writing emerged in response to economic needs, people soon grasped its utility for commemorative and religious purposes. As soon as literacy took hold, Mesopotamians and Egyptians were drafting historical records and literary compositions.

Ancient Egyptians used two forms of writing. Elaborate *hieroglyphs* (from the Greek "sacred carving") served in formal temple, royal, or divine contexts. More common, however, was *hieratic* writing, a cursive script written with ink on papyrus or pottery. (*Demotic* writing, from the Greek *demotika*, meaning "popular" or "in common use," developed much later and became the vital transitional key on the Rosetta Stone that ultimately allowed the nineteenth-century decipherment of hieroglyphics. (See **Analyzing Global Developments: The Development of Writing**.) Used for record keeping, hieratic writing also found uses in letters and works of literature—including narrative fiction, manuals of instruction and philosophy, cult and religious hymns, love poems, medical and mathematical texts, collections of rituals, and mortuary books.

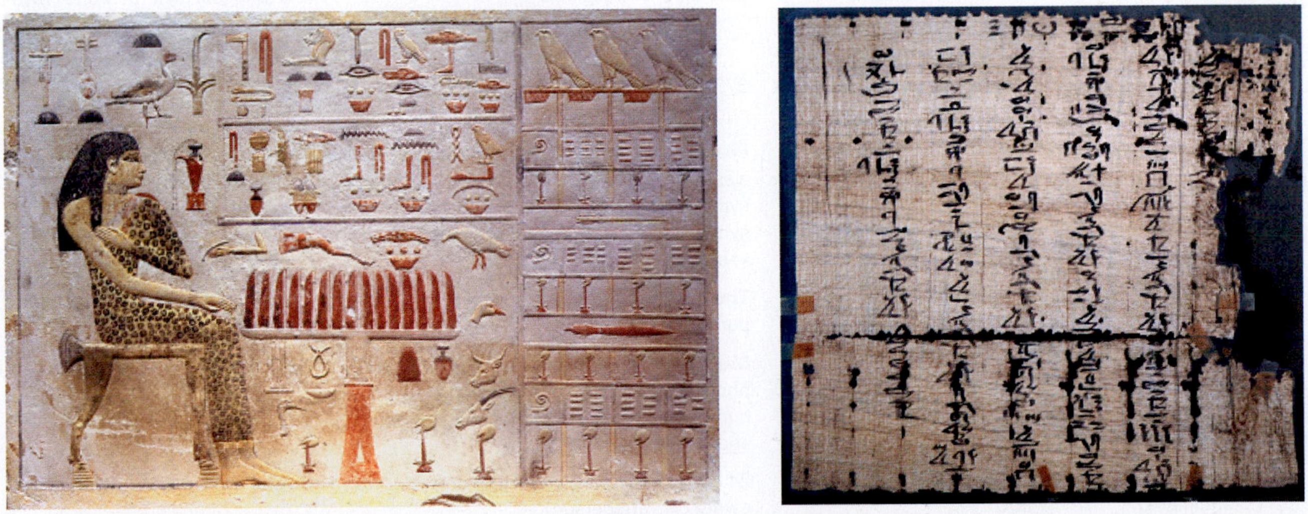

Egyptian Hieroglyphs and "Cursive Script" The Egyptians wrote in two distinctive types of script. The more formal is hieroglyphs, which is based on pictorial images that carry values of either ideas (logograms) or sounds (phonemes). All royal and funerary inscriptions, such as this funerary relief from the Old Kingdom, are rendered in hieroglyphic script. Daily documents, accountings, literary texts, and the like were most often written in a cursive script called hieratic, which was written with ink on papyrus. The form of the cursive signs is based on the hieroglyphs but is more abstract and can be formed more quickly.

Analyzing Global Developments

The Development of Writing

Agricultural surplus, and the urbanization and labor specialization that accompanied it, prompted the earliest development of writing and the profession of the scribes whose job it was to write. Early forms of writing were employed for a variety of purposes such as keeping economic and administration records, recording the reigns of rulers, and preserving religious events and practices (calendars, rituals, and divinatory purposes). By the third millennium BCE, some early societies (Mesopotamia and Egypt, in particular) used writing to produce literature, religious texts, and historical documents. Different types of writing developed in early societies, in part because each society developed writing for different purposes (see table below):

- Ideographic/Logographic/Pictographic Systems: symbols represent words (complex and cumbersome).
- Logophonetic and Logosyllabic Systems: symbols represent sounds, usually syllables (alphabetic, fewer symbols).
- Syllabic Systems: symbols represent syllables.
- Non-alphabetic Systems: symbols are letters that are assembled to create words.

Scholars know more about early cultures whose writing has since been deciphered. Undeciphered scripts, such as the Indus Valley script and Rongorongo, offer intrigue and promise to those who would attempt their decipherment.

QUESTIONS FOR ANALYSIS

- What is the relationship between writing and the development of earliest river basin societies? (See also Map 2.1.)
- To what extent does the type of society (river basin, seafaring, etc.) seem to impact the development of writing in that region (date, type, purpose, etc.)?
- How has the decipherment, or lack thereof, of these scripts impacted scholars' understandings of the societies that produced them?

NAME/TYPE OF SOCIETY	WRITING FORM AND DATE OF EMERGENCE	TYPE OF WRITING AND PURPOSE	DATE AND MEANS OF DECIPHERMENT
Mesopotamia (Sumer)/Riverine (Tigris-Euphrates)	Cuneiform, 3200 BCE	Transitions from c. 1,000 pictographs to about 400 syllables (record keeping)	Deciphered in 19th century via Behistun/Beisitun inscription
Egypt (Old Kingdom)/Riverine (Nile)	Hieroglyphs, 3100 BCE	Mixture of thousands of logograms and phonograms (religious)	Deciphered in early 19th century via trilingual Rosetta Stone (written in hieroglyphs, demotic script, and Greek)
Harappa/Riverine (Indus)	Indus Valley script, 2500 BCE	375–400 logographic signs (nomenclature and literature)	Undeciphered
Minoan/Mycenaean Greece/Seafaring micro-society	Phaistos Disk and Linear A (Minoan Crete); Linear B (Mycenaean, Crete and Greece) 1900–1300 BCE	Phaistos Disk (45 pictographic symbols in a spiral); Linear A (90 logographic-syllabic symbols); Linear B (roughly 75 syllabic symbols with some logographs) (record keeping)	Phaistos (undeciphered); Linear A (undeciphered); Linear B (deciphered in mid-20th century)
Shang Dynasty/Riverine (Yellow River)	Oracle bone script, 14th–11th century BCE	Thousands of characters (divinatory purposes)	Deciphered in early 20th century
Maya/Central American rainforest	Mayan glyphs, 250 BCE	Mixture of logograms (numeric glyphs) and phonograms (around 85 phonetic glyphs), and hundreds of "emblem glyphs" (record of rulers and calendrical purposes)	Decipherment begun in 20th century
Vikings/Seafaring (Scandinavia)	Futhark (runic alphabet), 200 CE	24 alphabetic runes (ritual use; or to identify owner or craftsperson)	Deciphered in 19th century
Inca/Andean highlands	Quipu, 3000? BCE	Knotted cords, essentially a tally system (record keeping)	Deciphered
Easter Island/Seafaring micro-society	Rongorongo, 1500 CE	120 glyphs (calendrical or genealogical)	Undeciphered

Sources: Chris Scarre (ed.), *The Human Past: World Prehistory and the Development of Human Societies* (2005); Luigi Luca Cavalli-Sforza, *Genes, Peoples, and Languages*, translated by Mark Selestad from the original 1996 French publication (2000).

Literacy spread first among upper-class families. Most students started training when they were young. After mastering the copying of standard texts in hieratic cursive or hieroglyphs, students moved on to literary works. The upper classes prized literacy as proof of high intellectual achievement. When they died, they had their student textbooks placed alongside their corpses as evidence of their talents. The literati produced texts mainly in temples, where these works were also preserved. Writing in hieroglyphs and the composition of texts in hieratic, and later demotic, script continued without break in ancient Egypt for almost 3,000 years.

PROSPERITY AND THE DEMISE OF OLD KINGDOM EGYPT

Cultural achievements, agrarian surpluses, and urbanization ultimately led to higher standards of living and rising populations. Under pharaonic rule, Egypt enjoyed spectacular prosperity. Its population swelled from 350,000 in 4000 BCE to 1 million in 2500 BCE and nearly 5 million by 1500 BCE. However, expansion and decentralization eventually exposed the weaknesses of the Old and Middle Kingdom dynasties.

The state's success depended on administering resources skillfully, especially agricultural production and labor. Everyone, from the most powerful elite to the workers in the field, was part of the system. In principle, no one possessed private property; in practice, Egyptians treated land and tools as their own—but submitted to the intrusions of the state. The state's control over taxation, prices, and the distribution of goods required a large bureaucracy that maintained records, taxed the population, appeased the gods, organized a strong military, and aided local officials in regulating the Nile's floodwaters.

Royal power, and the Old Kingdom, collapsed with the death of Pepy II in 2184 BCE. Local magnates assumed hereditary control of the government in the provinces and treated lands previously controlled by the royal family as their personal property. An extended drought strained Egypt's extensive irrigation system, which could no longer water the lands that fed the region's million inhabitants. (See **Current Trends in World History: Climate Change at the End of the Third Millennium BCE in Egypt, Mesopotamia, and the Indus Valley**.) In this so-called First Intermediate Period (2181 to 2055 BCE), local leaders plunged into bloody regional struggles to keep the irrigation works functioning for their own communities until the century-long drought ended. Although the Old Kingdom declined, it established institutions and beliefs that endured and were revived several centuries later.

The Indus River Valley: A Parallel Culture

Cities emerged in the Indus River valley in South Asia in the third millennium BCE. The urban culture of the Indus area is called "Harappan" after the urban site of Harappa that arose on the banks of the Ravi River, a tributary of the Indus. Developments in the Indus basin reflected local tradition combined with strong influences from Iranian plateau peoples, as well as indirect influences from distant Mesopotamian cities. Villages appeared around 5000 BCE on the Iranian plateau along the Baluchistan Mountain foothills, to the west of the Indus. By the early third millennium BCE, frontier villages had spread eastward to the fertile banks of the Indus River and its tributaries. (See Map 2.5.) The river-basin settlements soon yielded agrarian surpluses that supported greater wealth, more trade with neighbors, and public works. Urbanites of the Indus region and the Harappan peoples began to fortify their cities and to undertake public works similar in scale to those in Mesopotamia, but strikingly different in function.

The Indus Valley ecology boasted many advantages—especially compared to the area near the Ganges River, the other great waterway of the South Asian landmass. The melting

Current Trends in World History

Climate Change at the End of the Third Millennium BCE in Egypt, Mesopotamia, and the Indus Valley

During the long third millennium BCE, the first urban centers in Egypt, Mesopotamia, Iran, central Asia, and South Asia flourished and grew in complexity and wealth in a wet and cool climate. This smooth development was sharply if not universally interrupted beginning around 2200 BCE. Both archaeological and written records agree that across Afro-Eurasia, most of the urban, rural, and pastoral societies underwent radical change. Those watered by major rivers were selectively destabilized, while the settled communities on the highland plateaus virtually disappeared. After a brief hiatus, some recovered, completely reorganized and used new technologies to manage agriculture and water. The causes of this radical change have been the focus of much interest.

After four decades of research by climate specialists working together with archaeologists, a consensus has emerged that climate change toward a warmer and drier environment contributed to this disruption. Whether this was caused solely by human activity, in particular agriculture on a large scale, or was also related to cosmic causes such as the rotation of the earth's axis away from the sun, is still a hotly debated topic. It was likely a combination of factors.

The urban centers dependent on the three major river systems in Egypt, Mesopotamia, and the Indus Valley, all experienced disruption. In Egypt, the hieroglyphic inscriptions tell us that the Nile no longer flooded over its banks to replenish the fields with fresh soil and with water for crops. Social and political chaos followed for more than a century. In southern Mesopotamia, the deeply down-cut rivers changed course, disrupting settlement patterns and taking fields out of cultivation. Other fields were poisoned by salts brought on through overcultivation and irrigation without fallow periods. Fierce competition for water and land put pressure on the central authority. To the east and west, transhumant pastoralists, faced with shrinking pasture for their flocks, pressed in on the river valleys, disrupting the already challenged social and political structure of the densely urban centers.

In northern Mesopotamia, the responses to the challenges of aridity were more varied. Some centers were able to weather the crisis by changing strategies of food production and distribution. Some fell victim to intraregional warfare, while others, on the rainfall margin, were abandoned. When the region was settled again, society was differently organized. Population did not drastically decrease, but rather it distributed across the landscape more evenly in smaller settlements that required less water and food. It appears that a similar solution was found by communities to the east on the Iranian plateau, where the inhabitants of the huge urban center of Shahr i Sokhta abruptly left the city and settled in small communities across the oasis landscape.

The solutions found by people living in the cities of the Indus Valley also varied. Some cities, like Harappa, saw their population decrease rapidly. It seems that the bed of the river shifted, threatening the settlement and its hinterland. Mohenjo Daro, on the other hand, continued to be occupied for another several centuries, although the large civic structures fell out of use, replaced by more modest structures. And to the south, on the Gujarat Peninsula,

snows in the Himalayas watered the semitropical Indus Valley, ensuring flourishing vegetation, plus the region did not suffer the yearly monsoon downpours that flooded the Ganges plain. The expansion of agriculture in the Indus basin, as in Mesopotamia, Egypt, and China, depended on the river's annual floods to replenish the soil and avert droughts. From June to September, the rivers inundated the plain. Once the waters receded, farmers planted wheat and barley, harvesting the crops the next spring. Villagers also improved their tools of cultivation. Researchers have found evidence of furrows, probably made by plowing, that date to around 2600 BCE. These developments suggest that, as in Mesopotamia and Egypt, farmers were cultivating harvests that yielded a surplus that allowed many inhabitants to specialize in other activities.

In time, rural wealth produced urban splendor. More abundant harvests, now stored in large granaries, brought migrants into the area and supported expanding populations. By 2500 BCE cities began to replace villages throughout the Indus River valley, and within a few generations towering granaries marked the urban skyline. Harappa and Mohenjo Daro, the two largest cities, each covered a little less than half a square mile and may have housed 35,000 residents.

population and the number of settlements increased. They abandoned wheat as a crop, instead cultivating a kind of drought-enduring millet that originated in West Africa. Apparently conditions there became even more hospitable, allowing farming and fishing communities to flourish well into the second millennium BCE.

The evidence for this widespread phenomenon of climate change at the end of the third millennium BCE is complex and contradictory. This is not surprising, because every culture and each community naturally had an individual response to environmental and other challenges. Those with perennial sources of freshwater were less threatened than those in marginal zones where only a slight decrease in rainfall can mean failed crops and herds. As important, certain types of social and political institutions were resilient and introduced innovations that allowed them to adapt, while others were too rigid or short-sighted to find local solutions. A feature of human culture is its remarkable ability to adapt rapidly. When faced with challenges, resilience, creativity, and ingenuity lead to cultural innovation and change. This is what we can see, even in our own times, during the period of environmental stress.

Millet This hardy grain, cultivated for its resistance to drought, persists in the desert environment of present-day western Pakistan.

QUESTIONS FOR ANALYSIS

- What technological innovations resulted from the drought in the Indus Valley? Why?
- Imagine that the climate during the third millennium BCE had not changed. How do you think this might have affected the development of ancient Egypt?
- How has our understanding of global climate change affected the way we study prehistory?

Explore Further

Wolfgang Behringer, *A Cultural History of Climate* (2010).

Barbara Bell, "The Dark Ages in Ancient History. 1. The First Dark Age in Egypt," *American Journal of Archaeology*, vol. 75, no. 1 (January 1971), pp. 1–26.

Max Weiss et al., "The Genesis and Collapse of Third Millennium North Mesopotamian Civilization," *Science*, New Series, vol. 261, no. 5124 (August 20, 1993), pp. 995–1004.

Harappan cities sprawled across a vast floodplain covering 500,000 square miles—two or three times the Mesopotamian cultural zone. At the height of their development, the Harappan peoples reached the edge of the Indus ecological system and encountered the cultures of northern Afghanistan, the inhabitants of the desert frontier, the nomadic hunter-gatherers to the east, and the traders to the west. Although scholars know less about Harappan society than about Mesopotamia or Ancient Egypt, what we know about their urban culture and trade routes is impressive.

HARAPPAN CITY LIFE AND WRITING

The well-planned layout of Harappan cities and towns included a fortified citadel housing public facilities alongside a large residential area. The main street running through the city had covered drainage on both sides, with house gates and doors opening onto back alleys. Citadels were likely centers of political and ritual activities. At the center of the citadel of Mohenjo Daro was the famous great bath. The location, size, and quality of

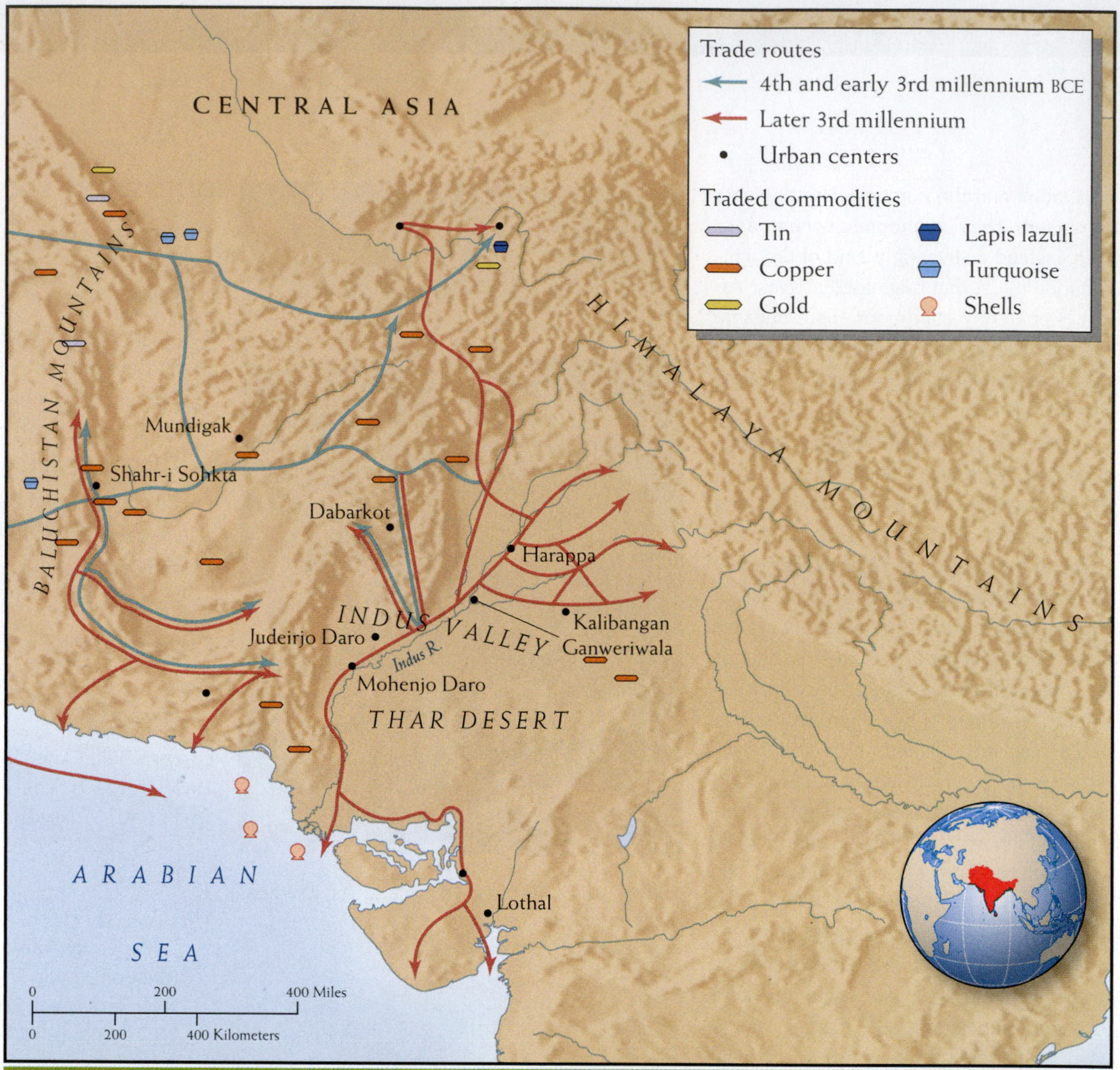

MAP 2.5 | The Indus River Valley in the Third Millennium BCE

Historians know less about the urban society of the Indus Valley in the third millennium BCE than they do about its contemporaries in Mesopotamia and Egypt. Recent scholarship has even suggested the importance of a second river, the Chagar-Hakra (Saraswati) to the east of the Indus, in this region. Archaeological evidence gives insight into this urban context.

- Where were cities concentrated in the Indus Valley?
- How did the region's environment shape urban development?
- What functions do you think outposts such as Lothal played in Harappan society?

the bath's steps, mortar and bitumen sealing, and drainage channel all suggest that the structure was used for public bathing rituals.

The Harappans used brick extensively—in houses for notables, city walls, and underground water drainage systems. Workers used large ovens to manufacture the durable construction materials, which the Harappans laid so skillfully that basic structures remain intact to this day. A well-built house had private bathrooms, showers, and toilets that drained into municipal sewers, also made of bricks. Houses in small towns and villages were made of less durable and less costly sun-baked bricks.

Many of the remains of Harappan culture lie buried under deep silt deposits accumulated over thousands of years of heavy flooding. Consequently, we know less about it than about

Mohenjo Daro Mohenjo Daro, the "mound of dead," is a large urban site of the Harappan culture. The view of the city demonstrates a neat layout of houses and civic facilities such as sewer draining.

other contemporary cultures of Afro-Eurasia. Additionally, scholars are still working to identify the Indus peoples' language and decipher the script of about 400 symbols. Although a ten-glyph-long public inscription has been found at the Harappan site of Dholavira, most of what remains of the Indus Valley script appears on a thousand or more stamp seals and small plaques excavated from the region, which may represent the names and titles of individuals rather than complete sentences. Moreover, because the Harappans did not produce King Lists (as the Mesopotamians and Egyptians did)—and may not even have had kings—scholars cannot chart a Harappan political history by tracing the rise and fall of dynasties and kingdoms. Relying only on fragmentary archaeological evidence, scholars have been unable to draw the rich portraits of Harappan life that they have supplied for the Mesopotamians and the Egyptians.

TRADE

The Harappans engaged in trade along the Indus River, through the mountain passes to the Iranian plateau, and along the coast of the Arabian Sea as far as the Persian Gulf and Mesopotamia. They traded copper, flint, shells, and ivory, as well as pottery, flint blades, and jewelry created by their craftworkers, in exchange for gold, silver, gemstones, and textiles. Carnelian, a precious red stone, was a local resource, but lapis lazuli had to come from what is now northern Afghanistan. Some of the Harappan trading towns nestled in remote but strategically important places. Consider Lothal, a well-fortified port at the head of the Gulf of Khambhat (Cambay). Although distant from the center of Harappan society, it provided vital access to the sea and to valuable raw materials. Its many workshops processed precious stones, both local and foreign. Because the demand for gemstones and metals was high on the Iranian plateau and in Mesopotamia, control of their extraction and trade was essential to maintaining the Harappans' economic power. So the Harappans built fortifications and settlements near sources of carnelian and copper mines.

Through a complex and vibrant trading system, the Harappans maintained access to mineral and agrarian resources. To facilitate trade, rulers relied not just on Harappan script but also on a system of weights and measures that they devised and standardized. Archaeologists have found Harappan seals, used to stamp commodities with the names of their owners or the nature of the goods, at sites as far away as the Persian Gulf, Mesopotamia, and the Iranian plateau.

COMPARISON

TRACE and **ANALYZE** the trade connections stretching from Mesopotamia to the Indus River Valley societies.

Dholavira inscription This is an artist's rendering of the 10 glyph-long inscription from Dholavira, an exceptional specimen of Indus Valley script both for its size, length, and inscription in stone. While Indus Valley script is still undeciphered, the excavator of this inscription has suggested it might record the name of a ruler or of the town, or even an incantation of some sort. Most examples of Indus Valley script are much briefer and appear on small seal stones along with images of animals and human figures.

The general uniformity in Harappan sites suggests a centralized and structured state. Unlike the Mesopotamians and the Egyptians, however, the Harappans apparently built neither palaces nor grand royal tombs. What the Indus River people show us is how much the urbanized parts of the world were diverging from one another, even as they borrowed from and imitated their neighbors.

The Yellow and Yangzi River Basins: East Asia

Like the Mesopotamians, Egyptians, and Harappans, East Asian peoples clustered in river basins. Their settlements along the Yellow River in the north and the Yangzi River to the south became the foundation of the future Chinese state. By 5000 BCE, both millet in the north and rice in the south were under widespread cultivation.

Yet in the following three millennia (when Mesopotamia, Egypt, and the Indus Valley were creating complex, city-based cultures), the Chinese moved slowly toward urbanization. (See Map 2.6.) Like the other regions' waterways, the Yellow and Yangzi rivers had annual floods and extensive floodplains suitable for producing high agricultural yields and supporting dense populations. In China, however, the evolution of hydraulic works, big cities, priestly and bureaucratic classes, and a new writing system took longer. A lack of easily domesticated animals and plants contributed to the different developmental path in China, as did geographic barriers. The Himalayan Mountains and the Taklamakan and Gobi deserts prevented large-scale migrations between East Asia and central Asia and hindered the diffusion of cultural breakthroughs occurring elsewhere in Afro-Eurasia.

FROM YANGSHAO TO LONGSHAN CULTURE

China's classical histories have claimed that China's cultural traditions originated in the Central Plains of the Yellow River basin and spread outward to less developed regions inside and even beyond mainland China. These histories place the beginnings of Chinese culture at the Xia dynasty, dating from 2200 BCE. Archaeological studies of river-basin environments in East Asia tell a different story, however. Whether or not the Xia existed as a historical dynasty, archaeological evidence suggests our study of the Yellow River basin and Yangzi delta should begin earlier—in the two millennia from 4000 to 2000 BCE.

China in 4000 BCE was very different geographically and culturally from what it is today. A warmer and moister climate divided its vast landmass into distinctive regions. Recent archaeological research records that at least eight distinct regional cultures appeared between 4000 and 2000 BCE, and only as these communities interacted did their institutions and ways of life come together to create a unified Chinese culture.

Although it was geographically divided, China was never devoid of outside influences. Some travelers did arrive via the ocean, but more came via the Mongolian steppe, through which nomads introduced important technologies such as metalworks. Nomads were drawn to the agricultural settlements (as they were in Mesopotamia), and they brought innovations, such as bronze and other goods, from the west. Through trade and migration, nomadic cultures and technologies filtered from the steppes to settled communities on the rivers.

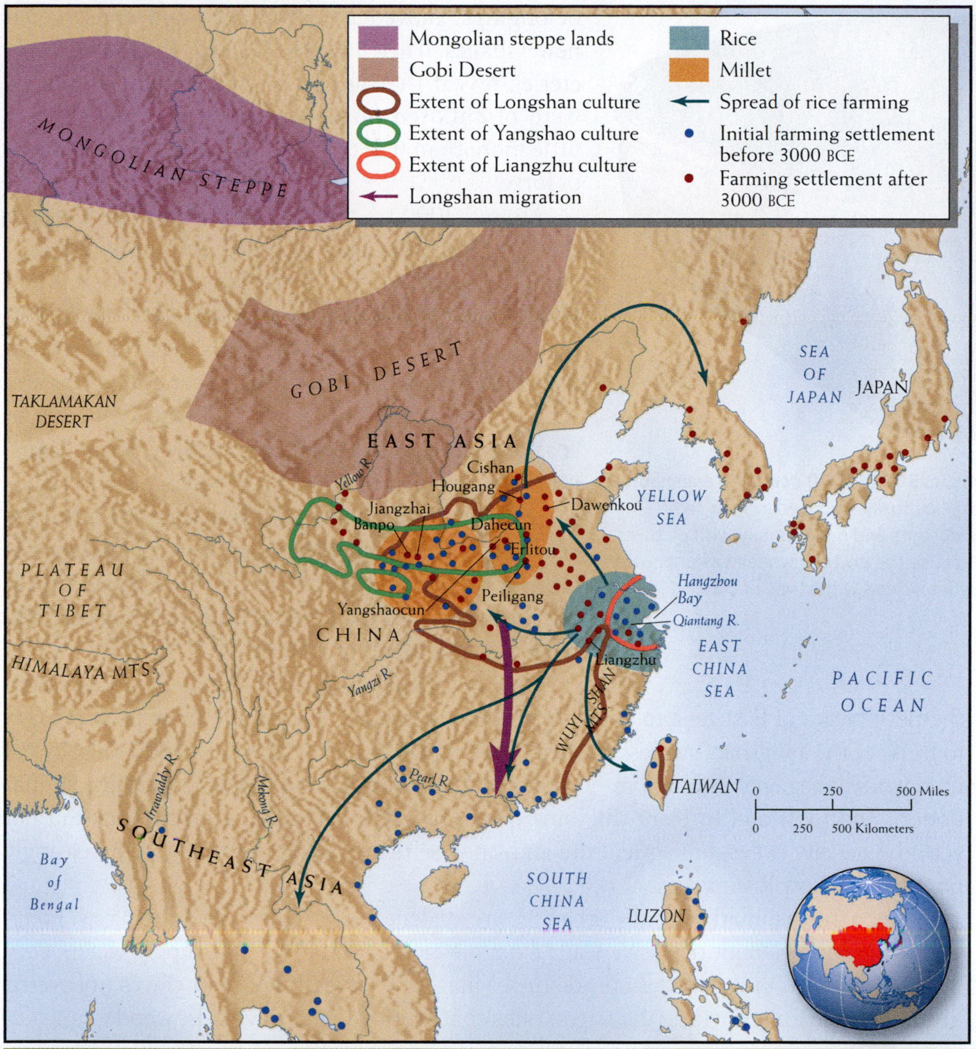

MAP 2.6 | River Basin Peoples in East Asia, 5000–2000 BCE

Complex agricultural societies emerged in East Asia during the third millennium BCE.

- What were the regional cultures that flourished here during this time?
- What are the major geographic differences between the northern and southern regions of China in this period?
- Based on geographic differences among the areas, how were these cultures different, and how were they similar?

The major divide in China was between the northern Yellow and more centrally located Yangzi river basins. Not only did these two regions rely on different crops—millet in the north and rice to the south—but they built their houses differently, buried their dead in different ways, and produced distinctive pottery styles. The best known of the early cultures developed along the Yellow River and in the Central Plains area and is known as the Yangshao culture.

Yangshao villages typically covered ten to fourteen acres and were composed of houses erected around a central square. Villagers had to move frequently because they practiced slash-and-burn agriculture. Once having exhausted the soil, residents picked up their

Yangshao Bowl with Dancing Figures, c. 5000–1700 BCE The Yangshao, also referred to as the "painted pottery" culture, produced gray or red pottery painted with black geometric designs and occasionally with pictures of fish or human faces and figures. Because the potter's wheel was unknown at the time, the vessels were probably fashioned with strips of clay.

belongings, moved to new lands, and constructed new villages. Their lives were hard. Excavated cemeteries reveal that nearly 20 percent of the burials were of children fifteen years and younger; only a little more than half of those buried lived past the age of forty.

Around 3000 BCE the Yangshao culture gave way to the Longshan culture, which had an even larger geographical scope and would provide some of the cultural foundations for the first strong states that emerged in the Central Plains. Longshan flourished from 3000 BCE to 2000 BCE, and had its center in Shandong Province. Although the Longshan way of life first took form in coastal and southern China, outside the Central Plains, it moved quickly into this hub of economic and political activity. Proof of its widespread cultural influence can be seen from the appearance of a unique style of black pottery, stretching all the way from Manchuria in the north through the Central Plains to the coast and beyond to the island of Taiwan.

The Longshan people likely migrated in waves from the peripheries of East Asia to the eastern China seashore. Their achievements, compared to those of the Yangshao, suggest marked development between 5000 and 2000 BCE. Several independent regional cultures in northern and southern China began to produce similar pottery and tools and to plant the same crops, probably reflecting contact. They did not yet produce city-states, but agriculture and small settlements flourished in the increasingly populated Yellow River valley.

Some of the hallmarks of early urban life are evident in the archaeological remains. Longshan communities built defensive walls for protection and dug wells to supply water. They buried their dead in cemeteries outside their villages. Of several thousand graves uncovered in southern Shanxi province, the largest ones contain ritual pottery vessels, wooden musical instruments, copper bells, and painted murals. Shamans performed rituals using jade axes. Jade quarrying in particular indicated technical sophistication, as skilled craftworkers incised jade tablets with powerful expressions of ritual and military authority. The threat of organized violence among Longshan villages was real. Discoveries at one Longshan site revealed a household whose members were scalped. At this same site, attackers filled the water wells with five layers of human skeletons, some decapitated. Clearly, the villages' defensive walls were essential.

As communities became more centralized, contact between regions increased. Links between northern and southern China arose when Longshan peoples began to migrate along the East Asian coast to Taiwan and the Pearl River delta in the far south. Similarities in artifacts found along the coast and at Longshan sites in northern China, such as the form and decoration of pottery and jade items, also point to a shared sphere of culture and trade.

Archaeologists also have found evidence of short-lived political organizations. Although they were nothing like the dynastic systems in Egypt, Mesopotamia, and the Indus Valley, they were wealthy—if localized—polities. They constituted what scholars call the era of Ten Thousand States (*Wan'guo*). One of them, the Liangzhu, has drawn particular interest for its remarkable jade objects and its sophisticated farming techniques. The Liangzhu grew rice and fruits and domesticated water buffalo, pigs, dogs, and sheep. Archaeologists have discovered the remains of net sinkers, wooden floats, and wooden paddles, which demonstrate a familiarity with watercraft and fishing. Artisans produced a black pottery from soft paste thrown on a wheel, and like the Longshan they created ritual objects from several varieties of jade. Animal masks and bird designs adorned many pieces, revealing a shared cosmology that informed the rituals of the Liangzhu elite.

In the late third millennium BCE, a long drought hit China (as it did Egypt, Mesopotamia, and India). Although the climate change limited progress and forced migrations to more dependable habitats, the Chinese recovered early in the second millennium BCE. Now they created elaborate agrarian systems along the Yellow and Yangzi rivers that were similar to earlier irrigation systems along the Euphrates, Indus, and Nile. Extensive trading networks and a stratified social hierarchy emerged; like the other river-basin complexes of Asia and North Africa, China became a centralized polity. Here, too, a powerful monarchy eventually united the independent communities. But what developed in China was a social and political system that emphasized an idealized past and a tradition represented by sage-kings, which later ages emulated. In this and other ways, China diverged from the rest of Afro-Eurasia.

Longshan Beaker, c. 2500 BCE Longshan has been called the "black pottery" culture, and its exquisite black pottery was not painted but rather decorated with rings, either raised or grooved. Longshan culture was more advanced than the Yangshao culture, and its distinctive pottery was likely formed on a potter's wheel.

Life Outside the River Basins

In 3500 BCE, the vast majority of humans lived outside of the complex cities that emerged in parts of Afro-Eurasia. At the other end of the spectrum, many peoples continued to live as hunters and gatherers, or in small agricultural villages or nomadic groups. In between were worlds such as those in the Aegean, Anatolia, Europe, and parts of China, where towns emerged and agriculture advanced, but not with the leaps and bounds of the great river-basin civilizations.

Some cultures outside the river basins—in the Aegean, Anatolia, and in Europe—had a distinctive warrior-based ethos, such that the top tiers of the social ladder held chiefs and military men instead of priests and scribes. In Europe and Anatolia especially, weaponry rather than writing, forts rather than palaces, and conquest rather than commerce dominated everyday life. Settlements in the Americas and sub-Saharan Africa were smaller and remained based around agriculture. Here, too, the inhabitants moved beyond stone implements and hunting and gathering, but they remained more egalitarian than river basin peoples.

AEGEAN WORLDS

Contact with Egypt and Mesopotamia affected the worlds of the Aegean Sea (the part of the Mediterranean Sea between the Greek Peloponnese and Anatolia), but it did not transform them. Geography stood in the way of significant urban development on the mountainous islands of the Aegean, on the Anatolian plateau, and in Europe. Even though people from Anatolia, Greece, and the Levant had populated the Aegean islands in the sixth

COMPARISON

COMPARE early urbanization with the ways of life in small villages and among pastoral nomads.

millennium BCE, their small villages, of 100 inhabitants or fewer, endured for 2,000 years before becoming more complex. On mainland Greece and on the Cycladic islands in the Aegean, fortified settlements housed local rulers who controlled a small area of agriculturally productive countryside. Metallurgy developed in both the island of Crete and the Cyclades. There is evidence of more formal administration and organizations in some communities by 2500 BCE, but the norm was scattered settlements separated by natural obstacles. By the early third millennium BCE, Crete had made occasional contact with Egypt and the coastal towns of the Levant, encountering new ideas, technologies, and materials as foreigners arrived on its shores. People coming by ship from the coasts of Anatolia and the Levant, as well as from Egypt, traded stone vessels and other luxury objects for the island's abundant copper. Graves of Aegean elites, such as those at Knossos on Crete, with their gold jewelry and other exotic objects, show that the elites did not reject the niceties of cultured life, but they knew that their power rested as much on their rugged landscape's resources as on self-defense and trade with others.

ANATOLIA

The highland plateau of Anatolia (in the region of modern-day Turkey) shows clear evidence of regional cultures focused on the control of trade routes and mining outposts. True cities did not develop here until the third millennium BCE, and even then they were not the sprawling population centers typical of the Mesopotamian plain. Instead, small communities emerged around fortified citadels housing local rulers who competed with one another. Two impressively fortified centers were Horoz Tepe and Alaça Hüyük, which have yielded more than a dozen graves—apparently royal—full of gold jewelry, ceremonial standards, and elaborate weapons. Similarly, the settlement at Troy was characterized by monumental stone gateways, stone-paved ramps, and high-status graves filled with gold and silver objects, vessels, jewelry, and other artifacts. Parallel grave finds on Crete, the Greek mainland, and as far away as Ur indicate that Troy participated in the trading system linking the Aegean and Southwest Asian worlds. At the same time, Troy faced predatory neighbors and pirates who attacked from the sea—an observation that explains its impressive fortifications.

EUROPE: THE WESTERN FRONTIER

At the western reaches of the Eurasian landmass was a region featuring cooler climates with smaller population densities. Its peoples—forerunners of present-day Europeans—began to make objects out of metal, formed permanent settlements, and started to create complex societies. Here, hierarchies began to undermine egalitarian ways. Yet, as in the Aegean worlds, population density and social complexity had limits.

More than in the Mediterranean or Anatolia, warfare dominated social development in Europe. Two contributing factors were the persistent fragmentation of the region's peoples and the type of agrarian development they pursued. The introduction of the plow and the clearing of woodlands expanded agriculture. Flint mining at an industrial level slashed the cost and increased the availability of raw materials needed to make tools for clearing forested lands and tilling them into arable fields. Compared to the river-basin societies, Europe was a wild frontier where violent conflicts over resources were common.

By 3500 BCE the more developed agrarian peoples had combined into large communities, constructing impressive monuments that remain visible today. In western Europe, large ceremonial centers shared the same model: enormous shaped stones, some weighing several tons each, set in common patterns—in alleyways, troughs, or circles—known as *megalithic* ("great stone") constructions. These daunting projects required cooperative planning and work. In the British Isles, where such developments occurred later, the

MAP 2.7 | Settlements on the Margins: The Eastern Mediterranean and Europe, 5000–2000 BCE

Urban societies in Southwest Asia had profound influences on peripheral societies.

- What three peripheral worlds did the urban societies of Southwest Asia influence?
- In what ways did the spread of flint and copper tools and weapons transform Aegean and European societies?
- How did agriculture spread from Southwest Asia to these worlds?

famous megalithic complexes at Avebury and Stonehenge probably reached their highest stages of development just before 2000 BCE.

By 2000 BCE, the whole of the northern European plain came to share a common material culture based on agriculture, the herding of cattle for meat and milk, the use of the plough, and the use of wheeled vehicles and metal tools and weapons, mainly of copper. Increasing communication, exchange, and mobility among the European communities led to increasing wealth but also sparked organized warfare over frontier lands and valuable resources. In an ironic twist, the integration of local communities led to greater friction and produced regional social stratification. The violent men who now protected their communities received ceremonial burials complete with their own drinking cups and weapons. Archaeologists have found these warrior burials in a swath of European lands extending from present-day France and Switzerland to present-day central Russia.

Stonehenge This spectacular site, located in the Salisbury Plain in Wiltshire in southwestern England, is one of several such megalithic structures found in the region. Constructed by many generations of builders, the arrangement of the large stone uprights enabled people to determine precise times in the year through the position of the sun. Events such as the spring and autumn equinoxes were connected with agricultural and religious activities.

Because the agricultural communities now were producing surpluses that they could store, residents had to defend their land and resources from encroaching neighbors.

An aggressive culture was taking shape based on violent confrontations between adult males organized in "tribal" groups. War cultures arose in all western European societies. Armed groups carried bell-shaped drinking cups across Europe, using them to swig beer and mead distilled from grains, honey, herbs, and nuts.

Warfare had the effect of accentuating the borrowing among the region's competing peoples. The violent struggles and emerging kinship groups fueled a massive demand for weapons, alcohol, and horses. Warrior elites borrowed from Anatolia the technique of combining copper with tin to produce harder-edged weapons made of the alloy bronze. Soon smiths were producing them in bulk—as evidenced by hoards of copper and bronze tools and weapons from the period found in central Europe. Traders used the rivers of central and northern Europe to exchange their prized metal products, creating one of the first commercial networks that covered the landmass.

THE AMERICAS

In the Americas, techniques of food production and storage, transportation, and communication restricted the surpluses for feeding those who did not work the land. Thus these communities did not grow in size and complexity. For example, in the Chicama Valley of Peru, which opens onto the Pacific Ocean, people still nestled in small coastal villages to fish, gather shellfish, hunt, and grow beans, chili peppers, and cotton (to make twined textiles, which they dyed with wild indigo). By around 3500 BCE, these fishermen abandoned their cane and adobe homes for sturdier houses, half underground, on streets lined with cobblestones.

Hundreds if not thousands of such villages dotted the seashores and riverbanks of the Americas. Some made the technological breakthroughs required to produce pottery; others devised irrigation systems and water sluices in areas where floods occurred. Some even began to send their fish catches inland in return for agricultural produce. Ceremonial structures highlighted communal devotion and homage to deities, and rituals to celebrate birth, death, and the memory of ancestors.

In the Americas, the largest population center was in the valley of Tehuacán (near modern-day Mexico City). Here the domestication of corn created a food source that enabled people to migrate from caves to a cluster of pit-house villages that supported a growing population. By 3500 BCE the valley held nothing resembling a large city. People lived in clusters of interdependent villages, especially on the lakeshores: here was a case of high population density, but not urbanization.

SUB-SAHARAN AFRICA

The same pattern occurred in sub-Saharan Africa, where the population grew but did not concentrate in urban communities. About 12,000 years ago, when rainfall and temperatures increased, small encampments of hunting, gathering, and fishing communities congregated around the large lakes and rivers flowing through the region that would later become the Sahara Desert. Large game animals roamed, posing a threat but also providing a source of food. Over the millennia, in the wetter and more temperate locations of this vast region—particularly the upland mountains and their foothills—permanent villages emerged.

As the Sahara region became drier, people moved to the desert's edges, to areas along the Niger River and the Sudan. Here they grew yams, oil palms, and plantains. In the savannah lands that stretched all the way from the Atlantic Ocean in West Africa to the Nile River basin in present-day Sudan, settlers grew grains such as millet and sorghum, which spread from their places of origin to areas along the lands surrounding the Niger River basin. Residents constructed stone dwellings and dug underground wells and food storage areas. As an increasing population strained resources, groups migrated south toward the Congo River and east toward Lake Nyanza, where they established new farms and villages. Although population centers were often hundreds or thousands of miles apart and were smaller than the urban centers in Egypt and Mesopotamia, the widespread use of the same pottery style, with rounded bottoms and wavy decoration, suggests that they maintained trading and cultural contacts. In these respects sub-Saharan Africa matched the ways of life in Europe and the Americas.

Conclusion

Over the fourth and third millennia BCE, the world's social landscape changed in significant ways. In a few key locations, where giant rivers irrigated fertile lands, complex human cultures began to emerge. These areas experienced all the advantages and difficulties of expanding populations: occupational specialization; social hierarchy; rising standards of living; sophisticated systems of art and science; and centralized production and distribution of food, clothing, and other goods. Ceremonial sites and trading crossroads became cities that developed centralized religious and political systems. As scribes, priests, and rulers labored to keep complex societies together, social distinctions within the city (including the roles of men and women) and the differences between country folk and city dwellers sharpened.

Although river-basin cultures shared basic features, each one's evolution followed a distinctive path. Where there was a single river—the Nile or the Indus—the agrarian hinterlands that fed cities lay along the banks of the waterway. In these areas cities were small; thus the Egyptian and Harappan worlds enjoyed more political stability and less rivalry. In contrast, cities in the immense floodplain of the Tigris and Euphrates needed large hinterlands to sustain their populations. Because of their growing power and need for resources, Mesopotamian cities vied for preeminence, and their competition often became violent.

In most areas of the world, however, people still lived in simple, egalitarian societies based on hunting, gathering, and basic agriculture—as in the Americas and sub-Saharan Africa. In Anatolia, Europe, and parts of China, regional cultures emerged as agriculture advanced and populations grew. Some of them, as in the Aegean and Europe, forged warrior societies. Beyond these frontiers, farmers and nomads survived as they had for many centuries. Thriving trading networks connected many, but not all, of these regions to one another.

Changes in climate affected everyone and could slow or even reverse development. How—and whether—cultures adapted depended on local circumstances. As the next chapter will show, the human agents of change often came from the fringes of larger settlements and urban areas.

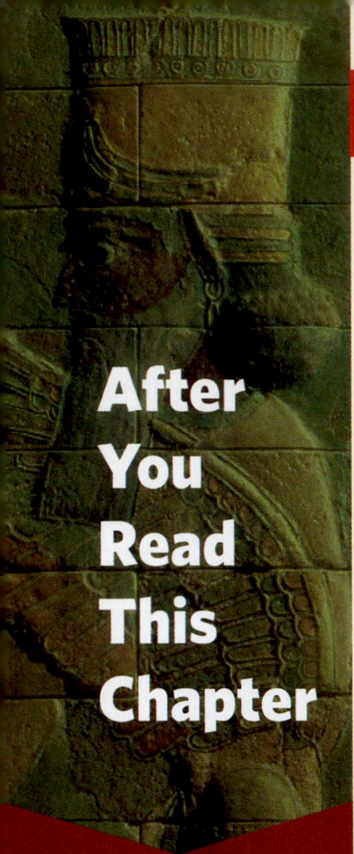

After You Read This Chapter

Go to INQUIZITIVE to see what you've learned—and learn what you've missed—with personalized feedback along the way.

TRACING THE GLOBAL STORYLINES

FOCUS ON: *Societies in the Great River Basins*

MESOPOTAMIA

- Peoples living along the Tigris River and Euphrates River control floodwaters and refine irrigation techniques.
- Mesopotamians establish the world's first large cities, featuring powerful rulers, social hierarchies, and monumental architecture.
- Mesopotamia is the birthplace of writing.

EGYPT

- Peoples of Egypt use Nile River waters to irrigate their lands and create a bountiful agriculture.
- Egyptian rulers known as pharaohs unify their territory, establish a powerful state, and develop a vibrant economy.
- Egyptians build magnificent burial chambers (pyramids) and worship a pantheon of gods.

INDUS VALLEY

- South Asian peoples harness the Indus River and create cities like Harappa and Mohenjo Daro.

EAST ASIA

- Peoples dwelling in the basins of the Yellow River and the Yangzi River control the waters' flow and expand agriculture.
- These people develop elaborate cultures, which scholars later label Yangshao and Longshan, respectively.

CHRONOLOGY

SOUTHWEST ASIA AND EGYPT	Earliest Sumerian cities appear in Mesopotamia 3500 BCE First Dynasty emerges in Egypt 3100 BCE
SOUTH ASIA	
EAST ASIA	Yangshao culture thrives along Yellow River 4000–3000 BCE
EUROPE AND THE MEDITERRANEAN	
THE AMERICAS	Chicama Valley culture thrives on Pacific coast of South America 3500 BCE Tehuacán Valley in Mexico thrives 3500 BCE
INNER AND CENTRAL ASIA	Dense village life along many lakes and rivers 3500 BCE Spread of nomadic pastoralism begins 3500 BCE

4000 BCE — **3000 BCE**

THINKING ABOUT GLOBAL CONNECTIONS

- ***Thinking about River-Basin Civilizations and the Environment*** Human interaction with the environment—including climate, geography, the characteristics of the rivers, and the continued cultivation of crops and herds—played a significant role in shaping each early river-basin civilization. Describe ways that these environmental factors influenced the unique characteristics of each river basin civilization.
- ***Thinking about Exchange Networks Among Early River-Basin Civilizations*** Carnelian from the Indus region buried in elite tombs of Egypt; lapis lazuli from the region of modern-day Afghanistan on necklaces adorning Harappan necks; shell from the Indus floodplain inlaid on Mesopotamian grave goods—these examples provide evidence of how trade in raw materials bound river-basin civilizations together in the third millennium BCE. What routes might such goods have traveled? What does this exchange of commodities suggest about other types of exchange that may have been taking place between these river basin societies?
- ***Thinking about Changing Power Relationships in River-Basin Civilizations*** From 3500–2000 BCE, as civilizations developed in the river basins of Mesopotamia, Egypt, South Asia, and East Asia, more intensive cultivation brought agricultural surpluses that ushered in a wide range of impacts. Explain, with examples from each of the river-basin civilizations, how food surpluses led to job specialization, wealth accumulation, and the resulting social hierarchies.

STUDY QUESTIONS

1. Where and how did **river basins** contribute directly to the emergence of cities, from 3500–2000 BCE? What were some similarities and differences in irrigation techniques among these early civilizations?
2. In what ways did cities in Mesopotamia, Egypt, and the Indus Valley differ from pastoral nomadic communities? How did the development of these cities introduce a hitherto unknown **urban-rural divide**?
3. What are some similarities and differences among the **cities** and **city-states** that developed in Mesopotamia, Egypt, and the Indus Valley? Compare, for example, developments in **social hierarchies**, religion, and the production of monumental architecture (including temples and palaces).
4. Compare technological developments, including writing (**scribes**) and other technologies (such as the use of **bronze** and jade), in the various river-basin societies. What might account for the regional variations in technologies?
5. How did long-distance trade influence the political, economic, and technological development of urban societies in Egypt, Mesopotamia, and the Indus Valley?
6. Contrast the agricultural developments in East Asia with those taking place in Mesopotamia, Egypt, and the Indus Valley at about the same time (3500–2000 BCE).
7. Identify shared characteristics of settlements in Europe, Anatolia, the Aegean, the Americas, and Africa between 5000 and 2000 BCE.

Old Kingdom Egypt 2649–2152 BCE

Sargon's Akkadian territorial state in Mesopotamia 2334–2103 BCE

Cities appear in Indus Valley 2500 BCE

Longshan Culture flourishes in Yellow River Valley 4000–2000 BCE

Fortified villages in the Aegean 2500 BCE

Stonehenge constructed 2000 BCE

2000 BCE **1000 BCE**

Going to the Source

Developing Complex Societies

As settled agriculture increased in river valleys across Afro-Eurasia, labor in these areas became more specialized, and eventually societies became more complex. With this increasing complexity came still further specialization of labor, along with increased social differentiation and inequality. Urban centers emerged, dramatically changing the ways of life of their inhabitants. These cities had a variety of functions ranging from religious to ceremonial to commercial. One of the most important developments was writing, which could recount anything, from political and economic transactions to religious beliefs. The documents presented here illustrate some of the complexities and tensions that emerged as cities grew in size and significance.

PRIMARY SOURCE 2.1

Sumerian Origins of Writing (c. 2100 BCE)

The world's first writing system developed in Mesopotamia. One Sumerian myth attributes this invention of cuneiform writing to Enmerkar, the lord [ruler] of Kulaba, who did not trust his messenger to remember a complicated message that he wanted to have delivered to another ruler, far away in Aratta. Writing thus had a political purpose, at least in this iteration. But this story, written in cuneiform characters, also points to the differentiation of labor.

*

His speech was substantial, and its contents extensive. The messenger, whose mouth was heavy, was not able to repeat it. Because the messenger, whose mouth was tired, was not able to repeat it, the lord of Kulaba patted some clay and wrote the message as if on a tablet. Formerly, the writing of messages on clay was not established. Now, under that sun and on that day, it was indeed so. The lord of Kulaba inscribed the message like a tablet. It was just like that. The messenger was like a bird, flapping its wings; he raged forth like a wolf following a kid. He traversed five mountains, six mountains, seven mountains. He lifted his eyes as he approached Aratta. He stepped joyfully into the courtyard of Aratta, he made known the authority of his king. Openly he spoke out the words in his heart. The messenger transmitted the message to the lord of Aratta:

"Your father, my master, has sent me to you; the lord of Unug, the lord of Kulaba, has sent me to you." "What is it to me what your master has spoken? What is it to me what he has said?"

"This is what my master has spoken, this is what he has said. My king is like a huge mesˇ tree . . . son of Enlil; this tree has grown high, uniting heaven and earth; its crown reaches heaven, its trunk is set upon the earth. He who is made to shine forth in lordship and kingship, Enmerkar, the son of Utu, has given me a clay tablet. O lord of Aratta, after you have examined the clay tablet, after you have learned the content of the message, say whatever you will say to me, and I shall announce that message in the shrine E-ana as glad tidings to the scion of him with the glistening beard. . . .

After he had spoken thus to him, the lord of Aratta received his kiln-fired tablet from the messenger. The lord of Aratta looked at the tablet. The transmitted message was just nails, and his brow expressed anger. The lord of Aratta looked at his kiln-fired tablet. At that moment, the lord worthy of the crown of lordship, the son of Enlil, the god Iškur, thundering in heaven and earth, caused a raging storm, a great lion, in. . . . He was making the mountains quake . . . , he was convulsing the mountain range . . . ; the awesome radiance . . . of his breast; he caused the mountain range to raise its voice in joy. (lines 500–551)

1. **How did the lord of Arrata react when he received the clay tablet?**
2. **Describe the connection between writing and political discussion in ancient Sumeria.**

PRIMARY SOURCE 2.2

The Debate between the Hoe and the Plough (2100 BCE)

"The Debate between the Hoe and the Plough" is one of seven major philosophical debates in Sumerian literature. Translated from cuneiform tablets found at the temple library in Nippur, this text illustrates the tension between the urban and rural elements of Sumerian society.

[1–6] O the Hoe, the Hoe, the Hoe, tied together with thongs; the Hoe, made from poplar, with a tooth of ash; the Hoe, made from tamarisk, with a tooth of sea-thorn; the Hoe, double-toothed, four-toothed; the Hoe, child of the poor . . . the Hoe started a quarrel . . . with the Plough.

[7–19] The Hoe having engaged in a dispute with the Plough, the Hoe addressed the Plough: "Plough, you draw furrows—what does your furrowing matter to me? You break clods—what does your clod-breaking matter to me? When water overflows you cannot dam it up. You cannot fill baskets with earth. You cannot spread out clay to make bricks. You cannot lay foundations or build a house. You cannot strengthen an old wall's base. You cannot put a roof on a good man's house. Plough, you cannot straighten the town squares. . . ."

[20–33] The Plough addressed the Hoe: "I am the Plough, fashioned by great strength, assembled by great hands, the mighty registrar of father Enlil. I am mankind's faithful farmer. . . ."

[41–51] "My threshing-floors punctuating the plain are yellow hillocks radiating beauty. I pile up stacks and mounds for Enlil. I amass emmer and wheat for him. I fill the storehouses of mankind with barley. The orphans, the widows and the destitute take their reed baskets and glean my scattered ears. People come to drag away my straw, piled up in the fields. The teeming herds of Cakkan thrive."

[52–56] "Hoe, digging miserably, weeding miserably with your teeth; Hoe, burrowing in the mud; Hoe, putting its head in the mud of the fields, spending your days with the brick-moulds in mud with nobody cleaning you, digging wells, digging ditches, digging! . . ."

[63–66] Then the Hoe addressed the Plough: "Plough, what does my being small matter to me, what does my being exalted matter to me, what does my being powerful matter to me?—at Enlil's place I take precedence over you, in Enlil's temple I stand ahead of you."

[67–75] "I build embankments, I dig ditches. I fill all the meadows with water. When I make water pour into all the reed-beds, my small baskets carry it away. When a canal is cut, or when a ditch is cut, when water rushes out at the swelling of a mighty river, creating lagoons on all sides (?), I, the Hoe, dam it in. Neither south nor north wind can separate it."

[76–79] "The fowler gathers eggs. The fisherman catches fish. People empty bird-traps. Thus the abundance I create spreads over all the lands. . . ."

[117–121] "I am the Hoe and I live in the city. No one is more honoured than I am. I am a servant following his master. I am one who builds a house for his master. I am one who broadens the cattle-stalls, who expands the sheepfolds."

122–126 "I spread out clay and make bricks. I lay foundations and build a house. I strengthen an old wall's base. I put a roof on a good man's house. I am the Hoe, I straighten the town-squares."

127–131 "When I have gone through the city and built its sturdy walls, have made the temples of the great gods splendid and embellished them with brown, yellow and decorative (?) clay, I build in the city of the palace where the inspectors and overseers live."

132–138 "When the weakened clay has been built up and the fragile (?) clay buttressed, they refresh themselves when the time is cool in houses I have built. When they rest on their sides by a fire which a hoe has stirred up, you do not come to the joyous celebration (?). They feed the labourer, give him drink and pay him his wages: thus I have enabled him to support his wife and children. . . ."

142–150 "I plant a garden for the householder. When the garden has been encircled, surrounded by mud walls and the agreements reached, people again take up a hoe. When a well has been dug, a water lift constructed and a water-hoist hung, I straighten the plots. I am the one who puts water in the plots. After I have made the apple-tree grow, it is I who bring forth its fruits. These fruits adorn the temples of the great gods: thus I enable the gardener to support his wife and children."

151–158 "After I have worked on the watercourse and the sluices, put the path in order and built a tower there on its banks, those who spend the day in the fields, and the field-workers who match them by night, go up into that tower. These people revive themselves there just as in their well-built city. The water-skins I made they use to pour water. I put life into their hearts again."

159–162 "Insultingly you call me 'Plough, the digger of ditches.' But when I have dug out the fresh water for the plain and dry land where no water is, those who have thirst refresh themselves at my well-head. . . ."

194–196 The Hoe having engaged in a dispute with the Plough, the Hoe triumphed over the Plough—praise be to Nisaba!

1. **What do the plough and the hoe represent?**
2. **Describe the conflict that this debate represents and discuss whether the same tensions exist today.**

PRIMARY SOURCE 2.3

"The Satire of the Trades" (c. 2025–1700 CE)

Written during Egypt's Middle Kingdom, *The Satire of the Trades* is a satirical poem written from the perspective of a father talking to his son. This excerpt portrays the father trying to convince his son that almost all of the newly specialized occupations are terrible.

I have seen many beatings—
Set your heart on books!
I watched those seized for labor-
There's nothing better than books . . .

But I have seen the smith at work
At the opening of his furnace;
With fingers like claws of a crocodile
He stinks more than fish roe.

The carpenter who wields an adze,
He is wearier than a field-laborer;
His field is the timber, his hoe is the adze.
There is no end to his labor . . .

The jewel-maker bores with his chisel
In hard stones of all kinds;
When he has finished the inlay of an eye,
His arms are spent, he's weary;
Sitting down when the sun goes down,
His knees and back are cramped . . .

The potter is under the soil,
Though as yet among the living;
He grubs in the mud more than a pig,
In order to fire his pots.
His clothes are stiff with clay . . .

The carpenter also suffers much . . .

The weaver in the workshop,
He is worse off than a woman;
With knees against his chest,
He cannot breathe air.
If he skips a day of weaving,
He is beaten fifty strokes;
He gives food to the doorkeeper,
To let him see the light of day . . .

See, there's no profession without a boss,
Except for the scribe; he is the boss
Hence if you know writing,
It will do better for you
Than those professions I've set before you,
Each more wretched than the other.

Lo I have set you on god's path,
A scribe's Renenet* is on his shoulder
On the day he is born.
When he attains the council chamber,
The court . . .
Lo, no scribe is short of food
And riches of the palace.

* Egyptian goddess of bounty and luck

1. **According to the author, which is the best profession? Why?**
2. **Compare this poem with Primary Source 2.2. How do both authors understand the change that comes with the creation of new kinds of jobs?**

PRIMARY SOURCE 2.4

Harappan Pot with Beads (c. 1700 BCE)

In 1996 archaeologists discovered this pot filled with beads at a Harappan site in Punjab, Pakistan. The beads shown here are made from a variety of materials including amazonite, banded agate, and jasper, with some made to resemble other natural stones like lapis lazuli and turquoise. Several beads have tapering holes drilled into them, which suggests the use of a tubular or tapered cylindrical tool. The pot also contained an unfinished bead with the hole only partially drilled. These beads illustrate the resources and craftsmanship available to Indus Valley jewelers.

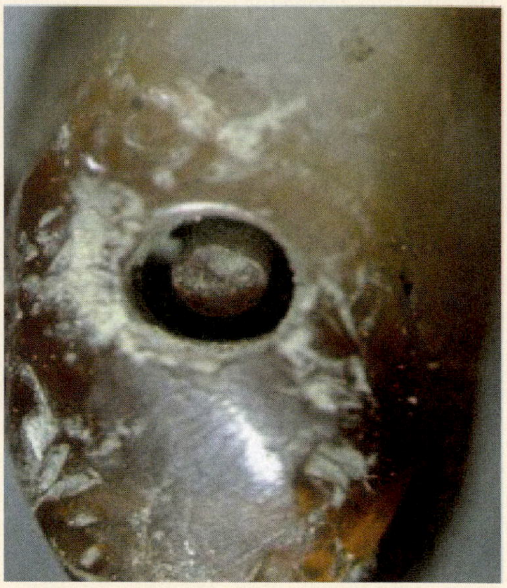

1. **What purpose might these beads have served beyond decoration?**
2. **What can these beads tell us about cultures in the Indus River Valley?**

PRIMARY SOURCE 2.5

Harappan Seal Stones

Writing developed around the same time that social hierarchies emerged and specialized labor became more prevalent. As early as 2500 BCE, Indus Valley scribes made notations—usually pictorial emblems and five to six abstract signs—on steatite seal stamps, pots, and even jewelry. The seal stamps shown here, which depict people and different kinds of animals, are still undeciphered.

1. **How might you interpret the varieties of human and animal images depicted in these seal stones?**
2. **What do these seals tell you about the emergence of complex societies?**

Questions for Analysis

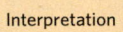

Interpretation

1. What is the connection between the rise of cities (or urbanization) and specialized labor?

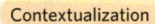

Contextualization

2. Why is writing important to understanding the social divisions that emerged along with the rise of sedentary agriculture and cities?

Long Essay Question

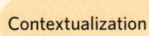

Contextualization

Identify the characteristics of complex societies and explain why such societies developed at the times and the places that they did.

Before You Read This Chapter

GLOBAL STORYLINES

- Climate change and environmental degradation lead to the collapse of river-basin societies.
- Transhumant migrants (with their animal herds in need of pasturage) and pastoral nomads (with their horse-drawn chariots) interact, in both destructive and constructive ways, with settled agrarian societies.
- A fusion of migratory and settled agricultural peoples produce expanded territorial states—in Egypt, Southwest Asia, the Indus River valley, and Shang China—that supplant earlier riverine societies.
- Microsocieties emerge in the eastern Mediterranean and South Pacific based on expanding populations and increased trade.

CORE OBJECTIVES

- **EXPLAIN** the relationship between climate change and human settlement patterns in the second millennium BCE.
- **DESCRIBE** the impact of transhumant herders and pastoral nomads on settled communities.
- **COMPARE** the varied processes by which territorial states formed and interacted with each other across Afro-Eurasia.
- **EXAMINE** the development of microsocieties in the South Pacific and the Aegean and **EXPLAIN** the relationship between geography and this development.

CHAPTER

3

Nomads, Territorial States, and Microsocieties

2000–1200 BCE

KEY TERMS

Amorites p. 97
chariot p. 88
Hammurapi's Code p. 98
Hittites p. 100
Hyksos p. 95
microsociety p. 109
oracle bones p. 108
pastoral nomads p. 88
territorial state p. 92
transhumant herders p. 88

Around 2200 BCE, the Old Kingdom of Egypt collapsed. The collapse did not occur because of incompetent rulers, of which there were many, or a decline in the arts and sciences, which is evident in unfinished building projects; the Old Kingdom fell because of radical changes in climate—namely, a powerful warming and drying trend that blanketed Afro-Eurasia between 2200 and 2150 BCE. The Mesopotamians and Harappans were as hard hit as the Egyptians.

In Egypt the environmental disaster yielded a series of low floods of the Nile because the usual monsoon rains did not arrive to feed the river's upper regions. With less water to irrigate crops, farmers could not grow enough food for the river basin's million inhabitants. Documents from this period reveal widespread suffering and despair. Consider the following tomb inscription: "All of Egypt was dying of hunger to such a degree that everyone had come to eating his children." Or another: "The tribes of the desert have become Egyptians everywhere. . . . The plunderer is everywhere, and the servant takes what he finds." Herders and pastoral nomads also felt the pinch. As these outsiders pressed upon permanent settlements in search of food, the governing structures in Egypt—and elsewhere, in Mesopotamia and the Indus Valley—broke down. The pioneering city-states may have created unprecedented differences between elites and commoners, between urbanites and rural folk, but everyone felt the effects of this disaster.

This chapter focuses on two related developments. The first focus is the impact of climate change on the peoples of Afro-Eurasia: famines occurred, followed by political and economic turmoil. The old order gave way as river-basin states in Egypt, Mesopotamia, and the Indus Valley collapsed. Herders and pastoral nomads, driven from grazing areas that were drying up, forced their way into the heartlands of these great states in pursuit of better-watered lands. Once there, they challenged the traditional ruling elites. The nomads also brought with them a new military weapon—the horse-drawn chariot. Nomads and their chariots form the second focus of this chapter, for chariots introduced a type of warfare that would dominate the plains of Afro-Eurasia for a half a millennium. The nomads' advantage proved only temporary, however. Soon the Egyptians, Mesopotamians, Chinese, and many others learned from their chariot-driving conquerors: they assimilated some of their foes into their own societies and drove others away, adopting the invaders' most useful techniques. This chapter also examines worlds apart from the expanding centers of population and politics, where climate change and chariot-driving nomads were shaping world history. The islanders of the Pacific and the Aegean did not interact with one another with such intensity—and therefore their political systems evolved differently. In these locales, microsocieties (small-scale, loosely interconnected communities) were the norm.

Nomadic Movement and the Emergence of Territorial States

As nomads and herders brought new pressures and new technologies to settled communities, innovations in governance spurred the rise of larger, expansionist territorial states. At the end of the third millennium BCE, drought and food shortages led to the overthrow of ruling elites throughout central and western Afro-Eurasia. Walled cities could not defend their hinterlands. Trade routes lay open to predators, and pillaging became a lucrative enterprise. Clans of horse-riding **pastoral nomads**—from the relatively sparsely populated and isolated Inner Eurasian steppes—swept across vast distances, eventually threatening settled people in cities. **Transhumant herders**—who lived closer to agricultural settlements and migrated seasonally to pasture their livestock—also advanced on populated areas in search of food and resources. These migrations of pastoral nomads and transhumant herders occurred across Eurasia, in the Arabian Desert and Iranian plateau in the west, and in the Indus River valley and the Yellow River valley in the east. (See Map 3.1.) Many transhumant herders and nomadic pastoralists settled in the agrarian heartlands of Mesopotamia, the Indus River valley, the highlands of Anatolia, Iran, China, and Europe. After the first wave of newcomers, more migrants arrived by foot or in wagons pulled by draft animals. Some sought temporary work; others settled permanently. They brought horses and new technologies that were useful in warfare; religious practices and languages; and new pressures to feed, house, and clothe an ever-growing population. This millennia-long process is sometimes referred to as Indo-European migrations.

COMPARISON

EXPLAIN the relationship between climate change and human settlement patterns in the second millennium BCE.

Perhaps the most vital breakthroughs that nomadic pastoralists transmitted to settled societies were the harnessing of horses and the invention of the **chariot**, a two-wheeled horse-drawn vehicle used in warfare and later in processions and races. On the vast steppe lands north of the Caucasus Mountains, during the late fourth millennium BCE,

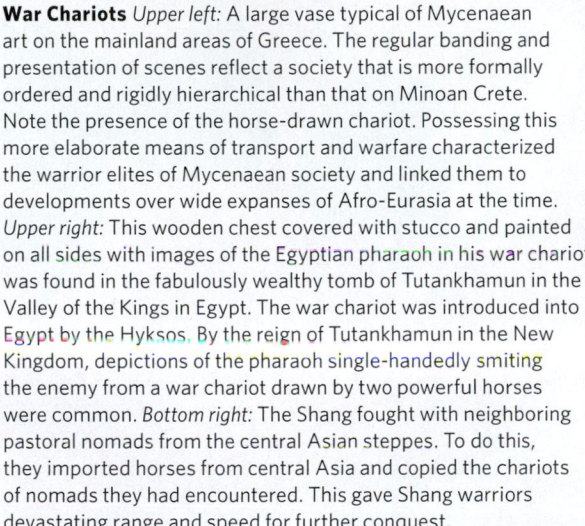

War Chariots *Upper left:* A large vase typical of Mycenaean art on the mainland areas of Greece. The regular banding and presentation of scenes reflect a society that is more formally ordered and rigidly hierarchical than that on Minoan Crete. Note the presence of the horse-drawn chariot. Possessing this more elaborate means of transport and warfare characterized the warrior elites of Mycenaean society and linked them to developments over wide expanses of Afro-Eurasia at the time. *Upper right:* This wooden chest covered with stucco and painted on all sides with images of the Egyptian pharaoh in his war chariot was found in the fabulously wealthy tomb of Tutankhamun in the Valley of the Kings in Egypt. The war chariot was introduced into Egypt by the Hyksos. By the reign of Tutankhamun in the New Kingdom, depictions of the pharaoh single-handedly smiting the enemy from a war chariot drawn by two powerful horses were common. *Bottom right:* The Shang fought with neighboring pastoral nomads from the central Asian steppes. To do this, they imported horses from central Asia and copied the chariots of nomads they had encountered. This gave Shang warriors devastating range and speed for further conquest.

settled people had domesticated horses in their native habitat. Elsewhere, as on the northern steppes of what is now Russia, horses were a food source. Only during the late third millennium BCE did people harness horses with cheek pieces and mouth bits in order to facilitate the control of horses and their use for transportation. Parts of horse harnesses made from wood, bone, bronze, and iron, found in tombs scattered across the steppe, reveal the evolution of headgear from simple mouth bits to full bridles with headpiece, mouthpiece, and reins.

Sometime around 2000 BCE, pastoral nomads in the mountains of the Caucasus joined the bit-harnessed horse to the two-wheeled chariot. Various chariot innovations began to unfold: pastoralists lightened chariots so their warhorses could pull them faster; spoked wheels made of special wood bent into circular shapes replaced solid-wood wheels that were heavier and prone to shatter; wheel covers, axles, and bearings (all produced by settled people) were added to the chariots; and durable metal went into the chariot's moving parts. Hooped bronze and, later, iron rims reinforced the spoked wheels. Initially iron was a decorative and experimental metal, and all tools and weapons were bronze.

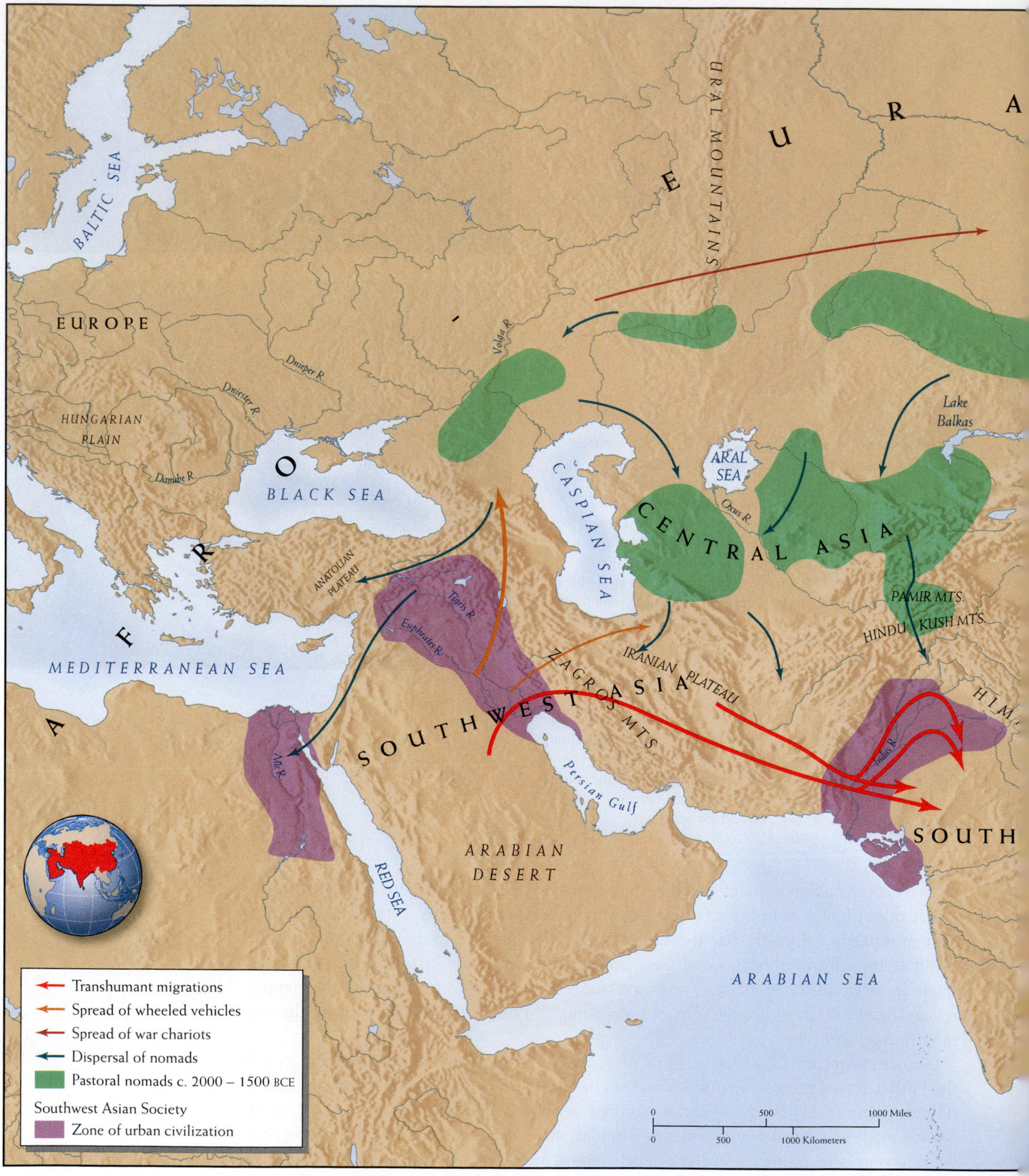
EURASIA
AFRO-EURASIA
EUROPE
BALTIC SEA
URAL MOUNTAINS
Volga R.
Dnieper R.
Dniester R.
HUNGARIAN PLAIN
Danube R.
BLACK SEA
CASPIAN SEA
ARAL SEA
Oxus R.
Lake Balkas
CENTRAL ASIA
PAMIR MTS.
HINDU KUSH MTS.
ANATOLIAN PLATEAU
Tigris R.
Euphrates R.
MEDITERRANEAN SEA
ZAGROS MTS.
IRANIAN PLATEAU
SOUTHWEST ASIA
Indus R.
Nile R.
Persian Gulf
ARABIAN DESERT
RED SEA
ARABIAN SEA
SOUTH
Transhumant migrations
Spread of wheeled vehicles
Spread of war chariots
Dispersal of nomads
Pastoral nomads c. 2000 – 1500 BCE
Southwest Asian Society
Zone of urban civilization
0 500 1000 Miles
0 500 1000 Kilometers

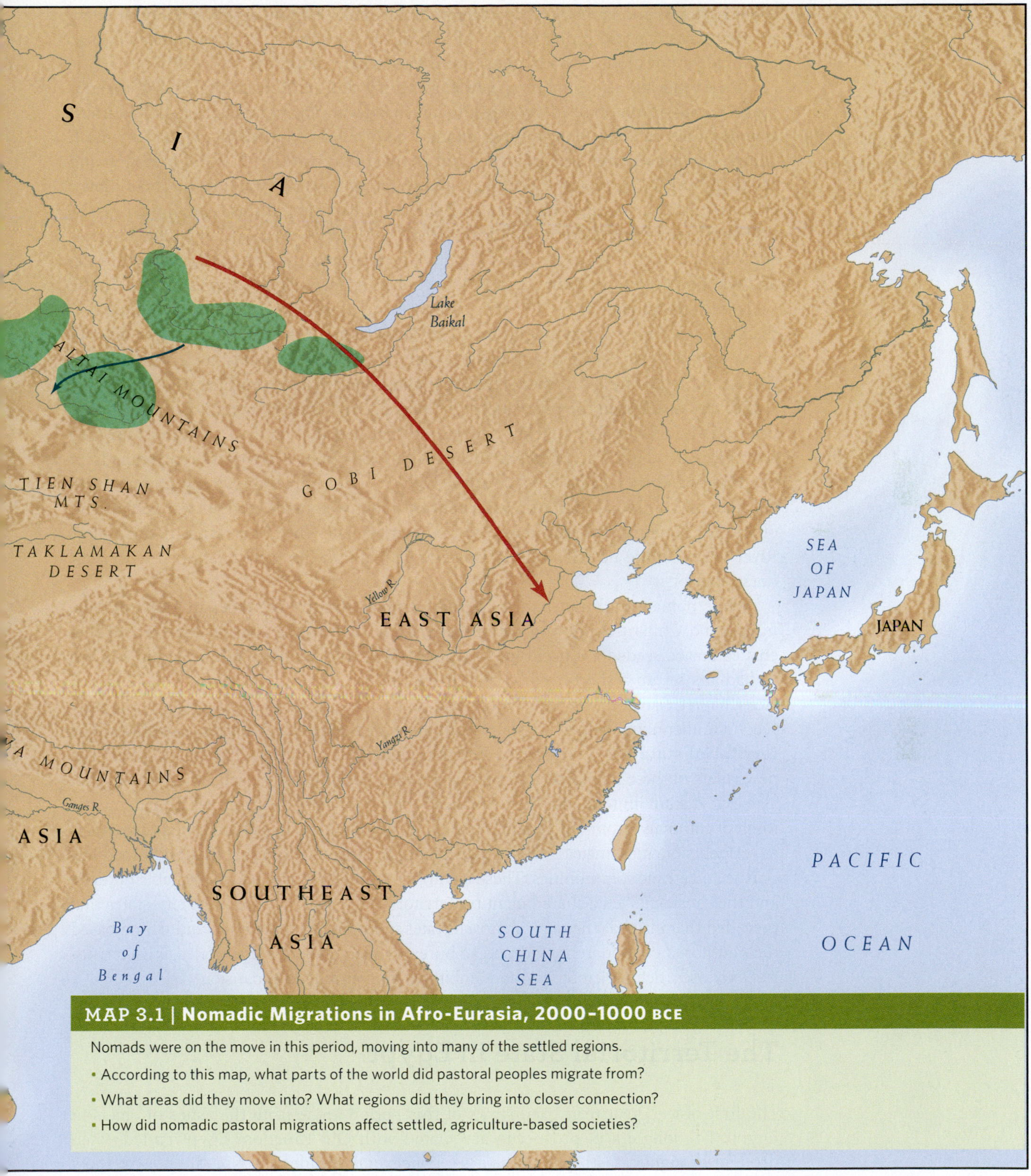

MAP 3.1 | Nomadic Migrations in Afro-Eurasia, 2000–1000 BCE

Nomads were on the move in this period, moving into many of the settled regions.

- According to this map, what parts of the world did pastoral peoples migrate from?
- What areas did they move into? What regions did they bring into closer connection?
- How did nomadic pastoral migrations affect settled, agriculture-based societies?

Iron's hardness and flexibility, however, eventually made it more desirable for reinforcing moving parts and protecting wheels, like those on the chariot. Thus the horse chariots combined innovations by both nomads and settled agriculturalists.

These innovations—combining new engineering skills, metalworking, and animal domestication—revolutionized the way humans made war. The horse chariot slashed travel time between capitals. Slow-moving infantry now ceded to battalions of chariots. Each vehicle carried a driver and an archer and charged into battle with lethal precision and ravaging speed. The mobility, accuracy, and shooting power of warriors in horse-drawn chariots tilted the political balance. After the nomads perfected this type of warfare (by 1600 BCE), they challenged the political systems of Mesopotamia and Egypt, and chariots soon became central to the armies of Egypt, Assyria, Persia, the Vedic kings of South Asia, and the Zhou rulers in China, and to local nobles as far west as Italy, Gaul, and Spain. Only with the development of cheaper armor made of iron (after 1000 BCE) did foot soldiers recover their military importance. And only after states developed cavalry units of horse-mounted warriors did chariots lose their decisive military advantage. For much of the second millennium BCE, then, charioteer elites prevailed in Afro-Eurasia.

For city dwellers in the river basins, the first sight of horse-drawn chariots must have been terrifying, but they quickly understood that war making had changed, and they scrambled to adapt. The pharaohs in Egypt probably copied chariots from nomads or neighbors, and they came to value them highly. For example, the young pharaoh Tutankhamun (r. c. 1336–1327 BCE) was a chariot archer who made sure his war vehicle and other gear accompanied him in his tomb. A century later the Shang kings of the Yellow River valley, in the heartland of agricultural China, likewise were entombed with their horse chariots.

While nomads and transhumant herders toppled the riverine cities in Mesopotamia, Egypt, and China through innovations in warfare such as the chariot, the turmoil that ensued sowed seeds for a new type of regime: the territorial state. While Sargon and the Akkadians set up a short-lived territorial state in earlier Mesopotamia (2334–2193 BCE) (see Chapter 2), the martial innovations and political and environmental crises of the early second millennium helped to spur their more enduring development elsewhere. The **territorial state** was a centralized kingdom organized around a charismatic ruler. The new rulers of these territorial states exerted power not only over localized city-states, but also over distant hinterlands. They enhanced their stability through rituals for passing the torch of command from one generation to the next. People no longer identified themselves as residents of cities; instead, they felt allegiance to large territories, rulers, and broad linguistic and ethnic communities. These territories for the first time had identifiable borders, and their residents felt a shared identity. Territorial states differed from the city-states that preceded them in that the new territorial states in Egypt, Mesopotamia, and China based their authority on monarchs, widespread bureaucracies, elaborate legal codes, large territorial expanses, definable borders, and ambitions for continuous expansion.

The Territorial State in Egypt

The first of the great territorial states of this period arose from the ashes of chaos in Egypt. The long era of prosperity associated with Old Kingdom Egypt ended when drought brought catastrophe to the area. For several decades the Nile did not overflow its banks, and Egyptian harvests withered. (See **Analyzing Global Developments: Climate Change and the Collapse of River-Basin Societies**.) As the pharaohs lost legitimacy and fell prey to feuding among rivals for the throne, regional elites replaced the

Analyzing Global Developments

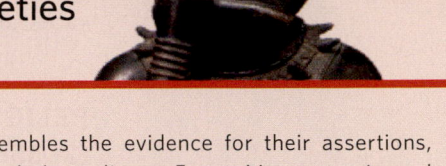

Climate Change and the Collapse of River-Basin Societies

The three great river-basin societies discussed in Chapter 2—Egypt, Mesopotamia, and the Indus Valley—collapsed at around the same time. The collapse in Egypt and Mesopotamia was almost simultaneous (roughly between 2200 BCE and 2100 BCE). In contrast, while the collapse was delayed in the Indus Valley for approximately 200 years, when it came, it virtually wiped out the Harappan state and culture. At first, historians focused on political, economic, and social causes, stressing bad rulers, nomadic incursions, political infighting, population migrations, and the decline of long-distance trade. In more recent times, however, a group of scientists that included paleobiologists, climatologists, sedimentationists, and archaeologists have studied these societies and found convincing evidence that a truly radical change in the climate—a 200-year-long drought spreading across the Afro-Eurasian land mass—was a powerful factor in the collapse of these cultures. But how can these researchers know so much about the climate 4,000 years ago? The following table assembles the evidence for their assertions, drawing on their scholarly studies on Egypt, Mesopotamia, and the Indus Valley.

QUESTIONS FOR ANALYSIS

- Why did more standard historical explanations for the collapse of the large river-basin societies precede the more recent emphases on climate change?
- Few scholars are willing to regard climate change as the overwhelming factor in the collapse of these river-basin societies. Why do you think that this is the case?
- On the basis of your reading, do you think that the evidence for climate change is convincing for all three societies? Which ones are the more persuasive, which the less convincing?

RIVER-BASIN SOCIETY	DATE OF COLLAPSE	CLIMATOLOGICAL EVIDENCE	ARCHAEOLOGICAL EVIDENCE	LITERARY EVIDENCE
Egypt	The Old Kingdom collapsed and ushered in a period of notable political instability, the First Intermediate Period (2184–2055 BCE).	Sedimentation studies reveal markedly lower Nile floods and an invasion of sand dunes into cultivated areas.	Much of the sacred sites of the Old Kingdom and their artwork is believed to have been destroyed in this period due to the political chaos.	An abundant literary record is full of tales of woe. Poetry and stelae call attention to famine, starvation, low Nile floods, even cannibalism.
Mesopotamia	The last effective ruler of the Kingdom of Akkad (2334–2193 BCE) was Naram Sin (r. 2254–2218 BCE).	Around 2100 BCE, inhabitants abruptly abandoned the Haabur drainage basin, whose soil samples reveal marked aridity as determined by the existence of fewer earthworm holes and wind-blown pellets.	Teil Leilan and other sites indicate that the large cities of this region began to shrink around 2200 BCE and were soon abandoned, and remained unoccupied for 300 years.	Later UR III scribes described the influx of northern "barbarians" and noted the construction of a wall, known as the Repeller of the Amorites, to keep these northerners out.
Indus Valley and the Harappan Society	Many of the Harappan peoples migrated eastward, beginning around 1900 BCE, leaving this region largely empty of people.	Hydroclimatic reconstructions show that precipitation began to decrease around 3000 BCE, reaching a low in 2000 BCE, at which point the Himalayan rivers stopped incising. Around 1700 BCE, the Ghaggar-Hakra rivers dried up.	Major Harappan urban sites began to shrink in size and lose their urban character between 1900 and 1700 BCE.	No literary source material because the Harappan script has still to be deciphered.

Sources: Barbara Bell, "The Dark Ages in Ancient History," *American Journal of Archaeology,* vol. 75, no. 1 (January, 1971), pp. 1–26; Max Weiss et al., "The Genesis and Collapse of Third Millennium North Mesopotamian Civilization," *Science, New Series,* vol. 261, no. 5124 (August 20, 1993), pp. 995–1004; H. M. Cullen et al., "Climate Change and the Collapse of the Akkadian Empire," *Geology,* vol. 28, no. 4, April 2000, pp. 379–82; Liviu Giosan et al., "Fluvial Landscapes of the Harappan Civilization," *Proceedings of the National Academy of Science, published online,* May 29, 2012; and Karl W. Butzer, "Collapse, Environment, and Society," *Proceedings of the National Academy of Science,* published online, March 6, 2012, vol. 109, no. 10, pp. 3632–39. For a general overview of climate change and historical studies, consult Wolfgang Behringer, *A Cultural History of Climate* (2010).

authority of the centralized state. Egypt, which had been one of the most stable corners of Afro-Eurasia, endured more than a century of tumult before a new order emerged. The pharaohs of the Middle Kingdom and, later, the New Kingdom reunified the river valley and expanded south and north.

RELIGION AND TRADE IN MIDDLE KINGDOM EGYPT (2055–1650 BCE)

Around 2050 BCE, after a century of drought, the Nile's floodwaters returned to normal and crops grew again. In the centuries that followed, pharaohs at Thebes consolidated power in Upper Egypt and began new state-building activity, ushering in a new phase of stability that historians call the Middle Kingdom. The rulers of this era developed Egypt's religious and political institutions in ways that increased state power, creating the conditions for greater prosperity and trade.

Religion and Rule Spiritual and worldly powers once again reinforced each other in Egypt. Gods and rulers together replaced the chaos that people believed had brought drought and despair. Amenemhet I (1985–1955 BCE), first pharaoh of the long-lasting Twelfth Dynasty (1985–1795 BCE), elevated a formerly less significant god, Amun, to prominence. The king capitalized on the god's name, which means "hidden," to convey a sense of his own invisible omnipresence throughout the realm. Because Amun's attributes of air and breath were largely intangible, believers in other gods were able to embrace his cult. Amun's cosmic power appealed to people in areas that had recently been impoverished.

The pharaoh's elevation of the cult of Amun unified the kingdom and brought even more power to Amun and the pharaoh. Consequently, Amun eclipsed all the other gods of Thebes. Merging with the formerly omnipotent sun god Re, the deity now was called Amun-Re: the king of the gods. Because the power of the gods and kings was intertwined, the pharaoh as Amun's earthly champion enjoyed enhanced legitimacy as the supreme ruler.

The massive temple complex dedicated to Amun-Re offers evidence of their joint power. Middle Kingdom rulers tapped into their kingdom's renewed bounty, their subjects' loyalty, and the work of untold slaves and commoners to build Amun-Re's temple complex at Thebes (present-day Luxor). For 2,000 years, Egyptians and slaves toiled to erect monumental gates, enormous courtyards, and other structures in what was arguably the largest, longest-lasting public works project ever undertaken. Middle Kingdom rulers also nurtured a cult of the pharaoh as the good shepherd whose prime responsibility was to care for his human flock. By instituting charities, offering homage to gods at the palace to ensure regular floodwaters, and performing ceremonies to honor their own generosity, the pharaohs portrayed themselves as these shepherds. As a result, the cult of Amun-Re was both a tool of political power and a source of spiritual meaning for Egyptians.

Amun This sculpture of the head of the god Amun was carved from quartzite during the Eighteenth Dynasty, around 1335 BCE. At Thebes in Upper Egypt, a huge temple complex was dedicated to the combined god Amun-Re. The powerful kings of the Middle and New Kingdoms each added a courtyard or a pylon, making this one of the largest religious structures in the ancient world.

Expanding Trade Networks Prosperity gave rise to an urban class of merchants and professionals who used their wealth and skills to carve out new opportunities for themselves. They indulged in leisure activities such as formal banquets with professional dancers and singers, and they honed their skills in hunting, fowling, and fishing. In a sign of their upward mobility and autonomy, some members of the middle class constructed tombs filled with representations of the material goods they would use in the afterlife as well as the occupations that would engage them for eternity. This new merchant class did not rely on the king's generosity and took burial privileges formerly reserved for the royal family and a few powerful nobles.

As they centralized power and consolidated their territorial state, Egyptians also expanded their trade networks (see Map 3.2). Because the floodplains had long since been deforested, the Egyptians needed to import massive quantities of wood by ship. Most prized were the cedars from Byblos (a city in the land soon known as Phoenicia, roughly present-day Lebanon), crafted into furniture and coffins. Commercial networks extended south through the Red Sea to present-day Ethiopia; importing precious metals, ivory, livestock, slaves, and exotic animals such as panthers and monkeys. Expeditions to the Sinai Peninsula searched for copper and turquoise. Expansion southward into Nubia for gold and other resources continued in the early New Kingdom. As part of Egyptian colonization southward, a series of forts extended as far south as the second cataract of the Nile River (just south of the modern-day border between Egypt and Sudan).

MIGRATIONS AND EXPANDING FRONTIERS IN NEW KINGDOM EGYPT (1550–1069 BCE)

The success of the new commercial networks lured pastoral nomads who were searching for work. Later, chariot-driving Hyksos invaders from Southwest Asia attacked Egypt, setting in motion the events marking the break between what historians call the Middle and New Kingdoms of Egypt. Although the invaders challenged the Middle Kingdom, they also inspired innovations that enabled the New Kingdom to thrive and expand.

Hyksos Invaders Sometime around 1640 BCE, a western Semitic-speaking people, whom the Egyptians called the **Hyksos** ("Rulers of Foreign Lands"), overthrew the unstable Thirteenth Dynasty (toward the end of Egypt's Middle Kingdom period). The Hyksos had mastered the art of horse chariots. Thundering into battle with their war chariots and their superior bronze axes and composite bows (made of wood, horn, and sinew), they easily defeated the pharaoh's foot soldiers. The victorious Hyksos did not destroy the conquered land, but adopted and reinforced Egyptian ways. Ruling as the Fifteenth Dynasty, the Hyksos asserted control over the northern part of the country and transformed the Egyptian military.

After a century of political conflict, an Egyptian who ruled the southern part of the country, Ahmosis (r. 1550–1525 BCE), successfully used the Hyksos weaponry—horse chariots—against the invaders themselves, and became pharaoh. This conquest marked the beginning of what historians call New Kingdom Egypt. Hyksos invasions had taught Egyptian rulers that they must vigilantly monitor their frontiers, for they could no longer rely on deserts as buffers. Ahmosis assembled large, mobile armies and drove the Hyksos "foreigners" back. Diplomats followed in the army's path, as the pharaoh initiated a strategy of interference in the affairs of Southwest Asian states. Such policies laid the groundwork for statecraft and an international diplomatic system that future Egyptian kings used to dominate the eastern Mediterranean world.

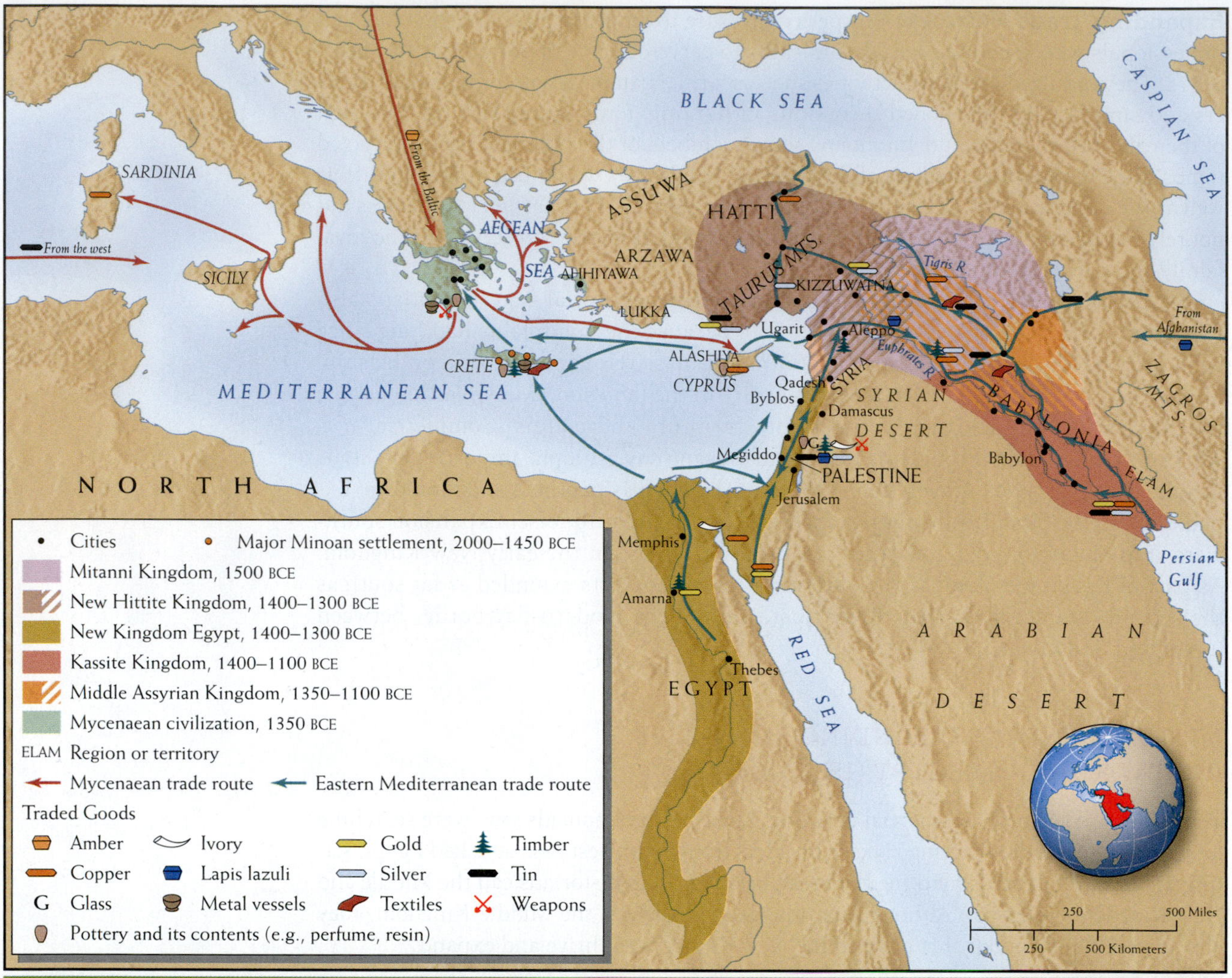

MAP 3.2 | Territorial States and Trade Routes in Southwest Asia, North Africa, and the Eastern Mediterranean, 1500–1350 BCE

Trade in many commodities brought the societies of the Mediterranean Sea and Southwest Asia into increasingly closer contact.

- What were the major trade routes and the major trading states in Southwest Asia, North Africa, and the eastern Mediterranean during this time?
- What were the major trade goods?
- Did trade enhance peaceful interactions among the territorial states?

Migrations and invasions introduced new techniques that the Egyptians adopted to consolidate their power. These included bronze working (which the Egyptians had not perfected), an improved potter's wheel, and a vertical loom. South Asian animals such as humped zebu cattle, as well as vegetable and fruit crops, now appeared on the banks of the Nile for the first time. Other significant innovations pertained to war: the horse and chariot, the composite bow, the scimitar (a sword with a curved blade), and other weapons from western Eurasia. These weapons transformed the Egyptian army from a standing infantry to a high-speed, mobile, and deadly fighting force. Egyptian troops extended the military frontier as far south as the fourth cataract of the Nile River (in northern modern-day Sudan), and the kingdom now stretched from the Mediterranean shores to Ethiopia.

Expanding Frontiers By the beginning of the New Kingdom, the territorial state of Egypt was projecting its interests outward: it defined itself as a superior, cosmopolitan society with an efficient bureaucracy run by competent and socially mobile individuals. As mentioned above, Egypt expanded its control southward into Nubia, as a source of gold, exotic raw materials, and manpower.

Historians identify this expansion most strongly with the reign of Egypt's most powerful woman ruler, Hatshepsut. She served as regent for her young son, Thutmosis III, who came to the throne in 1479 BCE. When he was seven years old, Hatshepsut proclaimed herself "king," ruling as coregent until she died two decades later. During her reign there was little military activity, but trade contacts into the Levant and Mediterranean and southward into Nubia flourished. When he ultimately came to power, Thutmosis III (r. 1479–1425 BCE) launched another expansionist phase, northeastward into the Levant, which lasted for 200 years. At the Battle of Megiddo (1469 BCE), the first recorded chariot battle in history, Thutmosis III, whose army employed nearly 1,000 war chariots, defeated his adversaries and established an Egyptian presence in Palestine. Having evolved into a strong, expansionist territorial state, Egypt was now poised to engage in commercial, political, and cultural exchanges with the rest of the region.

Hatshepsut The only powerful queen of Egyptian pharaonic history was Hatshepsut, seen here in a portrait head created during her reign. Because a woman on the throne of Egypt would offend the basic principles of order (*ma'at*), Hatshepsut usually portrayed herself as a man, especially late in her reign. This was reinforced by the use of male determinatives in the hieroglyphic renditions of her name.

Territorial States in Southwest Asia

Climatic change and invasions by migrants also transformed the societies of Southwest Asia, and new territorial kingdoms arose in Mesopotamia and Anatolia. Here, as in Egypt, the drought at the end of the third millennium BCE was devastating. Harvests shrank, the price of basic goods rose, and the social order broke down. In southern Mesopotamia cities were invaded by transhumant herders (not chariot-driving nomads) who sought grazing lands to replace those swallowed up by expanding deserts. A millennium of intense cultivation, combined with severe drought, brought disastrous consequences: rich soil in the river basin was depleted of nutrients; saltwater from the Persian Gulf seeped into the marshy deltas, contaminating the water table; and the main branch of the Euphrates River shifted to the west. Many cities lost access to their fertile agrarian hinterlands and withered away. Mesopotamia's center of political and economic gravity shifted northward, away from the silted, marshy deltas of the southern heartland.

COMPARISON

COMPARE the varied processes by which territorial states formed and interacted with each other in Egypt and Southeast Asia.

As scarcities mounted, transhumant peoples began to press in upon settled communities more closely. Mesopotamian city dwellers were scornful of the rustic migrants, whom they called **Amorites** ("westerners"), invading their cities. While these transhumant herders may have been western "foreigners" to those living in the urban centers of Mesopotamia, they were not strangers. These rural folk had wintered in villages close to the rivers to water their animals, which grazed on fallow fields. In the scorching summer, they retreated to the cooler highlands. Their flocks provided wools, leather, bones, and tendons to the artisan-based industries of the urban centers of Mesopotamia. In return, the herders purchased crafted products and agricultural goods. They also paid taxes, served as warriors, and labored on public works projects, but had few political rights within city-states.

Around 2000 BCE, Amorites from the western desert joined allies from the Iranian plateau to bring down the Third Dynasty of Ur, which had controlled all of Mesopotamia and southwestern Iran for more than a century. These Amorites and their allies founded the Old Babylonian kingdom, centered on the southern Mesopotamian city of Babylon, near modern-day Baghdad. Other territorial states arose in Mesopotamia in the millennium that followed, sometimes with one dominating the entire floodplain and sometimes with multiple powerful kingdoms vying for territory. As in Egypt, a century of political instability followed the demise of the old city-state models. Here, too, pastoralists played a role in the restoration of order, increasing the wealth of the regions they conquered and helping the cultural realm to flourish. The Old Babylonian kingdom expanded trade and founded territorial states with dynastic ruling families and well-defined frontiers. As we will see, pastoralists also played a key role in the development of territorial kingdoms in Anatolia.

Hammurapi's Code The inscription on the shaft of Hammurapi's Code is carved in a beautiful rendition of the cuneiform script. Because none of the laws on the code were recorded in the thousands of judicial texts of the period, it is uncertain if Hammurapi's Code presented actual laws or only norms for the proper behavior of Babylonian citizens.

MESOPOTAMIAN KINGSHIP

The new rulers of Mesopotamia changed the organization of the state and promoted a distinctive culture, as well as expanding trade. Herders-turned-urbanite-rulers mixed their own nomadic social organization with that of the once dominant city-states to create the structures necessary to support much larger territorial states. The basic social organization of the Amorites, out of which the territorial states in Mesopotamia evolved, was tribal (dominated by a ruling chief) and clan-based (claiming descent from a common ancestor). Over time, chieftains drew on personal charisma and battlefield prowess to become kings; kings allied with the merchant class and nobility for bureaucratic and financial support; and kingship became hereditary.

Over the centuries, powerful Mesopotamian kings expanded their territories and subdued weaker neighbors, inducing them to pay tribute in luxury goods, raw materials, and manpower as part of a broad confederation of city-states under the kings' protection. Control over military resources (metals for weaponry and, later, herds of horses for pulling chariots) was necessary for dominance. The ruler's charisma also mattered. Unlike the more institutionalized Egyptian leadership, Mesopotamian kingdoms could vacillate from strong to weak, depending on the leader's personality.

The most famous Mesopotamian ruler of this period was Hammurapi (or Hammurabi) (r. 1792–1750). Continuously struggling with powerful neighbors, he sought to centralize state authority and to create a new legal order. Using diplomatic and military skills to become the strongest king in Mesopotamia, he made Babylon his capital. He implemented a new system to consolidate power, appointing regional governors to manage outlying provinces and to deal with local elites. Like the Egyptian pharaohs of the Middle Kingdom, Hammurapi was shepherd and patriarch of his people, responsible for proper preparation of the fields and irrigation canals and for his followers' well-being. Balancing elite privileges with the needs of the lower classes, the king secured his power. **Hammurapi's Code**, with its "eye-for-an-eye" reciprocity of crime and punishment, is an example of this balancing act.

Its compilation of more than 300 edicts outlines crimes and their punishments. The Code places an emphasis on the king's control, as divine agent, over public matters; the vital role of the family in orderly relations; and the rights and responsibilities of each social class (free, dependent, and slave). Such an overarching legal code underscored the authority of the king as well as the hierarchies of power within the territorial state.

Power and Culture Mesopotamian rulers commissioned public art and works projects and promoted institutions of learning. The court supported workshops for skilled artisans and schools for scribes, the transmitters of an expanding literary culture. To dispel their image as rustic foreigners and to demonstrate their familiarity with the region's core values, new Mesopotamian rulers valued the oral tales and written records of the earlier Sumerians and Akkadians. Scribes copied the ancient texts and preserved their tradition. Royal hymns portrayed the king as a legendary hero of quasi-divine status.

Heroic narratives about legendary founders, based on traditional stories about the rulers of ancient Uruk, legitimized the new rulers. The most famous tale was the *Epic of Gilgamesh*, one of the earliest surviving works of literature. Originally composed more than a millennium earlier, in the Sumerian language, this epic narrated the heroism of the legendary king of early Uruk, Gilgamesh. Preserved by scribes in royal courts through centuries, the epic offers an example of how the Mesopotamian kings invested in cultural production to explain important political relations, unify their people, and distinguish their subjects from those of other kingdoms.

Trade and the Rise of a Private Economy Another feature of the territorial state in Mesopotamia was its shift away from economic activity dominated by the city-state and toward independent private ventures. Mesopotamian rulers designated private entrepreneurs rather than state bureaucrats to collect taxes. People paid taxes in the form of commodities such as grain, vegetables, and wool, which the entrepreneurs exchanged for silver. They, in turn, passed on the silver to the state after pocketing a percentage for their profit. This process generated more private economic activity and wealth, and more revenues for the state.

Gilgamesh This terra-cotta plaque is one of the few depictions of Gilgamesh (on the left wielding the knife) and his sidekick, Enkidu. It illustrates one of the episodes in their shared adventures, the killing of Humwawa, the monster of the Cedar Forest. The style of the plaque indicates that it was made during the Old Babylonian period, between 2000 and 1600 BCE.

Mesopotamia was a crossroads for caravans leading east and west. Peace and good governance allowed trade to flourish. The ability to move exotic foodstuffs, valuable minerals, textiles, and luxury goods across Southwest Asia won Mesopotamian merchants and entrepreneurs a privileged position as middlemen. Merchants also used sea routes for trade with the Indus Valley. Before 2000 BCE, mariners had charted the waters of the Red Sea, the Gulf of Aden, the Persian Gulf, and much of the Arabian Sea. And during the second millennium BCE, shipbuilders figured out how to construct larger vessels and to rig them with towering masts and woven sails—creating seaworthy craft that could carry bulkier loads. Shipbuilding required wood (particularly cedar from Phoenicia) as well as wool and other fibers (from the pastoral hinterlands) for sails. Such reliance on imported materials reflected a growing regional economic specialization and an expanding sphere of interaction across western Afro-Eurasia. The benefits and risks of trade in Mesopotamia are evident from royal edicts of debt annulment (to help merchants who had overstretched) and formalized commercial rules governing taxes and duties. In trade and other exchanges, Mesopotamia became a crucial link between Egypt, Anatolia, and southwestern Iran. Centralized control of the region facilitated a thriving trade in such precious commodities as horses, chariots, and lapis lazuli, which was exchanged for gold, wood, and ivory.

THE OLD AND NEW HITTITE KINGDOMS (1800–1200 BCE)

Chariot warriors known as the Hittites established territorial kingdoms in Anatolia, to the northwest of Mesopotamia. Anatolia (modern-day Turkey) was an overland crossroads that linked the Black and Mediterranean seas. Like other plateaus of Afro-Eurasia, it had high tablelands, was easy to traverse, and was hospitable to large herding communities. During the third millennium BCE Anatolia had become home to numerous communities run by native elites. These societies combined pastoral ways of life, agriculture, and urban commercial centers. Before 2000 BCE, peoples speaking Indo-European languages began to enter the plateau, probably coming from the steppe lands north and west of the Black Sea. The newcomers lived in fortified settlements and often engaged in regional warfare, and their numbers grew. Splintered into competing clans, they fought for regional supremacy. They also borrowed extensively from the cultural developments of the Southwest Asian urban cultures, especially those of Mesopotamia.

In the early second millennium BCE, the chariot warrior groups of Anatolia grew powerful on the commercial activity that passed through their region. Chief among them were the **Hittites**. Hittite lancers and archers rode chariots across vast expanses to plunder their neighbors and demand taxes and tribute. In the seventeenth century BCE, the Hittite leader Hattusilis I unified these chariot aristocracies, secured his base in Anatolia, defeated the kingdom that controlled northern Syria, and then campaigned along the Euphrates River, even sacking Babylon in 1595 BCE.

Two centuries later, the Hittites enjoyed another period of political and military success. In 1274 BCE, they fought the Egyptians at the Battle of Qadesh (in modern Syria), the largest and best-documented chariot battle of antiquity. Hittite control—spanning from Anatolia across the region between the Nile and Mesopotamia—was central to balancing power among the territorial states that grew up in the river valleys.

A COMMUNITY OF MAJOR POWERS (1400–1200 BCE)

Between 1400 and 1200 BCE, the major territorial states of Southwest Asia and Egypt perfected instruments of international diplomacy. A cache of 300 letters discovered at the present-day Egyptian village of Amarna offers intimate views of the interactions among the powers of Egypt and Southwest Asia. The letters include communications between Egyptian pharaohs and various leaders of Southwest Asia, including Babylonian and Hittite kings. The leaders of these powers settled their differences through treaties and diplomatic negotiations rather than on the battlefield. Each state knew its place in the political pecking order. It was an order that depended on constant diplomacy, based on communication, treaties, marriages, and the exchange of gifts. As nomadic peoples combined with settled urban polities to create new territorial states in Egypt, Mesopotamia, and Anatolia, and as those territorial states came into contact with one another through trade, this diplomacy was vital to maintaining the interactions among this community of major powers in Southwest Asia.

COMPARISON

DESCRIBE the impact of transhumant herders and pastoral nomads on settled communities in Egypt, Southwest Asia, and the Indus River Valley.

Nomads and the Indus River Valley

Compared with those in Egypt and Mesopotamia, territorial states emerged more slowly in the Indus River valley. Late in the third millennium BCE, drought ravaged the Indus River valley as it did other regions. By 1700 BCE, the population of the old Harappan heartland had plummeted. Here, too, around 1500 BCE, yet another group of nomadic peoples, calling themselves Aryans ("respected ones"), emerged from their homelands in the steppes of Inner Eurasia. In contrast to Egypt, Anatolia, and Mesopotamia, these pastoral nomads did not immediately establish large territorial states. Crossing the northern highlands of central Asia through the Hindu Kush, they descended into the fertile Indus River basin (see Map 3.3) with large flocks of cattle and horses. They sang chants called Rig Veda as they sacrificed some of their livestock to their gods. Known collectively as the Veda ("knowledge"), these hymns served as the most sacred texts for the newcomers, who have been known ever since as the *Vedic peoples*. Sanskrit, the spoken language of the Vedic peoples, is one of the earliest known Indo-European languages and a source for virtually all of the European languages, including Greek, Latin, English, French, and German. (See **Current Trends in World History: How Languages Spread**.)

Like other nomads from the northern steppe, they brought domesticated animals—especially horses, which pulled their chariots and established their military superiority. Not only were Vedic peoples superb horse charioteers, but they were also masters of copper and bronze metallurgy and wheel making. Their expertise in these areas allowed them to produce the very chariots that transported them into their new lands.

The Vedic peoples were deeply religious. They worshipped a host of deities, the most powerful of which were the sky god and the gods that represented horses. They were confident that their chief god, Indra (the deity of war), was on their side. The Vedic peoples also brought elaborate rituals of worship, which set them apart from the indigenous populations.

Indra with Buddha The Vedic peoples worshipped their gods by sacrificing and burning cows and horses and by singing hymns and songs, but they never built temples or sculptured idols. Therefore we do not know how they envisioned Indra and their other gods. However, when Buddhists started to make images of Buddha in the early centuries CE, they also sculpted Indra and Brahma as attendants of the Buddha. Indra in Buddhist iconography evolved into Vajrapani, the Diamond Lord. In this plate, the one on the left holding a stick with diamond-shaped heads is Indra/Vajrapani.

MAP 3.3 | Indo-European Migrations, Second Millennium BCE

One of the most important developments of the second millennium was the movement of Indo-European peoples.

- Where did the Indo-European migration originate?
- Where did Indo-European migrations spread to during this time?
- How did widespread drought push or draw the migrants into more settled agricultural regions, such as the Indus Valley?

As with many Afro-Eurasian migrations, the outsiders' arrival led to fusion as well as to conflict. While the native-born peoples eventually adopted the newcomers' language, the newcomers themselves took up the techniques and rhythms of agrarian life. The Vedic peoples used the Indus Valley as a staging area for migrations throughout the northern plain of South Asia. As they mixed agrarian and pastoral ways and borrowed technologies (such as iron working) from farther west, their population expanded and they began to look for new resources. With horses, chariots, and iron tools and weapons, they marched south and east. By 1000 BCE, they reached the southern foothills of the Himalayas and began to settle in the Ganges River valley. Five hundred years later, they had settlements as far south as the Deccan plateau.

Each wave of occupation involved violence, but the invaders did not simply dominate the indigenous peoples. Instead, the confrontations led them to embrace many of the ways of the vanquished. In particular, the Vedic newcomers were impressed with inhabitants' farming skills and knowledge of seasonal weather. These they adapted even as they continued to expand their territory. They moved into huts constructed from mud, bamboo, and reeds. They refined the already sophisticated production of beautiful carnelian stone beads, and they further aided commerce by devising standardized weights. In addition to raising domesticated animals, they sowed wheat and rye on the Indus plain, and they learned to plant rice in the marshy lands of the Ganges River valley. Later they mastered the use of plows with iron blades, an innovation that transformed the agrarian base of South Asia. This turn to settled agriculture was a major shift for the nomadic pastoral Vedic peoples. After all, their staple foods had always been dairy products and meat, and they were used to measuring their wealth in livestock (horses were most valuable, and cows were more valuable than sheep). Moreover, because they could not breed their prized horses in South Asia's semitropical climate, they initiated a brisk import trade from central and Southwest Asia.

As the Vedic peoples filled the relative void left by the collapse of the Harappans and adapted to their new environment, their initial political organization took a somewhat different course from those of Southwest Asia. Whereas competitive kingdoms dominated the landscape in Southwest Asia, competitive and balanced regimes were slower to emerge in South Asia. The result was a slower process of political integration.

The Shang Territorial State in East Asia (1600–1045 BCE)

China's first major territorial state combined features of earlier Longshan culture with new technologies and religious practices. Climatic change affected East Asia much as it had central and Southwest Asia. Stories supposedly written on bamboo strips and later collected into what historians call the "Bamboo Annals" tell of a time at the end of the legendary Xia dynasty when the sun dimmed, frost and ice appeared in summer, and a long drought followed heavy rainfall and flooding. According to Chinese mythology, the first ruler of the Shang dynasty defeated a despotic Xia king and then offered to sacrifice himself so that the drought would end. This leader, Tang, survived to found the territorial state called Shang, around 1600 BCE in northeastern China.

The Shang state was built on four elements that the Longshan peoples had already introduced: a metal industry based on copper; pottery making; walled towns; and divination using animal bones. To these Longshan foundations the Shang dynasty added hereditary rulers whose power derived from their relation to ancestors and gods; written records; large-scale metallurgy; tribute; and various rituals.

COMPARISON

COMPARE state formation in Shang China to Mesopotamia and Egypt.

STATE FORMATION

A combination of these preexisting Longshan strengths and Shang innovations produced a strong Shang territorial state and a wealthy and powerful elite, noted for its intellectual achievements and aesthetic sensibilities.

Current Trends in World History

How Languages Spread: The Case of Nomadic Indo-European Languages

Linguistics, or the study of language, is an important tool in world history. Language arose independently in a number of places around the world. All languages change with time, and their divergence from a mother tongue serves as a tool in determining at what point different languages, like German or French, broke apart. Scholars call related tongues with a common origin "language families." Even though members of the same language family diverged over time, they all share grammatical features and root vocabularies.

While technically there are more than a hundred language families, a much smaller number have influenced vast geographic areas. For example, the *Altaic* languages spread from Europe to central Asia. The *Sino-Tibetan* language family includes Mandarin, the most widely spoken language in the world. The *Uralic* family, which includes Hungarian and Finnish, occurs mainly in Europe. The *Afro-Asiatic* language family contains several hundred languages spoken in North Africa, sub-Saharan Africa, and Southeast Asia, Hebrew and Arabic among them.

One language family that linguists have studied extensively, and the one with the largest number of speakers today, is *Indo-European.* It was identified by scholars who recognized similarities in grammar and vocabulary among classical Sanskrit, Persian, Greek, and Latin. Living languages in this family include English, Irish, German, Norwegian, Portuguese, French, Russian, Persian, Hindi, and Bengali. For the past 200 years, comparative linguists have sought to reconstruct Proto-Indo-European, the parent of all the languages in the family. They have drawn conclusions about its grammar, hypothesizing a highly inflected language with different endings on nouns and verbs according to their use. They have also made suggestions about its vocabulary.

For example, after analyzing patterns of linguistic change, scholars have proposed that the basic Indo-European root that means "horse"—in Sanskrit, *a'sva;* Persian, *aspa;* Latin, *equus;* and Greek, *hippos* (ίππος)—is *ekwo-. Table 3-1 demonstrates the similarity of words in some of the major Indo-European languages. We have emphasized numbers, which are especially stable in language systems because people do not like to change the way they count. We have also provided the equivalents in two Semitic languages (Arabic and Hebrew) to show how different these basic words are in another language family (the Afro-Asiatic).

Attempts to locate the homeland of the original speakers of Proto-Indo-European involve mapping the reconstructed vocabulary onto a matching geography. For example, some of the vocabulary contains words for "snow," "mountain," and "swift river," as well as for animals that are not native to Europe, such as "lion," "monkey," and "elephant." Other words describe agricultural practices and farming tools that date back as far as 5000 BCE. Many linguists believe that nomadic and pastoral peoples of the Eurasian steppes took this language—along with their precious horses and chariots—as far as the borderlands of what is now Afghanistan and eastern Iran.

We know that the early speakers of Indo-European languages used chariots and had words for "wheel," "yoke," and "axle." In fact, the earliest pictures of horse-drawn chariots, used in battle, came from the steppe region east of the Ural Mountains. Indo-European-speaking nomads inhabited this area and subsequently migrated to South Asia and the Iranian plateau. Thus, the chariot was literally the vehicle for cultural mingling and, ultimately, the spread of the people's language.

Migration is only one of the possible reasons that languages move and change over vast areas and periods of time. Other influential factors are invasions, climatic conditions, natural resources, and ways of life. Even within one language, words can change through generations of use. And words from a common root can sometimes take on very different meanings while remaining similar phonetically. (To use an Indo-European root as an example, the Sanskrit *a'sura* means "demonic creature" whereas the Persian *ahura* means "Supreme God.")

Linguistic analysis sheds light on the geographic and demographic details of language penetration into different regions. Part of its allure is the fact

Shang kings used a personalized style of rule, making regular trips around the country to meet, hunt, and conduct military campaigns. With no rival territorial states on its immediate periphery, the Shang state did not create a strongly defended, permanent capital, but rather moved its capital as the frontier expanded and contracted. Bureaucrats used written records to oversee the large and expanding population of the Shang state.

Advanced Shang metalworking—the beginnings of which appeared in northwestern China at pre-Shang sites dating as early as 1800 BCE—was vital to the Shang territorial state. Shang bronze work included weapons, fittings for chariots, and ritual vessels.

that some issues defy resolution (for example, in some cases whether a given language was the dialect of the conquerors or the conquered). Nonetheless, the study of language families and their history underscores the key role of language in the intermingling of cultures throughout time.

QUESTIONS FOR ANALYSIS

- What relationships does Table 3.1 suggest among the Semitic languages and the Indo-European languages?
- How does the study of linguistics enhance our understanding of human geography?

Explore Further

David W. Anthony, *The Horse, the Wheel, and Language: How Bronze-Age Riders from the Eurasian Steppes Shaped the Modern World* (2007).

Joseph T. Shipley, *The Origins of English Words: A Discursive Dictionary of Indo-European Roots* (2001).

TABLE 3.1 | Similarity of Words in Some Major Indo-European Languages

	WORDS OF COMMON ORIGIN IN INDO-EUROPEAN LANGUAGES						SEMITIC LANGUAGES	
	SANSKRIT	HINDI	GREEK	LATIN	FRENCH	GERMAN	ARABIC	HEBREW
Numbers								
one	eka	ek	hen	unus	un	ein	wahid	ehad
two	dva	do	duo	duo	deux	zwei	ithnin	shnayim
three	tri	teen	treis	tres	trois	drei	thalatha	shlasha
four	catur	chār	tessara	quattuor	quatre	vier	arba'a	arba'a
five	pañca	pānch	penta	quinque	cinq	fünf	khamsa	hamisha
ten	daśa	das	deka	decem	dix	zehn	ashra	asara
hundred	śata	sau	hekaton	centum	cent	hundert	mi'a	me'a
Other common words								
father	pitṛ	pitā	pater	pater	père	vater	abu	aba
mother	mātṛ	mātā	mêter	mater	mère	mutter	umm	em
son	sūnu	betā	huios	filius	fils	sohn	ibn	ben
heart	hṛdaya	dil	kardia	cor	coeur	herz	qalb	lev
foot	pada	pair	pous	pes	pied	fuss	qadam	regel
god	deva	dev	theos	deus	dieu	gott	Allah	yahweh

Because copper and tin were available from the North China plain, only short-distance trade was necessary to obtain the resources that a bronze culture needed. (See Map 3.4.) Shang bronze-working technique involved the use of hollow clay molds to hold the molten metal alloy, which, when removed after the liquid had cooled and solidified, produced firm bronze objects. The casting of modular components that artisans could assemble later promoted increased production and permitted the elite to make extravagant use of bronze vessels for burials. The bronze industry of this period shows the high level not only of material culture (in the practical function of the physical objects) but also of cultural development (in the

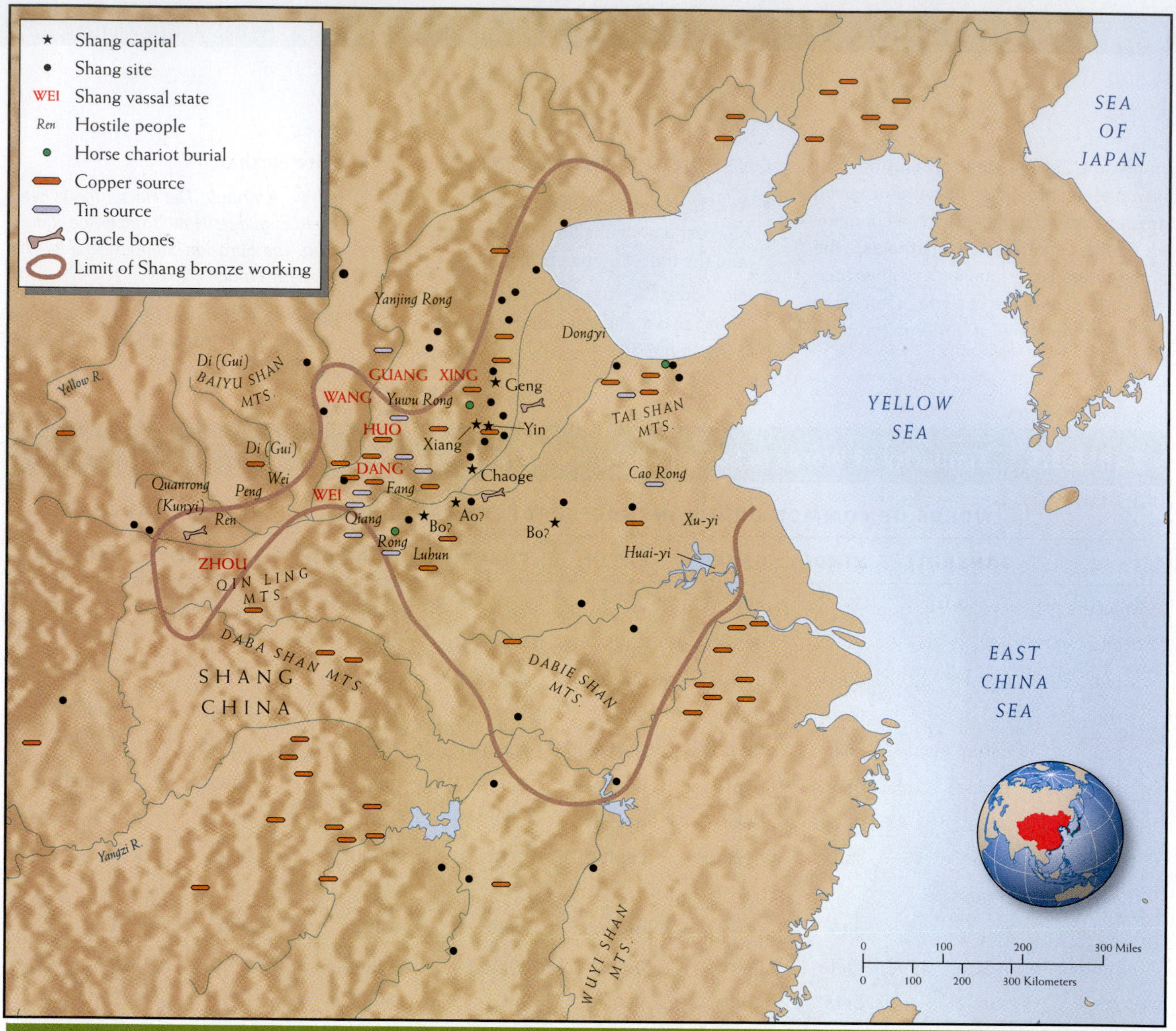

MAP 3.4 | Shang Dynasty in East Asia

The Shang state was one of the most important and powerful of early Chinese dynasties.

- Based on your analysis of this map, what raw materials were the most important to the Shang state?
- Why were there so many Shang capitals?
- Why were there no clear territorial boundaries for the Shang state?

aesthetic sense of beauty and taste conveyed by the choice of form). Since Shang metalworking required extensive mining, it necessitated a large labor force, efficient casting, and a reproducible artistic style. Although the Shang state highly valued its artisans, it treated its copper miners as lowly tribute laborers. By controlling access to tin and copper and to the production of bronze, Shang kings prevented their rivals from forging bronze weapons and thus increased their own power and legitimacy. With their superior weapons, Shang armies by 1300 BCE could easily destroy armies wielding wooden clubs and stone-tipped spears.

Chariots entered the Central Plains of China with nomads of the north around 1200 BCE, much later than their appearance in Egypt and Southwest Asia. They were quickly adopted by the upper classes. Chinese chariots were larger (fitting three men standing in a box mounted on eighteen- or twenty-six-spoke wheels) and much better built than those of their neighbors. As symbols of power and wealth, they were often buried with their owners. Yet, unlike elsewhere in Afro-Eurasia, they were at first little used in warfare during the Shang era, perhaps because of the effectiveness and shock value of large Shang infantry forces, composed mainly of foot soldiers, armed with axes, spears, arrowheads, shields, and helmets, all made of bronze. The chariot's primary purposes in Shang China were hunting and as a marker of high status. Shang metalworking and their incorporation of the chariot gave the Shang state a huge advantage and unprecedented power over its neighbors.

Bronze At the height of the Shang state, circa 1200 BCE, its rulers erected massive palaces at the capital of Yin, which required bronze foundries for its wine and food vessels. In these foundries, skilled workers produced bronze weapons and ritual objects and elaborate ceremonial drinking and eating vessels, like the one pictured.

AGRICULTURE AND TRIBUTE

The Shang dynastic rulers also understood the importance of agriculture for winning and maintaining power, so they did much to promote its development. The activities of local governors and the masses revolved around agriculture. Rulers controlled their own farms, which supplied food to the royal family, craftworkers, and the army. Farmers drained low-lying fields and cleared forested areas to expand the cultivation of millet, wheat, barley, and possibly rice. Their tools included stone plows, spades, and sickles. Farmers also cultivated silkworms and raised pigs, dogs, sheep, and oxen. Thanks to the twelve-month, 360-day lunar calendar developed by Shang astrologers, farmers were better able to track the growing season. By including leap months, this calendar maintained the proper relationship between months and seasons, and it relieved fears about solar and lunar eclipses by making them predictable.

The ruler's wealth and power depended on tribute from elites and allies. Elites supplied warriors and laborers, horses and cattle. Allies sent foodstuffs, soldiers, and workers and "assisted in the king's affairs"—perhaps by hunting, burning brush, or clearing land—in return for his help in defending against invaders and making predictions about the harvest. Commoners sent their tribute to the elites, who held the land as grants from the king. Farmers transferred their surplus crops to the elite landholders (or to the ruler if they worked on his personal landholdings) on a regular schedule. Tribute could also take the form of turtle shells and cattle scapulas (shoulder blades), which the Shang used for divination (see below). Divining the future was a powerful way to legitimate royal power—and then to justify the right to collect more tribute. By placing themselves symbolically and literally at the center of all exchanges, the Shang kings reinforced their power over others.

SOCIETY AND RITUAL PRACTICE

The advances in metalworking and agriculture gave the state the resources to sustain a complex society, in which religion and rituals reinforced the social hierarchy. The core organizing principle of Shang society was familial descent traced back many generations to a common male ancestor. Grandparents, parents, sons, and daughters lived and worked together and held property in common, but male family elders took precedence. Women from other male family lines married into the family and won honor when they became mothers, particularly of sons.

The death ritual, which involved sacrificing humans to accompany the deceased in the next life, reflected the importance of family, male dominance, and social hierarchy. Members of the royal elite were often buried with full entourage, including wives, consorts, servants, chariots, horses, and drivers. The inclusion of personal slaves and servants indicates a belief that the familiar social hierarchy would continue in the afterlife.

The Shang state was a full-fledged theocracy: it claimed that the ruler at the top of the hierarchy derived his authority through guidance from ancestors and gods. Shang rulers practiced ancestral worship, which was the major form of religious belief in China during this period. Ancestor worship involved performing rituals in which the rulers offered drink and food to their recently dead ancestors with the hope that they would intervene with their more powerful long-dead ancestors on behalf of the living. Divination was the process by which Shang rulers communicated with ancestors and foretold the future. The technique involved diviners' applying intense heat to the shoulder bones of cattle or to turtle shells and interpreting the cracks that appeared on these objects as auspicious or inauspicious signs from the ancestors regarding royal plans and actions. On these so-called **oracle bones**, scribes subsequently inscribed the queries asked of the ancestors to confirm the diviners' interpretations. Thus, Shang writing began as a dramatic ritual performance in which the living responded to their ancestors' oracular signs.

The oracle bones and tortoise shells offer a window into the concerns and beliefs of the elite groups of these very distant cultures. The questions put to diviners most frequently as they inspected bones and shells were about the weather, hardly surprising in communities so dependent on growing seasons and good harvests, about family health and well-being, and especially about the prospects of having male children, who would extend the family line.

In Shang theocracy, because the ruler was the head of a unified clergy and embodied both religious and political power, no independent priesthood emerged. Diviners and scribes were subordinate to the ruler and the royal pantheon of ancestors he represented. Ancestor worship sanctified Shang control and legitimized the rulers' lineage, ensuring that the ruling family kept all political and religious power. Because the Shang gods were ancestral deities, the rulers were deified when they died and ranked in descending chronological order. Becoming gods at death, Shang rulers united the world of the living with the world of the dead.

SHANG WRITING

In the process of scribes' and priests' using their script on oracle bones for the Shang king, the formal character-based writing of East Asia developed over time. So although Shang scholars did not invent writing in East Asia, they perfected it. Evidence for writing in this era comes entirely from oracle bones, which were central to political and religious authority under the Shang. Other written records may have been on materials that did not survive. This accident of preservation may explain the major differences between the ancient texts in China (primarily divinations on bones) and in the Southwest Asian societies that impressed cuneiform on clay tablets (primarily for economic transactions, literary and religious documents, and historical records). In comparison with Mesopotamia and Egypt, the transition of Shang record keeping (for example, questions to ancestors, lineages of rulers, or economic transactions) to literature (for example, myths about the founding of states) was slower. Shang rulers initially monopolized writing through their scribes, who positioned the royal families at the top of the social and political hierarchy. And priests wrote on the oracle bones to address the otherworld and gain information about the future so that the ruling family would remain at the center of the political system.

As Shang China cultivated developments in agriculture, ornate bronze metalworking and divinatory writing on oracle bones, the state did not face the repeated waves of pastoral nomadic invaders seen in other parts of Afro-Eurasia. It was nonetheless influenced by the chariot culture that eventually filtered into East Asia. Given that so many of the developments in Shang China bolstered the authority of the dynastic rulers and elite, it is perhaps not surprising that the chariot in China was initially more a marker of elite status than an effective tool for warfare.

Microsocieties in the South Pacific and in the Aegean

As environmental circumstances drove pastoral nomads and transhumant herders toward settled agriculturalists, leading ultimately to the development of powerful and somewhat intertwined territorial states in Egypt, Southwest Asia, the Indus River Valley, and Shang China, other pressures drove migrations across the South Pacific and Aegean. These maritime migrations led to the development after 2000 BCE, in such places as Austronesia and the Aegean, of **microsocieties**: small-scale, fragmented, and dispersed communities that had limited interaction with others.

COMPARISON

EXAMINE the development of microsocieties in the South Pacific and the Aegean and **EXPLAIN** the role geography played in their development.

THE SOUTH PACIFIC (2500 BCE–400 CE)

Austronesian-speaking peoples with origins in coastal South China migrated into the South Pacific during this period and formed microsocieties there. Using their double-outrigger canoes, which were 60 to 100 feet long and bore huge triangular sails, the early Austronesians crossed the Taiwan Straits and colonized key islands in the Pacific. Their vessels were much more advanced than the simple dugout canoes used in inland waterways. In good weather, double-outrigger canoes could cover more than 120 miles in a day. The invention of a stabilization device for deep-sea sailing sometime after 2500 BCE triggered further Austronesian expansion into the Pacific. By 400 CE, these nomads of the sea had reached most of the islands of the South Pacific. Their seafaring skills enabled the Austronesians to monopolize trade wherever they went.

By comparing the vocabularies and grammatical similarities of languages spoken today by the remaining tribal peoples in Taiwan, the Philippines, and Indonesia, scholars have traced the ancient Austronesian-speaking peoples back to coastal South China in the fourth millennium BCE. Pottery, stone tools, and domesticated crops and pigs also provide markers for tracking Austronesian settlements throughout the coastal islands and in the South Pacific. According to archaeologists, the same cultural features had spread from Taiwan to the Philippines (by 2500 BCE), to Java and Sumatra (by 2000 BCE), and parts of Australia and New Guinea (by 1600 BCE). The Austronesians then ventured farther eastward into the South Pacific, apparently arriving in Samoa and Fiji in 1200 BCE

Austronesian Canoe Early Austronesians crossed the Taiwan Straits and colonized key islands in the Pacific using double-outrigger canoes from 60 to 100 feet long equipped with triangular sails. In good weather, such canoes could cover more than 120 miles in a day.

and on mainland Southeast Asia in 1000 BCE. (See Map 3.5.) The Austronesians reached the Marquesas Islands, strategically located for northern and southern exploration, in the central Pacific around 200 CE. Over the next few centuries, some moved on to Easter Island to the south and Hawaii to the north. The immense thirty-ton stone structures on Easter Island represent the monumental Polynesian architecture produced after their arrival.

Equatorial lands in the South Pacific have a tropical or subtropical climate and, in many places, fertile soils containing nutrient-rich volcanic ash. In this environment the Austronesians cultivated dry-land crops (yams and sweet potatoes), irrigated crops (more yams, which grew better in paddy fields or in rainy areas), and tree crops (breadfruit, bananas, and coconuts). In addition, colonized areas beyond the landmass, such as the islands of Indonesia, had labyrinthine coastlines rich in maritime resources, including coral reefs and mangrove swamps teeming with wildlife. Island hopping led the adventurers to encounter new food sources, but the shallow waters and reefs offered sufficient fish and shellfish for their needs.

In the South Pacific, the Polynesian descendants of the early Austronesians shared a common culture, language, technology, and stores of domesticated plants and animals. These later seafarers came from many different island communities (hence the name *Polynesian,* "belonging to many islands"), and after they settled down, their numbers grew. Their crop surpluses allowed more densely populated communities to support craft specialists and soldiers. Most settlements boasted ceremonial buildings to promote local solidarity and forts to provide defense. On larger islands, communities often cooperated and organized workforces to enclose ponds for fish production and to build and maintain large irrigation works for agriculture. In terms of political structure, Polynesian communities ranged from tribal or village units to multi-island alliances that sometimes invaded other areas.

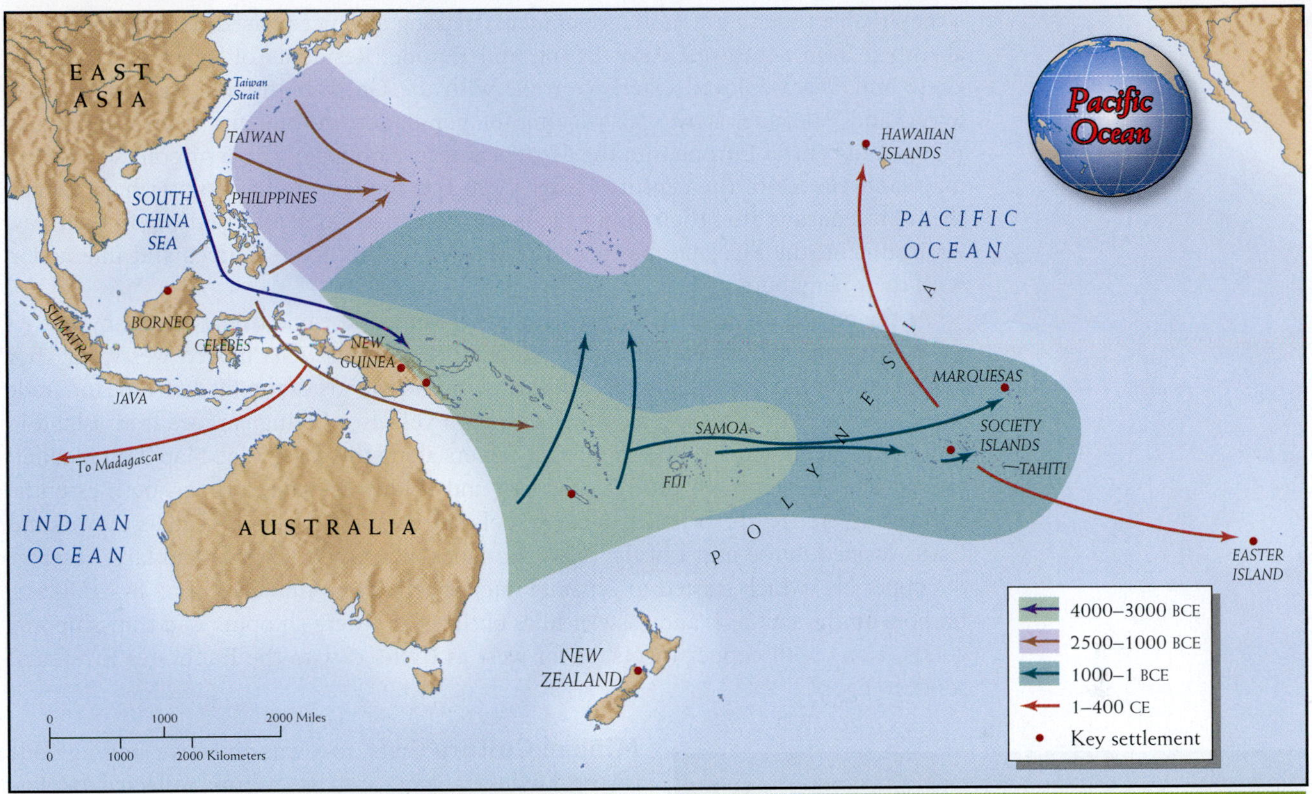

MAP 3.5 | Austronesian Migrations

The Pacific Ocean saw many migrations from East Asia.

- Where did the Austronesian migrants come from?
- What were the boundaries of their migration?
- Why, unlike other migratory people during the second millennium, did Austronesian settlers in Polynesia become a world apart?

The expansion of East Asian peoples throughout the South Pacific and their trade back and forth, however, did not integrate the islands into the mainland culture. Expansion could not overcome the tendency of these Austronesian microsocieties, dispersed across a huge ocean, toward fragmentation and isolation.

THE AEGEAN WORLD (2000–1200 BCE)

In the region around the Aegean Sea (the islands and the mainland of present-day Greece), no single power emerged before the second millennium BCE, but island microsocieties (the Minoans and the Mycenaeans) developed an expanding trade network and distinctive cultures. Settled agrarian communities were linked only by trade and culture. Fragmentation was the norm—in part because the landscape had no great riverine systems or large common plain. In its fragmentation, the island world of the eastern Mediterranean initially resembled that of the South Pacific.

As an unintended benefit of the lack of centralization, there was no single regime to collapse when the droughts arrived. Thus, in the second millennium BCE, peoples of the eastern Mediterranean did not struggle to recover lost grandeur. Rather, they enjoyed a remarkable though gradual development, making advances based on influences they absorbed from Southwest Asia, Egypt, and Europe. Residents of Aegean islands like Crete and Thera enjoyed extensive trade with the Greek mainland, Egypt, Anatolia, Syria, and Palestine. It was also a time of population movements from the Danube region and central Europe into the Mediterranean. Groups of these migrants settled in mainland Greece in the centuries after 1900 BCE; modern archaeologists have named them Mycenaeans after their famous palace at Mycenae. Soon after settling in their new environment, the Mycenaeans turned to the sea to look for resources and interaction with their neighbors.

At the outset, the main influence on the Aegean world came from the east by sea. As the institutions and ideas that had developed in Southwest Asia moved westward, they found a ready reception along the coasts and on the islands of the Mediterranean. Trade was the main source of eastern influences, with vessels carrying cargoes from island to island and up and down the commercial centers along the coast. (See Map 3.6.) Mediterranean trade centered on tin from the east and readily available copper, both essential for making bronze (the primary metal in tools and weapons). Islands such as Cyprus and Crete, located in the midst of the active sea-lanes, flourished. Cyprus had large reserves of copper ore, which started to generate intense activity around 2300 BCE. By 2000 BCE, harbors on the southern and eastern sides of the island were shipping and transshipping goods, along with copper ingots, as far west as Crete, east to the Euphrates River, and south to Egypt.

Seaborne Trade The size of the seaborne trade is revealed most spectacularly in the shipwrecks recovered by underwater archaeologists. One of these ships, sunk off the southern coast of Anatolia around 1325 BCE, was transporting ten tons of copper in 354 oxhide-shaped ingots, as well as more than a hundred amphorae (large, two-handled jars) containing all kinds of high-value commodities.

Minoan Culture Crete, too, was an active trading node in the Mediterranean, and its culture reflected outside influences as well as local traditions. Around 2000 BCE, a large number of independent palace centers began to emerge on Crete, at Knossos (ultimately the most impressive of them) and elsewhere. Scholars have named the people who built these elaborate centers the Minoans, after the legendary King Minos who may have ruled Crete at this time. The Minoans sailed back and forth across the Mediterranean, and by 1600 BCE they were colonizing other Aegean islands as trading and mining centers. The Minoans' wealth soon became a magnet for the Mycenaeans, their mainland competitors, who took over Crete around 1400 BCE.

As the island communities traded with the peoples of Southwest Asia, they borrowed some ideas but also kept their own cultural traditions. In terms of borrowing, the monumental architecture of Southwest Asia found small-scale echoes in the Aegean world—notably in the palace complexes built on Crete between 1900 and 1600 BCE.

In terms of a distinctive cultural element, worship on the islands focused on a female deity, the "Lady," but there are no traces of large temple complexes similar to those in Mesopotamia, Anatolia, and Egypt. Nor, apparently, was there any priestly class of the type that managed the temple complexes of Southwest Asian societies. Moreover, it is unclear whether these societies had full-time scribes.

Perhaps not surprisingly for a fragmented microsociety, there was significant regional diversity within this small

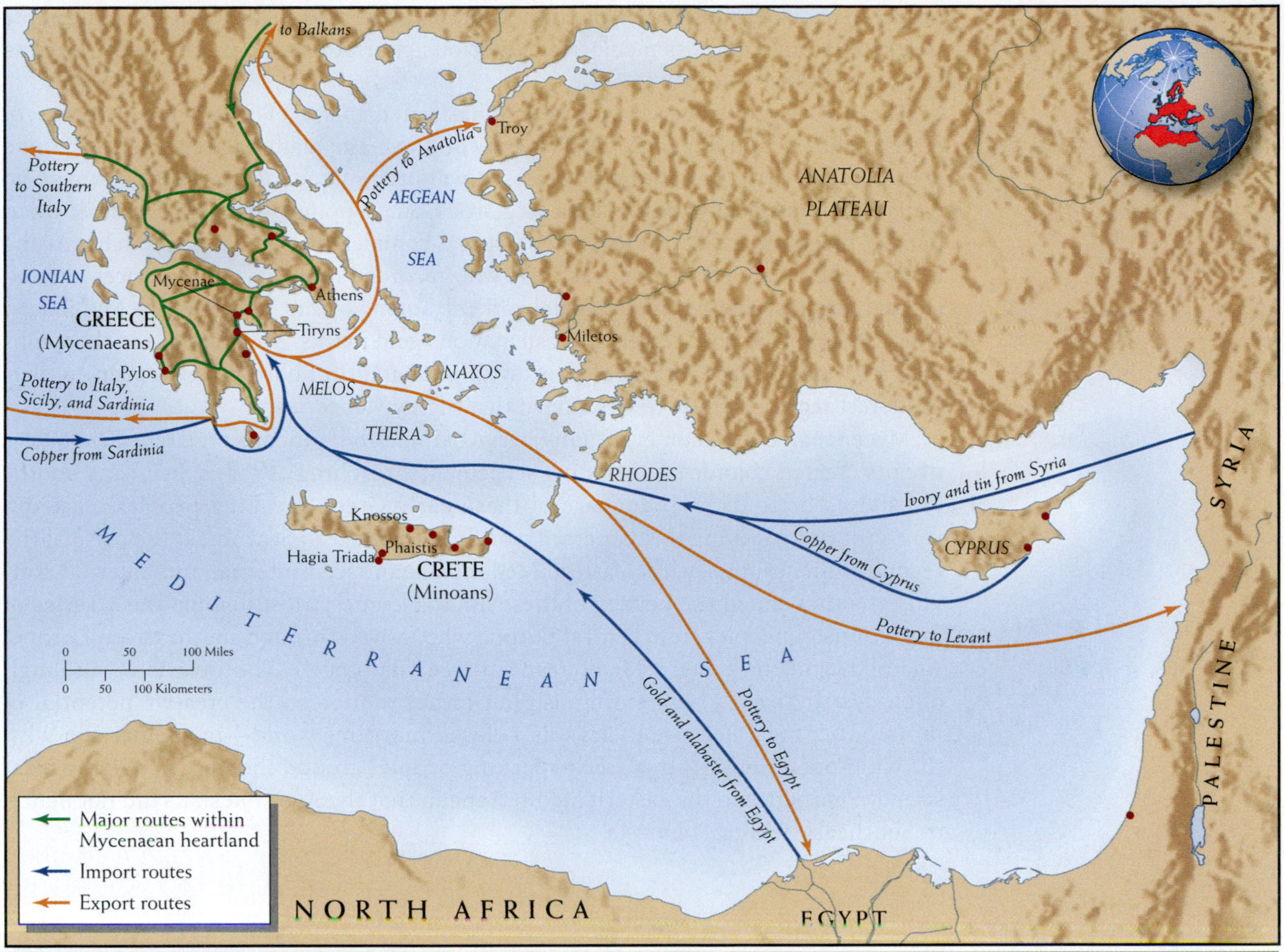

MAP 3.6 | Trade in the Eastern Mediterranean World

Greece, Egypt, and Cyprus were trade hubs in the eastern Mediterranean.

- What were the major commodities that were traded in the eastern Mediterranean?
- Why did trade originally move from east to west?
- What role did geographic location play in terms of the Mycenaeans eventually conquering the Minoans?

Aegean world. On Crete, the large, palace-centered communities controlled centrally organized societies with a high order of refinement. Confident in their wealth and power, the sprawling, airy palaces had no fortifications and no natural defenses. On Thera, a small island to the north of Crete, a trading city centered not on a major palace complex, but rather featured private houses, with bathrooms including toilets and running water and other rooms decorated with exotic wall paintings.

Mycenaean Culture The Mycenaean culture was more war-oriented than that of the peaceful, seafaring Minoans. When the Mycenaeans migrated to Greece from central Europe, they brought their Indo-European language, their horse chariots, and their metalworking skills. Their move was gradual, lasting from about 1850 to 1600 BCE, but ultimately they dominated the indigenous population. They maintained their dominance with their powerful weapon, the chariot, until 1200 BCE. The battle chariots and festivities of chariot racing described in the centuries-later epic poetry of Homer express memories of glorious chariot feats that echo Vedic legends from South Asia.

The Mycenaean material culture emphasized displays of weaponry, portraits of armed soldiers, and illustrations of violent conflicts. The main palace centers at Tiryns and Mycenae were the hulking fortresses of warlords surrounded by rough-hewn stone walls and strategically located atop large rock outcroppings. In these fortified urban hubs, a preeminent ruler (*wanax*) stood atop a complex bureaucratic hierarchy. At the heart of the palace society were scribes, who recorded the goods and services allotted to local farmers, shepherds, and metalworkers, among others. Tombs of the Mycenaean elite contain many gold vessels and ostentatious gold masks. Amber beads in the tombs indicate that the warriors had contacts with inhabitants of northern European coniferous forest regions, whose trees secreted that highly valued resin.

Mycenaean expansion eventually overwhelmed the Minoans on Crete. The Mycenaeans created colonies and trading settlements, reaching as far as Sicily and southern Italy. The trade and language of these early Greek-speaking peoples created a veneer of unity linking the dispersed worlds of the Aegean Sea. Yet, at the close of the second millennium BCE, the eastern Mediterranean faced internal and external convulsions that ended the heyday of these microsocieties. Most notable was a series of migrations of peoples from central Europe who moved through southeastern Europe, Anatolia, and the eastern Mediterranean (see Chapter 4). The invasions, although often destructive, did not extinguish but rather reinforced the creative potential of this frontier area. Because theirs was a closed maritime world—in comparison with the wide-open Pacific—the Greek-speaking peoples around the Aegean quickly reasserted dominance in the eastern Mediterranean that the Austronesians did not match in Southeast Asia or Polynesia.

Aegean Fresco This is one of the more striking wall paintings, or frescoes, discovered by archaeologists in the 1970s and 1980s at Akrotiri on the island of Thera (Santorini) in the Aegean Sea. Its brilliant colors, especially the blue of the sea, evoke the lively essence of Minoan life on the island. Note the houses of the wealthy along the port and the flotilla of ships that reflects the seaborne commerce that was beginning to flourish in the Mediterranean in this period.

Conclusion

The second millennium BCE was an era of migrations, warfare, and territorial state building in Afro-Eurasia. Whereas river-basin societies had flourished in the fourth and third millennia BCE in Mesopotamia, Egypt, the Indus Valley, and East Asia, now droughts shook the agrarian foundations of their economies. Old states crumbled; from the steppes and plateaus pastoral nomads and transhumant herders descended in search of food, grazing lands, and other opportunities. As transhumant herders pressed into the river-basin societies, the social and political fabric of these communities changed. Likewise, horse-riding nomads from steppe communities in Inner Eurasia conquered and settled in the agrarian states, bringing key innovations. Foremost were the horse chariots, which became a military catalyst sparking the evolution from smaller states to larger territorial states encompassing crowded cities, vast hinterlands, and broadened trade networks. The nomads and herders also adopted many of the settled peoples' beliefs and customs. On land and sea, migrating peoples created zones of long-distance trade that linked agrarian societies.

Through a range of trade, migrations, and conquest throughout the second millennium BCE, the Nile Delta, the basin of the Tigris and Euphrates rivers, the Indus Valley, and the Yellow River basin were brought into even closer contact than before. In Southwest Asia and the Nile River basin, the interaction led to an elaborate system of diplomatic relations. The first territorial states appeared in this millennium, composed of multiple communities living under common laws and customs. An alliance of farmers and warriors united agrarian production with political power to create and defend territorial boundaries. The new arrangements overshadowed the nomads' historic role as predators and enabled them to become military elites within these new states. Through taxes and drafted labor, villagers repaid their rulers for local security and state-run diplomacy. The rhythms of state formation differed where regimes were not closely packed together. In East Asia, for example, the absence of strong rivals allowed the emerging Shang dynasty to develop more gradually. Where landscapes had sharper divisions—as in the island archipelagos of the South Pacific and in the Mediterranean—small-scale, decentralized, and fragmented microsocieties emerged. But fragmentation is not the same as isolation. Even peoples in the worlds apart from the developments across Afro-Eurasia were not entirely secluded from the increasing flows of technologies, languages, goods, and migrants.

After You Read This Chapter

Go to INQUIZITIVE to see what you've learned—and learn what you've missed—with personalized feedback along the way.

TRACING THE GLOBAL STORYLINES

FOCUS ON: *The Emergence of Territorial States*

EGYPT AND SOUTHWEST ASIA

- Invasions by nomads and transhumant herders lead to the creation of larger territorial states: New Kingdom Egypt, Hittites, Mesopotamian states.
- A centuries-long peaceful era, a community of major powers, emerges among the major states as the result of shrewd statecraft and diplomacy.

INDUS RIVER VALLEY

- Migratory Vedic peoples from the steppes of Inner Eurasia use chariots and rely on domesticated animals to spread out and begin integrating the northern half of South Asia.

SHANG STATE (CHINA)

- Shang dynastic rulers promote improvements in metalworking, agriculture, and the development of writing, leading to the growth of China's first major state.

MICROSOCIETIES

- Substantial increases in population, migrations, and trade lead to the emergence of microsocieties among peoples in the South Pacific (Austronesians) and the Aegean world (Minoans and Mycenaeans).

CHRONOLOGY

EGYPT AND SOUTHWEST ASIA

Middle Kingdom in Egypt 2055–1650 BCE

SOUTH ASIA

EAST ASIA

THE MEDITERRANEAN

SOUTH PACIFIC

Austronesian migrations 2500 BCE–400 CE

2500 BCE

2000 BCE

THINKING ABOUT GLOBAL CONNECTIONS

- ***Thinking about Environmental Impacts and Territorial States*** Around 2000 BCE, a series of environmental disasters helped to destroy the civilizations that had thrived in parts of Afro-Eurasia in the third millennium BCE. What were the short-term and long-term impacts of these environmental troubles? How did they influence the movement of peoples and the formation of territorial states in the second millennium BCE?
- ***Thinking about Transformation & Conflict and Territorial States*** The second millennium BCE witnessed large-scale migrations of nomadic peoples who brought with them their domesticated horses and their chariot technology. These people are referred to by scholars as Indo-Europeans, largely on the basis of their languages (see Current Trends in World History: How Languages Spread). Contrast the impact of migrations into Southwest Asia (Anatolia and Mesopotamia), Egypt, South Asia, and East Asia. To what extent did conflict play a role in the impact of Indo-European-language speakers on the formation of territorial states?
- ***Thinking about Interconnection & Divergence and Territorial States*** While territorial states formed in Egypt, Mesopotamia, South Asia, and East Asia, microsocieties formed in the South Pacific and in the Aegean Sea. What factors influenced whether a region might host a territorial state as opposed to a microsociety? What areas of the planet were still worlds apart? What ways of life continued to predominate in those worlds apart from the territorial states and microsocieties discussed in this chapter?

STUDY QUESTIONS

1. Explain the differences between **pastoral nomads** and **transhumant herders**. How did each shape Afro-Eurasian history during the second millennium BCE?
2. Analyze the impact on Afro-Eurasia of the domestication of horses and the invention of the **chariot**. How did these developments affect both nomadic and settled peoples?
3. Define the term **territorial state**. In what areas of Afro-Eurasia did this new form of political organization emerge and thrive?
4. How do Amun-Re, Ahmosis, and Hatshepsut contribute to an understanding of Egypt as a territorial state? Explain the role of the **Amorites** and **Hammurapi's Code** in the formation of territorial state in Mesopotamia. What do these developments suggest about the religious, political, and legal dimensions of territorial states?
5. In what ways did the **Hyksos** and **Hittites** influence territorial state formation in Egypt and Mesopotamia? How does the Battle of Qadesh offer an example of that interaction?
6. Contrast the formation of territorial states in Egypt and Mesopotamia with the impact of Vedic peoples in South Asia.
7. Contrast the formation of the Shang state in East Asia with developments happening at the same time in Egypt, Mesopotamia, and South Asia. Explain the role of metallurgy and **oracle bones** in supporting Shang authority.
8. Define the term **microsociety**. Compare and contrast Polynesian microsocieties of the South Pacific with the Minoans and Mycenaeans of the Aegean.

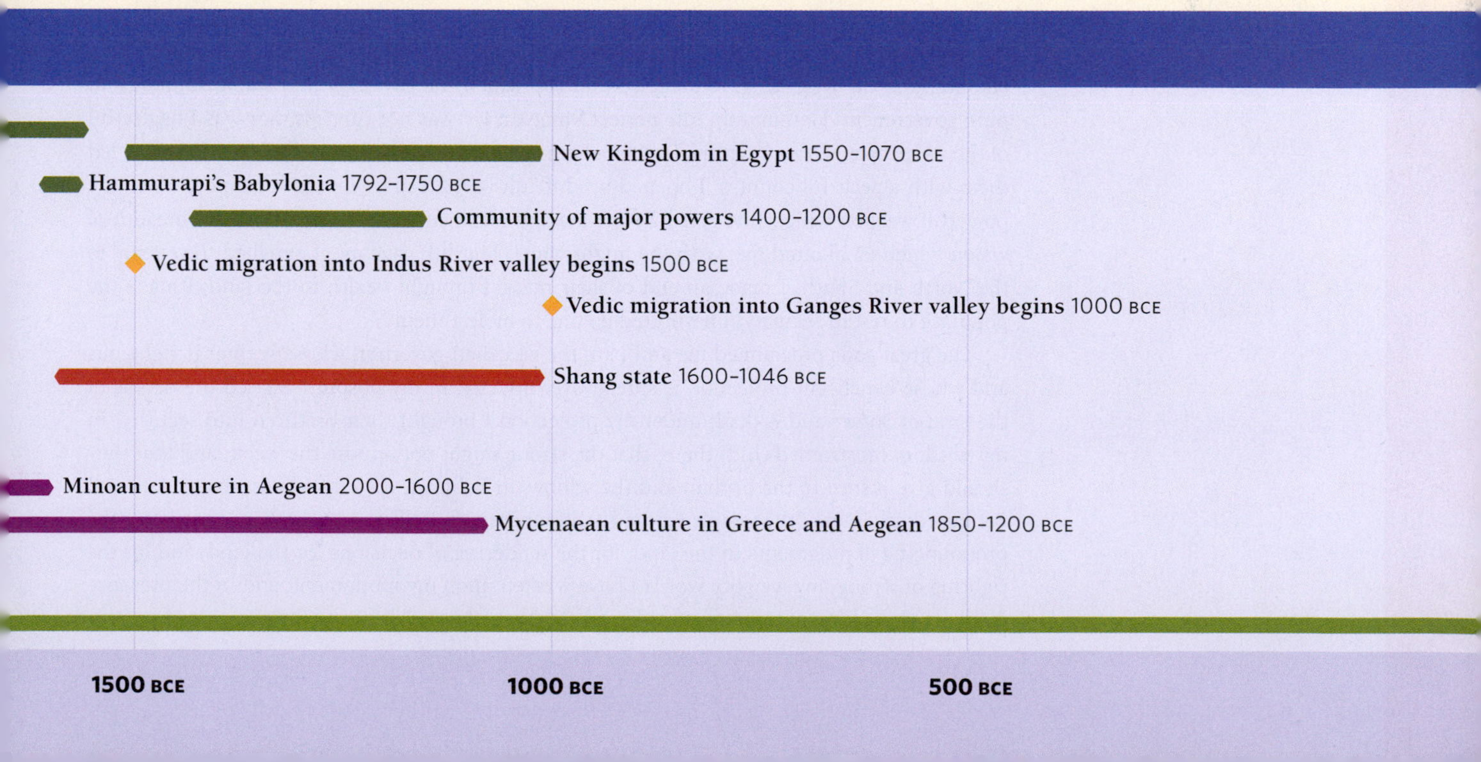

Going to the Source

Legal Authority in Expanding Territorial States

During the second millennium BCE and afterward, the control and expansion of territorial states required negotiating new relationships with those who lived under their rule, or who would come under their authority through treaty or through conquest. These new interactions, whether in the form of economic, military, or political alliances, or through imposed legal codes, can be considered part of the process of state building. In all cases, a certain amount of diplomacy was involved to demonstrate legitimacy either to subjects or people outside the territory. These documents come from throughout Asia and from Egypt. They cover a fairly long time period, but certain commonalities, or continuities, across the years are clearly evident.

PRIMARY SOURCE 3.1

Epilogue to the Code of Hammurapi (c. eighteenth century BCE)

Hammurapi's Code is generally considered to be one of the oldest existing legal codes, if not the oldest. Its concise laws dictate acceptable and unacceptable behavior, and suggest penalties for those who break the laws. Used as a backbone of early government, legal codes such as Hammurapi's suggest that people required appropriate standards of conduct in order to regulate their own behavior. Hammurapi, as well as other lawgivers, also needed to explain how and from where they derived their authority. The selection below, from the code's epilogue, provides such an explanation. It was engraved along with the rest of the code.

*

The Laws of justice which Hammurabi, the wise king, established. The righteous laws, which Hammurabi, the wise king, established and (by which) he gave the land stable support and pure government. Hammurabi, the perfect king, am I. I was not careless, nor was I neglectful of the . . . people, whose rule [the Gods] Bel presented and Marduk delivered to me. I provided them with a peaceful country. I opened up difficult barriers and lent them support. With the powerful weapon which [the gods] Za-má-má and Nana entrusted to me, with the breadth of vision which Ea allotted me, with the might which Marduk gave me, I expelled the enemy to the North and South; I made an end of their raids; I brought health to the land; I made the populace to rest in security; I permitted no one to molest them

The great gods proclaimed me and I am the guardian governor, whose scepter is righteous and whose beneficent protection is spread over my city. In my bosom I carried the people of the land of Sumer and Akkad; under my protection I brought their brethren into security; in my wisdom I restrained (hid) them; that the strong might not oppose the weak, and that they should give justice to the orphan and the widow, in Babylon, the city whose turrets Anu and Bel raised; in Esagila, the temple whose [101] foundations are firm as heaven and earth, for the pronouncing of judgments in the land, for the rendering of decisions for the land, and for the righting of wrong, my weighty words I have written upon my monument, and in the presence of my image as king of righteousness have I established.

The king, who is pre-eminent among city kings, am I. My words are precious, my wisdom is unrivaled. By the command of Shamash, the great judge of heaven and earth, may I make righteousness to shine forth on the land. By the order of Marduk, my lord, may no one efface my statues, may my name be remembered with favor in Esagila forever. Let any oppressed man, who has a cause, come before my image as king of righteousness! Let him read the inscription on my monument! Let him give heed to my weighty words! And may my monument enlighten him as to his cause and may he understand his case! May he set his heart at ease! (and . . . exclaim):

"Hammurabi indeed is a ruler who is like a real father to his people; he has given reverence to the words of Marduk, his lord; he has obtained victory for Marduk in North and South; he has made glad the heart of Marduk, his lord; he has established prosperity for the people for all time and given a pure government to the land."

1. **How does Hammurapi justify his rule?**
2. **Why might Hammurapi believe he needs to justify his rule?**

PRIMARY SOURCE 3.2

Instruction to Vizier Rekhmire (c. fifteenth century BCE)

No comprehensive law codes survive from Middle or New Kingdom Egypt, but a set of instructions to Rekhmire, a pharaoh's vizier (chief minister) from around 1450 BCE gives a keen sense of how judgments were made at the Egyptian court. In addition to revealing the existing power structure, these instructions convey a strong sense of hierarchy and authority. It is clear that laws required enforcement, and perhaps even intimidation, for them to be effective.

[L]et one be afraid of thee, (for) a prince is a prince of whom one is afraid. . . . Be not known to the people; and they shall not say: "He is (only) a man." . . . As for every act of this official, the vizier while hearing in the hall of the vizier, he shall sit upon a chair, with a rug upon the floor, and a dais upon it, a cushion under his back, a cushion under his feet, . . . and a baton at his hand. . . . Then the magnates of the South (shall stand) in the two aisles before him, while the master of the privy chamber is on his right, the [receiver of income] on his left, the scribes of the vizier at his (either) hand; one [corresponding] to another, with each man at his proper place. One shall be heard after another, without allowing one who is behind to be heard before one who is in front. . . . Let not any official be empowered to judge [against a superior] in his hall. . . . It is the vizier who shall punish him, in order to expiate his fault. Let not any official have power to punish in his hall. . . . It is he who dispatches the official staff, to attend to the water-supply in the whole land. It is he who dispatches the mayors and village sheiks to plow for harvest time. It is he who [appoints] the overseers of hundreds in the hall of the king's-house. It is he who [arranges] the hearing of the mayors and village sheiks who go forth in his name, of South and North. Every matter is reported to him; there are reported to him the affairs of the southern fortress. . . . It is he who takes every deposition; it is he who hears [it]. It is he who dispatches the [district] soldiers and scribes to carry out the [administration] of the king. The records of the nome are in his hall. . . . It is he who makes the boundary of every nome . . . all divine offerings and every contract. . . . It is he who appoints every appointee to the hall of judgment, when any litigant comes to him from the king's-house. It is he who hears every edict.

1. **Why is it important for the vizier to have so much power, and for that power to be so visible to all?**

2. **Compare these instructions to Primary Source 3.1. Which representation of the law and its enforcement do you find more effective? Why?**

PRIMARY SOURCE 3.3

Egyptian and Hittite Peace Treaty (1258 BCE)

After several years of open conflict and fifteen years after the battle of Qadesh, the largest chariot battle in history, the Egyptians and Hittites managed to make peace in this treaty between Ramses II and Hattusili III. The treaty addresses the relationship between the two kingdoms and represents an early example of foreign policy negotiation.

The treaty which the great [Hittite] chief of Kheta, Khetasar, the valiant, the son of Merasar, the great chief of Kheta, the valiant, the grandson, of Seplel, [the great chief of Kheta, the valiant, made, upon a silver tablet for Usermare-Setepnere (Ramses II), the great ruler of Egypt, the valiant, the son of Menmare (Seti II), the great ruler of Egypt, the valiant, the grandson of Menpehtire (Ramses I), the great ruler of Egypt, the valiant]; the good treaty of peace and of brotherhood, setting peace [between them], forever.

Now, at the beginning, since eternity, the relations of the great ruler of Egypt with the great chief of Kheta were (such) that the god prevented hostilities between them, by treaty. Whereas, in the time of Metella, the great chief of Kheta, my brother, he fought w[ith Ramses II], the great ruler of Egypt, yet afterward, beginning with this day, behold, Khetasar, the great chief of Kheta, is [in] a treaty-relation for establishing the relations which the Re made, and which Sutekh made, for the land of Egypt, with the land of Kheta, in order not to permit hostilities to arise between them, forever.

Behold . . , Khetasar, the great chief of Kheta, is in treaty relation with Usermare-Setepnere (Ramses II), the great ruler of Egypt, beginning with this day, in order to bring about good peace and good brotherhood between us forever, while he is in brotherhood with me, he is in peace with me; and I am in brotherhood with him, and I am in peace with him, forever. . . . The children of the children of the great chief of Kheta shall be in brotherhood and peace with the children of the children of Ramses-Meriamon, the great ruler of Egypt, being in our relations of brotherhood and our relations [of peace], that the [land of Egypt] may be with the land of Kheta in peace and brotherhood like ourselves, forever.

There shall be no hostilities between them, forever. The great chief of Kheta shall not pass over into the land of Egypt, forever, to take anything therefrom. Ramses-Meriamon, the great ruler of Egypt, shall not pass over into the land of Kheta, to take anything] therefrom, forever. . . .

If another enemy come against the lands of Usermare-Setepnere (Ramses II), the great ruler of Egypt, and he shall send to the great chief of Kheta, saying; "Come with me as reinforcement against him," the great chief of Kheta shall [come], and the great chief of Kheta shall slay his enemy. But if it be not the desire of the great chief of Kheta to come, be shall send his infantry and his chariotry, and shall slay his enemy.

Or if Ramses-Meriamon, [the great ruler of Egypt], be provoked against [delinquent] subjects, when they have committed some other fault against him, and he come to slay them, then the great chief of Kheta shall act with the lord of Egypt. . . .

1. **What are the terms of this peace treaty?**
2. **What provisions does the treaty make for mutual defense against an outside aggressor?**

PRIMARY SOURCE 3.4

Treaty between Tudhaliya IV and Shaushga-muwa of Amurru

Tudhaliya IV, who ruled from 1237 BCE–1209 BCE, was a Hittite king and the son of Hattusili III. Tudhaliya's peace treaty with the Amorite kingdom of Amurru, just south of modern-day Turkey, contained both political and economic provisions. Consider how this treaty derived its authority, as well as how that authority was used to create political, military, and economic alliances. The reference to "Sun" is believed to indicate a familial tie or an honorary title.

*

Great Kings, [Hittite King] Hatti, hero, beloved of the Sun-goddess of Arinna . . .

I, my Sun, [have taken you] Great King Shausgha-muwa [by the hand], and have made you my brother-in-law. And you [shall not change the words] on this treaty tablet.

When [the king] of Egypt is my Sun's [friend], he will also be your friend. [But] when he is my Sun's enemy, he shall also be [your enemy]. And the kings who are equal to me in rank—the King of Egypt, the King of Babylon, the King of Assyria, and the King of Ahhiyawa. When the King of Egypt is my Sun's friend, he shall also be your friend. But when he is my Sun's enemy, he shall also be your enemy. When the King of Babylon is my Sun's friend, he shall also be your friend. But when he is my Sun's enemy, he shall also be your enemy. Since the King of Assyria is my Sun's enemy, he shall also be your enemy. Your merchant shall not go to Assyria, and you shall not let his merchant into your country. He shall not pass through your country. If he would enter your country, take him and send him to my Sun. This matter [is placed] under an oath for you.

Since I, my Sun, am at war with the King of Assyria, gather together an army and a chariot . . . unit, as my Sun has done. Just as it is for my Sun an issue of urgency and . . . , it shall be for you an issue of urgency and . . . This matter is placed under an oath for you.

No ship of Ahhiyawa shall go to him (King of Assyria).

1. **Explain the relationship between the two kings who entered into this treaty. How are they supposed to treat each other's friends and enemies?**
2. **Why would a peace treaty such as this have been a significant document for people living in territory controlled by these two rulers?**

PRIMARY SOURCE 3.5

The Code of Manu (c. 200 BCE)

The Code of Manu is believed to represent some of the earliest laws of the nomadic Vedic peoples of South Asia. The code's nearly 2,700 verses were written down in Sanskrit sometime after 200 BCE, but the laws about social interactions in the excerpt below may date to a much earlier time. Pay particular attention to the kinds of relationships on which this code focuses, as well as the authority upon which the laws that it sets out are based.

*

CHAPTER I. 1. The great sages approached Manu, who was seated with a collected mind, and, having duly worshipped him, spoke as follows: 2. 'Deign, divine one, to declare to us precisely and in due order the sacred laws of each of the (four chief) castes (varna) and of the intermediate ones. 3. 'For thou, O Lord, alone knowest the purport, (i.e.) the rites, and the knowledge of the soul, (taught) in this whole ordinance . . . which is unknowable and unfathomable.' 4. He [Manu], whose power is measureless, being thus asked by the high-minded great sages, duly honoured them, and answered, 'Listen!'. . .

CHAPTER IX. 1. I [Manu] will now propound the eternal laws for a husband and his wife who keep to the path of duty, whether they be united or separated. 2. Day and night women must be kept in dependence by the males (of) their (families). . . . 3. Her father protects (her) in childhood, her husband protects (her) in youth, and her sons protect (her) in old age; a woman is never fit for independence. 4. Reprehensible is the father who gives not (his daughter in marriage) at the proper time; reprehensible is the husband who approaches not (his wife in due season), and reprehensible is the son who does not protect his mother after her husband has died. 5. Women must particularly be guarded against evil inclinations, however trifling (they may appear); for, if they are not guarded, they will bring sorrow on two families. 6. Considering that the highest duty of all castes, even weak husbands (must) strive to guard their wives. 7. He who carefully guards his wife, preserves (the purity of) his offspring, virtuous conduct, his family, himself, and his (means of acquiring) merit. . . . 10. No man can completely guard women by force; but they can be guarded by the employment of the (following) expedients: 11. Let the (husband) employ his (wife) in the collection and expenditure of his wealth, in keeping (everything) clean, in (the fulfilment of) religious duties, in the preparation of his food, and in looking after the household utensils. 12. Women, confined in the house under trustworthy and obedient servants, are not (well) guarded; but those who of their own accord keep guard over themselves, are well guarded. 13. Drinking (spirituous liquor), associating with wicked people, separation from the husband, rambling abroad, sleeping (at unseasonable hours), and dwelling in other men's houses, are the six causes of the ruin of women.

1. **Describe the laws surrounding women in this document. Why do you think women are singled out as in special need of protection?**
2. **Based on the five documents above, do you think laws and codes can sufficiently regulate human behavior to create order and stability? Why or why not?**

PRIMARY SOURCE 3.6

Compilation of Laws (c. sixth century BCE), Advisor Zichan of Zheng

This Chinese text from the sixth century BCE suggests that, unlike other societies reflected in the documents above, Chinese rulers may not have publicized a legal code, but they did create a clear system of punishments. It seems to imply that rulers had to negotiate with their populations over how those people should behave and be governed.

In the third month, the people of Zheng cast a penal text. Shu Xiang dispatched to Zichan a text. It stated, "Formerly, I had hope for you, but have now given it up. In the past, former kings consulted on affairs to decide them but did not make penal compilations, for they feared that the people would grow litigious. Still unable to control them, they restrained them with rightness, bound them with [good] governance, and raised them with humanness. They institutionalized emoluments and ranks to encourage their obedience and determined strict punishments so as to overawe their perversity. Fearing that that was not enough, they taught them of loyalty, rewarded good conduct, instructed them in their duties, deployed them with harmony, supervised them respectfully, supervised them with might, and adjudged them with firmness. Still they sought sagacious and erudite superiors, intelligent and astute officials, loyal and trustworthy elders, and kind and beneficent masters. It was only under such conditions that the people could be employed without disaster or disorder resulting. When the people are aware of a legal compilation, they will have no wariness of their superiors. All become contentious, appealing to the texts, and achieve their goals through lucky conniving. They cannot be governed. When the Xia had a disorderly government, they composed the *Punishments of Yu*. When the Shang had disorderly administration, they composed the *Punishments of Tang*. When the Zhou had disorderly administration, they composed the *Nine Punishments*. All three of these penal compilations arose in terminal ages. Now as advisor to the kingdom of Zheng you have rectified fields and ditches, established a reviled administration, instituted the tripartite compilation, and cast the penal text [in bronze], in order to calm the populace. Is this not difficult?"

1. **According to this description, what is the danger of letting people know the laws under which they are governed?**
2. **In your view, is it better to state the authority under which rules are made or to avoid discussing any laws with those who have to live by them? Why?**

Questions for Analysis

Comparison

1. Compare the source of authority in the societies represented in these documents. Which authority do you think would have been most effective at governing local populations?

Interpretation

2. Treaties often connected disparate peoples. In your view, what types of agreements should treaties put into writing? Are there specific areas that should not be written down? If so, what might they be?

Long Essay Question

Synthesis

Based on what you have read in this chapter and the documents above, explain the connection between laws, treaties, and the expansion of territorial states. What role do you think culture might have played in creating and implementing these laws and treaties?

Before You Read This Chapter

GLOBAL STORYLINES

- Climate change, migrations, technological advances, and administrative innovations contribute to the development of the world's first great empires.
- The Neo-Assyrians and then the Persians employ two different approaches to consolidate and maintain empires in Southwest Asia.
- South Asia becomes more culturally integrated despite the absence of a strong, centralized political authority.
- The Zhou dynasty establishes loose political integration in East Asia.

CORE OBJECTIVES

- **DESCRIBE** the factors that contributed to the rise of early empires in 1250–325 BCE and the characteristics of these empires.
- **COMPARE** empire formation, or the lack thereof, in Southwest Asia, South Asia, and East Asia in this period.
- **EVALUATE** the connection between empires and war, religion, and trade.
- **ANALYZE** the relationships between empires and the peoples on their peripheries.

CHAPTER

4

First Empires and Common Cultures in Afro-Eurasia

1250–325 BCE

KEY TERMS

alphabet p. 142
empire p. 126
mandate of heaven p. 150
monotheism p. 142
Phoenicians p. 142
satrapies p. 136
Sea Peoples p. 140
Upanishads p. 147
varna p. 146
Vedas p. 144
Zoroastrianism p. 136

Sennacherib—ruler of the Neo-Assyrian Empire early in the seventh century BCE—writes that at the end of one successful campaign he took "200,150 people, great and small, male and female, horses, mules, asses, camels, and sheep without number, I brought away from them and counted them my spoil." The booty about which Sennacherib boasts was unheard of in earlier ages. The immensity of such conquest highlights the arrival of a new era that involved empires with even larger geographical, political, economic, and cultural ambitions and achievements than the territorial states that preceded them (see Chapter 3). Given the nature and process of their formation, these early empires arguably replaced, rather than descended from, the earlier territorial states.

One key factor shaping these developments was warfare spurred by military innovation. Additionally, radical climate change drove many of the warrior/political leaders from the fringes of formerly powerful territorial states to the centers of power. There they established hybrid societies uniting cities and their hinterlands, among the Neo-Assyrians and Persians of Southwest Asia, Vedic parts of South Asia, and Zhou China. Imperial ideologies and religious beliefs supported the new empires. Farming yields increased and populations grew. On the fringes of empires, microsocieties arose and made significant contributions to human development: the seafaring Phoenicians developed a simplified alphabet, the Israelites espoused a strict monotheism, and Greek city-states came to the fore and even began to challenge the power of the Persian Empire.

Forces of Upheaval and the Rise of Early Empires

COMPARISON

DESCRIBE the factors that contributed to the rise of early empires in 1250–325 BCE and the characteristics of these empires.

Four related forces shaped the development of early empires in the first millennium BCE: climate change, migrations, new technologies, and administrative innovations. Migrants driven by climate change mingled with settled peoples. Ambitious leaders used innovations in technology and administration to create new states that went on to conquer other kingdoms. Gradually, a new political organization came into being: the **empire**. An empire is a group of states or different ethnic groups brought together under a single sovereign power. With varying degrees and types of centralization (as we will see in Southwest Asia, South Asia, and East Asia), empires connected distant regions through common languages, unifying political systems, trade, and shared religious beliefs. While most regions of Afro-Eurasia did not experience the rise of empire, those which did, and their neighbors, were profoundly impacted by the development.

CLIMATE CHANGE

Beginning around 1200 BCE, another prolonged period of drought gripped Afro-Eurasia, causing social upheavals and migrations and utterly destroying settled societies and long-established governments. Many regions that had enjoyed rapid population growth in the second millennium BCE now found themselves unable to support such large numbers, forcing peoples to leave their homes in search of food and fertile land. (See Map 4.1.)

From the Mediterranean to East Asia, this wave of drought led to dramatic political shifts. In Egypt, low Nile floods forced pharaohs to spend their time securing food supplies and repelling Libyans from the desert and "Sea People" marauders from the coast. In Anatolia, Hittite kings dispatched envoys to the rulers of all of the major agricultural areas, pleading for grain shipments to save their starving people. Even taking the drastic step of moving their capital to northern Syria, where food was more plentiful, did not prevent Hittite collapse. In mainland Greece, Mycenaean culture disintegrated when diminished rains made it impossible for farmers there to export wine, olives, and timber. Likewise in East Asia, radical climate change was a major factor in political developments. Arid conditions on the plains of central Asia resulted in powerful hot and dry winds carrying immense quantities of dust onto the North China plain. The dust storms reduced the soil's ability to retain moisture and led to a sharp decline in soil fertility. Some groups, like the Zhou peoples, went on the move in search of arable land.

MIGRATIONS

The violent movement of peoples, driven in part by climate change, disrupted urban societies and destroyed the administrative centers of kings, priests, and dynasties. Invaders, moving out of loosely organized peripheral societies, assaulted the urban centers and

Camels Dromedary camels (*left*) are good draft animals for travel and domestic work in the deserts of Arabia, Afghanistan, and India. Two-hump camels (*right*) are much bigger than dromedary camels. They are more suited to the extreme dry and cold weather in Iran and central Asia.

territorial kingdoms of mainland Greece, Crete, Anatolia, Mesopotamia, Egypt, and East Asia, causing the collapse of many of these once powerful states. Marauders from the Mediterranean basin and the Syrian desert upset the diplomatic relations and the elaborate system of international trade that had linked Southwest Asia and North Africa. In East Asia, the Zhou peoples, who by the twelfth century BCE were settled in the valley of the Yellow River's most important tributary, the Wei River in northwestern China, tangled with the Shang authorities and eventually overwhelmed the regime. In the Indus Valley, waves of nomads pressed down from the northwest, lured by fertile lands to the south. The upheavals caused by these migrations opened the way for new empires to develop, but only after centuries of turmoil and decline.

NEW TECHNOLOGIES

Technological innovations were crucial in reconstructing communities that had been devastated by drought and violent population movements. Advances in the use of pack camels, seaworthy vessels, iron tools for cultivation, and iron weapons for warfare facilitated the rise of empires.

The camel—first the one-humped Saharan dromedary and later the hardier two-humped Bactrian camel—helped to open up trade routes across Afro-Eurasia. The fat stored in camels' humps allows them to survive long journeys and harsh desert conditions, and thick pads under their hoofs enable them to walk smoothly over the difficult terrain that had previously hindered such long-distance exchange. Similarly, new shipbuilding technologies made a significant impact. Whereas boats had once been designed for limited transport on rivers and lakes and along shorelines, new ships boasted larger and better-reinforced hulls. Stronger masts and improved rigging allowed billowing sails to harness wind power more effectively. These innovations, along with improvements in ballast and steering, propelled bold mariners to venture out across large bodies of open water like the Mediterranean Sea.

Innovations in metalworking, in which bronze was supplanted by the harder iron, also facilitated the rise of empires. Iron became the most important and widely used metal from this time onward (hence the term Iron Age, sometimes used to describe this period). Although far

URAL MOUNTAINS
NORTH SEA
BALTIC SEA
EUROPE
Dnieper R.
Dniester R.
Volga R.
ARAL SEA
Danube R.
BLACK SEA
CASPIAN SEA
MYCENAEANS
AEGEAN SEA
Troy
Tiryns
ANATOLIA
HITTITES
Tigris R.
Nineveh
MITANNI
Ashur
CRETE
CYPRUS
SYRIAN DESERT
Euphrates R.
ELAMITES
ZAGROS MTS.
IRANIAN PLATEAU
MEDITERRANEAN SEA
Tyre
LEVANT
Jericho
Jerusalem
Babylon
SOUTHWEST ASIA
CENT
NORTH AFRICA
Amarna
EGYPT
Thebes
Persian Gulf
ARABIAN PENINSULA
RED SEA
NUBIA
Nile R.
SAHARA
Sub-Saharan periphery: Increased population and gradual adoption of agriculture
Niger R.
SUB-SAHARAN AFRICA
Congo R.
Lake Victoria
ATLANTIC OCEAN
Tropical woodlands: Yams and palm nuts cultivated
Urban cores
Vedic settlement by 900 BCE
Nomadic incursions (sea peoples)
Nomadic incursions (pastoralists)
Destroyed site
City

MAP 4.1 | Afro-Eurasia, 1200 BCE—Urban Cores and Nomadic Invaders

Nomadic incursions shattered the social and political status quo in Afro-Eurasia at this time. While destroying old polities, these migrations fostered a new social and political order in a variety of regions.

- Where did nomadic groups originate, and to where did they migrate?
- What is a major difference between the invasions of the Sea Peoples in this period versus pastoral invasions?
- Why do you think that so many of the nomadic movements were toward populated areas?

Current Trends in World History

Big Forces in Early Empires

Conflict has always been a part of the human condition. But organized warfare and the use of "big force," that is large, well-disciplined armies, appears only with the formation of complex societies. The military units created in these complex societies became crucial vehicles for expanding the lands and peoples under the control of single states and broadcasting the influence of these states well beyond the territories that they controlled militarily.

Evidence for intermittent conflict among the city-states of Sumer in the fourth millennium BCE and in Old Kingdom Egypt (2649–2152 BCE) shows that local populations were drafted into a common army when needed. Permanent forces, first recorded in the Old Akkadian period in the third millennium BCE, were used to forge unity, dominate trade routes, and repel threatening "barbarians." Over the next two millennia, across the full extent of Afro-Eurasia, the technologies and structure of war machines developed along similar paths, leading to large standing armies equipped with new and improved weapons, marked by continual innovation and addition of new capabilities.

The earliest armies of Sumer were soldiers on foot arranged in a box-like (*phalanx*) formation. The men were protected by the same types of leather capes and helmets and carried the same large shields to deflect spears and arrows. This mass-formation fighting of infantry that was enabled by uniform training, uniform armaments, and state provisioning became the norm for land forces in Egypt, Assyria and, later, the Greek city-states. By the early second millennium, horse-drawn chariots were added to the force, adding mobility and the potential of surprise to an ever-larger infantry force (see Chapter 3). Mounted cavalry was introduced late in the middle of the first millennium BCE in Assyria when fighting in mountainous terrain rendered the chariot impractical. Camels, long used as pack animals, were also used in warfare, primarily by Arab tribesmen conscripted into the Assyrian army. And elephants were one of the four components of the South Asian Vedic armies, combined with cavalry, infantry, and chariots into a highly effective fighting force.

Even before the rise of complex societies and large military forces, the weapons of warfare had been those of the hunter: bows and arrows, spears, and slings. Like these weapons, knives, daggers, axes and maces were also incorporated into armies and were wielded by infantries in hand-to-hand combat. The compound bow, first used in warfare by the Sumerians, was refined by the Assyrians into a powerful projectile that could achieve an arc of more than 200 yards, raining destruction down on the opposing infantry. Although bronze was the most important metal for weapons, the introduction of iron toward the end of the second millennium BCE expanded the availability of metal for these state war machines. Since war was often conducted to acquire land, cities had to be conquered by force. Battering rams, first documented in Egypt, were added to mobile siege machines; towers supporting archers are pictured on the Assyrian stone sculptures. Levers and breaking-bars as well as tunneling were used to undermine the integrity of the walls. And scaling ladders were thrown against the fortification for the final assault.

In China, the same elements of infantry, chariots, and archers were at the core of the army from as early as the Shang dynasty.

more abundant than the tin and copper used to make bronze, iron is more difficult to extract from ore and to fabricate into useful shapes. When the technology to smelt and harden iron advanced, iron tools and weapons replaced those made of bronze. This revolution in metallurgy brought shifts in agrarian techniques, such as forged-iron-edged plows that allowed farmers to cultivate crops far beyond the traditional floodplains of riverbanks. Farmers could now till more difficult terrain to remove weeds, break up sod, and unearth fertile subsoil. These technological innovations supported larger, more integrated societies.

ADMINISTRATIVE INNOVATIONS

The expansion of the first empires depended on military might, and control of expanded territories required new administrative techniques. Beginning in the ninth

While their original goal was to capture prisoners needed for sacrifice to the ancestors, soon defensive forces were needed to protect them against their neighbors. The Zhou gradually defeated the Shang through their superior forces and more ingenious and agile tactics. A fundamental advance was made with the invention around 475 BCE of the crossbow, a far more powerful personal killing machine, and the torsion catapult, which threw both heavy projectiles and fiery masses onto the enemy. From the beginning, the techniques and technologies of war were rapidly shared across cultural boundaries as a natural result of adapting and improving on the achievements of the enemy. What mattered most for success was the ability to integrate and coordinate the increasing number of elements that went into a fighting force. The Persians learned at the hands of the Greeks that numbers and sheer firepower could not overcome agility, communication, and integration.

Towards the end of the second millennium BCE, new forms of force were appearing not just on land but also on the sea. The construction of purpose-built ships for the conduct of war on water—the world's first "battleships"—occurred over the course of the eighth century BCE in the eastern Mediterranean. These special ships were built mainly by the Phoenician and the Greek city-states whose livelihood depended on commerce on the high seas. They were not designed like the slow-sailing bulky ships used for the transport of large cargoes but were sleek and slim—about 120 feet long and only 15 wide—with little room for anything other than the men rowing them. With up to 170 rowers, they were designed and constructed for speed and power. They had no purpose other than the deliberate sinking of other ships. At first, the rowers in ships were arranged with two banks (called "biremes" by the Greeks) and later with three (called "triremes"). The ships were armed with bronze "beaks" or rams that were used to cave in the sides of enemy ships. These ships were costly to construct, to man, to provision, and to command. As with the maintenance, training, and arming of large land forces, only relatively wealthy states and governments could afford to mount this kind of power on the high seas.

Lachisch relief Advancing forces from reliefs in Sennacherib's palace at Nineveh commemorating the brutal Neo-Assyrian assault of Lachish in 701 BCE.

QUESTIONS FOR ANALYSIS

- What are some of the military innovations that are characteristic of "Big Forces"?
- From your reading of this chapter, what other ways could you compare empires in addition to "Big Forces"?
- Why is the comparison of empires useful for historians?

Explore Further

Pierre Briant, *From Cyrus to Alexander: A History of the Persian Empire* (2002).

Harold M. Tanner, *China: A History: From Neolithic Cultures through the Great Qing Empire (10,000 BCE – 1799 CE)*, (2009).

century BCE, fierce Neo-Assyrian soldiers, equipped with iron weaponry and armor, established their king's rule over the countryside. The Neo-Assyrians used mass deportations to break resisters' unity, to provide slave labor in parts of the empire that needed manpower, and to integrate the realm. Over 300 years, they constructed an infrastructure of roads, garrisons, and relay stations throughout the entire territory, making it easier to communicate and to move troops. Moreover, they forced subject peoples to send tribute in the form of grains, animals, raw materials, and people, in addition to precious goods such as gold and lapis lazuli, which they used to build imperial cities and to enrich the royal coffers. In later centuries, such innovations—well-equipped armies, deportation, road systems for transit and communication, and tribute—became common among empires. (See **Current Trends in World History: Big Forces in Early Empires**.)

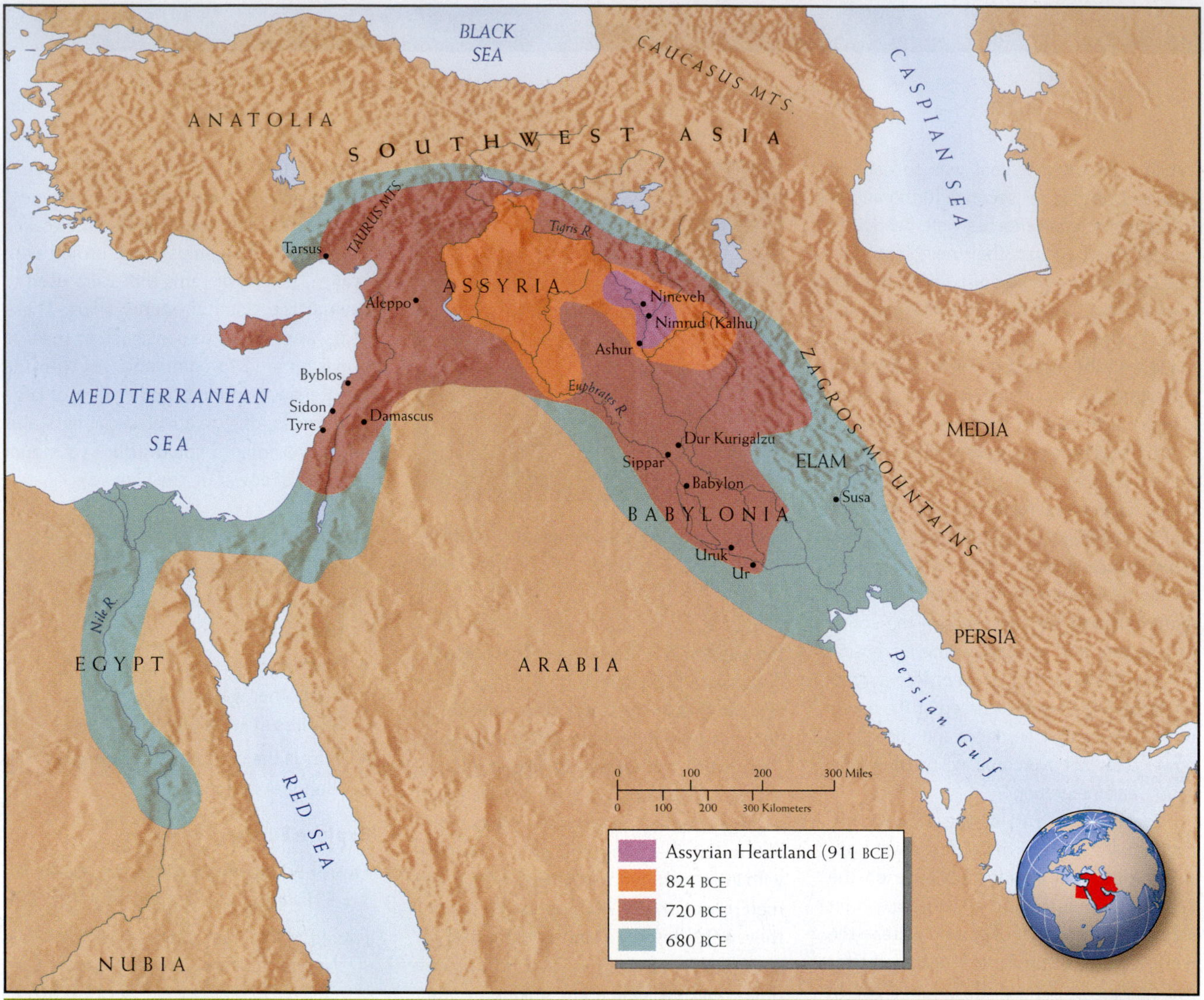

MAP 4.2 | The Neo-Assyrian Empire

The Neo-Assyrians built the first strong regional empire in Afro-Eurasia. In the process, they faced the challenge of promoting order and stability throughout their diverse realm.

- Where did the Neo-Assyrian Empire expand?
- Which parts of the empire were "the Land of Ashur," and which were "the Land under the Yoke of Ashur"?
- Why do you think expansion after 720 BCE led to the empire's destruction?

COMPARISON

COMPARE empire formation, or the lack thereof, in Southwest Asia, South Asia, and East Asia between 1250–325 BCE.

Empire in Southwest Asia: The Neo-Assyrian and Persian Empires

In Southwest Asia, the Neo-Assyrians and then the Persians offered some of the world's first experiments with true imperial control. The Neo-Assyrians (911–612 BCE) perfected early techniques of imperial rule, many of which became standard in later empires. The Neo-Assyrians also revealed the raw military side of imperial rule: constant, harsh warfare and the brutal exploitation of subjects. On the other hand, the Persians (ca. 560–331 BCE), who took control of Southwest Asia after the Neo-Assyrians, balanced their vast multicultural empire through a gentler combination of centralized administration and imperial ideology.

THE NEO-ASSYRIAN EMPIRE (911-612 BCE)

Defining features of the Neo-Assyrian empire included deportations, forced labor, and a rigid social hierarchy. Neo-Assyrian rulers divided their empire into two parts and ruled them in different ways. The core of empire, which the Assyrians called the "Land of Ashur," included such ancient cities as Ashur and Nineveh on the upper reaches of the Tigris River, and the lands between the Zagros Mountains and the Euphrates River. (See Map 4.2.) The king's appointees governed these interior lands, whose inhabitants had to supply food for the temple of the national god Ashur, manpower for the god's residence in the city of Ashur, and officials to carry out the state's business. Outside of Assyria proper lay "the Land under the Yoke of Ashur," whose inhabitants were not considered Assyrians. In these peripheral territories, local rulers held power as subjects of Assyria. These subordinated states were expected to deliver massive amounts of tribute in the form of gold and silver, as opposed to the manpower or agricultural goods supplied by those in the "Land of Ashur." Tribute went directly to the king, who used it to pay for his extravagant court and ever-increasing military costs.

Forced labor—including serving in the military—and deportations helped integrate the empire and undermine local resistance. The Neo-Assyrian armies were hardened and disciplined professional troops led by officers promoted on the basis of merit, not birth. Their military combined infantry, cavalry, iron weapons, horse-drawn chariots armored with iron plates and carrying expert archers, and siege warfare (complete with massive wheeled siege towers and iron-capped battering rams). The Neo-Assyrian army evolved over time from an all-Assyrian army that conducted annual summer campaigns to a several-hundred-thousand-strong, year-round force composed of Assyrians and conquered peoples. By the seventh century BCE, different ethnic groups in the Neo-Assyrian army performed specialized military functions: Phoenicians provided ships and sailors; Medes served as the king's bodyguards; and Israelites supplied charioteers. In addition to a military force, the Neo-Assyrian state needed huge labor forces for agricultural work and for enormous building projects. The Neo-Assyrians recruited most agricultural and construction workers from conquered peoples. Over three centuries the Neo-Assyrian Empire relocated more than 4 million people—a practice that not only supported its stupendous work projects but also undermined local resistance efforts.

Tiglath Pileser III The walls of the Neo-Assyrian palaces were lined with stone slabs carved with images of the victories of the king. This fragmentary slab from the palace of Tiglath Pileser III (r. 745–728 BCE) originally decorated the wall of his palace at Nimrud. It shows the inhabitants and their herds being forced to leave after the defeat of their town by the Assyrians. Below is Tiglath Pileser III, shaded by his royal umbrella, in his war chariot.

Neo-Assyrian Ideology and Propaganda Neo-Assyrian imperial ideology supported and justified its system of expansion, exploitation, and inequality. Even in the early stages of expansion, Assyrian inscriptions and art expressed a divinely determined destiny that drove the regime to expand westward toward the Mediterranean Sea. The national god Ashur had commanded all Assyrians to support the forcible growth of the empire, whose goal was

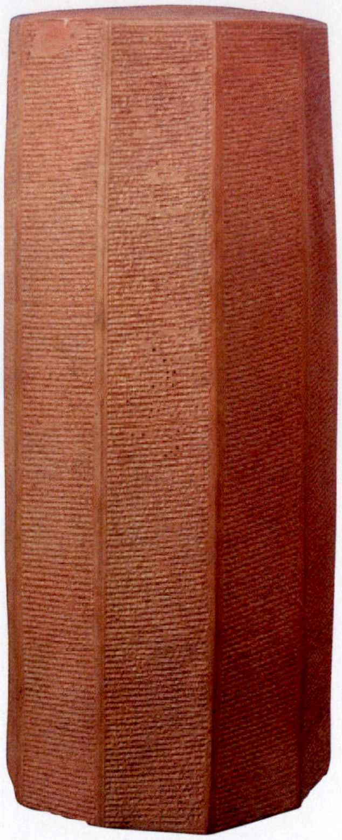

The Annals of Ashurbanipal This ten-sided baked clay cylinder carries a portion of the annals of the Neo-Assyrian king, Ashurbanipal (r. 668–627 BCE). It was found at Nineveh along with thousands of other tablets preserved in his famous library. The annals of Ashurbanipal were detailed, almost novelistic accounts of his military and civic achievements. Unlike earlier annals, there is first-person discourse, indirect discourse, flashbacks, and lively description of events and places.

to establish and maintain order and keep an ever-threatening cosmic chaos at bay. Only the god Ashur and his agent, the king, could bring universal order. The king conducted holy war to transform the known world into the well-regulated Land of Ashur, intensifying his campaign of terror and expansion with elaborate propaganda. A three-pronged propaganda program—including elaborate architectural complexes and ceremonies, texts such as inscriptions and year-by-year accounts (annals) of kings' achievements, and vivid images of the army's brutal campaigns—proclaimed that Neo-Assyria's triumph was inevitable.

Neo-Assyrian Social Structure The Neo-Assyrians also exploited a rigid social hierarchy. At the top was the king, who as the sole agent of the god Ashur conducted war to expand the Land of Ashur. Below the king were military elites, rewarded through gifts of land, silver, and exemptions from royal taxes. Over time, these military elites became the noble class and controlled vast estates that included both the land and the local people who worked it. The king and the elites owned the most populous part of the society, the peasantry, in which various categories of workers had differing privileges. Many workers were enslaved because they could not pay their debts, but they were allowed to marry nonslave partners, conduct financial transactions, and even own property with other slaves attached to it. Foreigners enslaved through conquest, however, had no rights and were forced to do hard manual labor on the state's monumental building projects. Those peoples forcibly relocated were not slaves but became attached to the lands that they had to work. Families were small and lived on modest plots of land, where they raised vegetables and planted vineyards.

Women in Neo-Assyria were far more restricted than their counterparts in the earlier periods of Sumerian and Old Babylonian Mesopotamia. Under the Neo-Assyrians' patriarchal social system, women had almost no control over their lives. Because all inheritance passed through the male line, it was crucial that a man be certain of the paternity of the children borne by his wives. As a result, all interactions between men and women outside of the family were highly restricted. The so-called "Middle Assyrians" of the thirteenth century BCE had introduced the practice of veiling, requiring it of all respectable women. Prostitutes who serviced the men of the army and worked in the taverns were forbidden to wear the veil, so that their revealed faces and hair would signal their disreputable status. Any prostitute found wearing the veil would be dragged to the top of the city wall, stripped of her clothing, flogged, and sometimes even killed.

The queens of Neo-Assyria obeyed the same social norms, but their lives were more comfortable and varied than the commoners'. They lived in a separate part of the palace with servants who were either women slaves or eunuchs (castrated males). Though Neo-Assyrian queens rarely wielded genuine power, they enjoyed respect and recognition, especially in the role of mother of the king. In fact, a queen could serve as regent for her son if the king died while his heir was still a child.

The Instability of the Neo-Assyrian Empire At their peak, the Neo-Assyrians controlled most of the lands stretching from Persia to Egypt. Yet their empire was unstable, as it required occupying armies to be spread across vast territories and a relentless propaganda machine. Discontent among nobles ultimately led to civil war, which made the Neo-Assyrian Empire vulnerable to external threats as well. The conquest of Nineveh by a combined force of Medes, Neo-Babylonians, and other groups contributed to the collapse of the Neo-Assyrian Empire in 612 BCE.

THE PERSIAN EMPIRE (CA. 560–331 BCE)

After a brief interlude of Neo-Babylonian rule, the Persians asserted power and created a gentler form of imperial rule in Southwest Asia, based more on persuasion and mutual

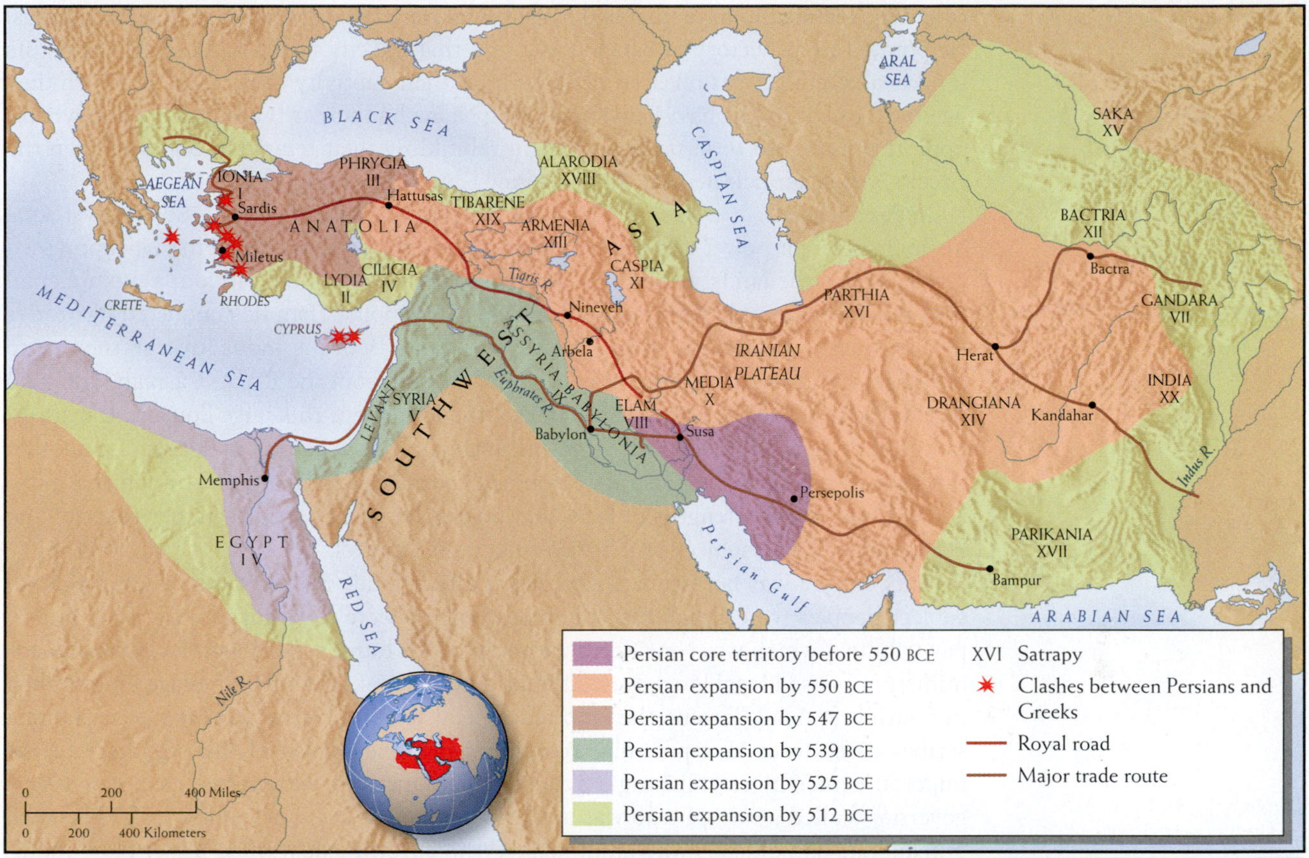

MAP 4.3 | The Persian Empire, 550–479 BCE

Starting in the sixth century BCE, the Persians succeeded the Assyrians as rulers of the large regional empire of Southwest Asia and North Africa. Compare the Persian Empire's territorial domains to those of the Neo-Assyrian Empire in Map 4.2.

- Geographically, how did the Persian Empire differ from the Neo-Assyrian state?
- Analyzing the map, how many Persian satrapies existed, and what role do you think they played in the success of the Persian Empire?
- How does geography help explain why the Greeks were able to defeat the Persians twice?

benefit than on raw power. A nomadic group speaking an Indo-Iranian language, the Persians had arrived on the Iranian plateau from central Asia during the second millennium and gradually spread to the plateau's southwestern part. These expert horsemen shot arrows from horseback with deadly accuracy in the midst of battle. After Cyrus the Great (r. 559–529 BCE) united the Persian tribes, his armies defeated the Lydians in southwestern Anatolia and took over their gold mines, land, and trading routes. He next overpowered the Greek city-states on the Aegean coast of Anatolia. In building their immense empire, the Persians, whose ancestors were pastoralists and had no urban traditions to build on, adapted the ideologies and institutions of the Babylonians, the Neo-Assyrians, and indigenous peoples, modifying them to fit their own customs and political aims.

The Integration of a Multicultural Persian Empire From their base on the Iranian plateau, the Persian rulers developed a centralized, yet multicultural empire that reached from the Indus Valley to northern Greece and from central Asia to the south of Egypt. (See Map 4.3.) Cyrus, the founder of the Persian Empire, presented himself as a benevolent ruler who claimed to have liberated his subjects from the oppression of their own kings. He pointed to his victory in Babylon as a sign that the city's gods had turned against its king as a heretic. Cyrus released the Jews from their captivity in Babylon, to which they had been exiled by the Neo-Babylonian king Nebuchadnezzar II around 587 BCE; whereupon they returned to Jerusalem to begin rebuilding their temple in 538 BCE. Even the Greeks, who later defeated the Persians, saw Cyrus as a model ruler.

In the aftermath of Cyrus's death on the battlefield, Darius I (r. 521–486 BCE) overcame his main rival for power and put the new empire on a solid footing. First he suppressed revolts across the lands, recording this feat on the Behistun Inscription, a monumental rock relief overhanging the road to his capital, Persepolis. Then he conquered territories held by dozens of different ethnic groups, stretching from the Indus River in the east to the Aegean and Mediterranean seas in the west, and from the Black, Caspian, and Aral seas in the north to the Nile River in the south. To manage this huge domain, Darius introduced dynamic administrative systems that enabled the empire to flourish for another two centuries. Its new bureaucracy combined central and local administration and made effective use of the strengths of local tradition, economy, and rule—rather than forcing Persian customs on subject people via rigid central control.

This empire was both centralized and multicultural. The Persians believed that all subject peoples were equal; the only requirements were to be loyal to the king and to pay tribute—which was considered an honor, not a burden. Although local Persian administrators used local languages, Aramaic (a dialect of a Semitic language long spoken in Southwest Asia) became the empire's official language because many of its literate scribes came from Mesopotamia. Darius brought the wealth of the periphery to the imperial center by establishing a system of provinces, or **satrapies**, each ruled by a governor (called a satrap) who was a relative or a close associate of the king. The local bureaucrats and officials who administered the government worked under close monitoring by military officers, central tax collectors, and spies (the so-called eyes of the king) who enforced the satraps' loyalty. Darius established a system of fixed taxation and formal tribute allocations. Moreover, he promoted trade throughout the empire by building roads, establishing a standardized currency including coinage, and introducing standard weights and measures. These strategies helped integrate and centralize the empire's vast territories.

Zoroastrianism, Ideology, and Social Structure The Persians built their ideology of kingship and their social structure on religious foundations. They drew their religious ideas from their pastoral and tribal roots, and thus their ideology reflected traditions of warrior and priestly classes similar to those preserved in the Vedic texts of the Indus Valley. Zoroaster (also known as Zarathustra), who most likely lived sometime after 1000 BCE in eastern Iran, crystallized the region's traditional beliefs into a formal religious system. The main source for the teachings of Zoroaster is the *Avesta*, a collection of holy works initially transmitted orally by priests and then, according to legend, written down in the third century BCE. **Zoroastrianism** ultimately became the religion of the empire.

Zoroaster promoted belief in the god Ahura Mazda, who had created the world and all that was good. In dualistic contrast, Ahura Mazda's adversary, Ahriman was deceitful and wicked. The Persians saw these two forces as engaged in a cosmic struggle for control of the universe. Zoroastrianism treated humans as capable of choosing between good and evil. Human choices had consequences: rewards or punishments in the afterlife.

Persians believed that their kings were appointed by Ahura Mazda as ruler over all peoples and all lands of the earth and charged by him with maintaining perfect order from which all creation would benefit. As such, kings enjoyed absolute authority. In return, they were expected to follow moral and political guidelines that reflected Zoroastrian notions

Persepolis. In the highland valley of Fars, the homeland of the Persians, Darius and his successors built a capital city and ceremonial center at the site of Persepolis. On top of a huge platform, there were audience halls, a massive treasury, the harem, and residential spaces. The building was constructed of mud brick. The roof was supported by enormous columns projecting the images of bulls.

of ethical behavior. Kings also had to show physical superiority that matched their moral standing. They had to be expert horsemen and peerless in wielding bows and spears. These were qualities valued by all Persian nobles, who revered the virtues of their nomadic ancestors. According to the ancient Greek historian Herodotus, Persian boys were taught three things only: "to ride, to shoot with the bow, and to tell the truth."

The Persian social order included four diverse groups with well-defined roles. A ruling class consisted of priests maintaining the ritual fire in temples, nobles administering the state, and warriors protecting and expanding the empire. An administrative and commercial class included scribes and bureaucrats who kept imperial records and merchants who secured goods from distant lands. The other two groups were made up of artisans and, finally, peasants who grew the crops and tended the flocks that fed the imperial machine.

The powerful Persian hereditary nobility surrounded and supported the king. These nobles had vast landholdings and often served the king as satraps or advisers. Also close to the king were wealthy merchants who directed trade across the vast empire. Royal gifts solidified the relations between king and nobles, reinforcing the king's place at the top of the political and social pyramid. In public ceremonies the king presented gold vessels, elaborate textiles, and jewelry to reward each recipient's loyalty and demonstrate dependence on the crown. Any kind of failure would result in the withdrawal of royal favor. Should such failures be serious or treasonous, the offenders faced torture and death. In Persian society, class and royal favor counted for everything.

Public Works and Imperial Identity The Persians undertook significant building projects that helped unify their empire and consolidate imperial identity. For one, the Persians engaged in large-scale road building and constructed a system of rapid and dependable communication. The key element in the system was the Royal Road, which followed age-old trade routes some 1,600 miles from western Anatolia to the heart of the empire in southwestern Iran, continuing eastward across the northern Iranian plateau and into central Asia. Traders used the Royal Road, as did the Persian army; subjects took tribute to the king, and royal couriers carried messages to the satraps and imperial armies over this road.

In addition to the Royal Road, the Persians devised other ways to connect the far reaches of the empire with its center. Darius oversaw the construction of a canal more

Persian Water-Moving Technique. The Persians perfected the channeling of water over long distances through underground channels called *qanats*. This technique, an efficient way to move water without evaporation, is still used today in hot, arid regions. In this example near Yazd, in central Iran, the domed structure leading to the underground tunnel is flanked by two brick towers called "badgir," an ancient form of air-conditioning that cools the water using wind (*bad* in Persian).

than 50 miles long linking the Red Sea to the Nile River. Additionally, Persians developed a system of *qanats,* underground tunnels through which water flowed over long distances without evaporating or being contaminated. Laborers from local populations toiled on these feats of engineering as part of their obligations as subjects of the empire.

Until Cyrus's time, the Persians had been pastoral nomads who lacked traditions of monumental architecture, visual arts, or written literature or history. Multiple capitals—at Persepolis, Pasargadae, and Susa—expressed a Persian imperial identity. Skilled craftsmen from all over the empire blended their distinct cultural influences into a new Persian architectural style. The Persians used monumental architecture with grand columned halls and huge open spaces to provide reception rooms for thousands of representatives bringing tribute from all over the empire and as a way to help integrate subject peoples by connecting them to one central, imperial authority. In the royal palace, three of the columned halls stood on raised platforms accessed via processional stairways that were lined with elaborate images of subjects bringing gifts and tribute to the king. This highly refined program of visual propaganda showed the Persian Empire as a society of diverse but obedient peoples. The carvings on the great stairway of Persepolis demonstrate the range of peoples each bringing distinctive tribute: the Armenians presenting precious metal vessels, the Lydians carrying gold armlets and bowls, the Egyptians offering exotic animals, and the Sogdians leading proud horses.

While the stream of tribute ebbed and flowed over time, the multicultural Persian Empire was able to hold power in Southwest Asia for more than 200 years, weakened by challenges posed by Greek city-states to their west in the fifth century and falling only to the invading army of Alexander the Great in 331 BCE. First the Neo-Assyrians, and then later the Persians, had fashioned their own brands of empire that used a combination of military force, rigid political and social organization, and religious ideology to maintain successive control over Southwest Asia. (See **Analyzing Global Developments: City-States to Empires**.)

Analyzing Global Developments

City-States to Empires

Dramatic developments in urban growth, agricultural production, military innovations, and governance in Southwest Asia in this period led to the emergence of the largest states known to that time, which we have called the first empires. Larger than either city-states or territorial states, empire represented a quantum leap in scale and size. In four distinct periods between 2900 and 350 BCE, this region was transformed from being governed by city-states, each covering less than 4 square miles with 30,000 people, to large-scale empires covering 3,000,000 square miles and governing 35,000,000 people. The Persian Empire (560–331 BCE) rivaled the Roman and Han empires in terms of its size and scale.

QUESTIONS FOR ANALYSIS

- By what scales of magnitude did each stage of empires increase? How much larger were the empires than the world's first states?
- When did the biggest leaps in development between stages occur?
- By what sort of mechanisms did these very large states come about?

STATE/EMPIRE	EST. AREA (SQ. MILES)	EST. POPULATION	NOTES
STAGE ONE: City States (2900–2100 BCE)			
Ur, Uruk, and Nipur	1–4 sq. miles	20–30,000 people	Uruk was the largest city-state for 2,000 years.
STAGE TWO: First Small Empire (c. 1800–1600 BCE)			
The Babylonian Empire	65,000 sq. miles	200,000 people	The city of Babylon was possibly the largest in the world, with 150,000 people.
STAGE THREE: First Large-Scale Empires (c. 910–540 BCE)			
The Neo-Assyrian Empire (c. 910–625 BCE)	540,000 sq. miles	15,000,000 people	Major cities included Kalhu, Nineveh, and Assur.
The Neo-Babylonian Empire (c. 625–540 BCE)	200,000 sq. miles	15,000,000 people	Babylon remained the largest city in the world, surrounded by 8–9 miles of walls.
STAGE FOUR: The Largest Empire in the Ancient World (c. 560–331 BCE)			
The Persian Empire (c. 560–331 BCE)	3,000,000 sq. miles	35,000,000 people	Largest empire ever (measured as a percentage of the global population).

Sources: T. Boiy, *Late Achaemenid and Hellenistic Babylon*; Pierre Briant, *Histoire de l'empire perse*, Paris, Fayard, 1996; Amélie Kuhrt, *The Ancient Near East, 3000–330 BCE*, 2 vols., London, RKP, 1995; J. N. Postgate, *Early Mesopotamia: Society and Economy at the Dawn of History*, London-New York, Routledge, 1992; M. Roaf, *Cultural Atlas of Mesopotamia and the Ancient Near East*, New York, Facts on File, 1990; W. Scheidel, "The Dynamics of Ancient Empires" New York, Oxford University Press, 2010; Marc van de Mieroop, A *History of the Ancient Near East, ca. 3000–323*, 2nd ed., Oxford, Blackwell, 2007; Marc van de Mieroop, *The Ancient Mesopotamian City*, Oxford, Clarendon Press, 1997.

Imperial Fringes in Western Afro-Eurasia

A very different world emerged on Afro-Eurasia's western edges. Although their powerful neighbors affected them, western peoples—such as the Sea Peoples, the Greeks, the Phoenicians, and the Israelites—retained their own languages, beliefs, and systems of rule. While their communities were smaller than those in Southwest Asia, each asserted power and had long-lasting influence disproportionate to their size.

COMPARISON

ANALYZE the relationships between empires and the peoples on their peripheries in Southwest Asia, South Asia, and East Asia.

SEA PEOPLES

New migrations brought violent change to long-established kingdoms and states in the Mediterranean and Southwest Asia. Beginning around 1200 BCE as the full effects of drought struck, new waves of Indo-European-speaking peoples left the Danube River basin in Central Europe. A rapid rise in population and the development of local natural resources, particularly iron, spurred this group, who came to be known as the **Sea Peoples** to move down the Danube toward the Black Sea. The invaders, armed with iron weaponry, brought turmoil to the peoples living in southeastern Europe, the Aegean, and the eastern Mediterranean.

The Hittites of Anatolia were the first to fall to their invasion. Once the invaders reached the Mediterranean, they mainly used boats for transportation, hence the label Sea Peoples (not a name they called themselves but rather one from the perspective of those whom they attacked). The Egyptians knew them as the Peleset, and only with great difficulty did the pharaohs repel them. The Sea Peoples ultimately settled along the southern coast of Southwest Asia, where they became known as the Philistines.

In the Mediterranean, the Sea Peoples' intrusion shook the social order of the Minoans on the island of Crete (see Chapter 3). Agricultural production in the region declined and, as the palace-centered bureaucracies and priesthoods of the second millennium BCE vanished, more violent societies emerged that relied on the newcomers' iron weapons. This was the culture of warrior-heroes described in the *Iliad,* an epic poem about the Trojan War, based on oral tales passed down for centuries before their compilation by Homer in the eighth century BCE. The Greek descendants of these warrior-heroes developed dynamic communities and, as we will see in the next section, offered one of the most significant challenges to the Persians.

THE GREEKS

Among the small-scale societies that emerged in Persia's shadow, the Greeks were particularly influential. Greek-speaking people in different cities sometimes cooperated with the Persians, even borrowing their ideas, but sometimes strongly resisted them. In 499 BCE, some Greek city-states and others in the eastern Mediterranean revolted against the Persians, who claimed control over the Greek islands and mainland. During the six-year struggle, some Greek communities sided with the Persians and suffered condemnation by other Greeks for doing so. On the mainland, most Greek cities resisted the Persian king's authority. In 490 BCE, Darius and his vast army invaded mainland Greece but suffered a humiliating defeat at the hands of the much smaller force of Athenians at Marathon, near Athens. The Persians retreated and waited another decade before challenging their western foe again. Meanwhile, however, Athens was becoming a major sea power.

Mycenaean Arms and Armor This Mycenaean vase illustrates the central role of arms and war to the societies on mainland Greece in the period down to 1200 BCE. The men bear common suits of armor and weapons—helmets, corsets, spears, and shields—most likely supplied to them by the palace-centered organizations to which they belonged. Despite these advantages, they were not able to mount a successful defense against the land incursions that destroyed the Mycenaean palaces toward the end of the thirteenth century BCE.

Under the leadership of Themistocles in the 480s BCE, Athens became a naval power whose strength was its fleet of triremes (battleships). When Greek and Persian forces clashed again in 480 BCE, Persian land forces led by Darius's successor Xerxes fought through Leonidas's 300 Spartans (and other Greeks) at Thermopylae only to have their navy lose the pivotal sea battle at Salamis. A year later, the

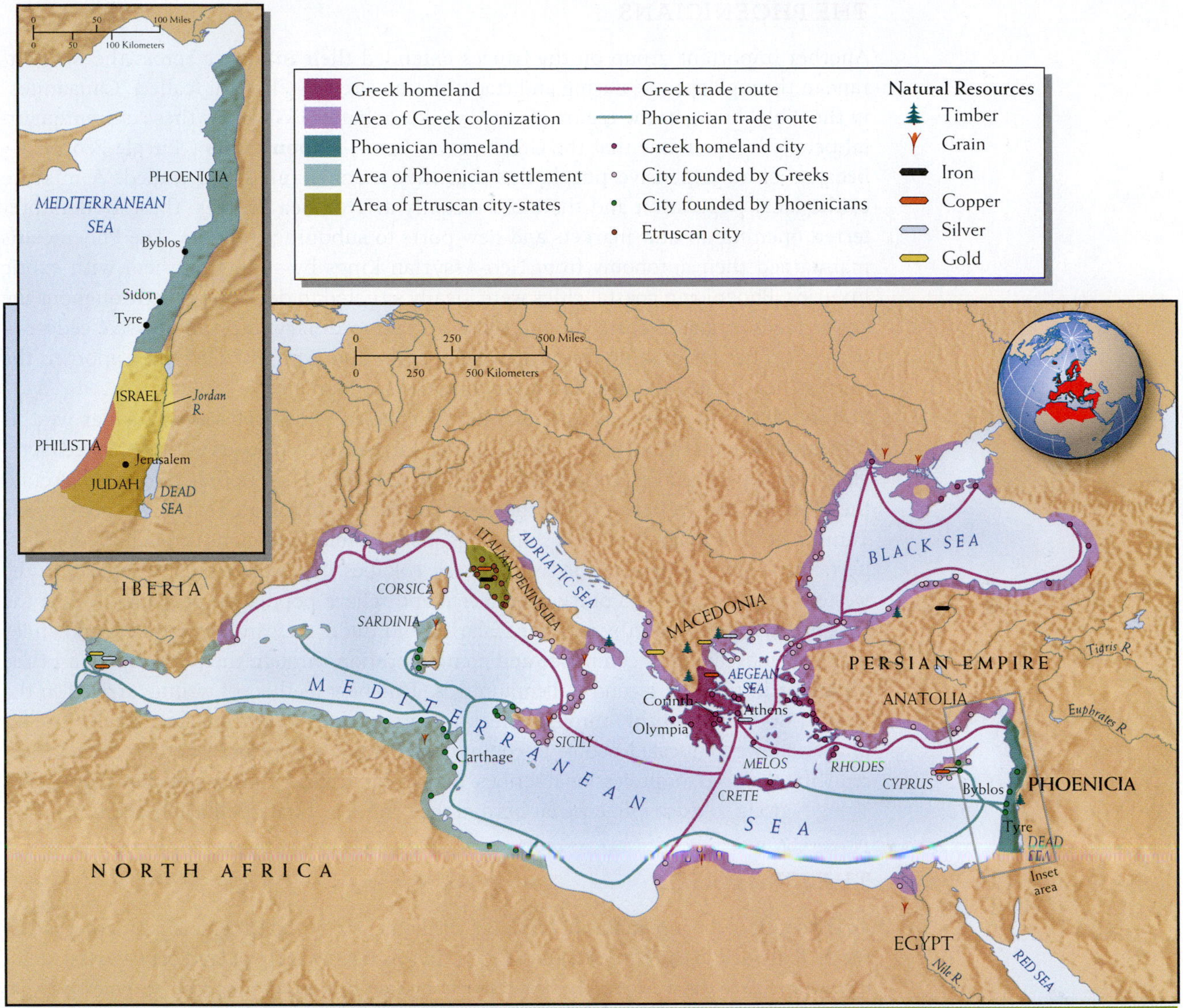

MAP 4.4 | The Mediterranean World, 1000–400 BCE

Peoples on the fringes of the great regional empires of Southwest Asia and North Africa had strong influences beyond their borders, despite their political marginalization. Though politically dwarfed by the Neo-Assyrian and Persian empires, various groups in the Mediterranean basin displayed strong cultural and economic power.

- What were the borderland communities and what did they trade?
- How far did their trading networks and settlement patterns extend?
- According to your reading, why were such small communities able to flourish in terms of trade and settlement?

Persians suffered a decisive defeat on land and eventually lost the war. Persian military defeats changed the balance of power. For the next 150 years Persia lost ground to the Greeks, who gradually regained territory in southeastern Europe and western Anatolia. That expanded territory, and its governance, would become in the fifth century BCE the root of Greek civil discord (see Chapter 5).

THE PHOENICIANS

Another important group on the fringes extended their influence across the Mediterranean through their seafaring and trade: these were the Chanani (called "Canaanites" in the Bible) living in the region of modern-day Lebanon. We know these entrepreneurial people by the name that the Greeks gave them—**Phoenicians** ("Purple People")—because of an expensive purple dye that they manufactured and traded. A mixture of the local population and the more recently arrived Sea Peoples, these traders preferred opening up new markets and new ports to subduing frontiers. The Phoenicians maintained their autonomy from Neo-Assyrian kings by supplying them with exotic luxuries. Phoenician coastal cities were ideally situated to develop trade throughout the entire Mediterranean basin. Inland stood an extraordinary forest of massive cedars—perfect timber for making large, seaworthy craft, and a highly desirable export to the treeless heartlands of Egypt and Mesopotamia (see Map 4.4).

Innovations in shipbuilding and seafaring enabled Phoenicians to sail as far west as present-day Morocco and Spain, carrying huge cargoes of such goods as timber, dyed cloth, glassware, wines, textiles, copper ingots, and carved ivory. Their trading colonies all around the southern and western rims of the Mediterranean (including Carthage in modern-day Tunisia) became major ports that shipped goods from interior regions throughout the Mediterranean. There they competed with Greek colonies that were similarly settling in the western Mediterranean to pursue commerce and relieve population pressures. While the Phoenicians are noteworthy for their seafaring and trade, they are perhaps best known for their revolutionizing of commerce and communication through their development of the **alphabet** in the mid second millennium BCE. This new method of writing arrived in the west in 800 BCE, probably through Greek traders working in Phoenician centers. The alphabet allowed educated people to communicate directly with one another, dramatically reducing the need for professional scribes. Phoenician trade and their alphabet allowed this "fringe" group to exert influence far beyond the confines of their political borders.

THE ISRAELITES

To the south of the mountains of Lebanon, the homeland of the Phoenicians, another minor region extended to the borderlands of Egypt. In this narrow strip of land between the Mediterranean Sea to the west and the desert to the east, an important microsociety emerged, that of the Israelites. The Israelites' own later stories emphasized their origins in Mesopotamia to the east, with the patriarch Abraham from Ur on the Euphrates. Later stories stressed connections with Egypt of the pharaohs to the west and the mass movement of a captive Israelite population out of Egypt under Moses in the late second millennium BCE. Archaeological evidence suggests that a local culture emerged in the area of present-day Israel between 1200 and 1000 BCE. These developments culminated in a kingdom centered at Jerusalem under King David (ca. 1000–960 BCE). The kingdom that David and his successor Solomon (ca. 960–930 BCE) established around Jerusalem, centered on the great temple that Solomon built in the city, did not last long. It fragmented immediately after Solomon's reign, forming the small kingdom of Israel in the north and the smaller Judah in the south.

Within the small kingdom founded by David and Solomon, profound religious and cultural changes took place. Solomon's great temple in Jerusalem outranked all other shrines in the land. The educated upper classes especially, who were linked to the temple, focused on one god, YHWH, over other regional deities in a form of reverence modern scholars call *henotheism* (the recognition of the power of one god over other spirits and deities that still exist). Gradually, however, there was a move to **monotheism** (the acceptance of only one god to the exclusion of all others).

PHENICIAN
ANCIENT GREEK
LATER GREEK
ROMAN
A
B
G
D
E
F
Z
H
Th
I
K
L
M
N
X
O
P
Q
R
S
T

The Phoenician Alphabet *Left*: The first alphabet was written on clay tablets using the cuneiform script. It was developed by Phoenician traders who needed a script that was easy to learn so that they could record transactions without specially trained scribes. This tablet was found at the port town of Ugarit (Ras Shamra) in Syria and is dated to the fourteenth century BCE. *Right*: The forms of the letters in the Phoenician alphabet of the first millennium BCE are based on signs used to represent the Aramaic language. These Phoenician letters were then borrowed by the ancient Greeks. Our alphabet is based on that used by the Romans, who borrowed their letterforms from the later Greek inscriptions.

The long transition to monotheism, completed by the seventh century BCE, did not take place without resistance. Challenging the power of kings and priests, prophets like Isaiah (ca. 720s BCE), Ezra (ca. 600s BCE), and Jeremiah (ca. 590s BCE) helped articulate the Israelites' monotheistic religion. Prophets threatened divine annihilation for groups that opposed the new idea of one temple, one god, and one moral system to the exclusion of all others. The Neo-Assyrians to the east figured large in many of the prophets' warnings. Ultimately, the Torah—a series of books that encapsulated the laws governing all aspects of life, including family and marriage, food, clothing, sex, and worship—became an exclusive "contract" between all these people and their one and only god. As Jewish people scattered over time across Afro-Eurasia, their monotheism would come to have a far-reaching impact.

Foundations of Vedic Culture in South Asia (1500–600 BCE)

In South Asia, language and belief systems—rather than a unified political system enforced and enlarged by military conquests—brought people together. Indo-European-speaking peoples, also known as Vedic peoples for the religious traditions they brought with them, entered South Asia through the passes in the Hindu Kush Mountains in the middle of the second millennium BCE and eventually occupied the whole of what are today Pakistan, Bangladesh, and northern India (see Chapter 3). Here the migrant population, together with the indigenous inhabitants, fostered a flourishing culture. Unlike societies in Southwest Asia, the new rulers in this region did not have previous states on which to found their power. Floods and earthquakes had weakened the earlier Harappan urban centers in the Indus River valley (see Chapter 2), and its urban culture had died out several centuries earlier. Vedic newcomers integrated this territory through a shared culture. Even though the Vedic migrants changed the social and cultural landscape of the region, they did not give it greater political coherence by creating a single, unified regional kingdom.

VEDIC CULTURE SETTLES DOWN

The men and women who migrated into the northern lands of South Asia were illiterate, chariot-riding, and cattle-keeping pastoral peoples, who lacked experience of cities and urban life. They brought with them much beloved and elaborate rituals, mainly articulated in hymns, called **Vedas** (Sanskrit for wisdom or knowledge), which they retained as they entered a radically different environment and which they relied on to provide a foundation for assimilating new ways. Transmitted orally, but eventually written down in Sanskrit, Vedic hymns reflected their earlier lives on the plains of central Asia and were infused with images of animals and gods. For example, in some of these Vedic poems storms "gallop" across the heavens, and thunder sounds like the "neigh of horses."

These Indo-European-speaking migrants, equipped with their Vedic traditions, encountered indigenous people who either lived in agricultural settlements or were herders like themselves. They allied themselves with some peoples and made enemies of others. In their interactions with local peoples, the Vedic migrants kept their own language and religious rituals but also absorbed local words and deities. Allies and defeated enemies who became part of their society had to accept Vedic culture. By the middle of the first millennium BCE, the Vedic peoples covered all of what is now northern India, and their language and rituals had become dominant in their new land (see Map 4.5).

Vedic elites, with their pastoral nomadic roots, never lost their passion for fine horses and they created trading routes to the northwest, beyond the Hindu Kush, to maintain a supply of these horses. But as the Vedic people entered the fertile river basins, they gradually settled down and turned to agriculture and herding. Indigenous farmers taught the Vedic newcomers farming techniques. For example, the iron plow was crucial for tilling the Ganges plain and transforming the Deccan plateau into croplands. In the drier north, the Vedic people grew wheat, barley, millet, and cotton; in the wet lowlands, they cultivated rice paddies. Farmers also produced tropical crops such as sugarcane and spices like pepper, ginger, and cinnamon. With farming success came increased populations and urban settlements across the region, fueled by agricultural surplus and trade in goods, both raw (grain) and manufactured (sugarcane into sugar).

SOCIAL DISTINCTIONS: CLANS AND *VARNA*

Over time, Vedic societies became more complex and less egalitarian than those of their pastoral ancestors. In the process of fanning out across the five tributaries of the Indus River and settling in the plain between the Ganges and Yamuna Rivers, the Vedic peoples created small regional governments and chieftainships. Jockeying for land and resources, they fought fiercely with the indigenous peoples and even more fiercely among themselves.

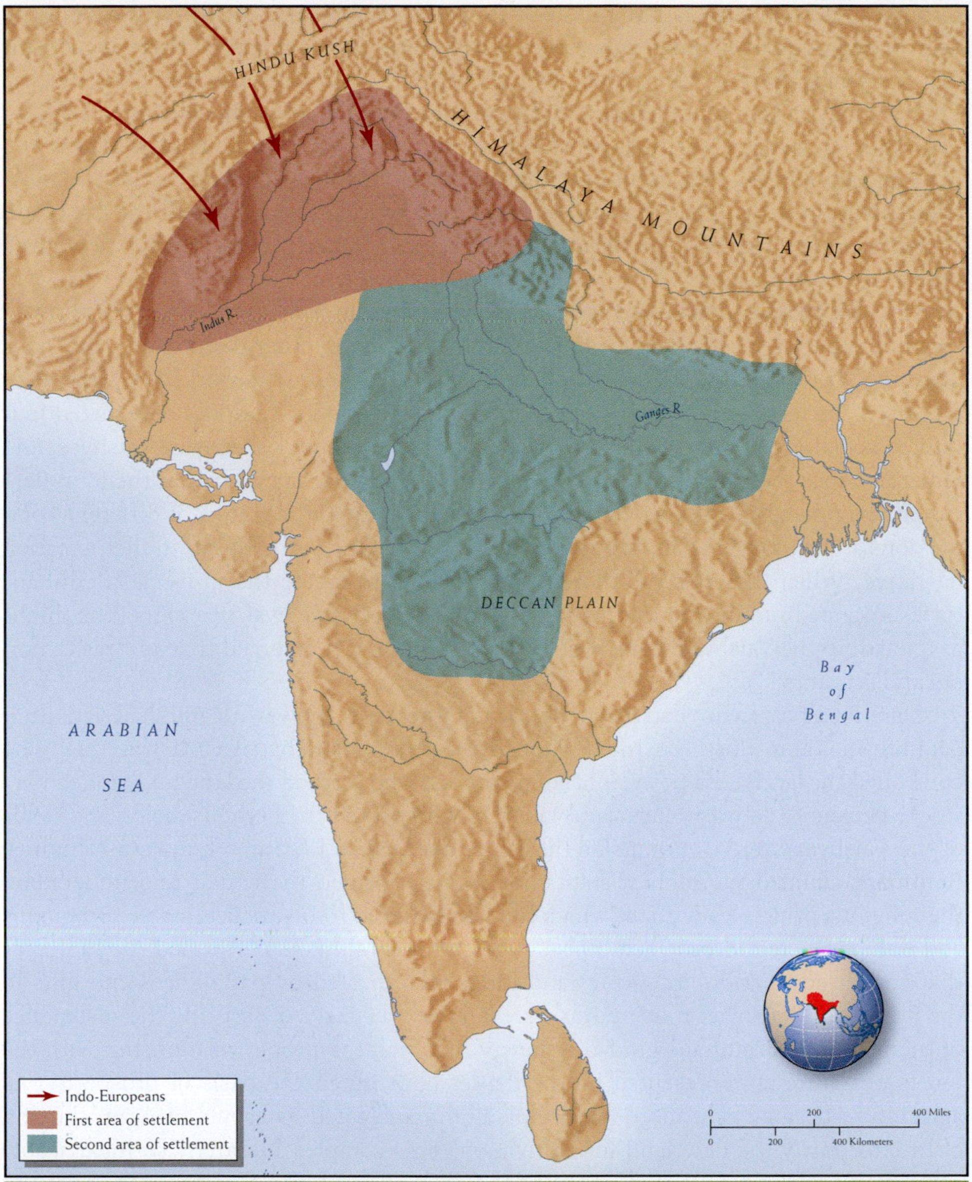

MAP 4.5 | South Asia, 1500–400 BCE

Indo-European peoples crossed over mountainous areas and entered northern South Asia, bringing with them their nomadic ways. They were, however, quick to learn settled agriculture from the local inhabitants.

- Where did the Indo-Europeans originally come from?
- Where did they settle? What geographical features may have influenced the stages of expansion southward?
- Based on your reading, why did Vedic culture prosper and provide a basis of unity for such large populations?

Vedic chieftainships eventually became small kingdoms with inhabitants bound to each other through lines of descent from a common ancestor. They traced their lineage—identified as either solar or lunar—through blood ties, marriage alliances, and invented family relations. The two lineages, solar and lunar, included many *clans* (groups of households claiming descent from a common ancestor) in which seniority determined one's power and importance. The Vedic peoples absorbed many local clans into their own lineages. Clans that adopted the Vedic culture became part of the lineage (through marriage or made-up ties) and were considered insiders. In contrast, clans that had other languages and rituals were considered to be uncivilized outsiders. These two lineages became less important over time, but were memorialized in the later *Mahabharata*, one of the two major Sanskrit epics of ancient India, which recalls the last phase of the lunar lineage, and the *Ramayana*, the second Sanskrit epic, which celebrates a hero of the solar lineage.

As Vedic peoples settled into agrarian communities after 1000 BCE, their social structure became even more complex and hierarchical. Among other distinctions, divisions developed between those who controlled the land and those who worked it. Vedic peoples used the term ***varna*** to refer to their rigid status distinction and recognized four ranked social groups into which one was born—Brahmans, Kshatriyas, Vaishyas, and Shudras. Since the Sankrit word *varna* means color, its use suggests that the four-class system originated in the encounter between clans and communities of different complexions and cultures. Vedic hymns described the origins of the *varnas* in their creation narrative. When the gods sacrificed Primeval Man to create the universe, Brahmans (priests) came from his mouth, his arms produced the Kshatriyas (warriors), the thighs gave birth to the Vaishyas (commoners), and from the feet emerged the Shudras (laborers and servants).

Clan members who had been politically the most powerful and had led their communities into northern India claimed the status of Kshatriyas. It was they who controlled the land. Less powerful clan members, who worked the land and tended livestock, became Vaishyas. Slaves and laborers who served in the households and fields of the Vaishyas came from outside the Vedic lineages and became known as Shudras. Brahmans claimed the highest status, for they performed the rituals and understood the religious principles without which life was believed to be unsustainable. Brahmans and Kshatriyas reinforced each other's high status. Brahmans performed the sacrifices that converted warriors into kings and kings reciprocated by paying fees and gifts to the Brahmans. Vaishyas and Shudras were left with the tasks of assuring the sustenance of the elite. The Brahmans guided a society in which the proper relationship with the forces of nature as represented by the deities constituted the basis of prosperity. As agriculture became ever more important, Brahmans acted as agents of Agni, the god of fire, to purify the new land for cultivation. This complex hierarchy so inextricably connected with Vedic religion provided the primary unifying structure for society in South Asia.

UNITY THROUGH THE VEDAS AND UPANISHADS

A Vedic culture, transmitted from generation to generation by the Brahmans, unified what political rivalries had divided. A common language (Sanskrit); belief in Agni, Indra, and other gods; and shared cultural symbols linked the dispersed communities and gave Vedic peoples a collective identity. Though Sanskrit was a language imported from central Asia, the people used it to transmit the Vedas orally. By expressing sacred knowledge in the rhythms and rhymes of Sanskrit, the Vedas effectively passed on their culture from one generation to the next.

The Vedas promoted cultural unity and pride through common ritual practices and support for hereditary leaders. As the priests of Vedic society, the Brahmans were responsible for memorizing the Vedic works. These included commentaries on sacred works from early nomadic times as well as new rules and rituals explaining the settled, farming way of life. The main body of Vedic literature includes the four Vedas: Rig-Veda, Sama-Veda, Yajur-Veda, and Atharva-Veda. The Rig-Veda, the earliest text, is a collection of hymns praising the gods, including Indra (god of war), Agni (god of fire), and Varuna (god of water). The Sama-Veda is a textbook of songs for priests to perform when making ritual sacrifices; most of their stanzas also appear in the Rig-Veda. The Yajur-Veda is a prayer book for the priest who conducted rituals for chariot races, horse sacrifices, or the king's coronation. The Atharva-Veda includes charms and remedies; many address problems related to agriculture, a central aspect of life. Although the Vedic period left no impressive buildings and artifacts, the Vedas laid the socio-religious foundations for South Asia.

Gold coin of Kumaragupta I Kumaragupta I's coin, dating from the fifth century CE, intentionally drew on much older Vedic concepts (including the *ashvamedha*, or horse sacrifice from the Yajur-Veda) and imagery (here, a Hindu goddess).

During the middle of the first millennium BCE, some thinkers (mostly Brahman ascetics dwelling in forests) felt that the Vedic rituals no longer provided satisfactory answers to the many questions of a rapidly changing society. The result was a collection of works known as the **Upanishads**, or the supreme knowledge, which expanded the Vedic cultural system. Taking the form of dialogues between disciples and a sage, the Upanishads offered insights into the ideal social order. The Upanishads teach that people are not separate from each other but belong to a cosmic universe called Brahma. While the physical world is always changing and is filled with chaos and illusion, *atman*, the eternal being, exists in all people and all creatures. Atman's presence in each living being makes all creatures part of a universal soul. Although all living beings must die, atman guarantees eternal life, ensuring that souls are reborn and transmigrate into new lives. This cycle continues with humans as they are reborn either as humans or as other living creatures, like cows, insects, or plants.

These unique views of life and the universe, as outlined in the Vedas and Upanishads, were passed along as principles of faith, bringing spiritual unity to the northern half of South Asia because local gods could easily be absorbed into the system. Unlike Southwest Asia, here in the kingdoms of the Indus Valley and the Ganges plain the common Vedic culture—rather than larger political units—was the unifying bond.

The Early Zhou Empire in East Asia (1045–771 BCE)

In China, the Zhou succeeded the Shang state, and Zhou rulers built a powerful tributary empire, claiming the "mandate of heaven." The Zhou had been only a minor state during the Shang's political preeminence, living side by side, trading and often allying with one another to fend off raiders from the northwest. The appearance of a dynamic leader among the Zhou peoples, King Wu, and the need to find more resources after drought-related dust storms swept across the North China plain emboldened the Zhou to challenge the Shang. At a battle in 1045 BCE, the Zhou prevailed. King Wu of the Zhou owed his success to his army of 45,000 troops and their superior weaponry, which included

COMPARISON

EVALUATE the connection between empires and war, religion, and trade in Southwest Asia and East Asia.

MAP 4.6 | The Shang and Zhou Dynasties, 2200–256 BCE

Toward the end of the second millennium BCE, the Zhou state supplanted the Shang dynasty as the most powerful political force in East Asia. Using the map above, compare and contrast the territorial reach of the Zhou state with that of the Shang.

- In what direction did the Zhou state expand the most dramatically?
- As you view the map, why do you think that the Zhou did not expand further northward and westward?
- Based on your reading, how did the Zhou integrate their geographically large and diverse state?

dagger axes, bronze armor, and 300 war chariots (small numbers by Southwest Asian standards, but overwhelming in East Asia). (See Map 4.6.) In the centuries that followed, innovations in politics, agriculture, and social structures helped the Zhou integrate their empire.

DYNASTIC INSTITUTIONS AND CONTROL OF THE LAND

When the Zhou took over from the Shang, their new state consisted of a patchwork of more than seventy small states, whose rulers, however, accepted the overarching authority of the Zhou kings. To solidify their power, the Zhou copied the Shang's patrimonial state structure, centered on ancestor worship in which the rulers' power passed down through a lineage of male ancestors reaching back to the gods. Thirty-nine Zhou kings followed one after the other, mostly in an orderly father-to-son succession, over a span of eight centuries.

Zhou Chariots This 17th-century painting (on silk) shows a pivotal Zhou king, emperor Mu Wang (of the 10th century BCE), riding in a chariot driven by a legendary charioteer. The Zhou adapted the use of chariots and archers from their predecessors to defeat the Shang around 1045 BCE. Regional lords who owed allegiance to the Zhou king distinguished themselves in the aristocratic hierarchy by using chariots for battle and travel.

Even though the Zhou drew heavily on Shang precedents, their own innovations produced some of the most significant contributions to China's distinctive cultural and political development. Regarding all those whom they governed as a single people, the Zhou employed the term *Huaxia*, or Chinese, when referring to their subjects. Contrary to political reality, Zhou leaders claimed that their territories were at heart unified, naming their lands *Zhongguo*, which at the time meant "the central states," but later came to mean "the middle kingdom" (and is a term still used for the modern state of China). Moreover, the Zhou kings of this middle kingdom, in addition to being required to rule justly, believed that they had a duty to extend their culture to "less civilized" peoples living in outlying regions.

Having defeated the Shang, and established Zhou control in northwestern China, King Wu (r. 1049–1043) and his successors expanded north toward what is now Beijing and south toward the Yangzi River valley. Seeking to retain the allegiance of the lords of older states and to gain the support of new lords, whom they appointed in annexed areas, Zhou kings rewarded their political supporters with lands that they could pass on to their descendants. As the Zhou expanded their territory, its new colonies often consisted of garrison towns where the Zhou colonizers lived, surrounded by fields (inhabited by local farmers). As under the Shang, Zhou regional lords supplied military forces as needed, paid tribute, and appeared at the imperial court to pledge their continuing allegiance.

Not only through dynastic institutions, but also through agricultural advances (including the iron plow, irrigation, and canals) did the Zhou leaders promote the integration of China. Wooden and, much later, iron plows enabled farmers to break the hard sod of lands beyond the river basins, and over time cultivators learned the practice of field rotation to prevent soil nutrients from being exhausted. In the middle of the first millennium BCE, regional states organized local efforts to regulate the flow of the main rivers. They built long canals to promote communication and trade, and they dug impressive irrigation networks to convert arid lands into fertile belts. This slow agrarian revolution enabled the Chinese population to soar, reaching perhaps 20 million by the late Zhou era.

Under the Zhou, landowners and rulers organized the construction of dikes and irrigation systems to control the floodplain of the Yellow River and Wei River valley surrounding the capital at Xianyang (present-day Xi'an). For centuries, peasants labored over this floodplain and its tributaries—building dikes, digging canals, and raising levees as the waters flowed to the sea. When their work was done, the bottom of the floodplain was a latticework of rich, well-watered fields, with carefully manicured terraces rising in gradual steps to higher ground. Eventually, irrigation works grew to such a scale that they required management by the Zhou rulers, centered in the Wei River valley, and their skilled engineers. The engineers also designed canals that connected rivers and supported commerce and other internal exchanges. Tens of thousands of workers spent countless days digging these canals, paying tribute in the form of labor.

The canals linked China's two breadbaskets: wheat and millet fields in the north and rice fields in the south. And as with the Yellow River in the north, engineers controlled the Yangzi River in the south. Nomads in mountainous areas or on the Zhou frontiers, who often fought with the Zhou ruler and his regional lords, began to depend on trade with the fertile heartlands. In these ways, the Zhou promoted greater unity within their territory and among the peoples living in and around it.

"MANDATE OF HEAVEN"

In addition to promoting a Chinese ethnic and political identity and cultivating advances in agriculture, Zhou rulers also introduced the long-enduring concept of the **mandate of heaven**, which provided a justification for their rule. Attributed by later Chinese intellectuals to King Wu's younger brother Zhou Gong (often referred to as the Duke of Zhou), the mandate asserted that Zhou moral superiority justified taking over Shang wealth and territories and that heaven had imposed a moral mandate on them to replace the Shang, whom they characterized as evil men whose policies brought pain to the people through waste and corruption, and return good governance to the people.

At first Zhou leaders presented the mandate of heaven as a religious compact between the Zhou people and their supreme "sky god" in heaven, but over time Zhou kings and the court detached the concept from the sky god and made the mandate into a free-standing Chinese political doctrine. The Zhou argued that since worldly affairs were supposed to align with those of the heavens, heavenly powers conferred legitimate rights to rule only on their chosen representative. In return, the ruler was duty-bound to uphold heaven's principles of harmony and honor. Any ruler who failed in this duty, who let instability creep into earthly affairs, or who let his people suffer, would lose the mandate. Under this system, spiritual authority withdrew support from any wayward dynasts and found other, more worthy, agents. The Zhou rulers had to acknowledge that any group of rulers, even they themselves, could be ousted if they lost the mandate of heaven because of improper practices.

As part of maintaining their mandate and their legitimacy as rulers, Zhou kings created royal calendars, official documents that defined times for undertaking agricultural activities and celebrating rituals. Unexpected events such as solar eclipses or natural calamities could throw into question the ruling house's mandate. Since rulers claimed that their authority came from heaven, the Zhou perfected the astronomical system on which they based their calendar. Zhou astronomers precisely calculated the length of a lunar month (29.53 days) and the solar year. To resolve the discrepancy between a solar year (365.25 days) and a lunar year (354.36 days), the Zhou occasionally inserted a leap month. Scribes dated the reigns of kings by days and years within a repeating sixty-year cycle.

Zhou legitimacy was also grounded in their use of bronze ritual vessels, statues, ornaments, and weapons, the large-scale production of which they borrowed from their Shang predecessors. Like the Shang, the Zhou developed an extensive system of bronze metalworking that required a large force of tribute labor. Many of its members were Shang, who were sometimes forcibly transported to new Zhou towns to produce the bronze ritual objects. These objects, sold and distributed across the lands and used in ceremonial rituals, symbolized Zhou legitimacy.

Zhou Wine Vessel Under the Zhou, bronze metallurgy depended on a large labor force. Many workers initially came from Shang labor groups, who were superior to the Zhou in technology. The use of bronze, such as for this wine vessel, exemplified dynastic continuity between the Shang and Zhou.

SOCIAL AND ECONOMIC CONTROLS

As the Chinese social order became more integrated, it also became more class-based. Directly under the Zhou ruler and his royal ministers were the hereditary nobles, divided into ranks. These regional lords had landholdings of different sizes. They all owed allegiance to the Zhou king, and they supplied warriors to fight in the king's army and laborers to clear land, drain fields, and do other work. The regional lords periodically appeared at court and took part in complex rituals to reaffirm their allegiance to the king. Below the regional lords were high officers at the Zhou court, as well as ministers and administrators who supervised the people's work. Aristocratic warriors stood at the bottom of the noble hierarchy.

Among commoners, an elaborate occupation-based hierarchy developed over time. Early on, most of the population worked as farmers on fields owned by great landholding families, while some commoners were artisans, such as bronze-workers or silk-weavers. The later occupation-based system, however, divided people more precisely by function—landholders who produced grain, growers of plants and fruit trees, woodsmen, breeders of cattle and chickens, artisans, merchants, weavers, servants, and those with no fixed occupation—and the central government exerted considerable control over how each group did its job. While reports of this control may be overstated, it does show a unique attempt by the Zhou government to assert power over the empire's diverse peoples.

The Zhou also made political and legal use of family structures. In their patrilineal society, the Zhou established strict hierarchies for both men and women. Both art and literature celebrated the son who honored his parents. Men and women had different roles in family and ceremonial life. On landholdings, men farmed and hunted, while women produced silk and other textiles and fashioned them into clothing. Wealth increasingly trumped other distinctions, however. In particular, rich women high in the Zhou aristocracy enjoyed a greater range of actions than other women. And wealthy merchants in emerging cities challenged the authority of local lords.

LIMITS AND DECLINE OF ZHOU POWER

The Zhou state relied on culture (its bronzes) and statecraft (the mandate of heaven) to maintain its leadership among competing powers and lesser principalities in its territories. Rather than having absolute control of an empire (like the Assyrians or Persians) or a primarily socio-religious unity (as among the Vedic peoples of South Asia), the Zhou state was first among many regional economic and political allies.

The Zhou dynasty was not highly centralized; instead, it expected regional lords to control the provinces. Military campaigns continued to press into new lands or to defend Zhou holdings from enemies. Rulers interacted with neighbors and allies by giving them power, protecting them from aggression, and intermarrying between dynastic family members and local nobles. Consequently, Zhou subordinates had more than autonomy; they had genuine resources that they could turn against the dynasts at opportune moments.

The power of the Zhou royal house over its regional lords declined in the ninth and eighth centuries BCE. In response, the Zhou court at Xianyang introduced ritual reforms with grandiose ceremonies featuring larger, standardized bronze vessels. Even this move could not reverse the regime's growing political weakness in dealing with its steppe neighbors and internal regional lords. In 771 BCE, northern steppe invaders forced the Zhou to flee their western capital, ushering in the beginning of what would come to be known as the Spring and Autumn Period of the Eastern Zhou dynasty centered at Luoyi (modern Luoyang).

The Zhou dynastic period, like the Shang, was later idealized by Chinese historians as a golden age of wise kings and officials. In fact, the Zhou model of government, culture, and society became the standard for later generations. Though the Neo-Assyrian and Persian superpowers were capable of greater expansion during this period, China was sowing the seeds of a more durable state.

Conclusion

Around 1000 BCE, dramatic changes in political and social structures took place across Afro-Eurasia. Consolidations of power, with varying degrees and types of centralization, formed in Southwest Asia (Neo-Assyrians and Persians), Vedic South Asia, and East Asia (among the Zhou). Driving these socio-political developments were changes in climate, invasions by nomadic peoples, technological innovations, and new administrative strategies.

A spectrum of power consolidation—from the highly centralized to the more culturally unified—occurred across Afro-Eurasia. The tightly consolidated Neo-Assyrian and Persian empires differed in fundamental ways from the earlier city-states and territorial states of this area. They created ideologies, political institutions, and economic ties that extended their power across vast regions. Their strong imperial institutions enabled them to exploit human and material resources at great distances from the imperial centers. At the other end of Afro-Eurasia, the Zhou in China established loose integration of diverse peoples and territories through a powerful dynastic arrangement buttressed by a mandate from heaven; but they could not overcome the power of local nobles or fully protect the western frontier from nomadic attacks. In the Vedic world of the Indus Valley and Ganges plain, shared values and revered texts did not lead to a single major state. An unparalleled degree of cultural, as opposed to political or economic, integration bound together northern South Asia. Many centuries would pass before a regime would layer a state over this shared cultural world.

Empire building did not occur everywhere. The majority of the world's people still lived in smaller political groupings. Even within Afro-Eurasia, some areas were completely untouched. And even where the Neo-Assyrian and Persian rulers, soldiers, and traders came into contact with certain groups, they did not necessarily crush them. For example, the nomadic peoples of the northern steppes and the southern desert locations throughout

Eurasia continued to be autonomous. But fewer and fewer were untouched by the technological, cultural, and political pulses of empires.

The peoples living in Southwest Asia (under the Neo-Assyrians and then Persians), in the Vedic society of South Asia, and in the Zhou kingdom of China made lasting contributions to the cultural and religious history of humanity. Late Vedic South Asia spun out the concept of cyclic universal time in the form of reincarnation. And in late Zhou China, an ideal of statecraft and social order took shape. On the fringes of these empires, other groups made lasting contributions. The Phoenicians traversed the whole of the Mediterranean basin and spread their simplified alphabet. From the land of Israel, a budding monotheism sprouted. All evolved into powerful cultural forms that in time spread their influences far beyond their sites of origin.

After You Read This Chapter

Go to INQUIZITIVE to see what you've learned—and learn what you've missed—with personalized feedback along the way.

TRACING THE GLOBAL STORYLINES

FOCUS ON: *First Empires and Smaller States*

ANCIENT NEAR EAST

- Neo-Assyrians use raw military power and massive population relocations to build and maintain the world's first empire.
- Persians rely on persuasion and tolerance to build a cosmopolitan empire.

MEDITERRANEAN WORLD

- Greeks, Phoenicians, and Israelites show the advantages of small-scale states with innovations in writing, trading, and religious thought.

SOUTH ASIA

- Vedic peoples build a unified common culture through religious and economic ties.

CHINA

- Zhou dynasty constructs a powerful tributary state and legitimates its rule via the mandate of heaven doctrine (good governance together with upright behavior equates to legitimate rule).

CHRONOLOGY

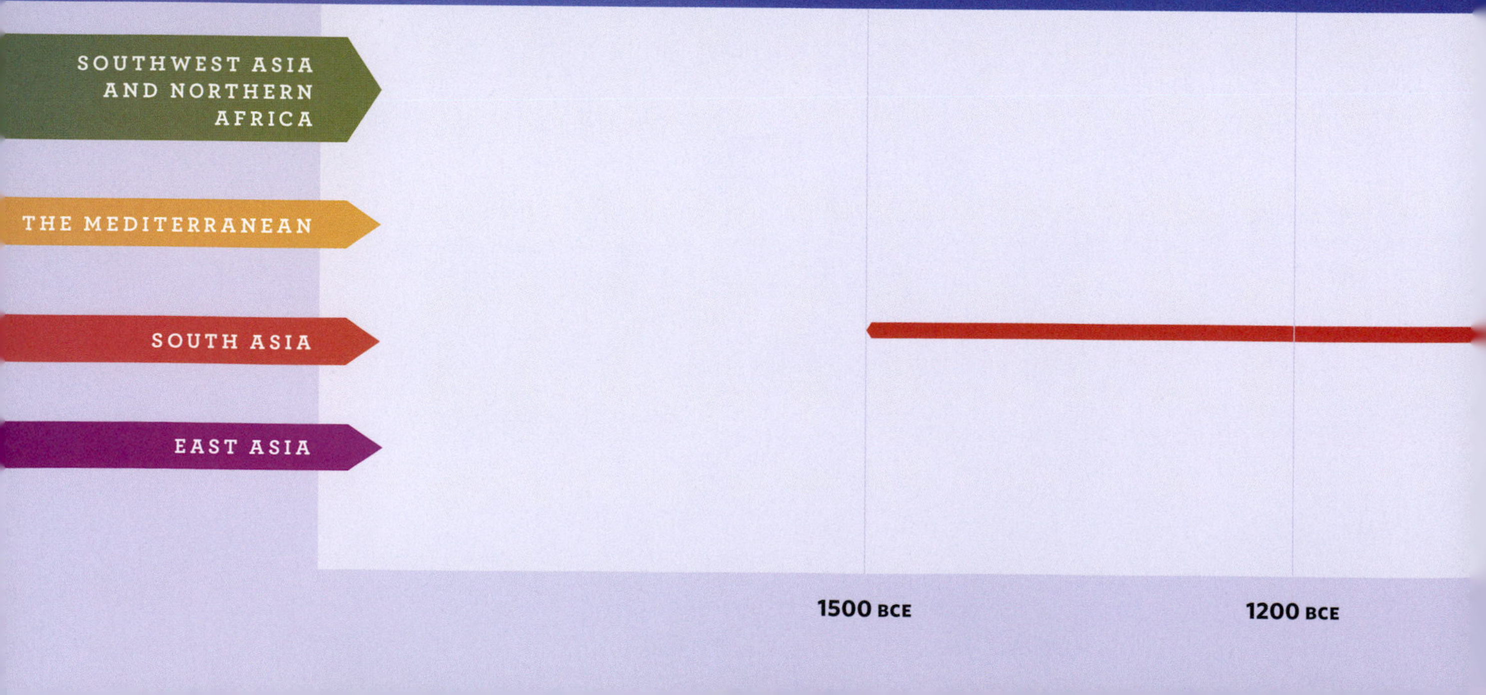

THINKING ABOUT GLOBAL CONNECTIONS

- ***Thinking about Power Relationships and the Formation of Empires*** From 1200 to 350 BCE, several regional empires with centralized rule developed: in Southwest Asia, the Neo-Assyrians and then Persians established tightly controlled empires; in East Asia, the Zhou achieved loose political unification; and a culturally integrated people thrived in South Asia. Compare the use of military force and its relationship to political centralization in each of these cases. How does religion help to bring unification?

- ***Thinking about the Environment and the Formation of Empires*** Just as climate change around 2000 BCE contributed to the demise of earlier civilizations, prolonged drought around 1200 BCE again brought dramatic changes to many areas. Compare the environmental crises in Egypt, Southwest Asia, and East Asia in the late second millennium BCE and their results, especially with respect to empire formation.

- ***Thinking about Exchange Networks and the Formation of Empires*** While this chapter focuses on the formation of empires, the majority of the world's people lived outside or on the fringes of these empires. The Sea Peoples, after disrupting the Hittites, Greeks, and Egyptians, settled down on the coast of Southwest Asia and became the Philistines; the Phoenicians expanded their trade across the Mediterranean; the Greeks effectively resisted Persian authority; and Jewish Israelites founded a kingdom centered on monotheism. Which had the most significant impact on human history: the centralized empires or the peoples on the fringes and beyond? Why?

STUDY QUESTIONS

1. Describe how climate change, migrations, technological developments, and administrative innovations contributed to the formation of empires in the later second millennium BCE.
2. What are the common features of **empires** across Eurasia from 1200–350 BCE? What are the similarities and differences in how empires formed, or did not form, in Southwest Asia, South Asia, and East Asia?
3. How did the Assyrian and Persian empires consolidate their imperial control over vast territories? What role did religious and political innovations such as **Zoroastrianism** and **satrapies** play in that consolidation?
4. How did peoples on the margins of Assyria and Persia—including the **Sea Peoples**, the **Phoenicians** (with their **alphabet**), the Israelites (and their **monotheism**), and the Greeks—interact with these imperial powers?
5. How did the Zhou Dynasty establish control in East Asia and what role did the **mandate of heaven** play in their maintenance of power?
6. How did socio-religious developments such as ***varna***, the **Vedas**, and the **Upanishads** enable South Asia to become integrated without a centralized imperial state?

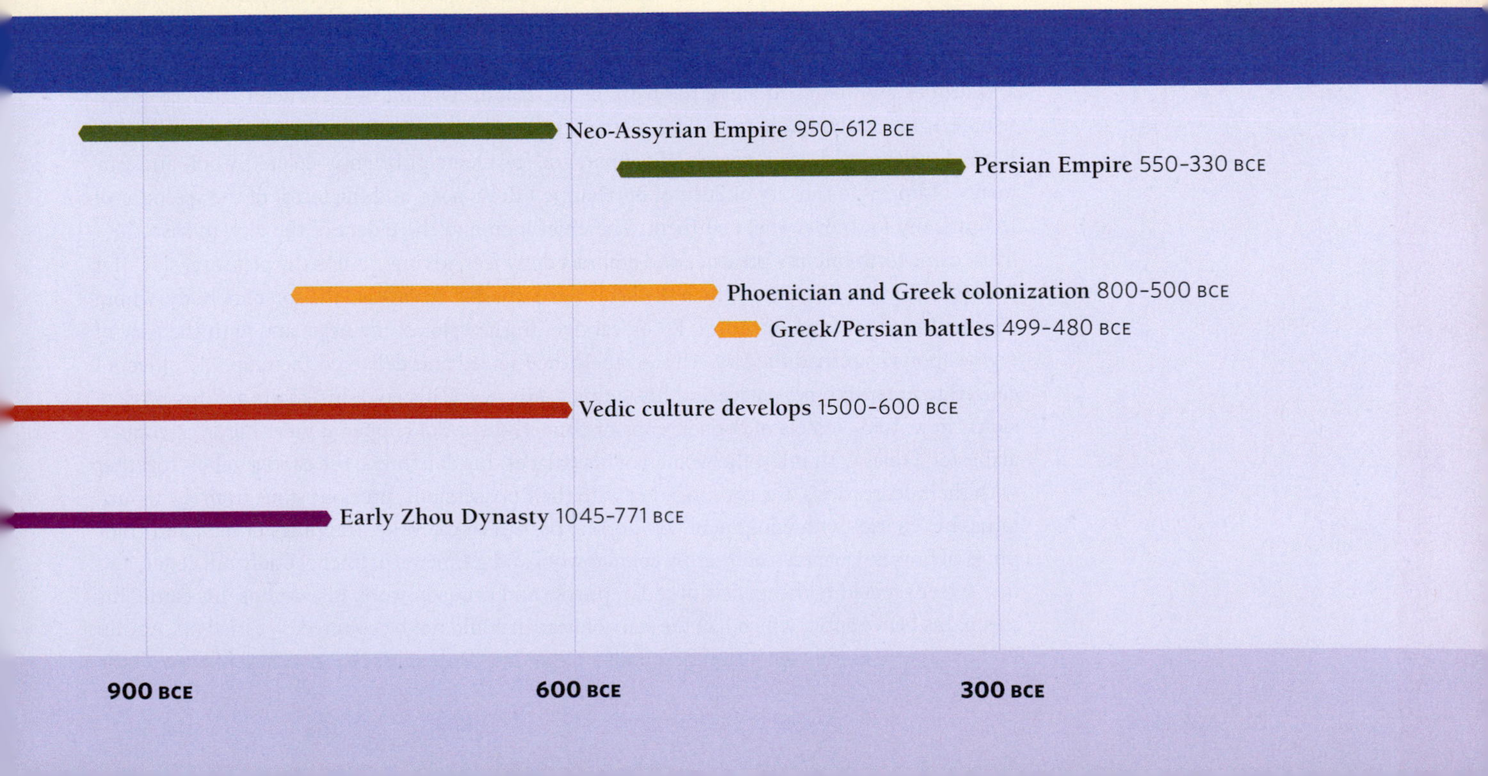

Going to the Source

Expanding Empires

Military control, political tolerance, and cultural control, especially through religion, are three methods that early empires used to acquire and justify their political power. The Assyrians relied on harsh political and military control, while others, such as the Persians, whose empire was linked through trade, pursued more lenient policies towards non-Persians. Early empires also used religion to justify their rule, and they often claimed to have the favor of their god(s) on their side. Leaders sometimes used religion as a way to explain why it was acceptable to conquer others. The sources below illustrate some of the ways in which the empires established in the first millennium BCE were able to maintain and justify their power, as well as how they demonstrated that power to others.

PRIMARY SOURCE 4.1

The Revolt of the City of Suru (c. 889–853 BCE)

This inscription from the Temple of Urta at Nimrud is part of the annals of Assurnasirpal II, who ruled as king of Assyria, during the ninth century BCE. It describes the various military victories of his regime. It recounts the Assyrian reaction to a revolt against Assyrian rule in Suru and also describes the tribute that Assyria demanded after Suru was defeated.

While I was staying in the land of Kutmuhi, they brought me the word: "The city of Suru of Bit-Halupe has revolted, they have slain Hamatai, their governor, and Ahiababa, the son of a nobody, whom they brought from Bit-Adini, they have set up as king over them." With the help of Adad and the great gods who have made great my kingdom, I mobilized [my] chariots and armies and marched along the bank of the Habur. During my advance I received much tribute from Shulmanu-haman-ilani of the city of Gardiganni, from Ilu-Adad of the city of Katna,—silver, gold, lead, vessels of copper, and garments of brightly colored wool, and garments of linen. To the city of Suru of Bit-Halupe I drew near, and the terror of the splendor of [Ashur], my lord, overwhelmed them. The chief men and the elders of the city, to save their lives, came forth into my presence and embraced my feet, saying: "If it is thy pleasure, slay! If it is thy pleasure, let live! That which thy heart desireth, do!" Ahiababa, the son of nobody, whom they had brought from Bit-Adini, I took captive. In the valor of my heart and with the fury of my weapons I stormed the city. All the rebels they seized and delivered them up. My officers I caused to enter into his palace and his temples. His silver, his gold, his goods and his possessions, iron, lead, vessels of copper, cups of copper, dishes of copper, a great horde of copper, alabaster, tables with inlay, the women of his palaces, his daughters, the captive rebels together with their possessions, the gods together with their possessions, precious stone from the mountains, his chariot with equipment, his horses, broken to the yoke, trappings of men and trappings of horses, garments of brightly colored wool and garments of linen, goodly oil, cedar, and fine sweet-scented herbs, panels of cedar, purple and crimson wool, his wagons, his cattle, his sheep, his heavy spoil, which like the stars of heaven could not be counted, I carried off. Azi-ilu I set over them as my own governor. I built a pillar over against his city gate, and I flayed all the chief men who had revolted, and I covered the pillar with their skins; some I walled up within the pillar, some I impaled upon the pillar on stakes, and others I bound to stakes round about the pillar; many within the border of my own land I flayed, and I spread their skins upon the walls; and I cut off the limbs of the officers, of the royal officers who had rebelled. Ahiababa I took to Nineveh, I flayed him, I spread his skin upon the wall of Nineveh. My power and might I established over the land of [Laqe]. While I was staying in the city of Suru, [I received] tribute from all the kings of the land of [Laqe],—silver, gold, lead, copper, vessels of copper, cattle, sheep, garments of brightly colored wool, and garments of linen, and I increased the tribute and taxes and imposed them upon them. At that time, the tribute of Haiani of the city of Hindani,—silver, gold, lead, copper, umu-stone, alabaster, purple wool, and [Bactrian] camels I received from him as tribute. At that time I fashioned a heroic image of my royal self, my power and my glory I inscribed thereon, in the midst of his palace I set it up. I fashioned memorial stelae and inscribed thereon my glory and my prowess, and I set them up by his city gate.

1. **Describe and evaluate Assurnasirpal's behavior towards the rebels.**
2. **On what grounds did Assurnasirpal base his authority?**

PRIMARY SOURCE 4.2

The Behistun Inscription (520 BCE), Darius I

To commemorate his consolidation of power over the Persian state, Darius I (r. 522–486 BCE) commissioned the trilingual Behistun inscription excerpted here. It was posted on a major road connecting Mesopotamia with what is now western Iran.

4.31–2. Saith Darius the King: These IX kings I took prisoner within these battles.

4.33–6. Saith Darius the King: These are the provinces which became rebellious. The Lie made them rebellious, so that these [men] deceived the people. Afterwards Ahuramazda put them into my hand; as was my desire, so I did unto them.

4.36–40. Saith Darius the King: Thou who shalt be king hereafter, protect thyself vigorously from the Lie; the man who shall be a Lie-follower, him do thou punish well, if thus thou shalt think, "May my country be secure!"

4.40–3. Saith Darius the King: This is what I did; by the favor of Ahuramazda, in one and the same year I did [it]. Thou who shalt hereafter read this inscription, let that which has been done by me convince thee; do not thou think it a lie.

4.43–5. Saith Darius the King: I turn myself quickly to Ahuramazda, that this [is] true, not false, [which] I did in one and the same year. . . .

4.52–6. Saith Darius the King: Now let that which has been done by me convince thee; thus to the people impart, do not conceal it: if this record thou shalt not conceal, [but] tell it to the people, may Ahuramazda be a friend unto thee, and may family be unto thee in abundance, and may thou live long!

4.57–9. Saith Darius the King: If this record thou shalt conceal, [and] not tell it to the people, may Ahuramazda be a smiter unto thee, and may family not be to thee!

4.59–61. Saith Darius the King: This which I did, in one and the same year by the favor of Ahuramazda I did; Ahuramazda bore me aid, and the other gods who are.

4.61–7. Saith Darius the King: For this reason Ahuramazda bore aid, and the other gods who are, because I was not hostile, I was not a Lie-follower, I was not a doer of wrong—neither I nor my family. According to righteousness I conducted myself. Neither to the weak nor to the powerful did I do wrong. The man who cooperated with my house, him I rewarded well; whoso did injury, him I punished well.

4.67–9. Saith Darius the King: Thou who shalt be king hereafter, the man who shall be a Lie-follower or who shall be a doer of wrong—unto them do thou not be a friend, [but] punish them well.

4.69–72. Saith Darius the King: Thou who shalt hereafter behold this inscription which I have inscribed, or these sculptures, do thou not destroy them, [but] thence onward protect them; as long as thou shalt be in good strength!

1. **From where did Darius the King derive his power?**
2. **Why do you think Darius inscribed this story on an important roadway from Mesopotamia to Persia?**

PRIMARY SOURCE 4.3

Persian Daric (sixth century BCE)

The Persian daric is a gold coin first minted by Darius the Great in the sixth century BCE and circulated throughout Persia and the Mediterranean. This daric shows an imprint of the Persian king Darius kneeling with a drawn bow.

1. **What impression of Darius does this military pose convey?**
2. **Why do you think Darius would have circulated a coin throughout the Persian Empire that showed him in this position?**

PRIMARY SOURCE 4.4

The Great Declaration (fourth century BCE)

The *Book of Documents,* one of *The Five Classics* of Chinese literature, was written before 300 BCE and is among the essential works of Confucianism. It contains speeches and documents attributed to the Zhou dynasty and earlier. In this excerpt, King Wu of the Zhou Empire explains the grievances against his predecessors, the Shang, and why he was compelled to overthrow them.

*

In the spring of the thirteenth year, there was a great assembly at [Mengjin]. . . . King [Wu] said, "Ah! ye hereditary rulers of my friendly states, and all ye my officers, managers of my affairs, listen clearly to my declaration. Heaven and earth is the parent of all creatures; and of all creatures man is the most highly endowed. The sincere, intelligent, and perspicacious *among men* becomes the great sovereign; and the great sovereign is the parent of the people. *But* now, [Shou], the king of Shang, does not reverence Heaven above, and inflicts calamities on the people below. He has been abandoned to drunkenness, and reckless in lust. He has dared to exercise cruel oppression. Along with criminals he has punishment all their relatives. He has put men into offices on the hereditary principle. He has made it his pursuit to have palaces, towers, pavilions, embankments, ponds, and all other extravagances, to the most painful injury of you, the myriad people. He has burned and roasted the loyal and good. He has ripped up pregnant women. Great Heaven was moved with indignation, and charged my deceased father [Wen] reverently to display its majesty; but *he died* before the work was completed . . . but [Shou] has no repentant heart. He abides squatting on his heels not serving God or the spirit of the heaven and earth, neglecting also the temple of his ancestors, and not sacrificing in it. . . . The iniquity of Shang is full. Heaven gives command to destroy it. If I did not comply with Heaven, my iniquity would be as great."

1. **What are King Wu's complaints about the Shang leader?**
2. **Why does King Wu believe that he is compelled to act? From where does he derive his authority?**

PRIMARY SOURCE 4.5

Tribute Scene at Palace of Persepolis

At the Persian capital of Persepolis, grand staircases leading to the main audience hall of the palace were decorated with scenes of the king and his courtiers as well as the delegations bringing tribute to the center of the empire. This image depicts tribute-bearers bringing animals and other items in bowls as gifts to the Persian king. Those delivering their tribute would have walked past these scenes on their way to pay respect to the Persian king.

1. **Why was paying tribute important to kings?**
2. **Why might this artwork and its location have been important for those who paid the tribute and for those who received it?**

PRIMARY SOURCE 4.6

War and Action in the Bhagavad Gita *(c. sixth century BCE)*

The *Bhagavad Gita* is perhaps the best-known work from the religious tradition that would become Hinduism. It is taken from a larger epic, known as the *Mahabharata*, which tells the story of two feuding families. In this selection, Arjuna, a member of one of the families, wonders why he should fight people on the other side of the feud, to whom he might be related. Lord Krishna, the Deity, who happens to be serving as Arjuna's chariot driver, offers his reply.

*

You have grieved for those who deserve no grief and you talk words of wisdom. Learned men grieve not for the living nor the dead. Never did I not exist, nor you, nor these rulers of men; nor will any one of us ever hereafter cease to be. As, in this body, infancy and youth and old age (come) to the embodied (self), so does the acquisition of another body; a sensible man is not deceived about that. The contacts of the senses . . . which produce cold and heat, pleasure and pain, are not permanent, they are ever coming and going. . . . There is no existence for that which is unreal; there is no non-existence for that which is real. And the (correct) conclusion about both is perceived by those who perceive the truth. . . .

These bodies appertaining to the embodied (self) which is eternal, indestructible, and indefinable, are said to be perishable; therefore do engage in battle, O descendant of Bharata! He who thinks it to be the killer and he who thinks it to be killed, both know nothing. It kills not, is not killed. It is not born, nor does it ever die, nor, having existed, does it exist no more. Unborn, everlasting, unchangeable, and primeval, it is not killed when the body is killed. . . . As a man, casting off old clothes, puts on others and new ones, so the embodied (self) casting off old bodies, goes to others and new ones. Weapons do not divide it (into pieces); fire does not burn it, waters do not moisten it; the wind does not dry it up. It is not divisible; it is not combustible; it is not to be moistened; it is not to be dried up. It is everlasting, all-pervading, stable, firm, and eternal. It is said to be unperceived, to be unthinkable, to be unchangeable. Therefore knowing it to be such, you ought not to grieve, But even if you think that it is constantly born, and constantly dies, still, O you of mighty arms! you ought not to grieve thus. For to one that is born, death is certain; and to one that dies, birth is certain. . . .

Therefore you ought not to grieve for any being. Having regard to your own duty also, you ought not to falter, for there is nothing better for a Kshatriya than a righteous battle. Happy those Kshatriyas, O son of Prithâ! who can find such a battle (to fight)—come of itself—an open door to heaven! But if you will not fight this righteous battle, then you will have abandoned your own duty and your fame, and you will incur sin. . . . All beings, too, will tell of your everlasting infamy; and to one who has been honoured, infamy is (a) greater (evil) than death. . . . Killed, you will obtain heaven; victorious, you will enjoy the earth. Therefore arise, O son of Kuntî! resolved to (engage in) battle. Looking alike on pleasure and pain, on gain and loss, on victory and defeat, then prepare for battle, and thus you will not incur sin.

1. **How might the Bhagavad Gita have motivated or discouraged people who were going to engage in fighting?**
2. **Describe the connection between religious practice and warfare.**

Questions for Analysis

Comparison

1. Compare the role that religious belief plays in conquest in these documents and analyze any similarities and differences that emerge.

Argumentation

2. Evaluate the ways in which empires consolidated their power.

Long Essay Question

Analyzing Evidence

Imagine that you were a ruler who sought to consolidate your power during this period. What problems would you have to consider before undertaking your efforts? What techniques would you use, and why would you choose them?

Before You Read This Chapter

GLOBAL STORYLINES

- A range of challenges—warfare, political upheaval, economic pressures, and social developments—transform the empires and states of Afro-Eurasia.
- "Second-generation" societies arise across Afro-Eurasia in a pivotal period sometimes called the "axial age."
- Complex new societies develop in the Americas and sub-Saharan Africa.
- Axial age thinkers in Afro-Eurasia reshape peoples' views of the world and their place in it.

CORE OBJECTIVES

- **DESCRIBE** the challenges that Afro-Eurasian empires and states faced in the first millennium BCE, and **COMPARE** the range of solutions they devised.
- **COMPARE** the political, cultural, and social developments across Afro-Eurasia with those occurring in the Americas and sub-Saharan Africa.
- **IDENTIFY** axial age thinkers and **ANALYZE** their distinctiv ideas.
- **EXPLAIN** the relationship between axial age thinkers acros Afro-Eurasia (East Asia, South Asia, and the Mediterranean) and the political and social situations to which they were responding.

KEY TERMS

axial age p. 166
Buddha p. 175
Chavín p. 184
Confucius p. 168
Daoism p. 168
Greek philosophers p. 181
Jainism p. 174
Meroe p. 190
Olmecs p. 185
second-generation societies p. 166

CHAPTER

5

Worlds Turned Inside Out

1000–350 BCE

In the midst of violent struggles for power and territory in China in the sixth century BCE, Master Kong Fuzi instructed his disciples on how to govern, saying: "Guide them by edicts, keep them in line with punishments, and the people will stay out of trouble but will have no sense of shame. Guide them by virtue, keep them in line with the rites, and they will, besides having a sense of shame, reform themselves" (Confucius, *The Analects*, II, 3).

Master Kong, also known as Confucius, represented a new breed of influential leaders who were teachers and thinkers, not kings, priests, or warriors. Nonetheless, it was the convulsions around them—incessant warfare, population growth, migrations, and the emergence of new cities—that motivated their search for insights. By viewing the world in innovative ways, these teachers instructed rulers on how to govern justly and showed ordinary individuals how to live ethically.

The teachers and founders of new ways of thinking from the first millennium BCE, who figure prominently in this chapter, were some of the most influential in history. In China, Confucius elaborated a set of principles for ethical living that has guided the Chinese population up to modern times. In South Asia, Siddhartha Gautama (the Buddha) laid out social and spiritual tenets that challenged

ROCKY MOUNTAINS
NORTH AMERICA
NOMADIC HUNTERS
Great Lakes
Mississippi R.
St. Lawrence R.
ATLANTIC OCEAN
Gulf of Mexico
OLMEC
MESOAMERICA
WEST INDIES
PACIFIC OCEAN
ANDES MOUNTAINS
NOMADIC HUNTERS
Amazon R.
CHAVÍN
SOUTH AMERICA
Rhine R.
CELTIC PEOPLES
IBERIANS
SAHARA
SAHARAN PEOPLES
SAHEL
Niger R.
NOK
NOK State
SLAVS People
0 1000 2000 Miles
0 1000 2000 Kilometers

MAP 5.1 | The World in an Axial Age, c. 500 BCE

By the middle of the first millennium BCE, complex agriculture-based societies beyond the regional empires of Southwest Asia and North Africa contributed to the flowering of new cultural pathways and ideas.

- According to your reading, where did these second-generation societies appear?
- Which societies had greater opportunities for cultural mixing, and which ones were more isolated?
- How did proximity to others or relative isolation shape these societies' development?

the traditional social hierarchy based on birth and with it, the power of the ruling priests and warriors. In Greece, Socrates, Plato, and Aristotle described a world that conformed to natural laws.

The philosophers, theologians, poets, political leaders, and merchants of this era founded literary traditions, articulated new belief systems, and established new political and economic institutions that spread well beyond the places that inspired them. While wars and havoc occurred within their societies and long-distance trade and travel linked societies, these centuries were dominated by a search for order and an appetite for new thinking.

An "Axial Age"

Some modern thinkers call the mid-first millennium BCE the **axial age**, to emphasize its pivotal and transitional role between the declining empires of ancient Egypt, Southwest Asia, northern India, and Zhou China, and the later empires of Alexander the Great, Rome, and the Han Chinese (see Chapters 6 and 7). This dynamic period gave rise to the ethical, philosophical, and religious underpinnings of cultures in India, China, and Europe.

In this axial age of the first millennium BCE, societies on the edges of regional empires or within declining empires of Afro-Eurasia started to follow innovative paths. (See Map 5.1.) These new communities were not just extensions of old ways of life. In each, dramatic innovations in cultural and religious beliefs were expanding people's social, political, and cultural options. Although each of the resulting cultures—in East Asia, South Asia, and the Mediterranean—was distinct from the others, we might call them all **second-generation societies**, given that they built on their predecessors yet represented a departure from ancient legacies.

While Afro-Eurasia experienced an axial age and the emergence of second-generation societies, other parts of the world saw complex, urban-based societies emerge for the first time.. The first of these in the Americas was established by the Olmecs in Mesoamerica, with artistic and religious reverberations well beyond their homelands. In Africa, distinct regional identities spread in the Upper Nile (in Nubia) and West Africa. One of the most striking features of the first millennium BCE is the long-lasting impact of both the axial age second-generation societies that stretched across Afro-Eurasia and the first complex societies isolated from them by oceans and desert.

Eastern Zhou China

COMPARISON

DESCRIBE the challenges that Afro-Eurasian empires and states faced in the first millennium BCE.

Destruction of the old political order paved the way for radical thinkers and cultural flourishing in Eastern Zhou China. Centered at Luoyang, the turbulent Eastern Zhou dynasty was divided by ancient Chinese chroniclers into the Spring and Autumn period (722–481 BCE) and the Warring States period (403–221 BCE). One writer from the Spring and Autumn period described over 500 battles among states and more than 100 civil wars within states, all taking place within 260 years. Fueling this warfare was the spread of cheaper and more lethal weaponry, made possible by new iron-smelting techniques, which in turn shifted influence from the central government to local authorities and allowed warfare to continue unabated into the Warring States period. Regional states became so powerful that they undertook large-scale projects, including dikes and irrigation systems, which had to this point been feasible only for empires. At the beginning of the Warring States period, seven large territorial states dominated the Zhou world. (See Map 5.2.) Their wars and shifting political alliances involved the mobilization of armies and resources on an unprecedented scale. Qin, the most powerful state, which ultimately replaced the Eastern Zhou dynasty in 221 BCE, fielded armies that combined huge infantries in the tens of thousands with lethal cavalries and skilled archers using state-of-the-art crossbows.

The conception of central power changed dramatically during this era, as royal appointees replaced hereditary officeholders. By the middle of the fourth century BCE, power was so concentrated in the major states' rulers that each began to call himself "king" (*wang*). Despite the constant warfare, scholars, soldiers, merchants, peasants, and artisans thrived in the midst of an expanding agrarian economy and interregional trade.

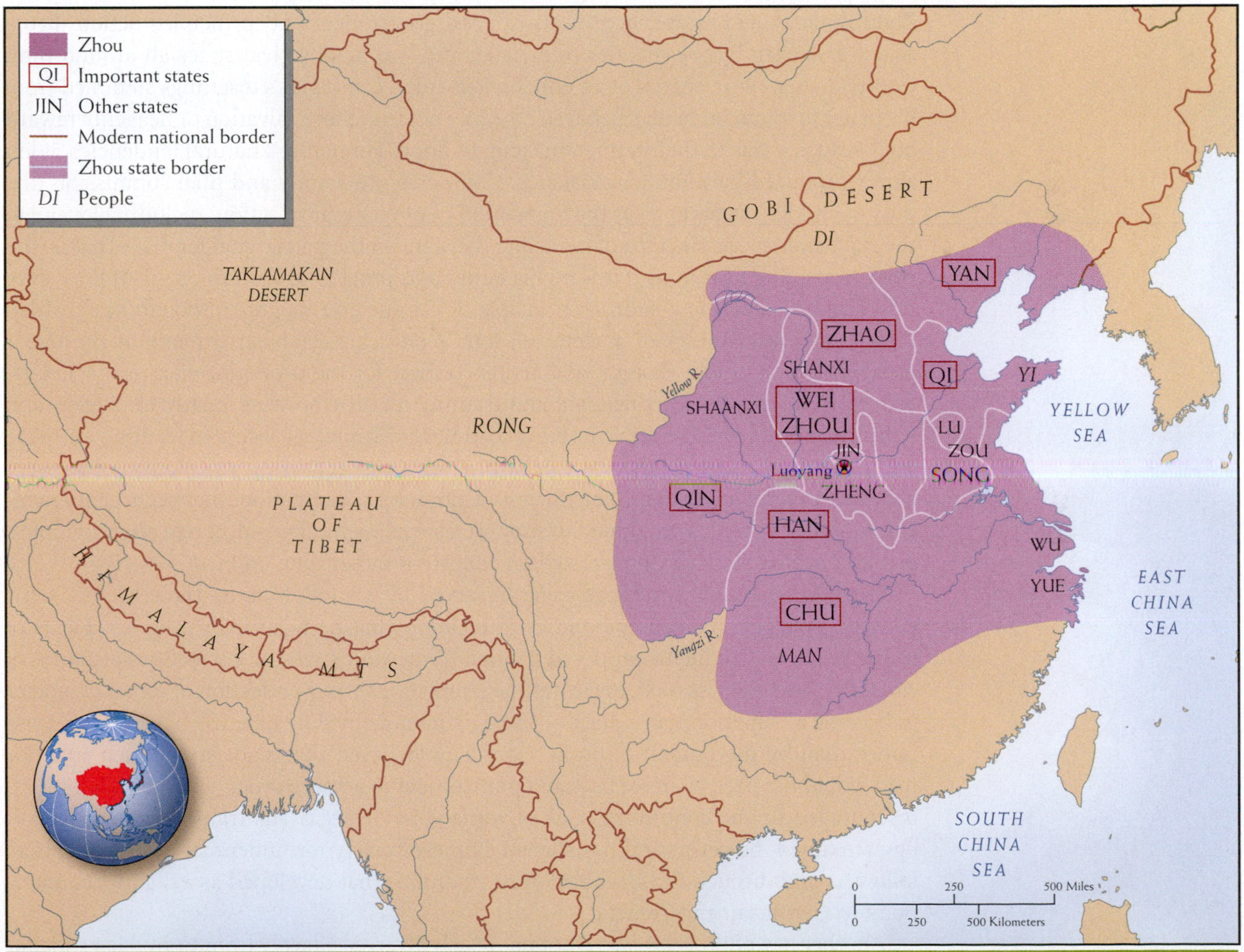

MAP 5.2 | Zhou China in the Warring States Period

The Warring States period witnessed a fracturing of the Zhou dynasty into a myriad of states.

- Find the Zhou capital of Luoyang on the map. Where was it located relative to the other key states?
- What about this map tells us why diplomacy was so important during this period?
- How do you think so many smaller states could survive when they were surrounded first by seven and then by three even larger and more powerful states (Qin, Qi, and Chu)?

COMPARISON

IDENTIFY axial age thinkers and **ANALYZE** their distinctive ideas.

INNOVATIONS IN THOUGHT

Out of this turmoil came new visions that would shape Chinese thinking about the individual's place in society and provided the philosophical underpinnings for the world's most enduring imperial system (lasting from the establishment of the Qin dynasty in 221 BCE until the abdication of China's last monarch in 1912). Often it was the losers among the political elites, seeking to replace their former advantages with new status gained through service, who sparked this intellectual creativity. Many important teachers emerged in China's axial age, each with disciples. The philosophies of these "hundred masters," a term mostly used at the time by itinerant scholars, constituted what came to be known as the Hundred Schools of Thought. Among the most influential were Confucianism and Daoism.

Confucius (551–479 BCE) was very much the product of the violent Spring and Autumn period. Serving in minor governmental positions, he believed the founders of the Zhou dynasty had established ideals of good government and principled action. Frustrated, however, by the realities of division and war among rival states all around him, Confucius set out in search of an enlightened ruler. Confucius's teachings stemmed from his belief that human beings behaved ethically not to achieve salvation or heavenly reward but because it was in their human makeup to do so. Humanity's natural tendencies, if left alone, produced harmonious existence. Confucius saw family and filial submission (the duty of children to parents) as the foundation of proper ethical action, including loyalty to the state and rulers. His idea of modeling the state on the patriarchal family—that is, the ruler respecting heaven as if it were his father and protecting his subjects as if they were his children—became a bedrock principle of Confucian thought. Although he regarded himself as a transmitter of ancient wisdom, Confucius established many of the major guidelines for Chinese thought and action: respect for the pronouncements of scholars, commitment to a broad education, and training for all who were highly intelligent and willing to work, whether noble or humble in birth. This equal access to training for those willing and able offered a dramatic departure from past centuries, when only nobles were believed capable of ruling. Nonetheless, Confucius's distinctions between gentlemen-rulers and commoners continued to support a social hierarchy—although an individual's position in that hierarchy now rested on education rather than on birth.

Confucius's ethical teachings were preserved by his followers in *The Analects*. In his effort to persuade his contemporaries to reclaim what he regarded as the lost ideals of the early Zhou, Confucius proposed a moral framework stressing correct performance of ritual (*li*), humaneness (*ren*), loyalty to the family (*xiao*), and perfection of moral character to become a "superior man" (*junzi*)—that is, a man defined by benevolence and goodness rather than by the pursuit of profit. Confucius believed that a society of such superior men would not need coercive laws and punishment to achieve order. Confucius left court, discouraged by the continuing state of warfare, in 484 BCE. His transformational ideology remained, however; and has shaped Chinese society for millennia, both through its followers and through those who adopted traditions that developed as a distinct counterpoint to Confucian engagement.

Another key philosophy was **Daoism**, which diverged sharply from Confucian thought by scorning rigid rituals and social hierarchies. Its ideas originated with a Master Lao (Laozi, "Old Master"), who—if he actually existed—may have been a contemporary of Confucius. His sayings were collected in *The Daodejing*, or *The Book of the Way and Its Power* (c. third century BCE). Master Lao's book was then elaborated by Master Zhuang (Zhuangzi, c. 369–286 BCE). Daoism stressed that the best path (*dao*) for living was to follow the natural order of things. Its main principle was *wuwei*, "doing nothing." Spontaneity, noninterference, and acceptance of the world as it is, rather than attempting to change it through politics and government, were what mattered. In Laozi's vision, the ruler who interfered least in the natural processes of change was the most successful. Zhuangzi focused on the enlightened individual living spontaneously and in harmony with nature, free of society's ethical rules and laws and viewing life and death simply as different stages of existence.

Apart from the philosophical discourse of the "hundred masters," with its far-reaching impact across Chinese society, elites and commoners alike tried to maintain stability in their lives through religion, medicine, and statecraft. The elites' rites of divination to predict the future and medical recipes to heal the body found parallels in the commoners' use of ghost stories and astrological almanacs to understand the meaning of their lives and the significance of their deaths. Elites recorded their political discourses on wood and bamboo slips, tied together to form scrolls. They likewise prepared military treatises, ritual texts, geographic works, and poetry. The growing importance of statecraft and philosophical discourse promoted the use of writing, with 9,000 to 10,000 graphs or signs required to convey these elaborate ideas.

What emerged from all this activity was a foundational alliance of scholars and the state. Scholars became state functionaries dependent on rulers' patronage. In return, rulers recognized scholars' expertise in matters of punishment, ritual, astronomy, medicine, and divination. Philosophical deliberations focused on the need to maintain order and stability by preserving the state. These bonds that rulers forged with their scholarly elites were a distinguishing feature of governments in Warring States China, as compared with other Afro-Eurasian societies at this time.

INNOVATIONS IN STATE ADMINISTRATION

Regional rulers of the Spring and Autumn period enhanced their ability to obtain natural resources, to recruit men for their armies, and to oversee conquered areas. This trend continued in the Warring States period, as the elites in the major states created administrative districts with stewards, sheriffs, and judges and a system of registering peasant households to facilitate tax collection and army conscription. These officials, who had been knights under the Western Zhou, were now bureaucrats in direct service to the ruler. These administrators were the "superior men" (*junzi*) of Confucian thought. They were paid in grain, titles, and gifts of gold and silver from the ruler. The most successful of these ministers was the Qin statesman Shang Yang (fourth century BCE). Lord Shang's reforms—including a head tax, administrative districts for closer bureaucratic control of hinterlands, land distribution for individual households to farm, and reward or punishment for military achievement—positioned the Qin to become the dominant state of its time.

Shang Yang of Qin An important statesman of Qin during the Warring States period, Shang Yang introduced administrative reforms that enhanced the power of the central government.

INNOVATIONS IN WARFARE

With administrative reforms came reforms in military recruitment and warfare. In earlier periods, nobles had let fly their arrows from chariots while conscripted peasants fought beside them on the blood-stained ground. The Warring States, however, relied on massed infantries of peasants, whose conscription was made easier by the registration of peasant households. Bearing iron lances and unconstrained by their relationships with nobles, these peasants fought fiercely. In addition to this conscripted peasant infantry, armies boasted elite professional troops equipped with iron armor and weapons, and wielding the recently invented crossbow. The crossbow's tremendous power, range, and accuracy enabled archers to kill lightly armored cavalrymen or charioteers at a distance. With improved siege technology, enemy armies assaulted the new defensive walls of towns and frontiers, either digging under them or using counterweighted siege ladders to scale them. Campaigns were no longer limited to an agricultural season, but now might stretch over a year or longer. The huge state armies contained as many as 1,000,000 commoners in the infantry, supported by 1,000 chariots and 10,000 bow-wielding cavalrymen. During the Spring and Autumn period, one state's entire army would face another state's; but by the Warring States period, armies could divide into separate forces and wage several battles simultaneously.

ECONOMIC, SOCIAL, AND CULTURAL CHANGES

While a growing population presented new challenges, the continuous warfare in these periods spurred economic growth in China. An agricultural revolution on the North China plain along the Yellow River led to rapid population growth, and the inhabitants of the Eastern Zhou reached approximately 20 million. Several factors contributed to increased agricultural productivity beginning in the Spring and Autumn period. Some rulers gave peasants the right to own their land in exchange for taxes and military service, which in turn increased productivity because the farmers were working to benefit themselves. Agricultural productivity was also enhanced by innovations such as crop rotation (millet and wheat in the north, rice and millet in the south) and oxen-pulled iron plowshares to prepare fields.

With this increased agricultural yield came the pressures of accompanying population growth. Ever-attentive peasant farmers tilling the fields of North and South China produced more rice and wheat than anyone else on earth, but that agricultural success was often outpaced by their growing families. As more people required more fuel, deforestation led to erosion of the fields. Many animals were hunted to extinction. Many inhabitants migrated south to domesticate the marshes, lakes, and rivers of the Yangzi River delta; here they created new arable frontiers out of former wetlands. When the expansion into arable land invariably hit its limits, Chinese families faced terrible food shortages and famines. The long-term economic result was a declining standard of living for massive numbers of Chinese peasants.

Despite these long-term cycles of population pressures and famine, larger harvests and advances in bronze and iron casting enabled the beginning of a market economy: trade in surplus grain, pottery, and ritual objects. Peasants continued to barter, but elites and rulers used minted coins. Grain and goods traveled along roads, rivers, and canals. Rulers and officials applied their military and organizational skills for public projects enhancing water works.

Economic growth had repercussions at all levels of society. Rulers attained a high level of cultural sophistication, as reflected in their magnificent palaces and burial sites. Archaeological evidence also suggests that commoners could purchase bronze metalwork, whereas previously only Zhou rulers and aristocrats could afford to do so. Social relations became more fluid as commoners gained power and aristocrats lost it. In Qin, for example, peasants who served in the ruler's army could be rewarded with land, houses, slaves, and even status change for killing enemy soldiers. While class relations had a revolutionary fluidity, gender relations became more rigid for elites and nonelites alike as male-centered kinship groups grew. The resulting separation of the sexes and male domination within the family affected women's position. An emphasis on monogamy, or at least the primacy of the first wife over additional wives and concubines, emerged. Relations between the sexes became increasingly ritualized and constrained by moral and legal sanctions against any behavior that appeared to threaten the purity of authoritarian male lineages.

Even with the endless cycles of warfare and chaos—or perhaps because of them—many foundational beliefs, values, and philosophies for later dynasties sprang forth during the Spring and Autumn and Warring States periods. By the middle of the first millennium BCE, China's political activities and institutional and intellectual innovations affected larger numbers of people, over a much broader area, than comparable developments in South Asia and the Mediterranean.

Knife Coin Zhou dynasty coins, like the later Han coin shown here, were made of bronze and produced in a variety of shapes, some resembling spades and knives, depending on the region. Each of the Warring States had its own currency.

The New Worlds of South Asia

While Chinese scholar-officials were theorizing about how to govern and organize their society, the Vedic peoples who settled in the Ganges valley were assimilating earlier residents and forging their own new political institutions, economic activities, and belief systems. The heartland of South Asian developments in this period was the mid-Ganges plain, a roughly 70,000-square-mile area in the northeast of present-day India and the southern tip of Nepal. (See Map 5.3.) Waves of Vedic peoples migrated into this region around 600 BCE, clearing land, establishing new cities and trade routes, expanding rice cultivation, and experimenting with new political forms. Abundant monsoon rains made the land suitable for rice farming, as opposed to the wheat and barley farming of the Indus Valley. Vedic migrants cleared land by setting fire to the forests and using iron tools—fashioned from ore mined locally—to remove what was left of the jungle. Two major kinds of states appeared in the mid- and lower Ganges plain: those ruled by hereditary monarchs and those ruled by a small elite (oligarchy). South Asian oligarchies were led by the Kshatriya class of warriors and officials. Kshatriya oligarchs controlled the land and other resources, overseeing the work of slaves and foreign workers.

In the kingdoms and oligarchic cities of northern India, a new system of hierarchy emerged alongside the old four-fold *varnas* (Brahman priests, Kshatriya warriors, Vaishya commoners, and Shudra laborers). *Varnas* remained the overarching theoretical basis for ranking the social order; but, since booming agriculture allowed for greater variation in professions, occupation and birth received new emphasis. Each occupational group established its own sublevels, called *jatis* (the Sanskrit word for birth). *Jatis* were organized not only by kinship and profession, but even by product. In the emerging urban centers, for instance, traders were regarded as "purer" than artisans, while those making gold utensils had higher status than those making copper or iron products. Yet members of each group colluded to restrict internal competition, and they closed ranks to preserve their status. Sub-*jatis* banned intermarriage to prevent other groups from accessing their knowledge. Religion buttressed this hierarchical system. Brahmanical texts, some from an earlier period and some from the present, invoked the principle of purity and pollution to rank *varnas* and *jatis* and to hinder movement between them. Occupations were made hereditary, and taboos were placed on intermarriage and interdining. These injunctions ensured that individuals did not move out of their inherited occupation. Thus, the basis of what would later become the caste system, which still plays an important role in Indian society, was laid at this time.

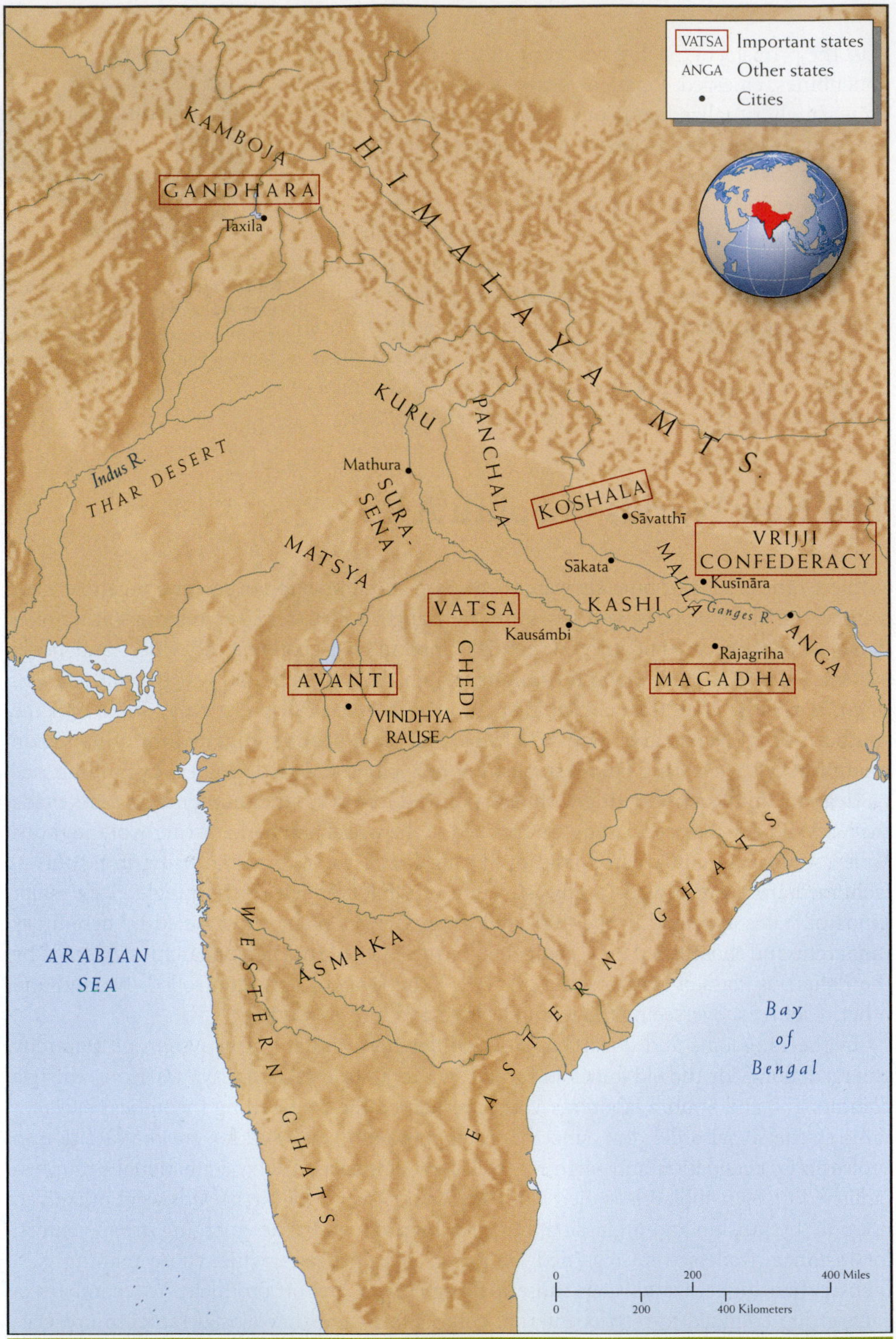

MAP 5.3 | Sixteen States in the First Millennium in South Asia

South Asia underwent profound transformations in the first millennium BCE that reflected growing urbanization, increased commerce, and the emergence of two types of states: monarchies and oligarchies.

- Where did the new states and cities appear?
- What geographic and environmental features encouraged social and cultural integration?
- According to this map, what other regions had influence on South Asia, and where might South Asian culture spread?

NEW CITIES AND A CHANGING ECONOMY

Supported by rice agriculture, cities began to emerge on the Ganges plain around 500 BCE and became centers of commercial and intellectual exchange. Some, such as Shravasti and Rajagriha, thrived as artisanal centers; while others, like Taxila, prospered through trade. These cities of the Ganges plain were dominated by men and women whose occupations—bankers, merchants, and teachers—did not fit easily into the old *varnas*. Precisely laid out streets were crowded with vendors, and wealthy residents employed elephants and horse-drawn chariots to move them about. Alleys leading from the main streets zigzagged between houses built with pebbles and clay. Although city expansion was often haphazard, civic authorities showed great interest in sanitation. The many squares dotting each city had garbage bins, and dirty water drained away in deep sink wells underground. Streets were graded so that rainfall would wash them clean.

The new cities offered exciting opportunities and innovations. Rural householders who moved into them prospered by importing rice and sugarcane from villages to sell in the markets; they then transported manufactured goods such as sugar, salt, and utensils back to their villages. The less affluent turned to craftwork, fashioning textiles, needles, fine pottery, copper plates, ivory decorations, and gold and silver utensils. Other professions included physicians, launderers, barbers, cooks, tailors, and entertainers. The elaborate division of labor suggests high degrees of specialization and commercialization. Those with money became bankers who financed trade and industry. As in Greece and China, coins came into use in these cities at about this time. Traders and bankers established municipal bodies that issued the coins and vouched for their worth. Made of silver, the coins had irregular shapes but specific weights, which determined their value; they also were punch-marked, or stamped with symbols of authority on one side.

Yet, the opportunities and innovations of the new cities did not ensure success for everyone. Many came to cities in search of work, and some fared better than others. As a whole, city dwellers had more material wealth, but their lives were far more uncertain. In addition, urban life created a new social class: those who did the dirtiest jobs, such as removing garbage and sewage, and were therefore viewed as physically and ritually impure "untouchables." Even though their work kept the cities clean, they were forced to live in

Taxila *(Left)* Taxila became the capital of Gandhara, a kingdom located in what is today northern Pakistan and eastern Afghanistan at the time that it was occupied by the Persian Empire in the fifth century BCE. Dharmarajika was one of the most important monasteries. The walkway around the stupa, a mound-like structure containing Buddhist relics, was covered with glass tiles, and the stupa itself was decorated with jewels. *(Right)* This corner of a stupa exhibits a variety of the architectural styles that prevailed in Gandharan art at its height. Both square and round columns are covered by Corinthian capitals. The right arch gate shows the style of Sanchi, the famous stupa in central India.

shantytowns outside the city limits. These outcasts became receptive audiences for those who would challenge Vedic rituals and Brahman priests.

BRAHMANS, THEIR CHALLENGERS, AND NEW BELIEFS

COMPARISON

COMPARE the range of solutions the axial age thinkers devised.

To the Brahmans, nothing about the cities seemed good, and their efforts to retain their superior status prompted new challenges to traditional beliefs. The Brahmans thought that *varnas* and *jatis* mixing indiscriminately polluted society. Moreover, lowborn persons grasping at higher status by acquiring wealth or skill skewed established hierarchies. When an alphabetic script appeared around 600 BCE, sacred knowledge became more accessible, and thus the Brahmans' ability to control the definition of right and wrong was undermined. Formerly, all of Vedic literature had been memorized, and only the brightest Brahmans could master the tradition. (See Chapter 4.)

Frightened by these urban threats, Brahmans sought to strengthen their relationships with the kings by establishing the idea of a monarch endowed with divine power. Kingship had been unnecessary in a long-ago golden age, according to Brahmanic scripts; a moral code and priests to uphold it had been enough to keep things in order. Over time, though, the world deteriorated due to rivalry for wealth. According to Brahmanic writings, the gods then decided that people on earth needed a king to maintain order. The gods enticed a reluctant Manu ("Man") with a range of promises, including one-tenth of the grain harvest, one-fiftieth of the cattle, merits for subjects' good behavior, and the most beautiful woman in his domain. In this Brahmanic account, royal power had a divine origin: the gods chose the king and protected him. Priests and Vedic rituals were essential to royal power, since kingly authority was validated through religious ceremonies carried out by Brahman priests. This emphasis on divine kingship solved some problems but created new ones. The Brahmans' claim to moral authority caused resentment among the Kshatriyas—especially those in the oligarchic republics, whose leaders did not assert divine power. Merchants and artisans also chafed at the Brahmans' claims to superiority. Such resentments provoked challenges to the Brahmans' domination. Some thinkers in South Asia believed that they were in an age of acute crisis because their culture's ancient harmony had been lost. And like many scholars and philosophers elsewhere in this axial era, a new group of South Asian scholars and religious leaders developed their own answers to questions about human existence.

Dissident South Asian thinkers challenged the Brahmans' worldview by refusing to recognize the gods that populated the Vedic world. Some of these rebels sprang from inside the Vedic tradition; though Brahmans, they rejected the idea that sacrificial rituals pleased the gods. To them, God was a universal concept, not a superhuman creature. Also, they felt that the many cows that priests slaughtered for ritual sacrifices could serve more practical uses, such as plowing the land and producing milk. Their discussions and teachings about the universe and life were later collected in the *Upanishads*. Other dissidents, such as Mahavira and the Buddha, came from outside the Vedic tradition.

Mahavira and Jainism Vardhamana Mahavira (c. 540–468 BCE) popularized the doctrines of **Jainism**, which had emerged in the seventh century BCE. Born a Kshatriya in an oligarchic republic, Mahavira left home at age thirty to seek the truth about life; he spent twelve years as an ascetic (one who rejects material possessions and physical pleasures) wandering throughout the Ganges valley before reaching enlightenment. He taught that the universe obeys its own everlasting rules and cannot be affected by any god or other supernatural being. He also believed that the purpose of life is to purify one's soul through asceticism and to attain a state of permanent bliss. The Jains' religious doctrines emphasized the idea that asceticism, rather than knowledge, would enable one to avoid harming other creatures and thereby purify the soul. Since the doctrine of *ahimsa* ("no hurt") held that every living creature has a soul—killing even an ant would result in an unfavorable rebirth—believers had to watch every step to avoid inadvertently becoming murderers. The extreme nonviolence of Jainism was impossible for peasants, who could not work the land without killing insects. Instead, Jainism became a religion of city dwellers and traders. Mahavira's teachings were transmitted orally for nearly a millennium before being compiled into writing by followers in the fifth century CE.

Buddha and Buddhism The most direct challenge to traditional Brahmanic thinking came from Siddhartha Gautama (c. 563–483 BCE), a contemporary of Mahavira and Confucius. Later known as the **Buddha** (Enlightened One), Gautama objected to Brahmanic beliefs, their rituals and sacrifices, and their preference for kingship that kept the priestly class in power. His axial age teachings provided the peoples of South Asia and elsewhere with alternatives to established traditions.

Gautama was born into a comfortable life, the son of a highly respected Kshatriya warrior, in a small oligarchic community nestled in the foothills of the Himalayas. Yet, at the age of twenty-nine, he walked away from everything, leaving behind his father, wife, and newborn son. Family and friends wept as he donned a robe and shaved his head and beard, symbols of the ascetic life that he intended to pursue. Gautama struggled with the belief that the life that he and most others were destined to live would consist of little more than endless episodes of suffering, which began with the pain of childbirth, followed by aging, illness, disease, and death, after which reincarnated beings would experience more of the same.

For six years, Gautama lived as an ascetic wanderer before a forty-nine-day meditation led him to the enlightened moment in which he realized that *nirvana* (spiritual contentment) could be achieved by finding a middle ground between self-indulgence and self-denial. He expressed this new credo as the Four Truths: (1) life, from birth to death, is full of suffering; (2) all sufferings are caused by desires; (3) the only way to rise above suffering is to renounce desire; and (4) the only way to rid oneself of desire is through adherence to the Noble Eightfold Path, which includes wisdom (right views and right intentions), ethical behavior (right conduct, right speech, and right livelihood), and mental discipline (right effort, right thought, and right meditation). This teaching represented a dramatic shift in thinking about humanity and correct behavior. Like the teachings of Mahavira, the Buddha's doctrines left no space for Brahmanic deities to dictate human lives. Buddha's logical explanation of human suffering and his guidelines for renouncing desire appealed to many people for their simplicity, accessibility, and challenge to the Vedic hierarchies. (See **Current Trends in World History: Prophets and the Founding Texts**.)

Like other dissident thinkers of this period, the Buddha delivered his message in a vernacular dialect of Sanskrit that all could understand. His many followers soon formed a community of monks called a *sangha* ("gathering"). The Buddha

Brahman Recluse When Buddhists started to tell stories in sculptures and paintings, Brahmans were included when appropriate. This character in Gandharan Buddhist art probably represents a Brahman who lived as a recluse, instead of as a priest. He is not shaved or dressed, but his expression is passionate.

Current Trends in World History

Prophets and the Founding Texts: Comparing Confucius and the Buddha

World history offers many opportunities to compare one society with another, and this chapter, with its emphasis on teachers, prophets, and intellectuals, in what we have called an axial age, provides an unparalleled moment to contrast the lives and the ideals of central figures whose teachings shaped spiritual movements, legal and political systems, and long-lasting traditions. In Confucianism and Buddhism, we find key leaders who inspired belief systems that were subsequently named for them.

Confucius (Kong Fuzi, 551–479 BCE) was one of the ancient world's great innovators. A government official in Zhou-era China, he elaborated a code of behavior that valued individual performance of traditional rituals and governmental morality based on correct social relationships, sincerity, and justice. Seeing division and war among rival states, he wished to restore order by promoting education, moral behavior, and the performance of rituals.

Over the centuries, the method and substance of his teaching, with many revisions, became the mainstream value system of imperial China. His idea of modeling the state on the patriarchal family—that is, the ruler should respect heaven as if it were his father and protect his subjects as if they were his children—became the foundation of Chinese political theory. Confucius wanted people to perform the rituals bequeathed by the early Zhou and to emulate the sages who had ordered the world according to principles of civility and culture.

Chinese philosophers did not always agree on how to interpret Confucius's ideas. Representing one school of Confucianists, Mencius (372–289 BCE) held that while recognizing the tendency of people to be led astray by worldly appetites and ambitions, he still believed in the inherent goodness of human nature. To recover that innate goodness required moral training. But according to Xunzi (310–237 BCE), Confucius saw humans as evil and lacking an innate moral sense. They therefore had to be controlled by education, ritual, and custom.

Nevertheless, both Mencius and Xunzi embraced Confucius's dictum that people were perfectible through education and the practice of proper conduct. All Confucians, whether pessimists or optimists, viewed moral cultivation through education as the heart of the civilizing process, and they ensured that his ideas remained a vital force throughout Chinese history.

The teachings of the Buddha (Siddhartha Gautama, c. 563–483 BCE), like those of Confucius, had far-reaching influence. The two thinkers were roughly contemporary, and both formulated their ideas in response

and his followers wandered from one city to another on the Ganges plain, where they found large audiences as well as the alms needed to sustain the expanding *sangha*. The Buddha's most influential patrons were urban merchants. In struggles between oligarchs and kings, the Buddha sided with the oligarchs, reflecting his upbringing in an oligarchic republic. He inevitably aroused opposition from the Brahmans, who favored monarchical government. While the Buddha himself did not seek to erase the Vedic hierarchies, Buddhism provided an escape from its oppressive aspects and the prestige that it afforded the Brahmans. Together with Jainism, Buddhism's challenge to Brahmanic thinking appealed particularly in the new urban contexts of South Asia and to those who felt disadvantaged by prevailing Vedic hierarchies in the first millennium BCE.

The Mediterranean World

COMPARISON

EXPLAIN the relationship between axial age thinkers across Afro-Eurasia, and the political and social situations to which they were responding.

Political, economic, and social changes also stimulated new thinking in the Mediterranean world. The violent upheavals that tore through the borderland areas of the northern Levant, the coastal lands of Anatolia, the islands of the Aegean and Mediterranean seas, and mainland Greece in the few centuries after 1000 BCE freed the people in these regions from the domination of Assyria and Persia (Chapter 4). These borderland communities encircling the Mediterranean basin also created second-generation societies that developed new social and political methods of organization and explored new axial age ideas.

to social chaos and degeneration. The Buddha presented a vision of society that challenged the Brahmanic order. Buddhism shaped the views of life and death and the scheme of time and space of the universe in South Asia. It also had a profound impact on peoples outside the region and even replaced Confucianism as the dominant religion in China for a few hundred years.

The Buddha offered a logical approach in the form of a unified system underlying the universe, instead of invoking divine intervention, to understand the universe and social life at a time of rapid political development. He believed that the universe and individual lives go through eternal cycles of birth, death, and rebirth, and he elaborated the concept of *karma* ("fate" or "action"), a universal principle of cause and effect. The birth of every living being, human or animal, reflects actions taken in his or her past lives. Karma embodies the sins and merits of each individual, establishing his or her status in the current life. In turn, deeds in the current life affect that karma and thus determine suffering and happiness in the next life. Buddhist believers therefore focused on the consequences of their actions: through their own behavior, they could attain better future lives.

Confucianism and Buddhism, much like the Vedic, Brahmin, and Judaic faiths discussed in Chapter 4, emerged in times of great turmoil. All the faiths were first transmitted orally; later, adherents created a written record to spread them more widely. But Buddhism and Confucianism stand out in that they have founders whose identification with their belief systems remains their most defining characteristic: the Buddha as an enlightened one, and Confucius as a sage teacher. We will see this phenomenon again with the rise of Christianity (from the teachings of Jesus) and Islam (from the teachings of Muhammad) as we continue our discussion of universalizing religions.

QUESTIONS FOR ANALYSIS

- What is the reward for good moral behavior for Confucius? For Buddha?
- What are the major similarities and differences between these two traditions?

Explore Further

David Schaberg, A *Patterned Past: Form and Thought in Early Chinese Historiography* (2002).

Karen Armstrong, *Buddha* (2001).

Lothar von Falkenhausen, *Chinese Society in the Age of Confucius (1000–250 BC): The Archaeological Evidence* (2006).

Phoenicians, Greeks, Cretans, Cypriots, Lydians, Etruscans, and many others exchanged not only trade goods but also ideas about the virtues of self-sufficient cities whose inhabitants shared power more widely than before. (See Map 5.4.)

FORMATION OF NEW CITY-STATES

In the ninth and eighth centuries BCE, as order returned to the eastern Mediterranean and the population rebounded, peoples who were clustered in more concentrated settlements formed city-states. Unlike the city-states of earlier Mesopotamia, which were governed by semidivine monarchs, or the great urban centers of Southwest Asian empires run by elite scribes, high priests, and monarchs, the Mediterranean city-states were governed by their citizens. These self-governing city-states were a new political form that profoundly influenced the Mediterranean region. This new urban entity—known first by the Phoenicians as a *qart*, then by the Greeks as a *polis*, and the Romans as a *civitas*—multiplied throughout the Mediterranean by the sixth century BCE.

The new principles of rulership were revolutionary. Ordinary residents, or "citizens," of these cities—such as Carthage and Gadir (modern-day Cádiz in Spain) among the western Phoenicians; Athens, Thebes, Sparta, and Corinth among the Greeks; Rome and Praeneste among the early Latins —governed themselves and selected their leaders. Their self-government took various forms, including tyranny (rule by a popularly approved individual), oligarchy (rule by the few), and democracy (rule by all free adult males).

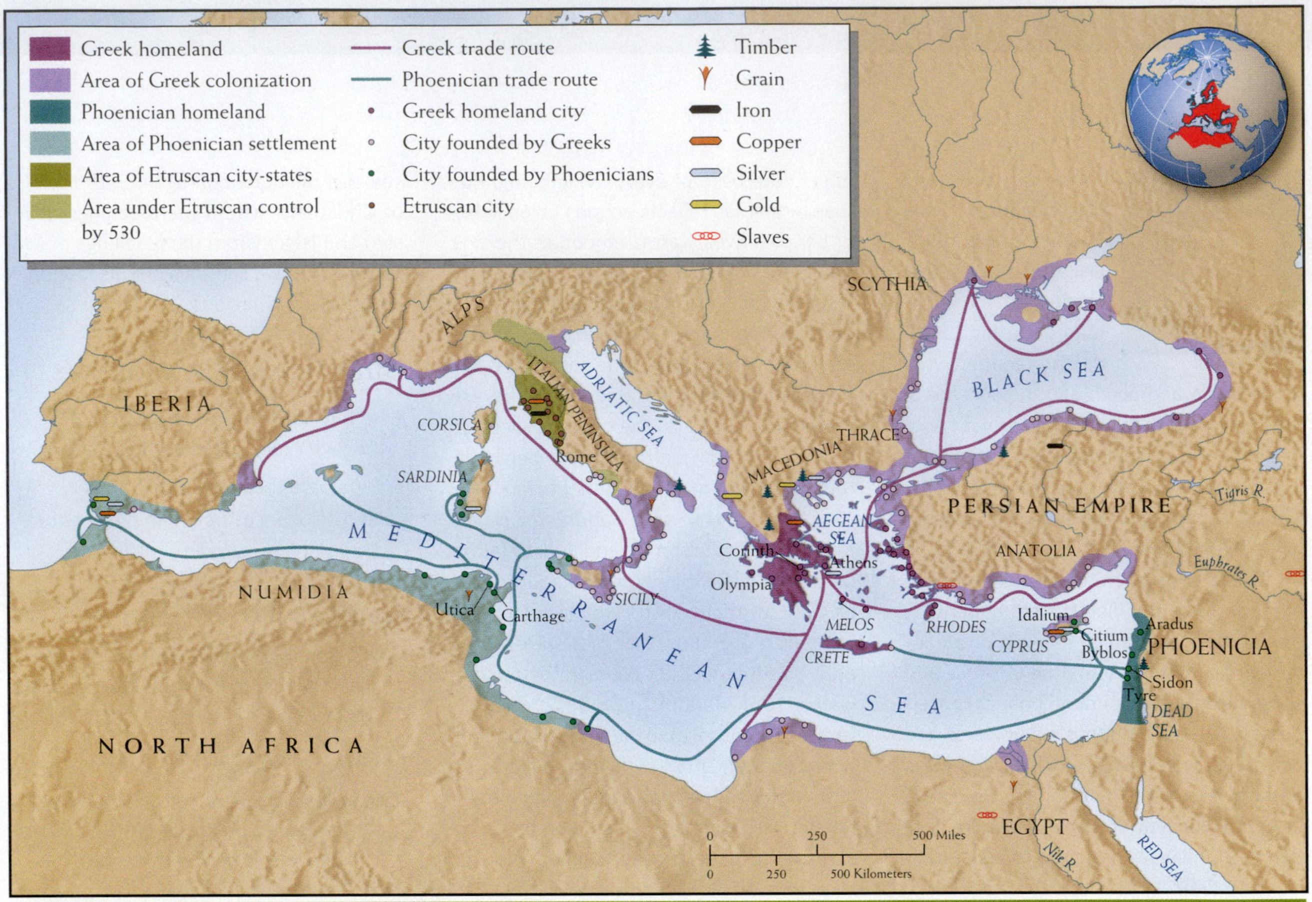

MAP 5.4 | The Mediterranean World

Phoenician and Greek city-states, as well as the colonies they founded, dotted the coastline of both the Mediterranean and Black seas.

- What were the main goods traded in the Mediterranean world in this period?
- What is the relationship between the sites of cities in areas of colonization and the resources and trade routes?
- What areas did the Greeks and Phoenicians control, and what was their main settlement pattern?

The new cities of the Mediterranean basin included adult male citizens, other free persons (including women, who could not vote or hold office), foreign immigrants, and large numbers of unfree persons (including slaves and people tied to the land who could not vote or fight for the polis). The small family unit, or household, was the most important social unit of the city-state and the city-state was seen as a natural outgrowth of the household. Thus, the free adult male was fully entitled to engage in the city's public affairs. In contrast, adult women of free birth remained enclosed within the private world of the family and had no standing to debate policy in public, vote, or hold office. Those enjoying full citizenship rights—the adult freeborn males—in each community decided what tasks, from warfare to public works, the city-state would undertake and what kind of government and laws it would adopt.

City-states were competitive places. Their histories relate rivalries between individuals, social classes, and other groups. Competition for honor and prestige was a value that shaped behavior in the city-states. This extreme competitive ethic found a benign outlet in organized sporting events. Almost from the moment that Greek city-states emerged, athletic contests sprang up. The greatest of these competitions were the Olympic Games, which began in 776 BCE at Olympia in southern Greece. The competitive spirit among communities also took the destructive form of armed conflicts over borderlands, trade, valuable resources, religious shrines, and prestige. The incessant battles among city-states fueled new developments in military equipment, such as the heavy armor that gave its name to the hoplites, or infantrymen, and in tactics, such as the standard block-like configuration (which the Greeks called a *phalanx*) in which the regular rank and file fought. These wars were so destructive that they threatened to destabilize the city-states' world. The most famous conflicts were the Peloponnesian War (431–404 BCE) between Athens and Sparta, and their respective allies, and the ongoing rivalry between the city-states of Rome and Phoenician Carthage (from c. 500 BCE onward). Despite the destabilizing effects of warfare, city-states prospered, and economic innovations facilitated trade and exchange throughout the Mediterranean.

ECONOMIC INNOVATIONS

Without an elaborate top-down bureaucratic and administrative structure, residents of the new cities devised other ways to run their commercial affairs. They developed open trading markets and a system of money that enabled buyers and sellers to know the precise value of commodities so that exchanges were efficient. At their center, the new city-states had a marketplace (*agora*), a large open area where individuals bought and sold commodities. These increasingly complex transactions required money, rather than barter or gift exchange. Like the states in Eastern Zhou China and Vedic South Asia, by the end of the fifth century BCE the Greek city-states were also issuing a striking variety of coins, and other peoples such as the Phoenicians, Etruscans, and Persians were using them. Coins bought services, as well, perhaps at first to hire mercenary soldiers. In the absence of large bureaucracies, Mediterranean cities relied on money to connect the producers and buyers of goods and services, especially as city-states became more far-flung.

The Agora The agora, or central open marketplace, was one of the core defining features of Mediterranean city-states. At its center, each city had one of these open-air plazas, the heart of its commercial, religious, social, and political life. When a new city was founded, the agora was one of the first places that the colonists measured out. The large, rectangular, open area in this picture is the agora of the Greek colonial city of Cyrene (in modern-day Libya).

Mediterranean Coins From the sixth century BCE onward, money in the form of precious metal coins began spreading through the city-states of the Mediterranean, beginning with the Greek city-states in the western parts of what is today Turkey, then spreading to the other Greek *poleis* and beyond. On the left here is the classic tetradrachm (four-drachma piece) coin of Athens with its owl of the goddess Athena; on the right is a silver coin of shekel weight produced by the city of Carthage in the western Mediterranean.

Indeed, the search for silver, iron, copper, and tin drove traders westward across the Mediterranean. By about 500 BCE the Phoenicians, Greeks, and others from the eastern Mediterranean had planted new city-states around the shores of the western Mediterranean and the Black Sea. Once established, these colonial communities became completely independent and transformed the coastal world. City-based life was common from southern Spain and western Italy to the Crimea on the Black Sea. With amazing speed, seaborne communications spread a Mediterranean-wide urban culture that bolstered the region's wealthy and powerful elites. Found among the local elites of Tartessos in southern Spain, the Gallic chiefs in southern France, and the Etruscan and Roman nobles of central Italy, a new aristocratic culture featured similar public displays of wealth: richly decorated chariots, elaborate armor and weapons, fine dining ware, elaborate houses, and public burials. From the western end of the Mediterranean to the Black Sea, the city-state communities developed a culture founded on market-based economies and private property.

In contrast to the privilege enjoyed by these elites was the traffic in human flesh: slavery. Treating men, women, and children as objects of commerce, to be bought and sold in markets, created a new form of commercial slavery called chattel slavery. When dangerous and exhausting tasks such as mining and farming required extra labor, freeborn citizens purchased slave laborers. These slaves were mainly war captives. In some city-states, slaves may have constituted up to a quarter of the population. In every one of the new city-states, slaves provided manual and technical labor of all kinds and produced the agricultural surpluses that supported the urban population.

NEW IDEAS

New ways of thinking about the world emerged from the competitive atmosphere that the Greek city-states fostered. In the absence of monarchical or priestly rule, ideas were free to arise, circulate, and clash. Individuals argued publicly about the nature of the gods, the best state, what is good, and whether to wage war. There was no final authority to give any particular idea a final stamp of approval and force its acceptance. New ideas emerged in science and the arts, and Greek philosophers proposed theories on human society and many other topics.

Naturalistic Science and Realistic Art In this competitive marketplace of ideas, some daring thinkers developed novel ways of perceiving the cosmos and representing the environment. Rather than seeing everything as the handiwork of all-powerful deities, they took a naturalistic view of humans and their place in the universe. This new thinking was evident in their art, which idealized the natural world. Artists increasingly represented humans, objects, and landscapes not in abstract, idealized, or formal ways but in "natural" ways, as they appeared to the human eye. Even their portrayals of gods became more humanlike. Later, these objective and natural views of humans and nature became the new ideals, the highest of which was the unadorned human figure: the nude became the centerpiece of Greek art. Individual artists—such as the vase painter Exekias, the sculptor Praxiteles, and the poet Sappho—began to sign their works in a clear manifestation of the new sense of the individual being freed from the restraints of an autocratic state or a controlling religious system.

The Human Form The human body as it appeared naturally, without any adornment, became the ideal set by Greek art. Even gods were portrayed in the same natural nude human form. This statue by Praxiteles is of the god Dionysus and the child Hermes. Such bold nude portraits of humans and gods were sometimes shocking to other peoples.

New Thinking and Greek Philosophers Axial age thinkers in city-states such as Miletus and Ephesus in western Anatolia did not accept traditional explanations of how and why the universe worked. Each thinker competed to outdo his peers in offering persuasive and comprehensive explanations of the cosmos, and their theories became ever more radical. For instance, Thales (c. 636–546 BCE) believed that water was the primal substance from which all other things were created. Xenophanes (c. 570–480 BCE) doubted the very existence of gods as they had been portrayed, asserting instead that only one general divine aura suffused all creation but that ethnic groups produced images of gods in their own likeness. Democritus (c. 460–370 BCE) claimed that everything was comprised of small and ultimately indivisible particles, which he called *atoma* ("uncuttables"). Pythagoras (c. 570–495 BCE), who devoted himself to the study of numbers, held that a wide range of physical phenomena, like musical sounds, were in fact based in numbers. This rich competition among ideas led to a more aggressive mode of public thinking, which the Greeks called *philosophia* ("love of wisdom").

In the fifth century BCE **Greek philosophers** (wisdom-lovers) were focusing on humans and their place in society. Some of these professional thinkers tried to describe an ideal state, characterized by harmonious relationships and free from corruption and political decline. One such thinker was Socrates (469–399 BCE), a philosopher who frequented the agora at Athens and encouraged people to reflect on ethics and morality, even as the Peloponnesian War raged on. (See **Analyzing Global Developments: Axial Age Thinkers and Their Ideas**.) He stressed the importance of honor and integrity as opposed

Analyzing Global Developments

Axial Age Thinkers and Their Ideas

In the mid-twentieth century, the German philosopher Karl Jaspers invented the term "axial age" to describe the importance of ideas that originated in the first millennium BCE. These thinkers and their ideas are characterized as "axial" because: 1) they were a pivot point, or axis, that seemed to turn the world in a new direction, 2) they occurred along an East-West axis stretching from the Mediterranean to East Asia, and 3) they are central to ethical thought even down to the present day. These axial age philosophers were both the product of, and a challenge to, the societies from which they came—in other words, they were spurred by complex social and political contexts to develop their new ideas, but these new ideas in many ways critiqued and offered alternatives to the status quo. The chart below does not represent every axial age tradition, but is meant to draw into relief the relationship between the innovative thinkers, their historical context, and the tenets of the new belief systems.

QUESTIONS FOR ANALYSIS

- What connections, if any, can be made between the geopolitical situation of a society and the axial age philosophy that sprang from that region? In what ways does each philosopher support or challenge the status quo?
- Jaspers was particularly impressed that societies he understood as being disconnected from one another would develop philosophical ideas so similar. How might the temporal and geographic relationship of the philosophers listed on the chart be explained? How do connections with other regions, or lack thereof, impact the development of these ideas? What might account for similarities and differences in these axial age philosophies?
- What are the similarities and differences in how these philosophers' ideas were transmitted through time?

THINKER	PHILOSOPHY	CORE TEXT	HISTORICAL CONTEXT	CENTRAL TENET	EXEMPLARY SAYINGS
Zoroaster, a.k.a. Zarathustra (1000–600 BCE)	Zoroastrianism	Avesta, the most sacred part of which is the Gathas, seventeen Middle Persian hymns purportedly written by Zoroaster himself	Southwest Asia, based in eastern Iranian nomadic culture, eventually becoming the central religion of Persian Empire	**Dualistic ethical system,** a world order based on the cosmic struggle between Ahura Mazda, the god of light (good), and Ahriman , the god of destruction (evil). Humans must choose between good and evil with reward or retribution doled out in the afterlife	**On dualism:** "There [are] . . . two spirits [present] in the primal [stage of one's existence], twins who have . . . [manifested themselves as] the two [kinds] of dreams, . . . thoughts and words, . . . [and] actions, the better and the evil." (30.3) **On rewards:** "Brilliant things . . . will be for the person who comes to the truthful one. But a long period of darkness, foul food, and the word 'woe'—to such an existence your religious view will lead you, O deceitful ones, of your own actions." (31.20)
Ezekiel (sixth century BCE), Isaiah (mid-6th century BCE), among other Jewish writers and prophets	Judaism	The Hebrew Bible, whose second part, Nevi'im, contains the writings of the prophets	Southwest Asia, with origins in Mesopotamian tribal cultures, eventually spreading to the early empires of Egypt and the Levant	A strict monotheistic tradition which dictates that its followers are the chosen people and have entered a **covenant,** or contractual relationship, with their god	**On monotheism:** "I am the first and I am the last; besides me there is no god." (Isaiah 44:6) **On the covenant:** "[. . .] I will make a new covenant . . . not like the covenant which I made with their fathers . . . to bring them out of the land of Egypt, my covenant which they broke, though I was their husband, says the Lord." (Jeremiah 31:31–32) **On individual responsibility:** "The righteousness of the righteous shall be upon himself, and the wickedness of the wicked shall be upon himself." (Ezekiel 18:20)

Sources: H. Humbach and I. Ichaporia, *The Heritage of Zarathustra* (Heidelberg, 1994); Helmut Humbach "Gathas, i. Texts," *Encyclopedia Iranica* (2000) vol. X, fasc. 3, pp. 321–27; William W. Malandra, "Gathas, ii. Translations," *Encyclopedia Iranica* (2000) vol. X, fasc. 3, pp. 327–30; Thomas G. West and Grace Starry West, *Four Texts on Socrates* (Cornell, 1984); D. C. Lau's translation of *Analects* in H. James, ed., *Norton Anthology of World Literature, vol. 1* (Norton, 2002), pp. 820–30; *The Dhammapada,* translated by Juan Mascaro (Penguin, 1973); *New Oxford Annotated Bible with Apocrypha,* Revised Standard Version (Oxford).

THINKER	PHILOSOPHY	CORE TEXT	HISTORICAL CONTEXT	CENTRAL TENET	EXEMPLARY SAYINGS
Siddhartha Gautama, later known as Buddha (c. 563–483 BCE)	Buddhism	Dhammapad, verse sayings of the Buddha, which were recorded in the third century BCE	India, as a challenge to Kshatriya oligarchy and the hierarchical system of the Vedic society	An ethical system governed by the **Four Noble Truths:** 1. Life is suffering 2. Suffering is rooted in attachment 3. Escape suffering by escaping attachment 4. Escape attachment via the **Eight-fold Path** of right view, intention, speech, action, livelihood, effort, mindfulness, and concentration	**On the Eight-fold Path:** The best of the paths is the path of eight. The best of the truths, the four sayings. The best of states, freedom from passions. The best of men, the one who sees. (*Dhammapada*, 273) **On extremes:** "He who lives not for pleasures, and whose soul is in self-harmony, who eats and fasts with moderation, and has faith and the power of virtue—this man is not moved by temptations, as a great rock is not shaken by the wind (8)
Kong Fuzi, also known as Confucius (551–479 BCE)	Confucianism	*Analects*, Confucius's dialogues with state leaders and students that were most likely recorded centuries later	China, during political turmoil toward the end of the Spring and Autumn period (722–481 BCE)	The code of moral behavior, as exemplified in the *junzi* (gentleman or superior man), centered on: ***ren*** (benevolence) ***li*** (proper ritual) ***xiao*** (filial piety)	**On virtue:** "The rule of virtue can be compared to the Pole Star which commands the homage of the multitude of stars without leaving its place." (II.1) **On respect:** "Duke Ai asked: 'What must I do before the common people will look up to me?' Confucius answered: 'Raise the straight and set them over the crooked and the common people will look up to you.'" (II.19)
Socrates (469–399 BCE)	Greek Philosophy	Dialogues recorded in the contemporary work of his students, especially Plato, and a collection of his sayings published later on	Greece, during a period of Greco-Perisan conflict and inter-city-state wars	Ethical code that encourages self-discovery through knowledge, the recognition of the limits to one's own faculties, and the questioning of authority to find truth	**On self-discovery:** "The unexamined life is not worth living for a human being." (*Apology* 38a) **On wisdom:** "I am wiser than this human being, for probably neither of us knows anything noble and good; but he supposes he knows something, when he does not know; while I, just as I do not know, do not even suppose that I do." (*Apology* 21d)
Jesus (6/4 BCE–ca. 30 CE)	Christianity	Sayings later known through canonical and noncanonical Christian Gospels, first put in writing in the late first century CE	Levant, specifically in Judea under Roman imperial rule, later spreads throughout the Indo-Mediterranean	God's personal relationship with humanity mediated by His son, Jesus, whose suffering expiates human sins and grants eternal life to believers	**On ethical thought:** "Blessed are you poor, for yours is the kingdom of God; Blessed are you that hunger now, for you shall be satisfied . . . Love your enemies, do good to those who hate you. . . ." (Luke 6:20–38) **On Judaism:** "'Love the Lord your God . . . ' This is the first . . . commandment. And the second is like it: 'Love your neighbor as yourself.' All the Law and the Prophets hang on these two commandments." (Matthew 22:37–40)

to wealth and power (just as Confucius had done in Eastern Zhou China and the Buddha in Vedic South Asia). Plato (427–347 BCE), a student of Socrates, presented Socrates's philosophy in a series of dialogues (much as Confucius's students had written down his thoughts). In *The Republic*, Plato envisioned a perfect city that philosopher-kings would rule. He thought that if fallible humans could imitate this model city more closely, their states would be less susceptible to the decline that was affecting the Greek city-states of his own day.

Plato's most famous pupil answered the same questions about nature and the acquisition of knowledge differently. Deeply interested in the natural world, Aristotle (384–322 BCE) believed that by collecting and studying all the facts one could about a given thing, one could achieve a better understanding. His main idea was that the interested inquirer can find out more about the world by collecting as much evidence as possible about a given thing and then making deductions from these data about general patterns. This was in stark contrast to Plato's claim that everything a person observes is in fact only a flawed copy of the "real" thing that exists in a thought-world of abstract patterns accessible only by pure mental meditation—completely the opposite of Aristotle's method. This competition of ideas raged on for centuries, with the new thinking of these Mediterranean axial age philosophers at times fueling the aspirations of the city-states and at other times challenging them.

Common Cultures in the Americas and Sub-Saharan Africa

COMPARISON

COMPARE the political, cultural, and social developments across Afro-Eurasia with those occurring in the Americas and sub-Saharan Africa.

During what we have termed the axial age in Eurasia and North Africa, peoples living in the Americas and most of sub-Saharan Africa built complex, urban-based societies for the first time. These regions did not have immense cities, elaborate written texts, domesticated animals, and the other ingredients that underlay the radical new ideas of this era. Nonetheless, among the Chavín of the Andes, the Olmecs of Mesoamerica, the peoples of Nubia, and the West African Nok, exciting new developments were taking place in the first millennium BCE. Since the written record from these communities is limited, however, knowledge of their societies and beliefs is based largely in archaeological remains.

THE CHAVÍN IN THE ANDES

Around 1400 BCE, as the **Chavín** peoples began to share a common belief system, they also began to organize their societies vertically along the steep mountainsides and deep fertile valleys of the Andes. (See Map 5.1.) Valley floors yielded tropical and subtropical produce; the mountains supported maize and other crops; and in the highlands, potatoes became a staple and llamas produced wool and dung (used as fertilizer and fuel) and, eventually, served as beasts of burden. Llamas could not transport humans, however, so the Chavín migratory and political reach remained limited. While most necessities were available nearby thanks to the ecological diversity of the region, the Chavín did undertake some long-distance trade—mainly in dyes and precious stones, such as obsidian. By 900 BCE, the Chavín were erecting elaborate stone carvings, using advanced techniques to weave fine cotton textiles, and making gold, silver, and copper metal goods. Scholars have found evidence that by 400 BCE trade in painted textiles, ceramics, and gold objects spanned the Pacific coast, the Andean highlands, and the watershed eastward to the tropical rainforests of the Amazon basin.

What unified the fragmented Chavín communities was a shared artistic tradition manifested in their devotion to powerful deities. Their spiritual capital was the central temple complex of Chavín de Huántar, in modern Peru's northeastern highlands. The temple boasted

El Lanzón The Chavín excelled at elaborate stone carvings with complex images of their deities. This image of El Lanzón is a good example. At the center of one of the Chavín peoples' greatest temples is a massive gallery with this giant monument in the middle, etched with images of snakes, felines, and humans combined into one hybrid supernatural form. Observe the hands and feet with claws and the eyebrows that turn into serpents. The rendering on the right makes it easier to see the details on the actual object.

a U-shaped platform whose opening to the east surrounded a sunken, circular plaza. From its passageways and underground galleries, priests—whom the Chavín believed were transformed into jaguars through their consumption of hallucinogenic drugs—could make dramatic entrances during ceremonies. Pilgrims brought tribute to Chavín de Huántar, where they worshipped and feasted together. The Chavín drew on influences from as far away as the Amazon and the Pacific coast as they created devotional cults that revered wild animals as representatives of spiritual forces. Carved stone jaguars, serpents, and hawks, baring their large fangs and claws to remind believers of nature's powers, dominated the spiritual landscape. The Chavín cult gave way around 400 BCE to local cultural heirs, but some elements of it survived in successor religions adopted by stronger states to the south.

THE OLMECS IN MESOAMERICA

Further to the north, the first complex society in Mesoamerica emerged around 1500 BCE between the highland plateaus of central Mexico and the Gulf Coast around modern-day Veracruz. (See Map 5.5.) The **Olmecs** are an example of a first-generation community that created new political and economic institutions while contemplating profound questions about the nature of humanity and the world beyond. The culture of the Olmecs—a name meaning "inhabitants in the land of rubber," one of their staples—sprang up from local village roots. The region's peoples formed a loose confederation of villages scattered from the coast to the highlands, mainly nestling in river valleys and along the shores of swampy lakes. Their residents traded with one another, shared a common language, and worshipped the same gods. Around 1500 BCE, the residents of hundreds of hamlets began to develop a single culture and to spread their beliefs, artistic achievements, and social structure far beyond their heartland.

At the core of Olmec culture were its decentralized villages, which housed hundreds—possibly thousands—of households apiece. In these settlements productive subsistence

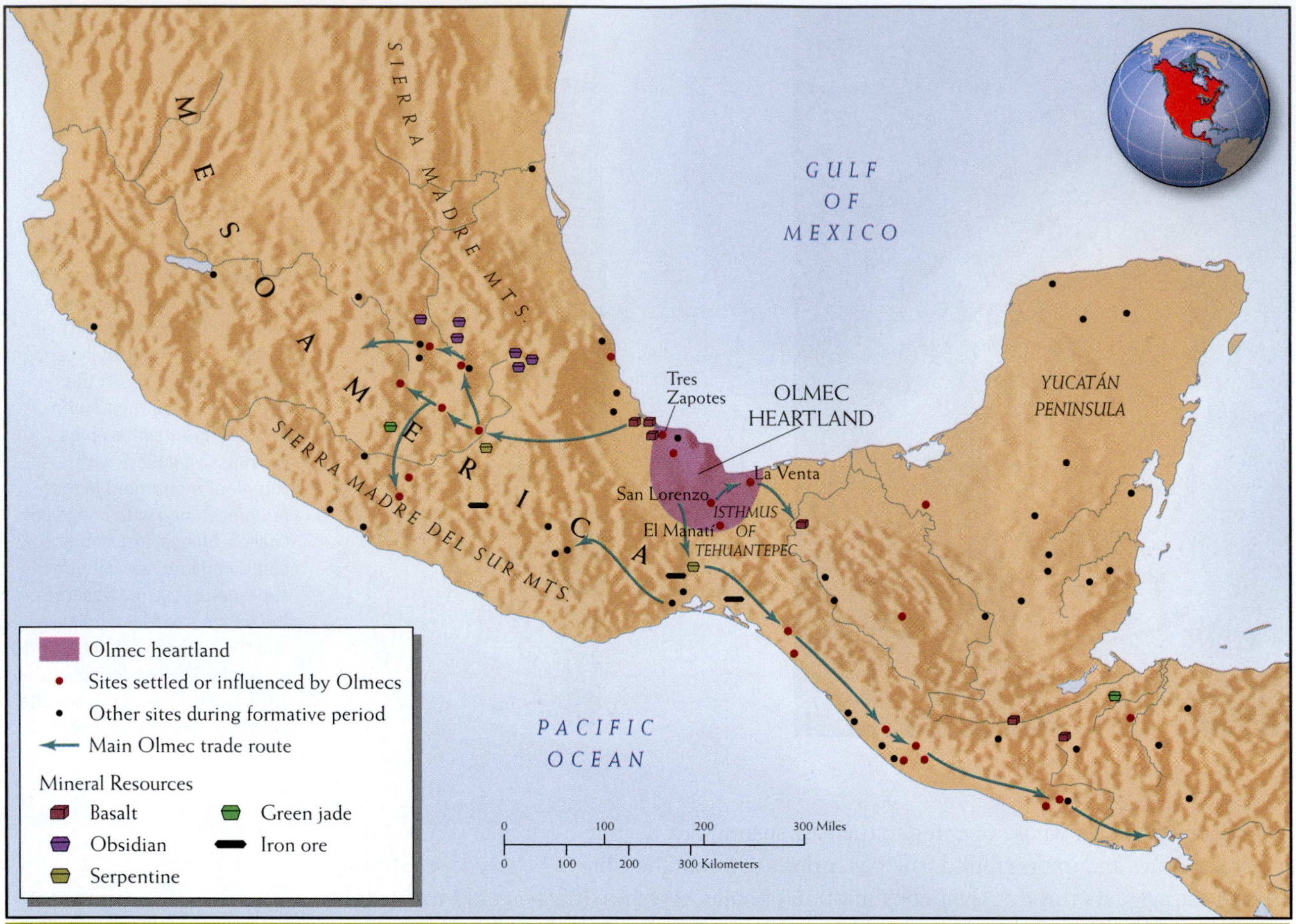

MAP 5.5 | The Olmec World

The Olmecs had a strong impact on Mesoamerica's early cultural integration.

- According to this map, how did they influence people living beyond the Olmec heartland?
- What geographical factors limited the extent of Olmec influence?
- What is the relationship between resources, trade routes, and Olmec settlements?

farmers cultivated most of the foodstuffs their communities needed (especially maize, beans, squash, and cacao), while shipping lightweight products including ceramics and precious goods (such as jade, obsidian, or quetzal feathers, used to create masks and ritual figurines) to other villages. Most of the precious objects were for religious purposes rather than everyday consumption. Despite their dispersed social landscape, the Olmec peoples created shared belief systems, a single language, and a priestly class who ensured that villagers and residents of the new urban centers followed highly ritualized practices.

Cities as Sacred Centers The primary Olmec cities, including San Lorenzo, La Venta, and Tres Zapotes, were small compared with the urban centers of Afro-Eurasia, but they served as devotional and secular hubs. The cities featured specialized structures that included massive earthen mounds, platforms, palaces, capacious plazas, and large stone monuments (colossal heads, jaguar sculptures, and basalt thrones). Beneath the mounds of the devotional centers, archaeologists have found axes, knives of sharpened obsidian, other tools, and jade figurines, buried as tokens for those who dwelled in the supernatural world. Olmec devotional art depicted natural and supernatural entities—not just snakes, jaguars, and crocodiles, but also certain humans called shamans, whom the Olmecs believed could commune with the supernatural and transform themselves wholly or partly into beasts. A common figurine is the "were-jaguar," a being that was part man, part animal. Shamans representing jaguars invoked the Olmec rain god, a jaguar-like being, to bring rainfall and secure the land's fertility.

A range of agriculture-linked devotional activity thrived in the Olmecs' major cities. Noble players competed in a complex ball game to honor the rain god, as fans cheered on. Olmec archaeological sites are filled with the remains of game equipment and trophies, some of which were entombed with dead rulers so they could play ball with the gods in the otherworld. It is likely that athletics and human sacrifice were blended in the same rituals. Many monuments depict a victorious and costumed ballplayer (sporting a jaguar headdress or a feathered serpent helmet) atop a defeated, bound human, though scholars are not sure whether the losers were literally executed. Nevertheless, rainmaking rites did include human sacrifice, which involved executing and dismembering captives. The Olmecs believed that the gods defined calendric passages, and thus the seasons and crucial rainfall patterns. Priests, charting celestial movements, devised a complex calendar that marked the passage of seasons and generations. Indeed, Olmecs' ceremonial life—from ball games to human sacrifice to calendars—was focused on agricultural and rainfall cycles.

A World of Social Distinctions Unlike many decentralized agrarian cultures that were simple and egalitarian, the Olmecs developed an elaborate cultural system marked by many tiers of social rankings. Daily labor kept village-focused Olmecs busy. The vast majority worked the fertile lands as part of household units, with children and parents toiling in the fields with wooden tools, fishing in streams with nets, and hunting turtles and other small animals. Most Olmecs juggled the needs of their immediate families, their village neighbors, and the taxes imposed by rulers.

The priestly class, raised and trained in the palaces at La Venta, San Lorenzo, and Tres Zapotes, directed the exchanges of sacred ritual objects among farming communities. Alongside the priestly elite emerged a secular elite composed of chieftains who supervised agrarian transactions, oversaw artisans, and accepted villagers' tribute. The highest-ranking chieftains commanded villages scattered over a large territory. The chieftains set up workshops, managed by foremen, where craftworkers created pots, painted, sculpted, and wove. Some of their work featured stones and gems imported from surrounding villages.

It is likely that a merchant class also developed to facilitate trade throughout Olmec territories and beyond. As the Olmecs' arts expanded, so did their demand for imported obsidian and jade, seashells, plumes, and other precious goods. The Olmecs exported rubber, cacao, pottery, ceramics, figurines, jaguar pelts, and crocodile skins throughout Mesoamerica. They also conveyed their belief system to neighbors—if not to convert them, at least to influence them and reinforce a sense of superiority.

The Loss of Centers The breakdown of the Olmec culture around the middle of the first millennium is shrouded in mystery. The decline was abrupt in some centers and drawn out in others. At La Venta, the altars and massive basalt heads were defaced and buried, indicating a dramatic shift. Yet there is little evidence of a spasm of war, a peasant uprising, a population shift, or conflict within the ruling classes. Indeed, in many parts of the heartland, the religious centers that had been the hubs of the Olmec world were abandoned but not destroyed. As the bonds between rulers and subjects weakened, so did the exchange of ritual objects that had enlivened the Olmec centers and made them magnets for obedience and piety. Although Olmec hierarchies collapsed, much of the Olmec hinterland remained heavily populated and highly productive. While it lasted, the Olmec combination of an integrated culture, a complex hierarchical social structure, and urban-centered devotional practice offered a degree of cohesion unprecedented in the Americas.

COMMON CULTURES IN SUB-SAHARAN AFRICA

In Africa, too, widespread common cultures emerged in a number of favorable locations. Africa's most significant climate-related historical development in the first millennium BCE was the continued drying up of the northern and central landmass and the sprawl of the great Sahara Desert. (See Map 5.6.) Large areas that had once supported abundant plant and animal life, including human settlements, now became sparsely populated. As a result, the African peoples began to coalesce in a few locations. Most important was the Nile Valley, which may have held more than half of the entire population of Africa at this time.

Climatic change divided Africa from the equator northward to the Sahara Desert into four zones. The first zone was the Sahara itself, which never completely emptied out despite its extreme heat and aridity. Its oases supported pastoral peoples, who raised livestock and promoted contacts between the northern and western parts of the landmass. South of the Sahara was the Sahel, literally the "coast" (Arabic *sahil*) of the great ocean of sand, which saw no city of great size in this period. The next zone was the Sudanic savanna, an area of high grasslands stretching from present-day Senegal along the Atlantic Ocean in the west to the Nile River and the Red Sea in the east. Many of West Africa's kingdoms later emerged there because the area was free of the tsetse fly, which was as lethal to animals as to humans, killing off cattle, horses, and goats. The fourth zone comprised the western and central African rain forests, a sparsely populated region characterized by small-scale societies.

Although there was contact across the Sahara, Africa below the Sahara differed markedly from North Africa and Eurasia. It did not develop plow agriculture; instead, its farmers depended on hoes. Also, except in densely populated regions, land was held communally and never carried as much value as labor, which was in short supply. African peoples could always move into new locations. They had more difficulty finding workers to turn the soil. In the savanna, millet and sorghum were the primary food crops; in the rain forests, yams and other root crops predominated. Relatively large populations inhabited the Sudanic savanna, the sole area for which substantial historical records exist. Here, in fact, a way of life that historians call Sudanic began to crystallize.

These Sudanic peoples were not completely dependent on their feet to get around (in contrast to their llama-reliant counterparts in the Americas). They had domesticated several animals, including cattle and goats, and even possessed small horses. Although their communities were scattered widely across this region of Africa, they had much in common. For example, they all possessed religious beliefs dominated by a high god, polities led by sacred kings, and burial customs of interring servants alongside dead rulers to serve them in the afterlife. Sudanic peoples were skilled cultivators and weavers of cotton, which they had domesticated. Archaeologists and historians used to believe that the Sudanic peoples borrowed their institutions, notably their sacred kingships, from their Egyptian neighbors; but linguistic evidence and their burial customs indicate that the Sudanic communities developed these practices independently.

Nubia: Kush and Meroe One of the most highly developed locations of common culture in sub-Saharan Africa was Nubia, a region lying between the first Nile cataract (a large waterfall) and the sixth, just north of where the Blue and White Niles come together. From at least the fourth millennium BCE onward, peoples in this region had contact with both the northern and southern parts of the African landmass. It was one of the few parts of sub-Saharan Africa known to the Eurasian world during this period.

By the second and first millennia BCE, complex societies formed and developed into states in Nubia. The first of the important Nubian states was Kush. It flourished between 1700 and 1500 BCE between the first and third cataracts, and had its capital at Kerma. Because of its proximity to Egypt, it adopted many Egyptian cultural and political practices, even as it was under constant pressure from the northern powerhouse. Its successor

MAP 5.6 | Africa, 500 BCE

The first millennium BCE was a period of cultural, economic, and political integration for North and sub-Saharan Africa.

- According to this map, what effect did the Mediterranean colonies have on Africa? What main factor integrated Kush, Nubia, and Egypt?
- Does the map reveal a relationship between the rise of Sudanic culture and the spread of iron working? If so, what is it?

states had to move farther south, up the Nile, to keep free from the powerful Egyptians; the kingdom's capitals were repeatedly uprooted and relocated upriver.

Nubia was Egypt's corridor to sub-Saharan Africa, a source of ivory, gold, and slaves; and an area that Egyptian monarchs wanted to dominate. To the Egyptians, the land of Kush and its people were there to be exploited, not conquered, as Egyptians had no desire to live there. Ramses II left his mark with his magnificent monuments at the Nubian site Abu Simbel around 1250 BCE.

Building on the foundations of earlier kings who had ruled Nubia, the **Meroe** kingdom arose in the fourth century BCE and flourished until 300 CE. Its rulers were influenced by the pharaonic culture, adapting hieroglyphs, erecting pyramids in which to bury their rulers, viewing their kings as divine, and worshipping the Egyptian god Amun. Meroe became a thriving center of production and commerce. Its residents were especially skilled in iron smelting and the manufacture of textiles, and their products circulated widely throughout Africa. However, Meroe was equally a part of the Sudanic savanna way of life—as evidenced by the distinctiveness of the language and the determination of its inhabitants to retain political autonomy from Egypt, including, if necessary, moving farther south, out of the orbit of Egypt and more into the orbit of Sudanic polities. Although they called their kings pharaohs, the influential leaders of Meroe selected them from among the many members of the royal family, attempting to ensure that their rulers were men of proven talents. In addition, the Nubian states had close commercial contacts with other merchants and commercial hubs in Sudanic Africa.

West African Kingdoms Complex societies also thrived in West Africa. The most spectacular West African culture of the first millennium BCE was the Nok culture, which arose in the sixth century BCE in an area that is today the geographical center of Nigeria. Though slightly south of the savanna lands of West Africa, the area was (and still is) in regular contact with that region. At Taruga, near the present-day village of Nok, early

Nubian pyramids at Meroe In imitation of Egyptian pharaohs more than a millennium ago, Meroitic royalty constructed pyramids for their burials. Smaller and steeper than Egyptian pyramids, they were decorated with reliefs on their interior walls and filled with grave goods from the Mediterranean world.

iron smelting occurred in 600 BCE. Taruga may well have been the first place in western Africa where iron ores were smelted. Ironworking was significant for the Nok peoples, who moved from using stone materials directly to iron, bypassing bronze and copper. They made iron axes and hoes, iron knives and spears, and luxury items for trade. The Nok achieved historical fame not for their iron-smelting prowess but for their magnificent terra-cotta figurines, discovered in the 1940s in the tin-mining region of central Nigeria. These naturalistic figures date to at least 500 BCE. They were likely altarpieces for a cult associated with the land's fertility. Placed next to new lands that were coming into cultivation, they were believed to bless the soil and enhance its productivity.

The Nok were not the only culture developing in this region. Peoples living in the Senegal River basin and Mande peoples around the western branch of the Niger River also began to establish large settlements, in which artisans smelted iron ore and wove textiles, and merchants engaged in long-distance trade. West Africa was also home to the Bantu-speaking peoples destined to play a major role in the history of the landmass. Around 300 BCE, small Bantu groups began to migrate southward into the equatorial rain forests, where they cleared land for farming; from there, some moved on to southern Africa. (See Chapter 8 for a discussion of the Bantu peoples.) As impressive as the iron working, figurines, and trade of West Africa were, these cultures were not yet producing—or at least there is no record of—the type of axial age developments that were happening in much of Eurasia.

Conclusion

Afro-Eurasia's great river-basin areas—the Nile, the Tigris-Euphrates, the Indus—were still important in the first millennium BCE, but their time as centers of world cultures was passing. Now they yielded some of their leadership to regions that had been on the fringes, whether the Mediterranean in the west or the Ganges in the east. Within the territorial states in China, the kingdoms and oligarchies in urbanizing South Asia, and the city-states in the Mediterranean world, great social and intellectual dynamism occurred.

During this axial age across much of Eurasia, influential thinkers came to the fore with perspectives quite different from those of the earlier river-basin civilizations and other contemporary developments elsewhere in worlds apart. In China, the political instability of the Warring States period propelled scholars such as Confucius to engage in political debate, where they stressed respect for social hierarchy. In South Asia, dissident thinkers challenged the Brahmanic spiritual and political order, and the Buddha articulated a religious belief system that was much less hierarchical than its Vedic predecessor. Mediterranean Greek philosophers offered new views about nature, their political world, and human relations and values—based primarily on secular rather than religious ideas.

Even where contacts with other societies were less intense, innovations occurred as first complex societies began to arise in the Americas and in sub-Saharan Africa. In the Americas, the Olmecs developed a worldview in which mortals had to appease angry gods through human sacrifice, and built elaborate temples where many peoples could pay homage to the same deities. In West Africa, the Nok peoples promoted interregional trade and cultural contact as they expanded their horizons. In sub-Saharan Africa, settled pockets devised complex cultural foundations for community life. One spectacular example of sub-Saharan and Egyptian synthesis was the Nubian culture of Meroe. As the world was coalescing into culturally distinct regions, many of the ideas newly forged in Eurasia, the Americas, and sub-Saharan Africa had a continuing impact on societies that followed.

After You Read This Chapter

Go to INQUIZITIVE to see what you've learned—and learn what you've missed—with personalized feedback along the way.

TRACING THE GLOBAL STORYLINES

FOCUS ON: *Innovative Societies*

CHINA

- Multistate system emerges from warfare, revolutionizing society and thought.
- Confucius and Master Lao outline new ideals of governing and living.

SOUTH ASIA

- Small monarchies and urban oligarchies emerge after the Vedic peoples' migrations and rule over societies organized around the varna system.
- Dissident thinkers like Mahavira and the Buddha challenge Brahman priests and the caste system.

THE MEDITERRANEAN WORLD

- Independent city-states emerge from social destruction and facilitate revolutionary principles in rulership, commerce, and thought.
- Thinkers like Socrates, Plato, and Aristotle challenge conventions and encourage public discourse about the role of the individual in society and the way the universe works.

THE AMERICAS

- Chavín peoples and the Olmecs produce increasingly hierarchical societies and connect villages via trade.
- Large-scale common cultures emerge.

SUB-SAHARAN AFRICA

- Expansion of the Sahara Desert and population migrations cause people to coalesce in a few locations.
- Early signs of a common culture appear across the Sudanic savanna.

CHRONOLOGY

EAST ASIA

SOUTH ASIA

THE MEDITERRANEAN

THE AMERICAS

- Olmec culture emerges and diffuses through Mesoamerica 1500–400 BCE
- Chavín culture flourishes in Central Andes of South America 1400–400 BCE

SUB-SAHARAN AFRICA

1600 BCE | 1400 BCE | 1200 BCE

THINKING ABOUT GLOBAL CONNECTIONS

- ***Thinking about Transformation & Conflict and the Axial Age*** In the first millennium BCE across Afro-Eurasia, axial age thinkers developed radical new ideas in response to their respective political and cultural situations. In what ways did axial age thinkers in East Asia (Confucius and Master Lao), South Asia (Mahavira and the Buddha), and the Mediterranean (naturalist philosophers and Socrates) address the unique transformations and conflicts that were taking place where they lived? How do Zoroaster of Persia and the Jewish prophets of Israel, discussed in Chapter 4, fit this model?

- ***Thinking about* Worlds Together, Worlds Apart *and the Axial Age*** From the mid-second through the mid-first millennium BCE, "second-generation" societies developed in Eastern Zhou China, the Ganges plain of South Asia, and the Mediterranean, while parts of South America, Mesoamerica, and sub-Saharan Africa birthed their first complex societies. What are the differences between the second-generation societies of Afro-Eurasia and the first complex societies elsewhere, and what might account for these very different, yet contemporary, developments across the globe?

- ***Thinking about Changing Power Relationships and the Axial Age*** Axial age thinkers in East Asia, South Asia, and the Mediterranean offered challenges to both political and social traditions. How did the innovative ideas of thinkers such as Confucius, the Buddha, and Socrates contest and help to reshape power relationships ranging from the political to the familial?

STUDY QUESTIONS

1. What specific problems faced Eastern Zhou China in the Spring and Autumn period (722–481 BCE) and Warring States period (403–221 BCE)? How did **Confucius** and Master Lao's **Daoism** address these issues?
2. How did urbanization influence the Vedic belief system of South Asia in the first millennium BCE? In what ways, and to whom, would Vedic beliefs as compared with **Jainism** and the ideas of **Buddha** have been appealing, especially considering the hierarchies (*varnas* and *jatis*) of South Asian society and urban versus rural contexts?
3. What forces shaped Mediterranean developments in the first millennium BCE, and how did innovative **Greek philosophers** address some of those forces?
4. What are some of the distinctive features of the Andean **Chavín** and the Mesoamerican **Olmecs**? In what ways were these complex societies in the Americas fragmented and in what ways were they unified?
5. How do sub-Saharan developments in Nubia, such as Kush and **Meroe**, compare and contrast with those taking place in West Africa?
6. What are some of the defining qualities of **axial age** thought and the innovative thinkers who inspired these ideas?
7. What is it about **second-generation societies** that seems to foster an environment in which the **axial age** develops?

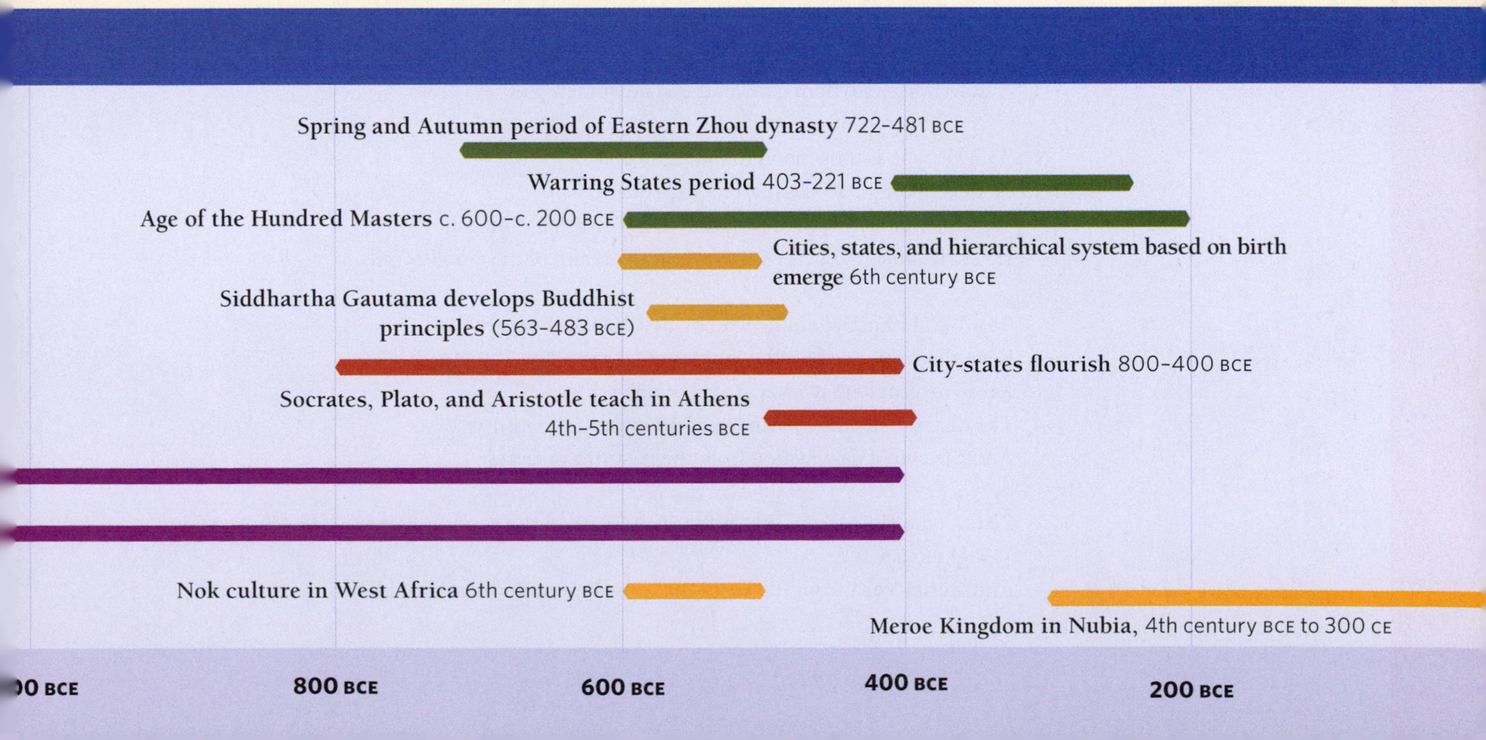

Spring and Autumn period of Eastern Zhou dynasty 722–481 BCE
Warring States period 403–221 BCE
Age of the Hundred Masters c. 600–c. 200 BCE
Cities, states, and hierarchical system based on birth emerge 6th century BCE
Siddhartha Gautama develops Buddhist principles (563–483 BCE)
City-states flourish 800–400 BCE
Socrates, Plato, and Aristotle teach in Athens 4th–5th centuries BCE
Nok culture in West Africa 6th century BCE
Meroe Kingdom in Nubia, 4th century BCE to 300 CE
00 BCE
800 BCE
600 BCE
400 BCE
200 BCE

Going to the Source

Ideas that Changed the World: 1000 to 350 BCE

The following documents all come from thinkers of the axial age, a term invented by German philosopher Karl Jaspers to describe the period in world history when important new (or "pivotal") ideas emerged in different parts of the world. Most of these ideas were not recorded by the thinkers themselves, but rather by their followers, either during their lifetimes or sometimes many years later. The documents all deal with religious beliefs, or at least universal ideas. These ideas were—and still can be—used to challenge the sociopolitical contexts in which they were created. It is thus important to consider not only the ideas themselves, but also how these ideas might be used outside of the specific contexts that led to their creation.

PRIMARY SOURCE 5.1

The Gathas from The Hymns of Zoroaster *(1000–600 BCE)*

In the *Gathas*, Zoroaster, also known as Zarathustra, outlines a philosophy in which forces of light and truth battle those of darkness and lies. These hymns, which Zoroaster addresses to Ahura Mazda, the god of light, praise the god and seek his guidance on how to behave. Initially a challenge to the spirit-focused tradition of the pastoral nomadic culture from which the Persians came, Zoroaster's ideas were eventually adopted by kings to undergird the Persian state and justify their rule.

In accordance with the Primeval Laws of this existence,
The Ratu (Judge) shall deal perfect justice to all;
To the good who chose the Truth,
To the evil who chose Falsehood,
And to those in whom good and evil are mixed . . .

33.3 He who is most good to the righteous,
Be he a noble, or a peasant, or a dependent,
He who zealously makes the good living creation flourish,
He shall come to dwell with Truth in the realm of the Good Mind.

33.4 I [Zarathustra] am he who by devotion and prayer shall
Keep disobedience and the Evil Mind far from Thee, O Mazda,
Keep insolent heresy away from the nobles,
The distrust spread by slanderers, from the community,
And the evil of destruction from the pastures of cattle . . .

33.6 I, who as Thy steadfast priest, have learned the straight path of Asha (Truth and Righteousness),
And would learn from the Best Mind how best to do what should be done,

Therefore I ask of Thee, My Lord,
Bless me with Thy Vision and grant me a consultation with Thee!

33.7 Come hither to me, in Thine own self, O Mazda!
Come unmistakably, O Thou Best One, with
The Spirit of Truth and The Good Mind!
Let my message be heard beyond the limits of the community of adherents.
Let the brilliant offerings of reverential prayers be manifest to all . . .

33.9 And with the blessings of these comrade Spirits of
Perfection and Immortality,
Let all advance to Thee, O Mazda!
Let all promote the cause of Truth! . . .

33.12 Arise for me, O Ahura!
Through my devotion give me steadfastness of purpose,
Through Thy Most Bounteous Spirit make me pure in goodness,
Through the Spirit of Righteousness grant me the courage of spiritual might,
And through the Good Mind give me the trust of the people.

33.14 To the Lord Mazda, as an offering,
Zarathustra dedicates the works of his life, even his very self.
The noblest essence of his Good Thought.
To Truth, he consecrates obedience to its principles
In word and deed, and all the might of his spiritual authority.

1. **Describe the relationship of Zoroaster and Ahura Mazda.**
2. **Why might this religious belief system have been important to Persian society and political life at the time that it first appeared?**

PRIMARY SOURCE 5.2

Ezekiel on Individual Responsibility *(sixth century BCE)*

Drawn from the Old Testament of the Bible, this selection from Ezekiel, one of the Jewish prophets who lived in the sixth century BCE, probably in exile in Babylon, describes the ways in which people who had accepted and were living under Jewish law needed to take individual responsibility for their actions.

*

If a man is righteous and does what is lawful and right, if he does not eat upon the mountains or lift up his eyes to the idols of the house of Israel, does not defile his neighbor's wife or approach a woman in her time of impurity, does not oppress any one, but restores to the debtor his pledge, commits no robbery, gives his bread to the hungry and covers the naked with a garment, does not lend at interest or take any increase, withholds his hand from iniquity, executes true justice between man and man, walks in my statutes, and is careful to observe my ordinances, he is righteous, he shall surely live, says the Lord God.

If he begets a son who is a robber, a shedder of blood, a man who does none of these duties, but eats upon the mountains, defiles his neighbor's wife, oppresses the poor and needy, commits robbery, does not restore the pledge, lifts up his eyes to the idols, commits abomination, lends at interest, and takes increase; shall he then live? He shall not live. He has done all these abominable things; he shall surely die; his blood shall be upon himself.

But if this man begets a son who sees all the sins which his father has done, and fears, and does not do likewise, who does not eat upon the mountains or lift up his eyes to the idols of the house of Israel, does not defile his neighbor's wife, he does not wrong any one, exacts no pledge, commits no robbery, but gives his bread to the hungry and covers the naked with a garment, withholds his hand from iniquity, takes no interest or increase, observes my ordinances, and walks in my statutes; he shall not die for his father's iniquity; he shall surely live. As for his father, because he practiced extortion, robbed his brother, and did what is not good among his people, behold, he shall die for his iniquity.

Yet you say, "Why should not the son suffer for the iniquity of the father?" When the son has done what is lawful and right, and has been careful to observe all my statutes, he shall surely live. The soul that sins shall die. The son shall not suffer for the iniquity of the father, nor the father suffer for the iniquity of the son; the righteousness of the righteous shall be upon himself, and the wickedness of the wicked shall be upon himself.

1. **Who determines who shall live and who shall die, and what criteria are used in this passage?**
2. **How would taking individual responsibility for one's actions affect government? Would it make a society that operated on such principles easier or harder to govern, and why?**

PRIMARY SOURCE 5.3

The Analects *(c. 400 BCE), Confucius*

In China, Confucius engaged in philosophical dialogues with his students in the transitional period of the 480s BCE, from the Spring and Autumn period to the Warring States period. Confucius's teachings about what it meant to be a superior gentleman (*junzi*), following the principles of practicing benevolence toward others (*ren*), proper ritual observance (*li*), and filial piety toward elders and ancestors (*xiao*)—as presented in the document here—eventually became the foundation for Chinese government and society for thousands of years. Moreover, these ideas diffused into other parts of eastern Asia, providing a framework for ordering both society and the state.

*

1.2. Master You said: "A man who respects his parents and his elders would hardly be inclined to defy his superiors. A man who is not inclined to defy his superiors will never foment a rebellion. A gentleman works at the root. Once the root is secured, the Way unfolds. To respect parents and elders is the root of humanity."

1.3. The Master said: "Clever talk and affected manners are seldom signs of goodness."

1.4. Master Zeng said: "I examine myself three times a day. When dealing on behalf of others, have I been trustworthy? In [dealings] with my friends, have I been faithful? Have I practiced what I was taught?"

1.5. The Master said: "To govern a state of middle size, one must dispatch business with dignity and good faith; be thrifty and love all men; mobilize the people only at the right times."

1.6. The Master said: "At home, a young man must respect his parents; abroad, he must respect his elders. He should talk little, but with good faith; love all people, but associate with the virtuous. Having done this, if he still has energy to spare, let him study literature."

1.7. Zixia said: "A man who values virtue more than good looks, who devotes all his energy to serving his father and mother, who is willing to give his life for his sovereign, who in [dealings] with friends is true to his word—even though some may call him uneducated, I still maintain he is an educated man."

1.8. The Master said: "A gentleman who lacks gravity has no authority and his learning will remain shallow. A gentleman puts loyalty and faithfulness foremost; he does not befriend his moral inferiors. When he commits a fault, he is not afraid to amend his ways."

1.9. Master Zeng said: "When the dead are honored and the memory of remote ancestors is kept alive, a people's virtue is at its fullest."

1.10. Ziqin asked Zigong: "When the Master arrives in another country, he always becomes informed about its politics. Does he ask for such information, or is it given him?"

Zigong replied: "The Master obtains it by being cordial, kind, courteous, temperate, and deferential. The Master has a way of enquiring which is quite different from other people's, is it not?" . . .

1.16. The Master said: "Don't worry if people don't recognize your merits; worry that you may not recognize theirs."

1. **Why are personal relationships so important to those who engage in politics?**
2. **Why does Confucius believe that filial piety is at the root of social and political relationships?**

PRIMARY SOURCE 5.4

The Republic *(360 BCE), Plato*

The Republic, written by Plato in 360 BCE, is a Socratic dialogue discussing the ideal version of government. A student of Socrates, Plato, who lived in Athens at the height of its Classical Age, was one of the foremost philosophers of ancient Greece.

Then you must not insist on my proving that the actual State will in every respect coincide with the ideal: if we are only able to discover how a city may be governed nearly as we proposed, you will admit that we have discovered the possibility which you demand; and will be contented. I am sure that I should be contented—will not you?

Yes, I will.

Let me next endeavour to show what is that fault in States which is the cause of their present maladministration, and what is the least change which will enable a State to pass into the truer form; and let the change, if possible, be of one thing only, or if not, of two; at any rate, let the changes be as few and slight as possible.

Certainly, he replied.

I think, I said, that there might be a reform of the State if only one change were made, which is not a slight or easy though still a possible one.

What is it? he said.

Now then, I said, I go to meet that which I liken to the greatest of the waves; yet shall the word be spoken, even though the wave break and drown me in laughter and dishonour; and do you mark my words.

Proceed.

I said: Until philosophers are kings, or the kings and princes of this world have the spirit and power of philosophy, and political greatness and wisdom meet in one, and those commoner natures who pursue either to the exclusion of the other are compelled to stand aside, cities will never have rest from their evils,—nor the human race, as I believe,—and then only will this our State have a possibility of life and behold the light of day. Such was the thought . . . , which I would . . . have uttered if it had not seemed too extravagant; for to be convinced that in no other State can there be happiness private or public is indeed a hard thing.

Socrates, what do you mean? I would have you consider that the word which you have uttered is one at which numerous persons, and very respectable persons too, in a figure pulling off their coats all in a moment, and seizing any weapon that comes to hand, will run at you might and main, before you know where you are, intending to do heaven knows what; and if you don't prepare an answer, and put yourself in motion, you will be prepared by their fine wits, and no mistake . . . you must do your best to show the unbelievers that you are right.

I ought to try, I said, since you offer me such invaluable assistance. And I think that, if there is to be a chance of our escaping, we must explain to them whom we mean when we say that philosophers are to rule in the State; then we shall be able to defend ourselves: There will be discovered to be some natures who ought to study philosophy and to be leaders in the State; and others who are not born to be philosophers, and are meant to be followers rather than leaders.

1. **Why does Plato support philosophers becoming leaders of government?**
2. **Why might this approach to rule have been controversial at the time that it was generated?**

PRIMARY SOURCE 5.5

The Dhammapada *(third century BCE), Buddha*

Siddhartha Gautama, later called the Buddha, offers his own wisdom in a text recorded by his followers in the third century BCE and known as the *Dhammapada*. The Buddha's ideas about suffering, desire, and how to escape both challenged the prevailing hierarchies of the *varna* system. In these excerpts, the Buddha defines the attributes of the foolish man and the virtues of peace.

Long is the night for the sleepless. Long is the road for the weary. Long is samsara (the cycle of continued rebirth) for the foolish, who have not recognized the true teaching.

If on one's way one does not come across one's better or an equal, then one should press on resolutely alone. There is no companionship with a fool.

"I've got children," "I've got wealth." This is the way a fool brings suffering on himself. He does not even own himself, so how can he have children or wealth?

A fool who recognises his own ignorance is thereby in fact a wise man, but a fool who considers himself wise—that is what one really calls a fool.

Even if a fool lived with a wise man all his life, he would still not recognise the truth, like a wooden spoon cannot recognise the flavour of the soup.

Even if a man of intelligence lives with a wise man only for a moment, he will immediately recognise the truth, like one's tongue recognises the flavour of the soup.

Stupid fools go through life as their own enemies, doing evil deeds which have bitter consequences.

A deed is not well done if one suffers after doing it, if one bears the consequences sobbing and with tears streaming down one's face.

But a deed is well done if one does not suffer after doing it, if one experiences the consequences smiling and contented. . . .

Better than a thousand pointless words is one saying to the point on hearing which one finds peace.

Better than a thousand pointless verses is one stanza on hearing which one finds peace.

Better than reciting a hundred pointless verses is one verse of the teaching (one dhammapada) on hearing which one finds peace.

Though one were to defeat thousands upon thousands of men in battle, if another were to overcome just one—himself, he is the supreme victor.

1. **According to the Buddha, why is inner peace more important than accumulating wealth and power?**
2. **What do you think the political and social implications might have been for those who followed the Buddha's teaching described here?**

PRIMARY SOURCE 5.6

The Suttas (third century BCE)

This excerpt from the Suttas, the discourses of the Buddha recorded by Buddhist monks between the third century BCE and the first century CE, chronicles an exchange between the Buddha and a young Brahmin, a representative from the highest varna in the Vedic system. Note that a follower of the Buddha likely wrote this, rather than the Buddha himself. Also consider the ways in which it challenges some of the ideas of the Vedic system then in place in the Indian subcontinent.

Once when the Lord [Buddha] was staying at Savatthi there were five hundred Brahmins from various countries in the city . . . and they thought: "This ascetic Gautama [the Buddha] preaches that all four castes are pure. Who can refute him?"

At the time there was a young brahman named Assadalayana in the city. . . a youth of sixteen, thoroughly versed in the Vedas . . . and in all brahmanic learning. "He can do it!" thought the brahmans, and so they asked him to try; but he answered, "The ascetic Gautama teaches a doctrine of his own, and such teachers are hard to refute. I can't do it!" They asked him a second time . . . and again he refused; and they asked him a third time, pointing out that he ought not admit defeat without giving battle. This time he agreed, and so, surrounded by a crowd of brahmans, he went to the Lord, and, after greeting him, sat down and said:

"Brahmins maintain that only they are the highest [varna], and the others are below them. They are white, the others black; only they are pure, and not the others. Only they are the true sons of Brahma, born from his mouth, born of Brahma, creation of Brahma, heirs of Brahma. Now what does the worthy Gautama say to that?"

"Do the Brahmins really maintain this, Assadalayana when they're born of women just like anyone else . . . ?"

"For all you say this is what they think . . ."

"Have you ever heard in the land of the Greeks and Kambojas [northern "Indians"] and other peoples on the borders there are only two classes, masters and slaves, and a master can become a slave and vice versa?"

"Yes, I've heard so."

"And what strength or support does that fact give to the Brahmins' claim?"
"Nevertheless, that is what they think."

"Again if a man is a murderer, a thief, or an adulterer, or commits other grave sins, when his body breaks up on death does he pass on to purgatory if he's a Kshatriya, Vaishya, or Shudra, but not if he's a brahman?"

"No, Gautama. In such a case the same fate is in store for all men, whatever their [varna]."

"And if he avoids great sin, will he go to heaven if he's a brahman, but not if he's a man of a lower [varna]?"

"No, Gautama. In such a case the same reward awaits all men, whatever their [varna]."

"And is a brahmin capable of developing a mind of love without hate or ill-will, but not a man of the other [varnas]?"

"No, all four [varnas] are capable of doing so."

"Can only a Brahmin go down to a river and wash away dust and dirt, and not men of the other [varnas]?"

"No, all four [varnas] can. . . ."

"Suppose there are two young Brahmin brothers, one a scholar and the other uneducated. Which would be served first at memorial feasts, festivals, and sacrifices, or when entertained as guest?"

"The scholar, of course; for what great benefit would accrue from entertaining the uneducated one?"

"But suppose the scholar is ill-behaved and wicked, while the uneducated is well-behaved and virtuous?"

"Then the uneducated one would be served first, for what great benefit would accrue from entertaining an ill-behaved and wicked man?"

"First, Assalayana, you based your claim on birth, then you gave up birth for learning, and finally you have come round to my way of thinking, that all four [varnas] are equally pure!"

At this Assalayana sat silent . . . his shoulders hunched, his eyes cast down, thoughtful in mind, and with no answer at hand.

1. **How does the Buddha explain the purity of all four castes?**
2. **What might the political and social consequences have been for teaching such beliefs?**

Questions for Analysis

Contextualization

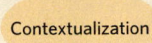

1. Compare the axial age thinkers whose ideas are represented in these documents. Could their ideas have been applied in societies other than the ones in which they were created? Why or why not?

Interpretation

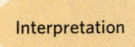

2. Evaluate which of the universalizing ideas expressed in these documents would have been most effective at governing a society, and explain why.

Long Essay Question

Synthesis

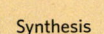

Based on these documents and your reading of the chapter, which is more important, equality or order? Explain your answer.

Before You Read This Chapter

GLOBAL STORYLINES

- Conquests by Alexander the Great and the influence of his successor states spread Hellenism across Southwest Asia and into South Asia.
- The Mauryan Empire accelerates the integration of South Asia and helps Buddhism spread throughout that region and beyond.
- "Silk Roads," both overland and by sea, facilitate the movement of commodities (spices, metals, and silks) and ideas (especially Buddhism and Hellenism) across Afro-Eurasia.

CORE OBJECTIVES

- **DESCRIBE** Hellenism and **EXPLAIN** its impact across Afro-Eurasia.
- **ANALYZE** the political changes that shaped central and South Asia in the aftermath of Alexander's incursion on the region.
- **EVALUATE** the forces that influenced the spread of Buddhism in this period.
- **TRACE** the early routes of the "Silk Roads" and **ASSESS** their importance in connecting Afro-Eurasia.

CHAPTER 6

Shrinking the Afro-Eurasian World

350–100 BCE

KEY TERMS

Bactria p. 217
bodhisattvas p. 219
caravan cities p. 224
cosmopolitans p. 208
Gandharan art p. 219
***koine* Greek** p. 208
Mahayana Buddhism p. 219
Mauryan Empire p. 213
The Periplus p. 230
Silk Roads p. 220

In the blistering August heat of 324 BCE, at a town on the Euphrates River that the Greeks called Opis (not far from modern Baghdad), Alexander the Great's experienced Macedonian troops declared that they had had enough. They had been fighting far from their homeland for more than a decade. They had marched eastward from the Mediterranean, forded wide rivers, traversed great deserts, trudged over high mountain passes, and slogged through rain-drenched forests. Along the way they had defeated massive armies, including those armed with fearsome war elephants. Some had taken wives from the cities and tribes they vanquished, so the army had become a giant swarm of ethnically mixed families. This was an army like no other. It did more than just defeat neighbors and rivals—it forcefully connected entire worlds, bringing together diverse peoples and lands.

Conquering in the name of building a new world, however, was not what the soldiers had bargained for. They loved their leader, but many thought he had gone too far. They had lost companions and grown weary of war. Some had mutinied at a tributary of the Indus, halting Alexander's advance into South Asia. Now they threatened to desert him altogether. Summoning up their courage, they voiced these resentments to their supreme commander. Alexander's response was immediate and inspired. In order to persuade his troops not to desert him, he evoked the astounding military triumphs and historic achievement they had accomplished: establishing his rule from Macedonia to the Indus Valley. This far-reaching political vision came to a sudden end with Alexander's death a year later, when he was thirty-two years old. Even in his short lifetime, though, he set in motion cultural and economic forces that would transform Afro-Eurasia.

In the aftermath of Alexander's conquests and the political developments that followed, two broad cultural movements came to link diverse populations across wide expanses of the Afro-Eurasian landmass: Hellenism and Buddhism. Buddhism, as an axial-age philosophy, was introduced in the previous chapter. Hellenism, briefly defined, was a shared Greek identity that spread throughout the lands in which Greeks settled and was expressed in their language, art, architecture, politics, and more. New empires—namely Alexander's successor states of the Mediterranean and the Mauryan Empire in South Asia—and broad new trade routes created the circuits through which Hellenism and Buddhism flowed. Imperial conquests and long-distance trade laid the foundations for widespread cultural systems that were far more enduring than the empires themselves.

One consequence of these developments was the emergence of the Silk Roads, a system of routes that for nearly a thousand years constituted the primary commercial network linking East Asia and the Mediterranean world. This system of trade routes, along which many different types of precious commodities were exchanged, extended over 5,000 miles and took its name from the huge quantities of precious silk that passed along it. Merchants, monks, and administrators helped to connect widespread parts of Afro-Eurasia, as the busy sea-lanes and Silk Roads flourished. Merely a few centuries after the conquests of Alexander and Mauryan kings, the world looked very different from the realms their armies had traversed.

Alexander and the Emergence of a Hellenistic World

COMPARISON

DESCRIBE Hellenism and **EXPLAIN** its impact across Afro-Eurasia.

The armed campaigns of the Macedonians led by Alexander the Great (356–323 BCE) began a drive for empire from the west that connected distant regions and spread a Hellenistic culture throughout the conquered lands. (See Map 6.1.) Alexander came from the frontier state of Macedonia to the north of Greece and commanded a highly mobile force armed with advanced military technologies that had developed during the incessant warfare among Greek city-states in the fifth and fourth centuries BCE. Under Alexander's predecessors—especially his father, Philip II—Macedonia had become a large ethnic and territorial state. Philip had unified Macedonia and then gone on to conquer neighboring states. Macedonia boasted gold mines that could finance Philip's new military technology and his disciplined army. Philip's troops included heavily armored infantry that maneuvered in closely arrayed units called phalanxes as well as large-scale cavalry formations for shock tactics. These infantry and cavalry forces were supported by income not only from Macedonian gold mines but also from the slave trade that passed through Macedonia. By the early 330s BCE, Philip had crushed the Greek city-states to the south, including Athens.

After Philip's assassination, his son Alexander used this new military machine in a series of daring attacks on the Persian Empire. Alexander owed much of his success to a readiness to take risks. In his initial forays into Southwest Asia he outpaced, outflanked, and outthought his adversaries. Through these rapid assaults he brought under the rule of his Greek-speaking elites all the lands of the former Persian Empire, extending from Egypt and the eastern Mediterranean to the Indus River valley.

The result of this expansion was hardly an empire, given that Alexander did not live long enough to establish institutions to hold the distant lands together. But his military campaigns continued a process that the Persians had already set in motion of smashing barriers that had separated peoples on the eastern and western ends of Afro-Eurasia. The conqueror saw himself as a new universal figure, a bridge connecting distant cultures.

Battle of Issus Mosaic of the Battle of Issus between Alexander the Great of Macedon and Darius, the king of Persia (found in a house at Pompeii in southern Italy). Alexander is the bareheaded figure to the far left; Darius is the figure to the right, gesturing with his right hand. The men represent two different types of warfare. On horseback, Alexander leads the cavalry-based shock forces of the Macedonian Greeks, while Darius directs his army from a chariot in the style of the great kings of Southwest Asia.

Alexander's conquests increased exposure of formerly Persian lands to the commodities of the Mediterranean and to cultural ideas associated with the Greek city-states. Alexander founded dozens of new cities named after himself, the most famous of which was Alexandria in Egypt, but also Iskandariya and Khandahar in modern-day Iraq and Afghanistan. Alexander seized the accumulated wealth that the Persian kings stored in their immense palaces, especially at Persepolis, and dispersed it into the money economies of the Mediterranean city-states. This massive redistribution of wealth fueled a widespread economic expansion in the Mediterranean and beyond.

ALEXANDER'S SUCCESSORS AND THE TERRITORIAL KINGDOMS

Alexander died in Babylon at age thirty-two, struck down by overconsumption of alcohol and other excesses that matched his larger-than-life personality and reflected the war culture of Macedonian warriors. His death in 323 BCE brought on the collapse of the regime he had personally held together. The conquered lands fragmented into large territories over which his generals squabbled for control.

Alexander's successors—his generals Seleucus, Antigonus, Ptolemy, Lysimachus, and others—thought of themselves not as citizens of a Greek city-state, but rather as absolute rulers over large blocks of territory, modeling themselves on the regional rulers they had defeated. One effect of powerful families controlling whole kingdoms was that some women could now hold great power, an unthinkable prospect in the democracies of the city-states. Queens in Macedonia, Syria, and Egypt—whether independent or as co-regents with their husbands—established new public roles for women. For example, Berenice of Egypt (c. 320–280 BCE) was the first in a series of powerful women who helped rule the kingdom of the Nile, a line that ended with the famous Cleopatra VII in the 30s BCE.

Berenice Portrait head of Berenice, wife and consort of Ptolemy I, the first Macedonian king of Egypt after its conquest by Alexander the Great. Berenice was one of the women who, as queens of huge empires, wielded power and commanded wealth in their own right.

Three large territorial states stood out in the new Hellenistic world: the Seleucid Empire (established by Seleucus), stretching from Syria to present-day

NORTH SEA
GERMANIC PEOPLES
BALTIC PEOPLES
CELTIC PEOPLES
CONQUESTS OF ALEXANDER THE GREAT, 323 BCE
GREEK CITY STATES
GREEK CITY STATES
GREEK CITY STATES
SCYTHIANS
STEPPES
ARAL SEA
CASPIAN SEA
CAUCASIAN PEOPLES
BLACK SEA
Massilia
Rome
Pella
MACEDONIA
Byzantium
Troy
Ancyra
Gordium
Sardis
Delphi
Athens
Sparta
Syracuse
Carthage
CARTHAGE
MEDITERRANEAN SEA
RHODES
Antioch
Tigris R.
Euphrates R.
Gaugamela
Ecbatana
SELEUCID EMPIRE
Seleucia
Babylon
Susa
Tyre
Jerusalem
Alexandria
Memphis
Siwa Oasis
PTOLEMAIC EMPIRE
Persepolis
Persian Gulf
Samarkand
Bukhara
Merv
Aï Khanoum
Bactra
Herat
Kandahar
ARABS
ARABIAN PENINSULA
RED SEA
Nile R.
KUSH
SAHARA DESERT
SAHARAN PEOPLES
Niger R.
SUB-SAHARAN AFRICA
NOK
Congo R.
BANTUS
ATLANTIC OCEAN
INDIAN
ARABIAN
MADAGASCAR
KALAHARI DESERT
0 500 1000 Miles
0 500 1000 Kilometers

MAP 6.1 | Afro-Eurasia in 250 BCE

Alexander of Macedonia did not live long enough to create one large politically unified empire, but his conquests integrated various Afro-Eurasian worlds culturally and economically. Trace the pathways that Alexander followed on his conquests.

- What were the names and locations of the Hellenistic successor states? What did these states have in common?
- Which states on the map did Greeks *not* rule? How did the spread of Hellenism affect them?

Afghanistan; Macedonia, ruled by the Antigonids (established by Antigonus); and Egypt, ruled by the Ptolemies (established by Ptolemy). In areas between these larger states, middle-sized kingdoms emerged. The old city-states of the Mediterranean, such as Athens and Corinth, still thrived, but now they functioned in a world dominated by these much larger power blocs. On mainland Greece, larger confederations of previously independent city-states formed.

Competition in war remained an unceasing fact of life, but the wars among the kingdoms of Alexander's successors were broader in scope and more complex in organization than ever before. Since the successor kingdoms were nearly equal in strength and employed the same advanced military technology, however, the near-constant state of wars between the new kings never achieved much. After battles that killed tens of thousands, and severely injured and wounded hundreds of thousands more, the three major kingdoms—and even the minor ones—remained largely unchanged.

The great powers therefore settled into a centuries-long game of watching one another and balancing threats with alliances. What emerged was a fierce competition that dominated international relations, in which diplomacy and treaty making sometimes replaced actual fighting. This equilibrium was reminiscent of the first age of international relations in the second millennium BCE (see Chapter 3). Long periods of peace began to grace the intervals between the new kingdoms' violent and destructive wars.

HELLENISTIC CULTURE

The unification of large blocks of territory under Alexander's successors helped spread a common Hellenistic culture. Following existing commercial networks, Hellenism was a shared Greek culture that extended across the entire Mediterranean basin and into Southwest Asia. Hellenistic culture included philosophical and political thinking, secular disciplines ranging from history to biology, popular entertainment in theaters, exercising and socializing in gymnasia, competitive public games, and art in many forms. Despite pockets of resistance, Hellenism was remarkably successful.

Common Language The core element of Hellenism was a common language known as *koine*, or "common," Greek. It replaced the city-states' numerous dialects with an everyday form that people anywhere could understand. ***Koine* Greek** quickly became the international language of its day. Peoples in Egypt, Judea, Syria, and Sicily, who all had distinct languages and cultures, could now communicate more easily with one another, and enjoy the same dramatic comedies and new forms of art and sculpture.

Cosmopolitan Cities Individuals were no longer citizens of a particular city (*polis*); instead they were the first **cosmopolitans**, that is, citizens (*polites*) belonging to the whole world or universe (*kosmos*). Much as Athens had been the model city of the age of the Greek city-state, Alexandria in Egypt became exemplary in the Hellenistic age. Whereas fifth-century BCE city-states had zealously maintained their exclusive civic identities (as Athenians, Spartans, or Corinthians, for example), Alexandria was a multiethnic city built by immigrants, who rapidly totaled half a million as they streamed in from all over the Mediterranean and Southwest Asia seeking new opportunities. Members of Alexandria's dynamic population, representing dozens of Greek and non-Greek peoples, communicated in the common language that supplanted their original dialects. Soon a new urban culture emerged to meet the needs of so diverse a population.

Hellenistic entertainment in this more connected world had to appeal to broad audiences and a wide variety of people. Plays were now staged in any city touched by Greek influence and had to translate to any environment. Consequently, the distinctive regional

The Theater at Syracuse
The great theater in the city-state of Syracuse in Sicily was considerably refurbished and enlarged under the Hellenistic kings. It could seat 15,000 to 20,000 persons. Here the people of Syracuse attended plays written by playwrights who lived on the far side of their world, but whose works they could understand as if the characters were from their own neighborhood. In the common culture of the Hellenistic period, plays deliberately featured typecast characters and situations, thereby broadening their audience.

humor and local characters of fifth-century Greek city-state drama gave way to dramas populated by the stock characters of standard sit-coms with which any audience could identify: the greedy miser, the old crone, the jilted lover, the golden-hearted whore, the boastful soldier, the befuddled father, the cheated husband, the rebellious son. At performances throughout the Mediterranean basin, laughter would be just as loud in Syracuse on the island of Sicily as in Scythopolis in the Jordan Valley of Judea.

A new political style of distant, almost godlike kings developed, in part due to the size of the territories over which they ruled. Instead of being accessible, which was not possible when Hellenistic kingdoms and states were so enormous, Hellenistic leaders became larger-than-life figures. Individuals related to political leaders primarily through the personality of the kings and their families. Rulership was personality, and personality could unite large numbers of subjects. For example, Demetrius Poliorcetes, the ruler of Macedonia, stood out in his high-platform shoes and heavy makeup, and he decorated his elaborate, flowing cape with images of the sun, the stars, and the planets. In the presence of a powerful sun-king like Demetrius, ordinary individuals felt small and inconsequential.

Philosophy and Religion Hellenistic religion and philosophy increasingly focused on the individual and his or her place in the larger world. This growing concern with the individual found expression in many new philosophical schools that proposed a range of ideas, including self-sufficiency (Cynicism), detachment (Epicureanism), and involvement (Stoicism). For instance, the Athenian Diogenes (c. 412–323 BCE), an early proponent of the Cynic school of philosophy, sought freedom from society's laws and customs, rejecting cultural norms as human-made inventions not in tune with nature and therefore false. Similarly turning thoughts to the self, Epicurus (c. 341–279 BCE), the founder of a school in Athens that he called The Garden, envisioned an ideal community of adherents regardless of their gender and social status, centered on his school. Seeking out pleasure and avoiding pain, these Epicureans contemplated the answer to the question "What is the good life?" and struggled to develop a sense of "not caring" (*ataraxia*) about their worries. More widespread than Diogenes's Cynicism and Epicurus's philosophy was Zeno's Stoicism. Zeno (c. 334–262 BCE), from the island of Cyprus, initiated it, and other cosmopolitan figures across the Hellenistic world—from Babylon in Mesopotamia to Sinope on the Black Sea—developed its beliefs. Named after the *Stoa Poikilē*, the roofed colonnade in the Athenian agora in which Zeno first presented his ideas, Stoicism argued that everything was grounded in nature. Stoicism regarded cities and kingdoms as human-made things, important but transient. Being in tune with nature and living a good life required understanding the rules of the natural order and being in control of one's passions, and thus indifference to pleasure and pain. Stoicism, Epicureanism, and Cynicism offered the individual a range of philosophical responses to the Hellenistic world developing all around.

Long-established religions were also shaped by Hellenism, and then reexported throughout the Mediterranean. For example, Greeks in Egypt drew on the indigenous cult of Osiris and his consort, Isis, to fashion a new narrative about Osiris's death and rebirth that represented personal salvation from death. Isis became a supreme goddess whose "supreme virtues" encompassed the powers of dozens of other Mediterranean gods and goddesses. Believers experienced personal revelations and out-of-body experiences (*exstasis*, "ecstasy"). A ritual of dipping in water (*baptizein*, "to baptize") marked the transition of believers, "born again" into lives devoted to a "personal savior" who delivered an understanding of a new life by direct revelation. These new beliefs, like the worship of Isis, emphasized the spiritual concerns of humans as individuals, rather than the collective worries of towns or cities. Other Hellenistic adaptations from earlier Greek religion, including cults of Demeter and Dionysus, similarly focused on the salvation of the individual as they spread throughout the Hellenistic world.

PLANTATION SLAVERY AND MONEY-BASED ECONOMIES

Ironically, philosophical and religious innovations focused on the self were accompanied by the rise of plantation slavery—the ultimate devaluing of an individual—as an engine of the Hellenistic economy. Large numbers of slaves were used in agricultural production—especially in Italy, Sicily, and North African regions close to Carthage. Alexander's conquests and Rome's political rise had produced unprecedented wealth for a small elite. These men and women used their riches to acquire huge tracts of land and to purchase slaves (either kidnapped individuals or conquered peoples) on a scale and with a degree of managerial organization never seen before. The slave plantations, wholly devoted to producing surplus crops for profit, helped to drive a new Mediterranean economy. The estates created vast wealth for their owners—though at a heavy price to others, as reliance on slave labor now left the free peasants who used to work the fields with no option but to move into overcrowded cities, where employment was hard to find.

The circulation of money reinforced the effects of forced labor. With more cash in the economy, wealthy landowners, urban elites, and merchants could more easily do business. The increasing use of Greek-style coins to pay for goods and services (in place of barter) promoted the importation of commodities such as wine from elsewhere in the Mediterranean. As coined money became even more available, it led to even more commercial exchanges. The forced transfer of precious metals to the Mediterranean from Southwest Asia by Alexander's conquests was so large that it actually caused the price of gold to fall.

In the west, Carthage began to mint its own coins—at first mainly in gold, but later in other metals. Rome moved to a money economy at the same time. By the 270s and 260s BCE, the Romans were issuing coins on a large scale under the pressures of their first war with Carthage (264–241 BCE). By the end of the third century, even borderland peoples such as the Gauls had begun to mint coins, imitating the galloping-horse images found on Macedonia's gold coins. So, too, did kingdoms in North Africa, where the coins of

Numidian kings bore the same Macedonian royal imagery. By around 100 BCE, inhabitants of the entire Mediterranean basin and surrounding lands were using coins to buy and sell all manner of commodities.

To pay for the goods that satisfied their newly acquired tastes, Celtic chieftains in the regions encompassing modern-day France began selling their own people in the expanding slave markets of the Mediterranean. Slavery and slave trading also became central to the economies of the Iberian Peninsula—especially in the hinterlands of large river valleys like the Ebro, where local elites founded urban centers imitating Greek styles.

Hellenistic Adaptation and Resistance The new high Greek culture spread far and wide, though it was not fully accepted everywhere in the Mediterranean. It appealed particularly to elites who sought to enhance their position by embracing Hellenistic culture over local values. Syrian, Jewish, and Egyptian elites in the eastern Mediterranean adopted this attitude, as well as Roman, Carthaginian, and African elites in the western Mediterranean.

The Hellenistic influences reached sub-Saharan Africa, where the kingdom of Meroe (see Chapter 5), already influenced by pharaonic forms, now absorbed characteristics of Greek culture as well. It is not surprising that Greek influences were extensive at Meroe, because continuous interaction with the Egyptians also exposed its people to the world of the Mediterranean. Both Meroe and its rival, Axum, located in the Ethiopian highlands, used Greek-style stelae (inscribed stone pillars) to boast of their military exploits. Citizens of Meroe worshipped Zeus and Dionysus. The rulers of Meroe, understanding the advantages of the Greek language, employed Greek scribes to record their accomplishments on the walls of Greek-Egyptian temples. In this way, Meroe developed a mix of Greek, Egyptian, and African cultural and political elements.

Not every community succumbed to the allure of Hellenism. The Jews in Judea offer a striking case of resistance and accommodation to its universalizing forces. Having been released from their Babylonian exile by the Persian monarch Cyrus in 538 BCE, the Jews returned to Judea—now a Persian province—and began rebuilding Jerusalem. While the Persians tolerated local customs and beliefs (see Chapter 4), the Hellenism brought by the Seleucid successor state that took Persia's place after Alexander's conquest brought a shock to Judaism. While some among the Jewish ruling elite began to adopt Greek ways—to wear Greek clothing, to participate in the gymnasium with its cult of male nudity, to produce images of gods as art—others rejected the push. Those who spurned assimilation rebelled against the common elements of Hellenism—its language, music, gymnasia, nudity, public art, and secularism—as being deeply immoral and threatening to their beliefs. Ultimately, this resistance to Hellenism led to full-scale armed revolt, headed up by the family of the Maccabees. In 167 BCE, the Seleucids provoked the Maccabees by forbidding the practice of Judaism (by outlawing worship and circumcision) and profaning the Jews' temple (by erecting an altar to Zeus in the sanctuary of the temple and sacrificing pigs on it). Though the Maccabees succeeded in establishing an independent Jewish state centered on the temple in Jerusalem, they did not entirely overcome the impact of the new universal culture on Judaism. A huge Jewish community in the Hellenistic city of Alexandria in Egypt embraced the new culture. Scholars there produced a version of the Hebrew scriptures in *koine* Greek, and historians (such as Jason of Cyrene) and philosophers (such as Philo of Alexandria) wrote in Greek, imitating Greek models.

Similar resistance and accommodation were taking place elsewhere. In the 330s and 320s BCE, when Alexander was uniting the eastern Mediterranean, the city-state of Rome took the first critical military actions to unify Italy. Rather than beginning as a kingdom like Macedonia, Rome went from being a city-state to flourishing as a large territorial state. During this transformation it adopted significant elements of Hellenistic culture: Greek-style temples, elaborately decorated Greek-style pottery and paintings, and an alphabet based on that of the Greeks. Many Roman elites saw immersion in Hellenistic ideals as a way to appear to the rest of the world as "civilized," while others resisted Greek ways as being overly luxurious and contrary to Roman ideals of manliness. The conservative Roman senator Cato the Elder (234–149 BCE) struggled with the tensions that Hellenism introduced to Roman ways. Although he was devoted to the Roman past, the Latin language, and the ideal of small-scale Roman peasant farmers and their families, Cato embraced many Hellenistic influences. He wrote a standard manual for the new economy of slave plantation agriculture, invested in shipping and trading, learned Greek rhetoric (both speaking and writing the language), and added the genre of history to Latin literature. Cato blended an extreme devotion to Roman tradition with bold Hellenistic innovations in most aspects of daily life.

Rome's long-time rival, the Phoenician colony of Carthage, also adopted Hellenism but with less internal conflict than at Rome. Carthaginian culture took on important elements of Hellenistic culture. For example, some Carthaginians went to Athens to become philosophers. Innovative ideas on political theory and warfare came from the Greek city-states. The design of their sanctuaries, temples, and other public buildings reveals a mix of Greek-style pediments and columns, Carthaginian designs and measurements, and local North African motifs and structures. Carthaginian women adorned themselves with jewelry that reflected styles from Egypt, such as ornate necklaces of gold and earrings of lapis lazuli.

Already well integrated into the Mediterranean economy, Carthage welcomed the increased communication and exchange that Hellenism facilitated. Carthaginian merchants traded with other Phoenician colonies in the western Mediterranean, with the towns of the Etruscans and the Romans in Italy, with the Greek trading city of Massilia (modern Marseilles) in southern France, and with Athens in the eastern Mediterranean. In addition, the Carthaginians expanded their commercial interests into the Atlantic, moving north along the coast of Iberia and south along the coast of West Africa, even establishing a trading post at the island of Mogador more than 600 miles down the Atlantic coast of Africa. Profoundly shaped by Alexander's conquests, Hellenism spread even further across Afro-Eurasia with Alexander's successors.

Converging Influences in Central and South Asia

COMPARISON

ANALYZE the political changes that shaped Central and South Asia in the aftermath of Alexander's incursion on the region.

During this period, tighter political organization in South Asia helped to spread new influences, like Hellenism and Buddhism, across the region. The high mountains of modern-day Afghanistan were a major geographical barrier to east-west exchange, but not impassable. Mountain passes—pinched like the narrow neck of an hourglass between the high plateau of Iran to the west and the towering ranges of Tibet to the east—offer the shortest route through the formidable Hindu Kush range. By crossing these passes, Alexander's armies expanded the routes between the eastern and western portions of Afro-Eurasia and brought about massive political and cultural changes in central and South Asia. Conquerors moved from west to east (like Alexander), from east to west (like the later nomads from central Asia) and from north to south, through the mountains, into the rich plains of the Indus and Ganges river valleys. At the same time, South Asian trade and religious influences, especially Buddhism, moved northward toward routes running west to east along what became known as the Silk Roads.

CHANDRAGUPTA AND THE MAURYAN EMPIRE

Alexander's brief occupation of the Indus Valley (327–325 BCE) paved the way for one of the largest empires in South Asian history, the Mauryan Empire. Before the arrival of Alexander's forces, South Asia had been a conglomerate of small warring states. This political instability came to an abrupt halt when, in 321 BCE, an ambitious young man named Chandragupta Mori (or Maurya), inspired by Alexander, ascended the throne of the Magadha kingdom and launched a series of successful military expeditions in what is now northern India.

The Magadha kingdom, located on the lower Ganges plain, held great strategic advantages over other states. For one thing, it contained rich iron ores and fertile rice paddies. Moreover, on the northeast Deccan plateau ample woods supported herds of elephants, a mainstay of the powerful Magadha mobile military forces, which used elephants to charge down and to terrify the enemy.

The Mori family, or Mauryans, did not start out as a distinguished ruling family, but economic strength and military skill elevated them over their rivals. Chandragupta (r. 321–297 BCE), though of lowly origins, probably from the Vaishya *varna*, grew up in the Punjab region of the Indus Valley observing Alexander's onslaught and aspiring to be an equally powerful military and political leader. When Alexander withdrew his forces from northern India, Chandragupta inserted himself into the political vacuum created by the Greek withdrawal.

Chandragupta's **Mauryan Empire** (321–184 BCE) constituted South Asia's first empire and served as a model for later Indian empire builders. After supplanting Magadha's Nanda monarchic dynasty, which had been in place for just over a century, Chandragupta used his military resources to reach westward beyond the Ganges plain into the area where four tributaries join the Indus. Here he pushed up to the border with the Seleucid kingdom, the largest successor kingdom of Alexander's empire, based in Mesopotamia.

Alexander's eastern successor, the Seleucid king Seleucus Nicator (358–281 BCE), responded by invading Mauryan territory—only to face Chandragupta's impregnable defenses. Soon thereafter, a treaty between the two powers gave a large portion of Afghanistan to the Mauryan Empire. One of the daughters of Seleucus went to the Mauryan court, accompanied by a group of Greek women. Seleucus also sent to Chandragupta's court an ambassador named Megasthenes, who lived in South Asia for years. In return for these gifts and diplomacy, the Mauryans sent Seleucus many South Asian valuables, including hundreds of elephants, which the Greeks soon learned to use in battles.

The Seleucid ambassador Megasthenes gathered his observations while at the Mauryan court into a book entitled *Indica,* after the Greek term for this region. Megasthenes's *Indica* depicted a well-ordered and highly stratified society divided into seven groups: philosophers, farmers, soldiers, herdsmen, artisans, magistrates, and councilors. People respected the boundaries between groups and honored rituals that reinforced their identities: members of different groups did not intermarry or even eat together. Megasthenes also noted the ways in which rulers integrated the region—for example, connecting major cities with extensive tree-lined roads, complete with mile markers. These roads facilitated both trade and the movement of troops. (See **Current Trends in World History: Building Roads**.) Contrary to Greek expectations of a military closely integrated into civil society, Megasthenes reported that soldiers in India were a profession separate from the rest of the population. Mauryan troops did not pursue any other occupation, but stood ready to obey their commander. This military force was huge, boasting cavalry divisions of mounted horses, war elephants, and scores of infantry.

Current Trends in World History

Building Roads: Early Highways for Communication, Trade, and Control

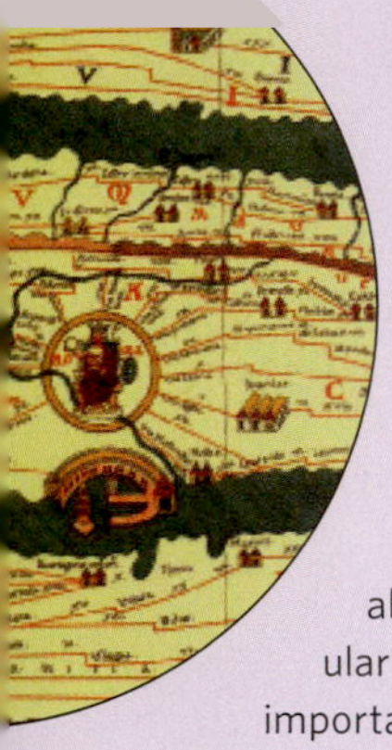

World historians have become fascinated with the history of roads because they provide insight into the way nations and empires functioned, and they allow us to study transnational forces that cross borders, like trade, migration, and the spread of ideas. Indeed, reliable communications and regular trade were among the most important forces that enabled the great regions of the world to be linked. If rivers and seas offered natural waterways to meet this demand, roads were the manmade answer that enabled soldiers, traders, and travelers to cross great stretches of land or go around high mountain ranges more quickly. Road building required huge financial and labor resources. Only empires had the incentives and resources to build large-scale roads and the networks that fed into them; these roads would aid in the empire's rule over their domain and in gathering the revenue that came from transregional trade.

The Persian empire was the largest state in the Afro-Eurasian world, which necessitated efficient communications over vast distances and terrain that was varied and forbidding. The problems were overcome by the construction of many "great" or "royal" roads across the empire to connect the royal capitals where the king resided from time to time. One of the best-known great roads connected the far western coast at Sardis in Asia Minor (present-day Turkey) with the heartland of the Persian empire around Susa (southern Iran) in the east, more than 1,700 miles away. The great roads featured way stations, supply depots, relays of horses and other pack animals, and state personnel, all to enable the local governors or satraps of the emperor to dispatch men and missions to the King of Kings.

If the royal Persian road communications system was a marvel of its age, the roads of the Roman Empire are rightly renowned for their extent and quality of construction. At its height, the empire boasted about 250,000 miles of roads; about 55,000 miles were of the formal stone-paved quality that most impresses us today. They were formally called "public roads" and were open to travel by anyone. Provincial, city, and municipal officials were in charge of upkeep. High standards of construction were imposed for the main paved highways—land was leveled and roadbeds were built up of layers of hard-packed sand and gravel, with careful gradients that allowed for drainage. The top layer was paved with heavy flagstones that provided long life.

It is easy to underestimate the amount of hard work and engineering required to construct the roadbeds, drainage, and bridges. The work and materials required to construct one major road in Italy, the Via Appia (the "Appian Way"), would be several times that required to build the great pyramids in Egypt. The major roads were marked with milestones that informed the traveler about the distance from the point of departure or to the next major town (5,000 or so of these have

The Regime of Aśoka The Mauryan Empire reached its height during the reign of its third king, Aśoka (r. 268–231 BCE), Chandragupta's grandson. Aśoka's lands comprised almost all of South Asia; only the southern tip of the peninsula remained outside his control. In 261 BCE, Aśoka launched the conquest of Kalinga, a kingdom on the east coast of the South Asian peninsula. The Mauryan army triumphed, but at a high price: about 100,000 soldiers died in battle, many more perished in its aftermath, and some 150,000 people endured forcible relocation. Aśoka was appalled and shamed by the brutal devastation his army had wrought. He vowed to cease inflicting pain on his people and pledged to follow the peaceful doctrines of Buddhism, issuing a famous edict that renounced brutal ways.

In this Kalinga edict Aśoka proclaimed his intention to rule according to the Indian concept of *dhamma*, a vernacular form of the Sanskrit word *dharma*, understood widely in Mauryan lands to mean tolerance of others, obedience to the natural order of things, and respect for all of earth's life forms. *Dhamma* was to apply to everyone, including the priestly Brahmans, Buddhists, members of other religious sects, and even Greeks. *Dhamma* became an all-encompassing moral code that all religious sects in South Asia accepted. With *dhamma* as a unifying symbol, Aśoka required all people, whatever their religious practices and cultural customs, to consider themselves his

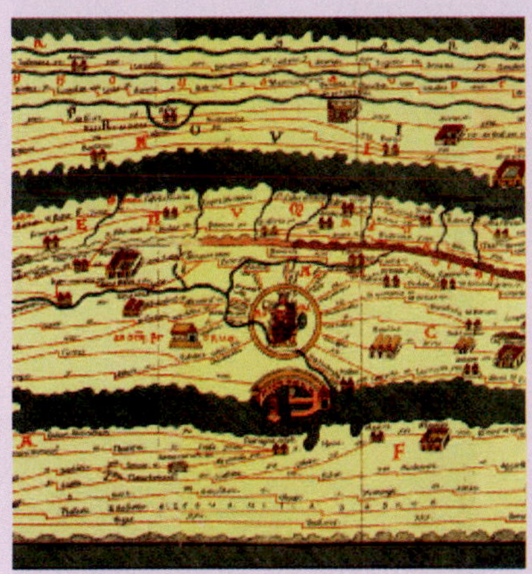

Roman Road System Coursing through Afro-Eurasia, the Roman road system is shown in all its complexity and glory in the only surviving copy of the ancient *Tabula Peutingeriana*. The icon of a seated ruler represents Rome.

survived). The English word "mile" comes from the Roman *milia passuum* (slightly less than our mile in length). The system of roads allowed the Roman state to maintain a public relay service called the *cursus publicus* along which imperial officials and units of the army, as well as information, could move efficiently and predictably from one part of the empire to another.

One of the singular achievements of the Qin dynasty was the building of a road system to create sufficient infrastructure to unify its far-flung empire. The Qin network of roads connected the capital at Xianyang to every part of the country. The Qin used peasants, soldiers, and some slaves as forced laborers to build new roads and widen existing ones, so that troops could move quickly and easily to put down revolts anywhere in the empire. These roads were expanded under the succeeding Han dynasty to facilitate travel not only for the military, but also for merchants and commoners.

The road system of Qin and Han China paralleled the Persian royal roads and the Roman road network in scale and magnitude. By 100 BCE, many roads were wide, surfaced with stone, and lined with trees; steep mountains were traversed by stone-paved stairways with broad treads and low steps. By the end of the sixth century CE, the internal road network, not counting the Silk Road from the Han and Tang capital of Chang'an to central Asia, had grown to encompass some 25,000 miles. This ingeniously engineered system of roads helped the Chinese—like other empires—to control an empire spanning a vast, geographically diverse area.

QUESTIONS FOR ANALYSIS

- What political and geographical motives did empires have to build road systems?
- What sort of people benefited most from these road systems? Who actually built the roads?

Explore Further

Xinru Liu, *The Silk Road in World History* (2010).

Wood, Francis, *The Silk Road: Two Thousand Years in the Heart of Asia* (2004).

subjects, to respect him as their father, and to conform to his moral code—starting with the precept that people of different religions or sects should get along with each other. He also praised the benefits of agrarian progress and banned large-scale cattle sacrifice as detrimental to agriculture. Meanwhile, he warned the "forest people," the hunters and gatherers living beyond the reach of government, to avoid making trouble.

To disseminate the ideals of *dhamma*, Aśoka regularly issued decrees, which he had chiseled on stone pillars and boulders in every corner of his domain, selecting locations where people were likely to congregate and where they could hear the words as read to them by the few who were literate. Occasionally he also issued edicts to explain his Buddhist faith. All were inscribed in local languages, including Sanskrit, as well as Greek and Aramaic in the Hellenistic- and Persian-influenced northwest.

The Mauryan Empire at its height encompassed 3,000,000 square miles, including all of what is today Pakistan, much of what is Afghanistan, the southeastern part of Iran, and the whole of the Indian subcontinent except for the lands at the southern tip. Its extraordinarily diverse geography consisted of jungles, mountains, deserts, and floodplains, and its equally disparate population of 50 to 60 million inhabitants was made up of pastoralists, farmers, forest dwellers, merchants, artisans, and religious leaders. Aśoka's promotion of

Aśoka Buddhist legend claims that Aśoka placed relics of the Buddha in the many stupas he had built. The stupa at Sarnath (*left*) is the best-preserved one from the time of Aśoka. Aśoka had his edicts carved on pillars like the one on the right all over India. The majestic lion at the top of the pillar shows the influence of Persian art, in which the lion was the symbol of royalty.

the Buddhist tenet of *dhamma* and his elaborate administrative structure were not enough to hold together his empire, which did not last long after his death in 231 BCE. The proliferation of Buddhism made possible by Aśoka's adoption and wholehearted sponsorship of the faith, however, was a lasting impact of his reign.

GREEK INFLUENCES IN CENTRAL ASIA

Hellenistic influences shaped politics and culture in the regimes that succeeded direct Greek control in central Asia. Alexander's military had thrust into Asia and reached as far as the Punjab. There he defeated several rulers of Gandhara in 326 BCE. In the course of this campaign he planted many garrison towns—especially in eastern Iran, northern Afghanistan, and in the Punjab, where he needed to protect his easternmost territorial acquisition. These garrison towns were originally stations for soldiers, but they soon became centers of Hellenistic culture. Many of these outposts displayed the characteristic features of a Greek city-state: a colonnaded main street lined by temples to patron gods or goddesses, a theater, a gymnasium for education, an administrative center, and a marketplace. Following Alexander's death, Seleucus Nicator built more of these Greek garrison towns before he concluded peace with Chandragupta and withdrew from the region.

The garrison towns founded by Alexander and Nicator remained and grew into Hellenistic centers. Once the Greek soldiers who had been stationed in them realized they would be spending their lives far from their homeland, they married local women and started families. Bringing their Hellenistic customs to the local populations, the soldiers established institutions familiar to them from the Greek city-states. *Koine* Greek was the official language; but because locals used their own languages in daily life, subsequent generations were bilingual. For centuries, traditional Greek institutions—especially Greek language and writing—survived many political changes and much cultural assimilation, providing a common basis of engagement in a long zone stretching from the Mediterranean to South Asia.

Hellenistic influences were even more pronounced in the regimes that succeeded Seleucid control in central Asia in the late third century BCE. The Seleucid state had taken over the entirety of the former Persian empire, including its central Asian and South Asian territory. The Hellenistic kingdom of **Bactria** broke away from the Seleucids around 200 BCE to establish a strong state that included the Gandhara region in modern Pakistan. As Mauryan power receded from the northwestern part of India, the Bactrian rulers extended their conquests into this area. Because the cities that the Bactrian Greeks founded included many Indian residents, they have been called "Indo-Greek." Those in Gandhara incorporated familiar features of the Greek polis, but inhabitants still revered Indian gods and goddesses.

Hellenistic Bactria served as a bridge between South Asia and the Greek world of the Mediterranean. Among the goods that the Bactrians sent west were elephants, which were vital to the Greek armies there. Not only did the Bactrian Greeks revive the cities in India left by Alexander but they also founded new Hellenistic cities in the Gandhara region. The Greek king Demetrius, who invaded India around 200 BCE, entrusted the extension of his empire in the northern region of India to his generals, many of whom became independent rulers after his death. Sanskrit literature refers to these Greek rulers as the Yavana kings—a word derived from "Ionia," a region whose name applied to all those who spoke Greek or came from the Mediterranean.

Two Coins *Top*: Wearing an elephant cap, Demetrius of Bactria titled himself the king of Indians as well as Greeks. On the other side of the coin is Hercules. *Bottom*: Another central Asian ruler, the Scythian king Maues used Greek to assert his position as "King of Kings" on one side of his coin. On the other side, the goddess Nike is surrounded by Kharoshthi letters.

Aï Khanoum, on the Oxus River (now the Amu) in present-day Afghanistan, was the site of an administrative center, possibly the capital of the Bactrian state. Unearthed by archaeologists in the 1960s, Aï Khanoum had avoided the devastations that befell so many other Hellenistic cities in this region. Greek-style architecture and inscriptions indicate that the original residents of Aï Khanoum were soldiers from Greece. Following the typical pattern, they married local women and established the basic institutions of a Greek polis. Aï Khanoum's characteristic Greek structures included a palace complex, a gymnasium, a theater, an arsenal, several temples, and elite residences. Featuring marble columns with Corinthian capitals, the palace contained an administrative section, storage rooms, and a library. A main road divided the city into lower and higher parts, with the main religious buildings located in the lower city. Though far from Greece, the elite Greek residents read poetry and philosophy and staged Greek dramas in the theater. Grape cultivation supported a wine festival associated with the god Dionysius. The remains of various statues indicate that the residents not only revered the Greek deity Athena and the demigod Heracles but also paid homage to the Persian Zoroastrian religion.

Perhaps the most adept ruler at mingling Greek and Indian influences was Menander (also known as Milinda), a Yavana city-state king of the mid-second century BCE. Using images and legends on coins to promote both traditions among his subjects, Menander claimed legitimacy as an Indian ruler who also cultivated Greek cultural forms. The face of his coins bore his regal image surrounded by the words "King, Savior, Menander," in Greek. The reverse side featured the Greek goddess Athena and the king's title in the local Pakrit language. This mixed Indo-Greek identity was not confined to coins. In his discussions with a Buddhist sage, King Menander debated the nature of the Buddha (was he human or divine?) and showed a keen interest in South Asian religious influences even as he embraced Hellenism. These "Indo-Greek" legacies persisted long after the Hellenistic regimes collapsed, because they remained essential to communication and trade around the rim of the Indian Ocean.

The Transformation of Buddhism

COMPARISON

EVALUATE the forces that influenced the spread of Buddhism in this period.

During this time of political and social change, South Asia also experienced upheavals in the religious sphere, as Hellenism and other east-west connections transformed Buddhism. Impressed by Hellenistic thought, South Asian peoples blended it with their own ethical and religious traditions. Beginning among the Yavana city-states in the northwest, where Buddhism's sway was most pronounced, this blended Buddhism rapidly spread to other regions that were experiencing the same changes. In addition to Hellenism, other layers of influence came together in South Asia through increased seafaring and interactions with nomadic peoples. This cultural fusion profoundly transformed and enriched Buddhism.

INDIA AS A SPIRITUAL CROSSROADS

Many land and sea routes now converged in India, rendering the region a melting pot of ideas and institutions. Improved mastery of the monsoon trade winds in this period opened the Indian Ocean to commerce and made India the hub for long-distance ocean traders and travelers. Another major influence on Buddhism was the Kushans, a horse-riding nomadic group who stabilized east-west connectivity through central Eurasia in the first century CE. With Kushan patronage and the thriving commerce their stability brought to the region, Buddhist communities grew so rich that monks began to live in elegant monastic complexes. (We will discuss the Kushans and their role in Silk Road trade later in this chapter.) The center of each monastic community was a stupa, with its Buddhist relics and sculptures depicting the Buddha's life and teachings. Such monasteries provided generously for the monks, furnishing them with halls where they gathered and worshipped and rooms where they meditated and slept. Buddhist monasteries were also open to the public as places for worship.

Stupa Staircase The risers from the staircase of a large stupa in the Gandhara region display scenes from Buddhist stories. The upper one shows men in nomads' clothing playing music, including the Greek-style lyre. On the middle one, men and women in Greek clothing drink and make merry. The pictures are Buddhist versions of performances in a Greek theater.

THE NEW BUDDHISM: THE MAHAYANA SCHOOL

This mixing of new ways—nomadic, Hellenistic, and Persian—with traditional Buddhism produced a spiritual and religious synthesis: **Mahayana** ("Great Vehicle") **Buddhism**. In the first two centuries of the Common Era, Mahayana Buddhists resolved a centuries-long dispute over whether the Buddha was a god or a wise human. They affirmed: the Buddha was indeed a deity. However, Mahayana Buddhism was accommodating; it offered a spiritual pluralism that incorporated outside influences and positioned Indian believers as a cosmopolitan people.

Mahayana Buddhism appealed especially to foreigners and immigrants who traded or settled in India because it made the Buddha easier to understand. The Buddha's preaching had stressed life's suffering and the renunciation of desire to end suffering and achieve nirvana. Newcomers to the region and to Buddhism—such as migrants or traders—saw no attraction in a belief that life consisted of painful cycles of birth, growth, death, and rebirth. This sharp dichotomy between a real world of hardship and the Buddha's abstract world of nirvana gave way to the Mahayana Buddhists' vision that **bodhisattvas**—enlightened demigods, ready to reach nirvana—delayed doing so in order to help others attain it. These bodhisattvas prepared spiritual halfway points to welcome deceased devotees not yet ready to release their desires and enter nirvana. The universe of the afterlife in Mahayana Buddhism presented an array of alternatives to the harsh real existence of worldly living. With its bodhisattvas, Mahayana Buddhism enabled all individuals—the poor and powerless as well as the rich and powerful—to move from a life of suffering into a happy existence.

NEW IMAGES OF BUDDHA IN LITERATURE AND ART

Just as Buddhism absorbed outside influences and became more appealing, it also inspired literature and art that appealed to diverse peoples. A new genre of literature dealing with the Buddha and the bodhisattvas emerged. Buddhist texts written in Sanskrit disseminated the life of the Buddha and his message far and wide, reaching far corners of Asia. Aśvaghosa (c. 80–c. 150 CE), a great Buddhist thinker and the first known Sanskrit writer, wrote a biography of the Buddha, which set the Buddha's life story within the commercial urban environment of the Kushan Empire (instead of in the rural Shakya republic in the Himalaya foothills, where he had actually lived). Aśvaghosa's largely fictive version of the Buddha's life story spread rapidly throughout India and beyond, introducing Buddha and his teachings to many potential converts.

The colorful images of Sanskrit Buddhist texts of the first centuries CE gave rise to a large repertoire of Buddhist sculptural art and drama. On Buddhist stupas and shrines, artisans carved scenes of the Buddha's life, figures of bodhisattvas, and statues of patrons and donors. Buddhist sculptures from the northern Kushan territory, fashioned from gray schist rock, are called **Gandharan art**. Those from the central region of India, created mainly from local red sandstone, are called Mathuran art. Gandharan Buddhist art shows strong Greek and Roman influences, whereas the Mathuran style evolved from the carved idols of South Asian folk gods and goddesses.

Despite their stylistic differences, the schools shared themes and cultural elements. Inspired by Hellenistic art and religious tradition, both took the bold step of sculpting the Buddha and bodhisattvas in realistic human, rather than symbolic, form (such as a bodhi tree, which symbolizes Buddha's enlightenment). Though the Buddha wore no decorations because he had cut off all links to the world, bodhisattvas were dressed as princes because they were still in this world, generously helping others. What was important was bringing the symbolic world of Buddhism closer to the people.

Buddhas The bronze Buddha on the left often strikes viewers as a Christlike figure. Greco-Roman influence on the iconography of Buddha was probably responsible for the Gandharan-style attire and facial expression of Buddhas and bodhisattvas. The Mathuran Buddha of the later Gupta period (*right*) is more refined than the Buddhas of the Kushan era. The robe is so transparent that the artist must have had very fine silk in mind when sculpting it.

Buddhist art reflected a spiritual system that appealed to people of diverse cultural backgrounds. Consider the clothes of the patron figures. For male and female figures alike, the garments were simple and well adapted to tropical climates. Those indigenous to the semitropical land had nude upper bodies and a wrapping like the modern *dhoti*, or loincloth, on their lower bodies. Jewelry adorned their headdresses and bodies. By contrast, the nomadic patron figures wore traditional cone-shaped leather hats, knee-length robes, trousers, and boots. Figures with Greek clothing demonstrate continuing Hellenistic influence, and those wearing Roman togas reveal imperial Rome's influence. The jumble of clothing styles illustrates that Buddhist devotees could share a faith while retaining their ethnic or regional differences.

COMPARISON

TRACE the early routes of the "Silk Roads" and **ASSESS** their importance in connecting Afro-Eurasia.

The Formation of the Silk Roads

In the first century BCE, trade routes stretching from China to central Asia and westward had merged into one big intertwined series of routes, famously referred to as the **Silk Roads** even though caravans transported many other precious commodities, such as incense, gemstones, and metals. Traders traveled segments of the route, passing their goods on to others who took them farther along the road and, in turn, passed them on again. The Silk Roads owed much to earlier overland routes through which merchants had exchanged frankincense and myrrh from the Arabian Peninsula for copper, tin, iron, gemstones, and textiles. (See Map 6.2.) During this period, seaborne trade also created closer connections between Afro-Eurasian worlds.

The effects of these long-distance exchanges altered the political geography of Afro-Eurasia. Egypt and Mesopotamia faded as sources of innovation and knowledge, becoming instead crossroads for peoples on either side of them. The former borderlands emerged as new imperial centers. What we now call the Middle East literally became a commercial middle ground between the Mediterranean and India. East Asia, principally China, finally connected indirectly with the Mediterranean via central and South Asia. Through China, whose traders reached Bali and other islands now in Indonesia, connections developed with Japan, Korea, and Southeast Asia. China, insulated from the west by the Himalayas and Pamir Mountains, remained politically and culturally a mysterious land to those from the Mediterranean. Yet products made from silk revealed to the Greeks and Romans that an advanced society lay far to the east.

NOMADS AND TRADE ROUTES

The horse-riding nomads of Inner Eurasia made long-distance trade possible. These scattered nomadic peoples already for centuries had linked entire regions and facilitated trade and interactions between distant communities. Responding to the drying out of their homelands in the second millennium BCE, they moved southward (see Chapter 3). Moving from place to place and being in close contact with their animals, the nomads were exposed to—and acquired resistance to—a greater variety of microbes than settled peoples did. Their relative immunity to disease made them ideal agents for linking distant settled communities. Nomads also raced into political vacuums and installed new regimes that linked northwest China and the Iranian plateau. Among the most important of these nomadic peoples were the Xiongnu (Hsiung-nu) pastoralists, originally from the eastern part of the Asian steppe in modern Mongolia. By the third century BCE their mastery of bronze technology made them the most powerful nomadic community in the area.

When Xiongnu power waned, a new empire, that of the Kushans, arose in their place around 50 CE. The Yuezhi, a nomadic group to the west of the Qin, unified the region's tribes, migrated southwestward, and established this Kushan empire in Afghanistan and the Indus River basin. The Kushans' empire embraced a large and diverse territory and was critical in the formation of the Silk Roads. The Kushans had been an illiterate people, but they adopted Greek as their official language. Kushan coinage, like the Indo-Greek coinage discussed earlier, blended Greek and Indian elements. Mediterranean traders arriving in the Kushan markets to purchase silks from China, as well as Indian gemstones and spices, conducted their transactions in Greek. The coins they used—struck to Roman weight standards (themselves derived from Greek coinage) and inscribed in Greek—served their needs perfectly. Kushan rule stabilized the trading routes through central Asia that stretched from the steppes in the east to the Parthian Empire in the west. This territory became a major segment of the Silk Roads.

CARAVAN CITIES AND THE INCENSE TRADE

As nomads moved southwestward, they produced a new kind of commercial hub: the caravan city. Established at strategic locations (often at the edges of deserts or in oases or

NORTH SEA
ROMAN EMPIRE
SCYTHIANS
URAL MTS.
ARAL SEA
BLACK SEA
CASPIAN SEA
from the West to India and China:
G
Rome
ANATOLIA
Athens
Carthage
Antioch
Oxus R.
Bukhara
Merv
Tigris R.
Dura Europos
PARTHIAN EMPIRE
ZAGROS MTS.
IRANIAN PLATEAU
Palmyra
Euphrates R.
MEDITERRANEAN SEA
Alexandria
Petra
NABATAEAN KINGDOM
Persepolis
Persian Gulf
from India to the West:
A/D
EGYPT
Myos Hormos
ARABIAN DESERT
Berenice
from Arabia to India:
Nile R.
NUBIA
from Arabia, Ethiopia and East Africa to the West:
I
LF
RED SEA
from Arabia and Ethiopia to India and China:
I
Meroe
ARABIAN STATES
AXUMITE KINGDOM
ARABIAN
from the West to India and Southeast Asia:
G
LT
Lake Victoria
INDIAN
Bhapta
MADAGASCAR
Silk Road
Incense trade route
Other trade routes
SCYTHS Nomad group
Boundary of empires, states, and kingdoms
Port/trading town
Buddhist heartland
Spread of Buddhism
Buddhist centers
Buddhist rock-carved temples
Sacred Buddhist mountains
Traded Goods
A/D Aromatics and drugs
Cu Copper
Coral
Everyday textiles
Fine cotton/garments
Fine stone and metal vessels
Furs
G Glassware
Gems
Gold
Grain
H Horses
I Incense
Ivory
Jewelry and cut gems
Lacquerware
LF Luxury foods
LT Luxury textiles
Peacocks
Pearls
Silk
Slaves
S Spices
Statuary
Sn Tin
Tortoiseshell
Wine
Wood

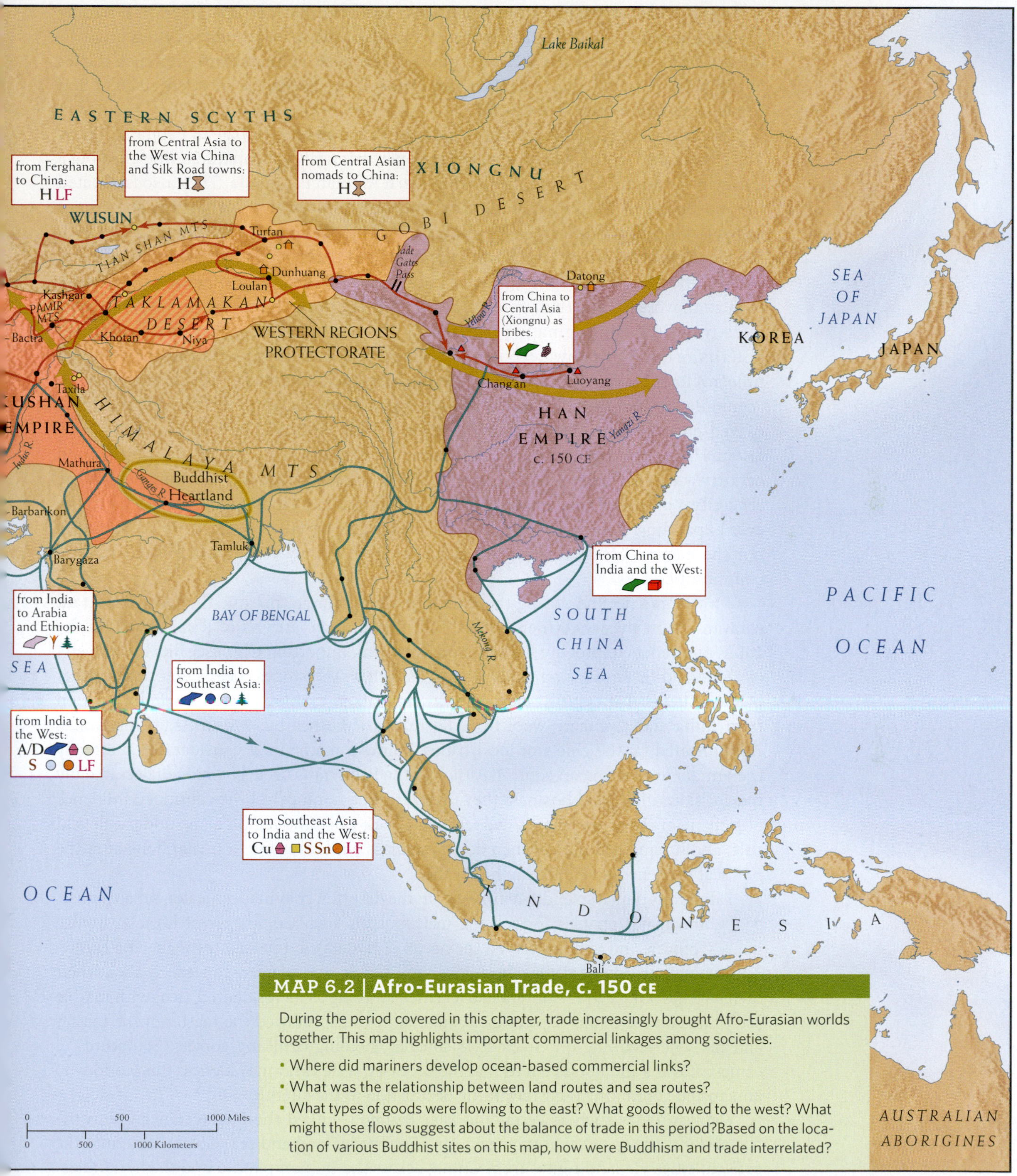

MAP 6.2 | Afro-Eurasian Trade, c. 150 CE

During the period covered in this chapter, trade increasingly brought Afro-Eurasian worlds together. This map highlights important commercial linkages among societies.

- Where did mariners develop ocean-based commercial links?
- What was the relationship between land routes and sea routes?
- What types of goods were flowing to the east? What goods flowed to the west? What might those flows suggest about the balance of trade in this period?Based on the location of various Buddhist sites on this map, how were Buddhism and trade interrelated?

at the end points of major trade arteries), these cities became locations where vast trading groups assembled before beginning their arduous journeys. Some caravan cities originating as Greek garrison towns became centers of Hellenistic culture, displaying such staples of the polis as public theaters. **Caravan cities** were among the most spectacular and resplendent urban centers of this era.

One of the most striking of these caravan cities was the Nabatean capital at Petra. The Nabateans were an Arabic-speaking people, primarily sheepherders who eked out a living in the Sinai Desert and the northwestern Arabian Peninsula. They also facilitated the movement of frankincense, myrrh, and other spices along what was sometimes called the Incense or Spice Road, linking the Arabian peninsula and Indian Ocean with the Mediterranean where Greeks and Romans used these goods to make perfumes and incense. Because the Greeks and later the Romans needed large quantities of incense to burn in worshipping their gods, the trade passing through this region was extremely lucrative. Although originating in Nabatean herders' practice of carving shelter and cisterns for catching rainwater out of the solid stone of the forbidding landscape, the magnificent "Rock City" of Petra (*petros* in Greek means rock) was made possible by the wealth accumulated from the spice trade. Houses, shrines, tombs, and even the vast theater—carved entirely from the sandstone terrain to seat 6,000–10,000 spectators—manifested Hellenistic influences. Petra's power and wealth lasted from the mid-second century BCE to the early second century CE. The caravan traders, the ruling elite of the rock city, controlled the supply of spices and fragrances from Arabia and India to the ever-expanding Roman Empire. Nabataean traders based in Petra traveled throughout the eastern Mediterranean, erecting temples wherever they established trading communities.

With Petra's decline during the Roman period, Palmyra became the most important caravan city at the western end of the Silk Roads. Rich citizens of Rome relied on the Palmyran traders to procure luxury goods for them, importing Chinese silks for women's clothing and incense for religious rituals, as well as gemstones, pearls, and many other precious items. Palmyran traders handled nonsilken textiles as well, including cotton from India and cashmere wool from Kashmir or the nearby central Asian highlands. Administered by the chiefs of local tribes, Palmyra maintained considerable autonomy even under formal Roman control. Although the Palmyrans used a Semitic dialect in daily life, for state affairs and business they used Greek, a reminder of the continued influence of Hellenism. Their merchants had learned Greek when the region came under Seleucid rule, and it remained useful when doing business with caravans from afar, long after the political influences of Hellenism had waned.

Palmyrans built a splendid marble city in the desert. A colonnade, theater, senate house, agora, and major temples formed the metropolitan area. Complexes of hostels, storage houses, offices, and temples served the needs of traders who passed through. The Palmyrans worshipped many deities, both local and Greek, and seemed concerned about their own afterlife. Like Petra, Palmyra had a cemetery as big as its residential area, with marble sculptures on the tombs depicting city life. Many tombs showed the master or the master and his wife reclining on Greek-style couches, holding drinking goblets. Sculptures of camel caravans and horses tell us that the deceased were caravan traders in this world who anticipated continuing their rewarding occupation in the afterlife.

Caravan cities such as Petra, and later Palmyra, linked the Mediterranean with the silk and incense routes that traversed Afro-Eurasia by land and sea. Goods came into the caravan cities via land routes from China, across the Iranian plateau and the Syrian desert, as well as through Afghanistan, the Indus, India's west coast, and across the Indian Ocean to the Red Sea.

Palmyran Tomb Sculpture This tombstone relief sculpture shows a wealthy young Palmyran, attended by a servant—probably a household slave. Palmyra was at the crossroads of the major cultural influences traversing Southwest Asia at the time. The style of the clothing—the flowing pants and top—and the couch and pillows reflect the trading contacts of the Palmyran elite, in this case with India to the east. The hairstyle and mode of self-presentation signal influences from the Mediterranean to the west.

CHINA AND THE SILK ECONOMY

China's flourishing economy owed much to the fact that Chinese silks were the most sought-after commodity in long-distance trade. As thousands of precious silk bales made their way to Indian, central Asian, and Mediterranean markets, silk became the ultimate prestige commodity of the regions' ruling classes. Over time, the exchange between eastern and western portions of the Silk Road was increasingly mediated by Persian, Xiongnu, Kushan, and other middlemen at the great oases and trading centers that grew up in central Asia. Local communities took profitable advantage of the silk trade from China based on their increased knowledge and contacts.

Silk was not only China's most valuable export, but it also served as a tool in diplomacy with the nomadic kingdoms on China's western frontiers and in funding the Chinese armies. The country's rulers used silk to pay off neighboring nomads and borderlanders, buying both horses and peaceful borders with the fabric. During the Zhou dynasty, it served as a precious medium of exchange and trade.

People valued silk as a material for clothing; as a filament made by spinning the protein fibers extracted from the cocoons of silkworms, it is smooth yet strong. Whereas cloth spun from hemp, flax, and other fibers tends to be rough, silk looks and feels rich. Moreover, it is cool against the skin in hot summers and warm in the winter. Silk also has immense tensile strength, being useful for bows, lute strings, and fishing lines. Artisans even wove it into a tight fabric to make light body armor or light bags for transporting liquids (particularly useful for traders crossing arid expanses). Before the Chinese invented paper, silk was a popular writing material that was more durable than bamboo or wood. Texts written on silk often joined other funerary objects in the tombs of aristocratic lords and wealthy individuals.

As the long-distance silk trade grew, commerce within China also expanded. Because of reforms in the Warring States period, economic life in China after 300 BCE centered increasingly on independent farmers producing commercial crops for the marketplaces along land routes as well as rivers, canals, and lakes. As this market economy grew, merchants organized themselves based on family lineages and occupational guilds. Power now shifted away from agrarian elites and into the hands of urban financiers and traders. The traders benefited from the improvement in roads and waterways, which eased the transportation of grain, hides, horses, and silk from the villages to the new towns and cities. Bronze coins of various sizes and shapes, as well as cloth and silk used in barter, spurred long-distance trade. By the second century BCE, wealthy merchants were ennobled as local magnates and wore clothing that marked their official status. As commerce further expanded, regional lords opened local customs offices along land routes and waterways to extract a share of the money and products for themselves.

Though China still had little intellectual interaction with the rest of Afro-Eurasia, its long-distance commercial exchanges skyrocketed due to the Silk Road trade. Southern silk was only the first of many Chinese commodities that reached the world beyond the Taklamakan Desert. China also became an export center for lacquer, hemp, and linen. From Sichuan came iron, steel, flint, hard stone, silver, and animals, while jade came from the northwest. At the same time, China was importing Mediterranean, Indian, and central Asian commodities.

Despite its early development of commerce, China still had no major ports that could compare to the caravan cities of Petra and Palmyra. Most cities in the landlocked north were administrative centers where farmers and traders gathered under the regional states' political and military protection. The larger cities had gates that closed between sunset and sunrise; during the night, mounted soldiers patrolled the streets. Newer towns along the southeastern seacoast still looked upriver to trade

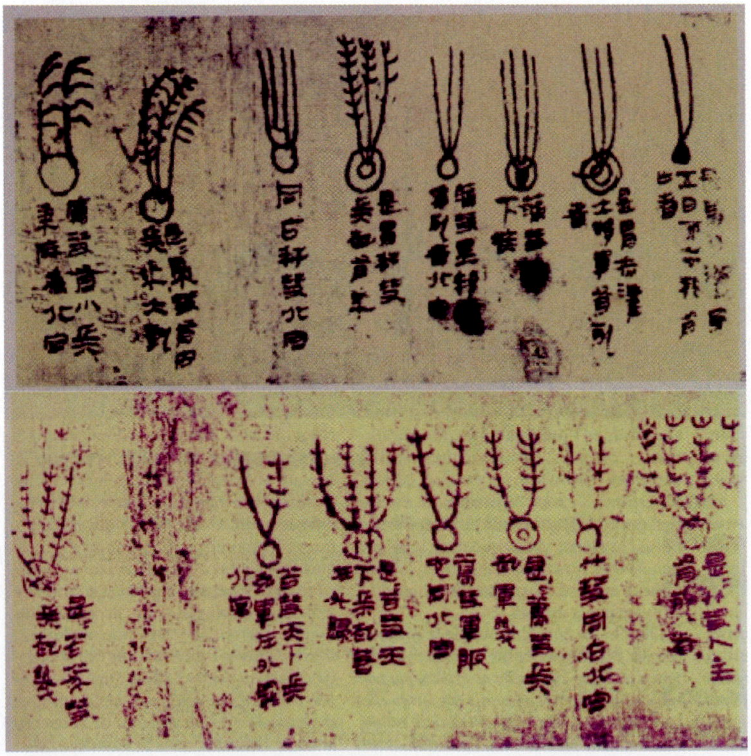

Silk Texts Before the invention of paper, silk was widely used as writing material because it was more portable and durable than bamboo or wood for correspondence, maps, illustrations, and important texts included as funerary objects in the tombs of aristocrats. The Mawangdui silk texts shown here are from a Hunan tomb that was closed in 168 BCE and opened in 1973.

with inland agrarian communities, which also produced silk for export. Facilitating oceanic trade became more of a concern for the state during this period, and merchant ships now enjoyed the protection of military boats. However, internal, interregional trade predominated, and it fed into the Silk Roads through decentralized networks.

THE SPREAD OF BUDDHISM ALONG THE TRADE ROUTES

In addition to silk traders, monks traveled along Afro-Eurasian trade arteries to spread the word of new religions. While Christians would later take advantage of these trade routes to spread their faith (see Chapter 8), Buddhism was the chief expansionist faith in this period. Under Kushan patronage during the first centuries CE, Buddhism reached out from India to China and central Asia, following the Silk Road. Monks from the Kushan Empire accompanied traders traveling to China. There they translated Buddhist texts into Chinese and other languages, aided by Chinese converts. Buddhist ideas were slow to gain acceptance everywhere they proselytized. It took several centuries, and a new wave of nomadic migrations, for Buddhism to take root in China.

Buddhism fared less well when it followed the commercial arteries westward. The religion never became established on the Iranian plateau and made no further headway toward the Mediterranean. The main barrier was Zoroastrianism, which had been a state religion in the Persian Empire during the fifth and fourth centuries BCE (see Chapter 4); by the time Buddhism began to spread, Zoroastrianism had long been established in Iran. Iranian Hellenism had done little to weaken the power of Zoroastrianism, whose adherents formed city-based religious communities affiliated primarily with traders. These Zoroastrian traders continued to adhere to their own faith while traveling along the Silk Roads and did nothing to help Buddhism spread westward.

COMMERCE ON THE RED SEA AND INDIAN OCEAN

Using new navigational techniques and larger ships, seafarers eventually expanded the transport of Silk Road commodities via the Red Sea and the Indian Ocean. Although land routes were the tried-and-true avenues for migrants, traders, and wayfarers, they carried only what could be borne on the backs of humans and animals. Travel on them was slow, and they were vulnerable to marauders. With time, some risk takers found ways of traversing waterways—eventually on an unprecedented scale and with an ease unimaginable to earlier merchants. These risk takers were Arabs, from the commercial middle ground of the Afro-Eurasian trading system.

Arab traders had long carried such spices as frankincense and myrrh to the Egyptians, who used them in religious and funerary rites, and later to the Greeks and Romans. Metals such as bronze, tin, and iron passed along overland routes from Anatolia, as did gold, silver, and chlorite from the Iranian plateau. Gold, ivory, and other goods from the northern part of India passed through Taxila (the capital of Gandhara) and the Hindu Kush Mountains into Persia as early as the sixth century BCE. Following the expansion of the Hellenistic world, however, ships increasingly conducted long-distance trade. Mastering the monsoons over time, they sailed down the Red Sea and across the Indian Ocean as they carried goods between the tip of the Arabian Peninsula and the ports of the Indian landmass.

Arab seafarers led the way into the Indian Ocean, forging links that joined East Africa, the eastern Mediterranean, and the Arabian Peninsula with India, Southeast Asia,

Analyzing Global Developments

The Cosmopolitan World of the *Periplus Maris Erythraei*

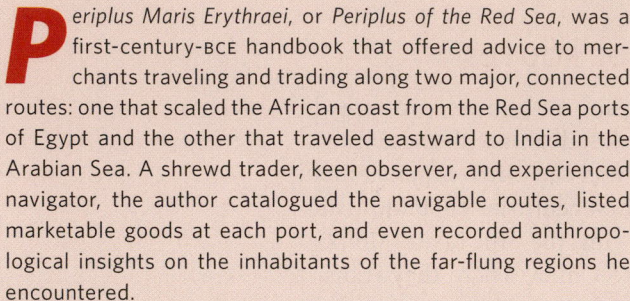

Periplus Maris Erythraei, or *Periplus of the Red Sea*, was a first-century-BCE handbook that offered advice to merchants traveling and trading along two major, connected routes: one that scaled the African coast from the Red Sea ports of Egypt and the other that traveled eastward to India in the Arabian Sea. A shrewd trader, keen observer, and experienced navigator, the author catalogued the navigable routes, listed marketable goods at each port, and even recorded anthropological insights on the inhabitants of the far-flung regions he encountered.

The author's voyage began in the Red Sea port of Berenice and moved southward to the tribal countries of modern-day Sudan and Eritrea. To the east, he found the placid waters of the Gulf of Aden and the frankincense of the Arabian coast. Though Indian products like rice and ghee were widely sold in Arabian market towns, the Indian port of Barygaza remained the most sought-after port of the time, despite its rugged coast, uneven sea bottom, and tidal waves. An important node in the Afro-Eurasian trade network, Barygaza proved to be a curious mix of the exotic and the familiar in the author's eyes, with its vendors hawking everything from Chinese silks to old Greek coins. Pragmatic in tone, the *Periplus* and its display of economic opportunity cannot help but dazzle even modern readers. The following table gives an overview of a few important ports in the *Periplus*, as well as a taste of the ancient world.

QUESTIONS FOR ANALYSIS

- What might these commodities imply about the socioeconomic status of the Greek trader and the status of the consumers of the goods that moved along these routes?
- What are some apparent patterns or commonalities in the goods that these market towns import and export? What goods exported at some of these ports are imported at other ports listed in the *PME*'s itinerary? What does that suggest about the nature of trade along this overseas route?
- Imagine that you are a merchant planning your first overseas venture. Based on the table, where should you stock up on supplies for your crew? With what ports would you want to trade and why? How would you come up with the capital investment needed to launch such a venture?
- What other types of evidence might help you interpret the nature of the trade that took place on these overseas routes? In what ways might that evidence add complexity to, or even complete the snapshot of trade offered by a *periplus* such as this one for Red Sea trade?

Source: Lionel Casson. *The Periplus Maris Erythraei: Text with Introduction, Translation, and Commentary* (Princeton, NJ: Princeton University Press, 1989).

and East Asia. Such voyages involved longer stays at sea and were far more dangerous than sailing in the Mediterranean. Yet by the first century CE, Arab and Indian sailors were transporting Chinese silks, central Asian furs, and fragrances from Himalayan trees across the Indian Ocean. The city of Alexandria in Egypt soon emerged as a key transit point between the Mediterranean Sea and the Indian Ocean. Boats carried Mediterranean exports of olives and olive oil, wine, drinking vessels, glassware, linen and wool textiles, and red coral up the Nile, stopping at Koptos and other port cities from which camel caravans took the goods to ports on the Red Sea. For centuries, Mediter-

	PORT	EXPORTS	IMPORTS	GIFTS FOR RULERS
Southern Arabia	Muza (Sect. 24)	myrrh, white marble, stacte (sweet spice for ancient Hebrew incense)	purple cloth; Arab-sleeved clothing, with no adornment, with checks, or interwoven with gold thread; herbs cyperus and saffron; blankets, with traditional local adornment or none; girdles with shaded stripes; ungent; money, considerable amount; wine; grain	horses, pack mules, expensive clothing, goldware, embossed silverware, copperware
East Africa	Opone (Sect. 13)	cinnamon, frankincense, cassia (Chinese cinnamon), better-quality slaves, tortoise shell	grain, rice, ghee, sesame oil, *monache* and *sagmatogene* (India cotton cloth), girdles, Indian cane sugar	
Persia	Omana, Apologos (Sect. 36)	purple cloth; native clothing; slaves; wine; dates; *madarate* (local sewn boats); pearls, in quantity but inferior to Indian	copper, teakwood beams, saplings, logs of sissoo (rosewood), ebony, frankincense from Kane	
Western India	Barygaza (Sect. 14, 47-8)	grain, rice, ghee, sesame oil, *monache* and *sagmatogene* (Indian cotton cloth), girdles, cane sugar, onyx, agate, molochinon, nard, costus, bedellium, ivory, lykion, Chinese ⌊sc. silk⌋ cloth, long pepper	Italian, Laodicean, and Arabian wine; copper, tin, lead; coral, peridot; printed and plain clothing; multicolored girdles, eighteen inches wide; storax, yellow sweet clover; raw glass; Roman money (gold and silver) commands an exchange at some profit against the local currency; inexpensive ungent	slave musicians, beautiful girls for concubinage, precious silverware, fine wine, expensive clothing with no adornment, choice ungent
Eastern India	Ganges (Sect. 63-4)	malabathron; Gangetic nard; pearls; cotton garments of the very finest quality, the so called Gangetic; *kaltis* (gold coins); finest tortoise shell; silk floss; yarn		

ranean merchants had considered the Arabian Peninsula to be the end of the Spice Road. But after Alexander's expedition and the establishment of colonies between Egypt and Afghanistan, they began to value the wealth and opportunities that lay along the shores of the Indian Ocean.

Arab sailors who ventured into the Indian Ocean benefited from new navigational techniques, especially celestial bearings (using the position of the stars to determine the position of the ship and the direction to sail). They used large ships called *dhows*, whose sails were rigged to easily capture the wind; these forerunners of modern cargo vessels were capable of long hauls in rough waters. Beginning about 120 BCE, mariners came to understand the seasonal rain-filled monsoon winds, which blow from the southwest between October and April and then from the northeast between April and October—knowledge that propelled the maritime trade connecting the Mediterranean with the Indian Ocean. Mariners accumulated the new sailing knowledge in books—each called a ***periplus*** ("sailing around")—in which sea captains recorded the landing spots and ports between their destinations, as well as their precious cargoes. (See **Analyzing Global Developments: The Cosmopolitan World of the *Periplus Maris Erythraei*.**) The revolution in navigational techniques and knowledge dramatically reduced the cost of long-distance shipping and multiplied the ports of call around large bodies of water. Some historians have argued that there were now two Silk Roads: one by land and oneby sea.

Conclusion

Alexander's territorial gains were awesome in their scale, but his empire was as transitory as it was huge. Though it crumbled upon his death, Alexander's conquest had effects more profound than those of any military or political regime before. Alexander's armies ushered in an age of thinking and practices that transformed Greek achievements into a common culture—Hellenism—whose influences, both direct and indirect, touched far-flung societies for centuries thereafter.

Hellenism offered a common language, both literally and figuratively, which linked culture, institutions, and trade. However, many Greek-speaking peoples and their descendants in parts of Southwest and central Asia integrated local cultural practices with their own ways, creating diverse and rich cultures. Thus the influences of culture flowed both ways. The economic story is equally complex. Following pathways forged by previous empires and kingdoms, Alexander's successors strengthened and expanded existing trade routes and centers of commercial activity, which ultimately led to the creation of the Silk Road.

Although the effects of this Hellenistic age lasted longer than most cultural systems and had a wider appeal than previous philosophical and spiritual ideas, they did not overwrite everything that came before. Some, like the Jewish people of Judea and elsewhere, like Alexandria, either fought against Hellenism with all their might or accommodated to it. Others, like the Romans and Carthaginians, took from the new common culture what they liked and discarded the rest.

In South Asia, the immediate successor to Alexander's military was the Mauryan Empire, which established its dominion over much of South Asia and even some of central Asia for close to a century and a half. Once Mauryan control receded, South Asia was opened up even more than before to currents moving swiftly across Afro-Eurasia, including the institutions and cultures of steppe nomads, seafarers, and Hellenists. The most telling South Asian responses occurred in the realm of spiritual and ethical norms, where Buddhist doctrines began to evolve toward a full-fledged world religious system.

Greater political integration helped fashion highways for commerce and enabled the spread of Buddhism. Nomads, like the Kushans, left their steppe lands and exchanged wares across great distances. As they found greater opportunities for business, their trade routes shifted farther south. Eventually merchants, rather than the trading nomads, seized the opportunities provided by new technologies, especially in sailing and navigation, and by thriving caravan cities. These commercial transformations connected distant parts of Afro-Eurasia. The Silk Roads and new sea-lanes connected ports and caravan cities from North Africa to South China, created new social classes, produced new urban settings, supported powerful new polities, and transported Hellenism and Buddhism well beyond their points of origin.

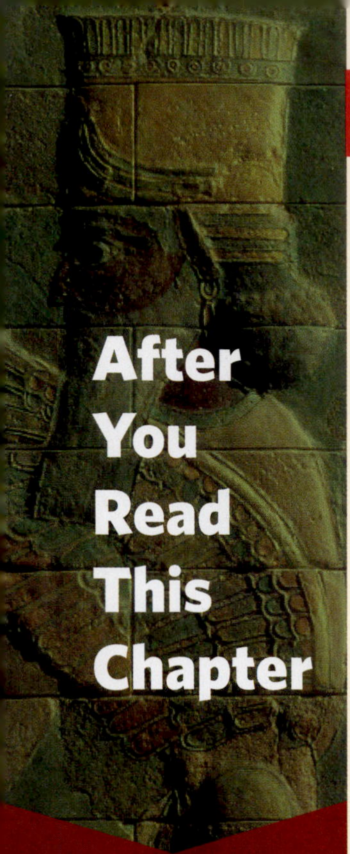

After You Read This Chapter

Go to INQUIZITIVE to see what you've learned—and learn what you've missed—with personalized feedback along the way.

TRACING THE GLOBAL STORYLINES

FOCUS ON: *Forces that Unify Afro-Eurasia*

THE MEDITERRANEAN WORLD

- The spread of Hellenism around the Mediterranean via Alexander's conquests leads to a common language, cosmopolitan cities, new types of philosophy and religion, plantation slavery, and money-based economies.

CENTRAL AND SOUTH ASIA

- Alexander's withdrawal from the Indus Valley leads to the creation of the Mauryan Empire, which integrates the northern half of India.
- The Seleucid and Bactrian kingdoms further solidify the spread of Hellenism into central Asia.

THE TRANSFORMATION OF BUDDHISM

- The combined influences of Hellenism, nomadism, and Indian Ocean seafaring transform Buddhism into a world religion.

FORMATION OF SILK ROADS

- Nomadic warriors from central Asia complete the final links of the overland Silk Roads, strengthening the ties that joined peoples across Afro-Eurasia.
- Overland traders carry spices, transport precious metals, and convey Buddhist thought along the Silk Roads into China.
- Seafaring traders use new navigation techniques and larger ships called *dhows* to expand the transport of Silk Road commodities to the Mediterranean world via the Indian Ocean.

CHRONOLOGY

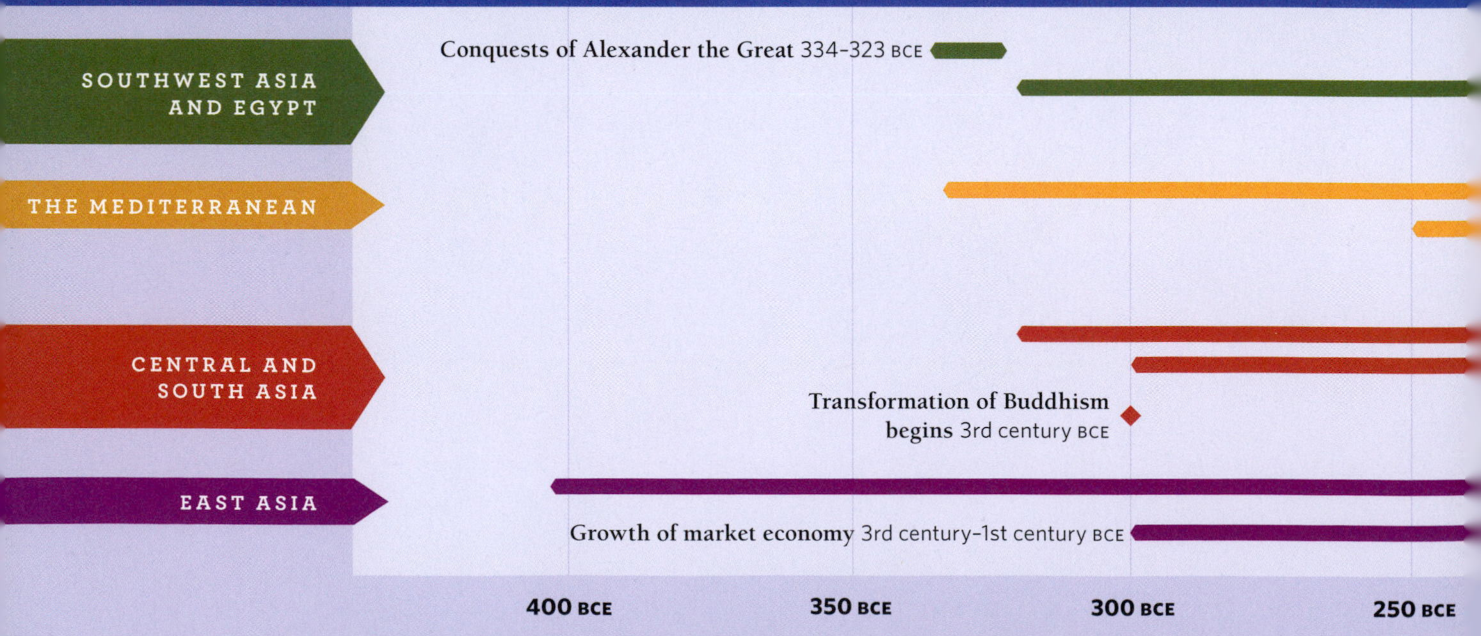

THINKING ABOUT GLOBAL CONNECTIONS

- ***Thinking about Crossing Borders and Shrinking the Afro-Eurasian World*** Alexander's conquests and the resulting Hellenistic kingdoms of his successors brought about a never-before-seen cultural unity across huge swaths of Afro-Eurasia. To what extent was this cultural diffusion—comparable in some ways to the globalization or "Americanization" of culture around the world in modern times—a positive development? In what ways might it have been seen by those living through it as a negative development?
- ***Thinking about Transformation & Conflict and Shrinking the Afro-Eurasian World*** Alexander and his successors brought about unity initially by brutal conquest, then later through diplomatic strategies and the spread of Hellenistic ideas. Likewise, as the Kalinga War demonstrated, Aśoka brutally conquered territories before his change of heart and promotion of *dhamma*. Compare and contrast the role of military conflict and cultural movements (like Hellenism and *dhamma*) in bringing unity to the Hellenistic world and South Asia.
- ***Thinking about* Worlds Together, Worlds Apart *and Shrinking the Afro-Eurasian World*** The long-distance trade routes known as the Silk Roads, and sometimes the Incense Roads, brought intensified interactions among societies across Afro-Eurasia in the last centuries BCE. Which societies were closely involved in this exchange? Which appear to have been less involved? What accounts for these regions' involvement, or lack thereof, in Silk Road exchange?

STUDY QUESTIONS

1. In what ways did Alexander's conquests, his successors, and Hellenism have an impact on Afro-Eurasia? In particular, how did ***koine* Greek, cosmopolitan** identity, new ways of thinking, and slavery shape the Hellenistic world?
2. In what ways did the **Mauryan Empire** bring continuity and change to South Asia? What role did *dhamma* play in Aśoka's uniting of South Asia?
3. Describe the long-term impact of Greek influence in central and South Asia. Consider garrison towns, the region of **Bactria**, and Yavana kings in your answer.
4. How did interregional contacts transform Buddhism in the aftermath of Hellenism and the Mauryan Empire? Consider the development of **Mahayana Buddhism**, the role of **bodhisattvas** in it, and the depictions of the Buddha in **Gandharan art** and Mathuran art.
5. To what extent were the **Silk Roads** a new development in this period 350 BCE–100 CE? What role did **caravan cities** and, later, the Kushans play in the development of these exchange routes? What new developments in interregional exchange do texts like the ***Periplus*** demonstrate?

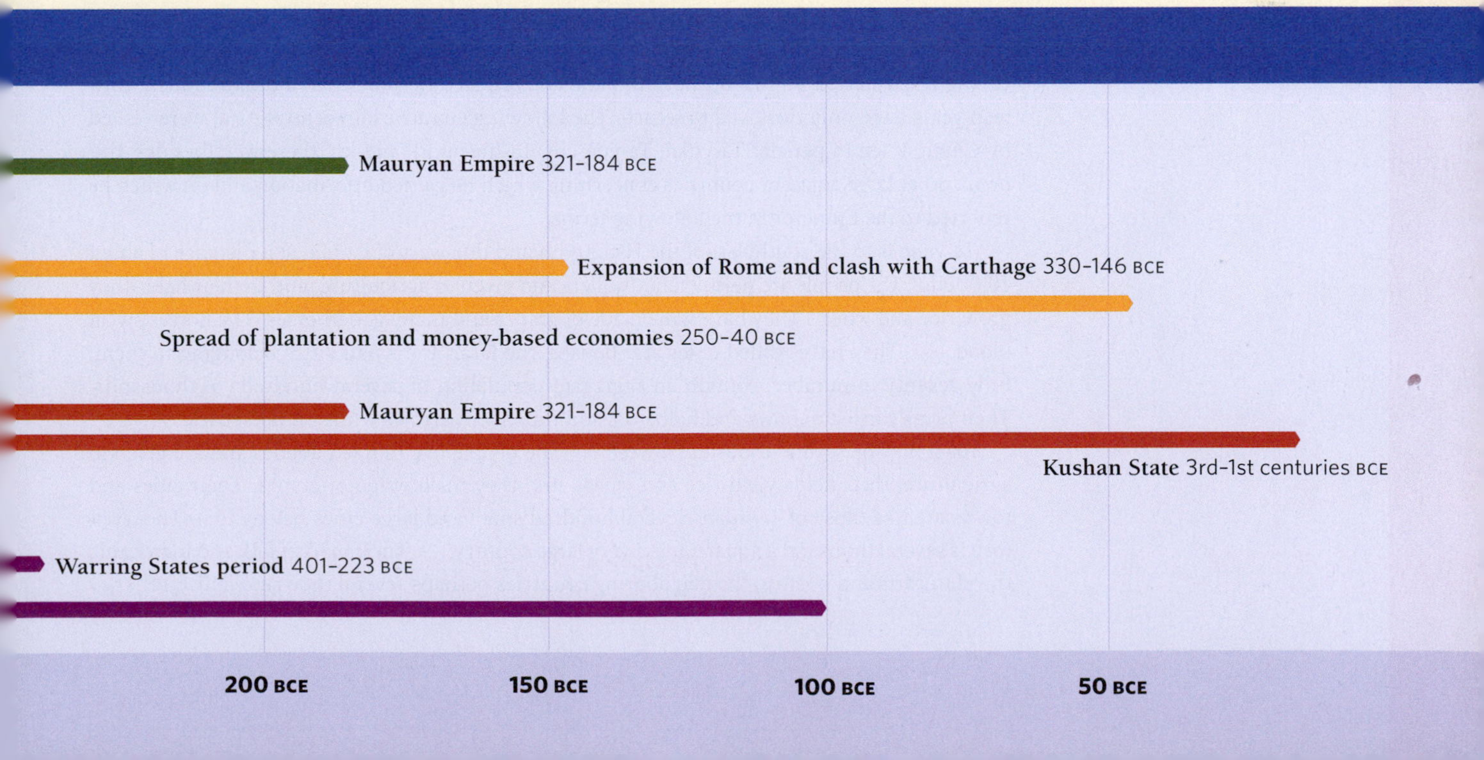

Going to the Source

Connecting Afro-Eurasia

In the aftermath of Alexander's conquests, Hellenistic successor states flourished in western Afro-Eurasia, Indo-Greek Bactrian states reigned in central Eurasia, and the Mauryans developed the first empire in South Asia. A web of trade routes through each of these regions joined together to form the Silk Roads, which included China in these networks of global interaction. The sources in this section, which address culture and commerce, provide a glimpse into this connected world. As with all travel, people from different places noticed different things on their journeys. As you read these descriptions, consider each author's point of view.

PRIMARY SOURCE 6.1

Reports (second century BCE*), Zhang Qian*

The Han dynasty sent Zhang Qian (200–114 BCE) as an envoy to other parts of Asia to explore possible alliances with nomadic states other than the Xiongnu that he encountered along the way. The reports that Zhang Qian compiled while traveling through central Asia provided the Han with a better political and economic understanding of the various peoples and lands to their west.

[The Emperor of] China appointed Chang K'ien [Imperial Chamberlain] and gave T'ang-i Fu the title *Fong-shi-kun* [The Gentleman attending the Embassy]. Chang K'ien was a man of strong physique, magnanimous and trustful, and popular with the foreign tribes in the south and west. T'ang-i Fu was formerly a Hu [Tartar; Xiongnu from the north and west]. Being an excellent bowman, he would, when supplies were exhausted, provide food by shooting game. When Chang K'ien started on his journey, his caravan consisted of more than a hundred men; thirteen years later, only two lived to return. The following countries [in central Asia] were visited by Chang K'ien in person: Ta-yuan, Ta-yue-chi, Ta-hia and K'ang-ku; there were besides, five or six other large adjacent countries concerning which he gained information and on which he reported to the Emperor in the following terms.

Ta-yuan is to the southwest of the Hsiung-nu and due west of China, at a distance of about 10,000 *li*.* The people are permanent dwellers and given to agriculture; and in their fields they grow rice and wheat. They have wine made of grapes and many good horses. The horses sweat blood. . . . They have walled cities and houses; the large and small cities belonging to them, fully seventy in number, contain an aggregate population of several hundreds of thousands. Their arms consist of bows and halberds, and they shoot arrows while on horseback. . . .

An-si may be several thousand *li* west. . . . The people live in fixed abodes and are given to agriculture; their fields yield rice and wheat; and they make wine of grapes. Their cities and towns are like those of Ta-yuan. Several hundred small and large cities belong to it. The territory is several thousand *li* square; it is a very large country. . . . Their market folk and merchants travel in carts and boats to the neighboring countries perhaps several thousand *li* distant. They make coins of silver; the coins resemble their king's face. Upon the death of a king the coins are changed for others on which the new king's face is represented. They paint [rows of characters] running sideways on [stiff] leather, to serve as records. . . .

The people [of Ta-Hia] have fixed abodes and live in walled cities and regular houses like the people of Ta-yuan. They have no great king or chief, but everywhere the cities and towns have their own petty chiefs. While the people are shrewd traders, their soldiers are weak and afraid to fight, so that, when the Ta-yue-chi migrated westward, they made war on the Ta-hia, who became subject to them. The population of Ta-hia may amount to more than a million. Their capital is called Lan-shi, and it has markets for the sale of all sorts of merchandise. To the southeast of it is the country of *Shon-tu* [India]. Chang K'ien says [in his report to the Emperor]: "When I was in Ta-hia, I saw there a stick of bamboo of Kiung [Kiung-chou in Ssi-ch'uan] and some cloth of Shu [Ssi-ch 'uan]. When I asked the inhabitants of Ta-hia how they had obtained possession of these, they replied: 'The inhabitants of our country buy them in Shon-tu [India].'" . . . The people there have fixed abodes, and their customs are very much like those of Ta-hia; but the country is low, damp, and hot. The people ride elephants to fight in battle. The country is close to a great river. According to my calculation, Ta-hia must be 12,000 *li* distant from China and to the southwest of the latter. . . .

The people occupying the tracts from Ta-yuan westward as far as the country of An-si talked different dialects, but their manners and customs being in the main identical, they understood each other. They had deepset eyes, most of them wore beards, and as shrewd merchants they would haggle about the merest trifles. They placed high value on women, and husbands were guided in their decisions by the advice of their wives. These countries produced no silk and varnish, and they did not know the casting of coins and utensils.

*A traditional unit of measurement, the distance covered by a li varied over time and often took into account the effort needed to cover the distance.

1. **How does Zhang Qian understand the world outside of China? What aspects of each region does he describe?**
2. **What do Zhang Qian's reports reveal about trade and commerce along the Silk Roads between China and India?**

PRIMARY SOURCE 6.2

The Kalinga Edict *(261 BCE), Aśoka*

After his vicious conquest of the region of Kalinga (261 BCE), the Mauryan emperor Aśoka issued this edict to express his regret over the miseries his conquest had caused. He also explained his conversion to Buddhism. His intent to rule by *dhamma* and to extend Buddhism's influence through his realm is preserved in rock edicts found at Dhauli and Jaugada in northeastern India. Pay particular attention to the language he uses to describe himself and others.

[Certainly] the slaughter, death and deportation of men which take place in the course of the conquest of an unconquered country are now considered extremely painful and deplorable by the Beloved of the Gods. But what is considered even more deplorable by the Beloved of the Gods is the fact that injury to or slaughter or deportation of the beloved ones falls to the lot of the Brahmans, *śramanas*, the adherents of other sects and the householders, who live in that country and among whom are established such virtues as obedience to superior personages, obedience to mother and father, obedience to elders and proper courtesy and firm devotion to friends, acquaintances, companions and relatives as well as to slaves and servants. And if misfortune befalls the friends, acquaintances, companions and relatives of persons who are full of affection towards the former, even though they are themselves well provided for, the said misfortune as well becomes an injury to their own selves. In war, this fate is shared by all classes of men and is considered deplorable by the Beloved of the Gods.

Excepting [among the Greeks], there is no country where . . . the Brahmans and the *śramanas* do not exist; and there is no place in any country where men are not indeed sincerely devoted to one sect or the other. Therefore, the slaughter, death or deportation of even a hundredth or thousandth part of all those people who were slain or who died or were carried away captive at that time in Kalinga, is now considered very deplorable by the Beloved of the Gods.

Now the Beloved of the Gods thinks that, even if a person should wrong him, the offense would be forgiven if it was possible to forgive it. And the forest [tribes] who live in the dominions of the Beloved of the Gods, even them he entreats and exhorts in regard to their duty. It is hereby explained to them that, in spite of his repentance, the Beloved of the Gods possesses power enough to punish them for their crimes, so that they should turn from evil ways and would not be killed for their crimes. [Certainly] the Beloved of the Gods desires the following in respect of all creatures[:] non-injury to them, restraint in dealing with them, and impartiality in the case of crimes committed by them.

So, what is conquest through *Dhamma* is now considered to be the best conquest by the Beloved of the Gods. And such a conquest has been achieved by the Beloved of the Gods not only here in his own dominions but also in the territories bordering on his dominions, as far away as . . . six hundred *yojanas* [about 1,500 miles], where the [Greek] king named Antiochus is ruling and where, beyond the kingdom of the said Antiochus, four other kings named Ptolemy, Antigonus, Magas, and Alexander are also ruling, and, towards the south, where the Colas and Pāndyas living as far as Ceylon. Likewise here in the dominion of His Majesty, the Beloved of the Gods—in the countries of the [Greeks] and the Kambojas, the Na-bhakas and Na-bhapanktis, the Bhojas and Pitinikas, the Andhras and Pa-rindas, everywhere the people are conforming to the instructions in *Dhamma* imparted by the Beloved of the Gods.

Even where the envoys of the Beloved of the Gods have not penetrated, there too men have heard of the practices of *Dhamma* and the ordinances issued and the instructions in *Dhamma* imparted by the Beloved of the Gods, and are conforming to *Dhamma* and will continue to conform to it.

[W]hatever conquest is achieved in this way, [certainly] that conquest creates an atmosphere of satisfaction everywhere both among the victors and the vanquished. In the conquest through *Dhamma*, satisfaction is derived by both the parties. But that satisfaction is indeed of little consequence. Only happiness of the people in the next world is what is regarded by the Beloved of the Gods as a great thing resulting from such a conquest.

And this record relating to *Dhamma* has been written on stone for the following purpose, [namely] that my sons and great-grandsons should not think of a fresh conquest by arms as worth achieving, that they should adopt the policy of forbearance and light punishment towards the vanquished even if they conquer a people by arms, and that they should regard the conquest through *Dhamma* as the true conquest. Such a conquest brings happiness to all concerned both in this world and in the next. And let all their intense joys be what is pleasure associated with *Dhamma*. For this brings happiness in this world as well as in the next.

1. **How does Aśoka understand his own conquest now that he has converted to Buddhism?**
2. **What does Aśoka think the role of Buddhism should be in the territories that he governs?**

PRIMARY SOURCE 6.3

"Sâgala: City of the Gods" (c. 150–130 BCE) from The Questions of King Menander

In *The Questions of King Menander*, the Indo-Greek king Menander, before raising questions about the divine nature of Buddha, describes his kingdom in the country of Yonakas, focusing on the trading city of Sâgala in present-day Pakistan. Sâgala was at the eastern end of the Greek empire established by Alexander the Great. When his army captured it, he destroyed the city, annexed the territory, and then built a new city in its place. It was known as a place where the Greek and local populations lived together peacefully and as an important commercial center.

*

Thus hath it been handed down by tradition—There is in the country of the Yonakas a great centre of trade, a city that is called Sâgala, situated in a delightful country well watered and hilly, abounding in parks and gardens and groves and lakes and tanks, a paradise of rivers and mountains and woods. Wise architects have laid it out, and its people know of no oppression, since all their enemies and adversaries have been put down. Brave is its defence, with many and various strong towers and ramparts, with superb gates and entrance archways; and with the royal citadel in its midst, white walled and deeply moated. Well laid out are its streets, squares, cross roads, and market places. Well displayed are the innumerable sorts of costly merchandise with which its shops are filled. It is richly adorned with hundreds of almshalls of various kinds; and splendid with hundreds of thousands of magnificent mansions, which rise aloft like the mountain peaks of the Himâlayas. Its streets are filled with elephants, horses, carriages, and foot-passengers, frequented by groups of handsome men and beautiful women, and crowded by men of all sorts and conditions, Brahmans, nobles, artificers, and servants. They resound with cries of welcome to the teachers of every creed, and the city is the resort of the leading men of each of the differing sects. Shops are there for the sale of Benares muslin, of Kotumbara stuffs and of other cloths of various kinds; and sweet odours are exhaled from the bazaars, where all sorts of flowers and perfumes are tastefully set out. Jewels are there in plenty, such as men's hearts desire, and guilds of traders in all sorts of finery display their goods in the bazaars that face all quarters of the sky. So full is the city of money, and of gold and silver ware, of copper and stone ware, that it is a very mine of dazzling treasures. And there is laid up there much store of property and corn and things of value in warehouses—foods and drinks of every sort, syrups and sweetmeats of every kind. In wealth it rivals Uttara-kuru, and in glory it is as, Âlakamandâ the city of the gods.

1. **How does Menander describe Sâgala? Which aspects of the city does he emphasize?**
2. **Compare Menander's description of Sâgala with the descriptions in Primary Source 6.1 and explain the similarities and differences that you discover.**

PRIMARY SOURCE 6.4

"The Ancient City of Alexandria" (early first century CE), Strabo

In this passage, the Greek geographer Strabo describes the thriving Egyptian port city of Alexandria, which had become an enormous transshipment center (or entrepôt) for goods from across the Mediterranean world as well as to points in Asia and Africa.

As for the Great Harbor at Alexandria, it is not only wonderfully well closed in and protected by artificial levees and by nature, it is also so deep that even the largest ships can be moored right at the stairs along its quayside. This Great Harbor is divided up into several minor harbors. . . . Even more exports are handled than imports. Anyone who might happen to be at Alexandria and at Dichaiarchia [the large Italian port on the Bay of Naples] would easily see for himself that the cargo ships sailing from here are bigger and more heavily laden. . . . The city itself is crisscrossed by streets that are wide enough for riding horses and driving chariots, and intersected by two main roads very much broader than the others. Its streets and avenues cut across each other at right angles. The city also boasts exceedingly beautiful public parks and its royal quarters take up a quarter, perhaps even a third of the whole city. . . . In earlier times, not even twenty ships would dare to go as far as the Arabian Gulf and manage to get a look outside its straits. But now large fleets of ships are sent out as far as India and to the furthest lands of the Ethiopians, from which the most valuable cargoes are brought to Egypt and then sent out again to other regions of the world. Double charges are collected on these shipments—both when they come in and when they go out—and the duties are especially high on luxury goods . . . for Alexandria alone does not just receive trade goods of this kind from all over the world, but it also furnishes supplies to the whole of the world outside.

1. **Based on this description, why was Alexandria an important city during the first century CE?**
2. **What aspects of the city does Strabo highlight and what do they reveal about the Hellenistic culture?**

PRIMARY SOURCE 6.5

The Voyage around the Erythraean Sea (first century CE)

The *Periplus Maris Erythraei* (*Voyage around the Erythraean [Red] Sea*) was written in the first century CE by an unknown, Greek-speaking Egyptian merchant. The *Periplus* details the trip along the Silk Road sea-lanes from Egypt to the east coast of India. In addition to providing sailors and merchants with safe ports and routes, the *Periplus* also advises them on the local populations and the goods they can obtain at various marketplaces along the route.

30. On this bay there . . . is an island. . . . The inhabitants are few and they live on the coast toward the north, which from this side faces the continent. They are foreigners, a mixture of Arabs and Indians and Greeks, who have emigrated to carry on trade there. . . .

38. Beyond this region, the continent making a wide curve from the east across the depths of the bays, there follows the coast district of Scythia, which lies above toward the north; the whole marshy; from which flows down the river Sinthus [Indus River], the greatest of all the rivers that flow into the Erythraean Sea. . . .

39. The ships lie at anchor at Barbaricum, but all their cargoes are carried up to the metropolis by the river, to the King. There are imported into this market a great deal of thin clothing, and a little spurious; figured linens, topaz, coral, storax, frankincense, vessels of glass, silver and gold plate, and a little wine. On the other hand there are exported costus, bdellium, lycium, nard [plant products], turquoise, lapis lazuli, Seric [silk] skins, cotton cloth, silk yarn, and indigo. And sailors set out thither with the Indian Etesian winds, about the month of July, that is Epiphi: it is more dangerous then, but through these winds the voyage is more direct, and sooner completed. . . .

41. Beyond the gulf of Baraca is . . . the Kingdom of Nambanus and of all India. . . . It is a fertile country, yielding wheat and rice and sesame oil and clarified butter, cotton and the Indian cloths made therefrom, of the coarser sorts. Very many cattle are pastured there, and the men are of great stature and black in color. . . . In these places there remain even to the present time signs of the expedition of Alexander, such as ancient shrines, walls of forts and great wells. . . .

47. The country inland from Barygaza is inhabited by numerous tribes . . . in which is Bucephalus Alexandria. Above these is the very war-like nation of the Bactrians, who are under their own king. And Alexander, setting out from these parts, penetrated to the Ganges . . . coming from this country, bearing inscriptions in Greek letters, and the devices of those who reigned after Alexander, Apollodotus and Menander. . . .

50. Beyond Barygaza . . . The inland country back from the coast toward the east comprises many desert regions and great mountains; and all kinds of wild beasts—leopards, tigers, elephants, enormous serpents, hyenas, and baboons of many sorts; and many populous nations. . . .

64. After this region under the very north, the sea outside ending in a land called This, there is a very great inland city called Thinae [China], from which raw silk and silk yarn and silk cloth are brought on foot through Bactria to Barygaza, and are also exported to Damirica by way of the river Ganges. But the land of This is not easy of access; few men come from there, and seldom. . . .

65. Every year on the borders of the land of This there comes together a tribe of men with short bodies and broad, flat faces, and by nature peaceable; they are called Besata, and are almost entirely uncivilized. They come with their wives and children, carrying great packs and plaited baskets of what looks like greengrape-leaves. They meet in a place between their own country and the land of This. There they hold a feast for several days, spreading out the baskets under themselves as mats, and then return to their own places in the interior. And then the natives watching them come into that place and gather up their mats; and they pick out from the braids the fibers which they call *petri*. They lay the leaves closely together in several layers and make them into balls, which they pierce with the fibers from the mats. And there are three sorts; those made of the largest leaves are called the large-ball malabathrum; those of the smaller, the medium-ball; and those of the smallest, the small-ball. Thus there exist three sorts of malabathrum, and it is brought into India by those who prepare it.

66. The regions beyond these places are either difficult of access because of their excessive winters and great cold, or else cannot be sought out because of some divine influence of the gods.

1. **Compare this account to Primary Source 6.1. What similarities and differences do the authors describe in the societies they observed?**
2. **Explain the connection between trade and the idea of being civilized as described by the author.**

PRIMARY SOURCE 6.6

Al Khazneh at Petra (c. first century CE)

Built as a mausoleum and crypt, Al Khazneh is carved directly out of a red sandstone cliff in the Nabatean city of Petra, now located in southwestern Jordan. Its interior is a simple, cave-like room. The exterior however suggests some of the grandeur that this city exhibited.

1. **What kinds of architectural influences do you see in this image? Why might they be present?**
2. **Imagine that you were a traveler encountering this building for the first time. What would you think about the building and the society that constructed it?**

Questions for Analysis

Comparison

1. Compare the primary sources in this set. What evidence of exchange (of goods or ideas) can you find in each source?

Interpretation

2. What do travelers' accounts contribute to historical knowledge?

Causation

3. Explain the connections between wealth and power during this era of Eurasian integration.

Long Essay Question

Argumentation

The development of the Silk Roads and other connections across Afro-Eurasia spread knowledge and facilitated commerce. In your view, which of these activities—knowledge or commerce—was more important to global integration? Explain your answer.

Before You Read This Chapter

GLOBAL STORYLINES

- Flourishing at roughly the same time, Han China and the Roman Empire become powerful and enduring "globalizing empires."
- The Han dynasty, building on Qin foundations, establishes a bureaucratic imperial model and social order in East Asia.
- The Roman Empire becomes a Mediterranean superpower exerting far-reaching political, legal, economic, and cultural influence.

CORE OBJECTIVES

- **IDENTIFY** the features that made Han China and imperial Rome globalizing empires.
- **DESCRIBE** the development of the Han dynasty from its beginnings through the third century CE.
- **EXPLAIN** the process by which Rome transitioned from a minor city-state to a dominating Mediterranean power.
- **COMPARE** Han China with imperial Rome in terms of their respective political authority, economy, cultural developments, and military expansion.

CHAPTER

7

Han Dynasty China and Imperial Rome

300 BCE–300 CE

KEY TERMS

Augustus p. 261
Christianity p. 264
commanderies p. 245
Emperor Wu p. 248
globalizing empire p. 244
Imperial University p. 249
Pax Romana p. 261
Pax Sinica p. 252
Punic Wars p. 259
res publica p. 259
Shi Huangdi p. 245

In third-century-BCE China, the Eastern Zhou state of Qin absorbed the remaining Warring States (see Chapter 5) and set the stage for the Han dynasty. The chief minister of the Qin state, Li Si, urged his king to seize the opportunity presented by the disarray of his opponents: by combining his fearsome armies and his own personal virtues, the king could sweep away his rivals as if dusting ashes from a kitchen hearth. "This is the one moment in ten thousand ages," Li Si whispered to the man who would become Qin Shi Huangdi. The king listened carefully. He followed the advice and laid the foundations for a mighty empire. Although Shi Huangdi's Qin Empire collapsed in 207 BCE after a mere two decades, his political innovations set the stage for the much more powerful Han Empire (206 BCE–220 CE), which became one of the most successful dynasties in Chinese history. Following the Qin model, the Han defeated other regional groups and established a Chinese empire that would last for four centuries.

At the other end of Afro-Eurasia another great state, imperial Rome, also met its rivals in war, emerged victorious, and consolidated its power into a vast empire. The Romans achieved this feat by using violent force on a scale hitherto unseen in their part of the globe. The result was a state of huge size, astonishingly unified and stable. Living in the Roman Empire in the mid-70s CE, Pliny the Elder wrote glowingly about the unity of the imperial Roman state. In his eyes, all the benefits that flowed from Rome's extensive reach derived from the greatness of a peace that joined diverse peoples under one benevolent emperor. In this chapter we will examine and compare the growth, politics, economies, and societies of the Han and Roman empires.

Globalizing Empires: The Han Dynasty and Imperial Rome

COMPARISON

IDENTIFY the features that made Han China and imperial Rome globalizing empires.

The Han and the Roman states became truly **globalizing empires**: they covered immense amounts of territory, included huge, diverse populations, and exerted influence far beyond their own borders. Their major innovation was not that they found new ways to plow resources into big armies and civil bureaucracies or because rulers gave new justifications for their rule. Rather, what distinguished the Romans and the Han from their predecessors was their commitment to integrating conquered neighbors and rivals into their worlds—by extending laws, offering systems of representation, exporting belief systems, colonizing lands, and promoting trade within and beyond their empires. Subject peoples became members of empires, not just the vanquished. Those who resisted not only waved away the benefits of living under imperial rule but also became the targets for military retribution.

In this period, an estimated one out of every four human beings in Afro-Eurasia fell directly under the authority of China or Rome. Their control shaped the identity of those living within their respective realms. To be "Han Chinese" meant that elites shared a common written language based on the Confucian classics, which qualified them for public office. It also meant that commoners from all walks of life shared the elites' belief system based on ancestor worship, ritual practices stressing appropriate decorum and dress for each social level, and a view that the agrarian-based Han Empire was a small-scale model of the entire cosmos. Those who lived beyond the realm of the Han were considered uncivilized.

What it meant to be "Roman" changed over time as Rome's imperial reach expanded. In the fifth century BCE, being Roman meant being a citizen of the city of Rome, speaking Latin (the regional language of central Italy), and eating and dressing like Latin-speaking people. By the late second century BCE, the concept of citizenship expanded to include not only citizens of the city but also anyone who had formal membership in the larger territorial state that the Romans were building. By the beginning of the third century CE, being Roman meant simply being a subject of the Roman emperors. This Roman identity became so deeply rooted that when the western parts of the empire disintegrated two centuries later, the inhabitants of the surviving eastern parts—who had no connection with Rome, did not speak Latin, and did not dress or eat like the original Romans—still considered themselves "Romans" in this broader sense.

The two empires reflected different patterns of development, types of public servants, and ideals for the best kind of government. For example, the civilian magistrate and the bureaucrat were typical of the Han Empire, whereas the citizen, the soldier, and the military governor were at the heart of the Roman Empire. In China, dynastic empires fashioned themselves according to the models of past empires. By contrast, Rome began as a collectively ruled city-state and pursued its road to domination as if creating something new. Nonetheless, like the Chinese, Romans were strongly traditional and also idealized their ancestors. Both new empires united huge landmasses and extraordinarily diverse populations.

While both China and Rome participated in Silk Road exchange, both economies were primarily agrarian-based; yet in China, free peasants worked the land, while a huge enslaved population worked the fields of the Roman Empire. At its height, the Han Empire included around 59 million inhabitants and covered 3 million square miles in China proper and, for a while, another 1 million square miles in central Asia. The Roman Empire governed an area and a population nearly as great as those of Han China.

Both empires left indelible legacies; following their collapses, both survived as models. Successor states in the Mediterranean sought to become the second Rome, and after the Han dynasty fell, the Chinese people identified themselves and their language simply as "Han." Both empires raised life to a new level of bureaucratic and military complexity and offered a common identity on a grander scale than ever before. It was a vision that would never be lost.

The Han Dynasty (206 BCE–220 CE)

The Han dynasty (206 BCE–220 CE) oversaw an unprecedented blossoming of peace and prosperity. Although supporters of the Han dynasty boasted of the regime's imperial uniqueness, in reality it owed much to its predecessor, the Qin state, which contributed vital elements of political unity and economic growth to its more powerful successor regime. (See Map 7.1.) Together, the Qin and Han created the political, social, economic, and cultural foundations that characterized imperial China thereafter.

COMPARISON

DESCRIBE the development of the Han dynasty from its beginnings through the third century CE.

THE QIN DYNASTY (221–207 BCE): A CRUCIAL FORERUNNER

Although it lasted only fourteen years, the Qin dynasty integrated much of China and made important administrative and economic innovations. The Qin were but one of many militaristic regimes during the Warring States period. What enabled the Qin to prevail over rivals was their expansion into the Sichuan region, which was remarkable for its rich mineral resources and fertile soils. There, a merchant class and the silk trade spurred economic growth, and public works fostered increased food production. These strengths enabled the Qin by 221 BCE to defeat the remaining warring states and unify an empire that covered roughly two-thirds of modern China.

Supported by able ministers and generals, a large conscripted army, and a system of taxation that financed all-out war, the Qin ruler King Zheng assumed the mandate of heaven from the Zhou. Declaring himself **Shi Huangdi**, or "First August Emperor" in 221 BCE, Zheng harkened back to China's mythical emperors of great antiquity. Forgoing the title of king (*wang*), which had been used by leaders of the Zhou and warring states, Zheng instead took the title of emperor (*di*), a term that had meant "ancestral ruler" for the Shang and Zhou.

Shi Huangdi centralized the administration of the empire. He forced the defeated rulers of the warring states and their families to move to Xianyang, the Qin capital—where they would be unable to gather rebel armies. The First August Emperor then parceled out the territory of his massive state into thirty-six provinces, called **commanderies** (*jun*). Each commandery had a civilian and a military governor, as well as an imperial inspector. Regional and local officials answered directly to the emperor, who could dismiss them at will. Civilian governors did not serve in their home areas, thus preventing them from building up power for themselves. These reforms provided China with a centralized bureaucracy and a hereditary emperor that later dynasties, including the Han, inherited.

The chief minister of the Qin Empire, Li Si, subscribed to the principles of Legalism developed during the Warring States period. This philosophy valued written law codes, administrative regulations, and inflexible punishments more highly than rituals and ethics (which the Confucians emphasized) or spontaneity and the natural order (which the Daoists stressed). Determined to bring order to a turbulent world, Li Si advocated strict laws and harsh punishments that included beheading, mutilation, and loss of rank and office.

MAP 7.1 | East Asia, 206 BCE–220 CE

Both the Qin and the Han dynasties consolidated much of East Asia into one large regional empire.

- According to the map, what physical features imposed a limit to this territorial expansion?
- Why was the Great Wall so long and why was it placed facing north?
- What impact did the pastoral Xiongnu have on each empire's effort to consolidate a large territorial state?
- According to your reading, why did the Han expand their influence farther west than the Qin?

Other methods of control further facilitated Qin rule. Registration of the common people at the age of sixteen provided the basis for taxation and conscription both for military service and public works projects. The Qin emperor established standard weights and measures, as well as a standard currency. The Qin also improved communication systems and administrative efficiency by constructing roads radiating out from their capital to all parts of the empire. Just as crucial was the Qin effort to standardize writing. Banning regional variants of written characters, the Qin required scribes and ministers throughout the empire to adopt the "small seal script," which later evolved into the less complicated style of bureaucratic writing known as "clerical script" that became prominent during the Han dynasty. In 213 BCE, a Qin decree ordered officials to confiscate and burn all books in private possession, except for technical works on medicine, divination, and agriculture. Education and learning were now under the exclusive control of state officials.

Intellectual Censorship This seventeenth-century painting depicts the infamous "Burning of the Books and Burying of the Scholars," edict enacted by Shi Huangdi at the suggestion of his advisor, Li Si. Unfortunately, even the state-approved texts were destroyed a mere six years later, during the fall of the Qin dynasty and sack of the capital.

The agrarian empire of the Qin yielded wealth that the state could tax. Increased tax revenues meant more resources for imposing order. The government issued rules on working the fields, taxed farming households, and conscripted laborers to build irrigation systems and canals so that even more land could come under cultivation. The Qin and later the Han dynasties relied on free farmers and conscripted their able-bodied sons into their huge armies. Working their own land and paying a portion of their crops in taxes, peasant families were the economic bedrock of the Chinese empire. Long-distance commerce thrived, as well. In the dynamic regional market centers of the cities, merchants peddled foodstuffs as well as weapons, metals, horses, dogs, hides, furs, silk, and salt—all produced in different regions and transported on the improved road system. Taxed both in transit and in the market at a higher rate than agricultural goods, these trade goods yielded even more revenue for the imperial government.

The Qin grappled with the need to expand and defend their borders, extending those boundaries in the northeast to the Korean Peninsula, in the south to present-day Vietnam, and in the west into central Asia. Relations between the settled Chinese and the nomadic Xiongnu to the north and west (see Chapter 6) teetered in a precarious balance until 215 BCE, when the Qin Empire pushed north into the middle of the Yellow River basin, seizing pasturelands from the Xiongnu and opening the region up for settlement. Qin officials built roads into these areas and employed conscripts and criminals to create a massive defensive wall that covered a distance of 3,000 miles along the northern border (the beginnings of the Great Wall of China—though north of the current wall, which was constructed more than a millennium later). In 211 BCE the Qin settled 30,000 colonists in the steppe lands of Inner Eurasia.

Despite its military power, the Qin dynasty collapsed quickly, due to constant warfare and the heavy taxation and exhausting conscription that war required. When conscripted workers mutinied in 209 BCE, they found allies in descendants of Warring States nobles, local military leaders, and influential merchants. The rebels swept up thousands of supporters with their call to arms against the "tyrannical" Qin. Shortly before Shi Huangdi died in 210, even the educated elite joined former lords and regional vassals in revolt. The second Qin emperor committed suicide in 207, and his weak successor surrendered to the leader of the Han forces later that year. The resurgent Xiongnu confederacy also reconquered their old pasturelands as the dynasty fell.

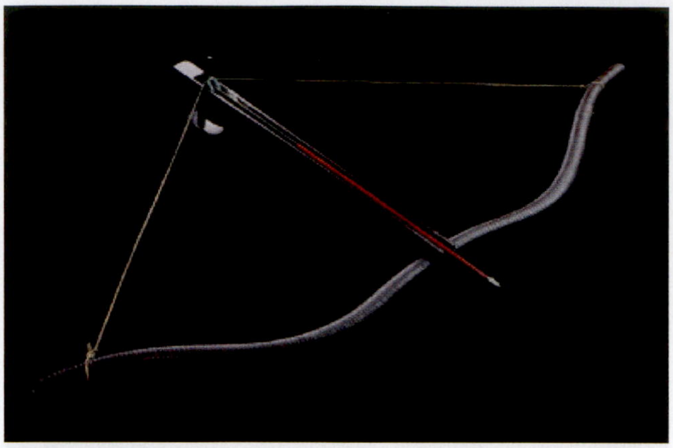

Qin Archer and Crossbow This kneeling archer was discovered in the tomb of the First Emperor. Notice his breastplate; its overlapping plates would have enhanced maneuverability. The wooden bow he was holding has disintegrated, but a replica appears above. The bronze arrowhead and trigger mechanism in this reproduction were found with the terra-cotta army.

BEGINNINGS OF THE WESTERN HAN DYNASTY

The civil war that followed the collapse of Qin rule opened the way for the formation of the Western Han dynasty. A commoner and former policeman named Liu Bang (r. 206–195 BCE) declared himself prince of his home area of Han. In 202 BCE, Liu proclaimed himself the first Han emperor. Claiming the mandate of heaven, the Han portrayed the Qin as evil; yet at the same time they adopted the Qin's bureaucratic system. In reality, Qin laws had been no crueler than those of the Han. Under Han leadership, China's armies swelled with some 50,000 crossbowmen who brandished mass-produced weapons made from bronze and iron. Armed with the crossbow, foot soldiers and mounted archers extended Han imperial lands in all directions. Following the Qin practice, the Han also relied on a huge conscripted labor force for special projects such as building canals, roads, and defensive walls.

The first part of the Han dynasty is known as the Western (or Former) Han dynasty (206 BCE–9 CE). The Han brought economic prosperity and the expansion of empire. This was especially the case under **Emperor Wu**, known also as Han Wudi, who presided over one of the longest and most eventful reigns in Chinese history (r. 140–87 BCE). Although called the "Martial Emperor" because of the state's many military campaigns, Emperor Wu rarely inspected his military units and never led them in battle. Wu followed the Daoist principle of *wuwei* (noninterference), striving to remain aloof from day-to-day activities and permitting the empire to function on its own as if it did not require intervention. Still, he used a stringent penal code to eliminate powerful officials who got in his way. In a single year, his court system prosecuted over a thousand such cases.

HAN POWER AND ADMINISTRATION

Undergirding the Han Empire was the tight-knit alliance between the imperial family and the new elite—the scholar-gentry class—who shared a determination to impose order on the Chinese population. Although the first Han emperors had no choice but to compromise with the aristocratic groups who had helped overthrow the Qin, in time the Han created the most highly centralized bureaucracy in the world. No fewer than 130,000 individuals staffed the central and local governments. That structure became the source of its enduring power. As under the Qin, the Han bureaucracy touched everyone because all males had to register, pay taxes, and serve in the military.

The Han court moved quickly to tighten its grip on regional administration. First it removed powerful princes, crushed rebellions, and took over the areas controlled by regional lords. According to arrangements instituted in 106 BCE by Emperor Wu, the empire consisted of thirteen provinces under imperial inspectors. Commanderies, each administered by a civilian and a military official, covered vast lands inhabited by countless ethnic groups totaling millions of people. These officials maintained political stability and ensured the efficient collection of taxes. However, given the immense numbers under their jurisdiction and the heavy duties they bore, in many respects the local administrative staff was still inadequate to the tasks facing them.

Han Coin After the Qin created the first standard imperial currency in China, the copper wuzhu coin was issued by Emperor Xuandi during the Western Han dynasty, 73–49 BCE. *Wuzhu,* which means "five grains," refers to the weight of the coin (1 wuzhu = 5 grains = 4 grams). The wuzhu was in circulation until 621 CE.

Government schools that promoted the scholar-official ideal became fertile sources for recruiting local officials. In 136 BCE, Emperor Wu founded what became the **Imperial University**, a college for classical scholars that supplied the Han need for well-trained bureaucrats. By the second century CE, the university boasted 30,000 students and faculty. Apart from studying the classics, Han scholars were naturalists and inventors. They made important medical discoveries, dealing with rational diagnoses of the body's functions and the role of wind and temperature in transmitting diseases. They also invented the magnetic compass and developed high-quality paper. Local elites encouraged their sons to master the classical teachings. This practice could secure future entry into the ruling class and firmly planted the Confucian classics at the heart of the imperial state.

Confucian thought slowly became the ideological buttress of the Han Empire. Under Emperor Wu, the bureaucracy deemed people's welfare to be the essential purpose of legitimate rule. By 50 BCE, the *Analects* containing Confucius's sayings was widely disseminated and three Confucian ideals reigned as the official doctrine of the Han Empire: honoring tradition, respecting the lessons of history, and the emperor's responsibility to heaven. Scholars used Confucius's words to tutor the princes. By embracing Confucian political ideals, Han rulers established an empire based on the mandate of heaven and crafted a careful balance in which the officials provided a counterweight to the emperor's autocratic strength. When the interests of the court and the bureaucracy clashed, however, the emperor's will was paramount.

ECONOMY AND THE NEW SOCIAL ORDER

Part of the Han leaders' genius was their ability to win the support of diverse social groups that had been squabbling for centuries. The basis of their success was their ability to organize daily life, create a stable social order, promote economic growth, and foster a state-centered religion. One important element in promoting political and social stability was how the Han allowed surviving Qin aristocrats to reacquire some of their former power. The Han also urged enterprising peasants who had worked the nobles' lands to become local leaders in the countryside. Successful merchants won permission to extend their influence in cities, and in local areas scholars found themselves in the role of masters when the state removed their lords.

Out of a massive agrarian base flowed a steady stream of tax revenues and labor for military forces and public works. The Han court drew revenues from many sources: state-owned imperial lands, mining, and mints; tribute from outlying domains; household taxes on the nobility; and taxes on surplus grains from wealthy merchants. Emperor Wu established state monopolies in salt, iron, and wine to fund his expensive military campaigns. His policies encouraged silk and iron production—especially iron weapons and everyday tools—and controlled profiteering through price

Model of a Han House Elite families in Chang'an and other Han cities typically lived in two-story houses with carved crossbeams and rafters and enclosed courtyards. The floors were covered with embroidered cushions, wool rugs, and mats for sitting. Screens were used for privacy. Women and children were cloistered in the inner quarters.

controls. He also minted standardized copper coins and imposed stiff penalties for counterfeiting.

Han cities were laid out in an orderly grid. Bustling markets served as public areas. Carriages transported rich families up and down wide avenues (and they paid a lot for the privilege: keeping a horse required as much grain as a family of six would consume). Court palaces became forbidden inner cities, off-limits to all but those in the imperial lineage or the government. Monumental architecture in China announced the palaces and tombs of rulers.

Domestic Life Daily life in Han China included new luxuries for the elite and reinforced traditional ideas about gender. Wealthy families lived in several-story homes with richly carved crossbeams and rafters and floors cushioned with embroidered pillows, wool rugs, and mats. Fine embroideries hung as drapes, and screens in the rooms secured privacy. Domestic space reinforced male authority as women and children stayed cloistered in inner quarters, preserving the sense that the patriarch's role was to protect them from a harsh society. Nonetheless, some elite women, often literate, enjoyed respect as teachers and managers within the family while their husbands served as officials away from home. Women who were commoners led less protected lives, working in the fields or even joining entertainment troupes.

Silk was abundant and available to all classes, though in winter only the rich wrapped themselves in furs while everyone else stayed warm in woolens and ferret skins. The rich also wore distinctive slippers lined with leather or silk. Wine and cooked meat came to the dinner tables of the wealthy on vessels fashioned with silver inlay or golden handles. Entertainment for those who could afford it included gambling, performing animals, tiger fights, foreign dancing girls, and even live music in private homes, performed by orchestras in the families' private employ. Although events like these had occurred during the Zhou dynasty, they had marked only public ritual occasions.

Social Hierarchy At the base of Han society was a free peasantry of farmers who owned and tilled their own land. The Han court upheld an agrarian ideal—which Confucians and Daoists supported—honoring the peasants' productive labors, while subjecting merchants to a range of controls (including regulations on luxury consumption) and belittling them for not doing physical labor. Confucians envisioned scholar-officials as working hard for the ruler to enhance a moral economy, which minimized profiteering by greedy merchants.

In reality, however, the first century of Han rule perpetuated the power of elites. At the apex were the imperial clan and nobles, followed, in order, by high-ranking officials and scholars, great merchants and manufacturers, and a regionally based class of local magnates. Below these elites, lesser clerks, medium and small landowners, free farmers, artisans, small merchants, poor tenant farmers, and hired laborers eked out a living. The more destitute became government slaves and relied on the state for food and clothing. At the bottom were convicts and private slaves.

Between 100 BCE and 200 CE, scholar-officials linked the imperial center with local society. At first, their political clout and prestige complemented the power of landlords and

Han Entertainment Han entertainment included dancing, particularly by foreign girls (*top left*), and acrobatics, for which the Chinese remain famous today (*bottom left*). Music was often played at the homes of rich families, who kept their own orchestras complete with bells and drums. Musical events became so popular, for both the entertainers (note the face in the Han statue on the right) and the entertained, that performances ceased being only somber ritual occasions.

large clans, but over time their autonomy grew as they gained wealth by acquiring private property. Following the fall of the Han, they emerged as the dominant aristocratic clans.

In the long run, the imperial court's struggle to limit the power of local lords and magnates failed. Rulers had to rely on local officials to enforce their rule, but those officials could rarely stand up to the powerful men they were supposed to be governing. And when central rule proved too onerous for local elites, they could rebel. Local uprisings against the Han that began in 99 BCE forced the court to relax its measures and left landlords and local magnates as dominant powers in the provinces. Below these privileged groups, powerless agrarian groups turned to Daoist religious organizations that crystallized into potent cells of dissent.

Religion and Omens Under Emperor Wu, Confucianism took on religious overtones. One treatise portrayed Confucius not as a humble teacher but as an uncrowned monarch, and even as a demigod and a giver of laws, which differed from the portrait in the *Analects* of a more modest, accessible, and very human Confucius.

Although Confucians at court championed classical learning, many local communities practiced forms of a remarkably dynamic popular Chinese religion. Imperial cults, magic, and sorcery reinforced the court's interest in astronomical omens—such as the appearance of a supernova, solar halos, meteors, and lunar and solar eclipses. Unpredictable celestial events, as well as earthquakes and famines, could be taken to mean that the emperor had lost the mandate of heaven. Powerful ministers exploited these occurrences to intimidate their ruler. People of high and low social position alike believed that witchcraft could manipulate natural events and interfere with the will of heaven. Religion in its many forms, from philosophy to witchcraft, was an essential feature of Han society from the elite to the poorer classes.

MILITARY EXPANSION AND THE SILK ROADS

The Han military machine was effective at expanding their borders and enforcing stability around the borderlands. Peace was good for business, specifically for creating stable conditions that allowed the safe transit of goods over the Silk Roads. Emperor Wu did much to transform the military forces. Following the Qin precedent, he made military service compulsory, resulting in a huge force: 100,000 crack troops in the Imperial Guard stationed in the capital and more than a million in the standing army.

Expanding Borders Han forces were particularly active along the borders. During the reign of Emperor Wu, Han control extended from southeastern China to northern Vietnam. When pro-Han Koreans appealed for Han help against rulers in their internal squabbles, Emperor Wu's expeditionary force defeated the Korean king and four Han commanderies sprang up in northern Korea. While incursions into Sichuan and the southwestern border areas were less successful due to mountainous terrain and malaria, a commandery nonetheless took root in southern Sichuan in 135 BCE, and soon it opened trading routes to Southeast Asia.

The Han Empire's most serious military threat, however, came from the Xiongnu and other nomadic peoples in the north. The Han inherited from the Qin a symbiotic relationship with these proud, horse-riding nomads: Han merchants brought silk cloth and thread, bronze mirrors, and lacquerware to exchange for furs, horses, and cattle. After humiliating defeats at the hands of the Xiongnu, the Han under Emperor Wu successfully repelled Xiongnu invasions around 120 BCE and ultimately penetrated deep into Xiongnu territory. The Xiongnu tribes were split in two, with the southern tribes surrendering and the northern tribes moving west, ultimately threatening Roman territory.

The Chinese Peace and the Silk Roads The retreat of the Xiongnu and other nomadic peoples introduced a glorious period of internal peace and prosperity some scholars have referred to as a ***Pax Sinica*** ("Chinese Peace," 149–87 BCE). During this period, long-distance trade flourished, cities ballooned, standards of living rose, and the population surged. As a result of their military campaigns, Emperor Wu and his successors enjoyed tribute from distant subordinate states, only intervening in their domestic policy if they rebelled. The Han instead relied on trade and markets to incorporate outlying lands as prosperous satellite states within the tribute system. The Xiongnu nomads even became key middlemen in Silk Road trade.

When the Xiongnu were no longer a threat from the north, the Han expanded westward. (See Map 7.2.) By 100 BCE, Emperor Wu had extended the northern defensive wall from the Tianshan Mountains to the Gobi Desert. Along the wall stood signal beacons for sending emergency messages, and its gates opened periodically for trading fairs. The westernmost gate was called the Jade Gate, since jade from the Taklamakan Desert passed through it. Wu also built garrison cities at oases to protect the trade routes. Soldiers at these oasis garrison cities settled with their families on the frontiers. When its military power expanded beyond the Jade Gate, the Han government set up a similar system of oases on the rim of the Taklamakan Desert. With irrigation, oasis agriculture attracted many more settlers. Trade routes passing through deserts and oases now were

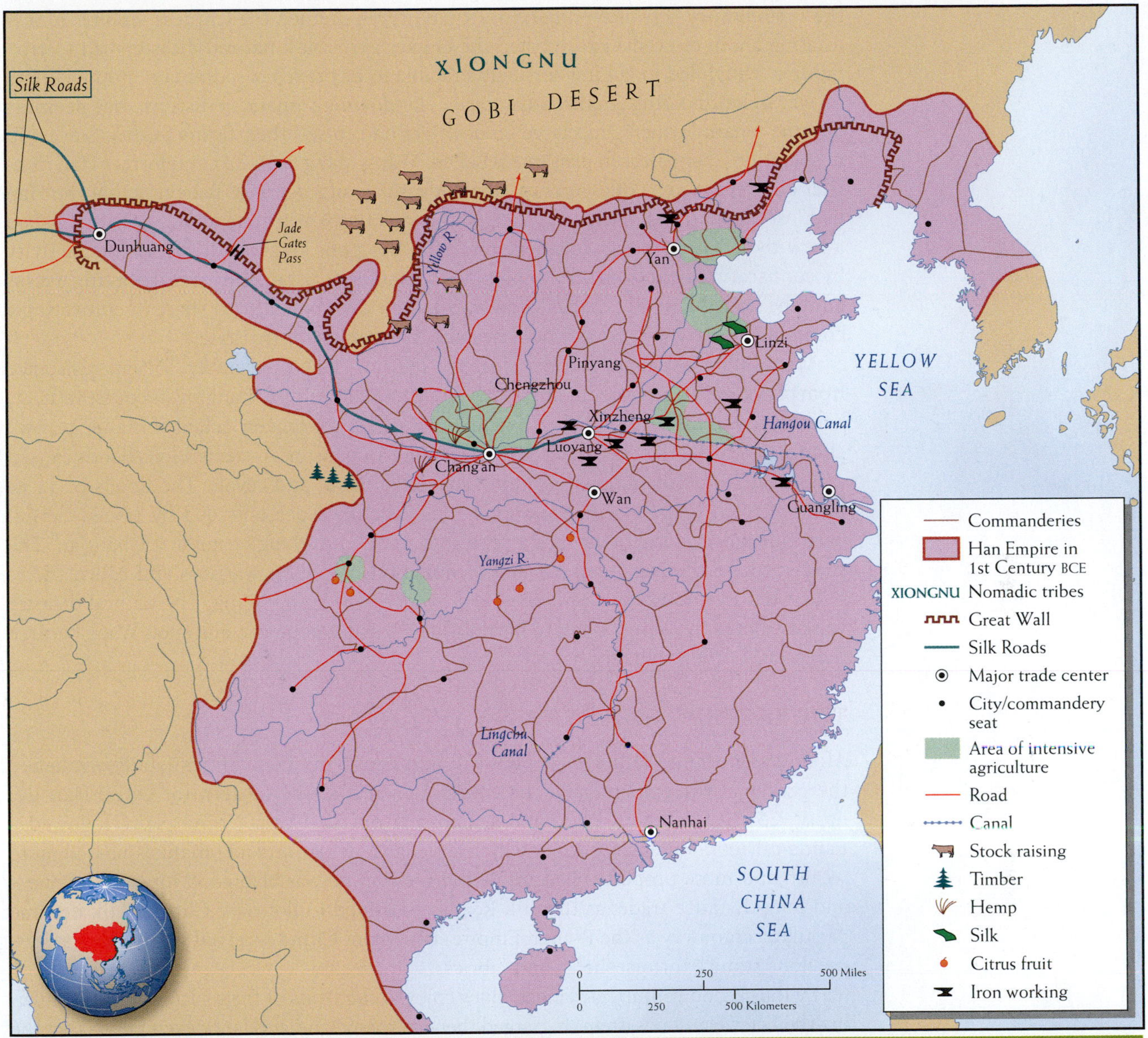

MAP 7.2 | *Pax Sinica*: The Han Empire in the First Century BCE

Agriculture, commerce, and industry flourished in East Asia under Han rule.

- According to the map, what were the main commodities that passed among the empire's regions?
- What type of administrative infrastructure integrated the vast domain?
- What other features united and/or marked off Han territory?

safer and more reliable—until fierce Tibetan tribes threatened them at the beginning of the Common Era—than the steppe routes, which they gradually replaced.

SOCIAL UPHEAVAL AND NATURAL DISASTER

The strain of military expenses and the tax pressures those expenditures placed on small landholders and peasants were more than the Han Empire could bear. By the end of the first century BCE, heavy financial expenditures drained the Chinese empire. A devastating chain of events exacerbated the empire's troubles: natural disasters led to crop failures, which led to landowners being unable to pay taxes based not on crop yield but on size of landholding. Taking advantage of landowners' financial distress, free peasants became tenant farmers, and large landowners had to sell their farms to their slaves. In desperation, dispossessed peasants rebelled. Wang Mang (r. 9–23 CE), a former Han minister and regent to a child emperor, took advantage of the crisis. Believing that the Han had lost the mandate of heaven, Wang Mang took over the throne in 9 CE and established a new dynasty. He designed reforms to help the poor and to foster economic activity by confiscating gold from wealthy landowners and merchants. By redistributing excess land, he hoped that all families would work their own parcels and share in cultivating a communal plot whose crops would become tax surplus for the state.

Wang Mang's regime, and his idealistic reforms, failed miserably. Violent resistance from peasants and large landholders, as well as the Yellow River changing its course in 11 CE, contributed to his demise. When the Yellow River, appropriately called "China's Sorrow," changed course—as it has many times in China's long history—tremendous floods caused mass death, vast migrations, peasant impoverishment, and revolt. The floods of 11 CE likely affected half the Chinese population. Rebellious peasants, led by Daoist clerics, used this far-reaching disaster as a pretext to march on Wang's capital at Chang'an. The peasants painted their foreheads red in imitation of demon warriors and called themselves Red Eyebrows. By 23 CE, they had overthrown Wang Mang. The natural disaster was attributed by Wang's rivals to his unbridled misuse of power, and soon Wang became the model of the evil usurper.

THE EASTERN HAN DYNASTY

After Wang Mang's fall, social, political, and economic inequalities fatally weakened the power of the emperor and the court. As a result, the Eastern (or Later) Han dynasty (25–220 CE), with its capital at Luoyang on the North China plain, followed a hands-off economic policy under which large landowners and merchants amassed more wealth and more property. Decentralizing the regime was also good for local business and long-distance trade, as the Silk Roads continued to flourish. Chinese silk became popular as far away as the Roman Empire. In return, China received glass, jade, horses, precious stones, tortoiseshells, and fabrics.

By the second century CE, landed elites enjoyed the fruits of their success in manipulating the Later Han tax system. It granted them so many land and labor exemptions that the government never again firmly controlled its human and agricultural resources as Emperor Wu had. As the court refocused on the new capital in Luoyang, local power fell into the hands of great aristocratic families. These elites acquired even more privately owned land and forced free peasants to become their rent-paying tenants, then raised their rents higher and higher.

Such prosperity bred greater social inequity—among large landholders, tenant farmers, and peasants working their small parcels—and a renewed source of turmoil. Simmering tensions between landholders and peasants boiled over in a full-scale rebellion in 184 CE. Popular religious groups championed new ideas among commoners and elites for whom the Daoist sage Master Laozi, the voice of naturalness and spontaneity, was an exemplary model. Daoist masters challenged Confucian ritual conformity and they advanced their ideas in the name of a divine order that would redeem all people, not just elites. Officials, along with other political outcasts, headed strong dissident groups and eventually formed local movements. Under their leadership, religious groups such as the Yellow Turbans—so called because they wrapped yellow scarves around their heads—championed Daoist millenarian movements across the empire. (A millenarian movement is a broad, popular upheaval calling for a just and ideal society, sometimes based on the restoration of a bygone moral age, led by charismatic spiritual prophets.) Their message received a warm welcome from a population that was increasingly hostile to Han rule.

Proclaiming the Daoist millenarian belief in a future "Great Peace," the Yellow Turbans demanded fairer treatment by the Han state and equal distribution of all farm lands. As agrarian conditions worsened, a widespread famine ensued. It was a catastrophe that, in the rebels' view, demonstrated the emperor's loss of the mandate of heaven. The economy disintegrated when people refused to pay taxes and provide forced labor, and internal wars engulfed the dynasty. After the 180s CE, three competing states replaced the Han: the Wei in the northwest, the Shu in the southwest, and the Wu in the south. A long-lasting unified empire did not return for several centuries.

The Roman Empire

At the other end of Afro-Eurasia from Han China, in a centuries-long process, Rome became a great power that ruled over as many as 60 million subjects. The Roman Empire at its height encompassed lands from the highlands of what is now Scotland in Europe to the lower reaches of the Nile River in modern-day Egypt and part of Sudan, and from the borders of the Inner Eurasian steppe in Ukraine and the Caucasus to the Atlantic shores of North Africa. (See Map 7.3.) Whereas the Han Empire dominated an enormous and unbroken landmass, the Roman Empire dominated lands around the Mediterranean Sea. Like Han China, though, the Romans acquired command over their world through violent military expansion. By the first century CE, almost unceasing wars against their neighbors had enabled the Romans to forge an unparalleled number of ethnic groups and minor states into a single, large political state. (See **Analyzing Global Developments: Great Empires Compared**.)

COMPARISON

EXPLAIN the process by which Rome transitioned from a minor city-state to a dominating Mediterranean power.

FOUNDATIONS OF THE ROMAN EMPIRE

Three major factors influenced the beginnings of Rome's imperial expansion: migrations of foreign peoples and Rome's military and political innovations.

Population Movements Between 450 and 250 BCE, migrations from northern and central Europe brought large numbers of Celts to settle in lands around the Mediterranean Sea. They convulsed the northern rim of the Mediterranean, staging armed forays into lands from what is now Spain in the west to present-day Turkey in the east. One of these migrations involved Gallic peoples from the region of the Alps and beyond launching a series of violent incursions into northern Italy that ultimately—around 390 BCE—led to the seizure of Rome. The important result for the Romans was not their city's capture, which was traumatic yet temporary, but rather the permanent dislocation that the invaders inflicted on the city-states of the Etruscans. These Etruscans, themselves likely a combination of indigenous people and migrations from Asia Minor centuries before, spoke their own language and were centered in what is now Tuscany. Before the Gallic invasions, the Etruscans had dominated the Italian peninsula. While the Etruscans with great difficulty drove the invading Gauls back northward, their cities never recovered nor did their ability to dominate other peoples in Italy, including their fledgling rival, the Romans. Thus the Gallic migrations removed one of the most formidable roadblocks to Roman expansion in Italy.

NORTH SEA
BALTIC SEA
ATLANTIC OCEAN
BRITANNIA
Londinium
GERMANIA INFERIOR
GERMANI
BELGICA
GALLIA LUGDUNENSIS
AGRI DECUMATES
Rhine R.
IUTHUNGI
RAETIA
GERMANIA SUPERIOR
GALLIA AQUITANIA
NORICUM
Danube R.
PANNONIA
GALLIA NARBONENSIS
DALMATIA
LUSITANIA
TARRACONENSIS
ITALIA
ADRIATIC SEA
CORSICA
Rome
Corduba
BAETIA
SARDINIA
MEDITERRANEAN
MAURETANIA TINGITANA
MAURETANIA CAESARIENSIS
SICILIA
Carthage
Syracuse
NUMIDIA
AFRICA
GAETULI
GARAMANTES
0 250 500 Miles
0 250 500 Kilometers
Mediterranean Sea current
Roman expansion to 201 BCE
Roman expansion 201–100 BCE
Roman expansion 100–44 BCE
Roman expansion 44 BCE–14 CE
Roman expansion 14–96 CE
Roman expansion 96–106 CE
GALLIA Roman province
GAETULI Border peoples
Roman provincial capital

MAP 7.3 | Roman Expansion to 120 CE

Roman expansion continued for several centuries before reaching its peak in the second century CE.

- According to the map, what were the first provinces to fall under Rome's power? What were the last two?
- Why did the Romans not expand their empire farther into eastern Europe or Southwest Asia?
- What were the geographic limits to Rome's expansion?

Analyzing Global Developments

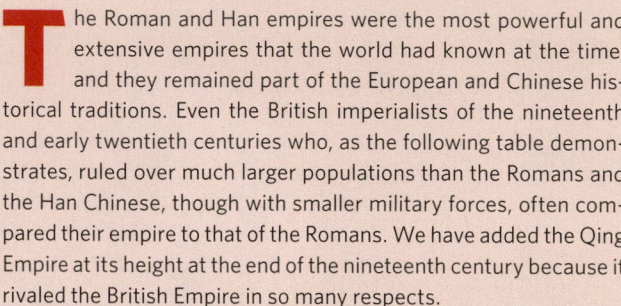

Great Empires Compared: The Han, the Roman, the Qing, and the British Empires after World War I

The Roman and Han empires were the most powerful and extensive empires that the world had known at the time, and they remained part of the European and Chinese historical traditions. Even the British imperialists of the nineteenth and early twentieth centuries who, as the following table demonstrates, ruled over much larger populations than the Romans and the Han Chinese, though with smaller military forces, often compared their empire to that of the Romans. We have added the Qing Empire at its height at the end of the nineteenth century because it rivaled the British Empire in so many respects.

While working with these population figures, it is important to keep in mind that the numbers for the early periods are based on conjecture rather than precise information. Although censuses were conducted in both the early Roman Empire and the Han dynasty, what they tabulated was different: Rome counted male citizens over the age of sixteen and China counted households. For instance, in an inscription boasting of his accomplishments over his forty-four-year reign, the Roman emperor Augustus claimed to have conducted censuses that counted over 4,063,000 citizens in 28 BCE, 4,233,000 in 8 BCE, and 4,937,000 in 14 CE. Assuming these reported census figures were correct, the modern demographer still must estimate how many people are represented by a male Roman citizen (wife, children, and slaves) and, in the case of the Han documents, a Chinese household (wife and children). Determining how many people lived in the rest of Afro-Eurasia is again based on conjecture and highly disputed. Nonetheless, these rough estimates offer some fascinating opportunities for comparison of empires.

QUESTIONS FOR ANALYSIS

- If you compare the modern-day British Empire with the empires of the Romans and the Han Chinese, what differences stand out in terms of land area and total population? How can we explain some of these differences?
- Can you explain why the Han Empire and the Qing Empire had much larger armies than the Roman and British empires?
- What does the population data on cities suggest about the place of cities in early world history versus modern world history?
- Given that these population figures, especially for the early period, are so conjectural and disputed, what is to be gained by estimating these numbers?

MAXIMUM LAND AREA	
Roman Empire	2,500,000 square miles, mainly land based
Han Empire	4,000,000 square miles, mainly land based
British Empire	1,800,000 square miles, mainly sea-borne
Qing Empire	4,500,000 square miles, mainly land based

TOTAL POPULATION	
Roman Empire	c. 60,000,000
Han Empire	c. 59,000,000
British Empire	459,307,735
Qing Empire	450,000,000

SIZE OF THE MILITARY FORCES	
Roman Empire	400,000
Han Empire	1,000,000
British Empire	330,000
Qing Empire	1,000,000

LARGEST CITIES	
Roman Empire	
Rome	1,100,000
Alexandria	600,000
Carthage	400,000
Athens	300,000
Antioch	250,000
Han Empire	
Chang'an City	400,000
Luoyang City	1,000,000
British Empire in 1920	
London	7,488,000
Calcutta	1,328,000
British Empire in 1920 (CONT.)	
Bombay	1,176,000
Glasgow	1,052,000
Birmingham	922,000
Cairo	791,000
Qing Empire in 1910	
Beijing	1,100,000
Guangzhou	739,000
Yangzhou	567,300
Shanghai	444,318
Suzhou	252,800
Hangzhou	120,000

Sources: Ping-Ti Ho, *Studies on the Population of China, 1368–1953* (1959); Susan Naquin, *Peking: Temples and City Life, 1400–1900* (2000); Tim Cornell and John Matthews, *Atlas of the Roman World* (1982); Greg Woolf, *Rome: An Empire's Story* (2012).

Military Manpower and the War Ethos The Romans achieved unassailable military power by organizing the communities that they conquered in Italy into a system that generated manpower for their army. This development began around 340 BCE, when the Romans faced a concerted attack by their fellow Latin city-states. By then, the other Latins viewed Rome not as an ally in a system of mutual defense, but as a growing threat to their own independence. After overcoming these nearby Latins, the Romans charged onward to defeat one community after another in Italy. Demanding from their defeated enemies a supply of men for the Roman army every year, Rome amassed a huge reservoir of military manpower.

In addition to their overwhelming advantage in manpower, the Romans cultivated an unusual war ethos. A heightened sense of honor drove Roman men to push themselves into battle again and again, and never to accept defeat. Guided by the example of great warriors and shaped by a regime of training and discipline, in which minor infractions of duty were punishable by death, the Roman army trooped out to war in annual spring campaigns beginning in the month—still called March today—dedicated to and named for the Roman god of war, Mars.

By 265 BCE, Rome controlled the Italian peninsula. It next entered into three great **Punic Wars** with Carthage, which had begun as a Phoenician colony and was now the major power centered in the northern parts of present-day Tunisia (see Chapters 4 and 5). The First Punic War (264–241 BCE) was a prolonged naval battle over the island of Sicily. With their victory, the Romans acquired a dominant position in the western Mediterranean. The Second Punic War (218–201 BCE), however, revealed the real strength and might of the Roman army. The Romans drew on their reserve force of nearly 750,000 men to ultimately repulse—with huge casualties and dramatic losses—the Carthaginian general Hannibal's invading force of 20,000 troops and their war elephants. They took the war to enemy soil, winning the decisive battle at Zama near Carthage in late 202 BCE. In a final war of extermination, waged between 149 and 146 BCE, the Romans used their overwhelming advantage in manpower, ships, and other resources to bring the five-centuries-long hegemony of Carthage in the western Mediterranean to an end.

With an unrelenting drive to war, the Romans continued to draft, train, and field extraordinary numbers of men for combat. Soldiers, conscripted at age seventeen or eighteen, served for up to ten years at a time. With so many young men devoted to war for such long spans of time, the war ethos became deeply embedded in the ideals of every generation. After 200 BCE, the Romans unleashed this successful war machine on the kingdoms of the eastern Mediterranean. In 146 BCE, the Romans annihilated what was left of Carthage—killing all its adult males and selling all its women and children into slavery—and obliterated the great Greek city-state of Corinth. Their monopoly of power over the entire Mediterranean basin was now unchallenged.

Roman military forces served under men who knew they could win not just glory and territory for the state, but also enormous rewards for themselves. They were talented men driven by burning ambition, from Scipio Africanus in the 200s BCE, the conqueror of Carthage, to Julius Caesar, the great general of the 50s BCE. Julius Caesar's eight-year-long cycle of Gallic wars resulted in the deaths of more than 1 million Gauls and the enslavement of another million. Western Afro-Eurasia had never witnessed war on this scale; it had no equal anywhere, except in China.

Political Institutions and Internal Conflict The conquest of the Mediterranean placed unprecedented power and wealth into the hands of a few men in the Roman social elite. The rush of battlefield successes had kept Romans and their Italian allies preoccupied with the demands of army service overseas. Once this process of territorial expansion slowed, social and political problems that had been lying dormant began to resurface.

Following the traditional date of its founding in 509 BCE, the Romans had lived in a state that they called the "public thing" or ***res publica*** (hence the modern word "republic"). In this state, policy issued from the Senate—a body of permanent members, 300 to 600 of Rome's

Roman Farmers and Soldiers In the late Republic most Roman soldiers came from rural Italy, where small farms were being absorbed into the landholdings of the wealthy and powerful. In the empire, soldiers were recruited from rural provincial regions. They sometimes worked small fields of their own and sometimes worked the lands of the wealthy—like the domain in the Roman province of Africa (in modern-day Tunisia) that is depicted in this mosaic.

most powerful and wealthy citizens—and from popular assemblies of the citizens. Every year the citizens elected the officials of state, principally two consuls who held power for a year and commanded the armies. In addition, the people annually elected ten men who, as tribunes of the plebs ("the common people"), had the special task of protecting the common people's interests against those of the rich and the powerful. In severe political crises, the Romans sometimes chose one man, a dictator, whose words, *dicta*, were law and who held absolute power over the state for no longer than six months. These institutions, originally devised for a city-state, were problematic for ruling a Mediterranean-sized empire.

By the second century BCE, Rome's power elite were exploiting the wealth from its Mediterranean conquests to acquire huge tracts of land in Italy and Sicily. They then imported enormous numbers of slaves from all around the Mediterranean to work this land. Free citizen farmers, the backbone of the army, were driven off their lands and into the cities. The result was a severe agrarian and recruiting crisis. In 133 and 123–121 BCE, two tribunes, the brothers Tiberius and Gaius Gracchus, tried—much as Wang Mang would in China more than a century later—to address these inequalities. The Gracchi brothers attempted to institute land reforms guaranteeing to all of Rome's poor citizens a basic amount of land that would qualify them for army service. But political enemies assassinated both men.

Thereafter, poor Roman citizens looked not to state institutions but to army commanders, to whom they gave their loyalty and support, to provide them with land and income. These generals became increasingly powerful and started to compete with one another, ignoring the Senate and the traditional rules of politics. As generals sought control of the state and their supporters took sides, a long series of civil wars began that lasted from 90 BCE to the late 30s BCE. The Romans now turned inward on themselves the tremendous resources built up during the conquest of the Mediterranean.

COMPARISON

COMPARE Han China with Imperial Rome in terms of their respective political authority, economy, cultural developments, and military expansion.

EMPERORS, AUTHORITARIAN RULE, AND ADMINISTRATION

Julius Caesar's adopted son, Octavian (63 BCE–14 CE) ultimately reunited the fractured empire and emerged as undisputed master of the Roman world. Octavian's authoritarian one-man rule marked the beginning of the ***Pax Romana*** ("Roman Peace," 25 BCE–235 CE). This peace depended on the power of one man with enough authority to enforce an orderly competition among Roman aristocrats.

Octavian concentrated immense wealth and the most important official titles and positions of power in his own hands. Signaling the transition to a new political order in which he alone controlled the army, the provinces, and the political processes in Rome, Octavian assumed a new title, ***Augustus*** ("the Revered One")—comparable to Qin Shi Huangdi's title—as well as the traditional republican roles of *imperator* (commander in chief, or emperor), *princeps* (first man), and *Caesar* (a name connoting his adoptive heritage, but which over time became a title assumed by imperial successors).

Rome's subjects tended to see these emperors as heroic or even semidivine beings in life, and to think of the good ones as becoming gods on their death. Yet emperors were always careful to present themselves as civil rulers whose power ultimately depended on the consent of Roman citizens and the might of the army. They contrasted themselves with the image of "king," a role the Romans had learned to detest from the monarchy they themselves had long ago overthrown to establish their Republic in 509 BCE. Nonetheless, the emperors' powers were immense.

Being a Roman emperor required finesse and talent, and few succeeded at it. Of the twenty-two emperors who held power in the most stable period of Roman history (between the first Roman emperor, Augustus, and the early third century CE), fifteen met their end by murder or suicide. As powerful as he might be, no individual emperor alone could govern an empire of such great size and population, encompassing a multitude of languages and cultures. He needed institutions and competent people to help him. In terms of sheer power, the most important institution was the army. So the emperors systematically transformed the army into a full-time professional force. Men now entered the imperial army not as citizen volunteers but as paid experts who enlisted for life and swore loyalty to the emperor and his family. It was part of the emperor's image to present himself as a victorious battlefield commander, inflicting defeat on the "barbarians" who threatened the empire's frontiers.

For most emperors, however, governance was largely a daily chore of listening to complaints, answering petitions, deciding court cases, and hearing reports from civil administrators and military commanders. At its largest in the second century CE, the Roman Empire encompassed more than forty administrative units, called provinces. As in Han China, each had a governor appointed or approved by the emperor; but unlike Han China, which had its formal Confucian-trained bureaucracy with ranks of senior and junior officials, the Roman Empire of this period was relatively understaffed in terms of central government officials. The emperor and his provincial governors depended very much on local help, sometimes aided by elite slaves and freedmen (former slaves) serving as government bureaucrats. With a limited staff of full-time assistants and an entourage of friends and acquaintances, each governor was expected to guarantee peace. For some essential tasks, though, the state had to rely on private companies, as with the collection of imperial taxes, where the profit motives of the publicans (the men in the companies that took up government contracts) were at odds with the expectations of fair government among the empire's subjects.

A Roman Town Roman towns featured many of the standard elements of modern towns and cities. Streets and avenues crossed at right angles; streets were paved; sidewalks ran between streets and houses. The houses were often several stories high and had wide windows and open balconies. All these elements can be seen in this street from Herculaneum, nicely preserved by the pyroclastic flow that ran down the slopes of nearby Mount Vesuvius when its volcano erupted in August of 79 CE, burying the town and its inhabitants.

TOWN AND CITY LIFE

Due to the conditions of peace and the wealth it generated, urban settlements were clustered in core areas of the empire—central Italy, southern Spain, northern Africa, and the western parts of present-day Turkey. The towns, whose municipal charters echoed Roman forms of government, provided the backbone of local administration for the empire. Towns often were walled, and inside those walls the streets and avenues ran at right angles. A large, open-air, rectangular area called the *forum* dominated the town center. Around it clustered the main public buildings: the markets, the main temples of principal gods and goddesses, and the building that housed city administrators. Residential areas featured regular blocks of houses, close together and fronting on the streets. Larger towns contained large apartment blocks that were not much different from the four- and five-story buildings in any modern city. In the smaller towns, sanitary and nutritional standards were reasonably good.

The imperial metropolis of Rome was another matter. With well over a million inhabitants, it was larger than any other urban center of its time; Xianyang and Chang'an—the Qin and Han capitals, respectively—each had a population of between 300,000 and 500,000. While Rome's inhabitants were privileged in terms of their access to government doles of wheat and aqueduct-supplied water, their living conditions could be appalling, with people jammed into ramshackle high-rise apartments prone to collapse in a fire. Apart from crime and violence, poor sanitary conditions and the diseases that accompany them were constant threats to the population.

Towns large and small tended to have two major entertainment venues: a theater, adopted from Hellenistic culture and devoted to plays, dances, and other popular events, and an amphitheater, a Roman innovation with a much larger seating capacity that surrounded the oval performance area at its center. In the amphitheaters, Romans could stage exotic beast hunts and gladiatorial matches for the enjoyment of huge crowds of appreciative spectators. These public entertainment facilities of Roman towns stressed the importance of citizens in civic life, as compared with the largely private entertainment of Han elite.

Deadly Roman Entertainment The huge amphitheater (left) is in the remains of the Roman city of Thysdrus in North Africa (the town of el-Jem in modern-day Tunisia). The wealth of the Africans under the empire enabled them to build colossal entertainment venues that competed with the one at Rome in scale and grandeur. Roman gladiators would fight, sometimes to the death, in such venues. In the brilliant mosaic from Rome (right), we see two gladiators at the end of a full combat in which Astacius has killed Astivus. The Greek letter theta, or "th" (the circle with crossbar through it) beside the names of Astivus and Rodan indicates that these men are dead—*thanatos* being the Greek word for "death."

SOCIAL AND GENDER RELATIONS

In Rome's civil society, laws and courts governed formal relationships, including those based on patronage and the family. By the last century BCE, the Roman state's complex legal system featured a rich body of written law, courts, and well-trained lawyers. Deeply entrenched throughout the empire, this legal infrastructure long outlasted the Roman Empire. Also firmly embedded in Roman society was a system of personal relationships that linked the rich and powerful with the mass of average citizens. Men and women of wealth and high social status acted as patrons, protecting and supporting dependents or "clients" from the lower classes. From the emperor at the top to the local municipal man at the bottom, the bonds between these groups in each city found formal expression in legal definitions of patrons' responsibilities to clients; at the same time, this informal social code raised expectations that the wealthy would be civic benefactors, sponsoring the construction of public libraries, bathhouses, and even theaters.

While patronage was important, the family was at the very foundation of the Roman social order. Legally speaking, the authoritarian *paterfamilias* ("father of the family") had nearly total power over his dependents, including his wife, children, grandchildren, and the slaves whom he owned. Despite this patriarchal system, Roman women, even those of modest wealth and status, had much greater freedom of action and much greater control of their own wealth and property when compared with women in most Greek city-states. As in Han China, some women in the Roman world could be well educated, literate, well connected, and in control of their own lives—despite what the laws and ideas of Roman males might suggest.

ECONOMY AND NEW SCALES OF PRODUCTION

Rome achieved staggering transformations in agriculture and mining. The area of land surveyed and cultivated rose steadily throughout this period, as Romans reached into arid lands on the periphery of the Sahara Desert to the south and opened up heavily forested regions in present-day France and Germany to the north. Roman agriculture and mining relied on chattel slaves—human beings purchased as private property (see Chapter 6). The massive concentration of wealth and slaves at the center of the Roman world led to the first large-scale commercial plantation agriculture and the first technical handbooks on how to run such operations for profit; it also led to dramatic slave rebellions, such as the Sicilian Revolt (135–132 BCE) and the Spartacus uprising (73–71 BCE), although the latter began among slaves in a school for gladiators. Slave-worked estates specialized in products destined for the big urban markets: wheat, grapes, and olives, as well as cattle and sheep. An impressive road system connected the far-flung parts of their empire. Milestones marked most of these roads and complex itineraries mapped major roads and distances between towns. (See Map 7.4.)

Coin Hoard The use of coins for a wide spectrum of economic exchanges became common in the Roman Empire. Looking at the batches buried for safekeeping gives us an idea of the range of coins in circulation at any one time. This coin hoard was found near Didcot in Oxfordshire, England. Buried about 165 CE, it contained about 125 gold coins minted between the 50s and 160s CE and represents the equivalent of about eleven years' pay for a Roman soldier. Gold coins were used for expensive transactions or to store wealth. Most ordinary purchases or payments were made with silver or brass coins.

Rome mined copper, tin, silver, and gold—out of which the Roman state produced the most massive coinage system known in western Afro-Eurasia before early modern times. Public and private demand for metals was so great that traces of the air pollution generated by their

MAP 7.4 | *Pax Romana*: The Roman Empire in the Second Century CE

The Roman Empire enjoyed remarkable peace and prosperity in the second century CE. Economic production increased, and Roman culture expanded throughout the realm.

- According to the map, what commodities were traded most widely?
- With what groups did Romans trade beyond their empire, and for what commodity in particular?
- Given what you know from your reading about the eastern Mediterranean origins of Christianity, how did the features of the *Pax Romana* shown on this map promote the spread of Christianity to the west?

mining operations remain in ice core samples taken from Greenland today. Rome's standardized currency facilitated taxation and the increased exchange of commodities and services. The economy functioned more efficiently due to this production of coins, which was paralleled only by the coinage output of Han dynasty China and its successors.

THE RISE OF CHRISTIANITY

Over centuries, Roman religion had cultivated a dynamic world of gods, spirits, and demons that was characteristic of earlier periods of Mediterranean history. **Christianity** took shape in this richly pluralistic world. Its foundations lay in a direct confrontation with Roman imperial authority: the trial of Jesus. After preaching the new doctrines of what was originally a sect of Judaism, Jesus was found guilty of sedition and executed by means of crucifixion—a standard Roman penalty—as the result of a typical Roman provincial trial overseen by a Roman governor, Pontius Pilatus.

No historical reference to Jesus survives from his own lifetime. Shortly after the crucifixion, Paul of Tarsus, a Jew and a Roman citizen from southeastern Anatolia, claimed to have seen Jesus in full glory outside the city of Damascus. Paul and the Mediterranean communities to whom he preached between 40 and 60 CE referred to Jesus as the Anointed One (the Messiah, in keeping with Jewish expectations) or the Christ—*ho Christos* in Greek (still the dominant language of the eastern Mediterranean region thanks to Hellenism). Only many decades later did accounts that came to be called the Gospels—such as Matthew, Mark, Luke, and John—describe Jesus's life and record his sayings. Jesus's preaching drew not only on Jewish models, but also on the Egyptian and Mesopotamian image of the great king as shepherd of his people (see Chapter 3). With Jesus, this image of the good shepherd took on a new, personal closeness. Not a distant monarch but a preacher, Jesus had set out on God's behalf to gather a new, small flock.

Through the writings of Paul and the Gospels, both written in Greek, this image of Jesus rapidly spread beyond Palestine (where Jesus had preached only to Jews and only in the local language, Aramaic) and entered the religious bloodstream of the Mediterranean. Core elements of Jesus's message, such as the responsibilities of the well-off for the poor and the promised eventual empowerment of "the meek," appealed to many ordinary people in the wider Mediterranean world. But it was the apostle Paul who was especially responsible for reshaping this message for a wider audience. While Jesus directed his teachings to villagers and peasants, Paul's message spoke to a world divided by religious identity, wealth, slavery, and gender differences: "There is neither Jew nor Greek, there is neither slave nor free, there is neither male nor female; for you are all one in Christ Jesus." This new message, universal in its claims and appeal, was immediately accessible to the dwellers of the towns and cities of the Roman Empire.

Just half a century after Jesus's crucifixion, the followers of Jesus saw in his life not merely the wanderings of a Jewish charismatic teacher, but a head-on collision between "God" and "the world." Jesus's teachings came to be understood as the message of a divine being—who, for thirty years had moved (largely unrecognized) among human beings. Jesus's followers formed a church: a permanent gathering committed to the charge of leaders chosen by God and by their fellow believers. For these leaders and their followers, death offered a defining testimony for their faith. Christians hoped for a Roman trial and the opportunity to offer themselves as witnesses (*martyrs*) for their faith.

Persecutions of Christians were sporadic and responses to local concerns. Not until the emperor Decius, in the mid-third century CE, did the state direct an empire-wide attack on Christians. But Decius died within the year, and Christians interpreted their persecutor's death as evidence of the hand of God in human affairs. By the last decades of the third century, Christian communities of various kinds, reflecting the different strands of their movement through the Mediterranean as well as the local cultures in which they settled, were present in every society in the empire.

THE LIMITS OF EMPIRE

The limitations of Roman force were a pragmatic factor in determining who belonged in, and was subject to, the empire as opposed to who was outside it and therefore excluded. The Romans pushed their authority in the west to the shores of the Atlantic Ocean, and to the south they drove it to the edges of the Sahara Desert. In both cases, there was little additional useful land available to dominate. (See Map 7.5.) Roman power was blocked, however, to the east

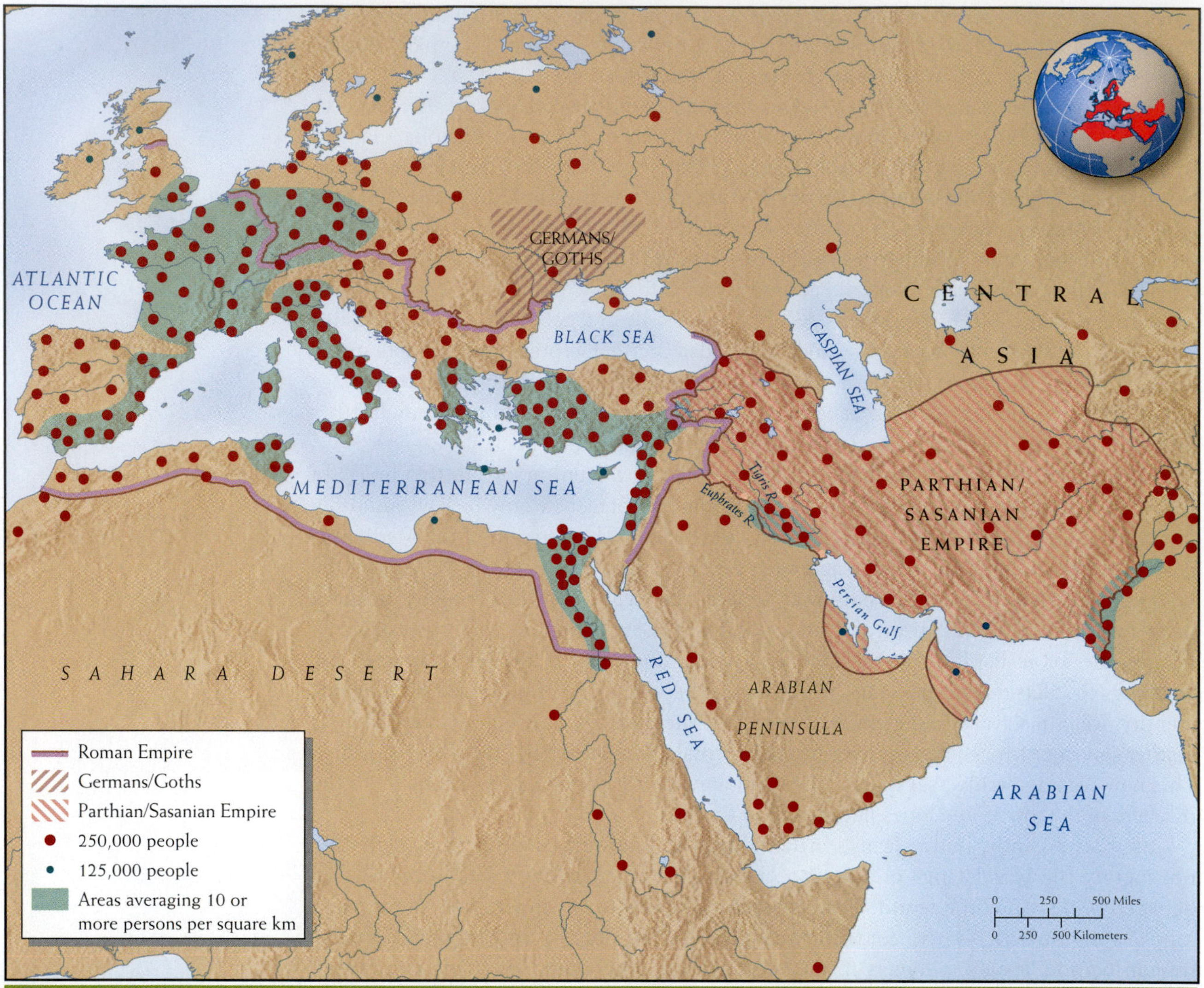

MAP 7.5 | Population of Roman World in 362 CE

Roman frontiers at the northern and eastern limits of the empire were persistent sources of anxiety and concern for imperial leaders. While not as densely populated as the Roman Empire, these regions contained large population centers as well.

- Name some of the major groups of peoples that lived just beyond Roman rule in the areas of eastern Europe and Southwest Asia.
- What were the geographical limits of the Roman Empire?
- According to your reading, why were Roman armies never able to subdue these neighboring peoples?

by the Parthians and then the Sasanians and to the north by the Goths and other Germanic peoples. (See **Current Trends in World History: Empires, Allies, and Frontiers**.)

The Parthians On Rome's eastern frontiers, powerful Romans such as Marcus Crassus in the mid-50s BCE and Mark Antony in the early 30s BCE wished to imitate the achievements of Alexander the Great and conquer the arid lands lying east of Judea and Syria. They failed miserably, stopped by the Parthian Empire and its successor the Sasanian Empire. The Parthian people had moved south from present-day Turkmenistan and settled in the region comprising the modern states of Iraq and Iran. Unlike the Persians before them, the Parthian social order was founded on nomadic pastoralism and a war capability based on technical advances in mounted horseback warfare. Reliance on horses made their style of fighting highly mobile and ideal for warfare on arid plains and deserts. They perfected the so-called Parthian shot: the arrow shot from a bow with great accuracy at long distance and from horseback at a gallop. On the flat, open plains of Iran and Iraq, the Parthians had a decisive advantage over slow-moving, cumbersome mass infantry formations that had been developed for war in the Mediterranean. Eventually the expansionist states of Parthia and Rome became archenemies: they confronted each other in Mesopotamia for nearly four centuries.

The Sasanians expanded the technical advances in mounted horseback warfare that the Parthians had used so successfully in open desert warfare against the slow-moving Roman mass infantry formations. King Shapur I (Shabuhr), their greatest monarch, exploited the weaknesses of the Roman Empire in the mid-third century, even capturing the Roman emperor Valerian. (See Chapter 8 for more on the Sasanians.) As successful as the Parthians and the Sasanians were in fighting the Romans, however, they could never challenge Roman sway over Mediterranean lands. Their decentralized political structure limited their coordination and resources, and their horse-mounted style of warfare was ill suited to fight around the more rocky and hilly environments of the Mediterranean world.

German and Gothic "Barbarians" In the lands across the Rhine and Danube, to the north, environmental conditions largely determined the limits of empire. The long and harsh winters, but excellent soil and growing conditions, produced hardy, dense population clusters scattered across vast distances. These illiterate, kin-based agricultural societies had changed little since the first millennium BCE.

As the Roman Empire fixed its northern frontiers along the Rhine and Danube rivers, two factors determined its relationship with the Germans and Goths on the rivers' other side. First, these small societies had only one big commodity for which the empire was willing to pay: human bodies. So the slave trade out of the land across the Rhine and Danube became immense: gold, silver, coins, wine, arms, and other luxury items flowed across the rivers in one direction in exchange for slaves in the other. Second, their wars were unremitting, as every emperor faced the expectation of dealing harshly with these so-called barbarians. Ironically, internal conflicts within the Roman Empire ultimately prompted increasing use of "barbarians" as soldiers and even as officers who served the empire.

While the Han Empire had fallen by 220 CE, the Roman Empire in the west continued to exist politically for 250 years, in which its history became intertwined with the rise of Christianity, one of the world's universalizing religions.

Soldier versus Barbarian On the frontiers of the Roman Empire, the legionary soldiers faced the non-Roman "barbarians" from the lands beyond. In this piece of a stone-carved picture from the northwestern frontier, we see a civilized and disciplined Roman soldier, to the left, facing a German "barbarian"—hair uncut and unkempt, without formal armor, his house a thatched hut. Frontier realities were never so clear-cut, of course. Roman soldiers, often recruited from the "barbarian" peoples, were a lot more like them than was convenient to admit, and the "barbarians" were influenced by and closer to Roman cultural models than this picture indicates.

Conclusion

China and Rome both constructed empires of unprecedented scale and duration, yet they differed in fundamental ways. Starting out with a less numerous and less dense population than China, Rome relied on slaves and "barbarian" immigrants to expand and diversify its workforce. While less than 1 percent of the Chinese population were slaves, more than 10 percent were slaves in the Roman Empire. The Chinese rural economy was built on a huge population of free peasant

Current Trends in World History

Empires, Allies, and Frontiers

Both the Han and the Roman empires faced threats on their frontiers and used allies as well as their own military prowess to counter such threats. Keeping good relations with frontier allies was essential to the statecraft of empires. It could also yield important intelligence for rulers in capitals.

THE HAN

Consider how the Han dealt with their enemies, the Xiongnu. Emperor Wu sent a special envoy to the Yuezhi, whom he thought would be willing to ally with him against the Xiongnu. His emissary was Zhang Qian, who had volunteered to undertake the journey into the dangerous steppe. In 139 BCE, Zhang set out with a group of 100 people; one was a former slave from the steppe, Ganfu, who guided the travelers and used his bow to kill wild animals when they ran out of food. Aware of the envoy's purpose, the Xiongnu chief detained the group when they tried to pass through his territory. The Xiongnu kept Zhang Qian for ten years, during which time he married a Xiongnu woman and had children. Zhang learned much of steppe life and geography, but he did not forget his mission; together with Ganfu, he eventually managed to escape. At last, they reached the Yuezhi camp on the northern bank of the Oxus River.

Unfortunately, Zhang Qian did not succeed in enlisting the support of the Yuezhi. Their surviving leaders had little inclination to return to the steppe to again battle the fierce Xiongnu, especially as they could see before them the fertile Bactrian plain dotted with Hellenistic cities (see Chapter 6). Zhang Qian accompanied the Yuezhi court in touring the land of Bactria. After consuming a year in futile negotiations with the Yuezhi leaders, Zhang set out for home, bearing much information about the cultures and products of Bactria and regions beyond, including India and Persia. He finally reached Chang'an, the Han capital, thirteen years after beginning his expedition. Although he had failed in his diplomatic mission, Zhang had collected invaluable information for Wudi about the frontier areas in central Asia.

THE ROMANS

The Romans also had to deal with their frontiers. To the north they contended with "barbarians," and to the east they ran up against the powerful kingdoms of the Parthians and the Sasanians. But the Romans did have occasional contacts with kingdoms far to the east. For example, in the reign of Augustus (r. 30 BCE–14 CE) an embassy came from Poros, a king in India. In a letter that his ambassadors carried, Poros described himself as the king over 600 other kings, and he offered any help that the emperor Augustus might want of him. With the letter came gifts carried by eight slaves, naked except for their scented loincloths: a "freak," a number of large snakes, a huge turtle, and a partridge larger than a vulture.

Although embassies of this sort did bring information from far afield, Rome knew little of communities outside the empire to the east except for the peoples and provinces of the Parthian and Sasanian empires, which were closest to its frontiers. Most of this knowledge was very local in nature, gained not through formal channels but in contacts between the two states over

farmers; this enormous labor pool, together with a remarkable bureaucracy, enabled the Han to achieve great political stability. In contrast, the millions of peasant farmers who formed the backbone of rural society in the Roman Empire were much more loosely integrated into the state structure. They never unified to revolt against their government and overthrow it, as did the mass peasant movements of Later Han China. In comparison with their counterparts in China, the peasants in the Roman Empire were not as well connected in their proximity or density, or as united in purpose. Here, too, the Mediterranean environment accented separation and difference.

By Chinese standards, the Roman Empire was relatively fragmented and underadministered. Moreover, no single philosophy or religion ever underpinned the Roman state in the way that Confucianism buttressed the dynasties of China. Both empires, however, benefited from the spread of a uniform language and imperial culture. The process was more comprehensive in China, which possessed a single language that the elites used, than in Rome, where officially a two-language world existed: Latin in the western Mediterranean, Greek in the east. Both states fostered a common imperial culture across all levels of society. Once entrenched, these cultures and languages lasted well after the end of empire.

military or territorial problems or from merchants and other travelers. Diplomacy did exist, but the Roman Empire had no centralized office to manage intelligence reports.

More important than statecraft were exchanges along the Silk Road that brought news, rumors, and impressions of distant empires. The Chinese were the source of the most expensive item in the Roman Empire: the highly valued commodity silk. But in Roman eyes, the Chinese were still very remote and unknown. As Pliny the Elder wrote, "Though mild in character, the Chinese still resemble wild animals in that they shun the company of the rest of humankind, and wait for trade to come to them." Although connected, the two empires that so dominated their own worlds were still worlds apart.

Zhang Qian This painting shows Zhang Qian crossing the Yellow River during his journey to the Yuezhi. Although he failed to forge an alliance for Emperor Wu, he returned home with valuable information about frontier areas of central Asia.

QUESTIONS FOR ANALYSIS

- Compare the ways in which the Han Chinese and Romans dealt with enemies on the fringes of their respective empires.
- What makes frontier zones useful for the study of world history?

Explore Further

Michael Loewe, *The Government of Qin and Han Empires: 221 BCE–220 CE* (2006).

Peter S. Wells, *The Barbarians Speak: How the Conquered Peoples Shaped Roman Europe* (1999).

Differences in human resources, languages, and ideas led the Roman and Han states to evolve in unique ways. In both places, however, the faiths of outsiders—Christians and Buddhists—eclipsed the classical and secular traditions that grounded their states' foundational ideals. Transmission of these new faiths benefited from expanded communications networks. The new religions added to the cultural mix that succeeded the Roman Empire and the Han dynasty.

At their height, both states surpassed their forebears by translating unprecedented military power into the fullest form of state-based organization. Each state's complex organization involved the systematic control, counting, and taxing of its population. In both cases, the general increase of the population, the growth of huge cities, and the success of long-distance trade contributed to the new scales of magnitude, making these the world's first two long-lasting global empires. The Han were not superseded in East Asia as the model empire until the Tang dynasty in the seventh century CE. In western Afro-Eurasia, the Roman Empire was not surpassed in scale or intensity of development until the rise of powerful European nation-states more than a millennium later.

After You Read This Chapter

Go to INQUIZITIVE to see what you've learned—and learn what you've missed—with personalized feedback along the way.

TRACING THE GLOBAL STORYLINES

FOCUS ON: *Comparing Han China and Imperial Rome*

- Han China and imperial Rome assimilate diverse peoples to their ways and regard outsiders as uncivilized.
- Both empires develop professional military elites, codify laws, and value the role of the state (not just the ruler) in supporting their societies.
- Both empires serve as models for successor states in their regions.
- The empires differ in their ideals and the officials they value: Han China values civilian bureaucrats and magistrates; Rome values soldiers and military governors.

CHRONOLOGY

EAST ASIA

- Qin Empire of Shi Huangdi 221–207 BCE
- Emperor Wu expands Han Empire 140–87 BCE

THE MEDITERRANEAN

- Roman state expands through Italian peninsula 350–265 BCE
- Rome eliminates Carthage (Punic Wars) 264–146 BCE
- Tiberius and Gaius Gracchus attempt agrarian reforms 133–121 BCE

300 BCE | 200 BCE | 100 BCE

THINKING ABOUT GLOBAL CONNECTIONS

- ***Thinking about* Worlds Together, Worlds Apart *and Globalizing Empires*** In the six centuries between 300 BCE and 300 CE, the Han dynasty and imperial Rome united huge populations and immense swaths of territory not only under their direct control but also under their indirect influence. In what ways did this expansive unity at each end of Afro-Eurasia have an impact on the connections between these two empires? In what ways did these two empires remain worlds apart?
- ***Thinking about Changing Power Relationships and Globalizing Empires*** Both the Han dynasty and the Roman Empire developed new models for heightened authoritarian control placed in the hands of a single ruler. In what ways did this authoritarian control at the top shape power relationships at all levels of these two societies? What were some potential challenges to this patriarchal, centralized control?
- ***Thinking about Transformation & Conflict and Globalizing Empires*** Both the Han dynasty and the Roman Empire faced intense threats along their borders. In what ways did Han interactions with nomadic groups like the Xiongnu and Roman interactions with Parthians to the east and Germans and Goths to the north impact these globalizing empires?

STUDY QUESTIONS

1. What are the characteristics of a **globalizing empire** and how do the Han dynasty and the Roman Empire fit that model?
2. How did developments begun under **Shi Huangdi**, such as **commanderies** and other Qin innovations, lay the foundations for the Han dynasty?
3. In what ways did **Emperor Wu** contribute to the creation of the Han dynasty?
4. What role did Confucianism and the **Imperial University** play in shaping the Han bureaucracy? What role did millenarian movements play in the demise of the Han dynasty?
5. What was the Roman war ethos and what role did it play in Roman imperialist endeavors, such as the **Punic Wars**?
6. What political features were central to the Roman ***res publica*** and in what ways did **Augustus** incorporate and challenge those in his formation of a model for empire?
7. Describe how hierarchies, such as the patron-client system and family structure, governed Roman life and in what ways **Christianity** challenged those structures.
8. Explain how Han and Roman leaders promoted long periods of peace—the ***Pax Sinica*** and ***Pax Romana***, respectively. What were some of the results of that long-lasting peace and what were the threats to preserving that peace?

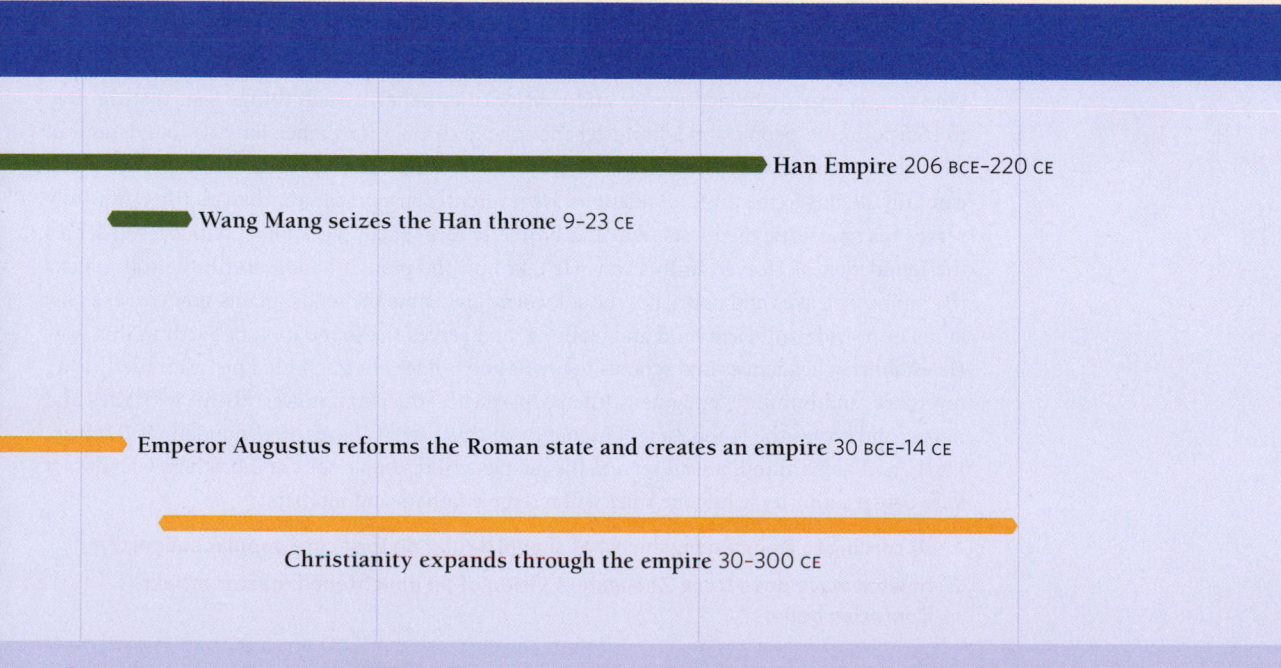

Han Empire 206 BCE–220 CE

Wang Mang seizes the Han throne 9–23 CE

Emperor Augustus reforms the Roman state and creates an empire 30 BCE–14 CE

Christianity expands through the empire 30–300 CE

1 CE | 100 CE | 200 CE | 300 CE

Going to the Source

Politics and Order in Rome and Han China, 300 BCE to 300 CE

Both Han China and Rome had agrarian-based economies, and both were expansionist states that faced challenges as a result of that expansion. Over time, the independent small farms of both empires gave way to large plantations with slave labor in the Roman world and tenant farming in Han China. This created economic as well as political problems in both empires. In Rome, it decreased the pool of potential soldiers, because only landed men could fight in the Roman army, and widened the wealth gap between the elite and non-elite. In Han China, monopolies on salt, iron, and wine funded military campaigns, but also encouraged people to move away from the ideal of productive farmers, supported by Confucian and Daoist philosophies. These social changes, along with changes in the relationships between men and women, prompted important questions about government's role in addressing issues that developed over growing inequality. Such questions continue to reverberate today.

PRIMARY SOURCE 7.1

Responsibilities of Han Rulership (second century BCE), Dong Zhongshu

The second-century BCE Han Chinese scholar Dong Zhongshu integrated a Confucian rationale into his justification of the legitimacy of Han rule. His critique of government landed him in trouble with the emperor, and at one point he was nearly executed. In this brief passage he talks about the relationship between government and the people, using familial language, perhaps related to Confucius's notion of ideal relationships.

One who is an enlightened master and worthy ruler believes such things [i.e., that the way to transform the people and administer the state is through reverence for "the foundation" of all living things, namely Heaven, Earth, and humankind]. For this reason he respectfully and carefully attends to the three foundations. He reverently enacts the suburban sacrifice, dutifully serves his ancestors, manifests filial and brotherly love, encourages filial conduct, and serves the foundation of Heaven in this way. He takes up the plough handle to till the soil, plucks the mulberry leaves and nourishes the silkworms, reclaims the wilds, plants grain, opens new lands to provide sufficient food and clothing, and serves the foundation of Earth in this way. He establishes academies and schools in towns and villages to teach filial piety, brotherly love, reverence, and humility, enlightens [the people] with education, moves [them] with rites and music, and serves the foundation of humanity in this way. If these three foundations [Heaven, Earth, and humankind] are all served, the people will resemble sons and brothers who do not dare usurp authority, while the ruler will resemble fathers and mothers.

1. **According to Dong Zhongshu, what should a ruler do to secure popular support?**
2. **In what ways does Dong Zhongshu's vision of an enlightened master reflect Confucian beliefs?**

PRIMARY SOURCE 7.2

The Life of Tiberius Gracchus (c. 75 CE), Plutarch

In the *Lives,* Plutarch's biographies of great men, the Roman plebeian tribune Tiberius Gracchus is described as a reformer who sought to address inequalities, especially through land reform. Such changes would ultimately take wealth and prestige away from the patrician families of Rome, though implementing them was difficult. In his efforts to pass and implement his reforms, Tiberius Gracchus made many political enemies. Before the laws could be fully implemented, his detractors assassinated him, along with his supporters, and unceremoniously dumped his body in the Tiber River.

Of the territory which the Romans won in war from their neighbours, a part they sold, and a part they made common land, and assigned it for occupation to the poor and indigent among the citizens, on payment of a small rent into the public treasury. And when the rich began to offer larger rents and drove out the poor, a law was enacted forbidding the holding by one person of more than five hundred acres of land. For a short time this enactment gave a check to the rapacity of the rich, and was of assistance to the poor, who remained in their places on the land which they had rented and occupied the allotment which each had held from the outset. But later on the neighbouring rich men, by means of fictitious personages, transferred these rentals to themselves, and finally held most of the land openly in their own names. Then the poor, who had been ejected from their land, no longer showed themselves eager for military service, and neglected the bringing up of children, so that soon all Italy was conscious of a dearth of freemen, and was filled with gangs of foreign slaves, by whose aid the rich cultivated their estates. . . . An attempt was therefore made to rectify this evil, and by Caius Laelius the comrade of Scipio; but the men of influence opposed his measures, and he, fearing the disturbance which might ensue, desisted, and received the surname of *Wise* or *Prudent*. Tiberius, however, on being elected tribune of the people, took the matter directly in hand. . . . When Tiberius came back from his campaign and found that his rival had far outstripped him in reputation and influence and was an object of public admiration, he determined, as it would seem, to outdo him by engaging in a bold political measure which would arouse great expectations among the people. However, the energy and ambition of Tiberius were most of all kindled by the people themselves, who posted writings on porticoes, house-walls, and monuments, calling upon him to recover for the poor the public land. . . .

Tiberius, striving to support a measure which was honourable and just with an eloquence that would have adorned even a meaner cause, was formidable and invincible, whenever, with the people crowding around the rostra, he took his stand there and pleaded for the poor. "The wild beasts that roam over Italy," he would say, "have every one of them a cave or lair to lurk in; but the men who fight and die for Italy enjoy the common air and light, indeed, but nothing else; houseless and homeless they wander about with their wives and children. And it is with lying lips that their imperators exhort the soldiers in their battles to defend sepulchres and shrines from the enemy; for not a man of them has an hereditary altar, not one of all these many Romans an ancestral tomb, but they fight and die to support others in wealth and luxury, and though they are styled masters of the world, they have not a single clod of earth that is their own." . . .

But the senate in its session accomplished nothing, owing to the prevailing influence of the wealthy class in it, and therefore Tiberius resorted to a measure which was illegal and unseemly, the ejection of Octavius from his office.

1. **Why had land become concentrated in the hands of wealthy Romans, and what argument did Tiberius make to address this inequality between the rich and poor?**
2. **According to Tiberius, what role should the government play in redistributing wealth?**

PRIMARY SOURCE 7.3

Debate on Salt and Iron (first century BCE)

This document contains excerpts from a debate about the economic policies that were in place during the Han dynasty. Emperor Zhao and his Confucian government officials reexamined the policies of the preceding emperor, Emperor Wu (r. 141–87 BCE), including the state monopolies on iron and salt. They were concerned that the previous emperor's policies harmed the important relationship between government and the people.

In the sixth year of the era Shiyuan [81 BCE], an imperial edict was issued directing the chancellor and the imperial secretaries to confer with the worthies and scholars who had been recommended to the government and to inquire into the grievances and hardships of the people.

The [scholars] responded: We have heard that the way to govern men is to prevent evil and error at their source, to broaden the beginnings of morality, to discourage secondary occupations* and open the way for the exercise of humaneness and rightness. Never should material profit appear as a motive of government. Only then can moral instruction succeed and the customs of the people be reformed. But now in the provinces the salt, iron, and liquor monopolies and the system of equitable marketing have been established to compete with the people for profit, dispelling rustic generosity and teaching the people greed. Therefore those who pursue primary occupations have grown few and those following secondary occupations numerous. As artifice increases, basic simplicity declines; and as the secondary occupations flourish, those that are primary suffer. When the secondary is practiced the people grow decadent, but when the primary is practiced they are simple and sincere. When the people are sincere then there will be sufficient wealth and goods, but when they become extravagant then famine and cold will follow. We recommend that the salt, iron, and liquor monopolies and the system of equitable marketing be abolished so that primary pursuits may be advanced and secondary ones suppressed. This will have the advantage of increasing the profitableness of agriculture.

His Lordship [the Imperial Secretary Sang Hongyang] replied: The Xiongnu have frequently revolted against our sovereignty and pillaged our borders. If we are to defend ourselves, then it means the hardships of war for the soldiers of China, but if we do not defend ourselves properly, then their incursions cannot be stopped. The former emperor [Wu] took pity upon the people of the border areas who for so long had suffered disaster and hardship and had been carried off as captives. Therefore he set up defense stations, established a system of warning beacons, and garrisoned the outlying areas to ensure their protection. But the resources of these areas were insufficient, and so he established the salt, iron, and liquor monopolies and the system of equitable marketing in order to raise more funds for expenditures at the borders. Now our critics, who desire that these measures be abolished, would empty the treasuries and deplete the funds used for defense. They would have the men who are defending our passes and patrolling our walls suffer hunger and cold. How else can we provide for them? Abolition of these measures is not expedient! . . .

His Lordship stated: In former times the peers residing in the provinces sent in their respective products as tribute, but there was much confusion and trouble in transporting them and the goods were often of such poor quality that they were not worth the cost of transportation.

For this reason transportation offices have been set up in each district to handle delivery and shipping and to facilitate the presentation of tribute from outlying areas. Therefore the system is called "equitable marketing." Warehouses have been opened in the capital for the storing of goods, buying when prices are low and selling when they are high. Thereby the government suffers no loss and the merchants cannot speculate for profit. . . .

The [scholars] replied: In ancient times taxes and levies took from the people what they were skilled in producing and did not demand what they were poor at. Thus the husbandmen sent in their harvests and the weaving women their goods. Nowadays the government disregards what people have and requires of them what they have not, so that they are forced to sell their goods at a cheap price in order to meet the demands from above. . . . The farmers suffer double hardships and the weaving women are taxed twice. We have not seen that this kind of marketing is "equitable." The government officials go about recklessly opening closed doors and buying everything at will so they can corner all the goods. With goods cornered prices soar, and when prices soar the merchants make their own deals for profit. The officials wink at powerful racketeers, and the rich merchants hoard commodities and wait for an emergency. With slick merchants and corrupt officials buying cheap and selling dear we have not seen that your level is "balanced." The system of equitable marketing of ancient times was designed to equalize the burden of labor upon the people and facilitate the transporting of tribute. It did not mean dealing in all kinds of commodities for the sake of profit.

* Farming is considered the primary occupation; artisans and merchants are secondary occupations.

1. **Why were the monopolies on salt, iron, and liquor established in Han China?**
2. **Why does the current government recommend abolishing the monopolies?**

PRIMARY SOURCE 7.4

The Role of the Roman State (44 BCE), Cicero

In this excerpt from his essay on ethics and public behavior, Marcus Tullius Cicero, a leading Roman politician from the 60s through the 40s BCE, presents his view on the responsibilities of political officeholders in the Roman state. Like others at this time, he was concerned with the relationship between government and the governed. He also considers the role of property in determining such relationships. Cicero himself came from a wealthy family, which may be why he did not support yet another attempt to pass an agrarian reform law.

That man who undertakes responsibility for public office in the state must make it his first priority to see that every person can continue to hold what is his and that no inroads are made into the goods or property of private persons by the state. It was a bad policy when Philippus, when he was tribune of the plebs [about 104 BCE], proposed an agrarian reform law. When his law was defeated, he took the defeat well and was moderate in his response. In the debates themselves, however, he tried to curry popular favor and acted in a bad way when he said, "In our community there are not more than two thousand men who have real property."

That speech ought to be condemned outright for attempting to advocate equality of property holdings. What policy could be more dangerous? It was for this very reason—that each person should be able to keep his own property—that states and local governments were founded. Although it was by the leadership of nature herself that men gathered together in communities, it was for the hope of keeping their own property that they sought the protection of states. . . .

Some men want to become known as popular politicians and for this reason they engage in making revolutionary proposals about land, with the result that owners are driven from their homes and money lent out by creditors is simply given free to the borrowers with no need for repayment. Such men are shaking the very foundations of the state. First of all, they are destroying that goodwill and sense of trust which can no longer exist when money is simply taken from some people and given to others [by the state]. And then they take away fairness, which is totally destroyed if each person is not permitted to keep what is his own. For, as I have already said, it is the peculiar function of the state and of local government to make sure that each person should be able to keep his own things freely and without any worry.

1. **According to Cicero, what is the state's role when it comes to private property?**
2. **Compare Cicero's thoughts on private property with those of Tiberius (Primary Source 7.2).**

PRIMARY SOURCE 7.5

Lessons for Women *(c. 100 CE), Ban Zhao*

Dong Zhongshu and Cicero were elite men and part of the political power structure, whereas writers from other backgrounds offer different ideas about what brings harmony to a community. In Han China an exceptional woman named Ban Zhao, whose father and brother were court historians working on the *Book of Han*, finalized the text herself after their deaths. Widowed at a young age, Ban Zhao was able to devote her attentions to literary and philosophical pursuits, including her *Lessons for Women*, which is excerpted below.

The Way of husband and wife is intimately connected with *yin* and *yang*, and relates the individual to gods and ancestors. Truly it is the great principle of Heaven and Earth, and the great basis of human relationships. Therefore the *Record of Rites* honors union of man and woman; and in the *Book of Odes* the First Ode manifests the principle of marriage. For these reasons the relationship cannot but be an important one. If a husband be unworthy, then he possesses nothing by which to control his wife. If a wife be unworthy, she possesses nothing with which to serve her husband. If a husband does not control his wife, then the rules of conduct manifesting his authority are abandoned and broken. If a wife does not serve her husband, then the proper relationship (between men and women) and the natural order of things are neglected and destroyed. As a matter of fact the purpose of these two (the controlling of women by men, and the serving of men by women) is the same.

Now examine the gentlemen of the present age. They only know that wives must be controlled, and that a husband's rules of conduct manifesting his authority must be established. They therefore teach their boys to read books and (study) histories. But they do not in the least understand that husbands and masters must (also) be served, and that the proper relationship and the rites should be maintained.

Yet only to teach men and not to teach women—is that not ignoring the essential relation between them? According to the *Record of Rites*, it is the rule to begin to teach children to read at the age of eight years, and by the age of fifteen years they ought then be ready for cultural training. Only why should it not be (that girls' education as well as boys' be) according to this principle?

1. **How does Ban Zhao describe the principle of marriage and the relationship between husband and wife?**

2. **What does Ban Zhao believe the role of education in society to be? How should the current system of education be changed?**

PRIMARY SOURCE 7.6

On Women in Rome (first century CE*), Musonius Rufus*

Musonius Rufus, a philosopher who lived in Rome during the first century CE, was exiled several times for his views. Generally associated with Stoic philosophy, he argued that individuals should pursue happiness through virtuous behavior. His philosophy focused on how to live well, but because he did not leave any written records, his ideas were collected by his students after his death. In this passage he addresses the place of women in Rome, as well as more generally.

(4) If a man knows something about a particular skill, and a woman doesn't, or if the reverse is true, this shows that there is no difference in their education. Only about all the important things do not let one know and the other not, but let them both know the same. If someone asks me, which doctrine requires such an education, I would answer him that without philosophy no man and no woman either can be well educated. I do not mean to say that women need to have clarity with or facility in argument, because they will use philosophy as women use it. But I do not recommend these skills particularly in men. My point is that women ought to be good and noble in their characters, and that philosophy is nothing other than the training for that nobility.

(13a) [Musonius Rufus] said that a husband and wife come together in order to lead their lives in common and to produce children, and that they should consider all their property to be common, and nothing private, not even their bodies. For the birth of a human being that such a union produces is a significant event, but it is not sufficient for the husband, because it could have come about without marriage, from some other conjunction, as in the case of animals. In marriage there must be complete companionship and concern for each other on the part of both husband and wife, in health and in sickness and at all times, because they entered upon the marriage for this reason as well as to produce offspring. When such caring for one another is perfect, and the married couple provide it for one another, and each strives to outdo the other, then this is marriage as it ought to be and deserving of emulation, since it is a noble union.

[12] But when one partner looks to his own interests alone and neglects the others, or (by Zeus) the other is so minded that he lives in the same house, but keeps his mind on what is outside it, and does not wish to pull together with his partner or to cooperate, then inevitably the union is destroyed, and although they live together their common interests fare badly, and either they finally get divorced from one another or they continue on in an existence that is worse than loneliness.

1. **How does Musonius Rufus describe the ideal relationship between a Roman husband and wife?**
2. **How does Musonius Rufus's description of marriage differ from that of Ban Zhao (Primary Source 7.5)?**

PRIMARY SOURCE 7.7

Roman Mosaic (second–third century CE)

This mosaic discovered in a home in Thugga, Tunisia, shows a slave in typical slave clothing pouring wine for guests from a large amphora. Slave labor was an important part of the Roman economy. While slaves served at every level of society and could even be physicians or teachers, most slaves were prisoners who were captured during Roman military conquest.

1. **How does this image depict Roman social order?**
2. **Why do you think a home would contain a mosaic such as this one?**

Questions for Analysis

Contextualization

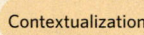

1. These documents all deal fundamentally with the problem of inequality in the social order, whether economic or between the sexes. Why might these issues have been so pressing in both Han China and in Rome during this period?

Analyzing Evidence

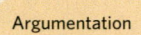

2. Using evidence from the documents, explain whether you believe that states should reflect the peoples' will or whether the peoples' will should instead be formed by the states in which they live.

Argumentation

3. Is equality more important than order and harmony? Or is order more important than equality? Explain your answer.

Long Essay Question

Argumentation

Compare the Roman and Han approaches to government in maintaining the social order. Explain which you prefer and the reasons for your preference.

Before You Read This Chapter

GLOBAL STORYLINES

- Universalizing religions—notably Christianity and Buddhism—appeal to diverse, widespread populations and challenge the power of secular rulers and thinkers.
- Across Afro-Eurasia, these universalizing religions offer continuity even as powerful empires, specifically the Roman Empire in the west and the Han dynasty in China, fall away.
- Along the Silk Roads, the merchants and rulers of Sasanian Persia, Sogdiana, and South Asia profoundly influence the exchange of goods, people, and ideas between east and west.
- In the "worlds apart," common cultural beliefs help unify newly organized polities in Mesoamerica and new communities of Bantu-speakers in sub-Saharan Africa.

CORE OBJECTIVES

- **DESCRIBE** the characteristics of universalizing religions, ar **EXPLAIN** why universalizing religions developed to varying degrees in Afro-Eurasia but did not develop elsewhere in the world.
- **ANALYZE** the relationship between empires and universalizing religions across Afro-Eurasia in this period.
- **ASSESS** the connections between political unity and religious developments in sub-Saharan Africa and Mesoamerica in the fourth to sixth centuries CE.
- **COMPARE** the unifying political and cultural developments in sub-Saharan Africa and Mesoamerica with those that took place across Eurasia in this period.

CHAPTER

8

The Rise of Universal Religions

300–600 CE

KEY TERMS

Bantu migrations p. 304
Byzantium p. 290
Code of Manu p. 299
creed p. 286
Hinayana Buddhism p. 298
Hinduism p. 296
Madhyamika (Middle Way) Buddhism p. 301
martyr p. 283
Sanskrit cosmopolis p. 298
universalizing religion p. 282

Around 180 CE, twelve Christians, seven men and five women, stood trial before the provincial governor at Carthage. Their crime was refusal to worship the gods of the Roman Empire. While the governor argued for the simplicity of his religion with its devotion to "the protecting spirit of our lord the emperor," one Christian retorted that his own lord was "the king of kings and emperor of all nations." This distinction was an unbridgeable gap between the governor and the Christians. The governor condemned them all. "Thanks be to God!" cried the Christians, and straightaway they were beheaded. As the centuries unfolded, the governor's old Roman ideas of the supremacy of an emperor-lord would give way to the martyrs' devotion to their Lord God as emperor over all. As with Christianity's claim of an "emperor of all nations," a religion's capacity for universalizing—particularly its broad appeal across diverse peoples and cultures—became ever more important to its success.

From 300 to 600 CE, the entire Afro-Eurasian landmass experienced a surge of religious activity. In the west, Christianity became the state faith of the Roman Empire. In India, Vedic religion (Brahmanism) evolved into a more formal spiritual system called Hinduism. Buddhism spread across northern India, central Asia, and China.

Around the same time, the peoples living in sub-Saharan Africa reached beyond their local communities, creating common cultures across wider geographical areas. The Bantu-speaking peoples, residing in the southeastern corner of present-day Nigeria, began to spread their way of life throughout the entire southern half of the landmass. Similarly, across the Atlantic Ocean, the Mayans established political and cultural institutions over a large portion of Mesoamerica. Across much of the world, spiritual concerns integrated scattered communities into shared faiths (see Map 8.1).

COMPARISON

DESCRIBE the characteristics of universalizing religions.

This integration was facilitated in Afro-Eurasia in part by the spread of what we might call universalizing religions. Two faiths in this era—Christianity and Buddhism—fit the model for this type of religion particularly well. Six main features characterize **universalizing religions**: their appeal to diverse populations (men and women, freeborn and slaves, rich and poor); their adaptability as they moved from one cultural and geographical area to another; their promotion of universal rules and principles to guide behavior that transcended place, time, and specific cultural practices; their proselytizing of new believers by energetic and charismatic missionaries; the deep sense of community felt by their converts despite, and perhaps because of, their many demands on followers; and—in the case of Christianity, though to a lesser extent Buddhism—the support given to them by powerful empires. Even as the Roman Empire and the Han dynasty began to crumble, these universalizing traditions continued to flourish.

Across Afro-Eurasia, universal religions were on the move (see Map 8.2). Religious leaders carrying written texts (books, scrolls, or tablets of wood or palm leaf) traveled widely. Christians from Persia went to China. Buddhists journeyed from South Asia to Afghanistan and used the caravan routes of central Asia to reach China. Voyages, translations, long-distance pilgrimages, and sweeping conversion campaigns remapped the spiritual landscape of the world. New religious leaders were the brokers of more universal but also more intolerant worldviews, premised on a distinct relationship between gods and their subjects. Religions and their brokers profoundly integrated societies. But they also created new ways to drive them apart.

Religious Change and Empire in Western Afro-Eurasia

COMPARISON

ANALYZE the relationship between empires and universalizing religions in the Roman and Sasanian empires, and the Gupta and Wei dynasties.

By the fourth century CE in western Afro-Eurasia, the Roman Empire was hardly the political and military juggernaut it had been 300 years earlier. Surrounded by peoples who coveted its wealth while resisting its power, Rome was fragmenting. So-called barbarians eventually overran the western part of the empire, but in many ways those areas still felt "Roman." Rome's endurance was a boon to the new religious activity that thrived in the turmoil of the immigrations and contracting political authority of the empire. Romans and so-called barbarians alike looked to the new faith of Christianity to maintain continuity with the past, eventually founding a central church in Rome to rule the remnants of empire.

THE APPEAL OF CHRISTIANITY

The spread of new religious ideas, including Christianity, in the Roman Empire changed the way people viewed their existence. Believing implied that an important otherworld loomed beyond the world of physical matter. Feeling contact with that other world gave worshippers a sense of worth; it guided them in this life, and they anticipated someday meeting their guides and spiritual friends there. No longer were the gods understood by believers as local powers to be placated by archaic rituals in sacred places. Many gods became omnipresent figures whom mortals could touch through loving attachment. As ordinary mortals now could hope to meet these divine beings in another, happier world, the sense of an afterlife glowed more brightly.

Christians' emphasis on obedience to their Lord God, rather than to a human ruler, sparked a Mediterranean-wide debate on the nature of religion. Christians, like the Jews from whose tradition their sect had sprung, possessed divinely inspired scriptures that told them what to believe and do, even when those actions went against the empire's laws. (See **Analyzing Global Developments: One God, Two Communities**.) Christians spoke of their scriptures as "a divine codex." Bound in a compact volume or set of volumes, this was the definitive code of God's law that outlined proper belief and behavior.

Another central feature of early Christianity was the figure of the **martyr**. Martyrs were women and men whom the Roman authorities executed for persisting in their Christian beliefs instead of submitting to emperor worship, as we saw in this chapter's opening story of the twelve Scillitan martyrs—so-called for the town in North Africa from which they came. While other religions, including Judaism and later Islam, honored martyrs who died for their faith, Christianity claimed to be based directly on "the blood of martyrs," in the words of the North African Christian theologian Tertullian (writing around 200 CE).

The story of Vibia Perpetua, a well-to-do mother in her early twenties, offers a striking example of martyrdom. Refusing to sacrifice to the Roman gods, Perpetua and her maidservant Felicitas, along with their companions, were condemned in 203 CE to face wild beasts in the amphitheater of Carthage, a venue small enough that the condemned and the spectators would have had eye contact with one another throughout the fatal encounter. The prison diary that Perpetua dictated before her death offered to Christians and potential converts a powerful religious message that balanced heavenly visions and rewards with her concerns over responsibility to her father, brother, and infant son. The remembered heroism of women martyrs like Perpetua and Felicitas offset the increasingly all-male leadership—bishops and clergy—of the institutionalized Christian church.

Christian Martyrs This detail from a mosaic found in a Roman circus in North Africa shows a criminal tied to a stake and being pushed on a little cart toward a lunging leopard. Christian martyrs were treated much the same as criminals: they were executed, sometimes thrown to wild animals. How might the treatment of martyrs like criminals have influenced those watching such "entertainment"?

Constantine: From Conversion to Creed Crucial in spurring Christianity's spread was the transformative experience of Constantine (c. 280–337 CE). Born near the Danubian frontier, he belonged to a class of professional soldiers whose careers took them far from the Mediterranean. Constantine's troops proclaimed him emperor after the death of his father, the emperor Constantius. In the civil war that followed, Constantine looked for signs from the gods. Before the decisive battle for Rome, which took place at a strategic bridge in 312 CE, he supposedly had a dream in which he saw an emblem bearing the words "In this sign

ROCKY MOUNTAINS
FOREST NOMADIC HUNTERS
NORTH AMERICA
Great Lakes
St. Lawrence R.
Mississippi R.
PLAINS NOMADIC HUNTERS
CELTIC PEOPLES
GERMAN
GOTHS
Carthage
KINGDOM OF THE VANDALS
SAHARA
SAHARAN PEOPLES
Niger R.
ATLANTIC OCEAN
Gulf of Mexico
Teotihuacán
WEST INDIES
MAYAN CITY STATES
PACIFIC OCEAN
ANDES MOUNTAINS
Amazon R.
CHAVIN
SOUTH AMERICA
Qi
Tuoba
Hephthalites
Sasanian
Gupta
Eastern Roman
Mayan
VANDALS Kingdom
BANTU People
City
0 1000 2000 Miles
0 1000 2000 Kilometers

MAP 8.1 | Empires and Universalizing Religions from 300 to 600 CE

The period from 300 to 600 CE was a time of tumultuous political change accompanied by the spread of adaptable and accessible universalizing faiths.

- Comparing this map with those in Chapters 6 and 7, which polities are new? Which polities have disappeared? Which ones have expanded or contracted?
- Where on the map are the world's empires located? How are peoples organized outside those empires?
- Looking at Map 8.2, what seems to be the relationship between these empires and religions or philosophies such as Christianity, Buddhism, Judaism, Hinduism, and Confucianism?

conquer." The "sign," which he then placed on his soldiers' shields, was the first two letters of the Greek *christos*, a title for Jesus meaning "anointed one." Constantine's troops won the ensuing battle and, thereafter, Constantine's visionary sign became known all over the Roman world. Constantine showered imperial favor on this once-persecuted faith, issuing an edict praising the work of Christian bishops and granting them significant tax exemptions.

By the time that Constantine embraced Christianity, it had already made considerable progress within the Roman Empire. It had prevailed in the face of stiff competition and periodically intense persecution from the imperial authorities. Apart from the new imperial endorsement, Christianity's success could be attributed to the sacred aura surrounding its authoritative texts, the charisma of its holy men and women, the fit that existed between its doctrines and popular preexisting religious beliefs and practices, and its broad, universalizing appeal to rich and poor, city dwellers and peasants, slaves and free people, young and old, and men and women.

In 325 CE, hoping to bring unity to the diversity of belief within Christian communities, Constantine summoned all bishops to Nicaea (modern Iznik in western Turkey) for a council to develop a statement of belief, or **creed** (from the Latin *credo,* "I believe"). The resulting Nicene Creed balanced three separate divine entities—God "the father," "the son," and "the holy spirit"—as facets of one supreme being. Also at Nicaea the bishops agreed to hold Easter, the day on which Christians celebrate Christ's resurrection, on the same day in every church of the Christian world. Writing near the end of Constantine's reign, an elderly bishop in Palestine named Eusebius noted that the Roman Empire of his day would have surprised the martyrs of Carthage, who had willingly died rather than recognize any "empire of this world."

Christianity in the Cities and Beyond After 312 CE, the large churches built in every major city, many with imperial funding, signaled Christianity's growing strength. These gigantic meeting halls were called basilicas, from the Greek word *basileus*, meaning king. They were modeled on Roman law-court buildings and could accommodate over a thousand worshippers. Inside a basilica's vast space, oil lamps shimmered on marble and brought mosaics to life. Rich silk hangings, swaying between rows of columns, increased the sense of mystery and directed the eye to the far end of the building—a splendidly furnished semicircular apse. Under the dome of the apse, which represented the dome of heaven, and surrounded by priests, the bishop sat and preached from his special throne, or *cathedra*.

Basilica Interior The interior of a basilica was dominated by rows of ancient marble columns and was filled with light from upper windows, so that the eye was led directly to the apse of the church, where the bishop and clergy would sit under a dome, close to the altar.

These basilicas became the new urban public forums, ringed with spacious courtyards where the city's poor would gather. In return for the tax exemptions that Constantine had granted them, bishops cared for the metropolitan poor. Bishops also became judges, as Constantine turned their arbitration process for disputes between Christians into a kind of small claims court. Offering the poor shelter, quick justice, and moments of unearthly splendor in grand basilicas, Christian bishops perpetuated "Rome" for centuries after the empire had disappeared.

The spread of Christianity outside the cities and into the hinterlands of Africa and Southwest Asia required the

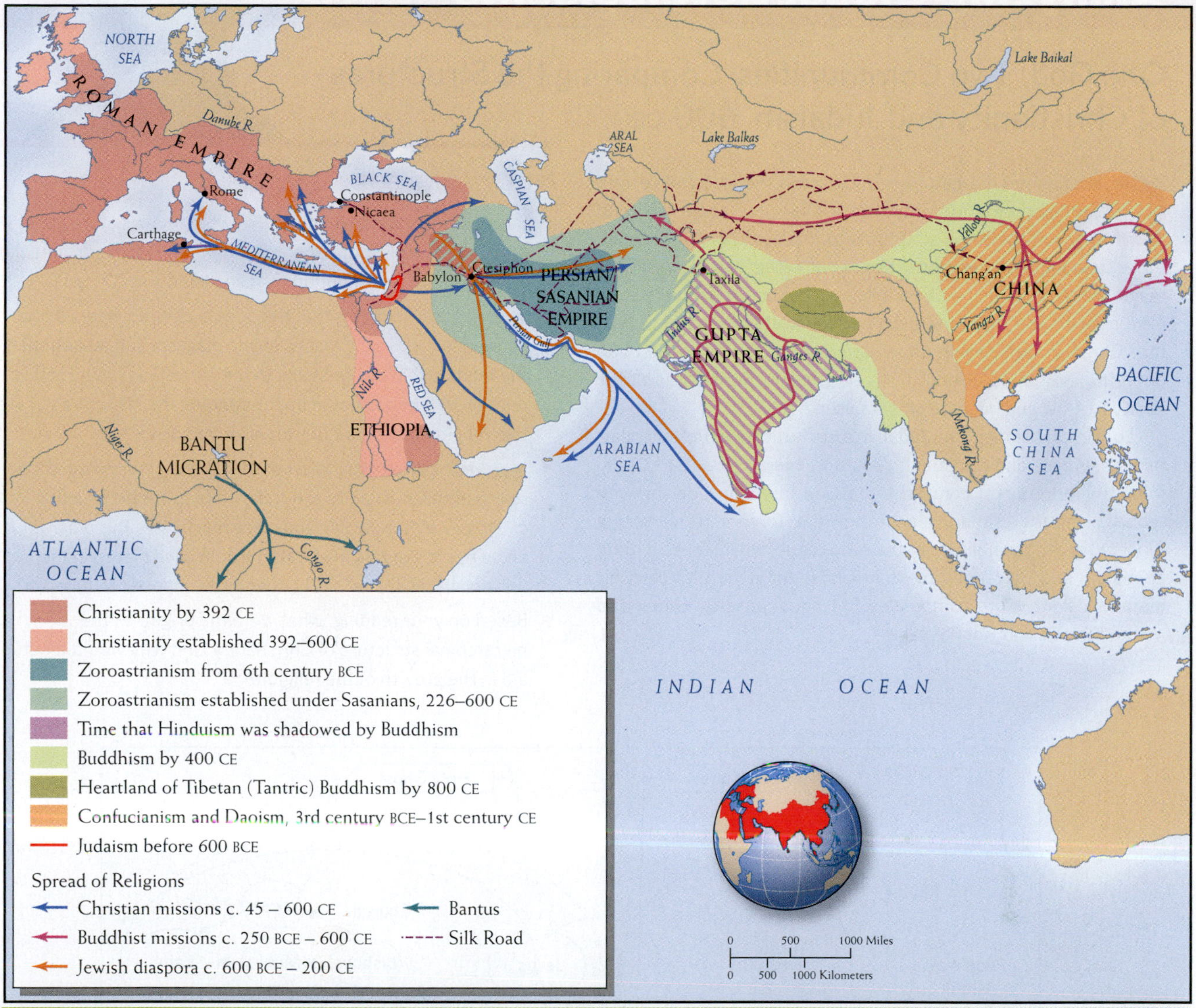

MAP 8.2 | The Spread of Universal Religions in Afro-Eurasia, 300–600 CE

The spread of universal religions and the shifting political landscape were intimately connected.

- Where did Hinduism, Buddhism, and Christianity emerge, and where did they spread?
- Along what routes did each religion spread?
- How did the rise and fall of empires affect the expansion of universal religions?

breaking of language barriers. In Egypt, Christian clergy replaced hieroglyphics with Coptic, a more accessible script based on Greek letters, in an effort to bridge the linguistic and cultural gap between town and countryside. In the crucial corridor that joined Antioch to Mesopotamia, Syriac, an offshoot of the Semitic language Aramaic, became a major Christian language. As Christianity spread farther north, to Georgia in the Caucasus and to Armenia, Christian clergy created written languages that are still used in those regions.

Analyzing Global Developments

One God, Two Communities: Comparing the Structures of Christianity and Judaism, 600 CE

Christianity emerged from Judaism in the first and second centuries ce and continues to share the same God and many of the same scriptures to this very day. Yet, despite these fundamental commonalities, what arose were two distinct religious communities, each with its own notions of God in relation to humanity. The following diagrams illustrate the major impact that Christian and Jewish understandings of the same God had upon the structures of their early religious institutions and their ability to grow and become universalizing.

Looking at the diagram, Judaism's institutional structure is flatter and simpler, and Christianity's is more hierarchical. One would think the more direct connection to God found in Judaism, with rabbis being the primary teachers of the Torah and overseeing most of the responsibilities at the synagogue, would make it more appealing and universalizing than Christianity, with its church's hierarchical structure composed of bishops, priests, monks, and nuns—but this was not the case.

QUESTIONS FOR ANALYSIS

- Based on your reading in the text, what factors more generally made religions like Christianity and Buddhism more appealing and universalizing than Judaism and Hinduism?
- The diagram suggests that the people of Israel had a direct connection to God. What does the diagram suggest about the relationship of Christians to the same God? Why is this relationship important in understanding the structures of the two religions and their universalizing appeal?
- Martyrs, like Perpetua (discussed in the chapter), played a big role in both Christianity and Judaism (e.g., rabbis resisting Rome c. 100 CE). Where would you place martyrs on this diagram, and why? What role might martyrdom have played in the universalizing appeal of Christianity as opposed to Judaism?
- Based on your reading, what were the origins of the hierarchical structure of Christianity, and why would it actually aid in the growth of the religion?

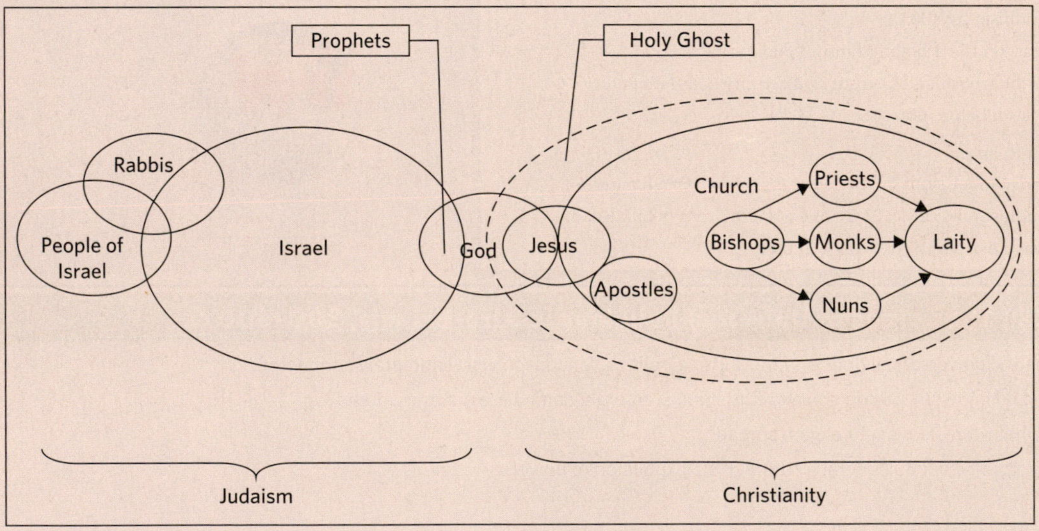

THE "FALL" OF ROME IN THE WEST

By the third and fourth centuries CE, the political and economic fabric of the old Roman world was unraveling (see Map 8.3). The so-called barbarian invasions of the late fourth and fifth centuries CE further contributed to that demise. These "invasions" were less an assault, and more a violent and chaotic immigration of young fighting men from the

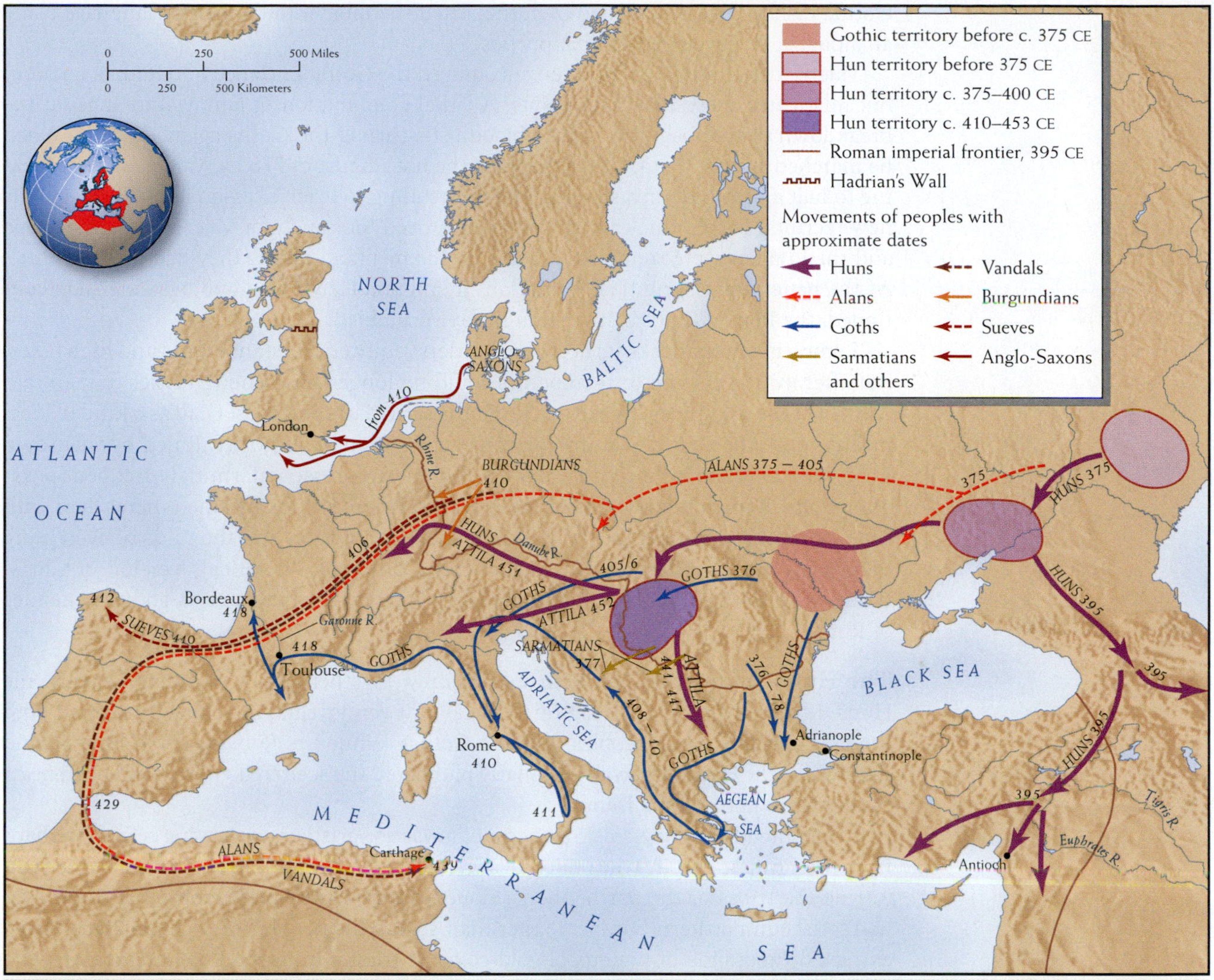

MAP 8.3 | Western Afro-Eurasia: War, Immigration, and Settlement in the Roman World, 375–450 CE

Invasions and migrations brought about the reconstitution of the Roman Empire at this time.

- Using the map, identify the people who migrated to or invaded the Roman Empire. Where were they from, and where did they go?
- How did these migrations and invasions reshape the political landscape of western Afro-Eurasia?
- Considering these effects, to what extent was the Roman depiction of these groups as "barbarians" a fair assessment?

frontiers of the empire. Today the term *barbarian* implies uncultivated or savage, but its meaning in antiquity was "foreigner" (with overtones of inferiority). Inhabitants of the empire's western provinces had become accustomed to non-Roman soldiers from across the frontiers, and for them *barbarian* was synonymous with "soldier." The popular image of bloodthirsty barbarian hordes streaming into the empire bears little resemblance to reality.

The Goths It was the Romans' need for soldiers that drew the barbarians in. The process reached a crisis point when tribes of Goths petitioned the emperor Valens (r. 365–378 CE) to let them immigrate into the empire. These Goths were no strangers to Roman influence: in fact, many had been evangelized into an anti-Nicene version of Christianity by the

Gothic bishop Ulfilas, who had even translated the Bible into the Gothic language using an alphabet he developed for that purpose.

Valens, desperate for manpower, encouraged the Goths' entrance into Roman territory but mistreated these new immigrants. A lethal combination of famine and anger at the breakdown of supplies—not innate bloodlust—turned the Goths against Valens. When he marched against them at Adrianople in the hot August of 378 CE, Valens was not seeking to halt a barbarian invasion but rather intending to teach a lesson in obedience to his new recruits. The Gothic cavalry, however, proved too much for Valens's imperial army, and the Romans were trampled to death by the men and horses they had hoped to hire. As the pattern of disgruntled "barbarian" immigrants, civil war, and overextension continued, the Roman Empire in western Europe crumbled.

Rome's maintenance of its northern borders required constant efforts and high taxes. But after 400 CE the western emperors could no longer raise enough taxes to maintain control of the provinces. In 418 CE, the Goths settled in southwest Gaul as a kind of local militia to fill the absence left by the contracting Roman authority. Ruled by their own king, who kept his military in order, the Goths suppressed alarmingly frequent peasant revolts. Roman landowners of Gaul and elsewhere anxiously allied themselves with the new military leaders rather than face social revolution and the raids of even more dangerous armies. Although they practiced a different, "heretical" version of Christianity, the Goths came as Christian allies of the aristocracy, not as godless enemies of Rome.

The Huns Romans and non-Romans also drew together to face a common enemy: the Huns. Led by their king Attila (406–453 CE) for twenty years, the Huns threatened both Romans and Germanic peoples (like the Goths). While the Romans could hide behind their walls, the Hunnish cavalry regularly plundered the scattered villages and open fields in the plains north of the Danube.

Attila intended to be a "real" emperor of a warrior-aristocracy. Having seized (perhaps from the Chinese empire) the notion of a "mandate of heaven"—in his case, a divine right to rule the tribes of the north—he fashioned the first opposing empire that Rome ever had to face in northern Europe. Rather than selling his people's services to Rome, Attila extracted thousands of pounds of gold coins in tribute from the Roman emperors who hoped to stave off assaults by his brutal forces. Drained both militarily and economically by this Hunnish threat, the Roman Empire in the west disintegrated only twenty years after Attila's death. In 476 CE, the last Roman emperor of the west, a young boy named Romulus Augustulus (namesake of both Rome's legendary founder and its first emperor), resigned to make way for a so-called barbarian king in Italy.

The political unity of the Roman Empire in the west now gave way to a sense of unity through the church. The Catholic Church (*Catholic* meaning "universal," centered in the bishops' authority) became the one institution to which all Christians in western Europe, Romans and non-Romans alike, felt that they belonged. The bishop of Rome became the symbolic head of the western churches. Rome became a spiritual capital instead of an imperial one. By 700 CE, the great Roman landowning families of the Republic and early empire had vanished, replaced by religious leaders with vast moral authority.

CONTINUITY OF ROME IN THE EAST: BYZANTIUM

Elsewhere the Roman Empire was alive and well. From the borders of Greece to the borders of modern Iraq, and from the Danube River to Egypt and the borders of Saudi Arabia, the empire survived undamaged. The new Roman Empire of the east—to which historians gave the name **Byzantium**—had its own New Rome, Constantinople. Founded in 324 CE by its namesake Constantine, on the Bosporus straits separating Europe from Asia, this strategically located city was well situated to receive taxes in gold and to control the sea-lanes of the eastern Mediterranean.

Constantinople was one of the most spectacularly successful cities in Afro-Eurasia, soon boasting a population of over half a million and 4,000 new palaces. Every year, more than 20,000 tons of grain arrived from Egypt, unloaded on a dockside over a mile long. A gigantic hippodrome echoing Rome's Circus Maximus straddled the city's central ridge, flanking an imperial palace whose opulent enclosed spaces stretched down to the busy shore. As they had for centuries before in Rome, emperors would sit in the imperial box, witnessing chariot races as rival teams careened around the stadium. The hippodrome also featured displays of eastern imperial might, as ambassadors came from as far away as central Asia, northern India, and Nubia.

Similarly, the future emperor Justinian came to Constantinople as a young man from an obscure Balkan village, to seek his fortune. When he became emperor in 527 CE, he considered himself the successor of a long line of forceful Roman emperors—and he was determined to outdo them. Most importantly, Justinian reformed the Roman laws. Within six years a commission of lawyers had created the *Digest,* a massive condensation and organization of the preexisting body of Roman law. Its companion volume was the *Institutes,* a teacher's manual for schools of Roman law. These works were the foundation of what later ages came to know as "Roman law," followed in both eastern and western Europe for more than a millennium.

Reflecting the marriage of Christianity with empire was the church of the Hagia Sophia, grandly rebuilt by Justinian on the site of two earlier basilicas. The basilica of Saint Peter in Rome, the largest church built by Constantine two centuries earlier, would have reached only as high as the lower galleries of Hagia Sophia. Walls of multicolored marble, gigantic columns of green and purple granite, audaciously curved semicircular niches placed at every corner, and a spectacular dome lined with gleaming gold mosaics inspired awe in those who entered its doors. Hagia Sophia represented the flowing together of Christianity and imperial culture that for another 1,000 years would mark the eastern Roman Empire centered in Constantinople.

Hagia Sophia The domed ceiling of Justinian's Hagia Sophia soared high above worshippers. Intricate mosaics decorated many of the walls and ceilings. The mosaic adorning the eastern apse, shown here, depicts Jesus sitting in the lap of the Virgin Mary.

Contacts between east and west, as well as internal discord, intensified during Justinian's reign. Not only did Justinian quell riots at the heart of Byzantium, he also undertook wars to reclaim parts of the western Mediterranean and to hold off the threat from Sasanian Persia in the east (see next section). Perhaps the most grisly reminder of this increased connectivity was a sudden onslaught in 541–542 CE of the bubonic plague from the east. One-third of the population of Constantinople died within weeks. Justinian himself survived, but thereafter he ruled an empire whose heartland was decimated. Nonetheless, Justinian's contributions—to the law, to Christianity, to the maintenance of imperial order—helped Byzantium last almost for nearly a millennium after Rome in the west had fallen away.

The Silk Roads

Although exchange along the Silk Roads had been taking place for centuries (see Chapter 6), the sharing of knowledge between the Mediterranean world and China began in earnest

MAP 8.4 | Exchanges Across Afro-Eurasia, 300–600 CE

Southwest Asia remained the crossroads of Afro-Eurasia in a variety of ways. Trade goods flowing between west and east passed through this region, as did universal religions. The question mark in eastern Africa indicates scholars' uncertainty about the origination of the plague.

- Using your finger, trace the principal trade routes and maritime routes. What were the areas of major religious influence? What was the relationship between trade routes and the areas of major religious influence?
- Then point out each area of religious influence. How did religious geography correspond to political geography?
- How was Southwest Asia affected by other regions, such as sub-Saharan Africa and central Asia, and how did it shape developments in these regions?

during this period. Wending their way across the difficult terrains of central Asia, a steady parade of merchants, scholars, ambassadors, missionaries, and other travelers transmitted commodities, technologies, and ideas between the Mediterranean worlds and China, and across the Himalayas into northern India, exploiting the commercial routes of the Silk Roads. Ideas, including the beliefs of the universalizing religions described in this chapter, traveled along with goods on these exchange routes. Christianity spread through the Mediterranean and beyond and, as we shall see later in this chapter, Buddhism and the Vedic religion (Brahmanism) also continued to spread.

The great oasis cities of central Asia played a crucial role in the effective functioning of the Silk Roads. While the Sasanians controlled the city of Merv in the west, nomadic rulers became the overlords of Sogdiana and Tukharistan and extracted tribute from the cities of Samarkand and Panjikent in the east. The tribal confederacies in this region maintained the links between west and east by patrolling the Silk Road between Iran and China. They also joined north to south as they passed through the mountains of Afghanistan into the plains of northern India. As a result, central Asia between 300 and 600 CE was the hub of a vibrant system of religious and cultural contacts covering the whole of Afro-Eurasia (see Map 8.4).

SASANIAN PERSIA

Beginning at the Euphrates River and stretching for eighty days of slow travel across the modern territories of Iraq, Iran, Afghanistan, and much of central Asia, the Sasanian Empire of Persia encompassed all the land routes of western Asia that connected the Mediterranean world with East Asia. In the early third century CE, the Sasanians had replaced the Parthians as rulers of the Iranian plateau and Mesopotamia. The Sasanian ruler called himself the "King of Kings of Iranian and non-Iranian lands," a title suggestive of the Sasanians' aspirations to universalism. The ancient, irrigated fields of what is modern Iraq became the economic heart of this empire. Its capital, Ctesiphon, arose where the Tigris and the Euphrates rivers come close, only twenty miles south of modern Baghdad.

Symbolizing the king's presence at Ctesiphon was the 110-foot-high vaulted Great Arch of Khusro, named after Justinian's rival, Khusro I Anoshirwan (Khusro of the Righteous Soul). As his name implied, Khusro Anoshirwan (r. 531–579 CE) exemplified the model ruler: strong and just. His image in the east as an ideal monarch was as glorious as that of Justinian in the west as an ideal Christian Roman emperor. For both Persians and Arab Muslims of later ages, the Arch of Khusro was as awe-inspiring as Justinian's Hagia Sophia was to Christians. (See **Current Trends in World History: Religious Conflict in Imperial Borderlands**.)

The Sasanian Empire controlled the trade crossroads of Afro-Eurasia and posed a military threat to Byzantium. Their Iranian armored cavalry was a fighting machine adapted from years of competition with the nomads of central Asia. These fearless horsemen fought covered from head to foot in flexible armor (small plates of iron sewn onto leather) and chain mail, riding "blood-sweating horses" draped in thickly padded cloth. Their lethal swords were light and flexible owing to steel-making techniques imported from northern India. With such cavalry, Khusro in 540 CE sacked Antioch, a city of great significance to early Christianity. The campaign was a warning, at the height of Justinian's glory, that Mesopotamia could reach out once again to conquer the eastern Mediterranean shoreline. Under Khusro II the confrontation between Persia and Rome escalated into the greatest war that had been seen for centuries. Between 604 and 628 CE, Persian forces under Khusro II conquered Egypt and Syria and even reached Constantinople before being defeated in northern Mesopotamia.

Politically united by Sasanian control, Southwest Asia also possessed a cultural unity. Syriac was the dominant language. While the Sasanians themselves were devout Zoroastrians (see Chapter 4), Christianity and Judaism enjoyed tolerance in Mesopotamia. Nestorian Christians—so named by their opponents for their acceptance of a hotly contested understanding of Jesus's divine and human nature, promoted by a former bishop of Constantinople named Nestorius—exploited Sasanian trade and diplomacy to spread their faith as far as Chang'an in China and the western coast of southern India. Protected by the Sasanian King of Kings, the Jewish rabbis of Mesopotamia compiled the monumental Babylonian Talmud at a time when their western peers, in Roman Palestine, were feeling cramped under the Christian state. The Sasanian court also embraced offerings from northern India, including the *Pancantantra* stories (moral tales played out in a legendary kingdom of the animals), polo, and the game of chess. In this regard Khusro's was truly an empire of crossroads, where the cultures of central Asia and India met that of the eastern Mediterranean.

THE SOGDIANS AS LORDS OF THE SILK ROADS

The Sogdians, who controlled the oasis cities of Samarkand and Panjikent, served as human links between the two ends of Afro-Eurasia. Their religion was a blend of Zoroastrian

Current Trends in World History

Religious Conflict in Imperial Borderlands

World historians often study borderland areas because it is in these zones that they can see most clearly the effects of cultural interaction. One example is the borderlands of the Sasanian Empire, which through the Persian Gulf reached out to control the trade on the Indian Ocean. This effort brought Persians into conflict with Roman merchants, who strove to reach India from the Red Sea. As a result, the entire region bounded by present-day Ethiopia (at the western end of the Red Sea), Yemen (in southern Arabia), and the Persian Gulf became a field of conflict between the Roman and Sasanian empires.

Their clash took religious as well as commercial and political form. Both Axum (modern-day Ethiopia) and Himyar (modern-day Yemen) had embraced monotheism, expressed in the worship of a Most High God known as al-Rahmānān (the Merciful One). In Axum, this monotheism was Christian: Christ was the protector of its kings, and the Cross of Christ was their talisman in battle. In contrast, the leaders of Himyar and the southern coast of Arabia were Jewish, and they dismissed Jesus as a crucified sorcerer.

The kings of Axum occupied the African side of the southern end of the Red Sea, looking down from the foothills of the well-watered and populous mountains of Ethiopia. Their formidable warrior-kingdom stretched as far as the Nile to the northwest, south into equatorial Africa, and eastward across the Red Sea to southern Arabia and Yemen. Axum's rulers, who became Christian around 340 CE, celebrated their victories on gigantic granite obelisks; they were monuments to a God that was very much a god of battles. Faced by the aggressive Christian kingdom of Axum, the Sasanians reached out to support the kings of Himyar, who since 380 CE had been Jewish. Thus, two monotheisms faced each other across the narrow southern opening of the Red Sea. Each was associated with a rich and aggressive kingdom. Each was backed by a great power—Axum by Christian Rome and Himyar by the Persians.

and Mesopotamian beliefs, touched with Brahmanic influences. Their language was the common tongue of the early Silk Roads, and their shaggy camels bore the commodities that passed through their entrepôts (transshipment centers). Moreover, their splendid mansions (excavated at Panjikent) show strong influences from the warrior-aristocracy culture of Iran. The palace walls display gripping frescoes of armored riders, reflecting the revolutionary change to cavalry warfare from Rome to China. The Sogdians were known as merchants as far away as China.

Through the Sogdians, products from western Asia and North Africa found their way to the eastern end of the landmass. Carefully packed for the long trek on jostling camel caravans, Persian and Roman goods rode side by side. Along with Sasanian silver coins and gold pieces minted in Constantinople, these exotic products found eager buyers as far east as China and Japan.

BUDDHISM ON THE SILK ROADS

South of the Hindu Kush Mountains, in northern India, nomadic groups made the roads into central Asia safe to travel, enabling Buddhism to spread northward and eastward via the mountainous corridor of Afghanistan into China. Buddhist monks were the primary missionary agents, the bearers of a universal message who traveled across the roads of central Asia, carrying holy books, offering salvation to commoners, and establishing themselves more securely in host communities than did armies, diplomats, or merchants.

At Bamiyan, a valley of the Hindu Kush—two gigantic statues of the Buddha, 121 and 180 feet in height, were carved from a cliffside during the fourth and fifth centuries CE (and stood there for 1,500 years until dynamited by the Taliban in 2001). Travelers found

Between 522 and 530 CE, a Jewish king of Himyar popularly known as Dhu Nuwas (the Man with the Forelock) drove the Ethiopian Christian garrisons out of southern Arabia. He turned churches into synagogues (just as, in the Christian empire far to the north, many synagogues had been turned into churches). In 523 CE, the Christians of the oasis city of Najran were ordered to become Jewish. Those who refused to do so Dhu Nuwas burned on pyres of brushwood piled into a deep trench.

Swept by these rivalries, the Arabian Peninsula was no longer a world apart, shut off from "civilization" by its cruel deserts and by its inhabitants' nomadic lifestyle. Far from it—Arabia had become a giant soundboard that amplified claims about the pros and cons of Judaism and Christianity, argued over with unusual intensity for an entire century. The "nonaligned" Arabs of the intermediate regions (between southern Arabia and Mesopotamia) still worshipped their ancestral tribal gods. But they had heard much, of late, about Jews and Christians, Romans and Persians. Arab tribes around Yathrib (modern Medina) adopted Judaism and remained in touch with the rabbis of Galilee along the caravan routes of northern Arabia. Here was a new kind of borderland between empires and between religions. In fact, it would be from this borderland that a new religion and a new prophet would emerge. His name was Muhammad.

QUESTIONS FOR ANALYSIS

- How did the geographical features of the Arabian Peninsula shape its religious development?
- What about borderlands makes them useful locations of analysis for world historians?

Explore Further

Fowden, Garth, *Empire to Commonwealth: The Consequences of Monotheism in Late Antiquity* (1993).

Yarshater, Ehsan, *Encyclopedia Iranica* (1982).

Bamiyan and Yungang Buddhas Compare the Buddhas at Bamiyan and Yungang. Note the Gandharan dress and standing pose of the Bamiyan Buddha, whose majesty and ornamentation the pilgrim Xuanzang described in the mid-seventh century CE. The Buddha in Yungang, one of five created under the emperors of the Northern Wei, sits at the foothills of the Great Wall, marking the eastern destination of the central Asian Silk Roads.

welcoming cave monasteries here and at oases all along the way from the Taklamakan Desert to northern China where—2,500 miles from Bamiyan—travelers also encountered five huge Buddhas carved from cliffs in Yungang, China. While those at Bamiyan stood tall with royal majesty, the Buddhas of Yungang sat in postures of meditation.

In the cliff face and clustered around the feet of the Bamiyan Buddhas various elaborately carved cave chapels housed intricate paintings with Buddhist imagery. Surrounding the Yungang Buddhas, over fifty caves sheltered more than 50,000 statues representing Buddhist deities and patrons. The Yungang Buddhas, seated just inside the Great Wall, welcomed travelers to the market in China and marked the eastern end of the central Asian Silk Road (see Map 8.5). The Bamiyan and Yungang Buddhas are a reminder that by the fourth century CE religious ideas were creating world empires of the mind, transcending kingdoms of this world and bringing a universal message contained in their holy scriptures.

Political and Religious Change in South Asia

COMPARISON

ANALYZE the relationship between empires and universalizing religions in South Asia and China.

South Asia, especially the area of modern India, enjoyed a surge of religious enthusiasm during the Gupta dynasty, the largest political entity in South Asia from the early fourth to the mid-sixth century CE. Its kings facilitated commercial and cultural exchange, much as the Roman Empire had done in the west. Chandragupta (r. c. 320–335 CE, not to be confused with Chandragupta Maurya from Chapter 6), calling himself "King of Kings, Great King," and his son expanded Gupta territory to the entire northern Indian plain and made a long expedition to southern India. The development of Hinduism out of the *varna*-bound Vedic Brahmanic religion and the continued spread of Buddhism helped unify a diverse region and the diverse peoples who lived there.

THE HINDU TRANSFORMATION

During this period, the ancient Brahmanic Vedic religion spread widely in South Asia. Because Buddhism and Jainism had many devotees in cities and commercial communities (see Chapter 5), conservative Brahmans turned their attention to rural India and brought their religion into accord with rural life and agrarian values. This refashioned Brahmanic religion emerged as the dominant faith in Indian society in the form of what we today call **Hinduism**.

In the religion's new, more accessible form, believers became vegetarians, abandoning the animal sacrifices that had been important to their earlier rituals. Their new rituals were linked to self-sacrifice—denying themselves meat rather than offering up slaughtered animals to the gods, as they had done previously. Three major deities—Brahma, Vishnu, and Shiva—formed a trinity representing the three phases of the universe—birth, existence, and destruction, respectively—and the three expressions of the eternal self, or *atma*. Vishnu was the most popular of the three and was thought by believers to reveal himself through various avatars (or incarnations).

Poets during the reign of Chandragupta, a generous patron of the arts, expressed the religious sentiments of the age. Working with the motifs and episodes from two early epics, *Mahabharata* and *Ramayana* (see Chapter 4), these poets addressed new problems and praised new virtues. What had once been lyric dramas and narrative poems written to provide entertainment now served as collective memories of the past and underscored Brahmanic religious beliefs about ideal behavior. The heroes and deeds that the poets praised in classical Sanskrit served as models for kings and their subjects.

A central part of the *Mahabharata* revolves around the final battle between two warring confederations of Vedic tribes. The hero Arjuna, the best warrior of one of these confederations, is unwilling to fight against his enemies because many of them are his cousins. At a crucial moment on the battlefield, Krishna—an avatar of Vishnu, who was Arjuna's charioteer and religious teacher—intervenes, commanding Arjuna to slay his

MAP 8.5 | Buddhist Landscapes, 300–600 CE

Buddhism spread from its heartland in northern India to central and East Asia at this time.

- Using your finger, trace the red lines of trade routes and then the red arrows showing the spread of Buddhism.
- According to the map, what role did increasingly extensive trade routes play in pushing this movement?
- What was the relationship among Buddhist centers and rock-carved temples, trade routes, and the spread of this universal faith?
- How did the travels of Xuanzang symbolize growing connections between East and South Asia?

foes, even those related to him. Krishna reminds Arjuna that he belongs to the Kshatriya *varna*, the warriors put on earth to govern and to fight against the community's enemies. The *Bhagavad Gita*, which preserves this tale of Krishna and Arjuna, became part of the authoritative literature of Hindu spirituality. It prescribed religious and ethical teachings and behaviors, called *dharma* in Hinduism, for people at every level of society.

Hindu Statue This huge statue of a three-headed god in a cave on a small island near Mumbai (Bombay) represents the theology of Hinduism. Brahma, the creator; Vishnu, the keeper; and Shiva, the destroyer are all from one *atma,* or the single soul of the universe.

Hindus also adopted the deities of other religions, even regarding the Buddha as an avatar of Vishnu. Thus the Hindu world of gods became larger and more accessible than the earlier Vedic one, enabling more believers to share a single faith. Hindus did not wish to approach the gods only through the sacrificial rituals at which Brahmans alone could officiate. Individuals, therefore, also developed an active relationship with particular gods through personal devotion, in a practice called *bhakti*. This individualized, personal *bhakti* devotion attracted Hindus of all social strata, while the mythological literature wove the deities into a heavenly order presided over by the trinity of Brahma, Vishnu, and Shiva as universal gods. During this period Hinduism lived side by side with Buddhism, competing for followers by building ornate temples and sculptures of gods and by holding elaborate rituals and festivals.

While the stories of human-divine interaction, the larger number of gods, and the development of *bhakti* devotion made Hinduism more personal than the old Vedic Brahmanism had been, Hinduism was still very much rooted in the hierarchical *varna* system. While Hinduism was more accessible to a wider audience than Brahmanism had been, there were limits to how universalizing this tradition could be since the *varna* system, with which it was closely intertwined, did not extend outside South Asia.

THE TRANSFORMATION OF THE BUDDHA

During the Gupta period, the two main schools of Buddhism—the Mahayana (Greater Vehicle) school and the Hinayana (Lesser Vehicle) school—acquired universalizing features that were different from what the Buddha had preached centuries earlier. The historical Buddha was a sage who was believed to enter *nirvana,* ending the pain of consciousness. In the earliest Buddhist doctrine, god and supernatural powers were not a factor (see Chapter 5). But by 200 CE a crucial transformation had occurred: his followers started to view the Buddha as a god. Mahayana Buddhism not only recognized Buddha as a god, but extended worship to the many bodhisattvas who bridged the gulf between the Buddha's perfection and the world's sadly imperfect peoples (see Chapter 6). It was especially in the Mahayana school that Buddhism became a universal religion, whose adherents worshipped divinities, namely the Buddha and the bodhisattvas, rather than recognizing them merely as great men.

Some Buddhists fully accepted the Buddha as god but could not accept the divinity of bodhisattvas; these adherents belonged to the more monkish school of old-fashioned **Hinayana Buddhism**, later called Theraveda in Ceylon and Southeast Asia. Rejecting Sanskrit authoritative scripture on the supernatural power of bodhisattvas, they remained loyal to the early Buddhist texts, which were probably based on the words of the Buddha himself. Hinayana temples barred all colorful idols of the bodhisattvas and other heavenly beings; they only contained images of the Buddha. Buddhism, with its vibrant competing Mahayana and Hinayana schools, spread along the Silk Roads far beyond its South Asian point of origin.

CULTURE AND IDEOLOGY INSTEAD OF AN EMPIRE

Unlike China and Rome, India did not have a centralized empire that could establish a code of laws and an overarching administration. Instead, what emerged to unify South Asia was a distinctive form of cultural synthesis—called by scholars the **Sanskrit cosmopolis**—based on Hindu spiritual beliefs and articulated in the Sanskrit language.

Spearheading this development from 300 to 1300 CE were priests and intellectuals well versed in the Sanskrit language and literary and religious texts. As Sanskrit spread, it stepped beyond religious scriptures and became the public language of politics, although local languages retained their prominence in day-to-day administration and everyday life. Kings and emperors used Sanskrit to express the ideals of royal power and responsibility. Rulers issued inscriptions in it, recording their genealogies and their prestigious acts. Poets celebrated ruling dynasties and recorded important moments in the language.

The emergence of Sanskrit as the common language of the elites in South and Southeast Asian societies also facilitated the spread of Brahmanism. Possessing an unparalleled knowledge of the language, Brahmans circulated their ideals on morality and society in Sanskritic texts, the most influential of which was the **Code of Manu**. This document records a discourse given by the sage, Manu, to a gathering of wise men seeking answers on how to organize their communities after the destruction wrought by a series of floods. The text lays out a set of laws designed to address the problems of assimilating strangers into expanding towns and refining the hierarchical Brahmanic order as the agricultural frontier expanded. Above all, the laws of Manu offered guidance for living within the *varna* and *jati* system, including whom to marry, which profession to follow, and even what to eat. The laws of Manu provided mechanisms for absorbing new groups into the system of *varnas* and *jatis*, thus propelling Hinduism into every aspect of life, far beyond the boundaries of imperial control.

During this period, settlers from northern India pushed southward into lands formerly outside the domain of the Brahmans. In these territories Brahmans encountered Buddhists and competed with them to win followers. The mixing of these two groups and the intertwining of their ideas and institutions ultimately created a common "Indic" culture organized around a shared vocabulary addressing concepts such as the nature of the universe and the cyclical pattern of life and death. Much of this mixing of ideas took place in schools, universities, and monasteries. The Buddhists already possessed large monasteries, such as Nalanda in northeast India, where 10,000 residential faculty and students assembled, and more than 100 smaller establishments in southeast India housing at least 10,000 monks. In these settings Buddhist teachers debated theology, cosmology, mathematics, logic, and botany. Brahmans also established schools where similar intellectual topics were discussed and where Buddhist and Brahmanic Hindu ideas were fused.

The resulting Indic cultural unity covered around 1 million square miles (an area as great as the extent of the Roman Empire) and a highly diverse population. Although India did not have a single governing entity like China and did not adhere to one religious system as in the Christian Roman Empire, it was developing a distinctive culture based on the intertwining of two shared, accessible, and—to varying degrees—universalizing religious traditions.

Political and Religious Change in East Asia

With the fall of the Han dynasty, China experienced a period of political disunity and a surge of new religious and cultural influences. In the first century CE, Han China was the largest state in the world, with as great a population as the Roman Empire had at its height. Its emperor extracted an annual income of millions of pounds of rice and bolts of cloth and conscripted millions of workers whose families paid tribute through their labor. Later Chinese regarded the end of the Han Empire as a disaster just as great as western Europeans regarded the end of the Roman Empire. In post-Han China, new influences arrived via the Silk Roads through contact with nomadic "barbarians" and the proselytizing of Buddhist monks and new forms of Daoism responded to a changing society.

THE WEI DYNASTY IN NORTHERN CHINA

After the fall of the Han in 220 CE, several small kingdoms—at times as many as sixteen of them—competed for control. Civil wars raged for roughly three centuries, a time called the Six Dynasties period, when no single state was able to conquer more than half of China's territory. The most successful regime was that of the Tuoba, a people originally from Inner Mongolia. In 386 CE the Tuoba founded the Northern Wei dynasty, which lasted 150 years and administered part of the Han territory. Although technically Mongolian "barbarians," the Northern Wei had lived for generations within the Chinese orbit as tributary states.

The Northern Wei maintained many Chinese traditions of statecraft and court life: they taxed land and labor on the basis of a census, conferred official ranks and titles, practiced court rituals, preserved historical archives, and promoted classical learning and the use of classical Chinese for record keeping and political discourse. Though they were nomadic warriors, they adapted their large standing armies to city-based military technology, which required drafting huge numbers of workers to construct dikes, fortifications, canals, and walls.

Among the challenges facing the Northern Wei rulers was the need to consolidate authority over their own highly competitive nomadic people. One strategy was to make their own government more "Chinese." Under Emperor Xiaowen (r. 471–499 CE), for example, the Tuoba royal family adopted the Chinese family name of Yuan and required all court officials to speak Chinese and wear Chinese clothing. However, the Tuoba warrior families resisted these policies. Xiaowen also rebuilt the old Han imperial capital of Luoyang based on classical architectural models dating from the Han dynasty (see Chapter 7) and made it the seat of his government.

Wei rulers sought stronger relationships with the Han Chinese families of Luoyang that had not fled south. The Wei offered them political power as officials in the Wei bureaucracy and more land. For example, the Dowager Empress Fang (regent for Xiaowen from 476–490 CE) attempted progressive land reforms that offered land to all young men—whether Han or Wei—who agreed to cultivate it. But even this plan failed to bridge the cultural divides between the "civilized" Han Chinese of Luoyang and the "barbarian" Tuoba Wei, because the latter showed no interest in farming.

Members of the Wei court supported Buddhist temples and monumental cave sites in an appeal to their Tuoba roots while also honoring Confucian traditions dating to the ancient Zhou period. Emperor Xiaowen's death cut short his efforts to unify the north. Several decades of intense fighting among military rulers followed, leading ultimately to the downfall of the Northern Wei dynasty.

CHANGING DAOIST TRADITIONS

Daoism, a popular Chinese religion under the Han and a challenge to the Confucian state and its scholar-officials (see Chapters 5 and 7), lost its political edge and adapted to the new realities in this period of disunity. Two new traditions of Daoist thought flourished in this era of self-doubt. The first was organized and community oriented, and involved heavenly masters who as mortals guided local religious groups or parishes. Followers sought salvation through virtue, confession, and ceremonies, including a mystical initiation rite. A second Daoist tradition was more individualistic, attempting to reconcile Confucian classical learning with Daoist religious beliefs in the occult and magic. It used trance and meditation to control human physiology. Through such mental and physical efforts, a skilled practitioner could accumulate enough religious merit to prolong his life. The concept of religious merit and demerit in Daoist circles echoed the Buddhist notion of karmic retribution (the cosmic assessment of one's acts in this life that determines one's rebirth into a better or worse next life; see Chapter 5). For the Daoists, however, eternal life was the ultimate goal, and not the Buddhists' ideal of release from the cycle of life, death, and rebirth.

BUDDHISM IN CHINA

Buddhism's universalizing message appealed to many people living in the fragmented Chinese empire. By the third and fourth centuries CE, travelers from central Asia who had converted to Buddhism had become frequent visitors in the streets and temples of the competing capitals: Chang'an, Luoyang, and Nanjing. Spreading the faith required intermediaries, endowed with texts and explanations, to convey its message. Kumarajiva (344–413 CE), a renowned Buddhist scholar and missionary, was the right man, in the right place, at the right time to spread Buddhism in China—where it already coexisted with other faiths.

Kumarajiva's influence on Chinese Buddhist thought was critical. Not only did he translate previously unknown Buddhist texts into Chinese, but he also clarified Buddhist terms and philosophical concepts. He and his disciples established a Mahayana branch known as **Madhyamika (Middle Way) Buddhism**, which used irony and paradox to show that reason was limited. For example, they contended that all reality was transient because nothing remained unchanged over time. They sought enlightenment by means of transcendental visions and spurned experiences in the material world of sights and sounds.

Kumarajiva represented the beginning of a profound cultural shift. After 300 CE Buddhism began to expand in northwestern China, taking advantage of imperial disintegration and the decline of Daoism and state-sponsored Confucian classical learning. The Buddhists stressed devotional acts, such as daily prayers and mantras, which included seated meditations in solitude requiring mind and breath control, as well as the saving power of the Buddha and the saintly bodhisattvas who postponed their own salvation for the sake of others. They even encouraged the Chinese to join a new class—the clergy. The idea that persons could be defined by faith rather than kinship was not new in Chinese society (see Chapter 7), but it had special appeal in a time of serious crisis like that of the turbulent Six Dynasties period. In the south, the immigrants from the north found that membership in the Buddhist clergy and monastic orders offered a way to restore their lost prestige.

Even more important, in the northern states—now part Chinese, part "barbarian"—Buddhism provided legitimacy. With Buddhists holding prominent positions in government, medicine, and astronomy, the Wei ruling houses could espouse a philosophy that was just as legitimate as that of the Han Chinese. As a Tuoba who ruled at the height of the Northern Wei in the early sixth century, Emperor Xuanwu was an avid Buddhist who made Mahayana Buddhism the state religion during his reign.

In 643 CE, the Chinese Buddhist Xuanzang brought back to Chang'an (then the world's largest city) an entire library of Buddhist scriptures—527 boxes of writings and 192 birch-bark tablets—that he had collected on a pilgrimage to Buddhist holy sites in South Asia. He lodged them in the Great Wild Goose Pagoda and immediately began to translate every line into Chinese. Although the importation of these texts from India was prfoundly important, Buddhism did not seek to be the same in all places and at all times. On the contrary, as the expression of a cosmic truth as timeless and varied as the world itself,

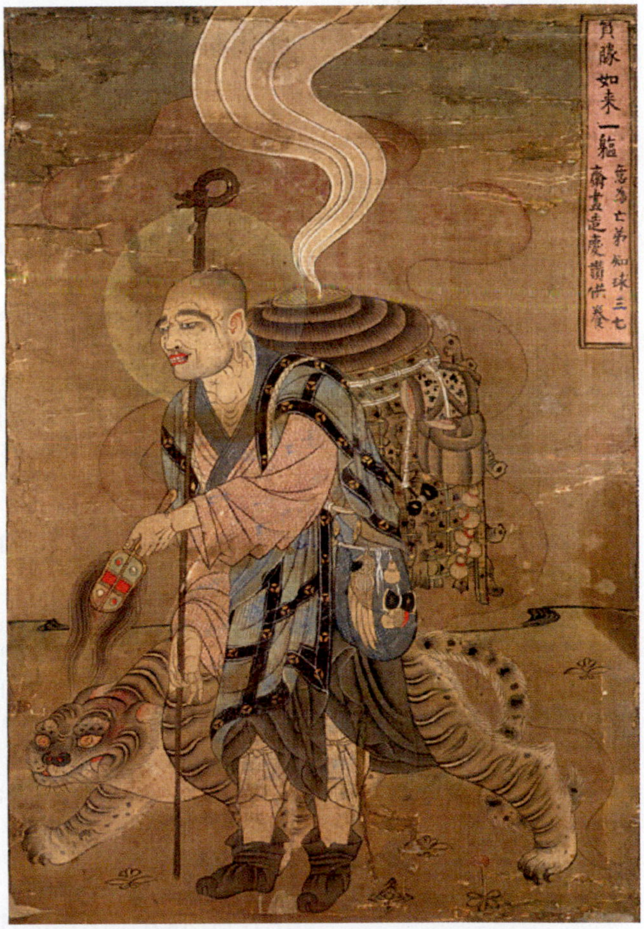

Xuanzang This painting, c. 900 CE, which survives in the caves of Dunhuang along the Silk Roads, portrays the Chinese pilgrim Xuanzang accompanied by a tiger on his epic travels in South Asia to collect important Buddhist scriptures.

Amitabha This exquisite tapestry is an illustration for the *Amitabha Sutra,* the "Sutra of the Western Pure Land." Since the text was translated into Chinese by Kumarajiva in the fourth century CE, Amitabha has been one of the most popular bodhisattvas in China. A devotee who invokes the name of Amitabha ten times before death would be saved to this Western Pure Land, where the Seven Treasures decorated the quiet landscape.

Buddhism showed a high level of adaptability, easily absorbing the gods and the wisdom of every country it touched.

By 400 CE China had more than 1,700 Buddhist monasteries and about 80,000 monks and nuns. By contrast, in 600 CE (after two centuries of monastic growth), Gaul and Italy—the two richest regions of western Europe—had, altogether, only 320 monasteries, many with fewer than 30 monks. Yet, in the two ends of Afro-Eurasia the principal bearers of the new religions were monks. Set apart from "worldly" affairs in their refuges, they enjoyed the pious support of royal courts and warriors whose lifestyles differed sharply from their own. Through their devoted faith in the divine and the support of secular rulers, these two universalizing religions—Buddhism and Christianity—would continue to grow, flourish, and revitalize themselves.

Faith and Cultures in the Worlds Apart

COMPARISON

ASSESS the connections between political unity and religious developments in sub-Saharan Africa and Mesoamerica in the fourth to sixth centuries CE.

In most areas of sub-Saharan Africa and Mesoamerica, it was not easy for ideas, institutions, peoples, and commodities to circulate broadly. Thus we do not see the development of universalizing faiths. Rather, belief systems and their associated deities remained local. Nonetheless, sub-Saharan Africans and peoples living in Mesoamerica revered prophetic figures who, they believed, communicated with deities and brought to humankind divinely prescribed rules of behavior. Peoples in both regions honored beliefs and rules that were passed down orally across generations. These unifying spiritual traditions guided behavior and established social customs.

BANTUS OF SUB-SAHARAN AFRICA

Today, most of Africa south of the equator is home to peoples who speak some variant of more than 400 Bantu languages. Although scholars using oral traditions and linguistic

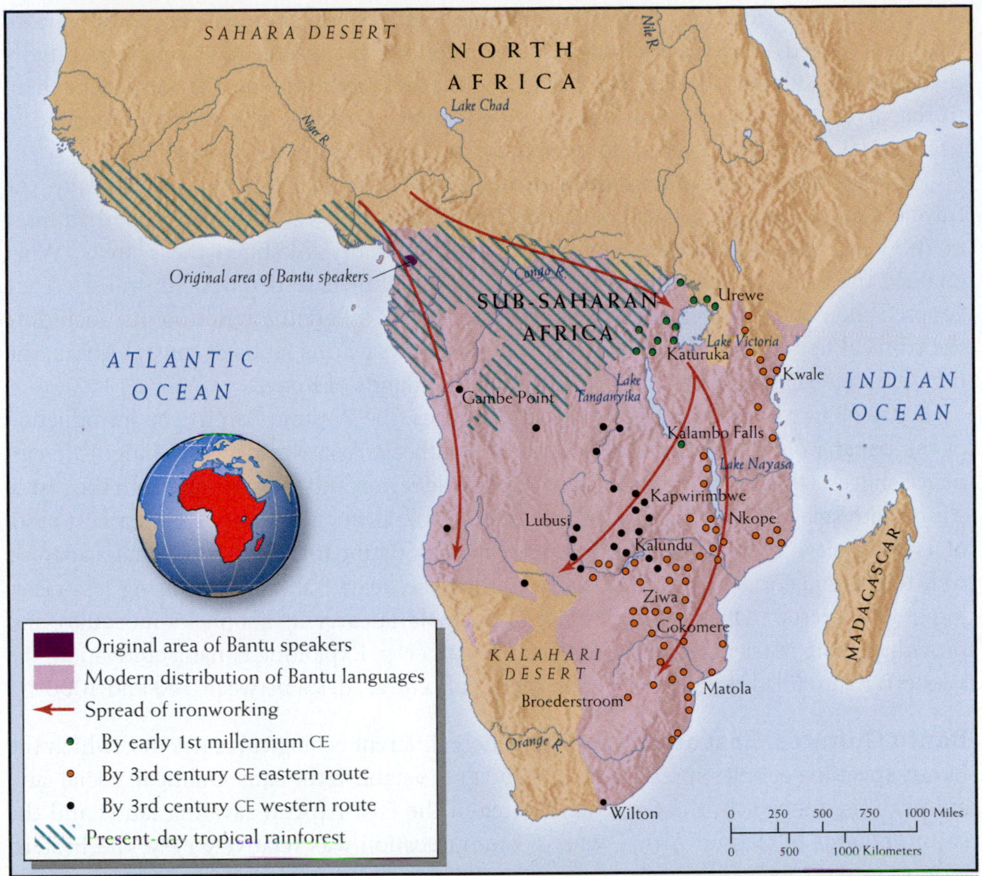

MAP 8.6 | Bantu Migrations

The migration of Bantu speakers throughout much of sub-Saharan Africa in the first millennium CE dramatically altered the cultural landscape.

- According to the map, where did the Bantu speakers originate? Into which areas did the Bantu speakers migrate?
- What skills did they have that enabled them to dominate the peoples already living there?
- According to your reading, did the Bantu migrations create a common culture below the Sahara Desert during this time?

evidence can trace a clear narrative of the Bantu people no further back than 1000 CE, it appears that the first Bantu speakers lived in the southeastern part of modern Nigeria, where about 4,000 or 5,000 years ago they likely shifted from hunting, gathering, and fishing to practicing settled agriculture. Preparing just one acre of tropical rain forest for farming required removing 600 tons of moist vegetation. To accomplish this arduous task, Bantus used mainly machetes, billhooks, and controlled burning. Bantus cultivated woodland plants such as yams and mushrooms, as well as palm oils and kernels. Yet the difficulties in preparing the land for settled agriculture did not keep the Bantus from being the most expansionist of African peoples (see Map 8.6).

Bantu Migrations Following riverbeds and elephant trails, Bantu migrants traveled out of West Africa in two great waves. One wave moved across the Congo forest region to East Africa. Their knowledge of iron smelting enabled them to deploy iron tools for agriculture. Because their new habitats supported a mixed economy of animal husbandry and sedentary agriculture, this group became relatively prosperous. A second wave of migrants moved southward through the rain forests in present-day Congo, eventually reaching the Kalahari Desert. The tsetse fly–infested environment did not permit them to rear livestock, so they were limited to subsistence farming. These Bantus learned to use iron later than those who had moved to the Congo region in the east.

Precisely when these **Bantu migrations** began is unclear, but once under way, the travelers moved rapidly. Genetic and linguistic evidence reveals that they absorbed most of the hunting-and-gathering populations who originally inhabited these areas. What enabled the Bantus to prevail and prosper was their skill as settled agriculturalists. They adapted their farming techniques and crops to widely different environments, including the tropical rain forests of the Congo River basin, the savanna lands of central Africa, the high grasslands around Lake Nyanza, and the highlands of Kenya.

For the Bantu of the rain forests of Central Africa (the Western Bantu), the introduction of the banana plant from tropical South and Southeast Asia was decisive. Linguistic evidence suggests that it first arrived in the Upper Nile region and then traveled into the rest of Africa with small groups migrating from one favorable location to another; the earliest proof of its presence is a record from the East African coast dating to 525 CE. The banana adapted well to the equatorial rain forests, withstanding the heavy rainfalls, requiring less clearing of rain forests, reducing the presence of the malaria-carrying anopheles mosquito, and providing more nutrients than the indigenous yam crop. Exploiting banana cultivation, the Western Bantu filled the equatorial rain forests of central Africa between 500 and 1000 CE.

Bantu Cultures, East and West The widely different ecological zones into which the Bantu-speaking peoples spread made it difficult to establish the same political, social, and cultural institutions. In the Great Lakes area of the East African savanna lands and the savanna lands of Central Africa, where communication was relatively easy, the Eastern Bantu speakers developed centralized polities whose kings ruled by divine right. They moved into heavily forested areas similar to those they had left in southeastern Nigeria. These locations supported a way of life that remained fundamentally unaltered until European colonialism in the twentieth century.

The Western Bantu-speaking communities of the lower Congo River rain forests formed small-scale societies based on family and clan connections. They organized themselves socially and politically into age groups, the most important of which were the ruling elders. Within these age-based networks, individuals who demonstrated talent in warfare, commerce, and politics provided leadership. Certain rights and duties were imposed on different social groups based mainly on their age. Males moved from child to warrior to ruling elder and females transitioned from child to married child-bearer. Bonds among age groups were powerful, and movement from one to the next was marked by meaningful and well-remembered rituals. So-called big men, supported by followers attracted by their valor and wisdom as opposed to inheritance, promoted territorial expansion. Individuals who could attract a large community of followers, marry many women, and sire many children could lead their bands into new locations and establish dominant communities.

These rain-forest communities held a common belief that the natural world was inhabited by spirits, many of whom were their own heroic ancestors. These spiritual beings intervened in mortals' lives and required constant appeasement. Diviners helped men and women understand the spirits' ways, and charms warded off the misfortune that aggrieved spirits might wish to inflict. Diviners and charms also protected against the injuries that living beings—witches and sorcerers—could inflict. In fact, much of the misfortune that occurred in the Bantu world was attributed to these malevolent forces. The Bantu migrations ultimately filled up more than half the African landmass. They spread a political and social order based on family and clan structures that rewarded

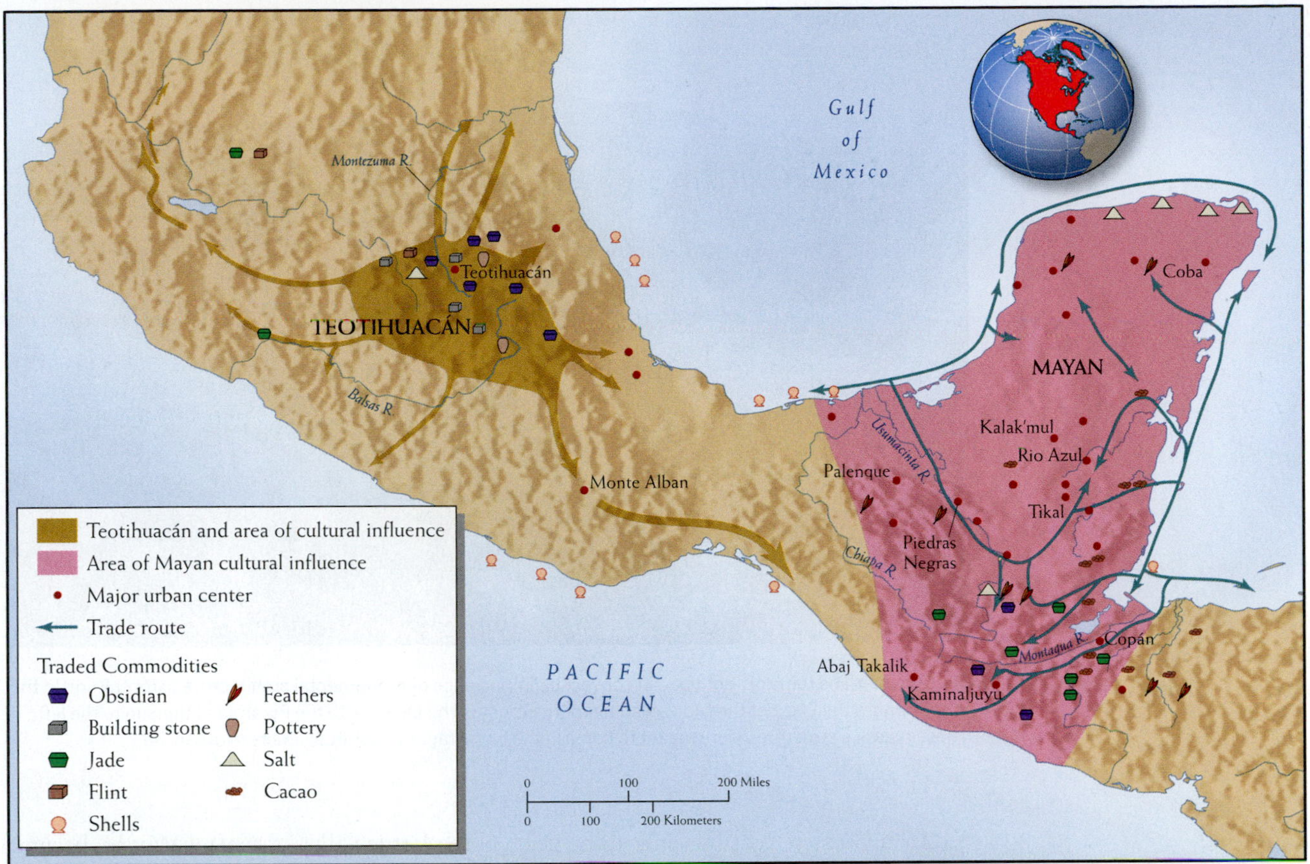

MAP 8.7 | Mesoamerican Worlds, 200–700 CE

At this time, two groups dominated Mesoamerica: one was located at the city of Teotihuacán in the center, and the other—the Mayans—was in the south.

- What commodities did these cultures trade? Look at the symbols for Traded Commodities in the map key, and find them all on the map.
- Judging by what you see, how did each group create a common culture in surrounding regions?
- To what extent do you believe the people of the Teotihuacán and Mayan worlds influenced each other?

individual achievement—and maintained an intense relationship to the world of nature that they believed was imbued with supernatural forces.

MESOAMERICANS

As in sub-Saharan Africa, the process of settlement and expansion in Mesoamerica differed from that in the large empires of Afro-Eurasia. Mesoamerica had no integrating artery of a giant river and its floodplain, and so it lacked the extensive resources that a state could harness for monumental ambitions. Nonetheless, some remarkable polities developed in the region, ranging from the city-state of Teotihuacán to the more widespread influence of the Mayans (see Map 8.7).

COMPARISON

COMPARE the unifying political and cultural developments in sub-Saharan Africa and Mesoamerica with those that took place across Eurasia in this period.

Teotihuacán Around 300 BCE, people in the central plateau and the southeastern districts of Mesoamerica where the dispersed villages of Olmec culture had risen and fallen (see Chapter 5) began to gather in larger settlements. Soon, political and social integration

Teotihuacán The ruins of Teotihuacán convey the importance of monumental architecture to its culture. In the foreground is the Plaza of the Moon leading to the Street of the Dead, with the Pyramid of the Sun to the left. These massive structures were meant to confirm the importance of spiritual affairs in urban life.

led to city-states. Teotihuacán, in the heart of the fertile valley of central Mexico, became the largest center of the Americas before the Aztecs almost 500 years later.

Fertile land and ample water from the valley's marshes and lakes fostered high agricultural productivity despite the inhabitants' technologically rustic methods of cultivation. The local food supply sustained a metropolis of between 100,000 and 200,000 residents, living in more than 2,000 apartment compounds lining the city's streets. At one corner rose the massive pyramids of the sun and the moon—the focus of spiritual life for the city dwellers. Marking the city's center was the huge royal compound; the grandeur and refinement of its stepped stone pyramid, the Temple of the Feathered Serpent, were famous throughout Mesoamerica.

The feathered serpent was the anchor for their spiritual lives. It was a symbol of fertility that governed reproduction and life. The feathered serpent's temple was the core of a much larger structure. From it radiated the awesome promenade known as the Street of the Dead, which culminated in the hulking Pyramid of the Moon, where foreign warriors and dignitaries were mutilated, sacrificed, and often buried alive to consecrate the holy structure.

Teotihuacán was a powerful city-state that flexed its military muscle to overtake its rivals. By 300 CE, Teotihuacán controlled the entire basin of the Valley of Mexico. It dominated its neighbors and demanded gifts, tribute, and humans for ritual sacrifice. Its massive public architecture displayed art that commemorated decisive battles, defeated neighbors, and captured fighters. While the city's political influence beyond the basin was limited, its cultural and economic diffusion were significant. Making use of porters, Teotihuacán's merchants traded their ceramics, ornaments of marine shells, and all sorts of decorative and valued objects (especially of green obsidian) far and wide. At the same time, Teotihuacán imported pottery, feathers, and other goods from distant lowlands.

This kind of expansion left much of the political and cultural independence of neighbors intact, with only the threat of force keeping them in check. In the fifth century CE, however, invaders burned Teotihuacán and smashed the carved figurines of the central temples and palaces, targeting Teotihuacán's institutional and spiritual core.

The Mayans In the Caribbean region of the Yucatán and its interior, the Mayan people flourished from about 250 CE to their zenith in the eighth century. The Mayans lived in an inhospitable region—hot, infertile, lacking navigable river systems, and vulnerable to hurricanes. Yet the Mayans achieved greatness without founding a single great central metropolis. Instead, they established hundreds, possibly thousands, of agrarian villages scattered across the diverse ecological zones of present-day southern Mexico to western El Salvador. Villages were linked by a shared Mayan language and through tribute payments, chiefly from lesser settlements to sacred towns. At their peak the Mayans may have numbered as many as 10 million.

Mayan Political and Social Structure The Mayans established a variety of kingdoms around major ritual centers—such as Palenque, Copán, and Piedras Negras—and their hinterlands. Such hubs were politically independent but culturally and economically interconnected through commerce. Some larger settlements, such as Tikal and Kalak'mul, became sprawling centers with dependent provinces. Ambitious rulers in these larger states frequently engaged in hostilities with one another.

Mayan culture encompassed about a dozen kingdoms that shared many features. Highly stratified, with an elaborate class structure, each kingdom was topped by a shamanistic king who legitimated his position via his lineage, reaching back to a founding father and, ultimately, the gods. The vast pantheon of gods included patrons of each subregion, as well as a creator god and deities for rain, maize, war, and the sun. Gods were neither especially cruel nor benevolent; but rather focused on the dance that sustained the axis connecting the underworld and the skies. What humans had to worry about was making sure that the gods got the attention and reverence they needed.

This was the job of Mayan rulers. Kings sponsored elaborate public rituals to reinforce their divine heritages, including ornate processions down their cities' main boulevards to honor gods and their descendants, the rulers. Lords and their wives performed ritual

Palenque Deep in the Lacandon jungle of present-day Mexico lies the ruin of the Mayan city of Palenque. Its pyramid, on the left, overlooks the site; on the right, the Tower of the Palace shadows a magnificent courtyard where religious figures and nobles gathered. There is no mistaking how a city like Palenque could command its hinterland with religious authority.

Wood Tablet This detail of a carved-wood tablet from a temple in the city of Tikal (c. 741 CE) is a fine example of the ornate form of scribal activity, which combined images and portraits with glyphs that tell a narrative.

blood sacrifice to feed their ancestors. A powerful priestly elite, scribes, legal experts, military advisers, and skilled artisans were vital to the hierarchy.

Most of the Mayan people remained tied to the land, which could sustain a high population only through dispersed settlements. Poor soil quality and limited water supply prevented large-scale agriculture: major rivers or irrigation systems were lacking. Through terraces, the draining of fields, and slash-and-burn agriculture, Mayans managed a subsistence economy of diversified agrarian production. Villagers cultivated maize, beans, and squash, rotating them to prevent the depletion of soil nutrients. Farmers supplemented these staples with root crops such as sweet potato and cassava. Cotton—the basic fiber used for clothing—frequently grew amid rows of other crops as part of a diversified mix.

Mayan Writing, Mathematics, and Architecture A common set of beliefs, codes, and values connected the dispersed Mayan villages. Sharing a similar language, Mayans developed writing and an important class of scribes who were vital to the society's integration. Rulers rewarded scribes for writing grand epics about dynasties and their founders, major battles, marriages, deaths, and sacrifices. Such writings offered to Mayans shared common histories, beliefs, and gods—always associated with the narratives of ruling families.

The best-known surviving text is the *Popol Vuh*, a "Book of Community." It narrates one community's creation myth, extolling its founders (twin heroes) and the experiences—wars, natural disasters, human ingenuity—that enabled a royal line to rule the Quiché Kingdom. The text begins with the gods' creation of the earth and ends with the rituals the kingdom's tribes must follow to avoid a descent into social and political anarchy, which had occurred several times throughout their history.

The Mayans also had skilled mathematicians, who devised a calendar and studied astronomy. They accurately charted regular celestial movements and marked the passage of time by precise lunar and solar cycles. The Mayans kept sacred calendars, by which they rigorously observed their rituals at the proper times. Each change in the cycle had particular rituals, dances, performances, and offerings to honor the gods with life's sustenance.

Cities reflected a ruler's ability to summon his subjects to contribute to the kingdom's greatness. Plazas, ball courts, terraces, and palaces sprawled out from neighborhoods. Activity revolved around grand royal palaces and massive ball courts, where competing teams treated enthusiastic audiences to contests that were more religious ritual than game. The Mayans also excelled at building monumental structures. In Tikal, for instance, surviving buildings include six massive, steep funerary pyramids featuring elaborately carved and painted masonry walls, vaulted ceilings, and royal burial chambers; the tallest temple soars more than 220 feet high (forty feet higher than Justinian's Hagia Sophia).

Mayan Bloodletting and Warfare Mayan elites were obsessed with spilling blood as a way to honor rulers and ancestors as well as gods. This gory rite led to frequent warfare, especially among rival dynasties, the goal of which was to capture victims for the bloody rituals. Rulers also would shed their own blood at intervals set by the calendar. Royal wives drew blood from their tongues and men had their penises perforated. Such bloodletting by means of elaborately adorned and sanctified instruments was reserved for those of noble descent. Carvings and paintings portray blood cascading from rulers' mutilated bodies.

Internal warfare doomed the Mayans, especially after devastating confrontations between Tikal and Kalak'mul during the fourth through seventh centuries CE. With each outbreak, rulers drafted larger armies and sacrificed greater numbers of captives. Crops perished. People fled. After centuries of misery, it must have seemed as if the gods themselves were abandoning the Mayan people. The cycle of violence destroyed the cultural underpinnings of elite rule that had held the Mayan world together. There was no single catastrophic event, no great defeat by a rival power. The Mayan people simply abandoned their spiritual centers, and cities became ghost towns. As populations declined, jungles overtook temples. Eventually, the hallmark of Mayan unity—the ability to read a shared script—vanished. While vibrant religious traditions thrived in sub-Saharan Africa and in Mesoamerica, they served more to reinforce the political and social situations from which they came rather than to spread a universalizing message far beyond their original context.

Conclusion

The breakdown of two imperial systems—Rome around the Mediterranean, and Han China in East Asia—introduced an era in which religion and shared culture rather than military conquest and political institutions linked large areas of Afro-Eurasia.

COMPARISON

EXPLAIN why universalizing religions developed to varying degrees in Afro-Eurasia but did not develop elsewhere in the world.

The Roman Empire gave way to a new religious unity, first represented by Christian dissenters and then co-opted by the emperor Constantine. In western Europe, the sense of unity unlimited by imperial frontiers gave rise to a universal, or "Catholic," church—the "true" Christian religion that believers felt all peoples should share. In the eastern Mediterranean, where the Roman Empire survived, Christianity and empire coalesced to reinforce one another. Christians here held that beliefs about God and Jesus found their most correct expression within the eastern Roman Empire and in its capital, Constantinople.

Similarly, in East Asia, the weakening of the Han dynasty enabled Buddhism to dominate Chinese culture. Without a unified state in China, Confucian officials lost their influence, while Buddhist priests and monks enjoyed patronage from regional rulers, local warriors, and commoners. In India, Brahman elites exploited population movements beyond the reach of traditional rulers as they established ritual forms for daily life on every level of society, while melding aspects of their own Vedic faith with those of Buddhism to create a new Hindu synthesis.

Not all regions felt the spread of universalizing religions, however. In most of sub-Saharan Africa belief systems were much more localized. Similarly in Mesoamerica, where long-distance transportation was harder and political authority more diffuse, religion was a unifying force but nothing like the widespread universalizing religions of Afro-Eurasia. Nevertheless, spiritual life was no less profound. Here, a strong sense of a shared worldview, a shared sense of purpose, and a shared sense of faith enabled common cultures to develop. Indeed, the Bantus and Mayans became large-scale common cultures—but ruled at the local level.

Thus, the period 300–600 CE saw the emergence of three great cultural units in Afro-Eurasia, each defined in religious terms: Christianity in the Mediterranean and parts of Southwest Asia, Hinduism in South Asia, and Buddhism in East Asia. They illustrate the ways in which peoples were converging under larger religious tents, while also becoming more distinct. Universalizing religions, whether Christian or Buddhist, and codes of behavior, such as the Brahmanic Code of Manu, gave people a new way to define themselves and their loyalties.

After You Read This Chapter

Go to INQUIZITIVE to see what you've learned—and learn what you've missed—with personalized feedback along the way.

TRACING THE GLOBAL STORYLINES

FOCUS ON: *Religions and Regions*

EUROPE AND SOUTHWEST ASIA

- Christianity moves from a minority, persecuted faith to a state religion in the Roman Empire.
- The Sasanian state in Iran provides fertile ground for a tolerant mixture of Zoroastrianism, Nestorian Christianity, Judaism, Buddhism, and Brahmanic religion.

SUB-SAHARAN AFRICA AND MESOAMERICA

- Large parts of Africa and the Americas develop common cultures based on religious beliefs shared by large, widely dispersed groups.

SOUTH ASIA AND EAST ASIA

- Brahmanism, or Hinduism, becomes the dominant religion among the Vedic peoples of South Asia.
- Buddhism spreads out of South Asia along the Silk Roads through central Asia and into East Asia.

CHRONOLOGY

THE MEDITERRANEAN AND SOUTHWEST ASIA

- Sasanian Empire flourishes in Iran and Mesopotamia 3rd–6th century CE
- Emperor Constantine legalizes Christianity in Roman Empire 313 CE
- "Barbarian" invasions of Roman Empire 4th and 5th centuries CE

CENTRAL ASIA

SOUTH ASIA

- Transformation of Brahmanism into Hinduism begins 1st or 2nd century CE

EAST ASIA

- Six Dynasties period 220–589 CE

SUB-SAHARAN AFRICA

- Bantu migrations from western Africa to south, central, and east

MESOAMERICA

- Maya culture dominates Yucatán Peninsula and surrounding area 3rd–9th century CE
- City of Teotihuacán dominates Valley of Mexico 4th–5th century CE

1 CE | 100 CE | 200 CE | 300 CE | 400 CE

THINKING ABOUT GLOBAL CONNECTIONS

- ***Thinking about Crossing Borders and Universalizing Religions*** Why did borders seem to infuse vitality into Christianity and Buddhism from the fourth through the sixth centuries CE? Which religions in this period did not seem to cross borders and why? What effect did this have on those religions?
- ***Thinking about Changing Power Relationships and Universalizing Religions*** Universalizing religions, like Christianity and Buddhism, were successful in part because of their diverse personalized appeal to men and women, rich and poor, and the upper and lower classes. How might this diverse appeal enable a universalizing religion like Christianity to undermine and alter traditional power relationships? In what ways did Buddhism do the same? Hinduism?
- ***Thinking about* Worlds Together, Worlds Apart *and Universalizing Religions*** Why did universalizing religions like Christianity and Buddhism develop in some parts of the world but not in others in the period 300 to 600 CE? How did these universalizing religions allow for continuity in Eurasia, even as empires fell away? In the "worlds apart," how might the lack of universalizing religion have influenced continuity, as political entities rose and fell over time?

STUDY QUESTIONS

1. What are the major characteristics of a **universalizing religion**, for the period from 300 to 600 CE? In what specific ways do Christianity, Buddhism, and other religious developments in this period fit this model? What traditions do *not*?
2. What factors contributed to the "fall" of the Roman Empire in the west? How do Christianity and the rise of **Byzantium** challenge the notion that Rome "fell"?
3. Explain the role of the Sasanians and the Sogdians in fostering connections along the Silk Roads.
4. What forces contributed to the development of **Hinduism** out of Brahmanism?
5. In what ways does the concept of the **Sanskrit cosmopolis** help to explain the nature of cultural unity in South Asia in this period?
6. What are some of the ways in which Buddhism universalized in this period, and what impact did this have on South Asia and East Asia?
7. In what specific ways did the Northern Wei dynasty attempt to fill the void left by the collapse of the Han dynasty?
8. What was the impact of the **Bantu migrations** on sub-Saharan Africa? What helped to unite the Bantu peoples?
9. In what ways did Teotihuacán and later the Mayans bring a degree of unity to parts of Mesoamerica? What factors impeded them?

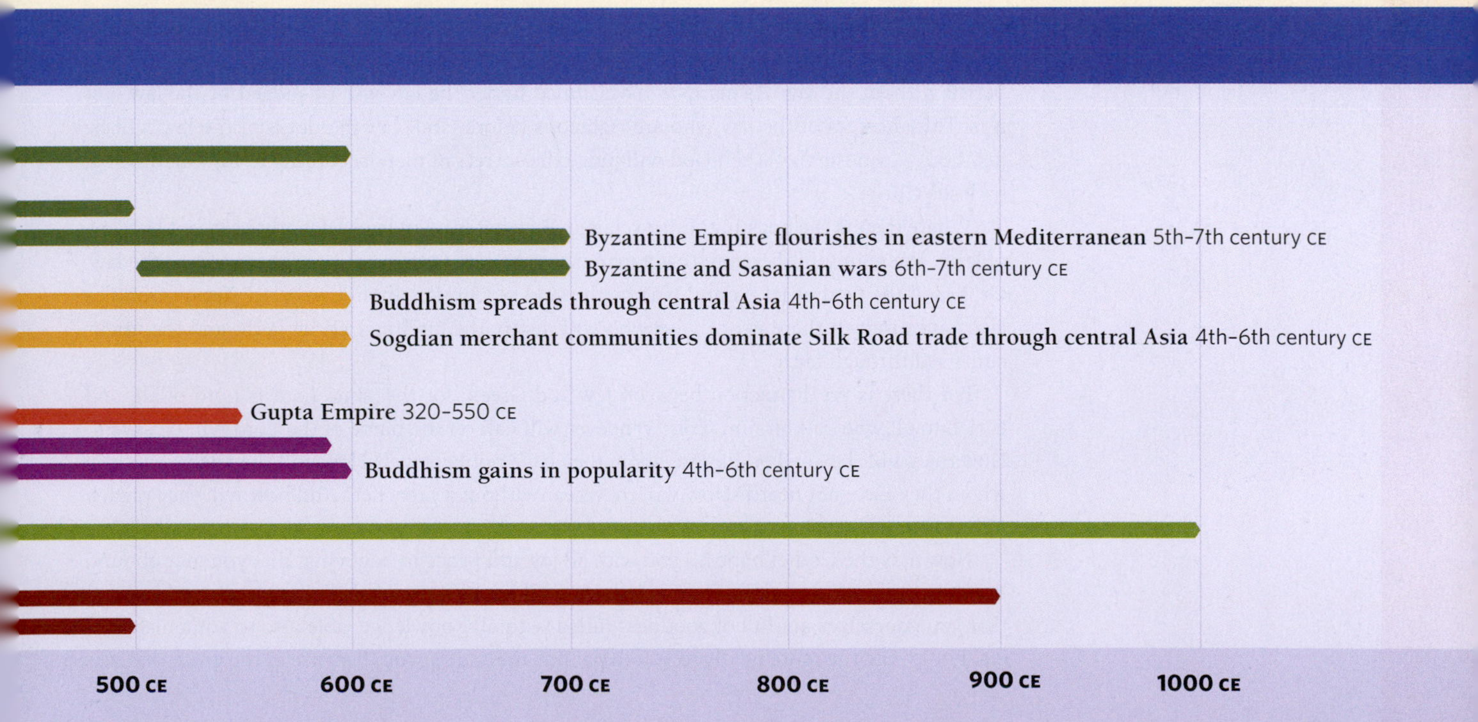

Byzantine Empire flourishes in eastern Mediterranean 5th–7th century CE
Byzantine and Sasanian wars 6th–7th century CE
Buddhism spreads through central Asia 4th–6th century CE
Sogdian merchant communities dominate Silk Road trade through central Asia 4th–6th century CE
Gupta Empire 320–550 CE
Buddhism gains in popularity 4th–6th century CE
500 CE
600 CE
700 CE
800 CE
900 CE
1000 CE

Going to the Source

The Diffusion of Universalizing Religions

The spread of universalizing religions, whether through trade or through pilgrimage, brought people of many societies across Eurasia into contact with each other. Though trading routes across the land mass made it easier for people to get from one place to another, sometimes religion spread from place to place outside of established trading networks. Christians, Buddhists, and Hindus traveled the religious geography of their faith, visiting sacred sites and relics and hearing stories of holy women and men. As they did so, they tried to make sense of what they saw and to make it relevant to those who received their descriptions. The documents here are almost all firsthand accounts that record some aspect of the spread of universalizing religions. Pay attention to the audience for these documents, as well as the types of things that the authors noticed.

PRIMARY SOURCE 8.1

Letter to the Romans *(first century CE), Paul of Tarsus*

Paul of Tarsus was a critical figure for early Christianity during the first century CE. After his conversion from Judaism to Christianity, Paul became the earliest proponent of expanding Christianity throughout the Roman Empire. As a result, he undertook several missionary journeys and is credited with founding several churches in Asia Minor and Europe. In this passage, he addresses the ways in which those living outside of Jewish law can still find access to God through faith.

But glory, honor, and peace go to every man who works good, to the Jew first, and also to the Greek. For there is no partiality with God. For as many as have sinned without law will also perish without the law. As many as have sinned under the law will be judged by the law. For it isn't the hearers of the law who are righteous before God, but the doers of the law will be justified . . . (in the day when God will judge the secrets of men, according to my Good News, by Jesus Christ . . .).

Where then is the boasting? It is excluded. By what kind of law? Of works? No, but by a law of faith. We maintain therefore that a man is justified by faith apart from the works of the law. Or is God the God of Jews only? Isn't he the God of Gentiles [non-Jews] also? Yes, of Gentiles also, since indeed there is one God who will justify the circumcised by faith, and the uncircumcised through faith. . . .

For there is no distinction between Jew and Greek; for the same Lord is Lord of all, and is rich to all who call on him. For, "Whoever will call on the name of the Lord will be saved." How then will they call on him in whom they have not believed? How will they believe in him whom they have not heard? How will they hear without a preacher? And how will they preach unless they are sent? . . .

Now may the God of hope fill you with all joy and peace in believing, that you may abound in hope, in the power of the Holy Spirit. I myself am also persuaded about you, my brothers, that you yourselves are full of goodness, filled with all knowledge, able also to admonish others. But I write the more boldly to you in part, as reminding you, because of the grace that was given to me by God, that I should be a servant of Christ Jesus to the Gentiles, serving as a priest the Good News of God, that the offering up of the Gentiles might be made acceptable, sanctified by the Holy Spirit. I have therefore my boasting in Christ Jesus in things pertaining to God. For I will not dare to speak of any things except those which Christ worked through me, for the obedience of the Gentiles, by word and deed, in the power of signs and wonders, in the power of God's Spirit; so that from Jerusalem, and around as far as to Illyricum, I have fully preached the Good News of Christ; yes, making it my aim to preach the Good News, not where Christ was already named, that I might not build on another's foundation.

1. **Why might Paul's message have appealed to gentiles living in the eastern Mediterranean?**
2. **What political dangers might Paul's ideas have posed to people who accepted his message and then converted to Christianity?**

PRIMARY SOURCE 8.2

Diary of a Pilgrimage (late fourth century CE), Egeria

Around 400 CE, Egeria, a religious woman from what is now Spain, traveled to Christian sites located in the eastern Mediterranean. She recorded her travels in a diary, an excerpt of which appears below. Only the middle sections of the diary have been located. Her notes were directed to her ladies, perhaps a group of nuns, as many scholars now believe that she may have been a nun herself.

On arriving there [Seleucia of Isauria, in what is now southern Turkey], I went to the bishop, a very holy man and a former monk. I also saw there in the same city a very beautiful church. Since it is around fifteen hundred feet from the city to the shrine of Saint Thecla, which lies beyond the city on a rather flat hill, I thought it best to go out there to make the overnight stop which I had to make. At the holy church there is nothing but countless monastic cells for men and women. I met there a very dear friend of mine, and a person to whose way of life everyone in the East bears witness, the holy deaconess Marthana, whom I had met in Jerusalem, where she had come to pray. She governs these monastic cells of *aputactitae*, or virgins. Would I ever be able to describe how great was her joy and how great mine when she saw me? But to return to the subject: There are many cells all over the hill, and in the middle there is a large wall which encloses the church where the shrine is. It is a very beautiful shrine. The wall is set there to guard the church against the Isaurians, who are evil men, who frequently rob and who might try to do something against the monastery which is established there. Having arrived there in the name of God, a prayer was said at the shrine and the complete Acts of Saint Thecla was read. I then gave unceasing thanks to Christ our God, who granted to me, an unworthy woman and in no way deserving, the fulfillment of my desires in all things. And so, after spending two days there seeing the holy monks and the *aputactitae*, both men and women, who live there, and after praying and receiving Communion, I returned to Tarsus and to my journey. [Egeria makes her way to Constantinople] . . . After arriving [in Constantinople], I did not cease giving thanks to Jesus our God, who had deigned to bestow His grace upon me, in the various churches, that of the apostles and the numerous shrines that are here. . . .

1. **Why do you think Egeria was traveling around Asia? What might she have been hoping to find?**
2. **Why do you think some historians believe that this diary was directed to other women, rather than to both men and women.**

PRIMARY SOURCE 8.3

A Record of Buddhistic Kingdoms (early fifth century CE*), Faxian*

Around the same time that Egeria traveled in western Asia, an elderly Chinese Buddhist monk named Faxian made his way from Chang'an in China to South Asia. He was trying to find Buddhist scriptures while visiting sites sacred to Buddhism. In his descriptions of his travels, Faxian offers a view into the varied worship practices within different schools of Buddhism as well as the many different regions—from China to India to Sri Lanka—where Buddhism flourished.

Chapter 31. Two *le* [Chinese unit of measure] north from this was the place where the Gramika girls presented to Buddha the rice gruel made with milk; and two *le* north from this (again) was the place where, seated on a rock under a great tree, and facing the east, he ate (the gruel). The tree and rock are there at the present day. The rock may be six cubits in breadth and length, and rather more than two cubits in height. . . . Half a yojana [Vedic unit of measure, approximately eight miles] from this place to the north-east there was a cavern in the rocks, into which the Bodhisattva entered, and sat cross-legged with his face to the west. (As he did so), he said to himself, "'If I am to attain to perfect wisdom (and become Buddha), let there be a supernatural attestation of it." [The text describes various signs that led him to the tree under which the Buddha attained enlightenment] . . . At the place mentioned above . . . men subsequently reared topes [Buddhist monuments] and set up images, which all exist at the present day. . . . At the place where Buddha attained to perfect Wisdom, there are three monasteries, in all of which there are monks residing. The families of their people around supply the societies of these monks with an abundant sufficiency of what they require, so that there is no lack or stint. The disciplinary rules are strictly observed by them. The laws regulating their demeanor in sitting, rising, and entering when the others are assembled are those which have been practiced by all the saints since Buddha was in the world down to the present day. . . .

Chapter 36. Faxian's original object had been to search for copies of the Vinaya. In the various kingdoms of North India, however, he had found one master transmitting orally (the rules) to another, but no written copies he could transcribe. He had therefore travelled far and come on to Central India. Here in the mahayana monastery, he found a copy of the Vinaya, containing the Mahasanghika rules—those which were observed in the first Great Council, while Buddha was still in the world.

1. **Describe the behavior of the monks that Faxian observes. How does their behavior relate to what you have read about Buddhism in this chapter?**
2. **Compare Faxian's journey with that of Egeria and explain the similarities and differences that you observe.**

PRIMARY SOURCE 8.4

Bhagavata Purana *(recorded c. 500* CE*)*

This passage comes from the *Bhagavata Purana*, a sacred text of Hinduism that exemplifies the *bhakti* devotion to Krishna, a human incarnation of the Hindu god Vishnu. Although this passage describes the travels of Vidura, a major character in the *Mahabharata* whose legendary storyline extends back to 1000 BCE, this text is thought to have been recorded in Sanskrit in the mid-first millennium ce as *bhakti* Hinduism became increasingly popular.

*

SB 3.1.17 By his piety, Vidura achieved the advantages of the pious Kauravas. After leaving Hastināpura, he took shelter of many places of pilgrimages, which are the Lord's lotus feet. With a desire to gain a high order of pious life, he traveled to holy places where thousands of transcendental forms of the Lord are situated. (18) He began to travel alone, thinking only of Krishna, through various holy places like Ayodhyā, Dvārakā and Mathurā [cities in India]. He traveled where the grove, hill, orchard, river and lake are all pure and sinless and where the forms of the Unlimited decorate the temples. Thus he performed the pilgrim's progress. (19) While so traversing the earth, he simply performed duties to please the Supreme Lord Hari. His occupation was pure and independent. He was constantly sanctified by taking his bath in holy places, although he was in the dress of a mendicant and had no hair dressing nor a bed on which to lie. Thus he was always unseen by his various relatives. (20) Thus, when he was in the land of Bhāratavarşa [i.e., India] traveling to all the places of pilgrimage, he visited Prabhāsakşetraśśś. At that time Mahārāja Yudhişţthira was the emperor and held the world under one military strength and one flag. . . . After this he proceeded west, where the river Sarasvatī flows. (22) On the bank of the river Sarasvatī there were eleven places of pilgrimage, namely (1) Trita, (2) Uśanā, (3) Manu, (4) Pŗŗthu, (5) Agni, (6) Asita, (7) Vāyu, (8) Sudāsa, (9) Go, (10) Guha and (11) ´Srāddhadeva. Vidura visited all of them and duly performed rituals. (23) There were also many other temples of various forms of the Supreme Personality of Godhead Vişnu, established by great sages and demigods. These temples were marked with the chief emblems of the Lord, and they reminded one always of the original Personality of Godhead, Krishna. (24) Thereafter he passed through very wealthy provinces like Surat, Sauvīra and Matsya and through western India, known as Kurujāngala. At last he reached the bank of the Yamunā, where he happened to meet Uddhava, the great devotee of Lord Krishna. Vidura asks Uddhava to give him updates on various family members of Lord Krishna. Vidura offers a profession of faith regarding the incarnation of Vishnu and asks Uddhava. . . . (45) O my friend, please, therefore, chant the glories of the Lord, who is meant to be glorified in the places of pilgrimage. He is unborn, and yet He appears by His causeless mercy upon the surrendered rulers of all parts of the universe. Only for their interest did He appear in the family of His unalloyed devotees the Yadus.

1. **Why did Vidari travel and what did he hope to accomplish?**
2. **Explain why the ideas of universalizing religion might be appealing to someone like Vidura?**

PRIMARY SOURCE 8.5

The Nestorian Stele (781 CE)

Nestorian Christians were a Christian sect that originated in the Byzantine Empire and migrated east to Persia during the fifth century CE after a schism with the religious leaders of Constantinople. They believed that the human and divine qualities of Christ could be separated. The Nestorian Stele was erected in 781 CE in northwest China. The inscription on the stele has text in both Chinese and Syriac, and it documents the spread of Christianity into China as early as 635 CE.

*

Thereupon, our Trinity being divided in nature, the illustrious and honorable Messiah, veiling his true dignity, appeared in the world as a man; angelic powers promulgated the glad tidings, a virgin gave birth to the Holy One in Syria; a bright star announced the felicitous event, and Persians observing the splendor came to present tribute. . . .

In the time of the accomplished Emperor Tai-tsung, the illustrious and magnificent founder of the dynasty, among the enlightened and holy men who arrived was the most-virtuous Olopun,* from the country of Syria. Observing the azure clouds, he bore the true sacred books; beholding the direction of the winds, he braved difficulties and dangers. In the year of our Lord 635 he arrived at Chang-an; the Emperor sent his Prime Minister, Duke Fang Hiuen-ling; who, carrying the official staff to the west border, conducted his guest into the interior; the sacred books were translated in the imperial library, the sovereign investigated the subject in his private apartments; when becoming deeply impressed with the rectitude and truth of the religion, he gave special orders for its dissemination.

In the seventh month of the year A.D. 638 the following imperial proclamation was issued: "Right principles have no invariable name, holy men have no invariable station; instruction is established in accordance with the locality, with the object of benefiting the people at large. The greatly virtuous Olopun, of the kingdom of Syria, has brought his sacred books and images from that distant part, and has presented them at our chief capital. Having examined the principles of this religion, we find them to be purely excellent and natural; investigating its originating source, we find it has taken its rise from the establishment of important truths; its ritual is free from perplexing expressions, its principles will survive when the framework is forgot; it is beneficial to all creatures; it is advantageous to mankind. Let it be published throughout the Empire, and let the proper authority build a Syrian church in the capital, which shall be governed by twenty-one priests. When the virtue of the Chau Dynasty declined, the rider on the azure ox ascended to the west; the principles of the great Tang becoming resplendent, the illustrious breezes have come to fan the East. . . ."

In A.D. 744 the priest Kih-ho, in the kingdom of Syria, looking toward the star [of China], was attracted by its transforming influence, and observing the sun [i.e., the emperor], came to pay court to the most honorable. The Emperor commanded the priest Lo-han, the priest Pu-lun, and others, seven in all, together with the greatly virtuous Kih-ho, to perform a service of merit in the Hing-king palace. Thereupon the Emperor composed mottoes for the sides of the church, and the tablets were graced with the royal inscriptions. . . .

[The following inscription appears in Syriac at the foot of the stone]

In the year of the Greeks one thousand and ninety-two, the Lord Jazedbuzid, Priest and Vicar-episcopal of Cumdan the royal city, son of the enlightened Mailas, Priest of Balkh a city of Turkestan, set up this tablet, whereon is inscribed the Dispensation of our Redeemer, and the preaching of the apostolic missionaries to the King of China.

* Syrian priest and missionary

1. **What is the significance of Olopun's reaching the Chinese Court?**
2. **What aspects of Nestorian Christianity might have been more appealing than Orthodox Christianity, at least from the perspective of the Chinese rulers?**

PRIMARY SOURCE 8.6

The Life of Hiuen-Tsiang

After traveling throughout China in search of sacred books, the Chinese Buddhist monk Hiuen-Tsiang (also known as Xuangzang) became famous for his seventeen-year journey to India, which was later recorded in the *Great Tang Records on the Western Regions*. The excerpts below come from a biography of the monk prepared by a student of his, the Shaman Hwui-Li, who describes Hiuen-Tsiang's journey from China to India. In this excerpt, he meets one of the rulers of Central Asia.

After leaving the mountains they arrived at the lake called Tsing. . . . Here he encountered the Khan of the Turks called Yeh-hu, who was then engaged on a hunting expedition. The horses of these barbarous people are very fine; the Khan's person was covered with a robe of green satin, and his hair was loose, only it was bound round with a silken band some ten feet in length, which was twisted round his head and fell down behind. He was surrounded by about 200 officers, who were all clothed in brocade stuff, with their hair braided. On the right and left he was attended by independent troops all clothed in furs and fine spun hair garments; they carried lances and bows and standards, and were mounted on camels and horses. The eye could not estimate their numbers.

When they saw each other, the Khan, full of joy, said: "Stay here for a while; after two or three days I will come back." He then directed one of his chief officers, Ta-mo-chi, to conduct him towards a large tent and to arrange things for his comfort. . . .

The tent of the Khan is a large pavilion adorned with golden flower ornaments which blind the eye with their glitter. All the officers had spread out in front long mats, in two rows, on which they sat; they were clad in shining garments of embroidered silk. The body-guard of the Khan stood behind them. Regarding these circumstances of state, although he was but the ruler of a wandering horde, yet there was a certain dignified arrangement about his surroundings. . . .

The Turks worship Fire: they do not use wooden seats, because wood contains fire, and so even in worship they never seat themselves, but only spread padded mats on the ground and so go through with it. But for the sake of the Master of the Law they brought an iron warming-pan covered with a thick padding, and requested him to be seated thereon. A short time afterwards they introduced the Chinese mission and the legates from Kau-chang with their letters of introduction and presents.

The Khan examined for himself the one and the other and was much pleased thereat; he then ordered the envoys to be seated, and caused wine to be offered to them with the sound of music . . ..

When the feast was over they sent round the grapewine again, and then asked the Master of the Law to expound (declare) the doctrines of religion. Then he, with a view to admonish them, spoke upon the subject of the ten precepts . . . love of preserving life, and the Paramitas,* and works that lead to final deliverance.

Raising his hands, he (the King) humbly prostrated himself to the ground, and joyously accepted the teaching of the Master.

And now having remained there several days, the Khan exhorted him to stop altogether, saying: "Sir; you have no need to go to India. . . ."

The Master replied: "Notwithstanding all this I desire to go and gaze on the sacred traces, and earnestly to search for the law. . . ."

The Master of the Law on his first arrival was treated disdainfully by the king, but after the first night's rest, he discoursed for the king's sake on the destiny (cause and consequence) of men and Devas: he lauded the meritorious qualities of Buddha: he set forth, by way of exhortation, the character of religious merit. . . .

Accordingly, having summoned a large assembly, he received many of them into the priesthood and established them in the convents. It was thus that he transformed their badly disposed (heretical) hearts, and corrected their evil customs. And so it was wherever he went.

* The perfection of certain virtues in Buddhism

1. **What was Hiuen Tsiang trying to accomplish, and why?**
2. **Why would the acceptance of Buddhist teachings by the Khan have been so significant at this time?**

Questions for Analysis

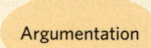

Argumentation

1. Why were travelers so important to these universalizing religions?

Comparison

2. Based on what you've read in the chapter and in these documents, compare the religions of Buddhism with Christianity; analyze similarities and differences in their diffusion.

Interpretation

3. Explain the role of rulers in facilitating the spread of religions from one place to another.

Long Essay Question

Argumentation

Based on these documents and your reading of the chapter, explain whether universalizing religions were more successful at integrating disparate societies or creating conflict among them.

Before You Read This Chapter

GLOBAL STORYLINES

- The universalizing religion of Islam, based on the message of the prophet Muhammad, originates on the Arabian Peninsula and spreads rapidly across Afro-Eurasia.
- The expanding Tang dynasty in East Asia consolidates its bureaucracy, struggles with religious pluralism, and extends its influence into Korea and Japan.
- Christianity splits over religious and political differences, leading to a divide between Roman Catholicism in the west and Greek Orthodoxy in the east.

CORE OBJECTIVES

- **DESCRIBE** and **EXPLAIN** the spread of Islam, Buddhism, and Christianity from 600 to 1000 CE.
- **COMPARE** the organizational structures of the Abbasids, Tang China, and Christendom.
- **COMPARE** the internal divisions within the Islamic, Tang, and Christian worlds.
- **EVALUATE** the relationships between religion, empire, and commercial exchange across Afro-Eurasia during this period.

CHAPTER 9

New Empires and Common Cultures

600–1000 CE

KEY TERMS

caliphate p. 326
civil service examinations p. 335
eunuchs p. 336
five pillars of Islam p. 323
Greek Orthodoxy p. 350
monasticism p. 347
Roman Catholic Church p. 347
sharia p. 327
Shiites p. 331
Sunnis p. 330
Vikings p. 349

In 754 CE al-Mansur, ruler of the new Muslim Abbasid dynasty, decided to relocate his capital city from Damascus (the capital of Islam's first dynasty) closer to the Abbasids' home region on the Iranian plateau. Islam was barely a century old, yet it flourished under this second dynasty. The caliph al-Mansur chose, for both practical and symbolic reasons, to build his capital near an unimposing village called Baghdad. Not only did the site lie between Mesopotamia's two great rivers, at the juncture of the canals that linked them, but it was also close to the ancient capital of the earlier Sasanian Empire and the site of ancient Sumerian and Babylonian power. By building at Baghdad, al-Mansur could reaffirm Mesopotamia's centrality in the world and promote the universalizing ambitions of Islam.

Al-Mansur's choice had enduring effects. Baghdad became a vital crossroads for commerce. Overnight, the city exploded into a bustling world entrepôt. Chinese goods arrived by land and sea; commodities from Inner Eurasia flowed in over the Silk Roads; and cargo-laden camel caravans wound across Baghdad's western desert, linking the capital with Syria, Egypt, North Africa, and southern Spain. The unity that the Abbasids imposed from Baghdad intensified the movement of peoples, ideas, innovations, and commodities.

While Islam was gaining ground in central Afro-Eurasia, Chinese might was surging in East Asia under the Tang dynasty. Yet, Islam and Tang China were clearly different worlds. The Islamic state had a universalizing religious mission: to bring humankind under the authority of the religion espoused by the Prophet Muhammad. In contrast, the Tang state had no such grandiose religious goals; the ruling elite supported religious variety within China, and they did not use Buddhism to expand their control into areas outside China. Instead, the Tang rulers expected that their neighbors would copy Chinese institutions and pay tribute as symbols of respect to the greatness of the Tang Empire. Though not as expansive as Islam and the Tang Empire, Christianity also strived in this period to extend its domain and add to its converts. With Islam's warriors, traders, and scholars crossing into Europe, Chinese influences taking deeper root in East Asia, and Christendom extending itself across Europe, religion and empire once again intertwined to serve as the social foundation across much of Afro-Eurasia.

The Origins and Spread of Islam

COMPARISON

DESCRIBE and **EXPLAIN** the spread of Islam, Buddhism, and Christianity from 600 to 1000 CE.

Islam began inside Arabia. Despite its remoteness and sparse population, by the sixth century CE Arabia was brushing up against exciting outside currents: long-distance trade, religious debate, and imperial politics. The Hijaz—the western region of Arabia bordering the Red Sea—knew the outside world through trading routes reaching up the coast to the Mediterranean. Mecca, located in the Hijaz, was an unimposing village of simple mud huts. Mecca's inhabitants included both merchants and the caretakers of a revered sanctuary called the kaaba, a dwelling place of deities. In this remote region, one of the world's major prophets emerged, and the universalizing faith he founded soon spread from Arabia through the trade routes stretching across Southwest Asia and North Africa.

Mecca At the great mosque at Mecca, which many consider the most sacred site in Islam, hundreds of thousands of worshippers gather for Friday prayers. Many are performing their religious duty to go on a pilgrimage to the holy places in the Arabian Peninsula.

A VISION, A TEXT, A NEW COMMUNITY

Born in Mecca around 570 CE into a well-respected tribal family, Muhammad enjoyed only moderate success as a trader. Then came a revelation that would convert him into a proselytizer of a new faith. In 610 CE, while Muhammad was on a month-long spiritual retreat in the hills near Mecca, he believed that God came to him in a vision and commanded him to recite a series of revelations.

The early revelations were short and powerful, emphasizing a single, all-powerful God (Allah), and instructions for Muhammad's fellow Meccans to carry this message to nonbelievers. Muhammad's early preaching had a clear message. He urged his small band of followers to act righteously, to set aside false deities, to submit themselves to the one and only true God, and to care for the less fortunate—for the Day of Judgment was imminent. Muhammad's most insistent message was the oneness of God, a belief that has remained central to the Islamic faith ever since.

These teachings, compiled into an authoritative version after the Prophet's death, constituted the foundational text of Islam: the Quran. Accepted as the word of God, the Quran's verses were understood to have flowed flawlessly through God's perfect instrument, the Prophet Muhammad. Muhammad believed that he was a prophet in the tradition of Moses, other Hebrew prophets, and Jesus, and that he communicated with the same God that they did. The Quran and Muhammad proclaimed the tenets of a new faith to unite a people and to expand its spiritual frontiers. Its message already had universalizing elements, though how far it was to be extended, whether to the tribesmen living in the Arabian Peninsula or well beyond, was not at all clear at first.

In 622 CE, Muhammad and a small group of followers, opposed by Mecca's leaders because of their radical religious beliefs and their challenge to the ruling elite's authority, escaped to Yathrib (later named Medina). The perilous 200-mile journey, known as *the hijra* ("breaking off of relations" or "departure"), yielded a new form of communal unity: the *umma* ("band of the faithful"). So significant was this moment that Muslims date the beginning of the Muslim era from this year.

Medina became the birthplace of a new faith called Islam ("submission"—in this case, to the will of God) and a new community called Muslims ("those who submit"). The city of Medina had been facing tribal and religious tensions, and by inviting Muhammad and his followers to take up residence there, its elders hoped that his leadership and charisma would bring peace and unity to their city. Early in his stay Muhammad put forth the Constitution of Medina, which required the community's people to refer all disputes to God and him. Now the residents were expected to replace traditional family, clan, and tribal affiliations with loyalty to Muhammad as the last and the truest Prophet of God.

Over time, the core practices and beliefs of every Muslim would crystallize as the **five pillars of Islam**. Muslims were expected to (1) *proclaim* the phrase "there is no God but God and Muhammad is His Prophet"; (2) *pray* five times daily facing Mecca; (3) *fast* from sunup until sundown during the month of Ramadan; (4) *travel* on a pilgrimage to Mecca at least once in a lifetime if their personal resources permitted; and (5) *pay* alms in the form of taxation that would alleviate the hardships of the poor. These clear-cut expectations gave the imperial system that soon developed a doctrinal and legal structure and a broad appeal to diverse populations.

MUHAMMAD'S SUCCESSORS AND THE EXPANDING *DAR AL-ISLAM*

In 632 CE, in his early sixties, the Prophet passed away; but Islam remained vibrant thanks to the energy of its early followers—especially Muhammad's first four successors, the "rightly guided caliphs" (the Arabic word *khalīfa* means successor). These caliphs ruled

NORTH SEA
ATLANTIC OCEAN
EUROPE
FRANKISH EMPIRE
Aachen
Tours 732
721
720
PYRENEES
720
714
KINGDOM OF THE VISIGOTHS
Toledo 712
Lisbon 711
Cordoba 711
711
Danube R.
BLACK
BYZANTINE EMPIRE
Constantinople
717
ANATOLIA
TAURUS MTS.
Rhodes 654
670, 674, 717
654
649
654
720 720
720
Carthage 697
MEDITERRANEAN SEA
ATLAS MOUNTAINS
Tripoli 647
Barca 643
Alexandria 642
Jerusalem 638
Al-Fustat (Cairo)
EGYPT
NORTH AFRICA
SAHARA DESERT
Nile R.
Niger R.
Muslim lands by 634 CE
Muslim lands by 656 CE
Muslim lands by 756 CE
Muslim raid
Muslim victory, with date
Muslim defeat, with date
656 Date of Muslim conquest
Further expansion of Islam
Byzantine Empire, 610 CE
Sasanian Empire, 610 CE
Frankish Empire, 610 CE
City

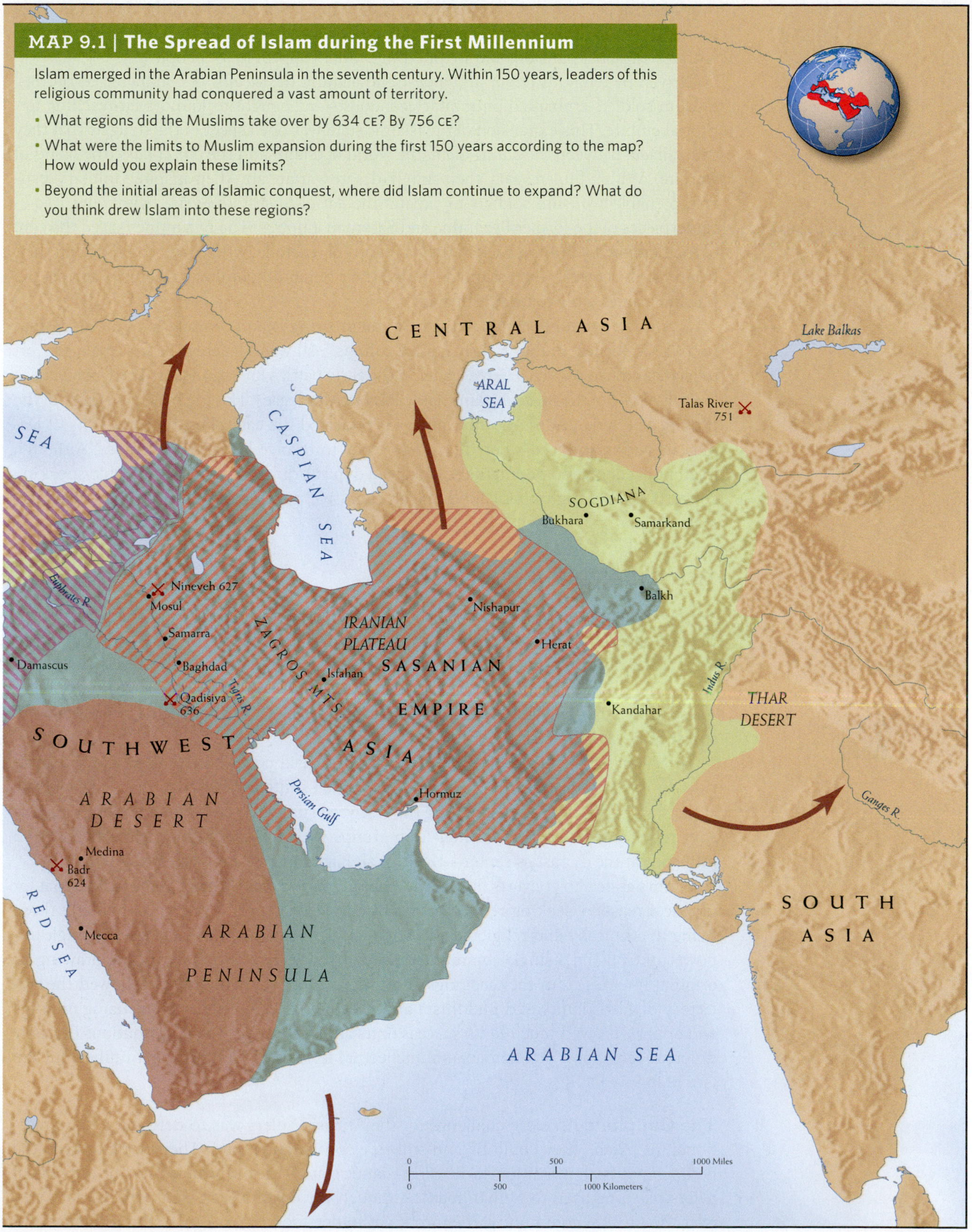

MAP 9.1 | The Spread of Islam during the First Millennium

Islam emerged in the Arabian Peninsula in the seventh century. Within 150 years, leaders of this religious community had conquered a vast amount of territory.

- What regions did the Muslims take over by 634 CE? By 756 CE?
- What were the limits to Muslim expansion during the first 150 years according to the map? How would you explain these limits?
- Beyond the initial areas of Islamic conquest, where did Islam continue to expand? What do you think drew Islam into these regions?

over Muslim peoples and the expanding state. They institutionalized the new faith. They set the new religion on the pathway to imperial greatness by linking religious uprightness with territorial expansion, empire building, and an appeal to all peoples.

Driven by religious fervor and a desire to acquire the wealth of conquered territories, Muslim soldiers embarked on military conquests and sought to found a far-reaching territorial empire. This expansion of the Islamic state was one aspect of the struggle that they called *jihad*, between the *dar al-Islam* (the world of Islam) and the *dar al-harb* (the world of warfare). Within fifteen years, their skill in desert warfare and their inspired military leadership enabled Muslim soldiers to expand the *dar al-Islam* into Syria, Egypt, and Iraq—centerpieces of the former Byzantine and Sasanian empires. The Byzantines saved the core of their empire by pulling back to the highlands of Anatolia, where they could defend their frontiers. In contrast, the Sasanians hurled their remaining military resources against the Muslim armies, only to be annihilated.

A political vacuum opened in the new and growing Islamic empire with the assassination of Ali, the last of the "rightly guided caliphs." Ali was arguably the first male convert to Islam and had proved a fierce leader in the early battles for expansion. The Umayyads, a branch of one of the Meccan clans, laid claim to Ali's legacy. Having been governors of the province of Syria under Ali, the Umayyads relocated the capital to the Syrian city of Damascus and introduced a hereditary monarchy to resolve leadership disputes. Although tolerant of conquered populations, Umayyad dynasts did not permit non-Arabic-speaking converts to hold high political offices, an exclusive policy that contributed to their ultimate demise.

THE ABBASID REVOLUTION

As the Umayyads spread Islam beyond Arabia, some peoples resisted what they experienced as Arab Umayyad repression and religious impurity. A new coalition emerged under the Abbasi family, which claimed descent from the Prophet. Disgruntled provincial authorities and their military allies, as well as non-Arab converts, joined the movement. These individuals had embraced Islam and learned Arabic, only to discover that they were still second-class citizens.

After amassing a sizable military force, the Abbasid coalition trounced the Umayyad ruler in 750 CE. The center of the Muslim state then shifted to Baghdad in Iraq (as we saw at the start of this chapter), signifying the eastward sprawl of the faith and its empire. This shift represented a success for non-Arab groups within Islam without eliminating Arab influence at the dynasty's center—the capital, Baghdad, in Arabic-speaking Iraq.

Islam's appeal to converts during the Abbasid period was diverse. Some turned to it for practical reasons, seeking reduced taxes or enhanced power. Others, particularly those living in ethnically and religiously diverse regions, welcomed the message of a single all-powerful God and a single community united by a clear code of laws. Islam, drawing its original impetus from the teachings and actions of a prophetic figure, followed the trajectory of Christianity and Buddhism and became a faith with a universalizing message and appeal. It owed much of its success to its ability to merge the contributions of vastly different geographic, economic, and intellectual territories into a rich yet unified culture (see Map 9.1).

The Caliphate An early challenge for the Abbasid rulers was to determine how traditional, or "Arab," they could be and still rule so vast an empire. They chose to keep the bedrock political institution of the early Islamic state—the **caliphate** (the line of political rulers reaching back to Muhammad). Although the caliphs exercised political authority over the Muslim community, they were not understood to have inherited Muhammad's prophetic powers or any authority in religious doctrine. That power was reserved for religious scholars, called *ulama*.

Abbasid rule borrowed practices from successful predecessors in its mixture of Persian absolute authority and the royal seclusion of the Byzantine emperors who lived in palaces far removed from their subjects. This blend of absolute authority and decentralized power involved a delicate and ultimately unsustainable balancing act. As the empire expanded it became increasingly decentralized politically, enabling wily regional governors and competing caliphates in Spain and Egypt to grab power. Even as Islam's political center diffused, though, its spiritual center remained fixed in Mecca, where many of the faithful gathered to fulfill their pilgrimage obligation.

The Army The Abbasids, like all rulers, relied on force to integrate their empire. Yet they struggled with what the nature of that military force should be: a citizen-conscript, all-Arab force or a professional, even non-Arab, army. In the early stages, leaders conscripted military forces from local Arab populations, creating citizen armies. Ultimately, however, the Abbasids recruited professional soldiers from Turkish-speaking communities in central Asia, and from the non-Arab, Berber-speaking peoples of North Africa and West Africans. Their reliance on foreign—that is, non-Arab—military personnel represented a major shift in the Islamic world. Not only did the change infuse the empire with dynamic new populations, but soon these groups gained political authority. Having begun as an Arab state and then incorporated strong Persian influence, the Islamic empire now embraced Turkish elements from the pastoral belts of central Asia.

Islamic Law (The *Sharia*) and Theology Islamic law, or the ***sharia***, began to take shape in the Abbasid period. The work of generations of religious scholars, the *sharia* covers all aspects of practical and spiritual life, providing legal principles for marriage contracts, trade regulations, and religious prescriptions such as prayer, pilgrimage rites, and ritual fasting. The most influential early scholar of the *sharia* was an eighth-century Palestinian-born Arab, al-Shafi'i, who insisted that Muhammad's laws as laid out in the Quran, in addition to his sayings and actions as written in later reports (*hadith*), provided all the legal guidance that Islamic judges needed. This shift gave *ulama* (Muslim scholars) a central place in Islam since only their spiritual authority, and not the political authority of the caliphs, was qualified to define religious law. The *ulama*'s ascendance opened a sharp division within Islam: between the secular realm of the caliphs and the religious sphere of religious judges, experts on Islamic law, teachers, and holy men.

Gender in Early Islam Pre-Islamic Arabia was one of the last regions in Southwest Asia where patriarchy had not triumphed. Instead, men still married into women's families and moved to those families' locations, as was common in tribal communities. Some women engaged in a variety of occupations and, if they became wealthy, even married more than one husband. But contact with the rest of Southwest Asia, where men's power over women prevailed, was already altering women's status in the Arabian Peninsula before the birth of Muhammad.

Muhammad's relations with women reflected these changes. As a young man, he married a woman fifteen years his senior—Khadija, an independent trader—and took no other wives before she died. It was Khadija to whom he went in fear following his first revelations. She wrapped him in a blanket and assured him of his sanity. She was also his first convert. Later in life, however, he took younger wives, some of whom were widows of his companions, and insisted on their veiling (partly as a sign of their modesty and privacy). He married his favorite wife, Aisha, when she was only nine or ten years old. As a major source for collecting Muhammad's sayings, Aisha became an important figure in early Islam.

By the time Islam reached Southwest Asia and North Africa, where strict gender rules and women's subordinate status were entrenched, the new faith was adopting a patriarchal outlook. Muslim men could divorce freely; women could not. A man could take four wives and numerous concubines; a woman could have only one husband. Well-to-do women, always veiled, lived secluded from male society. Still, the Quran did offer women some protections. Men had to treat each wife with respect if they took more than one. Women could inherit property (although only half of what a man inherited). Marriage dowries went directly to the bride rather than to her guardian, indicating women's independent legal standing; and while a woman's adultery drew harsh punishment, its proof required eyewitness testimony. The result was a legal system that reinforced men's dominance over women but empowered magistrates to oversee the definition of male honor and proper behavior.

THE BLOSSOMING OF ABBASID CULTURE

COMPARISON

EVALUATE the relationships between religion, empire, and commercial exchange across Afro-Eurasia during this period.

The arts flourished during the Abbasid period, a blossoming that left its imprint throughout society. Within a century of Abbasid rule, Arabic had superseded Greek as the Muslim world's preferred language for poetry, literature, medicine, science, and philosophy. Arabic spread beyond native speakers to become the language of the educated classes. Arabic scholars preserved and extended Greek and Roman thought, in part through the transmission of treatises by Aristotle, Hippocrates, Galen, Ptolemy, and Archimedes, among others. To house such manuscripts, patrons of the arts and sciences—including the caliphs—opened magnificent libraries.

The Muslim world absorbed scientific breakthroughs from China and other areas: they incorporated the use of paper from China, adopted siege warfare from China and Byzantium, and assimilated knowledge of plants from the ancient Greeks. From Indian sources, scholars borrowed a numbering system based on the concept of zero and units of ten—what we today call Arabic numerals. Arab mathematicians were pioneers in arithmetic, geometry, algebra, and trigonometry. Since much of Greek science had been lost in the West and later was reintroduced via the Muslim world, the Islamic contribution to the West was of immense significance. Thus, this intense borrowing, translating, storing, and diffusing of ideas brought worlds together.

ISLAM IN A WIDER WORLD

As Islam spread and decentralized, it generated dazzling and often competitive dynasties in Spain, North Africa, and points farther east. Each dynastic state revealed the Muslim talent for achieving high levels of artistry far from its heartland. But growing diversity led to a problem: Islam fragmented politically. No single political regime could hold its widely dispersed believers together (see Map 9.2).

Cities in Spain One extraordinary Muslim state arose in Spain under Abd al-Rahman III (r. 912–961 CE), the successor ruler of a Muslim kingdom founded there over a century earlier. Abd al-Rahman brought peace and stability to a violent frontier region where civil conflict had disrupted commerce and intellectual exchange. His evenhanded governance promoted amicable relations among Muslims, Christians, and Jews, and his diplomatic relations with Christian potentates as far away as France, Germany, and Scandinavia generated impressive commercial exchanges between western Europe and North Africa. He expanded and beautified the capital city of Cordoba, and his successor made the Great Mosque of Cordoba one of Spain's most stunning sites. In the nearby city Madinat al-Zahra, Abd al-Rahman III surrounded the city's administrative offices and mosque

The Great Mosque of Cordoba The great mosque of Cordoba was built in the eighth century by the Umayyad ruler Abd al-Rahman I and added to by other Muslim rulers. Built on the site of a Gothic church, which had been placed on the site of an earlier Roman temple, the mosque's most striking features were alternating red and white arches, made of jasper, onyx, marble, and granite and fashioned from materials from the Roman temple and other buildings in the vicinity. Around the doors and across the walls Arabic calligraphy proclaimed Muhammad's message and asserted the superiority of Arabic as God's chosen language.

with verdant gardens of lush tropical and semitropical plants, tranquil pools, fountains that spouted cooling waters, and sturdy aqueducts that carried potable water to the city's inhabitants.

Talent in Central Asia In the eastern regions of the Islamic empire, Abbasid rulers in Baghdad surrounded themselves with learned men from Sogdiana, the central Asian territory where Greek learning had flourished. The Barmaki family, who for several generations held high administrative offices under the Abbasids, came from the central Asian city of Balkh. Loyal servants of the caliph, the Barmakis made sure that wealth and talent from the crossroads of Asia were funneled into Baghdad. Devoted patrons of the arts, the Barmakis promoted and collected Arabic translations of Persian, Greek, and Sanskrit manuscripts. They also encouraged central Asian scholars to enhance their learning by moving to Baghdad. These scholars included the Islamic cleric al-Bukhari (d. 870 CE), who was a renowned collector of *hadith*; the mathematician al-Khwarizmi (c. 780–850 CE), who modified Indian digits into Arabic numerals and wrote the first book on algebra; and the philosopher al-Farabi (d. 950 CE), from a Turkish military family, who also made his way to Baghdad, where he studied eastern Christian teachings and promoted the Platonic ideal of a philosopher-king. Even when the Abbasid caliphate began to decline, intellectual vitality continued under the patronage of local rulers. The best example of this is, perhaps, the polymath Ibn Sina (known in the West as Avicenna, 980–1037), whose *Canon of Medicine* stood as the standard medical text in both Southwest Asia and Europe for centuries.

Trade in Sub-Saharan Africa Islam also crossed the Sahara Desert and penetrated well into Africa, carried by traders and scholars (see Map 9.3), where merchants exchanged weapons and textiles for gold, salt, and slaves. Trade did more than join West Africa to North Africa. It generated prodigious wealth, which allowed centralized political kingdoms to develop. The most celebrated was Ghana, which lay at the terminus of North Africa's major trading routes and was often hailed in Arab sources for its gold, as well as its pomp and power. Seafaring Muslim traders carried Islam into East Africa via the Indian Ocean. As early

MAP 9.2 | Political Fragmentation in the Islamic World, 750–1000 CE

By 1000 CE, the Islamic world was politically fractured and decentralized. The Abbasid caliphs still reigned in Baghdad, but they wielded very limited political authority. Looking at the map, first point to Baghdad and then point out all the areas under Abbasid control.

- What are the regions where major Islamic powers emerged?
- What areas were Sunni? Which were Shiite?
- Why were the Abbasids unable to sustain political unity in the Islamic world?

as the eighth century CE, coastal trading communities in East Africa were exporting ivory and possibly slaves. By the tenth century, the East African coast featured a mixed African-Arab culture. The region's evolving Bantu language absorbed Arabic words and before long gained a new name, Swahili (derived from the Arabic plural of the word meaning "coast").

OPPOSITION WITHIN ISLAM: SHIISM AND THE FATIMIDS

Islam's whirlwind rise generated internal tensions from the start. It is hardly surprising that a religion that extolled territorial conquests and created a large empire in its first decades would also spawn dissident religious movements that challenged the existing imperial structures. Muslims shared a reverence for a basic text and a single God, but often had little else in common. Religious and political divisions only grew deeper as Islam spread into new corners of Afro-Eurasia.

Sunnis and Shiites Early division within Islam was fueled by disagreements about who should succeed the Prophet, how the succession should take place, and who should lead Islam's expansion into the wider world. **Sunnis** (from the Arabic word meaning

The Jenne Mosque and the Al-Azhar Mosque The Jenne Mosque *(left)* arose in the kingdom of Mali when that kingdom was at the height of its power. The mosque speaks to the depth and importance of Islam's roots in the Malian kingdom. The mosque of al-Azhar *(right)* is Cairo's most important ancient mosque. Built in the tenth century by the Fatimid conquerors and rulers of Egypt, it quickly became a leading center for worship and learning, frequented by Muslim clerics and admired in Europe.

"tradition") accept that the political succession from the Prophet to the four "rightly guided caliphs" and then to the Umayyad and Abbasid dynasties was the correct one. The vast majority of Muslims today are Sunni. Dissidents, like the Shiites, contest the Sunni understanding of political and spiritual authority. **Shiites** ("members of the party of Ali") felt that the proper successors should have been Ali, who had married the Prophet's daughter Fatima, and then his descendants. Ali was one of the early converts to Islam and one of the band of Meccans who had migrated with the Prophet to Medina. The fourth of the "rightly guided caliphs," he ruled over the Muslim community from 656 to 661 CE, dying at the hands of an assassin who struck him down as he was praying in a mosque in Kufa, Iraq. Shiites believe that Ali's descendants, whom they call *imams,* have religious and prophetic power as well as political authority—and thus should be spiritual leaders.

Shiism appealed to regional and ethnic groups whom the Umayyads and Abbasids had excluded from power; it became Islam's most potent dissident force and created a permanent divide within Islam. Shiism was well established in the first century of Islam's existence, and over time the Sunnis and Shiites diverged even more than these early political disputes over succession might have indicated. Both groups had their own versions of the *sharia*, their own collections of *hadith*, and their own theological tenets.

The Fatimids Repressed in what is present-day Iraq and Iran, Shiite activists made their way to North Africa, where they joined with dissident Berber groups to topple several rulers. In 909 CE, a Shiite religious and military leader, Abu Abdallah, overthrew the Sunni ruler there. Thus began the Fatimid regime.

After conquering Egypt in 969 CE, the Fatimids set themselves against the Abbasid caliphs of Baghdad, refusing to acknowledge their legitimacy and claiming to speak for the whole Islamic world. The Fatimid rulers established their capital at al-Qahira (or Cairo). Early on they founded al-Azhar mosque, which attracted scholars from all over Afro-Eurasia and spread Islamic learning outward. They also built other elegant mosques and centers of learning. The Fatimid regime lasted until the late twelfth century, though its rulers made little headway in persuading the Egyptian population, most of whom remained Sunnis, to embrace their Shiite beliefs.

MAP 9.3 | Islam and Trade in Sub-Saharan Africa, 700–1000 CE

Islamic merchants and scholars, not Islamic armies, carried Islam into sub-Saharan Africa. Trace the trade routes in Africa, being sure to follow the correct direction of trade.

- According to the map key and icons, what commodities were Islamic merchants seeking below the Sahara?
- What were the major trade routes and the direction of trade in Africa?
- How did trade and commerce lead to the geographic expansion of the Islamic faith?

By 1000 CE Islam, which had originated as a radical religious revolt in a small corner of the Arabian Peninsula, had grown into a vast political and religious empire. It had become the dominant force in the middle regions of Afro-Eurasia. Like its rival in this part of the world, Christianity, it aspired to universality. But unlike Christianity, it was linked from its outset to political power. Muhammad and his early followers created an empire to facilitate the expansion of their faith, while their Christian counterparts inherited an empire when Constantine embraced the new faith. A vision of a world under the jurisdiction of Muslim caliphs, adhering to the dictates of the *sharia,* drove Muslim armies, merchants, and scholars to territories thousands of miles away from Mecca and Medina. Yet as Islam's reach stretched thin, political fragmentation within the Muslim world meant that Islam's reach could not extend to much of western Europe and China.

The Tang State

COMPARISON

COMPARE the organizational structures of the Abbasids, Tang China, and Christendom.

The rise of the powerful Tang Empire (618–907 CE) in China paralleled Islam's explosion out of Arabia and its impact throughout Afro-Eurasia. Once again the landmass had two centers of power, as Islam replaced the Roman Empire in counterbalancing the power and wealth of China. Like the Umayyads and the Abbasids, the Tang dynasty promoted a cosmopolitan culture. Under Tang rule Buddhism, medicine, and mathematics from India gave China's chief cities an international flavor. China became a hub for East Asian integration, and spread its influence to Korea and Japan.

TERRITORIAL EXPANSION UNDER THE TANG DYNASTY

The Tang dynasty expanded the boundaries of the Chinese state and reestablished its dominance in East and central Asia. After the fall of the Han, China had faced a long period of political fragmentation (see Chapter 8). As had happened several times before, yet another sudden change in the course of the Yellow River caused extensive flooding on the North China plain and set the stage for the emergence of the Tang dynasty. Revolts ensued as the population faced starvation. Li Yuan, the governor of a province under the short-lived Sui dynasty (589–618 CE) marched on Chang'an and took the throne in 618. He promptly established the Tang dynasty and began building a strong central government by increasing the number of provinces and doubling the number of government offices. By 624 CE the initial steps of establishing the Tang dynasty were complete; but Li Yuan's ambitious son, Li Shimin, forced his father to abdicate and took the throne in 627 CE.

An expanding Tang state required a large and professionally trained army, capable of defending far-flung frontiers and squelching rebellious populations. Toward these efforts the Tang built a military organization of aristocratic cavalry and peasant soldiers. The cavalry regularly clashed on the northern steppes with encroaching nomadic peoples, who also fought on horseback; at its height the Tang military had 700,000 horses. At the same time, between 1 and 2 million peasant soldiers garrisoned the south and toiled on public works projects.

Much like the Islamic forces, the Tang's frontier armies increasingly relied on pastoral nomadic soldiers from the Inner Eurasian steppe. Notable were the Uighurs, Turkish-speaking peoples who had moved into western China and by 750 CE constituted the empire's most potent military force. These warriors mobilized fearsome cavalries, fired longbows at distant range, and wielded steel swords and knives in hand-to-hand combat. The Tang military also pushed the state into Tibet, the Red River valley in northern Vietnam, Manchuria, and Bohai (near Korea).

At the empire's height, Tang armies controlled more than 4 million square miles of territory (see Map 9.4)—an area as large as the entire Islamic world in the ninth and tenth centuries. Once the Tang administrators brought South China's rich farmlands under

MAP 9.4 | The Tang State in East Asia, 750 CE

The Tang dynasty, at its territorial peak in 750 CE, controlled a state that extended from central Asia to the East China Sea.

- What foreign areas are under Tang control? What areas were heavily influenced by Tang government and culture?
- How can we tell from the map that China was undergoing an economic revolution during the Tang period?
- How did the Tang maintain order and stability in such a large, dynamic realm?

cultivation (by draining swamps, building an intricate network of canals and channels, and connecting lakes and rivers to the rice lands), the state was able to collect taxes from roughly 10 million families, representing 57 million individuals. Most of these taxes took the form of agricultural labor, which propelled the expansion of cultivated frontiers throughout the south.

ORGANIZING THE TANG EMPIRE

The Tang Empire emulated the Han in many ways, but its rulers also introduced new institutions. The heart of the agrarian-based Tang state was the magnificent capital city of Chang'an, the population of which reached 1 million, half of whom lived within its impressive city walls. The outer walls enclosed a thirty-square-mile area. Internal security arrangements made it one of the safest urban locales for its age. Its more than 100 quarters were separated from each other by interior walls with gates that were closed at night, after which no one was permitted on the streets. Horsemen patrolled the streets until the gates reopened in the morning. Chang'an had a large foreign population, estimated at one-third of its total, and a diverse religious life. Zoroastrian fires burned as worshippers sacrificed animals and chanted temple hymns. Nestorian Christians from Syria found a welcoming community, and Buddhists could boast ninety-one of their own temples in Chang'an in 722 CE.

Confucian Administrators Despite the Tang's reliance on the fruits of agriculture and a military force, the day-to-day control of the empire required an efficient and loyal civil service. Entry into the Tang ruling group required knowledge of Confucian ideas and all of the commentaries on the Confucian classics. It also required skill in the intricate classical Chinese language, in which this literature was written.

The Tang state introduced the world's first fully written **civil service examinations**, which tested sophisticated literary skills and knowledge of the Confucian classics. The Tang also allowed the use of Daoist classics as texts for the exams, believing that the early Daoists represented another important stream of ancient wisdom. Candidates for office, whom local elites recommended, gathered in the capital triennially to take qualifying exams. They had been trained since the age of three in the classics and histories, either by their families or in Buddhist temple schools. Most failed, but those who were successful underwent further trials to evaluate their character and determine the level of their appointments. New officials were selected from the pool of graduates on the basis of social conduct, eloquence, skill in calligraphy and mathematics, and legal knowledge.

Although official careers were in theory open to anyone of proven talent, in practice they were closed to certain groups. Women were not permitted to serve, nor were sons of merchants, nor those who could not afford a classical education. Over time, though, Tang civil examinations forced aristocrats to compete with commoner southern families, whose growing wealth gave them access to educational resources that made them the equals of the old elites. Through examinations, this new elite eventually outdistanced the sons of the northern aristocracy in the Tang government in effect by out-studying them.

The system underscored education as the primary avenue for success. Even impoverished families sought the best classical education they could afford for their sons. Although few succeeded in the civil examinations, many boys and even some girls learned the fundamentals of reading and writing. The Buddhists played a crucial role in extending education across society: as part of their charitable mission, their temple schools introduced many children to primers based on classical texts. Many Buddhist monks, in fact, entered the clergy only after not qualifying for or failing the civil examinations.

China's Female Emperor Not all Tang power brokers were men. The wives and mothers of emperors wielded influence in the court—usually behind the scenes, but sometimes publicly. The most striking example is the Empress Wu.

Born into a noble family, Wu Zhao played music and mastered the Chinese classics as a young girl. Because she was witty, intelligent, and beautiful, Wu was recruited before age thirteen to Li Shimin's court and became his favorite concubine. When Li Shimin died, his son assumed power and became the Emperor Gaozong. Wu became the new emperor's favorite concubine and gave birth to the sons he required to succeed him. As the mother of the future emperor, Wu enjoyed heightened political power. Subsequently, she took the place of Gaozong's Empress Wang by accusing her of killing Wu's newborn daughter.

After Gaozong suffered a stroke, Wu became administrator of the court, a position equal to the emperor's. She created a secret police force to spy on her opposition, and she jailed or killed those who challenged her. Following her husband's death, she made

The Tang Court This tenth-century painting of elegant ladies of the Tang imperial court enjoying a feast and music (*left*) tells us a great deal about the aesthetic tastes of elite women in this era. It also shows the secluded "inner quarters," where court ladies passed their daily lives far from the hurly-burly of imperial politics. Castrated males, known as eunuchs (*right*), guarded the women and protected the royal family of Tang emperors. By the late eighth century, eunuchs were fully integrated into the government and wielded a great deal of military and political power.

herself Empress Wu (r. 684–705 CE). She expanded the military and recruited her administrators from the civil examination candidates to oppose her enemies at court.

Wu ordered scholars to write biographies of famous women, and she empowered her mother's clan by assigning high political posts to her relatives. Later, she moved her court from Chang'an to Luoyang, where she tried to establish a new "Zhou dynasty," seeking to imitate the widely admired era of Confucius. Empress Wu elevated Buddhism over Daoism as the favored state religion, invited the most gifted Buddhist scholars to her capital at Luoyang, built Buddhist temples, and subsidized spectacular cave sculptures. In fact, Chinese Buddhism achieved its highest officially sponsored development in this period.

Eunuchs Tang rulers protected themselves, their possessions, and especially their women, with loyal and well-compensated **eunuchs** (men surgically castrated as youths and thus sexually impotent). By the late eighth century, more than 4,500 eunuchs were fully entrenched in the Tang Empire's institutions, wielding significant power not only within the imperial household but at the court and beyond. For instance, the Chief Eunuch controlled the military. Through him, the military power of court eunuchs extended to every province and garrison station in the empire, forming an all-encompassing network. This eunuch bureaucracy mediated between the emperor and the provincial governments.

Under Emperor Xianzong (r. 806–820 CE), eunuchs acted as a third pillar of the government, working alongside the official bureaucracy and the imperial court. Yet by 838 CE, the delicate balance of power among throne, eunuchs, and civil officials had evaporated. Eunuchs became an unruly political force in late Tang politics, and their competition for influence produced political instability.

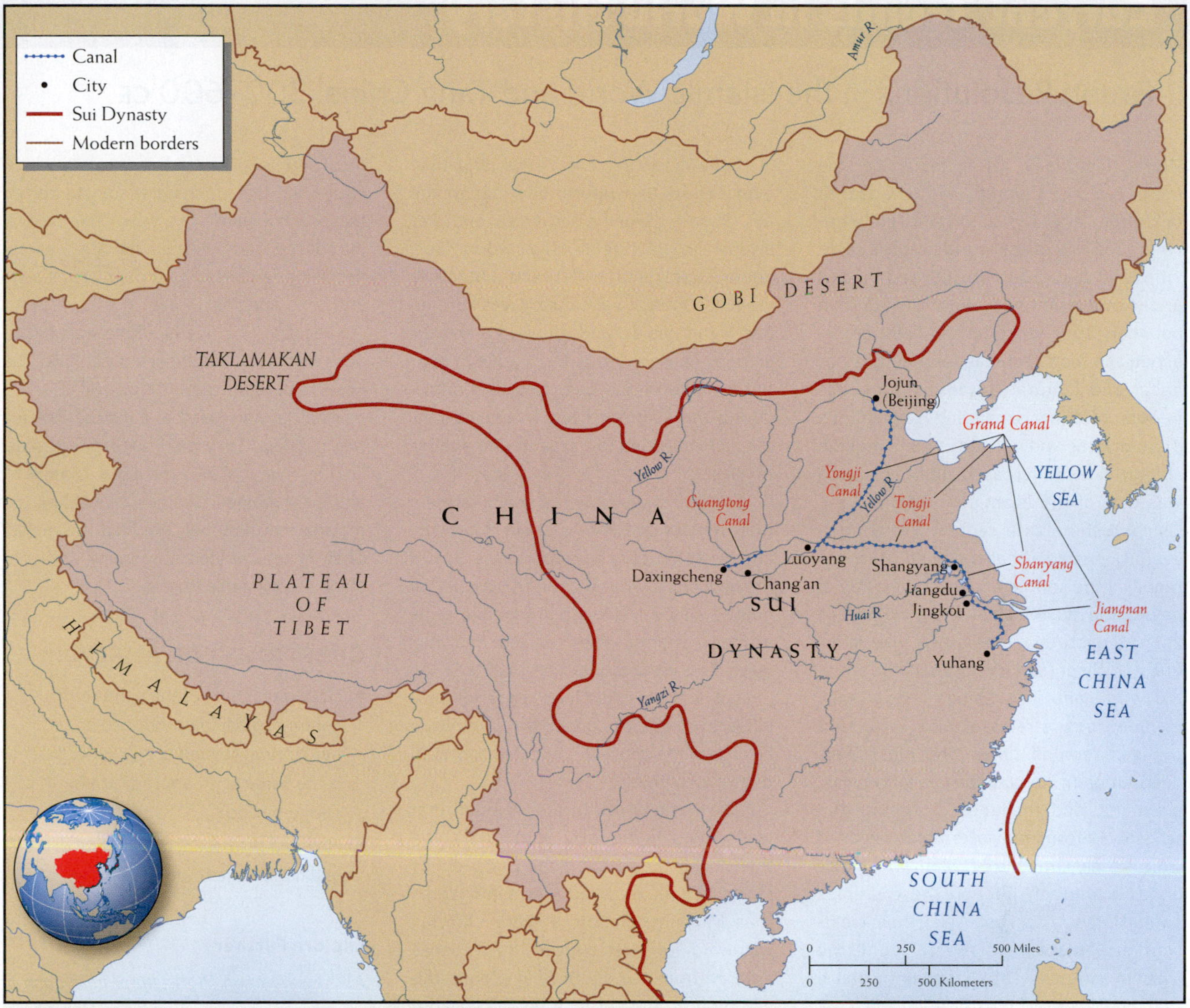

MAP 9.5 | The Sui Dynasty Canals

China, like the Islamic world, experienced a population explosion during this period.

- Where are the Sui dynasty canals on the map and the two areas showing population concentration?
- Why do you think the population concentrations are located along the canals? What major cities did the canals connect and what role did the canals play in integrating China under the Sui dynasty and its successor state, the Tang Empire?

AN ECONOMIC REVOLUTION

At its height, Tang China's economic achievements included agricultural production based on an egalitarian land allotment system, an increasingly fine handicrafts industry, a diverse commodity market, and a dynamic urban life. The earlier short-lived Sui dynasty had started this economic progress by reunifying China and building canals, especially the Grand Canal linking the north and south (see Map 9.5). The Tang continued by centering their efforts on the Grand Canal and the Yangzi River, which flows from west to east. These waterways aided communication and transport throughout the empire. The south grew richer, largely through the backbreaking labor of immigrants from the north.

Current Trends in World History

Green Revolutions in the Islamic World and Tang China, 300–600 CE

World historians often focus on the more famous Columbian Exchange to talk about how the sharing of foods between regions of the world created revolutions in diet. The Afro-Eurasian world underwent a food revolution of its own between 300 and 600 CE. New crops, especially food crops, leaped across political and cultural borders during this period, offering expanding populations more diverse and nutritious diets and the ability to feed increased numbers. Such was true of the Islamic world and Tang China in the eighth century. Now, however, it was India that replaced Mesopotamia as the source of a dazzling array of new cultigens. Most of them originated in Southeast Asia, made their way to India, and dispersed throughout the Muslim world and into China. These crops included new strains of rice, taro, sour oranges, lemons, limes, and most likely coconut palm trees, sugarcane, bananas, plantains, and mangoes. Sorghum and possibly cotton and watermelons arrived from Africa. Only the eggplant was indigenous to India. Although these staples spread quickly to East Asia, their westward movement was slower. Not until the Muslim conquest of Sindh in northern India in 711 CE did territories to the west fully discover the crop innovations pioneered in Southeast Asia.

India fascinated the Arabs, and they exploited its agricultural offerings to the hilt. Soon a revolution in crops and diet swept through the Muslim world. Sorghum supplanted millet and the other grains of antiquity because it was hardier, had higher yields, and required a shorter growing season. Citrus trees added flavor to the diet and provided refreshing drinks during the summer heat. Increased cotton cultivation led to a greater demand for textiles.

For over three hundred years, farmers from northwest India to Spain, Morocco, and West Africa made impressive use of the new crops. They increased agricultural output, slashed fallow periods, and grew as many as three crops on lands that formerly had yielded one (see Map 9.6). As a result farmers could feed larger communities; even as cities grew, the countryside became more densely populated and even more productive.

The same agricultural revolution that was sweeping through South Asia and the Muslim world also took East Asia by storm. China received the same crops that Muslim cultivators were carrying westward. Rice was critical. New varieties entered from the south, and groups migrating from the north (after the collapse of the Han Empire) eagerly took them up. Soon Chinese farmers became the world's most intensive wet-field rice cultivators. Early- and late-ripening seeds supported two or three plantings a year. Champa rice, introduced from central Vietnam, was especially popular for its drought resistance and rapid ripening.

Because rice needs ample water, Chinese hydraulic engineers went into the fields to design water-lifting devices, which peasant farmers used to construct hillside rice paddies. They also dug more canals, linking rivers and lakes (see Map 9.6) and even drained swamps, alleviating the malaria that had long troubled the region. Their efforts yielded a booming and constantly moving rice frontier.

QUESTIONS FOR ANALYSIS

- Historians think of the eighteenth century as having produced an agricultural revolution. To what extent is the same term appropriate for this earlier period?
- How did the new crops change diets and contribute to population growth?

Explore Further

Andrew Watson, *Agricultural Innovation in the Early Islamic World: The Diffusion of Crops and Farming Techniques, 700–1100* (1983).

Fertile land along the Yangzi became China's new granary, and areas south of the Yangzi became its demographic center.

Chinese merchants took full advantage of the Silk Roads to trade with India and the Islamic world; when rebellions in northwest China and the rise of Islam in central Asia jeopardized the land route, the "silk road by sea" became the avenue of choice. From all over Asia and Africa, merchant ships arrived in South China ports bearing spices, medicines, and jewelry in exchange for Chinese silks and porcelain. (See **Current Trends in World History: Green Revolutions in the Islamic World and Tang China, 300–600 CE.**)

In the large cities of the Yangzi delta, workshops produced rich brocades (silk fabrics), fine paper, intricate wood-block prints, unique iron casts, and exquisite porcelains. Art collectors all across Afro-Eurasia especially valued Tang "tricolor pottery," decorated with brilliant hues. Chinese artisans transformed locally grown cotton into highest-quality

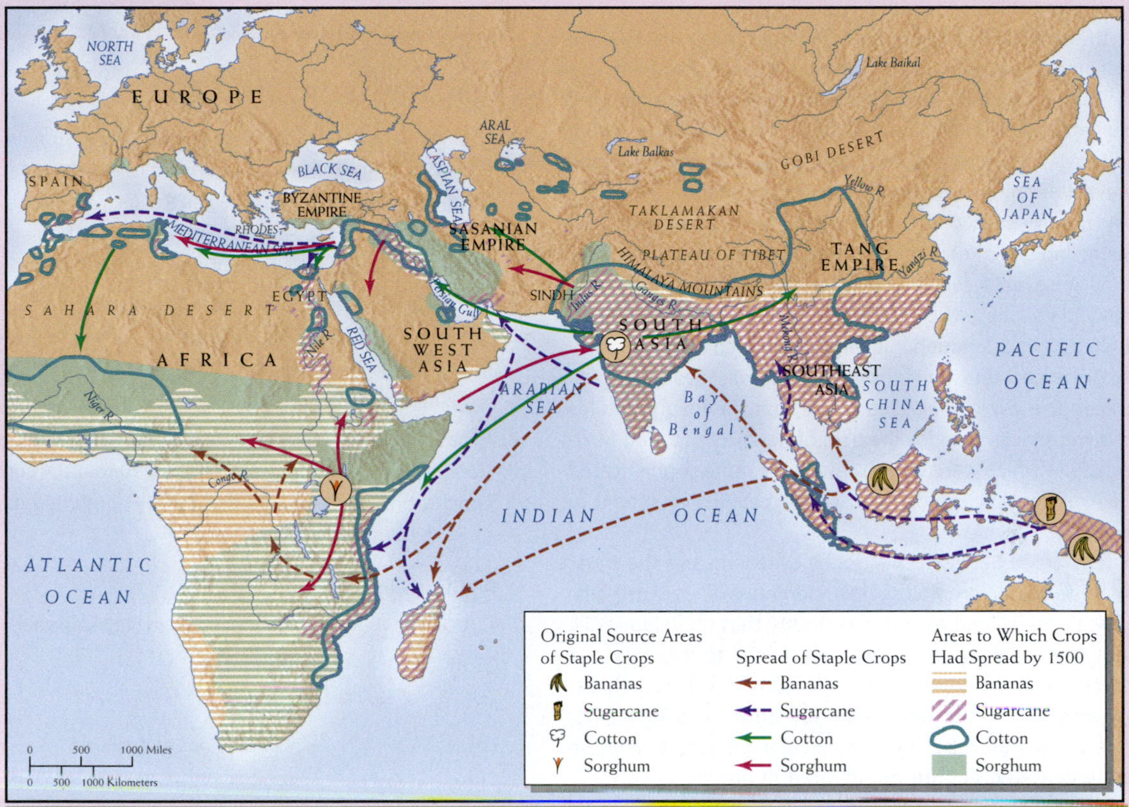

MAP 9.6 | Agricultural Diffusion in the First Millennium

The second half of the first millennium saw a revolution in agriculture throughout Afro-Eurasia. Agriculturalists across the landmass increasingly cultivated similar crops.

- Where did most of the crops originate? In what direction and where did most of them flow?
- What role did the spread of Islam and the growth of Islamic empires (see Map 9.1) play in the process?

clothing. Painting and dyeing technology improved and the resulting superb silk products generated significant tax revenue. These Chinese luxuries dominated the trading networks that reached Southwest Asia, Europe, and Africa via the Silk Roads and the Indian Ocean. (See **Analyzing Global Developments: Islam and the Silk Trade**.)

ACCOMMODATING WORLD RELIGIONS

The early Tang emperors tolerated remarkable religious diversity. Nestorian Christianity, Zoroastrianism, and Manichaeanism (a radical Christian sect) had entered China from Persia during the time of the Sasanian Empire. Islam came later. These spiritual impulses—together with Buddhism and the indigenous teachings of Daoism and Confucianism—spread throughout the Tang Empire and at first were widely used to enhance state power.

Analyzing Global Developments

Islam and the Silk Trade: Adapting Religion to Opulence

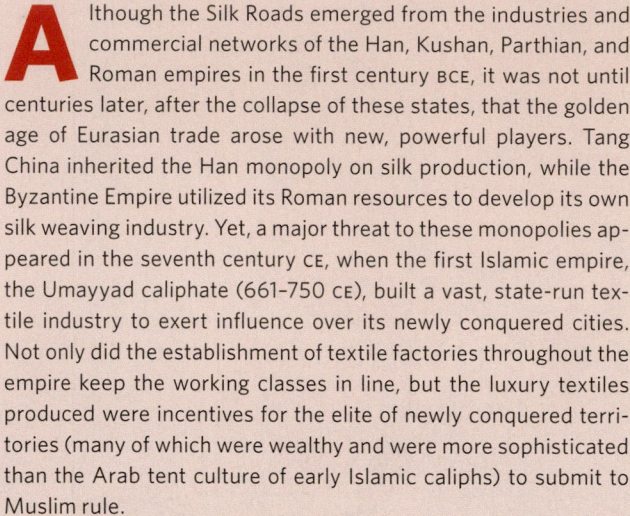

Although the Silk Roads emerged from the industries and commercial networks of the Han, Kushan, Parthian, and Roman empires in the first century BCE, it was not until centuries later, after the collapse of these states, that the golden age of Eurasian trade arose with new, powerful players. Tang China inherited the Han monopoly on silk production, while the Byzantine Empire utilized its Roman resources to develop its own silk weaving industry. Yet, a major threat to these monopolies appeared in the seventh century CE, when the first Islamic empire, the Umayyad caliphate (661–750 CE), built a vast, state-run textile industry to exert influence over its newly conquered cities. Not only did the establishment of textile factories throughout the empire keep the working classes in line, but the luxury textiles produced were incentives for the elite of newly conquered territories (many of which were wealthy and were more sophisticated than the Arab tent culture of early Islamic caliphs) to submit to Muslim rule.

Tensions arose between this opulent lifestyle and the Muslim way of life, which prohibited its adherents from wearing silk. The political, social, and religious authority that the Islamic silk trade lent the caliphate, however, was crucial to its unity and longevity. What's more, the Islamic silk industry was rapidly expanding, with no limits in sight, unlike Byzantine and Tang silks, which were restricted by their respective emperors. And so this textile-centered culture proliferated in an unbridled fashion, eventually infiltrating even religious rituals. The Abbasid caliphate (749–1258 CE) became one of the wealthiest medieval states, and its capital, Baghdad, the most cosmopolitan. To illustrate the sheer extent of the impact that the Islamic silk trade had upon the values of its people, the following table is a record of the goods that caliph Harun al-Rashid, upon whom several *Arabian Nights* stories are based, left behind upon his death in 809 CE.

QUESTIONS FOR ANALYSIS

- Looking back at Map 6.2 (see p. 223) and assuming that the exports of each region remained relatively constant throughout the history of the Silk Roads, with which cities and empires did the Abbasid Empire conduct most of its trade? The least? What might account for these differences?
- What can this list tell us about the values and activities of a caliph c. 800 CE? What, if anything, does the inventory reveal about the values and activities of the nonelite or working classes?
- What kind of evidence from contemporary Tang China or Western Christendom would allow you to draw comparable conclusions to arguments that can be constructed from al-Rashid's inventory?

Textiles: Silk Items	
4,000	silk cloaks, lined with sable and mink
1,500	silk carpets
100	silk rugs
1,000	silk cushions and pillows
1,000	cushions with silk brocade
1,000	inscribed silk cushions
1,000	silk curtains
300	silk brocade curtains
Everyday Textile Items	
4,000	small tents with their accessories
150	marquees (large tents)

Source: Xinru Liu, *The Silk Road in World History* (New York: Oxford University Press, 2010).

The Growth of Buddhism Buddhism, in particular, thrived under Tang rule. Initially, Emperor Li Shimin distrusted Buddhist monks because they avoided serving the government and paying taxes. Yet after Buddhism gained acceptance as one of the "three ways" of learning—joining Daoism and Confucianism—Li endowed huge monasteries, sent emissaries to India to collect texts and relics, and commissioned Buddhist paintings and statuary. Caves along the Silk Roads, such as those at Dunhuang, provided ideal venues for monks to paint the inside walls where religious rites and meditation took place.

Luxury Textile Items	
4,000	embroidered robes
500	pieces of velvet
1,000	Armenian carpets
300	carpets from Maysan (present-day eastern Iraq)
1,000	carpets from Darabjird (present-day Darab, Iran)
500	carpets from Tabaristan (southern coast of the Caspian sea)
1,000	cushions from Tabaristan
Fine Cotton Items and Garments	
2,000	drawers of various kinds
4,000	turbans
1,000	hoods
1,000	capes of various kinds
5,000	kerchiefs of different kinds
10,000	caftans (long robes)
4,000	curtains
4,000	pairs of socks
Fur and Leather Items	
4,000	boots lined with sable and mink
4,000	special saddles
30,000	common saddles
1,000	belts

Metal Goods	
500,000	dinars (cash)
2,000	brass objects of various kinds
10,000	decorated swords
50,000	swords for the guards and pages (*ghulam*)
150,000	lances
100,000	bows
1,000	special suits of armor
10,000	helmets
20,000	breastplates
150,000	shields
300	stoves
Aromatics and Drugs	
100,000	mithqals of musk (1 mithqual = 4.25 grams)
100,000	mithqals of ambergris (musky perfume ingredient)
	many kinds of perfume
1,000	baskets of India aloes
Jewelry and Cut Gems	
	jewels valued by jewelers at 4 million dinars
1,000	jeweled rings
Fine Stone and Metal Vessels	
1,000	precious china vessels
1,000	ewers

Anti-Buddhist Campaigns By the mid-ninth century, however, the growing influence of China's hundreds of thousands of Buddhist monks and nuns threatened Confucian and Daoist leaders, who responded by arguing that Buddhism's values conflicted with native traditions. One Confucian-trained scholar-official, Han Yu, even attacked Buddhism as a foreign doctrine of barbarian peoples who were different in language, culture, and knowledge. Although Han Yu was exiled for his objections, two decades later the state began suppressing Buddhist monasteries and confiscating their wealth, fearing that religious loyalties would undermine political ones. Increasingly intolerant Confucian

One of the Four Sacred Mountains This monastery on Mount Song is famous because in 527 CE an Indian priest, Bodhidharma, arrived there to initiate the Zen school of Buddhism in China.

scholar-administrators argued that the Buddhist monastic establishment threatened the imperial order.

By the mid-ninth century CE, the Tang state openly persecuted Buddhism. Emperor Wuzong (814–846 CE), for instance, closed more than 4,600 monasteries and destroyed 40,000 temples and shrines. More than 260,000 Buddhist monks and nuns endured a forced return to secular life, after which the state parceled out monastery lands to taxpaying landlords and peasant farmers. To expunge the cultural impact of Buddhism, classically trained literati revived ancient prose styles and the teachings of Confucius and his followers. Their efforts reversed some of the early Buddhist successes in China.

Although Buddhism remained important, the Tang era represented the triumph of homegrown ideologies (Confucianism and Daoism) over a foreign universalizing religion (Buddhism). In addition, by permanently dismantling huge monastic land holdings, the Tang ensured that no religion would rival its power. Successor dynasties continued to keep religious establishments weak and fragmented, although Confucianism maintained a more prominent role within society as the basis of the ruling classes' ideology and as a quasi-religious belief system for a wider portion of the population. The result was persistent religious diversity within China.

TANG INTERACTIONS WITH KOREA AND JAPAN

While China was opening up to the cultures of its western regions, its own culture was reaching out to the east—to Korea and, eventually, to Japan (see Map 9.7). Chinese influence, both indirect and direct, had reached into Korea for more than a millennium, and later into Japan; but not without local resistance and the flourishing of entirely indigenous and independent political and religious developments.

Early Korea Interactions with China played a fundamental role in the history of the Korean peninsula. Unification in 668 CE under the Silla—one of three rival states in

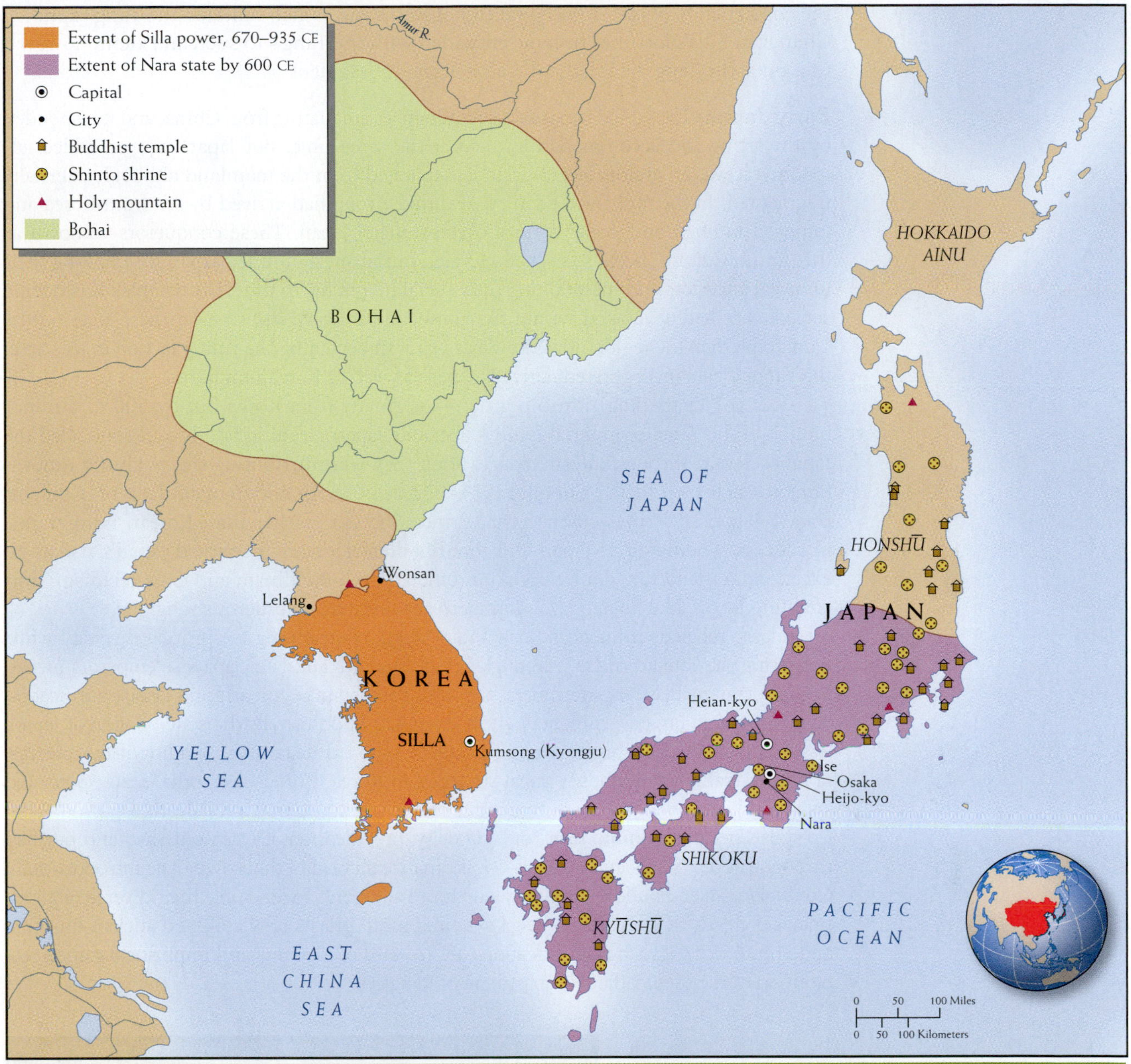

MAP 9.7 | Borderlands: Korea and Japan, 600–1000 CE

The Tang dynasty held great power over emerging Korean and Japanese states, although it never directly ruled either region.

- Based on the map, what connections do you see between Korea and Japan and the Tang Empire?
- What, if any, relationship do you see between the proliferation of Buddhist temples and Shinto shrines?

Korea—enabled Koreans to establish an autonomous government, but their opposition to the Chinese did not deter them from modeling their government on the Tang imperial state. The Silla rulers dispatched annual emissaries bearing tribute payments to the Chinese capital and regularly sent students and monks. As a result, literary Chinese—not their own dialect—became the written language of Korean elites. Chinese influence extended to the way in which the Silla state organized its court and bureaucracy and to the construction of the Silla capital city of Kumsong, which imitated the Tang capital of Chang'an. Silla's fortunes became entwined with the Tang's to such an extent, however, that once the Tang declined, Silla also began to fragment.

Early Japan Like Korea, Japan also felt influences emanating from China, and it responded by thwarting and accommodating them at the same time. But Japan enjoyed added autonomy: it was an archipelago of islands, separated from the mainland although internally fragmented. In the mid-third century, a warlike group had arrived by sea from Korea and imposed military and social control over southern Japan. These conquerors—known as the "Tomb Culture" because of their elevated burial sites—unified Japan by extolling their imperial ancestors and maintaining their social hierarchy. In time, the complex aristocratic society that had developed within the Tomb Culture gave rise to a Japanese state on the Yamato plain in the region now known as Nara. In becoming the ruling faction in this area, the Yamato clan incorporated native Japanese as well as Korean migrants.

After 587 CE the Soga kinship group—originally from Korea but by 500 CE a minor branch of the Yamato imperial family—became Japan's leading family and controlled the Japanese court through intermarriage. Soon they were attributing their cultural innovations to their own Prince Shotoku (574–622 CE), of Soga and Yamato descent. Contemporary Japanese scribes claimed that Prince Shotoku, rather than Korean immigrants, introduced Buddhism to Japan and that his illustrious reign sparked Japan's rise as an exceptional island kingdom. Shotoku promoted both Buddhism and Confucianism, thus enabling Japan, like its neighbor China, to accommodate numerous religions.

Indeed, religious influences flowed into Japan, contributing to spiritual diversity while bolstering the Yamato rulers. Although Prince Shotoku and later Japanese emperors turned to Confucian models for government, they also dabbled in occult arts and Daoist purification rituals. In addition, governmental edicts promoted Buddhism as the state religion of Japan. Association with Buddhism gave the Japanese state extra status by lending it the prestige of a universal religion whose appeal stretched to Korea, China, and India. State-sponsored spiritual diversity led native Shinto cults—which believed that after death a person's soul (or spirit) became a Shinto *kami,* or local deity, provided that it was nourished and purified through proper rituals and festivals—to formalize a creed of their own. The introduction of Confucianism and Buddhism motivated Shinto adherents to assemble their diverse religious practices into a well-organized belief system. Shinto priests now collected ancient liturgies, and Shinto rituals (such as purification rites to ward off demons and impurities) gained recognition in the state's official Department of Religion.

Horyuji Temple The main hall of the Horyuji Temple in Nara, Japan (*left*), built in the seventh century CE. The fresco (*right*) from the Horyuji Temple depicts gauze-draped celestial beings (known as *apsara* or *tennin* in Japanese Buddhism), flying above the Buddha's Pure Land burning incense.

Political integration under Prince Shotoku did not mean political stability, however. In 645 CE, the Nakatomi kinship group seized the throne and eliminated the Soga and their allies. Via intermarriage with the imperial clan, the Nakatomi became the new spokesmen for the Yamato tradition. Thereafter Nakatomi no Kamatari (614–669 CE) enacted a series of reforms that reflected Confucian principles of government allegedly enunciated by Shotoku. These reforms enhanced the power of the ruler, no longer portrayed simply as an ancestral kinship group leader but now depicted as an exalted "emperor" (*tenno*) who ruled by the mandate of heaven, as in China, and exercised absolute authority.

THE FALL OF TANG CHINA

Hence, at the eastern end of Afro-Eurasia, the Tang, as well as the Silla of Korea and the Yamato state of Japan, interacted with one another and blended both religious and political authority to maintain stability. The peak of Chinese power in East Asia occurred just as the Abbasids were expanding into Tang portions of central Asia. Yet, despite the Abbasid Empire's spread, China in 750 CE was still the most powerful and best-administered empire in the world. When Muslim forces drove the Tang from Turkistan in 751 CE at the battle of Talas River, however, their success emboldened groups such as the Sogdians and Tibetans to challenge the Tang and even take their capital. As a result, the Tang gradually retreated into the old heartlands along the Yellow and Yangzi rivers. Thereafter misrule, court intrigues, economic exploitation, and popular rebellions weakened the empire, but the dynasty held on for over a century more until northern invaders toppled it in 907 CE.

The Emergence of European Christendom

Although western Europe lacked a highly developed political empire like that of the Abbasids or the Tang dynasty, Christianity increasingly unified the peoples of Europe. In fifth-century western Europe, the mighty Roman military machine gave way to a multitude of warrior leaders whose principal allegiances were local. The political ideal of the Roman Empire certainly influenced western Europeans, but the true inheritor of Rome in the west was the Roman Catholic Church, with its priests, missionaries, and monks. In northern Europe, a frontier mentality and the Viking threat shaped Christianity. In eastern Europe and Byzantium, a form of Christianity known as Greek Orthodoxy had become dominant by 1000 CE. Together, these two major strands of the faith—the western Roman Catholic Church and eastern Greek Orthodoxy—constituted the realm of Christendom, the entire portion of the world in which Christianity prevailed as a unifying institution (see Map 9.8).

COMPARISON

COMPARE the internal divisions within the Islamic, Tang, and Christian worlds.

CHARLEMAGNE'S FLEDGLING EMPIRE

Far removed from the old centers of high culture, Charlemagne (r. 768–814 CE), ruler of the Franks, expanded his western European kingdom through constant warfare and plunder. In 802 CE, Harun al-Rashid, the Abbasid ruler of Baghdad, sent the gift of an elephant to Charlemagne, already the king of the Franks for three decades and recently crowned by the pope in Rome as "Holy Roman Emperor" (on Christmas Day in 800 CE). While the Franks interpreted the caliph's gift as an acknowledgment of Charlemagne's power, al-Rashid more likely sent the rare beast as a gracious reminder of his own formidable sway. In al-Rashid's eyes, Charlemagne's "empire" was a minor principality. Although Charlemagne claimed the lofty title of emperor and ultimately controlled much of western Europe, compared with the Islamic world's rulers and vast domain he was a political lightweight.

MAP 9.8 | Christendom, 600–1000 CE

The end of the first millennium saw much of Europe divided between two versions of Christianity, each with different traditions. On the map, locate Rome and Constantinople, the two seats of power in Christianity.

- According to the map, what were the two major regions where Christianity held sway?
- In what directions did Roman Catholic Christianity and Greek Orthodox Christianity spread?
- The map suggests that missionaries played important roles in spreading Roman Catholicism and Greek Orthodoxy. Why do you think that this was the case?

Charlemagne's empire had a population of less than 15 million; he rarely commanded armies larger than 5,000; and his tax system was rudimentary. At a time when the caliph's palace at Baghdad covered nearly 250 acres, Charlemagne's palace at Aachen was merely 330 by 655 feet. Baghdad itself was almost forty square miles in area, whereas there was no "town" outside the palace at Aachen. The palace was essentially a large country house set in open countryside, where Charlemagne and his Franks hunted wild boar from horseback.

Charlemagne and his men were representatives of the warrior class that dominated post-Roman western Europe. After Roman control faded away, war became once again the duty and joy of the aristocrats. Although the Franks vigorously engaged in trade, even that trade was based on war. Europe's principal export at this time was Europeans, and the massive sale of prisoners of war, in markets at Alexandria, Tunis, and southern Spain, financed the Frankish empire. The main victims of this trade were Slavic-speaking peoples, tribal hunters and cultivators from eastern Europe. This trade in Slavs gives us the modern term "slave."

Yet Charlemagne's seemingly uncivilized and inhospitable empire offered fertile ground for Christianity to sink down roots. As Christianity grew in western and northern Europe, the rough frontier mentality fueled its expansionist ambitions.

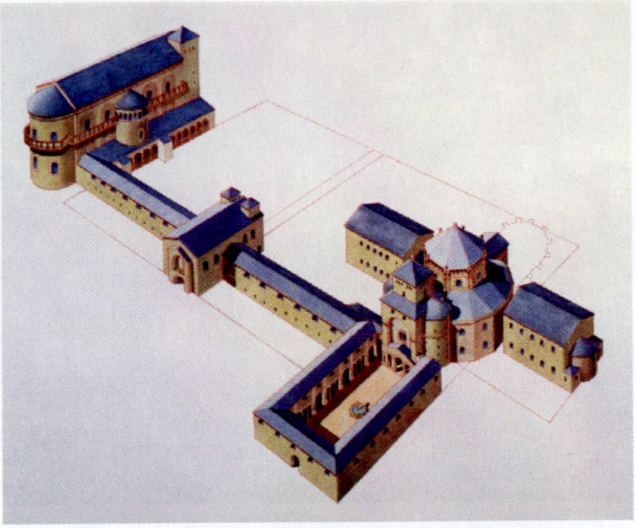

Charlemagne's Palace and Chapel Though not large by Byzantine or Islamic standards, Charlemagne's palace and chapel were heavy with symbolic meaning. A royal hall for banqueting in Frankish, "barbarian" style was linked by a covered walkway to the imperial domed chapel, which was meant to look like a miniature version of the Hagia Sophia of Constantinople. Outside the chapel was a courtyard, like that outside the shrine of Saint Peter at Rome.

CHRISTIANITY IN WESTERN EUROPE

Christians of the west, including those in northern Europe, felt that theirs was the one truly universal religion. Their goal was to bring rival groups into a single **Roman Catholic Church** that was replacing a political unity lost in western Europe when the Roman Empire fell. Drawing on the ideas of Augustine of Hippo (c. 410 CE), the western Christians believed that the "city of God" would take earthly shape in the form of the Catholic Church, and that the Catholic Church was not just for Romans—it was for all times and for all peoples.

The arrival of Christianity in northern Europe provoked a cultural revolution. Preliterate societies now encountered a sacred text—the Bible—in a language that seemed utterly strange. Latin had become a sacred language, and books themselves were vehicles of the holy. The bound codex, which had replaced the clumsy scroll, was still messy: it had no divisions between words, no punctuation, no paragraphs, no chapter headings. Readers who knew Latin as a spoken language could understand the script. But Irishmen, Saxons, and Franks could not, for they had never spoken Latin. Consequently, great care was lavished on the few parchment texts—like the Gospels in the Book of Kells (c. 800 CE)—that were prepared with words separated, sentences correctly punctuated and introduced by uppercase letters, and chapter headings.

Those producing these stunning Bibles were starkly different from ordinary men and women. They were monks and nuns. Christian **monasticism** had originated in Egypt, but it suited well the missionary tendencies of Christianity in northern Europe. The root of "monastic" and "monk" is the Greek *monos,* "alone": a man or a woman who chose to live alone, without the support of marriage or family. In Muslim (and Jewish) communities, religious leaders emphasized what they had in common with those around them. Many Islamic scholars, theologians, and mystics were married men, even merchants and courtiers. In the Christian West, the opposite was true: warrior societies honored small groups of monks and nuns who were utterly unlike themselves: unmarried, unfit for warfare, and intensely literate in an incomprehensible tongue.

Monasticism appealed to a deep sense that the very men and women who had little in common with ordinary people were best suited to mediate between believers and God. Laypersons (common believers, not clergy) gave gifts to the monasteries and offered them protection. In return, they gained the prayers of monks and nuns and the reassurance that

Monasticism The great monasteries of the age of Charlemagne, such as the St. Gallen Monastery (*left*), were like Roman legionary settlements. Placed on the frontiers of Germany, they were vast stone buildings, around which entire towns would gather. Their libraries, the largest in Europe, were filled with parchment volumes, carefully written out and often lavishly decorated in a "northern," Celtic style. Monasticism was also about the lonely search for God at the very end of the world, which took place in these Irish monasteries (*right*) on the Atlantic coast. The cells, made of loose stones piled in round domes, are called "beehives."

although they themselves were warriors and men of blood, the monks' and nuns' interventions on their behalf would keep them from going to hell. Payment for human sin, the atoning power of Jesus's crucifixion, and the efficacy of monastic prayers were significant theological emphases for western Roman Catholics.

The Catholic Church of northern Europe was a religion of monks, whose communities represented an otherworldly alternative to the warrior societies of the time. By 800 CE, most regions of northern Europe held great monasteries, many of which were far larger than the local villages. Supported by thousands of serfs donated by kings and local warlords, the monasteries became powerhouses of prayer that kept the regions safe.

Northern Christianity also gained new ties to an old center: the city of Rome. The Christian bishop of Rome had always enjoyed much prestige, but often took second place to other bishops in Carthage, Alexandria, Antioch, and Constantinople. Though people spoke of him with respect as *papa* ("the grand old man"), many others shared that title.

By the ninth century, this picture had changed. Believers from the distant north saw only one *papa* left in western Europe: Rome's pope. New Christians in northern borderlands wanted to find a religious leader for their hopes, and the Catholic Church of western Europe united behind the symbolic center of Rome and its popes. Charlemagne fed this desire when, in 800 CE, he went out of his way to celebrate Christmas Day by visiting the shrine of Saint Peter at Rome. There, Pope Leo III acclaimed him as the new "emperor" of the west. A "modern" Rome—inhabited by popes, famous for shrines of the martyrs, and protected by a "modern" Christian monarch from the north—was what Charlemagne's subjects wanted.

VIKINGS AND CHRISTENDOM

Vikings from Scandinavia exposed the weakness of Charlemagne's Christian empire. When al-Rashid's elephant died in 813 CE, the Franks viewed it as an omen of coming disasters. The great beast keeled over when his handlers marched him out to confront a Viking army from Denmark. Charlemagne died the next year. In the next half century, Charlemagne's empire of borderland peoples met its match on the wide border between the European landmass and the Atlantic (see Map 9.9).

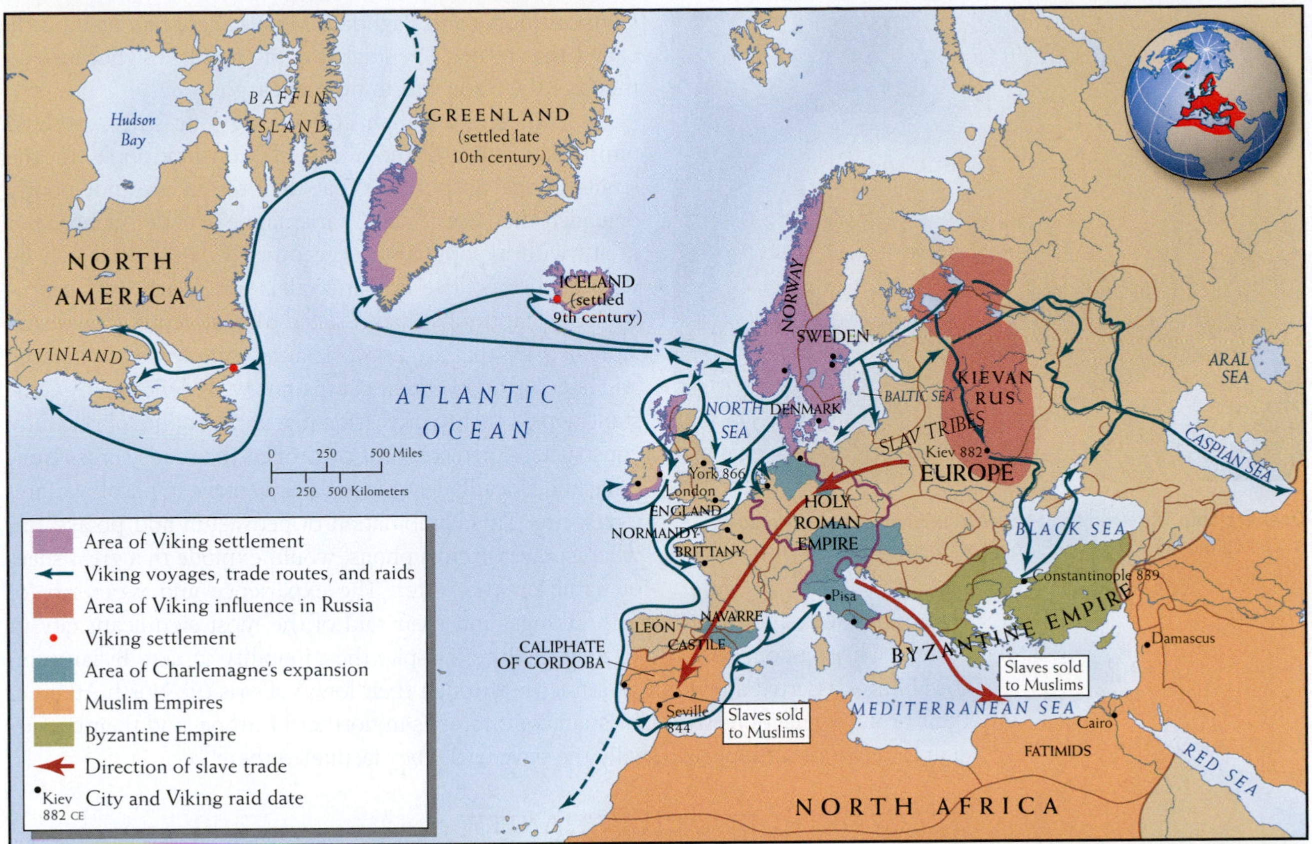

MAP 9.9 | The Age of Vikings and the Slave Trade, 800–1000 CE

Vikings from Scandinavia dramatically altered the history of Christendom.

- In what directions did the Vikings carry out their voyages, trade routes, and raids?
- What were the geographic limits of the Viking explorations in each direction?
- In what direction did the slave trade move, and what role did the Vikings and the Holy Roman emperors play in expanding the slave trade?

The **Vikings**' motives were announced in their name, which derives from the Old Norse *vik*, "to be on the warpath." The Vikings sought to loot the now-wealthy Franks and replace them as the dominant warrior class of northern Europe. They succeeded in their plundering and enslaving because of a deadly technological advantage: ships of unparalleled sophistication. Light and agile, Viking ships traveled far up the rivers of northern Europe and could even be carried overland from one river system to another. Under sail, the same boats could tackle open water and cross the North Atlantic. In the ninth century, the Vikings set their ships on both courses. They sacked the great monasteries along the coasts of Ireland and Britain and overlooking the Rhine and Seine rivers. At the same time, Norwegian adventurers colonized the uninhabited island of Iceland, and then Greenland. By 982 CE, they had even reached continental North America and established a settlement at L'Anse aux Meadows on the Labrador coast.

More long-lasting than their settlements in North America was the Viking incursion into eastern Europe. The Vikings sailed east along the Baltic and then turned south, edging up the rivers that crossed the watershed of central Russia. Here the Dnieper, the Don, and the Volga rivers flow south into the Black Sea and the Caspian. Consequently, the Vikings created an avenue of commerce that linked Scandinavia and the Baltic directly to

Oseberg Ship The Viking ship was a triumph of design. It could be rowed up the great rivers of Europe, or its sails could take it across the Atlantic.

Constantinople and Baghdad. Muslim geographers bluntly called this route "The Highway of the Slaves" because so much of the trade was in human cargo.

In 860 CE, more than 200 Viking long ships gathered ominously beneath the walls of Constantinople in the straits of the Bosporus. What they found was not poorly defended monasteries or Charlemagne's rustic Aachen, but a city with a population exceeding 100,000 protected by well-engineered late-Roman walls. For nearly two centuries, Constantinople had resisted almost yearly campaigns launched by the successive Islamic empires of Damascus and later Baghdad. These campaigns were deflected by Constantinople's highly professional generals, a line of skillfully constructed fortresses that controlled the roads across Anatolia, and a deadly technological advantage in naval warfare: Greek fire. This combination of petroleum and potassium, when sprayed from siphons, would explode in a great sheet of flame on the water. The experience and weaponry of Byzantium were too much for the Vikings, and their raid of the most significant city in eastern Christendom was a spectacular failure. Despite their inability to take Byzantium, the Vikings asserted an enduring influence through their forays across the North Atlantic, their brutal interactions with Christian communities in northern Europe, and their expansion into eastern Europe, especially the slave trade they facilitated there.

GREEK ORTHODOX CHRISTIANITY

Outlasting so many military emergencies bolstered the morale of the eastern Christians and led to a flowering of Christianity in this region. Not just Constantinople but Justinian's Hagia Sophia—its heart—had survived significant threats. That great building and the solemn Greek divine liturgy that reverberated within its domed spaces symbolized the branch of Christian belief that dominated in the east: **Greek Orthodoxy**. Greek Orthodox theology held that Jesus became human, less to atone for humanity's sins (as emphasized in Roman Catholicism) and more to facilitate *theosis* (a transformation of humans into divine beings). This was a truly distinct message from that which prevailed in the Roman Catholicism of the west.

In the tenth century CE, as Charlemagne's empire collapsed in western Europe, large areas of eastern Europe became Greek Orthodox, not Roman Catholic. In addition, Greek Christianity gained a spiritual empire in Southwest Asia. The conversion of Russian peoples, Balkan Slavs, and Arab peoples to Greek Orthodox Christianity was a complex process. It reflected a deep admiration for Constantinople on the part of Russians, Bulgarians, Arabs, and Slav princes. It was an admiration as intense as that of any western Catholic for the Roman popes.

By the year 1000 CE, then, there were two Christianities: the new and confident "borderland" Roman Catholicism of western Europe, and an ancient Greek Orthodoxy. Western Roman Catholics believed that their church was destined to expand everywhere. Greek Orthodox Christians were less euphoric but believed that their church would forever survive the regular ravages of invasion. This was a significant difference in attitude; Greek Orthodox Christians considered the Franks barbarous and grasping, and western Roman Catholics contemptuously called the eastern Christians "Greeks" and condemned them for "Byzantine" cunning.

Thus, like Islam, the Christian world was divided, with differences in heritage, theology, customs, and levels of civilization. At that time, the Orthodox world was considerably more ancient and more cultured than the world of the Catholic west. And each dealt with Islam differently. At Constantinople, eastern Christianity held off Muslim forces that constantly threatened the great city and its Christian hinterlands. In the west, by contrast, Muslim expansionism reached all the way to the Iberian Peninsula. Western Christendom, led by the Roman papacy, set about spreading Christianity to pagan tribes in the north, and it began to contemplate retaking lands from the Muslims. Yet in spite of their deep political, ethnic, and theological differences, the two regions of Christianity conducted a brisk trade in commodities and ideas.

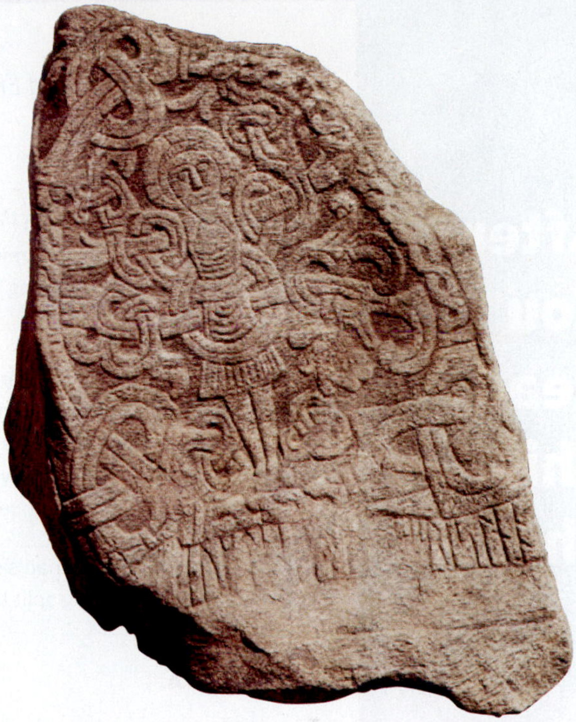

Jelling Stone Carved on the side of this great stone, Christ appears to be almost swallowed up in an intricate pattern of lines. For the Vikings, complicated interweaving like serpents or twisted gold jewelry was a sign of majesty: hence, in this, the first Christian monument in Denmark, Christ is part of an ancient pattern of carving, which brought good luck and victory to the king.

Conclusion

Despite the intermixing of peoples, ideas, and goods across Afro-Eurasia, new political and cultural boundaries were developing that would split this landmass in ways previously unimaginable. The most important dividing force was religion, as Islam challenged and slowed the spread of Christianity and as Buddhism challenged the ruling elite of Tang China. As a consequence, Afro-Eurasia's major cultural zones began to compete in terms of religious and cultural doctrines. The Islamic Abbasid Empire pushed back the borders of the Tang Empire. But the conflict grew particularly intense between the Islamic and Christian worlds, where the clash involved faith as well as frontiers.

The Tang Empire revived Confucianism, insisting on its political and moral primacy as the foundation of a new imperial order, and it embraced the classical written language as another unifying element. By doing so the Tang counteracted universalizing foreign religions—notably Buddhism but also Islam—spreading into the Chinese state. The same adaptive strategies influenced new systems on the Korean peninsula and in Japan.

In some circumstances, faith followed empire and relied on rulers' support or tolerance to spread the word. This was the case especially in East Asia. At the opposite extreme, empire followed faith—as in the case of Islam, whose believers endeavored to spread their empire in every direction. The Islamic empire and its successors represented a new force: expanding political power backed by one God whose instructions were to spread his message. In the worlds of Christianity, a common faith absorbed elements of a common culture (shared books, a language for the learned classes). But in the west, political rulers never overcame inhabitants' intense allegiance to local authority.

While universalizing religions expanded and common cultures grew, debate raged within each religion over foundational principles. In spite of the diffusion of basic texts in "official" languages, regional variations of Christianity, Islam, and Buddhism proliferated as each belief system spread. The period from 600 to 1000 CE demonstrated that religion, reinforced by prosperity and imperial resources, could bring peoples together in unprecedented ways. But it could also, as the next chapter will illustrate, drive them apart in bloody confrontations.

After You Read This Chapter

Go to INQUIZITIVE to see what you've learned—and learn what you've missed—with personalized feedback along the way.

TRACING THE GLOBAL STORYLINES

FOCUS ON: *Faith and Empire*

THE ISLAMIC EMPIRE

- Warriors from the Arabian Peninsula defeat Byzantine and Sasanian armies and establish an Islamic empire stretching from Morocco to South Asia.
- The Abbasid state takes over from the Umayyads, crystallizes the main Islamic institutions of the caliphate and Islamic law, and promotes cultural achievements in religion, philosophy, and science.
- Disputes over Muhammad's succession lead to a deep and enduring split between Sunnis and Shiites.

TANG CHINA

- The Tang dynasty dominates East Asia and exerts a strong influence on Korea and Japan.
- Tang rulers balance Confucian and Daoist ideals with Buddhist thought and practice.
- A common written language and shared philosophy, rather than a universalizing religion, integrate the Chinese state.

CHRISTIAN EUROPE

- Monks, nuns, and Rome-based popes spread Christianity throughout western Europe.
- Constantinople-based Greek Orthodoxy survives the spread of Islam.

CHRONOLOGY

THE ISLAMIC WORLD

- Life of Muhammad 570–632 CE
- Umayyad caliphate 661–750 CE

EAST ASIA

- Prince Shotoku initiates reforms in Japan 574–622 CE
- Tang dynasty in China 618–906 CE
- Silla unify Korean state 668–935 CE

EUROPE

- Arab armies conquer much of Byzantine Empire but the empire survives 632–661 CE

600 CE

700 CE

THINKING ABOUT GLOBAL CONNECTIONS

- ***Thinking about Crossing Borders and Faith & Empire*** As Islam spread outside its initial Arabian context, the faith underwent a range of developments. As Christianity and Buddhism continued to spread, these traditions underwent changes as well. Compare the shifts that took place within Islam as it expanded (600–1000 CE) with those within Buddhism and Christianity, not only in their earlier periods (see Chapter 8) but also during the period from 600 to 1000 CE.

- ***Thinking about Changing Power Relationships and Faith & Empire*** As each of the empires discussed in this chapter matured, divisions developed within the faiths that initially had helped to bring unity to their respective regions. In the Abbasid world, a split developed between Sunni and Shiite Muslims. In Tang China, Buddhism and Confucianism vied for political influence. Christendom divided into the Roman Catholic west and the Greek Orthodox east. What was the exact nature of each religious disagreement? How do these divisions compare in terms of the root of the internal rifts and their impact in the political realm?

- ***Thinking about* Worlds Together, Worlds Apart** The empires described in this chapter reached across wide swaths of territory and interacted with vibrant societies on their margins. The peoples of Europe struggled with the onslaught of the fierce Vikings. The peoples of Tang China interacted with neighboring Korea and Japan. How does the interaction of Europe and the Vikings compare with the relations of the Tang and the external influences that they experienced? To what extent did the Abbasids contend with similar exchanges?

STUDY QUESTIONS

1. Describe the origins and basic beliefs of Islam, including Muhammad, the Quran, and the **five pillars of Islam.** To what extent does this tradition fit the model for a universalizing religion (as described in Chapter 8)?
2. Trace the process, including jihad, by which Islam expanded from a new, localized religious tradition on the Arabian Peninsula to a dominant political power in western Afro-Eurasia. How did that expansion require a balancing act between political powers (such as the **caliphate** and religious authority (such as the *ulama* and ***sharia*** law)?
3. Although the Abbasid dynasty brought a great degree of integration across western Afro-Eurasia, what were some of the regional distinctions (in Spain, central Eurasia, and Africa) as well as internal divisions (such as between **Sunnis** and **Shiites**)?
4. How did the Tang Dynasty establish its control over East Asia? What role did the army, **civil service examinations**, and **eunuchs** play in Tang political organization?
5. How did the Tang interact with foreign ideas (including Zoroastrianism, Christianity, and Buddhism) and influence other polities (as in Korea and Japan)?
6. Identify some of the distinctive features of Christendom in western, northern, and eastern Europe. Compare the **Roman Catholic Church** and **Greek Orthodoxy.**
7. Explain the role of **monasticism** within Christian Europe. How does that compare with the role of monasticism in Tang China?
8. Analyze the impact of the **Vikings** in this period of world history, both in Europe and beyond.

Abbasid caliphate 750–1250 CE

Fatimid Shiite regime founded in Egypt 969 CE

Catholic Church based in Rome begins converting much of northern Europe into Christian communities 8th century CE

Charlemagne unites much of western Europe into a short-lived Christian kingdom 768–814 CE

Vikings raid much of Europe and establish strong commercial links across eastern Europe 9th and 10th centuries CE

800 CE | **900 CE** | **1000 CE**

Going to the Source

Thinking about Women

Despite comprising half the world's population, women are often omitted from historical narratives. Thinking about politics or economics, it is easy to see why, as women historically had very limited economic power and were restricted from holding office in most societies. Even so, women found ways to express themselves, and they prompted men to contemplate the differences between the sexes. The documents in this section all consider women—the ways in which they were seen by men, as well as the ways in which they were able to carve out places for themselves within particular societies. The documents refer to religion, as well as to the political and social realities with which women had to cope during the seventh to ninth centuries.

PRIMARY SOURCE 9.1

Surah 4, An-Nisa' ("On Women"), from the Quran (seventh century CE)

As the Abbasids extended their control from Southwest Asia across North Africa and into Spain, Islamic ideas about women moved with them. Surah 4 of the Quran ("On Women") outlines rules about marriage, inheritance, and the treatment of orphans, among other family-oriented topics. Recorded in the seventh century CE, the Quran, along with the *hadith* (the sayings of Muhammad), was the basis for the *sharia, or Islamic law,* regulating community matters within the Islamic world.

1. O mankind! Be careful of your duty to your Lord who created you from a single soul and from it created its mate and from two has spread abroad a multitude of men and women. Be careful of your duty toward God in whom you claim (your rights) of one another . . . God has been a watcher over you. . . .

3. [M]arry of the women, who seem good to you, two or three or four; and if you fear that you cannot do justice (to so many) then one (only) or (the captives) that your right hands possess. . . .

4. And give to the women (whom you marry) free gift of their marriage portions; but if they of their own accord remit to you any part of it, then you are welcome to absorb it (in your wealth).

23. Forbidden to you are your mothers, and your daughters, and your sisters, and your father's sisters, and your mother's sisters, and your brother's daughters and your sister's daughters, and your foster-mothers, and your foster-sisters, and your mothers-in-law, and your step-daughters who are under your protection (born) of your women to whom you have gone in. . . .

25. And whoever is not able to afford to marry free, believing women, let them marry from the believing slave girls whom your right hands possess. . . . This is for him among you who fears to commit sin. But to have patience would be better for you. God is forgiving, merciful. . . .

34. Men are in charge of women, because God has made the one of them to excel the other, and because they spend of their property (for the support of women). So good women are the obedient, guarding in secret what God has guarded. As for those from whom you fear rebellion, admonish them and banish them to beds apart, and scourge them. Then if they obey you, do not seek a way against them. God is ever high exalted, great.

1. **According to this passage from the Quran, how were women to be treated and why?**
2. **To whom is this document addressed?**

PRIMARY SOURCE 9.2

Law of Adamnan *(c. 700 CE), Adamnan*

The *Law of Adamnan*, a Christian text, describes how lay leaders and the Christian clergy had to address the brutality of tribal warfare as Christianity expanded into Ireland. In response to that brutality and to protect noncombatants, such as women, children, and the clergy, a monk named Adamnan created the *Cáin Adamnáin* (Law of Adamnan) around 700 CE. This passage describes how Adamnan, inspired by his mother and an angel, developed a law to protect noncombatants, which was then signed by kings, nobles, and religious authorities.

33. After fourteen years Adamnan obtained this Law of God, and this is the cause. On Pentecost eve a holy angel of the Lord came to him, and again at Pentecost after a year, and seized a staff, and struck his side and said to him: "Go forth into Ireland, and make a law in it that women be not in any manner killed by men, through slaughter or any other death, either by poison, or in water, or in fire, or by any other beast, or in a pit, or by dogs, but that they shall die in their lawful bed. Thou shalt establish a law in Ireland and Britain for the sake of the mother of each one, because a mother has borne each one, and for the sake of Mary mother of Jesus Christ, through whom all are. . . . For whoever slays a woman shall be condemned to a twofold punishment, that is, his right hand and his left foot shall be cut off before death, and then he shall die, and his kindred shall pay seven full *cumals*, and one-seventh part of the penance. If, instead of life and amputation, a fine has been imposed, the penance is fourteen years, and fourteen *cumals* shall be paid. But if a host has done it, every fifth man up to three hundred shall be condemned to that punishment; if few, they shall be divided into three parts. The first part of them shall be put to death by lot, hand and foot having been first cut off; the second part shall pay fourteen full *cumals*; the third shall be cast into exile beyond the sea, under the rule of a hard regimen; for the sin is great when any slays the mother and sister of Christ's mother and the mother of Christ, and her who carries a spindle and who clothes every one. . . .

34. The enactment of this Law of Adamnan is a perpetual law on behalf of clerics and women and innocent children until they are capable of slaying a man, and until they take their place in the tribe, and their (first) expedition is known.

1. **Why are those who kill women subject to the punishments described in this passage?**
2. **How might you explain the disparate treatment of men and women in this law?**

PRIMARY SOURCE 9.3

The Buddhist Grotto at Lung-men (late seventh century CE)

This large statue of the Buddha is believed to have been carved in the likeness of Empress Wu Zetian, who was China's only female ruler. During her reign, China expanded its territory greatly, moving north and west from its capital at Xian. This Buddha is located near Luo-yang, which from time to time served as the Chinese capital.

1. **Why might the artists have made the Buddha's face resemble the Empress?**
2. **Why might this image have been carved in a grotto near an area that had been the capital of earlier Chinese dynasties?**

PRIMARY SOURCE 9.4

Analects for Women *(800 CE), Song Ruoxin and Song Ruozhao*

Early Chinese thinkers such as Confucius had little to say about the expectations for women in society. In the late eighth century CE, two young women, the sisters Song Ruoxin and Song Ruozhao, who lived in the Tang emperor's court, composed their *Analects for Women*. The sisters were the daughters of a high-ranking court official. Song Ruozhao later served as the instructor of the royal princesses. This text adapted Confucian thought into a set of advice for women living around 800 CE.

Book One: On Deportment

The first thing for any woman to learn is the principle of deportment: that of purity and chastity. If you are pure, then chastity will follow; if you are chaste, then you will be honored. . . . Indoors or out, men and women should be in separate groups. . . . Hide your face when watching something. When going outside you must cover yourself.

Book Eleven: On Conciliation and Yielding

The rules for managing a household for a wife are to prize harmony and filial piety above all else. When your mother-in-law rebukes you, don't feel hurt. When your father-in-law has any criticism, listen to it quietly. In the upper rooms, and in the lower chambers, with nephews and nieces, you should behave harmoniously. Whether [disagreements are] right or wrong, don't get involved. [Whether an issue involves] good or bad, don't argue. Shameful family matters should never be exposed to the public. Be as good as you can in etiquette to neighbors both to the east and west. Greet them as they come and go, and behave cordially to them; [offer] a cup of tea or water, exchange pleasantries joyfully; say only what needs to be said; do whatever needs to be done. Idle talk of right or wrong should not enter your door. Don't learn from those stupid women who gossip in vile language without knowing the truth of the matter, thus offending and insulting the venerable elders. I venture to advise women to look to the past and to think ahead.

Book Twelve: On Preserving Chastity

. . . The bonds of the first marriage weigh more than a thousand pieces of gold. If there occurs the misfortune of the husband dying at a young age, wear mourning clothes for three years, and remain firm in your will to preserve your chastity. Protect your family and manage your property. Clean and sweep your husband's tomb. In life or in death, it is one life shared.

This essay "Book of Analects" discusses all topics exhaustively. Women from now on should follow this, day after day and month after month, remembering it always, taking unquestioned guidance from it. If you persist in this, you will enjoy boundless happiness

1. **What are Song Ruoxin and Song Ruozhao trying to convey in these comments on women's behavior?**
2. **Compare Song Ruoxin and Song Ruozhao's prescriptions for the roles of women with the descriptions in Primary Sources 9.1 and 9.2.**

PRIMARY SOURCE 9.5

Ecclesiastical History of England *(eighth century), Bede*

The English monk Bede resided in the North of England in the late seventh and early eighth centuries. His most famous work, the *Ecclesiastical History*, tells the story of Christianity in England. In this passage he writes about Hilda of Whitby, who founded a monastery and later became a saint. We know very little about Hilda; in fact, almost everything we know comes from Bede's account of her in this document—and he was born only a few years before she died.

In . . . the year of our Lord 680, the most religious handmaid of Christ, Hilda, abbess of the monastery that is called Streanaeshalch . . . after having done many heavenly deeds on earth, passed thence to receive the rewards of the heavenly life. . . . Her life falls into two equal parts, for the first thirty-three years of it she spent living most nobly in the secular habit; and still more nobly dedicated the remaining half to the Lord in the monastic life. For she was nobly born, being the daughter of Hereric, nephew to King Edwin, and with that king she also received the faith and mysteries of Christ, at the preaching of Paulinus, of blessed memory, the first bishop of the Northumbrians, and preserved the same undefiled till she attained to the vision of our Lord in Heaven.

When she had resolved to quit the secular habit, and to serve Him alone, she withdrew into the province of the East Angles, for she was allied to the king there; being desirous to cross over thence into Gaul, forsaking her native country and all that she had, and so to live a stranger for our Lord's sake in the monastery of Cale, that she might the better attain to the eternal country in heaven. . . .

After this she was made abbess in the monastery called Heruteu, which monastery had been founded, not long before, by the pious handmaid of Christ, Heiu, who is said to have been the first woman in the province of the Northumbrians who took upon her the vows and habit of a nun, being consecrated by Bishop Aidan; but she, soon after she had founded that monastery, retired to the city of Calcaria, which is called Kaelcacaestir by the English, and there fixed her dwelling. Hilda, the handmaid of Christ, being set over that monastery, began immediately to order it in all things under a rule of life, according as she had been instructed by learned men; for Bishop Aidan, and others of the religious that knew her, frequently visited her and loved her heartily, and diligently instructed her, because of her innate wisdom and love of the service of God.

When she had for some years governed this monastery, wholly intent upon establishing a rule of life, it happened that she also undertook either to build or to set in order a monastery in the place called Streanaeshalch, and this work which was laid upon her she industriously performed; for she put this monastery under the same rule of monastic life as the former; and taught there the strict observance of justice, piety, chastity, and other virtues, and particularly of peace and charity; so that, after the example of the primitive Church, no one there was rich, and none poor, for they had all things common, and none had any private property. Her prudence was so great, that not only meaner men in their need, but sometimes even kings and princes, sought and received her counsel; she obliged those who were under her direction to give so much time to reading of the Holy Scriptures, and to exercise themselves so much in works of justice, that many might readily be found there fit for the priesthood.

1. **Why do you think Hilda joined the monastery and how did she come to be in charge of it?**
2. **Why do you think that powerful men would choose to follow Hilda's direction?**

PRIMARY SOURCE 9.6

Visiting the Southern Tower of Chong-zhen Temple: Seeing Where the Recent Graduates of the Examination have written their Names *(mid-ninth century CE), Yu Xuan-ji*

Yu Xuan-ji was one of the few women poets of the Tang dynasty in China. She was a concubine who later became a Daoist nun. She was executed in her twenties after being accused of murdering her maid. In this poem, she learns about a party given to honor the men who passed the famed examinations that were required to become a government official. Her poem provides an unusually frank social commentary on the limitations of women.

Cloud-covered hilltops fill my eyes,
    I revel in springtime light,
Here clearly ranged are the silver hooks*
    that grew at their fingertips,
I have bitter regret that skirts of lace
    hide the lines of my poems,
and lifting my head in vain I covet
    the publicly posted name.

* Fine calligraphy

1. **What does Yu Xuanji regret and why? What does her regret say about the place of women in Tang China?**
2. **Compare Yu Xuanji's feelings about her position with of the sentiments expressed by the women in Primary Source 9.4.**

Questions for Analysis

Comparison

1. How would you characterize the roles and positions of women in these societies?

Argumentation

2. Why do you think religion figured so prominently in these women's lives?

Interpretation

3. Why do you think many of these documents are framed as rules? Do they apply more to women or to men? Explain your answer.

Long Essay Question

Argumentation

Based on these documents and your reading of the chapter, analyze the role of women in these societies and explain which society you think would have been most comfortable for women.

Before You Read This Chapter

GLOBAL STORYLINES

- Advances in maritime technology lead to increased sea trade, transforming coastal cities into global trading hubs and elevating Afro-Eurasian trade to unprecedented levels.
- Intensified trade and religious integration shape four major cultural "spheres": the Islamic world, India, China, and Europe.
- Sub-Saharan Africa is drawn into Eurasian exchange resulting in a true Afro-Eurasia–wide network, while the Americas experience more limited political, economic, and cultural integration.
- The Mongol Empire integrates many of the world's major cultural spheres.

CORE OBJECTIVES

- **IDENTIFY** technological advances of this period, especiall in ship design and navigation, and **EXPLAIN** how they facilitated the expansion of Afro-Eurasian trade.
- **DESCRIBE** the varied social and political forces that shape the Islamic world, India, China, and Europe, and **EVALUAT** the degree to which these forces integrated cultures and geographic areas.
- **COMPARE** both the internal integration and external interactions of sub-Saharan Africa with those of the Americas.
- **ASSESS** the impacts that the Mongol Empire had on Afro-Eurasian peoples and places.

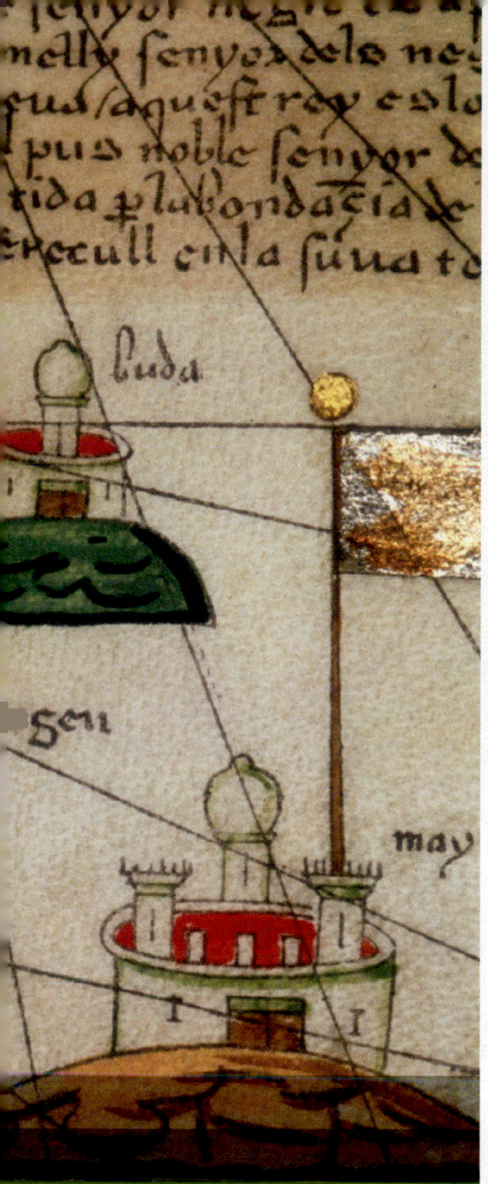

CHAPTER

10

Becoming "The World"

1000–1300 CE

KEY TERMS

Cahokia p. 386
Chimú Empire p. 384
Delhi Sultanate p. 370
entrepôts p. 363
flying cash p. 372
jizya p. 365
Mali p. 382
manorialism p. 377
Sufism p. 367
Toltecs p. 386

In the late 1270s two Christian monks, Bar Sāwmā and Markōs, voyaged into the heart of the Islamic world. They were not Europeans. They were Uighurs, a Turkish people of central Asia, many of whom had converted to Christianity centuries earlier. The monks hoped to make pilgrimage to Jerusalem in order to visit the tombs of the martyrs.

On their journey westward, Bar Sāwmā and Markōs traveled a world bound together by economic and cultural exchange. The two monks lingered at the magnificent trading hub of Kashgar in what is now western China, where caravan routes converged in a market for jade, exotic spices, and precious silks. Unable to continue on to Jerusalem due to the route's dangers (including murderous robbers), at Baghdad the monks parted ways. Bar Sāwmā was appointed an ambassador by the Buddhist Mongol il-Khan of Persia to drum up support among European leaders for an attack on Jerusalem to wrest it from Muslim control. He visited Constantinople (where the Byzantine emperor gave him gold and silver), Rome (where he met with the pope at the shrine of Saint Peter), and Paris (where he saw that city's vibrant university). In the end, neither monk ever reached Jerusalem or returned to China. Bar Sāwmā ended his days in Baghdad and Markōs became patriarch of the Nestorian branch of Christianity, centered in modern-day Iran.

Yet their voyages exemplified the crisscrossing of people, money, goods, and ideas along the trade routes and sea-lanes that connected the world's regions.

Three related themes dominate the period from 1000 to 1300 CE. First, trade along sea-based routes increased and coastal trading cities began to expand dramatically. Second, greater trade and religious integration generated the world's four major cultural "spheres," whose inhabitants were linked by shared institutions and beliefs: the Islamic world, India, China, and Europe. During this period sub-Saharan Africa and the Americas also thrived; however, they remained more fragmented, experiencing more limited political and economic integration. Third, the Mongol Empire, stretching from China to Persia and as far as eastern Europe, ruled over huge swaths of land in many of the world's major cultural spheres. Each of these three themes contributes to an understanding of how Afro-Eurasia became a "world" unified through trade, migration, and even religious conflict.

COMPARISON

IDENTIFY technological advances of this period, especially in ship design and navigation, and **EXPLAIN** how they facilitated the expansion of Afro-Eurasian trade.

Development of Maritime Trade

By the tenth century CE, sea routes were becoming more important than land networks for long-distance trade. Improved navigational aids, better mapmaking, refinements in shipbuilding, and new political support for shipping made seaborne trade easier and slashed its cost. These developments also fostered the growth of maritime commercial hubs (called anchorages), which further facilitated the expansion of maritime trade.

A new navigational instrument spurred this boom: the magnetic needle compass. This Chinese invention initially identified promising locations for houses and tombs, but eleventh-century sailors from Guangzhou (Canton) used it to find their way on the high seas. The use of this device eventually spread among navigators. Not only did the compass allow sailing under cloudy skies, but it also improved mapmaking.

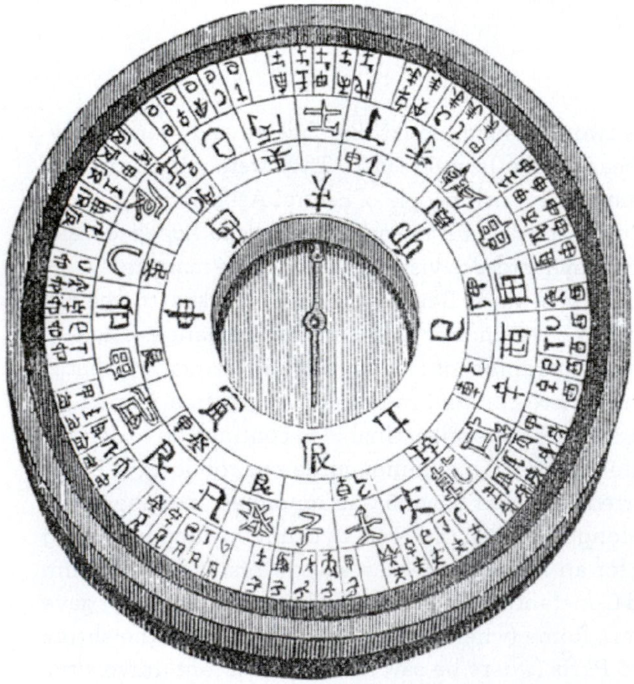

Antique Chinese Compass Chinese sailors from Canton started to use magnetic needle compasses in the eleventh century. By the thirteenth century, magnetic needle compasses were widely used on ships in the Indian Ocean and were starting to appear in the Mediterranean.

An array of new ship types—dhows, junks, and cogs—allowed for more impressive mastery of the seas. Maximizing monsoon trade winds on the Arabian Sea and the wider Indian Ocean were dhows, ships with triangular sails, called lateens. Sailing the South China seas were junks, large, flat-bottomed ships with internal sealed bulkheads, stern-mounted rudders, as many as four decks, six masts with a dozen sails, and the space to carry as many as 500 men. And, in the Atlantic, cogs, with their single mast and square sail, linked Genoa to locations as distant as the Azores and Iceland. The numbers testify to the power of the maritime revolution: while a porter could carry about 10 pounds over long distances, and animal-drawn wagons could move 100 pounds of goods over small distances, the Arab dhows could transport up to 5 tons of cargo, Atlantic cogs as much as 200 tons, and Chinese junks more than 500 tons.

Maritime traders enjoyed the protection of political authorities such as the Song rulers in China, who maintained a standing navy that protected traders and lighthouses that guided trading fleets in and out of harbors. The Fatimid

Dhow This modern dhow in the harbor of Zanzibar displays the characteristic triangular sail. The sail can make good use of the trade monsoon and thus has guided dhows on the Arabian Sea since ancient times.

caliphate in Egypt profited from maritime trade and defended merchant fleets from pirates, using armed convoys of ships to escort commercial fleets and regulate the ocean traffic. The system of protection soon spread to North Africa and southern Spain.

Long-distance trade spawned the growth of commercial cities. These cosmopolitan **entrepôts** where ships could drop anchor served as transshipment centers, located between borders or in ports, where traders exchanged commodities and replenished supplies. Beginning in the late tenth century CE, several regional centers became major anchorages of the maritime trade: in the west, the Egyptian port city of Alexandria on the Mediterranean (and Cairo, just up the Nile); near the tip of the Indian subcontinent, the port of Quilon (now Kollam); in the Malaysian Archipelago, the city of Melaka; and in the east, the Chinese city of Quanzhou (see Map 10.1) These hubs thrived under the political stability of powerful rulers who recognized that trade would generate wealth for their regimes.

Cairo and Alexandria were the Mediterranean's main maritime commercial centers. Cairo was home to numerous Muslim and Jewish trading firms, and Alexandria was their lookout post on the Mediterranean. The Islamic legal system prevalent in Egypt promoted a favorable business environment. Through Alexandria, Europeans acquired silks from China, especially the coveted *zaytuni* (satin) fabric from Quanzhou. But the Egyptian anchorage handled much more: from the Mediterranean, olive oil, glassware, flax, corals, and metals; from India, gemstones and aromatic perfumes; and from elsewhere, minerals and chemicals for dyeing or tanning, and raw materials such as timber and bamboo. Paper and books (including hand-copied Bibles, Talmuds, and Qurans) traveled along this network as well.

In south India during the tenth century CE, the Chola dynasty supported the port of Quilon, which was the nerve center of maritime trade between China and the Red Sea and the Mediterranean. Trade through Quilon continued to flourish long after the Chola golden age passed away. Personal relationships were key to trade at this anchorage as elsewhere; for instance, when striking a deal with a local merchant, a Chinese trader would mention his Indian neighbor in Quanzhou and that family's residence in Quilon. At Quilon, dhows arrived laden not only with goods from the Red Sea and Africa but

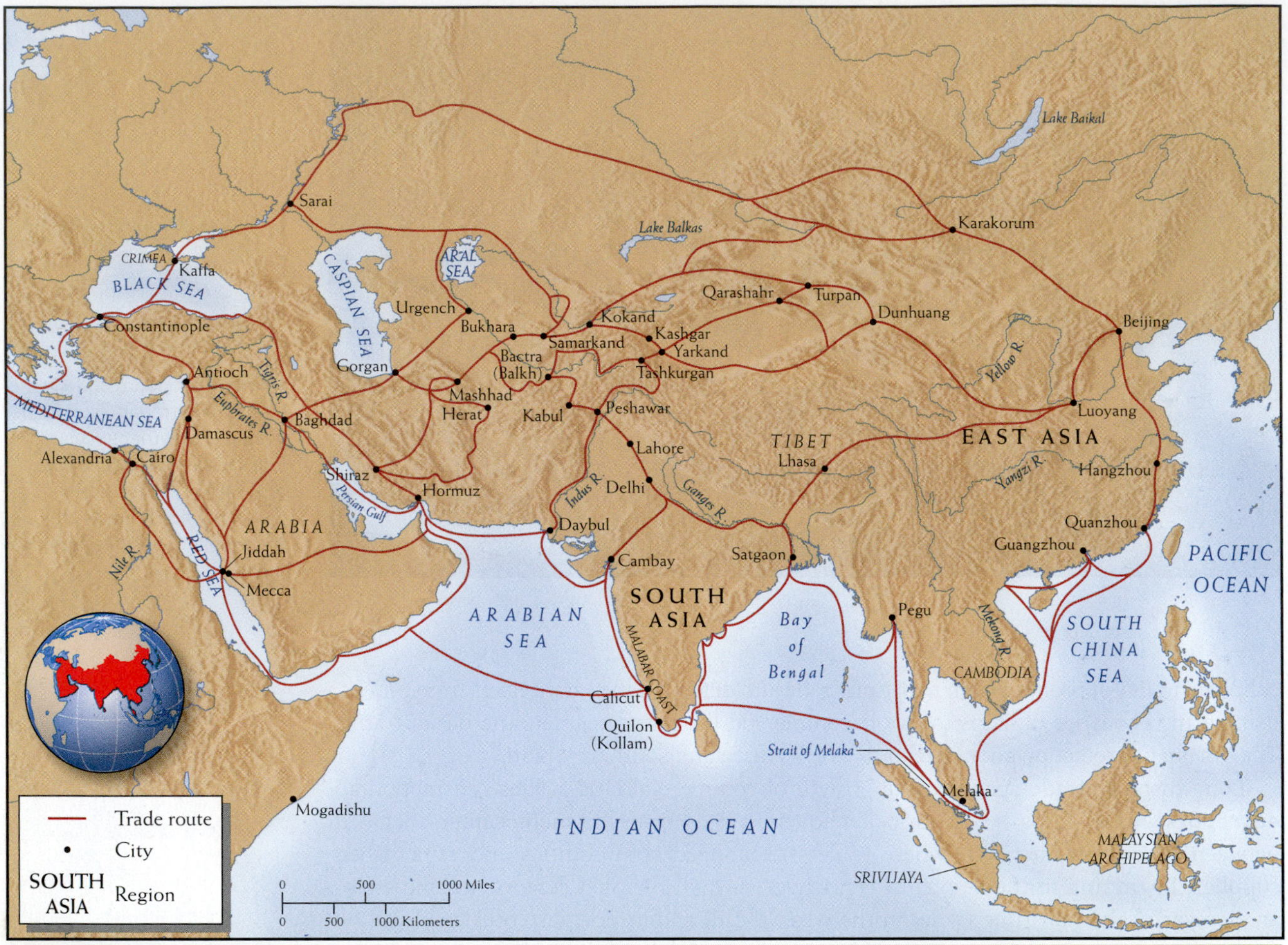

MAP 10.1 | Afro-Eurasian Trade, 1000–1300

During the early second millennium, Afro-Eurasian merchants increasingly turned to the Indian Ocean to transport their goods. Locate the global hubs of Quilon, Alexandria, Cairo, Melaka, and Quanzhou on this map.

- What regions do each of these global hubs represent?
- Based on the map, why would sea travel have been preferable to overland travel?
- According to the text, what revolutions in maritime travel facilitated this development?

also with traders, sojourners, and fugitives. Chinese junks unloaded silks and porcelain, and picked up passengers and commodities for East Asian markets. Muslims, the largest foreign community in Quilon, lived in their own neighborhoods and shipped horses from Arab countries to India and the southeast islands, where kings viewed them as symbols of royalty. There was even trade through Quilon in elephants and cattle from tropical countries, though the most common goods were spices, perfumes, and textiles.

East of Quilon, across the Bay of Bengal, Melaka became a key cosmopolitan entrepôt because of its strategic location and proximity to Malayan tropical produce. Indian, Javanese, and Chinese merchants and sailors spent months in such ports selling their goods, purchasing return cargo, and waiting for the winds to change so they could reach their next destination. During peak season, Southeast Asian ports were crowded with colorfully dressed foreign sailors, local Javanese artisans who produced finely textured batik handicrafts, and traders eager for profit. The traders converged from all over Asia to flood the markets with their merchandise and to search for pungent herbs, aromatic spices, and agrarian staples such as quick-ripening strains of rice to ship out.

In China, the Song government set up offices of seafaring affairs in its three major ports: Quanzhou, Guangzhou (Canton), and a third near present-day Shanghai. In return for a portion of the taxes, these offices registered cargoes, sailors, and traders, while guards kept a keen eye on the traffic. All foreign traders in Song China were guests of the governor, who doubled as the chief of seafaring affairs. Every year, the governor conducted a wind-calling ritual. Traders of every origin—Arabs, Persians, Jews, Indians, and Chinese—witnessed the ceremony, then joined together for a sumptuous banquet. Although most foreign merchants did not reside apart from the rest of the city, they did maintain buildings for religious worship according to their faiths. A mosque from this period still stands on a busy street in Quanzhou. Hindu traders living in Quanzhou worshipped in a Buddhist shrine where statues of Hindu deities stood alongside those of Buddhist gods. Each bustling port teemed with a cosmopolitan mix of peoples, goods, and ideas that flowed through the growing maritime networks thanks to improved ships and better navigational tools.

COMPARISON

DESCRIBE the varied social and political forces that shaped the Islamic world, China, and Europe, and **EVALUATE** the degree to which these forces integrated cultures and geographic areas.

The Islamic World in a Time of Political Fragmentation

While the number of Muslim traders began to increase in commercial hubs from the Mediterranean to the South China Sea, it was not until the ninth and tenth centuries CE that Muslims became a majority within their own Abbasid Empire (see Chapter 9), and even then rulers struggled to unite the diverse Islamic world. From the outset, Muslim rulers and clerics dealt with large non-Muslim populations, even as these groups were converting to Islam. Rulers accorded non-Muslims religious toleration as long as the non-Muslims accepted Islam's political dominion. Jewish, Christian, and Zoroastrian communities within Muslim lands were free to choose their own religious leaders and to settle internal disputes in their own religious courts. They did, however, have to pay a special tax, the ***jizya***, and defer to their rulers. While tolerant, Islam was an expansionist, universalizing faith. Intense proselytizing—especially by Sufi missionaries—carried the sacred word to new frontiers and, in the process, reinforced the spread of Islamic institutions that supported commercial exchange.

Slave Market Slaves were a common commodity in the marketplaces of the Islamic world. Turkish conquests during the years from 1000 to 1300 put many prisoners on the slave market.

POLITICAL DIVISIONS

As the Islamic faith increased its reach across Afro-Eurasia, its political institutions had begun to fragment. From 950 to 1050, it appeared that Shiism would be the vehicle for uniting the Islamic world. The Fatimid Shiites had established their authority over Egypt and much of North Africa (see Chapter 9), and the Abbasid state in Baghdad was controlled by a Shiite family, the Buyids. Each group created

MAP 10.2 | The Islamic World, 900–1200

The Islamic world experienced political disintegration in the first centuries of the second millennium.

- According to the map key, what were the two major types of Muslim states in this period and what were the two major empires?
- What were the sources of instability in this period according to the map?
- As Islam continued to expand in this period, what challenges did it face?

universities, in Cairo and Baghdad respectively, ensuring that leading centers of higher learning were Shiite. But divisions also sapped Shiism, as Sunni Muslims began to challenge Shiite power and establish their own strongholds. In Baghdad, the Shiite Buyid family surrendered to a group of Sunni strongmen in 1055. A century later, the last of the Shiite Fatimid rulers gave way to a new Sunni regime in Egypt (see Map 10.2).

The new strongmen were mainly Turks. Their people had been migrating into the Islamic heartland from the Asian steppes since the eighth century CE, bringing superior military skills and an intense devotion to Sunni Islam. Once established in Baghdad, they founded outposts in Syria and Palestine, and then moved into Anatolia after defeating Byzantine forces in 1071. But this Turkish state also crumbled, as tribesmen quarreled for preeminence.

By the thirteenth century the Islamic heartland had fractured into three regions. In the east (central Asia, Iran, and eastern Iraq), the remnants of the old Abbasid state persevered, with a succession of caliphs claiming to speak for all of Islam yet deferring to their Turkish military commanders. In the core of the Islamic world—Egypt, Syria, and the Arabian Peninsula—where Arabic was the primary language, military men of non-Arab origin held the reins of power. Farther west in North Africa, Arab rulers prevailed, but the influence of Berbers, some from the northern Sahara, was extensive. Islam was a vibrant faith, but its polities were splintered.

THE SPREAD OF SUFISM

Even in the face of this political splintering, Islam's spread was facilitated by a popular form of the religion, highly mystical and communal, called **Sufism.** The term *Sufi* comes from the Arabic word for wool (*suf*), which many of the early mystics wrapped themselves in to mark their penitence. Seeking closer union with God, Sufis performed ecstatic rituals such as repeating over and over again the name of God. In time, groups of devotees gathered to read aloud the Quran and other religious tracts. Sufi mystics' desire to experience God's love found ready expression in poetry. Most admired of Islam's mystical love poets was Jalal al-Din Rumi (1207–1273), spiritual founder of the Mevlevi Sufi order that became famous for the ceremonial dancing of its whirling devotees, known as dervishes.

Although many *ulama* (scholars) despised the Sufis and loathed their seeming lack of theological rigor, the movement spread with astonishing speed and offered a unifying force within Islam. Sufism's emotional content and strong social bonds, sustained in Sufi brotherhoods, added to its appeal for many. Sufi missionaries carried the universalizing faith to India, to Southeast Asia, across the Sahara Desert, and to many other distant locations. It was from within these brotherhoods that Islam became truly a religion for the people. As trade increased and more converts appeared in the Islamic lands, urban and peasant populations came to understand the faith practiced by the political, commercial, and scholarly upper classes even while they remained attached to their Sufi brotherhood ways. Over time, Islam became even more accommodating, embracing Persian literature, Turkish ruling skills, and Arabic-language contributions in law, religion, literature, and science.

WHAT WAS ISLAM?

Buoyed by Arab dhows on the high seas and carried on the backs of camels, following commercial networks, Islam had been transformed from Muhammad's original goal of creating a religion for Arab peoples. By 1300, its influence spanned Afro-Eurasia and reached multitudes of non-Arab converts (see Map 10.3). While Arabic remained the primary language of religious devotion, Persian became the language of Muslim philosophy and art and Turkish the language of law and administration. Islam attracted city dwellers and rural peasants alike, as well as its original audience of desert nomads. As other cities joined Cairo and Baghdad as centers of Islamic learning, Islam's extraordinary universal appeal generated an intense cultural flowering around 1000 CE.

That cultural blossoming in all fields of high learning was marked by diversity in both language and ideas. Representing the new Persian ethnic pride was Abu al-Qasim Firdawsi (920–1020), a devout Muslim who believed in the importance of pre-Islamic Sasanian traditions. In the epic poem *Shah Namah,* or Book of Kings, he celebrated the origins of Persian culture and narrated the history of the Iranian highland peoples from the dawn of time to the Muslim conquest. Indicative of the enduring prominence of the Islamic faith and the Arabic language in thought was the legendary Ibn Rushd (1126–1198), known as Averroës in the western world. Steeped in the writings of Aristotle, Ibn Rushd's belief that faith and reason were compatible even influenced the thinking of the Christian world's leading philosopher and theologian, Thomas Aquinas (1225–1274).

During this period, the Islamic world became one of the four cultural spheres that would play a major role in world history, laying the foundation for what would become

MAP 10.3 | Islamic and Hindu States and the Byzantine Empire, 1200–1300

Islam continued to expand during the thirteenth century.

- Where were Islam's largest and most important gains according to the map?
- What are some of the internal divisions within the Islamic world?
- What other religious communities existed under Islamic rule in this period? Based on the map, what might account for the location where these communities prospered?

known as the Middle East up through the middle of the twentieth century. Islam became the majority religion of most of the inhabitants of Southwest Asia and North Africa, Arabic language-use became widespread, and the Turks began to establish themselves as a dominant force, ultimately creating the Ottoman Empire, which would last into the twentieth century. The Islamic world became integral in transregional trade and the creation and transmission of knowledge.

India as a Cultural Mosaic

With its pivotal location along land- and sea-based trade routes, India became an intersection for the trade, migration, and culture of Afro-Eurasian peoples. With 80 million inhabitants in 1000 CE, it had the second-largest population in the region, not far behind China's 120 million. (See **Analyzing Global Developments: Growth in the World Population to 1340**.) Turks ultimately spilled into India as they had into the Islamic heartlands, bringing their newfound Islamic beliefs. But the Turkish newcomers encountered an ethnic and religious mix of which they were just one part (see Map 10.4).

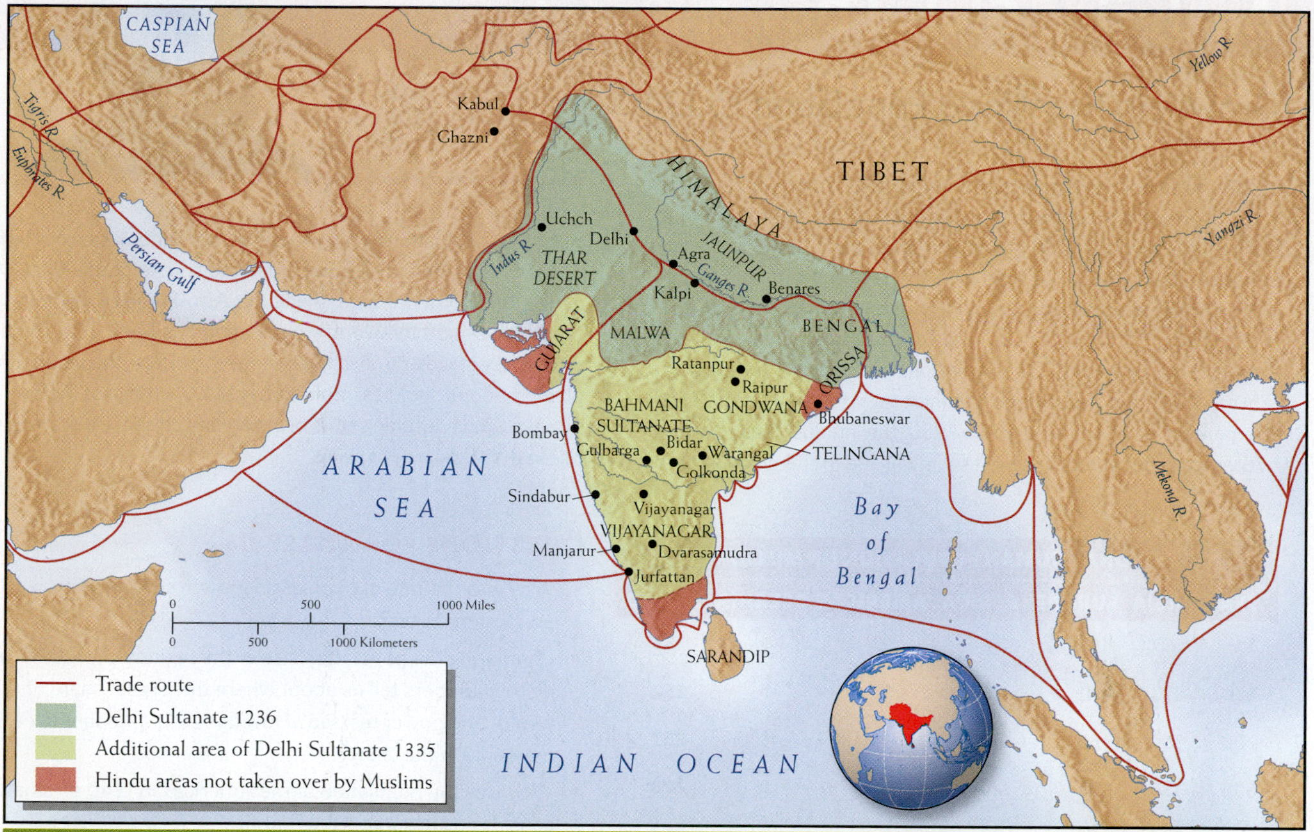

MAP 10.4 | South Asia in 1300

As the fourteenth century began, India was a blend of many cultures. Politically, the Turkish Muslim regime of the Delhi Sultanate dominated the region. Use the map key to identify the areas dominated by the Delhi Sultanate.

- How do you suppose the trade routes helped to spread the Muslims' influence in India?
- Now use the key to find the Hindu areas. Based on your reading, what factors accounted for Hinduism's continued appeal despite the Muslims' political power?

Before the Turks arrived, India was splintered among rival chiefs called *rajas*. These leaders gained support from Brahmans by doling out land grants to them. Since much of the land was uncultivated, the Brahmans first built temples, then converted the indigenous hunter-gatherer peoples to the Hindu traditions, and finally taught the converts how to cultivate the land. In this way, Brahmans simultaneously spread their faith and expanded the agrarian tax base for themselves and the rajas. They also repaid the rajas' support by compiling elaborate genealogies for them and endowing them with lengthy and legitimizing ancestries. In return, the rajas demonstrated that they, too, were well versed in Sanskrit culture, including equestrian skills and courtly etiquette, and were prepared to patronize artists and poets.

When the Turkish warlords began entering India, the rajas had neither the will nor resources to resist them after centuries of fighting off invaders. For example, Mahmud of Ghazna (971–1030) launched many expeditions from the Afghan heartland into northern India and, eager to win status within Islam, made his capital, Ghazni, a center of Islamic learning. Later, in the 1180s, Muhammad Ghuri led another wave of Islamic Turkish invasions from Afghanistan across the Delhi region in northern India. Wars raged between

Analyzing Global Developments

Growth in the World Population to 1340

The world experienced considerable human population growth during the first millennium of the Common Era in spite of occasional downturns, such as in Asia and Europe between 200 and 600 CE that were the result of climate change, movement of peoples, and the decline of the Roman and Han empires. Overall, however, an upward trajectory occurred though it averaged out to a mere .06 percent per year. For the period from 1750 to 1950 that percentage has increased to a little more than 0.5 percent per year, and since 1950 the number has risen to 1.75 percent per year. Even so, as we will see in the next chapter, the major populations in the Afro-Eurasian landmass were terrified by the loss of life that accompanied the spread of the Black Death across this immense area. Since the Afro-Eurasian recovery from the Black Death, the world's population has been on a steady increase, spectacularly so in the twentieth century, the result of more abundant food supplies, more accurate knowledge of the spread of diseases and a resulting control of epidemic diseases, and a general rise in the standards of living.

REGIONAL HUMAN POPULATION (IN MILLIONS)						
YEAR	**ASIA**	**EUROPE**	**AFRICA**	**AMERICAS**	**OCEANIA**	**WORLD**
	97	30	17	8	1	**153**
1 CE	172	41	26	12	1	**252**
200	160	55	30	11	1	**257**
600	136	31	24	16	1	**208**
1000	154	41	39	18	1	**253**
1200	260	64	48	26	2	**400**
1340	240	88	80	32	2	**442**

Source: Massimo Livi-Bacci, *A Concise History of World Population* (2012), p. 25.

QUESTIONS FOR ANALYSIS

- Why was the rate of population growth so limited in premodern times?
- Comparing the population size of the regions in 1340, what do the numbers tell us about where the largest share of wealth and power resided? How does this compare to earlier moments in the chart?
- Why was the population of the Americas in 1340 so small considering its large territorial size?
- How do changes in global population relate to the developments tracked in this chapter: a maritime revolution; a more integrally connected Africa; a thriving Abbasid caliphate; and an expanding Mongol Empire?

the Indus and Ganges rivers until, one by one, all the way to the lower Ganges valley, the fractured kingdoms of the rajas toppled. The Turks introduced their own customs while accepting local social structures, such as the hierarchical *varna* system The Turks constructed grand mosques and built impressive libraries where scholars could toil and share their wisdom with the court.

The most powerful and enduring of the Turkish Muslim regimes of northern India was the **Delhi Sultanate** (1206–1526), whose rulers brought political integration but also strengthened the cultural diversity and tolerance that were already a hallmark of the Indian social order. Sultans recruited local artisans for numerous building projects, and palaces and mosques became displays of Indian architectural tastes adopted by Turkish newcomers. But Islam never fully dominated South Asia because the sultans did not force their subjects to convert. Nor did they display much interest in the flourishing commercial life along the Indian coast. The sultans permitted these areas to develop on their own: Persian Zoroastrian traders settled on the coast around modern-day Mumbai (Bombay) while farther south, Arab traders controlled the Malabar coast. The Delhi Sultanate was a rich and powerful regime that brought political integration but did not enforce cultural homogeneity.

Hindu Temple When Buddhism started to decline in India, Hinduism was on the rise. Numerous Hindu temples were built, many of them adorned with ornate carvings like this small tenth-century temple in Bhubaneshwar, east India.

WHAT WAS INDIA?

During the eleventh, twelfth, and thirteenth centuries India became the most diverse and, in some respects, most tolerant region in Afro-Eurasia. India in this era arose as an impressive but fragile mosaic of cultures, religions, and ethnicities. When the Turks arrived, the local Hindu population, having had much experience with foreign invaders and immigrants, assimilated these intruders as they had done earlier peoples. Before long, the newcomers thought of themselves as Indians who, however, retained their Islamic beliefs and steppe ways. They continued to wear their distinctive trousers and robes and flaunted their horse-riding skills. At the same time, the local population embraced some of their conquerors' ways, donning the tunics and trousers that characterized Central Asian peoples.

Diversity and cultural mixing became most visible in the multiple languages that flourished in India. Although the sultans spoke Turkish languages, they regarded Persian literature as a high cultural achievement and made Persian their courtly and administrative language. Meanwhile, most of their Hindu subjects spoke local languages, adhered to the regulations of the *varna* system of hierarchies, and practiced diverse forms of Hindu worship. The rulers in India did what Muslim rulers in Southwest Asia and the Mediterranean did with Christian and Jewish communities living in their midst: they collected the *jizya* tax and permitted communities to worship as they saw fit and to administer their own communal law. Ultimately, Islam proved in India that it did not have to be an intolerant conquering religion to prosper.

Although Buddhism had been in decline in India for centuries, it, too, became part of the cultural intermixing of these centuries. As Vedic Brahmanism evolved into Hinduism (see Chapter 8), it had absorbed many Buddhist doctrines and practices, such as nonviolence (*ahimsa*) and vegetarianism. The two religions became so similar in India that Hindus simply considered the Buddha to be one of their deities—an incarnation of the great god Vishnu. Many Buddhist moral teachings mixed with and became Hindu stories. Artistic motifs reflected a similar process of adoption and adaptation. Goddesses, some beautiful and others fierce, appeared alongside Buddhas, Vishnus, and Shivas as their consorts.

The Turkish invaders' destruction of major monasteries in the thirteenth century deprived Buddhism of local spiritual leaders. Lacking dynastic support, Buddhists in India were more easily assimilated into the Hindu population or converted to Islam.

Once the initial disruptive effects of the Turkish invasions were absorbed, India remained a highly diverse and tolerant region during this period. Most importantly, India also emerged as one of the four major cultural spheres, enjoying a tremendous level of integration as Turkish-Muslim rulership and their traditions and practices were successfully intermixed with the native Hindu society, leading to a more integrated and peaceful India.

Song China: Insiders versus Outsiders

The preeminent world power in 1000 CE was still China, despite its recent turmoil. In 907 CE the Tang dynasty splintered into regional kingdoms, mostly led by military generals. In 960 CE one of these generals, Zhao Kuangyin, ended the fragmentation, reunified China, and assumed the mandate of heaven for the Song dynasty (960–1279). The following three centuries witnessed many economic and political successes, but northern nomadic tribes kept the Song dynasty from completely securing their reign (see Map 10.5 and Map 10.6). Ultimately, one of those nomadic groups, the Mongols, would bring the Song dynasty to an end; but not before Song influence had fanned out into Southeast Asia, helping to create new identities in the polities that developed there.

ECONOMIC AND POLITICAL DEVELOPMENTS

Chinese merchants, like those from India and the Islamic world, participated in Afro-Eurasia's powerful long-distance trade. Yet China's commercial successes could not have occurred without the country's strong agrarian base—especially its vast wheat, millet, and rice fields, which fed a population that reached 120 million. Crop cultivation benefited from breakthroughs in metalworking that produced stronger iron plows, which Song farmers harnessed to sturdy water buffalo to extend the agricultural frontier.

Manufacturing also flourished. With their piston-driven bellows to force air into furnaces, Song iron production in the eleventh century equaled that of European iron production in the early eighteenth century. In the early tenth century, Chinese alchemists mixed saltpeter with sulfur and charcoal to produce a product that would burn and could be deployed on the battlefield: gunpowder. Song entrepreneurs were soon inventing a remarkable array of incendiary devices that flowed from their mastery of techniques for controlling explosions and high heat. At the same time, artisans were producing increasingly light, durable, and exquisitely beautiful porcelains. Before long, their porcelain was the envy of all Afro-Eurasia (hence the modern term "china" for fine dishes). Also flowing from the artisans' skillful hands were vast amounts of clothing and handicrafts, made from the fibers grown by Song farmers. In effect, the Song Chinese oversaw the world's first manufacturing revolution, producing finished goods on a large scale for consumption far and wide.

Expanding commerce transformed the role of money and its wide circulation. By now the Song government was annually minting nearly 2 million strings of currency, each containing 1,000 copper coins. As the economy grew, the supply of metal currency could not match the demand, which fueled East Asia's desire for gold from East Africa. At the same time, merchant guilds in northwestern Shanxi developed the first letters of exchange, or paper money, which they called **flying cash**. These letters linked northern traders with their colleagues in the south. Before long, printed money became more common than minted coins for trading purposes. Eventually, the Song dynasty began to issue more notes to pay its bills—a practice that ultimately contributed to runaway inflation.

MAP 10.5 | East Asia in 1000

Several states emerged in East Asia between 1000 and 1300, but none were as strong as the Song dynasty in China. Using the key to the map, try to identify the factors that contributed to the Song state's economic dynamism.

- What external factors kept the Song dynasty from completely securing their reign?
- What factors drove the Chinese commercial revolution in this period?

Song emperors built on Tang political institutions by expanding a central bureaucracy of scholar-officials chosen even more extensively through competitive civil service examinations. Zhao Kuangyin, or Emperor Taizu (r. 960–976 CE), himself administered the final test for all who had passed the highest-level palace examination. In subsequent dynasties, the emperor was the nation's premier examiner, symbolically demanding oaths of allegiance from successful candidates. By 1100 these ranks of learned men had accumulated sufficient power to become China's new ruling elite. This expansion of the civil service examination system was crucial to a shift in power from the still significant hereditary aristocracy to a less wealthy but more highly schooled class of scholar officials.

COMPARISON

DESCRIBE the social and political forces that shaped Song China, and **EVALUATE** the degree to which they integrated the cultures of East Asia.

CHINA'S NEIGHBORS: NOMADS, JAPAN, AND SOUTHEAST ASIA

China's prosperity influenced its neighbors and its interactions with them. As Song China flourished, nomads on the outskirts eyed the Chinese successes closely. To the north, nomadic

MAP 10.6 | East Asia in 1200

The Song dynasty regularly dealt with "barbarian" neighbors. What were the major "barbarian" tribes during this period?

- Approximately what percentage of Song China was lost to the Jin in 1126?
- How did the "barbarian" tribes affect the Chinese identity in this period?

societies formed their own dynasties and adopted Chinese institutions. Located within the "greater China," as defined by the Han and Tang dynasties, these non-Chinese nomads sought both to conquer and to copy China proper. Despite their sophisticated weapons, the Song army could not match their enemies on the steppe when the nomads united against them. Steel tips improved the arrows that Song soldiers shot from their crossbows, and flame throwers and "crouching tiger" catapults sent incendiary bombs streaking into their enemies' ranks. But none of these breakthroughs was secret. Warrior neighbors on the steppe mastered the new arts of war more fully than did the Song military. Consequently, China drew on its economic success (and the innovation of paper money) to "buy off" the borderlanders. This short-term solution, however, led to economic instability (particularly inflation) and military weakness, especially as the Song forces were cut off from their supply, via the steppe nomads, of horses for warfare purposes.

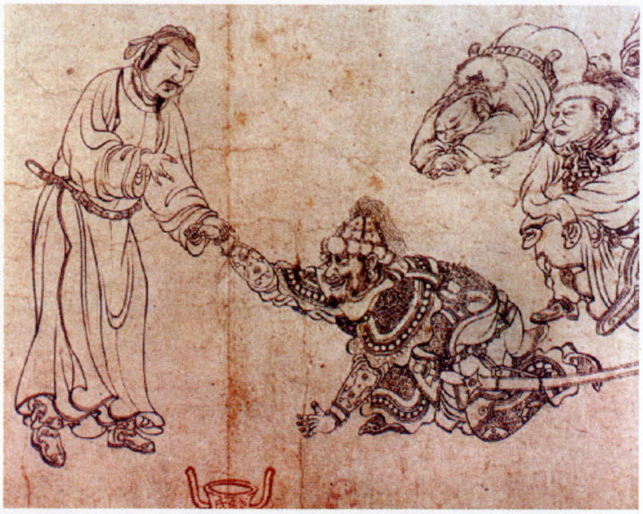

Chinese and Barbarian After losing the north, the Han Chinese grew resentful of outsiders. They drew a dividing line between their own agrarian society and the nomadic warriors, calling them "barbarians." Such identities were not fixed, however. Chinese and so-called barbarians were mutually dependent.

Feeling the pull of China's economic and political gravity, cultures around China consolidated their own internal political authority and defined their own identities in order to keep from being swallowed up by China. At the same time, they increased their commercial transactions with China. In Japan, for instance, leaders distanced themselves from Chinese influences, but they also developed a strong sense of their islands' distinctive identity. Even so, the long-standing dominance of Chinese ways remained apparent at virtually every level of Japanese society, and was most pronounced at the imperial court in the capital city of Heian (present-day Kyoto), which was modeled after the Chinese capital city of Chang'an. Outside Kyoto, however, a less China-centered way of life existed and began to impose itself on the center. Here, local notables, mainly military leaders and large landowners, began to challenge the imperial court for dominance. This challenge was accompanied by the arrival of an important new social group in Japanese society—samurai warriors. By the beginning of the fourteenth century, Japan had multiple sources of political and cultural power: an imperial family with prestige but little authority; an endangered and declining aristocracy; powerful landowning notables based in the provinces; and a rising and increasingly ambitious class of samurai.

During the Song period, Southeast Asia became a crossroads of Afro-Eurasian influences. The Malay Peninsula became home to many entrepôts for traders shuttling between India and China, because it connected the Bay of Bengal and the Indian Ocean with the South China Sea (see Map 10.7). Consequently, Southeast Asia was characterized by a fusion of religio-cultural influences: Vedic Brahmanism in Bali and other islands, Islam in Java and Sumatra, and Mahayana Buddhism in Vietnam and other parts of mainland Southeast Asia. Important Vedic and Buddhist kingdoms emerged in Southeast Asia. The most powerful and wealthy of these kingdoms was the Khmer Empire (889–1431), with its capital at Angkor, in present-day Cambodia. Public works and magnificent temples

Angkor Wat Mistaken by later European explorers for a remnant of Alexander the Great's conquests, the enormous temple complexes built by the Khmer people in Angkor borrowed their intricate layout and stupa (a mound-like structure containing religious relics) architecture from the Brahmanist Indian temples of the time. As the capital, Angkor was a microcosm of the world for the Khmer, who aspired to represent the macrocosm of the universe in the magnificence of Angkor's buildings and their geometric layout.

MAP 10.7 | Southeast Asia, 1000–1300

Cross-cultural influences affected Southeast Asian societies during this period.

- What makes Southeast Asia unique geographically compared to other regions of the world?
- Based on the map, why were the kingdoms of Southeast Asia exposed to so many cross-cultural influences?
- How does the system of regional kingdoms in Southeast Asia compare with that in India (Map 10.4)?

dedicated to the revived Vedic gods from India went hand in hand with the earlier influence of Indian Buddhism. One of the greatest temple complexes in Angkor—Angkor Wat—exemplified the Khmers' heavy borrowing from Vedic Indian architecture and the revival of the Hindu pantheon within the Khmer royal state. Kingdoms like the Khmer Empire functioned as political buffers between the strong states of China and India and brought stability and further commercial prosperity to the region.

WHAT WAS CHINA?

Paradoxically, the increasing exchange between outsiders and insiders within China hardened the lines that divided them and gave residents of China's interior a highly developed sense of themselves as a distinctive people possessing a superior culture. Exchanges with outsiders nurtured a "Chinese" identity among those who considered themselves true insiders and referred to themselves as Han. Song Chinese grew increasingly suspicious and resentful toward the outsiders living in their midst. They called these outsiders "barbarians" and treated them accordingly.

Print culture crystallized the distinct Chinese identity. Of all Afro-Eurasian societies in 1300, the Chinese were the most advanced in their use of printing and book publishing and circulation. Their books established classical Chinese as the common language of educated classes in East Asia. The Song government used its plentiful supply of paper to print books, especially medical texts, and to distribute calendars. The private publishing industry expanded and printing houses throughout the country produced Confucian classics, works on history, philosophical treatises, and literature—all of which figured in the civil examinations. Buddhist publications, too, were available everywhere.

China's huge population base coupled with a strong agrarian base and manufacturing innovations made it the wealthiest of the four major cultural spheres, and its common language and Confucian civil service system, which enabled a transfer of power from hereditary aristocrats to Confucian scholars, made it the most unified. China's influence on the surrounding region was tremendous.

Christian Europe

Europe, from 1000–1300, was a region of strong contrasts. Intensely localized power was balanced by a shared sense of Europe's place in the world, especially with respect to Christian identity. Some inhabitants even began to believe in the existence of something called "Europe" and increasingly referred to themselves as "Europeans" (see Map 10.8), especially in contrast to the world of Islam to the east and south.

COMPARISON

COMPARE the role that religions and migration played in forging unified identities in Europe, India, and the Islamic worlds.

LOCALIZATION OF POWER

From the agriculture-based manors of western Europe to the cities of Russia, power structures were localized. For example, in western Europe of the eleventh and twelfth centuries, the Franks became the unchallenged rulers after the collapse of Charlemagne's empire, yet they oversaw a somewhat fragmented manor-based economy and social structure. The peasantry's subjugation to this knightly class was at the heart of a system scholars have called feudalism (emphasizing the power of the local lords over the peasantry); but a more accurate term for the system is **manorialism**, which emphasizes instead the manor's role as the basic unit of economic power. The manor comprised the lord's fortified home (or castle), the surrounding fields controlled by the lord but worked by peasants (as free tenants or as serfs tied to the land), and the village in which those peasants lived. Although manorialism was driven by agriculture, limited manufacturing and trade augmented the manor economy. This system harnessed agrarian energy and helped western Europe shed its identity as a somewhat "barbarian" appendage of the Mediterranean.

Between 1100 and 1200, as many as 200,000 pioneering peasants emigrated from the regions of Belgium, Holland, and northern Germany to the frontiers of Europe (now Poland, the Czech Republic, Hungary, and the Baltic states). Despite the harsh climate and landscape, the area offered the promise of freedom from feudal lords' arbitrary justice and the imposition of forced labor that the peasants had experienced in western Europe. In a fragile balance between the native elites and liberty-seeking newcomers, castles and villages echoing the landscape of manorial France now replaced local economies that had been based on gathering honey, hunting, and the slave trade. For a thousand miles along the Baltic Sea, forest clearings dotted with new farmsteads and small towns edged inward from the coast up the river valleys.

MAP 10.8 | Latin Christendom in 1300

Catholic Europe expanded geographically and integrated culturally during this era.

- According to this map, into what areas did Western Christendom successfully expand?
- What factors contributed to the growth of a widespread common culture and shared ideas?
- How did long-distance trade shape the history of the region during this time?

Russian lands modeled themselves after Byzantium, not Rome or western Europe. A giant borderland between the steppes of Eurasia and the booming centers of Europe, Russia's cities lay at the crossroads of overland trade and migration. These cities were not agrarian centers, but hubs of expanding long-distance trade. Kiev became one of the region's greatest urban centers, a small-scale Constantinople with its own miniature Hagia Sophia. Russian Christians looked not to the Roman Catholic faith associated with the popes in Rome, but rather to Byzantium's Hagia Sophia and the Orthodoxy of the east as the source of religious authority. Russian Christianity remained that of a borderland—vivid oases of high culture set against the backdrop of vast forests and widely scattered settlements. Like the agricultural manors of western Europe, these Russian cities demonstrate the highly localized nature of power in Europe in this period.

WHAT WAS CHRISTIAN EUROPE?

Christianity in this era—primarily the Roman Catholicism of the west, but also the Orthodoxy of the east—became a universalizing faith that transformed the region becoming known as "Europe." The Christianity of post-Roman Europe had been a religion of monks, and its most dynamic centers were great monasteries. Members of the laity were expected to revere and support their monks, nuns, and clergy, but not to imitate them. By 1200, all this had changed. The internal colonization of western Europe—the clearing of woods and founding of villages—ensured that parish churches arose in all but the wildest landscapes. Now the clergy reached more deeply into the private lives of the laity. Marriage and divorce, previously considered family matters, became the domain of the church.

New understandings of religious devotion and innovative institutions for learning developed in the west. For instance, the followers of Francis of Assisi (1182–1226) emerged as an order of preachers who brought a message of repentance. Franciscans encouraged the laity—from the poorest to the elite—to feel remorse for their wrongdoings, to confess their sins to local priests, and to strive to be better Christians. At nearly the same time, intellectuals were beginning to gather in Paris to form the first European university, a sort of trade guild of scholars. These professional thinkers endeavored to prove that Christianity was the only religion that fully addressed the concerns of all rational human beings. Such was the message of Thomas Aquinas, who wrote *Summa contra Gentiles* (Summary of Christian Belief against Non-Christians) in 1264. The growing number of churches, new religious orders, and universities began to change what it meant to live in a "Christian Europe."

Crusader Kneeling, this Crusader promises to serve God (as he would serve a feudal lord) by going to fight on a Crusade (as he would fight for any lord to whom he had sworn loyalty). The two kinds of loyalty—to God and to one's lord—were deliberately confused in Crusader ideas. Both were about war. But fighting for God was unambiguously good, while fighting for a lord was not always so clear-cut.

RELATIONS WITH THE ISLAMIC WORLD

In the late eleventh century, western Europeans launched the Crusades, a wave of attacks against the Muslim world. The First Crusade began in 1095, when Pope Urban II appealed to the warrior nobility of France to put their violence to good use: they should combine their role as pilgrims to Jerusalem with that of soldiers, in order to free Jerusalem from Muslim rule. Such a just war, the clergy proposed, was a means for absolution, not a source of sin.

Starting in 1097, an armed host of around 60,000 men set out from northwestern Europe to seize Jerusalem. Crusading forces included knights in heavy armor, as well as people drawn from Europe's impoverished masses, who joined the movement to help besiege cities and construct a network of castles as the Christian knights drove their frontier forward. The fleets of Venice, Genoa, and Pisa helped transport later Crusaders and supplied the kingdoms they created as they moved eastward. Later Crusaders, especially those from the upper class, brought their wives, who found a degree of autonomy away from their homeland. There are even accounts of a children's crusade (1212), inspired by the visions of a boy. Over time, the Crusades drew together a range of peoples from varied walks of life in common purpose.

Current Trends in World History

The Crusades from Dual Perspectives

World history promotes comparative historical study, and when two cultures come together, as they did in the European crusades, their meeting offers unique opportunities to see how different societies view one another, and it provides a clear sense for their own self-identity. Such a confrontation took place during the crusades between European Christians and Muslims between 1095 and 1272.

In 1095, Pope Urban II called for the First Crusade in the following words:

> Oh, race of Franks, race from across the mountains, race chosen and beloved by God, as shines forth in very many of your works, set apart from all nations by the situation of your country, as well as by your Catholic faith and the honor of the Holy Church! To you our discourse is addressed, and for you our exhortation is intended. We wish you to know what a grievous cause has led us to your country, what peril, threatening you and all the faithful, has brought us.

The "grievous cause" was the occupation of the Holy City of Jerusalem by the Islamic empire. Formed within the complex relationship between the Byzantine Empire and the western Christian papacy and kingdoms of Europe, the religious motivation behind the Crusades became the subject of many literary renditions of the tumultuous events. It also generated emotionally stirring and argumentative writing, depicting either a Muslim or Christian enemy (depending on the work's author).

These written attacks are often passionate, harsh, and emotional. They also inspire and reinforce the conviction of fellow believers, with little concern for accuracy. Thus, some authors in the time of the Crusades were usually too biased or too misinformed to present accurate portraits of their enemies. But occasionally, firsthand accounts in the form of chronicles and histories offer us unique glimpses into Christian-Muslim relations in the age of the Crusades.

Consider Usāmah ibn Munqidh (1095–1188), the learned ruler of the city of Shaizar in western Syria. Skirmishes, truces, and the ransoming of prisoners were part of his daily life, and Usāmah socialized with his Frankish neighbors as much as he fought with them. He offers a dismissive opinion of his enemies. Basically, they struck him as "animals possessing the virtues of courage and fighting, but nothing else." In particular, their medical practice appalled him. More strange, the Franks allowed their wives to walk about freely and to talk to strangers unaccompanied by male guardians. How could men be at once so brave and yet so lacking in a proper, Arab sense of honor, which would lead a man to protect his women? Unlike other Muslim authors of his time, however, Usāmah does not refer to the Franks in derogatory terms such as "infidels" or "devils." In fact, he occasionally refers to some of them as his companions and writes of a Frank who called him "my brother."

No fewer than nine Crusades were fought over the two centuries that followed Urban II's call; but none of the coalitions, in the end, created lasting Christian kingdoms in the lands they "reconquered." Most knights returned home, their epic pilgrimage completed. The remaining fragile network of Crusader lordships barely threatened the Islamic heartland. The real prosperity and the capital cities of Muslim kingdoms lay inland, away from the coast—at Cairo, Damascus, and Baghdad. The assaults' long-term effect was to harden Muslim feelings against the Franks and the millions of nonwestern Christians who had previously lived peacefully in Egypt and Syria (see **Current Trends in World History: The Crusades from Dual Perspectives**).

Other campaigns of Christian expansion, like the Iberian efforts to drive out the Muslims, were more successful. Beginning with the capture of Toledo in 1061, the Christian kings of northern Spain slowly pushed back the Muslims. Eventually they reached the heart of Andalusia in southern Iberia and conquered Seville, adding more than 100,000 square miles of territory to Christian Europe. Another force, from northern France, crossed Italy to conquer Muslim-held Sicily, ensuring Christian rule in the strategically located mid-Mediterranean island. Unlike the Crusaders' fragile foothold at the edge of the Middle East, these two conquests

Christian authors had similar interests in documenting the customs of their enemies in battle. Jean de Joinville (1224/1225–1317) was a chronicler of medieval France. During one crusade, while in the service of the king, Joinville had occasion to note the Muslims' social behavior:

> Whenever the Sultan was in the camp, the men of the personal Guard were quartered all round his lodging, and appointed to guard his person. At the door of the Sultan's lodging there was a little tent for the Sultan's door-keepers, and for his musicians, who had Arabian horns and drums and kettledrums; and they used to make such a din at daybreak and at nightfall that people near them could not hear one another speak, and that they could be heard plainly all through the camp. The musicians never dared sound their instruments in the daytime unless by the order of the Chief of the Guard. Thus it was, that whenever the Sultan had a proclamation to make he used to send for the Chief of the Guard, and give him the order; and then the Chief would cause all the Sultan's instruments to be sounded; and thereupon all the host would come to hear the Sultan's commands.

Jean de Joinville Joinville offering his history, in which he described the Seventh Crusade, to Louis X of France (r. 1314–1316).

Although scholars regard such literary renditions with caution, they are useful for gleaning personal details that other types of works omit. The colorful accounts by authors such as Usāmah ibn Munqidh and Joinville are invaluable resources for the social history of the Crusaders.

QUESTIONS FOR ANALYSIS

- What customs or practices of their opponents did the Muslim and the Christian writers select to write about? Why?
- What aspects of the other side's customs does the writer seem to see as good or praiseworthy? What does that tell us about their perceptions of the strangers that they encountered?
- If a historian uses polemical written sources like this to analyze societies from the past, what can he or she say that is trustworthy about them?

Explore Further

Natasha, Hodgson, *Women, Crusading and the Holy Land in Historical Narrative* (2007).

Amin Maalouf, *The Crusades Through Arab Eyes*, trans. Jon Rothschild (1984).

Edward Peters (ed.), *The First Crusade: The Chronicle of Fulcher of Chartres and Other Source Materials* (1971).

were a turning point in relations between Christian and Muslim power in the Mediterranean. Christianity—and in particular the rise of the Roman Catholic Church, the spread of universities, and the fight against the Muslims in their native and spiritual homelands—were forces that helped create a cultural sphere known as Europe, whose peoples would become known as European, at the western end of the Afro-Eurasian landmass during this period.

Worlds Coming Together: Sub-Saharan Africa and the Americas

COMPARISON

COMPARE both the internal integration and external interactions of sub-Saharan Africa with those of the Americas.

From 1000 to 1300, sub-Saharan Africa and the Americas became far more internally integrated—culturally, economically, and politically—than before. Islam's spread and the growing trade in gold, slaves, and other commodities brought sub-Saharan Africa more fully into the exchange networks of the Eastern Hemisphere; yet the Americas remained isolated from Afro-Eurasian networks for several more centuries.

SUB-SAHARAN AFRICA COMES TOGETHER

During this period sub-Saharan Africa's relationship to the rest of the world changed dramatically. While sub-Saharan Africa had never been a world entirely apart before 1000 CE, now its integration with Eurasia became much stronger. Increasingly, interior hinterlands found themselves touched by the commercial and migratory impulses emanating from the Indian Ocean and Arabian Sea transformations (see Map 10.9).

West Africa and the Mande-Speaking Peoples Once trade routes bridged the Sahara Desert (see Chapter 9), the flow of commodities and ideas linked sub-Saharan Africa to North Africa and Southwest Asia. As the savanna region became increasingly connected to developments in Eurasia, Mande-speaking peoples became the primary agents for integration within and beyond West Africa. Exploiting their expertise in commerce and political organization, the Mande edged out rivals. The Mande homeland was a vast area, 1,000 miles wide between the bend in the Senegal River to the west and the bend of the Niger River to the east, stretching more than 2,000 miles from the Senegal River in the north to the Bandama River in the south.

By the eleventh century, Mande-speaking peoples were spreading their cultural, commercial, and political hegemony from the high savanna grasslands southward into the woodlands and tropical rain forests stretching to the Atlantic Ocean. Those dwelling in the rain forests organized small-scale societies led by local councils, while those in the savanna lands developed centralized forms of government under sacred kingships. Mande-speakers believed that their kings had descended from the gods and that they enjoyed the gods' blessing.

As the Mande broadened their territory to the Atlantic coast, they gained access to tradable items that residents of Africa's interior were eager to have—notably kola nuts and malaguetta peppers, for which the Mande exchanged iron products and manufactured textiles. Mande-speaking peoples, with their far-flung commercial networks and highly dispersed populations, dominated trans-Saharan trade in salt from the northern Sahel, gold from the Mande homeland, and slaves. By 1300 the Mande-speaking merchants had followed the Senegal River to its outlet on the coast and then pushed their commercial frontiers farther inland and down the coast. Thus, even before European explorers and traders arrived in the mid-fifteenth century, West African peoples had created dynamic networks linking the hinterlands with coastal trading hubs.

The Empire of Mali In the early thirteenth century, the empire of **Mali** became the Mande successor state to the kingdom of Ghana (see Chapter 9). The origins of the Mali Empire and its legendary founder are enshrined in *The Epic of Sundiata*. Sundiata's triumph, which occurred in the first half of the thirteenth century, marked the victory of new cavalry forces over traditional foot soldiers. Horses—which had always existed in some parts of Africa—now became prestige objects of the savanna peoples, symbols of state power.

Under the Mali Empire, commerce was in full swing. With Mande trade routes extending to the Atlantic Ocean and spanning the Sahara Desert, West Africa was no longer an isolated periphery of the central Muslim lands. The Mali king Mansa Musa (r. 1312–1332), made a celebrated hajj, or pilgrimage to Mecca, in 1325–1326, traveling through Cairo and impressing crowds with the size of his retinue—including soldiers, wives, consorts, and as many as 12,000 slaves—and his displays of wealth, especially many dazzling items made of gold. Mansa Musa's stopover in Cairo, one of Islam's primary cities, astonished the Egyptian elite and awakened much of the world to the fact that Islam had spread far below the Sahara and that a sub-Saharan state could mount such an impressive display of power and wealth.

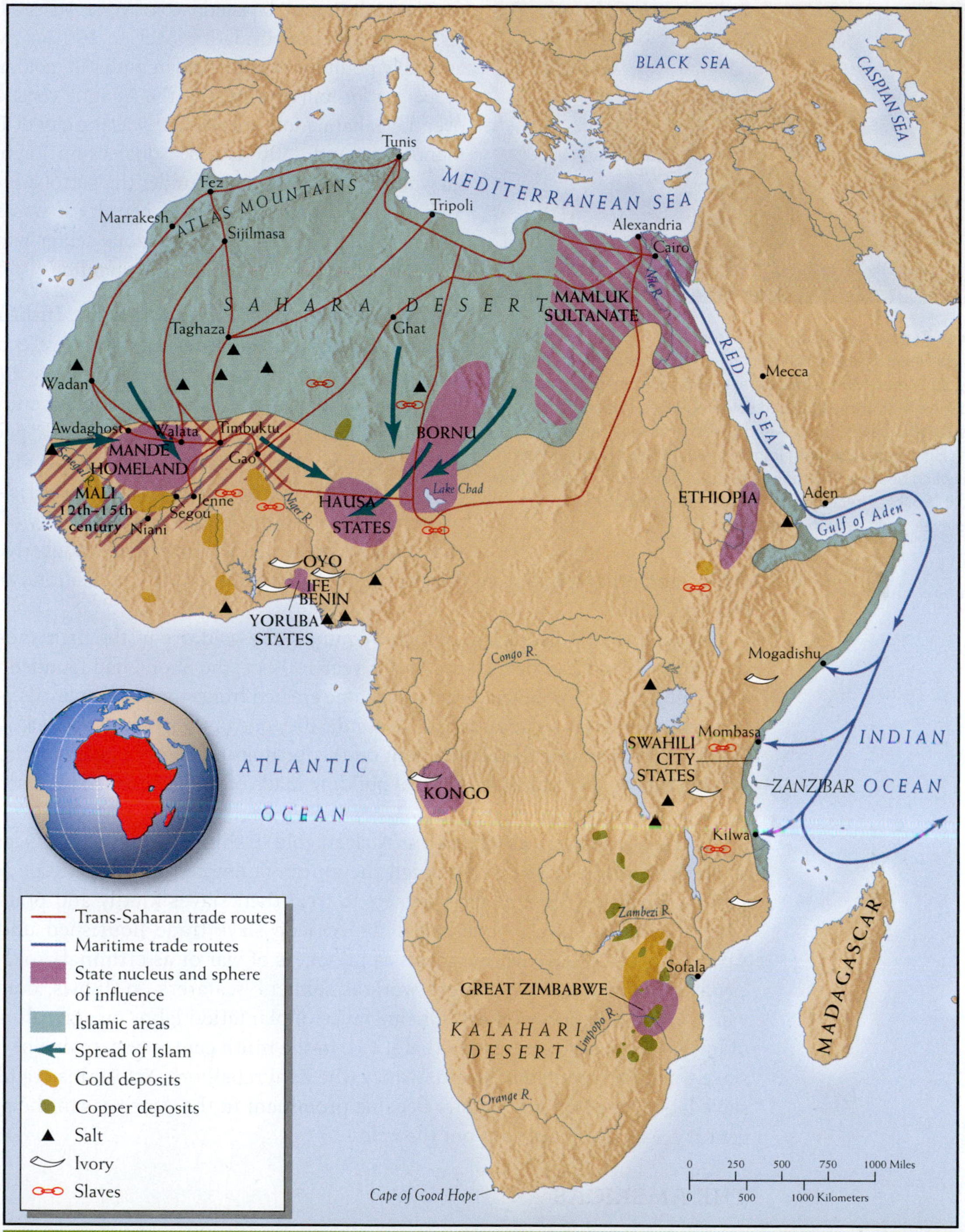

MAP 10.9 | Sub-Saharan Africa, 1300

Increased commercial contacts influenced the religious and political dimensions of sub-Saharan Africa at this time. Compare this map to Map 9.3 (p. 314).

- Where had strong Islamic communities emerged by 1300?
- According to this map, what types of activity were affecting the Mande homeland?
- To what extent had sub-Saharan Africa "come together"?

West African Asante Gold This picture from the 1375 Catalan Atlas shows Mansa Musa, the king of Mali, on his throne, surrounded by images of gold. When Mansa Musa traveled on pilgrimage to Mecca (1324–1325), his entourage included soldiers, wives, consorts, and as many as 12,000 slaves, many wearing rich brocades woven of Persian silk. His caravan brought immense quantities of gold—nearly 100 camels each bearing 300-pound sacks of gold—and Mansa Musa distributed it lavishly. Preceding his retinue as it crossed the desert were 500 slaves, each carrying a golden staff.

The Mali Empire boasted two of West Africa's largest cities. Jenne, an entrepôt dating back to 200 BCE, was a vital assembly point for caravans laden with salt, gold, and slaves preparing for journeys west to the Atlantic coast and north over the Sahara. More spectacular was the city of Timbuktu; founded around 1100 as a seasonal camp for nomads, it grew in size and importance under the patronage of various Malian kings. By the fourteenth century it was a thriving commercial, intellectual, and religious center famed for its three large mosques, which are still standing.

Trade Between East Africa and the Indian Ocean

Africa's eastern and southern regions were also integrated into long-distance trading systems. Because of monsoon winds, East Africa was a logical end point for much of the Indian Ocean trade. Swahili peoples living along that coast became brokers for trade from the Arabian Peninsula, the Persian Gulf territories, and the western coast of India. Merchants in the city of Kilwa on the coast of present-day Tanzania brought ivory, gold, slaves, and other items from the interior and shipped them to destinations around the Indian Ocean.

Shona-speaking peoples grew rich by mining the gold ore in the highlands between the Limpopo and Zambezi rivers. By the year 1000 CE, the Shona had founded up to fifty small religious and political centers, each one erected from stone to display its power over the peasant villages surrounding it. Around 1100, one of these centers, Great Zimbabwe, stood supreme among the Shona. Built on the fortunes made from gold, its most impressive landmark was a massive elliptical building made of stones fitted so expertly that they needed no grouting.

African slaves were as valuable as African gold in shipments to Indian Ocean as well as Mediterranean markets. Although the Quran attempted to mitigate the severity of slavery, requiring Muslim slave owners to treat their slaves kindly and praising those who freed their slaves, nonetheless the African slave trade flourished under Islam. Africans became slaves either taken as prisoners of war or as criminals sold into slavery as punishment. Slaves might work as soldiers, seafarers on dhows, domestic servants, and plantation workers. One instance of plantation labor on agricultural estates of lower Iraq was so oppressive that it led, in the ninth century CE, to one of the largest slave wars documented in world history (the Zanj rebellion). Yet in this era plantation-slave labor, like that which later became prominent in the Americas in the nineteenth century, was the exception, not the rule.

THE AMERICAS

During this period, the Americas were untouched by the connections reverberating across Afro-Eurasia. Apart from limited Viking contacts in North America (see Chapter 9), navigators still did not cross the large oceans that separated the Americas from other lands. Yet, here, too, commercial and expansionist impulses fostered closer contact among peoples who lived there.

Andean States of South America Growth and prosperity in the Andean region gave rise to South America's first empire. The **Chimú Empire** developed in the early second millennium in the fertile Moche Valley bordering the Pacific Ocean (see Map 10.10). Ultimately the Moche people expanded their influence across numerous valleys and ecological zones, from pastoral highlands to rich valley floodplains to the fecund fishing grounds of the Pacific Coast. As their geographical reach grew, so did their wealth.

The Chimú economy was successful because it was highly commercialized. Agriculture was its base, and complex irrigation systems turned the arid coast into a string of fertile oases capable of feeding an increasingly dispersed population. Cotton became a lucrative export to distant markets along the Andes. Parades of llamas and porters lugged these commodities up and down the steep mountain chains that are the spine of South America. A well-trained bureaucracy oversaw the construction and maintenance of canals, with a hierarchy of provincial administrators watching over commercial hinterlands.

MAP 10.10 | Andean States

Although the Andes region of South America was isolated from Afro-Eurasian developments before 1500, it was not stagnant. Indeed, political and cultural integration brought the peoples of this region closer together.

- Where are the areas of the Chimú Empire and Tiahuanaco influence on the map?
- What kinds of ecological niches did they govern?
- According to your reading, how did each polity encourage greater cultural and economic integration?

The Chimú Empire's biggest city, Chan Chan, held a core population of 30,000 inhabitants. A sprawling walled metropolis, covering nearly ten square miles with extensive roads circulating through neighborhoods, Chan Chan boasted ten huge palaces at its center. Protected by thick walls thirty feet high, these opulent residence halls symbolized the rulers' power. Within the compound, emperors erected burial complexes for storing their accumulated riches: fine cloth, gold and silver objects, splendid *Spondylus* shells, and other luxury goods. Around the compound spread neighborhoods for nobles and artisans; farther out stood rows of commoners' houses. The Chimú regime, centered at Chan Chan, lasted until Incan armies invaded in the 1460s and incorporated the Pacific state into their own immense empire.

Chan Chan The image shows what remains of Chan Chan. The city covered fifteen square miles and was divided into neighborhoods for nobles, artisans, and commoners, with the elites living closest to the hub of governmental and spiritual power.

Toltecs in Mesoamerica Additional hubs of regional trade developed farther north. By 1000 CE, Mesoamerica had seen the rise and fall of several complex societies, including Teotihuacán and the Mayans (see Chapter 8). Caravans of porters bound the region together, working the intricate roads that connected the coast of the Gulf of Mexico to the Pacific, and the southern lowlands of Central America to the arid regions of modern Texas (see Map 10.11). The **Toltecs** filled the political vacuum left by the decline of Teotihuacán and tapped into the commercial network radiating from the rich valley of central Mexico.

The Toltecs were a combination of migrant groups, farmers from the north and refugees from the south fleeing the strife that followed Teotihuacán's demise. These migrants settled northwest of Teotihuacán as the city waned, making their capital at Tula. They relied on a maize-based economy supplemented by beans, squash, and dog, deer, and rabbit meat. Their rulers made sure that enterprising merchants provided them with status goods such as ornamental pottery, rare shells and stones, and precious skins and feathers.

Tula was a commercial hub, a political capital, and a ceremonial center. While its layout differed from Teotihuacán's, many features revealed borrowings from other Mesoamerican peoples. Temples consisted of giant pyramids topped by colossal stone soldiers, and ball courts where subjects and conquered peoples alike played their ritual sport were found everywhere. The architecture and monumental art reflected the mixed and migratory origins of the Toltecs: a combination of Mayan and Teotihuacáno influences. At its height, the Toltec capital teemed with 60,000 people, a huge metropolis by contemporary European standards (if small, by Song Chinese and Abbasid Islamic world standards).

Toltec Temple Tula, the capital of the Toltec Empire, carried on the Mesoamerican tradition of locating ceremonial architecture at the center of the city. The Pyramid of the Morning Star cast its shadow over all other buildings. And above them stood columns of the Atlantes, carved Toltec god-warriors, the figurative pillars of the empire itself. The walls of this pyramid were likely embellished with images of snakes and skulls. The north face of the pyramid has the image of a snake devouring a human.

Cahokians in North America As in South America (Chan Chan of the Chimú) and Mesoamerica (Tula of the Toltecs), cities took shape at the hubs of trading networks across North America, as well. The largest was **Cahokia**, along the Mississippi River near modern-day East St. Louis. A city of about 15,000, it approximated the size of London at the time. Farmers and hunters had settled in the region around 600 CE, attracted by its rich soil, its woodlands for fuel and game, and its access to trade via the Mississippi. Eventually, fields of maize and other crops fanned out toward the horizon. The hoe replaced the trusty digging stick, and satellite towns erected granaries to hold the growing harvests.

Cahokia became a commercial center for regional and long-distance trade. The hinterlands produced staples for Cahokia's urban consumers, and in return its crafts rode inland on the backs of porters and to distant markets in canoes. Woven fabrics and ceramics from Cahokia were exchanged for mica from the Appalachian Mountains, seashells and sharks' teeth from the Gulf of Mexico, and copper from the upper Great Lakes. Cahokia became more than an

MAP 10.11 | Commercial Hubs in Mesoamerica and North America, 1000

Both Cahokia and Tula were commercial hubs of vibrant regional trade networks.

- Where are Cahokia and Tula on the map?
- According to the map, what kinds of goods circulated through these cities?
- How important do cities appear to be in North America and Mesoamerica?

importer and exporter: it was the exchange hub for an entire regional network trading in salt, tools, pottery, woven stuffs, jewelry, and ceremonial goods.

Dominating Cahokia's urban landscape were enormous earthen mounds of sand and clay (thus the Cahokians' nickname of "mound people"). It was from these artificial hills that the people honored spiritual forces. Building these types of structures without draft animals, hydraulic tools, or even wheels was labor-intensive, so the Cahokians recruited neighboring people to help. A palisade around the city protected the metropolis from marauders.

Ultimately Cahokia's success bred its downfall. As woodlands fell to the axe and soil lost nutrients, timber and food became scarce. In contrast to the sturdy dhows of the Arabian Sea and the bulky junks of the China Sea, Cahokia's river canoes could carry only limited cargoes. Cahokia's commercial networks met their limits. When the creeks that fed its water system could not keep up with demand, engineers changed their course, but to no avail. By 1350 the city was practically empty. Cahokia represented the growing networks of trade and migration, and the ability of North Americans to organize vibrant commercial societies.

Two forces contributed to greater integration in sub-Saharan Africa and the Americas, from 1000 to 1300: commercial exchange (salt, gold, ivory, and slaves in sub-Saharan Africa, and shells, pottery, textiles and metals in the Americas) and urbanization (at Jenne, Timbuktu, and Great Zimbabwe in sub-Saharan Africa, and Chan Chan, Tula, and Cahokia in the Americas). By 1300, trans-Saharan and Indian Ocean exchange had brought Africa into full-fledged Afro-Eurasian networks of exchange and, as we will see in Chapter 12, transatlantic exchange would soon bring the Americas into a global network.

The Mongol Transformation of Afro-Eurasia

COMPARISON

ASSESS the impacts that the Mongol Empire had on Afro-Eurasian peoples and places.

Commercial networks were clearly one way to integrate the world. But just as long-distance trade connected people, so could conquerors. The Inner Eurasian steppes had already unleashed horse-riding warriors such as the Kushans and Xiongnu (see Chapters 6 and 7). Now, the Mongols created an empire that straddled east and west (see Map 10.12), expanding their reach not only through brutal conquest but also through intensified trade and cultural exchange.

WHO WERE THE MONGOLS?

The Mongols were a combination of forest and prairie peoples. Residing in circular, felt-covered tents, which they shared with some of their animals, they lived by hunting and livestock herding. They changed campgrounds with the seasons. Life on the steppes was such a constant struggle that only the strong survived. Their food, primarily animal products, provided high levels of protein, which built up their muscle mass and their strength. Always on the march, their society resembled a perpetual standing army with bands of well-disciplined military units led by commanders chosen for their skill.

Wielding heavy compound bows made of sinew, wood, and horn, Mongol archers were deadly accurate at over 200 yards—even at full gallop. Their small but sturdy horses, capable of withstanding extreme cold, bore saddles with high supports in front and back, enabling the warriors to maneuver at high speeds. With their feet secure in iron stirrups, the archers could rise in their saddles to aim their arrows without stopping. These expert horsemen often remained in the saddle all day and night, even sleeping while their horses continued on. Each warrior kept many horses, replacing tired mounts with fresh ones so that the armies could cover up to seventy miles per day.

Mongol tribes solidified their conquests by extending kinship networks, building an empire out of an expanding confederation of familial tribes. Women were a vital link in those networks. Households sealed alliances by the exchange of daughters in marriage. In addition to their role in linking kinship networks, women in Mongol society were responsible for child-rearing, shearing and milking livestock, and processing pelts for clothing. But they also took part in battles. Although women could be bought and sold, Mongol wives had the right to own property and to divorce. Elite women, such as the mother and wife of the Mongol ruler Kubilai Khan, even played important political roles.

CONQUEST AND EMPIRE

The Mongols' need for grazing lands contributed to their desire to conquer the distant fertile belts and rich cities. The Mongols depended on settled peoples for grain and manufactured

Mongol Warriors This miniature painting is one of the illustrations for *History* by Rashid al Din, the most outstanding scholar under the Mongol regimes. Note the relatively small horses and strong bows used by the Mongol soldiers.

goods, including iron for tools, wagons, weapons, bridles, and stirrups. Their first expansionist forays followed caravan routes.

The Mongol expansion began in 1206 under a united cluster of tribes. These tribes were unified by a gathering of clan heads who chose one of those present as Chinggis (Genghis) Khan, or Supreme Ruler. This Chinggis (c. 1155–1227) launched a series of conquests southward across the Great Wall of China, and westward to Afghanistan and Persia. The Mongols even invaded Korea in 1231. The armies of Chinggis's sons reached both the Pacific Ocean and the Adriatic Sea. Chinggis's grandsons founded dynasties in Persia, in China, and on the southern Eurasian steppes. Thus, a realm took shape that touched all four of Afro-Eurasia's main worlds.

Mongols in Abbasid Baghdad In the thirteenth century, Mongol tribesmen were streaming out of the steppes, crossing the whole of Asia and entering the eastern parts of Europe. Mongke Khan, a grandson of Chinggis, made clear the Mongol aspiration for world domination: he commanded his brother, Hulagu, to conquer Iran, Syria, Egypt, Byzantium, and Armenia, and he appointed another brother, Kubilai, to rule over China, Tibet, and the northern parts of India.

When Hulagu reached Abbasid Baghdad in 1258, he encountered a feeble foe and a city that was a shadow of its former glorious self. Merely 10,000 horsemen faced his army of 200,000 soldiers, who were eager to acquire the booty of a wealthy city. Even before the battle had taken place, Baghdadi poets were composing elegies for their dead and mourning the defeat of Islam. The slaughter was vast. Hulagu himself boasted of taking the lives of at least 200,000 people. The Mongols hunted their adversaries in wells, latrines, and sewers and followed them into the upper floors of buildings, killing them on rooftops until, as an Iraqi Arab historian observed, "blood poured from the gutters into the streets. . . . The same happened in the mosques." In a few weeks of sheer terror, the Abbasid caliphate was demolished. Hulagu's forces showed no mercy to the caliph himself, who was rolled up in a carpet and trampled to death by horses. With Baghdad crushed, the Mongol armies pushed on to Syria, slaughtering Muslims along the way.

BALTIC SEA
POLAND
Leigritz
Moscow
RUSSIAN PRINCIPALITIES
Kiev
UKRAINE
Buda
Pest
KHANATE OF THE GOLDEN HORD
URAL MOUNTAINS
New Sarai
Old Sarai
Lake Balkas
ARAL SEA
BLACK SEA
CAUCASUS MTS.
CASPIAN SEA
Constantinople
BYZANTINE EMPIRE
KHANATE OF TH
Samarkand
Tabriz
Aleppo
Balkh
HINDU KUSH MTS.
MEDITERRANEAN SEA
Damascus
Herat
Baghdad
IL-KHANATE
HIMALAYA
Jerusalem
SULTANAT OF DELH
ARABIA
RED SEA
INDIAN OCEAN

MAP 10.12 | Mongol Campaigns and Conquests, 1200–1300

Mongol campaigns and conquests brought Afro-Eurasian worlds together as never before. Trace the outline of the entire area of Mongol influence shaded on this map.

- What cultural groups did the Mongol armies conquer, partially conquer, or invade?
- How many different Khanates did the Mongols establish across Eurasia, and what were they?
- What role did geography play in limiting the spread of their influence?

Mongols in China In the east, Mongol forces under Chinggis Khan had entered northern China at the beginning of the thirteenth century, defeating the Jin army that was no match for the Mongols' superior cavalry on the North China plain. Despite some serious setbacks from the climate (including malaria for the men and the death of horses from the heat), Chinggis's grandson Kubilai Khan (1215–1294) seized southern China from the Song dynasty beginning in the 1260s. The southern Song army fell before his warriors brandishing the latest gunpowder-based weapons, which the Mongols had borrowed from Chinese inventors and now used against them.

Hangzhou, the last Song capital, fell in 1276. Kubilai Khan's most able commander, Bayan, led his crack Mongol forces in seizing town after town, ever closer to the capital, while the Empress Dowager tried to buy them off, proposing substantial tribute payments, but Bayan was uncompromising. Once conquered, the Empress Dowager and Hangzhou were treated well by the Mongols. In fact, Hangzhou was still one of the greatest cities in the world when it was visited by the Venetian traveler Marco Polo in the 1280s and by the Muslim traveler Ibn Battuta in the 1340s. Both men agreed that neither Europe nor the Islamic world had anything like it.

Kubilai Khan founded his Yuan dynasty, with a capital at Dadu, present-day Beijing. The Mongol conquest both north and south changed the political and social landscape. But Mongol rule did not impose rough steppe-land ways on the "civilized" urbanite Chinese. While non-Chinese outsiders took political control, they were a conquering elite that ruled over a vast Han majority. The result was a divided ruling system in which incumbent Chinese elites governed locally, while newcomers managed the unifying central dynasty and collected taxes for the Mongols.

Southeast Asia also felt the whiplash of Kubilai Khan's conquest. Circling Song defenses in southern China, the Mongols galloped southwest and conquered states in Yunnan and in Burma. From there, in the 1270s, the armies headed directly back east into the soft underbelly of the Song state. In this sweep, portions of mainland Southeast Asia became annexed to China for the first time. Kubilai Khan used the conquered Chinese fleets to push his expansionism onto the high seas—meeting with failure during the unsuccessful 1274 and 1281 invasions of Japan from Korea. An ill-fated Javanese expedition to extend Mongol reach beyond the South China Sea in 1293 was Kubilai Khan's last.

In the end, the Mongol Empire reached its outer limits. In the west, the Egyptian Mamluks stemmed the advancing Mongol armies and prevented Egypt from falling into their hands. In the east, the waters of the South China Sea and the Sea of Japan foiled Mongol expansion into Java and Japan. Better at conquering than governing, the Mongols struggled to rule their vast possessions in makeshift states. Bit by bit, they yielded control to local administrators and rulers who governed as their surrogates. There was also frequent feuding among the Mongol rulers themselves. In China and in Persia, Mongol rule collapsed in the fourteenth century. Ultimately, the Mongols would meet a deadly adversary even more brutal than they were—the plague of the fourteenth century (see Chapter 11).

Mongol conquest reshaped Afro-Eurasia's social landscape. Islam would never again have a unifying authority like the caliphate or a powerful center like Baghdad. China, too, was divided and changed by the Mongols' introduction of Persian, Islamic, and Byzantine influences into China's architecture, art, science, and medicine. The Yuan policy of benign tolerance brought elements from Christianity, Judaism, Zoroastrianism, and Islam into the Chinese mix. The Mongol thrust also facilitated the flow of fine goods, traders, and technology from China to the rest of the world. Finally, the Mongol conquests encouraged an unprecedented Afro-Eurasian interconnectedness, surpassing even the Hellenistic connections that Alexander's conquests had brought in the late fourth century BCE (see Chapter 6).

Out of Mongol conquest and warfare would come centuries of trade, migration, and increasing contacts among Africa, Europe, and Asia.

Conclusion

Between 1000 and 1300, Afro-Eurasia was forming large cultural spheres. As trade and migration spanned longer distances, these spheres prospered and became more integrated. In central Afro-Eurasia, Islam was firmly established, and its merchants, scholars, and travelers acted as commercial and cultural intermediaries joining the landmass together, as they spread their universalizing faith. As seaborne trade expanded, India, too, became a commercial crossroads. Merchants in its port cities welcomed traders arriving from Arab lands to the west, from China, and from Southeast Asia. China also boomed, pouring its manufactures into trading networks that reached throughout Afro-Eurasia and even into Africa. Christian Europe had two centers—at Rome and at Constantinople—both of which were at war with Islam.

Neither sub-Saharan Africa nor the Americas saw the same degree of integration, but trade and migration in these areas had profound effects. Certain African cultures flourished as they encountered the commercial energy of trade on the Indian Ocean. Africans' trade with one another linked coastal and interior regions in an ever more integrated world. American peoples also built cities that dominated cultural areas and thrived through trade. American cultures shared significant features: reliance on trade, maize, and the exchange of goods such as shells and precious feathers. And larger areas honored the same spiritual centers.

By 1300, trade, migration, and conflict were connecting Afro-Eurasian worlds in unprecedented ways. When Mongol armies swept into China, into Southeast Asia, and into the heart of Islam, they applied a thin coating of political integration to these widespread regions and built on existing trade links. At the same time, most people's lives remained quite localized, driven by the need for subsistence and governed by spiritual and governmental representatives acting at the behest of distant authorities.

Still, locals noticed the evidence of cross-cultural exchanges everywhere—in the clothing styles of provincial elites, such as Chinese silks in Paris or Quetzal plumes in northern Mexico; in enticements to move (and forced removals) to new frontiers; in the news of faraway conquests or advancing armies. Worlds were coming together within themselves and across territorial boundaries, while remaining apart as they sought to maintain their own identity and traditions. In Afro-Eurasia especially, as the movement of goods and peoples shifted from ancient land routes to sea-lanes, these contacts were more frequent and far-reaching. Never before had the world seen so much activity connecting its parts. Nor within them had there been so much shared cultural similarity. By the time the Mongol Empire arose, the regions composing the globe were those that we now recognize as the cultural spheres of today's world.

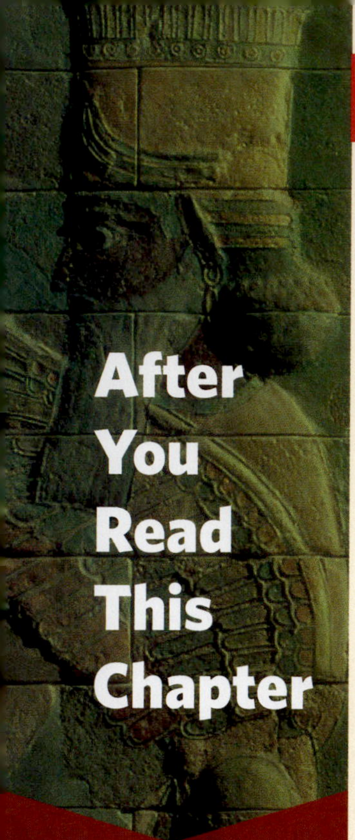

After You Read This Chapter

Go to INQUIZITIVE to see what you've learned—and learn what you've missed—with personalized feedback along the way.

TRACING THE GLOBAL STORYLINES

FOCUS ON: *Foundational Cultural Spheres*

THE ISLAMIC WORLD

- The Islamic world undergoes a burst of expansion, prosperity, and cultural diversification but remains politically fractured.
- Arab merchants and Sufi mystics spread Islam over great distances and make it more appealing to other cultures, helping to transform Islam into a foundational world.
- Islam travels across the Sahara Desert; the powerful gold- and slave-supplying empire of Mali arises in West Africa.

CHINA

- The Song dynasty reunites China after three centuries of fragmented rulership, reaching into the past to reestablish a sense of a "true" Chinese identity as the Han, through a widespread print culture and denigration of outsiders.
- Agrarian success and advances in manufacturing—including the production of both iron and porcelain—fuel an expanding economy, complete with paper money.

INDIA

- India remains a mosaic under the canopy of Hinduism despite cultural interconnections and increasing prosperity.
- The invasion of Turkish Muslims leads to the Delhi Sultanate, which rules over India for three centuries, strengthening cultural diversity and tolerance.

CHRISTIAN EUROPE

- Roman Catholicism becomes a "mass" faith and helps to create a common European cultural identity.
- Feudalism organizes the elite-peasant relationship, while manorialism forms the basis of the economy
- Europe's growing confidence is manifest in the Crusades and the reconquering of Iberia, an effort to drive Islam out of Christian lands.

CHRONOLOGY

SUB-SAHARAN AFRICA
- Kingdom of Mali emerges (King Mansa Musa 1312–1332) 1100 CE
- Great Zimbabwe flourishes 1100 CE

THE AMERICAS
- Cahokia flourishes as a commercial hub in North America 1000 CE
- Moche people found city of Chan Chan in South America 900 CE
- Toltecs dominate valley of Mexico 900–1100 CE

THE ISLAMIC WORLD
- Turkish migrants and armies spread into Islamic world's heartland 1000 CE

SOUTH ASIA
- Central Asian invasions begin 1000 CE

EAST ASIA
- Song dynasty in China 906–1279 CE

SOUTHEAST ASIA

EUROPE
- Reconquering of the Iberian Peninsula 1061–1492 CE

900 1000 1100

THINKING ABOUT GLOBAL CONNECTIONS

- ***Thinking about* Worlds Together, Worlds Apart** From 1000 to 1300 CE, a range of social and political developments contributed to the consolidation of four cultural spheres that still exist today: Europe, the Islamic world, India, and China. In what ways did these spheres interact with one another? In what ways was each sphere genuinely distinct from the others? To what extent were sub-Saharan Africa and the Americas folded into these spheres and with what result?

- ***Thinking about Transformation & Conflict and Becoming the World*** As the four cultural spheres of Afro-Eurasia consolidated, shocking examples of conflict between them began to take place. Whether Pope Urban II's call in 1095 to reclaim the "holy land" from Muslims or the Mongol Hulagu's brutal sack of Baghdad in 1258, this period was marked by large-scale warfare between rival cultural spheres. To what extent was such conflict inevitable? In what ways did conflict transform the groups involved?

- ***Thinking about Crossing Borders and Becoming the World*** Major innovations facilitated economic exchange in the Indian Ocean and in Song China. The magnetic needle compass, better ships, and improved maps shrank the Indian Ocean to the benefit of traders. Similarly, paper money in Song China changed the nature of commerce. How did these developments shift the axis of Afro-Eurasian exchange? What evidence suggests that bodies of water and the routes across them became more significant than overland exchange routes in binding together Afro-Eurasia? What might be the longer-term implications of these developments?

STUDY QUESTIONS

1. How did technological advances, such as the magnetic needle compass, junks, and dhows, fuel the maritime revolution in 1000–1300?
2. What political forces contributed to the fragmentation of the Islamic world in this period? What cultural forces provided a unifying force within Islam?
3. Compare raja-ruled India with that of Muslim-Turkish regimes such as the **Delhi Sultanate**.
4. How did economic and manufacturing developments, coupled with political developments, cement the power of the Song dynasty? How did Song interactions with nomads and neighbors lead to distinctive identities for both the Song and their neighbors?
5. How did developments such as **manorialism**, universities, and the Crusades contribute to Europe's identity as a fragmented yet distinctive cultural sphere?
6. Compare the trans-Saharan trade of the Mande-speaking peoples of West Africa and later **Mali** Empire that developed there with the Indian Ocean trade of the Shona-speaking peoples of East Africa. What goods were traded and what was the impact of that trade on these two regions of Africa?
7. Compare the degrees of integration in various regions of the Americas: South America (**Chimú Empire**), Mesoamerica (**Toltecs**), and North America (**Cahokia**).
8. What enabled the Mongols to conquer such huge swaths of territory across Eurasia? Contrast the expansion of Hulagu into the west with that of Kubilai Khan in the east?

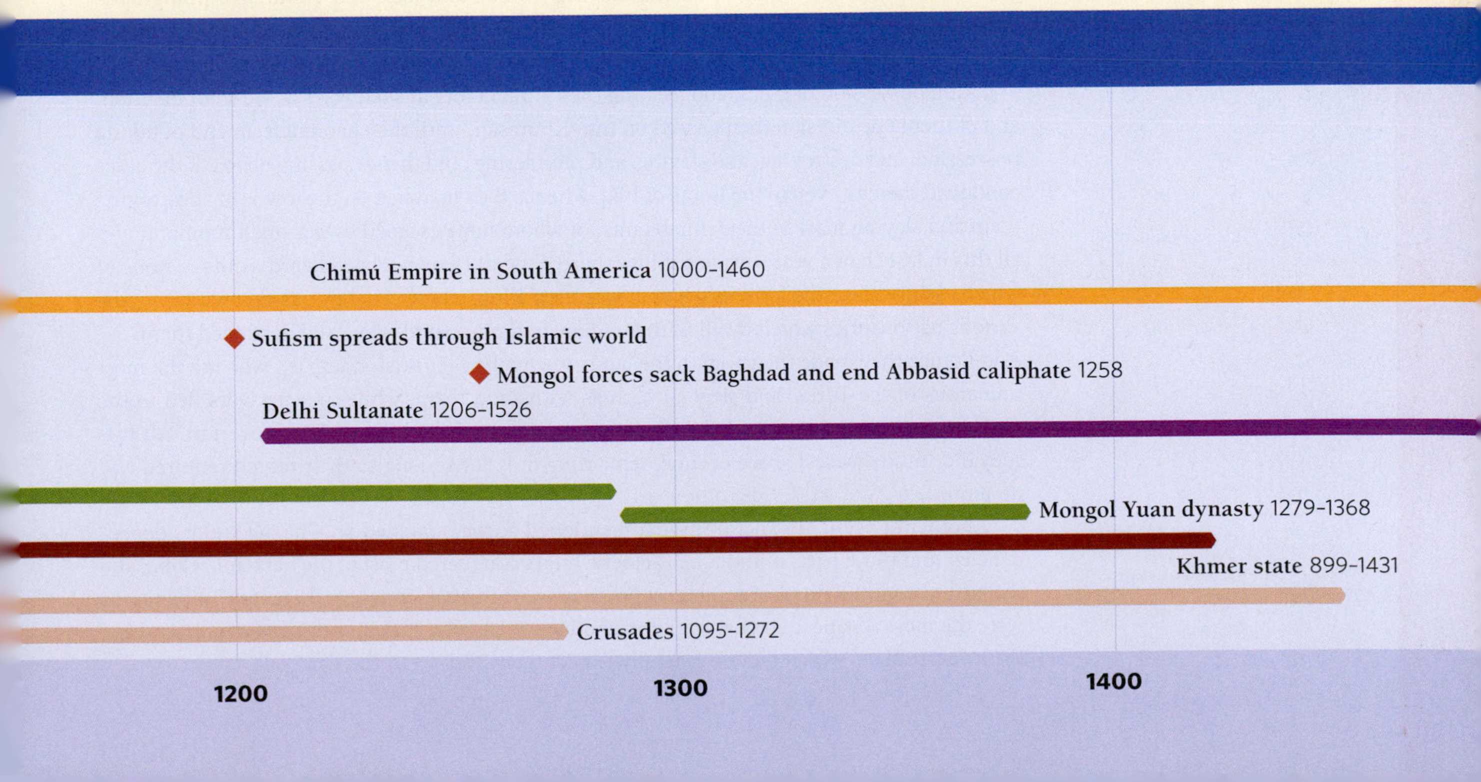

Going to the Source

Traveling around the Mongol World: The *Pax Mongolica*

The Mongols began their expansion from their territories, which were north and west of China's Great Wall, around 1206, moving south into China and west into central Asia. They eventually conquered both Muslim and Christian lands to the west and Chinese lands to the south. They even tried to conquer Japan and Java by sea, but were unsuccessful. The Mongols were fierce and effective fighters who used both horses and compound bows in their conquests. Once conquered, a kind of stability, or Pax Mongolica, prevailed in their territories, even controlling the Silk Roads. Their rule, however, came to an end in China with the rise of the Ming Empire.

PRIMARY SOURCE 10.1

On the Mongols (1220–1221), Ibn al-Athir

Ibn al-Athir (1160–1233) was a historian and biographer who lived in what is now modern-day Iraq. He wrote about the Mongol incursions into the Islamic empires of Southwest Asia in the thirteenth century, and the story he tells is one of war and Muslim defeat, but it also describes the conflict for control of the Eurasian landmass between the Islamic and Mongol empires. Eventually, some of the khanates would adopt Islam as their official language, but the Mongol territories generally permitted all religions to be practiced.

[T]hese Tatars [Mongols] spared none, slaying women and men and children, ripping open pregnant women and killing unborn babes. . . . For these were a people who emerged from the confines of China, and attacked the cities of Turkestan . . . and thence advanced on the cities . . . taking possession of them, and treating their inhabitants in such ways as we shall mention; and of them one division then passed on into Khurasan, until they had made an end of taking possession, and destroying, and slaying, and plundering, and thence passing on to . . . the cities contained therein, even to the limits of Iraq, whence they marched on the towns . . . destroying them and slaying most of their inhabitants, of whom none escaped save a small remnant; and all this in less than a year; this is a thing whereof the like has not been heard. And . . . none of which escaped save the fortress wherein was their King; wherefore they passed by it to . . . the various nationalities which dwell in that region, and plundered, slew, and destroyed them. . . . And thence they made their way to the lands of Qipchaq [Turkish nomads], who are the most numerous of the Turks, and slew all such as withstood them, while the survivors fled to the fords and mountain-tops, and abandoned their country, which these Tatars overran. All this they did in the briefest space of time, remaining only for so long as their march required and no more.

Another division, distinct from that mentioned above, marched on Ghazna and its dependencies, and those parts of India. . . . [T]hese Tatars conquered most of the habitable globe, and the best, the most flourishing and most populous part thereof, and that whereof the inhabitants were the most advanced in character and conduct, in about a year; nor did any country escape their devastations which did not fearfully expect them and dread their arrival.

Moreover they need no commissariat, nor the conveyance of supplies, for they have with them sheep, cows, horses, and the like quadrupeds, the flesh of which they eat, naught else. As for their beasts which they ride, these dig into the earth with their hoofs and eat the roots of plants, knowing naught of barley. And so, when they alight anywhere, they have need of nothing from without. As for their religion, they worship the sun when it rises, and regard nothing as unlawful, for they eat all beasts, even dogs, pigs, and the like. . . .

Therefore Islam and the Muslims have been afflicted during this period with calamities wherewith no people hath been visited. These Tatars (may God confound them!) came from the East, and wrought deeds which horrify all who hear of them. . . . We ask God to vouchsafe victory to Islam and the Muslims, for there is none other to aid, help, or defend the True Faith. But if God intends evil to any people, naught can avert it, nor have they any ruler save Him. As for these Tatars, their achievements were only rendered possible by the absence of any effective obstacle.

1. **According to Ibn al-Athir, why were the Mongols so powerful?**
2. **What was Ibn al-Athir's greatest fear, as expressed in this account, and why was he fearful?**

PRIMARY SOURCE 10.2

Letter from Guyuk Khan to Pope Innocent IV (c. 1246)

In 1237, Mongol armies began sacking several major Russian cities, and by 1241 the Mongols had defeated the Polish and German armies and the Hungarians, and were threatening Austria in the heart of Europe. This expansion worried European leaders and prompted Pope Innocent IV to send an envoy to learn the Mongol intentions. In 1245–1246 the pope and Guyuk Khan, leader of the Mongol Empire, exchanged letters through Catholic emissaries. The following letter is Guyuk Khan's response to Pope Innocent IV.

Having taken counsel for making peace with us. You Pope and all Christians have sent an envoy to us, as we have heard from him and as your letters declare. Wherefore, if you wish to have peace with us, You Pope and all kings and potentates, in no way delay to come to me to make terms of peace and then you shall hear alike our answer and our will. The contents of your letters stated that we ought to be baptized and become Christians. To this we answer briefly that we do not understand in what way we ought to do this. To the rest of the contents of your letters, viz: that you wonder at so great a slaughter of men, especially of Christians and in particular Poles, Moravians, and Hungarians, we reply likewise that this also we do not understand. However, lest we may seem to pass it over in silence altogether, we give you this for our answer.

Because they did not obey the word of God and the command of Chingis Khan . . . but took council to slay our envoys, therefore God ordered us to destroy them and gave them into our hands. For otherwise if God had not done this, what could man do to man? But you men of the West believe that you alone are Christians and despise others. But how can you know to whom God deigns to confer His grace? But we worshipping God have destroyed the whole earth from East to West in the power of God. And if this were not the power of God, what could men have done? Therefore if you accept peace and are willing to surrender your fortresses to us, You Pope and Christian princes, in no way delay coming to me to conclude peace and then we shall know that you wish to have peace with us. But if you should not believe our letters and the command of God nor hearken to our counsel then we shall know for certain that you wish to have war. After that we do not know what will happen: God alone knows.

1. **Why do you think Chingis Khan responded in this way to the pope?**
2. **Compare Primary Sources 10.1 and 10.2, which both portray the Mongols as violent and warlike people. Why might the authors have portrayed Mongols that way?**

PRIMARY SOURCE 10.3

Pilgrimage to Jerusalem (c. 1300), Bar Sāwmā

Born in Yuan China, the Nestorian Christian monk Rabban Bar Sāwmā traveled primarily across land routes from China through Mongol-controlled territory, all the way to Europe. On this journey he set out for Jerusalem but faced trouble on the roads and got only as far as Baghdad, then controlled by the Mongols. His goal, as this narrative indicates, was both religious and diplomatic. He describes his travels with his companions, as recorded in a Syriac text shortly after his death in Baghdad in 1294.

Chapter 3. One day they meditated, saying, "It would be exceedingly helpful to us if we were to leave this region and set out for the West, for we could then [visit] the tombs of the holy martyrs and Catholic Fathers and be blessed [by them]. And if Christ, the Lord of the Universe, prolonged our lives, and sustained us by His grace, we could go to Jerusalem, so that we might receive complete pardon for our offences, and absolution for our sins of foolishness. Now although Rabban Sâwmâ opposed Rabban Mark, and [tried to] frighten him with the toil of the journey, and the fatigue of travelling, and the terror of the ways, and the tribulations that would beset him in a foreign country, Rabban Mark burned to set out on the road. . . . And they arrived in Baghdad, and thence they went to the Great Church of Kôkê. . . . And they went to the monastery of Mâr Mârî, the Apostle, and received a blessing from the sepulchers (or relics?) of that country. And from there they turned back and came to the country of Bêth Garmai, and they received blessings from the shrine (or tomb) of Mâr Ezekiel [the prophet, near Dâḳôḳ], which was full of helps and healings. And from there they went to Arbîl, and thence to Mâwsil (i.e., Môṣul on the Tigris). And they went Shîgar (Sinjâr), and Nisibis, and Merdâ (Mardîn); and were blessed by the shrine [containing] the bones of Mâr Awgîn, the second Christ. And thence they went . . . and they were blessed by all the shrines and monasteries, and the religious houses, and monks, and the Fathers (i.e., Bishops) in their dioceses. . . . [W]hen they arrived there they heard from the inhabitants of the country that the road was cut because of the murders and robberies which had taken place along it.

Chapter 4. And the two monks turned back and came to Mâr Catholicus, who rejoiced [at the sight of] them, and said unto them, "This is not the time for a journey to Jerusalem. The roads are a disturbed state, and the ways are cut. Now behold, ye have received blessings from all the Houses of God, and the shrines (or relics?) which are in them, and it is my opinion that when a man visits them with a pure heart, the service thus paid to them is in no way less than that of a pilgrimage to Jerusalem.

1. **What dangers did the travelers encounter on their journey?**
2. **What role did religion play in this journey, both for those who traveled and those who controlled the territory through which they passed?**

PRIMARY SOURCE 10.4

Mongol Divination (c. 1300), Marco Polo

The Venetian merchant Marco Polo traveled at nearly the same time as Rabban Bar Sāwmā , but in the opposite direction. Long after his voyages were completed, Marco Polo recounted his twenty-four years of travel (1271–1295), including his time in the Mongol court of China. As this passage indicates, he described the connection that he observed between Mongol victory and what must have seemed like superstition, given Mongol control of so much territory on the Eurasian landmass.

*

Chapter 45. Chingis-khan commanded his astrologers and magicians to declare to him which of the two armies, in the approaching conflict, should obtain the victory. Upon this they took a green reed, and dividing it lengthways into two parts, they wrote upon one the name of their master, and upon the other the name of Un-khan. They then placed them on the ground, at some distance from each other, and gave notice to the king that during the time of their pronouncing their incantations, the two pieces of reed, through the power of their idols, would advance towards each other, and that the victory would fall to the lot of that monarch whose piece should be seen to mount upon the other. The whole army was assembled to be spectators of this ceremony, and whilst the astrologers were employed in reading their books of necromancy, they perceived the two pieces begin to move and to approach, and after some small interval of time, that inscribed with the name of Chingis-khan to place itself upon the top of its adversary. Upon witnessing this, the king and his band of Tartars marched with exultation to the attack of the army of Un-khan, broke through its ranks and entirely routed it. Un-khan himself was killed, his kingdom fell to the conqueror, and Chingis-khan espoused his daughter. After this battle he continued during six years to render himself master of additional kingdoms and cities; until at length, in the siege of a castle named Thaigin, he was struck by an arrow in the knee, and dying of the wound, was buried in the mountain of Altai.

1. **What does this account tell us about Mongol religious belief?**
2. **According to Chingis-khan's belief, what is the connection between success on the battlefield and the supernatural?**

PRIMARY SOURCE 10.5

Manifesto of Accession as First Ming Emperor (1372), Zhu Yuan-zhang (Hongwu Emperor)

Kublai Khan, a grandson of Chingis Khan, established the Yuan dynasty in China in 1271, which made China part of the Mongol Empire. Eventually the Yuan were replaced with the Ming dynasty in 1368. This letter sent by the Ming dynasty's new emperor, known as Hongwu, to the Byzantine emperor proclaims the end of Mongol rule in China and describes the factors that contributed to the Mongol's removal from power.

*

Since the Sung dynasty had lost the throne and Heaven had cut off their sacrifice, the Yuan dynasty had risen from the desert to enter and rule over Zhongguo [China] for more than a hundred years, when Heaven, wearied of their misgovernment and debauchery, thought also fit to turn their fate to ruin, and the affairs of Zhongguo were in a state of disorder for eighteen years. But when the nation began to arouse itself, We, as a simple peasant . . . conceived the patriotic idea to save the people, and it pleased the Creator to grant that Our civil and military officers effected their passage across eastward to the left side of the River. We have then been engaged in war for fourteen years; We have, in the west, subdued the king. . . . We have, in the east, bound the king. . . . We have, in the south, subdued Min and Yueh [Fukien and Kuang-tung], and conquered Pa and Shu [Sze-chuan]; We have, in the north, established order. . . . We have established peace in the Empire, and restored the old boundaries of Zhongguo. We were selected by Our people to occupy the Imperial throne of Zhongguo under the dynastic title of "the Great Ming," commencing with Our reign styled Hung-wu, of which we now are in the fourth year. We have sent officers to all the foreign kingdoms with this Manifesto except to you, Fu-lin [Byzantium], who, being separated from us by the western sea, have not as yet received the announcement. We now send a native of your country, Nieh-ku-lun [Fra. Nicolaus de Bentra, Archbishop of Peking], to hand you this Manifesto.

Although We are not equal in wisdom to our ancient rulers whose virtue was recognized all over the universe, We cannot but let the world know Our intention to maintain peace within the four seas. It is on this ground alone that We have issued this Manifesto.

1. **Why do you think it was so important for the Hongwu Emperor to write to the Byzantine Emperor?**
2. **How is the transition away from Yuan rule depicted in this letter?**

PRIMARY SOURCE 10.6

The Siege of Baghdad (1258), Persian Manuscript

This image depicts the Mongol siege of Baghdad, which lasted about twelve days. The Abbasids did not surrender to the besieging Mongols, but they were ultimately defeated and the Mongols sacked the city, executing many.

1. **How does this image depict the residents of Baghdad?**
2. **Explain how technology was used by both the Mongols and the Abbasids.**

Questions for Analysis

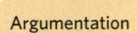

Continuity and Change over Time

1. Explain the ways in which Europe and Asia became integrated during this period.

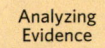

Argumentation

2. Explain the role of religion in integrating disparate places and peoples.

Analyzing Evidence

3. Based upon these documents, compare the way that Muslims, Christians, and Mongols approached the relationship between violence and empire.

Long Essay Question

Synthesis

Based on these documents and your reading of the chapter, assess whether the Mongol Empire had more of a positive or a negative impact on those who lived under its rule.

Before You Read This Chapter

GLOBAL STORYLINES

- The spread of the Black Death and the collapse of the Mongol Empire sets off crises across Afro-Eurasia, with major demographic, political, economic, and cultural consequences.
- Across Afro-Eurasia, continuity in religious beliefs and cultural institutions accompanies changes in political structures in Europe, the Muslim world, and China.
- In central Eurasia, new rulers—most notably the Ottomans—rebuild dynasties in place of the Mongols, using a blend of religion, military expansion, administrative control, and cultural tolerance.
- In Western Christendom, new monarchies establish political order, and the Renaissance brings a cultural rebirth to societies devastated by plague.
- In East Asia, the Ming dynasty replaces the Mongol Yuan dynasty, using an elaborate Confucian bureaucracy to oversee infrastructure and long-distance exchange.

CORE OBJECTIVES

- **DESCRIBE** the nature and origins of the crises spanning Afro-Eurasia during the fourteenth century and **ASSESS** the magnitude of the crises' effects, locally and trans-regionally.
- **EXPLAIN** the continuities of religious belief systems from the fourteenth through the fifteenth century.
- **COMPARE** the ways in which regional rulers in post-plague Afro-Eurasia attempted to construct unified states and **ANALYZE** the extent and nature of their successes.
- **EXAMINE** the ways in which the art and/or architecture of different regions reflected political realities, and **DESCRIBE** the specific themes that communicate these messages to viewers.
- **COMPARE** the means by which the Iberian kingdoms, the Ottoman Empire, the Ming Dynasty, and European polities each extended their territory and regional influence.

CHAPTER

11

Crises and Recovery in Afro-Eurasia

1300–1500

KEY TERMS

Black Death p. 405
devshirme p. 415
dynasty p. 410
humanism p. 422
Inquisition p. 421
monarchy p. 419
Ottoman Empire p. 412
Red Turban Movement p. 408
Renaissance p. 422
Topkapi Palace p. 414
Zheng He p. 429

When Mongol armies besieged the Genoese trading outpost of Caffa on the Black Sea in 1346, they not only damaged trading links between East Asia and the Mediterranean but also unleashed a devastating disease: the bubonic plague. Defeated Genoese merchants and soldiers withdrew, unknowingly taking the germs with them aboard their ships. By the time they arrived in Messina, Sicily, half the passengers were dead. The rest were dying. People waiting on shore for the ships' trade goods were horrified at the sight and turned the ships away. Desperately, the captains went to the next port, only to face the same fate. Despite these efforts at isolation, Europeans could not keep the plague (called the Black Death) from reaching their shores. As it spread from port to port, it eventually contaminated all of Europe, killing more than half of the population.

This story illustrates the disruptive effects of the Mongol invasions and the long-distance trade routes that the Mongol invasions foisted on Afro-Eurasian societies. In the thirteenth and early fourteenth centuries, Mongol armies swept into and took control of vast regions of Afro-Eurasia. Although the invasions ushered in an age of intensified cultural and political contact, the channels of exchange—the land trails and sea-lanes of human voyagers—became accidental conduits for deadly microbes. These germs devastated societies far more decisively than did Mongol warfare. They were the real "murderous hordes" of world history, infecting people from every community, class, and culture they encountered. So staggering was the Black Death's toll that population densities did not recover for 200 years. The most severely affected regions were those that the Mongols had brought together: settlements and commercial hubs along the old Silk Road and around the Mediterranean Sea and the South China Sea. While segments of the Indian Ocean trading world experienced death and disruption, South Asian societies, which had escaped the Mongol conquest, also escaped the dying and political disruptions associated with the Black Death.

This chapter explores the ways in which Afro-Eurasian peoples restored what they thought was valuable from old traditions while discarding what they thought had failed them, in favor of radically new institutions and ideas. Much of the recovery across Afro-Eurasia had striking similarities, as societies reaffirmed their most deeply held and long-standing beliefs. Chinese rulers looked to Confucian thought and well-known dynastic institutions to provide guidance going forward. In the Muslim heartland a small band of Turkish-speaking warriors—the Ottomans—channeled the energies of a revived Islam to expand their own territory and the Muslim world. Europeans also invoked their traditions. In the Iberian Peninsula political elites used a resurgent Catholicism to spread their political power and drive Muslim communities out of Europe. Europeans also created new dynastic monarchies and looked to their distant past in Greek and Roman culture for inspiration.

Radically new institutions and ideas appeared across Afro-Eurasia in the aftermath of the Black Death. Notable among these was the outburst of cultural activity that took place in western Europe. Historians have called this flourishing the Renaissance ("rebirth"), for during this era Europeans rediscovered their Greek and Roman pasts and used their inspiration drawn from classical antiquity to bring about far-reaching innovations in art, architecture, thought, and political and financial institutions. While recognizing significant changes to institutions and ideas in this period, this chapter stresses continuities. Considering how grievously people suffered and how many died, it is surprising how much of the old—particularly religious beliefs and institutions—survived the aftermath of Mongol rule and the Black Death. Rulers altered but did not transform their inherited traditions.

Collapse and Consolidation

COMPARISON

DESCRIBE the nature and origins of the crises spanning Afro-Eurasia during the fourteenth century.

Although the Mongol invasions overturned political systems, the plague devastated society itself. The pandemic killed millions, disrupted economies, and threw communities into chaos. Rulers could explain to their people the assaults of "barbarians," but it was much harder to make sense of an invisible enemy. Nonetheless, in response to the upheaval, new ruling groups moved to reorganize their states. By making strategic marriages and building powerful armies, these rulers enlarged their territories, formed alliances, and built dynasties.

THE BLACK DEATH

The spread of the Black Death was the fourteenth century's most significant historical development (see Map 11.1). Originating in Inner Asia, the disease afflicted peoples from China to Europe and killed 25 to 65 percent of infected populations.

How did the **Black Death** move so far and so fast? One explanation may lie in climatic changes. A cooler climate—scholars refer to a "Little Ice Age"—may have weakened populations and left them vulnerable to disease. In Europe, for instance, beginning around 1310, harsh winters and rainy summers shortened the growing seasons and ruined harvests. Exhausted soils no longer supplied the resources required by growing urban and rural populations, while nobles squeezed the peasantry in an effort to maintain their luxurious lifestyle. The ensuing famine lasted from 1315 to 1322, during which time millions of Europeans died of starvation or of diseases against which the malnourished population had little resistance. This climate change and famine laid the groundwork for the Black Death that soon followed. Another climate-related factor in the spread of the plague lay in the drying up of the central Asian steppe borderlands, where bubonic plague had existed for centuries. This drought may have forced rodents out of their usual dwelling places and pressed pastoral peoples, who carried the infectious strains, to move closer to settled agricultural communities. Fleas transmitted plague from rodent to rodent, and to humans. The resulting epidemic was terrifying, for its causes were unknown at the time. Infected victims died quickly—sometimes overnight—and in agony, coughing up blood and oozing pus and blood from black sores the size of eggs.

Plague Victim The plague was highly contagious and quickly led to death. Here the physician and his helper cover their noses to avoid the unbearable stench emanating from the patient. What strategies, other than medical, do you see the individuals in this image using against the plague?

But it was the trading network that spread the germs across Afro-Eurasia into famine-struck western Europe. This wider Afro-Eurasian population was vulnerable because its members had no immunities to the disease. The first outbreak in a heavily populated region occurred in the 1320s in southwestern China. From there, the disease spread through China and then took its death march along the major trade routes. Many routes terminated at the Italian port cities, where ships with dead and dying people aboard arrived in 1347. From there, what Europeans called the Pestilence or the Great Mortality engulfed the western end of the landmass. In China, the Muslim world, and Europe, societies suffered the disastrous effects of the Black Death.

Plague in China China was ripe for the plague's pandemic. Its population had increased under the Song dynasty (960 CE–1279) and subsequent Mongol rule. But by 1300, hunger and scarcity spread as resources were stretched thin. The weakened population was especially vulnerable. For seventy years, the Black Death ravaged China, reduced the size of the already small Mongol population, and shattered the Mongols' claim to a mandate from heaven. In 1331, plague may have killed 90 percent of the population in Bei Zhili (modern Hebei) province. From there it spread throughout other provinces, reaching Fujian and the coast at Shandong. By the 1350s, most of China's large cities suffered severe outbreaks.

COMPARISON

COMPARE the impact of the Black Death on China, Islam, and Europe.

SCANDINAVIA 1349
NORTH SEA
BALTIC SEA
Novgorod
Moscow
MUSCOVY 1351
Edinburgh (1350)
BRITAIN
Dublin (1349)
Oxford (1348)
London (1348)
Lübeck (1349)
Danzig
Bremen (1349)
Cologne (1349)
Amiens (1348)
Paris (1348)
EUROPE
Cracow
Kiev
KHANATE OF THE GOLDEN HORDE
Rostov
New Sarai
ARAL SEA
CASPIAN SEA
Buda (1349)
Venice (1347)
Genoa (1347)
Florence (1347)
Siena (1347)
Pisa (1347)
Bordeaux (1348)
Avignon (1347)
Marseille
Barcelona (1348)
Madrid
SPAIN 1348
Lisbon (1349)
BLACK SEA
Caffa (1346)
Constantinople (1347)
Trebizond
ANATOLIA
Naples
Palermo (1347)
Messina (1347)
Athens (1347)
Tabriz
Maraghah
Bukhara
Samar
Silk route
Aleppo (1347)
Baghdad (1347)
Isfahan
PERSIA
IL-KHANATE
Damascus (1347)
Jerusalem (1347)
Alexandria (1347)
Cairo (1347)
Basra
Shiraz
Hormuz
Persian Gulf
Ceuta
Fez
Algiers
Tunis
MEDITERRANEAN SEA
Tripoli (1348)
Marrakesh (1349)
Medina
Mecca (1348)
ARABIA
RED SEA
AFRICA
ARABIAN SEA
Aden (1351)
Mogadishu
INDIAN
ATLANTIC OCEAN
Progress of bubonic plague
Trade routes
Known areas of major outbreaks
Modern Chinese provincial names for regions affected by outbreak of plague

MAP 11.1 | The Spread of the Black Death

The Black Death was an Afro-Eurasian pandemic of the fourteenth century.

- What was the origin point of the Black Death?
- What were the main trade routes that allowed the Black Death to spread across Afro-Eurasia?
- Based on your reading, what factors made some areas more vulnerable to plague than others?

Even as the Black Death was engulfing China, bandit groups and dissident religious sects were undercutting the power of the last Yuan Mongol rulers. Popular religious movements warned of impending doom. Most prominent was the **Red Turban Movement**, which blended China's diverse cultural and religious traditions, including Buddhism, Daoism, and other faiths. Its leaders emphasized strict dietary restrictions, penance, and ceremonial rituals, and made proclamations that the world was drawing to an end.

Plague in the Islamic World The plague devastated parts of the Muslim world as well. The Black Death reached Baghdad by 1347. By the next year, the plague overtook Egypt, Syria, and Cyprus, with as many as 1,000 deaths a day according to a Tunisian report. Animals, too, were afflicted. One Egyptian writer commented: "The country was not far from being ruined. . . . One found in the desert the bodies of savage animals with the bubos under their arms. It was the same with horses, camels, asses, and all the beasts in general, including birds, even the ostriches." In the eastern Mediterranean, plague left much of the Islamic world in a state of near political and economic collapse. The great Arab historian Ibn Khaldun (1332–1406), who lost his mother and father and a number of his teachers to the Black Death in Tunis, underscored the desolation: "Cities and buildings were laid waste, roads and way signs were obliterated, settlements and mansions became empty, dynasties and tribes grew weak," he wrote. "The entire world changed."

Plague in Europe In Europe, the Black Death first ravaged the Italian Peninsula; then it seized France, the Netherlands, Belgium, Luxembourg, Germany, and England in its deathly grip. Overcrowded and unsanitary cities were particularly vulnerable. All levels of society—the poor, craftspeople, aristocrats—were at risk, although flight to the countryside offered some protection from infection. Nearly 50 million of Europe's 80 million perished between 1347 and 1351. After 1353, the epidemic waned, but the plague returned every seven years or so for the rest of the century, and sporadically through the fifteenth century. Consequently, the European population continued to decline, until by 1450 many areas had only one quarter the number of a century earlier.

In the face of the Black Death, some Europeans turned to debauchery, determined to enjoy themselves before they died. Others, especially in urban settings in Flanders, the Netherlands, and parts of Germany, claimed to find God's grace outside what they saw as a corrupt Church. Semimonastic orders like the Beghards held that a good layman could perform sacraments as well as a priest and that people should trust their own "interior instinct" more than the Gospel as then preached. By contrast, the Flagellants were so convinced that man had incurred God's wrath that they whipped themselves to atone for human sin.

For many who survived the plague, disappointment with the clergy smoldered. Famished peasants resented priests and monks for living lives of luxury. In addition, they despaired at the absence of clergy when they were so greatly needed. While many clerics had perished attending to their parishioners during the Black Death, others had fled to rural retreats far from the ravages of the plague, leaving their followers to fend for themselves.

The Black Death wrought devastation throughout Afro-Eurasia. The Chinese population plunged from around 115 million in 1200 to 75 million or less in 1400, the result of the Mongol invasions of the thirteenth century and the disease and disorder of the fourteenth century (see **Analyzing Global Developments: Population Changes in Fourteenth-Century Afro-Eurasia**). Over the course of the fourteenth century, Europe's population shrank by more than 50 percent. In the most densely settled Islamic territory—Egypt—a population that had totaled around 6 million in 1400 was cut in half. When farmers fell ill with the plague, food production collapsed. Famine followed and killed off the survivors.

Bubonic Plague and the Destruction of Society Bubonic plague devastated the countries of Western Christendom. Here, in Pieter Bruegel the Elder's *The Triumph of Death* (1562), we see skeletons murdering indiscriminately, rich and poor alike. Notice the role of religious imagery in this painting. Notice also the representation of social class. How does the artist convey distinctions of rank and status?

Worst afflicted were the crowded cities, especially coastal ports. Some cities lost up to two-thirds of their population. Refugees from urban areas fled their homes, seeking security and food in the countryside. The shortage of food and other necessities led to rapidly rising prices, work stoppages, and unrest. Political leaders added to their unpopularity by repressing the unrest. Everywhere, regimes trembled and collapsed. The Mongol empire, which had held so much of Eurasia together commercially and politically, disintegrated. Thus, the way was prepared for experiments in state building, religious beliefs, and cultural understandings.

REBUILDING STATES

Starting in the late fourteenth century, Afro-Eurasians began the task of reconstructing both their political order and their trading networks. By then the plague had died down, though it continued to afflict peoples for centuries. However, the rebuilding of military and civil administrations—no easy task—also required political legitimacy. With their

Analyzing Global Developments

Population Changes in Fourteenth-Century Afro-Eurasia

Famine, warfare, and disease led to vast population declines all across Afro-Eurasia in the fourteenth century. The Mongols were instrumental players in spreading disease across the landmass starting in China and moving westward along land- and sea-based trading routes towards the Mediterranean world and, ultimately, northern Europe (see Map 11.1). While the effects of these destructive forces were felt across the Afro-Eurasian landmass, some states and regions were less affected than others. The population data below come from the best historical studies of the last forty years and are based on painstaking archival research. They serve as one of the best ways for us to gain historical insight into this tumultuous century.

QUESTIONS FOR ANALYSIS

- Identify the regions or cities where population loss seems to have been lower or higher. Why might those variations in death rates have occurred?
- Compare the losses in urban areas with the losses in the region where those urban areas are located. What might that comparison suggest about the impact of fourteenth-century disasters on urban versus other populations?
- Explain why population decline was more severe and widespread in Europe than in Asia.
- Explain how the great loss of population in Europe and China marked a turning point in their histories.

LOCATION	POPULATION FIGURES	ACROSS THE 14TH CENTURY	% CHANGE
By Regions			
Europe	80M in 1346	30M in 1353	−60%
Asia	230M in 1300	235M in 1400	+2%
Islam	(regional data are not available)		
By Countries			
Spain	6M in 1346	2.5M in 1353	−60%
Italy	10M in 1346	4.5M in 1363	−55%
France	18M in 1346	7.2M in 1353	−60%
England	6M in 1346	2.25M in 1353	−62.5%
China	115M in 1200 85M in 1300	75M in 1400	−35% overall
Japan	9.75M in 1300	12.5M in 1400	+28%
Korea	3M in 1300	3.5M in 1400	+17%
India	91M in 1300	97M in 1400	+6.5%
By Cities			
London	100,000 in 1346	37,000 in 1353	−62.5%
Florence	92,000 in 1346	37,250 in 1353	−59.5%
Sienna	50,000 in 1346	20,000 in 1353	−60%
Bologna	50,000 in 1346	27,500 in 1353	−45%
Cairo	500,000 in 1300	300,000 in 1400	−40%
Damascus	80,000 in 1300	50,000 in 1400	−37%

Sources: Ole J. Benedictow, *The Black Death, 1346–1353: The Complete History* (Woodbridge, England, 2004); Michael Dols, *The Black Death in the Middle East* (Princeton, 1974): Colin McEvedy and Richard Jones, *Atlas of World Population History* (Hammondsworth, England, 1978); Ping-ti Ho, *Studies on the Population of China, 1368–1953 (Cambridge, MA, 1959).*

people deeply shaken by the extraordinary loss of life, rulers needed to revive confidence in themselves and their regimes, which they did by fostering beliefs and rituals that confirmed their legitimacy and by increasing their control over subjects.

The basis for power was a political institution well known to Afro-Eurasians for centuries, the **dynasty**—the hereditary ruling family that passed control from one generation to the next. As in the past, the new dynasties sought to establish their legitimacy in three ways. First, ruling families insisted that their power derived from a divine calling: Ming emperors in China claimed for themselves what previous dynastic rulers had asserted—the "mandate of heaven"—while European monarchs claimed to rule by "divine right." From their base in Anatolia, Ottoman warrior-princes asserted that they now carried the banner of Islam. In these ways, ruling households affirmed that God or the heavens intended for them to hold power. Second, leaders prevented squabbling among potential heirs by establishing clear rules about succession to the throne. Many European states tried to standardize succession by passing titles to the eldest male heir, thus ensuring political stability at a potential time of crisis, but in practice there were countless complications and quarrels. In the Islamic world, successors could be designated by the current ruler or elected by the community; here, too, struggles over succession were frequent. Third, ruling families elevated their power through conquest or alliance—by ordering armies forcibly to extend their domains, or by marrying their royal offspring to rulers of other states or members of other elite households, a technique widely practiced in Europe. Once it established legitimacy, the typical royal family would consolidate power by enacting coercive laws and punishments and sending emissaries to govern distant territories. A ruling family would also establish standing armies and new administrative structures to collect taxes and to oversee building projects that proclaimed royal power.

As we will see in the next three sections of this chapter, the innovative state building that occurred in the wake of the plague's devastation would not have been as successful had it not drawn on older traditions. In Europe, a cultural flourishing based largely on ancient Greek and Roman models gave rise to thinkers who proposed new views of governance. The peoples of the Islamic world held fiercely to their religion as successor states, notably the Ottoman Empire, absorbed numerous Turkish-speaking groups. The Ming, having failed in their attempts to control northern Vietnam and Korea, renounced the Mongol expansionist legacy and emphasized a return to Han rulership consolidating control of Chinese lands and concentrating on internal markets rather than overseas trade. Many of these regimes lasted for centuries, promoting political institutions and cultural values that became deeply embedded in the fabric of their societies.

The Islamic Heartland

The devastation of the Black Death followed hard on the heels of the Mongol destruction of Islam's most important city, Baghdad, and Islam's old political order. Nonetheless, these two catastrophes prepared the way for new Islamic states to emerge. The old, Arabic-speaking Islamic world remained vital, still at the heart of Islam geographically, but it now had to yield authority to new rulers and religious men. These societies now included large Turkish- and Persian-speaking populations as well. The new Islamic world occupied a vast geographical triangle. It stretched from Anatolia in the west to the Khurasan region of Persia and Afghanistan in the east and to the southern point at Baghdad.

The Ottomans, the Safavids, and the Mughals emerged as the dominant states in the old Islamic world in the early sixteenth century. They exploited the rich agrarian resources of the Indian Ocean regions and the Mediterranean Sea basin, and they benefited from a brisk seaborne and overland trade. By the mid-sixteenth century the Mughals controlled the northern Indus River valley; the Safavids occupied Persia; and the Ottomans ruled Anatolia, the Arab world, and much of southern and eastern Europe. Here we will explore in depth the Ottoman Empire, which emerged first and endured the longest of the three. (See Chapter 12 for a fuller discussion of the Mughals and Chapter 14 for more on the Safavids.)

THE OTTOMAN EMPIRE

The rise of the **Ottoman Empire** owed as much to innovative administrative techniques and religious tolerance as to military strength. Although the Mongols considered Anatolia to be a borderland region of little economic importance, their military forays in the late thirteenth century opened up the region to new political forces. The ultimate victors here were the Ottoman Turks. They transformed themselves from warrior bands roaming the borderlands between Islamic and Christian worlds into rulers of a settled state and, finally, into sovereigns of a far-flung highly bureaucratic empire (see Map 11.2). Under their chief, Osman (r. 1299–1326), the Turkish Ottomans formalized a stern and disciplined warrior ethos. They triumphed over their rivals by adapting the techniques of administration from their neighbors and by attracting these groups to their rule. In time, not only did the Ottoman state win the favor of Islamic clerics, but it also became the champion of Sunni Islam throughout the Islamic world.

MAP 11.2 | The Ottoman Empire, 1300-1566

This map charts the expansion of the Ottoman state from the time of its founder, Osman, through the reign of Suleiman, the empire's most illustrious ruler. Identify the earliest part of the empire under Osman. Then identify all the areas of conquest under Suleiman.

- Against whom did the Ottomans fight between the years 1326 and 1566?
- What were the geographic limits of the empire?
- According to your reading, how did Ottoman rulers promote unity among such a diverse population?

By the mid-fourteenth century, the Ottomans had expanded into the Balkans, becoming the most powerful force in the eastern Mediterranean and western Asia. By the early sixteenth century, the state controlled a vast territory, stretching in the west to the Moroccan border, in the north to Hungary and Moldavia, in the south through the Arabian Peninsula, and in the east to the Persian border. What was impressive and new within the Islamic world was the Ottomans' elaborate administrative hierarchy, atop which stood the sultan. Below him was a military and civilian bureaucracy, whose task was to demand obedience and revenue from subjects. The bureaucracy's discipline enabled the sultan to expand his realm, which in turn forced him to invest in an even larger bureaucracy.

The empire's spectacular expansion was primarily a military affair. To recruit followers, the Ottomans promised wealth and glory to new subjects. This was an expensive undertaking, but territorial expansion generated vast financial and administrative rewards. Moreover, by spreading the spoils of conquest and lucrative administrative positions, rulers bought off potentially unhappy subordinates. Still, without military might, the Ottomans would not have enjoyed the successes associated with the brilliant reigns of Murad II (r. 1421–1451) and his appropriately named successor, Mehmed the Conqueror (r. 1451–1481).

Mehmed's most spectacular triumph was the conquest of Constantinople, an ambition for Muslim rulers ever since the birth of Islam. Mehmed left no doubt that this was his primary goal: shortly after his coronation he vowed to capture the capital of the Byzantine Empire, a city of immense strategic and commercial importance, which had withstood Muslim efforts at conquest for centuries. First he built a fortress of his own to prevent European vessels from reaching the capital. Then, by promising his soldiers free access to booty and portraying the city's conquest as a holy cause, he amassed a huge army that outnumbered the defending force of 7,000 by more than ten times. For forty days his troops bombarded Constantinople's massive walls with artillery that included enormous cannons built by Hungarian and Italian engineers. On May 29, 1453, Ottoman troops overwhelmed the surviving soldiers and took the ancient Roman and Christian capital of Byzantium—which Mehmed promptly renamed Istanbul.

The Fall of Constantinople The use of heavy artillery in the forty-day siege of Constantinople was instrumental to the Ottoman victory. At the center of this Turkish miniature is one such cannon, possibly of Hungarian origin, which required hundreds of men and oxen to transport and secure outside the city walls.

The Tools of Empire Building The Ottomans adopted Byzantine administrative practices to unify their enlarged state and incorporated many of Byzantium's powerful families into it. Their dynastic power was, however, not only military; it also rested on a firm religious foundation. At the center of this empire were the sultans, who combined a warrior ethos with an unwavering devotion to Islam. Describing themselves as the "shadow of God" on earth, they claimed to be caretakers for the welfare of the Islamic faith. Throughout the empire, the sultans devoted substantial resources to the construction of elaborate mosques and to the support of Islamic schools. As self-appointed defenders of the faithful, the sultans assumed the role of protectors of the holy cities on the Arabian Peninsula and of Jerusalem, while working to unite the realm's diverse lands and peoples and constantly striving to extend the borders of Islam. During the reign of Suleiman (r. 1520–1566), the Ottomans reached the height of their territorial expansion. Under his administration, the Ottoman state ruled over 20 to 30 million people. By the time Suleiman died, the Ottoman

The Suleymaniye Mosque Built by Sultan Suleiman in the mid-sixteenth century to crown his achievements, the Suleymaniye Mosque was designed by the architect Sinan to dominate the city. What message do you think Suleiman was attempting to convey in building the mosque across a park from the Hagia Sophia, a formerly Christian basilica built in the sixth century by Justinian upon foundations going back 200 years earlier to the time of Constantine and his sons?

Empire bridged Europe and the Arab world. Istanbul by then was a dynamic imperial hub, dispatching bureaucrats and military men to oversee a vast domain.

Istanbul's **Topkapi Palace** exhibited the Ottomans' view of governance, the sultans' emphasis on religion, and the continuing influence of Ottoman familial traditions. Laid out by Mehmed II, the palace complex projected a vision of Istanbul as the center of the world. As a way to promote the sultan's magnificent power, architects designed the complex so that the buildings containing the imperial household were nestled behind layers of outer courtyards, in a mosaic of mosques, courts, and special dwellings for the sultan's harem. The harem had its own hierarchy of thousands of women, from the sultan's mother and consorts to the slave women who waited on them, and it became a formidable political force at the heart of Ottoman power.

The growing importance of Topkapi Palace as the command post of empire represented a crucial transition in the history of Ottoman rulers. Not only was the palace the place where future bureaucrats received their training; it was also the place where the chief bureaucrat, the grand vizier, carried out the day-to-day running of the empire. Whereas the early sultans had led their soldiers into battle personally and had met face-to-face with their kinsmen, the later rulers withdrew into the sacredness of the palace, venturing out only occasionally for grand ceremonies. Still, every Friday, subjects lined up outside the palace to introduce their petitions, ask for favors, and seek justice. If they were lucky, the

The Topkapi Palace A view of the inner courtyard of Topkapi's seraglio (sequestered living space), where the sultan and his harem lived. What does this image suggest about how the sultan used the palace to run his empire?

sultans would be there to greet them—but they did so behind grated glass, issuing their decisions by tapping on the window. The palace thus projected a sense of majestic, distant wonder, a home fit for semidivine rulers.

Diversity and Control The fact that the Ottoman Empire endured into the twentieth century owed much to the ruling elite's ability to gain the support and employ the talents of exceedingly diverse populations. After all, neither conquest nor conversion eliminated cultural differences in the empire's distant provinces. Thus, for example, the Ottomans' language policy was one of flexibility and tolerance. Although Ottoman Turkish was the official language of administration, Arabic was the primary language of the Arab provinces, the common tongue of street life. Within the empire's European corner, many people spoke their own languages. From the fifteenth century onward, the Ottoman Empire was perhaps more multilingual than any of its rivals.

In politics, as in language, the Ottomans showed flexibility and tolerance. The imperial bureaucracy permitted extensive regional autonomy. In fact, Ottoman military cadres perfected a technique for absorbing newly conquered territories into the empire by parceling them out as revenue-producing units among loyal followers and kin. Regional appointees could collect local taxes, part of which they earmarked for Istanbul and part of which they pocketed for themselves. (This was a common administrative device for many world dynasties ruling extensive domains.)

Like other empires, the Ottoman state was always in danger of losing control over its provincial rulers. Local potentates—the group that the imperial center allowed to rule in their distant regions—found that great distances enabled them to operate independently from central authority. These authorities kept larger amounts of tax revenues than Istanbul deemed proper. So, to limit their autonomy, the Ottomans established the janissaries, a corps of infantry soldiers and bureaucrats who owed direct allegiance to the sultan. The system at its high point involved a conscription of Christian youths from the empire's European lands. This conscription, called the ***devshirme***, required each village to hand over a certain number of males between the ages of eight and eighteen. Uprooted from their families and villages, selected for their fine physiques and good looks, these young men were converted to Islam and sent to farms to build up their bodies and learn Turkish. A select few were moved on to Topkapi Palace to learn Ottoman military, religious, and administrative techniques. Some of these men later enjoyed exceptional careers in the arts and sciences—such as the architect Sinan, who designed the Suleymaniye Mosque. Recipients of the best education available in the Islamic world, and trained in Ottoman ways, instructed in the use of modern weaponry, and deprived of family connections, the *devshirme* recruits were prepared to serve the sultan (and the empire as a whole) rather than the interests of any particular locality or ethnic group.

Thus, the Ottomans established their legitimacy via military skill, religious backing, and a loyal bureaucracy. They artfully balanced the decentralizing tendencies of the outlying regions with the centralizing forces of the imperial capital. Relying on a careful mixture of religious faith, imperial patronage, and cultural tolerance, the sultans curried loyalty and secured political stability. Indeed, the Ottoman Empire was so strong and stable that it dominated the coveted and highly contested trading crossroads between Europe and Asia for many centuries. Thus, its consolidation had powerful consequences for European efforts to rebuild their societies after the plague; above all, it closed off traditional overland trade routes to India and China.

Western Christendom

No region suffered more from the Black Death than Western Christendom, and no region made a more spectacular comeback. From 1100 to 1300, Europe had enjoyed a surge in population, rapid economic growth, and significant technological and intellectual innovations, only to see these achievements halted in the fourteenth century by famine and the Black Death. Europeans responded by creating new political and cultural forms. New dynastic states arose, competing with one another, and a movement called the Renaissance revived Europe's connections with its Greek and Roman past and produced masterpieces of art, architecture, and other forms of thought.

THE CATHOLIC CHURCH, STATE BUILDING, AND ECONOMIC RECOVERY

In the aftermath of famine and plague, the peoples of Western Christendom, like those in the Muslim world, looked to their religious beliefs and institutions as foundations for recovery. The faith of many had been severely tested, and religious authorities had to struggle to reclaim their power. To begin with, the late medieval western church found itself divided at the top (at one point during this period there were three popes) and challenged from below, both by individuals pursuing alternative kinds of spirituality and by increasing demands on the clergy and church administration. Disappointment with the clergy smoldered. The peasantry despaired at the absence of clergy when they were so greatly needed during the famines and Black Death. With groups like the Beghards challenging the clergy's right to define religious doctrine and practices, the church fought back, identifying all that was suspect and demanding strict obedience to the true faith. This entailed the persecution of heretics, Jews, Muslims in the Iberian Peninsula, homosexuals, prostitutes, and "witches." During this period the church expanded its charitable and bureaucratic functions, providing alms to the urban poor and registering births, deaths, and economic transactions. Crucially, faced with challenges to its authority, the church associated itself with secular rulers, lending moral authority to kings who claimed to rule "by divine right."

COMPARISON

COMPARE the role religious belief systems played in rebuilding Europe and Islam in the fourteenth and fifteenth centuries.

Europe's political rulers aligned themselves with church leaders to rebuild their states and consolidate their power. One royal family, the Habsburgs, drew on their Catholic religious traditions and established a powerful, long-lasting dynasty that would rule large parts of central Europe for centuries to follow. Habsburg leaders were elected to head the federation of states known as the Holy Roman Empire almost continuously from 1438 to 1806, and for a time they ruled Spain and its New World colonies. Yet even at the height of its power in the early sixteenth century, the Habsburg monarchy never succeeded in restoring an integrated empire to western Europe.

In 1450 Western Christendom had no central government, no official tongue, and only a few successful commercial centers, mostly in the Mediterranean basin (see Map 11.3).

MAP 11.3 | Western Christendom, 1400–1500

Europe was a region divided by dynastic rivalries during the fifteenth century. Locate the most powerful regional dynasties on the map: Portugal, Castile, Aragon, France, Burgundy, England, and the Holy Roman Empire.

- Which areas witnessed the greatest warfare during this period?
- On the basis of this map and the reading, why do you think that was the case?
- Contrast the size of political units in this map with those in Maps 11.2 and 11.4. Explain the significance of the differences.

Current Trends in World History

Joan of Arc: A Charismatic Leader in a Time of Social Turmoil

The immense historical impact of a French peasant girl, Joan of Arc, demonstrates the importance of charismatic individuals—even women in male-dominated societies—during periods of social turmoil. As Europe endured plagues, famines, and war, its people sought help through the special talents of women, even in areas like warfare. Indeed, if not for Joan of Arc, the country we know today as France might not exist. Gender is also a useful approach to study the relations between men and women in a society. World historians use it as a comparative theme across cultures and time, which makes it an even more useful lens for historical analysis.

Appearing on the scene in 1429, as the English seemed to be winning the Hundred Years' War, she rallied the French against the English occupiers and turned the tide of the war. By giving religious sanction, as well as military succor, to the Valois monarch Charles VII, she made possible the consolidation of France and left Europe an inspiring image of the female warrior-saint.

The world of Joan's childhood was a chaotic one, in which English lords were laying claim to various French-speaking principalities. By 1420, Valois authority had been greatly eroded, and English armies were conquering more and more French towns. In 1428, the English laid siege to Orléans, a large town in north-central France. To contemporaries, it seemed a symbolic battle: as Orléans went, they thought, so the war would go—and so would God wish it to go.

This is the point at which the paths of a seventeen-year-old peasant girl and the monarch of France crossed. Beginning at about age thirteen, the shy girl had received visions of saints who instructed her to rescue Orléans and bring France's ruler to be crowned king at Reims Cathedral. (He had not been crowned there, in the tradition of all French kings, because the English armies controlled Reims, Paris, and northern France.) For five years Joan resisted, but at last she obeyed her celestial advisers. Granted an audience with Charles VII in 1429, Joan impressed him with her piety and her passionate devotion to the Valois crown. He concluded that God really had sent her to serve France's cause—and his own. Joan won command of 7,000 to 8,000 men; then, wearing a suit of armor and brandishing a sword, she marched to relieve Orléans. Joan directed the assault with brilliance and inspired the French forces; her charisma came not only from a tradition of female Christian "seers," but also from the peculiarity of her appearance (a young woman in male attire) and her appeal to French speakers who resented rule by English "outsiders." After driving the English from Orléans, she then pressed on to Reims; here, thanks to her military victories, Charles VII was crowned, fulfilling her visions. He was now king of France—and though the war continued, the tide now turned in favor of the French.

The tide for Joan, however, turned for the worse. Although she continued to direct the troops with remarkable savvy, she failed to force open the gates of Paris, and jealous courtiers around Charles began to question her divine authority. She was wounded, then taken prisoner. After a year in English captivity she faced the

The feudal system of a lords' control over the peasantry (see Chapter 10), which was now in decline, left a legacy of political fragmentation and enduring elite privileges, which made the consolidation of a unified Christian Europe even more difficult to achieve. Europe's linguistic diversity reflected its political fragmentation. No single ruler or language united peoples, even when they shared a religion. Latin lost ground as rulers chose various regional dialects (e.g., French, Spanish, English) to be their official state language, whereas the written literary Chinese script remained a key administrative tool for China's dynasts, and in the Islamic world Arabic was the common language of faith and Turkish the language of administration.

Those who sought to rule the emerging states faced numerous obstacles. For example, rival claimants to the throne financed threatening private armies. Also, the clergy demanded and received privileges in the form of access to land and relief from taxation; they often meddled in politics themselves, and the church became a formidable economic

Inquisition and was found guilty of heresy, on the grounds that her visions were false and misleading. On May 30, 1431, she was burned at the stake in the marketplace in the town of Rouen. Since that time she has stood as a heroic and charismatic martyr, and the French have often invoked her name to awaken patriotism against foreign threats.

The fact that this young, illiterate woman played such an important role in the history of European warfare and state formation testifies to the fact that male aristocrats, intellectuals, and clerics were not the only important actors. At the right place, at the right time, a woman could use courage, faith, and intelligence to make her visions prevail.

QUESTIONS FOR ANALYSIS

- What other heroic figures, male or female, does Joan of Arc remind you of and why?
- Why do you think Charles VII failed to rescue Joan of Arc from her English prison?

Explore Further

Régine Pernoud and Marie-Véronique Clin, *Joan of Arc: Her Story*, trans. Jeremy Adams (1999).

powerhouse. And once the printing press became available in Europe in the 1460s, printers circulated anonymous pamphlets criticizing the court and the clergy. Some states had consultative political bodies—such as the Estates General in France, the Cortes in Spain, and Parliament in England—in which princes formally asked representatives of their people for advice and, in the case of the English Parliament, for consent to new forms of taxation. Such political bodies gave no voice to common men and no representation to women. But they did allow the collective expression of grievances against overbearing policies.

Out of the chaos of famine, disease, and warfare, the diverse peoples of Europe found a political way forward. This path involved the formation of centralized dynastic monarchies. A **monarchy** is a political system in which one individual holds supreme power and passes that power on to his or her next of kin. Often in competition with the new monarchies, a handful of European city-states, in which a narrow group of wealthy and influential voters selected their leaders, survived right up to the nineteenth century and in some cases into the twentieth. Consolidation of these states occurred sometimes through strategic marriages but more often through warfare, both between princely families and with local aristocratic allies and foreign mercenaries (see **Current Trends in World History: Joan of Arc**). Political stabilization was swiftest in southern Europe, where economies rebounded through seaborne trade with Southwest Asia. The stabilization of Italian city-states such as Venice and Florence, and of monarchical rule in Portugal and Spain, led to an economic and cultural flowering known as the Renaissance. In northern and western Europe, the process took longer. In England and France, in particular, internal feuding, regional warfare, and religious fragmentation delayed recovery for decades (see Chapter 12).

POLITICAL CONSOLIDATION AND TRADE IN THE IBERIAN PENINSULA

War and overseas trade played a central role in the emergence of new dynasties in Portugal and Spain. Through the fourteenth century, Portuguese Christians devoted themselves to fighting the Moors, who were Muslim occupants of North Africa, the western Sahara, and the Iberian Peninsula. After the Portuguese crossed the Strait of Gibraltar and seized the Moorish fortresses at Ceuta, in Morocco, their ships could sail between the Mediterranean and the Atlantic without Muslim interference. With that threat diminished, the Portuguese perceived their neighbor, Castile (part of which is now Spain), as their chief foe. Under João I (r. 1385–1433) Portugal defeated the Castilians, becoming the dominant power on the Iberian peninsula. No longer preoccupied with Castilian competition, the Portuguese sought new territories and trading opportunities in the North Atlantic and along the West African coasts. João's son Prince Henrique, known later as Henry the Navigator, further expanded the royal family's domain by supporting expeditions down the coast of Africa and offshore to the Atlantic islands of the Madeiras and the Azores. The west and central coasts of Africa and the islands of the North and South Atlantic, including the Cape Verde Islands, São Tomé, Principe, and Fernando Po, soon became Portuguese ports of call.

Portuguese monarchs granted the Atlantic islands to nobles as hereditary possessions on condition that the grantees colonize them, and soon the colonizers were establishing lucrative sugar plantations. In gratitude, noble families and merchants threw their political weight behind the king. Subsequent monarchs continued to cultivate local aristocrats' support for monarchical authority, thus ensuring smooth succession to the crown for members of the royal family.

In Spain, a new dynasty also emerged, though the road was difficult. Medieval Spain comprised rival kingdoms that quarreled ceaselessly. Within those kingdoms, several religions coexisted: Muslims, Jews, and Christians lived side by side in relative harmony, and Muslim armies still occupied strategic posts in the south. Over time, marriages and the formation of kinship ties among nobles and between royal lineages yielded a new political order. One by one, the major houses of the Spanish kingdoms intermarried, culminating in the wedding of Isabella of Castile and Ferdinand of Aragon (1469). This marriage linked Castile, wealthy and populous, to Aragon, which enjoyed an extended trading network in the Mediterranean. Together, the monarchs brought unruly nobles and distant towns under their control. They topped off their achievements by marrying their children into other European royal families—especially the Habsburgs, central Europe's most powerful dynasty.

Thus, Spain's two most important provinces were joined, and Spain later became a state to be reckoned with.

The new Spanish rulers sent Christian armies south to push Muslim forces out of the Iberian Peninsula. By the mid-fifteenth century only Granada, a strategic linchpin overlooking the straits between the Mediterranean and the Atlantic, remained in Muslim hands. After a long and costly siege, Christian forces captured the fortress there in 1492. This was a victory of enormous symbolic importance, as joyous as the fall of Constantinople was depressing (for Christians).

The Inquisition and Westward Exploration Isabella and Ferdinand sought to drive all non-Catholics out of Spain. Terrified by Ottoman incursions into Europe, they launched the **Inquisition** in 1481, taking aim especially against *conversos*—converted Jews

Ferdinand and Isabella Entering Granada This altar relief, sculpted by Felipe Vigarny in the early sixteenth century, depicts the triumphant entrance of King Ferdinand and Queen Isabella into the city of Granada after their conquest of this last Muslim stronghold in Spain. Why would such an image be depicted on an altar? In what ways does the image show power and distinction among the individuals depicted?

and Muslims, whom they suspected were Christians only in name. When Granada fell, the crown ordered the expulsion of all Jews from Spain. After 1499, a more tolerant attempt to convert the Moors (Muslims) by persuasion gave way to forced conversion—or emigration. All told, almost half a million people were forced to flee the Spanish kingdoms. This lack of tolerance meant that Spain, like other European states in this era, became increasingly homogenous. With fewer groups vying for influence within their territories, rulers turned their attention outward, fueling rivalries between the various European states.

So strong was the tide of Spanish fervor by late 1491 that the monarchs listened now to a Genoese navigator whose pleas for patronage they had previously rejected. Christopher Columbus promised them unimaginable riches that could finance their military campaigns and bankroll a crusade to liberate Jerusalem from Muslim hands. Off he sailed with a royal patent that guaranteed the monarchs a share of all he discovered. Soon the Spanish economy was reorienting itself toward the Atlantic, and Spain's merchants, missionaries, and soldiers were preparing for conquest and profiteering in what had been, just a few years before, a blank space on the map.

THE RENAISSANCE

Just as the Ming harkened back to Han Chinese traditions and the Ottomans looked to Sunni Islam to point the way forward, so European elites looked to their own traditions for guidance as they rebuilt after the devastation of the plague. They found inspiration in ancient Greek and Roman institutions and ideas. Europe's extraordinary political and economic revival also involved a powerful outpouring of cultural achievements, led by Italian scholars and artists and financed by bankers, churchmen, and nobles. Much later, scholars coined the word **Renaissance** to characterize the cultural flourishing of the Italian city-states, France, the Netherlands, England, and the Holy Roman Empire in the period 1430–1550. What was being "reborn" was ancient Greek and Roman art and learning—knowledge that could help people understand an expanding world and support the rights of secular individuals to exert power in it. Although the Renaissance was largely funded by popes and Christian kings, it challenged the authority of traditional religious elites, breaking the medieval church's monopoly on answers to the big questions. The movement emphasized secular forms of learning rather than just Christian doctrine and a more human-centered understanding of the cosmos.

The Renaissance was all about new exposure to the old—to classical texts and ancient art and architectural forms. Although some Greek and Roman texts were known in Europe and the Islamic world, the use of the printing press made others accessible to western scholars for the first time. Scholars now realized that the pre-Christian Greeks and Romans had developed powerful means of representing and caring for the human body. Having studied the world directly, without the need to square their observations with biblical information, the ancients had much to teach about geography, astronomy, and architecture and about how to govern states and armies. For Renaissance scholars it was no longer enough to understand Christian doctrine and to concern themselves with the next world. One had to go back to the original, classical sources in order to understand the human condition. This in turn required the learning of languages and history. Scholarship that attempted to return to Greek and Roman sources became known as **humanism**.

COMPARISON

COMPARE the way art and architecture reflected the political realities of Europe and Islam after the Black Death.

Because political and religious powers were not united in Europe (as they were in China and the Islamic world), scholars and artists seeking sponsors for their work could play one side against the other, or, alternatively, could suffer both clerical and political

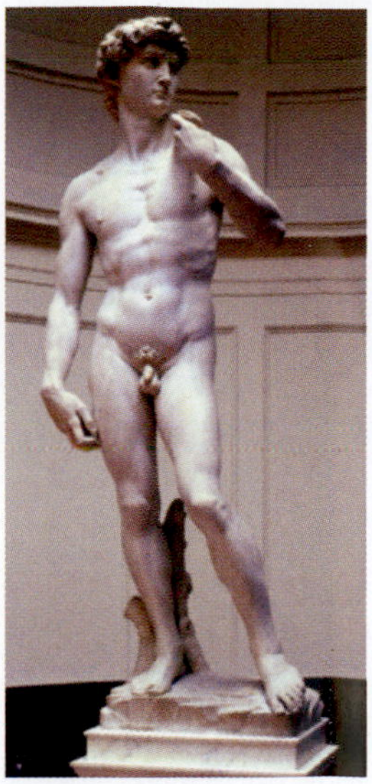

Renaissance Masterpieces Leonardo da Vinci's *The Last Supper* (*left*) depicts Christ's disciples reacting to his announcement that one of them will betray him. Michelangelo's *David* (*right*) stands over thirteen feet high and was conceived as an expression of Florentine civic ideals. In what ways do these Renaissance masterpieces draw on the principles of humanism and reflect a return to western "classics" of the Greco-Roman world?

persecution. Michelangelo (1475–1564), a leading painter, sculptor, architect, and engineer of the age, completed commissions for the famous Florentine bankers and political leaders of the Medici family, for the Florentine Wool Guild, and for Pope Julius II. Peter Paul Rubens painted for the courts of France, Spain, England, and the Netherlands, as well as selling paintings on the open market. These two painters, renowned for showing a great deal of flesh, frequently offended conservative church officials. Most support for the arts, however, came either from the church or individual clergymen, and virtually all secular donors were devout believers who commissioned works with religious themes. The Dutch scholar Desiderius Erasmus ridiculed corrupt popes and the clergy with the patronage of English, Dutch, and French supporters, while remaining a Catholic, an ordained cleric, and an opponent of Reformation doctrines. Conflicts within the Catholic Church, between the church and secular leaders, and among secular leaders and wealthy private citizens enabled artists to present challenging images and ideas with an unusual independence.

Gradually, a network of educated men and women took shape that was not wholly dependent on either the church or the state or a single princely patron. Classical knowledge gave individuals the means to challenge political, clerical, and aesthetic authority. Moreover, rivalries between Europe's relatively small states and city-states allowed many of these scholars to dodge the authorities by fleeing to neighboring communities. Of course, they could also use their learning to defend the older elites: for example, numerous lawyers and scholars continued to work for the popes in defending the papacy. At the same time, in contrast, men like Erasmus and later Martin Luther (the leading figure of the Reformation in the sixteenth century) looked to secular princes to support their critical scholarship. In Florence, Niccolò Machiavelli wrote the most famous treatise on authoritarian power, ***The Prince*** (1513). Machiavelli argued that political leadership required mastering the rules of modern statecraft, even if in some cases this meant disregarding moral imperatives. Holding and exercising power were vital ends in themselves, he claimed; traditional ideas of civic virtue should not deter rulers, like those of the Medici family, from maintaining control over society.

With Renaissance ideas challenging traditional authority and rulers facing a range of internal and external obstacles, the new monarchies of Europe were not all immediately successful in consolidating power and unifying peoples. In France and England, for example, the great age of monarchy had yet to dawn. Even when stable states did arise in Europe, they were fairly small compared to the Ottoman and Ming empires. In the mid-sixteenth century, Portugal and Spain, Europe's two most expansionist states, had populations of 1 million and 9 million, respectively. England, excluding Wales, was a mere 3 million in 1550. Only France, with 17 million, had a population close to the Ottoman Empire's 25 million. And these numbers paled in comparison with Ming China's population of nearly 200 million in 1550. But in Europe, small could be advantageous. Portugal's relatively small population meant that the crown had fewer groups to control. In the world of finance, the most successful merchants were those inhabiting the smaller Italian city-states and, a bit later, the cities of the northern Netherlands. The Florentines developed sophisticated banking techniques, created extensive networks of agents throughout Europe and the Mediterranean, and served as bankers to the popes. At the same time, the Renaissance—which flourished in the city-states and newly stabilized monarchies—made elite European culture more cosmopolitan and independent from government authority, even if it could not unify the states and peoples who cultivated it.

Ming China

Like the Europeans, the Chinese saw their stable worldview and political order crumble under the catastrophes of human and bacterial invasions. Moreover, like the Europeans, people in China had long regarded outsiders as "barbarians" and balked at being ruled by outsiders. Together, the Mongols and the Black Death upended the political and intellectual foundations of what had appeared to be the world's most integrated society. The Mongols brought the Yuan dynasty to power; then the plague devastated China and prepared the way for the emergence of the Ming dynasty. The Ming dynasty, ruled by ethnically Han Chinese, defined itself against its foreign predecessors. Ming emperors sought to reinforce everything Chinese. In particular, they supported China's vast internal agricultural markets in an attempt to minimize dependence on merchants and foreign trade.

RESTORING ORDER

In the chaotic fourteenth century, as plague and famine ravaged China and the Mongol Yuan dynasty collapsed, only a strong military movement capable of overpowering other groups could restore order. That intervention began at the hands of a poor young man who had trained in the Red Turban Movement: Zhu Yuanzhang.

It soon became clear that Zhu had a much grander design for China than the ambitions of most warlords. When he took Nanjing in 1356, he renamed it Yingtian ("In response to Heaven"). Lifted by subsequent successful military campaigns, Zhu (r. 1368–1398) took the imperial title of Hongwu ("expansive and martial") Emperor and proclaimed the founding of the Ming ("brilliant") dynasty in 1368. Soon thereafter, his troops met little resistance when they seized the Yuan capital of Beijing, causing the Mongol emperor to flee to his homeland in the steppe. It would, however, take Hongwu almost another twenty years to reunify the entire country.

CENTRALIZATION UNDER THE MING

Hongwu and successive Ming emperors had to rebuild a devastated society from the ground up. Although in the past China had experienced natural catastrophes, wars, and social dislocation, the plague's legacy was devastation on an unprecedented scale. It left the new rulers with the formidable challenge of rebuilding the great cities, restoring respect for ruling elites, and reconstructing the bureaucracy.

COMPARISON

COMPARE the ways rulers rebuilt unified states and their levels of success in China, Islam, and Europe.

Imperial Grandeur and Kinship The rebuilding began with the Hongwu Emperor, whose capital at Nanjing reflected imperial grandeur. When the dynasty's third emperor, the Yongle ("perpetual happiness") Emperor, relocated the capital to Beijing, he flaunted an even more grandiose style, employing around 100,000 artisans and 1 million laborers to build this new capital, including its Forbidden City. The city had three separate walled enclosures. Inside the outer city walls sprawled the imperial city; within its walls lay the palace city, the Forbidden City. Traffic within the walled sections navigated through broad boulevards leading to the different gates, above which imposing towers soared. The palace compound, where the imperial family resided, had more than 9,000 rooms. Anyone standing in the front courts, which measured more than 400 yards on a side and boasted marble terraces and carved railings, would gasp at the sense of awesome power. That was precisely the effect the Ming emperors wanted, just as the Ottoman sultans did in building Topkapi Palace.

Marriage and kinship buttressed the power of the Ming imperial household, much like the dynastic strategies of Europe. The Ming dynasty's founder married the adopted daughter of a leading Red Turban rebel (her father, according to legend, was a convicted murderer), thereby consolidating his power and eliminating a threat. Empress Ma, as she was known, became Hongwu's principal wife and was praised for her compassion. Emerging as the kinder face of the regime, she tempered the harsh and sometimes cruel disposition of her spouse. He had numerous other consorts as well, including Korean and Mongol women, who bore him twenty-six sons and sixteen daughters (similar to, although on smaller scale than, the sultan's harem at Ottoman Topkapi).

The Forbidden City The Yongle Emperor relocated the capital to Beijing, where he began the construction of the Forbidden City, or imperial palace, in the early fifteenth century. The palace was designed to inspire awe in all who saw it. In what ways do the partitions of space and the activities of people within that space appear to support imperial grandeur?

Building a Bureaucracy Faced with the challenge of reestablishing order out of turmoil, Hongwu initially sought to rule through his kinsmen—by giving imperial princes generous stipends, command of large garrisons, and significant autonomy in running their domains. However, when the princes' power began to threaten the court, Hongwu slashed their stipends, reduced their privileges, and took control of their garrisons. No longer dependent on these men, he established an imperial bureaucracy beholden only to him and to his successors. These officials won appointments through their outstanding performance on a reinstated civil service examination.

In addition, Hongwu took other steps to install a centralized system of rule. He assigned bureaucrats to oversee the manufacture of porcelain, cotton, and silk products, as well as tax collection. He reestablished the Confucian school system as a means of selecting a cadre of loyal officials (not unlike the Ottoman janissaries and administrators). He also set up local networks of villages to rebuild irrigation systems and to supervise reforestation projects to prevent flooding—with the astonishing result that the amount of land reclaimed nearly tripled within eight years. For water control, over 40,000 reservoirs underwent repairs or new construction. Historians estimate that Hongwu's reign oversaw the planting around Nanjing of about 1 billion trees, which were later used in building a maritime expedition fleet in the early fifteenth century.

Ming Deities A pantheon of deities worshipped during the Ming dynasty, demonstrating the rich religious culture of the period. In what ways does this document show Ming religious beliefs?

The imperial palace not only projected the image of a power center, it *was* the center of power. Every official received his appointment by the emperor through the Ministry of Personnel. Hongwu eliminated the post of prime minister (he executed the man who held the post) and ruled directly. Ming bureaucrats had to kneel before the emperor. The drawback of this centralized control, of course, was that the Ming emperor had to keep tabs on this immense system. Hongwu constantly moved his bureaucrats around, sometimes fortifying the administration, sometimes undermining it lest it become too autonomous. Over time, Hongwu nurtured a bureaucracy far more extensive than that of the Ottomans. The Ming thus established the most highly centralized system of government of all the monarchies of this period.

Religion under the Ming Just as the Ottoman sultans projected themselves as Muslim rulers, calling themselves the shadow of God, and European monarchs claimed to rule by divine right, so the Ming emperors enhanced their legitimacy by drawing on ancient Chinese religious traditions. Citing the mandate of heaven, the emperor revised and strengthened the elaborate rites and ceremonies that had supported dynastic power for centuries. Official rituals, such as those related to the gods of soil and grain, reinforced political and social classes, portraying the rulers as the moral and spiritual benefactors of their subjects. In lavish ceremonies, the emperor engaged in sacrificial rites, cultivating his image as mediator between the human and the spiritual worlds. The message was clear: the gods were on the side of the Ming household.

MING RULERSHIP

Conquest and defense helped establish the realm, and bureaucracy kept it functioning. The empire's scale (see Map 11.4) required complex administration. To many outsiders

MAP 11.4 | Ming China, 1500s

The Ming state was one of the largest empires at this time—and the most populous. Using the scale, determine the length of its coastline and its internal borders.

- What were the two Ming capitals and the three main seaport trading cities and how far are they from one another?
- According to the map, where did the Ming rulers expect the greatest threat to their security?
- How did the Ming rulers view foreign contact and exchange during this period?

(especially Europeans, whose region was in a state of constant war), Ming stability and centralization appeared to be political wizardry.

Ming rulers worried in particular about maintaining the support of ordinary people in the countryside. The emperor wished to be seen as the special guardian of his subjects. He wanted their allegiance as well as their taxes and labor. But during hard times, poor farmers were reluctant to provide resources—taxes or services—to distant officials. For these reasons and because the emperor distrusted state bureaucrats, Hongwu preferred to entrust management of the rural world to local leaders, whom he appointed as village chiefs, village elders, or tax captains. A popular Chinese proverb was: "The mountain is high and the emperor is far away." Within these communities, the dynasty created a social hierarchy based on age, sex, and kinship. While women's labor remained critical for the village economy, the government reinforced a gender hierarchy by promoting women's chastity and constructing commemorative arches for widows who honored their husbands by refraining from remarrying.

Like the European and Islamic states, the Ming Empire also faced periodic unrest and rebellion. Rebels often proclaimed their own brand of religious beliefs, just as local elites resented central authority. Outright terror helped stymie threats to central authority. In a massive wave of carnage, Hongwu slaughtered anyone who posed a threat to his authority, from the highest of ministers to the lowliest of scribes. From 1376 to 1393, four of his purges condemned close to 100,000 subjects to execution. Yet, despite the emperor's immense power, the Ming Empire remained undergoverned. Indeed, as the population multiplied, there were too few loyal officials to handle local affairs. By the sixteenth and early seventeenth centuries, for example, some 10,000 to 15,000 officials shouldered the responsibility of managing a population exceeding 200 million people. Nonetheless, Hongwu bequeathed to his descendants a set of tools for ruling that drew on subjects' direct loyalty to the emperor and on the intricate workings of an extensive bureaucracy. His legacy enabled his successors to balance local sources of power with the needs of dynastic rulership.

TRADE AND EXPLORATION UNDER THE MING

COMPARISON

COMPARE the ways that the Ming, Iberian, and Ottoman rulers extended their territories and influence.

In the fourteenth century, China began its economic recovery from the devastation of disease and political turmoil. Gradually, political stability allowed trade to revive. Now the new dynasty's merchants reestablished China's preeminence in long-distance commercial exchange. Chinese silk and cotton textiles, as well as fine porcelains, ranked among the world's most coveted luxuries. When a Chinese merchant ship sailed into port, trading partners and onlookers crowded the docks to watch the unloading of precious cargoes. Although Ming rulers' support for overseas ventures wavered and eventually declined, this period saw important developments in Chinese trade and exploration.

Overseas Trade: Success and Suspicion During the Ming period, Chinese traders based in ports such as Hangzhou, Quanzhou, and Guangzhou (Canton) were as energetic as their Muslim counterparts in the Indian Ocean. These ports were home to prosperous merchants and the point of convergence for vast sea-lanes. Leaving the mainland ports, Chinese vessels carried precious wares to offshore islands, the Pescadores, and Taiwan. From there, they sailed on to the ports of Southeast Asia. As entrepôts for global goods, East Asian ports flourished. Former fishing villages developed into major urban centers.

The Ming dynasty viewed overseas expansion with suspicion, however. Hongwu feared that too much contact with the outside world would cause instability and undermine his rule. In fact, he banned private maritime commerce in 1371. But enforcement was lax, and by the late fifteenth century maritime trade once again surged. Because much of the thriving business took place in defiance of official edicts, it led to constant friction between government officials and maritime traders. Although the Ming government ultimately agreed to issue licenses for overseas trade in the mid-sixteenth century, its policies continued to vacillate. To Ming officials, unlike their counterparts in Portugal and Spain, the sea represented problems of order and control rather than opportunities.

The Expeditions of Zheng He One spectacular exception to the Ming's attitude toward maritime trade was a series of officially sponsored expeditions in the early fifteenth century. It was the ambitious third Ming emperor, the Yongle Emperor, who took the initiative. One of his loyal followers was a Muslim whom the Ming army had captured as a boy. The youth was castrated and sent to serve at the court (as a eunuch, he could not continue his family line and so theoretically owed sole allegiance to the emperor). Given the name **Zheng He** (1371–1433), he grew up to be an important military leader. The emperor entrusted him with venturing out to trade, collect tribute, and display China's power to the world.

From 1405 to 1433, Zheng He commanded the world's greatest armada and led seven naval expeditions. His larger ships stretched 400 feet in length (Columbus's Santa Maria was 85 feet), carried hundreds of sailors on four tiers of decks, and maneuvered with sophisticated rudders, nine masts, and watertight compartments. The first expedition set sail with 28,000 men aboard a flotilla of sixty-two large ships and over 200 lesser ones. Zheng He and his entourage aimed to establish tributary relations with far-flung territories—from Southeast Asia to the Indian Ocean ports, to the Persian Gulf, and to the east coast of Africa (see Map 11.5). These expeditions did not seek territorial expansion, but rather control of trade and tribute. When the Yongle Emperor died in 1424, the expeditions lost their most enthusiastic patron. Moreover, by the mid-fifteenth century, there was a revival of military threats from the north, recalling how the maritime-oriented Song

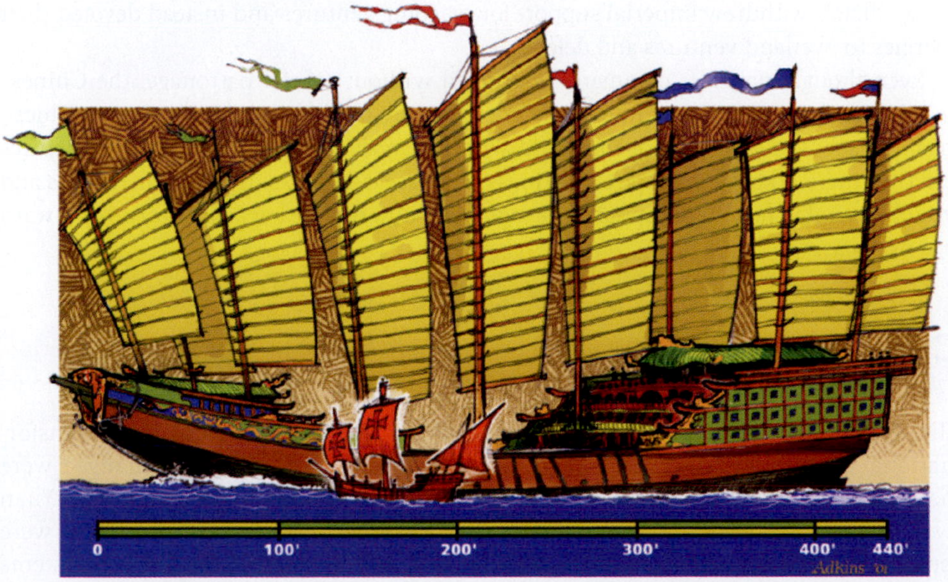

Zheng He's Ship The largest ship in Zheng He's armada had nine staggered masts and twelve silk sails, all designed to demonstrate the grandeur of the Ming dynasty. How much larger was Zheng He's ship compared to Columbus's *Santa Maria* (pictured in the foreground)? How might the differences in size and construction reflect differences in the capabilities and goals of European and Chinese seafaring?

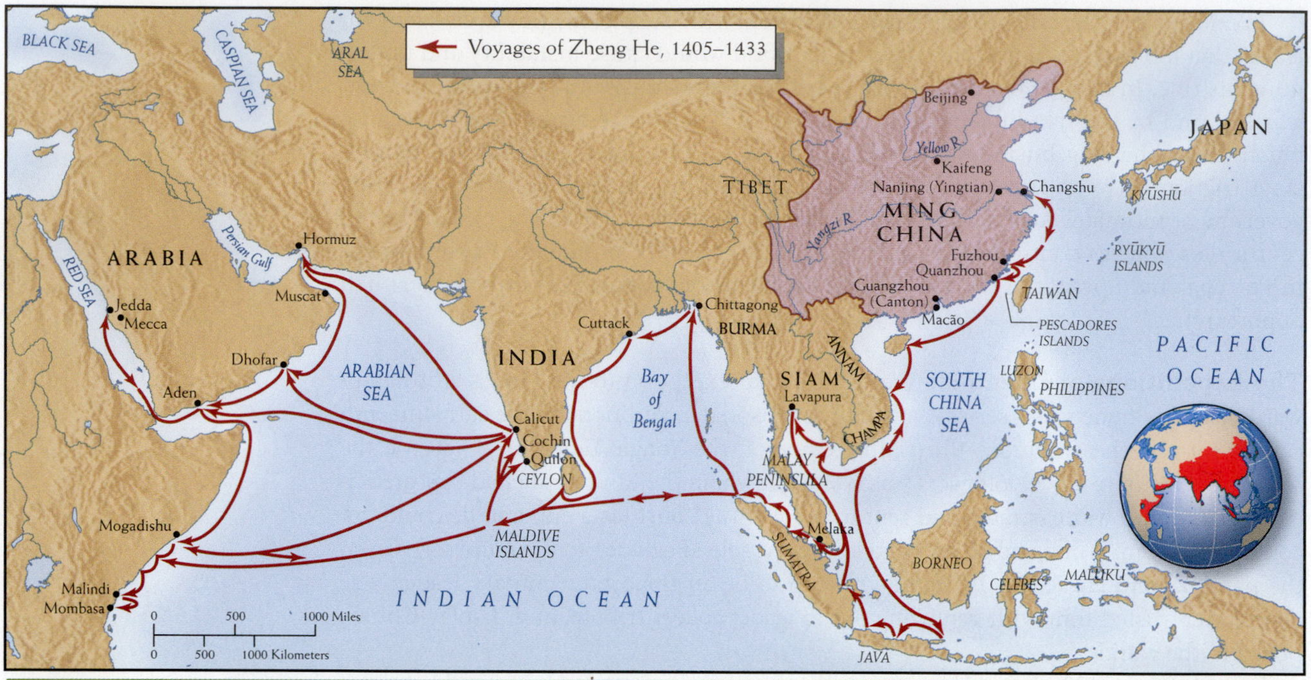

MAP 11.5 | Voyages of Zheng He, 1405–1433

Zheng He's voyages are some of the most famous in world history. Many have speculated about how history might be different if the Chinese emperors had allowed the voyages to continue.

- For how many years did Zheng's voyages go on?
- How far did Zheng go?
- Based on your reading, why did Chinese expeditions not have the same impact as European voyages of exploration toward the end of the fifteenth century, such as those of Columbus?

dynasty had been overrun by invaders from the north (see Chapter 10). Consequently, Ming officials withdrew imperial support for seagoing ventures and instead devoted their energies to overland ventures and defense.

Even though maritime commerce continued without official patronage, the Chinese decision to forgo overseas ventures was momentous. If China remained the wealthiest, most densely settled region of the world with the most fully developed state structures and thriving markets, the empire's wariness of overseas projects deprived merchants and would-be explorers of vital support in an age when others were beginning to look outward and overseas.

Conclusion

The dying and devastation that came with the Black Death caused many transformations, but certain underlying ideals and institutions endured. What changed were mainly the political regimes, which took the blame for the catastrophes. The Yuan dynasty collapsed and regimes in the Muslim world and Western Christendom were replaced by new political forms. In contrast, universal religions and cultural systems persisted even though they underwent vast transformations. A fervent form of Sunni

Islam found its champion in the Ottoman Empire. In Europe, centralizing monarchies appeared in Spain, Portugal, France, and England. The Ming dynasts in China set the stage for a long tenure by claiming the mandate of heaven and stressing China's place at the center of their universe.

The new states and empires had notable differences. These were evident in the ambition of a Ming warlord who established a new dynasty, the military expansionism of Turkish households bordering the Byzantine Empire, and the desire of various European rulers to consolidate power. But interactions among peoples also mattered; this era saw an eagerness to reestablish and expand trade networks, and a desire to convert unbelievers to "the true faith"—be it a form of Islam or an exclusive Christianity.

All of the dynasties surveyed in this chapter faced similar problems. They had to establish legitimacy, ensure smooth succession, deal with religious groups, and forge working relationships with nobles, townspeople, merchants, and peasants. Yet each state developed a distinctive identity; they all combined political innovation, traditional ways of ruling, and ideas borrowed from neighbors. European monarchies achieved significant internal unity, often through warfare with competing states. Ottoman rulers perfected techniques for ruling an ethnically and religiously diverse empire: they moved military forces swiftly, allowed local communities a degree of autonomy, and trained a bureaucracy dedicated to the Ottoman and Sunni Islamic way of life. The Ming fashioned an imperial system based on a Confucian-trained bureaucracy and intense subordination to the emperor so that it could manage a mammoth population. The rising monarchies of Europe and the Ottoman state all blazed with religious fervor and sought to eradicate or subordinate the beliefs of other groups.

The new states displayed unprecedented political and economic powers. All demonstrated military prowess, a desire for stable political and social hierarchies and secure borders, and a drive to expand. Each legitimized its rule via dynastic marriage and succession, state-sanctioned religion, and administrative bureaucracies. Each supported vigorous commercial activity. The Islamic regimes, especially, engaged in long-distance commerce and, by conquest and conversion, extended their holdings.

For Western Christendom, the Ottoman conquests were decisive. They provoked Europeans to establish commercial connections to the east, south, and west. The consequences of their new toeholds would be momentous—just as the Chinese decision to turn away from overseas exploration and commerce meant that China's contact with the outside world would be overland and eastward. As we shall see in Chapter 12, both decisions were instrumental in determining which worlds would come together and which would remain apart.

After You Read This Chapter

Go to INQUIZITIVE to see what you've learned—and learn what you've missed—with personalized feedback along the way.

TRACING THE GLOBAL STORYLINES

FOCUS ON: *Crisis and Recovery in Afro-Eurasia*

COLLAPSE AND CONSOLIDATION

- Bubonic plague originates in Inner Asia and afflicts people from China to Europe.
- Climate change and famine leaves people vulnerable, while commerce facilitates the spread of disease.
- The plague kills 25 to 65 percent of infected populations and leaves societies in turmoil.

ISLAMIC HEARTLAND

- Ottomans overrun Constantinople and become the primary Sunni regime in the Islamic world.
- The Ottomans establish their legitimacy with military prowess, religious backing, and a loyal bureaucracy.
- Sultans manage decentralizing tendencies of outlying provinces with flexibility and tolerance, relying on religious faith, patronage, and bureaucracy.

WESTERN CHRISTENDOM

- New dynastic monarchies that claim to rule by divine right appear in Portugal, Spain, France, and England.
- The Inquisition takes aim against *conversos*—converted Jews and Muslims.
- A rebirth of classical learning, known as the Renaissance, originates in Italian city-states and spreads throughout western Europe.

MING CHINA

- The Ming dynasty replaces the Mongol Yuan dynasty and rebuilds a strong state from the ground up, claiming a mandate from heaven.
- An elaborate, centralized bureaucracy oversees the revival of infrastructure and long-distance trade.
- The emperor and bureaucracy concentrate on developing internal markets and overland trade at the expense of overseas commerce.

CHRONOLOGY

ISLAMIC WORLD

Osman begins Ottoman Empire 1299

The Black Death arrives in Baghdad 1347

WESTERN CHRISTENDOM

Black Death reaches Italian port cities 1347

EAST ASIA

Black Death begins in China 1320

Hongwu founds Ming dynasty 1368

1200 | 1300

THINKING ABOUT GLOBAL CONNECTIONS

- ***Thinking about Exchange Networks*** By the fourteenth century, most of the Afro-Eurasian landmass was bound together by multiple exchange networks that functioned on many levels—political, cultural, and commercial. How did these exchange networks facilitate the spread of the plague? In what ways did the spread of the Black Death correspond with and diverge from existing political, cultural, and commercial networks?
- ***Thinking about Changing Power Relationships*** Fourteenth-century famine, plague, and the accompanying political, economic, and natural crises together triggered powerful, often differing, responses in western Europe, the Ottoman lands, and Ming China. How did men and women at different levels of society respond to the fourteenth-century crises? How did their responses reshape their societies? Pay special attention to the relationships among ordinary men and women, elites, and imperial bureaucracies in all three regions.
- ***Thinking about Environmental Impacts*** Climatic changes laid the groundwork for the devastation of the Black Death. What environmental developments in Europe, central Asia, and China set the stage for the Black Death?

STUDY QUESTIONS

1. Identify the fourteenth-century crisis that had the greatest impact throughout Afro-Eurasia and explain why: the **Black Death** (and accompanying famine of 1315 and climate change), the Mongol collapse, or political turmoil?
2. Analyze the role of philosophical and religious developments—both elite, like **humanism**, and popular movements, like the **Red Turban Movement** in China—in politics from 1300–1500 and explain how they provided both continuity and change in each society.
3. Explain how the Ottomans employed institutions such as **Topkapi Palace** and the ***devshirme*** system to consolidate their power?
4. Describe the ways in which regional monarchies and the **Renaissance** responded to the impact of the plague in western Europe? Analyze the role of the **Inquisition** in that process.
5. Explain how the Ming dynasty centralized power in China in the fourteenth and fifteenth centuries? What roles did emperors, bureaucrats, and ordinary people play? Compare Chinese efforts at bureaucratic centralization with those of the Ottomans.

Ottoman armies conquer Constantinople 1453

Suleiman expands and consolidates Ottoman Empire 1520–1566

Castile and Aragon unite to form Spain 1469

Spain conquers Granada 1492

Zheng He's voyages 1405–1433

00 | 1500 | 1600

Going to the Source

Diversity and Control: Cultural Responses to State Power

The devastation and dying across Afro-Eurasia in the fourteenth century was unprecedented. According to the most recent analysis of the impact of the Black Death on Europe, more than 60 percent of Europe's 80 million people died from the first onslaught of the disease between 1346 and 1353. In China and much of the Islamic world, the loss of life was also staggering, though perhaps not on such a large scale. Men and women who had previously prospered were stunned and often could not believe that the horrors of this disease could be visited upon them. They desperately sought explanations. At the same time, the states in which they lived had to find ways to consolidate their power and, at times, expand their authority, given the changing demographics.

The four documents and three illustrations here all consider the role that religion played in the lives of individuals and the states in which they lived. Identify and compare the ways in which different states and religions interacted with their subjects, and consider the historical context in which these interactions took place.

PRIMARY SOURCE 11.1

Flagellants in England (1350s), Robert of Avesbury

European Flagellants renounced the world and engaged in public self-punishment in reaction to the warfare, famines, and plagues of the fourteenth century. The Flagellants carried whips (*flagella*) with metal pieces run through knotted thongs, which they used to beat themselves until they were bruised, swollen, and bloody. Historian Robert of Avesbury here describes the actions of Flagellants in England during the reign of King Edward III.

*

In that same year of 1349, about Michaelmas [September 29], more than 120 men, for the most part from Zeeland or Holland, arrived in London from Flanders. These went barefoot in procession twice a day in the sight of the people, sometimes in St Paul's church and sometimes elsewhere in the city, their bodies naked except for a linen cloth from loins to ankle. Each wore a hood painted with a red cross at front and back and carried in his right hand a whip with three thongs. Each thong had a knot in it, with something sharp, like a needle, stuck through the middle of the knot so that it stuck out on each side, and as they walked one after the other they struck themselves with these whips on their naked, bloody bodies; four of them singing in their own tongue and the rest answering in the manner of the Christian litany. Three times in each procession they would all prostrate themselves on the ground, with their arms outstretched in the shape of a cross. Still singing, and beginning with the man at the end, each in turn would step over the others, lashing the man beneath him once with his whip, until all of those lying down had gone through the same ritual. Then each one put on his usual clothes and, always with their hoods on their heads and carrying their whips, they departed to their lodgings. It was said that they performed a similar penance every night.

1. **Why might the flagellants' self-punishment be a response to the demographic disaster that resulted from the plague epidemic?**
2. **Why do you think that only men participated in this ritual?**

PRIMARY SOURCE 11.2

Ming Shi-Lu *(1384), Veritable Records*

The *Ming Shi-Lu* is a history of China's Ming dynasty. It is organized according to the events within each emperor's reign. When each emperor died, official records and documents were collected into a history of the state under that emperor. When the Ming dynasty itself fell, the *Ming Shi-Lu* became their official history. It is, therefore, an official collection of primary sources. This selection explains the ways in which legal officials worked in provincial China under the Hongwu Emperor.

The Yun-nan Provincial Administration Commission advised: "Of the major and minor native officials under our jurisdiction, some have inherited their posts and some have been appointed. . . . Those who have inherited posts have long lived in their territories and they have their own stores and means of livelihood. It is thus not necessary to provide them with salaries and allowances. Those who are appointed have generally come to sojourn in these areas and because they have won the support of the local people we are employing them for a time. If we do not give them salaries, they will have no means of sustaining a livelihood. The law officials are more likely to accept bribes. They are also divided into the two grades of salaried and unsalaried. At present, there is no basis on which to apply the laws in handling crimes by the native officials. It is requested that the fixing of regulations be deliberated upon."

The Emperor ordered the six ministries to jointly deliberate upon this. They proposed: "Appointed native officials who commit offences should have their punishments decided in accordance with those for circulating officials, while in respect of the offences committed by those who inherit posts, the offices should not be permitted to arbitrarily punish them. First, depositions should be taken so as to ascertain the facts, and final deliberations should be memorialized. When due punishment is flogging or a lesser punishment, details should be recorded in their files. When banishment is due, they should be transferred to another place." These proposals were set down as orders.

1. **Why might some officials have inherited their posts?**
2. **Why might the different kinds of officials mentioned here have received different kinds of punishments for committing the same kinds of offenses? Do you think that this was a fair administration of justice? Why or why not?**

PRIMARY SOURCE 11.3

The Tribute of Children (fourteenth century), Anonymous

Sometime before the Ottoman conquest of Constantinople in 1453, the Ottoman sultan's prime minister suggested that the sultan should take not just 20 percent of the spoils of battle, but also 20 percent of those captured in battle. This was the origin of the janissary corps. To add to its numbers, every four years the sultan's agents went to every Christian village in the empire. All boys between the ages of about six and nine were brought to them and the sultan's agents selected a fifth of them, making sure to choose the strongest and most intelligent.

*

The advice of the vizier [prime minister] was followed; the edict was proclaimed; many thousands of the European captives were educated in the Mohammedan religion and arms, and the new militia was consecrated and named by a celebrated dervish. Standing in the front of their ranks, he stretched the sleeve of his gown over the head of the foremost soldier, and his blessing was delivered in the following words "Let them be called Janizaries [yingi-cheri, or 'new soldiers']; may their countenances be ever bright; their hand victorious; their swords keen; may their spear always hang over the heads of their enemies." . . . Such was the origin of these haughty troops, the terror of the nations.

They were kept up by continual additions from the sultan's share of the captives, and by recruits, raised every five years, from the children of the Christian subjects. Small parties of soldiers went from place to place. Wherever they come, they assembled the inhabitants with their sons. The leader of the soldiers had the right to take away all the youth who are distinguished by beauty or strength, activity or talent, above the age of seven. He carried them to the court of the grand seignior, a tithe, as it were, of the subjects. The captives taken in war and presented to the sultan, include Poles, Bohemians, Russians, Italians, and Germans.

These recruits are divided into two classes. Those who compose the first, were sent to Anatolia, where they were trained to agricultural labor, and instructed in the Mussulman faith; or they were retained about the seraglio [palace], where they carried wood and water, and were employed in the gardens, in the boats, or upon the public buildings, always under the direction of an overseer, who with a stick compelled them to work. Others, in whom traces of a higher character are discernible, were placed in one of the four seraglios of Adrianople or Galata, or the old or new one at Constantinople. Teachers come every morning, who remain with them until evening, and teach them to read and write. . . . Those who have performed hard labor are made Janizaries. Those who are educated in the seraglios become higher officers of state.

Both classes were kept under a strict discipline. The former especially were accustomed to privation of food, drink, and comfortable clothing and to hard labor. They were exercised in shooting with the bow and arquebuse by day, and spent the night in a long, lighted hall, with an overseer, who walks up and down, and permitted no one to stir. When they were received into the corps of the Janizaries, they are placed in cloister-like barracks. . . . Here not only the younger continued to obey the elders in silence and submission, but all were governed with such strictness that no one is permitted to spend the night abroad, and whoever was punished was compelled to kiss the hand of him who inflicted the punishment.

1. **Why were the janissaries selected from boys who came from territory far from the Ottoman palaces and courts?**
2. **Why do you think that conversion to Islam was a necessary part of their training?**

PRIMARY SOURCE 11.4

Saint Dominic Presiding over an Auto da Fe (fifteenth century), Pedro Berruguete

This painting by a Spanish Renaissance artist depicts a scene in which Spanish authorities burned people at the stake for their alleged heretical beliefs. Note the members of the Church hierarchy and soldiers who were loyal to the crown watching those accused by the Spanish Inquisition perform their acts of penance before they were executed.

1. **Why might the artist have placed the Church representatives at the highest level in the painting?**
2. **Why might the Catholic Church have supervised executions such as this one? What did it hope to gain from doing so?**

PRIMARY SOURCE 11.5

Qalandar Dervishes in the Islamic World (1548), Menavino

The Qalandar dervish order sprang up in Damascus, Syria, and in Egypt in the thirteenth century and spread rapidly throughout the Islamic world. Reacting to the period's widespread unrest, its members engaged in highly individualistic practices as they moved about, going so far as to renounce the world. The educated elite criticized the dervishes as ignorant hypocrites who lived on alms obtained from gullible common folk. In this excerpt, Giovan Antonio Menavino, a European observer of Ottoman society, describes the Qalandars, whom he called the torlaks.

Dressed in sheepskins, the torlaks [Qalandars] are otherwise naked, with no headgear. Their scalps are always clean-shaven and well rubbed with oil as a precaution against the cold. They burn their temples with an old rag so that their faces will not be damaged by sweat. Illiterate and unable to do anything manly, they live like beasts, surviving on alms only. For this reason, they are to be found around taverns and public kitchens in cities. If, while roaming the countryside, they come across a well-dressed person, they try to make him one of their own, stripping him naked. Like Gypsies in Europe, they practice chiromancy [palm-reading], especially for women who then provide them with bread, eggs, cheese, and other foods in return for their services.

Amongst them there is usually an old man whom they revere and worship like God. When they enter a town, they gather around the best house of the town and listen in great humility to the words of this old man, who, after a spell of ecstasy, foretells the descent of a great evil upon the town. His disciples then implore him to fend off the disaster through his good services. The old man accepts the plea of his followers, though not without an initial show of reluctance, and prays to God, asking him to spare the town the imminent danger awaiting it. This time-honored trick earns them considerable sums of alms from ignorant and credulous people.

1. **What is the author's impression of the Qalanders?**
2. **Why might people in the towns that the dervishes visited find their message and practices appealing, especially at this time?**

PRIMARY SOURCE 11.6

The Devshirme *System (1558)*

This miniature painting depicts the *devshirme* system in the Ottoman Empire (see p. 415). The parents are lined up on the right to present their boys to the Ottoman official selecting them for service to the empire. The boys are in the foreground in red.

1. **Describe the reaction of the parents who appear on the right side of the painting.**
2. **Why might the adults have been willing to part with their children?**

PRIMARY SOURCE 11.7

Confucian Scholars (c. 1540), Ch'iu Ying

This painting on silk depicts a group of scholars waiting for the results of their civil service exam. Candidates spent three days and two nights taking examinations as they sought to enter the Ming bureaucracy.

1. **Describe the figures that you see in the painting. How might you interpret what you observe?**
2. **Why were the results of the Chinese civil service exam so important for so many people?**

Questions for Analysis

Comparison

1. How was religion used differently in the societies that these documents discuss?

2. Explain any changes in the relationship between the states and their peoples that you have detected over the time period that the documents consider.

Analyzing Evidence

3. Based on these documents and your reading of the chapter, which government—China, the Ottoman Empire, or those in Europe—was likely to have the most consistent policies, and why?

Argumentation

4. How might the Black Death, discussed in this chapter, have prompted divergent responses from people who held varying views and beliefs?

Long Essay Question

Synthesis

Explain which method of state control depicted in these sources was most effective and why.

Before You Read This Chapter

GLOBAL STORYLINES

- The European "discovery" of the Americas begins a complex process that changes the ways peoples around the world interact with one another.
- For the first time, major world empires are oceanic, overseas empires rather than continental empires.
- Despite the long-term significance of European activity in the Americas, most Africans and Asians are barely aware of the Americas or the expansion of long-distance trade.
- Within Europe, dynastic states concentrate attention and resources on their own internal rivalries. Religious revolts, especially the Protestant Reformation, intensify those rivalries.
- Asian empires thrive in the sixteenth century, thanks to commercial expansion and political consolidation.

CORE OBJECTIVES

- **DESCRIBE** the broad patterns of world trade after 1450 and **COMPARE** major features of world trade in Asia, the Americas, Africa, and Europe.
- **ANALYZE** the factors that enabled Europeans to increase their trade relationships with Asian empires in the fifteenth and sixteenth centuries and **ASSESS** their significance.
- **COMPARE** the practices and the impact of European explorers in Asia and the Americas.
- **ANALYZE** the social and political relationships and **EXPLAIN** the sources of conflict within the Afro-Eurasian polities.
- **ASSESS** how European colonization of the Americas affected African and Amerindian peoples and **DESCRIBE** their responses.

CHAPTER

12

Contact, Commerce, and Colonization

1450–1600

KEY TERMS

Atlantic system p. 458
Aztec Empire p. 449
Jean Calvin p. 459
Columbian exchange p. 452
conquistadors p. 448
Counter-Reformation p. 459
encomenderos p. 448
Holy Roman Empire p. 461
Incan Empire p. 449
Jesuits p. 460
Martin Luther p. 459
Mughal Empire p. 462
Protestant Reformation p. 458

In 1519, five ships under the command of Ferdinand Magellan set out from the Spanish mainland. Nearly three years later a single vessel returned, having successfully sailed around the globe. This achievement came at a high cost: four ships had been lost, and only 18 men out of 265 had fought off scurvy, starvation, and stormy seas to complete the journey. Magellan himself had died. But the survivors had become the first true world travelers. Unlike earlier adventurers who made forays into Eurasia and Africa, Magellan's transoceanic passage connected these worlds with others that, from an Afro-Eurasian viewpoint, had been apart—the Americas.

Magellan's voyages were part of a wave of explorations that included one of the most momentous events in the narrative of world history: Christopher Columbus's voyages of discovery, which opened up worlds about which Afro-Eurasians had no previous knowledge. Although Christopher Columbus did not intend to "discover" America when he went looking for Asia, his voyages convinced Europeans that there were still new territories to exploit and peoples to convert to Christianity. For the first time since the Ice Age migrations, large numbers of people moved from Afro-Eurasian landmasses to the Americas. So did animals, plants, commercial products, and—most momentous—deadly germs.

It was enormously significant that Europeans, rather than Asians or Africans, first stumbled upon the Americas and then exploited their resources. For Europeans, too, now became empire builders—but of a different nature. Their empires were overseas. While the new colonies generated vast riches, they also brought unsettling changes to the rulers and the ruled.

Despite the significance of Europeans' activity in the Americas, most Africans and Asians were barely aware of its importance to them. Asian empires continued to flourish after recovering from the Black Death. Nor was Europe's attention exclusively on the Americas, for its royal houses competed with one another for power and territory at home. Religious revolt in the form of the Protestant Reformation intensified these rivalries. In the wake of Columbus, the drive to build and protect empires across oceans scattered peoples, splattered blood, and shattered worlds.

The Old Trade and the New

COMPARISON

DESCRIBE the broad patterns of world trade after 1450.

Well before commodities from the Americas entered Afro-Eurasian trade networks, commerce recovered from the destruction wrought by the Black Death. Just as political leaders rebuilt states by mixing traditional and innovative ideas, merchant elites revived old trade patterns while establishing new networks. Increasingly, traffic across seas supplemented the overland transportation of goods. The Indian Ocean and China seas emerged as the focal points of Afro-Eurasia's maritime commerce. Across these waters moved an assortment of goods, coordinated by Arab, Persian, Indian, and Chinese merchants who often settled in foreign lands to facilitate trade.

European mariners and traders, searching for new routes to South and East Asia, began exploring the Atlantic coast of Africa. Lured by spices, silks, and slaves, and aided by new maritime technology, Portuguese expeditions made their way around Africa and onward to India. Although Europeans still had little to offer would-be trading partners in Asia, their developing capability in overseas trade laid the foundations for a new kind of global commerce.

THE REVIVAL OF ASIAN ECONOMIES

Trade all across Afro-Eurasia benefited enormously from China's economic dynamism, which was driven primarily by China's vast internal economy. But the Chinese demand for silver fueled a revival of trade across the Indian Ocean and traditional overland routes. After the Ming dynasty relocated its capital from Nanjing in the prosperous south to the northern city of Beijing, Chinese merchants, artisans, and farmers exploited the surging domestic market. Reconstruction of the Grand Canal now opened a major artery that allowed food and riches from the economically vibrant lower Yangzi area to reach the capital region of Beijing. Urban centers, such as Nanjing with a population approaching a million and Beijing at half a million, became massive and lucrative markets. Despite official restrictions on trade, merchants thrived, and coastal cities remained active harbors. (See Map 12.5.)

Chinese Porcelain Box The shape, coloring, and texture of this Chinese porcelain writing box are a tribute to the exquisite craftsmanship that went into its production. This box was also a symbol of flourishing world trade and a typical example of what the French called "chinoiserie," the possession of which was a hallmark of taste and cultivation among the rich and the status-conscious in Europe.

What did foreign buyers have to trade with the Chinese? The answer was silver, which became essential to the Ming monetary system. Whereas their predecessors had used paper money, Ming consumers and traders mistrusted anything other than silver or gold for commercial dealings. Once the rulers adopted silver as a means of tax payment in the 1430s, it became the predominant medium for larger transactions.

China, however, did not produce sufficient silver for its booming economy. Indeed, silver and other precious metals were about the only commodities for which the Chinese would trade their precious manufactures. Through most of the sixteenth century, China's main source of silver was Japan, which one Florentine merchant called the "silver islands." After the 1570s, however, the Philippines, now under the control of the Spanish, became a gateway for silver coming from the New World. One-third of all silver mined in the Americas during the sixteenth and seventeenth centuries wound up in Chinese hands.

China's economic expansion contributed to the revival of Indian Ocean trade. Long-distance merchants developed a brisk commerce that tied the whole of the Indian Ocean together. Ports as far off as East Africa and the Red Sea enjoyed links with coastal cities of India, South Asia, and the Malay Peninsula. Muslims dominated this trade. India was the geographic and economic center of numerous trade routes. With a population expanding as rapidly as China's, its large cities (such as Agra, Delhi, and Lahore) each boasted nearly half a million residents. India's manufacturing center, Bengal, exported silk and cotton textiles and rice throughout South and Southeast Asia. Like China, India exported more than it imported, selling textiles and pepper in exchange for silver.

Overland commerce also thrived anew. One well-trafficked route linked the Baltic Sea, Muscovy, the Caspian Sea, the central Asian oases, and China. Other land routes carried goods to the ports of China and the Indian Ocean; from there, they crossed to the Ottoman Empire's heartland and went by land farther into Europe. Ottoman authorities took a keen interest in the caravan trade, since the state gained considerable tax revenue from it. To facilitate the caravans' movement, the government maintained refreshment and military stations along the route. The largest had individual rooms to accommodate the chief merchants and could provide lodging for up to 800 travelers, as well as care for all their animals. But gathering so many traders, animals, and cargoes could also attract marauders, especially desert tribesmen. To stop the raids, authorities and merchants offered cash payments to tribal chieftains as "protection money." This was a small price to pay in order to protect the caravan trade, whose revenues ultimately supported imperial expansion.

Overland Caravans and Caravanserais Muslim governments and merchants' associations constructed inns, or caravanserais, along the major trading routes. These areas were capable of accommodating a large number of traders and their animals in great comfort.

EUROPEAN EXPLORATION AND EXPANSION

COMPARISON

ANALYZE the factors that enabled Europeans to increase their trade relationships with Asian empires and **ASSESS** their significance.

The emergence of the Ottoman Empire prompted Europeans to probe unexplored links to the east in the sixteenth century. When the Ottomans took control of traditional overland trade routes from Europe to Asia, Europeans began to look south and west—and ventured across the seas. (See Map 12.1.) Taking the lead were the Portuguese, whose search for new routes to Asia led them first to Africa. Europeans had long believed that Africa was a storehouse of precious metals. In fact, a fourteenth-century map, the Catalan Atlas, had depicted a single black ruler controlling a vast quantity of gold in the interior of Africa. As the price of gold skyrocketed during and after the Black Death, ambitious men decided to venture southward in search of this commodity and its twin, silver. Having found sea routes around Africa, European merchants sought to reap the riches abounding in Asian ports, especially once Asian states were firmly established across the Indian Ocean in the seventeenth century.

Innovations in maritime technology and information from other mariners helped Portuguese sailors navigate the treacherous waters along the African coast. New vessels included the carrack, a three- or four-masted ship, developed by the Portuguese to deal with rough waters like the Atlantic Ocean and the Mediterranean. Equally important was the caravel, with specially designed triangular sails, which enabled European sailors to nose in and out of estuaries and navigate unpredictable currents and winds. By using highly maneuverable caravels and perfecting the technique of tacking (sailing into the wind rather than before it), the Portuguese advanced far along the West African coast. In addition, newfound expertise with the compass and the astrolabe helped navigators determine latitude.

The Catalan Atlas This 1375 map shows the world as it was then known. Not only does it depict the location of continents and islands, but it also includes information on ancient and medieval tales, regional politics, astronomy, and astrology.

Portuguese seafarers ventured from the coasts of Africa into the Indian Ocean and inserted themselves into its thriving commerce. In Asia, Portugal did not attempt to rule directly or to establish colonies. Rather, it aimed to exploit Asian commercial networks and trading systems. To do so, the Portuguese took advantage of a technology developed centuries earlier in China: gunpowder. Mounting small cannons on their warships, they bombarded ports and rival navies or merchant vessels.

The first Portuguese mariner to reach the Indian Ocean was Vasco da Gama (1469–1524). Like Columbus, da Gama was relatively unknown before his extraordinary voyage commanding four ships around the Cape of Good Hope. He found a network of commercial ties spanning the Indian Ocean, as well as skilled Muslim mariners who knew the currents, winds, and ports of call. Once established in the key ports, the Portuguese attempted to take over the trade or, failing this, to tax local merchants. From Sofala, Kilwa, and other important ports on the East African coast, Goa and Calicut in India, and Macao in southern China, the Portuguese soon dominated the most active sealanes of the Indian Ocean. The Portuguese did not interrupt the flow of luxuries among Asian and African elites; rather, their naval captains simply kept a portion of the profits for themselves, content to benefit from Asian prosperity without imposing Portuguese rule. Only with the discovery of the Americas and the conquest of Brazil did Portugal become an empire with large overseas colonies. For this to transpire, mariners would have to traverse the Atlantic Ocean itself.

The Atlantic World

By opening new sea-lanes in the Atlantic, European explorers set the stage for a major transformation in world history: the establishment of overseas colonies. After the discovery of the Americas, Europeans conquered the native peoples and created colonies for the purpose of enriching themselves and their monarchs.

COMPARISON

COMPARE the practices and the impact of European explorers in Asia and the Americas.

Crossing the Atlantic was a feat of monumental importance. It did not occur, however, with an aim to discover new lands. Columbus set out to open a more direct—and more lucrative—route to Japan and China. As we saw in Chapter 11, Ferdinand and Isabella hoped Columbus would bring them riches that would finance a crusade to liberate Jerusalem. Neither they nor Columbus expected he would find a "New World."

Europeans arrived in what they soon called the New World with cannons, steel weapons and body armor, horses, and, above all, deadly diseases that caused a catastrophic decline of Amerindian populations. Europeans arrived at a time of political upheaval and took advantage of divisions among the indigenous peoples. The combination of material advantages and local allies enabled Europeans to conquer and colonize the Americas, as they could not do in Asia or Africa, where long-standing patterns of trade had resulted in the development of shared immunities and stable states resisted outside incursions.

The devastation of the Amerindian population also resulted in severe labor shortages. Thus began the large-scale introduction of slave laborers imported from Africa, which led to the "Atlantic system" that connected Europe, the Americas, and Africa. The precious metals of the New World now gave Europeans something to offer their trading partners in Asia and enabled them to grow rich. In the process, they brought together peoples and ecosystems that had developed separately for thousands of years.

FIRST ENCOUNTERS

Christopher Columbus set sail from Spain in early 1492, stopped in the Canary Islands for supplies and repairs, and cast off into the unknown. When he stepped onto the beach of San Salvador (in the Bahamas) on October 12, 1492, the explorer ushered in a new era in world history. Like other expansion-minded Europeans, once established in the Americas, Columbus and the other mariners aimed to Christianize the world while enriching themselves and their backers. These goals—to save souls and to make money—drove the European colonization of the Americas and the formation of an Atlantic system. They also shaped Europeans' early interactions with Amerindians and Africans captured in the slave trade.

Columbus As Columbus made landfall and encountered Indians, he planted a cross to indicate the spiritual purpose of the voyage and read aloud a document proclaiming the sovereign authority of the king and queen of Spain. Quickly, he learned there was barter for precious stones and metals.

When Columbus made landfall in the Caribbean Sea, he unfurled the royal standard of Ferdinand and Isabella and claimed the "many islands filled with people innumerable" for Spain. It is fitting that the first encounter with Caribbean inhabitants, in this case the Tainos, drew blood.

GREENLAND
NORTH AMERICA
SOUTH AMERICA
ATLANTIC OCEAN
PACIFIC OCEAN
FROBISHER 1576
CARTIER 1534–1541
NEWFOUNDLAND (1497)
CABOT 1497–1498
ENGLAND
FRANCE
SPAIN
PORTUGAL
Lisbon
Seville
Cadiz
Ceuta (1415)
AZORES
MADEIRA
CANARY ISLANDS
CAPE VERDE ISLANDS
St. Augustine
SAN SALVADOR
COLUMBUS 1492
COLUMBUS 1493–1494
CORTÉS 1519
Zacatecas
Havana (1492)
CUBA
Tenochtitlán
YUCATAN
AZTEC EMPIRE
HISPANIOLA (1482)
VESPUCCI 1501–1502
MAGELLAN 1519
CABRAL 1500
DIAZ 1487–1488
FERNANDO PO
GOLD COAST
Elmina
SÃO TOMÉ
DEL CANO (after Magellan's death) 1521–1522
VASCO DA GAMA 1497–1498
DRAKE 1577–1580
Panama
Quito (1534)
Lima (1535)
Cuzco
Potosí
INCA EMPIRE
Bahia
Rio de Janeiro
PIZARRO 1531
Santiago
Buenos Aires (1535)
MAGELLAN AND DEL CANO 1520
CABRAL 1500
Line of Tordesillas 1494
Cape Horn
Straits of Magellan
Portuguese exploration
Spanish exploration
English exploration
French exploration
Portuguese controlled islands
Spanish controlled islands
Portuguese controlled cities
Spanish controlled cities

MAP 12.1 | European Exploration, 1420–1580

In the fifteenth and sixteenth centuries, sailors from Portugal, Spain, England, and France explored and mapped the coastline of most of the world.

- Explain why Europeans would have chosen sea routes to reach Asia rather than land routes.
- Trace the voyages that started from Portugal, and then the voyages that started from Spain. Explain why Portuguese explorers concentrated on Africa and the Indian Ocean, whereas their Spanish counterparts focused on the Americas.
- Contrast the different patterns of exploration in the New World with those in the Indian Ocean and the South China Sea.

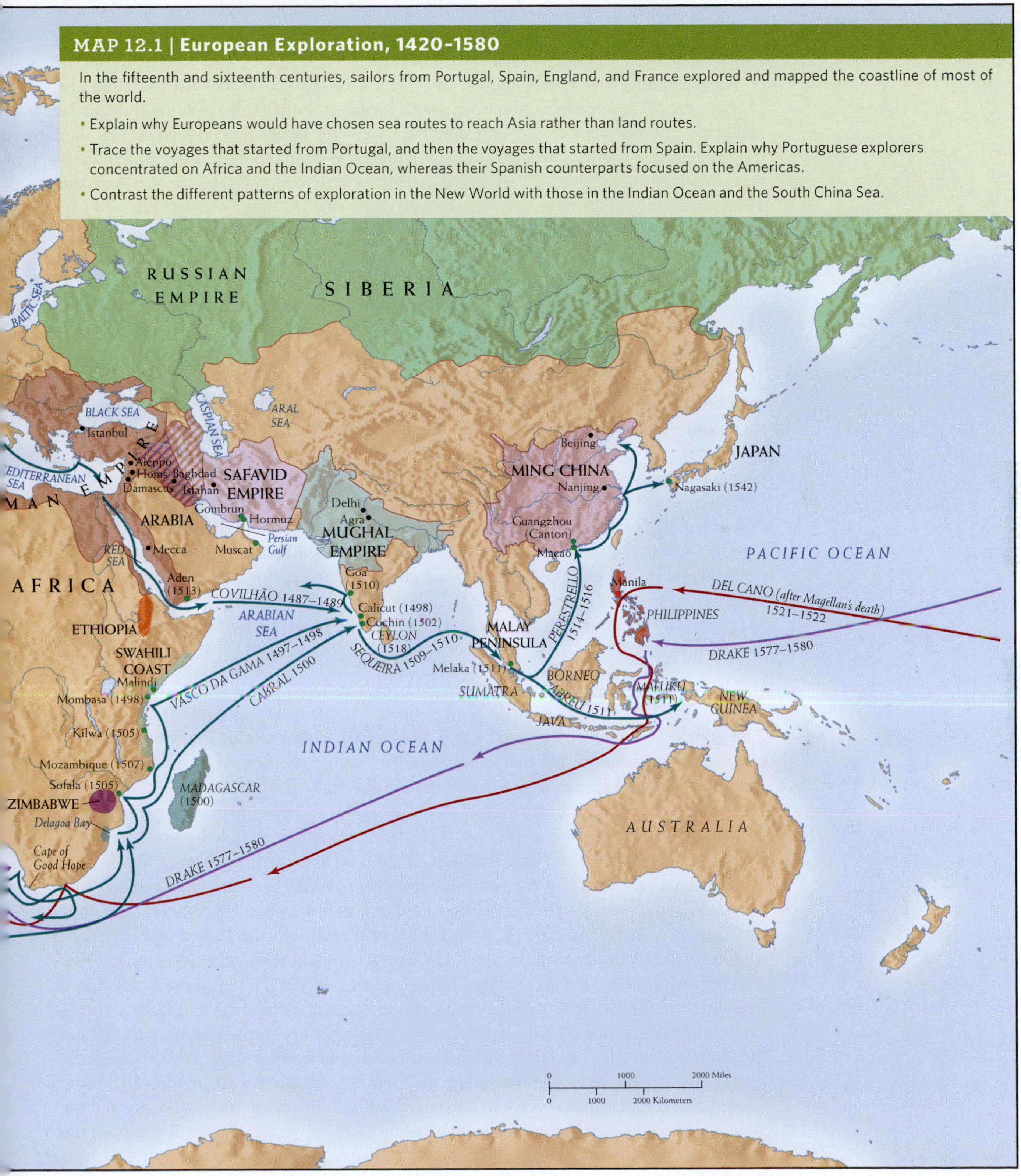

Columbus noted, "I showed them swords and they took them by the edge and through ignorance cut themselves." The Tainos had their own weapons but did not forge steel—and thus had no knowledge of such sharp edges.

For Columbus, the Tainos' naïveté in grabbing his sword symbolized the child-like primitivism of these people, whom he would mislabel "Indians" because he thought he had arrived off the coast of Asia. In Columbus's view the Tainos had no religion, but they did have at least some gold (found initially hanging as pendants from their noses). Likewise, Pedro Alvares Cabral, a Portuguese mariner whose trip down the coast of Africa in 1500 was blown off course across the Atlantic, wrote that the people of Brazil had all "the innocence of Adam." He also noted that they were ripe for conversion and that the soils "if rightly cultivated would yield everything." But, as with Africans and Asians, Europeans also developed a contradictory view of the peoples of the Americas. From the Tainos, Columbus learned of another people, the Caribs, who (according to his informants) were savage, warlike cannibals. For centuries, these contrasting images—innocents and savages—structured European (mis)understandings of the native peoples of the Americas.

We know less about what the Indians thought of Columbus or other Europeans on their first encounters. Certainly they were impressed with the Europeans' appearance and their military prowess. The Tainos fled into the forest at the approach of European ships, which they thought were giant monsters; others thought they were floating islands. European metal goods, in particular weaponry, struck them as otherworldly. The Amerindians found the newcomers different not for their skin color (only Europeans drew the distinction based on skin pigmentation), but for their hairiness. Indeed, the Europeans' beards, breath, and bad manners repulsed their Indian hosts. The newcomers' inability to live off the land also stood out. In due course, the Indians realized not just that the strange, hairy people bearing metal weapons were odd trading partners, but that they meant to stay and to force the local population to labor for them. The explorers had become **conquistadors** (conquerors).

FIRST CONQUESTS

First contacts between peoples gave way to dramatic conquests in the Americas; then conquests paved the way to mass exploitation of native peoples. After the first voyage, Columbus claimed that on Hispaniola (present-day Haiti and the Dominican Republic) "he had found what he was looking for"—gold. That was sufficient to persuade the Spanish crown to invest in larger expeditions. Whereas Columbus first sailed with three small ships and 87 men, ten years later the Spanish outfitted an expedition with 2,500 men.

Between 1492 and 1519, the Spanish experimented with institutions of colonial rule over local populations on the Caribbean island that they renamed Hispaniola. Ultimately they created a model that the rest of the New World colonies would adapt. But the Spaniards faced problems that would recur. The first was Indian resistance. As early as 1494, starving Spaniards raided and pillaged Indian villages. When the Indians revolted, Spanish soldiers replied with punitive expeditions and began enslaving them to work in mines extracting gold. As the crown rewarded conquistadors with grants (*encomiendas*) giving them control over Indian labor, a rich class of ***encomenderos*** arose who enjoyed the fruits of the system. Although the surface gold mines soon ran dry, the model of granting favored settlers the right to coerce Indian labor endured. In return, those who received the labor rights paid special taxes on the precious metals that were extracted. Thus, both the crown and the *encomenderos* benefited. The same cannot be said of the Amerindians, who perished in great numbers from disease, malnutrition, and overwork.

As Spanish colonists saw the bounty of Hispaniola dry up, they set out to discover and conquer new territories. Finding their way to the mainlands of the American landmasses, they encountered larger, more complex, and more militarized societies than those they had overrun in the Caribbean. Great civilizations had arisen there centuries before, boasting large cities, monumental buildings, and riches based on wealthy agrarian societies. In both Mesoamerica, starting with the Olmecs (see Chapter 5), and the Andes, with the Chimú (see Chapter 10), large states had laid the foundations for subsequent Aztec and **Incan empires**. These empires were powerful. But they had evolved untouched by Afro-Eurasian developments; as worlds apart, they were unprepared for the kind of assaults that European invaders had honed. In pre-Columbian Mesoamerica and then the Andes, warfare was more ceremonial, less inclined to wipe out enemies than to make them pay tribute. As a result, the wealth and vulnerability of these empires made them irresistible to outside conquerors.

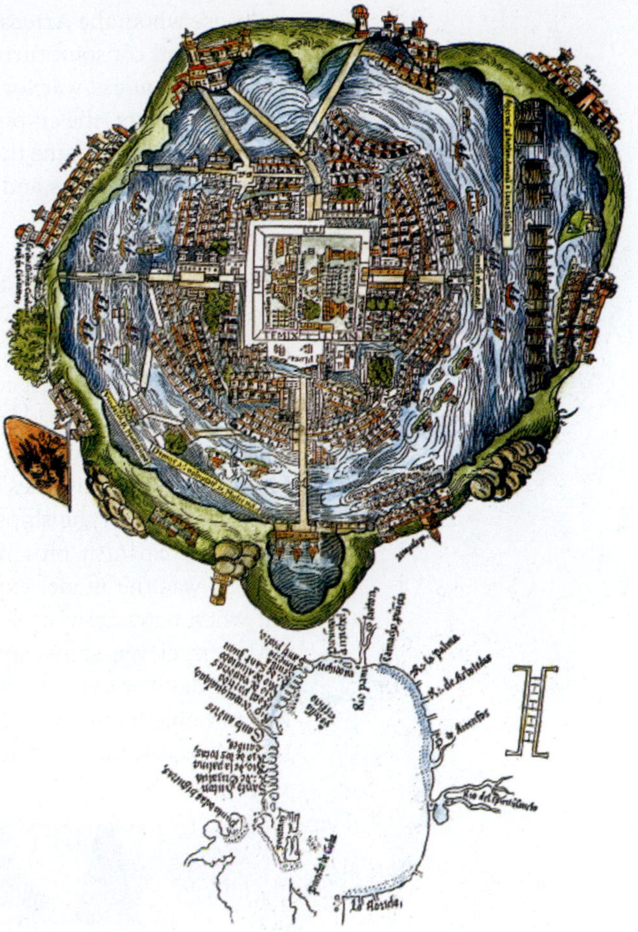

Tenochtitlán At its height, the Aztec capital Tenochtitlán was as populous as Europe's largest city. As can be seen from this map, it spread in concentric circles, with the main religious and political buildings in the center and residences radiating outward.

Aztec Society In Mesoamerica, the Mexicas had created an empire known to us as "Aztec." Around Lake Texcoco, Mexica cities grew and formed a three-city league in 1430, which then expanded through the Central Valley of Mexico to incorporate neighboring peoples. Gradually the **Aztec Empire** united numerous small, independent states under a single monarch who ruled with the help of counselors, military leaders, and priests. By the late fifteenth century, the Aztec realm may have embraced 25 million people. Tenochtitlán, situated on an immense island in Lake Texcoco, ranked among the world's largest cities.

Tenochtitlán spread in concentric circles, with the main religious and political buildings in the center and residences radiating outward. The city's outskirts connected a mosaic of floating gardens producing food for urban markets. Canals irrigated the land, waste served as fertilizer, and high-yielding produce found easy transport to markets. Entire households worked: men, women, and children all had roles in Aztec agriculture.

Extended kinship provided the scaffolding for Aztec statehood. Marriage of men and women from different villages solidified alliances and created clan-like networks. In Tenochtitlán, powerful families married their children to each other or found nuptial partners among the prominent families of other important cities. Soon a lineage emerged to create a corps of "natural" rulers. Priests legitimized new emperors in rituals to convey the image of a ruler close to the gods and to distinguish the elite from the lower orders.

Ultimately Aztec power spread though much of Mesoamerica, but the empire's constant wars and conquests deprived it of stability. In military campaigns, the Aztecs defeated their neighbors, forcing the conquered peoples to pay tribute of crops, gold, silver, textiles, and other goods that financed Aztec grandeur. Such conquests also provided a constant supply of humans for sacrifice, because the Aztecs believed that the great god of the sun required human hearts to keep on burning and blood to replace that given by the gods to moisten the earth through rain. Priests escorted captured warriors up the temple steps and tore out their hearts, offering their lives and blood as a sacrifice to the sun god.

Those whom the Aztecs sought to dominate did not submit peacefully. From 1440, the empire faced constant turmoil as subject populations rebelled. Tlaxcalans and Tarascans waged a relentless war for freedom, holding at bay entire divisions of Aztec armies. To pacify the realm, the empire diverted more and more men and money into a mushrooming military. By the time the electoral committee chose Moctezuma II as emperor in 1502, divisions among elites and pressures from the periphery placed the Aztec Empire under extreme stress.

Cortés and Conquest Not long after Moctezuma became emperor, news arrived from the coast of ships bearing pale, bearded men and monsters (horses and dogs). Here distinguishing fact from fiction is difficult. Some accounts left after the conquest by indigenous witnesses reported that Moctezuma consulted with his ministers and priests, wondering if these men were the god Quetzalcoátl and his entourage. Most historians dismiss the importance of these omens as the effort of rival elites to blame Moctezuma for their own inaction. In any case, Moctezuma sent emissaries bearing gifts, but he did not prepare for a military engagement.

Aboard one of the ships was Hernán Cortés (1485–1547), a former law student from one of the Spanish provinces. He would become the model conquistador, just as Columbus was the model explorer. For a brief time, Cortés was an *encomendero* in Cuba; but when news arrived of a potentially wealthier land to the west, he set sail with over 500 men, eleven ships, sixteen horses, and artillery. When the expedition arrived near present-day Veracruz, Cortés acquired two translators, including the daughter of a local Indian noble family, who became known as Doña Marina, also known as La Malinche. With the assistance of Doña Marina and other native allies, Cortés marched his troops to

Cortés Meets Mesoamerican Rulers *(Left)* This colonial image depicts the meeting of Cortés (second from right) and Moctezuma (seated on the left), with Doña Marina serving as an interpreter and informer for the Spanish conquistador. Notice at the bottom what are likely Aztec offerings for the newcomer. *(Right)* This detail from a twentieth-century Mexican mural depicts the meeting of Cortés and the king of Tlaxcala, enemy of the Aztecs. As Mexicans began to celebrate their mixed-blood heritage, Doña Marina (in the middle) became the symbolic mother of the first mestizos.

Tenochtitlán. Upon entering, he gasped in wonder that "this city is so big and so remarkable" that it was "almost unbelievable." One of his soldiers wrote, "It was all so wonderful that I do not know how to describe this first glimpse of things never heard of, seen or dreamed of before."

How was this tiny force to overcome an empire of many millions with an elaborate warring tradition? Crucial to Spanish conquest was their alliance, negotiated through translators, with Moctezuma's enemies—especially the Tlaxcalans. After decades of yearning for release from the Aztec yoke, the Tlaxcalans and other Mesoamerican peoples embraced Cortés's promise of help. The Spaniards' second advantage was their method of warfare. The Aztecs were seasoned fighters, but they fought to capture, not to kill. Nor were they familiar with gunpowder or sharp steel swords. Although outnumbered, the Spaniards killed their foes with abandon, using superior weaponry, horses, and war dogs. When Cortés arrived at Tenochtitlán, the Aztecs were still unsure who these strange men were and allowed Cortés to enter their city. With the aid of the Tlaxcalans and a handful of his own men, in 1519 Cortés captured Moctezuma, who became a puppet of the Spanish conqueror.

The Aztecs quickly changed their approach to fighting. When Spanish troops massacred an unarmed crowd in Tenochtitlán's central square while Cortés was away, they provoked a massive uprising. The Spaniards led Moctezuma to one of the palace walls to plead with his people for a truce, but the Aztecs kept up their barrage of stones, spears, and arrows—striking and killing Moctezuma. Cortés returned to reassert control; but realizing this was impossible, he gathered his loot and escaped. He left behind hundreds of Spaniards, many of whom were dragged up the temple steps and sacrificed by Aztec priests.

With the Tlaxcalans' help, Cortés regrouped. This time he bombarded Tenochtitlán with artillery, determined to defeat the Aztecs completely. Even more devastating was the spread of smallpox, brought by the Spanish, which ran through the Aztec soldiers and commoners like wildfire. In the end, starvation, disease, lack of artillery, and Cortes's ability to rally Amerindian allies to his side vanquished the Aztec forces. More died from disease than from fighting—the total number of Aztec casualties may have reached 240,000. As Spanish troops retook the capital, now in ruins, the Spaniards and their allies had to engage in house-to-house combat to secure control over Tenochtitlán. The Aztecs lamented their defeat in verse: "We have pounded our hands in despair against the adobe walls, for our inheritance, our city, is lost and dead." Cortés became governor of the new Spanish colony, renamed "New Spain." He promptly allocated *encomiendas* to his loyal followers and dispatched expeditions to conquer the more distant Mesoamerican provinces.

The Mexica experience taught the Spanish an important lesson: an effective conquest had to be swift—and it had to remove completely the symbols of legitimate authority. Their winning advantage, however, was disease. The Spaniards unintentionally introduced germs that made their subsequent efforts at military conquest much easier.

The Incas The other great Spanish conquest occurred in the Andes, where Quechua-speaking rulers, called Incas, had established an impressive state. Sometime around 1200, a band of Andean villagers settled into the valleys near what is now Cuzco, in Peru, which soon became the hub of South America's greatest empire. A combination of raiding neighbors and intermarrying into elite families raised the Incas to regional supremacy. Their power radiated along the valley routes that carved up the chain of great mountains until they finally ran up against the mighty warrior confederacy of the Chanca. After defeating the Chanca rivals around 1438, the Inca warrior Yupanqui renamed himself Pachacuti and began the royal line of Inca emperors. They eventually ruled a vast domain from what is now Chile to southern Colombia. At its center was the capital, Cuzco, with the magnificent fortress of Sacsayhuaman as its head. Built of huge boulders, the citadel was the nerve center of a complex network of strongholds that held the empire together.

As in most empires of the day, political power depended on a combination of tribute and commercial exchange to finance an extensive communication and military network. The empire developed an elaborate system of sending messages by runners who relayed up and down a system of stone highways carrying instructions to allies and roving armed divisions. None of this would have been possible without a wealthy agrarian base. Peasants paid tribute to village elders in the form of labor services to maintain public works, complex terraces, granaries, and food storage systems in case of drought or famine. In return, Inca rulers were obliged to shelter their people and allies in case of hardship. They oversaw rituals, festivals, and ceremonies to give spiritual legitimacy to their power. At their peak, the Incas may have governed a population of up to 6 million people. But as the empire stretched into distant provinces, especially into northern frontiers, ruling Incas lost touch with their base in Cuzco. Fissures began to open in the Andean empire as European germs and conquistadors appeared on South American shores.

When the Spaniards arrived in 1532 they found a divided empire, a situation they quickly learned to exploit. Francisco Pizarro, who led the Spanish campaign, had been inspired by Cortés's victory and yearned for his own glory. Commanding a force of about 600 men, he invited Atahualpa, the Incan ruler, to meet at the town of Cajamarca. There he laid a trap, intending to overpower the Incas and capture their ruler. As columns of Inca warriors and servants covered with colorful plumage and plates of silver and gold entered the main square, the Spanish soldiers were awed. One recalled, "many of us urinated without noticing it, out of sheer terror." But Pizarro's plan worked. His guns and horses shocked the Inca forces. Atahualpa himself fell into Spanish hands, later to be decapitated. Pizarro's conquistadors overran Cuzco in 1533 and then vanquished the rest of the Inca forces, a process that took decades in some areas.

The defeat of the New World's two great empires had enormous repercussions for world history. First, it set the Europeans on the road to controlling the human and material wealth of the Americas and opened a new frontier that the Europeans could colonize. Second, it gave Europeans a market for their own products—goods that found little favor in Afro-Eurasia. Now, following the Portuguese push into Africa and Asia (as well as a Russian push into northern Asia; see Chapter 13), the New World conquests introduced Europeans to a new scale of imperial expansion.

COMPARISON

ASSESS how European colonization of the Americas affected African and Amerindian peoples, and **DESCRIBE** their responses.

The Columbian Exchange The Spanish came to the Americas for gold and silver, but in the course of conquest and settlement they also learned about crops such as potatoes and corn. They brought with them horses, wheat, grapevines, and sugarcane, as well as devastating diseases. Historians call this transfer of previously unknown plants, animals, people, and products in the wake of Columbus's voyages the **Columbian exchange**. Over time, this exchange transformed environments, economies, and diets in both the new and the old worlds.

The first and most profound effect of the Columbian exchange was a destructive one: the decimation of the Amerindian population by European diseases. For millennia, the isolated populations of the Americas had been cut off from Afro-Eurasian microbe migrations. Africans, Europeans, and Asians had long interacted, sharing disease pools and gaining immunities; in this sense, in contrast, the Amerindians were indeed worlds apart. Sickness spread from almost the moment the Spaniards arrived. One Spanish soldier noted, upon entering the conquered Aztec capital, "the streets were so filled with dead and sick people that our men walked over nothing but bodies." As each wave of disease retreated, it left a population weaker than before, even less prepared for the next wave. The scale of death was unprecedented: imported pathogens wiped out up to 90 percent of the Indian population. A century after smallpox arrived

Analyzing Global Developments

The European Conquest of the Americas and Amerindian Mortality

If the fourteenth century was an age of dying across Afro-Eurasia, the sixteenth century saw even higher mortality rates in the Americas. As a result of European conquest, the exposure to virulent diseases, and the hyperexploitation of their labor under miserable conditions, the Native American populations saw their numbers reduced by 85 percent. The numbers themselves, however, are highly controversial and have sparked intense debates. Some scholars believe that no reliable numbers can be found for the population of the Americas when Europeans first arrived. Others have used a range of methods and data sources to establish population figures, including European firsthand accounts from that period, archaeological and anthropological evidence, estimates of the maximum number of people that the land could hold at that time (carrying capacity), and projections built backward from more recent censuses. These estimates vary widely from as little as 8 million to as high as more than 100 million.

AREA	POPULATION IN 1492	LATER POPULATIONS	MORTALITY RATES
The Americas	53.9 m	8 m in 1650	85%
The Caribbean			
Hispaniola	1.0 m	extinct by 1600	100%
The other islands	2.0 m	extinct by 1600	100%
Mexico	17.2 m	3.5 m in 1600	80%
The Andes	15.0 m	3.0 m in 1650	80%
Central America	5.63 m	1.12 m in 1700	80%
North America	3.79 m	1.5 m in 1700	60%
		250,000 in 1900	84%

QUESTIONS FOR ANALYSIS

- List the areas of the Americas that were most severely affected by population decline and explain why.
- Explain how the Portuguese and Spanish attempted to exploit the resources of the Americas and describe what effect this had on Amerindians and Africans.
- Explain why Native American population growth never recovered from the initial encounter with Europeans as Afro-Eurasian population growth eventually recovered from the Black Death.

Sources: Suzanne Austin Alchon, *A Pest in the Land: New World Epidemics in a Global Perspective* (2003); David Noble Cook, *Born to Die: Disease and New World Conquest, 1492 to 1650* (1998); William M. Denevan, *The Native Populations of the Americas in 1492* (1992); David Henige, *Numbers from Nowhere: The Amerindian Contact Population Debate* (1998);"La catastrophe demographique," *L'histoire*, July–August, 2007, no. 322, p. 17; Russell Thornton, *American Indian Holocaust: A Population History since 1492 (1987)*, p. xvii.

on Hispaniola in 1519, no more than 5 to 10 percent of the island's population was alive. (See **Analyzing Global Developments: The European Conquest of the Americas and Amerindian Mortality**.) Diminished and weakened by disease, Amerindians could not resist European settlement and colonization of the Americas. Thus were Europeans the unintended beneficiaries of a horrifying catastrophe.

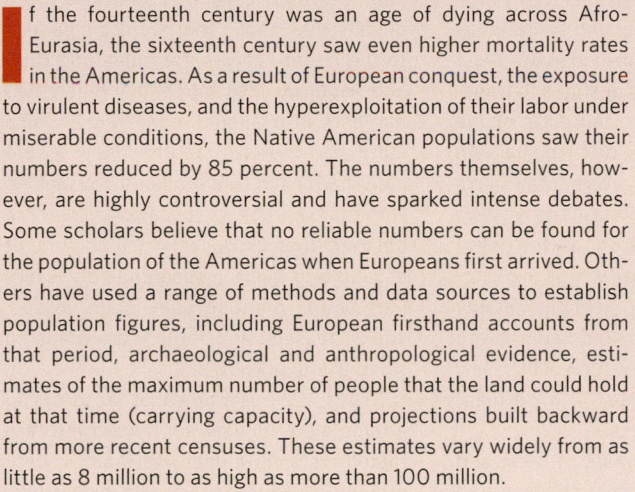

As time passed, all sides adopted new forms of agriculture from one another. After Amerindians taught Europeans how to grow potatoes and corn, the crops became staples all across Afro-Eurasia. The Chinese found that they could grow corn in areas too dry for rice and too wet for wheat, and in Africa, corn gradually replaced sorghum, millet, and rice to become the continent's principal food crop by the twentieth century. (See **Current Trends in World History: Corn and the Rise of Slave-Supplying Kingdoms in West Africa**.) Europeans also took away tomatoes, beans, cacao, peanuts, tobacco, and squash, while importing livestock such as cattle, swine, and horses to the New World. The environmental effects of the introduction of livestock to the Americas were significant. For example, in regions of central Mexico where Native Americans had once cultivated maize

Current Trends in World History

Corn and the Rise of Slave-Supplying Kingdoms in West Africa

New World varieties of corn spread rapidly throughout the Afro-Eurasian landmass soon after the arrival of Columbus in the Americas. Its hardiness and fast- ripening qualities made it more desirable than many of the Old World grain products. In communities that consumed large quantities of meat, it became the main product fed to livestock.

Corn's impact on Africa was as substantial as it was in the rest of Eurasia. Seeds made their way to western regions more quickly than to the south of the Sahara along two routes. One was via European merchants calling into ports along the coast; the second was West African Muslims returning across the Sahara after participating in the pilgrimage. The first evidence of corn cultivation in sub-Saharan Africa comes from a Portuguese navigator who identified the crop being grown on the island of Cape Verde in 1540. By the early seventeenth century, corn was replacing millet and sorghum as the main grain being grown in many West African regions and was destined to transform the work routines and diets of the peoples living in the region's tropical rain forests all the way from present-day Sierra Leone in the east to Nigeria in the west. In many ways this area, which saw the rise of a group of powerful slave-supplying kingdoms in the eighteenth century, notably Asante, Dahomey, Oyo, and Benin, owed its prosperity to the cultivation of this New World crop. (See Chapter 14 for a fuller discussion of these states.)

The tropical rain forests of West and central Africa were thick with trees and ground cover in 1500. Clearing them so that they could support intensive agriculture was exhausting work, requiring enormous outlays of human energy and man-hours. Corn, a crop first domesticated in central Mexico 7,000 years ago, made this task possible. It added much-needed carbohydrates to the carbon-deficient diets of rain-forest dwellers. In addition, as a crop that matured more quickly than those that were indigenous to the region (millet, sorghum, and rice) and required less labor, it yielded two harvests in a single year. Farmers also cultivated cassava, another New World native, which in turn provided households with more carbohydrate calories. Yet corn did more than produce more food per unit of land and labor. Households put every part of the plant to use—grain, leaves, stalks, tassels, and roots were made to serve useful purposes.

Thus, at the very time that West African groups were moving southward into the rain forests, European navigators were arriving along the coast with new crops. Corn gave communities of cultivators the caloric energy to change their forest landscapes, expanding the arable areas. In a select few of these regions, enterprising clans emerged to dominate the political scene, creating centralized kingdoms like Asante in present-day Ghana, Dahomey in present-day Benin, and Oyo and Benin in

and squash, Spanish settlers introduced large herds of sheep and cattle. Without natural predators, these animals reproduced with lightning speed, destroying entire landscapes with their hooves and their foraging.

As Europeans cleared trees and other vegetation for ranches, mines, or plantations, they undermined the habitats of many indigenous mammals and birds. On the islands of the West Indies, described by Columbus as "roses of the sea," the Spanish chopped down lush tropical and semitropical forests to make way for sugar plantations. Before long, nearly all of the islands' tall trees as well as many shrubs and ground plants were gone, and residents lamented the absence of birdsong. Over ensuing centuries, the plants and animals of the Americas took on an increasingly European appearance. At the same time, the interactions between Europeans and Native Americans would continue to shape societies on both sides of the Atlantic.

THE IBERIAN EMPIRES IN THE AMERICAS

The European presence in the New World went beyond the control of commercial outposts. Unlike their activities in the Indian Ocean—where they had to contend with stable, powerful states—European colonizers in the Americas controlled large amounts of territory, and ultimately the entire landmass (see Map 12.2). Those Native

Corn Plantation This nineteenth-century engraving by famed Italian explorer Savorgnan de Brazza shows women of the West African tribe Bateke working in corn plantations. Brazza would later serve as the governor general of the French colony in the Congo.

present-day Nigeria. These elites transformed what had once been thinly settled environments into densely populated states, with elaborate bureaucracies, big cities, and large and powerful standing armies.

There was much irony in the rise of these states, which owed so much of their strength to the linking of the Americas with Afro-Eurasia. The armies that they created and the increased populations that the new crops allowed were part and parcel of the Atlantic slave trade. That which the Americas gave with one hand (new crops), it took back with the other in warfare, captives, and New World slavery.

QUESTIONS FOR ANALYSIS

- What were the major effects of growing corn in West Africa?
- How did the growing of corn reshape the history of the Atlantic world during this period?

Explore Further

McCann, James, *Maize and Grace: Africa's Encounter with a New World Crop, 1500–2000* (2005).

Americans who survived the original encounters were harnessed as a means to siphon tribute payments to the new masters.

By fusing traditional tribute-taking with their own innovations, Spanish masters made villagers across their new American empire deliver goods and services. But because the Spanish authorities also bestowed *encomiendas*, those favored individuals could demand labor from their lands' Indian inhabitants—for mines, estates, and public works. Whereas Aztec and Inca rulers had used conscripted labor to build up their public wealth, the Spaniards did so for private gain.

Spanish migrants and their descendants preferred towns to the countryside. With the exception of ports, the major cities of Spanish America were the former centers of Indian empires. Mexico City took shape on the ruins of Tenochtitlán; Cuzco arose from the razed Inca capital. In their architecture, economy, and family life, the Spanish colonies adopted as much as they transformed the worlds they encountered.

Silver Silver was an important discovery for Spanish conquerors in Mesoamerica and the Andes. Conquerors expanded the customs of Inca and Aztec labor drafts to force the natives to work in mines, often in brutal conditions.

MAP 12.2 | The Spanish and Portuguese Empires in the Americas, 1492–1750

This map examines the growth of the Spanish and Portuguese empires in the Americas over two and a half centuries.

- Identify the natural resources that led the Spaniards and Portuguese to focus their empire building where they did. What were the major export commodities from these colonized areas?
- Looking back to Map 12.1, explain why Spanish settlement covered so much more area than Portuguese settlement.
- According to your reading, describe how the production and export of silver and sugar shaped the labor systems that evolved in both empires.

The next European power to seize land in the Americas, the Portuguese, were no less interested in immediate riches than the Spanish. Disappointed by the absence of tributary systems and precious metals in the area they controlled, Brazil, they found instead abundant, fertile land, which they doled out with massive royal grants. These estate owners governed their plantations like feudal lords (see Chapter 10). Failing to find established cities, the Portuguese created enclaves along the coast and lived in more dispersed settlements than the Spanish settlers.

The problem was where to find labor to work the rich lands of Brazil. Because there was no centralized government to deal with the labor shortage, Portuguese settlers initially tried to enlist the dispersed native population; but when recruitment became increasingly coercive, Indians turned on the settlers. Some Indians fought; others fled to the vast interior. Reluctant to pursue the Indians inland, the Portuguese hugged their beachheads, extracting brazilwood (the source of a beautiful red dye) and sugar from their coastal enclaves.

Silver, Sugar, and Slaves The Iberian empires in the Americas concentrated on three commodities that would transform Europe's relationship to the rest of the world: silver, sugar, and slaves. Silver enabled Spain and Portugal to enter established trade networks in Asia. The slave trade was a big business in itself: it subsidized shipbuilding and new insurance schemes. Above all, the use of slave labor made sugar cultivation fantastically profitable, fueling economic growth and political instability around the world.

The first Europeans in the Americas hoarded vast quantities of gold and silver for themselves and their monarchs. But they also introduced precious metals into the world's commercial systems, which electrified them. In the twenty years after the fall of Tenochtitlán, conquistadors took more gold and silver from Mexico and the Andes than all the gold accumulated by Europeans over the previous centuries.

Having looted Indian coffers, the Spanish entered the business of mining directly, opening the Andean Potosí mines in 1545. Between 1560 and 1685, Spanish America sent 25,000 to 35,000 tons of silver annually to Spain. From 1685 to 1810, this sum doubled. The two mother lodes were Potosí in present-day Bolivia and Zacatecas in northern Mexico. Silver brought bounty not only to the crown but also to a privileged group of families based in Spain's colonial capitals; thus private wealth funded the formation of local aristocracies.

Colonial mines epitomized the Atlantic world's new economy. They relied on an extensive network of Amerindian labor, at first enslaved, subsequently drafted. Here again, the Spanish adopted Inca and Aztec practices of requiring labor from subjugated villages. Each year, under the *mita*, the local system for recruiting labor, village elders selected a stipulated number of men to toil in the shafts, refineries, and smelters. Under the Spanish, the digging, hauling, and smelting taxed human limits to their capacity—and beyond. Mortality rates were appalling. The system pumped so much silver into European commercial networks that it transformed Europe's relationship to all its trading partners, especially those in China and India. It also shook up trade and politics within Europe itself.

Along with silver, sugar emerged as the most valuable export from the Americas. It also was decisive in rearranging relations between peoples around the Atlantic. Cultivation of sugarcane had originated in India, spread to the Mediterranean region, and then reached the coastal islands of West Africa. The Portuguese, the Spanish, and other European settlers transported the West African model to the Americas, first, in the sixteenth century in Brazil, and then in the Caribbean. By the early seventeenth century, sugar had become a major export from the New World. Because Amerindians resisted recruitment and their numbers were greatly reduced by disease, European plantation owners began importing African slaves. By the eighteenth century, sugar production required continuous and enormous transfers of labor from Africa, and its value surpassed that of silver as an export from the Americas to Europe.

At first most sugar plantations were fairly small, employing between 60 and 100 slaves. But they were efficient enough to create an alternative model of empire, one that resulted in more complete and dislocating control of the existing population. The slaves lived in wretched conditions: their barracks were miserable, and their diets were insufficient to keep them alive under backbreaking work routines. Moreover, these slaves were disproportionately men. As they rapidly died off, the only way to ensure replenishment was to import more Africans. This model of settlement relied on the transatlantic flow of slaves.

As European demand for sugar increased, the slave trade expanded. Although African slaves were imported into the Americas starting in the fifteenth century, the first direct voyage carrying them from Africa to the Americas occurred in 1525. From the time of Columbus until 1820, five times as many Africans as Europeans moved to the Americas: approximately 2 million Europeans (voluntarily) and 10 million Africans (involuntarily) crossed the Atlantic.

Well before European merchants arrived off its western coast, Africa had known long-distance slave trading. In fact, the overall number of Africans sold into captivity in the Muslim world exceeded that of the Atlantic slave trade. Moreover, Africans maintained slaves themselves. African slavery, like its American counterpart, was a response to labor scarcities. In many parts of Africa, however, slaves did not face permanent servitude. Instead, they were assimilated into families, gradually losing their servile status.

With the additional European demand for slaves to work New World plantations alongside the ongoing Muslim slave trade, pressure on the supply of African slaves intensified. Only a narrow band stretching down the spine of the African landmass, from present-day Uganda and the highlands of Kenya to Zambia and Zimbabwe, escaped the impact of African rulers engaged in the slave trade and Asian and European slave traders.

By the late sixteenth century, important pieces had fallen into place to create a new Atlantic world, one that could not have been imagined a century earlier. This was the three-cornered **Atlantic system**, with Africa supplying labor, the Americas land and minerals, and Europeans the technology and military power to hold the system together. In time, the wealth flows to Europe and the slave-based development of the Americas would alter the world balance of power.

The Transformation of Europe

COMPARISON

ANALYZE the social and political relationships and **EXPLAIN** the sources of conflict within the Afro-Eurasian polities.

Despite the flow of American silver into Spanish coffers, most European rulers and their subjects were focused on Europe, not the New World, in the sixteenth century. The period's frequent warfare centered on purely European concerns, above all on a religious split within the Roman Catholic Church, known as the Reformation. This conflict led to profound religious rifts among states and brought additional political rivalries to the continent.

THE REFORMATION

Like the Renaissance, the **Protestant Reformation** in Europe began as a movement devoted to returning to ancient sources—in this case, to biblical scriptures. Yet returning to the sources and interpreting Christian doctrine for oneself was dangerous in the fourteenth and fifteenth centuries, for the church feared that challenges to its authority would arise if laypersons were allowed to read the scriptures as they pleased. The church was right: when Luther and his followers seized the right to read and interpret the Bible in a new way, they paved the way for a "Protestant" Reformation that split Christendom for good.

The opening challenge to the authority of the Catholic Church originated in Germany. Here a monk and a professor of theology, **Martin Luther** (1483–1546), used his knowledge of the Bible to criticize the church's ideas and practices. For Luther, God's gift of forgiveness did not depend on taking sacraments or performing good deeds. This faith was something Christians could obtain from reading the Bible—rather than by having a priest tell them what to believe. Finally, Luther concluded that Christians did not need specially appointed mediators to speak to God for them; all believers were equally bound by God's laws and obliged to minister to one another's spiritual needs.

These became the three main principles that launched Luther's reforming efforts: (1) belief that faith alone saves, (2) belief that the scriptures alone hold the key to Christian truth, and (3) belief in the priesthood of all believers. Luther also reacted against corrupt practices in the church, such as the keeping of mistresses by monks, priests, and even popes; and the selling of indulgences, certificates that would supposedly shorten the buyer's time in Purgatory. In the 1510s, clerics were hawking indulgences across Europe in an effort to raise money for the sumptuous new Saint Peter's basilica in Rome. In 1517, Luther formulated ninety-five statements, or theses, and posted them on the doors to the Wittenberg cathedral, hoping to stir up his colleagues in debate.

In response, Pope Leo X and the Habsburg emperor, Charles V, demanded that Luther take back his criticisms and theological claims. When he refused, he was declared a heretic and narrowly avoided being burned at the stake. Luther wrote many more pamphlets attacking the church and the pope, whom he now described as the anti-Christ. Luther also translated the New Testament from Latin into German so that laypersons could have direct access, without the clergy, to the word of God. This act spurred many other reformers across Europe to undertake translations of their own, and it encouraged the Protestant clergy to teach children (and adults) to read their local languages.

Spread by printed books and ardent preachers in all the common languages of Europe, Luther's doctrines and those put forward by other reformers won widespread support in some regions, particularly among urban populations. In France and Switzerland, the reformer **Jean Calvin** (1509–1564) emphasized moral regeneration through church teachings and laid out a doctrine of predestination—the notion that each person is "predestined for damnation or salvation even before birth." Those who followed the new faith of Luther and Calvin identified themselves as "Protestants." They promised that their reformed version of Christianity provided both an answer to individual spiritual needs and a new moral foundation for community life. The renewed Christian creed appealed to commoners as well as elites, especially in communities that resented rule by Catholic "outsiders." For example, Protestantism was popular among the Dutch, who resented being ruled by Philip II, an Austrian Catholic who lived in Spain. The new ideas gained a wide following, although rarely a majority before the seventeenth century, in the German states, France, Switzerland, the Low Countries, England, and Scotland (see Map 12.3).

Counter-Reformation The Catholic Church responded to Luther and Calvin by embarking on its own renovation, which became known as the **Counter-Reformation**. At the Council of Trent, whose twenty-five sessions stretched from 1545 to 1563, Catholic leaders reaffirmed the church's doctrines. But the council also enacted reforms to answer the Protestants' assaults on clerical corruption. Like the Protestants, the reformed Catholics carried their message overseas—especially through an order established by the Spaniard, Ignatius Loyola (1491–1556). Loyola founded a brotherhood of priests, the Society of Jesus, or

MAP 12.3 | Religious Divisions in Europe after the Reformation, 1590

The Protestant Reformation divided Europe religiously and politically.

- Within the formerly all-Catholic Holy Roman Empire, list the Protestant groups that took hold.
- Looking at the map, can you identify any geographic patterns in the distribution of Protestant communities.
- List the regions in which you would expect Protestant-Catholic tensions to be the most intense, and explain why.

Jesuits, dedicated to the revival of the Catholic Church. From bases in Lisbon, Rome, Paris, and elsewhere in Europe, the Jesuits opened missions as far as South and North America, India, Japan, and China. The Reformation split European society deeply as both Catholics and Protestants vigorously promoted their faiths.

RELIGIOUS WARFARE IN EUROPE

The religious revival led Europe into another round of ferocious wars. Their ultimate effect was to weaken the **Holy Roman Empire**—a loose confederation of principalities that mainly clustered in central Europe, presided over in this period by the Habsburgs (see Chapter 11)—and strengthen the English, French, and Dutch. Already in the 1520s, the circulation of books presenting Luther's ideas sparked peasant revolts across central Europe. Some peasants, hoping that Luther's assault on the church's authority would help liberate them, rose up against repressive feudal landlords. In contrast to earlier wars in which one noble's retinue fought a rival's, the defense of the Catholic mass and the Protestant Bible brought crowds of simple folk to arms. Now wars between and within central European states raged for nearly forty years.

Religious conflicts weakened European dynasties. Spain, with its massive empire and its silver mines in the New World, spent much of its new fortune waging war in Europe. Most debilitating was its costly effort to subdue recently acquired Dutch territories. After a series of wars spanning nearly a hundred years, Catholic Spain finally conceded the Protestant Netherlands its independence. Wars took their toll on the Spanish Empire, which was soon wallowing in debts; not even the riches of its American silver mines could bail out the court. In the late 1550s, Philip II could not meet his obligations to creditors, and, within two decades, Spain was declared bankrupt three times. Its decline opened the way for the Dutch and the English to extend their trading networks into Asia and the New World, and the center of power within Europe shifted to the north.

Religious conflicts also sparked civil wars. In France, the divide between Catholics and Protestants exploded in the St. Bartholomew's Day Massacre of 1572. Catholic crowds rampaged through the streets of Paris murdering Huguenot (Protestant) men, women, and children and dumping their bodies into the Seine River. The number of dead reached 3,000 in Paris and 10,000 in provincial towns. Slaughter on this scale did not break the Huguenots' spirit, but it did bring more disrepute to the monarchy for failing to ensure peace. Another round of warfare exhausted the French and brought Henry of Navarre, a Protestant prince, to the throne. To become king, Henry IV converted to Catholicism. Shortly thereafter he issued the Edict of Nantes, a proclamation that declared France a Catholic country but also tolerated some Protestant worship.

St. Bartholomew's Day Massacre An important wedding between French Catholic and Huguenot families in Paris was scheduled for August 24, 1572, St. Bartholomew's Day; but instead of reconciliation, that day saw a massacre, as Catholics tried to stamp out Protestantism in France's capital city.

As princes sought to resolve religious questions within their domains, states increasingly became identified with one or another form of Christian faith—and, for Protestants, with a local language. (Protestants translated the Bible from Latin so that more people could read it.) In this way, religious strife propelled forward the process of state building and the forming of national identities. At the same time, religious conflict fueled rivalries for wealth and territory overseas. Thus, Europe entered its age of overseas exploration as a collection of increasingly powerful yet irreconcilably competitive rival states, whose differences stemmed not just from language but from the ways they worshipped the Christian God.

Prosperity in Asia

COMPARISON

COMPARE the major features of world trade in Asia, the Americas, Africa, and Europe.

While Europe was experiencing religious warfare, Asian empires were expanding and consolidating their power, and trade was flourishing. If anything, the arrival of European sailors and traders in the Indian Ocean strengthened trading ties across the region and enhanced the political power and expansionist interests of Asia's imperial regimes. The Mughal ruler of India, Akbar, and the Ottoman sultan, Suleiman the Magnificent (see Chapter 11), were effective and esteemed rulers. The Ming dynasty's elegant manufactures enjoyed worldwide renown, and its ability to govern vast numbers of highly diverse peoples led outsiders to consider China the model imperial state.

MUGHAL INDIA AND COMMERCE

The **Mughal Empire** became one of the world's wealthiest just when Europeans were establishing sustained connections with India. These connections, however, only touched the outer layer of Mughal India, one of Islam's greatest regimes. Established in 1526, it was a vigorous, centralized state whose political authority encompassed most of modern-day India. During the sixteenth century, it had a population of between 100 and 150 million.

The Mughals' strength rested on their military power. The dynasty's founder, Babur, had introduced horsemanship, artillery, and field cannons from central Asia, and gunpowder had secured his swift military victories over northern India. Under his grandson, Akbar (r. 1556–1605), the empire enjoyed expansion and consolidation that continued (under his own grandson, Aurangzeb) until it covered almost all of India (see Map 12.4). Known as the "Great Mughal," Akbar was skilled not only in military tactics but also in the art of alliance making. Deals with Hindu chieftains through favors and intermarriage also undergirded his empire.

Mughal rulers were flexible toward their realm's diverse peoples, especially in spiritual affairs. Though its primary commitment to Islam stood firm, the imperial court also patronized other beliefs, displaying a tolerance that earned it widespread legitimacy. The contrast with Europe, where religious differences drove deep fractures within and between states, was stark. Unlike European monarchs, who tried to enforce religious uniformity, Akbar studied comparative religion and hosted regular debates among Hindu, Muslim, Jain, Parsi, and Christian theologians. His tolerance kept a multifaceted spiritual kingdom under one political roof.

During the sixteenth century, expanded trade with Europe brought more wealth to the Mughal polity, while the empire's strength limited European incursions. Although the Portuguese occupied Goa and Bombay on the Indian coast, they had little presence elsewhere and dared not antagonize the Mughal emperor. In 1578, Akbar recognized

MAP 12.4 | Expansion of the Mughal Empire, 1556–1707

Under Akbar and Aurangzeb, the Mughal Empire expanded and dominated much of South Asia. Yet, by looking at the trading ports along the Indian coast, one can see the growing influence of Portuguese, Dutch, French, and English interests.

- Look at the dates for each port, and identify which traders came first and which came last.
- Compare this map with Map 12.2 (showing the earlier period 1492–1750). To what extent do the trading posts shown here reflect increased European influence in the region?
- According to your reading, explain how these European outposts affected Mughal policies.

the credentials of a Portuguese ambassador and allowed a Jesuit missionary to enter his court. Thereafter, commercial ties between Mughals and Portuguese intensified, but the merchants were still restricted to a handful of ports. In the 1580s and 1590s, the Mughals ended the Portuguese monopoly on trade with Europe by allowing Dutch and English merchantmen to dock in Indian ports.

Centered in northern India, the Mughal Empire used surrounding regions' wealth and resources—military, architectural, and artistic—to glorify the court. Over time, the enhanced wealth caused friction between wealthy and poorer Indian regions, and even between merchants and rulers. Yet as long as merchants relied on rulers for their commercial gains, and as long as rulers balanced local and imperial interests, the realm maintained a formal unity and kept Europeans on its margins.

PROSPERITY IN MING CHINA

China also prospered from increased commerce in the late sixteenth century. Like the Mughals, the Ming seemed unconcerned with the increasing appearance of foreigners, including Europeans bearing silver. As in India, the Ming confined European traders to port cities. Silver from the Americas did, however, circulate widely in China. It allowed employers to pay their workers with money rather than with produce or goods, which in turn motivated those workers to produce more. China also experienced soaring production in agriculture and handicrafts. A cotton boom, for example, made spinning and weaving China's largest industry.

One measure of greater prosperity under the Ming was its population surge. By the mid-seventeenth century, China's population probably accounted for more than one-third of the total world population. Although 90 percent of Chinese people lived in the countryside, large numbers filled the cities. Beijing, the Ming capital, grew to over 1 million; Nanjing, the secondary capital, nearly matched that number. Cities offered diversions ranging from literary and theatrical societies to schools of learning, religious societies, urban associations, and manufactures from all over the empire. The elegance and material prosperity of Chinese cities dazzled European visitors. One Jesuit missionary described Nanjing as surpassing all other cities "in beauty and grandeur. . . . It is literally filled with palaces and temples and towers and bridges. . . . There is a gaiety of spirit among the people who are well mannered and nicely spoken."

Urban prosperity fostered entertainment districts where people could indulge themselves anonymously and in relative freedom. Some Ming women found a place here as refined entertainers and courtesans, others as midwives, poets, sorcerers, and matchmakers. Female painters, mostly from scholar-official families, emulated males who used the home and garden for creative pursuits. The expanding book trade also accommodated women, who were writers as well as readers, not to mention literary characters and archetypes (especially of Confucian virtues). But Chinese women made their greatest fortunes inside the emperor's Forbidden City as healers, consorts, and power brokers. The vitality that commerce brought to Ming society continued even after the dynasty's fall in 1644, laying the foundation for further population growth and territorial expansion.

ASIAN RELATIONS WITH EUROPE

Europeans' overseas expansion had originally looked toward Asia, and now the products from their New World colonies enabled them to realize some of those dreams. The Portuguese led the way. In 1557, their arrival at Macao, a port along the southern coast of

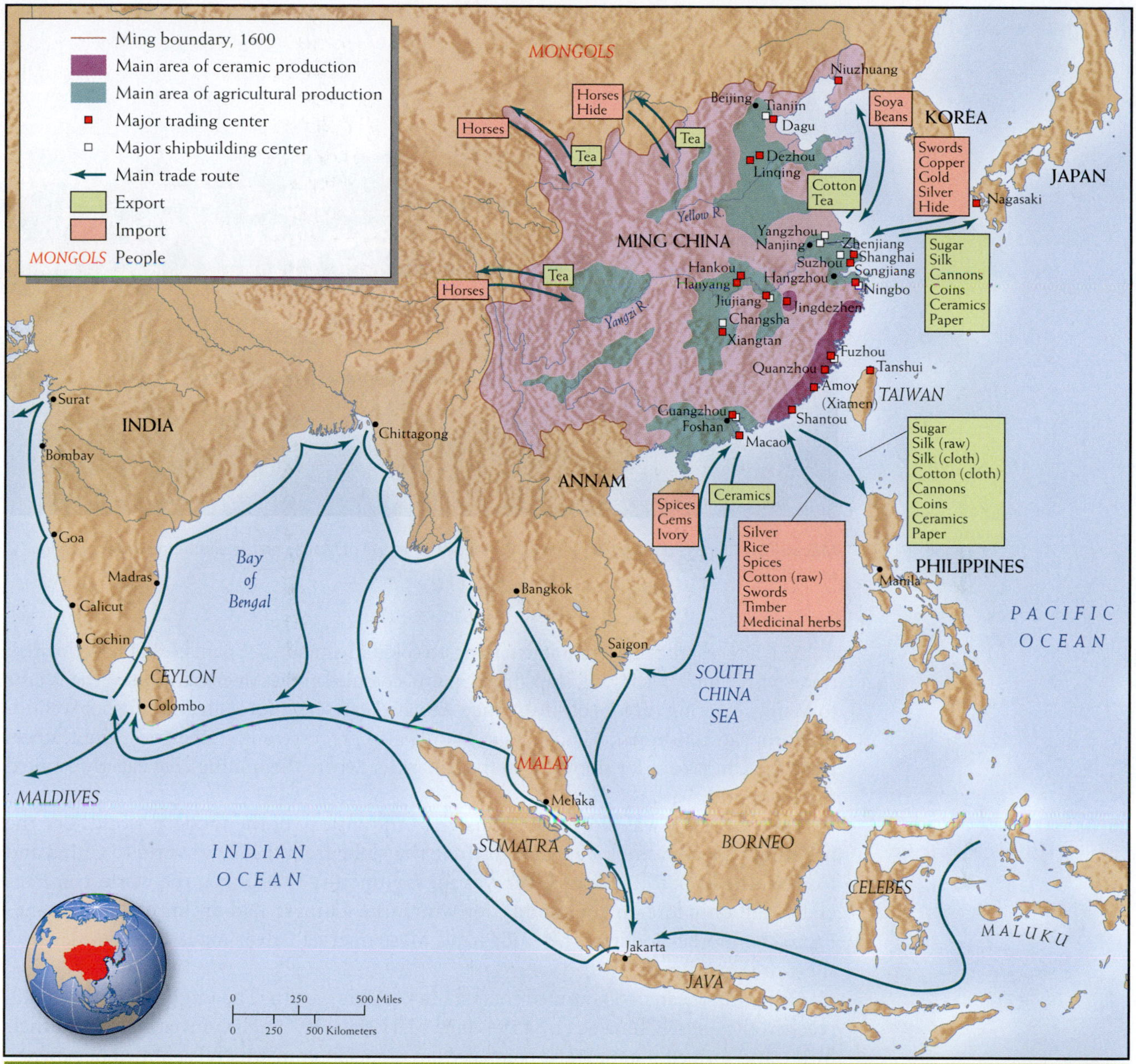

MAP 12.5 | Trade and Production in Ming China

The Ming Empire in the early seventeenth century was the world's most populous state and arguably its wealthiest.

- According to this map, list the main items involved in China's export-import trade, and identify some of the regions that purchased its exports.
- Evaluate the relative importance of China's internal and overland trade, and contrast it with overseas commerce.
- Locate the major trading and shipbuilding centers, and then explain how important the export trade was to the Ming Empire's prosperity.

China, enabled them to participate in China's expanding import-export trade. Within five years the number of Portuguese in Macao neared 1,000 (see Map 12.5).

Seeing how much the Portuguese were earning on Asian trade, the Spanish, English, and Dutch also ventured into Asian waters. With its monopoly on American silver, Spain enjoyed a competitive advantage. In 1565, the first Spanish trading galleon reached the Philippines;

Macao This Chinese painting depicts the Portuguese enclave of Macao on the southern border of China around 1800.

in 1571, after capturing Manila and making it a colonial capital, the Spanish established a brisk trade with China. Each year, ships from Spain's colonies in the Americas crossed the Pacific to Manila, bearing cargoes of silver. They returned carrying porcelain and silks for well-to-do European consumers. Merchants in Manila also procured silks, tapestries, and feathers from the China seas for shipment to the Americas, where the mining elite eagerly awaited these imports.

The year 1571 was altogether decisive in the history of the modern world. For the first time, Spanish ships were able to circle the globe from the New World to China and from China back to Europe. Silver was the commodity that linked the world commercially, the only foreign commodity for which the Chinese had an insatiable demand. From the mother lodes of the Andes and Mesoamerica, silver made the commerce of the world go round.

Other Europeans, too, wanted their share of Asia's wealth. The English and the Dutch reached the South China Sea by 1594. Five years later, 101 English investors pooled their funds and formed a joint-stock company (an association in which each member owned shares of capital). This English East India Company soon won a royal charter granting it exclusive rights to import East Indian goods. The company displaced the Portuguese in the Arabian Sea and the Persian Gulf. Doing a brisk trade in indigo, saltpeter, pepper, and cotton textiles, the English East India Company eventually acquired control of ports on both coasts of India—Fort St. George at the coastal city of Madras (1639), Bombay (1661), and Calcutta (1690).

The Europeans' arrival in the South China Sea and the Indian Ocean hardly spelled the beginning of the end of Asian autonomy. Confined to the coasts and a limited number of trading posts, the Europeans forged very weak connections to the ruling elites of Asian societies. For the moment, the Europeans' increased presence enhanced the wealth and might of Asian dynasties.

Conclusion

In the multicentered world of the fifteenth century, Europe was a poor cousin. However, a new spirit of adventure and achievement animated its peoples, stirred up by the rediscovery of antiquity (the Renaissance), the ambitions of merchants and other elites, and the spiritual fervor of the Reformation and Counter-Reformation. Desiring Asian luxury goods, European merchants and mariners were eager to exploit trade routes leading eastward, and new navigational techniques enabled them to sail into dangerous waters. More important, Europe's location promoted expansion across the largely unknown Atlantic Ocean. With the Ottomans controlling Constantinople and the eastern Mediterranean, Atlantic sea-lanes offered an alternative route to Asia. As Europeans searched for routes around Islamic territory, they first sailed down the coast of Africa and then across the Atlantic.

Encountering the "New World" was an accident of monumental significance. In the Americas, Europeans found riches. Mountains of silver and rivers of gold gave them the currency they needed for dealing with Asian traders. Europeans also found opportunities for exchange, conquest, and colonization. Yet, establishing these transatlantic empires heightened tensions within Europe, as rivals fought over the spoils and a religious schism turned into a divisive political and spiritual struggle.

Thus two conquests characterize this age of increasing world interconnections. The Islamic conquest of Constantinople drove Europeans to find new links to Asia. In turn, the Spanish conquest of the Aztecs and the Incas gave Europeans access to silver, which bought them an increased presence in Asian trading networks.

Amerindians also played an important role, as Europeans sought to conquer their lands, exploit their labor, and confiscate their gold and silver. Sometimes Amerindians worked with Europeans, sometimes under Europeans, sometimes against Europeans—and sometimes none were left to work at all. Then Europeans brought in African laborers, compounding the calamity of the encounter with the tragedy of slavery. Out of the catastrophe of contact, a new oceanic system arose to link Africa, America, and Europe. This was the Atlantic system. Unlike the tributary and trading orders of the Indian Ocean and China seas, the Atlantic Ocean supported a system of formal imperial control and settlement of distant colonies. These would become more important to how worlds connected and collided in the following centuries.

After You Read This Chapter

Go to INQUIZITIVE to see what you've learned—and learn what you've missed—with personalized feedback along the way.

TRACING GLOBAL STORYLINES

FOCUS ON: *Regional Developments in the Age of Exploration*

EUROPE

- Portugal creates a trading empire in the Indian Ocean and the South China Sea.
- Spain and Portugal establish colonies in the Americas, discover silver, and establish export-oriented plantation economies.
- The Protestant Reformation breaks out in northern and western Europe, splitting the Catholic Church.

THE AMERICAS

- Millions of Amerindians, lacking immunity to European diseases, perish in every region of the New World.
- Spanish conquest and disease destroy the two great Native American empires in Mexico (the Aztecs) and Peru (the Incas).

AFRICA

- Trade in African captives fuels the Atlantic slave trade, which furnishes labor for European plantations in the Americas.

ASIA

- Asian empires—the Mughals in India, the Ming in China, and the Ottomans in western Asia and the eastern Mediterranean—barely notice the Americas but profit economically from enhanced global trade.

CHRONOLOGY

EUROPE

Luther begins Protestant Reformation 1517

THE AMERICAS

Columbus discovers the New World 1492

Cortés conquers Aztec Empire 1522

Pizarro conquers Inca Empire 1533

SOUTH ASIA

Da Gama sails to India 1498

Portuguese establish bases around Indian Ocean 1508–1511

EAST ASIA

1500

THINKING ABOUT GLOBAL CONNECTIONS

- ***Thinking about Exchange Networks and the Age of Exploration*** In the fifteenth and sixteenth centuries, the densest trade networks and most powerful states remained centered in Asia. How did Columbus's "discovery" of the New World alter the terms on which peoples across Afro-Eurasia interacted with one another? What commodities and trade networks brought peoples together, on what terms, and what new inequalities did those contacts create around the world?
- ***Thinking about Changing Power Relationships and the Age of Exploration*** The effort to expand empires and trading networks differed substantially across Afro-Eurasia and the Americas in the fifteenth and sixteenth centuries. How did men and women at all levels of society contribute to this expansion? How did that participation shape or reshape their societies? Pay particular attention to the relationship between lower classes and elites.
- ***Thinking about Environmental Impacts and the Age of Exploration*** The Columbian exchange led to demographic catastrophe and environmental transformation in the New World. Why did the indigenous populations of the Americas get sick so much more often than Europeans? Why did the plants and animals of the New World increasingly come to resemble those of Afro-Eurasia?

STUDY QUESTIONS

1. Describe the obstacles to consolidating power in the **Aztec** and **Inca** empires before the arrival of European **conquistadors**.
2. Describe the **Columbian exchange** and explain how it influenced the different regions of the world.
3. Compare the **Atlantic system** with European trading in Asia.
4. Analyze the influence of religion on politics in **Mughal India** and Europe, including the **Holy Roman Empire**.
5. Explain how the **Jesuits** of the **Counter-Reformation** responded to the challenge posed by **Martin Luther** and **Jean Calvin** in the **Protestant Reformation**, both in Europe and around the world.

Religious and dynastic wars 1520s–1570s

Expansion and consolidation of Mughal empire 1556–1605

◆ **Portuguese establish trading port in Macao** 1557

◆ **Spanish make Manila their major port in the Pacific Ocean** 1571

1600

Going to the Source

Global Interactions and Cultural Contact

Overseas exploration and commerce brought new contacts between Europeans, Amerindians, Africans, and Asians during the fifteenth and sixteenth centuries. These primary sources document important examples of cultural interactions in this era and allow us to see how people from radically different cultures perceived one another and responded to people whose appearance and behaviors were unfamiliar to them.

As people from different cultures began to interact with each other, a variety of approaches and responses became evident. Some interactions led to new and constructive engagement, even consent, while others led to death and devastation. Thinking about these experiences in this time frame also allows us to contemplate the range of behaviors in both earlier and later periods.

PRIMARY SOURCE 12.1

Commentary on Foreigners *(c. 1420), Ming Official He Ao*

He Ao (Ho Ao) was a Ming official in the mid-fifteenth century. In this commentary he writes about his views of European traders. In much of Asia, the word "Feringi" is used to refer to Europeans. It comes from the Arabic word for Frank, and emerged during earlier European crusades. Of course, the Franks, or the French, are not the Europeans that He Ao would have encountered in fifteenth-century China.

The Feringis are most cruel and crafty. Their arms are superior to those of other foreigners. Some years ago they came suddenly to the city of Canton, and the noise of their cannon shook the earth [these were cannon-shots fired as a salute by the fleet of Fernão Peres]. Those who remained at the post-station [places where foreigners were lodged] disobeyed the law and had intercourse [dealings] with others. Those who came to the Capital were proud and struggled [among themselves?] to become head. Now if we allow them to come and go and to carry on their trade, it will inevitably lead to fighting and bloodshed, and the misfortune of our South may be boundless.

In the time of our ancestors, foreigners came to bring tribute only at fixed periods, and the law provided for precautionary measures, therefore the foreigners who could come were not many. But some time ago the Provincial Treasurer, Wu T'ing-chü, saying that he needed spice to be sent to the Court, took some of their goods no matter when they came. It was due to what he did that foreigner ships have never ceased visiting our shores and that barbarians have lived scattered in our departmental cities. Prohibition and precaution having been neglected, the Feringis became more and more familiar with our fair ways. And thus availing themselves of the situation the Feringis came into our port. I pray that all the foreign junks in our bay and the foreigners who secretly live (in our territory) be driven away, that private intercourse be prohibited and that our strategical defence be close, so that that part of our country will have peace.

1. **How does He Ao describe the European traders?**
2. **Why might this Ming official have been upset with the continued presence of foreign traders in Chinese ports?**

PRIMARY SOURCE 12.2

Approaching Tenochtitlán (1521), Hernán Cortés

As Hernán Cortés and a small band of Europeans made their way across Mexico in 1521, they encountered many different Amerindian groups. Most of them lived in states that paid tribute to the Aztec empire, with its capital in Tenochtitlán, in what is now Mexico City. Sometimes the tribute was in the form of humans, often captured in war and sacrificed to the Aztec's gods. Some Aztec warriors also believed they would gain strength and courage by eating those they had killed in battle. After Cortés reached Tenochtitlán, he recorded his observations in a letter to the Spanish monarch.

*

This great city of Tenochtitlán is built on the salt lake. . . . It has four approaches by means of artificial causeways. . . . The city is as large as Seville or Cordoba. Its streets . . . are very broad and straight, some of these, and all the others, are one half land, and the other half water on which they go about in canoes. . . . There are bridges, very large, strong, and well constructed, so that, over many, ten horsemen can ride abreast. . . . The city has many squares where markets are held. . . . There is one square, twice as large as that of Salamanca, all surrounded by arcades, where there are daily more than sixty thousand souls, buying and selling. . . . [I]n the service and manners of its people, their fashion of living was almost the same as in Spain, with just as much harmony and order; and considering that these people were barbarous, so cut off from the knowledge of God and other civilized peoples, it is admirable to see to what they attained in every respect. . . .

It happened . . . that a Spaniard saw an Indian . . . eating a piece of flesh taken from the body of an Indian who had been killed. . . . I had the culprit burned, explaining that the cause was his having killed that Indian and eaten him, which was prohibited by Your Majesty, and by me in Your Royal name. I further made the chief understand that all the people . . . must abstain from this custom. . . . I came . . . to protect their lives as well as their property, and to teach them that they were to adore but one God . . . that they must turn from their idols, and the rites they had practised until then, for these were lies and deceptions which the devil . . . had invented. . . . I, likewise, had come to teach them that Your Majesty, by the will of Divine Providence, rules the universe, and that they also must submit themselves to the imperial yoke, and do all that we who are Your Majesty's ministers here might order them. . . .

1. **How does Cortés indicate that he is impressed by the city of Tenochtitlán?**
2. **Why do you think Cortés chose to report on the actions of this individual? What do you think he was trying to accomplish?**

PRIMARY SOURCE 12.3

Letter to the Royal Audience of Santo Domingo (1533), Hernando Pizarro

This letter, written by the brother of Francisco Pizarro, the conqueror of the Inca Empire, describes the first meeting of the Spanish with the relatively newly installed Inca ruler Atahualpa. Like Mexico, this large empire was conquered by just a few Spaniards and their superior technology. Atahualpa had much of his gold brought to the Spanish, at their request. After he had done so, the Spanish killed him, offering him a chance to die as a Christian or remain unconverted.

[Atahualpa] came in a litter, and before him went three or four hundred Indians in liveries, cleaning the straws from the road and singing. Then came Atahualpa in the midst of his chiefs and principal men, the greatest among them being also borne on men's shoulders. When they entered the open space, twelve or fifteen Indians went up to the little fortress that was there and occupied it, taking possession with a banner fixed on a lance. When Atahualpa had advanced to the centre of an open space, he stopped, and a Dominican friar, who was with the [Spanish] Governor [Francisco Pizarro], came forward to tell him . . . that [Pizarro] waited for him in his lodging. . . . The friar then told Atahualpa that he was a priest, and that he was sent there to teach the things of the faith if they should desire to be Christians. He showed Atahualpa a book which he carried in his hands, and told him that that book contained the things of God. Atahualpa asked for the book, and threw it on the ground, saying: "I will not leave this place until you have restored all that you have taken in my land. I know well who you are and what you have come for." Then he rose up in his litter and addressed his men, and there were murmurs among them and calls to those who were armed. The friar went to the Governor and reported what was being done and that no time was to be lost. The Governor sent to me; and I had arranged with the captain of the artillery that, when a sign was given, he should discharge his pieces, and that, on hearing the reports, all the troops should come forth at once. This was done, and as the Indians were unarmed they were defeated without danger to any Christian. Those who carried the litter and the chiefs who surrounded Atahualpa were all killed, falling round him. The Governor came out and seized Atahualpa, and in protecting him he received a knife-cut from a Christian in the hand. . . . All were [then] brought into the town where the Governor was quartered.

1. **How does Pizarro describe Atahualpa's arrival and reception by the Spanish?**
2. **Explain whether religious belief or technology played the more important role in the Spanish conquest of the Inca Empire.**

PRIMARY SOURCE 12.4

Letter to the King of France (1535–1536), Jacques Cartier

French explorer Jacques Cartier and his men traveled into the interior of North America, in what is now Canada. His second voyage reached as far inland as present-day Montreal. This letter, which he sent to the King of France, describes his encounter with an Amerindian community who were probably Iroquois.

As we drew near to their village, great numbers of the inhabitants came out to meet us and gave us a hearty welcome, according to the custom of the country. And we were led by our guides and those who were conducting us into the middle of the village, where there was an open square between the houses. . . . They signaled to us that we should come to a halt here, which we did. And at once all the girls and women of the village, some of whom had children in their arms, crowded about us, rubbing our faces, arms, and other parts of the upper portions of our bodies which they could touch, weeping for joy at the sight of us and giving us the best welcome they could. They made signs to us also to be good enough to put our hands upon their babies. After this the men made the women retire, and themselves sat down upon the ground round about us, as if we had been going to perform a miracle play. And at once several of the women came back, each with a four-cornered mat, woven like tapestry, and these they spread upon the ground in the middle of the square, and made us place ourselves upon them. When this had been done, the ruler and chief of this country, whom in their language they call Agouhanna, was carried in, seated on a large deer-skin, by nine or ten men, who came and set him down upon the mats near the Captain, making signs to us that this was their ruler and leader. This Agouhanna, who was some fifty years of age, was in no way better dressed than the other Indians except that he wore about his head for a crown a sort of red band made of hedgehog's skin. This chief was completely paralyzed and deprived of the use of his limbs. When he had saluted the Captain and all his men, by making signs which clearly meant that they were very welcome, he showed his arms and his legs to the Captain motioning to him to be good enough to touch them, as if he thereby expected to be cured and healed. On this the Captain set about rubbing his arms and legs with his hands. Thereupon this Agouhanna took the band of cloth he was wearing as a crown and presented it to the Captain. And at once many sick persons, some blind, others with but one eye, others lame or impotent [of their legs] and others again so extremely old that their eyelids hung down to their cheeks, were brought in and set down or laid out near the Captain, in order that he might lay his hands upon them, so that one would have thought Christ had come down to earth to heal them. Seeing the suffering of these people and their faith, the Captain read aloud the Gospel of St. John, namely, "In the beginning," etc., making the sign of the cross over the poor sick people, praying God to give them knowledge of our holy faith and of our Savior's passion, and grace to obtain baptism and redemption. Then the Captain took a prayer-book and read out, word for word, the Passion of our Lord, that all who were present could hear it, during which all these poor people maintained great silence and were wonderfully attentive, looking up to heaven and going through the same ceremonies they saw us do. After this the Captain had all the men range themselves on one side, the women on another, and the children on another, and to the headmen he gave hatchets, to the others, knives, and to the women, beads and other small trinkets. . . . The Captain next ordered the trumpets and other musical instruments to be sounded, whereat the people were much delighted. We then took leave of them and proceeded to set out upon our return."

1. **How did the Amerindian community receive Cartier and his men?**
2. **Compare this exchange between Europeans and Amerindians with the interactions between Pizarro's men and the Inca leader in Primary Source 12.4.**

PRIMARY SOURCE 12.5

The Conquest of the Aztecs (late sixteenth century)

This drawing, made several years after the conquest of the Aztecs by an Amerindian who had converted to Christianity, shows the Spanish and their Amerindian allies fighting against the Aztecs. The Aztecs, themselves a conquering people, were not beloved by those whom they had conquered, especially as they exacted tribute and ruled through force.

1. **Describe the different types of military technology used in this image.**
2. **Based on this image, why do you think the Spanish were able to conquer the Aztec Empire?**

PRIMARY SOURCE 12.6

Letter to Ignatius Loyola (1549), Francis Xavier

Ignatius Loyola and Francis Xavier are generally regarded as the founders of the Society of Jesus, or Jesuit order. Focusing on education and evangelization, both men, of Spanish Basque origin, were made saints in the seventeenth century. Loyola became the first Father General of the order, while Xavier spent much of his time traveling in Asia.

The experience which I have of these countries makes me think that . . . there is no prospect of perpetuating our Society [Jesuits] out here by means of the natives themselves, and that the Christian religion will hardly survive us who are now in the country; so that it is quite necessary that continual supplies of ours should be sent out from Europe. We have now some of the Society in all parts of India where there are Christians. Four are in the Moluccas, two at Malacca, six in the Comorin Promontory, two at Coulan, as many at Bazain, four at Socotra. The distances between these places are immense. . . . The Portuguese in these countries are masters only of the sea and of the coast. On the mainland they have only the towns in which they live. The natives themselves are so enormously addicted to vice as to be little adapted to receive the Christian religion. They so dislike it that it is most difficult to get them to hear us if we begin to preach about it, and they think it like death to be asked to become Christians. So for the present we devote ourselves to keeping the Christians whom we have. Certainly, if the Portuguese were more remarkable for their kindness to the new converts, a great number would become Christians; as it is, the heathen see that the converts are despised and looked down upon by the Portuguese, and so, as is natural, they are unwilling to become converts themselves. For all these reasons there is no need for me to labour in these countries, and as I have learnt from good authorities that there is a country near China called Japan, the inhabitants of which are all heathen, quite untouched by Mussulmans or Jews, and very eager to learn what they do not know both in things divine and things natural. I have determined to go . . . as soon as I can.

1. **Why did Francis Xavier believe that Christianity could not take hold in India?**
2. **Why did Francis Xavier think Japan might be a better prospect for conversions?**

PRIMARY SOURCE 12.7

Akbar Hears a Petition (late sixteenth century)

In this image the individuals gathered before Akbar represent the diversity of people who sought help from the Mughal emperor. This miniature could thus reflect the multiethnic and multireligious character of the Mughal Empire, which was generally considered to be an example of a large territory in which rulers maintained some measure of social cohesion.

1. **Describe the audience in the painting. What can you determine about the different groups in attendance?**
2. **What types of items do the petitioners seem to be offering to Akbar, and why might they be doing so?**

Questions for Analysis

Analyzing Evidence

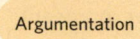

1. Explain the ways in which different American and Asian societies understood and reacted to the European presence in their territories.

Argumentation

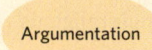

2. How did Christianity inform Europeans' interactions with the peoples they encountered around the globe?

Argumentation

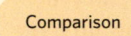

3. Why did Europeans expand beyond their boundaries beginning in the fifteenth century, and how would you evaluate their success or failure in the years before 1600?

Long Essay Question

Comparison

Based on what you have read in the chapter and the documents above, do you think that trade or religion was more important as a motivating force for people to behave the way that they did towards those who were unfamiliar to them? Explain why.

Before You Read This Chapter

GLOBAL STORYLINES

- Transoceanic trade networks (on an unprecedented scale) created vast wealth and new kinds of inequality.
- Silver gave Europeans a commodity to exchange with Asians and began to tilt the balance of wealth and power from Asia toward Europe.
- New World sugar also accelerated the shift of power in the Atlantic world from the Spanish and Portuguese to the British and French.
- European merchants and African leaders radically increased the volume and violence of the slave trade, destabilizing African societies.
- Asian rulers in India, China, and Japan, and Russian tsars enlarged their empires.
- The Ottoman, Safavid, and Mughal dynasties all struggled to resist European assaults.

CORE OBJECTIVES

- **IDENTIFY** and **EXPLAIN** the major steps in the integration of global trade networks in the seventeenth and eighteenth centuries, and **ANALYZE** examples of resistance to this integration.
- **ANALYZE** the consequences of the Atlantic slave trade for African societies.
- **EXPLAIN** the effects of New World silver and increased trade on the Asian empires and their response to it.
- **COMPARE** the impact of trade and religion on state power in various regions.
- **EXPLAIN** the significance of European consumption of goods (like tobacco, textiles, and sugar) for the global economy.

CHAPTER

13

Worlds Entangled

1600–1750

KEY TERMS

absolute monarchy p. 510
Canton system p. 502
chartered companies p. 484
enclosure p. 509
Mamluks p. 497
Manchus p. 500
mercantilism p. 484
Muscovy p. 506
Qing dynasty p. 502
Seven Years' War p. 512
Thirty Years' War p. 508
Tokugawa shogunate p. 503

In 1720, a financial panic engulfed Europe, making rich men into paupers and ruining many political careers. The panic arose from dashed hopes for huge profits from trade with the Americas. A group of British merchants established the South Sea Trading Company to compete with French firms and obtained privileged trading rights with all of Spanish America. Most coveted was the exclusive right to sell African slaves to Spanish colonies. As enthusiasm for such companies soared, eager investors sent share prices skyrocketing. But rumors of fantastic gains gave way to word that the original investors were dumping their shares and that the companies were worthless. Then the bubble burst. Share prices plummeted, nearly all the new companies went bankrupt, and many older firms collapsed. The so-called South Sea Bubble reflected the excitement—and the risks—of global trade and investment.

From 1600 to 1750, global trading networks propelled commerce across the world's oceans. New World silver was crucial to these networks in the early stages: it gave Europeans a commodity to exchange with Asians. From about 1600, however, other goods became as important as silver, as tobacco and then sugar flowed from Brazil and the Caribbean, spices from Southeast Asia, cotton textiles from India, and silks from China. The cumulative result was to tilt the balance of wealth and power towards Europe.

Current Trends in World History

Stimulants, Sociability, and Coffeehouses

While armies, travelers, missionaries, and diseases have breached the world's main political and cultural barriers, commodities have been the least respectful of the lines that separate communities. It has been difficult for ruling elites to curtail the desire of their populations to dress themselves in fine garments, to possess jewelry, and to consume satisfying food and drink no matter where these products may originate. The history of commodities, thus, is a core area for world historical research, for products span cultural barriers and connects peoples over long distances. As the world's trading networks expanded in the seventeenth and eighteenth centuries, merchants in Europe, Asia, Africa, and the Americas distributed many new commodities. By far the most popular were a group of stimulants—coffee, cocoa, sugar, tobacco, and tea—all of which (except for sugar) were addictive and also produced a sense of well-being. Previously, many of these products had been grown in isolated parts of the world: the coffee bean in Yemen, tobacco and cocoa in the New World, and sugar in Bengal. Yet, by the seventeenth century, in nearly every corner of the world, the well-to-do began to congregate in coffeehouses, consuming these new products and engaging in sociable activities.

Coffeehouses everywhere served as locations for social exchange, political discussions, and business activities. Yet they also varied from cultural area to cultural area, reflecting the values of the societies in which they arose.

The coffeehouse first appeared in Islamic lands late in the fifteenth century. As coffee consumption caught on among the wealthy and leisured classes in the Arabian Peninsula and the Ottoman Empire, local growers protected their advantage by monopolizing its cultivation and sale and refusing to allow any seeds or cuttings from the coffee tree to be taken abroad.

Despite some religious opposition, coffee spread into Egypt and throughout the Ottoman Empire in the sixteenth century. Ottoman bureaucrats, merchants, and artists assembled in coffeehouses to trade stories, read, listen to poetry, and play chess and backgammon. Indeed, so deeply connected were coffeehouses with literary and artistic pursuits that people referred to them as schools of knowledge.

From the Ottoman territories, the culture of coffee drinking spread to western Europe. The first coffeehouse in London opened in 1652, and within sixty years the city claimed no fewer than 500 such establishments. In fact, the Fleet Street area of London had so many that the English essayist Charles Lamb commented, "[T]he man must have a rare recipe for melancholy who can be dull in Fleet Street." Although coffeehouses attracted people from all levels of society, they especially appealed to the new mercantile and

COMPARISON

IDENTIFY and **EXPLAIN** the major steps in the integration of global trade networks in the seventeenth and eighteenth centuries.

Imperial expansion and transoceanic trade now brought the world together as never before. Europeans conquered and colonized more of the Americas, the demand for African slaves to work New World plantations leaped upward, and global trade intensified. Conquest, colonization, and commerce created riches for some but also provoked bitter rivalries. In the Americas, Spain and Portugal faced new competitors—primarily England and France. With religious tensions added to the mix, the stage was set for decades of bloody warfare in Europe and the Americas. At the same time, in the East, rulers in India, China, and Japan enlarged their empires, while Russia's tsars incorporated Siberian territories into their domain. Meanwhile, the Ottoman, Safavid, and Mughal dynasties, though resisting most European intrusions, found their stability profoundly shaken by the forces that entangled the world.

Economic and Political Effects of Global Commerce

Global trade affected not only merchant groups and their sponsoring nations but also individual rulers and common people. Increasing economic ties brought new places and products into world markets. (See **Current Trends in World History: Stimulants, Sociability,**

Coffee Coffee drinkers at an Ottoman banquet (left) and in an English coffeehouse (right).

professional classes as locations where stimulating beverages like coffee, cocoa, and tea promoted lively conversations. Here, too, opponents claimed that excessive coffee drinking destabilized the thinking processes and even caused conversions to Islam. But against such opposition, the pleasures of coffee, tea, and cocoa prevailed. These bitter beverages in turn required liberal doses of the sweetener sugar. A smoke of tobacco topped off the experience. In this environment of pleasure, patrons of the coffeehouses indulged their addictions, engaged in gossip, conducted business, and talked politics.

QUESTIONS FOR ANALYSIS

- What factors drove the consumption of stimulants like coffee on a global scale?
- What other commodities from earlier in world history played a similar role? Were there differences in the underlying factors such as scale of consumption between the different periods?

Explore Further

Ralph S. Hattox, *Coffee and Coffeehouses: The Origins of a Social Beverage in the Medieval Near East* (1985).

and Coffeehouses.) Closer economic contact enhanced the power of certain states and destabilized others. It bolstered the legitimacy of England and France, and it prompted strong local support of new rulers in Japan and parts of sub-Saharan Africa. But also in England, France, Japan, Russia, and Africa, linkages led to civil wars and social unrest. In the Ottoman state, outlying provinces slipped from central control; the Safavid regime foundered and then collapsed; the Ming dynasty gave way to the Qing. In India, rivalries among princes and merchants eroded the Mughals' authority, compounding the instability caused by peasant uprisings.

COMPARISON

EXPLAIN the significance of European consumption of goods (like tobacco, textiles, and sugar) for the global economy.

EXTRACTING WEALTH: MERCANTILISM

Transformations in global relations began in the Atlantic, where the extraction and shipment of gold and silver siphoned wealth from the New World (the Americas) to the Old World (Afro-Eurasia). (See Map 13.1.) American exports were so lucrative for Spain and Portugal that other European powers wanted a share in the bounty, so they too launched colonizing ventures in the New World. Although these latecomers found few precious minerals, they devised other ways to extract wealth, for the Americas had fertile lands on which to cultivate sugarcane, cotton, tobacco, indigo, and rice.

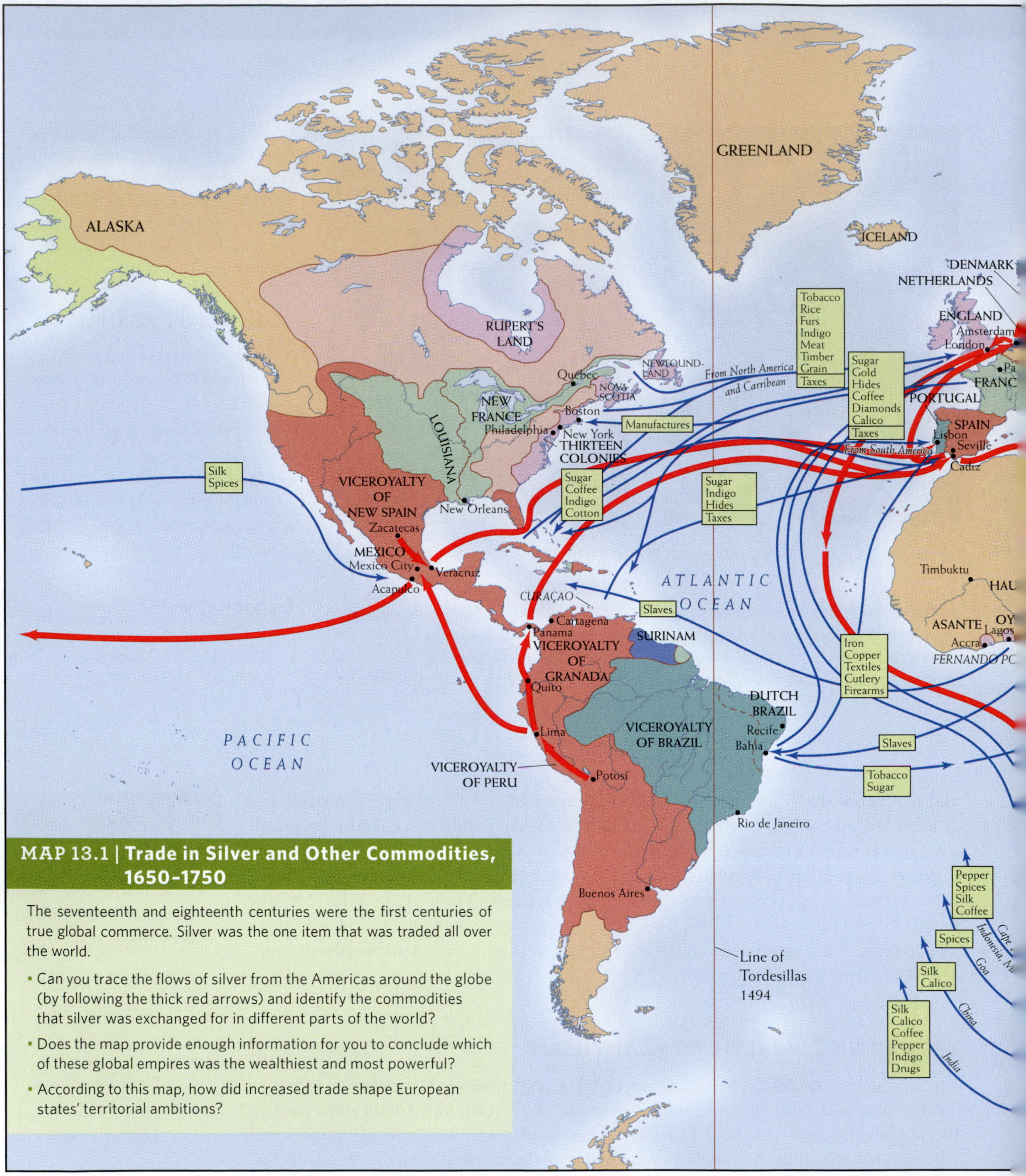

MAP 13.1 | Trade in Silver and Other Commodities, 1650–1750

The seventeenth and eighteenth centuries were the first centuries of true global commerce. Silver was the one item that was traded all over the world.

- Can you trace the flows of silver from the Americas around the globe (by following the thick red arrows) and identify the commodities that silver was exchanged for in different parts of the world?
- Does the map provide enough information for you to conclude which of these global empires was the wealthiest and most powerful?
- According to this map, how did increased trade shape European states' territorial ambitions?

ARCTIC OCEAN
SWEDEN
RUSSIAN EMPIRE
St. Petersburg
Danzig
POLAND
STRIA
OTTOMAN EMPIRE
Aleppo
Baghdad
SAFAVID EMPIRE
Isfahan
Basra
Hormuz
Alexandria
Suez
ARABIA
Muscat
ETHIOPIA
ENIN
Delhi
MUGHAL EMPIRE
Plassey
BENGAL
BIHAR
Calcutta
Diu
DECCAN PLATEAU
Bombay
Goa
Tellicherry
Madras
Pondicherry
Cochin
CEYLON
QING CHINA
JAPAN
Guangzhou
Rangoon
Da Nang
ANNAM (VIETNAM)
PHILIPPINES
Manila
Silk
Spices
PACIFIC OCEAN
Melaka
SUMATRA
BORNEO
MALUKU
NEW GUINEA
Banten
Batavia
JAVA
TIMOR
BANDA
Mogadishu
Malindi
Mombasa
ZANZIBAR
Luanda
Kilwa
Mozambique
Sofala
MADAGASCAR
MAURITIUS
RÉUNION
INDIAN OCEAN
Delagoa Bay
Cape Town
Cape of Good Hope
0 1000 2000 Miles
0 1000 2000 Kilometers
Spanish territory
Portuguese territory
English territory
French territory
Dutch territory
Anglo-French contested area
Silver flow
Trade route
Battle
Silk Commodity

If silver quickened the pace of global trade, sugar transformed the European diet. First domesticated in Polynesia, sugar rarely appeared in European diets before the New World plantations started exporting it. Previously, Europeans had used honey as a sweetener, but they soon became insatiable consumers of sugar. Between 1690 and 1790, Europe imported 12 million tons of sugar—approximately one ton for every African enslaved in the Americas.

No matter what products they supplied, colonies were supposed to provide wealth for their "mother countries"—according to the economic theory of mercantilism, which drove European empire builders. The term **mercantilism** describes a system that saw the world's wealth as fixed, meaning that any one country's wealth came at the expense of other countries. Mercantilism further assumed that overseas possessions existed solely to enrich European motherlands. Thus, colonies should ship more "value" to the mother country than they received in return. Colonies were supposed to be closed to competitors, so that foreign traders would not drain precious resources from an empire's exclusive domain. As the mother country's monopoly over its colonies' trade generated precious metals for royal treasuries, European states grew rich enough to wage almost unceasing wars against one another. Ultimately, mercantilists believed, as did the English philosopher Thomas Hobbes (1588–1679), that "wealth is power and power is wealth."

The mercantilist system required an alliance between the state and its merchants. Mercantilists understood economics and politics as interdependent, with the merchant needing the monarch to protect his interests and the monarch relying on the merchant's trade to enrich the state's treasury. **Chartered companies**, such as the (English) Virginia Company and the Dutch East India Company were the most visible examples of the collaboration between the state and the merchant classes. European monarchs awarded these firms monopoly trading rights over vast areas.

Exchanges and Expansions in North America

As rulers in England, France, and Holland granted monopolies to merchant companies, they began to dominate the settlement and trade of new colonies in the Americas and compete with the established colonies of Spain and Portugal. (See Map 13.2.) Although the search for precious metals or water routes to Asia had initially spurred British, French, and Dutch efforts to establish New World colonies, they soon learned that only by exploiting other resources could they generate profits.

EXPANDING MAINLAND COLONIES

While the Dutch relied primarily on commerce, the British and the French exploited natural resources in their North American colonies: the British established farms in a number of ecological zones, while the French relied primarily on the fur trade, especially in the interior.

In their colonies along the Atlantic seaboard, the English established one model for new colonies in the Americas. Although these territories failed to yield precious metals or a waterway across the continent, they did boast land suitable for growing a variety of crops. Different climates and soils made for very different agricultural possibilities: wheat, rye, barley, and oats in the Middle Colonies; tobacco in Virginia and North Carolina; and rice and indigo further south. In all of England's North American colonies, population growth fed greater hunger for farmlands, which put pressure on Indian holdings. The result: a souring of relations between Native Americans and colonists, often ferocious wars

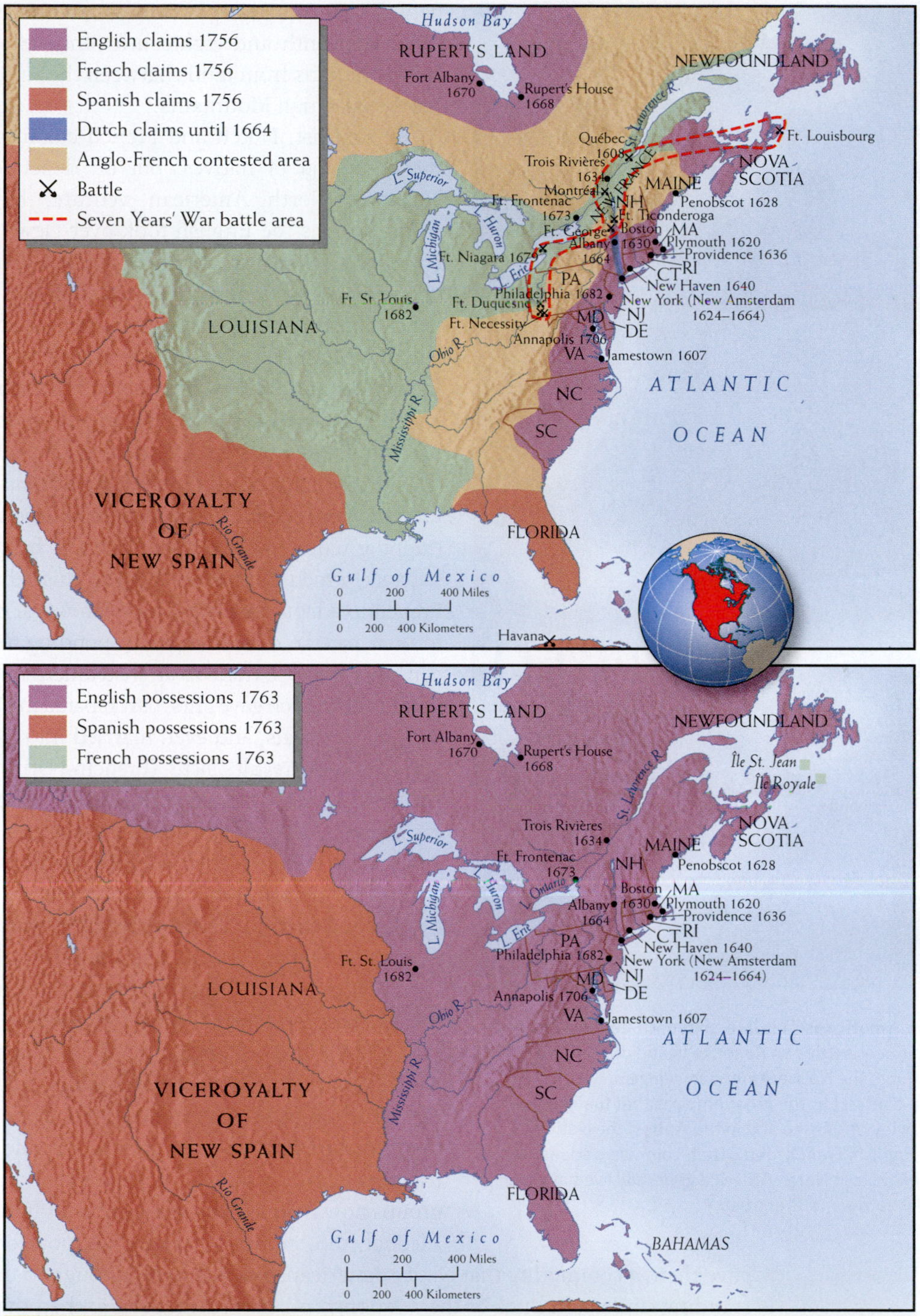

MAP 13.2 | Colonies in North America, 1607–1763

France, England, and Spain laid claim to much of North America at this time.

- Where was each of these colonial powers strongest before the outbreak of the Seven Years' War in 1756? (See p. 512 for a discussion of the Seven Years' War.)
- Which empire gained the most North American territory, and who lost the most at the end of the war in 1763?
- How do you think Native American peoples reacted to the territorial arrangements agreed to by Spain, France, and England at the Peace of Paris, which ended the war?

between natives and newcomers, and, over the course of the seventeenth and eighteenth centuries, the dispossession of Indians from lands between the Atlantic Ocean and the Appalachian Mountains.

By contrast, Dutch and French colonies rested not on the expulsion of natives, but on dependence on them. Holland's North American venture, however, proved short-lived, as the English took over New Netherland and renamed it New York in 1664. French claims were more enduring and extended across a vast swath of the continent, encompassing eastern Canada, the Great Lakes, and the Mississippi Valley. Crucial to the trade between Europeans and Native Americans in the northern parts of North America was the beaver, an animal for which Native Americans previously had little use.

Woodlands Native Americans This late-sixteenth-century drawing by John White, a pioneer settler on Roanoke Island off the coast of North Carolina, depicts the Native American village of Secoton in eastern Virginia. In contrast to the great empires that the Spanish conquered in the valley of Mexico and in the Andes, the Native Americans whom English, French, and Dutch colonizers encountered in the woodlands of eastern North America generally lived in villages that were politically autonomous entities.

The distinctive aspect of the fur trade was the Europeans' utter dependence on Native American know-how. After all, trapping required familiarity with the beavers' habits and habitats, which Europeans lacked. This reliance forced the French to adapt to Native American ways, which is evident in their pattern of exchange. Responding to Native American desires to use trade as an instrument to cement familial bonds, the French gave gifts, participated in Native American diplomatic rituals, and even married into Native American families. As a result, *métis* (French–Native American offspring) played an important role in New France as interpreters, traders, and guides. Thus, the French colonization of the Americas—owing to their reliance on Native Americans as trading partners, military allies, and mates—rested more on cooperation than conquest, especially compared to the empires built by their Spanish and English rivals.

As French (and English) traders introduced guns into the exchange networks, however, they initiated an arms race among Native Americans. To get more guns, Native Americans had to collect more skins, which resulted in the depletion of beavers in heavily trapped areas. That, in turn, pushed Native Americans to expand their hunting/trapping zones, which heightened conflicts between groups now increasingly competing for hunting territories. Alcohol, too, became a potent weapon for Europeans. It gave them a commodity that Native Americans wanted badly enough to undermine long-standing understandings of the relationship between humans and animals and to overwhelm strictures against overhunting.

The initial agricultural endeavors in the New World were modest. They relied on crops like tobacco that required relatively modest capital investments and could be profitably farmed on a small scale, with few workers. Sugar, by contrast, required major investments. It had to be processed near the cane fields, which meant mills had to be built; and it required massive amounts of labor. Produced on a large scale with slave labor, sugar was enormously profitable. From the middle of the seventeenth century, the British and French devoted their energies to replicating the Portuguese sugar plantations of Brazil on the islands they controlled in the Caribbean. All was not sweet there, however.

The Fur Trade For Europeans in northern North America, no commodity was as important as beaver skins. For the French especially, the fur trade determined the character of their colonial regime in North America. For Native Americans, it offered access to European goods, but overhunting depleted resources and provoked intertribal conflicts.

The Plantation Complex in the Caribbean

Large European plantations in the Caribbean relied on slave labor to produce sugar for export. Sugar was a killing crop. So deadly was the hot, humid environment in which sugarcane flourished (as fertile for disease as for sugarcane) that many sugar barons spent little time on their plantations. Management fell to overseers, who worked their slaves to death. Despite having immunities to yellow fever and malaria from their homeland's similar environment, the African slaves who worked on the plantations could not withstand the regimen. Inadequate food, atrocious living conditions, and a lack of sanitation added to their miseries. Moreover, plantation managers on large sugar plantations treated their slaves as nonhumans: one English gentleman commented that slaves were like cows, "as near as beasts may be, setting their souls aside."

More than disease and inadequate rations, the work itself decimated the enslaved. Average life expectancy was three years. Six days a week slaves rose before dawn, labored until noon, ate a short lunch, and then worked until dusk. At harvest time, sixteen-hour days saw hundreds of men, women, and children doubled over to cut the sugarcane and transport it to refineries, sometimes seven days per week. Under this brutal schedule, slaves occasionally dropped dead from exhaustion.

Amid disease and toil, the enslaved resisted as they could. The most dramatic expression of resistance was violent revolt. A more common form of resistance was flight. Seeking refuge from overseers, thousands of slaves took to the hills—for example, to the remote mountains of Caribbean islands or to Brazil's vast interior. Those who remained on the plantations resisted via foot dragging, pilfering, and sabotage.

Caribbean settlements and slaveholdings were not restricted to any single European power. But it was the latecomers—especially the English and the French—who concentrated on the islands of the Caribbean. (See Map 13.3.) The English took Jamaica from the Spanish and made it the premier site of Caribbean sugar by the 1740s. When the French seized half of Santo Domingo in the 1660s (renaming it Saint-Domingue, which is present-day Haiti), they created one of the wealthiest societies based on slavery of all time. This French colony's exports eclipsed those of all the Spanish and English islands combined. By 1789, French

Tobacco The cultivation of tobacco saved the Virginia colony from ruin and brought prosperity to increasing numbers of planters. The spread of tobacco plantations also pushed Native Americans off their lands and led planters to turn to Africa for a labor force.

Saint-Domingue produced nearly half of the world's supply of sugar and coffee. Its principal port city, Cap Français, was among the richest in the Atlantic world. The colony's merchants and planters built immense mansions worthy of the highest European nobles. Thus the Atlantic system benefited elite Europeans, who amassed new fortunes by exploiting the colonies' rich soil (which they eroded) and tropical climate, and the African slaves' labor.

The Slave Trade and Africa

COMPARISON

DESCRIBE the consequences of the Atlantic slave trade for African societies.

Although the slave trade began in the mid-fifteenth century, only in the seventeenth and eighteenth centuries did the numbers of human exports from Africa begin to soar. (See Map 13.4.) By 1820, four slaves had crossed the Atlantic for every European. (See **Analyzing Global Developments: The Atlantic Trade in Slaves from Africa**.) Those numbers were essential to the prosperity of Europe's American colonies. At the same time, the departure of so many inhabitants depopulated and destabilized many parts of Africa.

CAPTURING AND SHIPPING SLAVES

Merchants in Europe and the New World prospered as the slave trade grew, but their fortunes depended on trading and political networks in Africa. In fact, before the nineteenth-century discovery of quinine, European slavers could not survive in the African interior. Instead they took advantage of Africans' rivalries. Using firearms supplied by Europeans, African elites controlled the capturing of slaves; their networks linked moneylenders and traders on the coast with allies in the interior.

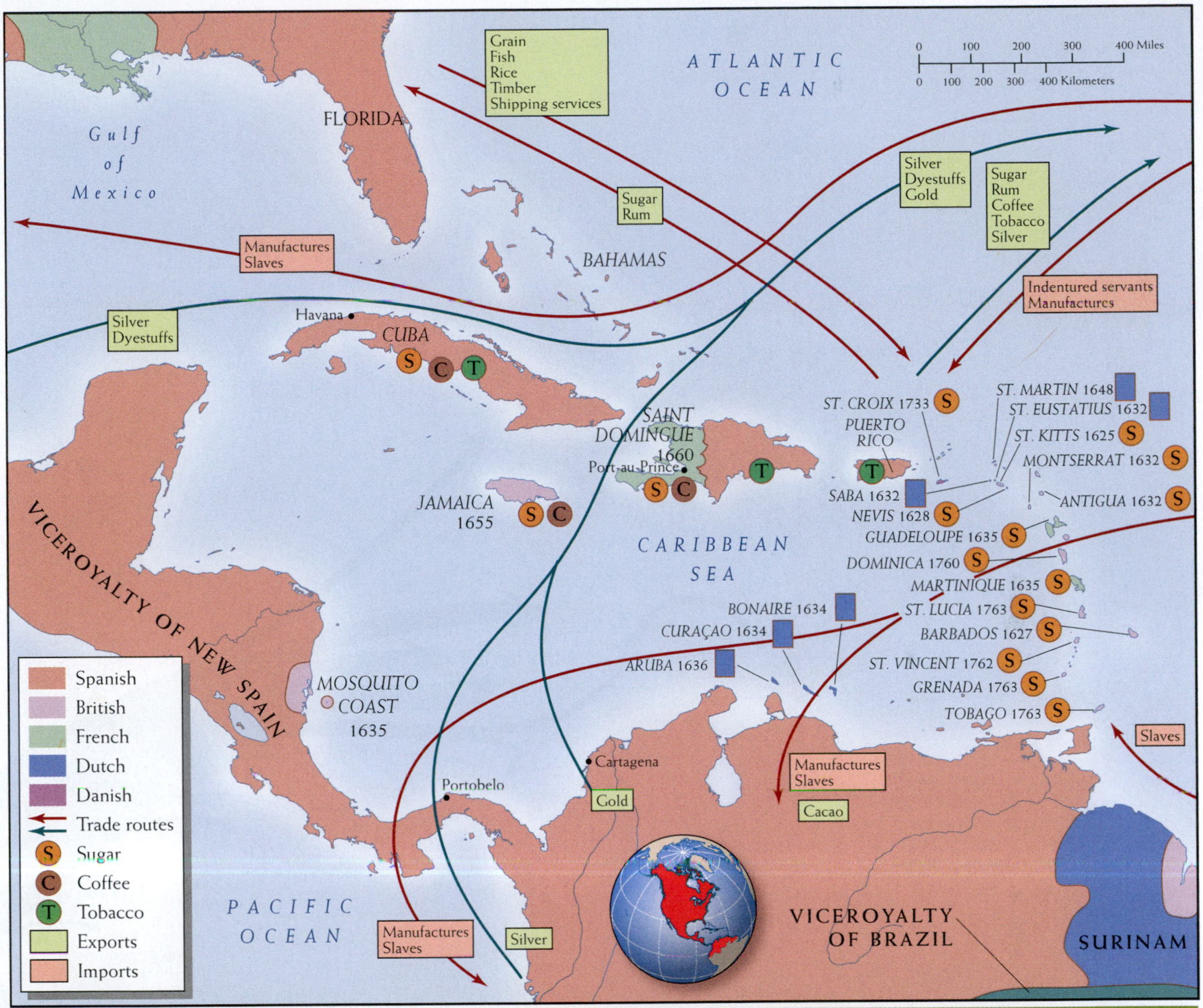

MAP 13.3 | Caribbean Colonies, 1625–1763

The Caribbean was a region of expanding trade in the seventeenth and eighteenth centuries.

- What were its major exports and imports?
- Who were its main colonizers and trading partners?
- According to your reading, how did the transformation of this region shape other societies in the Atlantic world?

Before the Europeans' arrival, Africa had an already existing system of slave commerce, mainly flowing across the Sahara to North Africa and Egypt and eastward to the Red Sea and the Swahili coast of East Africa. From the Red Sea and Swahili coast destinations, Muslim and Hindu merchants shipped slaves to ports around the Indian Ocean. However, the number of these slaves could not match the volume destined for the Americas once plantation agriculture began to spread. Indeed, 12.5 million Africans survived forcible enslavement and shipment to Atlantic ports from 1525 (the date of the first direct voyage from Africa to the Americas) until 1867 (when the last voyage took place).

Now the slave ports along the African coast became gruesome holding pens. Many slaves who perished did so before losing sight of Africa. Stuck in vast camps where disease

MAP 13.4 | The African Slave Trade, 1440–1867

The Atlantic slave trade flourished in the seventeenth, eighteenth, and nineteenth centuries, linking many parts of Africa with the Americas.

- What were the main areas in Africa from which the slaves were taken?
- What were the main areas that they were taken to in the Americas?
- Based on your reading, how and where did the slave trade reshape African societies?

NORTH SEA
EUROPE
BLACK SEA
CASPIAN SEA
ARAL SEA
ASIA
MEDITERRANEAN SEA
ALGERIA
TUNISIA
MOROCCO
LIBYA
EGYPT
PERSIA
Persian Gulf
RED SEA
ARABIA
SAHARA
2 million (1700–1900)
1.32 million
YEMEN
SENEGAMBIA
SIERRA LEONE
WINDWARD COAST
GOLD COAST
ASANTE STATE
BIGHT OF BENIN
BIGHT OF BIAFRA
AFRICA
ETHIOPIA
892,000
280,000
533,000
ARABIAN SEA
756,000
389,000
337,000
1.2 million
1.99 million
1.6 million
AMERICAS
12.57 million
(1501–1867)
5.7 million
KONGO KINGDOM
WEST CENTRAL AFRICA
SWAHILI COAST
INDIAN OCEAN
SOUTHEAST AFRICA
200,000
MADAGASCAR
MASCARENE ISLANDS
359,000
0 500 1000 1500 Miles
0 500 1000 1500 Kilometers

Analyzing Global Developments

The Atlantic Trade in Slaves from Africa (1501–1900)

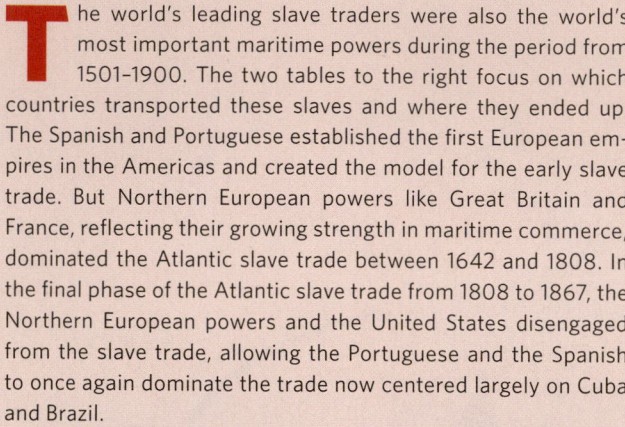

The world's leading slave traders were also the world's most important maritime powers during the period from 1501–1900. The two tables to the right focus on which countries transported these slaves and where they ended up. The Spanish and Portuguese established the first European empires in the Americas and created the model for the early slave trade. But Northern European powers like Great Britain and France, reflecting their growing strength in maritime commerce, dominated the Atlantic slave trade between 1642 and 1808. In the final phase of the Atlantic slave trade from 1808 to 1867, the Northern European powers and the United States disengaged from the slave trade, allowing the Portuguese and the Spanish to once again dominate the trade now centered largely on Cuba and Brazil.

In recent decades, scholars of the Atlantic slave trade have created the Trans-Atlantic Slave Trade Database, which can be accessed at the Voyages Web site (www.slavevoyages.org). Constructed from nearly 35,000 documented voyages during this period, this database incorporates roughly 80 percent of the slave ventures that set out for Africa to obtain slaves from all around the Atlantic world during this era. Through painstaking research historians have been able to reconstruct the Atlantic world slave trade and offer a clear insight into the experiences of all those involved and the impact of this trade on the global economy during these four centuries.

QUESTIONS FOR ANALYSIS

- Identify the countries that were the most heavily invested in the Atlantic slave trade based on the data in the first table. How do you know?
- Explain the relationship between the slave-trading countries and the colonies in the New World based on the entries in both tables.
- Why is the total number of slaves traded different from the number of slaves that disembarked? Did you expect the difference between these two numbers to be greater? If so, why?

Number of Slaves Taken from Africa to Americas by Nationality of Vessels That Carried Them (1501–1867)

VESSEL NATIONALITY	NUMBER OF SLAVES
Portugal/Brazil	5,849,300
Great Britain	3,259,900
France	1,380,970
Spain/Uruguay	1,060,900
Netherlands	555,300
United States	305,800
Baltic States	110,400
Total Atlantic World	**12,522,570**

Disembarkation of Slaves from Africa to the Americas 1501–1900

DISEMBARKING COUNTRY/COLONY	NUMBER OF SLAVES
Brazil (Portugal)	4.72 million
Smaller Caribbean Islands (mix)	1.75 million
Jamaica (Spain then Great Britain)	1.00 million
St.-Domingue (Spain then France)	792,000
Cuba (Spain)	779,000
Spanish Caribbean Mainland	390,000
United States	389,000
Dutch Guiana	294,000
Amazonia	142,000
Total	**10,703,000**

Source: David Eltis and David Richardson, Atlas of the Transatlantic Slave Trade *(New Haven, 2010).*

and hunger were rampant, the slaves were then forced aboard vessels in cramped and wretched conditions. These ships waited for weeks to fill their holds while their human cargoes wasted away below deck. Crew members tossed dead Africans overboard as they loaded on other Africans from the shore. When the cargo was complete, the ships set sail.

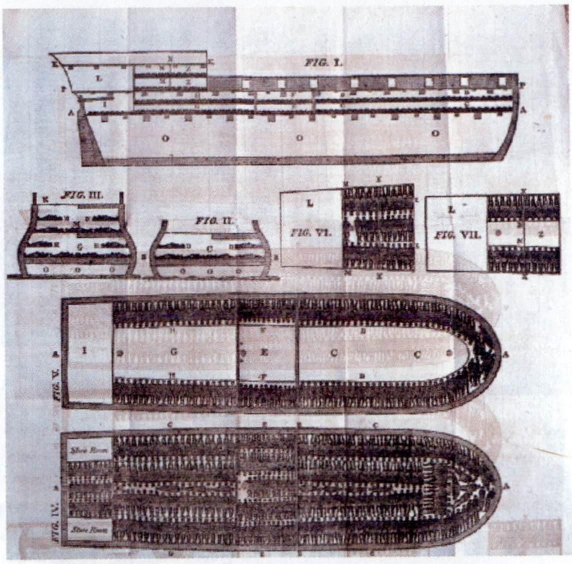

The Slave Trade (*Left*) Africans were captured in the interior and then bound and marched to the coast. Note that there is only one woman among the men (and a couple of children), reflecting the gender imbalance among those captured. (*Right*) After reaching the coast, the captured Africans would be crammed into the holds of slave vessels, where they suffered grievously from overcrowding and unsanitary conditions. Long voyages were especially deadly. If the winds failed or ships had to travel longer distances than usual, many of the captives would die en route to the slave markets across the ocean.

In their wake, crews continued to dump bodies. Most died of dehydration brought on by gastrointestinal diseases and a lack of fresh water. Smallpox and dysentery were also scourges. Either way, death was slow and agonizing.

SLAVERY'S GENDER IMBALANCE

In moving so many Africans to the Americas, the slave trade played havoc with the ratios of men to women in both places because most of the slaves shipped to the Americas were adult men. Although the numbers indicated Europeans' preferences for male laborers, they also reflected African slavers' desire to keep female slaves, primarily for household work. The gender imbalance made it difficult for slaves to reproduce in the Americas. So planters and slavers had to return to Africa to procure more captives—especially for the Caribbean islands, where slaves' death rates were so high.

Male slaves outnumbered females in the New World, but in the slave-supplying regions of Africa women outnumbered men. Female captives were especially prized in Africa because of their traditional role in the production of grains, leathers, and cotton. Moreover, the slave trade reinforced the traditional practice of polygamy—allowing relatively scarce men to take several wives, which helped minimize the loss of population.

AFRICA'S NEW SLAVE-SUPPLYING STATES

Africans did not passively let captives fall into the arms of European slave buyers; instead, local political leaders and merchants were active suppliers. This activity promoted the growth of centralized political structures, particularly in West African rain forest areas. The trade also shifted control of wealth away from households owning large herds or lands to those who profited from the capture and exchange of slaves—urban merchants and warrior elites.

The Port of Loango Partly as a result of the profits of the slave trade, African rulers and merchants were able to create large and prosperous port cities such as Loango, pictured here, which was on the west coast of south-central Africa.

In some parts of Africa, the booming slave trade created chaos as local leaders feuded over control of the traffic. In the Kongo kingdom, for example, civil wars raged for over a century after 1665, and captured warriors were sold as slaves. As members of the royal family clashed, entire provinces saw their populations vanish. Europeans fueled these conflicts and provided weapons to their African allies. Moreover, kidnapping became so prevalent that farmers worked their fields bearing weapons, leaving their children behind in guarded stockades.

As some African merchants and warlords sold other Africans, their commercial success enabled them to consolidate political power and grow wealthy. Their wealth financed additional weapons, with which they subdued neighbors and extended political control. Among the most durable new polities was the Asante state, which arose in the West African tropical rain forest in 1701 and expanded through 1750. This state benefited from its access to gold, which it used to acquire firearms (from European traders) to raid nearby communities for captives to be sold into slavery in the Americas. From its capital city at Kumasi, the state eventually encompassed almost all of present-day Ghana. Main roads spread out from the capital like spokes of a wheel, each approximately twenty days' travel from the center. Through the Asante trading networks African traders bought, bartered, and sold captives, who wound up in the hands of European merchants waiting in ports with vessels carrying manufactures and weaponry.

Slavery and the emergence of new states enriched and empowered some Africans, but they cost Africa dearly. For the princes, warriors, and merchants who organized the slave trade, their business enabled them to obtain European goods—especially alcohol, tobacco, textiles, and guns. The Atlantic system also tilted wealth away from rural dwellers and village elders and increasingly toward port cities. Across the landmass, the slave trade thinned the population. True, Africa was spared a demographic catastrophe equal to the devastation of American Indians. The introduction of American food crops—notably maize and cassava, producing many more calories per acre than the old staples of millet and sorghum—blunted the trade's depopulating aspects. Yet some areas suffered grievously from three centuries of heavy involvement in the slave trade. The Atlantic trade enhanced the warrior class, who carried out raids for captives; the dislocations, internal power struggles, and economic hardships that followed precipitated the rise and fall of West African kingdoms.

Asia in the Seventeenth and Eighteenth Centuries

Global trading networks grew as vigorously in Asia as they did in the Americas. In Asia, however, the Europeans were less dominant. Although they could gain access to Asian markets with American silver, they could not conquer Asian empires or colonize vast portions of the region. Nor were they able to enslave Asian peoples as they had Africans. The Mughal Empire continued to grow, and the Qing dynasty, which had wrested control from the Ming, significantly expanded China's borders. China remained the richest state in the world, but in some places the balance of power was tilting in Europe's direction. Not only did the Ottomans' borders contract, but by the late eighteenth century Europeans had established economic and military dominance in parts of India and much of Southeast Asia.

COMPARISON

EXPLAIN the effects of New World silver and increased trade on the Asian empires, and their responses to them.

THE DUTCH IN SOUTHEAST ASIA

In Southeast Asia the Dutch already enjoyed considerable influence by the seventeenth century. Although the Portuguese had seized the vibrant port city of Melaka in 1511 and the Spaniards had taken Manila in 1571, neither was able to monopolize the lucrative spice trade. To challenge them, the Dutch government persuaded its merchants to charter the Dutch East India Company (abbreviated as VOC) in 1602. Benefiting from Amsterdam's position as the most efficient money market with the lowest interest rates in the world, the VOC raised ten times the capital of its English counterpart—the royal chartered English East India Company. The advantages of chartered companies were evident

Attack on Bantam This engraving depicts a Dutch attack on Bantam in the late seventeenth century as part of the VOC's effort to expand its empire in Southeast Asia.

in the VOC's scale of operation: at its peak the company had 257 ships and employed 12,000 persons. Throughout two centuries it sent ships manned by a total of 1 million men to Asia.

The VOC's main impact was in Southeast Asia, where spices, coffee, tea, and teak wood were key exports (see again Map 13.1). The company's objective was to secure a trade monopoly wherever it could, fix prices, and replace the local population with Dutch planters. Under the leadership of Jan Pieterszoon Coen (who once said that trade could not be conducted without war nor war without trade), the Dutch swept into the Javanese port of Jakarta in 1619 and took over the nearby Bandanese Islands two years later. In Banda, the traditional chiefs and almost the entire population were killed outright, left to starve, or taken into slavery. Dutch planters and their slaves replaced the decimated local population and sent their produce to the VOC. The motive for such rapacious action was the huge profit to be made by buying nutmeg at a low price in the Bandanese Islands and selling it at many times that price in Europe. Although this aggressive expansion met widespread resistance from the local population and other merchants involved in the region's trade, by 1670 the Dutch had also taken Melaka from the Portuguese and controlled all of the lucrative spice trade from the Maluku islands. Next, the VOC set its sights on pepper. However, the Dutch had to share this commerce with Chinese and English competitors. Moreover, since there was no demand for European products in Asia, the Dutch had to participate more in inter-Asian trade as a way to reduce their need to make payments in precious metals.

TRANSFORMATIONS IN THE ISLAMIC HEARTLAND

Compared with Southeast Asia, the major Islamic empires did not feel such direct effects of European intrusion. They did, however, face internal difficulties, which were exacerbated by trade networks that eluded state control. From its inception, the Safavid Empire had always required a powerful, religiously inspired ruler to enforce Shiite religious orthodoxy and to hold together the realm's tribal, pastoral, mercantile, and agricultural factions. With a succession of weak rulers and declining tax revenues, the state foundered, and ultimately collapsed in 1722 (see Chapter 14). The Ottoman and Mughal empires, in contrast, remained more resilient.

The Ottoman Empire Having attained a high point under Suleiman (see Chapter 11), the Ottoman Empire ceased expanding. After Suleiman's reign, Ottoman armies and navies tried unsuccessfully to expand the empire's borders—losing, for example, on the western flank to the European Habsburgs. As military campaigns and a growing population strained the realm's limited resources, Ottoman intellectuals worried that the empire's glory was ebbing. A series of administrative reforms in the seventeenth century reinvigorated the state, but it never recaptured the vast power it enjoyed at its height.

Even as the empire's strength waned, by the seventeenth century its sultans faced a commercially more connected world. The introduction of New World silver into Ottoman networks of commerce and money lending eventually destabilized the empire. Although early Ottoman rulers had avoided trade with the outside world, the lure of silver broke through state regulations. Now Ottoman merchants established black markets for commodities that eager European buyers paid for in silver—especially wheat, copper, and wool. Because these exports were illegal, their sale did not generate tax revenues to support the state's civilian and military administration. So Ottoman rulers had to rely on loans of silver from the merchants. Some European royal houses, notably the Dutch and English, would grant those who bankrolled them a say in government, which vastly increased their credit and ultimately their power. Ottoman sultans, by contrast, feuded with their financiers, which undermined their authority.

More silver and budget deficits were a recipe for inflation. Prices tripled between 1550 and 1650. Runaway inflation caused hard-hit peasants in Anatolia, suffering from high food prices, shortages, and increasing taxes (used to pay off dynastic debts), to join together in uprisings that threatened the state's stability. Moreover, disorder at the center of the empire was accompanied by difficulties in the provinces, where breakaway regimes appeared.

The most threatening of the breakaway pressures occurred in Egypt beginning in the seventeenth century. In 1517, Egypt had become the Ottoman Empire's greatest conquest. As the wealthiest Ottoman territory, it was an important source of revenue, and its people shouldered heavy tax burdens. The group that asserted Egypt's political and commercial autonomy were military men, known as **Mamluks** (Arabic for "owned" or "possessed"), who had ruled Egypt as an independent regime until the Ottoman conquest (see Chapter 10). Although the Ottoman army had routed Mamluk forces on the battlefield, Ottoman governors in Egypt allowed the Mamluks to reform themselves. By the seventeenth century, these military men were nearly as powerful as their ancestors had been in the fifteenth century when they ruled Egypt independently. Mamluk leaders enhanced their power by aligning with Egyptian merchants and catering to the religious elites of Egypt, the *ulama*. Turning the Ottoman administrator of Egypt into a mere figurehead, this new provincial elite kept much of the area's fiscal resources for themselves at the expense not only of the imperial coffers but also of the local peasantry.

Amid new economic pressures and challenges from outlying territories, the Ottoman system also had elements of resilience—especially at the center, where decaying

Siege of Vienna This seventeenth-century painting depicts the Ottoman siege of Vienna, which began on July 14, 1683, and ended on September 12. The city might have fallen if the Polish king, John III, had not answered the pope's plea to defend Christendom and sent an army to assist German and Austrian troops in defeating the Ottomans.

leadership provoked demands for reform from administrative elites. Known as the Koprulu reforms, a combination of financial reform and anticorruption measures gave the state a new burst of energy and enabled the military to reacquire some of its lost possessions. Revenues again increased, and inflation decreased. Fired by revived expansionist ambitions, Istanbul decided to renew its assault on Christianity (see Chapter 11)—beginning with rekindled plans to seize Vienna. Although the Ottomans gathered an enormous force outside the Habsburg capital in 1683, both sides suffered heavy losses and the Ottoman forces ultimately retreated. Under the treaty that ended the Austro-Ottoman war, the Ottomans lost major European territorial possessions, including Hungary.

Thus, the Ottoman Empire began the eighteenth century dealing with serious economic challenges. Whereas in the sixteenth century rulers of the Ottoman Empire had wanted to create a self-contained and self-sufficient imperial economy, silver undermined this vision as it had elsewhere in the global economy. Indeed, the influx of silver opened Ottoman-controlled lands to trade with the rest of the world, producing breakaway regimes, widespread inflation, social discontent, and conflict between the state and its financiers that made these problems difficult to manage.

The Mughal Empire In contrast to the Ottomans' military reversals, the Mughal Empire reached its height in the 1600s. The period saw Mughal rulers extend their domain over almost all of India and enjoy increased domestic and international trade. But they, too, eventually had problems governing dispersed and resistant provinces, where many villages retained traditional religions and cultures.

Before the Mughals, India had never had a single political authority. Akbar and his successors had conquered territory in the north (see Chapter 12, Map 12.4), so now the Mughals turned to the south and gained control over most of that region by 1689. As the new provinces provided an additional source of resources, local lords, and warriors, the Mughal bureaucracy grew better at extracting services and taxes.

Imperial stability and prosperity did not depend entirely on the Indian Ocean trading system. Indeed, although the Mughals profited from seaborne trade, they never undertook overseas expansion. The main source of their wealth was land rents, which increased via incentives to bring new land into cultivation. But the imperial economy also benefited from Europeans' increased demand for Indian goods, including a sixfold rise in the English East India Company's textile purchases.

Eventually, Mughals were victims of their own success. More than a century of imperial expansion, commercial prosperity, and agricultural development placed substantial resources in the hands of local and regional authorities. As a result, local warrior elites became more autonomous. By the late seventeenth century, many regional leaders were well positioned to resist Mughal authority. As in the Ottoman Empire, then distant provinces began to challenge central rulers. Now the Indian peasants (like their counterparts in Ming China, Safavid Persia, and the Ottoman Empire) capitalized on weakening central authority. Many rose in rebellions; others took up banditry.

At this point the Mughal emperors had to accept diminished power over a loose unity of provincial states. Most of these areas accepted Mughal control in name only, administering semiautonomous regimes through access to local resources. Yet India still flourished, and landed elites brought new territories into agrarian production. Cotton, for instance, supported a thriving textile industry as peasant households focused on weaving and cloth production. Much of their production was destined for export as the region deepened its integration into world trading systems.

The Mughals themselves paid scant attention to commercial matters, but local rulers welcomed Europeans into Indian ports. As more European ships arrived, these authorities struck deals with merchants from Portugal and, increasingly, from England and Holland. Some Indian merchants formed trading companies of their own to control the sale of regional produce to competing Europeans; others established intricate trading networks that reached as far north as Russia. Mercantile houses grew richer and gained greater political influence over financially strapped emperors. Thus, even as global commercial entanglements enriched some in India, the effects undercut the Mughal dynasty.

FROM MING TO QING IN CHINA

Like India, China prospered in the seventeenth and eighteenth centuries; but here, too, growing wealth undermined central control and contributed to the fall of a long-lasting dynasty. As in Mughal India, local power holders in China increasingly defied the Ming government. Moreover, because Ming sovereigns discouraged overseas commerce and forbade travel abroad, they did not reap the rewards of long-distance exchange. Rather, such profits went to traders and adventurers who evaded imperial edicts. Together, the persistence of local autonomy and the accelerating economic and social changes brought unprecedented challenges until finally, in 1644, the Ming dynasty collapsed.

COMPARISON

ANALYZE examples of resistance in Southeast Asia and China to the growth of global trade networks.

Administrative and Economic Problems How did a dynasty that in the early seventeenth century governed the world's most economically advanced society (and perhaps a third of the world's population) fall from power? As in the Ottoman Empire, responsibility often lay with the rulers and their inadequate response to economic change. Zhu Yijun, the Wanli Emperor (r. 1573–1620) was secluded despite being surrounded by a staff of 20,000 eunuchs and 3,000 women. The "Son of Heaven" rarely ventured outside the palace compound, and when he moved within it a large retinue accompanied him, led by eunuchs clearing his path with whips. Ming emperors like Wanli quickly discovered that despite the elaborate arrangements and ritual performances affirming their position as the Son of Heaven, they had little control over the vast bureaucracy. An emperor frustrated with his officials could do little more than punish them or refuse to cooperate.

The timing of administrative breakdown in the Ming government was unfortunate, because expanding opportunities for trade led many individuals to circumvent official rules. From the mid-sixteenth century, bands of supposedly Japanese pirates ravaged the Chinese coast. Indeed, the Ming government had difficulties regulating trade with Japan and labeled all pirates as Japanese, but many of the marauders were in fact Chinese who flouted imperial authority. In tough times, the roving gangs terrorized sea-lanes and harbors. In better times, some functioned like mercantile groups: their leaders mingled with elites, foreign trade representatives, and imperial officials. What made these predators so resilient—and their business so lucrative—was their ability to move among the mosaic of East Asian cultures.

Silver This seventeenth-century helmet from the Ming (1368–1633) or the Qing (1644–1911) dynasties features steel, gold, silver, and textiles, all of which were vital to the Chinese economy during this century. Silver was especially important, for its large influx from Japan and the Americas led to severe economic problems, political unrest, and the overthrow of the Ming dynasty.

Just like in the Islamic empires, the influx of silver from the New World and Japan, while at first stimulating the Chinese economy, led to severe economic (and, eventually, political) problems. As we saw in Chapter 12, Europeans used New World silver to pay for their purchases of Chinese goods. As a result, by the early seventeenth century silver imports exceeded domestic bullion production (uncoined gold or silver) in China by some twentyfold. Increasing monetization of the economy, which entailed silver currency becoming the primary medium of exchange, bolstered market activity and state revenues at the same time.

Yet the use of silver pressured peasants, who now needed that metal to pay their taxes and purchase goods. When silver supplies were abundant, the peasants faced inflationary prices. When supplies were low, the peasants could not meet their obligations to state officials and merchants, and they took up arms in rebellion.

The Collapse of Ming Authority By the seventeenth century, the Ming's administrative and economic difficulties were affecting their subjects' daily lives. This was particularly evident when the regime failed to cope with devastation caused by natural disasters, as in the northwestern province of Shanxi after a drop in average temperatures shortened growing seasons and reduced harvests. As the price of grain soared there in 1627–1628, the poor and the hungry fanned out to find food by whatever means they could muster. To deal with the crisis, the government imposed heavier taxes and cut the military budget. Bands of dispossessed Chinese peasants and mutinous soldiers then vented their anger at local tax collectors and officials.

Now the cycle of rebellion and weakened central authority that played out in so many other places took its predictable toll. Outlaw armies grew large under charismatic leaders. The most famous rebel leader, the "dashing prince" Li Zicheng, arrived at the outskirts of Beijing in 1644. Only a few companies of soldiers and a few thousand eunuchs were there to defend the capital's twenty-one miles of walls, so Li Zicheng seized Beijing easily. Two days later, the emperor hanged himself. On the following day, the triumphant "dashing prince" rode into the capital and claimed the throne.

News of the fall of the Ming capital sent shock waves around the empire. One hundred and seventy miles to the northeast, where China meets Manchuria, the army's commander received the news within a matter of days. His task in the area was to defend the Ming against their menacing neighbor, a group that had begun to identify itself as Manchu. Immediately the commander's position became precarious. Caught between an advancing rebel army on the one side and the Manchus on the other, he made a fateful decision: he appealed for the Manchus' cooperation to fight the "dashing prince," promising his new allies that "gold and treasure" awaited them in the capital. Thus, without shedding a drop of blood, the Manchus joined the Ming forces. After years of coveting the Ming Empire, the Manchus were finally on their way to Beijing (see Map 13.5).

The Qing Dynasty Asserts Control Despite their small numbers, the Manchus overcame early resistance to their rule and oversaw an impressive expansion of their realm. The **Manchus**—the name was first used in 1635—were descendants of a Turkic-speaking group known as the Jurchens. They emerged as a force early in the seventeenth century, when their leader claimed the title of khan after securing the allegiance of various Mongol groups in northeastern Asia, paving the way for their eventual conquest of China.

When the Manchus defeated Li Zicheng and seized power in Beijing, they numbered around 1 million. Assuming control of a domain that included perhaps 250 million people, they were keenly aware of their minority status. Taking power was one thing; keeping it was another. But keep it they did. In fact, during the eighteenth century, the Manchu

MAP 13.5 | From Ming to Qing China, 1644–1760

Qing China under the Manchus expanded its territory significantly during this period. Find the Manchu homeland and then the area of Manchu expansion after 1644, when the Manchus established the Qing dynasty.

- Where did the Qing dynasty expand? Explain what this tells us about the priorities of the ruling elite, in particular with respect to global commerce.
- Explain the significance of the chronology of Chinese expansion. Does this qualify your answer to the first question?
- What does it tell us about the evolution of the ruling elite's priorities?
- Consider the scope of Chinese territorial expansion in this period, and, based on your reading, explain the challenges this posed for central authorities.

Qing ("pure") dynasty (1644–1911) incorporated new territories, experienced substantial population growth, and sustained significant economic growth.

The key to China's relatively stable economic and geographic expansion lay in its rulers' shrewd and flexible policies. The early Manchu emperors were able and diligent administrators. They also knew that to govern a diverse population they had to adapt to local ways. At the same time, Qing rulers were determined to convey a clear sense of their own majesty and legitimacy. Rulers relentlessly promoted patriarchal values. Widows who remained "chaste" enjoyed public praise, and women in general were urged to lead a "virtuous" life serving male kin and family. To the majority Han population, the Manchu emperor represented himself as the worthy upholder of familial values and classical Chinese civilization. However, insinuating themselves into an existing order and appeasing subject peoples did not satisfy the Manchu yearning to leave their imprint. They also introduced measures that emphasized their authority, their distinctiveness, and the submission of their mostly Han Chinese subjects. For example, Qing officials composed or translated important documents into Manchu and banned intermarriage between Manchu and Han, although this proved difficult to enforce.

Manchu impositions fell mostly on the peasantry, for the Qing financed their administrative structure through taxes on peasant households. In response the peasants sought new lands to cultivate in border areas, often planting New World crops that grew well in difficult soils. This move introduced an important change in Chinese diets: while rice remained the staple of the wealthy, peasants increasingly subsisted on corn and sweet potatoes.

While officials redoubled their reliance on an agrarian base, trade and commerce flourished. Chinese merchants continued to ply the waters stretching from Southeast Asia to Japan, exchanging textiles, ceramics, and medicine for spices and rice. Although the Qing state vacillated about permitting maritime trade with foreigners in its early years, it sought to regulate external commerce more formally as it consolidated its rule. In 1720, in Canton, a group of merchants formed a monopolistic guild to trade with Europeans seeking coveted Chinese goods and peddling their own wares. Although the guild disbanded in the face of opposition from other merchants, it revived after the Qing restricted European trade to Canton. The **Canton system**, officially established by imperial decree in 1759, required European traders to have guild merchants act as guarantors for their good behavior and payment of fees.

Despite public disregard for certain imperial edicts, the Qing dynasty enjoyed a heyday during the eighteenth century. It forced Korea, Vietnam, Burma, and Nepal to pay tribute, and its territorial expansion reached far into central Asia, Tibet, and Mongolia. China, in sum, negotiated a century of upheaval without dismantling established ways in politics and economics. The peasantry continued to practice popular faiths, cultivate crops, and stay close to fields and villages. Trade with the outside world was marginal to overall commercial life; like the Ming, the Qing cared more about the agrarian than the commercial health of the empire, believing the former to be the foundation of prosperity and tranquility. As long as China's peasantry could keep the dynasty's coffers full, the government was content to squeeze the merchants when it needed funds. Some historians view this practice as a failure to adapt to a changing world order, as it ultimately left China vulnerable to outsiders—especially Europeans. But this view projects later developments onto the past. By the mid-eighteenth century, Europe still needed China more than the other way around. For the majority of Chinese, no superior model of belief, politics, or economics was conceivable. Indeed, although the Qing had taken over a crumbling empire in 1644, a century later China was enjoying a new level of prosperity.

TOKUGAWA JAPAN

Integration with the Asian trading system exposed Japan to new external pressures, even as the islands grappled with internal turmoil. But the Japanese dealt with these pressures more successfully than the mainland Asian empires (Ottoman, Safavid, Mughal, and Ming), which saw political fragmentation and even the overthrow of ruling dynasties. In Japan, a single ruling family emerged. This dynastic state, the **Tokugawa shogunate**, accomplished something that most of the world's other regimes did not: it regulated foreign intrusion. While Japan played a modest role in the expanding global trade, it remained free of outside exploitation.

Unification of Japan During the sixteenth century, Japan had suffered from political instability as banditry and civil strife disrupted the countryside. Regional ruling families, called *daimyos,* had commanded private armies of warriors known as samurai. The daimyos sometimes brought order to their domains, but no one family could establish preeminence over others. Although Japan had an emperor, his authority did not extend beyond the court in Kyoto.

Following an effort by military leaders to unify Japan, one of the daimyos, Tokugawa Ieyasu seized power. This was a decisive moment. In 1603, Ieyasu assumed the title of shogun (military ruler), retaining the emperor in name only while taking the reins of power himself. He also solved the problem of succession, declaring that rulership would be hereditary and that his family would be the ruling household. Administrative authority shifted from Kyoto to the site of Ieyasu's domain headquarters: the castle town called Edo (later renamed Tokyo; see Map 13.6). By the time Ieyasu died, Edo had become a major urban center with a population of 150,000. This hereditary Tokugawa shogunate lasted until 1867.

The Tokugawa shoguns ensured a flow of resources from the working population to the rulers and from the provinces to the capital. Villages paid taxes to the daimyos,

Edo in the Rain This facsimile of an *ukiyo-e* ("floating world") print by Hiroshige (1797–1858) depicts one of several bridges in the bustling city of Edo (later Tokyo), with Mount Fuji in the background.

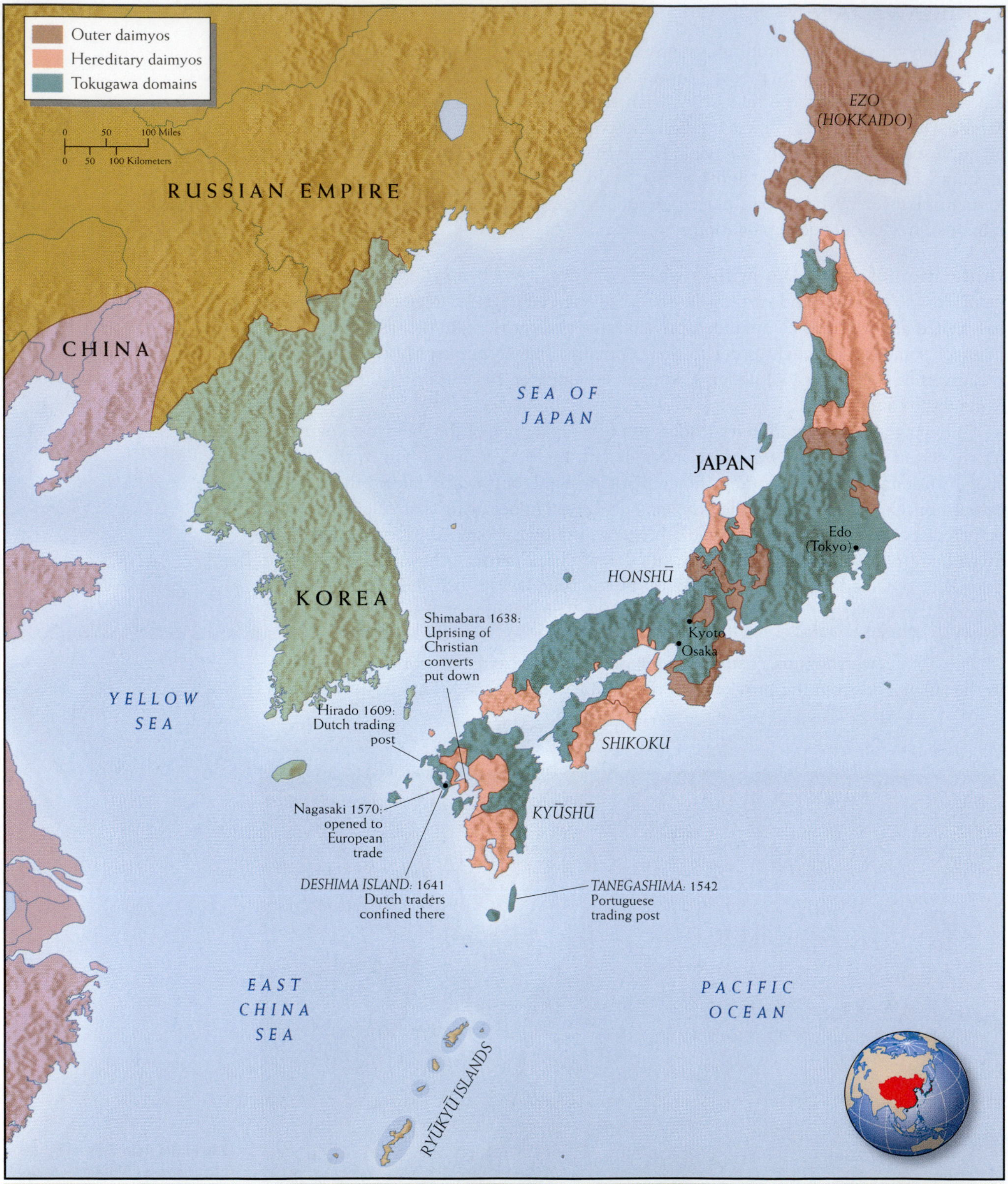

MAP 13.6 | Tokugawa Japan, 1603–1867

The Tokugawa shoguns created a strong central state in Japan at this time.

- According to this map, how extensive was their control?
- Based on your reading, what foreign states were interested in trade with Japan?
- How, according to the chapter, did Tokugawa leaders attempt to control relations with foreign states and other entities?

who transferred resources to the seat of shogunate authority. No longer engaged in constant warfare, the samurai became administrators. Peace brought prosperity. Agriculture thrived. Improved farming techniques and land reclamation projects enabled the country's population to grow from 10 million in 1550 to 16 million in 1600 and 30 million in 1700.

Foreign Affairs and Foreigners Internal peace and prosperity did not insulate Japan from external challenges. When Japanese rulers tackled foreign affairs, their most pressing concern was the intrusion of Christian missionaries and European traders. Initially, Japanese officials welcomed these foreigners out of an eagerness to acquire muskets, gunpowder, and other new technology. But once the ranks of Christian converts swelled, Japanese authorities realized that Christians were intolerant of other faiths, believed Christ to be superior to any authority, and fought among themselves. The government suppressed Christianity and drove European missionaries from the country.

Even more troublesome was the lure of trade with Europeans. The Tokugawa knew that trading at various Japanese ports would pull the commercial regions in various directions, away from the capital. When it became clear that European traders preferred the ports of Kyūshū (the southernmost island), the shogunate restricted Europeans to trade only in ports under Edo's direct rule in Honshū. Then, Japanese authorities expelled all European competitors. Only the Protestant (and nonproselytizing) Dutch won permission to remain in Japan, confined to an island near Nagasaki. The Dutch were allowed to unload just one ship each year, under strict supervision by Japanese authorities.

These measures did not close Tokugawa Japan to the outside world, however. Trade with China and Korea flourished, and the shogun received missions from Korea and the Ryūkyū islands. Edo also gathered information about the outside world from the resident Dutch and Chinese (who included monks, physicians, and painters). A few Japanese were permitted to learn Dutch and to study European technology, shipbuilding, and medicine (see Chapter 14). By limiting such encounters, the authorities ensured that foreigners would not threaten Japan's security.

The arrival of New World silver provided at least an initial boost to the major Asian economies. The Mughal Empire achieved its greatest influence in the seventeenth century. Despite a change in the ruling dynasty, China remained the world's center of wealth and power, although there, as elsewhere in Asia, silver caused inflation and altered relations between center and periphery. Ottoman domains shrank, and Europeans achieved important commercial footholds in parts of India and Southeast Asia.

Transformations in Europe

Between 1600 and 1750, religious conflict, commercial expansion, and the consolidation of dynastic power transformed Europe. Commercial centers shifted northward, and Spain and Portugal lost ground to England and France. To the east, the state of Muscovy expanded dramatically to become the sprawling Russian Empire.

COMPARISON

COMPARE the impact of trade and religion on state power in Europe and the Mughal Empire.

EXPANSION AND DYNASTIC CHANGE IN RUSSIA

During this period the Russian Empire expanded to become one of the world's largest-ever states. It gained positions on the Baltic Sea and the Pacific Ocean, and it established political borders with both the Qing Empire and Japan. These momentous shifts involved the elimination of steppe nomads as an independent force. Culturally, Europeans as well as Russians debated whether Russia belonged more to Europe or to Asia. The answer was both.

Muscovy Becomes the Russian Empire The principality of Moscow, or Muscovy, like Japan and China, used territorial expansion and commercial networks to consolidate a powerful state. This was the Russian Empire, the name given to Muscovy by Tsar Peter the Great around 1700. ("Tsar" was a Russian word derived from the Latin *Caesar* to refer to the Russian ruler.) Originally a mixture of Slavs, Finnish tribes, Turkic speakers, and many others, **Muscovy** spanned parts of Europe, much of northern Asia, numerous North Pacific islands, and even—for a time—a corner of North America (Alaska).

Like Japan, Russia emerged out of turmoil. Security concerns inspired the Muscovy regime to seize territory in the fifteenth and sixteenth centuries. Because the steppe, which stretches deep into Asia, remained a highway for nomadic peoples (especially descendants of the powerful Mongols), Muscovy sought to dominate the areas south and east of Moscow. Beginning in the 1590s, Russian authorities built forts and trading posts along Siberian rivers, and by 1639 the state's borders reached the Pacific. Thus, in just over a century Muscovy had claimed an empire straddling Eurasia and incorporating peoples of many languages and religions (see Map 13.7).

Much of this expansion occurred despite dynastic chaos that followed the death of Tsar Ivan IV in 1584. Ultimately, a group of prominent families reestablished central authority and threw their weight behind a new family of rulers. These were the Romanovs, court barons who set about reviving the Kremlin's fortunes. (The Kremlin was a medieval walled fortress where the Muscovite grand princes—later, tsars—resided.) Like the Ottoman and Qing dynasts, Romanov tsars and their aristocratic supporters would retain power into the twentieth century.

Absolutist Government and Serfdom In the seventeenth and eighteenth centuries, the Romanovs created an absolutist system of government. Only the tsar had the right to make war, tax, judge, and coin money. The Romanovs also made the nobles serve as state officials. Now Russia became a despotic state that had no political assemblies for nobles or other groups, other than mere consultative bodies like the imperial senate. Indeed, away from Moscow, local aristocrats enjoyed nearly unlimited authority in exchange for loyalty and tribute to the tsar.

During this period, Russia's peasantry bore the burden of maintaining the wealth of the nobility and the monarchy. Most peasant families gathered into communes, isolated rural worlds where people helped one another deal with the harsh climate, severe landlords, and occasional poor harvests. Communes functioned like extended kin networks in which members supported one another. In 1649, peasants were legally bound as serfs to the nobles and the tsar, meaning that, in principle, they had to perform obligatory services and deliver part of their produce to their lords.

Imperial Expansion and Migration A series of military victories in the eighteenth century made it possible to consolidate the empire and sparked significant population movements. The conquest of Siberia brought vast territory and riches in furs. Victory in a prolonged war with Sweden and then the incorporation of the fertile southern steppes, known as Ukraine, proved decisive. Peter the Great (r. 1682–1725) accomplished the victory in Sweden, after which he founded a new capital at St. Petersburg. Under Peter's successors, including the brilliant and ruthless Catherine the Great, Russia, already a harsh and colossal space, added even more territory. By the late eighteenth century, Russia's grasp extended from the Baltic Sea, Ukraine, and the Crimea on the Black Sea, and stretched eastward all the way to Siberia.

Many people migrated eastward to Siberia. Some were fleeing serfdom; others were being deported for rejecting religious reforms. Battling astoundingly harsh temperatures (falling to –40 degrees Centigrade/Fahrenheit) and frigid Arctic winds, these individuals traveled on horseback and trudged on foot to resettle in the east. But the difficulties of clearing forested lands or planting crops in boggy Siberian soils, combined with extraordinarily harsh

MAP 13.7 | Russian Expansion, 1462-1795

The state of Muscovy incorporated vast territories through overland expansion as it grew and became the Russian Empire.

- Using the map key, identify how many different expansions the Russian Empire underwent between 1462 and 1795 and in what directions generally.
- With what countries and cultures did the Russian Empire come into contact?
- According to the text, what drove such dramatic expansion?

winters, meant that many settlers died or tried to return. Isolation was a problem, too. There was no established land route back to Moscow until the 1770s, when exiles completed the Great Siberian Post Road through the swamps and peat bogs of western Siberia. The writer Anton Chekhov later called it "the longest and ugliest road in the whole world."

ECONOMIC AND POLITICAL FLUCTUATIONS IN CENTRAL AND WESTERN EUROPE

During this period European economies became more commercialized, especially after recovering from the Thirty Years' War. As in Asia, developments in distant parts of the world shaped the region's economic upturns and downturns. Compounding these pressures was the continuation of dynastic rivalries and religious conflicts.

The Thirty Years' War For a century after Martin Luther broke with the Catholic Church (see Chapter 12), religious warfare raged in Europe. So did contests over territory, power, and trade. The **Thirty Years' War** (1618–1648) was all three of these—a war between Protestant princes and the Catholic emperor for religious predominance in central Europe; a struggle for regional control among Catholic powers (the Spanish and Austrian Habsburgs and the French); and a bid for independence (from Spain) by the Dutch, who wanted to trade and worship as they liked.

The brutal conflict began as a struggle between Protestants and Catholics within the Habsburg Empire, but it soon became a war for preeminence in Europe. It took the lives of civilians as well as soldiers. In total, fighting, disease, and famine wiped out a third of the German states' urban population and two-fifths of their rural population. Ultimately the Treaty of Westphalia (1648) stated that as there was a rough balance of power between Protestant and Catholic states, they would simply have to put up with each other. The Dutch won their independence, but the war's enormous costs provoked severe discontent in Spain, France, and England. Central Europe was so devastated that it did not recover in economic or demographic terms for more than a century.

The Thirty Years' War The mercenary armies of the Thirty Years' War were renowned for pillaging and tormenting the civilians of central Europe. Here, the townsfolk exact revenge on some of these soldiers, hanging, as the engraving's caption claims, "damned and infamous thieves, like bad fruit, from this tree."

The Thirty Years' War transformed war making. Whereas most medieval struggles had been sieges between nobles leading small armies, centralized states fielding standing armies now waged decisive, grand-scale campaigns. The war also changed the ranks of soldiers: local enlisted men defending their king, country, and faith gave way to hired mercenaries or criminals doing forced service. Even officers, who previously obtained their stripes by purchase or royal decree, now had to earn them. Gunpowder, cannons, and muskets became standardized. By the eighteenth century, Europe's wars featured huge standing armies boasting a professional officer corps, deadly artillery, and long supply lines bringing food and ammunition to the front. The costs—material and human—of war began to soar.

Western European Economies In spite of the toll that warfare took on economic activity, the European states enjoyed significant commercial expansion in the seventeenth century. Northern Europe gained more than did the south, however. Spain, for example, started losing ground to its rivals as the costs of defending its empire soared and merchants from Northern Europe cut in on its trading networks. The weighty costs of its involvement in the Thirty Years' War dealt the Spanish economy a final, disastrous blow.

As European commercial dynamism shifted northward, the Dutch led the way with innovative commercial practices and a new mercantile elite. They specialized in shipping and in financing regional and long-distance trade. Their famous *fluitschips* carried heavy, bulky cargoes (like Baltic wood) with relatively small crews. Now shipping costs throughout the Atlantic world dropped as Dutch ships transported their own and other countries' goods. Amsterdam's merchants founded an exchange bank, established a rudimentary stock exchange, and pioneered systems of underwriting and insuring cargoes.

England and France also became commercial powerhouses, establishing aggressive policies to promote national business and drive out competitors. By stipulating that only English ships could carry goods between the mother country and its colonies, the English Navigation Act of 1651 protected English shippers and merchants—especially from the Dutch.

Economic development was not limited to port towns: the countryside, too, enjoyed breakthroughs in production. Most important was expansion in the production of food. In northwestern Europe, investments in water drainage, larger livestock herds, and improved cultivation practices generated much greater yields. Also, a four-field crop rotation involving wheat, clover, barley, and turnips kept nutrients in the soil and provided year-round fodder for livestock. As a result (and as we have seen many times before), increased agricultural output supported a growing urban population.

Production rose most where the organization of rural property changed. In England, in a movement known as **enclosure**, landowners took control of lands that traditionally had been common property serving local needs. Claiming exclusive rights to these lands, the landowners planted new crops or pastured sheep with the aim of selling the products in distant markets—especially cities. The largest landowners put their farms in the hands of tenants, who hired wage laborers to till, plant, and harvest. Thus, in England, peasant agriculture gave way to farms run by wealthy families who exploited the marketplace to buy what they needed (including labor) and to sell what they produced. In this regard, England led the way in a Europe-wide process of commercializing the countryside.

Dynastic Monarchies: France and England European monarchs had varying success with centralizing state power. In France, Louis XIII (r. 1610–1643) and especially his chief minister, Cardinal Richelieu, concentrated power in the hands of the king. Instead of sharing power with the aristocracy, much less commoners, the king and his counselors wanted him to rule free of external checks, to create an **absolute monarchy**. The ruler was not to be a tyrant, but his authority was to be complete and thorough, and his state free of bloody disorders. The king's rule would be lawful; but he, not his jurists, would dictate the last legal word. If the king made a mistake, only God could call him to account. Thus the Europeans believed in the "divine right of kings," a political belief not greatly different from imperial China where the emperor was thought to rule with the mandate of heaven.

In absolutist France, privileges and state offices flowed from the king's grace. All patronage networks ultimately linked to the king: that included financial supports the crown provided directly as well tax exemptions and a wide array of permissions—to publish a book or work in a regulated trade, from lawyers and professors to apothecaries, bookbinders, and butchers. The great palace Louis XIV built at Versailles teemed with nobles from all over France seeking favor, dressing according to the king's expensive fashion code, and attending the latest tragedies, comedies, and concerts.

The French dynastic monarchy provided a model of absolute rule for other European dynasts, like the Habsburgs of the Holy Roman Empire, the Hohenzollerns of Prussia, and the Romanovs of Muscovy. The king and his ministers controlled all public power, while other social groups, from the nobility to the peasantry, had no formal body to represent their interests. Nonetheless, French absolutist government was not as absolute as the king would have wished. Pockets of stalwart Protestants practiced their religion secretly in the plateau villages of central France, despite Louis XIV's discriminatory measures against them. Peasant disturbances continued. Criticism of court life, wars, and religious policies filled anonymous pamphlets, jurists' notebooks, and courtiers' private journals. Members of the nobility also grumbled about their political misfortunes, but since the king had suppressed the traditional advisory bodies they had dominated, they had no formal way to express their concerns.

England might also have evolved into an absolutist regime, but there were important differences between England and France. Queen Elizabeth (r. 1558–1603) and her successors used many policies similar to those of the French monarchy, such as control of patronage and elaborate court festivities. Above all, the English Parliament remained an important force. Whereas the French kings did not consult the Estates-General to enact taxes, the English monarchs had to convene Parliament to raise money.

Under Elizabeth's successors, fierce quarrels broke out over taxation, religion, and royal efforts to rule without parliamentary consent. Tensions ran high between Puritans (who preferred a simpler form of worship and more egalitarian church government) and Anglicans (who supported the state-sponsored, hierarchically organized Church of England headed by the king). Those tensions erupted in the 1640s into civil war that saw the victory of the largely Puritan parliamentary army and the beheading of the king, Charles I. Although the monarchy was restored a dozen years later, in 1660, the king's relation to Parliament and the relationship between the crown and religion remained undecided (in particular the right of Protestants to assume the throne).

Subsequent monarchs who aspired to absolute rule came into conflict with Parliament, whose members insisted on shared sovereignty and the right of Protestant succession. This dispute culminated in the Glorious Revolution of 1688–1689. In a bloodless upheaval, King James II fled to France and Parliament offered the crown to William of Orange and his wife, Mary (both Protestants). The outcome of the conflict established the principle that English monarchs must rule in conjunction with Parliament. Although the Church of England was reaffirmed as the official state church, Presbyterians and Jews were allowed to practice their religions. Catholic worship, still officially forbidden,

Versailles Louis XIV's Versailles, just southwest of Paris, was a hunting lodge that was converted at colossal cost in the 1670s–1680s into a grand royal chateau with expansive grounds. Much envied and imitated across Europe, the palace became the epicenter of a luxurious court life that included entertainments such as plays and musical offerings, state receptions, royal hunts, boating, and gambling. Thousands of nobles at Versailles vied with each other for closer proximity to the king in the performance of court rituals.

was tolerated as long as the Catholics kept quiet. By 1700, then, England's nobility and merchant classes had a guaranteed say in public affairs and assurance that state activity would privilege the propertied classes as well as the ruler. As a result, English rulers could borrow money much more effectively than their rivals.

Mercantilist Wars The rise of new powers in Europe, especially France and England, intensified rivalries for control of Atlantic trade. As conflicts over colonies and sea-lanes replaced earlier religious and territorial struggles, commercial struggles became worldwide wars. Across the globe, European empires constantly skirmished over control of trade and territory. English and Dutch trading companies took aim at Portuguese outposts in Asia and the Americas, and then at each other. Ports in India suffered repeated assaults and counterassaults. In response, European powers built huge navies to protect their colonies and trade routes and to attack their rivals.

After 1715, a series of wars occurred mainly outside Europe, as empires feuded over colonial possessions. These conflicts were especially bitter in border areas, particularly in the Caribbean and North America. Each round of warfare ratcheted up the scale and cost of fighting.

The **Seven Years' War** (known as the French and Indian War in North America) marked the culmination of this rivalry among European empires around the globe. Fought from 1756 to 1763, it saw Native Americans, African slaves, Bengali princes, Filipino militiamen, and European foot soldiers dragged into a contest over imperial possessions and control of the seas. The battles in Europe were relatively indecisive (despite being large), except in the hinterlands. After all, what sparked the war was a skirmish of British colonial troops (featuring a lieutenant colonel named George Washington) allied with Seneca warriors against French soldiers in the Ohio Valley (see Map 13.2 for North American references). In India, the war had a decisive outcome, for here the East India Company trader Robert Clive rallied 850 European officers and 2,100 Indian recruits to defeat the French (there were but 40 French artillerymen) and their 50,000 Maratha allies at Plassey. The British seized the upper hand—over everyone—in India. Not only did the British drive off the French from the rich Bengali interior, but they also crippled Indian rulers' resistance against European intruders (see Map 12.4 for India references).

The Seven Years' War changed the balance of power around the world. Britain emerged as the foremost colonial empire. Its rivals, especially France and Spain, took a pounding; France lost its North American colonies, and Spain lost Florida (though it gained the Louisiana Territory west of the Mississippi in a secret deal with France). In India, as well, the French were losers and had to acknowledge British supremacy in the wealthy provinces of Bihar and Bengal. But overwhelmingly, the biggest losers were indigenous peoples everywhere. With the rise of one empire over all others, it was harder for Native Americans to play the Europeans off against each other. Maratha princes faced the same problem. Clearly, as worlds became more entangled, the gaps between winners and losers grew more pronounced.

Conclusion

By the 1750s, the world's regions were more economically connected than they had been a century and a half earlier. The process of integrating the resources of previous worlds apart that had begun with Christopher Columbus's voyages intensified during this period. Traders shipped a wider variety of commodities—from Baltic wood to Indian cotton, from New World silver and sugar to Chinese silks and porcelain—over longer distances. People increasingly wore clothes manufactured elsewhere, consumed beverages made from products cultivated in far-off locations, and used imported guns to settle local conflicts.

Everywhere, this integration and the consumer opportunities that it made possible came at a heavy price. Nowhere was it more costly than in the Americas, where colonization and exploitation led to the expulsion of Native Americans from their lands and the decimation of their numbers. The cost was also very high for the millions of Africans forced across the Atlantic to work New World plantations and for the millions more who did not survive the journey.

Silver was the product from the Americas that most transformed global trading networks and that showed how greater entanglements could both enrich and destabilize. Although Spanish colonizers mined New World silver and shipped it to western Europe and Asia, it was Spain's main competitors in Europe that gained the upper hand in the seventeenth and eighteenth centuries. Nearly one-third of the silver from the New World ended up in China as payment for products like porcelains and silks that consumers still regarded as the world's finest manufactures. But if China's economy remained vibrant, silver did play a part in the fall of one dynasty and the rise of another. For the Ottoman and Mughal empires, the influx of silver created rampant inflation and undermined their previous economic autonomy.

Certain societies coped with increased commercial exchange and internal challenges more successfully than others. The Safavid and Ming dynasties could not withstand the pressures; both collapsed. The Spanish, Ottoman, and Mughal dynasties managed to survive but faced increasing pressure from aggressive rivals. For newcomers to the integrating world, the opportunity to trade helped support new dynasties. Japan, Russia, and England emerged on the world stage. But even in these newer regimes, commerce and competition did not erase conflict. To the contrary, while the world was more fully integrated in economic terms than ever before, greater prosperity for some hardly translated into peace for most.

After You Read This Chapter

Go to INQUIZITIVE to see what you've learned—and learn what you've missed—with personalized feedback along the way.

TRACING THE GLOBAL STORYLINES

FOCUS ON: *Regional Impact of World Trade*

THE AMERICAS

- England, France, and Holland join Spain and Portugal as colonial powers in the Americas.
- The English and French colonies in the Caribbean become the world's major exporters of sugar.

AFRICA

- The Atlantic slave trade increases to record proportions, creating gender imbalances, impoverishing some regions, and elevating the power of slave-supplying states.

SOUTHEAST ASIA

- The Dutch East India Company takes over the major islands of Southeast Asia.

THE ISLAMIC WORLD

- World trade destabilizes the Safavid, Ottoman, and Mughal empires.

EAST ASIA

- The Ming dynasty in China loses the mandate of heaven and is replaced by the Qing.
- The Tokugawa shogunate unifies Japan and limits the influence of Europeans in the country.

EUROPE

- Tsarist Russia expands toward the Baltic Sea and the Pacific Ocean and becomes the largest state in the world.
- Europe recovers from the Thirty Years' War (1618–1648), with Holland, England, and France emerging as economic powerhouses.

CHRONOLOGY

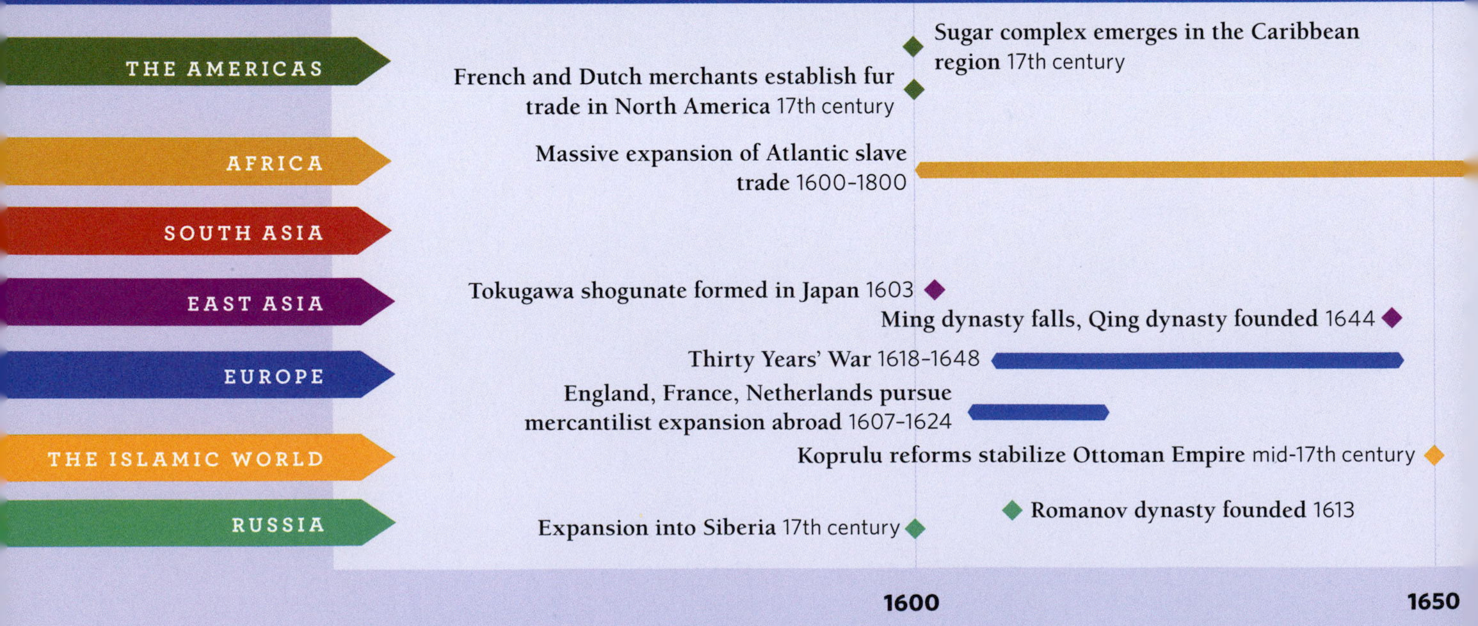

THE AMERICAS
Sugar complex emerges in the Caribbean region 17th century
French and Dutch merchants establish fur trade in North America 17th century
AFRICA
Massive expansion of Atlantic slave trade 1600–1800
SOUTH ASIA
EAST ASIA
Tokugawa shogunate formed in Japan 1603
Ming dynasty falls, Qing dynasty founded 1644
EUROPE
Thirty Years' War 1618–1648
England, France, Netherlands pursue mercantilist expansion abroad 1607–1624
THE ISLAMIC WORLD
Koprulu reforms stabilize Ottoman Empire mid-17th century
RUSSIA
Romanov dynasty founded 1613
Expansion into Siberia 17th century
1600
1650

THINKING ABOUT GLOBAL CONNECTIONS

- ***Thinking about Exchange Networks and World Trade*** How did silver, and then sugar, transform world trade? What political and cultural forces benefited from the development of long-distance trading networks? Which groups suffered and how? Contrast the effects of long distance trade in major world regions.

- ***Thinking about Changing Power Relationships and World Trade*** The seventeenth and eighteenth centuries witnessed the rise of new powers in England, Japan, and Russia, as well as regional powers on the west coast of Africa. Several established empires continued to expand but confronted powerful new challenges to their authority. How did leaders of the Ottoman, Mughal, and Qing empires respond to challenges to their authority? What major challenges did they face? How would you characterize the new powers that emerged around the world in this period?

- ***Thinking about the Impact of World Trade on Gender Relations*** The Atlantic slave trade wreaked havoc on sex ratios both in Africa and in the slave societies of the New World because most slaves taken from Africa were men. How did this affect social life on New World plantations? What strategies did African communities utilize to mitigate the loss of so many men? Elsewhere around the world, increased trade challenged established social hierarchies. How did ruling elites mobilize gender to reinforce their authority?

STUDY QUESTIONS

1. List the commodities that most transformed world trade in the sixteenth and seventeenth centuries, and analyze their significance.
2. Explain how **chartered companies**, the **enclosure** movement, and the **Seven Years' War** influenced European economic growth in this period.
3. How did Asian leaders respond to challenges to their efforts to centralize authority? Analyze the **Tokugawa shogunate**'s treatment of foreign influences and contrast it with the Ottoman rulers' relationship to the **Mamluks** and the **Manchu**'s relationship to the Han Chinese.
4. Explain how the slave trade changed African societies both in social and political terms, and on the coast as opposed to the interior. What roles did European traders and African rulers play?
5. Define **mercantilism**. Whose interests did it serve, both in core regions and their peripheries, at whose expense? Consider both elites and common people in your answer.

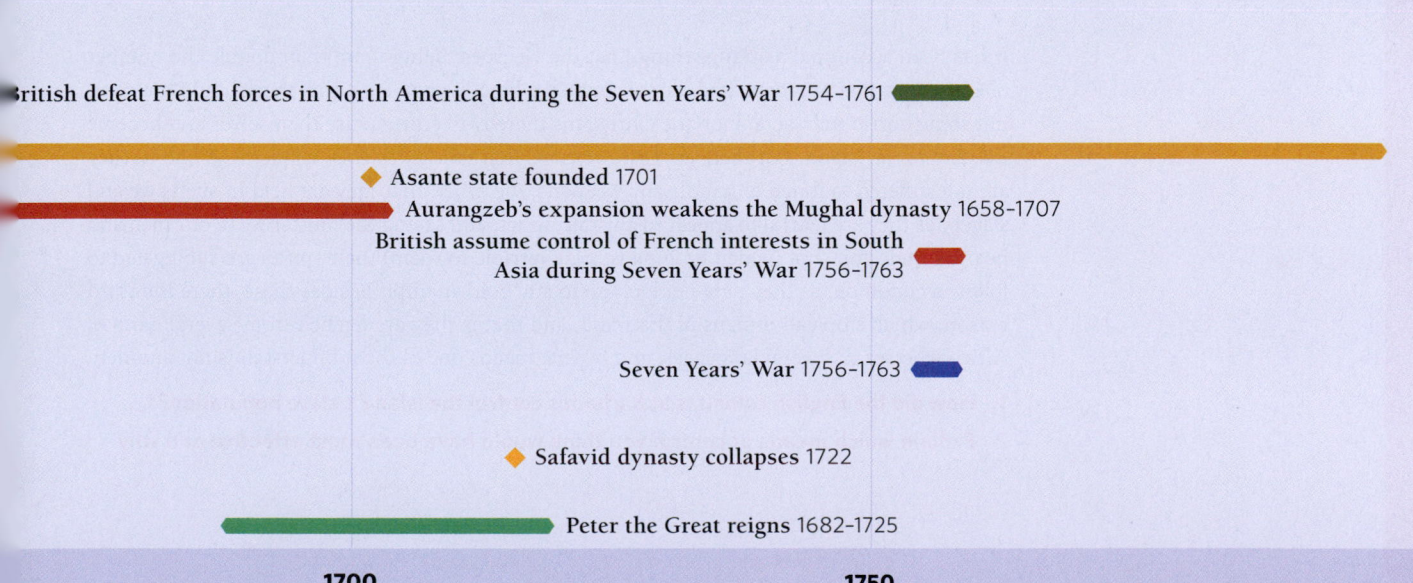

ritish defeat French forces in North America during the Seven Years' War 1754–1761

Asante state founded 1701

Aurangzeb's expansion weakens the Mughal dynasty 1658–1707

British assume control of French interests in South Asia during Seven Years' War 1756–1763

Seven Years' War 1756–1763

Safavid dynasty collapses 1722

Peter the Great reigns 1682–1725

1700 | 1750

Going to the Source

Slavery in the Atlantic World

Slavery in the Atlantic world was nothing new, as the labor regime had existed in many places around the world in earlier centuries. Foreigners or those who were captured in wars frequently found themselves enslaved in many societies. Historians have struggled to figure out what distinguished slavery in the Atlantic world from other systems of slavery in world history. Some suggest that it was the great distance involved, while others have said that it was the development of a system that had little or no possibility for freedom after enslavement. Others have discussed the Atlantic system's brutality.

The documents in this section all deal with aspects of slavery in the Atlantic world, particularly Africa and the Caribbean colonies. They endeavor to link production and consumption, and depict the range of African experiences on both sides of the Atlantic. And they do so across more than a century, which provides ample opportunity to explore changes and continuities over time.

PRIMARY SOURCE 13.1

A True and Exact History of the Island of Barbadoes *(1673)*, *Richard Ligon*

Richard Ligon wrote the most famous history of Barbados, England's first Caribbean colony. In this passage, he considers how a small group of European residents could control the large slave population without the threat of revolt. Books such as Ligon's regularly appeared in the seventeenth and eighteenth centuries, but they were designed for readers in Europe rather than colonists. Historians believe that such books were meant to encourage European migration across the Atlantic, despite the different tropical climate and large black majority populations.

It has been accounted a strange thing, that the Negroes, being more than double the number of Christians that are there, and they accounted a bloody people . . . that they should not commit some horrid massacre upon the Christians thereby to enfranchise themselves and become masters of the island. But there are three reasons that take away this wonder: the one is, they are not suffered to touch or handle any weapons; the other, that they are held in such awe and slavery as they are fearful to appear in any daring act; and seeing the mustering of our men and hearing their gun shot (which nothing is more terrible to them) their spirits are subjugated to follow a condition, as they dare not look up to any bold attempt. Besides these, there is a third reason, which stops all designs of that kind, and that is they are fetched from several parts of Africa who speak several languages, and by that means one of them understands not another.

1. **How did the English colonists at Barbados control the island's slave population?**
2. **Explain which means of control you think would have been most effective and why.**

PRIMARY SOURCE 13.2

Buying Slaves at Whydah *(1694), Thomas Phillips*

Thomas Phillips was captain of a slave ship owned by the Royal African Company. The English crew regularly purchased slaves in Africa, and after transporting them to the Caribbean they sold the survivors to colonists in places like Barbados and Jamaica. In this passage, Phillips describes the process of purchasing slaves from slave traders at Whydah, in present-day Benin, which is located on what Europeans then referred to as the "slave coast."

The best goods to purchase slaves here are cowries [sea snail shells], the smaller the more esteem'd. . . .

The next in demand are brass neptunes or basons [plates], very large, thin, and flat; for after they have brought them they cut them in pieces to make anilias or bracelets, and collars for their arms legs and necks.

The other preferable goods are blue paper sletias, cambricks or lawns, caddy chints, broad ditto [various types of cloth], coral, large, smooth, and of a deep red, rangoes [beads] large and red, iron bars, [gun] powder, and brandy. . . .

[B]ut without the cowries and brass they will take none of the last goods, and but small quantities at best, especially if they can discover that you have good store of cowries and brass aboard, then no other goods will serve their turn, till they have got as much as you have; and after, for the rest of the goods they will be indifferent, and make you come to their own terms, or else lie [offshore] a long time for your slaves, so that those you have on board are dying while you are buying others ashore; therefore every man that comes here, ought to be very cautious in making his report to the king at first, of what sorts and quantities of goods he has, and be sure to say his cargo consists mostly in iron, coral, rangoes, chints, etc. so that he may dispose of those goods as soon as he can, and at last his cowries and brass will bring him slaves as fast as he can buy them. . . .

1. **What types of goods did the English use to purchase slaves from local slave traders?**
2. **In your view, who controlled of the sale of slaves at Whydah? Use evidence to support your answer.**

PRIMARY SOURCE 13.3

Slaves on a Sugar Plantation (mid-eighteenth century)

This image depicts slaves on a Caribbean sugar plantation in the middle of the eighteenth century. Producing sugar cane was an involved process that required grueling labor for much of the year. Refining sugar from the cane after it was cut was also extremely labor intensive and required significant labor on almost every day of the year.

1. **How many different tasks are depicted in this image?**
2. **What does this illustration tell us about sugar production in the Caribbean?**

PRIMARY SOURCE 13.4

The History of Jamaica *(1774), Edward Long*

Edward Long was born and educated in Britain, but he spent time in Jamaica, where he married into a wealthy Jamaican family, became a planter, and joined the island's political establishment. Though he returned to England permanently after only eight years in the colony, he wrote what was considered the best and most accurate history of the island to that time. In this passage, Long explains the reasons for Jamaica's impressive growth between 1670 and 1768.

*

[T]he progressive settlement and opulence of [Jamaica] had kept even pace at least; and, therefore, must be deemed to have influenced the price of necessaries. . . . In 1670 were in this island only seventy sugar-works. In 1739, viz. sixty-nine years, they were increased to four hundred and twenty-nine, or six times the number. In 1768, viz. twenty-nine years, they were increased to six hundred and fifty-one; or above one half more than in 1739, and above nine times more than in 1670. And the stock of [slaves increased] about one third in the twenty-nine years; and to above sixteen times the number computed in 1670. This great progressive augmentation of property and wealth had, doubtless, a correspondent effect upon the trade and commerce of the island, internal and external, and consequently enlarged, to a prodigious degree, all the business of every public office, whether for matters of transfer, sale, debt, law, records, or trade and navigation. From 1728 to 1764 (thirty-six years), the export of sugar was increased three-fourths; and the shipping proportionably. Thus we may reasonably, and upon the most moderate average, say, that property in the island has augmented, since 1711, in the ratio of at least three to one; and that provisions of the island growth have not, on an average, advanced so much as one half their price since 1693. In other words, the business of the public offices has increased, with our augmentation of trade and property, to three times more, and the necessaries of life have not risen to more than one half, what they were.

1. **According to Long, how did the increase in slaves in Jamaica affect the island's sugar industry?**
2. **Why might Edward Long have made the claims that he did about economic growth in Jamaica?**

PRIMARY SOURCE 13.5

The Interesting Narrative of the Life of Olaudah Equiano *(1789), Olaudah Equiano*

Equiano's narrative is perhaps the most famous of the slave narratives that appeared in the late eighteenth and early nineteenth centuries when slavery began to fall out of favor in Europe. Equiano eventually purchased his freedom and became a fierce antislavery advocate. Though he lived in London as a free man, he continued to travel to the Americas, where he encountered African slaves and constantly had to provide proof of his freedom. In this passage he describes his own enslavement and conditions aboard the ship that would carry him to the Americas.

The first object which saluted my eyes when I arrived on the coast was the sea, and a slave ship, which was then riding at anchor, and waiting for its cargo. These filled me with astonishment, which was soon converted into terror when I was carried on board. . . . When I looked round the ship too and saw a large furnace of copper boiling, and a multitude of black people of every description chained together, every one of their countenances expressing dejection and sorrow, I no longer doubted of my fate; and, quite overpowered with horror and anguish, I fell motionless on the deck and fainted. When I recovered a little I found some black people about me, who I believed were some of those who brought me on board, and had been receiving their pay; they talked to me in order to cheer me, but all in vain. I asked them if we were not to be eaten by those white men with horrible looks, red faces, and loose hair. They told me I was not. . . .

In a little time after, amongst the poor chained men, I found some of my own nation, which in a small degree gave ease to my mind. I inquired of these what was to be done with us; they gave me to understand we were to be carried to these white people's country to work for them. I then was a little revived, and thought, if it were no worse than working, my situation was not so desperate: but still I feared I should be put to death, the white people looked and acted, as I thought, in so savage a manner; for I had never seen among any people such instances of brutal cruelty; and this not only shewn towards us blacks, but also to some of the whites themselves. . . .

At last, when the ship we were in had got in all her cargo, they made ready with many fearful noises, and we were all put under deck, so that we could not see how they managed the vessel. But this disappointment was the least of my sorrow. . . . The closeness of the place, and the heat of the climate, added to the number in the ship, which was so crowded that each had scarcely room to turn himself, almost suffocated us. This produced copious perspirations, so that the air soon became unfit for respiration, from a variety of loathsome smells, and brought on a sickness among the slaves, of which many died, thus falling victims to the improvident avarice, as I may call it, of their purchasers. This wretched situation was again aggravated by the galling of the chains, now become insupportable; and the filth of the necessary tubs [latrines], into which the children often fell, and were almost suffocated. The shrieks of the women, and the groans of the dying, rendered the whole a scene of horror almost inconceivable.

1. **How does Equiano describe his experience aboard the slave ship?**
2. **How does Equiano's experience of being transported across the Atlantic compare to the ideas of slavery presented in Primary Sources 13.2, 13.3, and 13.4?**

PRIMARY SOURCE 13.6

A Voyage to Saint Domingue *(1797), Francis Alexander Stanislaus, Baron de Wimpffen*

Baron de Wimpffen, a European aristocrat, reported on his visit to the French colony of Saint-Domingue, the richest colony in the world. He observed the colony in the years just before the slave revolt began. He describes a rigidly organized society with clear racial distinctions that he believes distort European social orders. His observations thus should be seen as connected to more than a century of African slavery that would soon come under attack.

The natural consequence of the order of things which prevails here, is, that all those titles of honour which are elsewhere the *pabula* [source] of emulation, of rivalry and of discord; which inspire so much pride, and create so many claims in some; so much ambition and envy in others; shrink to nothing, and entirely disappear before the sole title of WHITE. It is by your skin, however branded it may be, and not by your parchment [titles of nobility], however worm-eaten, that your pretensions to gentility are assessed. Thus you see that vanity, which on your side of the water torments and turns herself a thousand ways, to impose on the public, and usurp the tribute of respect which it accords to the claims of birth, would here lose both her time and her labor.

Each of the different classes of the inhabitants of St. Domingo has, as you will readily imagine, a turn of thinking, a style of living, more or less approximate or distinct; which, after all, has little resemblance to what you will find elsewhere; because the climate, the regimen, the manners, the wants, the occupations, the degree of reciprocal dependency, establish here connections of the slightest nature; very different from those which, with you, Sir, bind together the members of the same society.

1. **What is Baron de Wimpffen's observation of the French colony of Saint-Domingue?**
2. **What purpose might the Baron's report have served?**

Questions for Analysis

Interpretation

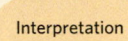

1. Explain the ways in which Africans, both in Africa and in the Americas, understood the trans-Atlantic slave trade.

Continuity and Change over Time

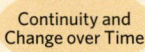

2. Explain the connection between sugar and slavery in the Atlantic world, paying attention to continuity and change over time.

Causation

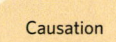

3. What roles did race and ethnicity play in the development of slave societies in the Caribbean islands?

Contextualization

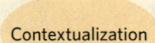

4. Explain the connection between African slavery and European and American freedoms.

Long Essay Question

Synthesis

Based on what you have read in the chapter and the documents above, do you think that slavery was a necessary system of labor for the economic growth of the Atlantic world? Why or why not? Provide evidence to support your answer.

Before You Read This Chapter

GLOBAL STORYLINES

- Growing global commerce enriches rulers and merchants, who express their power through patronage for the arts.
- Distinctive cultures flourish in the major regions of the world, blending new influences with local traditions to varying degrees.
- While the Islamic and Asian worlds confidently retain their own belief systems, the Americas and Oceania increasingly face European cultural pressures.

CORE OBJECTIVES

- **EXPLAIN** the connections between cultural growth and th creation of a global market.
- **DESCRIBE** and **COMPARE** how each culture in this period reflected the ideas of the state in which it was produced.
- **ANALYZE** the different responses to foreign cultures acro Afro-Eurasia in the period from 1500 to 1700.
- **DESCRIBE** how hybrid cultures emerged in the Americas, and **EXPLAIN** the connection between these cultures and Enlightenment ideology.
- **ANALYZE** the role that race and cultural difference playec in the process of global integration.

CHAPTER

14

Cultures of Splendor and Power

1500–1780

KEY TERMS

creoles p. 545
Enlightenment p. 536
Forbidden City of Beijing p. 530
great plaza at Isfahan p. 531
Oceania p. 545
Palace of Versailles p. 530
peninsulares p. 545
philosophes p. 538
scientific method p. 537
Taj Mahal p. 528

In 1664, a sixteen-year-old girl from the provinces of New Spain asked her parents for permission to attend the university in the capital. Although she had mastered Greek logic, taught Latin, and become a proficient mathematician, she had two strikes against her: she was a woman, and her thinking ran against the grain of the Catholic Church. So keen was she to pursue her studies that she proposed to disguise herself as a man. But her parents denied her requests, and instead of attending the university she entered a convent in Mexico City, where she would spend the rest of her life. The convent turned out to be a sanctuary for her. There she studied science and mathematics and composed remarkable poetry. Sor (Sister) Juana Inés de la Cruz was her name, and she spoke for a new world where people mixed in faraway places, where new wealth created new customs, and where new ideas began to take hold.

Sor Juana's story attests to the conflicts between new ideas and old orders that occurred as commerce and the consolidation of empires intensified contact between diverse cultures. On the one hand, global commerce created riches that supported arts, architecture, and scientific ventures. On the other, experiments with new ways caused discomfort among defenders of the old order and provoked backlashes against innovation.

This chapter explores how global commerce enriched and reshaped cultures in the centuries after the Americas ceased to be worlds apart from Afro-Eurasia. As New World commodities invigorated global trade and states consolidated power, rulers and merchants on both sides of the Atlantic displayed their power by commissioning fabulous works of art and majestic palaces and sprawling plazas. These cultural splendors were meant to impress, which they surely did. They also demonstrated the growing connections between distant societies, reflecting how foreign influences could blend with domestic traditions. Book production and consumption soared, with some publications finding their way around the world. The spread of books and ideas and increasing cultural contact led to experiments in religious toleration and helped foster cultural diversity. Yet even as Europeans, who were the greatest beneficiaries of New World riches, claimed to advance new universal truths, cultures around the globe still showed the resilience of inherited traditions.

Trade and Culture

COMPARISON

EXPLAIN the connections between cultural growth and the creation of a global market.

New wealth amassed by global commerce in the aftermath of Columbus's "discovery" created the conditions for cultural dynamism from 1500 to 1800. With newfound wealth, rulers promoted learning and the arts in order to legitimize their power and show their sophistication. In Europe, monarchs known as enlightened absolutists restricted the clergy and nobility and hired loyal bureaucrats who championed the knowledge of the new age. Mughal emperors, Safavid shahs, and Ottoman sultans glorified their regimes by bringing artists and artisans from all over the world to give an Islamic flavor to their major cities and buildings. Rulers in China and Japan also looked to artists to extol their achievements. In Africa, the wealth garnered from slave trading underwrote cultural productions of extraordinary merit.

Some rulers were more eager for change than others. Moreover, certain societies—in the Americas and the South Pacific, for example—found that contact, conquest, and commerce undermined indigenous cultural life. Although Europeans and native peoples often exchanged ideas and practices, these transfers were not equal. Native Americans, for example, adapted to European missionizing by creating mixed forms of religious worship—but only because they were under pressure to do so. And as the Europeans swallowed up new territories, it was *their* culture that spread and diversified. Indeed, the Europeans absorbed much from Native Americans and African slaves but offered them little share of sovereignty or wealth in return.

Despite the unifying aspects of world trade, each society retained core aspects of its individuality. Ruling classes disseminated values based on cherished classical texts and long-established moral and religious principles. They used space in new ways to establish and project their power. They mapped their geographies and wrote their histories according to their traditional visions of the universe.

It is not surprising that in 1500 the world's most dynamic cultures remained in Asia, in areas profiting from the Indian Ocean and China Sea trades. It was in China and the Islamic world that the spice and luxury trades first flourished; here, too, rulers had successfully established political stability and centralized control of taxation, law making, and military force. Although older ways did not die out, both trade and empire building contributed to the spread of knowledge about distant people and foreign cultures.

Culture in the Islamic World

As the Ottoman, Safavid, and Mughal empires gained greater expanses of territory in the sixteenth and seventeenth centuries, they acquired new resources to fund cultural development. Rulers supported new schools and building projects, and the elite produced books, artworks, and luxury goods. Cultural life was connected to the politics of empire building, as emperors and elites sought greater prestige by patronizing intellectuals and artists.

Forged under different empires, Islamic cultural and intellectual life now reflected three distinct worlds. In place of an earlier Islamic cosmopolitanism, unique cultural patterns prevailed within each empire. Although the Ottomans, the Safavids, and the Mughals shared a common faith, each developed a relatively autonomous form of Muslim culture.

COMPARISON

DESCRIBE and **COMPARE** how each Islamic culture in this period reflected the ideas of the state in which it was produced.

THE OTTOMAN CULTURAL SYNTHESIS

By the sixteenth century, the Ottoman Empire enjoyed a remarkably rich culture that reflected a variety of mixing influences. As the Ottoman Empire absorbed more cultures and territories, its blend of ethnic, religious, and linguistic elements exceeded the diversity of previous Islamic empires. It also balanced the interests of military men and administrators with those of clerics. Finally, it allowed autonomy to the minority faiths of Christianity and Judaism. That ability to balance a wide array of local traditions and interests and yet maintain authority in the center, supported by new revenues drawn from global trade, constituted the Ottoman synthesis.

Religion and Education A sophisticated educational system was crucial for the empire's religious and intellectual integration and for its cultural achievements. Here, as in religious affairs, the Ottomans tolerated difference. They encouraged three educational systems that produced three streams of talent—civil and military bureaucrats, *ulama*, and Sufi religious masters. The administrative elite attended hierarchically organized schools that culminated in the palace schools at Topkapi (see Chapter 11). In the religious sphere, an equally elaborate system took students from elementary schools (where they learned reading, writing, and numbers) on to higher schools, or *madrasas* (where they learned law, religion, the Quran, and the natural sciences). These graduates became *ulama* who served as judges, experts in religious law, or teachers. Yet another set of schools, *tekkes*, taught the devotional strategies and religious knowledge for students to enter Sufi orders.

Science and the Arts During this period, the Ottomans integrated some foreign elements into their culture, especially in science and philosophy, while furthering their own traditions in architecture, literature, and music. Most of the foreign influences came from Europe, with which the Ottomans were in constant contact. The Ottomans' most impressive effort to spread European knowledge occurred when a Hungarian convert to Islam, Ibrahim Muteferrika, set up a printing press in Istanbul in 1729. Muteferrika published works on science, history, and geography. One included sections on geometry; others, the works of Copernicus, Galileo, and Descartes; and a plea to the Ottoman elite to learn from Europe. When his patron was killed, however, the *ulama* promptly closed off this avenue of contact with western learning.

The Ottomans and the Tulip From the earliest times, the Ottomans admired the beauty of the tulip. (*Left*) Sultan Mehmed II smelling a tulip, symbol of the Ottoman sultans. (*Right*) The Ottomans used tulip motifs to decorate tiles in homes and mosques and pottery wares, as on the plate shown here.

The Ottomans combined inherited traditions with new elements in art as well. For example, portraiture became popular after the Italian painter Gentile Bellini visited Istanbul and composed a portrait of Mehmed II. In other areas, though, the Ottomans kept their own styles. The magnificent architectural monuments built in the sixteenth through eighteenth centuries, including mosques, gardens, tombs, forts, and palaces, showed scant western influence. Nor were the Ottomans interested in western literature or music. For the most part, they believed that God had given the Islamic world a monopoly on truth and enlightenment and that their military successes proved his favor.

The Ottomans' capacity to celebrate their well-being and prosperity spread from elites to the broader public during the so-called Tulip Period, which occurred in the first half of the eighteenth century. The elite had long admired the tulip's bold colors and graceful blooms, and for centuries the flower served as the sultans' symbol. In fact, both Mehmed the Conqueror and Suleiman the Magnificent grew tulips in the most secluded and prestigious courtyards at Topkapi Palace in Istanbul. And many Ottoman warriors heading into battle wore undergarments embroidered with tulips to ensure victory. By the early eighteenth century, tulip designs appeared on tiles, fabrics, and public buildings, and authorities sponsored elaborate tulip festivals. Indeed, Ottoman enjoyment of luxury goods (including lemons, soap, pepper, metal tools, coffee, and wine) grew so extensive that a well-traveled diplomat looked askance at the supposed wealth of Europe. He wrote, "In most of the provinces [of Europe], poverty is widespread, as a punishment for being infidels. Anyone who travels in these areas must confess that goodness and abundance are reserved for the Ottoman realms." Thus, despite challenges from western Europe and fears that their best days were behind them, the Ottomans' cultural traditions flourished into the eighteenth century and beyond.

SAFAVID CULTURE, SHIITE STATE

If global trade ultimately strengthened Safavid rivals both within the empire and without (see Chapter 13), it also provided the wherewithal for a period of spectacular artistic and architectural creativity, especially at the height of Safavid power in the seventeenth century. The Safavid Empire in Persia (1501–1722) was not as long-lived as the Ottoman Empire, but it was significant for giving the Shiite branch of Islam a home base and a location for displaying Shiite culture. The brilliant culture that emerged during the Safavid period provided a unique blend of Shiism and Persia's distinctive historical identity.

The Safavids created a mixed political and religious system based on Shiism and loyalty to the royal family. The most effective architect of a cultural life based on Shiite religious principles and Persian royal absolutism was Shah Abbas I (r. 1587–1629). The location that he chose to display the wealth and royal power of his state, its Persian and Shiite heritages, and its artistic sensibility was Isfahan, the capital city from its creation in 1598 until the empire's end in 1722.

Architecture and the Arts The Safavid shahs were unique among Afro-Eurasian rulers of this era, for they sought to project both absolute authority and accessibility. Their dwellings were unlike those of other rulers—such as Topkapi Palace in Istanbul, the Citadel in Cairo, and the Red Forts of the Mughals. Those were enclosed and fortified buildings, designed to enhance rulers' power by concealing them from their subjects. In contrast, the buildings of Isfahan were open to the outside, demonstrating the Safavid rulers' desire to connect with their people. Isfahan's centerpiece was the great plaza next to the royal palace and the royal mosque at the heart of the capital.

Other aspects of intellectual life reflected the elites' aspirations, wealth, and commitment to Shiite principles. Safavid artists perfected the illustrated book, the outstanding example being *The King's Book of Kings*, which contained 250 miniature illustrations. Here, artists demonstrated their mastery of three-dimensional representation and their ability to harmonize different colors. Weavers produced ornate silks and carpets for trade throughout the world; artisans painted tiles in vibrant colors and created mosaics that adorned mosques and other buildings. Moreover, the Safavids developed an elaborate calligraphy that was the envy of artists throughout the Islamic world. All of these works celebrated Shiite visions of the sacred while at the same time reinforcing the authority and prestige of the empire's ruling elite.

POWER AND CULTURE UNDER THE MUGHALS

Like the Safavids and the Ottomans, the Mughals fostered a lavish high culture, supported primarily by taxes on agriculture but reliant on silver for its currency and, at its high point, open to global trade. Because the Mughals ruled over a large non-Muslim population, the culture they developed in South Asia was initially broad and open, welcoming non-Muslims into its circle. Thus, while Islamic traditions dominated the empire's political and judicial systems, Hindus shared with Muslims the flourishing of learning, music, painting, and architecture, especially from the middle of the sixteenth century to the middle of the seventeenth.

Religion, Architecture, and the Arts In the sixteenth and early seventeenth centuries, Mughal culture mixed diverse elements from within South Asia and the broader Islamic world. The promise of an open Islamic high culture found its greatest fulfillment under the

Akbar Leading Religious Discussion This miniature painting from 1604 shows Akbar receiving Muslim theologians and Jesuits. The Jesuits (in the black robes on the left) hold a page relating, in Persian, the birth of Christ. A lively debate will follow the Jesuits' claims on behalf of Christianity.

Mughal emperor Akbar (r. 1556–1605). This skillful military leader was also a popular ruler who allowed common people as well as nobles from all ethnic groups to converse with him at court. His quest for universal truths outside the strict *sharia* led him to develop a religion of his own, which incorporated many aspects of Hindu belief and ritual practice (see Chapter 12).

In architecture, too, the Mughals produced masterpieces that blended styles. This was already evident as builders combined Persian, Indian, and Ottoman elements in tombs and mosques built by Akbar's predecessors. But Akbar enhanced this mixture in the elaborate city he built at Fatehpur Sikri, beginning in 1571. The buildings included residences for nobles (whose loyalty Akbar wanted), gardens, a drinking and gambling zone, and even an experimental school devoted to studying language acquisition in children.

Akbar's descendant Shah Jahan was also a lavish patron of architecture and the arts. In 1630, Shah Jahan ordered the building in Agra of a magnificent white marble tomb for his beloved wife, Mumtaz Mahal. Like many other women in the Mughal court, she had been an important political counselor. Designed by an Indian architect of Persian origin, this structure, the **Taj Mahal**, took twenty years and 20,000 workers to build. The forty-two-acre complex included a main gateway, a garden, minarets, and a mosque. The translucent marble mausoleum lay squarely in the middle of the structure, enclosed by four identical facades and crowned by a majestic central dome rising to 240 feet. The stone inlays of different types and hues, organized in geometrical and floral patterns, and featuring Quranic verses inscribed in Arabic calligraphy, gave the surface an appearance of delicacy and lightness. Blending Persian and Islamic design with Indian materials and motifs, this poetry in stone represented the most splendid example of Mughal high culture and the combining of cultural traditions.

Foreign Influences versus Islamic Culture Although later emperors were less tolerant than Akbar, Mughal culture remained vibrant. Well into the eighteenth century, the Mughal nobility lived in unrivaled luxury. The presence of foreign scholars and artists enhanced the courtly culture, and the elite eagerly consumed exotic goods from China and Europe. Foreign trade also brought in more silver, advancing the money economy and supporting the nobles' sumptuous lifestyles. In addition, the Mughals assimilated European military technology: they hired Europeans as gunners and military engineers in their armies, employed them to forge guns, and bought guns and cannons from them.

For all their openness to outside influences, the Mughals, like the Ottomans, remained supremely confident of their own traditions. The centers of the Islamic world were still Istanbul, Cairo, and Delhi. Even while incorporating a few new European elements into their cultural mix, most Muslims regarded Europeans as rude barbarians. Elites in Persia, India, and the Ottoman Empire looked to China and the east, not to Europe and the west, for inspiration.

Culture and Politics in East Asia

In East Asia, prosperity, facilitated by China's vast importation of silver from Japan and the Americas, promoted cultural dynamism in the sixteenth through eighteenth centuries. Still, it was China's booming internal market, more than global trade, that fueled a Chinese culture inspired mainly by its own traditions. China had long been a renowned center of learning, with its emperors and elites supporting artists, poets, musicians, scientists, and teachers. But in late Ming and early Qing China, a growing population and extensive commercial networks propelled the circulation of ideas as well as goods.

In Japan, too, economic growth supported elite and popular culture. Because of its giant neighbor across the sea, the Japanese people had always been aware of outside influences. Like the Chinese government, the Tokugawa shogunate tried to promote Confucian notions of a social hierarchy organized on the basis of social position, age, gender, and kin. It also tried to shield the country from egalitarian ideas that would threaten the strict social hierarchy. But the forces that undermined governmental control of knowledge in China proved even stronger in Japan.

COMPARISON

ANALYZE the different responses to foreign cultures across Afro-Eurasia in the period from 1500–1700.

CHINA: THE CHALLENGE OF EXPANSION AND DIVERSITY

While China had become increasingly connected with the outside world in the sixteenth and seventeenth centuries, the sources for its cultural flourishing during the period came primarily from within. The circulation of books spread ideas among the literate, and religious rituals instilled cultural values among the broader population. Advances in cartography reflected the distinctive worldview of Chinese elites.

Publishing and the Transmission of Ideas The decentralization of book production and the domestic market helped circulate ideas within China. Woodblock and moveable type printing had been present in China for centuries. Although initially the state had spurred book production by printing Confucian texts, before long the economy's increasing commercialization weakened government controls over what got printed. Even as officials clamped down on unorthodox texts, there was no centralized system of censorship, and unauthorized opinions circulated freely.

By the late Ming era, a burgeoning publishing sector catered to the diverse social, cultural, and religious needs of educated elites and urban populations. European visitors admired the vast collections of printed materials housed in Chinese libraries, describing them as "magnificently built" and "finely adorn'd." Perhaps more important, books and other luxury goods were now more affordable. Increasingly, publishers offered a mix of wares: guidebooks for patrons of the arts, travelers, or merchants; handbooks for performing rituals, choosing dates for ceremonies, or writing proper letters; almanacs and encyclopedias; morality books; medical manuals; and, above all, study guides.

Study aids for the civil service examination dominated the literary marketplace. In 1595, Beijing reeled with scandal over news that the second-place graduate had reproduced verbatim several model essays published by commercial printers. Ironically, then, the increased circulation of knowledge led critics to bemoan a decline in real learning; instead of mastering the classics, they charged, examination candidates were simply memorizing the work of others.

Elite women also joined China's literary culture. Anthologies of women's poetry were especially popular, not only in the market but when issued in limited circulation to

Current Trends in World History

The Political Uses of Space

The use of space for political purposes is a theme we can trace across world history. In the early modern period, many kings and emperors opted to build grand palaces to create lavish power centers, from which they could project their influence over their kingdoms; petitioners and potential rivals would have to come to *them* to ask for favors or to complete their business. Monarchs sculpted these environments, creating a series of spaces, each of them open to a smaller and smaller number of the king's favorites. Both palaces and their surrounding grounds were ornate and splendid, were expensive to construct, and involved the best craftsmen and artists available, which often meant borrowing ideas and designs from neighboring cultures. Palace complexes of this type, built in Beijing, in Istanbul, in Isfahan, and just outside of Paris, used space to project the rulers' power and to show who was boss.

The **Forbidden City of Beijing** was the earliest of these impressive sites of royal power (see illustration on p. 425). Its construction took about four years—from 1416 to 1420—although the actual name "Forbidden City" did not appear until 1576. The entrance of the City was straddled by the Meridian Gate, the tallest structure of the entire complex, which towered over all other buildings at more than thirty-five meters above the ground. It was from this lofty position that the emperor extended his gaze toward his empire, as he oversaw various court ceremonies, including the important annual proclamation of the calendar that governed the entire country's agricultural and ritual activities. Foreign emissaries received by the court were also often allowed to use one of the passageways through the gate, where they were expected to be duly awed. As for the officials' daily audience with the emperor, they had to line up outside the Meridian Gate around three a.m. before proceeding to the Hall of Supreme Harmony. It was typical of the entire construction project that this impressive hall with vermilion walls and golden tiles was built at considerable cost. For the columns of the hall, fragrant hardwood had to be found in the tiger-ridden forests of the remote southwest, while the mountain forests of the south and southwest were searched for other timbers that eventually made their way to the capital through the Grand Canal.

The Topkapi Palace in Istanbul, capital of the Ottoman Empire, began to take shape in 1458 under Mehmed II and underwent steady expansion over the years (see illustration on p. 415. Topkapi projected royal authority in much the same way as the Forbidden City emphasized Chinese emperors' power: governing officials worked enclosed within massive walls, and monarchs rarely went outside their inner domain.

More than two centuries later, in the 1670s and 1680s, the French monarch Louis XIV built the **Palace of Versailles** on the site of a royal hunting lodge eleven miles from Paris, the French capital (see illustration on p. 511). This enormously costly complex was built to house Louis's leading clergymen and nobles, who were obliged to visit at least twice a year. Louis hoped that by taking wealthy and powerful men and women away from their local power bases, and by diverting them with entertainments, he could keep them from plotting new forms of religious schism or challenging his right to rule. Going to Versailles also allowed him to escape the pressures and demands of the population of Paris. Many European monarchs—including Russia's Peter the Great—would build palace complexes modeled on Versailles.

If in China, the Ottoman Empire, and France, emperors built what were essentially private spaces in which to conduct and dominate state business, Shah Abbas (r. 1587–1629) of the Safavid Empire chose to create a great new public space instead. In the early seventeenth century,

celebrate the refinement of the writer's family. Men of letters soon recognized the market potential of women's writings; some also saw women's less regularized style (usually acquired through family channels rather than state-sponsored schools) as a means to challenge stifling stylistic conformity. On rare occasions, women even served as publishers themselves.

Although elite women enjoyed success in the world of culture, the period brought increasing restrictions on their lives. The practice of footbinding (which elite women first adopted at least as far back as the twelfth century) continued to spread among common people, as small, delicate feet came to signify femininity and respectability. The thriving

Shah Abbas oversaw the construction of the **great plaza at Isfahan**, a structure that reflected his desire to bring trade, government, and religion together under the authority of the supreme political leader. An enormous public mosque, the Shah Abbas Mosque, dominated one end of the plaza, which measured 1,667 feet by 517 feet. At the other end were trading stalls and markets. Along one side sat government offices; the other side offered the exquisite Mosque of Shaykh Lutfollah. If the other rulers of this era devoted their (considerable) income to creating rich *private* spaces, Shah Abbas used the vast open space of the plaza to open up his city to all comers, keeping only the Mosque of Shaykh Lutfollah for his personal use.

The royal use of space says a great deal about how monarchs in this era wished to be seen and remembered, and about how they wanted to rule. While some wanted to retreat from the rest of society, Shah Abbas wanted to create an open space for trade and the exchanging of ideas. World history is full of palaces and plazas (the Piazza San Marco in Venice might be compared to the royal plaza at Isfahan); we can still visit and admire them. But when we do, we should also remember that space, and the architecture that either opens up to the public or sets aside privileged spaces, has always had political as well as cultural functions.

Isfahan On the great plaza at Isfahan, markets and government offices operated in close proximity to the public Shah Abbas Mosque, shown here, and the shah's private mosque. This structure represented Shah Abbas's desire to unite control of trade, government, and religion under one leader.

QUESTIONS FOR ANALYSIS

- Choose one of the places discussed in this feature. Explain how the architectural layout shaped the political power exercised by that space.
- Contrast private spaces, like the palace at Versailles, with public spaces, like the great plaza at Isfahan. What political goals could be accomplished by each?

Explore Further

Babaie, Sussan, *Isfahan and Its Palaces: Statecraft, Shi'ism and the Architecture of Conviviality in Early Modern Iran* (2008).

Necipoğlu, Gülru, *Architecture, Ceremonial, and Power: The Topkapi Palace in the Fifteenth and Sixteenth Centuries* (1991).

publishing sector indirectly promoted stricter morality by printing plays and novels that echoed the government's conservative attitudes.

Popular Culture and Religion Important as the book trade was, it had only an indirect impact on most men and women in late Ming China. Those who could not read well or at all absorbed cultural values through oral communication, ritual performance, and daily practices.

Villagers participated in various religious and cultural practices, such as honoring local guardian spirits, patronizing Buddhist and Daoist temples, or watching performances

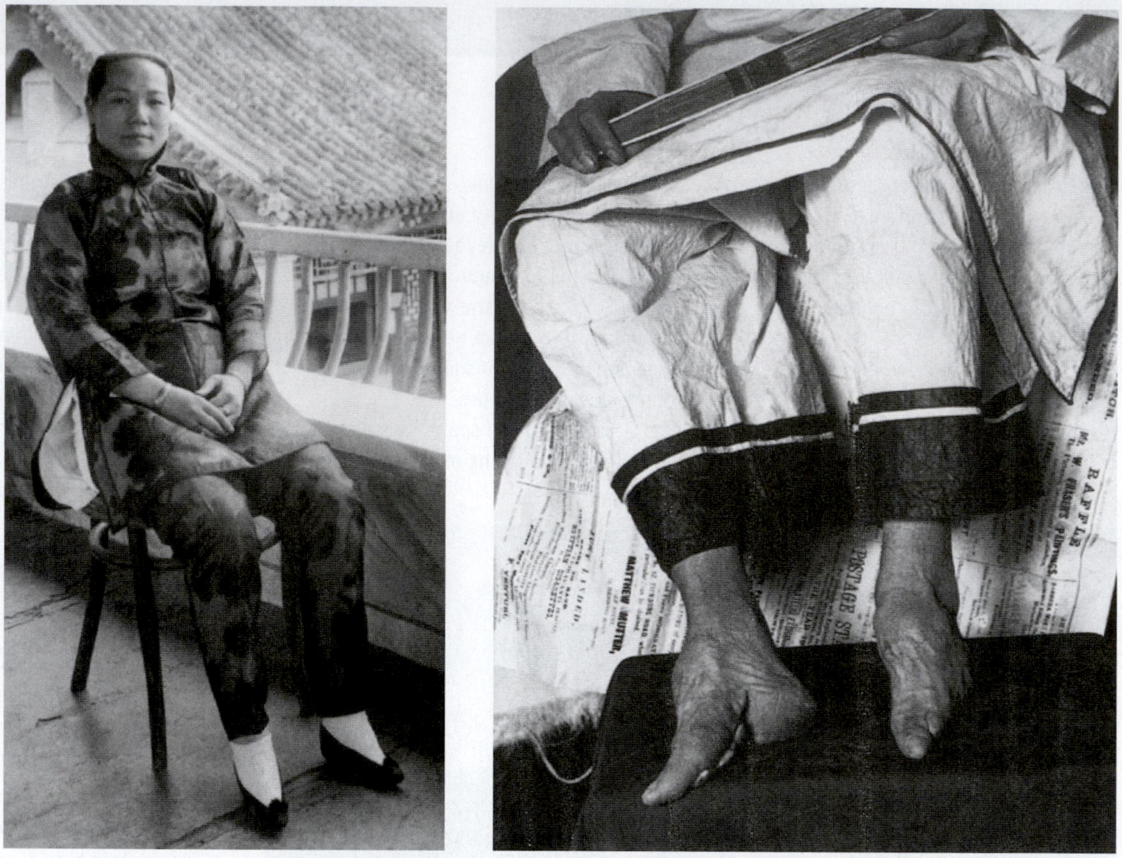

Footbinding Two images of bound feet: (*left*) as an emblem of feminine respectability when wrapped and concealed, as on this well-to-do Chinese woman; (*right*) as an object of curiosity and condemnation when exposed for the world to see.

by touring theater groups. At the grassroots level, there was little distinction among Buddhist, Daoist, and local cults. The Chinese believed in cosmic unity, and although they celebrated spiritual forces, they did not consider any of them to be a Supreme Being who favored one sect over another. They believed it was the emperor, rather than any religious group, who held the mandate of heaven. (See **Current Trends in World History: The Political Uses of Space**.) Unless sects posed an obvious threat, the emperor had no reason to regulate their spiritual practices. This situation promoted religious tolerance and avoided the sectarian warfare that plagued post-Reformation Europe.

Technology and Cartography Belief in cosmic unity did not prevent the Chinese from devising technologies to master nature's operations in this world. For example, the magnetic compass, gunpowder, and the printing press were all Chinese inventions. Chinese astronomers also compiled accurate records of eclipses, comets, novas, and meteors. In part, the emperor's needs drove their interest in astronomy and calendrical science. It was the emperor's job as the Son of Heaven, and thus mediator between heaven and earth, to determine the best dates for planting, holding festivities, scheduling mourning periods, and convening judicial court sessions.

Convinced that their sciences were superior, Christian missionaries in China tried to promote their own knowledge in areas such as astronomy and cartography (mapmaking).

In 1583, the Jesuit missionary Matteo Ricci brought European maps to China, hoping to impress the elite with European learning. Challenging their belief that the world was flat, his maps demonstrated that the earth was spherical—and that China was just one country among many others. Chinese critics complained that Ricci treated the Ming Empire as "a small unimportant country." As a concession, he placed China closer to the center of the maps and provided additional textual information. Still, his maps had a negligible impact, as neither the earth's shape nor precise scale was particularly important to most Chinese geographers.

Before the nineteenth century, the Chinese had fairly incomplete knowledge about foreign lands despite a long history of contact. Chinese writers, for example, often identified groups of other people through distinctive and, to them, odd physical features. A Ming geographical publication portrayed the Portuguese as "seven feet tall, having eyes like a cat, a mouth like an oriole, an ash-white face, thick and curly beards like black gauze, and almost red hair." Chinese elites glorified their "white" complexions against the peasants' dark skin; against the black, wavy-haired "devils" of Southeast Asia; and against the Europeans' "ash-white" pallor. Qing authors in the eighteenth century confused France with the Portugal known during Ming times, and they characterized England and Sweden as dependencies of Holland. During this period of cultural flourishing, in short, most Chinese did not feel compelled to revise their view of the world.

CULTURAL IDENTITY AND TOKUGAWA JAPAN

The culture that developed in Japan in this period drew on local traditions and, increasingly, foreign influences from China and Europe. Chinese cultural influence had long crossed the Sea of Japan, but under the Tokugawa shogunate there was also interest in European culture. This interest grew via the Dutch presence in Japan and limited contacts with Russians. At the same time, there was a surge in the study of Japanese traditions and culture. Thus, Tokugawa Japan engaged in a three-cornered conversation among time-honored Chinese ways, European teachings, and distinctly Japanese traditions.

Native Arts and Popular Culture Elite and popular culture featured elements that were distinctly Japanese. Until the seventeenth century, the main patrons of Japanese culture were the imperial court in Kyoto, the hereditary shogunate, religious institutions, and a small upper class. These groups developed an elite culture of theater and stylized painting. Samurai (former warriors turned bureaucrats) and daimyo (regional lords) favored a masked theater, called Nō, and an elegant ritual for making tea and engaging in contemplation.

Alongside the elite culture arose a rougher urban one that artisans and merchants patronized. Urban dwellers could purchase works of fiction and colorful prints made from carved wood blocks, and they could enjoy the company of female entertainers known as geisha. These women were skilled (*gei*) in playing the three-stringed instrument (*shamisen*), storytelling, and performing; some were also prostitutes. Geisha worked in the cities' pleasure quarters, which were famous for their geisha houses, public baths, brothels, and theaters. Kabuki—a type of theater that combined song, dance, and skillful staging to dramatize conflicts between duty and passion—became wildly popular. This art form featured dazzling acting, brilliant makeup, and sumptuous costumes.

Much popular entertainment chronicled the world of the common people rather than politics or high society. The urbanites' pleasure-oriented culture was known as "the floating world" (*ukiyo*), and the woodblock prints depicting it as *ukiyo-e* (*e* meaning

Artist and Geisha at Tea The erotic, luxuriant atmosphere of Japan's urban pleasure quarters was captured in a new art form, the *ukiyo-e*, or "pictures from a floating world." In this image set in Tokyo's celebrated Yoshiwara district, several geisha flutter about a male artist.

"picture"). Here, the social order was temporarily turned upside down. Those who were usually considered inferior—actors, musicians, courtesans, and others seen as possessing low morals—became idols.

Literacy in Japan now surged, especially among men. The most popular novels sold 10,000 to 12,000 copies. In the late eighteenth century, Edo had some sixty booksellers and hundreds of book lenders. In fact, the presence of so many lenders allowed books to spread to a wider public that previously could not afford to buy them. By the late eighteenth century, as more books circulated and some of them criticized the government, officials tried to censor certain publications. The government's response testified to the uncommon power wielded by people of modest means and the relative significance of popular culture in Japan.

Religion and Chinese Influence In the realm of higher culture and religion, China loomed large in the Tokugawa world. Japanese scholars wrote imperial histories of Japan in the Chinese style, and Chinese law codes and other books attracted a significant readership. Some Japanese traveled south to Nagasaki to meet Zen Buddhist masters and Chinese residents there. Buddhism originally came to Japan from China and remained associated with Chinese monks. A few of those monks even won permission to found monasteries outside Nagasaki and to give lectures and construct temples in Kyoto and Edo.

Although Buddhist temples grew in number, they did not displace the native Japanese practice of venerating ancestors and worshipping gods in nature. Later called Shintō ("the way of the gods"), this practice boasted a network of shrines throughout the country. Shintō developed from time-honored beliefs in spirits, or *kami*, who were associated with places (mountains, rivers, waterfalls, rocks, the moon) and activities (harvest, fertility). Seeking healing or other assistance, adherents appealed to these spirits in nature and daily life through incantations and offerings. Some women under Shintō served as *mikos*, a kind of shaman with special divinatory powers.

Reacting to the influence of Chinese Buddhism and desiring to honor their own country's greatness, some thinkers promoted intellectual traditions from Japan's past. These efforts stressed "native learning," Japanese texts, and Japanese uniqueness. In so doing, they formalized a Japanese religious and cultural tradition, and they denounced Buddhism as a foreign contaminant.

European Influences Not only did Chinese intellectual influences compete with revived native learning, but by the late seventeenth century Japan was also tapping other sources of knowledge. By 1670 a guild of Japanese interpreters in Nagasaki who could speak and read Dutch accompanied Dutch merchants on trips to Edo. As European knowledge spread to high circles in Edo, in 1720 the shogunate lifted its ban on foreign books. Thereafter European ideas, called "Dutch learning," circulated more openly.

Scientific, geographical, and medical texts appeared in Japanese translations and in some cases displaced Chinese texts. A Japanese-Dutch dictionary appeared in 1745, and the first official school of Dutch learning followed. Students of Dutch and other European teachings remained a limited segment of Japanese society, but the demand for translations intensified.

Japan's internal debates about what to borrow from the Europeans and the Chinese illustrate the changes that the world had undergone in recent centuries. A few hundred years earlier, products and ideas generally did not travel beyond coastal regions and had only a limited effect (especially inland) on local cultural practices. By the eighteenth century, though, expanded networks of exchange and new prosperity made the integration of foreign ideas feasible and, sometimes, desirable. The Japanese did not consider the embracing of outside influences as a mark of inferiority or subordination, particularly when they could put those influences to good use. This was not the case for the cultures that thrived within the great Asian land-based empires, which were eager lenders but hesitant borrowers.

African Cultural Flourishing

The wealth that spurred artistic achievement and displays of power in Asia and the Islamic world did not bypass African states. Proceeds from the slave trade enabled African upper classes to fund cultural activities and invigorate strong artisanal and artistic traditions that dated back many centuries. African artisans, like those in East Asia, maintained local forms of cultural production, such as woodcarving, weaving, and metalworking.

COMPARISON

DESCRIBE and **COMPARE** how Chinese, African, and Japanese cultures in this period reflected the ideas of the state in which it was produced.

Cultural traditions in Africa varied from kingdom to kingdom, but there were patterns among them. For example, all West African elites encouraged craftsmen to produce carvings, statues, masks, and other objects that would glorify the power and achievements of rulers. (Royal patrons in Europe, Asia, and the Islamic world did the same with architecture and painting.) There was also a widespread belief that rulers and their families had the blessing of the gods. Arts and crafts not only celebrated royal power but also captured the energy of a universe that people believed was suffused with spiritual beings. Starting in the 1500s and continuing through the eighteenth century when the slave trade reached its peak, African rulers who benefited from that trade had even more reason—and means—to support cultural pursuits.

THE ASANTE, OYO, AND BENIN CULTURAL TRADITIONS

The kingdom of Asante led the way in cultural attainments, and the Oyo Empire and Benin also promoted rich artistic traditions.

The Asante kingdom's access to gold and the revenues that it derived from selling captives made it the richest state in West Africa, perhaps even in the whole of sub-Saharan Africa. The citizens of Asante accorded the highest respect to entrepreneurs who made money and were able to surround themselves with retainers and slaves. The adages of the age were inevitably about becoming rich: "money is king" or "nothing is as important as money" or "money is what it is all about."

Asante's artisans celebrated these traditions through the crafting of magnificent seats or stools coated with gold as symbols of authority; the most ornate were reserved for the head of the Asante federation, the Asantehene, who ruled this far-flung empire

Brass Oba Head The brass head of an Oba, or king, of Benin. The kingdom's brass and bronze work was among the finest in all of Africa.

from the capital city of Kumasi. By the eighteenth century, these monarchs ventured out from the secluded royal palace only on ceremonial and feast days, when they wore sumptuous silk garments featuring many dazzling colors and geometric patterns all joined together in interwoven strips. Known as Kente cloth, this fabric could be worn only by the rulers. Kings also had a golden elephant tail, which was carried in front of them. It symbolized the highest level of wealth and power. Also held aloft on these celebratory occasions were maces, spears, staffs, and other symbols of power fashioned from the kingdom's abundant gold supplies. These reminded the common people of the Asantehene's connection to the gods.

Equally resplendent were rulers of the Oyo Empire and Benin, located in the territory that now constitutes Nigeria. Elegant, refined metalwork in the form of West African bronzes reflects these rulers' power and their peoples' high esteem. In the Oyo Empire, the Yoruba people drew on craft and artistic traditions dating back to the first millennium CE. The bronze heads of Ife, capital city of the Yoruba Oyo Empire, are among the world's most sophisticated pieces of art. According to one commentator, "little that Italy or Greece or Egypt ever produced could be finer, and the appeal of their beauty is immediate and universal." Artisans fashioned the best known of these works in the thirteenth century (before the slave-trade era), but the tradition continued and became more elaborate in the seventeenth and eighteenth centuries.

Stunning bronzes were produced in Benin as well. Although historical records have portrayed Benin as one of Africa's most brutal slave-trading regimes, it produced art of the highest order. Whether Benin's reputation for brutality was deserved or simply part of Europeans' desire to label African rulers as "savage" in order to justify their intervention in African affairs, it cannot detract from the splendor of its artisans' creations.

Although supported by funds from the Atlantic slave trade, the cultural traditions of western Africa remained little influenced by intellectual and artistic influences from the wider world. African culture during this period was relatively autonomous, even as Africa became increasingly entangled in the global webs of economic exchange and political domination.

The Enlightenment in Europe

An extraordinary cultural flowering also blossomed in Europe during the seventeenth and eighteenth centuries, driven by trade and internal commerce. Often the **Enlightenment** is defined purely in intellectual terms as the spreading of faith in reason and in universal rights and laws, but this era encompassed broader developments, such as the expansion of literacy, the spread of critical thinking, and the decline of religious persecution. Contact between Europe and the wider world after the fifteenth century played a formative role in Europeans' view of the world and their place in it. They quickly became eager consumers of other people's goods and practices. From Amerindian trapping methods to African slaves' cultivation techniques, from Chinese porcelain to New World tobacco and chocolate, contact with others influenced Europe in the seventeenth and eighteenth centuries. The more they learned, the more European intellectuals became convinced not only that their culture was superior—for that was hardly rare—but that they had discovered a set of universal laws that applied to everyone, everywhere around the world.

Abandoning the Christian belief in divine intervention, Enlightenment thinkers sought universal, objective knowledge that did not reflect any particular religion, political view, class, gender, or culture. These scholars struggled to formulate universal, natural laws, although most of these thinkers were unaware of how culture-bound their vision was. They ignored the extent to which European, upper-class male perspectives colored their "objective" knowledge.

THE NEW SCIENCE

Interest in scientific discoveries increased gradually over the seventeenth and eighteenth centuries. While the sixteenth century had brought new prosperity, the seventeenth century produced civil and religious wars, dynastic conflicts, and famines that devastated central Europe. These events bankrupted the Spanish, caused chaos in France, led to the execution of the English king, and saw the Dutch break free from Spanish control. They also contributed to the spread of Protestantism in Europe. At the same time, the crises made some intellectuals wish to turn their backs on religious strife and develop useful ways for understanding and improving *this* world—by imposing order on the chaos and instability they saw around them. By 1750, in some western countries, a significant minority of the population was eager to join in these discussions, which concentrated on the natural sciences, especially physics and astronomy.

The search for new, testable knowledge began centuries before the Enlightenment, in the efforts of Nicolaus Copernicus (1473–1542) and Galileo Galilei (1564–1642) to understand the behavior of the heavens. These men were both astronomers and mathematicians. Making their own mathematical calculations and observations of the stars and planets, they came to conclusions that contradicted age-old assumptions. This entailed considerable risk: when Galileo confirmed Copernicus's claims that the earth revolved around the sun, he was tried for heresy.

In the seventeenth century, a small but influential group of scholars committed themselves, similarly, to experimentation, calculation, and observation. They adopted a method for "scientific" inquiry laid out by the philosopher Sir Francis Bacon (1561–1626), who claimed that real science entailed the formulation of hypotheses that could be tested in carefully controlled experiments. Bacon was chiefly wary of classical and medieval authorities, but his principle also applied to traditional knowledge that European scientists were encountering in the rest of the world. Confident of their calculations performed according to the new **scientific method**, scientists like Isaac Newton (1642–1727) sought universal laws that applied to all matter and motion; they criticized older conceptions of nature (from Aristotelian ideas to folkloric and foreign ones) as absurd and obsolete. Thus, in his *Principia Mathematica* Newton set forth the laws of motion—including the famous law of gravitation, which simultaneously explained falling bodies on earth and planetary motion.

Most historians no longer call these changes a scientific revolution, for European thinking did not change overnight. Only gradually did thinkers come to see the natural world as operating according to inviolable laws that experimenters could figure out, like gravity and inertia. But by the late seventeenth century many rulers had developed a new interest in science, and they established royal academies to encourage research. This patronage, of course, had a political function. By incorporating the British Royal Society in 1662, for example, Charles II hoped to show not only that the crown backed scientific progress but also that England's great minds backed the crown. Similar reasoning lay behind Louis XIV's founding of the French Royal Academy of Sciences.

Gradually, the new science expanded beyond the court to gain popularity among elite circles. Marquise de Chatelet-Lomont built a scientific laboratory in her home and translated Newton's *Principia* into French, which her lover, Voltaire, one of the most influential of the Enlightenment figures, popularized. By about 1750, even artisans and journalists were applying Newtonian mechanics to their practical problems and inventions. In Italy, numerous female natural philosophers emerged, and the genre of scientific literature for "ladies" took hold. A consensus emerged among proponents of the new science that useful knowledge came from collecting data and organizing them into universally valid systems, rather than from studying revered classical texts.

By no means, however, did the scientific worldview dominate European thinking. Most people still understood their relationships with God, nature, and fellow humans via Christian doctrines and local customs. Although literacy was increasing, it was far from universal; schools remained church-governed or elite, male institutions. All governments employed censors and punished radical thinkers, peasants still suffered under arbitrary systems of taxation, and judicial regimes were as harsh as during medieval times. Nonetheless, the promise of universal scientific truths inspired Enlightenment thinkers, who in turn held them out as an ideal.

ENLIGHTENMENT THINKERS

Enlightenment thinkers, called ***philosophes*** in France, applied scientific reasoning to human interaction, to society as opposed to nature. Such thinkers included the French writers Voltaire (1694–1778) and Denis Diderot (1713–1784) and the Scottish moral philosopher and political economist Adam Smith (1723–1790). These writers also called attention to the evils and flaws of human society: Voltaire criticized the torture of criminals, Diderot denounced the despotic tendencies of the French kings Louis XIV and Louis XV, and Smith exposed the inefficiencies of mercantilism. Other Enlightenment thinkers, similarly, criticized contemporary European conditions, and they often suffered imprisonment or exile for writing about what they considered to be superstitious beliefs and corrupt political structures.

The Enlightenment touched all of Europe, but the extent of its reach varied. In France and Britain, enlightened learning spread widely; in Spain, Poland, and Scandinavia, enlightened circles were small and had little influence on rulers or the general population. Enlightened thought flourished in commercial centers like Amsterdam and Edinburgh and in colonial ports like Philadelphia and Boston. (See **Analyzing Global Developments: How Can We Measure the Impact of an Idea?**)

Popular Culture In the emerging marketplace for new books and new ideas, some of the most popular works were not from high intellectuals. Pamphlets charging widespread corruption, fraudulent stock speculation, and insider trading circulated widely. Sex, too, sold well. Works like *Venus in the Cloister, or the Nun in a Nightgown* racked up as many sales as the now-classic works of the Enlightenment. Bawdy and irreligious, these vulgar best-sellers exploited consumer demand—but they also seized the opportunity to mock authority figures, such as nuns and priests. Some even dared to go after the royal family, portraying Marie Antoinette as having sex with her court confessor. Such works displayed the seamier side of the Enlightenment, but they also revealed a willingness on the part of high- and low-brow intellectuals alike to challenge established beliefs and institutions and to undermine royal authority.

The reading public itself helped generate new cultural institutions and practices. In Britain and Germany, book clubs and coffeehouses sprang up to cater to sober men of business and learning; here, aristocrats and well-to-do commoners could read news sheets or discuss stock prices, political affairs, and technological novelties. The same sort of noncourtly socializing occurred in Parisian salons, where aristocratic women presided. The number of female readers, and writers, soared, and the relatively new genre of the novel, as well as specialized women's journals, appealed especially to them. A public sphere emerged that was radically democratic and beyond the control of kings or any corporate body: all it took to participate was the ability to read and the willingness to debate the issues of the day.

Challenges to Authority and Tradition Even though they took the aristocracy's money, many Enlightenment thinkers tried to overturn the status distinctions that characterized European society. They emphasized merit rather than birth as the basis for status. In his *Treatise on Human Understanding* (1690), John Locke claimed that man was born with a mind that was a clean slate (*tabula rasa*) and acquired all his ideas through experience. Locke stressed that cultural differences were not the result of unequal natural abilities, but of unequal opportunities to develop one's abilities. Similarly, in *The Wealth of Nations,* Adam Smith remarked that there was little difference (other than education) between a philosopher and a street porter: both were born, he claimed, with the ability to reason, and both should be free to rise in society according to their talents. Yet Locke and Smith still believed that a mixed set of social and political institutions was necessary to regulate relationships among ever-imperfect humans. Moreover, they did not believe that women could act as independent, rational individuals in the same way that all men, presumably, could. Although educated women like Mary Wollstonecraft and Olympe de Gouges took up the pen to protest these inequities (see Chapter 15 for further discussion), the Enlightenment did little to change the subordinate status of women in European society.

Universal Laws and Religious Tolerance Efforts to discover the "laws" of human behavior linked up with criticism of existing governments. Explaining the laws of economic relations was chiefly the work of Adam Smith, whose book *The Wealth of Nations* described universal economic principles. According to Smith, all people have what he called the propensity to truck, barter, and exchange—an innate desire to trade with one another. He objected that mercantilist controls and guild restrictions stifled economic growth and argued instead that a division of labor, spurred on by free and fair competition, provided the best conditions for producing wealth (though he did not advocate completely free, unregulated markets). Assuming that all people, everywhere shared Protestant notions of thrift and discipline, Smith claimed that by pursuing their own rational self-interest, virtuous individuals would advance the common good without meaning to do so—as if, as he put it, by an "invisible hand." Smith was conscious of growing economic gaps between "civilized and thriving" nations and "savage" ones. Yet he believed that until the poorer nations learned to abide by nature's laws and behaved virtuously, they could not expect a happy fate.

One of the most controversial areas for applying universal laws was religion. Although few Enlightenment thinkers were atheists (people who do not believe in any god), most of them called for religious toleration. They insisted that the use of reason, not force, was the best way to create a community of believers and morally good people. Governments often reacted by censoring books or exiling writers who criticized the authority of the church, but the arguments managed to persuade some rulers. Thus, in the late eighteenth century, governments from Denmark to Austria passed acts offering religious minorities some freedom of worship. However, toleration did not mean full civil rights—especially for Catholics in England or Jews anywhere in Europe. Religious minorities enjoyed much greater freedom in this period in the Ottoman Empire than they did in any European country.

Analyzing Global Developments

How Can We Measure the Impact of an Idea?

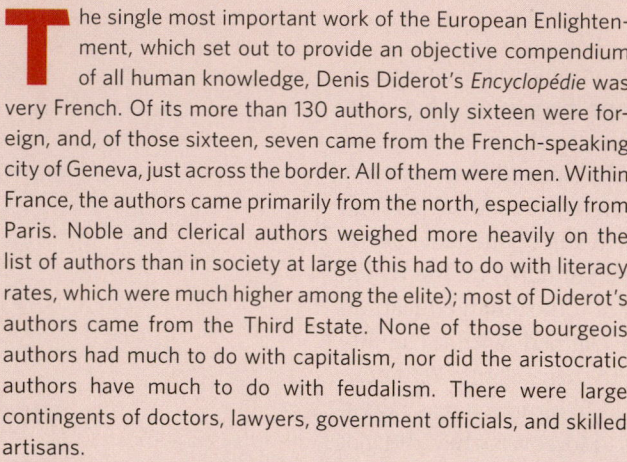

The single most important work of the European Enlightenment, which set out to provide an objective compendium of all human knowledge, Denis Diderot's *Encyclopédie* was very French. Of its more than 130 authors, only sixteen were foreign, and, of those sixteen, seven came from the French-speaking city of Geneva, just across the border. All of them were men. Within France, the authors came primarily from the north, especially from Paris. Noble and clerical authors weighed more heavily on the list of authors than in society at large (this had to do with literacy rates, which were much higher among the elite); most of Diderot's authors came from the Third Estate. None of those bourgeois authors had much to do with capitalism, nor did the aristocratic authors have much to do with feudalism. There were large contingents of doctors, lawyers, government officials, and skilled artisans.

We know very little about the production and diffusion of the first edition of the *Encyclopédie*, produced from 1751 to 1772 under Diderot's direction. The first four editions, in fact, were expensive luxury items, relatively unimportant in terms of diffusion. The great mass of *Encyclopédies* that circulated in prerevolutionary Europe came from cut-rate quarto and octavo editions published between 1777 and 1782, when the final, revised version, the *Encyclopédie méthodique*, began to appear. For these later editions, thorough records have survived, raising far-reaching questions about how ideas circulated and where during the Enlightenment, at least within Europe. (We know very little about the circulation of the *Encyclopédie* beyond Europe.) Where did the writers come from, where did their ideas go, and how, if at all, did their origins influence the content and ultimate significance of their project? We include a table of key words and their classification in thematic categories from the original edition, to give a sense of its contents and priorities.

TERMS	WORD COUNT	PRINCIPAL CATEGORIES
Commerce	5,713	Commerce, Geography
Science	2,095	[Multiple Categories]
Christ	1,821	Theology, Holy Scripture
African	1,772	Geography, History, Natural History, Botany
Slavery	238	Natural Law, Ethics, Religion, Ancient History
African Slavery (*La traite des nègres*)	15	Commerce
Negro	536	Natural History, Commerce
Saint-Domingue	96	Geography, Botany
China	957	Agriculture, Chemistry, History, Natural History, Geography, Metaphysics, Tapestry
Turk or Turkey	701	Geography, History
Muhammad	356	Theology, History, Philosophy

QUESTIONS FOR ANALYSIS

- What does the diffusion of the *Encyclopédie* within France and across Europe tells us about its influence? How should we evaluate the influence of a book?
- Do you think the *Encyclopédie*'s local origins compromise its universal ambitions?
- How do you think the social origins of the contributors shaped the kinds of topics covered by the *Encyclopédie*?

Source: Robert Darnton, *The Business of the Enlightenment: A Publishing History of the Encyclopédie, 1775–1800* (1979).

Seeking Universal Knowledge The Enlightenment produced numerous works that attempted to encompass universal knowledge. Most important was the French *Encyclopédie*, which ultimately comprised twenty-eight volumes containing essays by nearly 200 intellectuals. It was popular among the elite despite its political, religious, and intellectual radicalism. Its purpose was "to collect all the knowledge scattered over the face of the earth" and to make it useful to men and women in the present and future. Indeed, the

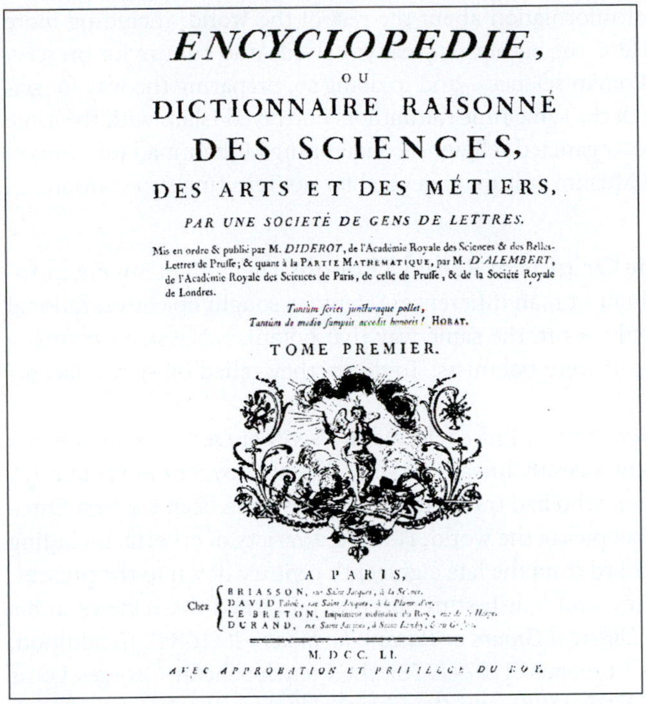
ENCYCLOPEDIE,
OU
DICTIONNAIRE RAISONNÉ
DES SCIENCES,
DES ARTS ET DES MÉTIERS,
PAR UNE SOCIETÉ DE GENS DE LETTRES.
Mis en ordre & publié par M. DIDEROT, de l'Académie Royale des Sciences & des Belles-Lettres de Prusse; & quant à la PARTIE MATHÉMATIQUE, par M. D'ALEMBERT, de l'Académie Royale des Sciences de Paris, de celle de Prusse, & de la Société Royale de Londres.
Tantùm series juncturaque pollet,
Tantùm de medio sumptis accedit honoris! HORAT.
TOME PREMIER.
A PARIS,
Chez BRIASSON, rue Saint Jacques, à la Science.
DAVID l'aîné, rue Saint Jacques, à la Plume d'or.
LE BRETON, Imprimeur ordinaire du Roy, rue de la Harpe.
DURAND, rue Saint Jacques, à Saint Landry, & au Griffon.
M. DCC. LI.
AVEC APPROBATION ET PRIVILEGE DU ROY.

The *Encyclopédie* Originally published in 1751, the *Encyclopédie* was the most comprehensive work of learning of the French Enlightenment. The title page (*left*) features an image of light and reason being dispersed throughout the land. The title itself identifies the work as a dictionary, based on reason, that deals not just with the sciences but also with the arts and occupations. It identifies two of the leading men of letters (*gens de lettres*), Denis Diderot and Jean le Rond d'Alembert, as the primary authors of the work. Contributors to the *Encyclopédie* included craftsmen as well as intellectuals. The detailed illustrations of a pin factory and the processes and machinery employed in pin making shown below are from a plate in the fourth volume of the *Encyclopédie* and demonstrate its emphasis on practical information.

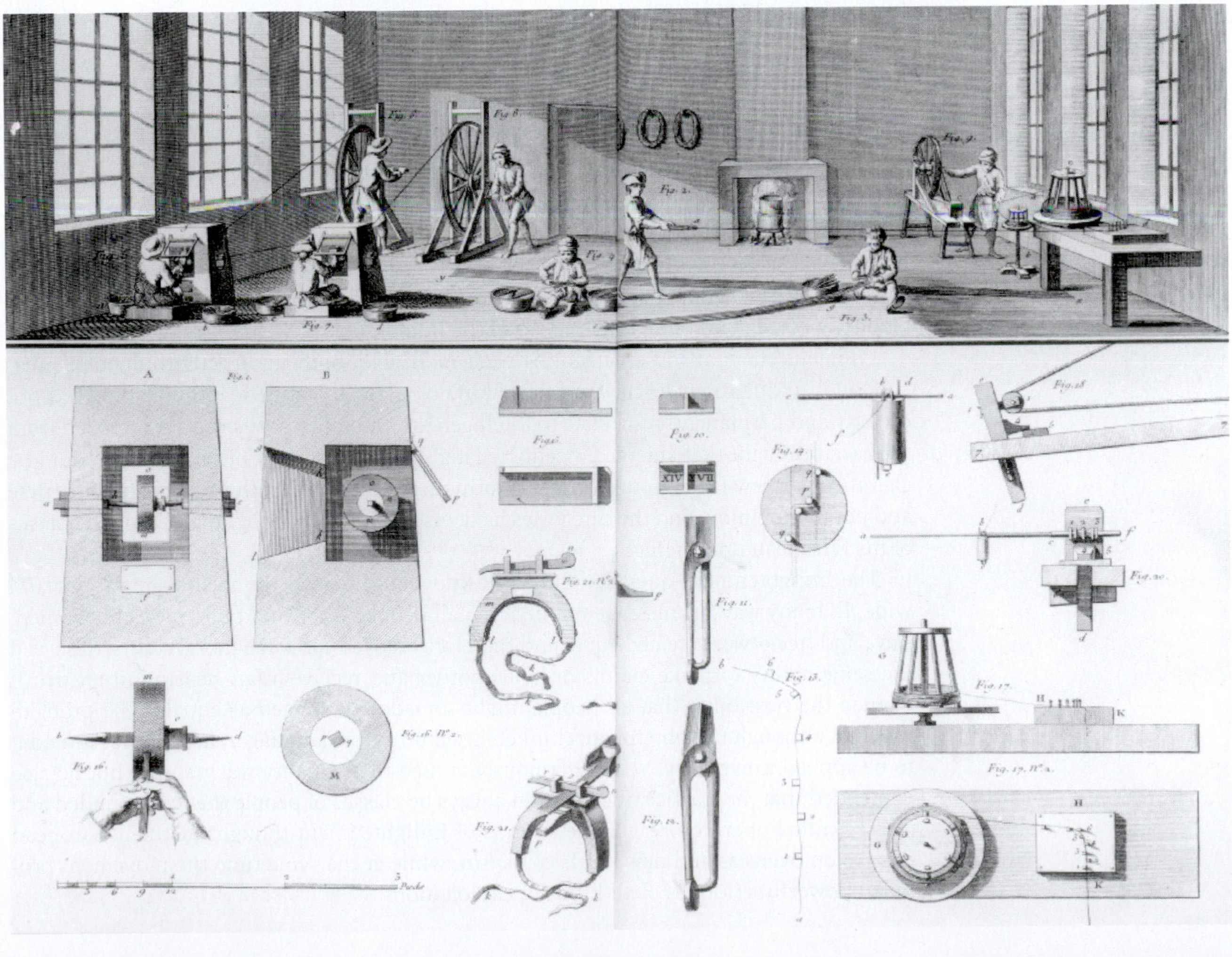

Encyclopédie offered a wealth of information about the rest of the world, including more than 2,300 articles on Islam. Here, the authors typically praised Arab culture for preserving and extending Greek and Roman science—and in doing so, preparing the way for scientific advances in Europe. But at the same time the authors portrayed Islam with the same ill will that they applied to other organized religions, condemning Muhammad for promoting a bloodthirsty religion and Muslim culture in general for not rejecting superstition.

COMPARISON

ANALYZE the role that race and cultural difference played in the process of global integration.

The Enlightenment and the Origins of Racial Thought The Enlightenment introduced new ways of thinking about human difference. Scientists sought objective, rational ways to classify peoples and cultures in the same way that botanists classified plants—indeed, many leaders in this field were botanists. To do so, they relied on new concepts of race.

Before the eighteenth century, the word *race* referred to a swift current in a stream or a test of speed; sometimes it meant a family lineage (mainly that of a royal or noble family). The Frenchman François Bernier, who had traveled in Asia, may have been the first European to attempt to classify the peoples of the world. He used a variety of criteria, including those that were to become standard from the late eighteenth century down to the present, such as skin color, facial features, and hair texture. Bernier published these views in his *New Division of the Earth by the Different Groups or Races Who Inhabit It* (1684). In addition, the Swedish naturalist Carolus Linnaeus (1707–1778), the French scholar Georges Louis LeClerc, the comte de Buffon (1707–1788), and the German anatomist Johann Friedrich Blumenbach (1752–1840) also were among the first to use racial principles to classify humankind.

In his *Systema Naturae* (first published in 1735), Europe's most accomplished naturalist, Carolus Linnaeus, identified five subspecies of *Homo sapiens*, or wise man. He gave each of the continents a subspecies: there was *Homo europaeus*; *Homo americanus*; *Homo afar*; and *Homo asiaticus*, to which he added a fifth category, *Homo monstrosus*, for "wild" men and "monstrous" types. He believed that each of these groups was marked by distinctive social and intellectual characteristics, contrasting light-skinned Europeans, who he believed were governed by laws, to "sooty" Asians, who were governed by opinion. Custom governed copper-skinned Americans, while only personal whim ruled Africans, whom he consigned to the lowest rung of the human ladder.

Linnaeus thought these categories were malleable, both under environmental pressure and mixing to create new species. Skin color, facial features, and hair type did not directly and permanently correlate to intelligence or morality—this was far removed from the racial thought that emerged a century later. But the idea that human beings could be classified in a few large groups proved enormously influential both in scientific discourse and popular opinion, and the categories he devised were profoundly marked by the biases of his European upbringing.

The Enlightenment quest for universal knowledge spread the idea of liberty far and wide. In many ways its message implied that all people—rich and poor, men and women, slave and free—were created equal and therefore enjoyed the same moral status, deserved the same ability to make claims on one another and receive a fair hearing in return. It opened the possibility that all people might someday be treated as equals. The problem was that although Enlightenment thinkers used universal language, they did not intend it to be applied universally. Voltaire famously argued that equality was natural, but he also contended that, in practice, there would always be classes of people that commanded and classes called upon to obey. Some strands of Enlightenment thought justified European expansion overseas and new kinds of racism, while at the same time the movement provided powerful critiques of all kinds of exploitation.

Creating Hybrid Cultures in the Americas

COMPARISON

DESCRIBE how hybrid cultures emerged in the Americas, and **EXPLAIN** the connection between these cultures and Enlightenment ideology.

As European empires expanded in the Americas, mingling between colonizers and native peoples, as well as African slaves, produced hybrid cultures. But the mixing of cultures grew increasingly unbalanced as Europeans imposed authority over more of the Americas. In addition to guns and germs, many European colonizers brought Bibles, prayer books, and crucifixes. With these, they set out to Christianize and "civilize" Amerindian and African populations in the Americas. Yet missionary efforts produced uneven and often unpredictable outcomes. Even as Amerindians and African slaves adopted Christian beliefs and practices, they often retained older religious practices too.

European colonists likewise borrowed from the peoples they subjugated and enslaved. This was especially true in the sixteenth and seventeenth centuries, when the colonists' survival in the New World often depended on adapting. New sorts of hierarchies emerged, and elites in Latin America and North America increasingly followed the tastes and fashions of European aristocrats. Yet, even as they imitated Old World ways, these colonials forged identities that separated them from Europe.

SPIRITUAL ENCOUNTERS

Although the Jesuits had little impact in China and the Islamic world, Christian missionaries in the Americas had armies and officials to back up their insistence that Native Americans and African slaves abandon their own deities and spirits for Christ. Nonetheless, their attempts to force conversions were rarely a complete success, and some European settlers became interested in Amerindian culture.

European missionaries, especially Catholics, used numerous techniques to bring Amerindians within the Christian fold. They smashed idols, razed temples, and whipped backsliders. Catholic orders (principally Dominicans, Jesuits, and Franciscans) also learned what they could about Indian beliefs and rituals—and then exploited that knowledge to make converts to Christianity. For example, many missionaries found it useful to demonize local gods, subvert indigenous spiritual leaders, and transform Indian iconography into Christian symbols.

Neither gentle persuasion nor violent coercion produced the results that missionaries desired. When conversions did occur, the Christian practices that resulted were usually syncretic: mixed forms in which indigenous deities and rituals merged with Christian ones. Those who did convert saw Christian spiritual power as an addition to, not a replacement for, their own religions.

Europeans also attempted to Christianize slaves from Africa, though many slave owners doubted the wisdom of converting persons they regarded as mere property. Sent forth with the pope's blessing, Catholic priests targeted slave populations in the American colonies of Portugal, Spain, and France. Applying many of the same techniques that missionaries used with Indian "heathens," these priests produced similarly mixed results.

More distressing to missionaries than the blending of beliefs or outright defiance were the Amerindians' successes in assimilating captured colonists. It deeply troubled the missionaries that quite a few captured colonists adjusted to their situation, accepted adoptions into local societies, and refused to return to colonial society when given the chance. Moreover, some Europeans voluntarily chose to live among the Amerindians. Comparing the records of cultural conversion, one eighteenth-century colonist suggested that "thousands of Europeans are Indians," yet "we have no examples of even one of those Aborigines having from choice become European." (Aborigines are original, native inhabitants of a region, as opposed to invaders, colonizers, or later peoples of mixed ancestry.)

Racial Mixing (*Left*) This image shows racial mixing in colonial Mexico—the father is Spanish, the mother Indian, and the child a mestizo. This is a well-to-do family, illustrating how Europeans married into the native aristocracy. (*Right*) Here too we see a racially mixed family. The father is Spanish, the mother black or African, and the child a mulatto. Observe, however, the less aristocratic and markedly less peaceful nature of this family.

While this calculation was no doubt exaggerated, it shows that despite the missionaries' intentions, cultural exchange went in more than one direction.

INTERMARRIAGE AND CULTURAL MIXING

In the early stages of colonization, Europeans mixed with Amerindians in part because there were many more men than women among the colonists. Almost all the early European traders, missionaries, and settlers were men (although the British North American settlements saw more women arrive relatively early on). In response to the scarcity of women and as a way to help Amerindians accept the newcomers' culture, the Portuguese crown authorized intermarriage between Portuguese men and local women. These relations often amounted to little more than rape, but longer-lasting relationships developed in places where Amerindians kept their independence—as among French fur traders and Amerindian women in Canada, the Great Lakes region, and the Mississippi Valley. Whether by coercion or consent, sexual relations between European men and Amerindian women resulted in offspring of mixed ancestry. In fact, the mestizos of Spanish colonies and the *métis* of French outposts soon outnumbered settlers of wholly European descent.

The increasing numbers of African slaves in the Americas complicated the mix of New World cultures even further. Unlike marriages between fur traders and Indian women, in which the women held considerable power because of their connections to Indian trading partners, sexual intercourse between European men and enslaved African women was almost always forced. Children born from such unions swelled the ranks of mixed-ancestry people in the colonial population, contributing to the new cultural mix that was emerging.

FORMING AMERICAN IDENTITIES

Over time, as European colonies in the Americas became more securely established, the colonists developed a sense of their own distinctive "American" identities. The colonization of the Americas brought Europeans, Africans, and Indians into sustained contact, though the nature of the colonies and the character of the contact varied considerably. Where European dominance was most secure, colonists imposed their ways on subjugated populations and imported what they took to be the chief cultural and institutional attributes of the countries they had left behind. Yet Europeans were not immune to cultural influences from the groups they dispossessed and enslaved.

The Creole Identity In Spanish America, ethnic and cultural mixing produced a powerful new class, the **creoles**—people born in the Americas. By the late eighteenth century, creoles increasingly resented the control that **peninsulares**—men and women born in Spain or Portugal but living in the Americas—had over colonial society. Creoles especially resented the exclusive privileges given to peninsular rulers, like those that forbade creoles from trading with other colonial ports. Also, they disliked the fact that royal ministers gave most official posts to peninsulares.

In many cities of the Spanish and Portuguese empires, reading clubs and salons hosted energetic discussions of fresh Enlightenment ideas and contributed to the growing creole identity. The Spanish crown, recognizing the role of printing presses in spreading troublesome ideas, strictly controlled the number and location of printers in the colonies. In Brazil, royal authorities banned them altogether. Nonetheless books, pamphlets, and simple gossip allowed new notions of science, history, and politics to circulate among literate creoles.

Anglicization In one important sense, wealthy colonists in British America were similar to the creole elites in Spanish and Portuguese America: they, too, copied European ways. For example, they constructed "big houses" (in Virginia and elsewhere—especially the Caribbean) modeled on the country estates of English gentlemen and imported opulent furnishings and fashions from the finest British stores. Imitating the British also involved tightening patriarchal authority. In seventeenth-century Virginia, men had vastly outnumbered women, which gave women some power (widows in particular gained greater control over property and more choices when they remarried). During the eighteenth century, however, sex ratios became more equal, and women's property rights diminished as British customs took precedence.

Intellectually, too, British Americans were linked to Europe. Importing enormous numbers of books and journals, these Americans played a significant role in the Enlightenment as producers and consumers of political pamphlets, scientific treatises, and social critiques. Indeed, drawing on the words of numerous Enlightenment thinkers, American intellectuals created the most famous of enlightened documents: the Declaration of Independence. It announced that all men were endowed with equal rights and were created to pursue worldly happiness. In this way Anglicized Americans showed themselves, like the creole elites of Latin America, to be products of both European and New World cultures.

The Influence of European Culture in Oceania

In the South Pacific as in the Americas, European influence had powerful consequences in the eighteenth century. Though in centuries past Hindu, Buddhist, and Islamic missionaries and Chinese traders had traveled to Malaysia and nearby islands, they had not ventured beyond Timor (see Map 14.1). Europeans began to do so in the years after 1770, turning their sights on **Oceania** (Australia, New Zealand, and the islands of the southwest Pacific). Using their new wealth to fund voyages with scientific and political objectives, Europeans invaded these remaining unexplored areas. The results were mixed: while some islands maintained their autonomy, the biggest prize, Australia, underwent thorough Anglicization.

Until Europeans colonized it in the late eighteenth century, Australia was, like the Americas before Columbus, truly a world apart. Separated by water and sheer distance from other regions, Australia's main features were harsh natural conditions and a sparse population. At the time of the European colonization, the island was home to around 300,000 people, mostly hunter-gatherers. Now the intrusion into Oceania presented Europeans with a previously unknown region that could serve as a laboratory for studying other peoples and geographical settings.

THE SCIENTIFIC VOYAGES OF CAPTAIN COOK

In Oceania and across the South Pacific, Europeans experimented with a scientific form of imperialism. The story of the region's most famous explorer, Captain James Cook (1728–1779), shows how closely related science and imperialist ventures could be. Cook's voyages and his encounter with the South Sea Islanders opened up the Pacific, and particularly Australia, to European colonizers.

Captain Cook has become a legendary figure in European cultural history, portrayed as one of the saintly scientists of enlightened progress. His first voyage had two objectives. The Royal Society charged him with the scholarly task of observing the movement of the planet Venus from the Southern Hemisphere, and the British government assigned him the secret mission of finding and claiming "the southern continent" for Britain. Cook set sail in 1768, and his voyage was so fruitful that he subsequently undertook two more scientific-imperial adventures.

The Voyages of Captain James Cook During his celebrated voyages to the South Pacific, Cook (*left*) kept meticulous maps and diaries. Although he had little formal education, he became one of the great exemplars of enlightened learning through experience and experiment. (*Right*) Kangaroos were unknown in the West until Cook and his colleagues encountered (and ate) them on their first visit to Australia. This engraving of the animal (which unlike most animals, plants, and geographical features actually kept the name the Aborigines had given it) from Cook's 1773 travelogue, *A Voyage Round the World in the Years 1768–1771*, lovingly depicts the kangaroo's environs and even emotions.

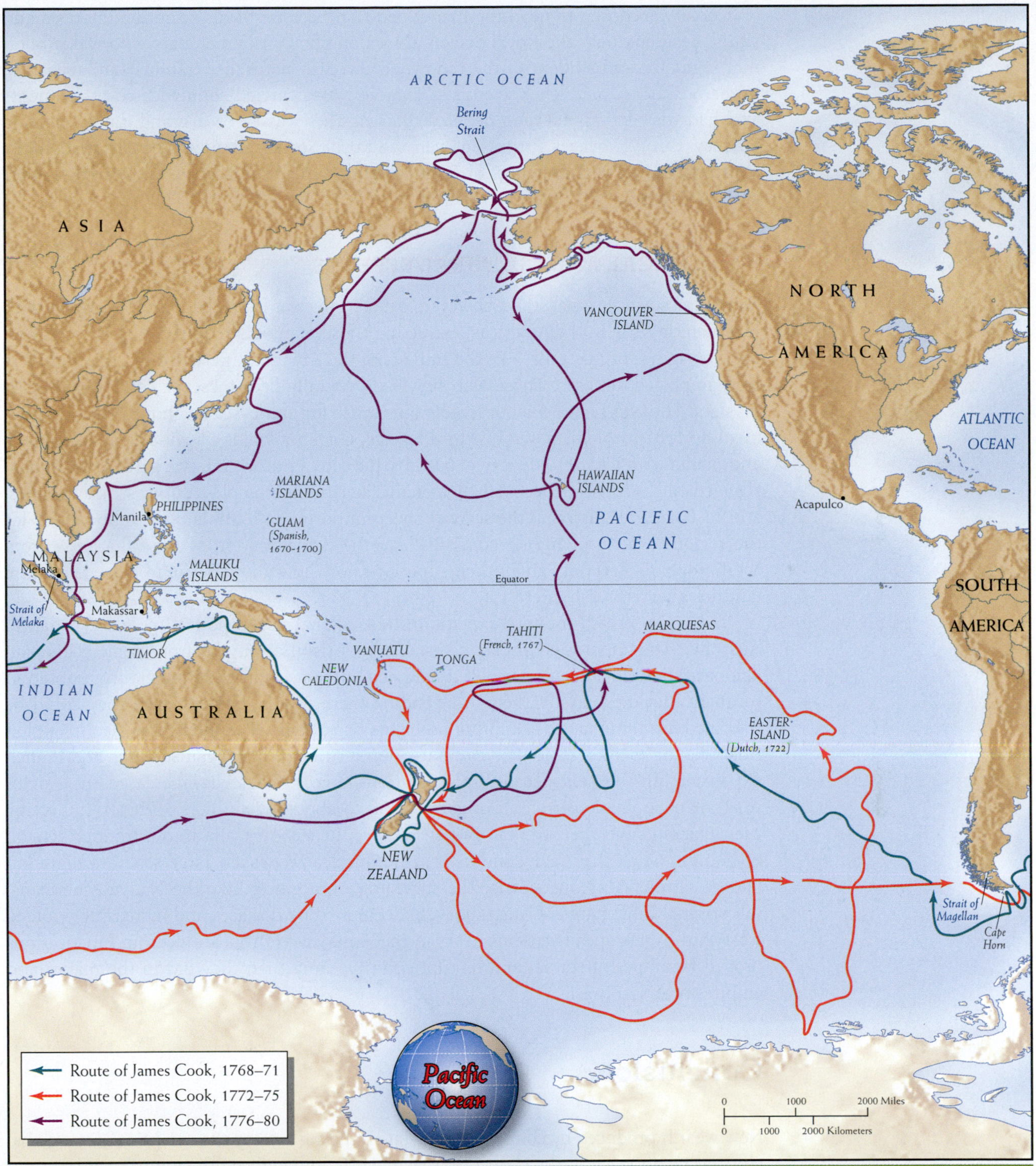

MAP 14.1 | Southeast Asia

Captain Cook's voyages throughout the Pacific Ocean symbolized a new era in European exploration of other societies.

- According to this map, how many voyages did Cook take?
- Where did Cook explore, and what peoples did he encounter?
- Contrast the routes Cook selected for his three voyages. How do they differ? What does that tell us about his project?

Cook was chosen to head the first expedition because of his scientific interests and skills. Besides Cook, the Royal Society sent along one of its members who was a botanist; a doctor and student of the renowned Swedish naturalist Carolus Linnaeus; and numerous artists and other scientists. The crew also carried sophisticated instruments and had instructions to keep detailed diaries. This was to be a grand data-collecting journey. Cook's voyages surpassed even the Royal Society's hopes. The scientists made approximately 3,000 drawings of Pacific plants, birds, landscapes, and peoples never seen in Europe.

ECOLOGICAL AND CULTURAL EFFECTS

More than science was at stake, however, for Australia was intended to supply Britain with raw materials. As in the Americas, extracting those materials required a labor force, and the Aborigines of Australia, like the Indians of the Americas, perished in great numbers from imported diseases. Those who survived generally fled to escape control by British masters. Thus, to secure a labor force, plans arose for grand-scale conquest and resettlement by British colonists. On his third voyage, Cook took along a wide array of animals and plants with which to turn the South Pacific into a European-style garden, with massive ecological consequences. His lieutenant later brought apples, quinces, strawberries, and rosemary to Australia; the seventy sheep imported in 1788 laid the foundations for the region's wool-growing economy. In fact, the domestication of Australia arose from the Europeans' certainty about their superior know-how and a desire to make the entire landmass serve British interests.

In 1788, a British military expedition took official possession of the eastern half of Australia. The intent was, in part, to establish a prison colony far from home. This plan belonged as well to the realm of "enlightened" dreams: removing people from an environment that did not suit them and sending them to new climes where they could be reformed, or, if not, at least limiting problems back home. The intent was also to exploit Australia for its timber and flax and to use it as a strategic base against Dutch and French expansion. In the next decades, immigration—free and forced—increased the Anglo-Australian population from an original 1,000 to about 1.2 million by 1860. Importing their customs and their capital, British settlers turned Australia into a frontier version of home, just as they had done in British America. Yet, such large-scale immigration had disastrous consequences for the surviving Aborigines. Like the Native Americans, the original inhabitants of Australia were decimated by diseases and increasingly forced westward by European settlement. As in the Americas, European ideas and institutions proved far more influential and disruptive in Oceania than they did in the major land empires of Afro-Eurasia.

Conclusion

New wealth produced by commerce and state building created the conditions for a global cultural renaissance in the sixteenth, seventeenth, and eighteenth centuries. It began in the Chinese and Islamic empires and then stretched into Europe, Africa, and previous worlds apart in the Americas and Oceania. Experiments in religious toleration encouraged cultural exchange; book production and consumption soared; grand new monuments took shape; luxury goods became available for wider enjoyment.

Although the Islamic and Chinese worlds confidently retained their own systems of knowing, believing, and representing, the Americas and Oceania increasingly faced

European cultural pressures. Here, while hybrid practices became widespread by the late eighteenth century, European beliefs and habits took over as the standards for judging degrees of "civilization." African cultures largely escaped this influence, though their homelands felt the impact of European expansionism because of the slave trade.

From a commercial standpoint, the world was more integrated than ever before. But the exposure and cultural borrowing that global trade promoted did not obliterate established cultural traditions. The Chinese, for instance, still believed in the superiority of their traditional knowledge and customs. Muslim rulers, confident of the primacy of Islam, allowed others to form subordinate cultural communities within their realm and adopted the Europeans' knowledge only when it served their own imperial purposes.

Only the Europeans were constructing knowledge that they believed was both universal and objective, enabling mortals to master the world of nature and all its inhabitants. This view would prove consequential, as well as controversial, in the centuries to come.

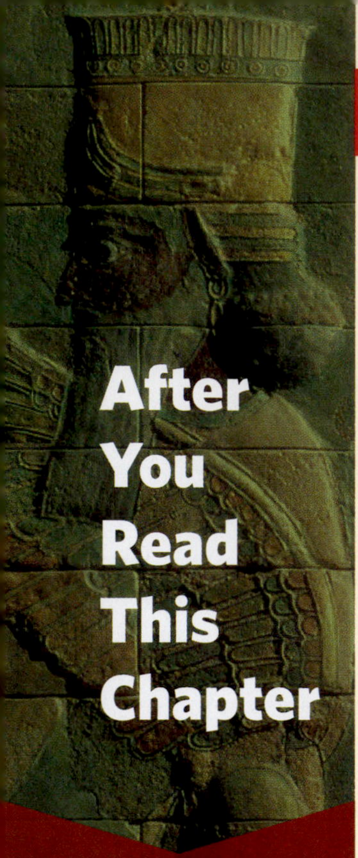

After You Read This Chapter

Go to INQUIZITIVE to see what you've learned—and learn what you've missed—with personalized feedback along the way.

TRACING GLOBAL DEVELOPMENTS

FOCUS ON: *The Flourishing of Regional Cultures*

THE ISLAMIC WORLD

- The Ottomans' unique cultural synthesis accommodates not only mystical Sufis and ultraorthodox *ulama* but also military men, administrators, and clerics.
- The Safavid state proclaims the triumph of Shiism and Persian influences in the sumptuous new capital, Isfahan.
- Mughal courtly culture values art and learning and, at its high point, welcomes non-Muslim contributions.

EAST ASIA

- China's cultural flourishing, coming from within, is evident in the broad circulation of traditional ideas, publishing, and mapmaking.
- Japan's imperial court at Kyoto develops an elite culture of theater, stylized painting, tea ceremonies, and flower arranging.

EUROPE

- Cultural flourishing known as the Enlightenment yields a faith in reason and a belief in humans' ability to fathom the laws of nature and human behavior.
- European thinkers articulate a belief in unending human progress.
- Europeans expand into Australia and the South Pacific.

AFRICA

- Slave-trading states such as Asante, Oyo, and Benin celebrate royal power and wealth through art.

THE AMERICAS

- Even as Euro-Americans participate in the Enlightenment, their culture reflects Native American and African influences.

CHRONOLOGY

THE ISLAMIC WORLD
Shah Abbas builds Isfahan 1587–1629

AFRICA
Oyo and Asante kingdoms produce vibrant artistic works 1600s

EUROPE

EAST ASIA
Growing circulation of books and ideas in China 1600s
Floating Worlds appear in Japanese cities 1600s

THE AMERICAS
Hybrid cultures appear 1600s

1500 1550 1600

THINKING ABOUT GLOBAL CONNECTIONS

- ***Thinking about Exchange Networks and Cultural Change*** How did increased exchanges of goods and ideas change established traditions? What institutions and ideas proved most hospitable to foreign influence, even in established cultures, and why? Which fields proved more resistant to outside ideas? Why were some regions more receptive to foreign influences than others? Consider religion, natural science, and art.
- ***Thinking about Changing Power Relationships and Cultural Change*** How did established cultures respond to the inclusion of the Americas into an increasingly integrated world? Which cultures flourished, and why? What relationship(s) can you see between new wealth and cultural change?
- ***Thinking about Environmental Impacts and Cultural Change*** The isolation of the Americas and Oceania paved the way for ecological catastrophe when Europeans arrived. How, in turn, did ecological catastrophes leave indigenous cultures vulnerable? Consider the nature of religious change in the Americas and the Afro-Eurasian core regions and population movements in Australia.

STUDY QUESTIONS

1. Explain how wealth and trade shaped cultural traditions. Where did established high cultures remain vibrant? Where did they come under attack? Where did innovations occur? What made innovation possible?
2. Define the **Enlightenment** and contrast it to the other cultural developments in this chapter. In what ways was it unique?
3. Explain the relationship between **creoles** and **peninsulares** and, more broadly, between the various social groups in the Spanish empire.
4. Compare different uses of monumental architecture as instruments of rule. Consider the **Forbidden City of Beijing**, the **great plaza at Isfahan**, the **Palace of Versailles**, and the **Taj Mahal**.
5. Analyze the relationship between the **scientific method**, concepts of racial difference, and established social hierarchies. Pay particular attention to Captain Cook's expedition to **Oceania**.

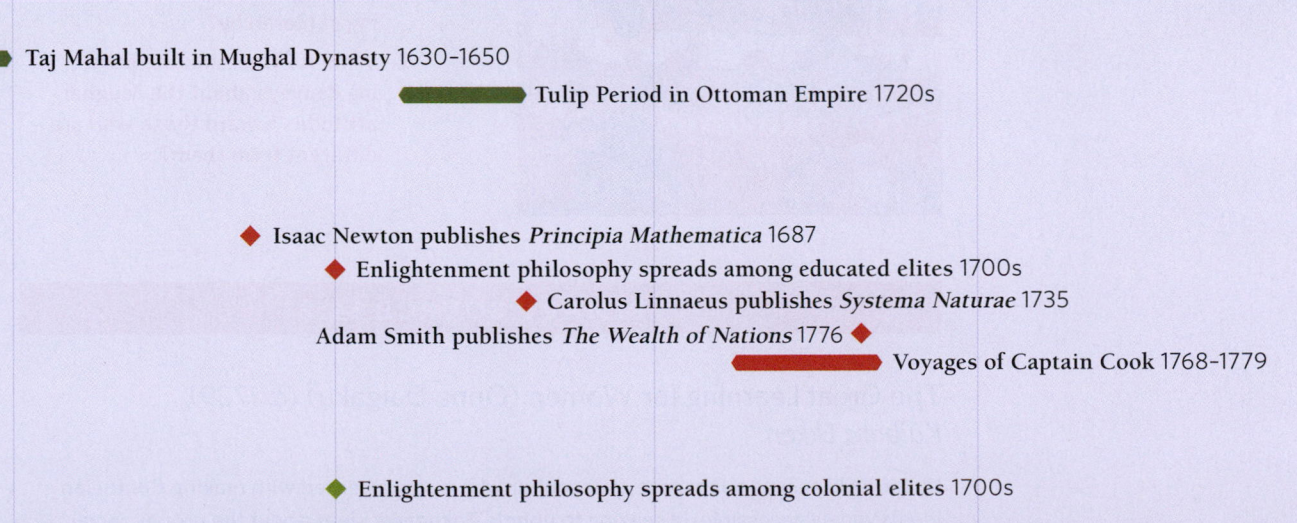

Taj Mahal built in Mughal Dynasty 1630–1650

Tulip Period in Ottoman Empire 1720s

Isaac Newton publishes *Principia Mathematica* 1687

Enlightenment philosophy spreads among educated elites 1700s

Carolus Linnaeus publishes *Systema Naturae* 1735

Adam Smith publishes *The Wealth of Nations* 1776

Voyages of Captain Cook 1768–1779

Enlightenment philosophy spreads among colonial elites 1700s

1650 | 1700 | 1750 | 1800

Going to the Source

Considering Difference and Inequality

As societies around the world expanded and interacted in the seventeenth century, they faced issues of what to do about people who looked and acted differently from them. They also discovered that these people sometimes had different ideas about what was important. The European Enlightenment of the eighteenth century also considered the ideas of difference and inequality. At the core of the Enlightenment was a belief that by using a process of rational inquiry, as opposed to emotions or religious explanations, universal principles could be uncovered. Enlightenment thinkers believed that these principles could be employed in all societies and all times.

PRIMARY SOURCE 14.1

The Mughal Court (c. 1615)

This painting by a Mughal artists shows the Mughal court in the seventeenth century. It depicts social order and inequality. For example, the Mughal emperor is at the center of the painting, surrounded by men of various ranks and ethnicities, who assume their proper place in the ordered world of the multicultural Mughal Empire.

1. **What does this image reveal about the Mughal Empire's understanding of hierarchy?**
2. **What do you think the painting conveys about the Mughal attitudes toward those who are different from them?**

PRIMARY SOURCE 14.2

The Great Learning for Women (Onna Daigaku) *(c. 1729), Kaibara Ekken*

Kaibara Ekken was a Japanese philosopher who was concerned with making Confucian ideals widely accessible. In seeking to uphold Tokugawa ideas about the proper social relationships at a time when people in Japan were being exposed to Western ideas, he

promoted older Confucian ideas by popularizing them in a series of "self-help" manuals designed to be read by a wide section of the population. The document was published several years after his death, which suggests that it might be a compilation of his lectures, transcribed by his students.

It is the duty of a girl living in her parents' house to practice filial piety toward her father and mother. But after marriage, her duty is to honor her father-in-law and mother-in-law, to honor them beyond her father and mother, to love and reverence them with all ardor and to tend them with a practice of filial piety. . . . Never should a woman fail, night and morning, to pay her respects to her father-in-law and mother-in-law. Never should she be remiss in performing any tasks they may require of her. With all reverence she must carry out, and never rebel against, her father-in-law's commands. On every point must she inquire of her father-in-law and mother-in-law and accommodate herself to their direction. . . .

A woman has no other lord; she must look to her husband as her lord and must serve him with all worship and reverence, not despising or thinking lightly of him. The Way of the woman is to obey her man. In her dealings with her husband, both the expression of her countenance and the style of her address should be courteous, humble, and conciliatory, never peevish and intractable, never rude and arrogant—that should be a woman's first and principal care.

When the husband issues his instructions, the wife must never disobey them. In doubtful cases she should inquire of her husband and obediently follow his commands. If her husband ever asks her a question, she should answer to the point; to answer carelessly would be a mark of rudeness. If her husband becomes angry at any time, she must obey him with fear and trembling and not oppose him in anger and forwardness. A woman should look on her husband as if he were Heaven itself and never weary of thinking how she may yield to him and thus escape celestial castigation. . . .

A woman must always be on the alert and keep a strict watch over her own conduct. In the morning she must rise early and at night go late to rest. Instead of sleeping in the middle of the days, she must be intent on the duties of her household; she must not grow tired of weaving, sewing, and spinning. She must not drink too much tea and wine, nor must she feed her eyes and ears on theatrical performances (kabuki, jōruri), ditties. In her capacity as a wife, she must keep her husband's household in proper order. If the wife is evil and profligate, the house will be ruined.

In everything she must avoid extravagance and in regard to both food and clothes, she must act according to her station in life and never give in to luxury and pride.

1. **According to Ekken, how are women supposed to behave after they are married?**
2. **How does Ekken understand the role of women within Japanese society?**

PRIMARY SOURCE 14.3

On Inequality (1755), Jean-Jacques Rousseau

The Enlightenment *philosophe* Jean-Jacques Rousseau spent years thinking about the problem of inequality, especially as he observed it in continental European societies. This selection, from his *Discourse on Inequality,* addresses the origins of inequality. Years later Rousseau would propose a solution to the problem of inequality in a book that was not well received in France, especially as it proposed a form of government different from France's absolute monarchy. Rousseau fled France to avoid being prosecuted for his ideas.

*

The man that had most strength performed most labour; the most dexterous turned his labour to best account; the most ingenious found out methods of lessening his labour; the husbandman required more iron, or the smith more corn, and while both worked equally, one earned a great deal by his labour, while the other could scarce live by his. It is thus that natural inequality insensibly unfolds itself with that arising from a variety of combinations, and that the difference among men, developed by the difference of their circumstances, becomes more sensible, more permanent in its effects, and begins to influence in the same proportion the condition of private persons. Things once arrived at this period, it is an easy matter to imagine the rest. I shall not stop to describe the successive inventions of other arts, the progress of language, the trial and employments of talents, the inequality of fortunes, the use or abuse of riches, nor all the details which follow these, and which every one may easily supply. . . .

It is thus that the most powerful or the most wretched, respectively considering their power and wretchedness as a kind of title to the substance of others, even equivalent to that of property, the equality once broken was followed by the most shocking disorders. It is thus that the usurpations of the rich, the pillagings of the poor, and the unbridled passions of all, by stifling the cries of natural compassion, and the as yet feeble voice of justice, rendered man avaricious, wicked and ambitious. There arose between the title of the strongest, and that of the first occupier a perpetual conflict, which always ended in battery and bloodshed. Infant society became a scene of the most horrible warfare: Mankind thus debased and harassed, and no longer able to retreat, or renounce the unhappy acquisitions it had made. . . .

1. **How would you characterize Rousseau's views about inequality?**
2. **What might be the limitations to creating a society of perfect equality?**

PRIMARY SOURCE 14.4

"What is Tolerance?" (1764), Voltaire

Voltaire approached one problem that arose from natural inequality: people have different opinions, and in this brief passage he asks his reader to consider how to deal with differences by being tolerant. One logical place to begin is with the premise that all are equal before God. That being said, Voltaire is quite critical of the ways in which Christians practiced the idea of tolerance, which he views as essential to the religion.

*

What is tolerance? It is the natural attribute of humanity. We are all formed of weakness and error: let us pardon reciprocally each other's folly. That is the first law of nature.

It is clear that the individual who persecutes a man, his brother, because he is not of the same opinion, is a monster. There is no difficulty here. . . .

Madmen, who have never been able to worship the God who made you! . . . Look at the Great Turk. He governs Guebres, Banians, Greek Christians, Nestorians, Romans. The first who tried to stir up tumult would be impaled; and everyone is at peace.

Of all the religions, the Christian is without doubt the one which should inspire tolerance most, although up to now the Christians have been the most intolerant of all men.

1. **How does Voltaire describe tolerance?**
2. **How might Voltaire have responded to Ekken's view of women (Primary Source 14.1)?**

PRIMARY SOURCE 14.5

"What is Enlightenment?" (1784), Immanuel Kant

The German philosopher Immanuel Kant (1724–1804) answered the question, "What is Enlightenment?" with the Latin *Sapere aude*!—meaning "Dare to know!" In this passage, Kant explains why he thinks people of all ranks must think and engage in rational enquiry, and how failing to do so has led to many social problems.

*

Enlightenment is the human being's emergence from his self-incurred minority. Minority is inability to make use of one's own understanding without direction from another. This minority is *self-incurred* when its cause lies not in lack of understanding but in lack of resolution and courage to use it without direction from another. *Sapere aude!* Have courage to make use of your *own* understanding! is thus the motto of enlightenment.

It is because of laziness and cowardice that so great a part of humankind, after nature has long since emancipated them from other people's direction (*naturaliter maiorennes*), nevertheless gladly remains minors for life, and that it becomes so easy for others to set themselves up as their guardians. It is so comfortable to be a minor! If I have a book that understands for me, a spiritual advisor who has a conscience for me, a doctor who decides upon a regimen for me, and so forth, I need not trouble myself at all. I need not think, if only I can pay; others will readily undertake the irksome business for me. That by far the greatest part of humankind (including the entire fair sex) should hold the step toward majority to be not only troublesome but also highly dangerous will soon be seen to by those guardians who have kindly taken it upon themselves to supervise them; after they have made their domesticated animals dumb and carefully prevented these placid creatures from daring to take a single step without the walking cart in which they have confined them, they then show them the danger that threatens them if they try to walk alone. Now this danger is not in fact so great, for by a few falls they would eventually learn to walk.

1. **Why does Voltaire criticize those who choose to remain "minors" for life?**
2. **Do you think that tolerance is required in a society that is rooted in inequality? Why or why not?**

PRIMARY SOURCE 14.6

On the Rights of Women (1792), Mary Wollstonecraft

Mary Wollstonecraft is known for her Enlightenment discussion of gender and the differences between men and women. She urges her readers not to ignore women, who had limited opportunities in many parts of the world. In this passage, she considers the ways in which women have been put into unwelcome positions and compares women to others who have been considered inferior despite higher social positions.

*

I love man as my fellow; but his sceptre, real or usurped, extends not to me, unless the reason of an individual demands my homage; and even then the submission is to reason, and not to man. In fact, the conduct of an accountable being must be regulated by the operations of its own reason; or on what foundation rests the throne of God?

It appears to me necessary to dwell on these obvious truths, because females have been insulated, as it were; and while they have been stripped of the virtues that should clothe humanity, they have been decked with artificial graces that enable them to exercise a short-lived tyranny. Love, in their bosoms, taking the place of every nobler passion, their sole ambition is to be fair, to raise emotion instead of inspiring respect; and this ignoble desire, like the servility in absolute monarchies, destroys all strength of character. Liberty is the mother of virtue, and if women be, by their very constitution, slaves, and not allowed to breathe the sharp invigorating air of freedom, they must ever languish like exotics, and be reckoned beautiful flaws in nature. Let it also be remembered, that they are the only flaw.

As to the argument respecting the subjection in which the sex has ever been held, it retorts on man. The many have always been enthralled by the few; and monsters, who scarcely have shown any discernment of human excellence, have tyrannized over thousands of their fellow-creatures. Why have men of superior endowments submitted to such degradation? For, is it not universally acknowledged that kings, viewed collectively, have ever been inferior, in abilities and virtue, to the same number of men taken from the common mass of mankind—yet have they not, and are they not still treated with a degree of reverence that is an insult to reason? China is not the only country where a living man has been made a God. *Men* have submitted to superior strength to enjoy with impunity the pleasure of the moment; *women* have only done the same, and therefore till it is proved that the courtier, who servilely resigns the birthright of a man, is not a moral agent, it cannot be demonstrated that woman is essentially inferior to man because she has always been subjugated.

1. **What does Wollstonecraft believe is the cause of women's subjugation?**
2. **Do you find Wollstonecraft's argument about women persuasive? Explain why or why not.**

Questions for Analysis

Comparison

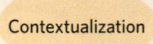

1. Compare and explain the ways in which these documents depict social and political order.

Argumentation

2. Do you think that inequality is a natural part of the human condition? Is it something that cannot (or should not) be solved? Explain your answer.

Analyzing Evidence

3. Compare and analyze the ways in which these documents address, or do not address, gender differences.

Long Essay Question

Contextualization

Based on these documents and your reading of the chapter, how did people in the seventeenth and eighteenth centuries attempt to deal with the problems of inequality and tolerance?

Before You Read This Chapter

GLOBAL STORYLINES

- A new era based on radically new ideas of freedom and the nation-state emerges in the Atlantic world.
- The industrious and industrial revolutions transform communities and the global economy.
- The worldwide balance of power shifts decisively towards northwestern Europe.

CORE OBJECTIVES

- **DESCRIBE** the new ideas of freedom and **EXPLAIN** how they differed from earlier understandings of this term.
- **COMPARE** political and economic developments in the Atlantic world with regions elsewhere around the globe during the period 1750–1850.
- **IDENTIFY** and **EXPLAIN** the key developments that constituted the Industrial Revolution.
- **EXPLAIN** patterns of global trade and economic growth and **CONNECT** them to political changes during the perio 1750–1850.
- **COMPARE** the groups of people who held power in each of the regions in 1750 and then in 1850, and **EXPLAIN** the changes that took place during this period in these societ

CHAPTER

15

Reordering the World

1750–1850

KEY TERMS

Muhammad Ali p. 582
Napoleon Bonaparte p. 567
bourgeoisie p. 576
East India Company p. 583
free trade (laissez-faire) p. 560
industrial revolution p. 576
industrious revolution p. 575
Opium War p. 586
popular sovereignty p. 560
social contract p. 564

In 1798, the French commander Napoleon Bonaparte invaded Egypt. At the time, Europeans regarded this territory as the cradle of a once-great culture, a land bridge to the Red Sea and trade with Asia, and an outpost of the Ottoman Empire. Occupying the country would allow Napoleon to introduce some of the principles of the French Revolution and to seize control of trade routes to Asia. Napoleon also hoped that by defeating the Ottomans, who controlled Egypt, he would augment his and France's historic greatness. But events did not go as Napoleon planned, for his troops faced a resentful Egyptian population. Although Napoleon soon returned to France and his dream of a French Egypt was short-lived, his invasion challenged Ottoman rule and threatened the balance of power in Europe. Indeed, Napoleon's actions in Africa, the Americas, and Europe, combined with the principles of the American and French revolutions, laid the foundations for a new era—one based on a radically new understanding of freedom as the absence of constraint, the opposite of privileges handed down by a lord or master.

That new idea of freedom first rang out across western Europe and the Americas and reverberated around the world. It destroyed the American colonial domains of Spain, Portugal, Britain, and France;

brought new nations to the stage; and challenged established elites everywhere, leading in some cases to the expansion of colonial rule. The impulse for change was a belief that governments should enact laws that apply to all people, though in practice there were significant exceptions (slaves, women, and colonized subjects). Free speech, free markets, free labor, and governments freely chosen by freeborn men, it was thought, would benefit everyone. In Europe and the Americas, though not elsewhere, the era also witnessed the emergence of the nation-state. This new form of political organization derived legitimacy from its inhabitants, often referred to as citizens, who, in theory, if not always in practice, shared a common culture, ethnicity, and language.

Yet, freedom in some corners of the globe set the stage for depriving people of freedom elsewhere and led inexorably to changes in the worldwide balance of power. Even as western European countries lost their New World colonies, they gained economic and military strength, which further challenged Asian and African governments.

Revolutionary Transformations and New Languages of Freedom

COMPARISON

DESCRIBE the new ideas of freedom and **EXPLAIN** how they differed from earlier understandings of this term.

In the eighteenth century, the circulation of goods, people, and ideas created pressures for reform around the Atlantic world. As economies expanded, many people felt that the restrictive mercantilist system prevented them from sharing in the new wealth and power. Similarly, an increasingly literate public called for their states to adopt just practices, including the abolition of torture and the accountability of rulers. In several places, power holders could not stamp out these demands before they became full-scale revolutions.

Reformers wanted to expand the franchise, to enable property holders to vote. Claims of **popular sovereignty**, the idea that political power depends on "the people," became rooted in the idea of the nation: people who shared a common language, common culture, and common history. This in turn gave rise to the nation-state as a form of political organization. Over the course of the nineteenth century, political movements began to emphasize nationalism, the idea that a fully fledged nation should have a state of its own, and democracy, the idea that the people, the *demos*, should choose their own representatives and be governed by them (see Chapter 16). In this chapter, we concentrate on the first expressions of this new thinking, in thirteen of Britain's North American colonies and in France. In both places, the "nation" and the "people" toppled their former rulers.

This chapter also concentrates on far-reaching economic developments that came in tandem with revolutionary political change. Economic reformers argued that unregulated economies would produce faster economic growth. Going well beyond the work of Adam Smith, they called for **free trade** (or **laissez-faire**), unencumbered by tariffs, quotas, and fees; free markets, which would be unregulated; and free labor, which meant using paid rather than slave labor. They insisted that these economic freedoms would yield more just and more efficient societies, ultimately benefiting everyone, everywhere in the world.

Yet, the same European and Euro-American elites who wanted a freer world often exploited slaves, denied women equal treatment, restricted colonial economies, and tried forcibly to open Asia's and Africa's markets to European trade and investment. In Africa, idealistic upheavals did not lead to free and sovereign peoples, but to greater enslavement.

Political Reorderings

Late in the eighteenth century, revolutionary ideas spread across the Atlantic world (see Map 15.1) following the trail of Enlightenment ideas about freedom and reason. As more newspapers, pamphlets, and books circulated in European countries and American colonies, readers began to discuss their societies' problems and to believe they had the right to participate in governance.

The slogans of independence, freedom, liberty, and equality seemed to promise an end to oppression, hardship, and inequities. In the North American colonies and in France, revolutions ultimately brought down monarchies and blossomed into republics. The examples of the United States and France soon encouraged other people in the Caribbean and Central and South America to reject the rule of monarchs. In these revolutionary environments, new institutions—such as written constitutions and permanent parliaments—claimed to represent the people.

COMPARISON

COMPARE political and economic developments in the Atlantic world with regions elsewhere around the globe during the period 1750–1850.

THE NORTH AMERICAN WAR OF INDEPENDENCE, 1776–1783

The American Revolution ended British rule in North America. It was the first of a series of revolutions to shake the Atlantic world, inspired by new ideas of freedom.

By the mid-eighteenth century, Britain's colonies in North America swelled with people and prosperity. Bustling port cities like Charleston, Philadelphia, New York, and Boston saw inflows of African slaves, European migrants, and manufactured goods, while agricultural staples flowed out. A "genteel" class of merchants and landowning planters dominated colonial affairs.

Land was a constant source of dispute. Planters struggled with independent farmers (yeomen). Sons and daughters of farmers, often unable to inherit or acquire land near their parents, moved westward, where they came into conflict with Amerindian peoples. To defend their lands, many Amerindians allied with Britain's rival, France. After losing the Seven Years' War (see Chapter 13), however, France ceded its Canadian colony to Britain to secure the return of its much more lucrative Caribbean colonies, especially Saint-Domingue. This left many Indians no choice but to turn to the British government to help them resist the aggressive advances of land-hungry colonists. British officials did make some concessions to Indian interests, but they did not have the troops or financial strength to enforce them.

Asserting Independence from Britain Despite these tensions, Britain stood supreme in the Atlantic world in the mid-1760s, with its greatest foes defeated and its empire expanding. Political revolution in North America seemed unimaginable. And yet, a decade later, that is what occurred.

The spark came from the government of King George III, which insisted that colonists contribute to the crown that protected them, notably in the Seven Years' War (known in North America as the French and Indian War). The king's officials imposed taxes on a variety of commodities and tried to put an end to smuggling by colonists who sought to evade mercantilist restrictions on trade. To the king's surprise and dismay, colonists objected to the new measures and protested having to pay taxes when they lacked political representation in the British Parliament.

Hudson Bay
RUSSIA
BRITISH NORTH AMERICA
OREGON (Claimed by Spain, Russia and Britain)
LOUISIANA
Quebec
Boston
New York
Philadelphia
Washington, D.C.
UNITED STATES 1776 (independence recognized by Great Britain 1783)
Charleston
Santa Fe
MEXICO 1821
FLORIDA
Gulf of Mexico
ATLANTIC OCEAN
PACIFIC OCEAN
CUBA
PUERTO RICO
Mexico City
BELIZE
JAMAICA
REPUBLIC OF HAITI 1804
GUADELOUPE (Fr.)
MARTINIQUE (Fr.)
UNITED PROVINCES OF CENTRAL AMERICA 1823
Cartagena
Caracas
TRINIDAD (Br.)
REPUBLIC OF COLOMBIA 1819
GUIANA
Quito
PERU 1821
Lima
BRAZIL 1822
BOLIVIA 1825
PARAGUAY 1811
Rio de Janeiro
CHILE 1818
PROVINCES OF LA PLATA 1816
URUGUAY 1828
Buenos Aires
Montevideo
British possessions
Spanish possessions
French possessions
Portuguese possessions
Dutch possessions
Ottoman possessions
Russian Empire
1776 Date of political independence from European (or Ottoman) colonial rule
0 1000 2000 Miles
0 1000 2000 Kilometers

MAP 15.1 | Revolutions of National Independence in the Atlantic World, 1776–1829

Influenced by Enlightenment thinkers and the French Revolution, colonies gained independence from European powers (and in the case of Greece, from the Ottoman Empire) in the late eighteenth and early nineteenth centuries.

- Which European powers granted independence to their colonial possessions in the Americas during this period?
- What were the first two colonial territories to become independent in the Americas?
- Based on the chronology presented here and on your reading, consider the relative importance of European influence and local developments in the Americas in accounting for the timing of independence in different countries. Why, in particular, did colonies in Spanish and Portuguese America obtain political independence decades after the United States won its independence?

The Boston Massacre Paul Revere's idealized view of the Boston Massacre of March 5, 1770. In the years after the Seven Years' War, Bostonians grew increasingly disenchanted with British efforts to enforce imperial regulations. When British troops fired on and killed several members of an angry mob in what came to be called the "Boston Massacre," the resulting frenzy stirred revolutionary sentiments among the populace.

In 1775, resistance in the form of petitions and boycotts turned into open warfare between a colonial militia and British troops in Massachusetts. Once blood was spilled, more radical voices came to the fore. Previously, leaders of the protest had claimed to revere the British Empire. Now calls for severing the ties to Britain became more prominent. Thomas Paine, a recent immigrant from England, captured the new mood in a pamphlet he published in 1776, arguing that it was "common sense" for people to govern themselves. Later that year, the Continental Congress (in which representatives from thirteen colonies gathered) adapted part of Paine's popular pamphlet for the Declaration of Independence.

Drawing on Enlightenment themes (see Chapter 14), the declaration written by Thomas Jefferson stated the people's "natural right" to govern themselves. It also drew inspiration from the writings of the British philosopher John Locke, notably the idea that governments should be based on a **social contract** in which the law binds both ruler and people. Locke had written nearly a century earlier that the people had the right to rebel against their government if it broke the contract and infringed on their rights. With the Declaration of Independence, the rebels announced their right to rid themselves of the English king and form their own government.

The Declaration's assertion that "all men are created equal" overturned former social hierarchies in the thirteen colonies (now calling themselves states). Thus, common men no longer automatically deferred to gentlemen of higher rank. Many women claimed that their contributions to the revolution's cause (by managing farms and shops in their husbands' absence) earned them greater equality in marriage, including property rights. However, the political arrangements Americans designed during their War of Independence gave voting rights only to white, male property owners—not women, not slaves, not Amerindians, not poor white men without property. Indeed, many slaves sided against the revolution, for it was the British who offered them freedom—most directly in exchange for military service. Their hopes for freedom were thwarted when Britain conceded the loss of its rebellious American colonies. With the Treaty of Paris (1783), the United States gained its independence.

Building a Republican Government With independence, the former colonists had to build a new government. They generally agreed that theirs was not to be a monarchy. But what it *was* to be remained through the 1780s a source of much debate, involving heated words and sometimes heated action. As a loose confederation of relatively autonomous states, the new national state struggled to deal with local rebellions, foreign relations, and crushing levels of debt. To save the young nation from falling into "anarchy," propertied men convened the Constitutional Convention in Philadelphia in 1787.

This gathering aimed to forge a document that would create a more powerful national government and a more unified nation. After fierce debate, the convention drafted a charter for a republican government in which power would rest with representatives of the people—not with a king. When it went before the states for approval, the Constitution was controversial. Its critics, known as anti-Federalists, feared the growth of a potentially tyrannical national government and insisted on including a Bill of Rights to protect individual liberties from abusive government intrusions. Ultimately the Constitution was ratified by the states and then amended by the Bill of Rights.

Ratification of the Constitution and the addition of the Bill of Rights did not end arguments about the scope and power of the national government of the United States. Some Americans called for the national government to abolish slavery. However, many others—especially leaders in the south, where slavery was a mainstay of the economy—argued that the national government did not have the power to do so. In an uneasy truce, political leaders agreed not to let the debate over whether to abolish slavery escalate into a cause for disunion. As the frontier pushed westward, however, the question of which new states would or would not allow slavery again sparked debates. Initially the existence of ample land postponed a confrontation. In 1800, Thomas Jefferson's election as the third president of the United States marked the triumph of a model of sending pioneers out to new lands in order to reduce conflict on old lands. In the same year, however, a Virginia slave named Gabriel Prosser raised an army of slaves to seize the state capital at Richmond and won support from white artisans and laborers for a more inclusive republic. His dream of an egalitarian revolution fell victim to white terror and black betrayal, though: twenty-seven slaves, including Prosser, went to the gallows. With them, for the moment, died the dream of a multiracial republic in which all men were truly created equal.

In the larger context of the Atlantic world, the successful defiance of Europe's most powerful empire and the establishment of a nonmonarchical, republican form of government sent shock waves through the Americas and Europe and even into distant corners of Asia and Africa. It also helped pave the way for other revolts over the next several decades.

THE FRENCH REVOLUTION, 1789–1799

Partly inspired by the American Revolution, French men and women soon began to call for liberty too—and the result profoundly shook Europe's dynasties and social hierarchies. Its impact, though, reached well beyond Europe, for the French Revolution, even more than the American, inspired rebels and terrified rulers around the globe.

Origins and Outbreak The French king himself opened the door to revolution. Eager to weaken his rival, England, Louis XVI spent huge sums in support of the American rebels—and thereby overloaded the state with debt. To restore his credit, Louis needed to raise taxes on the privileged classes; to do so, he was forced to convene the Estates-General, a medieval advisory body that had not met for over a century. Like the American colonists, French nobles argued that taxation gave them the right of representation.

When the delegates assembled in 1789, however, a procedural dispute spun out of control. The delegates of the clergy (the First Estate) and the aristocracy (the Second Estate) hoped to vote by estate and overrule the delegates representing everyone else (the Third Estate). But the Third Estate, which had more representatives than the first two estates combined, refused to be outvoted. It demanded that all delegates sit together in one chamber and vote as individuals. Soon delegates of the Third Estate declared themselves to be the "National Assembly," the body that should determine France's future.

Afraid that the King would crush the reform movement, a Parisian crowd attacked a medieval armory in search of weapons on July 14, 1789. Not only did this armory—the Bastille—hold gunpowder, but it was also an infamous prison for political prisoners.

The "Tennis Court Oath" Locked out of the chambers of the Estates-General, the deputies of the Third Estate reconvened at a nearby indoor tennis court in June 1789; there they swore an oath not to disband until the king recognized the sovereignty of a national assembly.

The crowd stormed the prison and murdered the commanding officer, then cut off his head and paraded it through the streets of Paris. On this day (Bastille Day), the king made the fateful decision not to call out the army, and the capital city belonged to the crowd. As news spread to the countryside, peasants torched manor houses and destroyed municipal archives containing records of feudal dues, payments they owed to landlords of specially designated properties. Barely three weeks later, the French National Assembly abolished the privileges of the nobility and the clergy. It declared a new era of liberty, equality, and fraternity. Liberty, like freedom, now meant the absence of constraint rather than a special privilege granted by the king.

Revolutionary Transformations The French Revolution connected the concept of a people more closely with a nation. The "Declaration of the Rights of Man and Citizen" (1789) echoed the Americans' Declaration of Independence, but in more radical terms. It guaranteed all citizens of the French nation inviolable liberties and gave all men equality under the law. It also proclaimed that "the principle of all sovereignty rests essentially in the nation." Both the rhetorical and the real war against old-regime privileges threatened to end dynastic and aristocratic rule in Europe.

Social relations changed too, as women felt that the new principles of citizenship should include women's rights. In 1791, a group of women demanded the right to bear arms to defend the revolution, but they stopped short of claiming equal rights for both sexes. In their view, women would become citizens by being good revolutionary wives and mothers, not because of any natural rights. In the same year, Olympe de Gouges composed the "Declaration of the Rights of Woman and Citizen," proposing rights to divorce, hold property in marriage, be educated, and have public careers. The all-male assembly did not take up these issues, believing that a "fraternity" of free *men* composed the nation.

As the revolution gained momentum, deep divisions emerged. In 1790, all clergy had to take an oath of loyalty to the new state—an action that bitterly divided the country. The most divisive, destructive turn in the revolution came in 1792, when the French declared a preemptive war against Austria, and then Prussia, Britain, and Russia. They soon had foreign armies on their soil and a civil war to contend with, when peasants outraged by the loyalty oath and city dwellers in major provincial cities rose up against the Revolutionary government and its wartime demands.

The Terror In response to this self-induced crisis, elite reformers made common cause with urban radicals in Paris, who demanded price controls, direct democracy, and the violent suppression of dissent. Together, they launched the Reign of Terror. The Committee of Public Safety, including the lawyer Maximilien Robespierre, oversaw the execution of as many as 40,000 so-called enemies of the people—mostly peasants and laborers who had taken up arms against them—justified in terms of defending the Republic. If most victims were of modest means, the term *aristocrat* was often equated with treason. Even before terror was declared as government policy, Louis XVI and his wife, Marie Antoinette, had lost their heads to the guillotine (itself a novel and supposedly rational, enlightened way to execute prisoners painlessly).

By 1794 France's army numbered some 800,000 soldiers, making it the world's largest. Most French officers now came from the middle classes, some even from the lower class. Foot soldiers identified with the French fatherland. Having vowed to wage a defensive war, they now pushed foreign armies off French soil and waged a war to "liberate" the disenfranchised from their rulers across Europe.

When the military emergency ended, enthusiasm for Robespierre's measures lost popular support, and Robespierre himself went to the guillotine on 9 Thermidor (according to the new, Revolutionary calendar, or July 28, 1794). His execution marked the end of the Terror but did not restore order. Several years later, following yet more political turmoil, a coup d'état brought to power a thirty-year-old general from the recently annexed Mediterranean island of Corsica.

The general, **Napoleon Bonaparte** (1769–1821), put security and order ahead of social reform. His regime retained significant revolutionary changes, especially those associated with more efficient state government. He eased religious tensions by working out an accord with the Vatican. However, Napoleon was determined not only to reform France but also to prevail over its enemies, and he retreated from republican principles. Taking the title Emperor of the French, he centralized government administration and established a system of rational tax collection. Most important, he created a civil legal code—the "Code Napoleon"—that applied throughout all of France (and the French colonies).

THE NAPOLEONIC ERA, 1799–1815

Determined to extend the reach of French influence, Napoleon launched a series of military campaigns in an effort to build a vast empire. He had his armies trumpet the principles of liberty, equality, and fraternity wherever they went. Many local populations initially embraced the French, regarding them as liberators from the old order. Although Napoleon thought the entire world would take up his cause, this was not always the case.

In Portugal, Spain, and Russia, French troops faced fierce popular resistance. Portuguese and Spanish soldiers and peasants formed bands of resisters called guerrillas, and British troops joined them to fight the French in the Peninsular War (1808–1813).

MAP 15.2 | Napoleon's Empire, 1812

Early in the first decade of the nineteenth century, Napoleon controlled almost all of Europe.

- What major states were under French control? What countries were allied to France?
- Compare this map with the European part of Map 15.1, and explain how Napoleon redrew the map of Europe. What major country was not under French control?
- According to your reading, how was Napoleon able to control and build alliances with so many states and kingdoms?

In Germany and Italy, as local inhabitants grew tired of paying tribute, many looked to their past for inspiration to oppose the French. Now they discovered something they had barely recognized before: *national* traditions and borders. One of the ironies of Napoleon's attempt to bring all of Europe under French rule was that it laid the foundations for nationalist strife.

In Europe, Napoleon extended his empire from the Iberian Peninsula to the Austrian and Prussian borders. (See Map 15.2.) By 1812, when he invaded Russia, however, his forces were too overstretched and undersupplied to survive the harsh winter. After his failed attack on Russia, all the major European powers united against him. At the Battle of

Waterloo in Belgium in 1815, armies from Prussia, Austria, Russia, and Britain crushed his troops as they made their last stand. The stage was now set for a century-long struggle on the continent between those who wanted to restore society as it was before the French Revolution and those who wanted to guarantee a more liberal order based on individual rights, limited government, and free trade.

Revolution in Saint-Domingue In 1791, slaves took up arms against white planters. This engraving was based on a German report on the uprising and reflects white fears of slave rebellion as much as the actual events themselves.

REVOLUTION IN SAINT-DOMINGUE (HAITI)

France also saw colonies break away in this age of new freedoms, notably Saint-Domingue. Unlike most of British North America, revolution here came from the bottom rungs of the social ladder: slaves. In this Caribbean colony, freedom therefore meant not just liberation from Europe, but emancipation from white planters. It posed a powerful question: how universal were these new rights?

At the outset of the French Revolution the island's black slave population numbered 500,000, compared with 40,000 white French settlers and about 30,000 free "people of color" (individuals of mixed black and white ancestry, as well as freed black slaves). Almost two-thirds of the slaves were relatively recent arrivals, brought to the colony to toil on its renowned sugar plantations, which were exceptional in their brutality. The slave population was an angry majority without local ties, producing wealth for rich absentee landlords of a different race.

The breakdown of authority in France unleashed conflict in Saint-Domingue, where local tensions were already high. White settlers sought self-government; they wanted to break free of the exclusive trade arrangement with France and to control the island themselves. Free blacks wanted to end racial discrimination among property holders without, initially, calling slavery into question. Slaves, by contrast, invoked revolutionary language to denounce their masters and air long-standing grievances. As civil war erupted, slaves fought French forces that had arrived to restore order. In 1793, the National Convention in France abolished slavery. In part, the motive was to declare the universality of liberty, equality, and fraternity within the French nation, which included colonies. In part, it was to restore order to the colony. Once liberated, the former slaves took control of the island. (See **Current Trends in World History: Two Case Studies in Political Change and Environmental Degradation**.)

The specter of a free country ruled by former slaves sent shudders across the Western Hemisphere, and above all in Britain and Spain, which had neighboring colonies. A version of martial law was declared in Venezuela. Thomas Jefferson, author of the Declaration of Independence and U.S. president at the time, refused to recognize Haiti. Like other American slave owners, he worried that the example of a successful slave uprising might inspire similar revolts in the United States and elsewhere in the Americas.

REVOLUTIONS IN SPANISH AND PORTUGUESE AMERICA

Revolutionary enthusiasm also spread through Spanish and Portuguese America. As in Haiti, subordinated people of color took advantage of the period's political instability;

Current Trends in World History

Two Case Studies in Political Change and Environmental Degradation

Overthrowing slavery and colonial domination did not necessarily halt environmental degradation. In fact, in two important New World countries, the new nations of Haiti and Brazil, the transition to independence aggravated environmental problems created by former colonial regimes.

Two hundred and fifty years ago, Haiti, which was under French colonial rule at that time and known as Saint-Domingue, was the richest colony in the Americas, perhaps even the richest colony in the world, accounting for two-thirds of France's worldwide investment. Saint-Domingue's extraordinary wealth came from large, white-owned sugar plantations that used a massive and highly coerced slave population. The slaves' lives were short and brutal, lasting on average only fifteen years; hence the wealthy planter class had to replenish their labor supplies from Africa at frequent intervals.

White planters on the island were eager to amass quick fortunes so that they could sell out and return to France. Vastly outnumbered by enslaved Africans at a time when abolitionist sentiments were gaining ground in Europe and even circulating among slaves in the Americas, the planters' families knew that their prosperity was unlikely to last. They gave little thought to sustainable growth and were not troubled that they were destroying their environment.

The planters greeted the onset of the French Revolution in 1789 with enthusiasm. They saw an opportunity to assert their independence from France, to engage in wider trading contacts with North America and the rest of the world, and thus to become even richer. They ignored the possibility that the ideals of the French Revolution—especially its slogan of liberty, equality, and fraternity—could inspire the island's free blacks, free mulattoes, and slaves. Indeed, no sooner had the white planters thrown in their lot with the Third Estate in France than a slave rebellion broke out in Saint-Domingue. From its beginnings in 1791, it led, after great loss of life to African slaves and French soldiers, to the proclamation of an independent state in Haiti in 1804, ruled by African Americans. Haiti became the Americas' second independent republican government. Although the revolt brought political independence to its black population, it only intensified the land's environmental deterioration. Not only did sugarcane fields become scorched battlefields, but freed slaves rushed to stake out independent plots on the old plantations and in wooded areas. In both places, the new peasant class energetically cleared the land. The small country became even more deforested, and intensive cultivation increased erosion and soil depletion. Haiti fell into a more vicious cycle of environmental degradation and poverty.

The second case study of political change leading to the destruction of the environment comes from the independent Brazilian state where the ruling elite, having achieved autonomy from Portugal, expanded the agrarian frontier. Landowners oversaw the clearing of ancient hardwood forests so that slaves and squatters could plant coffee trees. The clearing process had begun with sugarcane in the coastal regions, but it accelerated with coffee plantings in the hilly regions of São Paulo.

In fact, coffee was a worse threat to Brazil's forests than any other invader in the previous 300 years. Coffee trees thrive on soils that are neither soggy nor overly dry. Therefore planters razed the virgin forest,

they mobilized European ideas against European colonizers and challenged the established order. (See Map 15.3.)

Even before the French Revolution, Andean Indians rebelled against Spanish colonial authority. In a major uprising in the 1780s, they demanded freedom from forced labor and compulsory consumption of Spanish wares. After an army of 40,000 to 60,000 Andean Indians besieged the ancient capital of Cuzco and nearly vanquished Spanish armies, it took Spanish forces many years to eliminate the insurgents.

After this uprising, Iberian American elites who feared their Indian or slave majorities renewed their loyalty to the Spanish or Portuguese crown. Ultimately, however, the French Revolution and Napoleonic wars shattered the ties between Spain and Portugal and their American colonies.

Brazil and Constitutional Monarchy Brazil was a prized Portuguese colony whose path to independence saw little political turmoil and no social revolution. In 1807, French troops stormed Lisbon, the capital of Portugal, but not before the royals and their associates

Slaves Cutting Cane Sugar was the preeminent agricultural export from the New World for centuries. Owners of sugarcane plantations relied almost exclusively on African slaves to produce the sweetener. Labor in the fields was especially harsh, as slaves worked in the blistering sun from dawn until dusk.

which contained a balanced variety of trees and undergrowth, and Brazil's once-fertile soil suffered rapid depletion by a single-crop industry. Within one generation the clear-cutting led to infertile soils and extensive erosion, which drove planters farther into the frontier to destroy even more forest and plant more coffee groves. The environmental impact was monumental: between 1788 and 1888, when slavery was abolished, Brazil produced about 10 million tons of coffee and lost 300 million tons of ancient forest biomass (the accumulated biological material from living organisms).

QUESTIONS FOR ANALYSIS

- Who intensified the deforestation and degradation in each case, and why did they do it?
- Why do you think deforestation increased in intensity after Haitians and Brazilians gained their autonomy/independence?

Explore Further

David Geggus (ed.), *The Impact of the Haitian Revolution in the Atlantic World* (2001).

Jared Diamond and James A. Robinson (eds.), *Natural Experiments of History* (2010).

fled to Rio de Janeiro, then the capital of Brazil. There they settled down, enacting reforms in administration, agriculture, and manufacturing and establishing schools, hospitals, and a library. Brazil now became the center of the Portuguese empire. Furthermore, the royal family willingly shared power with the local planter aristocracy, so the economy prospered, and slavery expanded.

When the King returned to Portugal in 1821, his son Pedro remained. Fearing an uprising among local elites, Pedro declared Brazil an independent state and established a constitutional monarchy. Local elites soon embraced Pedro's rule and cooperated to minimize conflict, lest a slave revolt erupt. By the 1840s, Brazil had achieved a political stability unmatched in the Americas.

Mexico's Independence When Napoleon occupied Spain, he sparked a crisis in the Spanish empire that eventually led Mexico to secede. Because the ruling Spanish monarchy fell captive to Napoleon in 1807, colonial elites in Buenos Aires (Argentina), Caracas (Venezuela), and Mexico City (Mexico) found themselves without an emperor.

MAP 15.3 | Latin American Nation Building

Creating strong, unified nation-states proved difficult in Latin America. The map shows where boundaries were drawn in Mexico, the United Provinces of Central America, and the Republic of Colombia. In each case, the governments' territorial and nation-building ambitions failed to some degree.

- During what period did a majority of the colonies in Latin America gain independence?
- Which European countries lost the most in Latin America during this period?
- Why did all these colonies gain their independence during this time?

After Napoleon's defeat, locally born creoles resented the fact that Spain reinstated *peninsulares* (people born in Spain) as colonial officials with the help of the royal army. Inspired by Enlightenment thinkers and chafing at the efforts to restore Iberian authority, the creoles wanted to keep their privileges and get rid of the peninsulares.

Mexico's creoles identified themselves more as Mexicans than as Spanish Americans, and as the Spanish king appeared less and less able to govern effectively, Mexican generals (with support of the creoles) proclaimed Mexican independence in 1821. Unlike the situation in Brazil, Mexican secession did not lead to stability.

Other South American Revolutions The loosening of Spain's grip on its colonies was more prolonged and militarized than Britain's separation from its American colonies. Venezuela's Simón Bolívar (1783–1830), the son of a merchant-planter family, who was educated on Enlightenment texts, dreamed of a land governed by reason. He revered Napoleonic France as a model state built on military heroism and constitutional proclamations. So did the Argentine leader General José de San Martín (1778–1850). Men like Bolívar, San Martín, and their many generals waged extended wars of independence against Spanish armies and their allies between 1810 and 1824.

What started in South America as a political revolution against Spanish colonial authority escalated into a social struggle among Indians, mestizos, slaves, and whites. The armed populace threatened the planters and merchants; rural folk battled against aristocratic creoles; Andean Indians fled the mines and occupied great estates. Popular armies, having defeated Spanish forces by the 1820s, fought civil wars over the new postcolonial order.

New states and collective identities of nationhood now emerged. A narrow elite led these political communities, and their guiding principles were often contradictory. Bolívar, for instance, urged his followers to become "American," to overcome their local identities. He wanted the liberated countries to form a Latin American confederation, urging Peru and Bolivia to join Venezuela, Ecuador, and Colombia in the "Gran Colombia." But local identities prevailed, giving way to unstable national republics. Bolívar died surrounded by opponents; San Martín died in exile. The real heirs to independence were local military chieftains, who often forged alliances with landowners. Thus the legacy of the Spanish American revolutions was contradictory and echoed developments elsewhere around the world: the triumph of wealthy elites under a banner of liberty, yet often at the expense of poorer, nonwhite, and mixed populations.

Change and Trade in Africa

Africa also was swept up in revolutionary tides, as increased domestic and world trade—including the selling of African slaves—shifted the terms of state building across the continent. The main catalyst for Africa's political shake-up was the rapid growth and then the demise of the Atlantic slave trade.

ABOLITION OF THE SLAVE TRADE

Even as it enriched and empowered some Africans and many Europeans, the slave trade became a subject of fierce debate in the late eighteenth century. Some European and American revolutionaries argued that slave labor was inherently less productive than free wage labor and ought to be abolished. At the same time, another group favoring abolition of the slave trade insisted that traffic in slaves was immoral. In London they created committees, often led by Quakers, to lobby Parliament for an end to the slave trade. Quakers in Philadelphia did likewise. Pamphlets, reports, and personal narratives denounced the traffic in people.

In response to abolitionist efforts, North Atlantic powers moved to prohibit the slave trade. Denmark acted first in its Caribbean colonies in 1803, Great Britain followed in 1807, and the United States joined the campaign in 1808. Over time, the British persuaded the French and other European governments to do likewise. To enforce the ban, Britain posted a naval squadron off the coast of West Africa to prevent any slave trade above the equator and compelled Brazil's emperor to end slave imports. After 1850, Atlantic slave-shipping dropped sharply, though slavery did not end for several decades due to the continued profitability of cotton in the southern United States, sugar in the Caribbean, and coffee in Brazil.

NEW TRADE WITH AFRICA

Even as the Atlantic slave trade died down, Europeans promoted commerce with Africa. Now they wanted Africans to export raw materials and to purchase European manufactured goods. What Europeans liked to call "legitimate" trade aimed to raise the Africans' standards of living by substituting trade in produce for trade in slaves. West Africans responded by exporting palm kernels and peanuts. The real bonanza was in vegetable oils to lubricate machinery and make candles and in palm oil to produce soap. European merchants argued that by becoming vibrant export societies, Africans would earn the wealth to profitably import European wares.

The new trade gave rise to a generation of successful West African merchants. There were many rags-to-riches stories, like that of King Jaja of Opobo (1821–1891). Kidnapped and sold into slavery as a youngster, he started out paddling canoes carrying palm oil to coastal ports. Ultimately becoming the head of a coastal canoe house, he founded the port of Opobo and could summon a flotilla of war canoes on command. Another freed slave, a Yoruba, William Lewis, made his way back to Africa and in 1828 settled in Sierra Leone (a British colony for freed slaves, notably Black Loyalists from the United States). Starting with a few utensils and a small plot of land, he became a successful merchant who sent his son Samuel to England for his education. Samuel eventually became an important political leader in Sierra Leone.

However, the rise of free labor in the Atlantic world and the dwindling foreign slave trade had an unanticipated effect. It strengthened slavery within Africa. In some areas, by the mid-nineteenth century slaves accounted for more than half the population. No longer did they comfortably serve in domestic employment; instead, they toiled on palm oil plantations or, in East Africa, on clove plantations. They also served in the military forces, bore palm oil and ivory to markets as porters, or paddled cargo-carrying canoes along rivers leading to the coast. In 1850, northern Nigeria's ruling class had more slaves than independent Brazil, and almost as many as the United States. As Africa ceased to be the world's supplier of slaves, it became in time the world's largest slave-holding region.

Economic Reordering

COMPARISON

IDENTIFY and **EXPLAIN** the key developments that constituted the Industrial Revolution.

Behind the political and social upheavals, profound changes were occurring in the world economy. Until the middle of the eighteenth century, global trade touched only the edges of most societies, which produced for their own subsistence. Surpluses of special goods, from porcelains to silks, entered trade arteries but did not change the cultures that produced

New Farming Technologies Although major technological changes in agriculture only emerged late in this period, the spread of more intensive cultivation led to increased yields.

them. A century later, by the middle of the nineteenth century, global trade networks had expanded their reach. The desire for cash, for silver or gold, drove market relations much further than they had ever reached before. People increasingly worked to produce goods they could sell, which transformed social relations in agricultural hinterlands as well as bustling urban centers.

AN INDUSTRIOUS REVOLUTION

Many of these developments took place first in northwestern Europe and British North America. Here, as elsewhere in the world, households had always produced mainly for themselves and made available for marketplaces only meager surpluses of goods and services. But dramatic changes occurred when family members, including wives and children, decided to work harder and longer in order to produce more for the market and purchase more in the market. In these locations, households devoted less time to leisure activities and more time to working, using the additional income from hard work to purchase products produced elsewhere. Scholars recently have come to call this change an **industrious revolution**. Beginning in the second half of the seventeenth century, it gained speed in the eighteenth century and laid the foundations for the industrial revolution of the late eighteenth and early nineteenth centuries.

The willingness on the part of families to work more and an eagerness to eat more diverse foods, to wear better clothes, and to consume products that had once been available as luxuries only to the wealthy classes led in turn to a large expansion in trade. Sugar and silver were the pioneering products. But by the eighteenth century, other staples joined the long-distance trading business, including tea: its leaves came from China, the sugar to cut its bitterness from the Caribbean, the slaves to harvest the sweetener from Africa, and the ceramics to serve a proper cup from the English Midlands. Even ordinary people could purchase imported goods with their earnings. Thus, the poor began to enjoy coffee, tea, and sugar. European artisans and farmers purchased tools, furnishings, and home decorations. Slaves and colonial laborers also used their meager earnings to buy imported cotton cloth made in Europe from the raw cotton they themselves had picked several seasons earlier.

The expansion of global trade had important social and political consequences. As new goods flowed from ever more distant corners of the globe, immense fortunes grew. To support their enterprise, traders needed new services in insurance, bookkeeping, and the recording of legal documents. Trade supported the growth of the liberal professions—accountants and lawyers. The new cities of the commercial revolution, hubs like Bristol, Bombay, and Buenos Aires, provided the homes and flourishing neighborhoods for the growing class of men and women known as the **bourgeoisie**: urban businessmen, financiers, and other property owners without aristocratic origins.

THE INDUSTRIAL REVOLUTION

Trade and finance repositioned western Europe's relationship with the rest of the world. So did the emergence of manufacturing. Like agricultural production, output of industrial commodities surged. The heart of this process was a gradual accumulation and diffusion of technical knowledge. Lots of little inventions, their applications, and their spread across the Atlantic world gradually built up a stock of technical knowledge and practice. Historians have traditionally called these changes the **industrial revolution**.

Nowhere was this industrial revolution more evident than in Britain. Britain had access to waterways, constructed a network of canals, and had large supplies of coal and iron—key materials used in manufactured products. It also had a political and social environment that allowed merchants and industrialists to invest heavily while also expanding their internal and international markets. Among their investments was the application of steam power to textile production, which enabled Britain's manufacturers to produce cheaper goods in larger quantities. Finally, Britain had access to New World lands as sources of financial investment, raw materials, and markets for manufactured goods. These factors' convergence promoted self-sustaining economic growth.

Consider the relationship between inventor and investor in the advent of the steam engine. Such engines burned coal to boil water, and the resulting steam drove mechanized devices. There were several tinkerers working on such an engine. But the most famous was James Watt (1736–1819) of Scotland, who managed to separate steam condensers from piston cylinders so that pistons could stay hot and run constantly; he joined forces with the industrialist Matthew Boulton, who marketed the steam engine and set up a laboratory where Watt could refine his device. The steam engine catalyzed a revolution in transportation. Steam-powered engines also improved sugar refining, pottery making, and other industrial processes, generating more products at lower cost than when workers had made them by hand.

Textile production was critical. Most raw cotton for the British cloth industry had come from colonial India until 1793, when the American inventor Eli Whitney (1765–1825) patented a "cotton gin" that separated cotton seeds from fiber. After that, cotton farming spread so quickly in the southern United States that by the 1850s it was producing more than 80 percent of the world's cotton supply. In turn, every black slave in the Americas and many Indians in British India were consumers of cheap, British-produced cotton shirts. The price of cotton cloth declined by nearly 50 percent between 1780 and 1850, as textiles became the

A Cotton Textile Mill in the 1830s The region of Lancashire became one of the major industrial hubs for textile production in the world. By the 1830s, mills had made the shift from artisanal work to highly mechanical mass production. Among the great breakthroughs was the discovery that cloth could be printed with designs, such as paisley or calico (as in this image), and marketed to middle-class consumers.

world's most dynamic industry. England became the world's largest cloth producer, driving most of the other centers of textile production, notably those in the Indian subcontinent, out of business.

Wherever the industrial revolution took hold, it allowed societies to outdistance rivals in manufacturing and elevated them to a new place in the emerging global economic order. (See Map 15.4.) But why did this revolution cluster mainly in the Atlantic world? This is an important question, because the unequal distribution of global wealth, the gap between the haves and have-nots, really took off in this era of revolutions. In much of Asia and Africa, technical change altered modes of production and business practices, but it was not followed by a continuous cascade of changes. The great mystery was China, the home of astronomical water clocks and gunpowder. Why did China not become the epicenter of the industrial revolution?

There are two reasons. China did not foster experimental science of the kind that allowed Watt to stumble onto the possibility of steam, or Whitney the cotton gin. Experimentation, testing, and the links between thinkers and investors were a distinctly Atlantic phenomenon. The Qing, like the Mughal and Ottoman dynasties, swept the great minds into the bureaucracy and reinforced the old agrarian system based on peasant exploitation and tribute. Second, Chinese, Mughal, and Ottoman rulers did not support overseas expansion and trade that helped create the commercial revolution in the Atlantic world. The agrarian dynasties of China and India neither showered favors on local merchants nor effectively shut out interlopers. This made them vulnerable to cheap manufactured imports from European traders backed by their governments extolling the virtues of free trade.

The effects were profound. Historically, Europe had a trade imbalance with partners to the east—furs from Russia, and spices and silks from Asia. It made up for this with silver from the Americas. But the new economic order meant that by the nineteenth century, western Europe not only had manufactures like cotton textiles to export to Asia, it

MAP 15.4 | Industrial Europe around 1850

By 1850 much of western Europe was industrial and urban, with major cities linked to one another through a network of railroads.

- According to this map, what natural resources contributed to the growth of the industrial revolution? What effects did it have on urban population densities?
- Compare the course of major rivers with those of the railways.
- According to your reading, why were the effects of the industrial revolution more rapidly apparent in Great Britain and in north-central Europe?

also had capital. One of Europe's biggest debtors was none other than the sultan of the Ottoman Empire, whose tax system could not keep up with the spending necessary to keep the realm together. More and more, Asian, African, and American governments found themselves borrowing from Europe's financiers just as their people were buying industrial products from Europe and selling their primary products to European consumers and producers.

WORKING AND LIVING

The industrial revolution brought more demanding work routines—not only in the manufacturing economies of western Europe and North America but also on the farms and plantations of Asia and Africa.

Urban Life and Work Routines Increasingly, Europe's workers made their livings in cities. London, Europe's largest city in 1700, saw its population nearly double over the next century to almost 1 million. By the 1820s, population growth was even greater in the industrial hubs of Leeds, Glasgow, Birmingham, Liverpool, and Manchester. (See **Analyzing Global Developments: Town and Countryside, Core and Periphery in the Nineteenth Century**.)

For most urban dwellers, cities were not healthy places. Water that powered the mills, along with chemicals used in dyeing, went directly back into waterways that provided drinking water. Overcrowded tenements shared just a few outhouses. Most European cities as late as 1850 had no running water, no garbage pickup, no underground sewer system. The result was widespread disease. (In fact, no European city at this time had as clean a water supply as the largest towns of the ancient Roman Empire once had.)

Changes in work affected the understanding of time. Whereas most farmers' workloads had followed seasonal rhythms, after 1800 industrial settings imposed a rigid concept of work discipline. To keep the machinery operating, factory and mill owners installed huge clocks and used bells or horns to signify the workday's beginning and end. Employers also measured output per hour and compared workers' performance.

Industrialization imposed numbing work routines and paltry wages. Worse, however, was having no work at all. As families abandoned their farmland and depended on wages, being idle meant having no income. Periodic downturns in the economy put wage workers at risk, and many responded by organizing protests.

Social Protest and Emigration While entrepreneurs accumulated private wealth, the effects of the industrial revolution on working-class families raised widespread concern, sometimes leading to protests or emigration. In the 1810s in England, groups of jobless craftsmen, called Luddites, smashed the machines that had left them unemployed. Social advocates sought protective legislation for workers, including curbing child labor, limiting the workday, and, in some countries, legalizing prostitution for the sake of monitoring the prostitutes' health.

Some people, however, could not wait for legislative reform. The period saw unprecedented emigration, as unemployed workers or peasants abandoned their homes to seek their fortunes in America, Canada, and Australia. During the Irish Potato Famine of 1845–1849, at least 1 million Irish citizens left their country (and a further million or so died) when fungi attacked their subsistence crop. Desperate to escape starvation, they booked cheap passage to North America on ships so notorious for disease and malnutrition that they earned the name "Coffin Ships."

Analyzing Global Developments

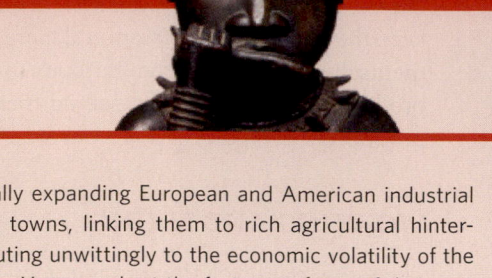

Town and Countryside, Core and Periphery in the Nineteenth Century

The textile industry was by far the most dynamic sector of the world economy in the nineteenth century. It was dependent on cotton, whose production was labor-intensive but required relatively little capital investment and benefited little from economies of scale. In the first half of the century, cotton was primarily produced by slaves in the southern United States. By the late 1850s, the United States accounted for 77 percent of the cotton consumed in Britain, for 90 percent in France, and for about 92 percent in Russia. After the U.S. Civil War and subsequent slave emancipations, sharecroppers continued to produce the crop, though cotton production began to flourish in Brazil, Egypt, West Africa, and India.

Wheat, on the other hand, was the basic staple of European and Mediterranean diets well into the nineteenth century, and it remains vitally important. Before the advent of railroads, most wheat was consumed locally. In the second half of the century, however, vast quantities of wheat came onto world markets as railroads spread through the midwest of the United States and the plains of central and eastern Europe. Grown on large, capital-intensive farms, that wheat—as well as rye, corn, millet, and other grains—fed radically expanding European and American industrial cities and factory towns, linking them to rich agricultural hinterlands and contributing unwittingly to the economic volatility of the nineteenth century. Here we chart the fortunes of two of the most important commodities of the nineteenth-century world—cotton and wheat—against the growth of cities and railroads.

QUESTIONS FOR ANALYSIS

- Which countries appear to be the most dynamic? Pay attention to relative change over time—not only in the biggest cities and most extensive rail networks but also in those growing the fastest.
- How does the growth of railroads and cities vary by country? What does this tell us about the relationship between economic core regions and their peripheries, and about patterns of inequality more generally?
- How did the extension of railroads, and the economic integration they fostered, influence patterns of inequality worldwide?

POPULATION OF MAJOR CITIES (IN THOUSANDS)

	1800	1830	1850	1880	1900
Alexandria	15		60	231	320
Delhi		150	152	173	209
Rio de Janeiro	43	125	166	360	523
London	1,117		2,685	4,770	6,586
Paris	576		1,053	2,269	2,714
Moscow	250		365	748	989
New York City	60	161	340	847	1,478
Tokyo	457			824	1,819

POPULATION ESTIMATES (IN THOUSANDS)

	1800	1825	1850	1875	1900
Egypt	3,854	4,541	4,752	6,961	10,186
India	255,000	257,000	285,000	306,000	
Brazil			7,678	9,930	17,438
England	8,893	12,000	17,928	22,712	32,528
France	27,349	30,462	35,783	36,906	38,451
Russia	35,500	52,300	68,500	90,200	132,900
America	5,297	11,252	23,261	45,073	76,094
Japan	25,622	26,602	27,201	25,037	44,359

OUTPUT OF COTTON (IN THOUSAND METRIC TONS)

	1800	1825	1850	1875	1900
Egypt				132	293
India			12	533	536
America	17	121	484	1,050	2,120

WHEAT PRODUCTION (IN THOUSAND METRIC TONS)

	1825	1850	1875	1900
France	4,580	6,600	7,550	8,860
Russia			53	136
America		2,722	8,546	16,302

LENGTH OF OPEN RAILWAY LINES (IN KILOMETERS)

	1825	1850	1875	1900
Egypt		1,184	1,410	2,237
India		32	10,527	39,834
Brazil		14	1,801	15,316
England	43	9,797	23,365	30,079
France	17	2,915	19,351	38,109
Russia	27	501	19,029	53,234
America	37	14,518	119,246	311,160
Japan		29	62	6,300

Sources: S. Beckert, "Emancipation and Empire: Reconstructing the Worldwide Web of Cotton Production in the Age of the American Civil War," *The American Historical Review* 109, no. 5 (December 2004): 1405–1438; B. R. Mitchell, *International Historical Statistics: Africa, Asia, and Oceania, 1750–2005, International Historical Statistics: The Americas, 1750–2005,* and International Historical Statistics: Europe, 1750–2005 (London: Palgrave Macmillan, 2007).

The industrial revolution produced wealth on an unprecedented scale, but that wealth was distributed unevenly. Enormous inequalities resulted, both within societies and between them. Free trade resulted, in the long run, not in the proliferation of ever-more-productive small workshops but in massive industrial concentration, a concentration that would prove dynamic, creative, and unstable.

Persistence and Change in Afro-Eurasia

Western Europe's military might, its technological achievements, and its economic strength represented a threat to the remaining Afro-Eurasian empires. Western European merchants and industrialists sought closer economic and (in some cases) political ties. They did so in the name of gaining "free" access to Asian markets and products. Rulers in Russia, the Ottoman Empire, India, and China all sought to borrow from the ideas and institutions emerging from western Europe, but they did so on their own terms, intent on defending the core of their social and political traditions.

COMPARISON

COMPARE the groups of people who held power in each of the regions in 1750 and then in 1850, and **EXPLAIN** the change that took place during this period in these societies.

REVAMPING THE RUSSIAN MONARCHY

Russian rulers responded to the pressures by strengthening their traditional authority through modest reforms and the suppression of domestic opposition. Tsar Alexander I (r. 1801–1825) was fortunate that Napoleon committed several blunders and lost his formidable army in the Russian snows. Yet the French Revolution and its massive armies struck at the heart of Russian political institutions, which rested upon a huge peasant population laboring as serfs. The tsars could no longer justify their absolutism by claiming that enlightened despotism was the most advanced form of government, since a new model, rooted in popular sovereignty and the concept of the nation, had arisen.

In December 1825, when Alexander died unexpectedly and childless, there was a question over succession. Some Russian officers launched a patriotic revolt. The Decembrists, as they were called, came primarily from elite families and were familiar with western European life and institutions. Some called for a constitutional monarchy to replace Russia's despotism; others favored a tsar-less republic and the abolition of serfdom. Their conspiracy failed to win over conservatives or the peasantry, who still believed in the tsar's divine right to rule. Nicholas (r. 1825–1855) became tsar and brutally suppressed the insurrectionists.

Still, Alexander's successors faced a world in which powerful European states had constitutions and national armies of citizens, not subjects. In trying to maintain absolutist rule, Russian tsars portrayed the monarch's family as the ideal historical embodiment of the nation with direct ties to the people. Nicholas himself prevented rebellion by expanding the secret police, enforcing censorship, conducting impressive military exercises, and maintaining serfdom. And in the 1830s he introduced a conservative ideology that stressed religious faith, hierarchy, and obedience. For the time being, the influence of the French Revolution was quashed in Russia.

REFORMING EGYPT AND THE OTTOMAN EMPIRE

Unlike Russia, where Napoleon's army had reached Moscow, the Ottoman capital in Istanbul never faced a threat by French troops. Still, Napoleon's invasion of Egypt shook the Ottoman Empire. Even before this trauma, Ottoman authorities faced the challenge posed by increased trade with Europe—and the greater presence of European merchants and missionaries. In addition, many non-Muslim religious communities in the sultan's empire wanted the European powers to advance their interests. In the wake of Napoleon, who had promised to remake Egyptian society, reformist energies swept from Egypt to the center of the Ottoman domain.

COMPARISON

EXPLAIN patterns of global trade and economic growth and **CONNECT** them to political changes during the period 1750–1850.

Reforms in Egypt In Egypt, far-reaching changes came with the rule of **Muhammad Ali**. After the French withdrawal in 1801, Muhammad Ali (r. 1805–1848) won a chaotic struggle for supreme power in Egypt and aligned himself with influential Egyptian families. Yet he looked to revolutionary France for a model of modern state building. As with Napoleon (and with Simón Bolívar in Latin America), the key to his hold on power was the army.

Muhammad Ali also made reforms in education and agriculture. He established a school of engineering and opened the first modern medical school in Cairo under the supervision of a French military doctor. And his efforts in the countryside made Egypt one of the world's leading cotton exporters. A summer crop, cotton required steady watering when the Nile's irrigation waters were in short supply. So Muhammad Ali's Public Works Department, advised by European engineers, deepened the irrigation canals and constructed a series of dams across the Nile. These efforts transformed Egypt, making it the most powerful state in the eastern Mediterranean and alarming the Ottoman state (which still controlled Egypt) and the great powers in Europe. At the same time, European merchants pressed for free access to Egyptian markets, just as they did in Latin America and Africa.

Ottoman Reforms Under political and economic pressures like those facing Muhammad Ali in Egypt, Ottoman rulers also made reforms. Indeed, military defeats and humiliating treaties with Europe were painful reminders of the sultans' vulnerability. In 1805 Sultan Selim III tried to create a new infantry, trained by western European officers. But before he could bring this force up to fighting strength, the janissaries stormed the palace, killed its officers, and deposed Selim in 1807. Over the next few decades, janissary military men and clerical scholars (*ulama*) cobbled together an alliance that thwarted reformers.

Why did reform falter in the Ottoman state before it could be implemented? Reform was possible only if the forces opposed to reform—especially in the military—were weak and the reformers strong. In the Ottoman Empire, the janissary class had grown powerful, providing the main resistance to change. Ottoman authority depended on clerical support, and the Muslim clergy also resisted change. Blocked at the top, Ottoman rulers hesitated to appeal for popular support. Such an appeal, in the new age of popular sovereignty and national feeling, would be dangerous for an unelected dynast in a multiethnic and multireligious realm.

Mahmud II (r. 1808–1839) broke the political deadlock, shrewdly manipulating his conservative opponents. Like Muhammad Ali in Egypt, Mahmud brought in European officers to advise his forces. Here, too, military reform spilled over into nonmilitary areas. The Ottoman modernizers created a medical college, then a school of military sciences. To understand Europe better and to create a first-rate diplomatic corps, the Ottomans schooled their officials in European languages and had European classics translated into Turkish. As Mahmud's successors extended reforms into civilian life, this era—known as the Tanzimat, or Reorganization period—saw legislation that guaranteed equality for all Ottoman subjects, regardless of religion.

The reforms, however, stopped well short of revolutionary change. Reform relied too much on the personal whim of rulers, and the bureaucratic and religious infrastructure

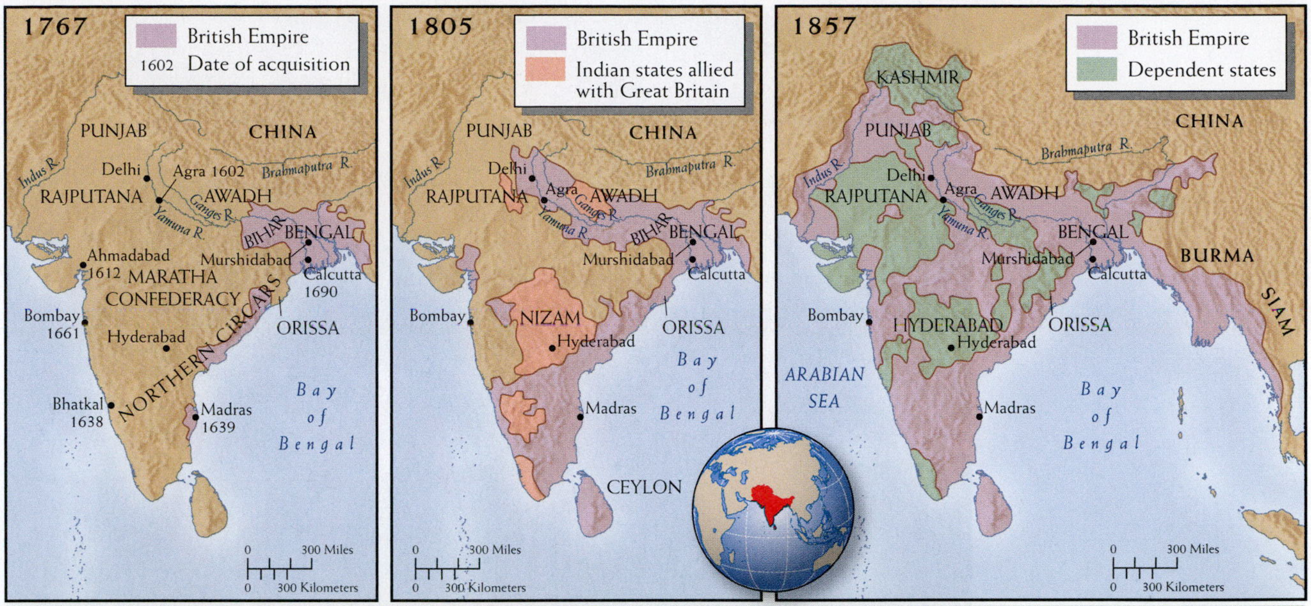

MAP 15.5 | The British in India, 1767–1857

Starting from locations in eastern and northeastern India, the British East India Company extended its authority over much of South Asia prior to the outbreak of the Indian Rebellion of 1857.

- What type of location did the British first acquire in India?
- According to your reading, how did the company expand into the interior of India and administer these possessions?
- Why did it choose a strategy of direct rule over some areas and indirect rule over other areas in India?

remained committed to old ways. Any effort to reform the rural sector met resistance by the landed interests. Finally, the merchant classes profited from business with a debt-ridden sultan. By preventing the empire's fiscal collapse through financial support to the state, bankers lessened the pressure for reform and removed the spark that had fired revolutions in Europe.

COLONIAL REORDERING IN INDIA

Europe's most important colonial possession in Asia between 1750 and 1850 was British India. Unlike in North America, the changes that the British fostered in Asia did not lead to political independence. Instead, India was increasingly dominated by the **East India Company**, which the crown had chartered in 1600. The company's control over India's imports and exports in the eighteenth and nineteenth centuries, however, contradicted British claims about their allegiance to a world economic system based on "free trade."

The East India Company's Monopoly In enforcing the East India Company's monopoly on trade, the British soon took control of much of the region. Initially, the British tried to control India's commerce by establishing trading posts along the coast without taking complete political control. After conquering the state of Bengal in 1757, the company began to fill its coffers and its officials began to amass personal fortunes. In spite of violent opposition, the British secured the right for the East India Company to collect tax

Indian Resistance to Company Rule Tipu Sultan, the Mysore ruler, put up a determined resistance against the British. This painting by Robert Home shows Cornwallis, the East India Company's governor, receiving Tipu's two sons as hostages after defeating him in the 1792 war. The boys remained in British custody for two years. Tipu returned to fighting the British and was killed in the war of 1799.

revenues in Bengal, Bihar, and Orissa and to trade free of duties throughout Mughal territory. In return, the Mughal emperor would receive a hefty annual pension. The company went on to annex other territories, bringing much of South Asia under its rule by the early 1800s. (See Map 15.5.)

To rule with minimal interference required knowing the conquered society. This led to orientalist scholarship: British scholar-officials wrote the first modern histories of South Asia, translated Sanskrit and Persian texts, identified philosophical writings, and compiled Hindu and Muslim law books. Through their efforts, the company-state presented itself as a force for revitalizing authentic Hinduism and recovering India's literary and cultural treasures. However, although the orientalist scholars admired Sanskrit language and literature, they still supported British colonial rule and did not necessarily agree with local beliefs.

Effects in India Company rule and booming trade altered India's urban geography. By the early nineteenth century, colonial cities like Calcutta, Madras, and Bombay became the new centers at the expense of older Mughal cities like Agra, Delhi, Murshidabad, and Hyderabad. As the colonial cities attracted British merchants and Indian clerks, artisans, and laborers, their populations surged. Calcutta's reached 350,000 in 1820; Bombay's jumped to 200,000 by 1825. In these cities, Europeans lived close to the company's fort and trading stations, while migrants from the countryside clustered in crowded quarters called "black towns."

India now became an importer of British textiles and an exporter of raw cotton—a reversal of its traditional pattern of trade. In the past, India had been an important textile manufacturer, exporting fine cotton goods throughout the Indian Ocean and to Europe.

But its elites could not resist the appeal of cheap British textiles. As a result, India's industrial sector declined. In addition, the import of British manufactures caused unfavorable trade balances that changed India from a net importer of gold and silver to an exporter of these precious metals.

Led by evangelical Christians and liberal reformers, the British did more than alter the Indian economy; they also advocated far-reaching changes in Indian culture. For example, they sought to stop the practice of *sati,* by which women burned to death on the funeral pyres of their dead husbands. Now the mood swung away from the orientalists' respect for India's classical languages, philosophies, cultures, and texts. In 1835, when the British poet, historian, and Liberal politician Lord Macaulay was making recommendations on educational policies, he urged that English replace Persian as the language of administration and that European education replace Oriental learning. The result, reformers hoped, would be a class that was Indian in blood and color but English in tastes and culture.

This was a new colonial order, but it was not stable. Most wealthy landowners resented the loss of their land and authority. Peasants, thrown to the mercy of the market, moneylenders, and landlords and subject to high taxation, were in turmoil. The non-Hindu forest dwellers and roaming cultivators, faced with the hated combination of a colonial state and moneylenders, revolted. Dispossessed artisans stirred up towns and cities. And merchants and industrialists chafed under the British-dominated economy. As freedom expanded in Europe, exploitation expanded in India.

PERSISTENCE OF THE QING EMPIRE

The remote Chinese empire was largely unaffected by the upheavals in Europe and America until the first Opium War (1839–1842) forced the Chinese to acknowledge their military weaknesses. The Qing dynasty, which had taken power in 1644, was still enjoying prosperity and territorial expansion as the nineteenth century dawned. Their sense of imperial splendor continued to rest on the political structure and social order inherited from the Ming (see Chapter 11). However, they could not resist European demands for access to their resources and markets.

The Qing had a talent for extending the empire's boundaries and settling frontier lands. Before 1750, they conquered Taiwan (the stronghold of remaining Ming forces), pushed westward into central Asia, and annexed Tibet. To secure these territorial gains, the Qing encouraged settlement of frontier lands like Xinjiang. New crops from the Americas aided this process—especially corn and sweet potatoes, which grow well in less fertile soils.

Like their European counterparts, Chinese peasants were on the move. But migration occurred in Qing China for different reasons. The state-sponsored westward movement into Xinjiang, for example, aimed to secure a recently pacified frontier region through military colonization, after which civilians would follow. So peasants received promises of land, tools, seed, and the loan of silver and a horse—all with the dual objectives of producing enough food to supply the troops and relieving pressure on the poor and arid northwestern part of the country. These efforts brought so much land under cultivation by 1840 that the region's ecological and social landscape completely changed.

Despite their success in expanding the empire, the Qing faced nagging problems. As a ruling minority, they looked warily at innovation, and only late in the eighteenth century did they deal with their rapidly expanding population. On the one hand, the tripling of China's population since 1300 demonstrated the realm's prosperity; on the other, a population of over 300 million severely strained resources—especially soil for growing crops and wood for fuel. In the late eighteenth and early nineteenth centuries, uprisings inspired by mystical beliefs in folk Buddhism, and at times by the idea of restoring the Ming, engulfed northern China.

By the mid-nineteenth century, extraordinary changes had made western European powers stronger than ever before, and the Qing could no longer dismiss their demands. The first clear evidence of an altered global balance of power was not the rise of Napoleon, but a British-Chinese war over a narcotic. Indeed, the **Opium War** exposed China's vulnerability in a new era of European ascendancy.

The Opium War and the "Opening" of China Europeans had been selling staples and intoxicants in China for a long time, and by the late eighteenth century opium, which had previously been used as a medicine or an aphrodisiac, was being smoked in long-stemmed pipes at every level of Chinese society. Sensing opium's economic potential, the East India Company established a monopoly over the export of opium from India in 1773 to help pay for a rapid growth in the company's purchase of tea from China. Because the Chinese showed little taste for British goods, the British had been financing their tea imports with exports of silver to China. But by the late eighteenth century, the company's tea purchases had become too large to finance with silver. Fortunately for the company, the Chinese were eager for Indian cotton and opium, and then mostly just opium.

Opium's impact on China's balance of trade was devastating. In a reversal from earlier trends, silver began to flow out of instead of into China. Once silver shortages occurred, the peasants' tax burden grew heavier. Consequently, long-simmering unrest in the countryside gained momentum. At the Qing court, some officials wanted to legalize the opium trade so as to eliminate corruption and boost revenues. (After all, as long as opium was an illegal substance, the government could not tax its traffic.) In 1838 the emperor sent

Opium (*Left*) A common sight in late Qing China was establishments catering specifically to opium smoking. Taken from a volume condemning the practice, this picture shows opium smokers idling their day away. (*Right*) Having established a monopoly in the 1770s over opium cultivation in India, the British greatly expanded their manufacture and export of opium to China to balance their rapidly growing import of Chinese tea and silk. This picture from the 1880s shows an opium warehouse in India where the commodity was stored before being transported to China.

MAP 15.6 | The Qing Empire and the Opium War

The Opium War demonstrated the superiority of British military technology. Their victory granted the British control of Hong Kong and established a series of treaty ports, which gave Europeans access to Chinese trade and which were subject to the laws of designated European countries.

- How many treaty ports were there after the Opium War? What was their significance?
- How were the treaty ports distributed along China's coastline?
- According to the text, how did the Opium War change relations between China and the western powers?

a special commissioner to Canton, the main center of the trade, to eradicate the influx of opium.

When British merchants in Canton resisted, war broke out. In June 1840, British warships bombarded coastal regions near Canton and sailed upriver for a short way. On land, Qing soldiers used spears, clubs, and a few imported matchlock muskets against the modern artillery of British troops, many of whom were Indians supplied with percussion cap rifles. Along the Yangzi River, outgunned Qing forces fought fiercely, as soldiers killed their own wives and children before committing suicide themselves. But they were no match for British military technology.

The Qing ruling elite capitulated, and through the 1842 Treaty of Nanjing, the British acquired the island of Hong Kong and the right to trade directly with the Chinese in five treaty ports and to reside there. (See Map 15.6.) They also forced the Chinese to repay the costs that the British had incurred in the war.

Subsequent treaties guaranteed that the British and other foreign nationals would be tried in their own courts for crimes, rather than in Chinese courts, and would be exempt from Chinese law. Moreover, the British insisted that any privileges granted through treaties with other parties would also apply to them. Other western nations followed the British example in demanding the same right, and the arrangement thus guaranteed all Europeans and North Americans a privileged position in China.

Still, China did not become a formal colony. To the contrary, in the mid-nineteenth century Europeans and North Americans were trading only on its outskirts. Most Chinese did not encounter Europeans. Daily life for most people went on as it had before the Opium War. Only the political leaders and urban dwellers were beginning to feel the foreign presence and wondering what steps China might take to acquire European technologies, goods, and learning.

Conclusion

During the period 1750–1850, changes in politics, commerce, industry, and technology reverberated throughout the Atlantic world and, to varying degrees, elsewhere around the globe. By 1850, the world was more integrated economically, with Europe increasingly at the center.

In the Americas, colonial ties broke apart. In France, the people toppled the monarchy. Dissidents threatened the same in Russia. Such upheavals introduced a new public vocabulary—the language of the nation—and made the idea of revolution empowering. In the Americas and parts of Europe, nation-states took shape around redefined hierarchies of class, gender, and color. Britain and France emerged from the political crises of the late eighteenth century determined to expand their borders. Their drive forced older empires such as Russia and the Ottoman state to make reforms.

As commerce and industrialization transformed economic and political power, European governments compelled others (including Egypt, India, and China) to expand their trade with European merchants. Ultimately, such countries had to participate in a European-centered economy as exporters of raw materials and importers of European manufactures. By the 1850s, many of the world's peoples became more industrious, producing less for themselves and more for distant markets. Through changes in manufacturing, some areas of the world also made more goods than ever before. With its emphasis on free trade, Europe began to force open new markets—even to the point of colonizing them. Gold and silver now flowed out of China and India to pay for European products like opium and textiles.

However, global reordering did not mean that Europe's rulers had uncontested control over other people, or that the institutions and cultures of Asia and Africa ceased to be dynamic. Some countries became dependent on Europe commercially; others became colonies. China escaped colonial rule but was forced into unfavorable trade relations with the Europeans. In sum, dramatic changes combined to unsettle systems of rulership and to alter the economic and military balance between western Europe and the rest of the world.

After You Read This Chapter

Go to INQUIZITIVE to see what you've learned—and learn what you've missed—with personalized feedback along the way.

TRACING THE GLOBAL STORYLINES

FOCUS ON: *The Global Effects of the "New Ideas"*

THE ATLANTIC WORLD

- North American colonists revolt against British rule and establish a nonmonarchical, republican form of government.
- In the wake of the American Revolution, the French citizenry proclaims a new era of liberty, equality, and fraternity and executes opponents of the revolution, notably the king and queen of France.
- Napoleon's French empire extends many principles of the French Revolution throughout Europe.
- In the midst of the French Revolution, Haitian slaves throw off French rule, abolish slavery, and create an independent state.
- Napoleon's invasion of Iberia frees Portuguese and Spanish America from colonial rule.
- The British lead a successful campaign to abolish the Atlantic slave trade and promote new sources of trade with Africa.
- An industrial revolution spreads outward from Britain to a few other parts of the Atlantic world.

AFRICA, INDIA, AND ASIA

- In Egypt, a military leader, Muhammad Ali, modernizes the country and threatens the political integrity of the Ottoman Empire.
- The British East India Company increasingly dominates the Indian subcontinent.
- The Qing Empire persists despite major European encroachments on its sovereignty.

CHRONOLOGY

THE AMERICAS

EUROPE — James Watt invents the steam engine 1769

AFRICA

OTTOMAN EMPIRE

SOUTH ASIA

EAST ASIA

1700

1750

THINKING ABOUT GLOBAL CONNECTIONS

- ***Thinking about Exchange Networks and Sociopolitical Change*** How did established dynasties respond to pressures created by increased exchanges of goods, ideas, and peoples? To what degree did established elites respond by forging a partnership with "the people"? Who defined "the people," on what terms?
- ***Thinking about Changing Power Relationships and Sociopolitical Change*** What new kinds of political organizations emerged in this period? Where did new political systems take root, and where did established elites resist most successfully?
- ***Thinking about Environmental Impacts and Sociopolitical Change*** Although new technologies only gradually transformed agriculture—by far the most common economic activity in the world—the spread of more intensive cultivation demanded considerable capital investment. How did the relationship between town and countryside change as a result? How did living conditions change in cities as their populations swelled?

STUDY QUESTIONS

1. Describe the political and social revolutions that occurred in the Atlantic world between 1750 and 1850. What ideas inspired these changes? Pay special attention to **free trade**, **popular sovereignty**, the **social contract**, and republican government. Who was included and who was excluded from revolutionary measures?
2. Explain how the Atlantic world's political and social revolution led to the end of the Atlantic slave trade. What economic, social, and political consequences did this development have on sub-Saharan Africa?
3. Explain the relationship between industrialization and the **industrious revolution**. How did industriousness spur economic growth? Where did the decisive changes take place, both in geographical terms but also in social terms? That is, which social groups were most important in effecting change? What role did the **bourgeoisie** play?
4. Evaluate how the **industrial revolution** altered the societies that began to industrialize during this time. What impact did this process have on the environment? How were gender roles and family relationships altered?
5. Compare responses to European influence in Egypt under **Muhammad Ali**; in India, under the rule of the **East India Company**; and in China during the **Opium War**.

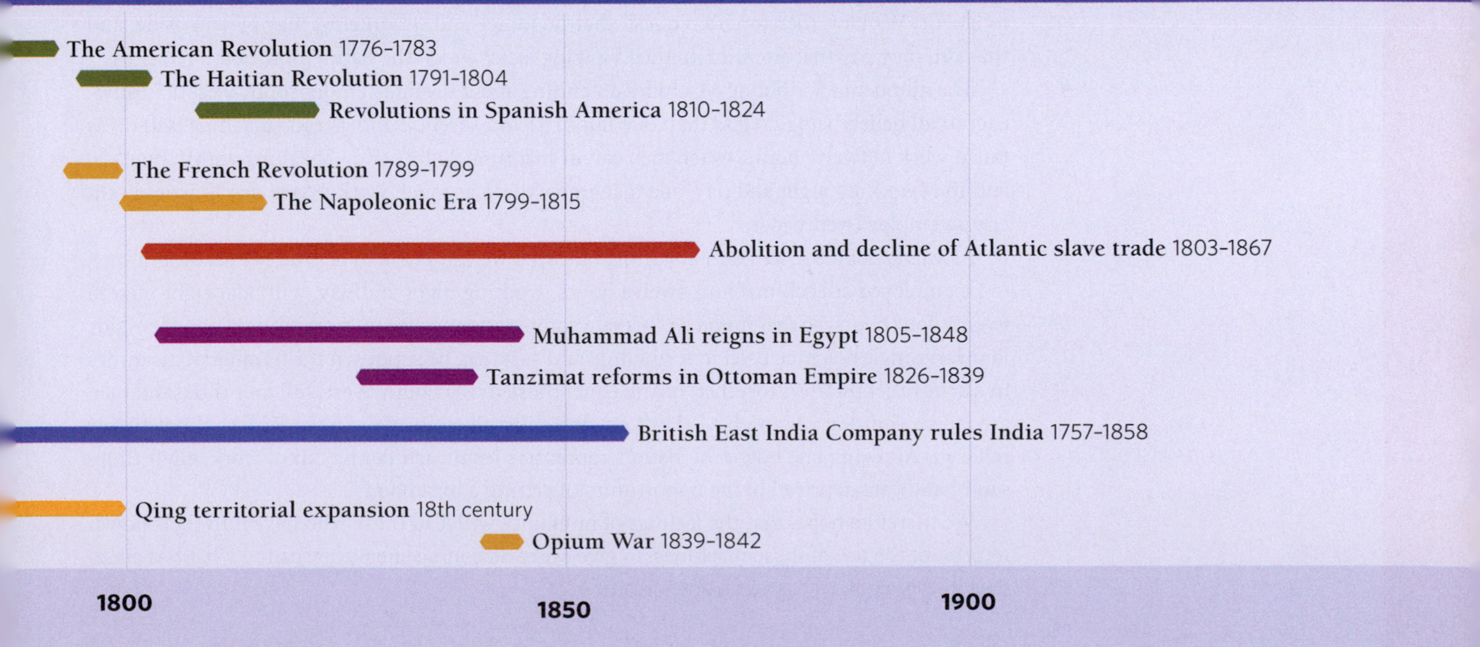

Going to the Source

Industrialization, Freedom, and Equality

Many historians argue that industrialization is one of the most important causes of change in the modern world. They claim that industrialization improved the lives of many, all around the world, by making cheap goods available to them—goods that would have been more expensive if produced by hand. Other historians counter that industrialization exacerbated inequality, degraded the environment, and generally made people more acquisitive than they otherwise would have been. The following documents reflect this debate. They present a variety of positions on the relationship between freedom, equality, and industry.

PRIMARY SOURCE 15.1

Yorkshire Cloth Workers Petition (1786)

This petition from a group of cloth manufacturers in Leeds, England, challenged the ways in which machines were taking over the work of human beings. It suggests that machines may impoverish workers, including children, who had previously made cloth. Because the machines were housed in factories and not in people's homes, the workers feared a loss of control over their work processes.

To the Merchants, Clothiers and all such as wish well to the Staple Manufactory of this Nation.

The Humble ADDRESS and PETITION of Thousands, who labour in the Cloth Manufactory.

SHEWETH, That the Scribbling-Machines have thrown thousands of your petitioners out of employ, whereby they are brought into great distress, and are not able to procure a maintenance for their families, and deprived them of the opportunity of bringing up their children to labour: We have therefore to request, that prejudice and self-interest may be laid aside, and that you may pay that attention to the following facts, which the nature of the case requires.

The number of Scribbling-Machines extending about seventeen miles south-west of LEEDS, exceed all belief, being no less than one hundred and seventy! and as each machine will do as much work in twelve hours, as ten men can in that time do by hand, (speaking within bounds) and they working night and day, one machine will do as much work in one day as would otherwise employ twenty men.

As we do not mean to assert any thing but what we can prove to be true, we allow four men to be employed at each machine twelve hours, working night and day, will take eight men in twenty-four hours; so that, upon a moderate computation twelve men are thrown out of employ for every single machine used in scribbling; and as it may be supposed the number of machines in all the other quarters together, nearly equal those in the South-West, full four thousand men are left to shift for a living how they can, and must of course fall to the Parish, if not timely relieved. Allowing one boy to be bound apprentice from each family out of work, eight thousand hands are deprived of the opportunity of getting a livelihood.

We therefore hope, that the feelings of humanity will lead those who have it in their power to prevent the use of those machines, to give every discouragement they can to what has a tendency so prejudicial to their fellow-creatures. . . .

Men of common sense must know, that so many machines in use, take the work from the hands employed in Scribbling,—and who did that business before machines were invented.

How are those men, thus thrown out of employ to provide for their families;—and what are they to put their children apprentice to, that the rising generation may have something to keep them at work, in order that they may not be like vagabonds strolling about in idleness? Some say, Begin and learn some other business.—Suppose we do; who will maintain our families, whilst we undertake the arduous task; and when we have learned it, how do we know we shall be any better for all our pains; for by the time we have served our second apprenticeship, another machine may arise, which may take away that business also; so that our families, being half pined whilst we are learning how to provide them with bread, will be wholly so during the period of our third apprenticeship. Signed, in behalf of THOUSANDS, by Joseph Hepworth, Thomas Lobley, Robert Wood, Thos. Blackburn.

1. **Why do you suppose that manufacturers were so concerned with the effects of new machines on their children?**
2. **Imagine that you lived in the late eighteenth century. Which would you prefer—more access to cheap cloth (and other products) or the ability to control how and when you worked? Explain your answer.**

PRIMARY SOURCE 15.2

History of the Cotton Manufacture (1823), Richard Guest

In this selection from his history of cotton production, Richard Guest explains how industrial production was changing not just manufacturing processes but social orders. Pay attention to the author's comparisons about the quantity and quality of cloth being produced, as well as about the greater efficiency of factory production.

It is a curious circumstance, that, when the Cotton Manufacture was in its infancy, all the operations, from the dressing of the raw material to its being finally turned out in the state of cloth, were completed under the roof of the weaver's cottage. The course of improved manufacture which followed, was to spin the yarn in factories and to weave it in cottages. At the present time, when the manufacture has attained a mature growth, all the operations, with vastly increased means and more complex contrivances, are again performed in a single building. The Weaver's cottage with its rude apparatus of peg warping, hand cards, hand wheels, and imperfect looms, was the Steam Loom factory in miniature. Those vast brick edifices in the vicinity of all the great manufacturing towns in the south of Lancashire, towering to the height of seventy or eighty feet, which strike the attention and excite the curiosity of the traveller, now perform labours which formerly employed whole villages. In the Steam Loom factories, the cotton is carded, roved, spun, and woven into cloth, and the same quantum of labour is now performed in one of these structures which formerly occupied the industry of an entire district.

A very good Hand Weaver, a man twenty-five or thirty years of age, will weave two pieces of . . . shirting per week, each twenty four yards long. . . . A Steam Loom Weaver, fifteen years of age, will in the same time weave seven similar pieces. A Steam Loom factory containing two hundred Looms, with the assistance of one hundred persons under twenty years of age, and of twenty-five men will weave seven hundred pieces per week, of the length and quality before described. To manufacture one hundred similar pieces per week by the hand, it would be necessary to employ at least one hundred and twenty-five Looms, because many of the Weavers are females, and have cooking, washing, cleaning and various other duties to perform; others of them are children and, consequently, unable to weave as much as the men. It requires a man of mature age and a very good Weaver to weave two of the pieces in a week, and there is also an allowance to be made for sickness and other incidents. Thus, eight hundred and seventy-five hand Looms would be required to produce the seven hundred pieces per week; and reckoning the weavers, with their children, and the aged and infirm belonging to them at two and a half to each loom, it may very safely be said, that the work done in a Steam Factory containing two hundred Looms, would, if done by hand Weavers, find employment and support for a population of more than two thousand persons.

1. **Explain the change in cotton production that Guest describes.**
2. **Does the author think that industrialization will benefit a majority of the population? Why or why not?**

PRIMARY SOURCE 15.3

American Labor, Industry, and Government (1835–1840), Alexis de Tocqueville

The French aristocrat Alexis de Tocqueville toured around the United States in the first half of the nineteenth century and recorded his impressions in *Democracy in America*. In this selection, Tocqueville comments on the developing industrial society as he observed it and the political ideology upon which American society rested.

Chapter 13, Why the Americans are so Restless in the Midst of their Prosperity

In America I saw the freest and most enlightened men placed in the happiest circumstances that the world affords, [yet] it seemed to me as if a cloud habitually hung upon their brow, and I thought them serious and almost sad, even in their pleasures.

The chief reason for this contrast is that the former [the Europeans] do not think of the ills they endure, while the latter [the Americans] are forever brooding over advantages they do not possess. It is strange to see with what feverish ardor the Americans pursue their own welfare, and to watch the vague dread that constantly torments them lest they should not have chosen the shortest path which may lead to it.

A native of the United States clings to this world's goods as if he were certain never to die; and he is so hasty in grasping at all within his reach that one would suppose he was constantly afraid of not living long enough to enjoy them. He clutches everything . . . but soon loosens his grasp to pursue fresh gratifications. . . .

When all the privileges of birth and fortune are abolished, when all professions are accessible to all, and a man's own energies may place him at the top of any one of them, an easy and unbounded career seems open to his ambition and he will readily persuade himself that he is born to no common destinies. But this is an erroneous notion, which is corrected by daily experience. The same equality that allows every citizen to conceive these lofty hopes renders all the citizens less able to realize them; it circumscribes their powers on every side, while it gives freer scope to their desires. Not only are they themselves powerless, but they are met at every step by immense obstacles, which they did not at first perceive. They have swept away the privileges of some of their fellow creatures which stood in their way, but they have opened the door to universal competition; the barrier has changed its shape rather than its position. When men are nearly alike and all follow the same track, it is very difficult for any one individual to walk quickly and cleave a way through the dense throng that surrounds and presses on him. This constant strife between the inclination springing from the equality of condition and the means it supplies to satisfy them harasses and wearies the mind. . . .

Chapter 14, How the Taste for Physical Gratifications Is United in America to Love of Freedom and Attention to Public Affairs

When the taste for physical gratifications among them has grown more rapidly than their education and their experience of free institutions, the time will come when men are carried away and lose all self-restraint at the sight of the new possessions they are about to obtain. In their intense and exclusive anxiety to make a fortune they lose sight of the close connection that exists between the private fortune of each and the prosperity of all. It is not necessary to do violence to such a people in order to strip them of the rights they enjoy; they themselves willingly loosen their hold. The discharge of political duties appears to them to be a troublesome impediment which diverts them from their occupations and business. If they are required to elect representatives, to support the government by personal service, to meet on public business, they think they have no time, they cannot waste their precious hours in useless engagements; such idle amusements are unsuited to serious men who are engaged with the more important interests of life. These people think they are following the principle of self-interest, but the idea they entertain of that principle is a very crude one; and the better to look after what they call their own business, they neglect their chief business, which is to remain their own masters.

1. **How does Tocqueville describe Americans' involvement in public affairs?**
2. **Why does Tocqueville see a conflict emerging between American laborers and their own happiness? How does he propose to solve this problem?**

PRIMARY SOURCE 15.4

Capital and Labour (1843)

This image depicts nineteenth-century British children working in the mines, as well as people of other classes. It originally appeared in the satirical magazine *Punch*; the author was responding to a British government report on limiting child labor.

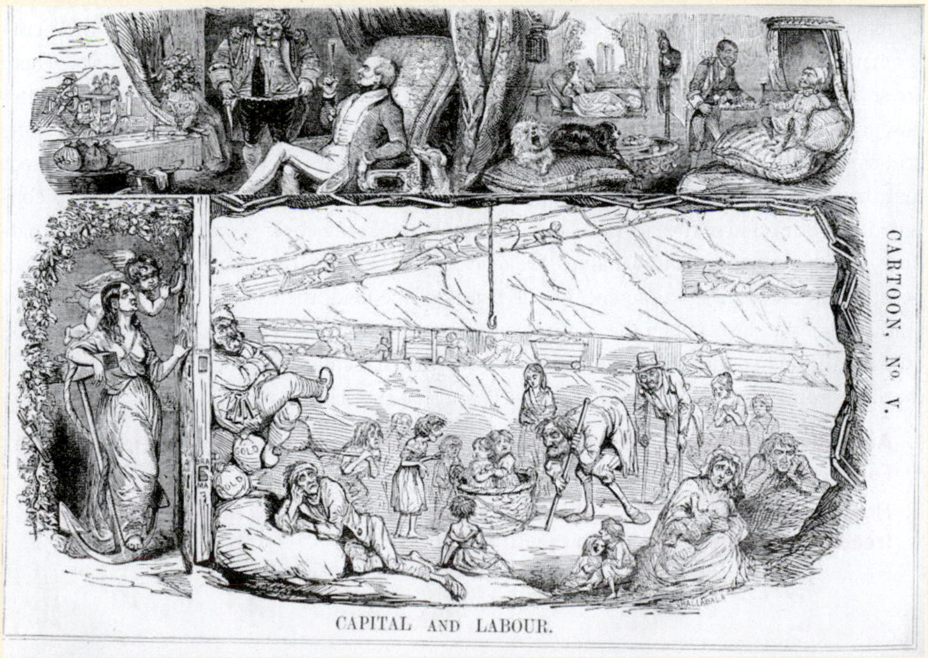

1. **What does this image reveal about working conditions for the poor?**
2. **Explain the connection between capitalists and laborers that the cartoonist is trying to make.**

PRIMARY SOURCE 15.5

"What to the Slave Is the Fourth of July?" (1852), Frederick Douglass

Frederick Douglass spent the first twenty years of his life as a slave before becoming a leading abolitionist in the United States. In an address delivered on July 5, 1852, Douglass contrasts the freedoms and natural rights championed in the American Declaration of Independence and celebrated on the Fourth of July with the substantial lack of freedom that African-American slaves, as well as freemen (to say nothing of women) endured throughout the country.

Fellow-Citizens—pardon me, and allow me to ask, why am I called upon to speak here today? What have I, or those I represent, to do with your national independence? Are the great principles of political freedom and of natural justice, embodied in that Declaration of Independence, extended to us? And am I, therefore, called upon to bring our humble offering to the national altar, and to confess the benefits, and express devout gratitude for the blessings, resulting from your independence to us? . . .

But, such is not the state of the case. I say it with a sad sense of the disparity between us. I am not included within the pale of this glorious anniversary! Your high independence only reveals the immeasurable distance between us. The blessings in which you this day rejoice, are not enjoyed in common. The rich inheritance of justice, liberty, prosperity, and independence, bequeathed by your fathers, is shared by you, not by me. The sunlight that brought life and healing to you, has brought stripes and death to me. This Fourth of July is *yours*, not *mine*. *You* may rejoice, *I* must mourn. . . .

Must I undertake to prove that the slave is a man? That point is conceded already. Nobody doubts it. The slaveholders themselves acknowledge it in the enactment of laws for their government. They acknowledge it when they punish disobedience on the part of the slave. There are seventy-two crimes in the state of Virginia, which, if committed by a black man (no matter how ignorant he be) subject him to the punishment of death; while only two of these same crimes will subject a white man to the like punishment. What is this but the acknowledgment that the slave is a moral, intellectual, and responsible being. The manhood of the slave is conceded. It is admitted in the fact that southern statute books are covered with enactments forbidding, under severe fines and penalties, the teaching of the slave to read or write. When you can point to any such laws, in reference to the beasts of the field, then I may consent to argue the manhood of the slave. When the dogs in your streets, when the fowls of the air, when the cattle on your hills, when the fish of the sea, and the reptiles that crawl, shall be unable to distinguish the slave from a brute, then will I argue with you that the slave is a man!

1. **According to Douglass, why does the existence of slavery undermine the ideals of the Fourth of July?**
2. **How would you characterize the relationship between slavery on the one hand and freedom and independence on the other hand?**

PRIMARY SOURCE 15.6

Observations on the Filth of the Thames (1855), Michael Faraday

The well-known British scientist Michael Faraday wrote this letter to the editor of the London *Times*, in which he observes a great deal of water pollution and suggests grave consequences if it is not stopped. Though he does not enumerate them, we assume that he is discussing the degradation of London's water and the effect on its large urban population.

SIR,

I traversed this day by steam-boat the space between London and Hungerford Bridges between half-past one and two o'clock; it was low water, and I think the tide must have been near the turn. The appearance and the smell of the water forced themselves at once on my attention. The whole of the river was an opaque pale brown fluid. In order to test the degree of opacity, I tore up some white cards into pieces, moistened them so as to make them sink easily below the surface, and then dropped some of these pieces into the water at every pier the boat came to; before they had sunk an inch below the surface they were indistinguishable, though the sun shone brightly at the time; and when the pieces fell edgeways the lower part was hidden from sight before the upper part was under water. This happened at St. Paul's Wharf, Blackfriars Bridge, Temple Wharf, Southwark Bridge, and Hungerford; and I have no doubt would have occurred further up and down the river. . . .

The smell was very bad, and common to the whole of the water; it was the same as that which now comes up from the gully-holes in the streets; the whole river was for the time a real sewer. Having just returned from out of the country air, I was, perhaps, more affected by it than others; but I do not think I could have gone on to Lambeth or Chelsea, and I was glad to enter the streets for an atmosphere which, except near the sink-holes, I found much sweeter than that on the river.

I have thought it a duty to record these facts, that they may be brought to the attention of those who exercise power or have responsibility in relation to the condition of our river; there's nothing figurative in the words I have employed, or any approach to exaggeration; they are the simple truth. If there be sufficient authority to remove a putrescent pond from the neighbourhood of a few simple dwellings, surely the river which flows for so many miles through London ought not to be allowed to become a fermenting sewer. . . . If we neglect this subject, we cannot expect to do so with impunity; nor ought we to be surprised if, ere many years are over, a hot season give us sad proof of the folly of our carelessness.

1. **What do you think was causing London's water pollution?**
2. **Why might Faraday have thought that it was important to stop this pollution?**

Questions for Analysis

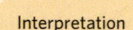

Argumentation

1. Do you believe that societies based on economic efficiency, such as industrialization, were improvements upon previous societies? Why or why not?

Interpretation

2. Some historians argue that individuals are the products of their environments. Do the documents in this chapter support or refute that assertion? Explain your answer.

Change and Continuity over Time

3. Analyze changes and continuities in the ideas of inequality between the eighteenth and nineteenth centuries.

Long Essay Question

Interpretation

Based on what you have read in the chapter and the documents above, evaluate the degree to which industry, free labor, and competition improved the lives of people in nineteenth-century Britain and America.

Before You Read This Chapter

GLOBAL STORYLINES

- Protest movements challenge the nineteenth-century order based on industrial capitalism, the nation-state, and colonization.
- Led by prophets, political radicals, and common people, the movements arise among marginal groups and regions and express visions of ideal, utopian futures.
- The movements differ markedly depending on distance from the centers of change (Europe and the Americas) and reflect local circumstances.
- Although most movements are defeated, they give voice to the views of peasants and workers and have a lasting effect on the policies of ruling elites.

CORE OBJECTIVES

- **DESCRIBE** the challenges to the ideals of industrial capitalism, colonialism, and nation-states in this period.
- **COMPARE** the utopian goals, immediate outcomes, and long-term influence of rebel movements around the world.
- **ANALYZE** the connection between nineteenth-century protest movements and organized religion.
- **ASSESS** the role religion played in these alternate social visions.

CHAPTER

16

Alternative Visions of the Nineteenth Century

KEY TERMS

Caste War of the Yucatan p. 621
Usman dan Fodio p. 605
liberalism p. 612
Marxism p. 616
***Mfecane* movement** p. 607
millenarian p. 609
proletarians p. 616
Taiping Rebellion p. 610
Tenskwatawa p. 617
utopian socialism p. 614
Wahhabism p. 603

By the late nineteenth century, territorial expansion in the United States confined almost all Native Americans to reservations. The buffalo that once supported many tribes disappeared: white settlers built towns, farms, and railroads throughout the buffalo's natural habitat, and Native Americans overhunted the shrinking herds. Across the American West, many Native Americans fell into despair. One was a Paiute Native American named Wovoka. But in 1889, he had a vision of a much brighter future. In his dream, the "Supreme Being" told Wovoka that if Native Americans lived harmoniously, shunned white ways (especially alcohol), and performed the cleansing Ghost Dance, then the buffalo would return, and Native Americans, including the dead, would be reborn to live in eternal happiness.

As word spread of Wovoka's vision, Native Americans from hundreds of miles around made pilgrimages to the lodge of this new prophet. Many proclaimed him the Native Americans' messiah or the "Red Man's Christ," an impression fostered by scars on his hands. Soon, increasing numbers joined in the ritual Ghost Dance, hoping it would restore the good life that European colonialism in the Americas had extinguished. Among the hopefuls was Sitting Bull, a revered Sioux chief who was himself famous for his visions. Yet, less than two years after Wovoka's vision, Sitting Bull died at the hands of police forces on a Sioux reservation. A few days later, on December 29, 1890, the U.S. Seventh Cavalry Regiment massacred Sioux Ghost Dancers at a South Dakota creek called Wounded Knee.

Though it failed, this movement was one of many prophetic crusades that challenged an emerging nineteenth-century order. The ideals of the French and American revolutions in politics—equality before the law, and government for and by property-holding citizens in a world of nation-states—now provided the dominant answers to age-old questions of who should govern and how. Emerging from the industrial revolution, the ideas of free-market (laissez-faire) capitalism, in which private owners competed against one another to maximize profits using new technologies and industrial organizations, provided the dominant answers to questions about how productive activity should be organized. But these political and economic answers were not powerful enough entirely to stamp out other views. A diverse assortment of political radicals, charismatic prophets, peasant rebels, and anticolonial insurgents put forward striking counterproposals to those that capitalists, colonial modernizers, and nation-state builders had developed. The people making these counterproposals were motivated by the impending loss of their existing worlds and were energized by visions of ideal, utopian futures.

This chapter presents the voices and visions of those who opposed a nineteenth-century world in which capitalism, colonialism, and nation-states held sway. It puts the spotlight on challengers who shared a dislike of global capitalism and European (and North American) colonialism. Beyond that similarity, these challengers differed in significant ways, for the alternatives they proposed reflected the local circumstances in which each of them developed. Although many of these challengers suffered devastating defeats, like the Ghost Dancers at Wounded Knee, the dreams that aroused their fervor did not always die with them. Some of these alternative visions of the nineteenth century endured to propel the great transformations of the twentieth.

Reactions to Social and Political Change

COMPARISON

ANALYZE the connections between nineteenth-century protest movements and organized religion in Islam, China, and the Americas.

The alternatives to the emerging order of the nineteenth century varied considerably. Some rebels and dissidents called for the revitalization of traditional religions; others wanted to strengthen village and communal bonds; still others imagined a society where there was no private property and where people shared goods equally. The actions of these dissenters depended on their local traditions and the degree of contact they had with the effects of industrial capitalism, European colonialism, and centralizing nation-states.

This era of rapid social change, when differing visions of power and justice vied with one another, offers unique opportunities to hear the voices of the lower orders—the peasants and workers, whose perspectives the elites often ignored or suppressed. While there are few written records that capture the views of the illiterate and the marginalized, we do have traditions of folklore, dreams, rumors, and prophecies. Handed down orally from generation to generation, these resources illuminate the visions of common people.

Prophecy and Revitalization in the Islamic World and Africa

In regions that experienced European and North American influence but not direct colonial rule, alternative perspectives were strongest far from the main trade and cultural routes. People outside the emerging capitalist world order led these movements. In the

Islamic world and Africa, leaders on the margins were especially important in articulating alternative views.

Even though much of the Islamic world and non-Islamic Africa had not been colonized and was only partially involved with European-dominated trading networks, these regions had reached turning points. By the late eighteenth century, the era of Islamic expansion and cultural flowering under the Ottomans, Safavids, and Mughals was over. Their empires had extended Muslim trading orbits, facilitated cross-cultural communication, and promoted common knowledge over vast territories. Their political and military decline, however, brought new challenges to the faithful. The sense of alarm intensified as Christian Europe's power spread from the edges of the Islamic world to its centers. While this perception of danger motivated military men in Egypt and the Ottoman sultans to modernize their states (see Chapter 15), it also bred religious revitalization movements that sought to recapture the glories of past traditions. Led by prophets who feared that the Islamic faith was in trouble, these movements spoke the language of revival and restoration as they sought to establish new religiously based governments across lands in which Muslims ruled and Islamic law prevailed.

Prophecy also exerted a strong influence in non-Islamic Africa, where long-distance trade and population growth were upending the social order. Just as Muslim clerics and political leaders sought solutions to unsettling changes by rereading Islamic classics, African communities looked to charismatic leaders who drew strength from their peoples' spiritual and magical traditions. Often uniting disparate groups behind their dynamic visions, prophetic leaders and other "big men" gained power because they were able to resolve local crises—mostly caused by drought, a shortage of arable land, or some other issue related to the harsh environment.

ISLAMIC REVITALIZATION

Movements to revitalize Islam took place on the peripheries—at a certain remove from trade networks and the changes wrought by global capitalism. (See Map 16.1.) Here, religious leaders rejected the westernizing influences they felt encroaching on their authority and way of life. Revitalization movements looked back to Islamic traditions and modeled their revolts on the life of Muhammad. But even as they looked to the past, they attempted to establish something new: full-scale theocracies. These reformers conceived of the state as the primary instrument of God's will and as the vehicle for purifying Islamic culture. (See **Current Trends in World History: Islam: An Enduring Alternative in Algeria**.)

Wahhabism One of the most powerful reformist movements arose on the Arabian Peninsula, the birthplace of the Muslim faith. In the Najd region, an area surrounded by mountains and deserts, a religious cleric named Muhammad Ibn abd al-Wahhab (1703–1792) galvanized the population by attacking what he regarded as lax religious practices. His message found a ready response among local inhabitants, who felt threatened by the new commercial activities and fresh intellectual currents swirling around them. Abd al-Wahhab demanded a return to the pure Islam of Muhammad and the early caliphs.

Although Najd was far removed from the centers of the expanding world economy, Abd al-Wahhab himself was not. Having been educated in Iraq, Iran, and the Hijaz (a region on the western end of modern Saudi Arabia, on the Red Sea), he believed that Islam had fallen into a degraded state, particularly in its birthplace. He railed against the polytheistic beliefs that had taken hold of the people, complaining that in defiance of Muhammad's tenets men and women were worshipping trees, stones, and tombs and making sacrifices to false images. Abd al-Wahhab's movement stressed the absolute oneness of Allah and severely criticized Sufi sects for extolling the lives of saints over the worship of God.

As **Wahhabism** swept across the Arabian Peninsula, the movement threatened the Ottomans' hold on the region. Wahhabism gained a powerful political ally in the Najdian

Current Trends in World History

Islam: An Enduring Alternative in Algeria

Many of the alternative movements featured in this chapter derived their impetus from deeply held religious beliefs. Religion played a role in the Indian mutiny and in the visions that spurred the Taiping rebels. In Muslim locations far from the main currents of Western influence, like the Arabian Peninsula and northern Nigeria, it generated revivalist movements. But elsewhere it became a political force, and one that developed a palpably anti-European nature as well as the power to endure long beyond the victory of European invaders. World historians like to study political and social movements because they bring into relief the relationship between the colonizer and the colonized and, in the case of these alternative movements, the relationship between peoples living on the peripheries of empires and those living in the center who are part of the ruling elite, including indigenous elites.

This was the case in particular along the old Ottoman periphery, one of the major targets for European colonization. Strikingly, in the first decades of the nineteenth century, in the Ottomans' Balkan domains of Serbia and Greece, Christianity had linked together opponents against the empire. In the decades to follow, as Ottoman power receded, it left behind it Islamic groups who also used religion as the glue that bound together otherwise diverse peoples. The example below highlights the importance of Islam in galvanizing resistance to French imperialism in Algeria. But it would also be possible to cite examples from the Caucasus Mountains, another Ottoman periphery, where Islam linked together Chechen and other groups in opposition to Russian colonization in the 1840s and 1850s; in the early twentieth century, Libyans attempted to oppose Italian colonization by rallying behind the green flag of the prophet. Unquestionably, the more Europeans sought to dominate lands inhabited by Muslims, the more they called forth in reaction Islamic alternatives and a politicized form of Islamic resistance.

In 1830, through a series of mishaps and miscalculations the French found themselves in possession of the Regency of Algiers, a territory of 60,000 square miles where previously 10,000 Ottoman Turks had ruled over 3 million Arab and Berber tribesmen. The French invasion had been an ill-considered adventure, designed to divert attention from the fact that the backward-looking French king, Charles X, had lost his legitimacy at home. In 1830, Charles was toppled by the so-called July Revolution, but his successor, King Louis Philippe, (r. 1830–1848), decided to pursue France's adventure abroad. This was a risky and in the long run costly plan, however, as the French controlled only a few costal enclaves and the capital city of Algiers; in 1831, the European civilian population was a mere 3,228. Moreover, although the French had driven out the Turks, they had emboldened Arab tribes in the western part of the land to found their own independent state.

In seeking a leader to unite them, the Arab tribes turned to Abd al-Qadir (1807–1883), a charismatic and domineering personality even though only twenty-five years of age. His father, head of the most important Sufi Brotherhood in Algeria, had groomed his son to be a leader, and taught him to despise the Ottoman overlords. Abd al-Qadir and his followers had already committed themselves to overthrowing the Ottomans; but once the French arrived, they were even more determined to rid their area of invaders they regarded as infidels, intent on seizing their lands and imposing their way of life on them. In organizing resistance to the French, it mattered greatly that Abd al-Qadir was also known as a holy man and a scholar, rather than as merely the head of one of the tribes. In preparation

House of Saud, a leading family whose followers, inspired by the Wahhabis' religious zeal, undertook a militant religious campaign in the final years of the eighteenth century. Frightened by the Wahhabi challenge, the Ottoman sultan persuaded the provincial ruler of Egypt to send troops to the Arabian Peninsula to suppress the movement. The Egyptians defeated the Saudis in 1818, but Wahhabism and the House of Saud continued to represent a pure Islamic faith that attracted clerics and ordinary people throughout the Muslim world.

Usman dan Fodio and the Fulani In West Africa, Muslim revolts erupted from Senegal to Nigeria in the early nineteenth century, partly in response to increased trade with the outside world and the circulation of religious ideas from across the Sahara Desert. In this region, the Fulani people were decisive in religious uprisings that sought, like the Wahhabi movement, to re-create a supposedly purer Islamic past. The majority were cattle-keepers, practicing a for battle, he called on his soldiers to follow him in a holy war (*jihad*) against Christian invaders, promising those who joined him in battle that "anyone of you who dies, will die a martyr; those of you who survive will gain glory and live happily." Tribes that might not have fought together, or fought together so long, did so because they were united by their loyalty to a religious as well as a political leader; Abd al-Qadir succeeded in part because he was a forceful personality, but in part, too, because he stood for Islam, something that the native Algerians shared, whatever their kinship ties or their loyalties to local leaders.

For fifteen years, Abd al-Quadir's forces held out, only surrendering to a massive French force of 108,000 men in 1847. Although often defeated in pitched battles, Abd al-Qadir used his superior knowledge of the terrain and his ability to wait in ambush for French columns to frustrate the French. The French government was finally compelled to send its most accomplished military man, Marshal Thomas Robert Bugeaud, and to provide him with one-third of its entire military force, to finish the job of "pacifying" Algeria.

The French conquest of Algeria marks one of the bloodiest episodes in the history of those two lands. No fewer than 300,000 Algerians perished during these years. Although the French portrayed Abd al-Qadir as a Muslim fanatic, determined to take his people back to a dark age, their message fell on deaf ears. The Algerians extolled him for resisting the French and later made him an iconic figure of the nationalist movement. One of the first acts carried out by the independent Algerian government in 1962 was to tear down the statue of Marshal Bugeaud and to replace it with one of Abd al-Qadir. The religiously motivated resistance leader had prevailed over the secular political conquerors after all.

Abd al-Qadir Polish artist Stanislaw Chlebowski painted Abd al-Qadir in 1866 during his exile in Constantinople.

QUESTIONS FOR ANALYSIS

- What impact did Algeria's geographic location play in determining its role in these revolutionary events?
- How did the native Algerians view their former Ottoman rulers compared to the French Europeans? What was their ultimate goal?

Explore Further

Julia Clancy-Smith, *Rebel and Saint: Muslim Notables, Populist Protest, Colonial Encounter (Algeria and Tunisia, 1800–1904)* (1994).

Raphael Danziger, *Abd al-Qadir: Resistance to the French and Internal Consolidation* (1977).

John Ruedy, *Modern Algeria: The Origins and Development of a Nation* (2005).

pastoral and nomadic way of life. But some were sedentary, living in settled communities, and people in this group converted to Islam, read the Islamic classics, and communicated with holy men of North Africa, Egypt, and the Arabian Peninsula. They concluded that West African peoples were violating Islamic beliefs and engaging in irreligious practices.

The most powerful of these reform movements flourished in what is today northern Nigeria. Its leader was a Fulani Muslim cleric, **Usman dan Fodio** (1754–1817), who ultimately created a vast Islamic empire. Dan Fodio's movement had all the trappings of the Islamic revolts of this period. It sought inspiration in the life of Muhammad and demanded a return to early Islamic practices. It attacked false belief and urged followers to wage holy war (*jihad*) against unbelievers.

Dan Fodio blamed local leaders for what he saw as their failure to respect Islamic law. He won the support of devout Muslims in the area, who agreed that the people were

MAP 16.1 | Muslim Revitalization Movements in the Middle East and Africa and the *Mfecane* Movement in Southern Africa

During the nineteenth century, a series of Muslim revitalization movements took place throughout the Middle East and North Africa.

- According to this map, in how many different areas did the revitalization movements occur?
- Based on their geographic location within their larger regions, did these movements occur in central or peripheral areas?
- According to your reading, were any of the same factors that led to Islamic revitalization involved in the *Mfecane* developments in southern Africa?

not properly practicing Islam. He also gained the backing of his Fulani tribes and many Hausa-speaking peasants, who had suffered under the rule of the Hausa landlord class. The revolt, initiated in 1804, resulted in the overthrow of the Hausa rulers and the creation of a confederation of Islamic emirates, almost all of which were in the hands of the Fulani allies of dan Fodio.

Fulani women of northern Nigeria made critical contributions to the success of the religious revolt. Although dan Fodio and other male leaders of the purification movement expected women to obey the *sharia* (Islamic law), being modest in their dress and their association with men outside the family, they also expected women to support the community's military and religious endeavors. In this effort, they cited women's important role in the first days of Islam. The best known of the Muslim women leaders was Nana Asma'u (1793–1864), daughter of dan Fodio. Fulani women of the upper ranks acquired an Islamic education, and Asma'u was as astute a reader of Islamic texts as any of the learned men in her society. Like other Muslim Fulani devotees, she accompanied the warriors on their campaigns, encamped with them, prepared food for them, bound up their wounds, and provided daily encouragement. According to many accounts, Asma'u inspired the warriors at their most crucial battle, hurling a burning spear into the midst of the enemy army. Her poem "Song of the Circular Journey" celebrates the triumphs of military forces that trekked thousands of miles to bring a reformed Islam to the area.

Usman dan Fodio considered himself a cleric first and a political and military man second. Although his political leadership was decisive in the revolt's success, thereafter he retired to a life of scholarship and writing. He delegated the political and administrative functions of the new empire to his brother and his son. An enduring decentralized state structure, which became known as the Sokoto caliphate in 1809, developed into a stable empire that helped spread Islam through the region. In 1800, on the eve of dan Fodio's revolt, Islam was the faith of a small minority of people living in northern Nigeria; a century later, it had become the religion of the vast majority, thanks to dan Fodio's military prowess and success in creating a stable political structure, and the increasing Fulani contacts with the broader Islamic world.

CHARISMATIC MILITARY MEN IN NON-ISLAMIC AFRICA

Non-Islamic Africa saw revolts, new states, and prophetic movements arise from the same combination of factors that influenced the rest of the world—particularly long-distance trade and population increase. Local communities here also looked to religious traditions and, as was so often the case in African history, expected charismatic clan leaders, known as "big men," to provide political leadership.

In southern Africa, early in the nineteenth century, a group of political revolts reordered the political map. Collectively known as the ***Mfecane*** ("the crushing" in Zulu) **movement**, its epicenter was a large tract of land lying east of the Drakensberg Mountains, an area where growing populations and land resources existed in a precarious balance (see again Map 16.1). Many branches of Bantu-speaking peoples had inhabited the southern part of the African landmass for centuries. At the end of the eighteenth century, however, their political organizations still operated on a small scale. These tiny polities could not cope with the competition for land that now dominated southern Africa. That competition intensified with the arrival of British colonizers, who fought both with Dutch settlers and indigenous African communities over natural resources. The import of European goods that flowed into southern Africa from Delagoa Bay also was a destabilizing factor. A branch of the Nguni, the Zulus, produced a fierce war leader, Shaka (1787–1828), who created a ruthless warrior state. It drove other populations out of the region and forced a shift from small clan communities to large, centralized monarchies throughout southern and central Africa.

Shaka and His Zulu Regiments *(Left)* This illustration, the only one from the time, may be an exaggeration, but it does not exaggerate the view that many had of the awesome strength and power of Shaka, the leader who united the Zulu peoples into an invincible warrior state. *(Right)* Shaka's Zulu state owed its political and military successes to its young warriors, who were deeply loyal to their ruler and whose training and discipline were exemplary. Shown here is a regimental camp in which the warriors slept in huts massed in a circular pattern and trained in military drill and close combat in the inside circle.

Shaka was the son of a minor chief who emerged victorious in the struggle for cattle-grazing and farming lands that arose during a severe drought. A physically imposing figure, Shaka used terror to intimidate his subjects and to overawe his adversaries. His enemies knew that the price of opposition would be a massacre, even of women and children. Nor was he kinder to his own people. Following the death of his beloved mother, he executed those who were not properly contrite and did not weep profusely. Reportedly, it took 7,000 lives to assuage his grief.

Shaka built a new Zulu state around his military and organizational skills and the fear that his personal ferocity produced. He drilled his men relentlessly in the use of short stabbing spears and in discipline under pressure. Like the Mongols, he had a remarkable ability to incorporate defeated communities into the state and to absorb young men into his military. His army of 40,000 men comprised regiments that lived, studied, and fought together. Forbidden from marrying until they were discharged from the army, Shaka's warriors developed an intense esprit de corps and regarded no sacrifice as too great in the service of the state. So overpowering were these forces that other peoples of the region fled from their home areas, and Shaka claimed their estates for himself and his followers. Peoples in nearby areas who weren't absorbed into the Zulu state adopted many of Shaka's military and political innovations, at first to defend themselves and then to take over new land as they fled their old areas. The new states of the Ndebele in what later became Zimbabwe and the Sotho of South Africa came into existence in this way in the mid-nineteenth century.

In turning southern Africa from a region of smaller polities into an area with larger and more powerful states, Shaka seemed very much a man of the modern, nineteenth-century world. Yet he was, in his own unique way, a familiar kind of African leader. He shared a charismatic and prophetic style with others who emerged during periods of acute social change. His new state built an enduring Zulu community and established its traditions against encroachments by outside, European forces.

Prophecy and Rebellion in China

In the mid-nineteenth century, China experienced an explosive popular rebellion that incorporated Christian beliefs into its long tradition of peasant revolts. Whereas movements promoting alternative visions in the Islamic world and Africa appeared in areas distant from western influences and drew substantially on their own traditions, China was no longer isolated. In fact, it had been conducting a brisk trade in opium with Europe. Until 1842, the Chinese had confined trade with Europeans to the port city of Canton. After the Opium War, however, westerners forced Qing rulers to open up a number of other ports to trade.

As in the Islamic world and other parts of sub-Saharan Africa, population increases in China—from 250 million in 1644 to around 450 million by the 1850s—were putting considerable pressure on land and other resources. Moreover, the rising consumption of opium, grown in India and brought to China by British traders, produced further social instability and financial crisis. As banditry and rebellions spread, the Qing rulers turned to the landed elites, the gentry, to maintain order in the countryside. But as the gentry raised its militia to suppress these troublemakers, it whittled away at the authority of the Qing Manchu rulers. Faced with these changes, the Qing dynasty struggled to maintain control.

Searching for an alternative present and future, hundreds of thousands of disillusioned peasants joined what became known as the Taiping Rebellion. Beginning in 1850, the uprising drew on China's long history of peasant revolts. Traditionally, these rebellions ignited within popular religious sects whose visions were egalitarian or **millenarian** (convinced of the imminent coming of a just and ideal society). Moreover, in contrast to orthodox institutions, here women played important roles. Inspired by Daoists, who revered a past golden age before the world was corrupted by human conventions, or by Buddhist sources, these sects threatened the established order.

THE DREAM OF HONG XIUQUAN

The story of the rebellion begins with a complex dream that inspired its founding prophet, Hong Xiuquan (1813–1864). A native of Guangdong province in the southernmost part of the country (see Map 16.2), Hong first encountered Christian missionaries in the 1830s. He was then trying, unsuccessfully, to pass the civil service examination. After failing the exam for the third time, Hong suffered a strange "illness" in which he had visions of combating demons; these dreams included a mysterious "Old Father" and an "Elder Brother." He also began proclaiming himself the Heavenly King. Relatives and neighbors thought he might have gone mad, but Hong gradually returned to his normal state.

In 1843, after failing the exam for the fourth time, Hong immersed himself in a Christian tract entitled *Good Words for Exhorting the Age*. Reportedly, reading this tract enabled Hong to realize the full significance of his earlier visions. All the pieces suddenly fell into place, and he began to grasp their meaning. The "Old Father," he concluded, was the Lord Ye-huo-hua (a Chinese rendering of "Jehovah"), the creator of heaven and earth. His visions of cleansing rituals in heaven foretold Hong's baptism. The "Elder Brother" was Jesus the Savior, the son of God. He, Hong Xiuquan, was the younger brother of Jesus—God's other son. Just as God had previously sent Jesus to save mankind, Hong thought that God was now sending *him* to rid the world of evil. What was once a series of dreams now became a prophetic vision.

THE REBELLION

Hong's prophecy tapped into a millenarian tradition, inspiring a movement that spread rapidly from southern China. Unlike earlier sectarian leaders whose plots for rebellion were

MAP 16.2 | The Taiping Rebellion in China, 1851-1864

The Taiping Rebellion started in the southwestern part of the country. The rebels, however, went on to control much of the lower Yangzi region and part of the coastal area.

- What cities did the rebels' march start and end in?
- Why do you think the Taiping rebels were so successful in southern China and not in northern regions?
- How did western powers react to the Taiping Rebellion? Would they have been as concerned if the rebellion took place farther to the north or west?

secret before exploding onto the public arena, Hong chose a more audacious path. Once convinced of his vision, he began to preach his doctrines openly, baptizing converts and destroying Confucian idols and ancestral shrines. Such assaults on the establishment testified to his conviction that he was carrying out God's will. Hong's message of revitalization of a troubled land and restoration of the "heavenly kingdom," imagined as a just and egalitarian order, appealed to the subordinate classes caught in the flux of social change. Drawing on a largely rural social base and asserting allegiance to Christianity, the **Taiping** ("Great Peace") **Rebellion** (1850–1864) claimed to herald a new era of economic and social justice.

Many early followers came from the margins of local society—those whose anger at social and economic dislocations caused by the Opium War was directed not at the Europeans, but at the Qing government. The Taiping identified the ruling Manchus as the "demons" and as the chief obstacle to realizing God's kingdom on earth. Taiping policies were strict: they prohibited the consumption of alcohol, the smoking of opium, or any indulgence in sensual pleasure. Men and women were segregated for administrative and residential purposes. At the same time, in a drastic departure from dynastic practice, women joined the army in segregated units.

By 1850, Hong's movement had amassed a following of over 20,000, giving Qing rulers cause for concern. When they sent troops to arrest Hong and other rebel leaders, Taiping forces repelled them and then took their turmoil beyond the southwestern part of the country. In 1851, Hong declared himself Heavenly King of the "Taiping Heavenly Kingdom" (or "Heavenly Kingdom of Great Peace"). By 1853, the rebels had captured major cities. Upon capturing Nanjing, the Taiping cleansed the city of "demons" by systematically killing all the Manchus they could find—men, women, and children. Then they established their own "heavenly" capital in the city.

But the rebels could not sustain their vision. Several factors contributed to the fall of the Heavenly Kingdom: struggles within the leadership, an excessively rigid code of conduct, and the rallying of Manchu and Han elites around the embattled dynasty. Disturbed by the Taiping's rejection of Confucianism and wanting to protect their property, landowning gentry led militias against the Taiping. Moreover, western governments also opposed the rebellion, claiming that its doctrines represented a perversion of Christianity. Thus, a mercenary army led by foreign officers took part in suppressing the rebellion. Hong himself perished as his heavenly capital fell in 1864. All told, at least 20 million people died in the Taiping Rebellion.

Taiping Rebellion A painting depicting the Taiping rebels attacking a town. Had the Taiping succeeded in overthrowing the Qing, it would have changed the course of Chinese history and profoundly affected the rest of the world.

Like their counterparts in the Islamic world and Africa, the Taiping rebels promised to restore lost harmony. Despite all the differences of cultural and historical background, what Abd al-Wahhab, dan Fodio, Shaka, and Hong had in common was the perception that the present world was unjust. Thus, they sought to reorganize their communities—an endeavor that involved confronting established authorities. In this regard, the language of revitalization used by prophets in Islamic areas and China was crucial, for it provided an alternative vocabulary of political and spiritual legitimacy. By mobilizing masses eager to return to an imagined golden age, these prophets and charismatic leaders gave voice to those dispossessed by global change, while producing new, alternative ways of organizing society and politics.

Socialists and Radicals in Europe

Europe and North America were the core areas of economic growth, based on the industrial revolution and free trade, nation-state building, and colonial expansion. But there, too, the main currents of thought and activity encountered challenges. Prophets of all stripes—political, social, cultural, and religious—voiced antiestablishment values and dreamed of alternative arrangements. Radicals, liberals, utopian socialists, nationalists, abolitionists, and religious mavericks made plans for better worlds to come.

COMPARISON

DESCRIBE the challenges to the ideals of industrial capitalism and nation states in this period in Europe and the Americas.

RESTORATION AND RESISTANCE

The social and political ferment of the efforts to restore the old order, known as the Restoration period (1815–1848) owed a great deal to the ambiguous legacies of the French Revolution and the Napoleonic wars. (See Map 16.3.) Kings had been toppled and replaced by republics, and then by Napoleon and his relatives; these experiments gave Restoration-era states and radicals many political options from which to choose in the years between Napoleon's downfall in 1815 and the revolutions of 1848.

This period has often been called the Age of Ideology because revolutionary upheavals forced everyone, even those in power, to justify their vision of the social order. Appeals to tradition no longer sufficed. Those called reactionaries or conservatives wanted a return to the world that existed before the French Revolution; they rejected change. Liberals, by contrast, accepted the French Revolution's overthrow of aristocratic privilege. They wanted to hold on to the principles of 1789—above all free trade and equality before the law—without accepting the price controls and political violence of the Terror. Free markets rather than government controls, they believed, would make the most sensible decisions. These proponents of **liberalism** insisted on the individual's right to think, speak, act, and vote as he or she pleased without government interference, so long as no harm came to people or property. Both reactionaries and liberals could find elements to their taste in all the states of the post-Napoleonic world. Much more threatening to the ruling elite were the radicals who believed that the French Revolution had not gone far enough. They longed for a grander revolution that would sweep away the Restoration's political *and* economic order.

RADICAL VISIONS

Reactionaries and liberals did not form the only alternative groups of importance at this time. Most discontented of all—and most determined to effect grand-scale change—were the radicals.

The term *radicals* refers to those who favored the total reconfiguration of the old regime's state system: going to the root of the problem and continuing the revolution, not reversing it or stopping reform. In general, radicals shared a bitter hatred for the status quo and an insistence on popular sovereignty, but beyond this consensus much disagreement remained. If some radicals demanded the equalization or abolition of private property, others—like Serbian, Greek, Polish, and Italian nationalists—were primarily interested in throwing off the oppressive overlordship of the Ottoman and Austrian empires and creating their own nation-states. It was the radicals' threat of a return to revolutions that ultimately reconciled both liberals and reactionaries to preserving the status quo.

Congress of Vienna Following the French Revolution and Napoleon's defeat, European kings and aristocrats revived most of their former powers. At the Congress of Vienna in 1815, the Austrian prime minister Clemens von Metternich took the lead in drafting a peace settlement that would balance power among the states of Europe.

Nationalists In the period before the revolutions of 1848, nationalism was a cause dear to both liberals and radicals, and it threatened conservative rulers who claimed to rule by divine right. The idea of popular sovereignty spread, especially during and after Napoleon's occupation of the continent, but who exactly were "the people"? The "people," or the nation, were generally considered to be those who shared a common language, culture, and history, but nationalists fought bitterly over which people counted and who decided. All nationalists believed that governments

MAP 16.3 | Civil Unrest and Revolutions in Europe, 1819–1848

Civil unrest and revolutions swept Europe after the Congress of Vienna established a peace settlement at the end of the French Revolution and Napoleon's conquests. Conservative governments had to fight off liberal rebellions and demands for change.

- How many sites of revolutionary activity can you locate on this map?
- What parts of Europe appear to have been politically stable, and what parts rebellious? Based on your reading and the map, can you explain the stability of some parts of Europe and the instability of others?

should represent the "people" and that each people—or, at least, their people—should have a state of their own.

Each fledgling nationalist movement—whether Polish, Czech, Greek, Italian, or German—had different contours, but they all drew backers from the liberal aristocracy and the well-educated, commercially active middle classes. Most nationalist movements were, at first, weak and easily crushed, such as attempted Polish uprisings inside tsarist Russia in 1830–1831 and 1863–1864. Unable to win political power, the movements' leaders instead pursued educational and cultural programs to arouse and unite their nation for eventual statehood. By contrast, the Greeks, inspired by religious revivalism and enlightened ideas, managed to wrest independence from the Ottoman Turks after a years-long series of skirmishes, in 1832.

Other nationalist movements were suppressed or at least slowed down with little bloodshed. In places like the German principalities, the Italian states, and the Hungarian parts of the Habsburg Empire, secret societies of young men—students and intellectuals—gathered to plan bright, republican futures. Regrettably for these patriots, however, organizations like Young Italy, founded in 1832 to promote national unification and renewal, had little popular or foreign support. Censorship and a few strategic executions suppressed them. Yet many of these movements ultimately succeeded in the century's second half, when conservatives and liberals alike in western Europe employed nationalist fervor to advance their own ambitions. Kings, aristocrats, and bourgeois businessmen realized that they could mobilize popular support in their capacity as Germans, Frenchmen, or Italians, even as they limited poor people's political rights. However, in central Europe, nationalism pitted many claimants for the same territories against one another, like the Czechs, Serbs, Slovaks, Poles, and Ruthenians (Ukrainians). They did not understand why they could not have a nation-state too. Indeed the term "nation," like that of the people, was so abstract and vague that it unleashed a series of competing claims that were incompatible with one another and would prove enormously destructive in the twentieth century.

Socialists and Communists Early socialists and communists (the terms were more or less interchangeable in the nineteenth century) insisted that political reforms offered no effective answer to the more pressing "social question": what was to be done about the inequalities so powerfully magnified by industrial capitalism? The socialists worried in particular about two things. One was the growing gap between impoverished workers and newly wealthy employers. The other concern was that the division of labor—that is, the dividing up and simplifying of tasks so that each worker performs most efficiently—might make people into soulless, brainless machines. Socialists believed that the whole free-market economy, not just the state, had to be transformed to save the human race from self-destruction. Liberty and equality, they insisted, could not be separated; liberal capitalism and free markets belonged on history's ash heap, in their view, along with aristocratic privilege.

No more than a handful of radical prophets hatched revolutionary plans in the years after 1815, but they were not the only participants in strikes, riots, peasant uprisings, and protest meetings. Indeed, ordinary workers, artisans, domestic servants, and women employed in textile manufacturing all joined in attempts to answer the "social question" to their satisfaction. A few socialists and feminists—like the English thinker John Stuart Mill and his wife, Harriet—campaigned for social and political equality of the sexes. In Britain in 1819, Manchester workers at St. Peter's Field demonstrated peacefully for increased representation in Parliament, but panicking guardsmen fired on the crowd, leaving 11 dead and 460 injured in an incident later dubbed the Peterloo Massacre. In 1839 and 1842, nearly half the adult population of Britain signed the People's Charter, which called for universal suffrage for all adult males, the secret ballot, equal electoral districts, and annual parliamentary elections. This mass movement, known as Chartism, like most such endeavors, ended in defeat. Parliament rejected the charter in 1839, 1842, and 1848.

Fourier and Utopian Socialism Despite their many defeats, the radicals kept trying. Charles Fourier's **utopian socialism** was perhaps the most visionary and influential of all Restoration-era alternative movements.

Fired by the egalitarian hopes and the cataclysmic failings of the French Revolution, Fourier (1772–1837) believed himself to be the scientific prophet of the new world to come. He was an imaginative, self-taught man who earned his keep in the cloth trade, an occupation that gave him an intense hatred for merchants and middlemen. Convinced that the division of labor and repressive moral conventions were destroying mankind's natural talents and passions, Fourier concluded that a revolution grander than that of 1789 was needed. But this utopian transformation of economic, social, and political conditions, he thought, could occur through organization, not through bloodshed. Indeed, by 1808 Fourier believed that the thoroughly corrupt world was on the brink of giving way to a new and harmonious age, of which he was the oracle.

First formulated in 1808, his "system" envisioned the reorganization of human communities into what he called phalanxes. In these harmonious collectives of 1,500 to 1,600 people, diversity would be preserved but efficiency maintained; best of all, work would become enjoyable. All members of the phalanx, rich and poor, would work, though not necessarily at the same tasks. All would work in short spurts of no more than two hours, so as to make labor more interesting and sleep, idleness, and overindulgence less attractive. Truly undesirable jobs, like sweeping out stables or cleaning latrines, would fall to young adolescents, who, Fourier argued, actually liked mucking about in filth.

Fourier's writings gained popularity in the 1830s, appealing to radicals who supported a variety of causes. In France, women were particularly active in spreading his ideas. Longing for social and moral reforms that would address problems such as prostitution, poverty, illegitimacy, and the exploitation of workers (including women and children), some women saw in Fourier's ideas a higher form of Christian communalism. By reshaping the phalanx to accommodate monogamous families and Christian values, women helped to make his work more respectable to middle-class readers. In Russia, Fourier's works inspired the imaginations of the young writer Fyodor Dostoevsky. He and fourteen others in the radical circle to which he belonged were sentenced to death for their views (though their executions were called off at the last minute). The German thinker Karl Marx read Fourier with great care, and there are many remnants of utopian thought in his work. In *The German Ideology* Marx describes life in an ideal communist society; in a postrevolutionary world, he predicts, people would no longer have to commit to a single profession or sphere of activity. Everyone could develop their talents in a range of areas. A well-ordered society would make it possible, as he put it in a famous phrase, "for me to do one thing today and another tomorrow, to hunt in the morning, fish in the afternoon, rear cattle in the evening, [and] criticize after dinner."

Marxism University-educated and philosophically radical, Karl Marx (1818–1883) elaborated what he called a scientific socialism. After being expelled from the university for

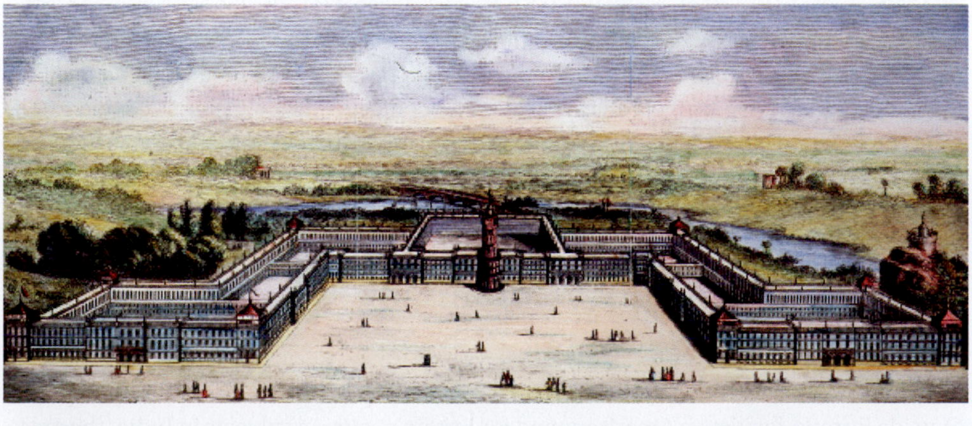

The Phalanx The Phalanx, as one of Fourier's German followers envisioned it. In this rendering, the idealized home for the residents of the cooperative social system is represented as a building architecturally similar to the home of the French kings, the Louvre.

Karl Marx The author (with Friedrich Engels) of *The Communist Manifesto*, Karl Marx argued that the exploitation of wage laborers would trigger a proletarian revolution and would lead to socialism supplanting capitalism.

his radical views, Marx took up a career in journalism. In that capacity, he covered legislative debates over property rights and taxation and developed an interest in economics. His understanding of capitalism, a term he was instrumental in popularizing, deepened through his collaboration with Friedrich Engels (1820–1895). Engels was a German-born radical who, after observing conditions in the factories owned by his wealthy father in Manchester, England, published a devastating indictment of industrial wage labor entitled *The Condition of the Working Class in England*.

Together, Marx and Engels developed what they called "scientific socialism," which they contrasted with the "utopian socialism" of others like Fourier. Scientific socialism was rooted, they argued, in a materialist theory of history: what mattered in history were the production of material goods and the ways in which society was organized into classes of producers and exploiters. History, they claimed, consisted of successive forms of exploitative production and rebellions against them. Capitalist exploitation of the wage worker was only the latest, and worst, version of class conflict, Marx and Engels contended. In industrialized societies, capitalists owned the means of production (the factories and machinery) and exploited wage workers. Marx and Engels were confident that the clashes between industrial wage workers with nothing to sell but their labor—or **proletarians**—and capitalists would end in a colossal transformation of human society and would usher in a new world of true liberty, equality, and fraternity. These beliefs constituted the fundamentals of **Marxism.** For Marx and Engels, history moved through stages: from feudalism to capitalism, and then, finally, to socialism (or communism).

From these fundamentals, Marx and Engels issued a comprehensive critique of post-1815 Europe. They identified a whole class of the exploited—the working class. They believed that more and more people would fall into this class as industrialization proceeded and that the masses would not share in the rising prosperity that capitalists monopolized. Marx and Engels predicted that there would be overproduction, and underconsumption of goods would lead to lower profits for capitalists and, consequently, to lower wages or unemployment for workers—which would ultimately spark a proletarian revolution. This revolution would result in a "dictatorship of the proletariat" and the end of private property. With the destruction of capitalism, the men claimed, exploitation would cease and the state would wither away.

After a decade of hardship across Europe known as the hungry forties, revolutions erupted in 1848 in France, Austria, Russia, Italy, Hungary, and the German states. After hearing that revolution had broken out in France, Marx and Engels published *The Communist Manifesto,* calling on the workers of all nations to unite in overthrowing capitalism. These were not proletarian revolutions. Modern industry had not developed beyond a few key locations by midcentury, mostly in northern and western Europe. Instead the revolutions were cross-class affairs, lead by an uneasy coalition of liberal doctors, lawyers, and university professors; often radical students and urban artisans; and a mass of poor peasants. As a group, they shared little more than a frustration with old elites and a desire for independent nations. Marx and Engels were sorely disappointed (not to mention exiled) by the reactionary crackdowns that quickly crushed the 1848 revolutions. The failure of those revolutions, however, did not doom their prophecy itself or diminish commitment to alternative social landscapes.

Insurgencies against Colonizing and Centralizing States

COMPARISON

DESCRIBE the challenges to the ideals of industrial capitalism in India and the Americas.

Outside Europe, for Native Americans and for Britain's colonial subjects in India, the greatest threat to traditional worlds was colonialism. While European radicals looked back to revolutionary legacies in imagining a transformed society, Native Americans insurgents and rebels in British India drew on their traditional cultural and political resources to imagine local alternatives to foreign impositions. Like the peoples of China, Africa, and the Middle East, native groups in the Americas and India met the period's challenges with prophecy, charismatic leadership, and rebellion. The insurgents all sought to defend their cultures and looked to an idealized past free from outside influences, but the new worlds they envisioned bore unmistakable marks of the present as well.

NATIVE AMERICAN PROPHETS

Like other native peoples threatened by imperial expansion, the Native Americans of North America dreamed of a world in which intrusive colonizers disappeared. Taking such dreams as prophecies, many Native Americans in the Ohio Valley flocked in 1805 to hear the revelations of a Shawnee Native American named Tenskwatawa. Facing a dark present and a darker future, they enthusiastically embraced the Shawnee Prophet's visions, which (like that of the Paiute prophet Wovoka nearly a century later) foretold how invaders would vanish if Native Americans returned to their customary ways and traditional rites.

Early Calls for Resistance and a Return to Tradition Tenskwatawa's visions—and the anticolonial uprising they inspired—drew on a long tradition of visionary leaders. Often these prophets inspired their followers not only to engage in cleansing ceremonies but also to cooperate in violent, anticolonial uprisings. In the 1760s, for example, the preachings of the Delaware shaman Neolin encouraged Native Americans of the Ohio Valley and Great Lakes to take up arms against the British, leading to the capture of several British military posts. Although the British put down the uprising, imperial officials learned a lesson from the conflict: they assumed a less arrogant posture toward Ohio Valley and Great Lakes Native Americans, and they forbade colonists from trespassing on lands west of the Appalachian Mountains. The British, however, were incapable of restraining the flow of settlers across the mountains, and the problem became much worse for the Native Americans once the American Revolution ended. With the Ohio Valley transferred to the new United States, American settlers crossed the Appalachians and flooded into Kentucky and Tennessee.

Despite the settlers' considerable migration, much of the territory between the Appalachian Mountains and the Mississippi River, which Americans referred to as the "western country," remained a Native American country. North and south of Kentucky and Tennessee, Native American warriors more than held their own against American forces. But in 1794 Native American warriors failed to repel invading American armies, and their leaders had to surrender lands in what is now the state of Ohio to the United States. (See Map 16.4.)

Tenskwatawa: The Shawnee Prophet The Shawnees, who lost most of their land, were among the most bitter—and bitterly divided—of Native American peoples living in the Ohio Valley. Some Shawnee leaders concluded that their people's survival now required that they cooperate with American officials and Christian missionaries. This strategy, they realized, entailed wrenching changes in Shawnee culture. European reformers, after all, insisted that Native American men give up hunting and take up farming, an occupation that the Shawnees and their neighbors had always considered "women's work." Moreover, the Shawnees were pushed to abandon communal traditions in favor of private property rights.

Among the demoralized Shawnees was **Tenskwatawa** (1775–1836), whose story of overcoming personal failures through religious visions and embracing a strict moral code has parallels with that of Hong Xiuquan, the Taiping leader. In his first thirty years, Tenskwatawa could claim few accomplishments. He had failed as a hunter and as a medicine man, had blinded himself in one eye, and had earned a reputation as an obnoxious braggart. All this changed in the spring of 1805, however, after he fell into a trance and experienced a vision. In this dream, Tenskwatawa encountered a heaven where the virtuous enjoyed the traditional Shawnee way of life and a hell where evildoers suffered punishments. Additional revelations followed, and Tenskwatawa soon stitched these together into a new social gospel that urged disciples to abstain from alcohol and return to traditional customs.

Like other prophets, Tenskwatawa exhorted Native Americans to avoid contact with outside influences, to reduce their dependence on European trade goods and to sever their connections to Christian missionaries. If Native Americans obeyed these dictates, Tenskwatawa promised, the deer, which "were half a tree's length under the ground," would come back in abundant numbers to the earth's surface. Likewise, he claimed, Native Americans killed in conflict with colonial intruders would be resurrected, while evil Americans would depart from the country west of the Appalachians.

Like the Qing's response to Hong's visions, American officials grew concerned as the Shawnee Prophet gathered followers. The spread of Tenskwatawa's message raised fears of a pan-Native American confederacy. Hoping to undermine the Shawnee Prophet's claims to supernatural power, territorial governor William Henry Harrison challenged Tenskwatawa to make the sun stand still. But Tenskwatawa one-upped Harrison. Having learned

MAP 16.4 | Native American Revolts in the United States and Mexico

The new world order of expanding nation-states and industrial markets strongly affected indigenous peoples in North America.

- According to this map, where did the fiercest resistance to centralizing states and global market pressures occur?
- What regions of the United States were Native Americans forced to leave?
- According to your reading, to what extent, if any, did the natives' alternative visions create or preserve an alternative to the new emerging order?

of an impending eclipse from white astronomers, Tenskwatawa assembled his followers on June 16, 1806. Right on schedule, and as if on command, the sky darkened. Claiming credit for the eclipse, Tenskwatawa saw his standing soar, as did the ranks of his disciples.

At the same time, however, Tenskwatawa had made plenty of enemies among his fellow Native Americans. His visions consigned drinkers to hell and singled out those who cooperated with colonial authorities for punishment in this world and the next. Indeed, Tenskwatawa condemned as witches those Native Americans who rejected his preaching in favor of the teachings of Christian missionaries and American authorities. (To be sure, Tenskwatawa's damnation of Christianized Native Americans was somewhat paradoxical, for missionary doctrines obviously influenced his vision of a burning hell for sinners and his crusade against alcohol.)

Tecumseh and the Wish for Native American Unity Although Tenskwatawa's accusations alienated some Native Americans, his prophecies gave heart to many more. This was particularly the case once his brother, Tecumseh (1768–1813), helped circulate the message of Native American renaissance among Native American villages from the Great Lakes to the Gulf Coast. On his journeys after 1805, Tecumseh did more than spread his brother's visions; he also wedded them to the idea of an enlarged Native American confederation. Moving around the Great Lakes and traveling across the southern half of the western country, Tecumseh preached the need for Native American unity. Always, he insisted that Native Americans resist any American attempts to get them to sell more land. In response, thousands of followers renounced their ties to colonial ways and prepared to combat the expansion of the United States.

By 1810, Tecumseh had emerged, at least in the eyes of American officials, as even more dangerous than his brother. Impressed by Tecumseh's charismatic organizational talents, William Harrison warned that this new "Indian menace" was forming "an Empire that would rival in glory" that of the Aztecs and the Incas. In 1811, while Tecumseh was traveling among southern tribes, Harrison had his troops attack Tenskwatawa's village, Prophet's Town, on the Tippecanoe River in what is now the state of Indiana. The resulting battle was evenly fought, but the Native Americans eventually gave ground and American forces burned Prophet's Town. That defeat discredited Tenskwatawa, who had promised his followers protection from destruction at American hands. Spurned by his former disciples, including his brother, Tenskwatawa fled to Canada. Tecumseh soldiered on, supporting the British in the War of 1812 in the hope that a British victory would check American expansionism. But in 1813, with the war's outcome still in doubt and the pan-Native American confederacy still fragile, he perished at the Battle of the Thames, north of Lake Erie.

Native American Removals The discrediting of Tenskwatawa and the death of Tecumseh damaged the cause of Native American unity; then British betrayal dealt it a fatal blow. Following the war's end in 1814, the British withdrew their support and left the Native Americans south of the Great Lakes to fend for themselves against land-hungry American settlers and the armies of the United States. By 1815, American citizens outnumbered Native Americans in the western country by a seven-to-one margin, and this gap dramatically widened in the next few years. Recognizing the hopelessness of military resistance, Native Americans south of the Great Lakes resigned themselves to relocation. During the 1820s, most of the peoples north of the Ohio River were removed to lands west of the Mississippi River. During the 1830s, the southern tribes were cleared out, completing what amounted to an ethnic cleansing of Native American peoples from the region between the Appalachians and the Mississippi.

In the midst of these final removals, Tenskwatawa died, though his dream of an alternative to American expansion had faded for his people years earlier. Through the rest of the

Visions of Native American Unification *(Left)* A portrait of Tenskwatawa, the "Shawnee Prophet," whose visions stirred thousands of Native Americans in the Ohio Valley and Great Lakes to renounce dependence on colonial imports and resist the expansion of the United States. *(Right)* A portrait of his brother, Tecumseh, who succeeded in building a significant pan-Native American confederation, although it unraveled following his death at the Battle of the Thames in 1813 and the end of warfare between the United States and Britain the following year.

nineteenth century, however, other Native American prophets emerged, and their visions continued to inspire followers with the hope of an alternative to life under the colonial rule of the United States. But like Wovoka and the Ghost Dancers in 1890, these dreams failed to halt the expansion of the United States and the contraction of Native American lands.

THE CASTE WAR OF THE YUCATAN

As in North America, the Spanish establishment of an expansionist nation-state in Mexico sparked widespread revolts by indigenous peoples. The most protracted was the Mayan revolt in the Yucatan peninsula. The revolt started in 1847, and its flames were not finally doused until the full occupation of the Yucatan by Mexican national troops in 1901.

The strength and endurance of the Mayan revolt stemmed in large measure from the unusual features of the Spanish conquest in southern Mesoamerica. Because this area lacked precious metals and fertile lands, Spain and its rivals focused elsewhere—on central and northern Mexico and the Caribbean islands. As a result, the Mayan Indians escaped forced recruitment for silver mines or sugar plantations. This does not mean that global processes sidestepped the Mayan Indians. In fact, the production of dyes and foodstuffs for shipment to other regions drew the Yucatan into long-distance trading networks. Nonetheless, cultivation and commerce were much less disruptive to indigenous lives in the Yucatan than elsewhere in the New World.

Growing Pressures from the Sugar Trade Local developments, however, encroached on the Mayan world in the nineteenth century. First, regional elites—mainly white, but often with the support of mixed race (mestizo) populations—bickered for supremacy so long as the central authority of Mexico City remained weak. Weaponry flowed freely through the peninsula, and some combatants even appealed for Mayan support. At the same time, regional and international trade spurred the spread of sugar estates, which threatened traditional corn cultivation in the Yucatan. Over the decades, plantations encroached on Mayan properties. Planters used several devices to lure independent Mayans to work, especially in the harvest. The most important device, debt peonage, involved giving small cash advances to Indian families, which obligated fathers and sons to work for meager wages to pay off the debts. In addition, Mexico's costly wars, culminating in a showdown with the United States in 1846, drove tax collectors and army recruiters into villages in search of revenues and soldiers.

The combination of material and physical threats was explosive. When a small band of Mayans, fed up with rising taxes and ebbing autonomy, used firearms to drive back white intruders in 1847, they sparked a war that took a half century to complete. The rebels were primarily free Mayans who had not yet been absorbed into the sugar economy. They wanted to dismantle old definitions of Indians as a caste—a status that deprived the Indians of legal and political equality with whites and that also subjected the Indians to special taxes. Thus, local Mayan leaders, like Jacinto Pat and Cecilio Chi, upheld a republican model in the name of formal equality of all political subjects and devotion to a spiritual order that did not distinguish between Christians and non-Christians. "If the Indians revolt," one Mayan rebel explained, "it is because the whites gave them reason; because the whites say they do not believe in Jesus Christ, because they have burned the cornfield."

The Caste War Horrified, the local white elites reacted to the uprising with vicious repression and dubbed the ensuing conflict a **caste war**. In their view, the bloody conflict was a struggle between forward-looking liberals and backward-looking Indians. At first, whites and mestizos were no match for the determined Mayans, whose forces seized town after town. They especially targeted symbols of white power. With relish they demolished the whipping posts where Indians had endured public humiliation and punishment.

In the end, fortune, not political savvy, saved the Yucatan's whites. Settlement of the war with the United States in 1848 enabled Mexico City to rescue local elites in the Yucatan. With the help of a $15 million payment from Washington for giving up its northern provinces, Mexico could spend freely to build up its southern armies. The Mexican government soon fielded a force of 17,000 soldiers and waged a scorched-earth campaign to drive back the depleted Mayan forces.

By 1849, the confrontation had entered a new phase in which Mexican troops engaged in mass repression of the Mayans. Mexican armies set Indian fields and villages ablaze. Between 30 and 40 percent of the Mayan population perished in the war and its repressive aftermath. The inhabitants of entire Mayan cities pulled up stakes and withdrew to isolated districts protected by fortified villages. War between armies degenerated into guerrilla warfare between an occupying Mexican army and mobile bands of Mayan squadrons, inflicting a gruesome toll on the invaders. As years passed, the war ground to a stalemate, especially once the U.S. funds ran out and Mexican soldiers began deserting in droves.

Caste War in the Yucatan The ruthless slaughter of Maya farmers by Mexican troops is captured in this 1850 painting. The intimacy of the bloodstained straw hats strewn on the road suggest this work was an eyewitness account.

Reclaiming a Mayan Identity Warfare prompted a spiritual transformation that reinforced a purely Mayan identity against the Mexican invaders' efforts to create a strong, centralized state. Thus, a struggle that began with demands for legal equality and relative cultural autonomy became a crusade for spiritual salvation and the complete cultural separation of the Mayan Indians. A particularly influential group under José María Barrera retreated to a hamlet called Chan Santa Cruz. There, at the site where he found a cross shape carved into a mahogany tree, Barrera had a vision of a divine encounter. Thereafter, people in a swath of Yucatan villages around Chan Santa Cruz refashioned themselves as moral communities. Leaders created a polity, with soldiers, priests, and tax collectors pledging loyalty to the Speaking Cross. Like the followers of Hong in China's Taiping Rebellion, Indian rebels forged an alternative religion: it blended Christian rituals, faiths, and icons with Mayan legends and beliefs. At the center was a stone temple, Balam Na ("House of God"), 100 feet long and 60 feet wide. Through pilgrimages to Balam Na and the secular justice of Indian judges, the Mayans soon governed their domain in the Yucatan autonomously, almost completely cut off from the rest of Mexico.

The Mexican government threw its weight behind the strong-arm ruler General Porfirio Díaz (r. 1876–1911). The general sent one of his veteran commanders, Ignacio Bravo, to do what no other Mexican could accomplish: vanquish Chan Santa Cruz. When General Bravo finally entered the town, he found the once imposing temple Balam Na covered in vegetation. Nature was reclaiming the territories of the Speaking Cross. Hunger and Bravo's soldiers finally drove the Mayans to work on white Mexican plantations; the alternative vision was vanquished. A combination of declining economic conditions and the soldiers under Ignacio Bravo brought an end to the Mayan revolt.

THE REBELLION OF 1857 IN INDIA

COMPARISON

DISTINGUISH the long-term influence of protest movements from their immediate political accomplishments in Asia, Islam, and Africa.

Like Native Americans, the peoples of nineteenth-century India had a long history of opposition to colonial domination. Armed revolts had occurred since the onset of rule by the British East India Company (see Chapter 15). Nonetheless, the uprising of 1857 was unprecedented in its scale, and it posed a greater threat than had any previous rebellion. (See **Analyzing Global Developments: Alternative Movements in Asia and Africa**.)

India under Company Rule During the first half of the nineteenth century the British rulers of India had dismantled most of the traditional powers of the nobility and the rights of peasants. Believing that the princely powers and landed aristocracies were out of date, the company instituted far-reaching changes in administration. Lord Dalhousie, upon his appointment as governor-general in 1848, immediately began annexing what had been independent princely domains and stripping native aristocrats of their privileges. Swallowing one princely state after another, the British removed their former allies.

The government also decided to collect taxes directly from peasants, displacing the landed nobles as intermediaries. In disarming the landed nobility, the British threw the retainers and militia of the notables into unemployment, and by demanding high taxes from peasants, the British forced them to rely on moneylenders, who could take ownership of land when peasant proprietors failed to pay. Meanwhile, the company transferred judicial authority to an administration that was insulated from the Indian social hierarchy.

The most prized object for annexation was the kingdom of Awadh in northern India (see Map 16.5). Founded in 1722 by an Iranian adventurer, it was one of the first successor states to have gained a measure of independence from the Mughal ruler in Delhi. With access to the fertile resources of the Ganges Plain, its opulent court in Lucknow was one place where Mughal splendor still survived. In 1765, the company imposed a treaty on Awadh under which the ruler paid an annual tribute for British troops stationed in his territory to "protect" his kingdom from internal and external enemies.

Analyzing Global Developments

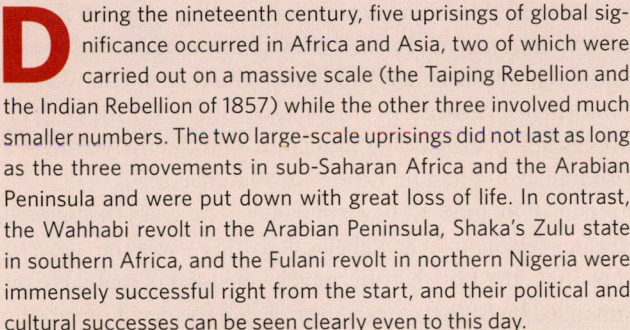

Alternative Movements in Asia and Africa

During the nineteenth century, five uprisings of global significance occurred in Africa and Asia, two of which were carried out on a massive scale (the Taiping Rebellion and the Indian Rebellion of 1857) while the other three involved much smaller numbers. The two large-scale uprisings did not last as long as the three movements in sub-Saharan Africa and the Arabian Peninsula and were put down with great loss of life. In contrast, the Wahhabi revolt in the Arabian Peninsula, Shaka's Zulu state in southern Africa, and the Fulani revolt in northern Nigeria were immensely successful right from the start, and their political and cultural successes can be seen clearly even to this day.

QUESTIONS FOR ANALYSIS

- How would you assess the influence of Europe on the uprisings discussed in this chapter and their role in shaping the outcomes?
- Although all five movements suffered stinging military defeats (the Fulani at the hands of the British in 1900, the Zulu state at the hands of the British in 1878, the Wahhabis at the hands of Egyptian troops at the beginning of the nineteenth century, the Taiping rebels at the hands of the Qing rulers, and the Indian rebels by British soldiers), were their long-term consequences markedly different?
- Is there anything that holds these diverse movements together and allows us to represent them as alternatives to the main developments under way in western Europe and North America, where rapid economic growth, nationhood, and the beginnings of democracy came to the fore?

Explore Further

William Dalrymple, *The Last Mughal: The Fall of a Dynasty: Delhi, 1857* (2007).

Carolyn Hamilton (ed.), *The Mfecane Aftermath: Reconstructive Debates in Southern African History* (1995).

Mervyn Hiskett, *The Sword of Truth: The Life and Times of the Shehu Usman dan Fodio* (1994).

Jonathan Spence, *God's Chinese Son: The Taiping Heavenly Kingdom of Hong Xiuquan* (1996).

MOVEMENT/LEADER	SHORT-TERM CONSEQUENCES	LONG-TERM CONSEQUENCES
Smaller-Scale Uprisings		
The Fulani Revolt Northern Nigeria (1804–1817) Usman dan Fodio (1754–1817)	• Created largest state in sub-Saharan Africa • Occupied two-thirds of present day Nigeria • British conquered it in early twentieth century	• Gained independence in 1960 • Fulani elite families who worked with British now rule over present-day Nigeria
Shaka's Zulu State Shaka (1787–1828)	• Created an army of 40,000 warriors • Created Zulu State covering 11,500 sq. miles in South Africa	• British conquered Zulu in 1878 • Zulu maintained their identity through apartheid • Population of 11 million today
The Wahhabi Rebellion Arabian Peninsula (1744–1818) Ibn Abd al-Wahhab (1703–1792)	• Ruled over much of the Arabian Peninsula • Defeated by Egyptian army in 1812	• Created the House of Saud, which rules over Saudi Arabia today • Retains commitment to Wahhab principles today
Larger-Scale Uprisings		
The Taiping Rebellion (1851–1864) Hong Xiuquan (1813–1864)	• Half a million members • Leader Hong and rebels ruled over central and southern China from Nanjing for 11 years	• Rebellion caused 20 million deaths by 1853 • Nearly toppled Qing Dynasty Mao viewed it as precursor to peasant-led Communist movement. Now viewed as threat to social order due to large-scale violence
The Indian Rebellion (1857–1858) Geographic Leaders, no monolithic figure	• Indian sepoys of East India Company started • Sepoys pledged support to Mughal emperor • Revolt included sepoys, peasants, small landholders, and religious leaders across north India	• British crown ended company rule after suppressing rebellion brutally • Laid the foundation for later Indian populist and nationalist resistance

Treaty Violations and Annexation In 1856, citing misgovernment and deterioration in law and order, the East India Company violated its treaty obligations and sent its troops to Lucknow to take control of the province. Nawab Wajid Ali Shah, the poet-king of Awadh, whom the British saw as weak and immoral, refused to sign the treaty ceding control to the British.

The annexation of princely domains and the abolition of feudal privileges formed part of the developing practices of European imperialism. To the policy of annexation, Dalhousie added an ambitious program of building railroads, telegraph lines, and a postal network to unify the disjointed territory into a single "network of iron sinew" under British control. Dalhousie saw these infrastructures as key to developing India into a productive colony—a supplier of raw materials for British industry, and a market for its manufactures.

A year after Dalhousie's departure in 1856, India went up in flames. The spark that ignited the simmering discontent into a furious rebellion—the Rebellion of 1857—was the "greased cartridge" controversy. At the end of 1856, the British army, which consisted of many Hindu and Muslim recruits (sepoys) commanded by British officers, introduced the new Enfield rifle to replace the old-style musket. To load the rifle, soldiers had to bite the cartridge open. Although manufacturing instructions stated that linseed oil and beeswax be used to grease the cartridge, a rumor circulated that cow and pig fat had been used. Biting into cartridges greased with animal fat meant violating the Hindu and Muslim sepoys' religious traditions. The sepoys became convinced that there was a plot afoot to defile them and to compel their conversion to Christianity. So a wave of rebellion spread among the 270,000 Indian soldiers, who greatly outnumbered the 40,000 British soldiers employed to rule over 200 million Indians.

Rebellion Breaks Out The mutiny broke out on May 10, 1857, at the military barracks in Meerut. The revolt soon turned from a limited military mutiny into a widespread civil rebellion that involved peasants, artisans, day laborers, and religious leaders. While the insurgents did not eliminate the power of the East India Company, which managed to retain the loyalty of princes and landed aristocrats in some places, they did throw the

The Indian Sepoys Pictured here are Indian soldiers, or sepoys, who were armed, drilled, and commanded by British officers. The sepoys were drawn from indigenous groups that the British considered to be "martial races." This photograph shows the Sikhs, designated as one such "race."

MAP 16.5 | Indian Rebellion of 1857

The Indian Rebellion of 1857 broke out first among the Indian soldiers of the British army. Other groups soon joined the struggle.

- According to this map, how many centers of rebellion were located in British territory and how many in dependent states?
- Why do you think the rebellion occurred in the interior of the subcontinent rather than along the coasts?
- In what way was the company's expansion into formerly autonomous areas during the first half of the nineteenth century a factor in the rebellion?

company into a crisis. Before long, the mutineers in Delhi issued a proclamation declaring that because the British were determined to destroy the religion of both Hindus and Muslims, it was the duty of the wealthy and the privileged to support the rebellion. To promote Hindu-Muslim unity, rebel leaders asked Muslims to refrain from killing cows in deference to Hindu sentiments.

Although the dispossessed aristocracy and petty landholders led the rebellion, leaders also appeared from the lower classes. Bakht Khan, who had been a junior noncommissioned officer in the British army, became commander-in-chief of the rebel forces in Delhi, replacing one of the Mughal emperor's sons. And Devi Singh, a wealthy peasant, set himself up as a peasant king. Dressed in yellow, the insignia of Hindu royalty, he constituted a government of his own, modeling it on the British administration. While his imitation of company rule showed his respect for the British bureaucracy, he defied British authority by leading an armed peasantry against the hated local moneylenders. The call to popular forces also marked the rebel career of Maulavi Ahmadullah Shah, a Muslim theologian. He stood at the head of the rebel forces in Lucknow, leading an army composed primarily of ordinary soldiers and people from the lower orders. Claiming to be an "Incarnation of the Deity," and thus inspired by divine will, he emerged as a prophetic leader of the common people. He voiced his undying hatred of the British in religious terms, calling on Hindus and Muslims to destroy British rule and warning his followers against betrayal by landed authorities.

Participation by the Peasantry The presence of popular leadership points to the important role of the lower classes. Although feudal chieftains often brought them into the rebellion, the peasantry made it their own. The organizing principle of their uprising was the common experience of oppression. Thus, they destroyed anything that represented the authority of the company: prisons, factories, police posts, railway stations, European bungalows, and law courts. Equally significant, the peasantry attacked native moneylenders and local power-holders who were seen as benefiting from company rule.

Vigorous and militant as the popular rebellion was, it was limited in its territorial and ideological horizons. To begin with, the uprisings were local in scale and vision. Peasant rebels attacked the closest seats of administration and sought to settle scores with their most immediate and visible oppressors. They generally did not carry their action beyond the village or collection of villages. Their loyalties remained intensely local, based on village attachments and religious, caste, and clan ties. Nor did popular militants seek to undo traditional hierarchies of caste and religion.

British Response Convinced that the rebellion was the result of plotting by a few troublemakers, the British reacted with brutal vengeance. Villages were torched, and rebels were tied to cannons and blown to bits to teach Indians a lesson in power.

By July 1858, the vicious campaign to restore British control had achieved its goal. Yet, in August, the British Parliament abolished company rule and the company itself, and transferred responsibility for the governing of India to the crown. In November, Queen Victoria issued a proclamation guaranteeing religious toleration, promising improvements, and allowing Indians to serve in the government. She promised to honor the treaties and agreements with princes and chiefs and to refrain from interfering in religious matters. The insurgents had risen up not as a nation, but as a multitude of communities acting independently; their determination to find a new order shocked the British and threw them into a panic. Having crushed the uprising, the British resumed the work of transforming India into a modern colonial state and economy. But the desire for radical alternatives and traditions of popular insurgency, though vanquished, did not vanish.

Conclusion

The nineteenth century was a time of turmoil and transformation. While powerful forces reconfigured the world as a place for capitalism, colonialism, and nation-states, so too did prophets, charismatic leaders, radicals, peasant rebels, and anticolonial insurgents arise to offer alternatives. Reflecting local circumstances and traditions, the struggles of these men and women for a different future opened up spaces for the ideas and activities of lower classes.

Conventional historical accounts either neglect these struggles or fail to view them as a whole. These individuals were not just romantic, last-ditch resisters, as some scholars have argued. Even after defeat, their messages remained alive within their communities. Nor were their actions isolated and atypical events, for when viewed on a global scale they bring to light a world that looks very different from the one that became dominant. To see the Wahhabi movement in the Arabian Peninsula together with the Shawnee Prophet in North America, the utopians and radicals in Europe with the peasant insurgents in British India, and the Taiping rebels with the Mayans in the Yucatan is to glimpse a world of marginalized regions and groups. It was a world that more powerful groups endeavored to suppress but could not erase.

In this world, prophets and rebel leaders usually cultivated power and prestige locally; the emergence of an alternative political or social movement in one region did not impinge on communities and political organizations in others. As much as these individuals had in common, they envisioned widely different kinds of futures. Even Karl Marx, who called the workers of the world to unite, was acutely aware that the call for a proletarian revolution applied only to the industrialized countries of Europe. Other dissenters had even more localized horizons. A world fashioned by movements for alternatives meant a world with multiple centers and different historical timelines.

What gave force to a different mapping of the world was the fact that common people were at the center of these alternative visions, and their voices, however muted, gained a place on the historical stage. The quest for various forms of equality defined efforts to reconstitute alternative worlds. In Islamic regions, the emphasis on equality in revitalization movements was evident in their mobilization of all Muslims, not just the elites. Likewise, charismatic military leaders in Africa, for all their use of raw power, used the framework of community to build new polities. The Taiping Rebellion distinguished itself by seeking to establish an equal society of men and women in service of the Heavenly Kingdom. Operating under very different conditions, European radicals imagined a society free from aristocratic privileges and bourgeois property. Anticolonial rebels and insurgents depended on local solidarities and proposed alternative moral communities. In so doing, these movements compelled ruling elites to adjust the way they governed. The next chapter explores this challenge.

After You Read This Chapter

Go to INQUIZITIVE to see what you've learned—and learn what you've missed—with personalized feedback along the way.

TRACING THE GLOBAL STORYLINES

FOCUS ON: *Regional Variations in Alternative Visions*

EUROPE

- European socialists and radicals envision a world free of exploitation and inequalities, while nationalists work to create new independent nation-states.

THE AMERICAS

- Native American prophets in the United States imagine a world restored to its customary ways and traditional rites.
- Mayans in the Yucatan defy the central Mexican government in a rebellion known as the Caste War.

THE ISLAMIC WORLD AND AFRICA

- Revivalist movements in the Arabian Peninsula and West Africa demand a return to traditional Islam.
- A charismatic warrior, Shaka, creates a powerful state in southern Africa.

SEMI-COLONIAL CHINA

- An inspired prophetic figure, Hong Xiuquan, leads the Taiping Rebellion against the Qing dynasty and European encroachment on China.

COLONIAL INDIA

- Indian troops mutiny against the British and attempt to restore Mughal rule.

CHRONOLOGY

THE ISLAMIC WORLD AND AFRICA

- Dan Fodio's movement in West Africa 1804–1809
- Wahhabis wage militant religious campaign in Arabian Peninsula 1813–1815
- Shaka creates Zulu State in South Africa 1818–1828

CHINA

- Taiping Rebellion 1851–1864

EUROPE

- Restoration period 1815–1848
- Fourier's utopian socialism gains popularity 1830s
- Revolutions across Europe; Marx and Engels publish *The Communist Manifesto* 1848

THE AMERICAS

- Tecumseh's Rebellion in North America 1810–1813

INDIA

- Indian revolt 1857–1858

1800 — 1850

THINKING ABOUT GLOBAL CONNECTIONS

- ***Thinking about Exchange Networks and Alternative Visions*** How did people around the world respond to the major changes of the French, American, and Industrial Revolutions? What difference did proximity to the European and American "core" make?
- ***Thinking about Changing Power Relationships and Alternative Visions*** What kind of challenges did the new order provoke? What kinds of traditions did those challenges draw on, and what kind of success did they have?
- ***Thinking about Gender and Alternative Visions*** Describe the role women played in millenarian protest movements during the nineteenth century, and explain the significance of gender to those movements.

STUDY QUESTIONS

1. Describe the global order that emerged in the nineteenth century, and identify its core values.
2. Explain the goals of Islamic revitalization movements such as **Wahhabism** in the Arabian Peninsula and **Usman dan Fodio's** movement in West Africa. How were these regions affected by the new world order? What alternative did Islamic revitalization propose?
3. Compare the **millenarian** aspirations of the **Taiping Rebellion**, and the Shawnee rebellion of **Tenskwatawa**.
4. Compare the role of state centralization in the ***Mfecane* movement** and the **Caste War** in the Yucatan, Mexico.
5. Explain the relationship between **liberalism**, **utopian socialism,** and **Marxism**.

Caste War in Yucatan, Mexico 1847–1901

Ghost Dance movement in North America 1889–1890

1900

1950

Going to the Source

Religion and Change in the Nineteenth Century

World historians often consider religion to be a tool that humans use to unite or exclude people. Many states and societies also employ religion as a basis for law or politics. Religious tenets thus are adapted to particular political circumstances, just as some political circumstances must adapt to the prevailing religious beliefs of the people who live in a particular time and place. The documents in this section illustrate a variety ways in which religion has interacted with government. Though the authors have quite different religious beliefs, they share a common way of considering political and social changes.

PRIMARY SOURCE 16.1

Differences between Muslim and Non-Muslim Governments (1806), Usman Dan Fodio

Usman dan Fodio criticized Muslim rule from within the faith. He believed that many Muslim elites were not living according to Muslim principles. In this selection from his many writings on reforming Islamic states and societies in Africa, he identified problems with the Hausa state where he lived, in present-day northern Nigeria. In 1800, Usman dan Fodio led the Fulani War, a rebellion that resulted in the founding of the Sokoto caliphate. That state expanded in West Africa until the 1830s.

[O]ne of the ways of their government is the building of their sovereignty upon three things: the people's persons, their honor, and their possessions; and whomsoever they wish to kill or exile or violate his honor or devour his wealth they do so in pursuit of their lusts, without any right in the Shari'a. One of the ways of their government is their imposing on the people monies not laid down by the Shari'a. One of the ways of their government is their intentionally eating whatever food they wish, whether it is religiously permitted or forbidden, and wearing whatever clothes they wish, whether religiously permitted or forbidden, and drinking what beverages they wish, whether religiously permitted or forbidden, and riding whatever riding beasts they wish, whether religiously permitted or forbidden, and taking what women they wish without marriage contract, and living in decorated palaces, whether religiously permitted or forbidden, and spreading soft carpets as they wish, whether religiously permitted or forbidden. . . .

One of the ways of their government is to place many women in their houses, until the number of women of some of them amounts to one thousand or more. One of the ways of their government is that a man puts the affairs of his women into the hands of the oldest one, and every one of the others is like a slave-woman under her. One of the ways of their government is to delay in the paying of a debt, and this is injustice. One of the ways of their government is what the superintendent of the market takes from all the parties to a sale, and the meat which he takes on each market day from the butchers . . . and one of the ways of their government is the cotton and other things which they take in the course of the markets. . . . One of the ways of their governments is the taking of people's beasts of burden without their permission to carry the sultan's food to him. Whoever follows his beast to the place where they unload it, they return it to him but he who does not follow, his beast is lost. . . .

One of the ways of their government, which is also well known, is that if you have an adversary in law and he precedes you to them, and gives them some money, then your word will not be accepted by them, even though they know for a certainty of your truthfulness, unless you give them more than your adversary gave. One of the ways of their government is to shut the door in the face of the needy. . . . Therefore do not follow their way in their government, and do not imitate them.

1. **What are Usman dan Fodio's main concerns about the Hausa government?**
2. **How does Usman dan Fodio use religion to frame his critique of Hausa society?**

PRIMARY SOURCE 16.2

Visions of the Great Good Spirit (1810), Tenskwatawa

In the first decade of the nineteenth century, Tenskwatawa, the Shawnee Native American religious leader and prophet, recalled an earlier, happier time for the Amerindian peoples of the areas around the Great Lakes and Ohio Valley, a time before the arrival of the Europeans. In the passage below, Tenskwatawa urges people to spurn the ways of white Americans and return to the authentic, pure ways of a precolonial past.

Our Creator put us on this wide, rich land, and told us we were free to go where the game was, where the soil was good for planting. That was our state of true happiness. We did not have to beg for anything. Our Creator had taught us how to find and make everything we needed, from trees and plants and animals and stone. We lived in bark, and we wore only the skins of animals.

Thus were we created. Thus we lived for a long time, proud and happy. We had never eaten pig meat, nor tasted the poison called whiskey, nor worn wool from sheep, nor struck fire or dug earth with steel, nor cooked in iron, nor hunted and fought with loud guns, nor ever had diseases which soured our blood or rotted our organs. We were pure, so we were strong and happy.

For many years we traded furs to the English or the French, for wool blankets and guns and iron things, for steel awls and needles and axes, for mirrors, for pretty things made of beads and silver. And for liquor. This was foolish, but we did not know it. We shut our ears to the Great Good Spirit. We did not want to hear that we were being foolish.

But now those things of the white men have corrupted us, and made us weak and needful. Our men forgot how to hunt without noisy guns. Our women don't want to make fire without steel, or cook without iron, or sew without metal awls and needles, or fish without steel hooks. Some look in those mirrors all the time, and no longer teach their daughters to make leather or render bear oil. We learned to need the white men's goods, and so now a People who never had to beg for anything must beg for everything!

And that is why Our Creator purified me and sent me down to you full of the shining power, to make you what you were before!

No red man must ever drink liquor, or he will go and have the hot lead poured in his mouth! . . . Do not eat any food that is raised or cooked by a white person. It is not good for us. Eat not their bread made of wheat, for Our Creator gave us corn for our bread. . . .

The Great Good Spirit wants our men to hunt and kill game as in the ancient days, with the silent arrow and the lance and the snare, and no longer with guns.

If we hunt in the old ways, we will not have to depend upon white men, for new guns and powder and lead, or go to them to have broken guns repaired. Remember it is the wish of the Great Good Spirit that we have no more commerce with white men! . . .

Our Creator told me that all red men who refuse to obey these laws are bad people, or witches, and must be put to death. . . .

The Great Good Spirit will appoint a place to be our holy town, and at that place I will call all red men to come and share this shining power. For the People in all tribes are corrupt and miserable! In that holy town we will pray every morning and every night for the earth to be fruitful, and the game and fish to be plentiful again.

1. **Why does Tenskwatawa object to the ways in which the Shawnee and other Native Americans are living?**
2. **How has the adaptation of European ways changed native peoples and what changes does Tenskwatawa suggest his followers make?**

PRIMARY SOURCE 16.3

Critique of Religion (1843), Karl Marx

Karl Marx, one of the nineteenth century's most prolific students of political economy, is best known for creating the idea of communism as a response to the problems that he observed in European industrial society. But Marx wrote more broadly about society, and in this passage he explains the ways in which religion is created and used by humans to avoid dealing with many contemporary problems—especially those that he observed in nineteenth-century Europe.

*

The basis of irreligious criticism is this: *man makes religion;* religion does not make man. Religion is indeed man's self-consciousness and self-awareness so long as he has not found himself or has lost himself again. But *man* is not an abstract being, squatting outside the world. Man is *the human world*, the state, society. This state, this society, produce religion which is an *inverted world consciousness*, because they are an *inverted world.* Religion is the general theory of this world, its encyclopedic compendium, its logic in popular form. . . . The struggle against religion is, therefore, indirectly, a struggle against *that world* whose spiritual *aroma* is religion.

Religious suffering is at the same time an expression of real suffering and a protest against real suffering. Religion is the sigh of the oppressed creature, the sentiment of a heartless world, and the soul of soulless conditions. It is the opium of the people.

The abolition of religion as the *illusory* happiness of men, is a demand for their *real* happiness. The call to abandon their illusions about their condition is *a call to abandon a condition which requires illusions*. The criticism of religion is therefore, the *embryonic criticism of this vale of tears* of which religion is the *halo.*

It is the *task of history*, therefore, once the *other-world of truth* has vanished to establish the *truth of this world.* The immediate *task of philosophy*, which is in the service of history, is to unmask human self-alienation in its secular form now that it has been unmasked in its sacred form. Thus the criticism of heaven is transformed into the criticism of earth, the *criticism of religion* into the *criticism of law* and the *criticism of theology* into the *criticism of politics.*

1. **According to Marx what role does religion play within society?**
2. **What does Marx mean when he says that religion "is the opium of the people"?**

PRIMARY SOURCE 16.4

The Principles of the Heavenly Nature (1854), Taiping Heavenly Kingdom

Inspired by their understanding of Christianity, the Taiping leadership confronted the central role of the family and ancestral worship in Chinese society by urging all its followers to regard themselves as belonging to a single family, as described in this excerpt from an official declaration. The Taiping's leader, Hung Xiuquan (1814–1864), became convinced that he was the younger brother of Jesus Christ.

We brothers and sisters, enjoying today the greatest mercy of our Heavenly Father, have become as one family and are able to enjoy true blessings; each of us must always be thankful. Speaking in terms of our ordinary human feelings, it is true that each has his own parents and there must be a distinction in family names; it is also true that as each has his own household, there must be a distinction between this boundary and that boundary.

Yet we must know that the ten thousand names derive from the one name, and the one name from one ancestor. Thus our origins are not different. Since our Heavenly Father gave us birth and nourishment, we are of one form though of separate bodies, and we breathe the same air though in different places. This is why we say, "All are brothers within the four seas." Now, basking in the profound mercy of Heaven, we are of one family. . . .

We brothers, our minds having been awakened by our Heavenly Father, joined the camp in the earlier days to support our Sovereign, many bringing parents, wives, uncles, brothers, and whole families. It is a matter of course that we should attend to our parents and look after our wives and children, but when one first creates a new rule, the state must come first and the family last, public interests first and private interests last.

Moreover, as it is advisable to avoid suspicion [of improper conduct] between the inner [female] and the outer [male] and to distinguish between male and female, so men must have male quarters and women must have female quarters; only thus can we be dignified and avoid confusion. There must be no common mixing of the male and female groups, which would cause debauchery and violation of Heaven's commandments. Although to pay respects to parents and to visit wives and children occasionally are in keeping with human nature and not prohibited, yet it is only proper to converse before the door, stand a few steps apart and speak in a loud voice; one must not enter the sisters' camp or permit the mixing of men and women. Only thus, by complying with rules and commands, can we become sons and daughters of Heaven.

1. **According to the Taiping leadership, what is the role of the state in relation to one's family?**
2. **Explain the ways in which this Taiping declaration blends ideas of Confucianism and Christianity.**

PRIMARY SOURCE 16.5

The Azamgarh Proclamation (1857), Bahadur Shah

Bahadur Shah, the last Mughal emperor, issued the Azamgarh Proclamation in August 1857 on behalf of the Indian rebels who had seized the garrison town of Azamgarh, sixty miles north of Benares. Though Shah's Mughal Empire, and thus his authority, was limited to Delhi only, he called on the rebellion's followers to restore the pre-British order—in this

case, a much larger Mughal Empire. For his involvement in this rebellion, the British tried, convicted, and exiled him from Delhi.

It is well known to all, that in this age the people of Hindoostan, both Hindoos and Mohammedans, are being ruined under the tyranny and oppression of the infidel and treacherous English. It is therefore the bounden duty of all the wealthy people of India, especially of those who have any sort of connection with any of the Mohammedan royal families, and are considered the pastors and masters of their people, to stake their lives and property for the well being of the public. . . .

Several of the Hindoo and Mussalman chiefs, who have long since quitted their homes for the preservation of their religion, and have been trying their best to root out the English in India, have presented themselves to me, and taken part in the reigning Indian crusade. . . . Parties anxious to participate in the common cause, but having no means to provide for themselves, shall receive their daily subsistence from me; and be it known to all, that the ancient works, both of the Hindoos and the Mohammedans, the writings of the miracle-workers and the calculations of the astrologers, pundits, and rammals, all agree in asserting that the English will no longer have any footing in India or elsewhere. . . .

Section I—Regarding Zemindars [large landholders, responsible for collecting land taxes for the government]. It is evident, that the British Government in making zemindary settlements have imposed exorbitant *Jumas* [taxes], and have disgraced and ruined several zemindars. . . . Such extortions will have no manner of existence in the Badshahi Government; but on the contrary, the *Jumas* will be light, the dignity and honour of the zemindars safe, and every zemindar will have absolute rule in his own zemindary. . . .

Section II—Regarding Merchants. It is plain that the infidel and treacherous British Government have monopolized the trade of all the fine and valuable merchandise, such as indigo, cloth, and other articles of shipping, leaving only the trade of trifles to the people, and even in this they are not without their share of the profits, which they secure by means of customs and stamp fees, & c. in money suits, so that the people have merely a trade in name. . . . When the Badshahi Government is established, all these aforesaid fraudulent practices shall be dispensed with, and the trade of every article, without exception, both by land and water, shall be open to the native merchants of India. . . .

Section IV—Regarding Artisans. It is evident that the Europeans, by the introduction of English articles into India, have thrown the weavers, the cotton dressers, the carpenters, the blacksmiths, and the shoemakers, &c., out of employ, and have engrossed their occupations, so that every description of native artisan has been reduced to beggary. But under the Badshahi Government the native artisan will exclusively be employed in the services of the kings, the rajahs, and the rich. . . .

Section V—Regarding Pundits, Fakirs and other learned persons. The pundits and fakirs being the guardians of the Hindoo and Mohammedan religions respectively, and the Europeans being the enemies of both the religions, and as at present a war is raging against the English on account of religion, the pundits and fakirs are bound to present themselves to me, and take their share in the holy war.

1. **Explain the ways in which Bahadur Shah used religion in his critique of British government in India.**
2. **According to Bahadur Shah, how has British rule affected local industry in India?**

Questions for Analysis

Comparison

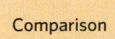

1. Compare the ways in which aspects of nineteenth-century society posed problems for many people around the world.

Contextualization

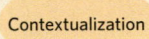

2. Explain and evaluate the connections between the governments and religious leaders described in the documents above.

Interpretation

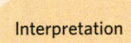

3. Do you think that religion was an effective tool against colonial rule? Why or why not?

Long Essay Question

Synthesis

Based on what you have read in the chapter and the documents above, evaluate the ways in which religion was used by those around the globe who sought changes to their societies in the nineteenth century.

Before You Read This Chapter

GLOBAL STORYLINES

- Nation-state building and imperial expansion change the map of the world.
- Industrialization, science, and technology enable states in North America and western Europe—and, to a lesser extent, Japan—to overpower other regions politically, militarily, and economically.
- European, American, and Japanese imperialists encounter significant opposition in Africa and Asia.

CORE OBJECTIVES

- **IDENTIFY** the institutions that enabled elites in western Europe, the Americas, and Japan to consolidate nation-states, and **ANALYZE** the degree to which they succeeded during this period.
- **EXPLAIN** the roles that industrialization, science, and technology played in the expansion of powerful states into the rest of the world.
- **COMPARE** the reactions to imperialism in Africa and Asia, and **EVALUATE** how effective these responses were.
- **ANALYZE** the extent to which colonies contributed to the wealth and political strength of the nation-states that controlled them.

CHAPTER

17

Nations and Empires

1850–1914

KEY TERMS

Charles Darwin p. 648
imperialism p. 638
limited-liability joint-stock company p. 641
Manifest Destiny p. 639
Meiji Restoration p. 659
natural selection p. 648
Raj p. 650
Self-Strengthening movement p. 664
steel p. 648

In 1895, the Cuban patriot José Martí launched a rebellion against the last Spanish holdings in the Americas. The anti-Spanish struggle continued until 1898, when Spain withdrew from Cuba and Puerto Rico. Martí hoped to bring freedom to a new Cuban nation and equality to all Cubans. But even as he helped secure freedom from the declining Spanish empire, he could not prevent military occupation and political domination of Cuba by the world's newest imperial power, the United States. Martí's hopes and frustrations found parallels around the world.

After 1850, the building of nation-states in Europe, the Americas, and Oceania and the expansion of their empires changed the map of the world, exhilarating some peoples and frustrating others. Those who benefited most were Europeans and peoples of European descent. During these decades the nation-states of Europe, now locked in intense political and economic rivalry, projected their power across the entire world. Much of the rivalry among European states intensified through disruptions in the European balance of power, caused by the unification of two new states (Italy and Germany). Across the Atlantic, the United States abandoned its anticolonial origins and annexed overseas possessions. Yet imperial expansion did not go unchallenged. It encountered resistance from communities being incorporated into the new empires. In Asia and Africa resisters struggled to repel their invaders, often demanding the right to govern themselves.

The second half of the nineteenth century witnessed the simultaneous—and entwined—advance of nationalism and imperialism. These decades also saw the further expansion of industrialization. Taken together, the era's political and economic developments allowed western Europe and the United States to attain primacy in world affairs. But tensions inside these states and their empires, as well as within other states, made the new world order anything but stable.

Consolidating Nations and Constructing Empires

COMPARISON

IDENTIFY the institutions that enabled elites in western Europe, the Americas, and Japan to consolidate nation-states.

During the second half of the nineteenth century, the idea of building nation-states engulfed the globe, and nationalism became closely linked to imperialism. Enlightenment thinkers had emphasized the importance of nations, defined as peoples who shared a common past, territory, culture, and traditions. To many people it seemed natural that once absolutist rulers had fallen, governments should draw their power and legitimacy from those who lived within their borders and that the body of institutions governing each territory should be uniquely concerned with promoting the welfare of that particular people. This seemed such a natural process that little thought was given to the relationship between "nation" and "state," between the people and their government; national states were simply supposed to well up from the people's longing for liberty and togetherness.

BUILDING NATIONALISM

More often than not, however, local elites created nations. They did so by compelling diverse groups of people and regions to accept a unified network of laws, a central administration, time zones, national markets, and a single regional dialect as the "national" language. To overcome strong regional identities, state administrators broadened public education in the national language and imposed universal military service to build a national army. In this way, dominant elites spread their values and institutions outward to regions throughout each nation and beyond their borders. While a handful of nation-states were already well established in the mid-nineteenth century, two of the most important—Italy and Germany—were newly created in this period, forged through strategic military contests.

EXPANDING THE EMPIRES

The processes of nation building also required the acquisition of new territories, often overseas, a development that was called **imperialism.** Rulers measured national strength not only by their people's unity but also by their economic power and the conquest of new territories. Thus, Germany, France, the United States, Russia, and Japan challenged Britain's leadership in overseas trade by developing their industries and seizing new territories.

Imperial rule facilitated a widespread movement of labor, capital, commodities, and information. As scholars studied previously unknown tribes and races, new schools taught colonized peoples the languages, religions, scientific practices, and cultural traditions of their colonizers. Publications and products from the "mother country" circulated widely among indigenous elites. Yet colonies were seen as subordinate to the mother country and were given little or no representation in home governments. In this sense, nation and empire were in tension with one another.

Expansion and Nation Building in the Americas

Once freed from European control, the elites of the Americas set about creating political communities of their own. By the 1850s they shared a desire both to create widespread loyalty to their political institutions and to expand territorial domains. This also meant finding ways to settle hinterlands that previously belonged to indigenous populations.

COMPARISON

ANALYZE the degree to which elites in the Americas succeeded in consolidating nation-states.

Although nation-states took shape throughout the world, the Americas saw the most complete assimilation of new possessions. Instead of treating outlying areas as colonial outposts, American nation-state builders turned them into new provinces. With the help of rifles, railroads, schools, and land surveys, frontiers became staging areas for the expanding populations of North and South American societies. For indigenous peoples, however, such national expansion meant the loss of traditional lands on a vast scale, and many lost lives.

THE UNITED STATES

Military might, diplomacy, and the power of numbers enabled the United States to claim territory that spanned the North American continent (see Map 17.1). At its independence, the new country established a barely united confederation of states. Native American resistance and Spanish and British rivalry hemmed in the Americans of European descent. At the same time, the disunited states threatened to break apart, as questions of states' rights and of slavery versus free labor intruded into national politics. Yet, rallying to the rhetoric of **Manifest Destiny**, which maintained that it was God's will for the United States to "overspread" North America, American whites pushed their territorial claims and boundaries westward. They acquired territories via purchase agreements and treaties with France, Spain, and Britain, and via warfare and treaties with diverse Native American nations and Mexico.

Civil War and States' Rights Westward expansion proved the undoing of the American nation. The question was whether newly acquired lands would be open to slavery or restricted to free labor. Following the 1860 election of Abraham Lincoln, who pledged to halt the expansion of slavery, the United States divided between North and South and plunged into a gruesome Civil War (1861–1865).

The bloody conflict led to the abolition of slavery, and the struggle to extend voting and citizenship rights to male freed slaves qualified the Civil War as a second American Revolution. Abraham Lincoln had promised a new model of freedom for a state reborn out of bloodshed. Its cornerstone would be the incorporation of freed slaves as citizens of the United States. Yet experiments in biracial democracy during the Reconstruction period (1867–1877) were short-lived. In the decades after the Civil War, counterrevolutionary pressure led to the denial of voting rights to African Americans and the restoration of (white, patriarchal) planter rule in the southern states. This pressure was spearheaded by the terrorism of some former Confederates who sought to reverse African Americans' legal and political gains and to restore white planters to power in the South.

MAP 17.1 | U.S. and Canadian Westward Expansion, 1803–1912

Americans and Canadians expanded westward in the second half of the nineteenth century, aided greatly by railways.

- How many railroad lines ultimately reached the western borders of Canada and the United States?
- By what years were the territorial expansions of Canada and the United States complete? How did territorial expansion strengthen Canadian and American nationalism?
- What were the major events that led to the annexation of the western half of the United States?

African American Gains and Losses In the immediate aftermath of the American Civil War, "Radical Republicans" asserted political control by passing laws and constitutional amendments ending slavery, guaranteeing equal rights, and enfranchising freed slaves, known as freedmen. One result was the election of African Americans (*above*) to the U.S. Congress. During the 1870s, however, white leaders retreated from the commitment to black rights, allowing ex-Confederates to reassert control over southern politics. (*Right*) The Ku Klux Klan terrorized African Americans in the post–Civil War South. Klan violence reversed many of the legal and political gains made by freedmen and helped restore planters to power in the South.

Nonetheless, the war brought enduring changes across the United States. The defeat of the South established the preeminence of the national government. After the Civil War, Americans learned to speak of their nation in the singular ("the United States is" in contrast to "the United States are"). With an invigorated nationalism came a stronger national government.

Economic and Industrial Development Even more dizzying were social and economic changes that followed the Civil War. Within ten years of the war's end, the industrial output of the United States had climbed by 75 percent. Americans made such impressive industrial gains that the United States soon joined Britain and Germany atop the list of economic giants.

A potent instrument of capital accumulation appeared at this time—the **limited-liability joint-stock company**. Firms such as Standard Oil and U.S. Steel attracted money from well-to-do investors via a stock market. These investors, called shareholders, in theory owned the company; nonetheless they left the running of these enterprises to paid managers. Intermediaries, like J. Pierpont Morgan, the New York financial giant who became the world's wealthiest man, loaned money and brokered big deals on the New York Stock Exchange. So great were the fortunes amassed by leading financiers and industrialists that by 1890 the richest 1 percent of Americans owned nearly 90 percent of the nation's wealth.

The expansion of railroad lines symbolized American economic and territorial growth. In 1865, the United States boasted 35,000 miles of track. By 1900, nearly 200,000 miles of track connected the Atlantic to the Pacific and crisscrossed the American territory in between. Americans continued their migrations west. Joined by throngs of immigrants from Europe, they were attracted by homestead acts promising nearly free acreage to settlers and by promoters from the railroads.

By now the United States had become a major world power. It boasted an economy that, despite troubles in the 1890s, had expanded rapidly over the last decades of the nineteenth century. It also was a more integrated nation after the Civil War, with an amended constitution that claimed to uphold the equality of all members of the American nation, even those men who were not white. But there was disagreement on what that equality should involve (for example, should it include women as voters?) or how the country would adjust to a new century in which the nation's "destiny" had already been fulfilled.

CANADA

Canadians also built a new nation, enjoyed economic success, and followed an expansionist course. Like the United States, Canada had access to a vast frontier prairie for growing agricultural exports. And as in the United States, these lands became the homes and farms of more European immigrants. However, whereas the United States had waged a war to gain independence, Canada's separation from Britain was peaceful. From the 1830s to the 1860s, Britain gradually passed authority to the colony, leaving Canadians to grapple with the task of creating a shared national community.

Building a Nation Sharp internal divisions made that task especially difficult. For one thing, there was a well-established French population. Wanting to keep their villages, their culture, their religion, and their language intact, these French Canadians did not feel integrated into the emerging Canadian national community. Nor were they eager to join the English-speaking population in settling new areas, lest such migration dilute their French-Canadian presence.

The English-speakers were equally unenthusiastic about creating an independent Canadian state. Fear of being absorbed into the American republic reinforced these Canadians' loyalty to the British crown and made them content with colonial status. Indeed, when Canada finally gained its independence in 1867, it was by an Act of Parliament in London and not by revolution.

Territorial Expansion Lacking cultural and linguistic unity, Canadians used territorial expansion to build an integrated state. In response to the U.S. purchase of Alaska from Russia in 1867 and the movement of settlers onto the American plains, Canadian leaders realized that they had to incorporate their own western territories, lest these, too, fall into American hands.

The Canadian state also faced friction with indigenous peoples. Frontier warfare threatened to drive away investors and settlers, who could always find property south of the border instead. To prevent the kind of bloodletting that characterized the United States' westward expansion, the Canadian government signed treaties with indigenous peoples to ensure strict separation between natives and newcomers.

The Canadian government acquired significant powers to intervene in, regulate, and mediate social conflict between Anglo and French residents, and among both groups and the Native American population. These powers, in fact, were fuller than those of the U.S. government. But even though the state was relatively strong, the sense of a national identity was comparatively weak. Expansionism helped Canada remain an autonomous state, but it did not solve the question of what it meant to belong to a Canadian nation.

LATIN AMERICA

Latin American elites also engaged in nation-state building and expanded their territorial borders. But unlike in the United States and Canada, expansion did not always create homesteader frontiers that could help expand democracy and forge national identities. Instead, civil conflict fractured certain countries in the region (see Chapters 15 and 16), although a few, most notably Brazil and Mexico, remained united.

Much of Latin America shared a common social history. Far more than in North America, the richest lands in Latin America went to large estate holders producing exports such as sugar, coffee, or beef. As a result, privileged elites monopolized power more than in North America's young democracies.

Amerindian and peasant uprisings were a major worry in new Latin American republics. Fearing insurrections, elites devised governing systems that protected private property while limiting the political rights of the poor. Likewise, the specter of slave revolts, driven home not just by earlier, brutal events in Haiti (see Chapter 15) but also by daily rumors of rebellions, kept elites in a state of alarm. Creating strong states, it seemed to many Latin American elites, required excluding large groups of people from power.

Brazil's "Exclusive" Nation-State Brazil illustrates the process by which Latin American rulers built nation-states that excluded much of the population from both the "nation" and the "state." Through the nineteenth century, rulers in Rio de Janeiro defused political conflict by allowing planters to retain the reins of power.

The official prohibition of the slave trade in 1830, coupled with slave resistance, began to choke the planters' system by driving up the price of slaves within the region. Thereafter, Brazilian elites retained some former slaves as gang-workers or sharecroppers (who received tools and seeds in return for a share of the crop), and they also imported new workers—especially from Italy, Spain, and Portugal—as seasonal migrant workers or indentured tenant farmers. Indeed, European and even Japanese migration to Brazil helped planters preserve their holdings in the post-slavery era. In all, 2 million Europeans and some 70,000 Japanese moved to Brazil.

The Brazilian state was deliberately exclusive. As in the United States, elites imposed severe restrictions on suffrage and set rules that reduced political competition. However, given the greater share of the black population in Brazil, restrictions there excluded a larger share of the potential electorate than in the United States.

Brazilian Expansion and Economic Development Like Canada and the United States, the Brazilian state extended its reach to distant areas and incorporated them as provinces. The largest land-grab occurred in the Amazon River basin, the world's largest drainage watershed and tropical forest. Here, the Brazilian state gave giant concessions to local capitalists to extract rubber latex. When combined with sulfur, rubber was a key raw material for tire manufacturing in European and North American bicycle and automobile industries.

For a time, Brazil became the world's exclusive exporter of rubber; as a result, its planters, merchants, and workers prospered. Rich merchants became lenders and financiers, not only to workers but also to landowners. The mercantile elite of Manaus, the capital of the Amazon region, designed and decorated their city to reflect their new fortunes. Although the streets were still paved with mud, the town's elite built a replica of the Paris Opera House, and Manaus

Opera House in Manaus The turn-of-the-century rubber boom brought immense wealth to the Amazon jungle. As in many boom-and-bust cycles in Latin America, the proceeds flowed to a small elite and diminished when the rubber supply outstripped the demand. But the wealth produced was sufficient to prompt the local elite to build temples of modernity in the midst of the jungle. Pictured here is the Opera House in the rubber capital of Manaus. Like other works built by Latin American elites of the period, this one emulated the original in Paris.

became a regular stopover for European opera singers on the circuit between Buenos Aires and New York. Rubber workers also benefited from the boom. Mostly either Amerindians or mixed-blood people, they sent their wages home to families elsewhere in the Amazon jungle or on the northeastern coast of Brazil.

One problem was the ecosystem. Such a diversified biomass could not tolerate a regimented form of production. Cultivating rubber trees at the expense of other vegetation made the forest vulnerable to nonhuman predators. Leaf blights and ferocious ants destroyed all experiments at creating more sustainable rubber plantations.

The Brazilian rubber boom, moreover, soon went bust. As competition led to increased supplies and reduced prices, Brazilian producers went bankrupt. Merchants called in their loans, landowners forfeited their titles, and rubber workers returned to their small subsistence farms. Tropical vines crept over the Manaus Opera House, and it gradually fell into disrepair.

Throughout the Americas, nineteenth-century elites, working with outdated ideas of who should wield power, nonetheless attempted to satisfy popular demands for inclusion. While the ideal was to construct nation-states that could reconcile differences among their citizens and pave the way for economic prosperity, political autonomy did not bring prosperity, or even the right to vote, to all. As each nation-state expanded its territorial boundaries, many inhabitants were left out of the political realm.

Consolidation of Nation-States in Europe

COMPARISON

COMPARE the challenges elites within Europe faced to those in the Americas in consolidating their nation-states and the degree to which they succeeded.

In Europe, no "frontier" existed into which new states could expand. Instead, nation-states took shape out of older monarchies and empires, and their borders were determined by diplomats or by battles. In the wake of the French Revolution, the idea caught on that "the people" should form the basis for the nation and that nations should share a common culture—but no one could agree on who "the people" should be. Yet, over the course of the nineteenth century, as literacy, cities, industrial production, and the number and prosperity of property owners expanded, ruling elites had no choice but to share power with a wider group of citizens. These citizens, in turn, increasingly defined themselves as, say, French or German, rather than as residents of Marseilles or subjects of the King of Bavaria.

DEFINING "THE NATION"

For a very long time, in most places, "the nation" was understood to comprise kings, clergymen, nobles—and occasionally rich merchants or lawyers—and no one else. Although some peoples, such as the English and the Spanish, were already self-conscious about their unique histories, only in the late eighteenth century were the crucial building blocks of European nationalism put in place.

Cultural changes laid the foundations of the nation. Increasingly literate urban populations met in coffee houses and other public places to discuss the issues of the day. Their collective debates—public opinion—weighed for the first time on the decisions of kings and statesmen. During the nineteenth century, a huge expansion of the periodical press made it possible for people all across Europe to read books and newspapers in their own languages. The emerging industrial economy made merchants anxious to standardize laws, taxation policies, and weights and measures. States invested huge sums in building roads and then railroads—and these linked provincial towns and bigger cities, laying the foundations for a closer political integration.

But who were the people, and what constituted a viable nation-state? For some, the nation was a collection of all those who spoke one language; for others, it was all those who

MAP 17.2 | Italian Unification and German Unification, 1815-1871

Italian unification and German unification altered the political map of Europe.

- What were the names of the two original states that grew to become Italy and Germany?
- Who were the big losers in these territorial transfers?
- According to your reading, what problems did the new Italian and German states face in creating strong national communities?

lived in a certain territory and who shared a common religious heritage. This was a particularly acute problem in multiethnic central and southeastern Europe, where many people were multilingual, rich and poor alike. But some who shared the same language objected to being lumped into one nation-state. The Irish, for example, spoke English but were predominately Catholics and wanted to be free from Anglican rule.

UNIFICATION IN GERMANY AND ITALY

Two of Europe's fledgling nation-states came into being when the dynastic states of Prussia and Piedmont-Sardinia incorporated their smaller, linguistically related neighbors, creating the German and Italian nation-states (see Map 17.2). In both regions, conservative prime ministers—Count Otto von Bismarck of Prussia and Count Camillo di Cavour of Piedmont—exploited liberal, nationalist sentiment to rearrange the map of Europe.

Building Unified States The unification of Germany and Italy posed all the familiar problems of who should be included in the new nation-states. To begin with, German-speakers were spread all across central and eastern Europe; for centuries they had lived in many different states. Similarly, Italians had lived separately in city-states and small kingdoms on the Italian peninsula and spoke a range of dialects. The historical experiences and economic developments had made Bavarian Germans (Catholic) quite different from Prussian Germans (Protestant); likewise, the Milanese (who lived in a wealthy urban industrial center) shared little, language included, with the typical Sardinian peasant. But liberal nationalists had made the case that their high culture—especially their literary, musical, and theatrical traditions—overrode these differences, and emotional appeals by poets, composers, and orators convinced many people that this was indeed the case. Bismarck and Cavour merged this nationalist rhetoric with clever diplomacy—and the use of military force in a series of small conflicts—to forge united German and Italian nation-states.

These "unified" states rejected democracy. In the new Italy, which was a constitutional monarchy, less than 5 percent of the 25 million people could vote. The new German empire (the Second Reich) had an assembly elected by all adult males (the Reichstag), but it had little power. The country was ruled by a combination of aristocrats and bureaucrats under a monarch. Liberals dominated in many localities, but only the emperor (the Kaiser) could depose the prime minister. In fact, Bismarck continued to dominate Prussian politics for twenty-eight years, until fired in 1890 by Kaiser Wilhelm II. By that time, unification had yielded brisk economic growth both in Italy and especially Germany, but conflict between regions and political groups continued.

NATION BUILDING AND ETHNIC CONFLICT IN THE AUSTRO-HUNGARIAN EMPIRE

Bismarck's unification of Germany came at the expense of Habsburg supremacy in central Europe and (as we will see in the next section) of French territory and influence in the west. After Germany won a victory over the Austrian army in 1866, the Hungarian nobles who controlled the eastern Habsburg Empire forced the weakened dynasts to grant them home rule. In the Compromise of 1867, the Habsburgs agreed that their state would officially be known as the Austro-Hungarian Empire. But this move did not solve Austria-Hungary's nationality problems. In both the Hungarian and the Austrian halves of the dual state, Czechs, Poles, and other Slavs now began to clamor for their own power-sharing "compromise" or autonomous national homelands. They would, however, have to wait until the end of World War I.

DOMESTIC DISCONTENTS IN FRANCE AND BRITAIN

Although already unified as nation-states, Britain and France faced major difficulties. For the French, dealing with defeat at the hands of the Germans was the primary national concern in the decades leading up to World War I. For the British, issues of Irish separatism, the rise of the working class, and feminists' demands troubled the political arena.

Destabilization in France The Franco-Prussian War of 1870–1871 completed the unification of Germany. Germany took the French provinces of Alsace and Lorraine, and its victory destabilized France. The German siege of Paris, which lasted for more than three months, devastated the capital. Unprepared, Parisians had no food stocks and were compelled to eat all sorts of things, including two zoo elephants. Under terrible conditions and without effective leadership, the French capital resisted until January 1871, when the government signed a humiliating peace treaty. The Germans left in place a weak provisional French government. Refusing the negotiated peace, furious Parisians vented their rage and established their own government, proclaiming the city a utopia for workers. The leftist commune they established lasted until the provisional national government's army stormed Paris a few months later. At least 25,000 Parisians died in the bloody mop-up that followed. A "Third Republic" took the place of Napoleon III's empire, but it struggled to achieve stability. In the years following the Franco-Prussian war, France saw increasing conflict between classes and the rise of anti-German nationalism.

Irish Nationalism in Great Britain Although the English had long thought of themselves as a nation, the idea that all British people belonged in the same state was much more problematic. The kingdom of England—which was originally composed of England, clearly the dominant state, and Wales—became the kingdom of Great Britain when it united with Scotland in 1707 and Ireland in 1801. It was home to peoples whose historical experiences, religious backgrounds, and economic opportunities were very different. In the nineteenth century, British leaders wrestled in particular with demands for independence from Irish nationalists and lower-class agitation, especially in England. Beginning in 1832, England responded to class conflict at home by extending political rights to most men but not women. England finally established universal suffrage for all adult males after World War I, in 1918; roughly one quarter of British women gained the right to vote at that time and the rest a decade later.

Yet Ireland remained Britain's Achilles' heel. The British government was widely condemned for its failure to relieve Irish suffering during the potato famine of 1845–1849 (see Chapter 15); even though millions of poor Irish and Scottish workers made their way to England, seeking either passage to North America or work in the English mill towns, they did not assimilate easily and often got the lowliest jobs. All of this, on top of 300 years of repressive English domination, fueled a mass movement for Irish home rule that continued into the twentieth century.

Born in opposition to the old monarchical regimes, European nationalism by the end of the nineteenth century had become a means used by liberal and conservative leaders alike to unite the people behind them. But just what they meant by "the people" remained bitterly contested. Continental powers increasingly resorted to an aggressive foreign policy and imperial expansion to maintain popular support without granting political power to ordinary people. France alone, of the European great powers, had a parliamentary democracy elected by universal manhood suffrage.

Industry, Science, and Technology

A powerful combination of industry, science, and technology shaped the emerging nation-states in North America and western Europe. It also reordered the relationships among different parts of the world. One critical factor was that after 1850 western Europe and North America experienced a new phase of industrial development—essentially a second industrial revolution. Japan, too, joined the ranks of industrializing nations as its state-led program of industrial development started to pay dividends. These changes transformed the global economy and intensified rivalries among industrial societies.

COMPARISON

EXPLAIN the roles that industrialization, science, and technology played in expansion of powerful states into the rest of the world.

NEW TECHNOLOGIES, MATERIALS, AND BUSINESS PRACTICES

New technologies and materials drove economic development in the late nineteenth century and led to new business practices. This period witnessed major technological changes with the arrival of new organic sources of power (like oil) and new ways to get old organic sources (like coal) to processing plants. These changes freed manufacturers from having to locate their plants close to their fuel sources. Not only did the most important new source of energy—electricity—permit factories to arise in areas with plenty of skilled workers, but it also slashed production costs. **Steel**, now cheaply produced because of technical innovations, became essential for shipbuilding and railways. They were part of a bundle of innovations that included chemicals and pharmaceuticals, which together transformed northwestern Europe, the United States, and Japan.

The breakthroughs of the second industrial revolution ushered in new business practices, especially mass production and the giant integrated firm. No longer would modest investments suffice, as they had in Britain a century earlier. Now large banks were the major providers of funds. In Europe, limited-liability joint-stock companies were as wildly successful in raising capital on stock markets as they were in the United States. Companies like Standard Oil, U.S. Steel, and Siemens mobilized investments from large numbers of shareholders. The scale of these firms was awesome. U.S. Steel alone produced over half of the world's steel ingots, castings, rails, and heavy structural shapes—and nearly half of all its steel plates and sheets, which were vital in the construction of buildings, railroads, ships, and the like.

INTEGRATION OF THE WORLD ECONOMY

Not only did industrial change concentrate power in North Atlantic societies, but it also reinforced their power on the world economic stage and created a more integrated global economy. Europe and the United States increased their exports in new products; they also grew eager to control the importation of tropical commodities such as cocoa and coffee. While the North Atlantic societies were still largely self-sufficient in coal, iron, cotton, wool, and wheat (the major commodities of the first industrial revolution), the second industrial revolution bred a need for rubber, copper, oil, and bauxite (an ore used to make aluminum), which were not available domestically. Equally important, large pools of money became available for investing overseas.

Movements of Labor and Technology Vast movements of workers took place to satisfy the labor demands of an increasingly integrated world economy. Indians moved thousands of miles from Asia to work on sugar plantations in the Caribbean, Mauritius, and Fiji, to labor in South African mines, and to build railroads in East Africa. Chinese workers constructed railroads in the western United States and toiled on sugar plantations in Cuba. The Irish, Poles, Jews, Italians, and Greeks flocked to North America to fill its burgeoning factories. Italians also moved to Argentina to harvest wheat and corn.

With steam-powered gunboats and breech-loading rifles, Europeans opened new territories for trade and conquest. At home and in their colonial possessions, imperial powers constructed networks of railroads that carried people and goods from hinterlands to the coasts. From there, steamships bore them across the seas. Completion of the Suez Canal in 1869 shortened ship voyages between Europe and Asia and lowered the costs of interregional trade. Information moved even faster than cargoes, thanks to the laying of telegraph cables under the oceans, supplemented by overland telegraph lines.

Charles Darwin and Natural Selection Although machines were the most visible evidence that humans could master the universe, perhaps the most momentous shift in the conception of nature derived from the travels of one British scientist: **Charles Darwin** (1809–1882).

Darwin's theory, articulated in his *Origin of Species* (1859), laid out the principles of **natural selection**. Inevitably, he claimed, populations grew faster than the food supply; this condition

Charles Darwin This image depicts Darwin testing the speed of a tortoise in the Galapagos Islands. It was during his visit to these islands that Darwin developed many of the ideas that he would put forth in his 1859 *Origin of Species*.

created a "struggle for existence" among species. In later work he showed how the passing on of individual traits was also determined by what he called sexual selection—according to which the "best" mates are chosen for their strength, beauty, or talents and the less fit fail to reproduce at comparable rates. Although Darwin's book dealt exclusively with animals (and mostly with birds), his readers immediately wondered what his theory implied for humans.

A passionate debate began among scientists and laymen, clerics and anthropologists. Some read Darwin's doctrine of natural selection to mean that it was natural for the strong nations to dominate the weak, or justifiable to allow disabled persons to die—something Darwin explicitly rejected. As more groups (mis)interpreted Darwin's theory to suit their own objectives, a set of beliefs known as social Darwinism legitimated the suffering of the underclasses in industrial society. In subsequent years Europeans would repeatedly suggest that they had evolved more than Africans and Asians. Extending Darwinian ideas far beyond the scientist's intent, some Europeans came to believe that therefore nature itself gave them the right to rule others.

Global Expansionism and an Age of Imperialism

Increasing rivalries among nations and social tensions within them produced an expansionist wave late in the nineteenth century. Although Africa became the primary focus of interest, a frenzy of territorial conquest overtook Asia as well. In China's territories, competition by foreign powers to establish spheres of influence heated up in the 1890s. And in India, imperial ambitions provoked the British to conquer Burma (present-day Myanmar). Moreover, Britain and Russia competed for preeminence from their respective outposts in Afghanistan and central Asia. In the Americas, new territories were usually incorporated as provinces of the expansionist state, making them integral parts of the nation. In Asia and Africa, however, European and American imperialism turned far-flung territories into colonial possessions.

COMPARISON

COMPARE the different western colonial models used in various regions of the world and the responses of those regions.

The Raj Strengthens Control (*Top*) In the aftermath of the Indian Rebellion of 1857, the British government, called the Raj (meaning "rule" in Hindi), intervened much more actively in India. It built an extensive system of railroads to develop India as a profitable colony and to maintain military security. This engraving shows the East India Railway around 1863. (*Bottom*) The British allowed several native princes to remain as long as they accepted imperial hegemony. This photograph shows a road-building project in one such princely state. Officials of the Muslim princely ruler and British advisers supervise the workers.

The inhabitants of these colonial possessions were generally designated as subjects of the empire without the rights and privileges of citizens.

INDIA AND THE IMPERIAL MODEL

Britain's rule in India provided a model for other imperialist governments by developing the colony's infrastructure in order to maximize British profits from trade. Having suppressed the Indian Rebellion of 1857 (see Chapter 16), authorities revamped the colonial administration. From the British point of view, Indians were not to be appeased—and certainly not brought into British public life. But they did have to be governed, and the economy had to be revived. So, after replacing the East India Company's rule by crown government in 1858, the British set out to make India into a more secure and productive colony. This period of British sovereignty was known as the **Raj** ("rule").

The most urgent tasks facing the British in India were those of modernizing its transportation and communication systems and transforming the country into an integrated colonial state. These changes had begun under the governor-general of the East India Company, Lord Dalhousie, who oversaw the development of India's modern infrastructure. After the British suppressed the revolt, they took up the construction of public works with renewed vigor.

Railways were a key element both in the pacification, shuttling troops to danger zones, and in the later reform project. The first railway line opened in 1853, and by 1910 India had 30,627 miles of track in operation—the fourth largest railway system in the world.

Construction of other public works followed. Engineers built dams across rivers to tame their force and to irrigate lands; workers installed a grid of telegraph lines that opened communication between distant parts of the region. These public works served imperial and economic purposes: India was to become a consumer of British manufactures and a supplier of primary staples such as cotton, tea, and wheat. On the hillsides of the island of Ceylon and the northeastern plains of India, the British established vast plantations to grow tea—which was then marketed in England as a healthier alternative to Chinese green tea. India also became an important consumer of British manufactures, especially textiles, in an ironic turnaround to its centuries-old tradition of exporting its own cotton and silk textiles.

The reform efforts of the Raj made India into a unified territory and enabled its inhabitants to begin to regard themselves as "Indians." These were the first steps to becoming a "nation" like Italy and the United States, but there were profound differences. Above all, as colonial subjects Indians did not enjoy basic civic and human rights, and even elites lacked the vote. Other European powers followed the British example in trying to modernize and integrate their colonies economically without welcoming colonial peoples into the life of the nation.

COLONIZING AFRICA

No region felt the impact of European colonialism more powerfully than Africa. In 1880, the only two large European colonial possessions there were French Algeria and two British-ruled South African states, the Cape Colony and Natal. But within a mere thirty years, seven European states had carved almost all of Africa into colonial possessions.

Partitioning the African Landmass In the context of heightened international rivalries, Portugal called for an international conference to discuss claims to Africa. Meeting in Berlin between 1884 and 1885, delegates from Europe, the United States, and the Ottoman Empire agreed to carve up Africa and to recognize the claims of the first European power that claimed control of a given territory. Colonizers rushed to plant their flags as widely as possible, lest they be outmaneuvered by their rivals (see Maps 17.3a and 17.3b).

The consequences for Africa were devastating. Nearly 70 percent of the newly drawn borders failed to correspond to older demarcations of ethnicity, language, culture, and commerce—for Europeans knew little of the landmass beyond its coast and rivers. They based their new colonial boundaries on European trading centers rather than on the location of African population groups (see Map 17.4).

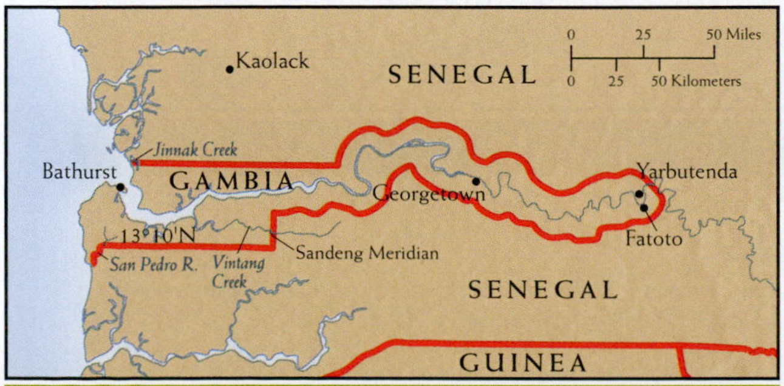

MAP 17.3A | Senegal and Gambia

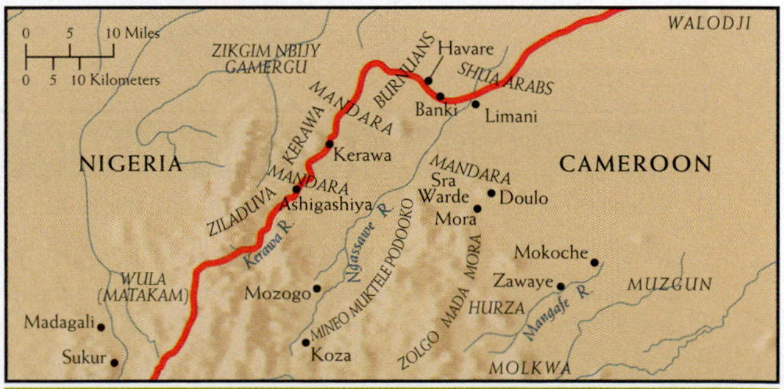

MAP 17.3B | Mandara Peoples

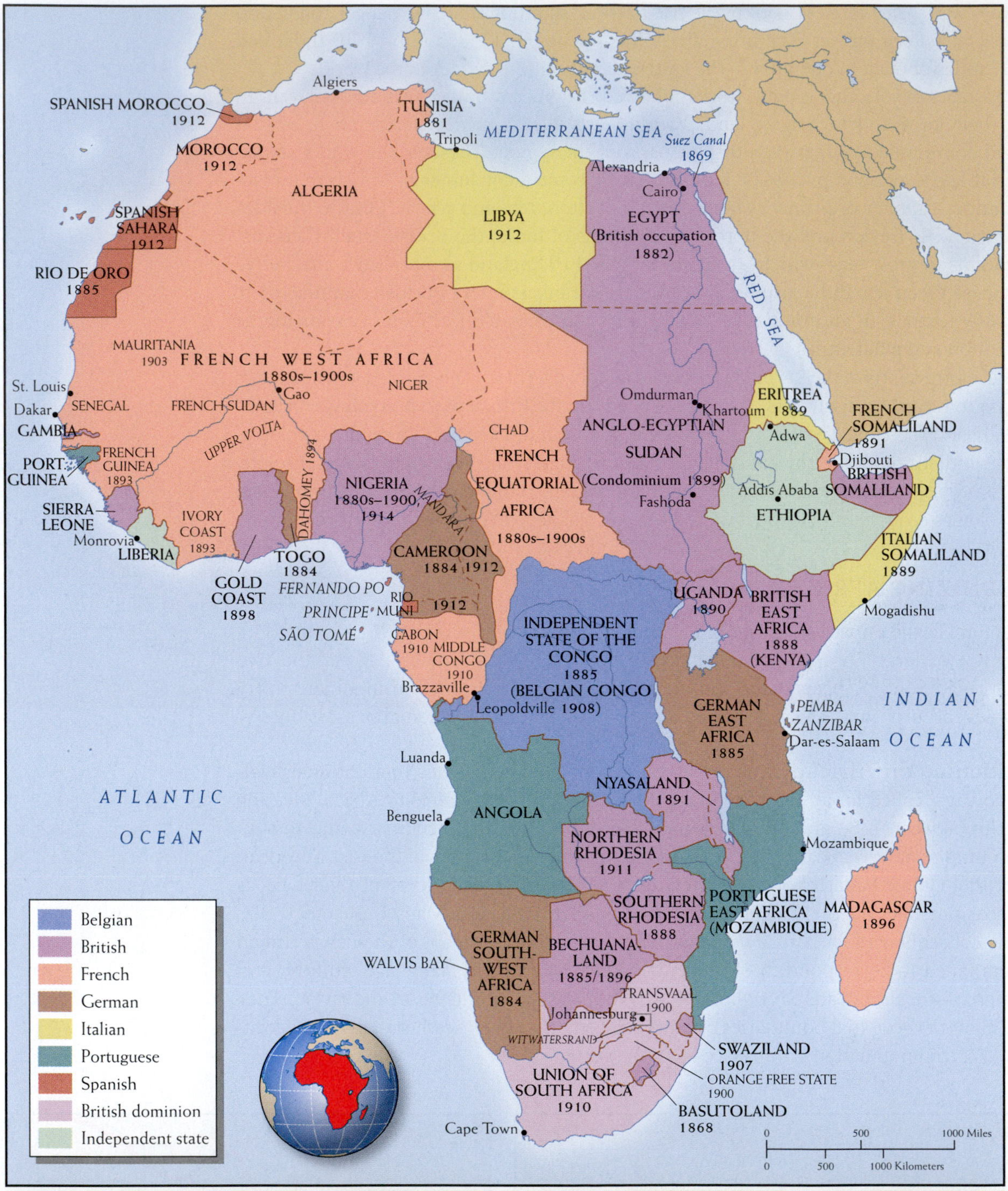

MAP 17.4 | Partition of Africa, 1880–1914

The partition of Africa took place between the early 1880s and the outbreak of World War I.

- Which two European powers gained the most territory in Africa?
- Which two African states managed to remain independent? What kind of economic and political gain did European powers realize through the colonization of Africa? Did any of the European states realize their ambitions in Africa?

Europeans in Africa (*Left*) Henry Morton Stanley was one of the most famous of the nineteenth-century explorers in Africa. He first made his reputation when he located the British missionary-explorer David Livingstone, feared dead, in the interior of Africa, uttering the famous words, "Dr. Livingstone, I presume." Stanley worked on behalf of King Leopold, establishing the Belgian king's claims to territories in the Congo and often using superior weaponry to cow African opponents. (*Right*) The ardent British imperialist Cecil Rhodes endeavored to bring as much of Africa as he could under British colonial rule. He had an ambition to create a swath of British-controlled territory that would stretch from the Cape in South Africa to Cairo in Egypt, as this cartoon shows.

Several motives led the European powers into their frenzied partition of Africa. Although European businesses were primarily interested in Egypt and South Africa, where their investments were lucrative, small-scale traders and investors harbored fantasies of great treasures locked in the vast uncharted interior. Politicians, publicists, and the reading public also took an interest. The writings of explorers like David Livingstone (1813–1873), a Scottish doctor and missionary, and Henry Morton Stanley (1841–1904), an adventurer in the pay of the *New York Herald*, excited readers with accounts of Africa as a continent of unlimited economic potential.

The most determined of the African empire builders was Leopold II (r. 1865–1909), king of the Belgians. (See **Current Trends in World History: Africa's Newest Hunters and Gatherers** for Leopold's activities in central Africa and their effects on Africans and the environment.) In southern Africa, the British champion of imperialism Cecil Rhodes (1853–1902) brought the Rhodesias, Nyasaland, Bechuanaland, the Transvaal, and the Orange Free State into the British Empire as part of a design to have British territories stretching all the way from the Cape of Good Hope in South Africa to Cairo in Egypt.

Other Europeans saw Africa as a grand opportunity for converting souls to Christianity. In fact, Europe's civilizing mission was an important motive in the scramble for African

Current Trends in World History

Africa's Newest Hunters and Gatherers: Greed, Environmental Degradation, and Resistance

Africa was the birthplace of hunting and gathering (see Chapter 1). Ironically, although the European colonizers justified their partition of Africa on the grounds of bringing civilization to a benighted people, in fact, in their quest to enrich themselves, the first generation of colonizers exploited the most available resources of the continent, enslaved and killed huge numbers of people, and returned parts of the continent to a hunting-and-gathering mode of production. The most driven and greediest of these figures was Leopold II, king of the Belgians, who was determined, in spite of sweet-sounding rhetoric, to do whatever it took to line his pockets and make himself a formidable figure in European politics. King Leopold's story and others like it fascinate world historians because it conveys in the starkest detail the nature of the relationship between the rulers and the Africans that they ruled. It also provides a strong point of comparison for the different models of ruling that each European power instituted in their colonies.

Even before ascending the throne in 1865, Leopold cast about for ways to become more than the constitutional monarch of a small, recently established, and neutral state. A voracious reader on colonialism, he was struck forcefully by one book: *How the Dutch Ruled Java*, published in 1861. By demonstrating how the Dutch colonial state had expropriated money from the East Indies (today called Indonesia) to spend on projects at home, the book fired his imagination. Could he not do the same? Could he not stake out a colony, take money from it to swell his own exchequer, and use some of it on public works at home—to beautify the cities of Belgium the way Paris had been beautified in the 1850s and 1860s?

Fixing his gaze on central Africa, in the 1880s Leopold manipulated the other European states into recognizing him as the sovereign head of a "Congo Free State," in which he lead a European effort to "civilize" (and especially to exploit) the Congo River basin. Leopold hired the world-famous explorer, Henry Stanley, to "pacify" the country and ready it for economic development.

But how to make these lands pay off? They were almost entirely unexplored and unsurveyed, and though in time they would yield some of the richest mineral deposits in the world, these prospects were unknown to Leopold and his administrators at first. What the rain forests of Africa had was wild products, especially rubber and ivory. But how to get Africans, who at that point hardly participated in world trade, to tap wild rubber vines and hunt elephants? The solution here and elsewhere in similar African environments was to create large armies (known in Leopold's state as the *Force Publique*), fix quotas for districts to procure, and compel villagers to bring in baskets of rubber and elephant tusks.

For Leopold the results were little short of astonishing. He extracted vast sums from the Congo, spending lavishly on himself and on Belgium. He sank millions

territory. In Uganda, northern Nigeria, and central and western Africa, missionaries went ahead of European armies, begging the European statesmen to follow their lead.

African Resistance Africans faced two unappealing options: they could capitulate to the Europeans and negotiate to limit the loss of their autonomy, or they could fight to preserve their sovereignty. Only a few chose to negotiate. Lat Dior, a Muslim warlord in Senegal, refused to let the French build a railway through his kingdom. "As long as I live, be well assured," he wrote the French commandant, "I shall oppose with all my might the construction of this railway. I will always answer no, no, and I will never make you any other reply. Even were I to go to rest, my horse, *Malay*, would give you the same answer." Conflict was inevitable, and Lat Dior lost his life in a battle with the French in 1886. Most Africans who resisted were unaware of the Europeans' superior military technology, and even those who adapted their tactics to meet the challenge were unable to keep the Europeans out indefinitely.

Only Menelik II of Ethiopia successfully repulsed the Europeans, for he knew how to play rivals off one another. By doing so, he procured weapons from the French, British, Russians, and Italians. He also had a united, loyal, and well-equipped army. In 1896, his of francs into making the seaside city of Ostend one of the finest resorts in the world. At Tervuren, while a choir sang the new Congo anthem, Leopold laid the foundation stone of a world college for overseas colonial administration. In Brussels he spent over $5 million renovating royal palaces and constructing parks, avenues, casinos, and racecourses.

For the Congolese, Leopold's state was nothing more than a reign of terror. Forced to roam farther and farther from their home villages in search of rubber and elephants to keep pace with ever-escalating quotas, villagers suffered an immense loss of life through famine and conflicts with the *Force Publique*. Perhaps as many as 10 million Africans perished in a population that had been roughly 20 million before Leopold's agents arrived.

Leopold's brutality did not go unobserved, however. Already in 1899, the writer Joseph Conrad took the Congo as his model of rapacious European imperialism in his novella, *Heart of Darkness*. African villagers rebelled, though unsuccessfully, and, by the first decade of the twentieth century, rumors and then detailed reports painted a stark picture of terror and environmental degradation as the villagers rooted out almost all of the wild rubber and began the hunt for elephants that would ultimately render them an endangered species. In 1908, just a year before his death, Leopold was compelled, against his wishes, to turn the administration of the Congo over to the Belgian parliament.

King Leopold Despite the inhumane way in which he funded his vast array of public buildings, Leopold is sometimes called, not unaffectionately, the "Builder King" by Belgians today.

QUESTIONS FOR ANALYSIS

- Why was King Leopold such an important figure in the European partition of Africa?
- While the Congo story is arguably one of the most brutal of all stories of colonial exploitation and environmental degradation, which other episodes in world history does it remind you of and why?

Explore Further

Herbst, Jeffrey, *States and Power in Africa: Comparative Lessons in Authority and Control* (2000).

Hochschild, Adam, *King Leopold's Ghost* (New York, 1998).

troops routed Italian forces at the Battle of Adwa, after which Adwa became a celebrated moment in African history. Its memory inspired many of Africa's later nationalist leaders.

Colonial Administrations in Africa Once the Europeans' euphoria over the gains of the partition and conquest had worn off, the power to rule the colonies fell to "men on the spot"—military adventurers, settlers, and entrepreneurs whose main goal was to get rich quick. As these individuals established little kingdoms in some areas, Africans (like Amerindians on the other side of the Atlantic) found themselves confined to territories where they could barely provide for themselves.

Eventually, these rough-and-ready systems led to violent revolts from aggrieved Africans, and in their aftermath the colonial rulers had to create more efficient administrations, dedicated to providing health care and education for the colonized. As in India, colonial powers in Africa laid the foundations for future nation-state organizations. Once information trickling out of Africa revealed that the imperial governments were not realizing their goal of bringing "civilization" to the "uncivilized" and creating easy profits, each European power implemented a new form of colonial rule, stripping the strongman conquerors of their absolute powers,

COMPARISON

ANALYZE the extent to which colonies contributed to the wealth and political strength of the nation-states that controlled them.

Battle of Adwa Portrait of King Menelik, who defeated the Italian forces at the battle of Adwa in 1896, thus saving his country from European colonization.

monitoring them more closely and assuming greater responsibility for the colonized peoples.

Eventually, stabilized colonies began to deliver on their economic promise. Whereas early imperialism in Africa had relied on the export of ivory and wild rubber, after these resources became depleted the colonies pursued other exports. From the rain forests came cocoa, coffee, palm oil, and palm kernels. From the highlands of East Africa came tea, coffee, sisal (used in cord and twine), and pyrethrum (a flower used to make insecticide). Another important commodity was long-staple, high-quality cotton, grown in Egypt and the Anglo-Egyptian Sudan. Indeed, tropical commodities from all across Africa (as from India and Latin America) flowed to industrializing societies. (See **Analyzing Global Developments: Imperialism and the African Trade Revolution**.)

Thus, European colonial administrators saw Africa as fitting into the world economy in the same way that British administrators viewed India—as an exporter of raw materials and an importer of manufactures. They expected Africa to profit from this role. But, in truth, African workers gained little from participating in colonial commerce, while the price they paid in disruption to traditional social and economic patterns was substantial.

To observers, the European empires in Africa seemed solid and durable, but in fact European colonial rule there was fragile. For all of British Africa, the only all-British force was 5,000 men garrisoned in Egypt. Elsewhere, European officers depended on African military and police forces. And prior to 1914, the number of British administrative officers available for the whole of northern Nigeria was less than 500. These were hardly strong foundations for colonial rule. It would not take much to destabilize the European order in Africa.

THE AMERICAN EMPIRE

The United States, like Europe, was drawn into the mania of overseas expansion and empire building. Echoing the earlier rhetoric of Manifest Destiny, the expansionists of the 1890s claimed that Americans still had a divine mission to spread their superior civilization and their Christian faith around the globe. However, America's new imperialists followed the European model of colonialism from Asia and Africa: colonies were to provide harbors for American vessels, supply raw materials to American industries, and purchase the surplus production of American farms and factories. These new territorial acquisitions were not intended for American settlement or statehood. Nor were their inhabitants to become American citizens, for nonwhite foreigners were considered unfit for incorporation into the American nation.

The pressure to expand came to a head in the late 1890s, when the United States declared war on Spain and invaded the Philippines, Puerto Rico, and Cuba. The United States annexed Puerto Rico after minimal protest, but Cubans and Filipinos resisted becoming colonial subjects. Bitterness ran particularly high among Filipinos, to whom American leaders had promised independence if they joined in the war against Spain. Betrayed, Filipino rebels launched a war for independence in the name of a Filipino nation. In two years of fighting, over 5,000 Americans and perhaps 200,000 Filipinos perished. The outcome: the Philippines became a colony of the United States.

Analyzing Global Developments

Imperialism and the African Trade Revolution

The colonial period initiated a trade revolution in Africa, which, as we have seen, had been a supplier of human labor to the Americas from the fifteenth century until the middle of the nineteenth century (see Chapter 13). Even as the Europeans endeavored to eradicate the African institution of slavery and slave trading within the continent, they also promoted the reintegration of African economies into the world economy. African exports included new cash crops like cocoa from West Africa and significant minerals like gold and diamonds from South Africa, while imports were mainly European manufactures. To promote trade, the colonial powers financed railways and deepened harbors. Already by the outbreak of World War I, West Africa had become the world's leading exporter of cocoa, South Africa the leading exporter of diamonds and gold, and Egypt, along with the United States, the leading exporter of high-quality cotton.

QUESTIONS FOR ANALYSIS

- Is there a correlation between the increase in the length of railway lines built and the quantity of natural resources taken out of Africa? If so, how can you tell?
- During what period were the largest increases in the construction of the railroads and the exportation of cocoa and gold, and why was this so?
- What, then, can we assume about the economic impact of colonial rule in this period, and who were the beneficiaries of the increased trade between Africa and the rest of the world?

LENGTH OF RAILWAY LINE OPENED (IN KILOMETERS)

Year	Africa
1880	4,579
1885	6,813
1890	9,202
1895	11,962
1900	16,319
1905	25,574
1910	37,768
1915	47,624

COCOA EXPORTS FROM THE GOLD COAST AND NIGERIA (IN TONS)

Year	Gold Coast	Nigeria
1900	536	202
1905	5,090	470
1910	22,600	2,932
1915	77,300	9,105
1920	125,000	17,155

UNION OF SOUTH AFRICA GOLD MINES (IN OUNCES)

Year	Total Output	Estimated % of World Output
1897	2,744	24%
1907	6,451	32.4%
1913	8,799	39.3%
1916	9,297	42.3%
1921	8,129	50.9%

Sources: B. R. Mitchell, *International Historical Statistics: Africa, Asia, and Oceania, 1750–2005* (2007), pp. 713–18; Polly Hill, *The Gold Coast Cocoa Farmer: A Preliminary Survey* (1965), p. 132; Sara Berry, *Cocoa, Custom and Socio-Economic Change in Western Nigeria*, Oxford Studies in African Affairs (1975), p. 221; S. Herbert Frankel, *Capital Investment in Africa: Its Course and Effects* (1938), pp. 83–84.

Colonies in the Philippines and Puerto Rico laid the foundations for a revised model of U.S. expansionism. The earlier pattern had been to turn Native American lands into privately owned farmsteads and to extend the Atlantic market across the continent. But now, in this new era, the nation's largest corporations (with government support) aggressively intervened in the affairs of neighbors near and far. Following the Spanish-American

War, the United States repeatedly sent troops to many Caribbean and Central American countries. The Americans preferred to turn these regimes into dependent states, rather than making them part of the United States itself (as with Alaska and Hawaii) or converting them into formal colonies (as the Europeans had done in Africa and Asia).

IMPERIALISM AND CULTURE

Europeans and Americans set out to bring "civilization" to the peoples of their colonies. At least since the Crusades, Europeans had regularly written and thought about others. These images and ideas had grown more numerous and varied as commerce and colonialism in Asia and the Atlantic world increased; they served various purposes, including those of informing, entertaining, flattering, and criticizing European culture. As Europeans and Americans grew more and more confident in their achievements, they became convinced that their arts and sciences were superior—and curiosity often turned to disdain. In time Europeans presumed that the only true modern civilization was their own; other peoples might have reigned over great empires in antiquity, but had since fallen into decadence and decline. Artists and writers portrayed nonwestern peoples as exotic, sensuous, and economically backward in a genre scholars have come to call "orientalism."

If Darwin remained ambivalent about the nature of race, his followers embraced the idea of stable racial differences that evolved only on the longest of time horizons, at a glacial pace, over thousands of years rather than decades or centuries. They ratified a view of "lower" and "higher" races, the former stuck in the past and the latter anointed by God (or in the case of social Darwinists, by nature itself) to define and dictate civilization's future. Europeans' relationship to others might now be one of condescending sympathy or of ruthless exploitation, but

The Women of Algiers in Their Apartment An oil painting by Eugène Delacroix (1798–1863) of Algerian women being attended by a black servant. European painters in the nineteenth century often used images of women to portray Arab Muslim society.

the result was that it was up to white Europeans and Americans to create modern culture. The darker people, social Darwinists argued, were not nearly as fully "evolved" as the Europeans, and could not hope to catch up. At best they could be taught European languages, sciences, and religions, and perhaps be made to evolve more quickly. It is telling that French colonial subjects who did well at French schools were known as *evolués*, "the evolved ones."

Celebrating Imperialism Especially in middle- and upper-class circles, Europeans celebrated their imperial triumphs. After the invention of photographic film and the Eastman Kodak camera in 1888, imperial images surfaced in popular forms such as postcards and advertisements. Imperial themes also decorated packaging materials; tins of coffee, tea, tobacco, and chocolates featured pictures highlighting the commodities' colonial origins. Cigarettes often had names like "Admiral," "Royal Navy," "Fighter," and "Grand Fleet." Some of this served as propaganda, produced by investors in imperial commodities or by colonial pressure groups.

Propaganda promoted imperialism abroad but also inspired changes at home. For example, champions of empire argued that if the British population did not grow fast enough to fill the world's sparsely settled regions, then the population of other nations would. Population was power, and the number of healthy children provided an accurate measure of global influence. "Empire cannot be built on rickety and flat-chested citizens," warned a British member of Parliament in 1905. Empire and imperialism carried European, American, and, to a lesser extent, Japanese power and culture throughout the world. In terms of the size of the populations they ruled, this era was the high point of European and Euro-American predominance.

Pressures of Expansion in Japan, Russia, and China

The challenge of integrating political communities and extending territorial borders was a problem not just for western Europe and the United States. Other societies also aimed to overcome domestic dissent and establish larger domains. Japan, Russia, and China provide three contrasting models; their differing forms of expansion eventually led them to fight over possessions in East Asia.

COMPARISON

COMPARE the challenges elites faced in Japan, China, and Russia in consolidating nation-states to those faced by western elites.

JAPAN'S TRANSFORMATION AND EXPANSION

Starting in the 1860s, Japanese rulers tried to recast their country less as an old dynasty and more like a modern nation-state. Since the early seventeenth century, the Tokugawa Shogunate had kept outsiders within strict limits and thwarted internal unrest. But after an American naval officer, Commodore Matthew Perry, entered Edo Bay in 1853 with a fleet of steam-powered ships, other Americans, Russians, Dutch, and British followed in his wake. These outsiders forced the Tokugawa rulers to sign humiliating treaties that opened Japanese ports, slapped limits on Japanese tariffs, and exempted foreigners from Japanese laws. Younger Japanese, especially among the military (samurai) elites, felt that Japan should respond by adopting, not rejecting, Western practices.

In 1868, a group of reformers toppled the Tokugawa Shogunate and promised to return Japan to its mythic greatness. Then Emperor Mutsuhito—the Meiji ("Enlightened Rule") Emperor—became the symbol of a new Japan. His reign (1868–1912) was called the **Meiji Restoration**. By founding schools, initiating a propaganda campaign, and revamping the army to create a single "national" fighting force, the Meiji government promoted a political

Perry arrives in Japan A Japanese wood-block print portraying the uninvited arrival into Edo (Tokyo) Bay on August 7, 1853, of a tall American ship, which was commanded by Matthew Perry. This arrival marked the end of Japan's ability to fully control the terms of its interactions with foreigners.

community that stressed linguistic and ethnic homogeneity, as well as superiority compared to others. In this way the Meiji leaders overcame age-old regional divisions, subdued local political authorities, and mobilized the country to face the threat from powerful Europeans.

Economic Development One of the Meiji period's remarkable achievements was the nation's economic transformation. After 1871, when the government banned the feudal system and allowed peasants to become small landowners, farmers improved their agrarian techniques and saw their standard of living rise. The energetic new government unified the currency around the yen, created a postal system, introduced tax reforms, and established an advanced civil service system. In 1889, the Meiji government introduced a constitution (based largely on the German model). The following year, 450,000 people—about 1 percent of the population—elected Japan's first parliament, the Imperial Diet.

As the government sold valuable enterprises to the people who had provided strong support, it created private economic dynasties. The new large companies (such as Sumitomo, Yasuda, Mitsubishi, and Mitsui) were trusted family organizations. Fathers, sons, cousins, and uncles ran different parts of large integrated corporations—some in charge of banks, some running the trade wing, some overseeing factories. Women played a crucial role, not just as custodians of the home but also as cultivators of important family alliances, especially among potential marriage partners. In contrast to American limited-liability firms, which issued shares on stock markets to anonymous buyers, Japan's version of large-scale managerial capitalism was a personal affair.

Expansionism and Conflict with Neighbors As in many other emerging nation-states, expansion was a tempting prospect to the Japanese. It offered the promise of more markets for selling goods and obtaining staples, and it was a way to burnish the image of national superiority and greatness. The Meiji moved first to take over the kingdom of the Ryūkyūs, southwest of Japan (see Map 17.5). A small show of force, only 160 Japanese soldiers, was enough to establish the new Okinawa Prefecture there in 1879. The Japanese regarded the people of the Ryūkyūs as an ethnic minority and refused to incorporate them into the nation-state on

MAP 17.5 | Japanese Expansion, 1870–1910

Under the Meiji Restoration, the Japanese state built a strong national identity and competed with foreign powers for imperial advantage in East Asia.

- According to the map, what were the first areas that the Japanese Empire acquired as it started to expand?
- What two empires' spheres of influence were affected by Japan's aggressive attempts at expansion?
- According to your reading, what were the new Japanese state's objectives? How were they similar to or different from European expansionism of the same period?

equal terms. In contrast with the British in India or the Americans in Puerto Rico, the Japanese conquerors refused to train a native Ryūkyūs governing class. Meiji intellectuals insisted that the "backward" Okinawans were unfit for local self-rule and representation.

The Japanese fixed upon Korea, which put their plans on a collision course with China. In a formal treaty, the Japanese recognized Korea as an independent state (expected to be no longer dominated by China), opened Korea to trade, and won the right to apply Japanese law in Korea. As a result, the Chinese worried that soon the Japanese would try to take over Korea. These fears were well founded, for Japanese designs on Korea eventually sparked the Sino-Japanese War of 1894–1895, in which the Chinese suffered a humiliating defeat.

The Sino-Japanese War accelerated Japan's rapid transformation into a nation-state and a colonial power with no peer in Asia. Having lost the war, China ceded the province of Taiwan to the Japanese. Japan also annexed Korea in 1910 and converted Taiwan and Korea into the twin jewels of its young empire. Like the British in India, the Japanese regarded their colonial subjects as racially inferior and unworthy of the privileges of citizenship. And like other imperial powers, the Japanese expected their possessions to serve the metropolitan center.

RUSSIAN TRANSFORMATION AND EXPANSION

Russia expanded out of a sense of a civilizing mission and a need to defend against other countries expanding along its immense borders. Facing an emerging Germany, a British presence in the Middle East and Persia, a consolidating China, and an increasingly powerful Japan, Russia knew it would have to extend its already large territorial domain. So it established a number of expansionist fronts simultaneously: southwest to the Black Sea, south into the Caucasus and Turkestan, and east into Manchuria (see Map 17.6). Success depended on annexing territories and establishing protectorates over conquered peoples.

Modernization and Internal Reform In the 1860s, Tsar Alexander II launched a wave of "Great Reforms" to make Russia more modern and to preserve its status as a great power. In 1861, for example, a decree emancipated peasants from serfdom. Other changes included a sharp reduction in the duration of military service, a program of education for the conscripts, and the beginnings of a mass school system to teach children reading, writing, and Russian culture. Starting in the 1890s, state-sponsored industrialization led to the building of railroads and factories and stimulated the expansion of the steel, coal, and petroleum industries. But while the reforms strengthened the state, they did not enhance the lives of common people. Workers in Russia were brutally exploited, even by the standards of the industrial revolution. Also, large landowners had kept most of the empire's fertile land, and the peasants had to pay substantial redemption fees for the poorer-quality plots they received.

Before long, in the press, courtrooms, and streets, men and women denounced the regime. Revolutionaries engaged in terror and assassination. In 1881, a terrorist bomb killed the tsar. In the 1890s, following a period of famine, the radical doctrines of Marxism (see Chapter 16) gained popularity in Russia. Even aristocratic intellectuals, such as the author of *War and Peace,* Count Leo Tolstoy, lamented their despotic government.

Territorial Expansion Yet the critics of internal reform did not hold back the Russian expansionists, who believed they had to take over certain lands to keep them out of rivals' hands. So they conquered the highland people of the Caucasus Mountains to prevent Ottomans and Persians from encroaching on Russia's southern flank. And they battled the British over areas between Turkestan and British India, such as Persia (Iran) and Afghanistan. Although some Russians moved to these lands, they never became a majority there. The new provinces were multiethnic, multireligious communities that were only partially integrated into the Russian nation.

MAP 17.6 | Russian Expansion, 1801–1914

The Russian state continued to expand in the nineteenth century.

- According to this map, what lands did Russia acquire during the period 1796–1855? What lands did it acquire next?
- Compare this map of Russian expansion with Map 13.7 (p. 481). How did the direction of Russia's expansion change in the nineteenth century?
- Which states did the expanding Russian Empire more resemble in this era, western Europe (such as Great Britain) or American states (such as the United States)?

Perhaps the most impressive Russian expansion occurred in East Asia, where the Amur River basin offered rich lands, mineral deposits, and access to the Pacific Ocean. The Chinese also wanted to colonize this area, which lay just north of Manchuria. After twenty years of struggle, Russia claimed the land north and south of the Amur River and in 1860 founded Vladivostok, a port on the Pacific Ocean whose name signified "Rule the East." Deciding to focus on these areas in Asia, the Russian government sold its one territory in North America (Alaska) to the United States. Then, to link central Russia and the western part of the country to its East Asian spoils, the government began construction of the Trans-Siberian Railroad. When it was completed in 1916, the new railroad bridged the east and the west.

Governing a Diverse Empire Russia was a huge empire whose rulers were only partially effective at integrating its diverse parts into a political community. Unlike the United States, which displaced or slaughtered native populations during its expansion across an entire continent, Russia tolerated and taxed many of the new peoples. The state's approach ranged from outright repression (of Poles and Jews) to favoritism (toward Baltic Germans and Finns), although the beneficiaries of favoritism often later lost favor if they became too strong. Further, unlike the United States, which managed to pacify borders with its weaker neighbors, Russia faced the constant suspicions of Persians and Ottomans and the menace of British troops in Afghanistan. In East Asia, a clash with expansionist Japan loomed on the horizon.

CHINA UNDER PRESSURE

While the Russians and Japanese scrambled to copy European models of industrialism and imperialism, the Qing were slower to mobilize against threats from the west. Even as the European powers were dividing up China into spheres of influence, Qing officials were much more worried about internal revolts and threats from their northern borders than European incursions.

Adopting Western Learning and Skills A growing number of Chinese officials recognized the superior armaments and technology of rival powers and were deeply troubled by the threat posed by European military might. Starting in the 1860s, reformist bureaucrats sought to adopt elements of western learning and technological skills—but with the intention of keeping the core Chinese culture intact.

This so-called **Self-Strengthening movement** included a variety of new ventures: arsenals, shipyards, coal mines, a steamship company to contest the foreign domination of coastal shipping, and schools for learning foreign ways and languages. Most interesting was the dispatch abroad of about 120 schoolboys under the charge of Yung Wing. The first Chinese graduate of an American college (Yale University, 1854), Yung believed that western education would greatly benefit Chinese students, so he took his charges to Connecticut in the 1870s to attend school and live with American families. Conservatives at the Qing court were soon dismayed by reports of the students' interest in Christianity and aptitude for baseball. In 1881, after the U.S. government refused to admit the boys into military academies, they summoned the students home.

Yung Wing's abortive educational mission was not the only setback for the Self-Strengthening movement, for skepticism about western technology was rife among conservative officials. Some insisted that the introduction of machinery would lead to unemployment; others worried that railways would facilitate western military maneuvers and lead to an invasion; still others complained that the crisscrossing tracks disturbed the harmony between humans and nature. The first short railway track ever laid in China was torn up in 1877 shortly after being built, and the country had only 179 miles of track prior to 1895.

Although they did not acknowledge the railroad's usefulness, the Chinese did adopt other new technologies to access a wider range of information. For example, by the early 1890s there were about a dozen Chinese-language newspapers (as distinct from the foreign-language press) published in major cities, with the largest ones having a circulation of 10,000 to 15,000. To avoid government intervention, these papers sidestepped political controversy; instead, they featured commercial news and literary contributions. In 1882, the newspaper *Shenbao* made use of a new telegraph line to publish dispatches within China.

Internal Reform Efforts China's defeat by Japan in the Sino-Japanese War (1894–1895), sparked by quarrels over Korea, prompted a more serious attempt at reform by the Qing. Known as the Hundred Days' Reform, the episode lasted only from June to September 1898. The force behind it was a thirty-seven-year-old scholar named Kang Youwei and his twenty-two-year-old student Liang Qichao. Citing rulers such as Peter the Great of Russia and the Meiji Emperor of Japan as their inspiration, the reformers urged Chinese leaders to develop a railway network, a state banking system, a modern postal service, and institutions to foster the development of agriculture, industry, and commerce. The reform failed when a group of conservative leaders placed the Dowager Cixi on the throne, rescinded the reformist laws, and executed six of the reform movement's major leaders. They did not, however, capture Kang Youwei, who fled to Japan.

But, in truth, the reforms of the Self-Strengthening movement were ineffectual, too modest and poorly implemented. Very few Chinese acquired new skills. Despite talk of modernizing, the civil service examination remained based on Confucian classics and still opened the only doors to government service. Governing elites were not yet ready to reinvent the principles of their political community, and they adhered instead to the traditional dynastic structure.

By the late nineteenth century, the success of the Qing regime in expanding its territories a century earlier seemed like a distant memory, as various powers repeatedly forced it to make economic and territorial concessions. Unlike Japan or Russia, however, the Qing government resisted comprehensive social reforms (until after the turn of the twentieth century), and its policies left the country vulnerable to both external aggression and internal instability.

Conclusion

Between 1850 and 1914, most of the world's people lived not in nation-states but in land empires or in the overseas colonies of nation-states. But leaders in colonial territories, often responding to popular upheavals and destabilizing economic changes, began to see independent nation-states as the most desirable form of governance for their regions.

Although the ideal of "a people" united by territory, history, and culture grew increasingly popular worldwide, it was not easy to make it a reality. Official histories, national heroes, novels, poetry, and music helped, but central to the process of nation formation were the actions of bureaucrats. Asserting sovereignty over what it claimed as national territory, the state "nationalized" diverse populations by creating a unified system of law, education, military service, and government.

Colonization beyond borders was another part of nation building in many societies. In these efforts, territorial conquests took place under the banner of nationalist endeavors. In Europe, the Americas, Japan, and to some extent Russia, the intertwined processes of nation building and territorial expansion were most effective. Expansion abroad consolidated national identities at home.

However, the integrating impulses of imperialist nation-states did not wipe out local differences, mute class antagonisms, or eliminate gender inequalities. Even as Europeans and Americans came to see themselves as chosen—by God or by natural selection—to rule the rest, they suffered deep divisions. Not everyone identified with the nation-state or the empire, or agreed on what it meant to belong or to conquer. But by the century's end, racist advocates and colonial lobbyists seem to have convinced many that their interests and destinies were bound up with their countries' unity, prosperity, and global clout.

Ironically, imperial expansion had an unintended consequence, for self-determination could also apply to racial or ethnic minorities at home and in the colonies. Armed with the rhetoric of progress and uplift, colonial authorities tried to subjugate distant people, but colonial subjects themselves often asserted the language of "nation" and accused imperial overlords of betraying their own lofty principles. As the twentieth century opened, Filipino and Cuban rebels used Thomas Jefferson's Declaration of Independence to oppose American invaders, Koreans defined themselves as a nation crushed under Japanese heels, and Indian nationalists made colonial governors feel shame for violating British standards of "fair play."

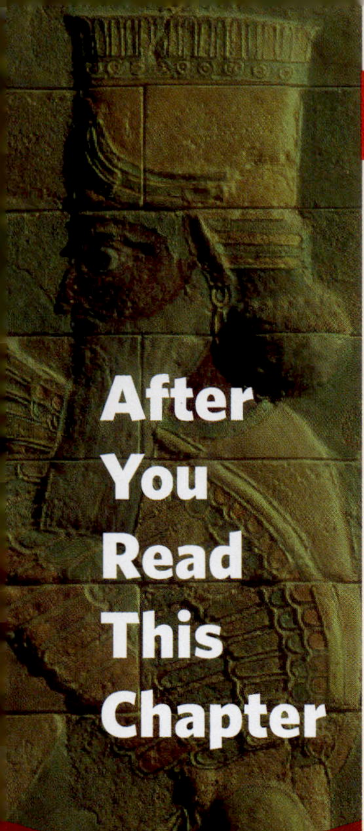

After You Read This Chapter

Go to INQUIZITIVE to see what you've learned—and learn what you've missed—with personalized feedback along the way.

TRACING THE GLOBAL STORYLINES

FOCUS ON: *Nationalism, Imperialism, and Technological Innovations*

THE AMERICAS AND EUROPE: CONSOLIDATING NATIONS

- Residents of the United States claim territory across the North American continent after fighting a bloody civil war to preserve the union and abolish slavery.
- Canadians also build a new nation and expand across the continent.
- Brazilians create a prosperous nation-state that excludes much of the population from the privileges of belonging to the "nation" and the "state."
- The dynastic states of Prussia and Sardinia-Piedmont create German and Italian nation-states at the expense of France and the Austrian Empire.

INDUSTRY, SCIENCE, AND TECHNOLOGY ON A GLOBAL SCALE

- Continued industrialization transforms the global economy.
- New technologies of warfare, transportation, and communication lead to greater global economic integration.
- Charles Darwin's *Origin of Species* overturns previous conceptions of nature, arguing that present-day life forms evolved from simpler ones over long periods.

EMPIRES

- After suppressing the Indian Rebellion of 1857, the British reorganize their rule in India, providing a model for other imperialist powers.
- European powers partition the entire African continent (except for Ethiopia and Liberia) despite intense African resistance.
- Americans win the Spanish-American War, annex Puerto Rico, and establish colonial rule over the Philippines.
- The expansionist aims of Japan, Russia, and China lead to clashes over possessions in East Asia, with Russia gaining much territory and Japan defeating the Chinese.
- Colonial rule spurs nationalist sentiments among the colonized.

CHRONOLOGY

THE AMERICAS
- U.S. Civil War 1861–1865
- Canada gains self-rule 1867

EUROPE
- *On the Origin of Species* published 1859

EAST ASIA AND SOUTHEAST ASIA
- Commodore Perry "opens" Japan 1853

AFRICA AND THE MIDDLE EAST

SOUTH ASIA

RUSSIA
- Crimean War 1853–1856
- Great Reforms to modernize Russia 1860s

1800 | 1850

THINKING ABOUT GLOBAL CONNECTIONS

- ***Thinking about* Worlds Together, Worlds Apart *and Nations & Empires*** Compare the eighteenth century empires of Spain, Portugal, and Britain with the new empires arising in Africa at the end of the nineteenth century. What were the sources of their wealth and power? How and to what degree were colonial territories and economies integrated with their imperialist states?
- ***Thinking about Changing Power Relationships and Nations & Empires*** How did the growth of Western influence and Japanese power lay the basis for opposition movements in Africa and Asia? How did people respond to imperialism? Where was resistance most effective?
- ***Thinking about Environmental Impacts and Nations & Empires*** Describe the the second industrial revolution and explain how it differed from the first industrial revolution. Pay special attention to the new technologies used in the late nineteenth century and especially to the sources of power and new materials that were used.

STUDY QUESTIONS

1. Compare **Manifest Destiny** in the United States with European **imperialism** in Africa. What common influences shaped both kinds of expansion? How did they differ?
2. Describe the challenges that mass nationalism and economic expansion posed for the multiethnic, multireligious empires of Austria-Hungary and Russia.
3. Compare the **Meiji Restoration** with China's **Self-Strengthening movement**. What values did they share? Can you explain their differences?
4. Explain the significance of **steel** and **limited-liability joint-stock companies** to the second industrial revolution.
5. Analyze the cultural impact of imperialist ambitions on imperialist nations. How did notions of race and ethnicity shape the colonial mentality of Europeans, Americans, and Japanese?

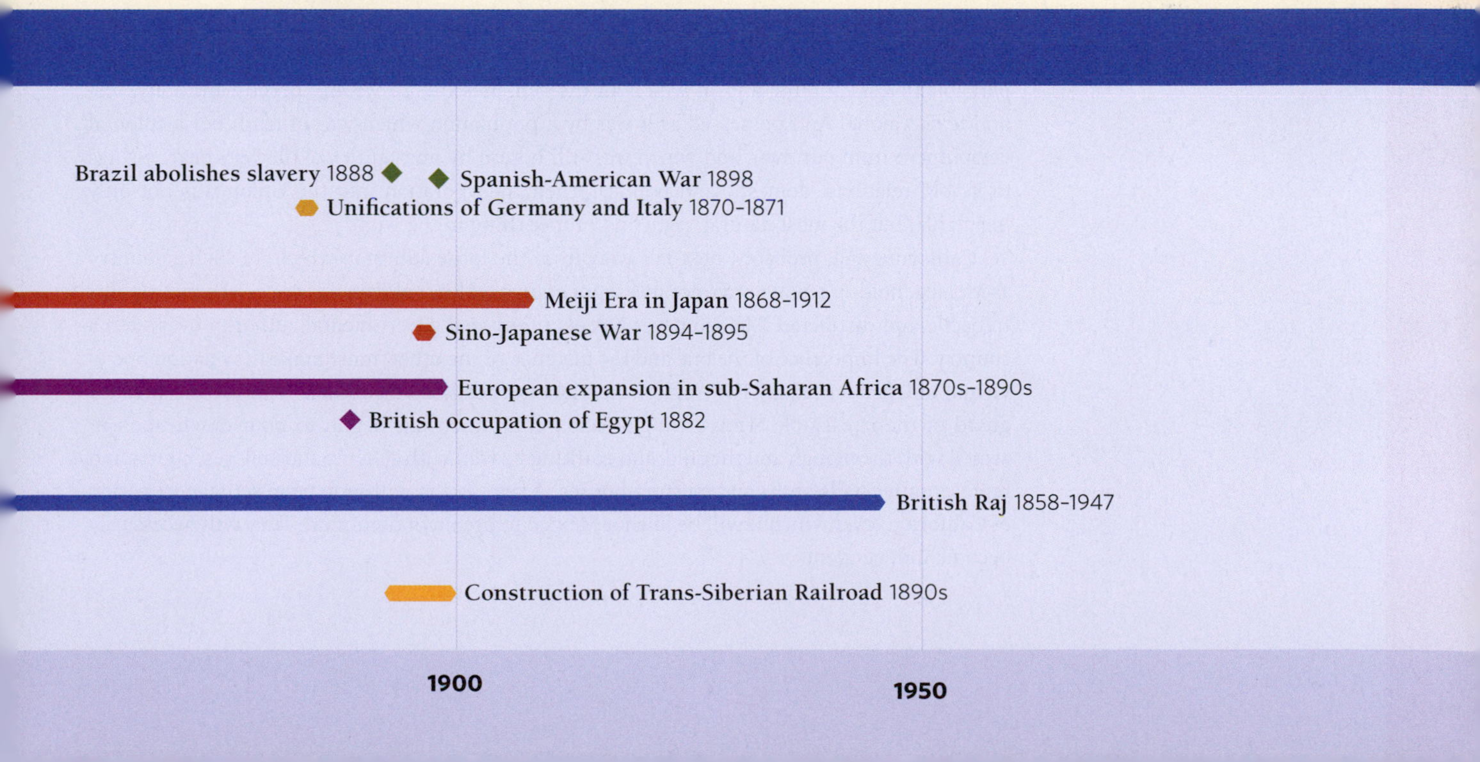

Going to the Source

Responses to Imperialism

Imperialism, the expansion of states outside their boundaries, is generally associated with the nineteenth century, when many European countries and the United States moved into Africa, Asia, and other lands beyond their official geographical borders. As more and more territories were brought under the control of outside governments, colonized peoples began to think about the colonizers—and vice versa. The documents here present a variety of ways to consider imperialism. Some clearly support such expansion, viewing it as inevitable and for the benefit of others. Others struggle with the process, suggesting that there may be costs as well as benefits.

PRIMARY SOURCE 17.1

"Manifest Destiny" (1845), John L. O'Sullivan

New York newspaper editor John L. O'Sullivan coined the term "manifest destiny" in 1845 to explain how the quasi-religious term "manifest design of Providence" could be used to support the territorial expansion of the United States as it took over territory from both indigenous Amerindians and other European powers.

Texas has been absorbed into the Union in the inevitable fulfillment of the general law which is rolling our population westward; the connexion of which with that ratio of growth in population which is destined within a hundred years to swell our numbers to the enormous population of *two hundred and fifty millions* (if not more), is too evident to leave us in doubt of the manifest design of Providence in regard to the occupation of this continent. It was disintegrated from Mexico in the natural course of events, by a process perfectly legitimate on its own part, blameless on ours; and in which all the censures due to wrong, perfidy and folly, rest on Mexico alone. And possessed as it was by a population which was in truth but a colonial detachment from our own, and which was still bound by myriad ties of the very heart strings to its old relations, domestic and political, their incorporation into the Union was not only inevitable, but the most natural, right and proper thing in the world. . . .

California will, probably, next fall away from the loose adhesion which, in such a country as Mexico, holds a remote province in a slight equivocal kind of dependence on the metropolis. Imbecile and distracted, Mexico never can exert any real governmental authority over such a country. The impotence of the one and the distance of the other, must make the relation one of virtual independence. . . . The Anglo-Saxon foot is already on its borders. Already the advance guard of the irresistible army of Anglo-Saxon emigration has begun to pour down upon it, armed with the plough and the rifle, and marking its trail with schools and colleges, courts and representative halls, mills and meeting-houses. A population will soon be in actual occupation of California, over which it will be idle for Mexico to dream of dominion. They will necessarily become independent.

1. **Why does O'Sullivan believe that the United States is destined to take over territories that belonged to other states, such as Mexico?**
2. **Why does O'Sullivan believe that California will become independent?**

PRIMARY SOURCE 17.2

On the Origin of Species *(1859), Charles Darwin*

Charles Darwin examined the evolution of different species in nature to determine how and why they were created. He described the process of natural selection, in which nature creates overabundance so that the "fittest" species survive and adapt themselves to their environments. Although his book says nothing about human beings, and Darwin himself was appalled by the human suffering and exploitation that resulted from imperialism, many of his contemporaries used Darwin's ideas to justify imperial expansion around the globe.

Again, it may be asked, how is it that varieties, which I have called incipient species, become ultimately converted into good and distinct species, which in most cases obviously differ from each other far more than do the varieties of the same species? How do those groups of species, which constitute what are called distinct genera, and which differ from each other more than do the species of the same genus, arise? All these results . . . follow inevitably from the struggle for life. Owing to this struggle for life, any variation, however slight and from whatever cause proceeding, if it be in any degree profitable to an individual of any species, in its infinitely complex relations to other organic beings and to external nature, will tend to the preservation of that individual, and will generally be inherited by its offspring. The offspring, also, will thus have a better chance of surviving, for, of the many individuals of any species which are periodically born, but a small number can survive. I have called this principle, by which each slight variation, if useful, is preserved, by the term of Natural Selection, in order to mark its relation to man's power of selection. We have seen that man by selection can certainly produce great results, and can adapt organic beings to his own uses, through the accumulation of slight but useful variations, given to him by the hand of Nature. But Natural Selection, as we shall hereafter see, is a power incessantly ready for action, and is as immeasurably superior to man's feeble efforts, as the works of Nature are to those of Art.

We will now discuss in a little more detail the struggle for existence. . . . I should premise that I use the term Struggle for Existence in a large and metaphorical sense, including dependence of one being on another, and including (which is more important) not only the life of the individual, but success in leaving progeny. Two canine animals in a time of dearth, may be truly said to struggle with each other which shall get food and live. But a plant on the edge of a desert is said to struggle for life against the drought, though more properly it should be said to be dependent on the moisture. . . .

A struggle for existence inevitably follows from the high rate at which all organic beings tend to increase. Every being, which during its natural lifetime produces several eggs or seeds, must suffer destruction during some period of its life, and during some season or occasional year, otherwise, on the principle of geometrical increase, its numbers would quickly become so inordinately great that no country could support the product. Hence, as more individuals are produced than can possibly survive, there must in every case be a struggle for existence, either one individual with another of the same species, or with the individuals of distinct species, or with the physical conditions of life. . . . Although some species may be now increasing, more or less rapidly, in numbers, all cannot do so, for the world would not hold them.

It may be said that natural selection is daily and hourly scrutinising, throughout the world, every variation, even the slightest; rejecting that which is bad, preserving and adding up all that is good; silently and insensibly working, whenever and wherever opportunity offers, at the improvement of each organic being in relation to its organic and inorganic conditions of life. We see nothing of these slow changes in progress, until the hand of time has marked the long lapses of ages, and then so imperfect is our view into long past geological ages, that we only see that the forms of life are now different from what they formerly were.

1. **According to Darwin, how do various species become distinct?**
2. **How might Darwin's concept of natural selection be applied to human beings in an age of imperialist expansion?**

PRIMARY SOURCE 17.3

Letter to Phan Đình Phùng (c. 1880), Hoàng Cao Khai

This letter is written by one Vietnamese friend to another; the two men had grown up together in the same village, but took different views of the French occupation of Indochina. While the writer is more accommodationist, his friend has taken a principled stand to fight against the colonizers.

Soon it will be seventeen years since we ventured upon different paths of life. Although matters have changed, the road . . . remains long and arduous. Nevertheless, in neither my dreams nor my thoughts do I ever feel that you are far. How sweet was our friendship when we both lived in our village.

From the day on which you decided to take up arms against the invasion, your courage and loyalty have grown so renowned that I have often heard the French administrators speak of you with high regard. It is therefore clear that loyal men command respect not only from their compatriots but also from persons of foreign countries. At the time when the capital was lost and after the royal carriage had departed, you courageously answered the appeals of the King by raising the banner of righteousness. It was certainly the only thing to do in those circumstances. No one will question that.

But now the situation has changed and even those without intelligence or education have concluded that nothing remains to be saved. How is it that you, a man of vast understanding, do not realize this? But I seem to perceive your reasoning. You are determined to do whatever you deem righteous. You give all your efforts and talents to the cause you consider just. And yet, although it is in a man's power to undertake any enterprise, its outcome depends upon the will of Heaven. All that matters indeed is the giving of one's life to one's country. No one therefore can deter you from your goal.

The subject I should now like to introduce is the suffering imposed upon our country. It distresses me and has prompted me, on several occasions, to write to you so as to discuss with you or at least impart to you some of my superficial ideas. Each time, however, I lacked the courage to complete my letter. Why? Because I knew your determination too well and knew that my words would certainly not induce you to change your mind. Moreover, the circumstances in which we now live are so unlike that I doubted you would want to understand my language.

But recently, in an interview with the French governor-general, we happened to discuss the situation in our province. Here are his views. He knows quite well that you are committed to your righteous cause and that you are also utterly selfless. But though you have no thoughts for you own person nor for your own family, you should at least attend to the sufferings of the population of a whole region. The governor mentioned this to me becaus he knew that I was from the same province as you and that we might together devise a plan to save it. His words are not worthless, and this is precisely the reason why I can no longer remain silent.

Are you not ashamed to see that the governor-general, who comes from a foreign country several thousand miles away, knows how to care for our people while we, who were born and raised in this country, remain blind to the sufferings of its people? How will they judge us, the generations a hundred years hence? I have always been taught that superior men should consider the care of the people as fundamental; who has ever heard of men who were loyal to their king but forgot the people's aspirations?

Until now, your actions have undoubtedly accorded with your loyalty. May I ask however what sin our people have committed to deserve so much hardship? I would understand your resistance did you involve but your family for the benefit of a large number! As of now, hundreds of families are subject to grief; how do you have the heart to fight on? I venture to predict that, should you pursue your struggle, not only will the population of our village be destroyed but our entire country will be transformed into a sea of blood and a mountain of bones. It is my hope that men of your superior morality and honesty will pause a while to appraise the situation.

Recently, Mr. Pham Tron Mu'u came to offer his surrender, and I personally presented him to various French officials who treated him like a precious guest. They immediately cabled the provincial authorities, requesting them to free his three sons and to permit him to attend to his ancestors' tombs. This alone will prove to you the tolerance and generosity of the government of the Protectorate. It will also prove to you that, though they come from a foreign country several thousand miles away, the French have the same heart and the same logic we have.

1. **What is the author's goal in writing to his long-time friend?**
2. **Explain why the author might believe that the Vietnamese would benefit from French imperialism.**

PRIMARY SOURCE 17.4

Address to the Indian National Congress (1907), Bal Gangdadhar Tilak

The British created the Indian National Congress Party in 1885 to give voice to Indians, who began to demand greater political representation and a say in their own political and economic affairs. In this address by the party's leader, Bal Gangdadhar Tilak is sensitive to how the nature of opposition to colonial rule changes over time.

Two new words have recently come into existence with regard to our politics, and they are Moderates and Extremists. These words have a specific relation to time, and they, therefore, will change with time. The Extremists of today will be Moderates tomorrow, just as the Moderates of today were Extremists yesterday. When the National Congress was first started and Mr. Dadabhai's views, which now go for Moderates, were given to the public, he was styled an Extremist, so that you will see that the term Extremist is an expression of progress. We are Extremists today and our sons will call themselves Extremists and us Moderates. Every new party begins as Extremists and ends as Moderates. The sphere of practical politics is not unlimited. We cannot say what will or will not happen 1,000 years hence—perhaps during that long period, the whole of the white race will be swept away in another glacial period. We must, therefore, study the present and work out a program to meet the present condition. . . .

One thing is granted, namely, that this government does not suit us. As has been said by an eminent statesman—the government of one country by another can never be a successful, and therefore, a permanent government. There is no difference of opinion about this fundamental proposition between the old and new schools. One fact is that this alien government has ruined the country. In the beginning, all of us were taken by surprise. We were almost dazed. We thought that everything that the rulers did was for our good and that this English government has descended from the clouds to save us from the invasions of Tamerlane and Chingis Khan, and, as they say, not only from foreign invasions but from internecine warfare, or the internal or external invasions, as they call it. . . . We are not armed, and there is no necessity for arms either. We have a stronger weapon, a political weapon, in boycott.

We have perceived one fact, that the whole of this administration, which is carried on by a handful of Englishmen, is carried on with our assistance. We are all in subordinate service. This whole government is carried on with our assistance and they try to keep us in ignorance of our power of cooperation between ourselves by which that which is in our own hands at present can be claimed by us and administered by us. The point is to have the entire control in our hands. I want to have the key of my house, and not merely one stranger turned out of it. Self-government is our goal; we want a control over our administrative machinery. We don't want to become clerks and remain [clerks]. At present, we are clerks and willing instruments of our own oppression in the hands of an alien government, and that government is ruling over us not by its innate strength but by keeping us in ignorance and blindness to the perception of this fact. . . . Every Englishman knows that they are a mere handful in this country and it is the business of every one of them to befool you in believing that you are weak and they are strong. This is politics. We have been deceived by such policy so long. What the new party wants you to do is to realize the fact that your future rests entirely in your own hands. If you mean to be free, you can be free; if you do not mean to be free, you will fall and be forever fallen. . . .

This is the way in which a nation progresses, and this is the lesson you have to learn from the struggle now going on. This is a lesson of progress, a lesson of helping yourself as much as possible, and if you really perceive the force of it, if you are convinced by these arguments, then and then only is it possible for you to effect your salvation from the alien rule under which you labor at this moment successful, that is, those who are unfit to tend to extinction, but that the issue of the struggle does not depend on mere physical force.

1. To what aspects of British colonial rule in India does Tilak object?

2. How might you connect Darwin's ideas about natural selection to Tilak's speech?

PRIMARY SOURCE 17.5

Fifty Years of New Japan *(1910), Okuma Shigenobu*

Okuma Shigenobu, a Japanese politician, wrote *Fifty Years of New Japan*, which explores the sources of Meiji Japan's power and the role of competition with the West. Okuma Shigenobu later served as Japanese prime minister from 1914 to 1916. He also founded Waseda University, and was a proponent of translating Western books and science into Japanese.

By comparing the Japan of fifty years ago with the Japan of today, it will be seen that she has gained considerably in the extent of her territory, as well as in her population, which now numbers nearly fifty million. Her government has become constitutional not only in name, but in fact, and her national education has attained to a high degree of excellence. In commerce and industry, the emblems of peace, she has also made rapid strides, until her import and export trades together amounted in 1907 to the enormous sum of 926,000,000 yen. Her general progress, during the short space of half a century, has been so sudden and swift that it presents a rare spectacle in the history of the world. This leap forward is the result of the stimulus which the country received on coming into contact with the civilization of Europe and America, and may well, in its broad sense, be regarded as a boon conferred by foreign [interaction]. Foreign [interactions] animated the national consciousness of our people, who under the feudal system lived localized and disunited, and [such connections have] enabled Japan to stand up as a world power. We possess today a powerful army and navy, but it was after Western models that we laid their foundations by establishing a system of conscription in pursuance of the principle "all our sons are soldiers," by promoting military education, and by encouraging the manufacture of arms and the art of shipbuilding. We have reorganized the systems of central and local administration, and effected reforms in the educational system of the empire. All this is nothing but the result of adopting the superior features of Western institutions. That Japan has been enabled to do so is a boon conferred on her by foreign [interactions], and it may be said that the nation has succeeded in this grand metamorphosis through the promptings and the influence of foreign civilization. For twenty centuries the nation has drunk freely of the civilizations of Korea, China, and India, being always open to the different influences impressed on her in succession. Yet we remain politically unaltered under one Imperial House and sovereign, that has descended in an unbroken line for a length of time absolutely unexampled in the world. We have welcomed Occidental civilization while preserving their old Oriental civilization. They have attached great importance to Bushido [samurai values], and at the same time held in the highest respect the spirit of charity and humanity. They have ever made a point of choosing the middle course in everything, and have aimed at being always well-balanced. We are conservative simultaneously with being progressive; we are aristocratic and at the same time democratic; we are individualistic while also being socialistic. In these respects we may be said to somewhat resemble the Anglo-Saxon race.

1. **According to Shigenobu, how has Japan benefited from its interactions with Westerners and Western institutions?**
2. **Why does Shigenobu believe that Japan is at once conservative and progressive?**

PRIMARY SOURCE 17.6

Ottoman Cartoon (1908–9)

This cartoon depicts Britain as a giant that controls access to the Ottoman province of Egypt by blocking the local populations. The giant is shown leaning on the pyramids.

1. **Why might the Ottomans have depicted Britain's presence in Egypt this way?**
2. **What are the locals doing in response to the British blockage, and why might they have been doing this?**

Questions for Analysis

Comparison

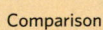

1. Compare the range of responses to imperialism presented in these documents.

Analyzing Evidence

2. Explain how Darwin's ideas have been used by imperialists to justify their actions, as well as by those who struggled against imperialism.

Contextualization

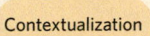

3. How is the concept of "manifest destiny" connected to global imperialism and why might that be important?

Long Essay Question

Argumentation

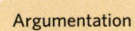

Based on what you have read in the chapter and the documents above, assess the degree to which imperialism in the nineteenth century either improved or worsened conditions for people who were affected by imperialist policies and actions.

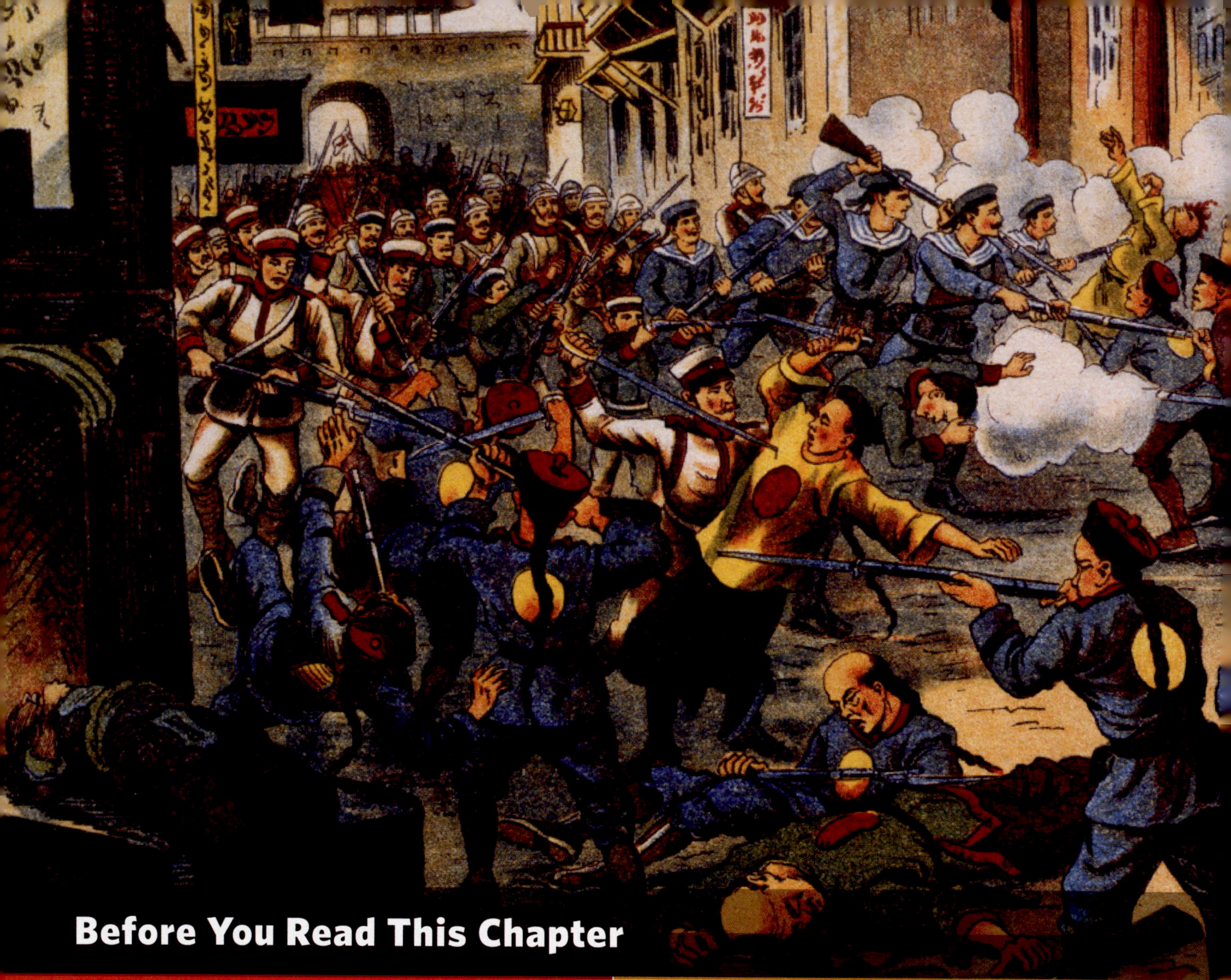

Before You Read This Chapter

GLOBAL STORYLINES

- Numerous factors lead to global instability: vast population movements, worldwide financial crises, class conflict, the rise of women's consciousness, and hatred of colonial domination.
- Class conflict, economic instability, and great power rivalry within Europe combine with growing protest from overseas to undermine Europe's dominant position in world affairs.
- New scientific thinking and artistic expression, known as cultural modernism, challenge the dominant Western view of progress and open Europe and North America to the cultural achievements of nonwestern societies.

CORE OBJECTIVES

- **EXPLAIN** the connections between migration and the development of nationalism in this period.
- **COMPARE** Chinese responses to imperialism with responses to imperialism in Africa.
- **IDENTIFY** and **DESCRIBE** political, economic, and social crise that swept through the world in this period, and **ANALYZE** the impact they had on different regions of the world.
- **EXPLAIN** the ways in which new cultural forms at the turn of the century reflected challenges to the world order as it then existed.
- **EVALUATE** the ways in which race, nation, and religion unified populations but also made societies more difficult to govern and economies more difficult to manage.

CHAPTER

18

An Unsettled World

1890–1914

KEY TERMS

anarchism p. 691
Boxer Uprising p. 685
Mexican Revolution p. 692
modernism p. 693
pan movements p. 703
popular culture p. 695
progressive reformers p. 693
Shanghai School p. 698
Sun Yat-sen p. 701
syndicalism p. 691

In 1905 a young African man, Kinjikitile Ngwale, began to move among various ethnic groups in German East Africa, spreading a message of opposition to German colonial authorities. In the tradition of visionary prophets (see Chapter 16), Kinjikitile claimed that by anointing his followers with blessed water (*maji* in Swahili), he could protect them from European bullets and drive the Germans from East Africa. Kinjikitile's reputation spread rapidly, drawing followers from across 100,000 square miles of territory. Although German officials soon executed Kinjikitile, they could not prevent a broad uprising, called the Maji-Maji Revolt. The Germans brutally suppressed the revolt, killing between 200,000 and 300,000 Africans.

The Maji-Maji Revolt and its aftermath revealed the intensity of opposition to the world of nations and their empires. In Europe and North America, critics who felt deprived of the full benefits of industrializing nation-states—especially women, workers, and frustrated nationalists—demanded far-reaching reforms. In Asia, Africa, and Latin America, anticolonial critics and exploited classes protested European domination. In the face of so much unrest from within their nations and from their colonies, Europeans' faith in the idea of progress and the superiority of their "civilization" was shaken. Ironically, this occurred at the very moment when Europeans and people of European descent seemed to have established preeminence in world affairs.

This chapter tackles the anxieties and insecurities that unsettled the world around the turn of the twentieth century. It ties them in particular to several key factors: (1) the uprooting of millions of people from countryside to city and from one continent to another, (2) discontent with the poverty that many suffered even as economic production increased, and (3) resentment of and resistance to European domination. Around the globe, this tumult caused a questioning of established ideas that led to a flowering of new thinking and fresh artistic expression under the label of "modernism." This unsettling movement was a defining feature of the era.

Progress, Upheaval, and Movement

COMPARISON

EXPLAIN the connections between migration and the development of nationalism in this period.

Rapid economic progress in the decades leading up to 1914 brought challenges to the established order and the people in power. In Europe and the United States, radicals and middle-class reformers agitated for political and social change. In areas colonized by European countries and the United States, resentment focused on either colonial rulers or indigenous elites. Even in nations such as China, which had not been formally colonized but which faced repeated intrusions, popular discontent targeted domination by Europeans. At the same time, millions of people migrated to cities and different countries in search of a better life.

In the late nineteenth century, whole new industries fueled economic growth, especially in the industrial countries and in territories that exported vital raw materials to Europe and the United States. But industrial capitalism also spurred inequalities within industrial countries and, especially, between the world's industrial and nonindustrial regions. Periodic economic downturns left thousands out of work. This led, in some cases, to organized opposition to authoritarian regimes or to the free market system; it also provoked new critiques of the new industrial order and the values that supported it.

In Europe and North America, a generation of young artists, writers, and scientists broke with older conventions and sought new ways of seeing and describing the world. In Asia, Africa, and South America as well, many of these innovators were energized by the idea of moving beyond traditional forms of art, literature, music, and science. But this generation's exuberance worried those who were not ready to give up their cultural traditions and institutions.

PEOPLES IN MOTION

If the world was being *unsettled* by political, economic, and cultural changes, it was also being *resettled* by mass emigration (see Map 18.1). The emigration of throngs of Europeans to temperate zones in the Americas and Oceania began after the Napoleonic wars and gathered momentum in the 1840s, when the Irish fled their starving communities to seek better lives in North America. After 1870, the flow of Europeans became a torrent. The United States was the favored destination, with six times as many European immigrants arriving there as in Argentina (the second-place receiving country) between 1871 and 1920. The high point occurred between 1901 and 1910, when over

6 million Europeans entered the United States. This was nothing less than a demographic revolution.

Emigration, Immigration, Internal Migration Europeans were not the only peoples on the move. Between the 1840s and the 1940s, 29 million South Asians migrated into the Malay Peninsula and Burma (British colonies), the Dutch Indies (Indonesia), East Africa, and the Caribbean. Most were recruited to labor on plantations, railways, and mines in British-controlled territories. Meanwhile, the Chinese, too, emigrated in massive numbers. Between 1845 and 1900, population pressure, a shortage of cultivable land, and social turmoil drove 800,000 Chinese to seek new homes in North and South America, New Zealand, Hawaii, and the West Indies. Nearly four times as many settled in Southeast Asia. Moreover, industrial changes caused millions to migrate *within* their own countries or to neighboring ones, seeking employment in the burgeoning cities or other opportunities in frontier regions.

From the 1860s until 1914, governments imposed almost no controls on immigration or emigration. In China, the Qing government failed in its effort to restrict emigration into the dominant Manchus' northeastern homelands. The United States allowed entry to anyone who was not a prostitute, a convict, or a "lunatic"; but in 1882, racist reactions spurred legislation that barred entry to almost all Chinese. Travel within Europe required no passports or work permits; foreign-born criminals were subject to deportation, but that was the extent of immigration policy. (See **Analyzing Global Developments: Migration and the Origin of Border Control Policies**.)

Urban Life Cities boomed, with both positive and negative effects. Tokyo's population climbed from 500,000 in 1863 to 1,750,000 in 1908, and London's passed 6.5 million.

Urban Transportation (*Left*) Streetcars in Tokyo, Japan's capital, are watched over by sword-bearing patrolmen in 1905, during the Russo-Japanese War. The first electric streetcar began running in Japan in 1895. Note the elevated electricity lines, which dated from the 1880s. (*Right*) Heavy traffic in London, about 1910, points to an urban population on the move. Note the many kinds of transportation—motor buses as well as horse-drawn wagons; the railings in the foreground mark the entrance to the Underground, or subway.

NORTH SEA
DENMARK
Copenhagen
Glasgow
BRITAIN
Bradford
Leeds
Manchester and Liverpool
Sheffield
Birmingham
London
Bristol
NETHERLANDS
Hamburg
Amsterdam
Rotterdam
Antwerp
GERMANY
Berlin
Wuppertal
Cologne
Leipzig
Dresden
BELGIUM
Brussels
Frankfurt
Paris
LUX.
Nuremberg
Munich
FRANCE
AUSTRIA-HUNGARY
SWITZ.
Lyons
Milan
Turin
Bordeaux
ITALY
Marseilles
NORWAY
Inset area
CANADA
IRELAND
Belfast
Dublin
BRITISH COLUMBIA
Pittsburgh
Cleveland
Montreal
32 million (1620–1914)
UNITED STATES
Detroit
Chicago
Buffalo
Boston
New York
Philadelphia
Baltimore
Washington, D.C.
Cincinnati
St. Louis
San Francisco
CALIFORNIA
PORTUGAL
Barcelona
Madrid
Lisbon
SPAIN
TUNISIA
ATLANTIC OCEAN
SPANISH MOROCCO
ALGERIA
MOROCCO
1.5 million (1850–1914)
New Orleans
7.4 million (1530–1914)
SPANISH SAHARA
FRENCH WEST AFRICA
CUBA
MEXICO
Mexico City
12 million (1530–1860)
CENTRAL AMERICA
TRINIDAD
GAMBIA
PORT. GUINEA
SIERRA LEONE
LIBERIA
NIGERIA
TOGO
GOLD COAST
SP. GUINEA
VENEZUELA
COLOMBIA
GUYANA
ECUADOR
PACIFIC OCEAN
BRAZIL
PERU
BOLIVIA
PARAGUAY
CHILE
Rio de Janeiro
ARGENTINA
URUGUAY
Santiago
Buenos Aires
Montevideo
Boundary in 1900
Percentage Population Increase 1700–1900
0–49%
50–99%
100–249%
250–1000%
Over 1000%
City Population in 1900
250,000–500,000
500,000–1,000,000
Over 1,000,000
Major Population Movements 1500–1914
Migration originating from:
Europe, Scandinavia, and western Russia
Asia
Africa
0 1000 2000 Miles
0 1000 2000 Kilometers
0 200 400 Miles
0 200 400 Kilometers

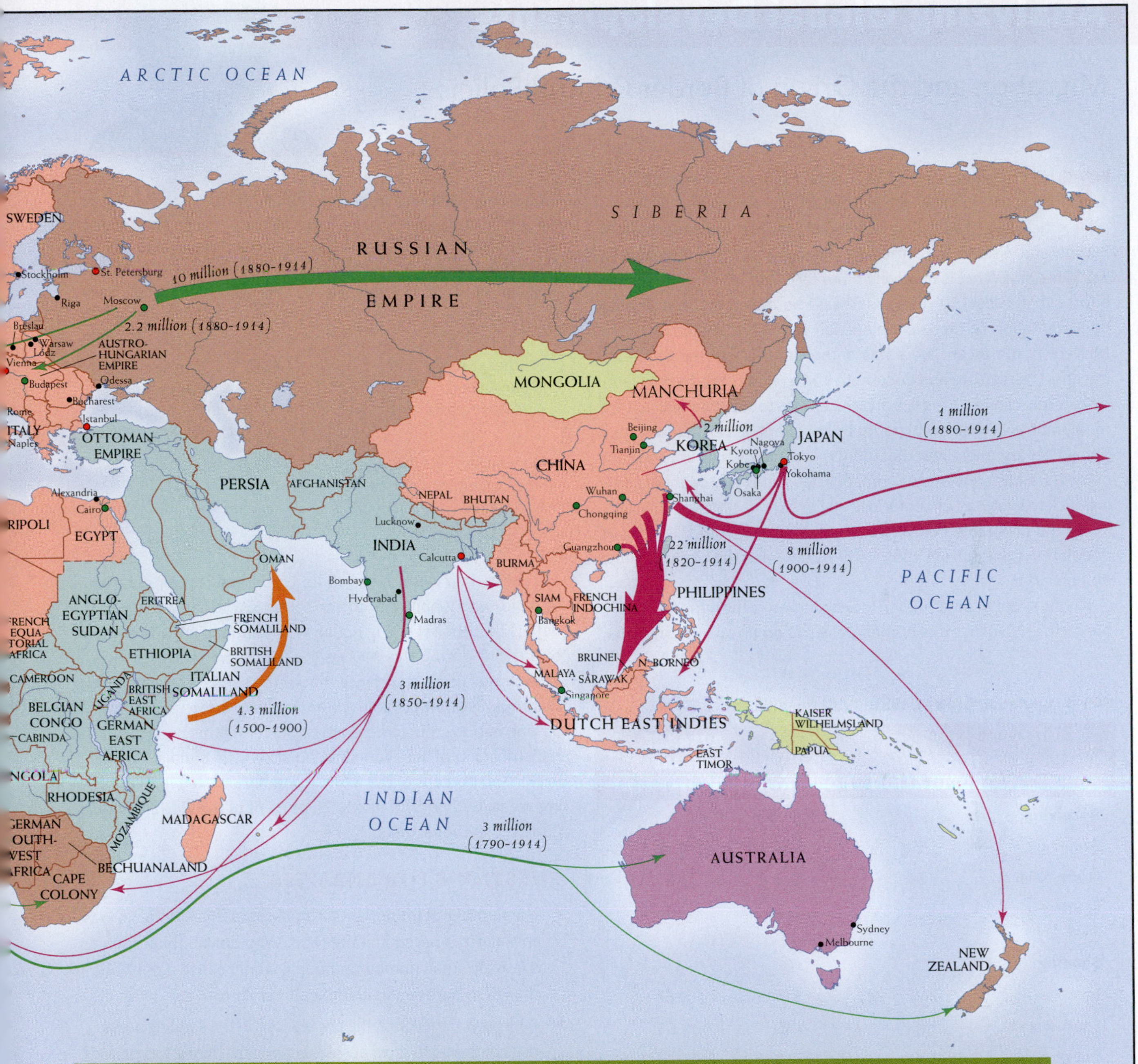

MAP 18.1 | Nineteenth-Century Migration

The nineteenth century witnessed a demographic revolution in terms of migration, urbanization patterns, and population growth. The world's population also rose from roughly 625 million in 1700 to 1.65 billion in 1900 (a two-and-a-half-fold increase).

- To what areas did most of the migrants from Europe go? What about the migrants from China, India, and Africa?
- What four areas saw the greatest population increase by 1900?
- How were migration flows and urbanization connected? What factors most accounted for these global population changes? Was internal growth more important than external migration in the case of the world's population growth? In what countries was population growth most affected by external or internal migration?

Analyzing Global Developments

Migration and the Origin of Border Control Policies

The movement of large numbers of people within and across regions—namely, the spread of the Mongols, the Atlantic slave trade, and nineteenth-century migrations from Europe and Asia to the Americas—is not a new phenomenon in world history. What is relatively more recent to world history is the effort over the last 150 years to increase border control and identity documentation of these people(s) on the move. Historian Adam McKeown in a recent work has demonstrated that the origins of the effort to regulate and document border control go back to late-nineteenth-century America and the efforts to substantially restrict the number of Asian immigrants trying to enter the United States. The earlier argument was that modern-day border control grew out of long-standing sovereignty practices of states and countries dating back to even earlier centuries.

In the first table below, we see a comparison of the rates of population growth from 1850 to 1950 between the major regions of the world.

In the second table, we see more concretely the number of people on the move in terms of their points of origin and destinations.

World Population Growth, 1850–1950 (in millions)

	1850 POPULATION	1950 POPULATION	AVERAGE ANNUAL GROWTH (%)
Receiving			
Americas	59	325	1.72
North Asia	22	104	1.57
Southeast Asia	42	177	1.45
Sending			
Europe	265	515	0.67
South Asia	230	445	0.66
China	420	520	0.21
Africa	81	205	0.93
World	1,200	2,500	0.74

Global Long-Distance Migration, 1840–1940

DESTINATION	ORIGINS	MIGRANTS (MILLIONS)	AUXILIARY ORIGINS
Americas	Europe	55–58	2.5 million from India, China, Japan, Africa
Southeast Asia, Indian Ocean Rim, Australasia	India S. China	48–52	5 million from Africa, Europe, NE Asia, Middle East
Manchuria, Siberia, Central Asia, Japan	NE Asia Russia	46–51	

These data were compiled from port and customs statistics at major entry points to major countries. What we see in the data is that the receiving nations' populations grew by a factor of 4.0–5.5 during this 100-year period, and that their overall growth was more than twice that of the sending regions during this time. Not only was the population growth rate of the receiving nations much more dramatic during this period, but the redistribution of the world's population was equally dramatic. In 1850 10 percent of the world's population lived in the receiving areas, but by 1950 nearly 25 percent of the world's population lived in those areas.

QUESTIONS FOR ANALYSIS

- The number of immigrants from Asia to the America's was only about 3 percent of the total. Why do you think such a relatively small number of people would cause a dramatic change in border and identification control?
- Why do you think that the populations in the sending areas also continued to grow at substantial rates during this period?
- Why do you think so many people were on the move from South China and India to other parts of the Indian Ocean world? From northeast Asia to East Asia and Inner Asia?

Sources: Adam McKeown, *Melancholy Order: Asian Migration and the Globalization of Borders (2008)*; Colin McEvedy and Richard Jones, *Atlas of World Population History* (1978); Adam McKeown, "Global Migration, 1846–1940," *Journal of World History* 15 (2004), p. 156.

Major cities faced housing shortages, despite governments' massive rebuilding and beautification projects. This was the era in which city planning came into its own—to widen and regularize thoroughfares for train and streetcar traffic, and to make crowded city life attractive to new inhabitants. City governments in New York, Cairo, Buenos Aires,

Bombay, and Brussels spent lavishly on opera houses, libraries, sewers, and parks, hoping to ward off disease and crime and to impress others with their modernity. And yet, for all those efforts, cholera and tuberculosis remained major killers, and suicide and alcoholism became growing problems. Population movement and the growth of cities were distinct features of the later nineteenth century all over the world, opening up new opportunities to become rich or to sink into poverty.

Discontent with Imperialism

In the decades before the Great War, opposition to European domination in Asia and Africa gathered strength. During the nineteenth century, as Europeans touted imperialism as a "civilizing mission," local prophets had voiced alternative visions contesting European supremacy (see Chapter 16). While imperialists consolidated their hold, suppression of unrest in the colonies required ever more force and bloodshed. As the cycle of resistance and repression escalated, many Europeans back home, mainly on the left and out of power, questioned the harsh means of controlling their colonies. By 1914, these questions were intensifying as colonial subjects across Asia and Africa challenged imperial domination.

COMPARISON

COMPARE Chinese responses to imperialism with responses to imperialism in Africa.

UNREST IN AFRICA

Africa witnessed many anticolonial uprisings in the first decades of colonial rule (see Map 18.2). Violent conflicts embroiled not only the Belgians and the Germans, who paid little attention to African political traditions, but also the British, whose colonial system left traditional African rulers in place. These uprisings made Europeans uneasy. Why, they wondered, were Africans resisting regimes that had huge advantages in firepower and transport and that were bringing medical skills, literacy, and other fruits of European civilization? Some Europeans concluded that Africans were too stubborn or unsophisticated to appreciate Europe's generosity. Others, shocked by colonial cruelty, called for reform. A few radicals even demanded an end to imperialism.

The Anglo-Boer War The continent's most devastating anticolonial uprising occurred in South Africa. This unique struggle pitted two white communities against each other: the British in the Cape Colony and Natal against the Afrikaners, descendants of original Dutch settlers who lived in the Transvaal and the Orange Free State (see Map 18.2 inset). Although two white regimes were the main adversaries, the Anglo-Boer War (1899–1902) involved the area's 4 million black inhabitants as fully as its 1 million whites.

The war's origins lay in the discovery of gold in the Transvaal in the mid-1880s. As the area rapidly became Africa's richest state, the prospect that Afrikaner republics might become the powerhouse in southern Africa was more than British imperialists could accept. Fearing that war was inevitable, the president of the Transvaal launched a preemptive strike against the British. In late 1899, Afrikaner forces crossed into South Africa. Fighting a relentless guerrilla campaign, Afrikaners waged a war that would last three years and cost Britain 20,000 soldiers and £200 million.

In a frustrated effort to respond to Afrikaner hit-and-run tactics, the British instituted a terrifying innovation: the concentration camp. At one moment in the war, at least 155,000 captured men, women, and children were held in camps surrounded by barbed wire. The British rounded up Afrikaners and Africans, whom they feared would side with the "anticolonial" Dutch descendants. Ultimately, the British won the war, bringing the Transvaal and the Orange Free State—with their vast gold reserves—into their empire.

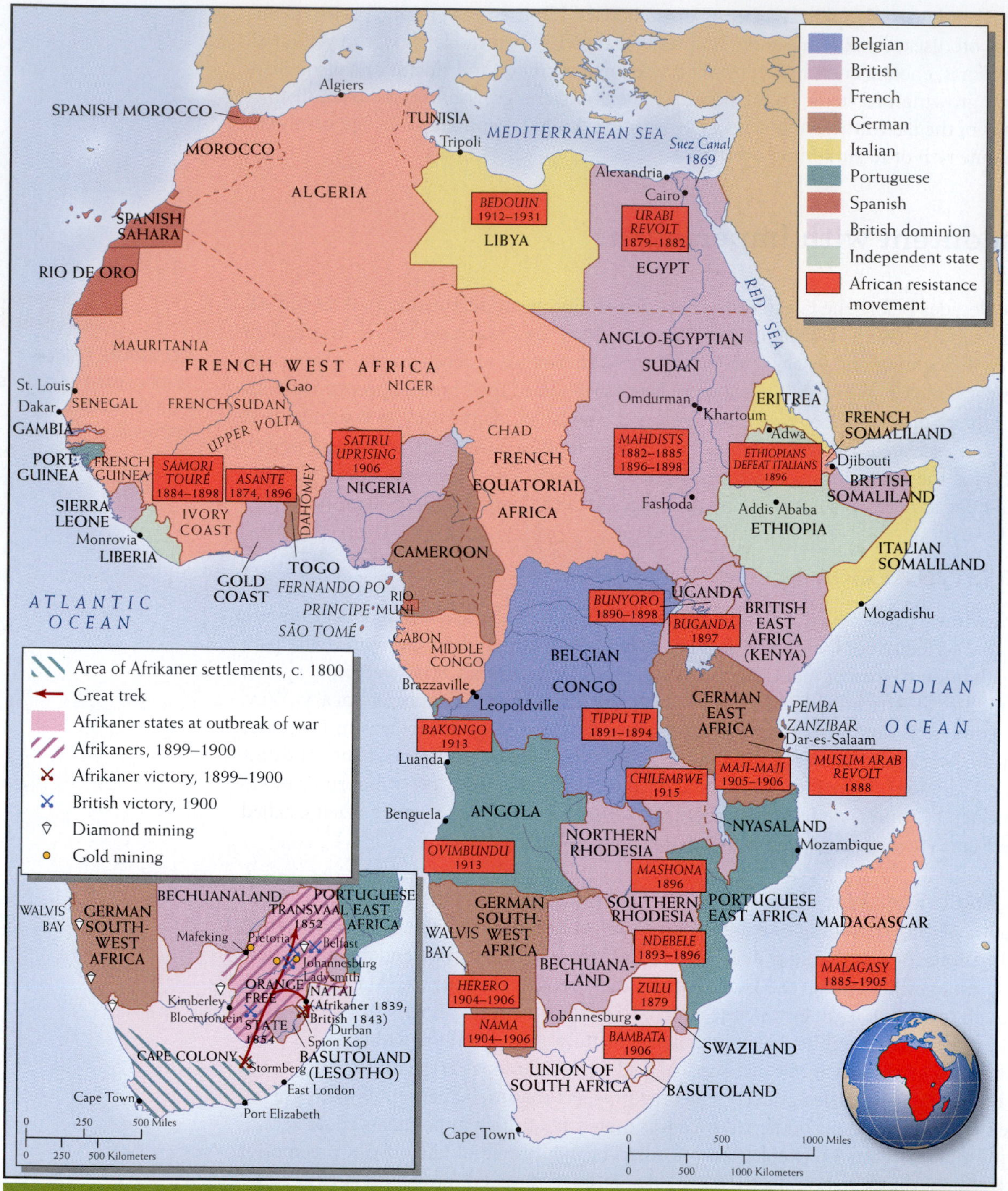

MAP 18.2 | Uprisings and Wars in Africa

The European partition and conquest of Africa were violent affairs.

- How many separate African resistance movements can you count on this map?
- Where was resistance the most prolonged?
- According to your reading, why were Ethiopians, who sustained their autonomy, able to do what other African opponents of European armies were not?

But the horrors of the war traumatized the British, who regarded themselves as Europe's most enlightened and efficient colonial rulers.

Other Struggles in Colonized Africa The disgust that some Europeans felt toward imperial violence deepened after Germany's activities in Africa also went brutally wrong. Germany had established colonies in Southwest Africa (present-day Namibia), Cameroon, and Togo in 1884 and in East Africa in 1885. In German Southwest Africa, the Herero and San people resisted the Germans, and in German East Africa (modern-day Tanzania), the Muslim Arab peoples rebelled. Between 1904 and 1906, fighting in German Southwest Africa escalated to such an extent that the German commander issued an extermination order against the Herero population.

Extermination of the Herero The Germans carried out a campaign of near-extermination against the Herero population in German Southwest Africa in 1904–1906. Nearly 90 percent of the Herero were killed.

According to those who favored European imperialism, however, the atrocities of the Boer War and German Southwest Africa, like the horrors of Leopold's Belgian Congo (see Chapter 17), were exceptions to what they considered their enlightened rule. Portraying Africans as either accepting subjects or childlike primitives—as in the Maji-Maji Revolt in German East Africa, described at the beginning of this chapter—Europeans redoubled their efforts to impose colonial order. The problem, in their view, was that they had not tried hard enough to bring civilization. In many cases, the number of officials stationed in the colonies increased.

THE BOXER UPRISING IN CHINA

Although not formally colonized, China too struggled against European intrusions. As the population swelled to over half a billion and outstripped the country's resources, problems of landlessness, poverty, and peasant discontent (long-standing concerns in China's modern history) left the established order vulnerable to internal revolts and foreign intervention.

The breakdown of dynastic authority originated largely with foreign pressure. For one thing, China's defeat in the Sino-Japanese War of 1894–1895 (see Chapter 17) was deeply humiliating. Japan acquired Taiwan as its first major colony, and European powers demanded that the weakened Qing government grant them specific areas within China as their respective "spheres of influence" (see Map 18.3). The United States argued instead for maintaining an "open door" policy in China that would keep access available to all traders, while supporting missionary efforts to spread Christianity.

Unrest and Revolt The most explosive reaction to these pressures, the **Boxer Uprising**, started within the peasantry. Like colonized peoples in Africa, the Boxers violently resisted European meddling. And like the Taiping Rebellion decades earlier (see Chapter 16), the story of the Boxers was tied to missionary activities. Whereas in earlier centuries Jesuit missionaries had sought to convert the court and the elites, by the mid-nineteenth century the missionary goal was to convert commoners. After the Taiping Rebellion, Christian missionaries had streamed into China, impatient to make new converts in the hinterlands and confident of their governments' backing.

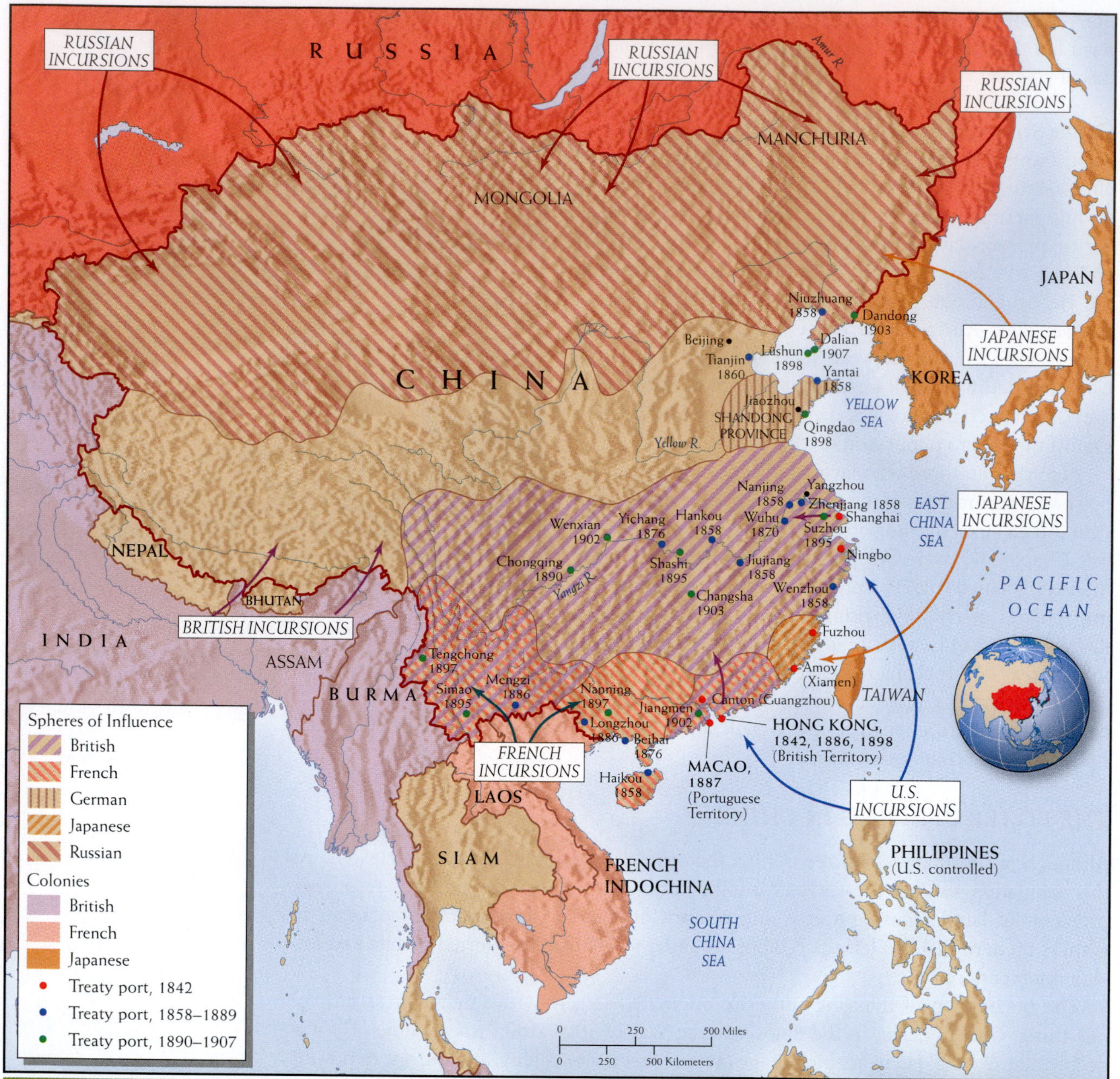

MAP 18.3 | Foreign Spheres of Influence in China, 1842–1907

While technically independent, the Qing dynasty could not prevent foreign penetration and domination of its economy during the nineteenth century.

- Which five powers established spheres of influence in China?
- At what time was the greatest number of treaty ports established?
- According to your reading, what did the foreign powers hope to achieve within their spheres of influence? What kinds of local opposition did the foreign influence inspire?

The Boxers rejected claims of Western superiority. Especially in regions suffering from natural disasters and economic hardship, activists provided assistance to the dispossessed. Women played a prominent role. The so-called Red Lanterns were mostly teenage girls and unmarried women who announced their loyalty by wearing red

The Boxer Uprising in China The Boxer Uprising was eventually suppressed by a foreign army made up of Japanese, European, and American troops that arrived in Beijing in August 1900. The picture here shows fighting between the foreign troops and the combined forces of Qing soldiers and the Boxers. After a period of indecision, the Qing court, against the advice of some of its officials, finally threw its support behind the struggle of the Boxers against the foreign presence, laying the ground for the military intervention of the imperialist powers.

garments. Although segregated from the male Boxers—Red Lanterns worshipped at their own altars and practiced martial arts at separate boxing grounds—they were important to the movement in counteracting the influence of Christian women. Indeed, one of the Boxers' greatest fears was that cunning Christian women would use their guile to weaken the Boxers' spirits. They claimed that the "purity" of the Red Lanterns could counter this threat. The Red Lanterns were supposedly capable of incredible feats: they could walk on water or fly through the air. Belief in their magical powers provided critical assistance for the uprising.

As the movement gained momentum, the Qing vacillated between viewing the Boxers as a threat to order and embracing them as a force to check foreign intrusion. Early in 1900, Qing troops clashed with the Boxers in an escalating cycle of violence. By spring, however, the Qing could no longer control the tens of thousands of Boxers roaming the vicinities of Beijing and Tianjin. Embracing the Boxers' cause, the empress dowager declared war against the foreign powers in June 1900.

Acting without any discernible plan or leadership, the Boxers attacked Christian and foreign symbols and persons. They harassed and sometimes killed Chinese Christians in parts of northern China, destroyed railroad tracks and telegraph lines, and attacked owners of foreign objects such as lamps and clocks. In Beijing, the Boxers besieged foreign embassy compounds where diplomats and their families cowered in fear. The Boxers also reduced the Southern Cathedral to ruins and then besieged the Northern Cathedral, where more than 3,000 Catholics and 40 French and Italian marines had sought refuge.

Foreign Involvement and Aftermath In August 1900, a foreign army of 20,000 troops crushed the Boxers. About half came from Japan; the rest came primarily from Russia, Britain, Germany, France, and the United States. Thereafter, the victors forced the Chinese to sign the punitive Boxer Protocol. It required the regime to pay an exorbitant compensation in gold (about twice the empire's annual income) for damages to foreign life and property. The protocol also authorized western powers to station troops in Beijing.

Even in defeat, the Boxers' antiwestern uprising showed how much had changed in China since the Taiping Rebellion. Although the Boxers were primarily peasants, even they had felt the unsettledness generated by European inroads into China. Indeed, the Europeans' commercial and spiritual reach, once confined to elites and port cities, had extended across much of China. Whereas the Taiping Rebellion had mobilized millions against the Qing, the Boxers remained loyal to the dynasty and focused their wrath on foreigners and Chinese Christians. The Boxer Rebellion, like the Maji-Maji Revolt in East Africa, revealed the widespread political opposition to westernization and the willingness of disaffected populations to resist western programs.

Worldwide Insecurities

COMPARISON

IDENTIFY and **DESCRIBE** political, economic, and social crises that swept through the world in this period, and **ANALYZE** the impact they had on different regions of the world.

While news of unrest in the distant colonies and in China generally did not lead Europeans to question their ways, conflicts closer to home tore at European confidence in this era. The rise of a European-centered world deepened rivalries within Europe. Numerous factors fostered conflict, including France's smoldering resentment at its defeat in the Franco-Prussian War (see Chapter 17), and led to a buildup of military forces, especially in Britain, Germany, and France. Tensions also increased as the European states competed for raw materials and colonial footholds. Not everyone, however, supported vast expenditures on the military. Many Europeans disapproved of spending on massive steam-powered warships. Others warned that the arms race would end in a devastating war. At the same time, the booms and busts of expanding industrial economies, challenges about the proper roles of women, and problems of uncontrolled urbanization shook the established order and had an impact across the globe (see again Map 18.1). These changes and insecurities transformed Europe and swept through the world.

FINANCIAL, INDUSTRIAL, AND TECHNOLOGICAL CHANGE

Economic developments helped make powers "great," but they could also unsettle societies. Indeed, pride about wealth and growth coincided with laments about changes in national and international economies. To begin with, Americans and Europeans recognized that the small-scale, laissez-faire capitalism championed by Adam Smith (see Chapter 14) was giving way to an economic order dominated by huge, heavily capitalized firms. Gone, it seemed, was Smith's vision of many small producers in vigorous competition with one another, all benefiting from efficient—but not exploitative—divisions of labor.

Instead of smooth progress, the economy of Europe and North America in the nineteenth century bounced between booms and busts: long-term business cycles of rapid growth followed by countercycles of stagnation. Late in the century, the pace of economic change accelerated. Large-scale steel production, railroad building, and textile manufacturing expanded at breakneck speed, while waves of bank closures, bankruptcies, and agricultural crises ruined many small property owners, including farmers. By the century's end, European and North American economies were dominated as never before by a few large-scale firms, such as John D. Rockefeller's Standard Oil and the large banking institutions in France, Britain, Germany, and the United States. The same was true in Japan, where *zaibatsu*—large companies with banking subsidiaries for finance and industrial wings dominating different sectors of the market—like Sumitomo, Mitsui, and Mitsubishi were the engine of Japan's extraordinary economic growth.

Financial Integration and Crises These were years of heady international financial integration. More and more countries joined the world system of borrowing and lending; more and more countries were linked financially through global loans and the fact that all of the major national currencies in the world, such as the American dollar, the British pound, and the French franc were exchanged at reliable rates. At the hub of this world system were the banks of London, which since the Napoleonic wars had been a major source of capital for international borrowers.

The rise of giant banks and huge industrial corporations caused alarm, for it seemed to signal an end to free markets and competitive capitalism. Rather than longing for the return of truly free markets, many critics sought reforms that would protect people from economic instability. The solution, many economists and politicians thought, was for the state to manage the national economies.

Banking especially seemed in need of closer government supervision. Many industrial societies already had central banks (banks that issued national currencies, fixed underlying interest rates, and in general controlled monetary policy); London's Bank of England had long since overseen local and international money markets. But governments did not have the resources to protect all—or even most—investments during times of crisis. Between 1890 and 1893, 550 American banks collapsed, and only the intervention of J. P. Morgan prevented the depletion of the nation's reserves of gold that stood behind the dollar.

The road to regulation of banking and finance, however, was hardly smooth. In 1907, a more serious crisis threatened. A panic on Wall Street led to a run on the banks. Once again, J. P. Morgan rescued the American economy from financial panic—by compelling financiers to commit unprecedented funds (eventually $35 million) to protect banks and trusts against depositors' panic. Morgan himself lost $21 million and emerged from the bank panic convinced that some sort of public oversight was needed. By 1913, the U.S. Congress ratified the Federal Reserve Act, creating boards to monitor the supply and demand of the nation's money. The crisis of 1907 also showed how national financial matters could quickly become international affairs as panicked American investors withdrew their funds from other countries, many of which relied on American capital.

Industrialization and the Modern Economy Backed by big banks, industrialists extended their enterprises to new places. For example, with loans from European investors, Russia built railways, telegraph lines, and factories. By 1900, Russia was producing half of the world's oil and a considerable amount of steel. Yet industrial development remained uneven: southern Europe and the American South continued to lag behind northern regions. The gap was even more pronounced in colonial territories, which contained few industrial enterprises aside from railroad building and mining.

By 1914, the factory and the railroad had become global symbols of the modern economy—and of its positive and negative effects. Everywhere, the coming of the railroad to one's town or village was a big event: for some, it represented an exhilarating leap into the modern world; for others, a terrifying abandonment of the past. Ocean liners, automobiles, and airplanes likewise could be both dazzling and disorienting.

For ordinary people, the new economy brought benefits and drawbacks. Factories produced cheaper goods, but they belched clouds of black smoke. Railways offered faster transport, but they ruined small towns unlucky enough to be left off the branch line. Machines (when operating properly) were more efficient than human and animal labor, but workers who used them felt reduced to machines themselves. Indeed, the American Frederick Winslow Taylor proposed a system of "scientific management" to make human bodies perform more like machines, maximizing the efficiency of workers' movements. But workers did not want to be managed or to cede control of the pace of production to employers. Labor's resistance to "Taylorization" led to numerous strikes. For strikers, as for those left out of the new economy, the course of progress had taken an unsettling turn.

THE "WOMAN QUESTION"

Complicating the situation was turmoil about the "woman question." In the West, female activists demanded that women be given more rights as citizens; more radical voices called for fundamental changes to the family and the larger society. At the same time, imperialists claimed that colonial rule was bringing great improvements to women in Asia and Africa. But the "woman question" was no more easily settled there than elsewhere.

Women's Issues in the West In western countries, for most of the nineteenth century, a belief in "separate spheres" had supposedly confined women to domestic matters, while leaving men in charge of public life and economic undertakings. (In practice, only women from middle- and upper-class families avoided working outside the home for wages.) However, as economic developments created new jobs for women and greater access to education, women increasingly found work as teachers, secretaries, typists, department store clerks, social workers, and telephone operators. These jobs offered greater economic and social independence. Some educated women spearheaded efforts to improve conditions for the urban poor and to expand the government's role in regulating economic affairs. Nonetheless much of the population continued to think that higher education and public activism were not suitable for women.

In one important change, many women began to assert control over reproduction. Although in numerous countries the use of contraceptive devices was illegal, women still found a variety of ways to limit the number of children they bore. In addition to marrying late and sleeping apart, some used spermicidal herbs, which sometimes worked but sometimes killed the woman; others relied a variety of sponges and other barriers; condoms; or insisted on the practice of *coitus interruptus* (withdrawal). When contraception failed, many women turned to abortion, even though it was illegal. Successful contraception, by whatever means, depended on cooperation and communication and tended to be more effective as educational levels increased.

Early in the twentieth century, the birthrate in America was half of what it had been a century before. By having fewer children, families could devote more income to education, food, housing, and leisure activities. Declining birthrates, along with improved medicine, also meant that fewer women died in childbirth; more would see their children reach adulthood.

Still, changes in women's social status did not translate into full political rights at the national level, such as the vote. By the mid-nineteenth century, women's suffrage movements had appeared in several countries, but these campaigns bore little immediate fruit. In 1868, women received the right to vote in local elections in Britain. Within a few years, Finland, Sweden, and some American states allowed single, property-owning women the right to cast ballots—again, only in local elections. Women obtained the right to vote in national elections in New Zealand in 1893, in Australia in 1902, in Finland in 1906, and in Norway in 1913.

Despite these gains, male alarmists portrayed women's suffrage and women's rights as the beginning of civilization's end. Among women, views on feminism varied. Most middle-class women in Europe and the Americas were not seeking to make women equal to men. Indeed, many bourgeois women recoiled from the close relationships between socialism and feminism. In Latin America, for example, anarchists championed a version of feminism arguing that the abolition of private property would liberate women from their misery and that the traditional family was a bourgeois convention. Other women feared becoming too "mannish," and a few worried that equality would destroy female sensuality. Most, probably, looked to reform less in terms of voting rights and more in terms of better treatment within families and local communities.

Women's Status in Colonies In the colonial world, the woman question was also a contentious issue—but it was mainly argued among men. European authorities liked to boast that colonial rule improved women's status. Citing examples of traditional societies' treatment of women, they criticized the veiling of women in Islamic societies, the binding of women's feet in China, widow burning (*sati*) in India, and female genital mutilation in Africa. Europeans believed that prohibiting such acts was a justification for colonial intervention.

And yet, colonialism only added to women's burdens. As male workers headed into the export economy, formerly shared agricultural work fell exclusively on women's shoulders. In Africa, for example, the opening of vast gold and diamond mines drew thousands of men away to work in the mines, leaving women to tend to the farmstead and to do colonial tasks that men once did. Similarly, the rise of European-owned agricultural estates in Kenya and Southern Rhodesia depleted surrounding villages of male family members, who went to work on the estates. In these circumstances, women kept the local, food-producing economy afloat.

Nor did colonial "civilizing" rhetoric improve women's political or cultural circumstances. In fact, European missionaries preached a message of domesticity to Asian and African families, emphasizing that women's place was in the home raising children and that women's education should be different from men's. Thus, males overwhelmingly dominated the new schools that Europeans built. Moreover, the chiefs who collaborated with colonial officials consistently favored men. As a result, African women often lost landholding and other rights that they had enjoyed before the Europeans' arrival.

CLASS CONFLICT

As capitalism's volatility shook confidence in free market economies and sharpened conflicts between classes, the tone of political debate was transformed as new voices called for radical change. Although living conditions for European and North American workers improved over time, widening inequalities in income and the slow pace of reform bred frustration. Most workers remained committed to peaceful agitation, but some radicals favored violence against the state and its agents.

Strikes and Revolts In the Americas and in Europe, radicals adopted numerous tactics for asserting the interests of the working class. In Europe, the franchise was gradually expanded in hopes that the lower classes would prefer voting to revolution—and indeed, most of the new political parties that catered to workers had no desire to overthrow the state. But conservatives feared them anyway, especially as they gained electoral clout. The Labour Party, founded in Britain in 1900, quickly boasted a large share of the vote. By 1912, the German Social Democratic Party was the largest party in the Reichstag though it lacked power since the Reichstag was only an advisory body. It was not the legally sanctioned parties that sparked violent street protests and strikes in the century's last decades. A whole array of **syndicalists** (labor activists), **anarchists** (who opposed government altogether), royalists, and socialists sprang up in this period, making work stoppages everyday affairs.

Although the United States had similar radical groups, they were few and small. Nonetheless, American workers were organizing. The labor movement's power burst forth

Labor Disputes The late nineteenth century witnessed a surge in industrial strife, worker strikes, and violent suppression of labor movements. (*Left*) One of the deadliest confrontations in the United States occurred in May 1892, when a strike against the Carnegie Steel Company escalated into a gunfight, which left ten dead and many more wounded. Here, a group of striking workers keeps watch over the steel mill in Homestead, Pennsylvania. (*Right*) Striking dockworkers rally in London's Trafalgar Square, 1911. By this time, residents of European cities were used to seeing crowds of protesters pressing for improved working conditions or political reform.

dramatically in 1894. Spawned by wage cuts and firings following an economic downturn, the Pullman strike (directed against the maker of railway sleeping cars, George Pullman) involved approximately 3 million workers. The strike's conclusion, however, revealed the enduring power of the status quo. After hiring replacement workers to break the strike, Pullman requested federal troops to protect his operation. After its leaders were jailed, the strike collapsed. Although strikes and protests in the United States and Europe often failed to achieve their immediate goals, they worried those in power and ultimately led to important changes.

Revolution in Mexico Perhaps the most successful turn-of-the-century revolution occurred in Mexico. This peasant uprising thoroughly transformed the country. Fueled by the unequal distribution of land and by disgruntled workers, the **Mexican Revolution** erupted in 1910 when political elites split over the succession of General Porfirio Díaz after decades of his strong-arm rule. Dissidents balked when Díaz refused to step down, and peasants and workers rallied to the call to arms.

From the north (led by the charismatic Pancho Villa) to the south (under the legendary Emiliano Zapata), peasants, farmers, and other rural workers helped topple the Díaz regime. In the name of providing land for farmers and ending oligarchic rule, peasant armies defeated Díaz's troops and proceeded to destroy many large estates. The fighting lasted for ten brutal years, during which almost 10 percent of the country's population perished.

Thereafter political leaders had to accept popular demands for democracy, respect for the sovereignty of peasant communities, and land reform. The revolution's most lasting legacy was perhaps the creation of rural communes for Mexico's peasantry. These communal village holdings, called *ejidos*, looked back to a precolonial heritage. The revolution spawned a set of new national myths based on the heroism of rural peoples, Mexican nationalism, and a celebration of the Aztec past.

Preserving Established Orders Although the Mexican Revolution succeeded in toppling the old elite, elsewhere in Latin America the ruling establishment remained united against assaults from below. Already, in 1897, the Brazilian army had mercilessly suppressed a peasant movement in the northeastern part of the country. Moreover, in Cuba, the Spanish and then the American armies crushed tenant farmers' efforts to reclaim land from sugar estates. In Guatemala, Mayan Indians lost land to coffee barons.

In Europe and the United States, the preservation of established orders did not rest on repression alone. Here, elites also grudgingly agreed to gradual change. Indeed, by the century's end, left-wing agitators, muckraking reporters, and middle-class reformers began to win meaningful social improvements. Unable to suppress the socialist movement, Otto von Bismarck, the German chancellor, defused the appeal of socialism by enacting social welfare measures in 1883–1884, insuring workers against illness, accidents, and old age and establishing maximum working hours. In the United States, it took lurid journalistic accounts of unsanitary practices in Chicago slaughterhouses (including tales of workers falling into lard vats and being rendered into cooking fat) to spur the federal government into action. (See **Current Trends in World History: Industrialization and Its Antidotes**.) In 1906, President Theodore Roosevelt signed a Meat Inspection Act that provided for government supervision of meatpacking operations. In other cases (banking, steel production, railroads), the federal government's enhanced supervisory authority served corporate interests as well.

These consumer and family protection measures reflected a broader reform movement, one dedicated to creating a more efficient society and correcting the undesirable consequences of urbanization and industrialization. At local and state levels, these **progressive reformers** attacked corrupt city governments that had allegedly fallen into the hands of immigrant-dominated "political machines." The progressives also attacked other vices, such as gambling, drinking, and prostitution—all associated with industrialized, urban settings. The creation of city parks preoccupied urban planners, who hoped parks' green spaces would serve as the city's "lungs" and offer healthier forms of entertainment than houses of prostitution, gambling dens, and bars. From Scandinavia to California, the proponents of old-age pensions and public ownership of utilities put pressure on lawmakers. Thousands of associations took shape against capitalism's harsher effects, and they occasionally succeeded in changing state policies. Indeed, the period leading up to World War I was one of rapid change, in which financial crises reverberated across the globe, European and American women pressed for their rights and also agitated for the rights of Asian and African women, and elites were forced to make reforms, though they tended to be limited, in the colonial and colonializers' worlds.

Cultural Modernism

As revolutionaries and reformers wrestled with the problems of progress, intellectuals, artists, and scientists struggled to make sense of change in their own societies and beyond. What we call **modernism**—the sense of having broken with tradition—came to prominence in many fields, from physics to architecture, from painting to the social sciences.

COMPARISON

EXPLAIN how European modernism drew on Afro-Asian influences and represented uncertainty about ideas inherited from the Enlightenment.

Current Trends in World History

Industrialization and Its Antidotes: Conservation and Regulation

As the impact of industrialization spread during the late nineteenth century, a few individuals, including those who championed rapid economic development, recognized that this progress brought unwanted consequences. A new awareness dawned that while industrialization allowed production to increase dramatically, it also resulted in the depletion of natural resources and the degradation of the quality of life for humans. Awakened to the ecological costs of economic progress, these environmentalist pioneers tried to reverse a trend, which we have highlighted throughout this study, of humankind's growing tendency to pollute the environment, overgraze marginal areas, and exploit resources to their exhaustion.

One of the first world leaders to take seriously industrialization's threats to the environment—and to national character—was President Theodore Roosevelt. A man who delighted in hunting, riding, and testing himself against the elements, Roosevelt worried that as the United States became an increasingly industrialized and urbanized society, the American people would lose the courage, the fitness, and the "rugged individualism" that the taming of wildernesses had supposedly imbued in them. In understanding the problem and formulating a response to it, he was especially struck by George Perkins Marsh's 1864 Man and Nature, which explored the ways in which the use and depletion of forests and other natural resources had determined the rise and fall of civilizations around the ancient Mediterranean. If the United States failed to curb its destruction of woodlands, that book suggested, it faced a collapse similar to Greece and Rome. Although several "national" parks and forests had been founded before Roosevelt became U.S. president in 1901, he was extremely active in pushing forward legislation to conserve more land, especially in the west. By offering visitors the opportunity to experience wilderness conditions, the national parks were to provide a partial antidote to what Roosevelt saw as the effeminizing tendencies of modern society.

In setting aside lands as national forests and parks, Roosevelt wanted to prevent what he feared might be the degeneration of the American character. But Roosevelt had other objects in view too in pressing the state to take a more activist role in the economy. Noting that on the European continent, "progressives" and urban-based reformers were augmenting the reach and power of the state to combat economic inequalities and to build infrastructures that benefited all, Roosevelt pushed for a departure from the laissez-faire principles that had dominated American political-economic discourse in the last decades of the nineteenth century. With European state-funded projects like the straightening of the Rhine River in mind, Roosevelt argued that the state should itself tackle projects that were too large to be built by private enterprises.

In yet another area, Roosevelt created a national, regulatory solution to a problem that the market could not solve by itself. In the decade or so before he came into office, newspaper reporters had exposed hundreds of schemes by sellers of home remedies such as Mrs. Winslow's Soothing Syrup to get rich by promising consumers that their "patent" medicines would cure any disease. In truth, many of these "medicines" contained alcohol, cocaine, or just cod-liver oil; some were

Modernist movements were notably international. Egyptian social scientists read the works of European thinkers, while French and German painters flocked to museums to inspect artifacts from Egypt and artworks from other parts of Africa, Asia, and Oceania. As education spread and political reforms enfranchised more Americans and Europeans, changes in the meaning of culture occurred, causing it to be less elitist and more popular. Yet European elites did not give up their opera houses and paintings in favor of arts and entertainments that were appealing to urban workers or colonized peoples. Instead, the arts became more abstract: musicians abandoned the comfort of harmonic and diatonic sound (the eight-tone scale standard in classical western music at the time); writers and visual artists left realistic representation behind.

Above all, modernism in arts and sciences replaced the certainties of the Enlightenment with the unsettledness of the new age. Modernists challenged claims to provide complete, coherent explanations and representations of all kinds. With growing doubts harmful, others were simply useless. Other investigators, such as the novelist Upton Sinclair, exposed horrors in the meatpacking industry. Sinclair's realist novel, *The Jungle* (1906), for example, contained reports of extremely unsanitary workplace conditions and of workers falling into fat-rendering machines and being canned along with the beef. In the same year that Sinclair's hugely influential novel appeared, Roosevelt oversaw the creation of the Food and Drug Administration and the passage of the Pure Food and Drug Act. The FDA's charge was to implement this act, and to look after public health—something that did not concern profit-hungry corporations—by regulating food and medicines against contamination. In the wake of the banking panic of 1907 (see Financial Integration and Crises, p. 689), too, Americans came to accept that they needed banking regulations as well, and in 1913 Congress enacted the Federal Reserve Act. Americans were not alone in beginning to temper capitalism with regulation, and industrialization with conservation. Europeans at last began to enact legislation to protect workers from dangerous workplaces and to create large green spaces in cities so that the industrialized world might have "lungs" with which to breathe. In Argentina, many were drawn to mountainous regions to escape becoming too "soft" in urban surroundings, and a conservationist movement began that would hit its stride in the 1930s. Although such developments only moderated—slightly—the industrialized world's contributions to environmental degradation and the exploitation of mass consumers, they did signal the reality that some, at least, had begun to recognize that progress, too, had its price.

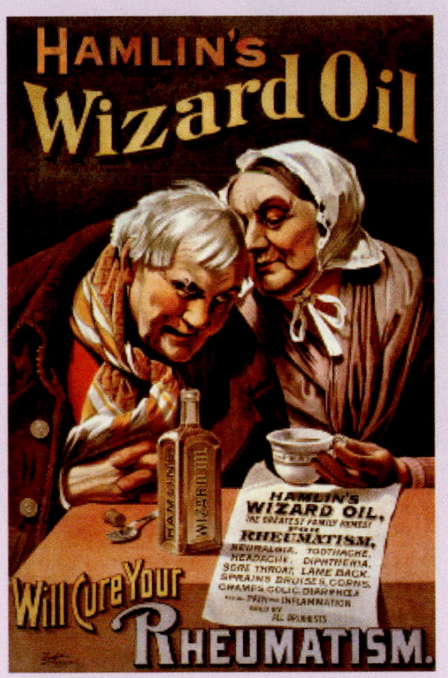

Patent Medicines Like Mrs. Winslow's Soothing Syrup, Hamlin's Wizard Oil claimed to cure anything from headaches to cancer, in humans and animals alike.

QUESTION FOR ANALYSIS

- Who benefited from Roosevelt's national parks and the Pure Food and Drug Act? Who may have suffered from these regulations?
- Roosevelt considered courage, fitness, and "rugged individualism" vital to the American identity. Why did he choose these traits specifically, and are these traits as vital today? Explain.

Explore Further

Douglas Brinkley, *Wilderness Warrior: Theodore Roosevelt and the Crusade to Save America* (2010).

Edmund Morris, *Theodore Rex* (2002).

about civilizing missions or urban and industrial "progress," artists and scientists struggled to understand a world in which human reason seamed inadequate.

POPULAR CULTURE COMES OF AGE

From the late eighteenth to the late nineteenth century, production and consumption of the arts, books, music, and sports changed dramatically. The change derived mainly from new urban settings, technological innovations, mass education, and increased leisure time. Middle-class art lovers eagerly purchased mass-produced engravings; millions attended dance halls and vaudeville shows (entertainment by singers, dancers, and comedians). For the first time, sports attracted mass followings. Soccer in Europe, baseball in the United States, and cricket in India had wildly devoted middle- and working-class fans. Thus did a truly **popular culture** emerge, delivering affordable and accessible forms of art and entertainment to "the masses."

Impressionism was an artistic movement, radical in its day, which emerged in Paris in the last third of the nineteenth century. Its members broke away from the conventional art community and its official, academic salons. With small, visible brushstrokes, the impressionists stressed the changing qualities of light, the passage of time, and movement. Rather than compete with photography and present a facsimile of a stable, static, coherent external reality, they sought to capture perceptions of a world in rapid flux. These two paintings, Claude Monet's *The Gare St-Lazare* (*left*) and Camille Pissarro's *Sunset over the Boieldieu Bridge at Rouen* (*right*), exemplify the impressionists' ambivalent view of nineteenth-century progress.

By the nineteenth century's close, the press stood as a major form of popular entertainment and information. This was partly because publishers were offering different wares to different classes of readers and partly because many more people could read, especially in Europe and the Americas. By that time, the English *Daily Mail* and the French *Petit Parisien* boasted circulations of over 1 million. In the United States, urban dwellers, many of them immigrants, avidly read newspapers—some in English, others in their native languages. Banner headlines, sensational stories, and simple language drew in readers with little education or poor English skills.

By now the kind of culture one consumed had become a reflection of one's real (or desired) status in society. For many Latin American workers, for example, reading one's own newspaper or comic strip was part of being a worker. Argentina's socialist newspaper, *La Vanguardia*, was one of Buenos Aires's most prominent periodicals, read and debated at work and in the cafés of working-class neighborhoods. Anyone seen reading the bourgeois paper, *La Prensa*, faced heckling and ridicule by fellow workers. As the community of cultural consumers broadened, and as ideas from across the globe flooded in, writers, artists, and scholars struggled to adapt.

MODERNISM IN EUROPEAN CULTURE

In intellectual and artistic terms, Europe at the turn of the twentieth century experienced perhaps its richest age since the Renaissance. Artists' work reflected their doubts about the modern world, as represented by the railroad, the big city, and the factory. While the artists and writers of the mid-nineteenth century had largely celebrated progress, the painters and novelists of the century's end took a darker view. They turned away from reason, which the Enlightenment had championed, and descriptive prose as they searched for meanings that came from instinct and emotion. The primitive came to symbolize both Europe's lost innocence and the forces that reason could not control, such as sexual drives, religious fervor, or brute strength.

New Forms of Subjectivity Jean-Auguste-Dominique Ingres, one of the great realist artists of the nineteenth century, was one of Pablo Picasso's idols. The portrait of the newspaper baron Louis-François Bertin (*left*) embodies the artist's confidence in his own ability to represent an external reality just as it appears. Picasso refined his technique by copying Ingres's works at the Louvre. He clearly used Ingres as a model for his 1910 portrait of his own art dealer, Ambroise Vollard (*right*), which built on the work of the impressionists, in an effort to challenge the two-dimensional realism of his master.

Europeans began to see the world in a fundamentally different way, aided by the experience of nonwestern visual arts. The painter who led the way in incorporating nonwestern themes into modern art was Pablo Picasso (1881–1973), who found in African art forms a radically new way of expressing human sentiments that was shocking to most European and American observers. Other artists were inspired by the sleekness and syncopation of machines, or by the irrational content of dreams. And painting was not the only art form that displayed a modern style. Arnold Schönberg (1874–1951) composed the first piece of music that rejected traditional western tonality. World-famous dancers like Isadora Duncan (1877–1927) pioneered the expressive, free-form movements that laid the foundations for modern dance.

However, the arts alone did not undermine older views of the world. Even science, in which the Enlightenment had placed so much faith, challenged the idea that the world functioned according to easily understood natural laws. After 1900, pioneering physicists and mathematicians like Albert Einstein (1879–1955) challenged the idea that a single scientific theory, like Newton's, could explain everything. They took apart the Enlightenment's conviction that man could achieve full knowledge of, and control over, nature. In a series of papers published between 1905 and 1915, Einstein worked out the special and general theories of relativity, which demonstrated that measurements of speed and gravitational pull were not purely objective, but always conditioned by the relative position and conditions of the observer. Although most scientists continued to collect data, feeling certain that they could plumb nature's depths, some of their colleagues began to question the arrogance of this view.

From the time of the Enlightenment, Europeans had prided themselves in their "reason." To be rational was to be civilized and to master irrational urges; respectable, middle-class nineteenth-century men were thought to embody these virtues. But in the late nineteenth century, faith in rationality began to falter. Perhaps reason was *not* man's highest attainment, said some; perhaps reason was impossible for man to sustain, said others. Friedrich Nietzsche (1844–1900) claimed that conventional European attempts to assert The Truth—including science and Judeo-Christian moral codes—were nothing more than life-destroying quests for power. Sigmund Freud (1856–1939) began to excavate layers of the human subconscious, where irrational desires and fears lay buried. For Freud, human nature was not as simple as it had seemed to Enlightenment thinkers. Instead, he asserted, humans were driven by sexual longings and childhood traumas. Neither Nietzsche nor Freud was well loved among nineteenth-century liberal elites. But in the new century, Nietzsche would become the prophet for many antiliberal causes, from nudism to Nazism; and Freud's dark vision would become central to the twentieth century's understanding of the self.

CULTURAL MODERNISM IN CHINA

What it meant to be modern sparked debate beyond western Europe. Europeans provided one set of answers; thinkers elsewhere offered quite different answers. Chinese artists and scientists at the turn of the century selectively engaged western ideas and transformed them. Indeed, some scholars have described the late Qing period as a time of competing cultural *modernities*, in contrast to the post-Qing era, which pursued a single, western-oriented *modernity*. These forms of modernity involved critical reflection on Chinese traditions and mixed reactions to Western culture.

As in the West, Chinese writers now had a wider readership. By the late nineteenth century, more than 170 presses in China were serving a potential readership of 2 to 4 million concentrated mostly in the urban areas. These cities were more economically and culturally vibrant than the hinterlands. Not only was there an expanding body of readers, but newly rich beneficiaries of the treaty-port economy now patronized the arts.

Painters from the lower Yangzi region, collectively known as the **Shanghai School**, adopted elements from both indigenous and foreign sources. Although classically trained, they appropriated new western techniques into their art.

Similarly, fantasy novels drew on both western science and indigenous supernatural beliefs. Some experimental writers explicitly addressed Chinese–western relations. Depicting China at war with western powers, the novel *New Era* (1908) celebrated conventional military themes but also introduced western inventions such as electricity-repellent clothing and bulletproof satin.

Although steamships, telegraphs, and railroads captured public attention, there was little interest in changing fundamental Chinese beliefs. Indeed, even as Chinese intellectuals recognized new modes of knowledge, many of the elite insisted that Chinese learning remain the principal source of all knowledge. What kind of balance should exist between western thought and Chinese learning, or even whether the ancient classics should keep their fundamental role, was an issue that would haunt generations to come. In this respect, the Chinese dilemma reflected a worldwide challenge to accepting the impulses of modernism.

Modernism arose at a time when intellectuals began to question the values that had sustained Europe and North America throughout most of the nineteenth century. It reflected discontent with industrialization, income inequality, and colonial repression. Even though modernism had its origins and most profound impact in Europe, in many ways, especially in art, it drew upon nonwestern traditions and spread its influence throughout Asia and Africa among the educated classes.

Rethinking Race and Reimagining Nations

Ironically, at this time of huge population transfers and shared technological modernization, many European and American elites embraced the idea that the identities of peoples and nations were deeply rooted and unchangeable and were based on physical and cultural characteristics. By the century's close, racial roots had become a crucial part of identity. People wanted to know who they (and their neighbors) were—especially in terms of *biological* ancestry. Now the idea of inheritance took on new weight, in both cultural and biological forms. Nationalists spoke of the uniqueness of the Slavic soul, the German mind, Hindu spirituality, the Hispanic race.

COMPARISON

EVALUATE the ways in which race, nation, and religion unified populations but also made societies more difficult to govern.

Nationalist and racial ideas were different in different parts of the world. In Europe and America, debates about race and national purity reflected several concerns: above all, fear of being overrun by the brown, black, and yellow peoples beyond the borders of "civilization." By contrast, in India these ideas were part of the anticolonial debate, and they helped to mobilize people politically. This was also the case in China, Latin America, and the Islamic world, where discussions of identity went hand in hand with opposition to western domination and corrupt indigenous elites.

As we will see, these new impulses produced a variety of national movements, from China's anti-Qing campaign to India's Swadeshi movement. At the same time, pan-ethnic movements looked beyond the nation-state, envisioning communities based on ethnicity. Behind these movements was the notion that political communities should be built on racial purity.

NATION AND RACE IN NORTH AMERICA AND EUROPE

Americans and Europeans greeted the end of the century with a combination of pride and pessimism, and this mood influenced attitudes about national identity, race, and religion. In the early 1890s, for example, Americans flocked to extravagant commemorations of the four-hundredth anniversary of Christopher Columbus's discovery. Yet, at the same time, Americans—like many Europeans—feared for their future.

Regulating the Environment and Immigration Americans especially worried that the United States had exhausted its supposedly infinite supply of new land and resources—as evidenced by the disappearance of the buffalo, the erosion of soils, and the depletion of timber stands by aggressive logging companies. Conservationists' alarm grew more intense with the Census Bureau's 1890 announcement that the American frontier had "closed." When Theodore Roosevelt became president of the United States in 1901, he translated concerns about conserving natural resources into government policy. The market, insisted Roosevelt and like-minded conservationists, could not be trusted to protect "nature." Instead, federal regulation was necessary. This led to the creation in 1905 of the National Forest Service to manage the development of millions of acres of permanent public lands.

Another issue troubled the Americans: the need to maintain the dominance of persons of European descent. As a result, the government initiated new forms of racial discrimination where old forms (like slavery) had broken down. In the American West, animosity toward Chinese workers led to the 1882 Exclusion Act, which prohibited almost all immigration from China. In the American South, where most of the nation's 7 million African Americans resided, a system of "Jim Crow" laws upheld racial segregation and inequality.

Americans from western Europe grew even more anxious as throngs of "swarthy" immigrants entered the United States from southern and eastern Europe. Even more threatening were darker peoples who were colonial subjects in the Philippines, Puerto Rico, and Cuba. Talk of the end of white America fueled support for more restrictive immigration policies.

Across the North Atlantic, European elites engaged in similar discussions. For them, the final divvying up of Africa was in many respects equivalent to the closing of the American frontier. The Germans and Italians, in particular, complained about the lack of new territories on which to plant their flags. The French and British, by contrast, worried about how to preserve their overseas empires in a period of intense international competition.

New Social Issues in Europe Darwinist theory provoked new anxieties about inherited diseases, racial mixing, and the dying out of white "civilizers." Sexual relations between European colonizers and indigenous women—and their mixed offspring—had always been a part of European expansionism, but as racial identities hardened, many saw racial mixing as harmful to the supposedly superior white races. In addition, medical attention focused on homosexuality, regarding it as a disease and a threat to civilization.

Some people debated whether Jews—defined by religious practice or, increasingly, by ethnicity—could be fully assimilated into European society. Even though Jews had gained rights as citizens in most European countries by the late nineteenth century, powerful prejudices persisted. In the 1880s and 1890s, violent attacks known as pogroms, often involving police complicity, targeted the large Jewish populations in the Russian Empire's western territories and pushed the persecuted farther westward. These emigrants' presence, in turn, stirred up fear and resentment, especially in Austria, Germany, and France. Rumors circulated about Jewish bankers' conspiratorial powers, and anxieties over the "pollution" of the European races became widespread.

RACE-MIXING AND THE PROBLEM OF NATIONHOOD IN LATIN AMERICA

In Latin America, debates about identity chiefly addressed ethnic intermixing and the legacy of a system of government that, unlike much of the North Atlantic world, excluded rather than included most people. Social hierarchies reaching back to the sixteenth century ranked whites born in Spain and Portugal at the top, creole elites in the middle, and indigenous and African populations at the bottom. Thus, the higher on the social ladder, the more likely people were to be white.

Contested Mixtures and Invented Traditions "Mixing" did not lead to a shared heritage. Nor did it necessarily lead to homogeneity. In fact, the "racial" order did not stick, since some Iberians occupied the lower ranks, while a few people of color managed to ascend the social ladder. Moreover, starting in the 1880s, the racial hierarchy saw further disruption by the deluge of poor European immigrants; they flooded into prospering Latin American countrysides or into booming cities like Buenos Aires in Argentina and São Paulo in Brazil. Latin American societies, then, did not easily become homogeneous "nations."

Latin American leaders began to exalt bygone glories as a way to promote national identity and foster unity. Inventing successful myths could make a government seem

Diego Rivera's History of Mexico This is one of the most famous works of Mexican art, a portrait of the history of Mexico by the radical nationalist painter Diego Rivera. In this chapter, and in previous chapters, we have shown parts of this mural. In stepping back to view the whole work, which is in the National Palace in Mexico City, we can see how Rivera envisioned the history of his people generally. Completed in 1935, this work seeks to show a people fighting constantly against outside aggressors, from their glorious preconquest days (lower center), winding like a grand epic through the conquest, colonial exploitation, the revolution for independence, nineteenth-century invasions from France and the United States, to the popular 1910 revolution. It culminates in an image of Karl Marx, framed by a "scientific sun"—pointing to a future of progress and prosperity for all, as if restoring a modern Tenochtitlán of the Aztecs. This work captured many Mexicans' efforts to return to the indigenous roots of the nation and to fuse them with modern scientific ideas.

more legitimate—as the heir to a rightful struggle of the past. In Mexico, many parades celebrated Aztec grandeur, thereby creating a mythic arc from the greatness of the Aztec past to the triumphal story of Mexican independence. As the government glorified the Aztecs with pageants, statues, and pavilions, however, it continued to ignore modern Aztec descendants, who lived in squalor. Thus, race in Latin America was a more fluid category than it was in North America and Europe.

SUN YAT-SEN AND THE MAKING OF A CHINESE NATION

Just as Latin Americans celebrated their past, Chinese writers emphasized the power and depth of Chinese culture—in contrast to the Qing Empire's failing political and social strength. Here, writers used race to emphasize the superiority of the Han Chinese. Here, too, the pace of change generated a desire to trace one's roots back to secure foundations. Moreover, traditions were reinvented in the hope of saving Chinese culture threatened by modernity.

Among those who thought most intensely about the future of China was **Sun Yat-sen** (1866–1925), whose life story symbolized the challenge of nation building. Sun was part of an emerging generation of critics of the old regime. Like his European counterparts, Sun dreamed of a political community reshaped along national lines. Born into a modest rural household in southern China, he studied medicine in the British colony of Hong Kong and then turned to politics during the Sino-Japanese War. When the Qing government rejected his offer of service to the Chinese cause, he became convinced that China's rulers were out of touch with the times. Subsequently he established an organization based in Hawaii to advocate the Qing downfall and the cause of republicanism. The cornerstone of his message was Chinese—specifically, Han—nationalism. Sun blasted the feeble rule by outsiders, the Manchus, and trumpeted a sovereign political community of "true" Chinese.

Replacing the Qing and Reconstituting a Nation Realizing that reforms were necessary, the Manchu court began overhauling the administrative system and the military in the aftermath of the Boxer Uprising. Yet these changes came too late. The old elites grumbled, and the new class of urban merchants, entrepreneurs, and professionals (who often benefited from business with westerners) regarded the government as outmoded. Peasants and laborers resented the high cost of the reforms, which seemed to help only the rulers.

A mutiny, sparked in part by the government's nationalization of railroads and its low compensation to native Chinese investors, broke out in the city of Wuchang in central China in 1911. As it spread to other parts of the country, Sun Yat-sen hurried home from traveling in the United States. Few people rallied to the emperor's cause, and the Qing dynasty collapsed—an abrupt end to a dynastic tradition of more than 2,000 years.

China was soon be reconstituted, and Sun's ideas, especially those regarding race, played a central role. The original flag of the republic, for example, consisted of five colors representing the citizenry's major racial groups: red for the Han, yellow for the Manchus, blue for the Mongols, white for the Tibetans, and black for the Muslims. But Sun had reservations about this multiracial flag, believing there should be only one Chinese race. The existence of different groups in China, he argued, was the result of incomplete assimilation—a problem that the modern nation now had to confront.

NATIONALISM AND INVENTED TRADITIONS IN INDIA

British imperial rule persisted in India, but the turn of the century saw cracks in its stranglehold. Four strands had woven the territory together: the consolidation of colonial administration, the establishment of railways and telegraphs, the growth of western education and ideas, and the development of colonial capitalism. Now it was possible to speak of India as a single unit. It was also possible for anticolonial thinkers to imagine seizing and ruling India by themselves. Thus a new form of resistance emerged, different from peasant rebellions of the past. Now, dissenters talked of Indians as "a people" who had both a national past and national traditions.

A Modernizing Elite Leaders of the nationalist opposition were western-educated intellectuals from colonial cities and towns. Although a tiny minority of the Indian population, they gained influence through their access to the official world and their familiarity with European knowledge and history. This elite group used their knowledge to develop modern cultural forms. For example, they turned colloquial languages (such as Hindi, Urdu, Bengali, Tamil, and Malayalam) into standardized, literary forms for writing novels and dramas. Now the publication of journals, magazines, newspapers, pamphlets, novels, and dramas surged, facilitating communication throughout British India.

Along with print culture came a growing public sphere where intellectuals debated social and political matters. By 1885, voluntary associations in big cities had united to establish a political party, the Indian National Congress. Lawyers, prominent merchants, and local notables dominated its early leadership. The congress demanded greater representation of Indians in administrative and legislative bodies, criticized the government's economic policies, and encouraged India's industrialization.

Underlying this political nationalism, embodied by the Indian National Congress, was cultural nationalism. The nationalists claimed that Indians might not be a single race but were at least a unified people, because of their unique culture and common colonial history.

Rewriting Traditions The recovery of traditions became a way to establish a modern Indian identity without acknowledging the recent subjugation by British colonizers. So Indian intellectuals (like those in Latin America) turned to the past and rewrote the histories of ancient empires and kingdoms. In this way, Indian intellectuals promoted the idea of India as a nation-state.

To portray Indians as a people with a unifying religious creed, intellectuals reconfigured Hinduism so that it resembled western religion. This was no easy task, for traditional Hinduism did not have a supreme textual authority, like the Bible or the Quran, a monotheistic God, an organized church, or an established creed. Nonetheless, nationalist Hindu intellectuals combined various philosophical texts, cultural beliefs, social practices, and Hindu traditions into a mix that they labeled the authentic Hindu religion. While fashioning hybrid forms, revivalists also narrowed the definition of Indian traditions. As Hindu intellectuals looked back, they identified Hindu traditions and the pre-Islamic past as the only sources of India's culture. Other contributors to the region's mosaic past were forgotten; the Muslim past, in particular, had no prominent role.

Hindu Revivalism Hindu revivalism became a powerful political force in the late nineteenth century, when the nationalist challenge to the colonial regime took a militant turn. New leaders rejected constitutionalism and called for militant agitation. The British decision to partition Bengal in 1905 into two provinces—one predominantly Muslim, the other Hindu—drew militants into the streets to urge the boycott of British goods. Rabindranath Tagore, a famous Bengali poet and future Nobel laureate, composed stirring nationalist poetry. Activists formed voluntary organizations, called Swadeshi ("one's own country") Samitis, which championed indigenous enterprises for manufacturing soap, cloth, medicine, iron, and paper, as well as schools for imparting nationalist education. Although few of these ventures succeeded, the efforts reflected the nationalist desire to assert Indians' autonomy as a people.

Unlike the insurgents of 1857, nationalist leaders in India at the turn of the twentieth century imagined a modern national community. Invoking religious and ethnic symbols, they formed modern political associations to operate in a national public arena. They did not seek a radical alternative to the colonial order; instead, they fought for the political rights of Indians as a secular, national community. In these new nationalists, British rulers discovered an enemy not so different from themselves.

THE PAN MOVEMENTS

India and China were not the only places where activists dreamed of founding new states. Across the globe, groups had begun to imagine new communities based on ethnicity or, in some cases, religion. **Pan movements** (from the Greek *pan*, "all") sought to link people across state boundaries. The grand aspiration of all these movements—which included pan-Asianism, pan-Islamism, pan-Africanism, pan-Slavism, pan-Turkism, pan-Arabism, pan-Germanism, and Zionism—was the rearrangement of borders in order to unite dispersed communities. But such remappings posed a threat to rulers of the Russian, Austrian, and Ottoman empires, as well as to overseers of the British and the French colonial empires.

Pan-Islamism Within the Muslim world, intellectuals and political leaders begged their fellow Muslims to put aside their differences and unite under the banner of Islam in opposition to European incursions. The leading spokesman for pan-Islamism was the well-traveled Jamal al-Din al-Afghani (1839–1897). Born in Iran and given a Shiite upbringing, he nonetheless called on Muslims worldwide to overcome their Sunni and Shiite differences so that they could work together against the West. Afghani called for unity and action, for an end to corruption and stagnation, and for acceptance of the true principles of Islam.

The pan-Islamic message only added to Muslims' confusion as they confronted the West. Indeed, Arab Muslims living as Ottoman subjects had many calls on their loyalties.

Religion and Reform Efforts in the Ottoman Empire Sultan Abdul Hamid bestows a constitution on the Ottoman Empire. The Sultan sponsored pan-Islamic sentiment in order to hold the empire together.

Should they support the Ottoman Empire to resist European encroachments? Or should they embrace the Islamism of Afghani? Most decided to work within the fledgling nation-states of the Islamic world, looking to a Syrian or Lebanese identity, for example, as the way to deal with the West and gain autonomy. But Afghani and his disciples had struck a chord in Muslim culture, and their Islamic message has long retained a powerful appeal.

Pan-Germanism and Pan-Slavism Pan-Germanism found followers across central Europe, where it often competed with a pan-Slavic movement that sought to unite all Slavs against their Austrian, German, and Ottoman overlords. This area had traditionally been ruled by German-speaking elites, who owned the land farmed by Slavic peasants. German elites began to feel increasingly uneasy as Slavic nationalisms (spurred by the midcentury revivals of traditional Czech, Polish, Serbian, and Ukrainian languages and cultures) became more popular. Even more threatening was the fact that the Slavic populations were growing faster than the German population. As pogroms in the Russian Empire's borderlands in the 1880s, as well as economic opportunities, drove crowds of eastern European Jews westward, German resentment toward these newcomers also increased.

The rhetoric of pan-Germanism inspired mass, grassroots political activism. It motivated central Europeans to think of themselves as members of a German *race*, their identities determined by blood rather than defined by state boundaries. This, too, was the lesson of pan-Slavism. Both movements led extremists to take actions that were dangerous to existing states. The organization of networks of radical southern Slavs, for example, unsettled Bosnia and Herzegovina (annexed by the Austrians in 1908). Indeed, it was a Serbian proponent of plans to carve an independent Slav state out of Austrian territory in the Balkans who assassinated the heir to the Habsburg throne in June 1914. By August, the whole of Europe had descended into mass warfare, bringing much of the rest of the world directly or indirectly into the conflict as well. Eventually, the war would fulfill the pan-Slav, pan-German, and anti-Ottoman Muslim nationalist longing to tear down the Ottoman and Habsburg empires. Intellectuals articulated the pan movements, but aspiring political leaders and secret societies took up their ideologies, leaving Europe and much of Asia at the end of the nineteenth century boiling with ideas of how to change the borders of states and the dominance of France and Britain.

Conclusion

Ever since the Enlightenment, Europeans had put their faith in "progress." Through the nineteenth century, educated, secular elites took pride in booming industries, bustling cities, and burgeoning colonial empires. Yet by the century's end, urbanization and industrialization seemed more disrupting than uplifting, more disorienting than reassuring.

Moreover, colonized people's resistance to the "civilizing mission" fueled doubts about the course of progress.

The realization that "the people" were developing ways to unseat them terrified ruling elites. In colonial settings, nationalists learned how to mobilize large populations. In Europe, socialist and right-wing leaders likewise challenged liberals by appealing to the idea of popular sovereignty. A politics that relied on closed-door negotiations between "rational" gentlemen was unprepared to deal with modern ideas and identities.

Nor were elites able to control the scope of change, for the expansion of empires had drawn ever more people into an unbalanced global economy. Everywhere, disparities in wealth appeared. Moreover, the size and power of industrial operations threatened small firms and made individuals seem insignificant. Even some cities seemed too big and too dangerous. All these social and economic challenges stretched the capacities of gentlemanly politics.

They also stimulated creative energy. Western artists borrowed nonwestern images and vocabularies; nonwestern intellectuals looked to the West for inspiration, even as they formulated antiwestern ideas. The upheavals of modern experience propelled scholars to study the past and to fabricate utopian visions of the future.

Even as these changes unsettled the European-centered world, they intensified rivalries among Europe's powers themselves. Although the world had become a smaller place and travel was easier and quicker, at least for those who had wealth and came from powerful societies, this increasing global integration had its limitations and contradictions. At its center—Europe—the global order was unstable. And in the massive conflict that destroyed this era's faith in progress, Europe would ravage itself. The Great War (described in Chapter 19) would yield an age of even more rapid change—with even more violent consequences.

After You Read This Chapter

Go to INQUIZITIVE to see what you've learned—and learn what you've missed—with personalized feedback along the way.

TRACING THE GLOBAL STORYLINES

FOCUS ON: *Sources of Global Anxieties and Expressions of Cultural Modernism*

GLOBAL TRENDS

- Mass migrations and unprecedented urban expansion challenge national identities.

AFRICA AND CHINA: ANTI-COLONIALISM

- The Anglo-Boer War and violent uprisings against colonial rule in Africa call Europe's imperializing mission into question.
- The Chinese rise up against European encroachments in the Boxer Uprising.

EUROPE AND NORTH AMERICA: MOUNTING TENSIONS

- Intense political rivalries, financial insecurities and crises, rapid industrialization, feminism, and class conflict roil Europe and spread to the rest of the world.

MEXICO: RESENTMENT TOWARD ELITES

- The most widespread revolution from below takes place in Mexico.

CULTURAL MODERNISM

- Increased earning power gives workers in wealthy nations the leisure to enjoy music, vaudeville shows, sports, and other forms of popular culture and to read mass-circulation newspapers.
- Elite culture explores new forms in painting, architecture, music, literature, and science in order to break with the past and differentiate itself more dramatically from popular culture.
- New ideas of race emerge, as does a renewed emphasis on the nation-state and nationalism.

CHRONOLOGY

AFRICA

THE AMERICAS
- Jim Crow laws in the United States 1890s
- Labor unrest 1880s–1910s

EUROPE

SOUTH ASIA
- Indian National Congress founded 1885

EAST ASIA

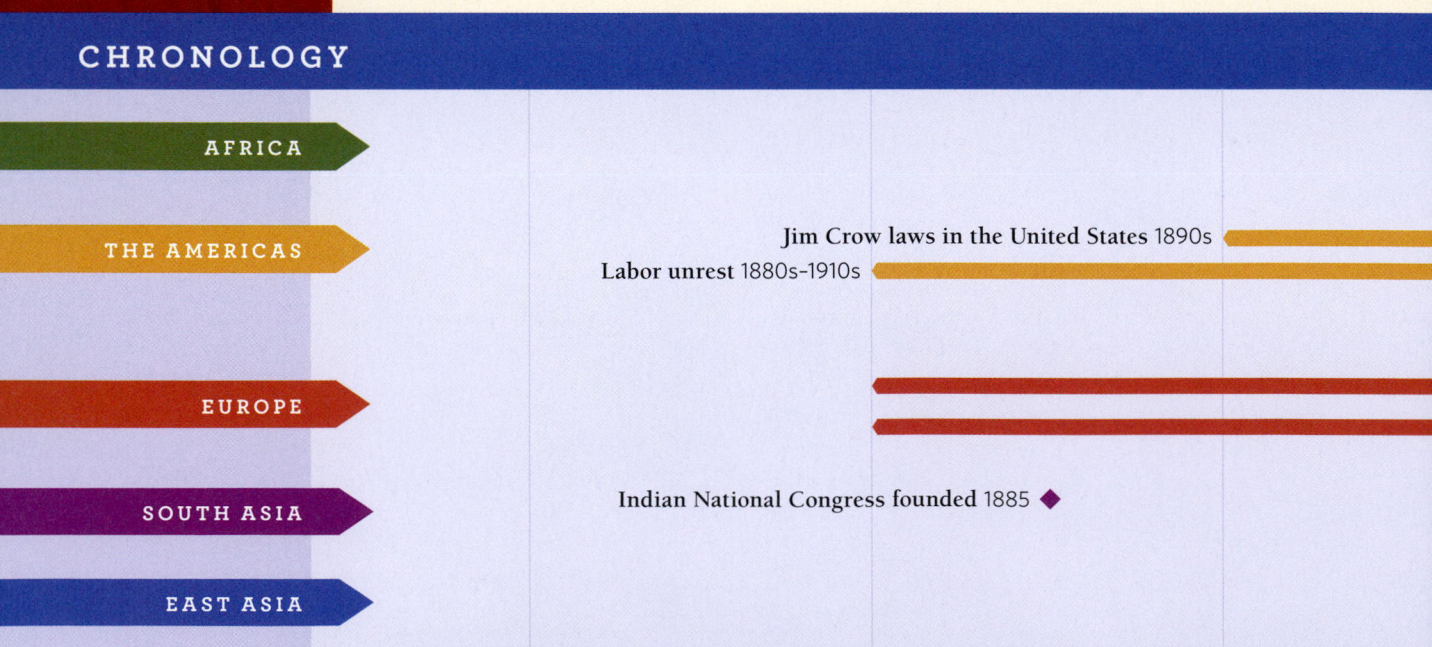

1870 1880 1890

THINKING ABOUT GLOBAL CONNECTIONS

- ***Thinking about Crossing Borders and an Unsettled World*** How did mobility of different kinds unsettle established certainties in this period? Think in particular of the massive flight of farmers towards cities, and the erosion of traditional social hierarchies; the prevalence of steamships and rail travel, making long-distance journeys easier than ever before; and the emergence of the telephone and telegraph, which revolutionized communications.
- ***Thinking about Changing Power Relationships and an Unsettled World*** To what extent were challenges to western influence internal to the western tradition, the product of growing doubts and contradictions within the Enlightenment project, articulated by Europeans like Nietzsche and Freud? To what degree were they external to that tradition, a reaction against the massive concentration of wealth and power centered in the West and the values that supported western dominance?
- ***Thinking about Women and Gender in an Unsettled World*** To what degree did the economic and technological breakthroughs of the nineteenth century improve women's lives? To what extent were women able to make claims on governments in different parts of the world? How did ordinary women take control of their bodies and their lives, and how did feminists challenge patriarchal cultures?

STUDY QUESTIONS

1. Identify different understandings of the term *progress* in Europe and the United States. What did the term mean and what were its sources for competing social and political groups? What were the views of **progressive reformers**, **anarchists**, and **syndicalists**.
2. Compare the challenges to the West posed by the **pan movements** and **Sun Yat-sen**.
3. Describe new forms of **popular culture** that emerged in this period and explain their significance.
4. Explain the significance of race and nation in this period.
5. Compare the goals and methods of revolutionary and reform movements in Latin America (especially the **Mexican Revolution**) and China (especially the **Boxer Uprising**) during this era.
6. To what extent did the challenges **modernism** posed grow out of the Enlightenment tradition and to what extent were they external to that tradition?

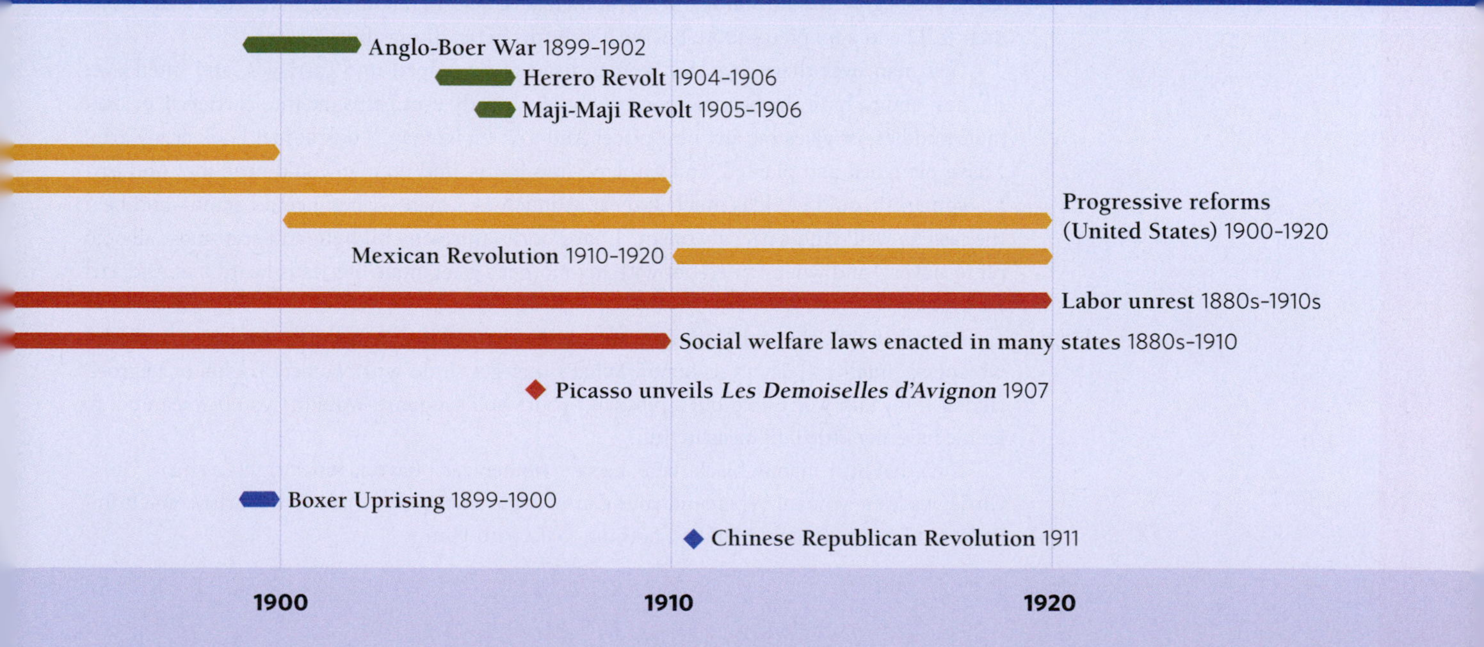

Going to the Source

Challenging Social Orders around the Globe

These documents each provide a way to reflect on what it means to be *within* a specific society, but also considered distinct, or unequal, by its policies and institutions. The documents come from diverse places around the world in the late nineteenth and early twentieth centuries: from the Islamic world within the British Empire, from the Americas, from Asia, and from Australia. Each document considers how people sought the promise of (and benefits from) the societies in which they found themselves, and how other members of those same societies sought to exclude them. Though many of these societies claimed to be based on the Enlightenment ideals of liberty and equality, these documents show us that not everyone who lived there found those principles to be universally applied. Expanding the definitions of who could be included frequently led to conflict. But so did excluding specific groups of people from full equality. That tension between the two poles of inclusion and exclusion is reflected in each of these documents.

PRIMARY SOURCE 18.1

"A'n't I A Woman?" (1851), Sojourner Truth

Sojourner Truth, born a slave in New York State, gained her freedom in 1827 and became well known as an abolitionist speaker and advocate for women's rights. This is an excerpt from an extemporaneous speech that she delivered to a women's convention in Akron, Ohio, in 1851.

Well, children, where there is so much racket there must be something out of kilter. I think that 'twixt the negroes of the South and the women at the North, all talking about rights, the white men will be in a fix pretty soon. But what's all this here talking about?

That man over there says that women need to be helped into carriages, and lifted over ditches, and to have the best place everywhere. Nobody ever helps me into carriages, or over mud-puddles, or gives me any best place! And a'n't I a woman? Look at me! Look at my arm! I have ploughed and planted, and gathered into barns, and no man could head me! And a'n't I a woman? I could work as much and eat as much as a man—when I could get it—and bear the lash as well! And a'n't I a woman? I have borne thirteen children, and seen most all sold off to slavery, and when I cried out with my mother's grief, none but Jesus heard me! And a'n't I a woman?

Then they talk about this thing in the head; what's this they call it? [member of audience whispers, "intellect"] That's it, honey. What's that got to do with women's rights or negroes' rights? If my cup won't hold but a pint, and yours holds a quart, wouldn't you be mean not to let me have my little half measure full?

Then that little man in black there, he says women can't have as much rights as men, 'cause Christ wasn't a woman! Where did your Christ come from? Where did your Christ come from? From God and a woman! Man had nothing to do with Him.

If the first woman God ever made was strong enough to turn the world upside down all alone, these women together ought to be able to turn it back, and get it right side up again! And now they is asking to do it, the men better let them.

1. **What inequities does Sojourner Truth profess about being a woman? About being black?**
2. **Explain why Sojourner Truth believed that women were equal citizens.**

PRIMARY SOURCE 18.2

Lecture on Teaching and Learning (1882), Sayyid Jamal al-din al-Afghani

Sayyid Jamal al-din al-Afghani was born in Iran and later moved across the border into Afghanistan. Though he came from a relatively conservative part of the world, he argued neither for isolation nor for maintaining the status quo. Indeed, he challenged Islamic society from within its own borders. Known as an early proponent of a pan-Islamic identity, he argued for reform in the Muslim world and for Muslim unity. In this passage from a lecture he delivered in India, he recognizes the significance of Western science in the world's increasing global interactions and challenges other conservative clerics to overcome their biases against it.

Jurisprudence among the Muslims includes all domestic, municipal, and state laws. Thus a person who has studied jurisprudence profoundly is worthy of being prime minister of the realm or chief ambassador of the state, whereas we see our *muftis* [experts on Muslim religious law] after studying this science, unable to manage their own households, although they are proud of their own foolishness.

The science of principles consists of the philosophy of the shar'ia or "philosophy of law." In it are explained the truth regarding right and wrong, benefit and loss, and the causes for the promulgation of laws. Certainly, a person who studies this science should be capable of establishing laws and enforcing civilization. However, we see that those who study this science among the Muslims, are deprived of understanding of the benefits of laws, the rules of civilization, and the reform of the world.

Since the state of these "ulama" [elite religious scholars] has been demonstrated, we can say that our ulama at this time are like a very narrow wick, on top of which is a small flame that neither lights its surroundings nor gives light to others. A scholar is a true light if he is a scholar. Thus, if a scholar is a scholar he must shed light on the whole world, and if his light does not reach the whole world, at least it should light up his region, his city, his village, or his home. What kind of scholar is it who does not enlighten even his own home?

The strangest thing of all is that our "ulama" these days have divided science into two parts. One they call Muslim science, and one European science. Because of this they forbid others to teach some of the useful sciences. They have not understood that science is that noble thing that has no connection with any nation, and is not distinguished by anything but itself. Rather, everything that is known, is known by science, and every nation that becomes renowned becomes renowned through science. Men must be related to science, not science to men. . . .

The father and mother of science is proof, and proof is neither Aristotle nor Galileo. The truth is where there is proof, and those who forbid science and knowledge in the belief that they are safeguarding the Islamic religion are really the enemies of that religion. The Islamic religion is the closest of religions to science and knowledge and there is no incompatibility between science and knowledge and the foundation of the Islamic faith.

The first education obtained by man was religious education, since philosophical education can only be obtained by a society that has studied some science and is able to understand proofs and demonstrations. Hence we can say that reform will never be achieved by the Muslims except if the leaders of our religion first reform themselves and gather the fruits of their science and knowledge.

1. **What is al-Afghani's understanding of science in the Muslim world?**
2. **Why does al-Afghani criticize Muslim legal experts?**

PRIMARY SOURCE 18.3

Chinese Exclusion in Australia (1902), Hugh H. Lusk

These excerpts come from an article written by Hugh H. Lusk, a former New Zealand Parliament member and regular contributor to the *North American Review* who frequently wrote about Britain's South Pacific empire, especially Australia and New Zealand. In this article he discusses Australia's wish to have an all-white colony. He wrote at a time when the British Empire, which included people of all races and ethnicities, was governed nearly exclusively by white European men. And he wrote just twenty years after the United States Congress passed the Chinese Exclusion Act (1882), which limited immigration from China into the United States.

There are already a good many Chinese in every one of the states of the Commonwealth, forming a percentage of the population at least five times as great as it does in America, and they are popular in none. That they are hard-working, frugal and, on the whole, fairly inoffensive and law-abiding people, is admitted everywhere; but they are essentially a people apart, incapable of really adopting, or adapting themselves to, the standards of the white race which holds the continent, and the feeling may be said to be universal which demands their exclusion.

The Japanese are more popular in Australia than the Chinese, but the same objections are felt to apply to them; and it is even probable that they owe any advantage they have in popular estimation rather to their smaller numbers than to anything else.

The question which had to be met, therefore, in dealing with the proposed exclusion of the Mongolian races from Australia, was not the propriety of their exclusion, but the method of giving effect to it. The re-enactment of a Chinese exclusion act in America is a simple thing. There is, of course, the question of Chinese or Japanese sensibility to be considered; but if the public sentiment is in favor of risking any loss of popularity at Peking or Tokio which may be involved, there is an end of the matter.

China may feel that America is, after all, not so very much more sympathetic than other foreign devils, and Japan may feel offended to think that even now her people are regarded as less desirable than certain European peoples whose arrival in Japan would hardly be esteemed a benefit. Yet, if Congress thinks fit to exclude them, little will be said on the subject. The position of Australia is different. It is one of the inevitable drawbacks of incorporation in an Empire so extended as that of Great Britain that questions of primarily local concern . . . cannot be dealt with independently of the interests of the other divisions. The Commonwealth of Australia has been accorded the fullest possible powers of self-government; yet, when its Parliament proceeded to legislate for the effectual exclusion of un-desirable emigration a difficulty presented itself.

The desire of the people and Parliament was to put a stop to the introduction of Chinese or Japanese immigrants by a statute that should say so in plain and unmistakable language. Other methods had been tried by the separate colonies [in Australia] already, such as the imposition of special poll taxes, and the requirement of capital in the hands of the immigrants; but all had been cleverly evaded. When the promised bill was brought before Parliament by the Government, however, it was found that it contained no mention of either of the countries intended to be specially affected by its provisions. Instead of this, it took the form of an act which applied, or at any rate might in the discretion of the Executive be made to apply, to immigrants from Germany, France, Italy or America, as well as from China and Japan. A very simple educational test is, in fact, the only safeguard provided. It is required that every immigrant shall be compelled to make a written application for admission in one of certain European languages, or in English, before the proper official. . . .

To the natural criticism, which was offered in no uncertain way by the Opposition, that it could certainly be evaded with ease by any smart Chinese or Japanese immigrant, the reply was that, in the interests of the trade of the Empire—which means, of course, of Great Britain—it was considered most unwise to antagonize either China or Japan at present.

1. **Why does Lusk propose excluding Chinese from Australia?**
2. **Why would an educational test be an effective method to exclude Asian and other undesirable immigrants?**

PRIMARY SOURCE 18.4

On Injustices to Chinese Women (early twentieth century), Qiu Jin

Qiu Jin was a revolutionary who advocated an overthrow of the Qing dynasty. Though she lived for a time in Japan, she returned to China and produced articles and journals that argued for women's equality in China. In 1907 she was executed for her role in aiding an uprising against the Qin government. In this document, she compares the treatment of Chinese women to slavery and ties the nation's future to the fate of women. It is worth noting that she spoke from personal experience, as she had her feet bound and experienced an unhappy marriage.

Alas! The greatest injustice in this world must be the injustice suffered by our female population of two hundred million. If a girl is lucky enough to have a good father, then her childhood is at least tolerable. But if by chance her father is an ill-tempered and unreasonable man, he may curse her birth: "What rotten luck: another useless thing." Some men go as far as killing baby girls while most hold the opinion that "girls are eventually someone else's property" and treat them with coldness and disdain. In a few years, without thinking about whether it is right or wrong, he forcibly binds his daughter's soft, white feet with white cloth so that even in her sleep she cannot find comfort and relief until the flesh becomes rotten and the bones broken. What is all this misery for? Is it just so that on the girl's wedding day friends and neighbors will compliment him, saying, "Your daughter's feet are really small"? Is that what the pain is for?

But that is not the worst of it. When the time for marriage comes, a girl's future life is placed in the hands of a couple of shameless matchmakers and a family seeking rich and powerful in-laws. A match can be made without anyone ever inquiring whether the prospective bridegroom is honest, kind, or educated. On the day of the marriage the girl is forced into a red and green bridal sedan chair, and all this time she is not allowed to breathe one word about her future. . . .

When Heaven created people it never intended such injustice because if the world is without women, how can men be born? Why is there no justice for women? We constantly hear men say, "The human mind is just and we must treat people with fairness and equality." Then why do they greet women like black slaves from Africa?

How did inequality and injustice reach this state? . . .

I hope that we all shall put aside the past and work hard for the future. Let us all put aside our former selves and be resurrected as complete human beings. Those of you who are old, do not call yourselves old and useless. If your husbands want to open schools, don't stop them; if your good sons want to study abroad, don't hold them back. Those among us who are middle-aged, don't hold back your husbands lest they lose their ambition and spirit and fail in their work. After your sons are born, send them to schools. You must do the same for your daughters and, whatever you do, don't bind their feet. As for you young girls among us, go to school if you can. If not, read and study at home. Those of you who are rich, persuade your husbands to open schools, build factories, and contribute to charitable organizations. Those of you who are poor, work hard and help your husbands. Don't be lazy, don't eat idle rice. These are what I hope for you. You must know that when a country is near destruction, women cannot rely on the men any more because they aren't even able to protect themselves. If we don't take heart now and shape up, it will be too late when China is destroyed.

Sisters, we must follow through on these ideas!

1. **What is Qiu Jin trying to accomplish by publicly speaking out?**
2. **What role does education play in women's rights for Qiu Jin?**

PRIMARY SOURCE 18.5

Industrialization and Women's Freedom in Egypt (1909), Bahithat al-Badiya

In a 1909 lecture in Cairo open only to women, Bahithat al-Badiya, an educated, upper-class Egyptian woman, insisted that female veiling in public was unnatural, absurd, and counterproductive.

Men say when we become educated we shall push them out of work and abandon the role for which God created us. But isn't it rather men who have pushed women out of work? Before, women used to spin and to weave cloth for clothes for themselves and their children, but men invented machines for spinning and weaving and put women out of work. . . . Since male inventors and workers have taken away a lot of our work should we waste our time in idleness or seek other work to occupy us? Of course, we should do the latter. . . . Obviously, I am not urging women to neglect their home and children to go out and become lawyers or judges or railway engineers. But if any of us wish to work in such professions our personal freedom should not be infringed. . . .

Men say to us categorically, "You women have been created for the house and we have been created to be bread-winners." Is this a God-given dictate? How are we to know this since no holy book has spelled it out? Political economy calls for a division of labor but if women enter the learned professions it does not upset the system. The division of labor is merely a human creation. . . . If men say to us that we have been created weak we say to them, "No it is you who made us weak through the path you made us follow." After long centuries of enslavement by men, our minds rusted and our bodies weakened. . . .

Men criticize the way we dress in the street. They have a point because we have exceeded the bounds of custom and propriety. . . . [But:] veiling should not prevent us from breathing fresh air or going out to buy what we need if no one can buy it for us. It must not prevent us from gaining an education nor cause our health to deteriorate. When we have finished our work and feel restless and if our house does not have a spacious garden why shouldn't we go to the outskirts of the city and take the fresh air that God has created for everyone and not just put in boxes exclusively for men.

1. **How does al-Badiya describe the position of women in Egyptian society?**
2. **Why do you think that al-Badiya attacks the patriarchal system that she observed in Egypt?**

PRIMARY SOURCE 18.6

Transport Worker's Strike (1911)

This photo shows transport workers at a meeting and rally in central London. Residents of European cities regularly encountered such protests at the time. Workers' demands varied from city to city and port to port, and the outcomes differed as well.

1. **How would you interpret the position of the woman in this photograph?**
2. **Why would transit workers unite in a strike at this time? What might they have been hoping to achieve?**

Questions for Analysis

Analyzing Evidence

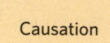

1. According to these documents, which groups of people sought to achieve greater equality within their societies? Compare the various approaches that they used to gain equality.

Causation

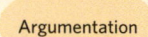

2. Explain why some of these groups of people were not given full access to power.

Argumentation

3. Based on what you've read in these documents, what is the relationship between science, universal truth, and political rights?

Long Essay Question

Synthesis

Based on what you have read in the chapter and the documents above, assess the degree to which countries around the world and their national institutions were able to treat all those who lived within them fairly during the late nineteenth and early twentieth centuries. Explain your answer.

Before You Read This Chapter

GLOBAL STORYLINES

- The Great War (World War I) engulfs the globe, exhausts Europe, and promotes production and consumption on a mass scale.
- The harsh terms of the peace settlement produce resentment in Germany and contribute to global economic problems.
- European countries' efforts to rebuild their economies after the Great War by cutting expenses and returning to the gold standard cause the Great Depression, which directly affects the entire global economy.
- Three strikingly different visions for building a better world arise: liberal democracy, authoritarianism, and anticolonialism.

CORE OBJECTIVES

- **IDENTIFY** the causes for World War I, and **ANALYZE** the effects of the war on regions both within and outside of Europe.
- **EXPLAIN** how the development of modern, mass societies both caused and were affected by the Great Depression.
- **COMPARE** the ideologies of liberal democracy, authoritarianism, and anticolonialism, and **EVALUATE** the success of each in this period.
- **EXPLAIN** how access to consumer goods and other aspect of mass society influenced political conflict in Asia, Africa, and Latin America.

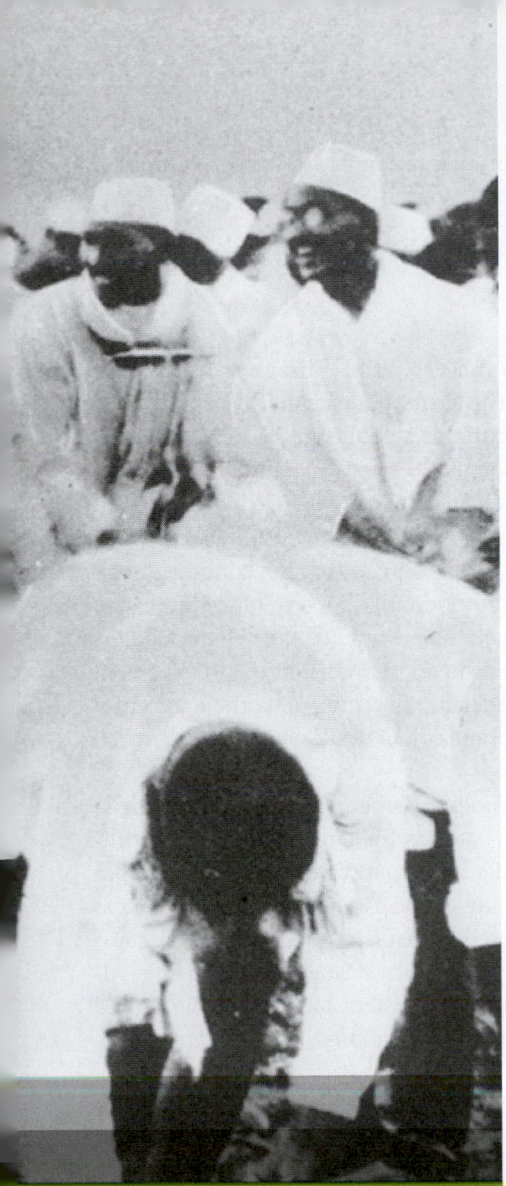

CHAPTER

19

Of Masses and Visions of the Modern

1910–1939

KEY TERMS

- **Mustafa Kemal Ataturk** p. 743
- **Bolsheviks** p. 723
- **Chiang Kai-shek** p. 743
- **fascism** p. 734
- **Mohandas Karamchand (Mahatma) Gandhi** p. 740
- **Great Depression** p. 729
- **Great War (World War I)** p. 718
- **Adolf Hitler** p. 735
- **Benito Mussolini** p. 734
- **Nazis** p. 735
- **Joseph Stalin** p. 732

Raging from August 1914 to November 1918, the Great War (World War I) shook the foundations of the European-centered world. Although most major battles occurred on European soil, multitudes of American, African, and Asian soldiers were ferried across oceans to join the war effort. Campaigns also bloodied the soil in Turkey, Egypt, Syria, and sub-Saharan Africa. The war's impact was thoroughly global. In addition to involving countless soldiers from Europe's colonies, it spread notions of freedom and self-determination and a growing disillusionment with European rule. Elsewhere, nations grappled with competing visions for building stable governments and strong economies.

This chapter deals with the Great War and its global impact. First, because the war was fought on a worldwide scale and to utter exhaustion in Europe, it required the resources of a large part of the world. It prompted production and consumption on a mass scale. Wartime leaders also used new media such as radio and film to promote national loyalties and to discredit enemies—and thereby helped to spread a mass culture. Second, the harsh terms of the peace settlement contributed to the outbreak of the Great Depression. Third, political turmoil surrounding the war inflamed disputes over how to manage mass societies and build a better world. To this end, three distinct visions arose:

liberal democracy, authoritarianism, and anticolonialism. These ideologies competed for preeminence in the decades leading up to World War II.

The Quest for the Modern

When people spoke of "being modern" in the 1920s and 1930s, they disagreed about what it meant. For culture and the arts (see Chapter 18), the term "modernism" has a fairly precise meaning. It emerged in the late nineteenth century as a challenge to the supposedly conservative values of realism in Europe, and to established artistic traditions elsewhere. In other fields, however, there was much less agreement. Reformers have always distinguished their ideas as modern or progressive while opposing accepted norms as backward or traditional. In the early twentieth century, most people agreed that in economic terms modernity involved mass production and mass consumption. In the West, for example, the automobile, the gramophone (record player), the cinema, and the radio reflected the benefits of economic progress and mass culture. In politics, being modern meant the involvement of the masses. Everywhere people favored strong leadership to reinvigorate their societies; some wanted more democracy to replace monarchical and colonial rule while others favored more authoritarian solutions.

The first political vision of being or becoming modern—the *liberal democratic* one—confronted economic failings that beset this period, such as the Great Depression, without sacrificing market economies or representative democracy. It widened participation in politics but also gave greater power to regulatory bureaucracies. After the Great Depression spread hard times and unemployment, this predominantly American and western European model linking capitalism and democracy no longer seemed so promising. Although many countries rejected the liberal perspective, the system survived in the United States, parts of western Europe, and several Latin American nations.

For many observers, liberal democracies failed to match the astonishing dynamism of a second perspective—*authoritarianism*. Authoritarian regimes rejected democracy, subordinated the individual to the state, managed and often owned most industries, used censorship and terror to enforce loyalty, and exalted an all-powerful leader. During this period, authoritarianism was evident in both right-wing dictatorships (including Fascist Italy, Nazi Germany, dictatorial Spain and Portugal, and militaristic Japan) and a left-wing dictatorship (the Soviet Union).

The third vision—*anticolonialism*—also questioned the liberal democratic order, primarily because of its connection to colonialism. However, many anticolonialists did not reject representative democracy, private property, or free markets. Resentful of European rulers who preached democracy but practiced despotism, anticolonial leaders sought to oust their colonial rulers and then find their own path to modernity, their own vision of progress. They generally favored mixing Western ideas with indigenous traditions.

Authoritarian and anticolonial visions of modernity both embraced technology and economic dynamism. They sought to take advantage of economic growth and mass support and redefine what freedom meant, while rejecting what they considered the hypocrisy and weakness of liberal democracy.

COMPARISON

IDENTIFY the causes for World War I, and **ANALYZE** the effects of the war on regions both within and outside of Europe.

The Great War

Few events were more decisive in drawing men and women worldwide into national and international politics than the **Great War**. For over four years, millions of soldiers from Europe, as well as from its dominions and colonies, killed one another. The war's carnage shook the hierarchies of prewar society around the world. Above all, the war made clear how much the power of the state now depended on the support of the people.

The war's causes were complex. At the heart of the European tensions, however, were nationalist rivalries, which pitted Britain and France against a rising Germany, and Austria-Hungary and Russia against each other as the Ottoman Empire began to crumble. Through most of the nineteenth century, Britain had been the preeminent power. By the century's end, however, German industrial output had surpassed Britain's, and Germany had begun building a navy. For the British, who controlled the world's seas, the German navy was an affront; for the Germans, it was a logical step in their expanding ambitions. This Anglo-German antagonism drew in the other powers in rival alliances. Germany joined Austria-Hungary to form the Central Powers; Britain affiliated itself with France and Russia in the Triple Entente (later called the Allied Powers after Italy joined).

THE FIGHTING

Despite hopes for a swift resolution, the war became infamous for its duration and horrors. Well-armed and secretly pledged to defend their partners in 1914, the rivals lacked only a spark to ignite open hostilities. That came in August, when the heir to the Habsburg throne was assassinated in Sarajevo, the capital of Austrian Bosnia. The assassin hoped to trigger an independence movement that would detach South-Slav territories from the Austro-Hungarian Empire (see Chapter 18) and unite them with independent Serbia. Russia backed the Serbs against Austria-Hungary, and the British, French, and Germans were drawn into the conflict to support their partners. The world war that followed dragged in Europe's colonies, too. For those who expected a short war, the fighting did not go as expected.

Stalemate The initial German offensive stalled thirty miles outside Paris at the First Battle of the Marne, in September 1914 (see Map 19.1). A stalemate ensued. Vast land armies dug trenches along the Western Front—from the English Channel through Belgium and France to the Alps—installing barbed wire and setting up machine-gun posts.

Trenches in World War I The expectation of a short, decisive war turned out to be an illusion; instead, armies dug trenches and filled them with foot soldiers and machine guns. To advance entailed walking into a hail of machine-gun fire. Life in the trenches meant cold, dampness, rats, disease, and boredom.

MAP 19.1 | World War I: The European and Middle Eastern Theaters

Most of the fighting in World War I, despite its designation as a world war, occurred in Europe. Although millions of soldiers fought on both sides, the territorial advances were relatively small. Look at the maps above, and identify all the countries where the Allies and Central Powers made advances.

- Which countries had to fight a two-front war?
- Did the armies of the Central Powers or the Allies gain the most territory during the war?
- According to your reading, how did those territorial gains affect the war's outcome?

Anything but glorious, life in the trenches mixed boredom, dampness, dirt, vermin, and disease, punctuated by the terror of being ordered to "go over the top" to attack the enemy's entrenched position. Doing so meant running across a "no man's land" in which machine guns mowed down almost all attackers. The war also witnessed new instruments of warfare, including poison gas; submarines; military aircraft, used primarily for reconnaissance; and, in the latter stages, tanks.

The death toll forced governments to call up more men than ever before. More than 70 million men worldwide fought in the war, including almost all of Europe's young adult males. From 1914 to 1918, 13 million served in the German army. In Russia, more than 15 million men took up arms. The British Empire mobilized nearly 9 million soldiers, and the 5.25 million troops of the United Kingdom (England, Scotland, Wales, and Ireland) constituted almost half the prewar population of men aged fifteen to forty-nine. In France around 8 million served, roughly 80 percent of men aged fifteen to forty-nine, a greater proportion than in any other major power. Over half of all the men mobilized for World War I were killed, injured, taken prisoner, or unaccounted for. (See **Analyzing Global Developments: Measuring Casualties in World War I**.)

Mass mobilization also undermined traditional gender boundaries. Tens of thousands of women served at or near the front as doctors, nurses, and technicians. Even more women mobilized on the "home front," taking on previously male occupations—especially in munitions plants. But women could also turn against the state. Particularly in central Europe and Russia, the war's demands for soldiers and supplies left farms untended and caused food shortages. Bread riots and peaceful protests by women, traumatized by loss and desperate to feed their children, put states on notice that their citizens expected compensation for their sacrifices. Indeed, civilian pressure forced many states to make promises they would have to fulfill after the war, in the form of welfare provisions, expanded suffrage, and pensions for widows and the wounded.

Empire and War The war's horrors reached around the globe (see Map 19.2). In 1915–1916, Ottoman forces (allied with the Central Powers) massacred or deported 1.3 million Armenians, who were accused as a group of collaborating with the Russians. Many analysts regard these attacks as the world's first genocide, the intentional elimination of a whole people. To increase their forces, the British and the French conscripted colonial subjects: India provided 1 million soldiers; over 1 million Africans fought in Africa and Europe for their colonial masters, and another 3 million transported war supplies. Even the sparsely populated British dominions of Australia, New Zealand, and Canada dispatched over a million young men to fight for the empire.

The Russian Revolution The war destroyed entire empires. The first to go was Romanov Russia. In February 1917, Tsar Nicholas II stepped down under pressure from his generals. They wanted to quash the mass unrest in the capital, St. Petersburg, which, they believed, threatened the war effort along the Eastern Front. Some members of the Russian parliament formed a provisional government; at the same time, grassroots councils (soviets) sprang up in factories,

Women's War Effort With armies drafting nearly every able-bodied man, women filled their places in factories, especially in those that manufactured war materials, such as the French plant pictured here in 1916.

Analyzing Global Developments

Measuring Casualties in World War I

You would think that tabulating historical data would be a fairly easy thing to do. At different points in this text, however, we have seen that it takes painstaking efforts on the part of historians and demographers first to figure out the best way to collect the data and second to accurately categorize and count the data. Figuring out the number of Africans that left on slave ships and where they embarked and disembarked during the Atlantic slave trade is a great example of this kind of work. Historian Jay Winter and others have worked tirelessly during the last thirty years to come up with accurate death tolls for the soldiers and civilians in World War I. In a landmark book, *The Great War and the British People*, Winter used a range of archival sources from government agencies' data and mortality rate tables from major insurance companies to estimate and calculate the number of deaths among people in Britain and Ireland. While the carnage in World War I seems beyond measure, Winter, in one paradoxical finding, demonstrated that death rates among civilians actually went down during World War I in Britain and Ireland. Winter suggests that the best explanation for this development was the efforts of the state to mobilize the civilian population, to provide health insurance, and, most importantly, to improve nutrition.

The table below builds on Winter's early efforts and shows the best estimates for the military death tolls across all the major participants in World War I.

QUESTIONS FOR ANALYSIS

- Based on data provided in the table, did the mobilization for the war have a greater impact on the societies of the Central Powers or the Allied Powers? Please justify your answer.
- While the Allies mobilized nearly twice as many men as the Central Powers, the latter suffered greater casualty rates. Why?
- The United States played a major role in World War I, but why were the number of its dead, wounded, and missing/POW so low compared to the other major combatants?

Military participation and military losses in World War I

COUNTRY	MOBILIZED	DEAD	WOUNDED	POW/MISSING	TOTAL CASUALTIES	% CASUALTIES
Allied Powers						
Russia	15,798,000	1,800,000	4,950,000	2,500,000	9,250,000	59
France	7,891,000	1,375,800	4,266,000	537,000	6,178,800	78
GB, Emp. and Dom.	8,904,467	908,371	2,090,212	191,652	3,190,235	36
Italy	5,615,000	578,000	947,000	600,000	2,125,000	38
USA	4,273,000	114,000	234,000	4,526	352,526	8
Japan	800,000	300	907	3	1,210	0
Romania	1,000,000	250,706	120,000	80,000	450,706	45
Serbia	750,000	278,000	133,148	15,958	427,106	57
Belgium	365,000	38,716	44,686	34,659	118,061	32
Greece	353,000	26,000	21,000	1,000	48,000	14
Portugal	100,000	7,222	13,751	12,318	33,291	33
Montenegro	50,000	3,000	10,000	7,000	20,000	40
Total	**45,899,467**	**5,380,115**	**12,380,704**	**3,984,116**	**22,194,935**	**46**
Central Powers						
Germany	13,200,000	2,037,000	4,216,058	1,152,800	7,405,858	56
Austria-Hungary	900,000	1,100,000	3,620,000	2,200,000	6,920,000	77
Turkey	2,998,000	804,000	400,000	250,000	1,454,000	48
Bulgaria	400,000	87,500	152,390	27,029	266,919	67
Total	**25,598,000**	**4,028,500**	**8,388,448**	**3,629,829**	**16,046,777**	**63**
Grand Total	**71,497,467**	**9,408,615**	**21,219,152**	**7,613,945**	**38,241,712**	**53**

Sources: John Horne (ed.), *A Companion to World War I* (2010); Tucker Spencer (ed.), *The European Powers in the First World War: An Encyclopedia* (1996); J. M. Winter, *The Great War and the British People* (1985).

The Russian Revolution (*Above*) The July 1917 demonstrations in Petrograd were among the largest in the Russian Empire during that turbulent year of war and revolution. In this photo, marchers carry banners, "Down with the Ministers-Capitalists" and "All Power to the Soviets of Worker, Soldier and Peasant Deputies." (*Left*) Vladimir Lenin died just six years and three months after the October 1917 revolution, but he lived on in his writings and images, such as in this painting by Pavel Kuznetsov. Artists and propagandists helped make Lenin an icon of the new Soviet order.

garrisons, and towns. The irony of Russia's February Revolution, which brought an end to the monarchy, was that the military and civilian elites wanted to restore order, not encourage a revolution. With the tsar removed, millions of peasants seized land, soldiers and sailors abandoned the front, and borderland non-Russian groups declared autonomy from the crumbling Russian Empire.

In October 1917, left-wing Socialists calling themselves **Bolsheviks** seized power. Led by Vladimir Lenin and Leon Trotsky, the Bolsheviks drew support among radicalized soldiers, sailors, and factory workers organized in the soviets. Arresting provisional government members and claiming power in the name of the soviets, the Bolsheviks proclaimed a socialist revolution to overtake the February "bourgeois" revolution. Several months later, Soviet Russia signed the Treaty of Brest-Litovsk, acknowledging German victory on the Eastern Front as the Russian army collapsed. For protection, the Bolshevik leadership relocated the capital to Moscow and set up a dictatorship. Lenin insisted on accepting the peace treaty and the loss of vast territories to safeguard the socialist revolution.

The Fall of the Central Powers On April 2, 1917, the United States declared war on Germany. This occurred after German submarines sank several American merchant ships and after a secret telegram came to light in which German officials sought Mexican support by promising to help Mexico regain territories it had lost to the United States in 1848.

With American support, the Allies turned the tide at the Second Battle of the Marne in July 1918 and forced the Germans to retreat into Belgium. German troops then began to surrender, and some announced a soldiers' strike as hunger and influenza became unbearable. Before long, Germany tottered on the edge of civil war as the Allied blockade caused food shortages. Faced with defeat and civil strife, the Central Powers fell one after

GREENLAND
CANADA
UNITED STATES
ATLANTIC OCEAN
PACIFIC OCEAN
FINLAND
NORWAY
SWEDEN
BALTIC SEA
DENMARK
UNITED KINGDOM
GERMANY
POLAND
AUSTRIA-HUNGARY
FRANCE
ITALY
SERBIA
ROMANIA
BLACK SEA
CAUCASUS
BULGARIA
PORTUGAL
SPAIN
MONTENEGRO
ALBANIA
GREECE
OTTOMAN EMPIRE
IRAQ
TUNISIA
MOROCCO
ALGERIA
LIBYA
EGYPT
ARABIA
RIO DE ORO
BRITISH HONDURAS
BAHAMAS
CUBA
JAMAICA
WEST INDIES
HONDURAS
NICARAGUA
COSTA RICA
PANAMA
VENEZUELA
BRITISH GUIANA
DUTCH GUIANA
FRENCH GUIANA
COLOMBIA
ECUADOR
PERU
BRAZIL
BOLIVIA
PARAGUAY
CHILE
ARGENTINA
URUGUAY
GAMBIA
GUINEA
SIERRA LEONE
GOLD COAST
TOGO
NIGERIA
CAMEROON
ANGLO-EGYPTIAN SUDAN
ETHIOPIA
UGANDA
BRITISH EAST AFRICA
GERMAN EAST AFRICA
NORTHERN RHODESIA
SOUTHERN RHODESIA
GERMAN SOUTH-WEST AFRICA
SOUTH AFRICA
Allied Powers, colonies and allies
Central Powers and colonies
Neutral nations throughout the war
Troop movements
0 1000 2000 Miles
0 1000 2000 Kilometers

MAP 19.2 | World War I: The Global Theater

This map illustrates the ways in which World War I was a truly global conflict.

- Which states outside Europe became involved?
- Other than Europe, which continent experienced the most warfare?
- Which parts of the world were spared the fighting, and why?

another. After Kaiser Wilhelm II slipped into exile, the German empire became a republic. The last Habsburg emperor also gave up the throne, and Austria-Hungary dissolved into several new states. With the collapse of the Ottoman Empire, the war claimed a fourth dynasty among its casualties.

THE PEACE SETTLEMENT AND THE IMPACT OF THE WAR

To decide the fate of vanquished empires and the future of the modern world, the victors convened five peace conferences, one for each of the Central Powers. Most important was the conference to negotiate peace with Germany, held at Versailles, France, in January 1919. Delegates drew many of their ideas from American president Woodrow Wilson's "Fourteen Points," a blueprint he had devised for making peace in Europe. Wilson especially insisted that postwar borders be redrawn by following the principle of "self-determination of nations" and that an international League of Nations be set up to negotiate further quarrels. Such high-minded ideas were appealing, but once delegates got down to the business of carving up Europe and doling out Germany's colonies, negotiations became tense and difficult. Over the objections of the Americans and British, the French insisted on a punitive treaty that assigned Germany sole blame for the war and forced it to pay reparations.

Applying the principle of self-determination was much more difficult in practice than Wilson had understood. Suddenly, 60 million people in central and eastern Europe emerged as inhabitants of new nation-states (see Map 19.3). The patchwork nature of the old multiethnic empires here meant that as many as 25 million now lived in states in which they were ethnic minorities and vulnerable to persecution in the tumultuous years after the armistice. Moreover, the peacemakers were not prepared to extend self-determination beyond Europe. Although political elites negotiated the Versailles peace treaty, its effects as well as those of the war were felt by anticolonial leaders and their followers around the world. One of them, a photographer's assistant living in Paris named Nguyen Ai Quoc, the future Ho Chi Minh, famously challenged the American delegation at Versailles to take their own principles seriously and support his people's liberation from French rule, to no avail.

Mass Society: Culture, Production, and Consumption

COMPARISON

EXPLAIN how the development of modern, mass societies both caused and were affected by the Great Depression.

The war dramatically extended the making of mass societies. Even before 1914, democratic regimes had begun to extend the right to vote, in many cases making non–property holders and women eligible to cast ballots. Authoritarian regimes, meanwhile, had begun to mobilize the people via rallies and mass organizations. And new technologies, such as radio, were helping to create mass cultures that spanned geographic and class divides.

MASS CULTURE

New forms of communication and entertainment contributed to the new mass culture. In an effort to mobilize populations for total war, leaders had disseminated propaganda as never before—through public lectures, theatrical productions, musical compositions, and (censored) newspapers. Indeed, the war's impact had politicized cultural activities while broadening the audience for nationally oriented information and entertainment.

MAP 19.3 | Outcomes of World War I in Europe, North Africa, and Some of the Middle East

The political map of Europe and the Middle East changed greatly after the peace treaty of 1919.

- Comparing this map with Map 19.1, which shows the European and Middle Eastern theaters of war, identify the European countries that came into existence after the war.
- What happened to the Ottoman Empire, and what powers gained control over many territories of the Ottoman state?
- What states emerged from the Austro-Hungarian Empire?

Josephine Baker Reacting to the Great War's carnage, many Europeans looked longingly for supposedly pristine worlds that their own corrupting civilization had not destroyed. The African American entertainer Josephine Baker was a sensation on the stage in Paris after the war. Many of her shows exoticized or even caricatured her African descent.

Postwar *mass culture* was distinctive. First, it differed from elite culture (opera, classical music, paintings, literature) because it reflected the tastes of the working and the middle classes, who now had more time and money to spend on entertainment. Second, mass culture relied on new technologies, especially film and radio, which could reach an entire nation's population and consolidate their sense of being a single state.

Radio Radio entered its golden age after World War I. Invented early in the twentieth century, it made little impact until the 1920s, when powerful transmitters permitted stations to reach much larger audiences—often with nationally syndicated programs. Radio "broadcasts" gave listeners a sense of intimacy with newscasters and stars, addressing consumers as personal friends and drawing them into the lives of serial heroes.

Radio also was a way to mobilize the masses, especially in authoritarian regimes. The Italian dictator Benito Mussolini pioneered the radio address to the nation; later, Soviet and Nazi propagandists used it to great effect, as did the right-wing Japanese government. But even dictatorships could not exert total control over mass culture. For example, although the Nazis regarded jazz as racially inferior music and the Soviets regarded it as "bourgeois," neither could prevent young or old from tuning in to foreign radio broadcasts, smuggling gramophone records over the borders, or creating their own jazz bands.

Film and Advertising Film, too, had profound effects. For traditionalists, Hollywood by the 1920s signified vulgarity and decadence because the silver screen prominently displayed modern sexual habits. Like radio, film served political purposes. Here, again, antiliberal governments took the lead. German filmmaker Leni Riefenstahl's movie of the Nazi Nuremberg rally of 1934, *Triumph of the Will,* is a key example of propagandistic cinema. Nazi-era films were comedies, musicals, melodramas, detective films, and adventure epics—sometimes framed by racial stereotypes and political goals. Soviet film studios also produced Hollywood-style musicals alongside didactic pictures about socialist triumphs.

In market economies, radio and film grew into big businesses, and with expanded product advertising they promoted other enterprises as well. Especially in the United States, advertising became a major industry, with radio commercials shaping national consumer tastes. Increasingly, too, American-produced entertainment, radio programs, and cinematic epics reached an international audience. Thanks to new media, America and the world began to share mass-produced images and fantasies.

MASS PRODUCTION AND MASS CONSUMPTION

The same factors that promoted mass culture also enhanced production and consumption on a mass scale. In fact, World War I had relied on industrial might, for machine technologies produced war materials with abundant and devastating effect.

Never before had armies had so much firepower at their disposal. Whereas in 1809 Napoleon's artillery had discharged 90,000 shells over two days during the largest battle waged in Europe to that point, by 1916 German guns were firing 100,000 rounds of shells per hour for twelve hours at a time in the Battle of Verdun. To sustain military production, millions of men and women worked in factories at home and in the colonies. Producing huge quantities of identical guns, gas masks, bandage rolls, and boots, these factories reflected the modern world's demands for greater volume, faster speed, reduced cost, and standardized output—key characteristics of *mass production*.

The war reshuffled the world's economic balance of power, boosting the United States as an economic powerhouse. As the United States' share of world industrial production climbed above one-third in 1929 (roughly equal to that of Britain, Germany, and Russia combined), people around the globe regarded it as a "working vision of modernity" in which not only production but also consumption boomed.

Triumph of the Will Though later denounced, this propaganda film of Adolf Hitler and the Nazi Party Congress won a Golden Lion at the 1935 Venice Biennale and an award at the 1937 World's Exhibition in Paris. Its poster featured the many mass rallies that projected an image of dynamism and collective will, which Hitler claimed to embody.

The Automobile Assembly Line The most outstanding example of the relationship between mass production and consumption in the United States was the motor car. Before World War I, the automobile had been a rich man's toy. Then came Henry Ford, who founded the Ford Motor Company in 1903. Seeking to make more cars more quickly and cheaper, Ford used mechanized conveyors to send the auto frame along a track, or assembly line, where each worker performed one simplified task. By standardizing the manufacturing process and substituting machinery for manual labor, Ford's assembly line brought a new efficiency to the mass production of automobiles.

By the 1920s, a finished car rolled off Ford's assembly line every ten seconds. Although workers complained about becoming "cogs" in a depersonalized labor process, the system boosted output and reduced costs. Altogether, nearly 4 million jobs related directly or indirectly to the automobile—an impressive total in a labor force of 45 million workers.

After World War I, automobile ownership became more common among Americans. Ford further expanded the market for cars by paying his own workers $5 per day—approximately twice the average manufacturing wage in the United States. He understood that without *mass consumption*, increased purchasing power in the middle classes, and appetite for goods there could be no mass production. Whereas in 1920 Americans owned 8 million motor cars, a decade later they owned 23 million. The automobile's rapid spread seemed to demonstrate that mass production worked.

The Great Depression However, it was not all easy listening and smooth motoring in countries where mass societies were taking root. On October 24, 1929—Black Tuesday—the American stock market collapsed, plunging not only the American economy and its consumers, heavily in debt, but also international financial and trading systems into crisis. This event led the world into the **Great Depression**.

The causes of the Depression went back to the Great War. The efforts by European governments to slash spending and return to the prewar gold standard (see Chapter 18) stifled growth and compromised their ability to pay their war debts. Political and economic instability in Germany, the linchpin of the European economy, made matters even more difficult. The financial terms of the Versailles treaty required Germany to pay reparations to compensate for the costs of the war. The German government, however, was unable or unwilling to tax citizens at the rates that prevailed in victor countries, which would have enabled them to meet their treaty obligations. They opted instead to print more money. The resulting hyperinflation destroyed both the German economy and democracy.

To restore stability, Europeans borrowed heavily from the United States. Germany borrowed more from the United States than it paid in reparations, but that assistance was insufficient and short-lived. In 1928 and 1929, American banks pulled their support. Starting in central Europe, banks began to collapse. The panic then spread to the world's stock markets, which led to the Wall Street crash of 1929, which spurred more bank closures.

Financial turmoil produced a major reduction in world trade. Striving to protect workers and investors from the influx of cheap foreign goods, governments raised tariffs against imports. After the United States enacted protective tariffs, other governments abandoned free trade in favor of protectionism. Manufacturers cut back production, laid off millions of workers, and often went out of business. By 1935, world trade had shrunk to one-third of its 1929 level. The producers of raw materials, mainly found in the less developed economies, felt the harshest effects, for their international markets shut down almost completely. For example, world prices for Argentine beef, Chilean nitrates, and Indonesian sugar all dropped sharply.

The Great Depression forced people to rethink the core of laissez-faire liberalism (see Chapter 15), the idea that free markets regulate themselves and free trade leads to economic progress. By the late 1930s, the exuberant embrace of private mass production had ceded to a new conviction: state intervention to regulate the economy was critical to prevent disaster. In 1936, the British economist John Maynard Keynes published a landmark treatise, *The General Theory of Employment, Interest, and Money.* He argued that the market could not always adjust to its own failures and that sometimes the state had to stimulate it by increasing the money supply and creating jobs. Although the "Keynesian Revolution" took years to transform economic policy, many governments had doubts whether capitalism could be saved. The Great Depression did more than any other event to challenge the belief that liberal democracy and capitalism were the best way to achieve political stability and economic progress.

Mass Politics: Competing Visions for Building Modern States

COMPARISON

COMPARE the ideologies of liberal democracy, authoritarianism, and anticolonialism, and **EVALUATE** the success of each in this period.

In the aftermath of World War I, societies grappled with the question of how to build modern, prosperous states. The war upset class, gender, and colonial relations, which were already unsettled in the prewar period. On battlefronts and home fronts, countless workers, peasants, women, and colonial subjects had sacrificed and now expected to share in the fruits of peace. Many, even in victorious nations, lost confidence in traditional authorities who had failed to prevent the cataclysm and allowed it to go on so long. Amid widespread political turmoil, the states that retained some form of democracy revised the liberal vision, while authoritarianism gained in popularity and anticolonial movements gathered steam.

LIBERAL DEMOCRACY UNDER PRESSURE

The demands of fighting a total war had a profound effect on all of the European states. All of them, including the democracies in Britain and France, seized the opportunity to experiment with illiberal policies. Indeed, the war brought both the suspension of many democratic rights and an effort by governments to manage industry and distribution. States on both sides of the conflict jailed many individuals who opposed the war. Governments regulated both production and, through rationing, consumption. Above all, the war and the economic crises that followed revolutionized the size and scope of the state.

British and French Responses to Economic Crises Britain and France retained their democracies, but even here, old-fashioned liberal democracy was on the run. Strife rippled across the British Empire, and in the home isles Britain gave independence to what became the Republic of Ireland in 1922. Britain's working-class Labour Party came to power twice between 1923 and 1931; but either alone or in coalition with Liberals and Conservatives, Labour could not lift the country out of its economic crisis.

Disorder was even more pronounced in France, which had lost 10 percent of its young men and seen the destruction of vast territory. In 1932–1933, six government coalitions came and went over the course of just nineteen months. Against the threat of a rightist coup, a coalition of the moderate and radical left, including the French Communist Party, formed the Popular Front government (1936–1938). It introduced the right of collective bargaining, a forty-hour workweek, two-week paid vacations, and minimum wages.

The American New Deal In the United States, too, markets and liberalism faced challenges. When the Great Depression shattered the nation's fortunes, pressure intensified to create a more secure political and economic system.

By the end of 1930, more than 4 million American workers had lost their jobs. As President Hoover insisted that citizens' thrift and self-reliance, not government handouts, would restore prosperity, the economic situation worsened. By 1933, industrial production had dropped by a staggering 50 percent since 1929. The hard times were even worse in the countryside, where farm income plummeted by two-thirds between 1929 and 1932.

In the 1932 presidential election, a Democrat, Franklin Delano Roosevelt, won in a landslide. He promptly launched what came to be called the New Deal, a set of programs and regulations that dramatically expanded the scope of the American national

"Jim Crow" The American New Deal left most African Americans behind. In the rural American South, "Jim Crow" laws mandated racial segregation, with African Americans forced to use separate, and usually unequal, facilities, including schools, hotels, and theaters, such as this one in Mississippi.

government and its role in the nation's economic life. In his first hundred days in office, Roosevelt obtained legislation to provide relief for the jobless and to rebuild the shattered economy. Among his administration's experiments were the Federal Deposit Insurance Corporation to guarantee bank deposits up to $5,000, the Securities and Exchange Commission to monitor the stock market, and the Federal Emergency Relief Administration to help states and local governments assist the needy. Subsequently, in 1935, the Works Progress Administration put nearly 3 million people to work building roads, bridges, airports, and post offices. In addition, the Social Security Act inaugurated old-age pensions supported by the federal government.

Never before had the U.S. federal government expended so much on social welfare programs or intervened so directly in the national economy. Yet the Depression lingered, and before long unemployment again climbed—from 7 million in 1937 to 11 million in 1938.

The New Deal did not substantially redistribute national income. Privately owned enterprises continued to dominate American society. Roosevelt's aim was not to destroy capitalism, but to save it. In this regard the New Deal succeeded, for it staved off authoritarian solutions to modern problems.

Collectivized Agriculture Soviet plans for the socialist village envisioned the formation of large collectives supplied with advanced machinery, thereby transforming peasant labor into an industrial process. The realities behind the images of smiling farmers—such as in this poster, proclaiming "Let's Achieve a Victorious Harvest"—were low productivity, enormous waste, and often broken-down machinery.

During the interwar years, liberal democratic regimes respected elections and defended private property against challenges from labor movements. But they intervened in markets and regulated people's lives in ways their prewar counterparts never would have contemplated.

AUTHORITARIANISM AND MASS MOBILIZATION

Like the liberal systems they challenged, authoritarian regimes came in various stripes. Right-wing dictatorships arose in Italy, Germany, and Japan. Although differing in important respects, they all disliked the left-wing dictatorship of the Soviet Union. The Soviets, in turn, hated the Fascists.

The Soviet Union and Socialism The most dramatic blow against liberal capitalism occurred in Russia when the Bolshevik Party seized power and established a socialist regime. Fearing the spread of socialist revolutions, Britain, France, Japan, and the United States sent armies to Russia to contain bolshevism. But after executing the tsar and his family, the Bolsheviks rallied support by defending the homeland against its invaders. They also mobilized people to fight (and win) a civil war (1918–1921) in the name of defending the revolution.

To revive the economy, which had been devastated by war, revolution, and civil war, the Bolsheviks grudgingly legalized private trade and private property. In 1924, with the country still recovering from civil war, the undisputed leader of the revolution, Lenin, died. No one had done more to shape the institutions of the revolutionary regime, including creating expectations for a single ruler. After eliminating his rivals, **Joseph Stalin** (1878–1953) emerged as the new leader of the Communist Party and the country, which soon became the Union of Soviet Socialist Republics (U.S.S.R.), or Soviet Union.

Since socialism as a fully developed social and political order did not exist anywhere in the 1920s, no one was sure how it would actually work. Stalin resolved this dilemma by defining Soviet or revolutionary socialism in opposition to capitalism. Since capitalism had "bourgeois" parliaments serving the interests of the rich, socialism, as elaborated by Stalinist leaders, would have soviets (councils) of worker and peasant deputies. Since capitalism had unregulated markets, which led to inefficiency and unemployment, socialism would have economic planning and full employment. And since capitalism relied on the "exploitation" of private ownership, socialism would outlaw private trade and private property. In short, socialism would eradicate capitalism and then invent socialist forms in housing, culture, values, dress, and even modes of reasoning.

The efforts to build a noncapitalist society required class war, and these efforts began in the heavily populated countryside. As Stalin solidified his control over the Soviet Union in the late 1920s, he sought to combine individual farms into larger units owned and worked collectively, and run by regime loyalists. Tens of thousands of urban activists

MAP 19.4 | The Soviet Union

The Union of Soviet Socialist Republics (U.S.S.R.) came into being after World War I.

- How did its boundaries compare with those of the older Russian Empire, as shown in Map 17.6 (p. 633)?
- Identify the other Soviet Socialist Republics.
- What does the large number of Soviet republics suggest about the ethnic diversity within the Soviet Union?

and Red Army soldiers led a drive to establish these collective farms and to compel farmers to sell all their grain and livestock at state-run collection points for whatever price the state was willing to pay (often very little).

In protest, many peasants burned their crops, killed their livestock, and destroyed their farm machinery. The government responded by deporting the protesters, along with many bystanders, to remote areas. Meanwhile, harvests again declined, and famine claimed millions more lives. Grudgingly, the regime allowed the collectivized peasants to have household plots. Here they could grow their own food and take some of their produce to approved markets. But few escaped the collectives, which depended on the state for seed, fertilizers, and machinery.

The year 1928 saw the beginning of a frenzied Five-Year Plan to "catch and overtake" the leading capitalist countries. As peasants were forced onto collective farms, millions of enthusiasts (as well as deported peasants) set about building a socialist urban utopia founded on advanced technology, almost all of it purchased from the Depression-mired capitalist countries. More than 10 million people helped build or rebuild hundreds of factories, hospitals, and schools. Huge hydroelectric dams, automobile and tractor factories, and heavy machine–building plants symbolized the promise of Soviet-style modernity, which eliminated unemployment during the capitalist Great Depression. Soviet authorities also started building socialism on the borderlands, and the U.S.S.R soon included several new republics (see Map 19.4), all of which acquired their own institutions—but under central rule from Moscow.

Mass Terror and Stalin's Dictatorship The Soviet political system became more ruthless as the state expanded. Police power grew the most, partly from forcing peasants into collectives and organizing mass deportations. As the party's ranks swelled, ongoing loyalty tests also led to the removal of party members, even when they professed absolute loyalty. From 1936 to 1938, trials of supposedly treasonous "enemies of the people" resulted in the execution of around 750,000 people and the arrest or deportation of several million more. They were sent to forced-labor camps, collectively known as the Gulag. Such purges decimated the loyal Soviet elite—party officials, state officials, intelligentsia, army officers, and even members of the police who had enforced the terror. Lenin and Stalin secured a communist regime based in Russia but did so through highly coercive and deeply resented methods. Nonetheless, Stalin's efforts at heavy industrialization were to pay off when Nazi Germany invaded the Soviet Union in World War II (see Chapter 20).

Italian Fascism Disillusionment with the costs of the Great War and fear of a communist takeover like that in Russia inspired violent political movements in many European countries, above all in Italy and Germany. In Italy, mass strikes, occupations of factories, and peasant land seizures swept the country in 1919 and 1920. Amid this disorder, authoritarian nationalists seized power. Their leader was **Benito Mussolini** (1883–1945), a former socialist journalist, who coined the term **fascism**. In the wake of the Russian Revolution of 1917, fascism represented a counterrevolution. It combined mass movements, which had emerged on the political left, with an aggressive, authoritarian nationalism and antisocialist and antiliberal values.

In 1919, Mussolini sought to organize alienated veterans into a mass political movement. In the early years, black-shirted vigilante squads received money from landowners and factory owners to beat up socialist leaders. Still, the Fascists presented themselves as champions of the little guy, of peasants and (nonsocialist) workers, as well as of war veterans, students, and white-collar professionals.

In 1922, Mussolini announced a march on Rome. The march was a bluff, since Mussolini had no military support, yet it intimidated the king, who opposed Fascist ruffians but feared bloodshed. So he withheld use of the army against the lightly armed marchers.

When the Italian government resigned in protest, the monarch invited Mussolini to become prime minister, despite the fact that Fascists had won only a small minority of seats in the 1921 elections. Soon a series of decrees transformed Italy from a constitutional monarchy into a dictatorship. Within a few years, all parties except that of the Fascists had been dissolved. The regime used parades, films, radio, and visions of recapturing Roman imperial grandeur to boost support during the troubled times of the Depression. Mussolini used his personal charisma to promote the idea that as *Il Duce* (the leader), he personified the power and unity of Italy.

Mussolini's dictatorship made deals with big business and the church. He left traditional elites in place and preserved their powerful institutions; thus, his regime fell short of a total social revolution. By the mid-1930s, Italian fascism had settled into a traditional form of conservatism. Nonetheless, as the first antiliberal, antisocialist alternative, the early phase of Italian fascism served as a model for other countries.

German Nazism In Germany, too, fear of bolshevism and anger over the war's outcome propelled a violent, authoritarian party to power. Here, the dictator was **Adolf Hitler** (1889–1945), backed by the nationalist workers' movement, whose name he changed to the National Socialist German Workers' Party (*Nationalsozialistische Deutsche Arbeiterpartei*, or **Nazis**).

Unlike Mussolini, the young Hitler was never a Socialist, but the Nazi's Twenty-Five Points (1920) combined nationalism with a heavy dose of anticapitalism. The party platform called for the renunciation of the Treaty of Versailles and discrimination against Jews. It was an assertion of Germany's grievances against the world and of the small man's grievances against those whom the Nazis perceived as the rich. At first, Hitler and the Nazis were unsuccessful, and Hitler himself was arrested. He was sentenced to five years in prison for treason, but served less than a year. While in prison he wrote an autobiographical and fanatically anti-Semitic treatise called *Mein Kampf* (My Struggle, 1925), which subsequently became wildly popular among Nazis.

As the Great Depression eroded popular support for the Weimar Republic (the democratic regime that came into existence after the Treaty of Versailles), conservative leaders sought to profit from Hitler's popularity. Germany's president appointed Hitler chancellor (prime minister) in 1933, even as the Nazi movement was declining as an electoral force. Like Mussolini, Hitler came to power legally, with the help of traditional elites. Yet neither leader won an electoral majority.

Hitler's first step as chancellor was to heighten fears of communist conspiracy. The burning of the Reichstag (parliament) building in Berlin gave the Nazis an opportunity to blame the fire on the Communists. They immediately suspended civil liberties, including free speech and freedom of association, and attacked and imprisoned their opponents, especially Communists. By July 1933, the Nazis were the only legal party and Hitler was dictator of Germany. Like Mussolini, Hitler relied on choreographed mass rallies, new mediums like film and radio, as well as his own personal charisma to mobilize a mass following.

Hitler also unleashed a campaign of persecution against Jews. Like many other right-wing Germans, he believed that a Jewish-socialist conspiracy had stabbed the German army in the back, causing its surrender in World War I, and that intermarriage with Jews was destroying the supposed purity of the Aryan race (which included northern, white Europeans). Hitler and the Nazis did not believe that religious practice defined Jewishness; instead, they held, it was transmitted biologically from parents to children. Hitler encouraged the use of terror against Jews, destroying their businesses, homes, and marriages with non-Jews, and ultimately eliminating all traces of Jewish life and culture in Nazi-dominated central Europe.

The Nazis won popular support for restoring order and reviving the economy, although the economic gains had more to do with timing than Nazi policy. In any case, Germany reemerged as a great power with expansionist aspirations. Just as Mussolini reached back to ancient Rome to connect fascism to the Italian past, Hitler, too, invoked history.

He called his state the Third Reich—he considered the Holy Roman Empire (or Reich) the first, and the Reich created by Bismarck in 1871 the second—to bolster its legitimacy.

Militarist Japan Unlike authoritarian regimes in Europe, the right-wing movement that emerged in Japan did not spring from wounded power and pride during World War I. In fact, because wartime disruptions reduced European and American competition, Japanese products found new markets in Asia. Although the government expanded the electorate and seemed headed towards liberal democracy in the early 1920s, Japan veered to the political right in 1926 when Emperor Hirohito came to power.

Adding Manchuria to its Korean and Taiwanese colonies (see Map 19.5), Japan established the puppet state of Manchukuo. Meanwhile, at home, "patriots" carried out a campaign of terror against uncooperative businessmen and critics of the military. Unlike Italian fascism and German Nazism, Japanese authoritarianism had an explicitly religious dimension. The state in Japan took on a sacred aura through the promotion of an official religion, Shinto, and of Emperor Hirohito's divinity. By 1940, Hirohito and his closest advisers had merged all political parties into the Imperial Rule Assistance Association, ending even the semblance of democracy, and they advocated a radical form of racial purity. The Imperial Army divided the peoples of Asia into "master races," "friendly races," and "guest races," reserving a dominant position for the Japanese "Yamato Race."

Common Features of Authoritarian Regimes All of the major authoritarian regimes of this period claimed that modern economies required state direction. In Japan, the government fostered huge business conglomerates (*zaibatsu*); in Italy, it encouraged big business to form cartels. The German state also regarded the private sector as the vehicle of economic growth, but it expected entrepreneurs to support the Nazis' racial, antidemocratic, and expansionist aims. The most thorough form of economic coordination occurred in the Soviet Union, which adopted American-style mass production while eliminating private enterprise. Instead, the Soviet state owned and managed all of the country's industry.

All of these states relied heavily on mass organizations. Russia, Italy, and Germany had single mass parties; Japan had various rightist groups until the 1940 merger. All promoted dynamic youth movements, such as the Hitler Youth and the Union of German Girls, the Soviet Communist Youth League, and the Italian squads marching to the anthem "Giovinezza" (Youth).

Three of the four adopted extensive social welfare policies. The Nazis emphasized full employment, built public housing, and provided assistance to needy Aryan families. The Italian National Agency for Maternity and Infancy provided services for unwed mothers and infant care. Soviet programs addressed maternity, disability, sickness, and old age. Although Japan did not enact innovative social welfare legislation, its Home Affairs Ministry enlisted helpmates among civic groups, seeking to raise savings rates and improve child-rearing practices.

All of these regimes, except the Soviet Union, were ambivalent about women in public roles. Even the Soviets, who claimed to support gender equality, eventually restricted abortion and rewarded mothers who had many children. Officials were eager to honor new mothers as a way to repair the loss of so many young men during the Great War. Yet many more women were also entering professional careers, and some were becoming their families' primary wage earners.

Finally, all the dictatorships used violence and terror as tools for remaking the sociopolitical order. The Italians and the Japanese were not shy about arresting political opponents, particularly in their colonies. However, it was the Nazis and especially the Soviets who filled concentration and labor camps with alleged enemies of the state, whether Jews or supposed counterrevolutionaries.

MAP 19.5 | The Japanese Empire in Asia, 1933

Hoping to become a great imperial power like the European states, Japan established numerous colonies and spheres of influence early in the twentieth century.

- What were the main territorial components of the Japanese Empire?
- How far did the Japanese succeed in extending their political influence throughout East Asia?
- According to your reading, what problems did the desire to extend Japanese influence in China present to Japanese leaders?

THE HYBRID REGIMES IN LATIN AMERICA

COMPARISON

EXPLAIN how access to consumer goods and other aspects of mass society influenced political conflict in Asia, Africa, and Latin America.

Latin American countries felt the same pressures that produced liberal democratic and authoritarian responses in Europe, Russia, and Japan. However, the Latin American leaders devised solutions that combined democratic and authoritarian elements.

Economic Turmoil Latin American states had stayed out of the fighting in World War I, but their export economies had suffered. As trade plummeted, popular confidence in oligarchic regimes fell, and radical agitation surged.

As in Europe, Latin American governments stepped in to manage volatile economic markets. More than in any other region, the Depression battered Latin America's trading and financial systems, as well as the standards of living of laborers, because all were so dependent on exports. Exporters of basic staples, from sugar to wheat, faced stiff competition from other exporters and evaporating demand for their commodities. The region in fact suffered doubly because it had borrowed so much money to invest in infrastructure and expansion. When the world's major banks failed, creditors called in their loans from Latin America. This move drove borrowers to default. In an effort to improve their economic prospects, Latin American governments—with enthusiastic backing from the middle classes, nationalist intellectuals, and urban workers—turned to their domestic rather than foreign markets as the main engine of growth. Here, too, the state took a much more interventionist role in market activity than the ideal of classical liberalism.

After the war, Latin American elites confronted the mass age by establishing mass parties and encouraging interest groups to associate with them. Collective bodies such as chambers of commerce, trade unions, peasant associations, and organizations for minorities like blacks and Indians all operated with state sponsorship. This form of modern politics, often labeled corporatist, used social groups to bridge the gap between ruling elites and the general population.

Samba dancers The dance started in the shantytowns of Rio de Janeiro and eventually became popular throughout the world, thanks to films, photographs, and long-playing records that featured samba music.

Corporatist Politics in Brazil Corporatist politics took hold especially in Brazil, where the old republic collapsed in 1930. In its place, a coalition led by the skilled politician Getúlio Vargas (1883–1954) cultivated a strong following by enacting socially popular reforms.

Dubbing himself the "father of the poor," Vargas encouraged workers to organize, erected monuments to national heroes, and supported the building of schools and the paving of roads. He made special efforts to appeal to Brazilian blacks, who had been excluded from public life since the abolition of slavery. Thus, he legalized many previously forbidden Afro-Brazilian practices, such as the ritual "candomblé" dance, whose African and martial overtones seemed threatening to white elites. Vargas also supported samba schools, organizations that not only taught popular dances but also raised funds for public works. Moreover, Vargas addressed maternity and housing policies and enfranchised women (although they had to be able to read, as did male voters). Although he condemned the old elites for betraying the country to serve the interests of foreign consumers and investors, he also arranged foreign funding and technical transfers to build steel mills and factories. However, he took this step to create domestic industry so that Brazil would not be so dependent on imports. In these and other ways, Brazil and other Latin American governments combined democratic and authoritarian institutions and methods as a response to the economic downturn of the depression.

ANTICOLONIAL VISIONS OF MODERN LIFE

Debates over liberal-democratic versus authoritarian models engaged the world's colonial and semicolonial regions as well. But here there was a larger concern: what to do about colonial authority? Throughout Asia, most educated members of these communities wanted to roll back the European and American imperial presence. Some Asians even accepted Japanese imperialism as an antidote, under the slogan "Asia for the Asians." In Africa, however, where the European colonial presence was more recent, intellectuals still questioned the real meaning of colonial rule: were the British and the French sincerely committed to African improvement, or were they obstacles to African peoples' well-being? (See **Current Trends in World History: Population Movements**.)

In Africa as well as Asia, then, the search for the modern encompassed demands for power sharing or full political independence. To overcome the contradictions of the democratic liberalism Europeans practiced at home and the authoritarianism they exercised in colonial areas, educated Asians and Africans proposed various forms of nationalism.

Behind the Asian and African nationalist movements were profound disagreements about how best to govern nations once they gained independence and how to define citizenship. The democratic ethos of the imperial powers appealed to many intellectuals. Others liked the radical authoritarianism of fascism and communism, with their promises of rapid change. Whatever their political preferences, most literate colonial subjects also regarded their own religious and cultural traditions as sources for political mobilization. Thus Muslim, Hindu, Chinese, and African nationalist leaders used traditional values to gain the support of the rank and file. The colonial figures involved in political and intellectual movements insisted that the societies they sought to establish were going to be modern *and* at the same time retain their indigenous characteristics.

African Stirrings Africa contained the most recent territories to come under the Europeans' control, so anticolonial nationalist movements there were quite young. The region's fate remained very much in the hands of Europeans. After 1918, however, African peoples probed more deeply for the meaning of Europe's imperial presence.

There was some room (but not much) for voicing African interests under colonialism. The French had long held to a vision of assimilating their colonial peoples into French culture. In France's primary West African colony, Senegal, four coastal cities had traditionally elected one delegate (of mixed African and European ancestry) to the French National Assembly. This practice, limiting African representation to men of mixed ancestry, lasted until 1914, when Blaise Diagne (1872–1934), an African candidate, ran for office and won the seat in the French National Assembly, invoking his African origins and garnering the African vote. While the British allowed Africans to elect delegates to municipal bodies, they refused to permit colonial representatives to sit in Parliament.

Opposition was still not widespread in Africa, for protests ran up against not only colonial administrators but also western-educated African elites. Yet, even this privileged group began to reconsider its relationship to colonial authorities. In Kenya, immediately after World War I, a small contingent of mission-educated Africans called on the British to provide more and better schools and to return lands they claimed European settlers had

Current Trends in World History

Population Movements: Filling Up the Empty Spaces and Spreading Capitalism

As we have seen in Chapters 12 and 13, the European discovery of the Americas resulted in a vast movement of peoples across the Atlantic Ocean from Europe and Africa into the Western Hemisphere. These population movements, among the largest in world history to that point, pale when measured against the long-distance migrations that occurred in the hundred years between 1840 and 1940. During these years, 150 million individuals of European and Asian descent filled up the less populated parts of the world, moving from Europe, South Asia, and China into the Americas, Southeast Asia, and northern Asia in unprecedented numbers and spreading a capitalist mode of production wherever they moved. A great many of the migrants went as laborers in the factories and on the plains of the Americas and on the rubber, sugar, tea, and coffee plantations springing up in the Dutch East Indies and East and southern Africa. They were as essential to the expansion of the capitalist system in these regions as the 12 million African captives transported to the Americas during the Atlantic slave trade were for the economic expansion of the Americas. Although the new watchword in economic relations was free labor, not all of the men and women who moved were in fact free workers. Indentured servitude—that is, agreeing to work for a certain number of years, usually between three and seven, in return for transportation to the region, food, housing, and clothing—was widely used with Chinese and Indian workers.

A good example of the movement and use of semi-coerced or indentured workers in less-developed regions comes from East Africa. There, the British and Germans were engaged in a furious political rivalry to extend their control over territories, and British officials believed that constructing a railway from the coast of East Africa at the port of Mombasa to Kisumu at Lake Victoria would enhance their territorial ambitions in East Africa. They also concluded that they would be unable to recruit a sufficient supply of African workers to accomplish the task. Not surprisingly, they looked to the government of India to assist them in providing the necessary work force.

The British government of India did more than help them. In all, it made available nearly 35,000 indentured South Asian workers on three-year contracts for the construction of what was known as the Uganda Railway, the track for which, covering a distance of 582 miles, was completed in a mere five years from 1896 to 1901. The work was arduous, the

stolen. Although defeated in this instance, the young nationalists drew important lessons from their confrontation with the authorities. Their new spokesperson, Jomo Kenyatta (1898–1978), invoked their precolonial Kikuyu traditions as a basis for resisting colonialism. These early anticolonial movements prepared the foundations for more widespread resistance to colonial rule after World War II.

Imagining an Indian Nation As Africans explored the use of modern politics against Europeans, the war and its aftermath brought full-blown challenges to British rule in India. Indeed, the Indian nationalist challenge provided inspiration for other anticolonial movements.

For over a century, Indians had heard British authorities extol the virtues of liberal democracy, yet they were excluded from participation. In 1919, the British did slightly enlarge the franchise in India and allowed more local self-government, but these moves did not satisfy Indians' nationalist longings. During the 1920s and 1930s, the nationalists, led by **Mohandas Karamchand (Mahatma) Gandhi** (1869–1948), laid the foundations for an alternative, anticolonial movement.

Gandhi and Nonviolent Resistance When Gandhi returned to India in 1915, after studying law in England and gaining a reputation for working on behalf of Indian immigrants in South Africa, he immediately became the focus of the Indian nationalist movement. He spelled out the moral and political philosophy of *satyagraha*, or nonviolent resistance, which he had developed while in South Africa. His message to Indians was simple:

The Uganda Railway Indian workers cut rock for the Uganda Railway in this 1905 photograph, taken in British East Africa.

living conditions in the work camps were horrific, yet the British official overseeing the construction concluded that had it not been for this work force, it is doubtful if the project could have been completed in less than twenty years. The building of the Uganda Railway is one of many examples where we see significant numbers of people moving to new places and regions, sometimes by their own choosing and sometimes not, to play an important role in the expansion of the capitalist system and the rivalries between colonial powers.

QUESTIONS FOR ANALYSIS

- Why do you think that in some cases, like the building of the Uganda Railway, governments had to be involved in forcibly moving workers to where they were needed rather than letting market forces draw the workers to where work was available?
- What do you see as some of the similarities and differences in the treatment of the African slaves versus the forced or indentured servants during this period?

Explore Further

Adam McKeown, *Melancholy Order: Asian Migration and the Globalization of Border* (2008).

develop your own resources and inner strength and control the instincts and activities that encourage participation in colonial economy and government, and you shall achieve *swaraj* ("self-rule"). Faced with Indian self-reliance and self-control pursued nonviolently, Gandhi claimed, the British eventually would have to leave.

Indian nationalists urged people to oppose cooperation with government officials, to boycott goods made in Britain, to refuse to send their children to British schools, and to withhold taxes. Gandhi added his voice, calling for an all-India *satyagraha*. He also formed an alliance with Muslim leaders and began turning the Indian National Congress from an elite organization of lawyers and merchants into a mass organization open to anyone who paid dues, even the illiterate and poor.

When the Depression struck India in 1930, Gandhi singled out salt as a testing ground for his ideas on civil disobedience. Every Indian used salt, whose production was a heavily taxed government monopoly. Thus, salt symbolized the Indians' subjugation to an alien government. To break the colonial government's monopoly, Gandhi began a 240-mile march from western India to the coast to gather sea salt for free. Accompanying him were seventy-one followers representing different regions and religions of India. News wire services and mass-circulation newspapers worldwide reported on the drama of the sixty-one-year-old Gandhi, wooden staff in hand, dressed in coarse homespun garments, leading the march. Thousands of people gathering en route were moved by the sight of the frail apostle of nonviolence encouraging them to embrace independence from colonial rule. By insisting

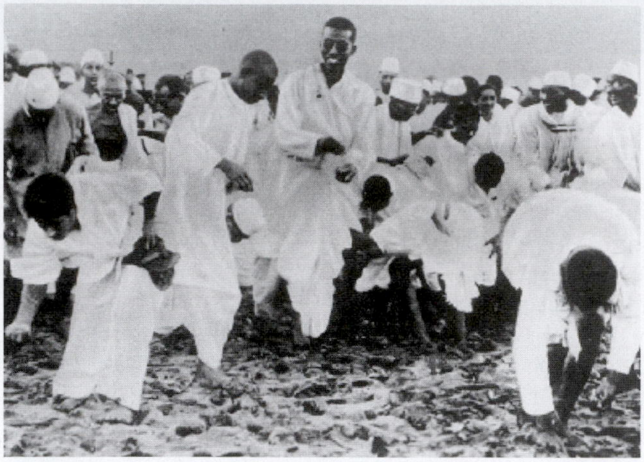

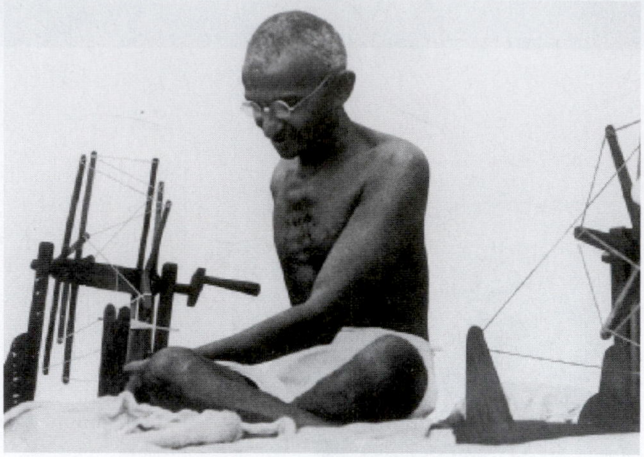

Gandhi and the Road to Independence *(Left)* Gandhi launched a civil disobedience movement in 1930 by violating the British government's tax on salt. Calling it "the most inhuman poll tax the ingenuity of man can devise," Gandhi, accompanied by his followers, set out on a month-long march on foot covering 240 miles to Dandi on the Gujarat coast. The picture shows Gandhi arriving at the sea, where he and his followers broke the law by scooping up handfuls of salt. *(Right)* Gandhi believed that India had been colonized by becoming enslaved to modern industrial civilization. Indians would achieve independence, he argued, when they became self-reliant. Thus, he made the spinning wheel a symbol of *swaraj* and handspun cloth the virtual uniform of the nation.

that Indians follow their conscience (always through nonviolent protest), by exciting the masses through his defiance of colonial power, and by using symbols like homespun cloth to counter foreign, machine-spun textiles, Gandhi instilled in the people a sense of pride, resourcefulness, and Indian national awareness.

A Divided Anticolonial Movement in India Although Gandhi gained a mass following, his program met opposition from within, for many in the Indian National Congress Party did not share his vision of community as the source of public life. Cambridge-educated Jawaharlal Nehru (1889–1964), for example, believed that only by embracing science and technology could India develop as a modern nation.

Even less enamored were radical activists who wanted a revolution, not peaceful protest. In the countryside, these radicals sought to organize peasants to overthrow colonial domination. Other activists galvanized the growing industrial proletariat by organizing trade unions. Their stress on class conflict ran against Gandhi's ideals of national unity.

Religion, too, threatened to fracture Gandhi's hope for anticolonial unity. The Hindu-Muslim alliance crafted by nationalists in the early 1920s splintered over who represented them and how to ensure their political rights. The Muslim community found an impressive leader in Muhammad Ali Jinnah, who set about making the Muslim League the sole representative organization of the Muslim community. In 1940, the Muslim League passed a resolution demanding independent Muslim states in provinces where they constituted a majority, on the grounds that Muslims were not a religious minority of the Indian nation, but a nation themselves.

In 1937, the British belatedly granted India provincial assemblies, a national legislature with two chambers, and an executive. By then, however, India's people were deeply politicized. The Congress Party, which inspired the masses to overthrow British rule, struggled to contain the different ideologies and new political institutions, such as labor unions, peasant associations, religious parties, and communal organizations. Seeking a path to economic modernization, Gandhi, on one side, envisioned independent India as an updated collection of village republics organized around the benevolent authority of male-dominated households. Nehru, on another side, hoped for a socioeconomic transformation powered by science and state-sponsored economic planning. Both believed that India's traditions of collective welfare and humane religious and philosophical practices set it apart from the modern West. By the outbreak of World War II, India was well on its way toward political independence, but British policies and India's divisions foretold a violent end to imperial rule (see Chapter 20).

Chinese Nationalism Unlike India and Africa, China was never formally colonized. But foreign powers' "concession areas" on Chinese soil compromised its sovereignty. Indeed, foreign nationals living in China enjoyed many privileges, including immunity from Chinese law. Furthermore, unequal treaties imposed on the Qing government had robbed China of its customs and tariff autonomy. Thus, the Chinese nationalists' vision of a modern alternative echoed that of the Indian nationalists: ridding the nation of foreign domination was the initial condition of national fulfillment. For many, the 1911 Revolution (as the fall of the Qing dynasty came to be known; see Chapter 18) symbolized the first step toward transforming a crumbling agrarian empire into a modern nation.

Despite high hopes, the new republic could not establish legitimacy. For one thing, factional and regional conflicts made the government little more than a loose alliance of rural elites, merchants, and military leaders. Its intellectual inspiration came from the ideas of Sun Yat-sen, founder of the nationalist political party, the Guomindang. Under the banner of anti-imperialism, the party sponsored large-scale organizations of workers' unions, peasant leagues, and women's associations that looked to students and workers as well as the Russian Revolution for inspiration.

In 1926, amid a renewed tide of anti-foreign agitation, **Chiang Kai-shek** (1887–1975) seized control of the party following Sun's death. Chiang launched a partially successful military campaign to reunify the country and established a new national government with its capital in Nanjing.

Peasant Populism in China: White Wolf For many Guomindang leaders, the peasant population represented a backward class. Thus, the leadership failed to tap into the revolutionary potential of the countryside, which was alive with grassroots movements such as that of White Wolf.

From late 1913 to 1914, Chinese newspapers circulated reports about a roving band of armed men led by a mysterious figure known as White Wolf. This figure terrified members of the elite. It is unlikely that the band, rumored to have close to a million followers, had more than 20,000 members even at its height. But the mythology surrounding White Wolf was so widespread that the movement's impact reverberated well beyond its physical presence.

Popular myth depicted White Wolf as a Chinese Robin Hood with the mission to restore order. The band's objective was to rid the country of government injustices. Raiding major trade routes and market towns, White Wolf's followers gained a reputation for robbing the rich and aiding the poor. Stories of helping the poor won the White Wolf army many followers in rural China, where local peasants joined temporarily as fighters and then returned home when the band moved on. Although the White Wolf army lacked the power to restore order in the countryside, its presence reflected the changes that had to come in China.

A Post-Imperial Turkish Nation Of all the postwar anticolonial movements, none was more successful or more committed to European models than that of **Mustafa Kemal Ataturk** (1881–1938), who helped forge the modern Turkish nation-state. Until 1914, the Ottoman Empire was a colonial power in its own right. But having fought on the losing German side, it saw its realm shrink to a part of Anatolia under the Treaty of Sèvres, which ended the war between the Allies and the Ottoman Empire.

In 1920, an Ottoman army officer and military hero named Mustafa Kemal harnessed an outpouring of Turkish nationalism into opposition to Greek troops who had been sent to enforce the peace treaty. Rallying his own troops to defend the fledgling Turkish nation, Kemal reconquered most of Anatolia and the area around Istanbul and secured international recognition for the new state in 1923 in the Treaty of Lausanne. Thereafter, a vast, forcible exchange of populations occurred. Approximately 1.2 million Greek Christians left Turkey to settle in Greece, and 400,000 Muslims relocated from Greece to Turkey.

With the Ottoman Empire gone, Kemal and his followers moved to build a state based on Turkish national identity. First they deposed the sultan. Then they abolished the Ottoman caliphate and proclaimed Turkey a republic, whose supreme authority would be an elected House of Assembly. Later, after Kemal insisted that the people adopt European-style surnames, the assembly conferred on Kemal the mythic name Ataturk, "father of the Turks."

In forging a Turkish nation, Kemal looked to construct a European-style secular state and to eliminate Islam's hold over civil and political affairs. The Turkish elite replaced Muslim religious law with the Swiss civil code, instituted the western (Christian) calendar, and abolished the once-powerful dervish religious orders. They also sought to eliminate Arabic and Persian words from Turkish, substituted Roman script for Arabic letters, forbade polygamy, made wearing the fez (a brimless cap associated in Kemal's mind with old-fashioned ways) a crime, and instructed Turks to wear European-style hats. The veil, though not outlawed, was denounced as a relic. In 1934, the government enfranchised Turkish women, granted them property rights in marriage and inheritance, and allowed them to enter the professions. Schools were taken out of the hands of Muslim clerics, placed under state control, and, along with military service, became the chief instrument for making the masses conscious of belonging to a Turkish nation. Yet, many villagers did not accept Ataturk's non-Islamic nationalism, remaining devoted to Islam and resentful of the prohibitions against dervish dancing.

In imitating Europe, Kemal also borrowed many of its antidemocratic models. Inspired by the Soviets, he inaugurated a five-year plan for the economy emphasizing centralized coordination by the government. During the 1930s, Turkish nationalists also drew on Nazi examples by advocating racial theories that celebrated central Asian Turks as the founders of all civilization. In another authoritarian move, Kemal occasionally rigged parliamentary elections, while using the police and judiciary to silence his critics. The Kemalist revolution in Turkey was the most far-reaching and enduring transformation that had occurred outside Europe and the Americas up to that point. It offered an important model for the founding of secular, authoritarian states in the Islamic world.

Nationalism and the Rise of the Muslim Brotherhood in Egypt Elsewhere in the Middle East, where France and Britain expanded their holdings at the Ottomans' expense, anticolonial movements borrowed from European models while putting their own stamp on nation-making and modernization campaigns. In Egypt, the British occupation predated the fall of the Ottoman Empire, but here, too, World War I energized the forces of anticolonial nationalism.

When the war ended, Sa'd Zaghlul (1857–1927), an educated Egyptian patriot, pressed for an Egyptian delegation to be invited to the peace conference at Versailles. He hoped to present Egypt's case for national independence. Instead, British officials arrested and exiled him and his most vocal supporters. When news of this action came out, Egypt burst into revolt. Rural rebels broke away from the central government, proclaiming local republics. Villagers tore up railway lines and telegraph wires, the symbols of British authority.

After defusing the conflict, British authorities tried to appease the Egyptian desire to control their own destiny. In 1922, Britain proclaimed Egypt independent, although it retained the right to station British troops on Egyptian soil. This provision was intended to protect traffic through the Suez Canal and foreign populations residing in Egypt, but it also enabled the British to continue to influence Egyptian politics. Two years later, elections placed Zaghlul's nationalist party, the Wafd, in office. But the British prevented the Wafd from exercising real power.

This subversion of independence and democracy provided an opening for antiliberal versions of anticolonialism in Egypt. During the Depression years, a fascist group, Young Egypt, garnered wide appeal. Much more influential and destined to have an enduring influence throughout the Arab world was an Islamic group, the Muslim Brotherhood, which attacked liberal democracy as a facade for middle-class, business, and landowning interests. The Muslim Brotherhood was anticolonial and anti-British, but its members considered mere political independence insufficient. Egyptians, they argued, must also renounce the lure of the West (whether liberal capitalism or godless communism) and return to a purified form of Islam. For the Muslim Brotherhood, Islam offered a complete way of life. A "return to Islam" through the nation-state created yet another model of modernity for colonial and semicolonial peoples.

Conclusion

The Great War and its aftermath accelerated the trend toward mass participation in a broad range of activities and the debate over how to define progress and organize the people. Because mass society meant production and consumption on a staggering scale, satisfying the populace became a pressing concern for rulers worldwide. Competing programs vied for influence in the new, broader, public domain.

Most programs fell into one of three categories: liberal democratic, authoritarian, or anticolonial. Liberal democracy defined the political and economic systems in most of western Europe and the Americas in the decade following World War I. Resting on faith in free enterprise and representative democracy (with a restricted franchise), liberal regimes had already been unsettled before the Great War. Turn-of-the-century reforms broadened electorates and brought government oversight and regulation into private economic activity. But during the Great Depression, dissatisfaction again deepened. Only far-reaching reforms, introducing greater regulation and more aggressive government intervention to provide for the citizenry's welfare, saved capitalist economies and democratic political systems in Britain, France, and North America from collapse.

Through the 1930s, liberal democracy was in retreat. Authoritarianism seemed better positioned to satisfy the masses while representing the dynamism of modernity. While authoritarians differed about the faults of capitalism, they joined in the condemnation of electoral democracy. Authoritarians mobilized the masses to put the interests of the nation above the individual. That mobilization often involved brutal repression, yet it seemed also to restore pride and purpose to a great number of people.

Meanwhile, the colonial and semicolonial world searched for ways to escape from European domination. In Asia and Africa, anticolonial leaders sought to eliminate foreign rule while turning colonies into nations and subjects into citizens. Some looked to the liberal democratic West for models of nation building, but others rejected liberalism because it was associated with colonial rule. Instead, socialism, communism, fascism, and a return to religious traditions offered more promising paths.

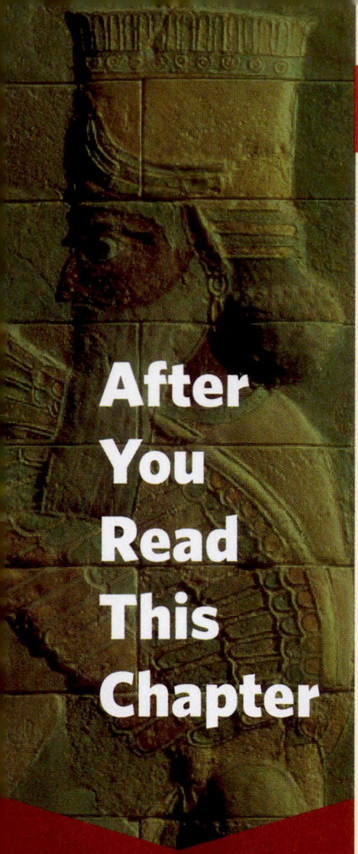

After You Read This Chapter

Go to INQUIZITIVE to see what you've learned—and learn what you've missed—with personalized feedback along the way.

TRACING THE GLOBAL STORYLINES

FOCUS ON: *World War I and Its Aftermath*

THE GREAT WAR

- The war destroys empires, starting with the Bolshevik Revolution against the tsarist regime in Russia, followed by the defeat and dissolution of the German, Austro-Hungarian, and Ottoman empires.
- Mass mobilization sees almost 70 million men join the fighting, undermines traditional gender boundaries, and forces states to recognize their peoples' demands for compensation afterward.
- Popular culture spreads as leaders use the new media of radio and film to promote national loyalties and discredit enemies.

THE AFTERMATH

- Liberal democracies in France, Britain, and the United States survive the Great Depression by enacting far-reaching changes in their political systems and free market economies.
- Authoritarian (communist and fascist) dictatorships with many political similarities emerge in the Soviet Union, Italy, and Germany, Spain, and Portugal.
- Latin American leaders devise hybrid solutions that combine democratic and authoritarian elements.
- Peoples living under colonial rule in Asia and Africa mobilize traditional values to oppose imperial rulers.
- Key individuals emerge in the struggle to define newly independent nations: Kenyatta, Gandhi, Chiang Kai-shek, and Ataturk.

CHRONOLOGY

THE AMERICAS
- U.S. enters World War I 1917

EUROPE
- World War I 1914–1918
- Mussolini takes over Italy 1922

SOVIET UNION
- Bolshevik Revolution 1917
- Russian civil war 1918–1921

EAST ASIA

SOUTH ASIA

MIDDLE EAST
- Mustafa Kemal creates modern Turkish nation state 1923

1900 | 1910 | 1920

THINKING ABOUT GLOBAL CONNECTIONS

- ***Thinking about Transformation & Conflict and Visions of the Modern*** What was the relationship between war and progress in the early twentieth century? What new political, social, and cultural movements grew out of the Great War? Think in particular of the role of former soldiers in politics; the adaptation in peacetime of production practices developed for the war effort; and governments' willingness and ability to regulate the economy and people's everyday lives.
- ***Thinking about Changing Power Relationships and Visions of the Modern*** What, if anything, was left in this period of the tradition of classical liberalism, which trusted markets to regulate themselves and believed progress would result from individuals pursuing their own self interest? What role did government intervention—in the economy and society—play for the three major traditions discussed in this chapter: liberal democratic, authoritarian, and anticolonial? How central was state intervention to their respective views of progress and modernity?
- ***Thinking about Gender and Visions of the Modern*** What role did women play in the social transformations of the early twentieth century, both as participants and as symbols? Pay special attention to the role of women workers in war production and, increasingly, in professional careers thereafter; to women consumers in an era of mass production; and to governments' commitment to the ideal of gender equality, and (faltering) willingness to abide by that ideal.

STUDY QUESTIONS

1. Explain the relationship between the **Great War** and the **Great Depression**, both in terms of origins and outcomes. What common sources did they share? What caused them? What values and assumptions did they both challenge?
2. Define the terms mass culture, mass production, and mass consumption. How, where, and why did they spread?
3. Distinguish **fascism** from traditional conservatism. Compare it to other political movements discussed in this chapter, especially **bolshevism**.
4. Explain how authoritarian leaders (**Stalin, Mussolini, and Hitler**) defined progress. What did it mean to them? What elements did they share with liberal democracy, and in what terms did they reject that tradition?
5. Contrast the visions of progress espoused by anticolonial leaders, including **Gandhi, Ataturk**, and **Chiang Kai-shek**. To what extent did they reflect borrowed elements versus local native traditions and ideas?
6. Describe how Latin American societies adjusted to economic instability. How did visions of becoming modern affect states and societies in that region of the world?

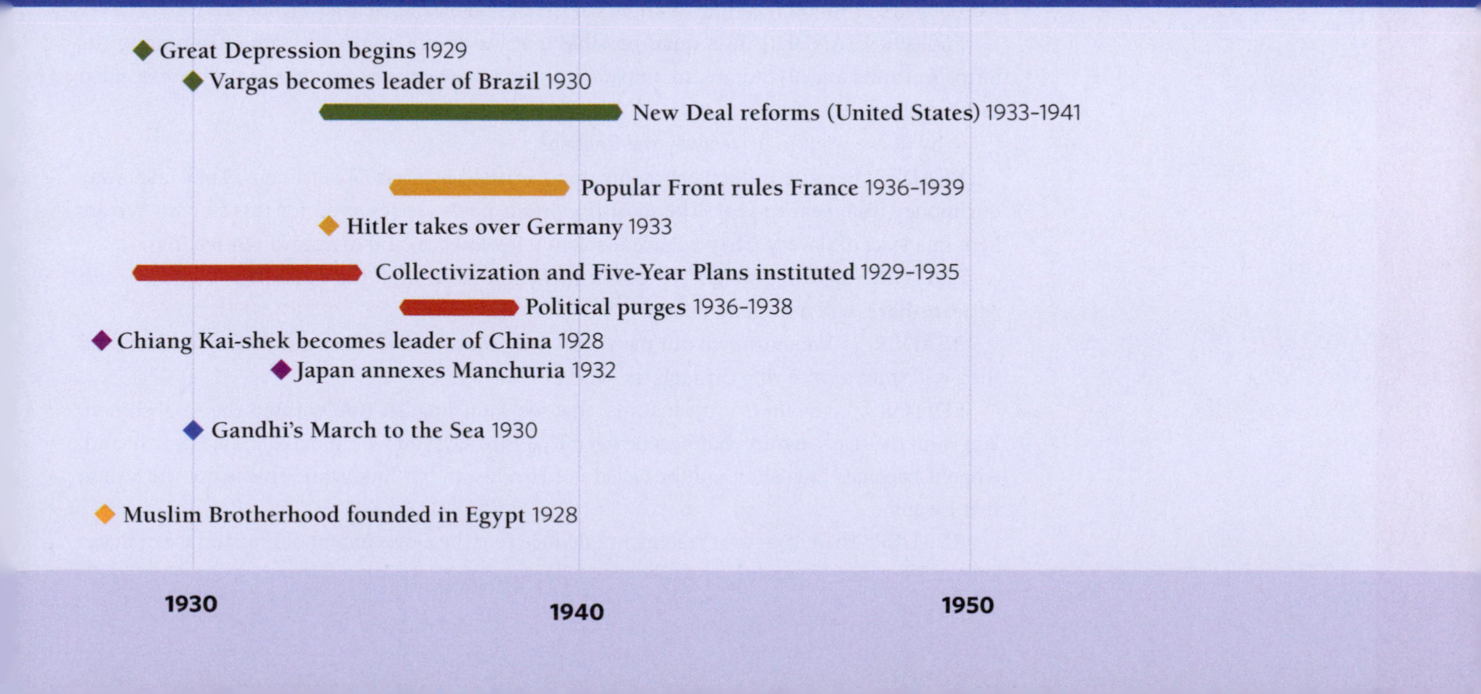
Great Depression begins 1929
Vargas becomes leader of Brazil 1930
New Deal reforms (United States) 1933–1941
Popular Front rules France 1936–1939
Hitler takes over Germany 1933
Collectivization and Five-Year Plans instituted 1929–1935
Political purges 1936–1938
Chiang Kai-shek becomes leader of China 1928
Japan annexes Manchuria 1932
Gandhi's March to the Sea 1930
Muslim Brotherhood founded in Egypt 1928
1930
1940
1950

Going to the Source

Competing Ideologies

The following documents all address at least one of the main ideologies discussed in this chapter: anticolonialism, with its clear desire to be rid of colonial rule, but certainly less clear ideas about what type of rule should replace it; liberalism, with its belief in a limited role for the state and a valorizing of the individual; and authoritarianism, which generally envisioned a much stronger role for the state and the subjugation of individual desires to the will of the government. Ideologies are not created in a vacuum, however: each of these documents is the product of a specific time and place. The documents in this section come from across the globe and deal with people who are trying to fix problems that they see in the societies where they live. Yet, in some ways each author offers a point of view that could be applied in other places, and perhaps even in other times.

PRIMARY SOURCE 19.1

Excerpt from Hind Swaraj *(1909), Mohandas Gandhi*

British rule fundamentally changed social and economic relations in India by bringing new technologies to the subcontinent. Gandhi wanted all Indians to be treated as equal citizens, and not simply machine operators. Here he is especially concerned about British ideas of government, the values that accompanied British rule, and what would happen to Indians once British colonialism ended. This document, in the form of an interview, proposes questions that the public might have asked if given the chance, with Gandhi in the role of editor.

*

READER: . . . I would now like to know your views on Swaraj [self-government]. . . .

EDITOR [GANDHI]: It is quite possible that we do not attach the same meaning to the term. You and I and all Indians are impatient to obtain Swaraj, but we are certainly not decided as to what it is. . . .

Why do we want to drive away the English?

READER: Because India has become impoverished by their Government. They take away our money from year to year. The most important posts are reserved for themselves. We are kept in a state of slavery. They behave insolently towards us, and disregard our feelings.

EDITOR: Supposing we get self-government similar to what the Canadians and the South Africans have, will it be good enough?

READER: . . .We must own our navy, our army, and we must have our own splendour, and then will India's voice ring through the world.

EDITOR: . . . In effect it means this: that we want English rule without the Englishman. You want the tiger's nature, but not the tiger; that is to say, you would make India English, and, when it becomes English, it will be called not Hindustan but Englistan. This is not the Swaraj that I want.

READER: Then from your statement I deduce that the Government of England is not desirable and not worth copying by us.

EDITOR: . . . If India copies England, it is my firm conviction that she will be ruined.

READER: To what do you ascribe this state of England?

EDITOR: It is not due to any peculiar fault of the English people, but the condition is due to modern civilisation. It is a civilisation only in name. Under it the nations of Europe are becoming degraded and ruined day by day.

READER: . . . I should like to know your views about the condition of our country.

EDITOR: . . . India is being ground down not under the English heel but under that of modern civilisation. It is groaning under the monster's terrible weight. . . . India is becoming irreligious. Here I am not thinking of the Hindu, the Mahomedan, or the Zoroastrian religion, but of that religion which underlies all religions. We are turning away from God.

READER: You have denounced railways, lawyers and doctors. I can see that you will discard all machinery. What, then, is civilisation?

READER: . . . The tendency of Indian civilisation is to elevate the moral being, that of the Western civilisation is to propagate immorality. The latter is godless, the former is based on a belief in God. So understanding and so believing, it behooves every lover of India to cling to the old Indian civilisation even as a child clings to its mother's breast.

READER: . . . What, then, . . . would you suggest for freeing India?

EDITOR: . . . Those alone who have been affected by Western civilisation have become enslaved. . . . If we become free, India is free. And in this thought you have a definition of Swaraj. It is Swaraj when we learn to rule ourselves.

1. What are Gandhi's objections to British rule?

2. What is the role of religion in Gandhi's version of swaraj?

PRIMARY SOURCE 19.2

An Open Letter from Ho Chi Minh to M. Albert Serraut, French Minister of Colonies (1922)

Vietnamese independence leader Ho Chi Minh spent his early career in France, where he saw firsthand how the French colonizers of Indochina understood his society. This open and sarcastic letter from Ho Chi Minh to the French Minister of Colonies, was published in the Intercolonial Union newspaper, *La Paria* (The Pariah), which Ho founded and edited, along with other unhappy colonists from French colonies in North Africa and Asia. Ho began to gravitate to communism when he lived in Paris, though this letter makes fewer references to the Communist Party than his later works contain.

*

Your Excellency,

We know very well that your affection for the natives, of the colonies in general, and the Annamese [the Vietnamese people] in particular is great. Under your proconsulate, the Annamese people have known true prosperity and real happiness, the happiness of seeing their country dotted all over with an increasing number of spirit and opium shops which, together with firing squads, prisons, "democracy" and all the improved apparatus of modern civilization, are combining to make the Annamese the most advanced of the Asians and the happiest of mortals.

These acts of benevolence save us the trouble of recalling all the others, such as enforced recruitment and loans, bloody repressions, the dethronement and exile of kings, profanation of sacred places, etc.

As a Chinese poem says, "The wind of kindness follows the movement of your fan, and the rain of virtue precedes the tracks of your carriage." As you are now the supreme head of all the colonies, your special care for the Indochinese has but increased with your elevation. You have created in Paris itself a service having the special task—with special regard to Indo-China, according to a colonial publication—of keeping watch on the natives, especially the Annamese, living in France.

But "keeping watch" alone seemed to Your Excellency's fatherly solicitude insufficient, and you wanted to do better. That is why for some time now, you have granted each Annamese—dear Annamese, as Your Excellency says—private *aides-de-camp*. Though still novices in the art of Sherlock Holmes, these good people are very devoted and particularly sympathetic. We have only praise to bestow on them and compliments to pay to their boss, Your Excellency. . . .

At a time when Parliament is trying to save money, and cut down administrative personnel; when there is a large budget deficit; when agriculture and industry lack labour; when attempts are being made to levy taxes on workers' wages; and at a time when repopulation demands the use of all productive energies: it would seem to us anti-patriotic at such a time to accept personal favours which necessarily cause loss of the powers of the citizens condemned—as *aides-de-camp*—to idleness and the spending of money that the proletariat has sweated hard for.

In consequence, while remaining obliged to you, we respectfully decline this distinction flattering to us but too expensive to the country.

If Your Excellency insists on knowing what we do every day, nothing is easier: we shall publish every morning a bulletin of our movements, and Your Excellency will have but the trouble of reading.

Besides, our timetable is quite simple and almost unchanging.

Morning: from 8 to 12 at the workshop.

Afternoon: in newspaper offices (leftist of course) or at the library.

Evening: at home or attending educational talks.

Sundays and holidays: visiting museums or other places of interest.

There you are!

Hoping that this convenient and rational method will give satisfaction to Your Excellency, we beg to remain.

1. **What is Ho Chi Minh's chief objection in this article?**
2. **Based on what you have read, what solution might Ho Chi Minh propose to address his concerns?**

PRIMARY SOURCE 19.3

The Man Nobody Knows *(1925), Bruce Barton*

Bruce Barton was the son of a Christian minister. He wrote a series of manuals and articles about ways that individuals could achieve success by pursuing their own good in their own way—a component of liberal thinking. The selection below comes from his most famous book, *The Man Nobody Knows*, in which he imagines Jesus as a contemporary American businessman. Barton worked as a journalist and an advertising executive and was twice elected to the U.S. Congress as a Republican representative from New York State on an anti–New Deal platform.

*

"If you're forever thinking about saving your life," Jesus said, "you'll lose it; but the man who loses his life shall find it." Because he said it and he was a religious teacher, because it's printed in the Bible, the world has dismissed it as high minded ethics but not hard headed sense. But look again! . . .

What did Henry Ford mean, one spring morning, when he tipped a kitchen chair back against the whitewashed wall of his tractor plant and talked about his career?

"Have you ever noticed that the man who starts out in life with a determination to make money, never makes very much?" he asked. It was rather a startling question; and without waiting for my comment he went on to answer it: "He may gather together a competence, of course, a few tens of thousands or even hundreds of thousands, but he'll never amass a really great fortune. But let a man start out in life to build something better and sell it cheaper than it has ever been built or sold before—let him have that determination, and, give his whole self to it—and the money will roll in so fast that it will bury him if he doesn't look out."

"When we were building our original model, do you suppose that it was money we were thinking about? Of course we expected that it would be profitable, if it succeeded, but that wasn't in the front of our minds. We wanted to make a car so cheap that every family in the United States could afford to have one. So we worked morning, noon and night, until our muscles ached and our nerves were so ragged that it seemed as if we just couldn't stand it to hear anyone mention the word automobile again. One night, when we were almost at the breaking point I said to the boys, 'Well, there's one consolation,' I said, 'Nobody can take this business away from us unless he's willing to work harder than we've worked.' And so far," he concluded with a whimsical smile, "nobody has been willing to do that."

1. **What do you think is Barton's chief concern in this passage?**
2. **How does Barton connect innovation to both happiness *and* profit? Do you find this argument compelling? Why or why not?**

PRIMARY SOURCE 19.4

The End of Laissez-Faire *(1926), John Maynard Keynes*

The economic theory of John Maynard Keynes, the founder of Keynesian economics, is generally credited with saving capitalism following the Great Depression crisis in the 1930s. This excerpt is from an essay in which he argues for greater state involvement in the economy, at least in general terms. Keynes suggests that individuals engaged in competition with each other may not actually benefit society as a whole. His later work *The General Theory of Employment, Interest, and Money* makes a much more specific economist's case for government intervention in particular areas.

The disposition towards public affairs, which we conveniently sum up as individualism and *laissez-faire,* drew its sustenance from many different rivulets of thought and springs of feeling. For more than a hundred years our philosophers ruled us because, by a miracle, they nearly all agreed or seem to agree on this one thing. We do not dance even yet to a new tune. But a change is in the air. We hear but indistinctly what were once the clearest and most distinguishable voices which have ever instructed political mankind. The orchestra of diverse instruments, the chorus of articulate sound, is receding at last into the distance. . . .

The most important *Agenda* of the State relates not to those activities which private individuals are already fulfilling, but to those functions which fall outside the sphere of the individual, to those decisions which are made by *no one* if the State does not make them. The important thing for government is not to do things which individuals are doing already, and to do them a little better or a little worse; but to do those things which at present are not done at all.

It is not within the scope of my purpose on this occasion to develop practical policies. I limit myself, therefore, to naming some instances of what I mean from amongst those problems about which I happen to have thought most. Many of the greatest economic evils of our time are the fruits of risk, uncertainty, and ignorance. It is because particular individuals, fortunate in situation or in abilities, are able to take advantage of uncertainty and ignorance, and also because for the same reason big business is often a lottery, that great inequalities of wealth come about; and these same factors are also the cause of the unemployment of labour, or the disappointment of reasonable business expectations, and of the impairment of efficiency and production. Yet the cure lies outside the operations of individuals; it may even be to the interest of individuals to aggravate the disease. I believe that the cure for these things is partly to be sought in the deliberate control of the currency and of credit by a central institution, and partly in the collection and dissemination on a great scale of data relating to the business situation, including the full publicity, by law if necessary, of all business facts which it is useful to know. These measures would involve society in exercising directive intelligence through some appropriate organ of action over many of the inner intricacies of private business, yet it would leave private initiative and enterprise unhindered. Even if these measures prove insufficient, nevertheless, they will furnish us with better knowledge than we have now for taking the next step.

1. **Why might Keynes have argued for greater government intervention in the economy in the years after World War I?**
2. **What does Keynes think the relationship between the individual and the government ought to be?**

PRIMARY SOURCE 19.5

Detroit Industry (1932), Diego Rivera

Mexican artist Diego Rivera's mural depicts workers on a Ford assembly line in Detroit, Michigan, which had been automated several years before Rivera painted the mural. It is part of a series of twenty-seven panels commissioned to honor the city's labor force.

1. **How did the moving assembly line change the way people worked?**
2. **Describe the relationship between workers and machines depicted in this mural.**

PRIMARY SOURCE 19.6

"What is Fascism?" (1935), Benito Mussolini (with Giovanni Gentile)

Italian Fascism is one of several authoritarian regimes (e.g., Nazism and Soviet Communism) that arose in the years between World Wars I and II. Determined to preserve private property, the Fascists, in contrast to the Bolsheviks in the Soviet Union, disagreed with the system of liberalism, in which individuals could pursue their own good in their own way. In this document, Mussolini articulates the Fascist program—the state is the supreme authority, but individuals contribute to the state and it carries out their will—thus ensuring perfect liberty.

Anti-individualistic, the Fascist conception of life stresses the importance of the State and accepts the individual only in so far as his interests coincide with those of the State, which stands for the conscience and the universal will of man as a historic entity. It is opposed to classical liberalism which arose as a reaction to absolutism and exhausted its historical function when the State became the expression of the conscience and will of the people. Liberalism denied the State in the name of the individual; Fascism reasserts the rights of the State as expressing the real essence of the individual. And if liberty is to be the attribute of living men and not of abstract dummies invented by individualistic liberalism, then Fascism stands for liberty, and for the only liberty worth having, the liberty of the State and of the individual within the State. The Fascist conception of the State is all embracing; outside of it no human or spiritual values can exist, much less have value. Thus understood, Fascism, is totalitarian, and the Fascist State—a synthesis and a unit inclusive of all values—interprets, develops, and potentates the whole life of a people. . . .

Fascism is therefore opposed to Socialism to which unity within the State (which amalgamates classes into a single economic and ethical reality) is unknown, and which sees in history nothing but the class struggle. Fascism is likewise opposed to trade unionism as a class weapon. But when brought within the orbit of the State, Fascism recognizes the real needs which gave rise to socialism and trade unionism, giving them due weight in the guild or corporative system in which divergent interests are coordinated and harmonized in the unity of the State. . . .

Grouped according to their several interests, individuals form classes; they form trade-unions when organized according to their several economic activities; but first and foremost they form the State, which is no mere matter of numbers, the sums of the individuals forming the majority. Fascism is therefore opposed to that form of democracy which equates a nation to the majority, lowering it to the level of the largest number; but it is the purest form of democracy if the nation be considered as it should be from the point of view of quality rather than quantity, as an idea, the mightiest because the most ethical, the most coherent, the truest, expressing itself in a people as the conscience and will of the few, if not, indeed, of one, and ending to express itself in the conscience and the will of the mass, of the whole group ethnically molded by natural and historical conditions into a nation, advancing, as one conscience and one will, along the self same line of development and spiritual formation. Not a race, nor a geographically defined region, but a people, historically perpetuating itself; a multitude unified by an idea and imbued with the will to live, the will to power, self-consciousness, personality. . . .

First of all, as regards the future development of mankind, and quite apart from all present political considerations, Fascism does not, generally speaking, believe in the possibility or utility of perpetual peace. It therefore discards pacifism as a cloak for cowardly supine renunciation in contradistinction to self-sacrifice. War alone keys up all human energies to their maximum tension and sets the seal of nobility on those peoples who have the courage to face it. All other tests are substitutes which never place a man face to face with himself before the alternative of life or death. Therefore all doctrines which postulate peace at all costs are incompatible with Fascism.

Equally foreign to the spirit of Fascism, even if accepted as useful in meeting special political situations—are all internationalistic or League superstructures which, as history shows, crumble to the ground whenever the heart of nations is deeply stirred by sentimental, idealistic or practical considerations. Fascism carries this anti-pacifistic attitude into the life of the individual.

1. **What is the role of the state according to the Fascist vision of society?**
2. **Compare Mussolini's statements to Primary Source 19.3 and analyze the similarities and differences between the two documents.**

PRIMARY SOURCE 19.7

Facing Mount Kenya *(1937), Jomo Kenyatta*

Jomo Kenyatta was a leading nationalist before Kenya gained its independence from Britain in 1963. He then served as its president until his death in 1978. In *Facing Mount Kenya*, he wrote an account of his own Kikuyu community. He stressed the cohesion of precolonial society and identified destructive consequences of colonialism in Africa.

And it is the culture which he inherits that gives a man his human dignity as well as his material prosperity. It teaches him his mental and moral values and makes him feel it worth while to work and fight for liberty.

But a culture has no meaning apart from the social organisation of life on which it is built. When the European comes to the Gikuyu country and robs the people of their land, he is taking away not only their livelihood, but the material symbol that holds family and tribe together. In doing this he gives one blow which cuts away the foundations from the whole of Gikuyu life, social, moral, and economic. When he explains, to his own satisfaction and after the most superficial glance at the issues involved, that he is doing this for the sake of the Africans, to "civilize" them, "teach them the disciplinary value of regular work," and "give them the benefit of European progressive ideas," he is adding insult to injury, and need expect to convince no one but himself.

There certainly are some progressive ideas among the Europeans. They include the ideas of material prosperity, of medicine, and hygiene, and literacy which enables people to take part in world culture. But so far the Europeans who visit Africa have not been conspicuously zealous in imparting these parts of their inheritance to the Africans, and seem to think that the only way to do it is by police discipline and armed force. They speak as if it was somehow beneficial to an African to work for them instead of for himself, and to make sure that he will receive this benefit they do their best to take away his land and leave him with no alternative. Along with his land they rob him of his government, condemn his religious ideas, and ignore his fundamental conception of justice and morals, all in the name of civilisation and progress.

If Africans were left in peace on their own lands, Europeans would have to offer them the benefits of white civilisation in real earnest before they could obtain the African labour which they want so much. They would have to offer the African a way of life which was really superior to the one his fathers lived before him, and a share in the prosperity given them by their command of science. They would have to let the African choose what parts of European culture would be beneficially transplanted, and how they could be adapted. He would probably not choose the gas bomb or the armed police force, but he might ask for some other things of which he does not get so much today. As it is, by driving him off his ancestral lands, the Europeans have robbed him of the material foundations of his culture, and reduced him to a state of serfdom incompatible with human happiness. The African is conditioned, by the cultural and social institutions of centuries, to a freedom of which Europe has little conception, and it is not in his nature to accept serfdom for ever. He realises that he must fight unceasingly for his own complete emancipation; for without this he is doomed to remain the prey of rival imperialisms, which in every successive year will drive their fangs more deeply into his vitality and strength.

1. **How does Kenyatta understand the relationship between individuals and their government, particularly in the African context?**
2. **Compare this document to Primary Source 19.1. Analyze their similarities and differences.**

Questions for Analysis

Comparison

1. Compare the anticolonial documents above. Do you find one approach more appealing than another? Why or why not?

Argumentation

2. Compare the documents that consider the relationship between individuals, their governments, and the economy. Do you find one approach to this relationship more compelling than another? Why or why not?

Causation

3. Explain the reasons that movements for social and political change developed in the years after World War I.

Long Essay Question

Synthesis

Imagine that you are creating a government of your own. What would be its goals and which ideology (or ideologies) would you find most useful to your state and why?

Before You Read This Chapter

GLOBAL STORYLINES

- World War II shatters the European-centered global order, weakening Europe and Japan, and unsettling empires.
- The United States and its liberal-democratic allies (the First World) engage in a cold war with the Soviet Union and its communist allies (the Second World).
- Decolonized states in Asia, Africa, and Latin America (the Third World) struggle to find a "third way" but find themselves caught between rival superpowers.

CORE OBJECTIVES

- **EXPLAIN** the relationship between World War II and the three-world order.
- **ANALYZE** the extent to which World War II was a global war.
- **ANALYZE** the roles that the United States and the Soviet Union played in the Cold War.
- **IDENTIFY** the goals of Third World states in this period, and **EVALUATE** the degree to which these goals were achieved.
- **COMPARE** the civil rights issues in the First, Second, and Third worlds, and **ASSESS** the ways each "world" address these and other basic rights.

CHAPTER 20

The Three-World Order

1940–1975

KEY TERMS

In February 1945, the three leaders of the World War II Allies—president Franklin Delano Roosevelt of the United States, prime minister Winston Churchill of Great Britain, and premier Joseph Stalin of the Soviet Union—met to prepare for the postwar world. By then, Germany, Italy, and Japan were losing the war. But the world's reordering was a source of deep contention, for the three leaders had profoundly different visions for the future. Roosevelt envisioned independent nation-states protected by an international body and had no interest in restoring the old European empires. Churchill, however, resisted decolonization of the British Empire. Stalin sought above all to secure Soviet influence in eastern Europe and to weaken Germany so that it could never again menace the Soviet Union. When the fighting stopped, the European-centered order, shocked by World War I, had been shattered by World War II. Empires lay in ruins and faced dismantling by independence movements. The nation-state had emerged as the prevailing global political organization.

With the weakening of western Europe, a new three-world order emerged. Heading the "First World," the United States championed capitalism and democracy as the best way to bring unprecedented prosperity in the decades after 1945. The United States' crucial ally

COMPARISON

EXPLAIN the relationship between World War II and the three-world order.

during World War II, the Soviet Union became its chief adversary in the decades that followed. As leader of the communist "Second World," the Soviet Union contested capitalist societies' claims and trumpeted socialism's accomplishments. As their spheres of influence expanded, the Americans and the Soviets (and their respective allies) engaged in a bitter ideological rivalry, known as the **Cold War** because no direct military conflict occurred between these two superpowers. Caught in between were formerly colonized and semicolonized people. Lumped together as the "Third World" by Western intellectuals and by Asian and African leaders who embraced the idea of an alternative to the dominant blocs, these nations emerged from the war eager to seek their own ways forward.

World War II and Its Aftermath

COMPARISON

ANALYZE the extent to which World War II was a global war.

World War II was truly a world conflict, a devastatingly total one. It grew out of unresolved problems connected to the Great War. World War I had not been, as many had prophesied, "the war to end all wars." Especially influential were the resentments bred by the harsh provisions and controversial state boundaries set out in the treaties signed at the war's end. World War II also resulted from the aggressive ambitions and racial theories of Germany and Japan. By the late 1930s, German and Japanese ambitions to become colonial powers brought these dictatorships (which along with Italy constituted the Axis powers) into conflict with France, Britain, the Soviet Union, and eventually the United States (the Allied powers). Fighting occurred in Europe, Africa, and Asia, and the Atlantic and Pacific oceans, as the warring nations mobilized millions of people and placed enormous demands on civilian populations.

THE WAR IN EUROPE

World War II began in September 1939 with Germany's invasion of Poland and the British and French decision to oppose it. Before it was all over in 1945, much of Europe, including Germany, had been leveled.

Blitzkrieg and Resistance Germany's early success was staggering. Nazi troops overran Poland, France, Norway, Denmark, Luxembourg, Belgium, and Holland. Within less than two years, the Germans controlled virtually all of Europe from the English Channel to the Soviet border (see Map 20.1). Only Britain escaped Axis control, although Nazi bombers pulverized British cities. In 1939, Germany signed a nonaggression pact with the Soviets, but in 1941 the German army broke the pact and invaded the Soviet Union with 170 divisions, 3,000 tanks, and 3.2 million men—an invasion force of a size unmatched before or since. Here, as elsewhere, the Germans fought a *blitzkrieg* ("lightning war") of tank-led assaults followed by motorized infantrymen and then foot soldiers. By October 1941, the Germans had reached the outskirts of Moscow. The Soviet Union seemed on the verge of a monumental defeat.

The Nazi war was not just a grab for land and raw materials; it was also a crusade for a new order based on race. Throughout Europe, Hitler established puppet governments that complied with deportation orders against Jews and dissidents. His new order made Europe a giant police state. It gave rise to collaborators, who worked with the Germans; resistance fighters, who opposed German occupiers for varying reasons; and a wide range

The Devastation of War (*Left*) In the Battle of Britain, Nazi warplanes strafed British cities in an effort to break British morale. But the devastating bombing raids, such as this one in Coventry in November 1940, helped rally the British, who refused to give in. (*Right*) In November 1942, Nazi troops entered Stalingrad, some 2,000 miles from Berlin. Hitler wanted to capture the city not only to exploit the surrounding wheat fields and the oil of the Caucasus but also for its very name. With handheld flamethrowers and sometimes just their fists, Soviet troops drove out the Germans in February 1943.

of options in between, as people struggled to make their way and take care of their families as best they could.

In the east, the tide turned against the Germans and their collaborators after the ferocious battles of Stalingrad in 1942–1943 and Kursk in 1943. At the battle of Stalingrad, the German army and its allies suffered 1.5 million men killed, wounded, or captured against 750,000 Soviet troops suffering the same fates. Only six months later, at the battle of Kursk, the largest tank conflict in world history, the Germans, boasting a tank force of more than 2,000, lost out to a Soviet tank force twice its size. Once the Soviet army blunted the initial German assault, it launched a massive counteroffensive. This move initiated the defeat of the German war effort on the Eastern Front, but full retreat took another two years as the Soviets drove Hitler's army slowly westward. The spectacular D-Day landing of western Allied forces in Normandy on June 6, 1944 (when the Germans had a mere 15 divisions in France, as compared with more than 300 on the Eastern Front), initiated defeat in the west. On April 30, 1945, as Soviet and Anglo-American forces converged on Berlin, Hitler committed suicide. Days later, Germany surrendered unconditionally.

The Bitter Costs of War The war in Europe had devastating human and material costs. This was particularly the case in eastern Europe, where German forces leveled more than 70,000 Soviet villages, obliterated one-third of the Soviet Union's wealth, and inflicted 7 million Soviet military deaths (by contrast, the Germans lost 3.5 million soldiers) and at least 20 million civilian deaths. German bombing of British cities, such as London, took a heavy toll on civilians and buildings, as did Allied bombing of war plants and Axis cities like Dresden and Tokyo. Tens of millions were left homeless.

Europe's Jews paid an especially high price. Hitler had long talked of "freeing" Europe of all Jews. At the war's outset, the Nazis herded Jews into ghettos and labor camps and then seized their property. As the German army moved eastward, more and more Jews came under their control.

At first the Nazi bureaucrats considered deportation but then ruled out transporting "subhumans" as too costly, and began instead to starve Jews and crowd them together in

MAP 20.1 | World War II: The European Theater

The Axis armies enjoyed great success during the early stages of World War II.

- Looking at the map, which states were within the Axis territory when World War II began in September 1939? What were the territorial boundaries when the Axis powers reached their greatest extent?
- When did the military balance begin to turn against Germany and Italy? Where do you think the outcome of the conflict was decided, eastern Europe or western Europe?

unsanitary ghettoes. By the summer of 1941, special troops operating behind the army on the Eastern Front had begun mass shootings of communists and Jewish civilians, and by fall 1941, Hitler and the S.S.—the *Schutzstaffel*, or special security forces—were building a series of killing centers. Cattle cars shipped Jews from all over Europe to the extermination sites in the east where Nazis used the latest technology, including the arsenic-based poison gas Zyklon B, to kill men, women, and children. The largest facility, Auschwitz, combined an extermination center and work camp in a single complex.

The deliberate racial extermination of the Jews, known as the **Holocaust**, claimed around 6 million lives. About half of this number died in the gas chambers of death camps; the others were shot or gassed in mobile vans, or they succumbed to starvation or disease. The shift to a policy of extermination was both unimaginably brutal and rapid. At its core, the Holocaust was brief, intense mass murder. In mid-March 1942, roughly three-quarters of all victims of the Holocaust were still alive and one-quarter had been killed; within a year—by March 1943—the proportions were reversed, with three-quarters of the victims dead. The Nazis also turned their mass killing apparatus against gypsies, homosexuals, communists, and Slavs, with deportations to the death camps continuing to the very end of the war.

Nazi genocides—enormous in scale and reliant on modern, "enlightened" administrative practices—stood as a powerful challenge to European claims that science, technology, and an efficient bureaucracy would make life better for everyone. Lamenting connections between European culture and the Holocaust, German philosopher Theodor Adorno wrote: "[t]o write poetry after Auschwitz is barbaric" (1949). Nazi crimes, he suggested, defied human understanding.

THE PACIFIC WAR

Like the war in Europe, the conflict in the Pacific transformed the military and political landscape (see Map 20.2). The war broke out when Japan's ambitions to dominate Asia targeted American interests and might.

Japan's Efforts to Expand Japanese efforts to expand in Asia were already under way in the 1930s, but the outbreak of war in Europe opened opportunities for further expansion. Japan's military invaded and occupied Manchuria in 1931 and then launched an offensive against the rest of China in 1937. Although the Japanese did not achieve China's complete submission, the invaders exacted a terrible toll on the population. Most infamous was the so-called rape of Nanjing, in which Japanese aggressors slaughtered at least 100,000 civilians and raped thousands of women in the Chinese city between December 1937 and February 1938.

Meanwhile, Germany's swift occupation of western Europe left defeated nations' Asian colonies at the mercy of Japanese forces. After concluding a pact with Germany in 1940, the Japanese occupied French Indochina in 1941 and made demands on the Dutch East Indies for oil and rubber. The chief remaining obstacle to further expansion in the Pacific was the United States, which already had imperial interests in places like China and the Philippines, as well as other Pacific islands. Hoping to strike the United States before it was prepared for war, the Japanese launched a surprise air attack on the American naval base at Pearl Harbor in Hawaii on December 7, 1941.

Now Japan's expansion shifted into high gear. With French Indochina already under their control, the Japanese turned against the American colony of the Philippines and against the Dutch East Indies, both of which fell in 1942. By coordinating their army, naval, and air force units and using tactical surprise, the Japanese seized a huge swath of territory that included British-ruled Hong Kong, Singapore, Malaya, and Burma, while threatening the British Empire's hold on India as well.

Japan justified its aggression on the grounds that it was anticolonial and pan-Asian; Japan promised to drive out the European imperialists and to build a new order reflecting "Asia for Asians." In practice, however, the Japanese made oppressive demands on fellow Asians for resources, developed myths of Japanese racial purity and supremacy, and treated Chinese and Koreans with brutality.

MAP 20.2 | World War II: The Pacific Theater

Like Germany and Italy, Japan experienced stunning military successes in the war's early years.

- In what directions did the Japanese direct their military offensives?
- Analyzing this map, why do you think the Japanese were so concerned about an American presence in East Asia, when the United States was so geographically distant?
- According to your reading, how did the Allied strategies to defeat the Japanese Empire shape postwar relations in the region?

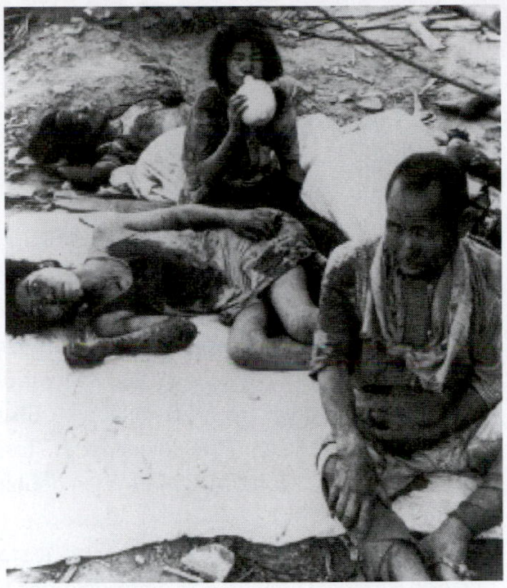

The Aftermath of the Atomic Bomb (*Left*) A view of Nagasaki less than half a mile from "ground zero" after the atomic bomb was dropped in August 1945. A few reinforced concrete buildings still stand. (*Right*) Thousands of people were immediately crushed or burned to death in the blast. Many died later from horrendous burns and radiation poisoning.

Allied Advances and the Atomic Bomb Like the Germans in their war against Russia, the Japanese could not sustain their military successes against the United States. By mid-1943, U.S. forces had put the Japanese on the defensive. Fighting from island to island, American troops recaptured the Philippines, and a combined force of British, American, and Chinese troops returned Burma to Britain. The Allies then moved toward the Japanese mainland. By summer 1945, American bombers had all but devastated the major cities of Japan. Yet Japan did not surrender.

Anticipating that an invasion of Japan would cost hundreds of thousands of American lives, U.S. president Harry Truman unleashed the Americans' secret weapon. It was the work of a team of scientists who were predominantly European refugees. On August 6, 1945, an American plane dropped an atomic bomb on the city of Hiroshima, killing or maiming over 100,000 people, and poisoning the air, soil, and groundwater for decades to come. Three days later, the Americans dropped a second atomic bomb on Nagasaki. Within days, Emperor Hirohito announced Japan's surrender, bringing the war to an official end. After the six years of World War II, much of East Asia and Europe lay in ruins; millions had died, and millions more were wounded, displaced, widowed, and orphaned. What the postwar world would look like, however, remained unclear. (See **Analyzing Global Developments: World War II Casualties**.)

The Beginning of the Cold War

The destruction of Europe and the defeat of Japan left a power vacuum, which the United States and the Soviet Union rushed to fill. Avoiding direct warfare, the Americans and Soviets vied for influence in postwar Europe and around the globe in a series of smaller conflicts.

> **COMPARISON**
>
> **ANALYZE** the roles that the United States and the Soviet Union played in the Cold War.

REBUILDING EUROPE

Communism and liberal democracy offered competing approaches to rebuilding states and societies in Europe after World War II. The task of political rebuilding was daunting, for

Analyzing Global Developments

World War II Casualties

World War II was the most destructive armed conflict in recorded history. It mobilized more than 120 million military personnel. More than 20 million died. The death toll on civilian populations was substantially greater. Civilian deaths from genocide, bombing, starvation, and disease were estimated to range from 30 million to 55 million, including the 6 million Jews killed in the Holocaust. Historians now put the total at roughly 60 million dead, more than double the number killed in World War I.

A total reordering of the globe was at stake from the outset of World War II. The war was a struggle not only for the control of resources and territory, as World War I had been, but it was also fought to decide which peoples would control the world's resources and which peoples would be destroyed because the aggressors decided that they were undesirable.

QUESTIONS FOR ANALYSIS

- Compare and contrast the casualties for World Wars I and II. (See the Analyzing Global Developments feature in Chapter 19.)
- Which countries endured the greatest loss of life in World War II and why? Which of the major participants in the war endured the fewest casualties and why?
- Contrast civilian and military casualties in World War II and explain why the civilian casualty rates were so much higher than military losses?
- Many historians, especially those specializing in modern European history, regard World War I as a greater turning point in European and Western history than World War II, with its extraordinarily high loss of life. Can you understand why these historians would hold to this view? What is your view of the relative global importance of the two wars?

NATION	POPULATION IN 1939	MAX. NO. MOBILIZED	MILITARY DEATHS	MISSING IN ACTION	CIVILIAN WAR-RELATED DEATHS	ESTIMATED TOTAL DEATHS
Belgium	8,386,000	800,000	22,651	55,513	76,000	88,000
Brazil	40,289,000	200,000		4,222		1,000
British Commonwealth		4,683,000	400,000	369,267	92,673	466,000
Australia	6,968,000	680,000	37,467	39,803		24,000
Canada	11,267,000	780,000	42,666	53,174		38,000
India	311,820,000	2,150,000	48,674	64,354		1,500,000
New Zealand	1,628,500	157,000	13,081	19,314		10,000
South Africa	10,160,000	140,000	8,681	14,363		7,000
UK	47,760,000	4,683,000	403,195	369,267	92,673	357,000
China	517,568,000	5,000,000	2,220,000	14,685,593		10,000,000
Czechoslovakia	15,300,000 (1938)	180,000	10,000	8,017	215,000	225,000
Denmark	3,795,000	15,000	6,400	2,000	2,000	4,000
France	40,000,000	5,000,000	245,000	390,000	350,000	563,000
Greece	7,221,900	414,000	88,300	42,290	325,000	413,000
Netherlands	8,729,000	500,000	7,900	2,860	200,000	208,000

Sources: Alan Axelrod (ed.), *Encyclopedia of World War II*, vol. 1. (2007); John Dower, *War without Mercy* (1986); Geoffrey Hosking, *Rulers and Victims: The Russians in the Soviet Union* (2006).

NATION	POPULATION IN 1939	MAX. NO. MOBILIZED	MILITARY DEATHS	MISSING IN ACTION	CIVILIAN WAR-RELATED DEATHS	ESTIMATED TOTAL DEATHS
Norway	2,944,900	25,000	3,000	364	7,000	10,000
Poland	34,775,700	1,000,000	597,320	766,606	5,675,000	5,800,000
Philippines	16,000,300	105,000	127,000		91,000	118,000
United States	131,028,000	16,353,659	292,000	671,801	6,000	298,000
USSR	108,377,000	12,500,000	8,700,000	14,685,593		27,000,000
Yugoslavia	5,510,100	500,000	305,000	425,000	1,200,000	1,505,000
Bulgaria	6,458,000	450,000	18,500	21,878	10,000	20,000
Finland	3,700,000	250,000	82,000	50,000	2,000	84,000
Germany	69,622,500	9,200,000	325,000	7,250,000	780,000	4,200,000
Hungary	9,129,000	350,000	200,000	89,313	290,000	490,000
Italy	44,394,000	4,000,000	380,000	225,000	152,941	395,000
Japan	71,380,000	6,095,000	1,740,955	326,000	672,000	2,700,000
Romania	19,933,800	600,000	300,000		200,000	500,000
Indonesia	69,435,000					4,000,000

Total World War II Deaths: 60 million (including 6 million Jews)

The Berlin Airlift In summer 1948, a new currency was issued for the united occupation zones of West Germany. It began to circulate in Berlin at more favorable exchange rates than the eastern zone's currency, and Berlin seemed poised to become an outpost of the West inside the Soviet occupation zone. The Soviets responded by blocking western traffic into Berlin; the West countered with an airlift, forcing the Soviets to back down in May 1949 but hastening the division of Germany into two countries.

the old order had been discredited. Liberal democrats had to distance themselves from their prewar predecessors. Communism, by contrast, gained new appeal. Many eastern Europeans, reacting to the horrors of fascism and not knowing the extent of Stalin's crimes, looked to the Soviets for answers.

Europe's leftward tilt alarmed U.S. policymakers. They feared that the Soviets would use their ideological influence and the territory taken over by the Red Army to spread communism. They also worried that Stalin might seize Europe's overseas possessions and create communist regimes outside Europe. But no one wished to fight another "hot" war. As President Truman began advocating a policy of containment to prevent the further advance of communism, an American journalist popularized the term *cold war* in 1946 to describe a new form of struggle in which both sides endeavored to avoid direct warfare.

Truman's containment policy was tested when the Soviets attempted to seize control of Berlin. Like the rest of Germany, Berlin had been partitioned into British, French, American, and Soviet zones of occupation; but the city itself was an island lying within the Soviet zone. In 1948, the Soviets attempted to cut the city off from western access by blocking western routes to the capital. The Allies responded with the Berlin Airlift, which involved transporting supplies in planes to western Berlin to keep the population from capitulating to the Soviets. This crisis lasted for almost a year, until Stalin allowed trucks to roll through the eastern zone in May 1949.

In that same year, occupied Germany was split into two hostile states: the democratic Federal Republic of Germany in the west, and the communist German Democratic Republic in the east. In 1961, leaders in the German Democratic Republic built a wall around West Berlin to insulate the east from capitalist propaganda and to halt a flood

MAP 20.3 | NATO and Warsaw Pact Countries

The Cold War divided Europe into two competing blocs: those joined with the United States in the North Atlantic Treaty Organization (NATO) and those linked to the Soviet Union under the Warsaw Pact.

- Which nations had borders with nations belonging to the opposite bloc?
- Comparing this map with Map 20.1, explain how combat patterns in World War II shaped the dividing line between the two blocs.
- According to the map, where would you expect Cold War tensions to be the most intense?

of émigrés fleeing communism. The Berlin Wall became the great symbol of a divided Europe and of the Cold War.

U.S. policymakers wanted to shore up democratic governments in Europe, so Truman promised American military and economic aid. Containing the spread of communism meant securing a capitalist future for Europe, a job that fell to Truman's secretary of state, General George C. Marshall. He launched the Marshall Plan, an ambitious program that provided over $13 billion in grants and credits to reconstruct Europe and facilitate an economic revival. U.S. policymakers hoped the aid would dim communism's appeal by fostering economic prosperity, muting class tensions, and integrating western European nations into an alliance of capitalist democracies.

Stalin saw the Marshall Plan as a threat to the Soviet Union and rejected the offer of support. He felt the same about the formation in 1949 of the **North Atlantic Treaty Organization (NATO)**, a military alliance between countries in western Europe and North America. He believed that the Soviet Union, having sacrificed millions of people to the war against fascism, deserved to be dominant in eastern Europe. Soviet troops had occupied eastern European nations at the war's end, and both communists and leftist members of other parties formed Soviet-backed coalition governments there. In 1955, the Soviets formally allied themselves with these communist nations in the **Warsaw Pact**, a military alliance of their own (see Map 20.3). The tense confrontations between NATO and the Warsaw Pact countries in Europe and in other parts of the world in the 1950s and 1960s brought the world to the brink of an atomic World War III.

WAR IN THE NUCLEAR AGE: THE KOREAN WAR

The dropping of the atomic bombs on Japan in 1945 changed military affairs forever. Spurred by the onset of the Cold War, the Soviets worked hard to catch up to the Americans, and in 1949 tested their first nuclear bomb. Thereafter, each side rushed to stockpile nuclear weapons and update its military technologies. By 1960, the explosive power of these weapons had increased so greatly that nuclear war might lead to the world's destruction without a soldier firing a single shot. This sobering realization changed the rules of the game. Each side now possessed the power to inflict total destruction on the other, a circumstance that inhibited direct confrontations but sparked smaller conflicts in parts of Asia such as Korea, where the postwar settlement was murky.

Atom Bomb Anxiety This photograph shows schoolchildren taking shelter under their desks during an A-bomb drill in Brooklyn, New York, 1951. The Soviets had exploded their first test bomb in 1949. Underground bomb shelters were built in many American urban areas as places in which to survive a doomsday attack.

In 1950, North Korean troops backed by the Soviet Union invaded U.S.-backed South Korea, setting off the Korean War (see Map 20.4). President Truman ordered American troops to drive back the North Koreans. The Security Council of the United Nations—established in 1945 to help prevent another world war—also sent troops from fifteen nations to restore peace. Within a year, the invaders had been routed and were near collapse. When U.N. troops advanced north to the Chinese border, however, Stalin maneuvered his communist Chinese allies into rescuing the communist regime in North Korea and driving the South Korean and U.N. forces back to the old boundary in the middle of the Korean peninsula. The fighting continued until 1953, when an armistice divided the country at roughly the same spot as at the start of the war.

MAP 20.4 | The Korean War

The Korean War was an early confrontation between the capitalist and communist blocs during the Cold War era.

- What were the dates of each side's farthest advance into the other side's territory?
- Why was this peninsula strategically important?
- According to your reading, how did the outcome of the war shape political affairs in East Asia for the next several decades?

The Korean War energized America's anticommunist commitments and spurred a rapid increase in NATO forces. The U.S. now saw Japan as a bulwark against communism and resolved to rebuild Japanese economic power. Like West Germany, Japan went from being the enemy in World War II to being a valued U.S. ally as the Cold War rivalry between the United States and the Soviet Union spurred both sides to shore up alliances around the globe.

Decolonization

COMPARISON

IDENTIFY the goals of Third World states in this period, and **EVALUATE** the degree to which these goals were achieved.

The unsettling of empires, including those established by Japan before and during World War II and the longer-standing colonies belonging to European states, inspired colonial peoples to reconsider their political futures. The process of **decolonization** and nation building followed four patterns: civil wars, wars of independence, negotiated independence, and incomplete decolonization.

THE CHINESE REVOLUTION

In China, the ousting of Japanese occupiers intensified a civil war that brought the communists to power. The communist movement in China had its origins in post–World War I hostility toward the western powers. In this period, communists had vowed to free China from colonialism, but had been outgunned by Chiang Kai-shek's Nationalist regime and driven from China's cities; they retreated into the interior, where they founded base camps. In 1934, under attack by Chiang's forces, the communists, led by **Mao Zedong** (1893–1976), abandoned their bases and undertook an arduous 6,000-mile journey through the rugged terrain of northwestern China (see Map 20.5). In the course of this great escape, glorified in communist lore as the Long March, fewer than 10,000 of the approximately 80,000 people who started the journey reached their destination. Fortunately for the communists, the Japanese invasion in 1937 diverted Nationalist troops and offered Mao and the survivors a chance to regroup.

Mao's followers cultivated popular support by advocating the lowering of taxes, cooperative farming, and policies aimed at women, such as the outlawing of arranged marriages and the legalization of divorce. Like many anticolonial reformers, Mao regarded women's emancipation as a key component in building a new nation, since he considered their oppression to be both unjust and an obstacle to progress.

Communist expansion in rural areas during World War II swelled the membership of the Communist Party from 40,000 in 1937 to over a million in 1945. After Japan's surrender, China's civil war between Nationalists and communists resumed. But communist forces now had the numbers, the guns (mostly supplied by the Soviet Union), and the popular support to assault Nationalist strongholds and seize power.

NEGOTIATED INDEPENDENCE IN INDIA AND AFRICA

In India and most of colonial Africa, gaining independence involved little bloodshed, although the aftermaths were often extremely violent. The British, realizing that they could no longer rule India without coercion, bowed to the inevitable and withdrew. The same happened in Africa, where nationalists also succeeded in negotiating independence from European empires; although, as we shall see, there were notable exceptions.

India Unlike China, India achieved political independence without an insurrection. But it did veer dangerously close to civil war. The leadership of the Indian National Congress

MAP 20.5 | The Long March, 1934–1935

During the Long March, which took place during the struggle for power between the Guomindang (Nationalists) and the communists within China, communist forces traveled over 6,000 miles to save their lives and their movement.

- What route did the communist forces take?
- Why did the communists take this particular route?
- How did this movement affect the outcome of this internal struggle in the long run?

retained tight control over the mass movement that it had mobilized in the 1920s and 1930s (see Chapter 19). Even Gandhi hesitated to leave the initiative to the common people, believing that they had not yet assimilated the doctrine of nonviolence. Gandhi and the leadership worked hard to convince the British that they, the middle-class leaders, spoke for the nation. At the same time, the threat of a mass peasant uprising with radical aims (like the communist revolution in China) encouraged the British to transfer power quickly.

As negotiations moved forward, Hindu-Muslim unity deteriorated. Whose culture would define the new nation? The Indian nationalism that had existed in the late nineteenth century reflected the culture of the Hindu majority. Yet this movement masked the multiplicity of regional, linguistic, caste, and class differences *within* the Hindu community, just as Muslim movements that arose in reaction to Hindu-dominated Indian nationalism overlooked divisions within their own ranks. Now the prospect of defining "India" created a grand contest between newly self-conscious communities. Riots broke out between Hindus and Muslims in 1946, which increased the mutual distrust between the Congress Party and Muslim League leaders. The specter of civil war haunted the proceedings, as outgoing colonial rulers decided to divide the subcontinent into two states: India and Pakistan.

On August 14, 1947, Pakistan gained independence from Britain; a day later, India did the same. The euphoria of decolonization, however, drowned in a frenzy of brutality. Shortly after independence, as many as 1 million Hindus and Muslims killed one another. Fearing further violence, 12 million Hindus and Muslims left their homes to relocate in the new countries where they would be in the majority. Although the British departed peacefully from India, the peoples inhabiting the subcontinent engaged in open warfare over differences that haunt the relationship between India and Pakistan to this day.

Africa for Africans Shortly after Indian independence, most African states also gained their sovereignty. Except in southern Africa, where minority white rule persisted, the old colonial states gave way to indigenous rulers.

The postwar years also saw Africans move to cities in search of a better life. As expanding educational systems produced a wave of primary and secondary school graduates, these educated young people and other new urban dwellers became disgruntled when attractive employment opportunities were not forthcoming. Three groups—former servicemen, the urban unemployed or underemployed, and the educated—led the nationalist agitation that began in the late 1940s and early 1950s (see Map 20.6).

Faced with rising nationalist demands and too much in debt to invest more in pacifying the discontented, European powers agreed to decolonize. The Soviet Union and the United States also favored decolonization. Thus decolonization in most of Africa was a rapid and relatively sedate affair. In 1957, the Gold Coast (renamed Ghana) under prime minister Kwame Nkrumah became tropical Africa's first independent state. Other British colonial territories followed in rapid succession, so that by 1963 all of British-ruled Africa except for Southern Rhodesia was independent.

Decolonization in much of French-ruled Africa followed a similarly smooth path, although the French were initially resistant. Instead of negotiating independence, they tried first to accord fuller voting rights to their colonial subjects, even allowing Africans and Asians to send delegates to the French National Assembly. In the end, however, the French electorate had no desire to share the privileges of French citizenship with African and Asian populations. Thus, France dissolved its political ties with French West Africa and French Equatorial Africa in 1960, having given protectorates in Morocco and Tunisia their independence in 1956. Algeria, considered an integral part of France, was a different

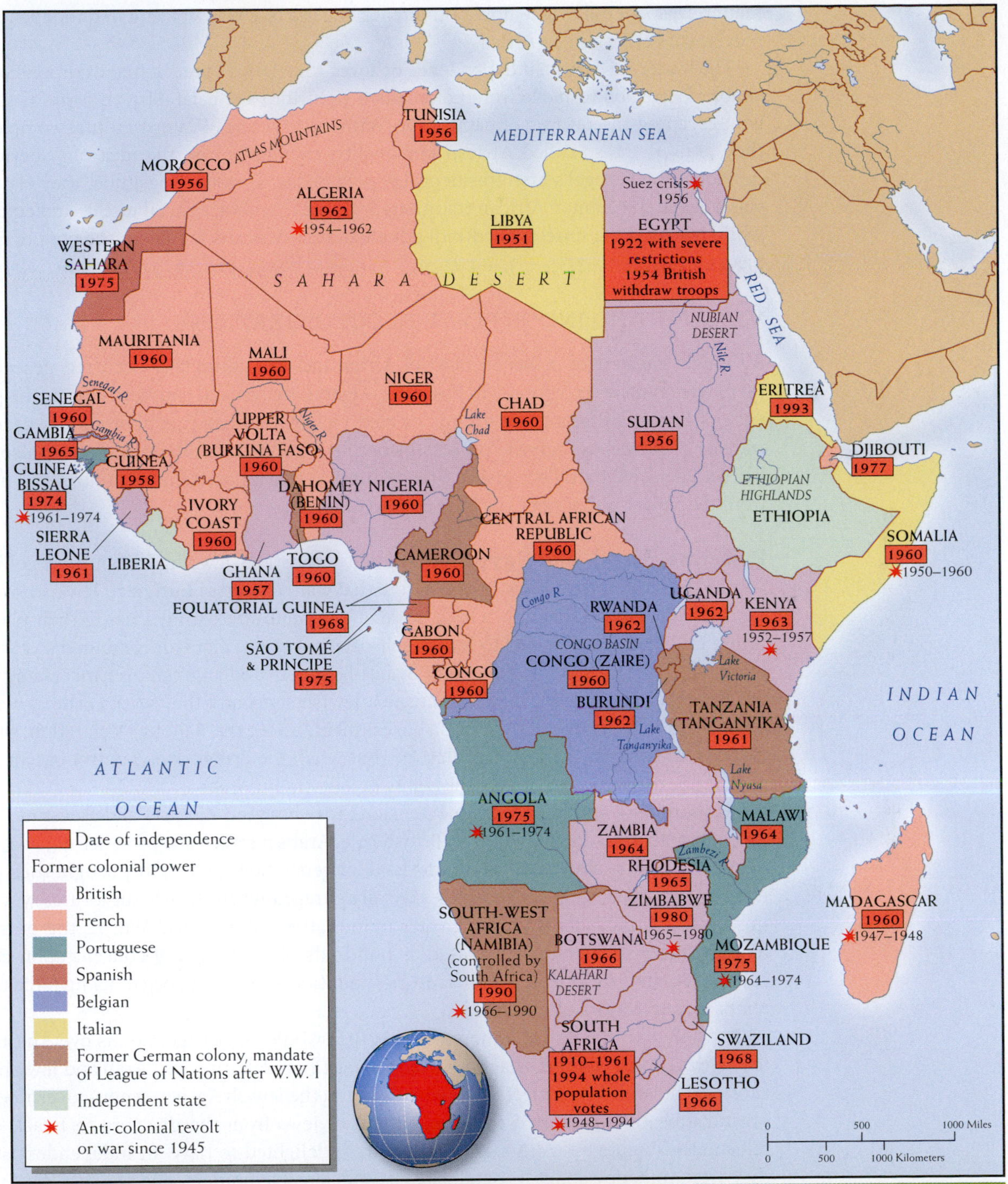

MAP 20.6 | Decolonization in Africa

African decolonization occurred after World War II, largely in the 1950s, 1960s, and 1970s.

- Find at least four areas that won independence in the 1950s, and identify which former colonial power had ruled each area.
- What areas took longer to gain independence?
- According to your reading, what problems and tensions contributed to this uneven process across Africa?

matter. Desperate efforts to hold onto French Algeria (see below) facilitated independence movements elsewhere in Africa.

The leaders of African independence believed that Africa's precolonial traditions would enable the region to move from colonialism right into a special African form of socialism, escaping the ravages of capitalism. Without rejecting Western culture completely, they praised the so-called African personality, exemplified by the idea of "Negritude" developed by Senegal's first president, Léopold Sédar Senghor. Negritude, they claimed, was steeped in common African traditions and able to embrace social justice and equality, while rejecting the unrestrained individualism that Africans felt lay at the core of European culture.

VIOLENT AND INCOMPLETE DECOLONIZATIONS

Although transfers of power in most of Africa and Asia ultimately occurred peacefully, there were notable exceptions. In Palestine, Algeria, Kenya, and southern Africa, the presence of European immigrant groups created violent conflicts that aborted any peaceful transfer of power—or left the process incomplete. In Vietnam, the process was also violent and delayed, partly because of France's desire to reimpose colonial control and partly from the power politics of Cold War competition.

Palestine, Israel, and Egypt In Palestine, Arabs and Jews had been on a collision course since the end of World War I. Before that war, a group of European Jews, known as Zionists, had argued that only a large-scale migration from existing states to their place of origin in Palestine could lead to Jewish self-determination. Zionism combined a yearning to return to the holy lands with a fear of anti-Semitism and anguish over increasing Jewish assimilation. Zionists wanted to create a Jewish state, and they won a crucial victory during World War I when the British government, under the Balfour Declaration, promised a homeland for the Jews in Palestine. But when the British took control of Palestine after 1918, they also guaranteed the rights of Palestinian Arabs.

As more Jews settled in Palestine, tensions rose between Zionists and Palestinian Arabs, and both grew dissatisfied with British rule. Arabs resented the presence of Jews, who displaced farmers who had lived on the land for generations and openly sought their own independent state. Zionists became especially enraged when British authorities wavered in supporting their demands for greater immigration. After World War II, the pressure to allow more immigration increased as hundreds of thousands of concentration camp survivors clamored for entry into Palestine, and Zionist militants began using force to attempt to gain control of the state.

In 1947, after the British announced that they would leave negotiations over the area's fate to the United Nations, that body voted to partition Palestine into Arab and Jewish territories. The Arab states rejected the partition, and the Jewish Agency, a non-governmental organization that supported the immigration of Jews from the diaspora to Israel, only reluctantly accepted it. Although the Jews were delighted to have an independent state, they were unhappy about its small size, its indefensible borders, and the fact that it did not include all the lands that had belonged to ancient Israel. For their part, the Palestinians were shocked at the partition, and they looked to their better-armed Arab neighbors to regain the territories set aside for the new state of Israel.

The ensuing Arab-Israeli War of 1948–1949 shattered the legitimacy of Arab ruling elites. Arab states entered the war poorly prepared to take on the well-run and enthusiastically supported Israeli Defense Force. By the time the United Nations finally negotiated a truce, Israel had extended its boundaries and more than 1 million Palestinians had become refugees in surrounding Arab countries.

Embittered by this defeat, a group of young army officers in Egypt plotted to overthrow the Egyptian regime, which they felt was corrupt and still under European influence. One of the officers, Gamal Abdel Nasser, became the head of a secret organization of junior military officers—the Free Officers Movement. These men had ties with communists and other dissident groups, including the Muslim Brotherhood, which favored a return to Islamic rule. They launched a successful coup in 1952, forcing the king to abdicate and leave the country. The new regime dissolved the parliament, banned political parties (including the communists and the Muslim Brotherhood), and stripped the old elite of its wealth.

In 1956, Nasser moved to nationalize the Suez Canal Company (an Egyptian company, mainly run by French businessmen and experts), inciting the Israelis, the British, and the French to invade Egypt and seize territory along the Suez Canal. Opposition by the United States and the Soviet Union forced the invading countries to withdraw, providing Nasser with a spectacular diplomatic triumph. As Egyptian forces reclaimed the canal, Nasser's reputation as leader of the Arab world soared. He became the chief symbol of a pan-Arab nationalism that swept across the Middle East and North Africa and especially through the camps of Palestinian refugees.

The Algerian War of Independence The appeal of Arab nationalism was particularly strong in Algeria, where a European settler population (the *colons*) of 1 million stood in the way of decolonization. Indeed, French leaders claimed that Algeria was an integral part of France. Although the *colons* were a minority, they held the best land and generally lived in the major cities near the coast. They controlled Algeria's finances and all of its major public institutions.

Anticolonial nationalism in Algeria gathered force after World War II. The Front de Libération Nationale (FLN) emerged as the leading nationalist party in the 1950s, using violence to provoke its opponents and to make the local population choose between supporting the nationalist cause or the *colons*. The full-fledged revolt that erupted in 1954 pitted FLN troops and guerrillas against thousands of French troops. Atrocities and terrorist acts occurred on both sides.

The war dragged on for eight years, at a cost of perhaps 300,000 lives. On the French mainland, the war came as a terrible shock, for many, though not all, French citizens had accepted the idea that Algeria was not a colonial territory but part of France itself. The *colons* insisted that they had emigrated to Algeria in response to their government's promises and that yielding power to the nationalists would be a betrayal. After an insurrection led by *colons* and army officers brought down the French government in 1958, the new French president, Charles de Gaulle, negotiated a peace accord. Shortly after handing over power to FLN leaders, 800,000 *colons* left Algeria. By late 1962, over nine-tenths of the European and indigenous Jewish population had departed.

Southern Africa The bloody conflict in Algeria highlights a harsh reality of African decolonization: the presence of European settlers often prevented the smooth transfer of power. South Africa, which held the continent's largest and wealthiest settler population (a mixture of Afrikaans- and English-speaking peoples of European descent), defied black majority rule longer than other African states. After winning the elections of 1948, the white Afrikaner–dominated National Party enacted an extreme form of racial segregation known as apartheid. Under apartheid, laws stripped Africans, Indians, and "colored" persons (those of mixed descent) of their few political rights. Racial mixing of any kind was forbidden, and schools were strictly segregated.

The ruling party tolerated no protest. Nelson Mandela, one of the leaders of the African National Congress (ANC) who campaigned for an end to discriminatory legislation, was repeatedly harassed, detained, and tried by the government, even though he had at first urged peaceful resistance. After the Sharpeville massacre in 1960, in which police killed demonstrators who were peacefully protesting the oppressive laws, Mandela and the ANC decided to oppose the apartheid regime with violence. A South African court sentenced Mandela to life imprisonment.

Women helped keep resistance flames burning. The most dynamic of these individuals was Winnie Mandela, wife of the imprisoned Nelson Mandela. Unlike many of the ANC leaders, who opposed the regime from exile, she remained behind and openly and courageously spoke out against the apartheid government. Nonetheless, whites retained external support. Through the 1950s and 1960s, Western powers (especially the United States) saw South Africa as a bulwark against the spread of communism in Africa.

Vietnam The same concern to contain communism also drew the United States into support for a conservative and pro-Western regime in South Vietnam. Vietnam had come under French rule in the 1880s, and by the 1920s approximately 40,000 Europeans were living among and ruling over roughly 19 million Vietnamese. To promote an export economy of rice, mining, and rubber, the colonial rulers granted vast land concessions to French companies and local collaborators, while leaving large numbers of peasants landless.

The colonial system also generated a new intelligentsia. Primarily schooled in French and Franco-Vietnamese schools, educated Vietnamese worked as clerks, shopkeepers, teachers, and petty officials. Yet they had few opportunities for advancement. Discontented, they turned from the traditional ideology of Confucianism to modern nationalism. Vietnamese intellectuals overseas, notably Ho Chi Minh, one of the original founders of the French Communist Party, took the lead in imagining a new Vietnamese nation-state.

When the French tried to restore their rule in Vietnam after Japan's defeat in 1945, Ho led the resistance. War with France followed (1946–1954), featuring guerrilla tactics to undermine French positions. The Viet Minh, the League for the Independence of Vietnam, were most successful in the north, but even in the south their campaign bled the French. Finally, in 1954, the anticolonial forces won a decisive military victory. At the Geneva Peace Conference, Vietnam (like Korea) was divided into two zones. Ho controlled the north, while a government with French and American support took charge in the south.

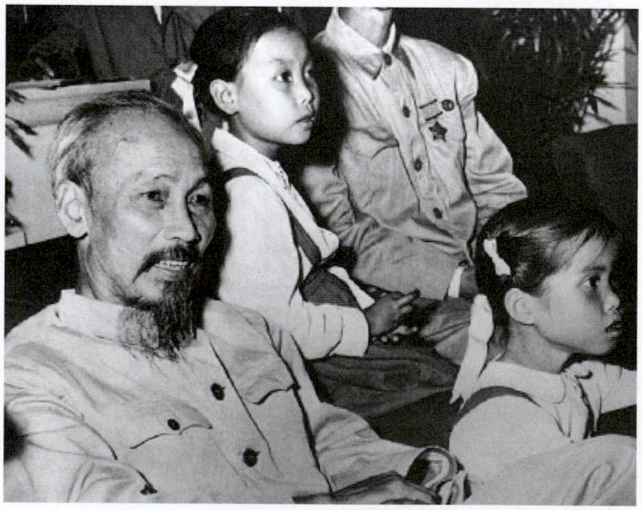

Ho Chi Minh Ho Chi Minh's formation of the League for the Independence of Vietnam, or Viet Minh, in 1941 set the stage for Ho's rise at the end of World War II. Here he attends a youth rally in October 1955, just over a year after the victory of his forces at Dien Bien Phu, which resulted in the ousting of the French from Vietnam.

During the early 1960s, U.S. involvement escalated as Ho's support for Viet Cong communist guerrillas heightened American concerns about the spread of communism. In 1965, large numbers of American troops entered the country to fight on behalf of South Vietnam, while communist North Vietnam turned to the Soviet Union for supplies. Over the next several years, the United States sent some 500,000 soldiers to fight the Vietnam War, but peasant support enabled the Viet Cong, a term meaning Vietnamese communists, to continue fierce guerrilla fighting. Even the bombing of villages and the deployment of counterinsurgency forces failed to prevent the spread of communism in Southeast Asia. In 1975, two years after the final withdrawal of American troops, the South Vietnamese government collapsed.

Thus, the process of decolonization varied across regions. Although most of the lands in Asia and Africa had gained independence by the mid-1960s, there were significant exceptions in Africa—South Africa, Southern Rhodesia, and the Portuguese colonies—and Asia, notably Vietnam. Although the British and French realized that they no longer had the resources to stem the nationalist tide that was spreading through the Third World, they tried to use military might to support European areas of settlement, like Algeria and Kenya.

Three Worlds

World War II and postwar decolonization created a three-world order, in which the liberal-democratic and capitalist First World and the communist Second World competed for global influence, notably among the newly decolonized Third World states. The war had made the Soviet Union and the United States into superpowers. Possessing nuclear weapons, superior armies, and industrial might, they vied for global influence. As decolonization spread, the two Cold War belligerents offered new leaders their models for modernization. The decolonized, however, had their own ideas. With the communist takeover in 1949, China had shrugged off semicolonial status, but Mao soon broke from Soviet direction. Other decolonized nations in Asia and Africa had underdeveloped economies and could not leap into either capitalist or communist industrial development. They drew some elements from communist and capitalist models, but politically tended to favor single-party states. Moreover, in some places colonial rule persisted, and civilians were not allowed even relative autonomy, because the colonizers remained in place.

THE FIRST WORLD

As the Cold War spread in the early 1950s, western Europe and North America became known as the First World, or "the free world." Later on, Japan joined this group. First World states sought to organize the world on the basis of capitalism and democracy. Yet, in struggling against communism, the free world sometimes aligned with Third World dictators, thereby sacrificing its commitment to freedom and democracy for the sake of propping up pro-Western regimes.

Western Europe The reconstruction of western Europe after World War II was a spectacular success. By the late 1950s, most nations' economies there were thriving, thanks in part to massive American economic assistance. Improvements in agriculture were particularly impressive. As industrial production boomed and wages rose, goods that had been luxuries before the war—refrigerators, telephones, automobiles, indoor plumbing—became commonplace. Prosperity and the dismantling of national military establishments allowed governments to expand social welfare systems; by the late 1950s education and health care were within the reach of virtually all citizens.

Western Europe's economic recovery blunted the appeal of socialism and communism. At the same time, the Cold War slowed down efforts to punish fascists, Nazis, and collaborators. Although war crimes trials brought the conviction of a number of prominent Nazis, the fear was that a complete purge of former Nazis would deprive Germany of political and economic leaders, leaving it susceptible to communist subversion.

The United States While Europe lay in ruins in 1945, the United States entered a period of economic expansion and a rising standard of living. Americans could afford more consumer goods than ever before—almost always U.S. manufactures. Home ownership became more common, especially in the burgeoning suburbs.

Yet anxieties about the future of the First World abounded. Following the Soviet Union's explosion of an atomic bomb, the Communist Revolution in China, and the outbreak of the Korean War, fear of the communist threat prompted increasingly harsh rhetoric. Anticommunist hysteria led the Republican senator from Wisconsin, Joseph McCarthy, to initiate a campaign to uncover closet communists in the State Department and in Hollywood in the 1950s. Televised congressional hearings broadcast his views to the entire nation, compelling elected officials to support a strong anticommunist foreign policy and a large military budget.

Postwar American prosperity did not benefit all citizens equally. During the 1950s, nearly a quarter of the American population lived in poverty. But many African Americans, a group disproportionately trapped below the poverty line, participated in a powerful movement for equal rights and the end of racial segregation. The National Association for the Advancement of Colored People (NAACP) won court victories that mandated the desegregation of schools. Boycotts, too, became a weapon of the growing civil rights movement, with Martin Luther King Jr. (1929–1968) leading a successful strike against injustices in the bus system of Montgomery, Alabama. Here and in subsequent campaigns against white supremacy King borrowed his most effective weapon—the commitment to nonviolent protest and the appeal to conscience—from Gandhi. As the civil rights movement spread, the federal government gradually supported programs for racial equality.

The Japanese "Miracle" Japan reemerged as an economic powerhouse in this period. The war had ended with Japan's unconditional surrender in 1945, its dreams of dominating East Asia dashed, and its homeland devastated. But after 1945, in an attempt to

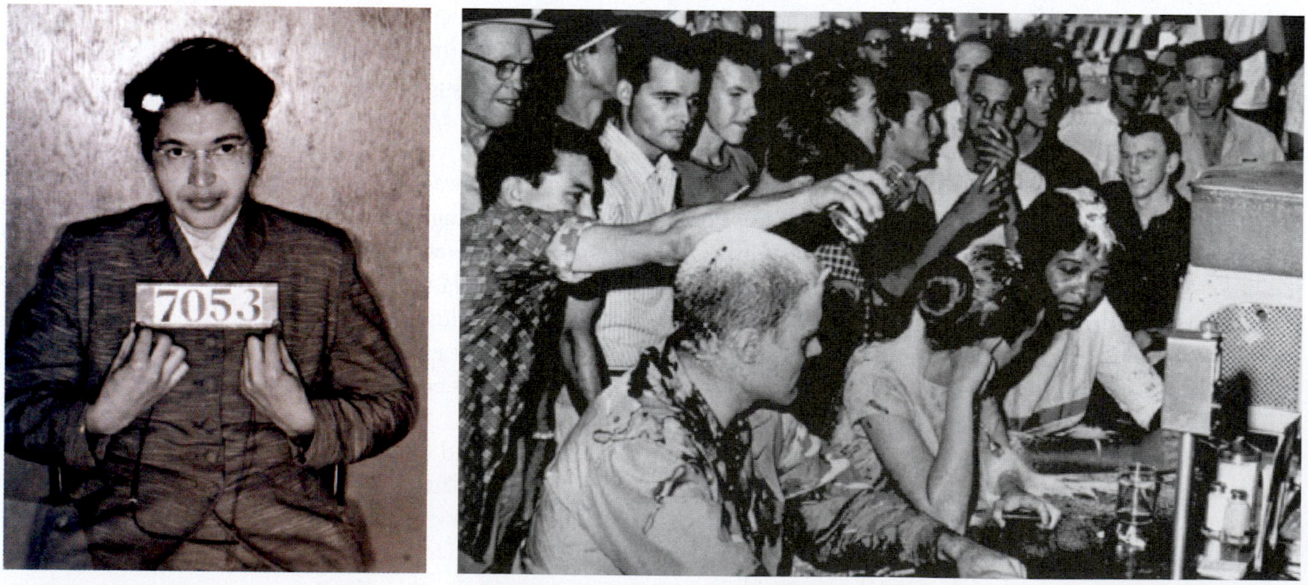

Civil rights movement The 1955 arrest of Rosa Parks (*left*), for refusing to give up her seat on a Montgomery, Alabama, bus, led to a boycott that brought Martin Luther King Jr. to prominence and galvanized the challenge to legal racial segregation in the American South. (*Right*) Borrowing from Gandhi's tactics of nonviolent civil disobedience, protesters staged "sit-ins" across the southern United States in the 1950s and early 1960s, as in this photograph of black and white students seated together at a segregated lunch counter in Jackson, Mississippi.

incorporate Japan into the First World, American military protection, investment, and transfers of technology helped to rebuild Japanese society. The Japanese government guided economic development through directed investment, partnerships with private firms, and protectionist trade policies. By the mid-1970s, Japan, formerly a dictatorship, became a politically stable civilian regime with a thriving economy, enjoying considerable American guidance and the replacement of the power of the emperor with a parliamentary system.

THE SECOND WORLD

The Soviet Union along with its eastern and central European allies as well as Mongolia and North Korea constituted the communist Second World. The scourge of World War II and the shadow of the Cold War fell heavily on the Soviets. Having suffered more deaths and more damage than any other industrialized nation, the Soviet Union was determined to insulate itself from future aggression from the West. That meant turning eastern Europe into a bloc of communist buffer states.

The Appeal of the Soviet Model The Soviet model's egalitarian ideology and success with rapid industrialization made it seem a worthy alternative to capitalism. Here, there was no private property and thus, in Marxist terms, no exploitation. Workers "owned" the factories and worked for themselves. The Soviet state promised full employment, boasting that a state-run economy would be immune from upturns and downturns in business cycles. Freedom from exploitation, combined with security, was contrasted with the capitalist model of owners hoarding profits and suddenly firing loyal workers when they were not needed.

The Soviet system touted protections for workers, inexpensive mass transit, paid maternity leave, free health care, and universally available education. Whereas under the tsarist regime less than one-third of the Russian Empire's population had been literate, by the 1950s the literacy rate soared above 80 percent. True, Soviet policies did not provide material abundance of the sort that First World nations were enjoying. But if consumer goods were often scarce, they were always cheap. Likewise, while it sometimes took ten years to obtain a small apartment through waiting lists at work, when one's turn finally came the apartment carried low annual rent and could be passed on to one's children.

Few Soviet citizens knew how people lived in the capitalist world, so it was easy to believe in the advantages of the Soviet system. Government censors skewed news about the First World and suppressed unfavorable information about the Soviet Union and the communist bloc. Critics did not typically seek to overthrow the system and restore capitalism. Rather, they wanted the Soviet regime to introduce reforms that would create "socialism with a human face."

Repression of Dissent Few people outside the Soviet sphere knew just how inhuman Soviet communism was, and few within knew the extent of the brutality. Under Stalin, anyone suspected of opposing the regime risked imprisonment, forced labor, and often torture or execution. By the time of Stalin's death in 1953, the vast Gulag (labor camp complex) confined several million people, who dug for gold and uranium and survived on hunks of bread and gruel.

In 1956, the new party leader, Nikita Khrushchev, delivered a speech at a closed session of the Communist Party Congress in which he attempted to separate Stalin's crimes from true communism. The speech was never published in the Soviet Union, but party members distributed it to party organizations abroad. The crimes that Khrushchev revealed came as a terrible shock.

Current Trends in World History

Soviet Ecocide

Before the twentieth century, the spread of peasant agriculture, as well as settlement in the steppe and forest zones and the hunting of fur-bearing forest animals, brought profound changes in the Russian environment, including soil degradation, deforestation, and depopulation of species. But the environmental impact of Soviet-era industrialization was staggering. No other industrial civilization poisoned its land, air, water, and people so systematically and over so long a time. Scholars have deemed the Soviet environmental catastrophe an "ecocide."

Soviet economic planners and propagandists celebrated the plumes of purple and orange smoke in their skies as evidence of the huge quantities of industrial production. Pollution-control devices remained unheard of well after their 1950s introduction in Europe and the United States; even when installed in Soviet factories, they were rarely turned on so as not to depress output. Sulfur dioxide, hydrogen sulfide, and solid phenols in water, the food supply, and the air caused epidemic levels of respiratory and intestinal ailments, blood diseases, and birth defects. The giant steel plant at Magnitogorsk, once the pride of Stalin's industrial leap, became a zone of atmospheric and soil devastation 120 miles long and 40 miles wide; inside, chronic bronchitis, asthma, and cancers attacked the population.

In agriculture, the Soviet Union continued to use the fertilizer DDT long after its 1972 banning in the United States. Despite the socialist country's overall development, in the 1970s Soviet life expectancy began to decline and infant mortality to rise. By 1989, Soviet men lived an average of 63.9 years from birth, down from 66.1 in 1965. Infant mortality by the late 1980s rose to 25.4 per 1,000, roughly the same as in Malaysia, a developing country, and Harlem. Alcoholism also contributed mightily to adverse health trends.

The April 1986 Chernobyl nuclear disaster exposed 20 million people in Ukraine and Belarus to excess radiation. Although there was no bomb concussion, the accident spewed more radioactive material into the atmosphere than had been released in the atomic bombs over Hiroshima and Nagasaki. The Chernobyl cleanup claimed around 7,000 lives.

Few symbols of Soviet ecocide surpassed the Aral Sea. Because of dams built for wasteful power plants and excess irrigation for cotton production, the Aral's volume shrank by two-thirds, and gave way to huge white, lifeless salt marshes. Soviet cosmonauts, looking down from space in 1975, were astonished to see immense storms of dust and salt over Central Asia. Toxic salt rain wreaked enormous damage on human and animal lungs. Soviet Uzbekistan, with twice the population of Soviet Belarus, was served by only one-third the hospitals.

Lake Baikal, the largest fresh body of water, and once among the cleanest, suffered the construction from the 1950s

Repercussions were far-reaching. Eastern European leaders interpreted Khrushchev's speech as an endorsement for political liberation and economic experimentation. Right away, Polish intellectuals began a drive to break free from the communist ideological straitjacket. Hungarian intellectuals and students held demonstrations demanding an uncensored press, free elections with genuine alternative parties, and the withdrawal of Soviet troops. But the seeming liberalization promised by Khrushchev's speech proved short-lived.

Rather than let eastern Europeans stray, the Soviet leadership crushed dissent. In Poland, the security police massacred strikers. In Hungary, tanks from the Soviet Union and other Warsaw Pact members invaded and installed a new government that aimed to smash all "counterrevolutionary" activities. The Second World remained very much the dominion of the Soviet Union.

Despite its repressive policies, the Soviet Union's status surged after the launching of Sputnik, the first satellite, into space in 1957. Students from Third World countries flocked to the Soviets' excellent education system for training as engineers, scientists, army commanders, and revolutionaries. The updated 1961 Communist Party program predicted euphorically that within twenty years the Soviet Union would surpass the United

Aral Sea Catastrophe What was once one of the largest lakes in the world shrank to less than 10 percent of its original size, due to the aggressive Soviet construction of irrigation canals in the sixties to bolster cotton production. Here, a shipping vessel is moored in the field of the former Aral Sea, in present-day Kazakhstan.

of factories on its perimeter, especially a cellulose cord plant (for tires on Soviet bombers) and pulp plant (for paper). The threat to Baikal, as well as the Aral Sea catastrophe, sparked grass-roots environmental groups in an otherwise tightly controlled Soviet society. Scientists led the way in breaking censorship taboos, and people from all walks of life turned up at unsanctioned meetings and signed their names to petitions to stop the damage and protect the environment.

QUESTIONS FOR ANALYSIS

- Why do you think environmental degradation was so much more severe in the Soviet Union compared to Western countries?
- Why do you think environmental awareness developed much sooner in the United States than in the Soviet Union?

Explore Further

Murray Feshbach and Alfred Friendly Jr., *Ecocide in the USSR: Health and Nation under Siege* (1992).

Douglas R. Wiener, *A Little Corner of Freedom: Russian Nature Protection from Stalin to Gorbachev* (2002).

States and eclipse the First World, but reckless industrialization left terrible scars both on the population and on the landscape. (See **Current Trends in World History: Soviet Ecocide**.)

THE THIRD WORLD

In the 1950s, the French demographer Alfred Sauvy coined the term **Third World** (*tiers monde*) to describe those countries that, like the "third estate" in the 1789 French Revolution, represented the majority of the population but were oppressed. By the early 1960s, the term characterized a large bloc of countries in Asia, Africa, and Latin America. All had experienced colonial domination and now aimed to create more just societies than those of the First and Second worlds.

Limits to Autonomy Charting a third way proved difficult. Both the Soviets and the Americans saw the Third World as "underdeveloped." The Western powers looked to two new instruments of global capitalism, the **World Bank** and the **International Monetary Fund (IMF)**.

Both raised capital from all participating nations, but the most from the United States, and provided economic guidance in the Third World. The World Bank funded loans for projects to lift poor societies out of poverty (such as providing electricity in India and building roads in Indonesia), while the IMF supported the new governments' monetary systems when they experienced economic woes (as in Ghana, Nigeria, and Egypt). Yet both institutions also intruded on these states' autonomy.

Another force that threatened Third World economic autonomy was the multinational corporation. In the rush to acquire advanced technology, Africans, Asians, and Latin Americans struck deals with multinational corporations to import their know-how. Owned primarily by American, European, and Japanese entrepreneurs, firms such as United Fruit, Firestone, and Volkswagen expanded cash-cropping and plantation activities and established manufacturing branches worldwide. But such corporations impeded the growth of indigenous firms. Although the world's nations were more economically interdependent, the West still made the decisions—and reaped most of the profits.

Whether dealing with the West or the Soviet Union, Third World leaders had limited options because they faced pressure to choose one side or the other in the Cold War. To create more subservient client states, the Soviet Union backed communist insurgencies around the globe, while the United States supported almost all leaders who declared their anticommunism. With the threat of nuclear war hanging over the United States and the Soviet Union, the two superpowers competed through proxy states that they armed to battle one another.

Nowhere was the militarization of Third World countries more threatening to economic development than in Africa. Whereas in the colonial era African states had spent little on military forces, this trend ended abruptly once the states became independent and were drawn into the Cold War. Civil wars, like the one that splintered Nigeria between 1967 and 1970, were opportunities for the great powers to wield influence. When the West refused to sell weapons to the Nigerian government so it could suppress the breakaway eastern province of Biafra, the Soviets supplied MIG aircraft and other vital weapons, contributing to a destructive conflict and the ultimate triumph of the federal government of Nigeria.

Revolutionaries and Radicals As postcolonial states increasingly found themselves mired in debt and dependency, dissatisfaction grew. While some radicals seized power in the 1950s and 1960s, revolutionary transformation of society proved elusive.

Third World revolutionaries drew on the pioneering writings of Frantz Fanon (1925–1961). While serving as a psychiatrist in French Algeria, Fanon (who was born in a French Caribbean colony) became aware of the psychological damage of European racism. He subsequently joined the Algerian Revolution and became a radical theorist of liberation. His 1961 book *The Wretched of the Earth* urged Third World peoples to achieve personal and national independence through violence against their European oppressors.

The Maoist Model While Fanon moved people with his writings, others did so by building political organizations and undertaking revolutionary social experiments. In 1958, Mao Zedong introduced the Great Leap Forward. Mao's program organized China into 24,000 social and economic units, called communes. Peasants took up industrial production in their own backyards. The campaign aimed to catapult China past the developed countries, but the communes failed to feed the people and the industrial goods were inferior. As many as 45 million people may have perished from famine and malnutrition, forcing the government to abandon the experiment.

The Cultural Revolution in China *(Left)* Young women were an important part of the Red Guards during the Cultural Revolution. Here female Red Guards march in the front row of a parade in the capital city of Beijing under a sign that reads "Rise." *(Right)* In their campaign to cleanse the country of undesirable elements, the Red Guards often turned to public denunciation as a way to rally the crowd. Here a senior provincial party official is made to stand on a chair wearing a dunce's cap, while the young detractors chant slogans and wave their fists in the air.

Fearing that China's revolution was losing spirit, in 1966 Mao launched the Great Proletarian Cultural Revolution. This time Mao turned against his associates in the Communist Party and appealed to China's young people. They enthusiastically responded. Organized into "Red Guards," over 10 million of them journeyed to Beijing to participate in huge rallies where they pledged to cleanse the party of corrupt elements and remake Chinese society.

With help from the army, the Red Guards set out to rid society of the "four olds"—old customs, old habits, old culture, and old ideas. They ransacked homes, libraries, museums, and temples. They destroyed classical texts, artworks, and monuments. With its rhetoric of struggle against American imperialism and Soviet revisionism, the Cultural Revolution also targeted anything foreign. Knowledge of a foreign language was enough to compromise a person's revolutionary credentials. The Red Guards attacked government officials, party cadres, or just plain strangers in an escalating cycle of violence. Even family members and friends were pressured to denounce one another; all had to prove themselves faithful followers of Chairman Mao.

Given the costs of the Great Leap Forward and the Cultural Revolution, many of Mao's revolutionary policies were hard to celebrate. But radicals in much of the Third World were unaware of these costs and found the style of a rapid and massive—if deeply undemocratic—appeal to the masses attractive.

Latin American Revolution Most Third World radicals did not go as far as Mao, but they still dreamed of overturning the social order. In Latin America, such dreams excited those who wished to throw off the influence of U.S.-owned multinational corporations and local elites.

Reform programs in Latin America addressed numerous concerns. Economic nationalists urged greater protection for domestic industries and sought to curb the multinationals. Liberal reformers wanted to democratize political systems and redistribute land, lest

Fidel Castro and Cuba's National Liberation The Cuban Revolution of 1958–1959 was a powerful model for many national liberation movements elsewhere in the world. No sooner did Cuban rebels force a break with the United States in 1959 than they discovered that they needed outside support to survive. The Soviet Union, eager to gain a toehold for communism close to the United States, began to provide economic and military help to their Caribbean ally. Here Castro grasps the hand of Nikita Khrushchev atop the Lenin Mausoleum in Moscow for the May Day parade in 1963.

discontent erupt into full-blown revolutions like China's. But when liberals and nationalists joined forces, as in Guatemala in the 1950s, their reforms met resistance from local conservatives and from the United States.

In Cuba, the failure to address political, social, and economic concerns spurred a revolution. Since the Spanish-American War of 1898, Cuba had been ruled by governments better known for their compliance with U.S. interests than with popular sentiment. In the 1930s, sugar planters, casino operators, and North American investors prospered, but middle- and working-class Cubans did not. In 1953, a group composed heavily of university students launched a botched assault on a military garrison. One of the leaders, a law student named **Fidel Castro**, gave a stirring speech at the rebels' trial, which made him a national hero. After his release from prison in 1955, he fled to Mexico. Several years later, he returned and started organizing guerrilla raids that brought him to power in 1959.

Castro then elbowed aside rivals and wrested control of the economy from the wealthy elite, who fled to exile. As his policies grew increasingly radical, American leaders began to plot his demise. It was over Cuba and its radicalizing revolution that the world came closest to nuclear Armageddon in the Cuban Missile Crisis of 1962. To deter U.S. attacks, Castro appealed to the Soviet Union to install nuclear weapons in Cuba—a mere ninety miles off the coast of Florida. When U.S. intelligence detected the weapons, president John F. Kennedy ordered a blockade of Cuba just as weapons-bearing Soviet ships were heading toward Havana. For several weeks, the world was paralyzed with anxiety as Kennedy, Khrushchev, and Castro matched threats. In the end, Kennedy succeeded in getting the Soviets to withdraw their nuclear missiles from Cuba.

By rejecting the power of capitalist industrial societies, Castro and his followers promoted revolution, not reform, as a way to achieve Third World liberation. The symbol of this new spirit was Castro's closest lieutenant, Ernesto "Che" Guevara (1928–1967). Shortly after receiving his medical degree in 1953, he arrived in Guatemala in time to witness the CIA-backed overthrow of the progressive Jacobo Arbenz government. Thereafter, Guevara became increasingly bitter about American influences in Latin America. He joined Castro's forces and helped topple the pro-American regime in Cuba in 1958. After 1959, he held several posts in the Cuban government but grew restive for more action. Latin America, he believed, should challenge the world power of the United States. Soon his casual military uniform, his patchy beard, his cigar, and his moral energy became legendary symbols of revolt.

To combat the germ of revolution, the Kennedy administration sent American advisers throughout Latin America to dole out aid, explain how to reform local land systems, and demonstrate the benefits of liberal capitalism. Working with American advisers, Latin American militaries were trained to root out radicalism. Even Salvador Allende's democratically elected socialist government in Chile was not spared; the CIA and U.S. policymakers aided General Augusto Pinochet's military coup against the regime in 1973 and looked the other way while political opponents were butchered. By 1975, protesters had been liquidated in Argentina, Uruguay, Brazil, Mexico, Bolivia, and Venezuela.

Tensions Within the Three Worlds

Each of the three "worlds" was beset by vulnerabilities and divisions. The United States experienced social unrest in this period on a scale not seen since the Great Depression, and other First World countries also experienced major protest movements. In the Second World, too, dissent challenged the Soviet Union's hold on world communism. In the Third World, the optimism generated at independence gave way quickly to discouragement and eventually despair. Finally, in the 1970s, the rising fortunes of oil-producing nations and of Japan introduced new problems in the relations within and among worlds.

COMPARISON

COMPARE the civil rights issues in the First, Second, and Third worlds, and **ASSESS** the ways each "world" addressed these and other basic rights.

TENSIONS IN THE FIRST WORLD

Although the First World enjoyed great prosperity in the decades after World War II, lingering inequality created friction within these societies and between allies.

Women's Issues, Civil Rights, and Environmental Concerns In the First World, groups that believed that they had been left behind in the surge of economic growth expressed deep unhappiness. One issue was women's economic and political opportunities. Women in Italy, France, and Belgium did not obtain the right to vote until the end of World War II. Although women made gains in employment outside the home, they still awaited a decrease in domestic responsibilities.

A second source of concern, especially articulated by students in Europe, was the deployment of nuclear weapons in their countries, as well as the rigid social and educational institutions that preserved power and high culture for the elite few. Protests reached their apex in Paris in 1968, when workers joined students in a general strike and clashed violently with police.

A rising crescendo of protests against racial discrimination in the United States propelled the U.S. federal government to enact civil rights legislation and to promote programs designed to end poverty. The Civil Rights Act of 1964 banned segregation in public facilities and outlawed racial discrimination in employment, and the Voting Rights Act of 1965 gave millions of previously disenfranchised African Americans an opportunity to exercise equal political rights. The Lyndon Baines Johnson administration also supported programs targeting social security, health, education, and assistance to the poor. Aided by impressive economic growth, the War on Poverty nearly halved the U.S. poverty rate.

But legacies of racism and inequality were not easy to overcome, and protest movements proliferated. In spite of Supreme Court decisions, most schools remained racially homogeneous not only in the South but across the United States, as "white flight" to the suburbs left inner-city neighborhoods and schools to minorities. Militant voices, like those of Malcolm X and the Black Panthers, became prominent. Instead of integration, these radicals advocated black separatism; instead of Americanism, they espoused embracing their African origins.

African American struggles inspired Native Americans, Mexican Americans, homosexuals, and women to initiate their own campaigns for equality and empowerment. Women now questioned a life built around taking care of home and family. In fact, the introduction of the birth control pill in 1960 and the publication of Betty Friedan's *The Feminine Mystique* in 1963 stand as watershed moments in American women's history. Because oral contraception allowed women to limit childbearing and to have sex with less fear of pregnancy, the resulting freedom helped unleash a sexual revolution. Moreover,

Friedan blasted the myth of middle-class domestic contentment, describing the idealized 1950s suburban home as a "comfortable concentration camp" from which women must escape. Despite rising numbers of married women and college-educated women in the workforce, their compensation and opportunity for advancement lagged far behind those of men.

A year before Friedan authored her challenge to the subordination of women, Rachel Carson published *Silent Spring*, a book that was equally revolutionary in its attack against long-held practices. In particular, Carson's book took on the use of synthetic pesticides such as dichlorodiphenyltrichloroethane (DDT), which she said caused cancer, devastated wildlife, and destroyed natural ecosystems. Although chemical manufacturers responded that pesticides had vastly multiplied agricultural yields, *Silent Spring* stirred opposition that ultimately led to the banning of DDT in the United States in 1972. More broadly, Carson's book spurred the development of an environmental movement that questioned many of the ideas about economic progress and material prosperity upon which the "American Dream" had rested.

The escalation of the Vietnam War prompted many white American college students to question the ideals of American society. As the United States increased troop levels there in the 1960s, it conscripted more and more men. After president Richard Nixon sent American troops into Cambodia in 1970 to root out North Vietnamese soldiers, students at over 500 campuses occupied buildings and closed down universities. At Kent State University in Ohio, National Guardsmen attempting to stop the protests killed four students. The United States withdrew from Vietnam in 1973, but not before the divisions created by the war had strained the country almost to the breaking point.

TENSIONS IN WORLD COMMUNISM

The unity of the communist world also came under increasing pressure. As early as 1948, Yugoslavia had broken free of the Soviet yoke and embarked on its own road to building socialism. Other satellite states within the Soviet bloc had more trouble freeing themselves. In 1956, Poland and Hungary were forced back in line. Twelve years later, Czechoslovakia experienced the Prague Spring, in which communist authorities experimented with creating a democratic and pluralist socialist world. Workers and students rallied behind the reformist government of Alexander Dubček, calling for more freedom of expression, more autonomy for workers and consumers, and more debate within the ruling party. Once again, Soviet tanks crushed what they branded a "counterrevolutionary" movement. As the tanks rolled into Prague, the Czech capital, one desperate student doused himself with gasoline and lit a match—his public suicide a gesture of defiance against communist rule.

Thereafter, the Prague Spring served as a symbol for dissenters, who were divided between those who still wanted to reform socialism and those who wanted to overturn it. Underground reading groups proliferated throughout eastern Europe, and many Russians renewed their faith in Orthodox Christianity, their prerevolutionary religion. Many dissidents were exiled from the Soviet Union. Most famous by the early 1970s was the Russian novelist Alexander Solzhenitsyn. His masterwork, *The Gulag Archipelago,* rejected the notion that socialism could be reformed by a turn away from Stalin's policies. Yet very few people in the Soviet Union could obtain copies of Solzhenitsyn's exposé, which had been published abroad and was a best-seller in the West. In 1974 the author himself was expelled from the USSR.

Still, there were important changes within the Second World. During the 1950s and 1960s, "national communism" became the rule throughout eastern Europe, even in countries that experienced Soviet invasions. National variations also arose within the Soviet

Hungarian Revolt Khrushchev's secret 1956 speech denouncing Stalin's crimes unintentionally destabilized the communist bloc. Tanks of the Soviet-led Warsaw Pact forces crossed into Hungary to put down a revolt that year, restoring the Soviet-style system but damaging Soviet prestige. Some American officials and especially American-supported radio had encouraged the Hungarians to rise up but then did nothing to support them, damaging U.S. prestige. The upshot was a turn to "national communism" in the Soviet satellites as a way to promote stability and loyalty.

Union, where Moscow conceded some autonomy to the communist party machines of its fifteen republics—in exchange for fundamental loyalty. Dissidents were still persecuted, but by the 1970s, many fewer were murdered outright, and the population of the gulags declined.

Widespread dislike of the United States created a Sino-Soviet alliance in the years just after the Chinese Revolution of 1949. By the late 1950s, the Soviet Union had contributed massive military and economic aid to China. But the Chinese increasingly sought to define their own brand of Marxism and criticized Khrushchev's efforts to reduce tensions with the United States and the West. The divide raised China's profile throughout Asia and even in eastern Europe. Indeed, Romania achieved a measure of autonomy in foreign policy by playing off China and the Soviet Union. Albania declared its allegiance to China. African nations, interested in Soviet aid, increased their demands with subtle hints that they might consider deepening ties with China instead. Clearly, the Second World was no monolith.

TENSIONS IN THE THIRD WORLD

In contrast to the First and Second worlds, the Third World was never unified by economic, military, or political alliances. The Cold War pushed Third World states to choose between alignment with the First World or the Second. Nonetheless, radicalism nourished new hopes for unifying and empowering the Third World.

One effort at collaboration was the formation in 1960 of an alliance of oil exporters. The Organization of Petroleum Exporting Countries (OPEC)—which included Algeria, Ecuador, Gabon, Indonesia, Iran, Iraq, Kuwait, Libya, Nigeria, Qatar, Saudi Arabia, the

United Arab Emirates, and Venezuela—had little impact in raising oil revenues through the 1960s, even though several members nationalized their oil fields. But after the fourth major Arab-Israeli war broke out in 1973, OPEC's Arab members decided to pressure Israel's First World allies by halting oil exports to them. Overnight, the embargo lifted oil prices more than threefold, a bonanza that enriched all oil producers and led to an oil crisis in the West. To many, the bulging treasuries of OPEC nations seemed like the Third World's revenge. Here were Saudi Arabian princes, Venezuelan magnates, and Indonesian ministers dictating world prices to industrial consumers.

But the realignment was not thorough. Third World producers of raw materials such as coffee and rubber tried unsuccessfully to duplicate OPEC's model, and OPEC itself had trouble controlling the world's oil market. During the 1970s, discoveries in the North Sea, Mexico, and Canada reduced pressures on the large oil-consuming states to be more fuel efficient. With supply up, prices fell. To compensate for lost revenue, various OPEC states raised their own production, putting further downward pressure on prices.

Nor did oil revenues help overcome poverty and dependency in the Third World as a whole. To the contrary, most revenue surpluses from OPEC simply flowed back to First World banks or were invested in real estate holdings in Europe and the United States. Some of these funds were in turn reloaned to the world's poorest countries in Africa, Asia, and Latin America, at high interest rates, to pay for more expensive imports—including oil! The biggest bonanza went to multinational petroleum firms whose control over production, refining, and distribution yielded enormous profits.

For all the talk in the mid-1970s of changing the balance of international economic relations between the world's rich and poor countries, fundamental inequalities persisted. Those few Third World nations that appeared to break out of the cycle of poverty, like South Korea and Taiwan, did not achieve success through free trade and private sector development. Rather, these states regulated domestic markets, nurtured new industries, educated the populace, and required multinationals to work with local firms.

Conclusion

The three-world order arose on the ruins of European empires and their Japanese counterpart. First, the Soviet Union and the United States became superpowers. Second, World War II affirmed the nation-state rather than the empire as the primary form for organizing communities. Third, in spite of the rhetoric of individualism and the free market, the war and postwar reconstruction enhanced the reach and functions of the modern state. In the Third World, too, leaders of new nations saw the state as the primary instrument for promoting economic development.

The organization of the world into three blocs lasted into the mid-1970s. This arrangement fostered the economic recovery of western Europe and Japan from the wounds inflicted by war. These nations' recovery grew out of a Cold War alliance with the United States, where anticommunist hysteria accompanied an economic boom. The Cold War also cast a shadow over the citizens of the Soviet Union and eastern Europe. Gulags and political surveillance became widespread, while the Soviets and their satellite regimes mobilized resources for military purposes. The Third World, squeezed by its inability to reduce poverty, on the one hand, and superpower rivalry, on the other, struggled to pursue a "third way." While some states maintained democratic institutions and promoted economic development, many tumbled into dictatorships and authoritarian regimes, marked by high levels of corruption. They also often suffered irreparable environmental damage.

In this context Third World revolutionaries sought radical social and political transformation, seeking paths different from both Western capitalism and Soviet communism. Though not successful, they energized considerable tensions in the three-world order. These tensions intensified in the late 1960s and early 1970s as Vietnamese communists defeated the United States, an oil crisis struck the West, and protests escalated in the First and Second worlds. Thirty years after the war's end, the world order forged after 1945 was beginning to give way.

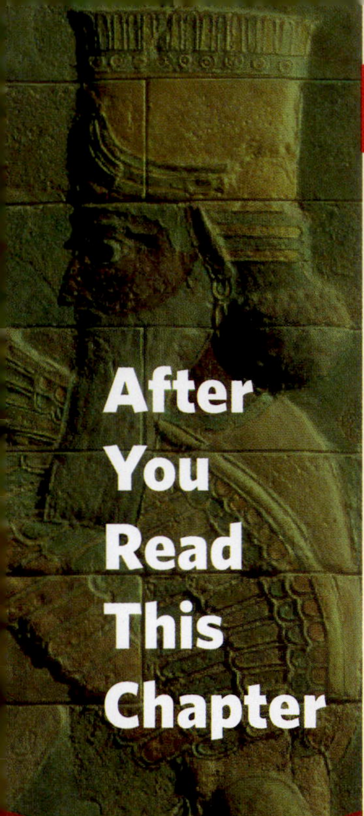

After You Read This Chapter

Go to INQUIZITIVE to see what you've learned—and learn what you've missed—with personalized feedback along the way.

TRACING THE GLOBAL STORYLINES

FOCUS ON: *World War II and a New Global Order*

WORLD WAR II

- World War II grows out of unresolved problems connected to World War I, especially the aggressive plans of Germany and Japan to expand their political and economic influence.
- The war brings huge human and material costs and ushers in an age of nuclear weapons.
- At war's end, the United States, fearing the spread of communism and Soviet influence, rebuilds war-torn Europe and Japan and creates military and political alliances to contain Soviet expansionist ambitions.

A NEW GLOBAL ORDER

- The Soviet Union and the United States become superpowers.
- Japan emerges as an economic powerhouse and a U.S. ally.
- A weakened Europe cannot resist demands for independence from Asian and African nationalists.
- Chinese communists engineer a revolution, while Indian nationalists and many African leaders achieve independence through negotiations.
- Elsewhere, especially in territories with large settler populations, decolonization is violent (Palestine, Israel, Egypt, Algeria, and Kenya) or incomplete (southern Africa).
- Actions by Latin American reformers and revolutionary insurgents spark counterinsurgency efforts by the United States and its regional allies.
- An insecure three-world order emerges after most Asian and African states achieve independence.

CHRONOLOGY

THE AMERICAS
- United States emerges as a global superpower 1945

EUROPE
- World War II 1939–1945
- NATO formed 1949

SOVIET UNION
- Soviet Union emerges as a global superpower, creates client states in Eastern Europe 1945
- Stalin dies 1953

AFRICA

MIDDLE EAST
- Decolonization 1940s and 1950s
- The United Nations partitions Palestine 1948

SOUTH ASIA
- British Raj ends, India and Pakistan declare independence 1947

EAST ASIA
- World War II 1937–1945
- Communist victory in Chinese civil war 1949
- Korean War 1950–1953
- Vietnamese fight for independence 1950–1975

1930 | 1940 | 1950

THINKING ABOUT GLOBAL CONNECTIONS

- ***Thinking about* Worlds Together, Worlds Apart *and the Three-World Order*** Explain how the collapse of a Europe-centered world changed how states interacted with one another. In what ways did the division of the globe into three rival worlds differ from the dominance of the European "great powers" that preceded it? Which world order do you think was more stable, the Europe-centered world or the three-world order that followed it? Do you think one system was more equitable than the other?

- ***Thinking about Changing Power Relationships and the Three-World Order*** Analyze Third World revolutionaries' ability to alter the dynamic of the Cold War. Where do you think power was located in this period? To what degree did Washington and Moscow determine the course of world affairs and to what degree were politicians in places like Havana, Ho Chi Minh City, or Cairo able to play the superpowers off against one another? How and to what degree were revolutionaries able to make claims on the First and Second worlds, in terms of economic, political, or military assistance?

- ***Thinking about Environmental Impacts and the Three-World Order*** In this period, for the first time, organized groups set out to defend the environment. What sparked their protests? Where were those organizations most fully developed? Where was ecological devastation most extreme? What force or forces opposed environmentalists?

STUDY QUESTIONS

1. Explain the relationship between the **Holocaust** and the Enlightenment tradition. In what sense were Nazi atrocities the result of modern technology, bureaucratic rationalization, and universalizing theories? To what extent did they violate the notions of tolerance, humanity, and justice that the *philosophes* promoted?
2. Compare and contrast the three worlds of the postwar order. What was each world attempting to achieve? How successful was each one in achieving these goals?
3. Analyze the roles played by OPEC, the **IMF**, and the **World Bank** in postwar economic competition.
4. Assess the impact of nuclear weapons on state rivalries and superpower relations during the **Cold War**, and evaluate the role played by **NATO** and the **Warsaw Pact**.
5. Evaluate the impact of **Third World** revolutionaries and radicals in transforming their societies. How successful were **Mao Zedong** and **Fidel Castro** in challenging the international status quo?
6. Analyze **decolonization**. Where and why did violence spiral out of control? Where and why did the process proceed smoothly?

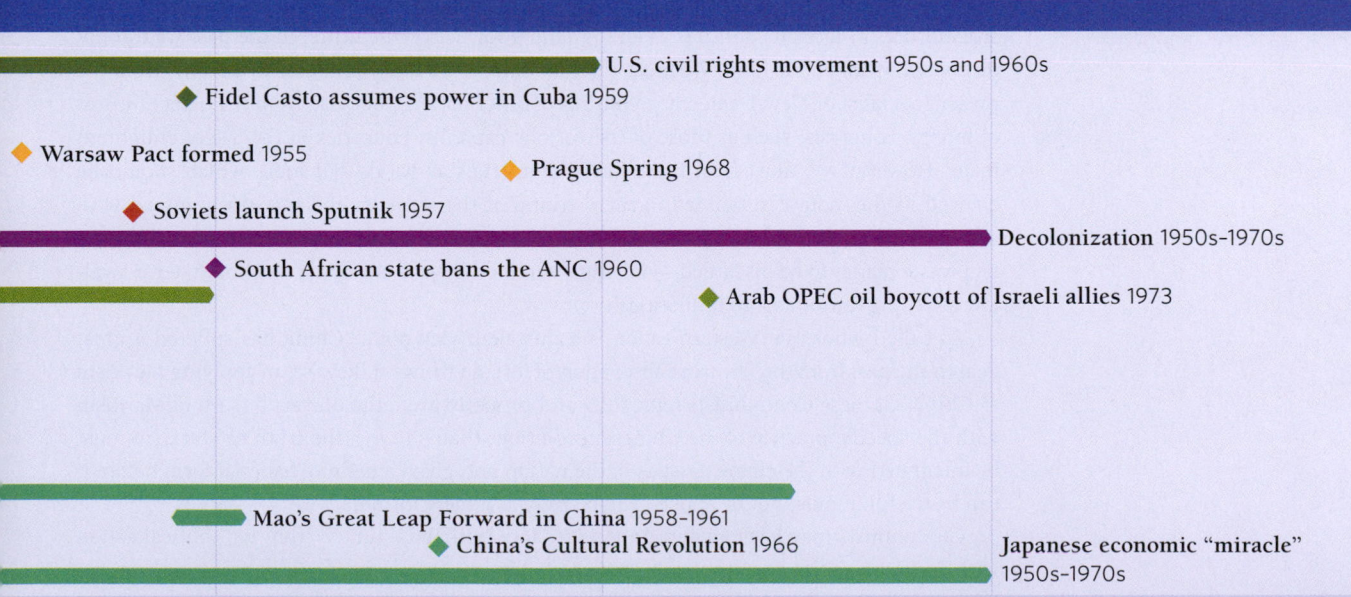

U.S. civil rights movement 1950s and 1960s

Fidel Casto assumes power in Cuba 1959

Warsaw Pact formed 1955

Prague Spring 1968

Soviets launch Sputnik 1957

Decolonization 1950s–1970s

South African state bans the ANC 1960

Arab OPEC oil boycott of Israeli allies 1973

Mao's Great Leap Forward in China 1958–1961

China's Cultural Revolution 1966

Japanese economic "miracle" 1950s–1970s

1960 **1970** **1980**

Going to the Source

Establishing the Third World

At the end of World War II, the United States and the Soviet Union were the two richest countries in the world. The two countries employed very different ideologies to run their governments and their economies. Each sought to extend its influence to other parts of the world using a variety of methods from military expansion to economic aid. The resulting Cold War saw states create new alliances. Those countries who allied themselves politically and economically with the United States were known as the First World. Those countries who allied themselves with the Soviet Union were known as the Second World. But not all countries were strictly allied with one camp or another; many actively sought to be non-aligned and were generally referred to as the Third World.

The documents in this section come from across the Third World: India, Indonesia, Cuba, Senegal; and the Chinas, both mainland China (before its 1949 revolution) and Taiwan, which compares itself to mainland (and Communist) China.

PRIMARY SOURCE 20.1

"New Democracy" (1940), Mao Zedong

Drawing on the European intellectuals Marx and Lenin, Mao Zedong, in his "New Democracy," set forth his proposals for a new democratic culture—nationalistic, scientific, and mass-based—that he regarded as a transitional stage to the communist utopia of the future. These ideas can be seen as his blueprint for Chinese development. Mao Zedong went on to become the first leader of Communist China.

New-Democratic culture is national. It opposes imperialist oppression and upholds the dignity and independence of the Chinese nation. . . . China should absorb on a large scale the progressive cultures of foreign countries as an ingredient for her own culture; in the past we did not do enough work of this kind. We must absorb whatever we today find useful, not only from the present socialist or New-Democratic cultures of other nations, but also from the older cultures of foreign countries, such as those of the various capitalist countries in the age of enlightenment. However, we must treat these foreign materials as we do our food, which should be chewed in the mouth, submitted to the working of the stomach and intestines, mixed with saliva, gastric juice, and intestinal secretions, and then separated into essence to be absorbed and waste matter to be discarded—only thus can food benefit our body; we should never swallow anything raw or absorb it uncritically.

So-called wholesale Westernization is a mistaken viewpoint. China has suffered a great deal in the past from the formalist absorption of foreign things. Likewise, in applying Marxism to China, Chinese Communists must fully and properly unite the universal truth of Marxism with the specific practice of the Chinese revolution; that is to say, the truth of Marxism must be integrated with the characteristics of the nation and given a definite national form before it can be useful; it must not be applied subjectively as a mere formula. . . .

Communists may form an anti-imperialist and anti-feudal united front for political action with certain idealists and even with religious followers, but we can never approve of their idealism or religious doctrines. A splendid ancient culture was created during the long period of

China's feudal society. To clarify the process of development of this ancient culture, to throw away its feudal dross, and to absorb its democratic essence is a necessary condition for the development of our new national culture and for the increase of our national self confidence; but we should never absorb anything and everything uncritically.

1. **What is Mao's approach to adopting Western ways?**
2. **Why did Mao believe that communist ideology could benefit China?**

PRIMARY SOURCE 20.2

"A Note to the Members of the National Planning Committee" (1940), Jawaharlal Nehru

Jawaharlal Nehru, who was the head of the Indian National Congress Party, argued that an independent India needed to modernize through the use of technology and science to create opportunities for economic growth. He was committed to the idea of development as a path forward both before and after independence. After India gained independence in 1947, Nehru served as its first prime minister until his death in 1964.

✷

The octopus of war grips and strangles the world and the energy of mankind is more and more directed to destroying what man has built up with infinite patience and labour. Yet it is clear that war by itself cannot solve any problem. It is by conscious, constructive and planned effort alone that national and international problems can be solved. In India many people thought, with reason, that it was premature to plan, so long as we did not have the power to give effect to our planning. The political and economic freedom of India was a prerequisite to any planning, and till this was achieved our national and international policy would continue to be governed, as heretofore, in the interests of the City of London and other vested interests. And yet we started, wisely I think, a National Planning Committee and we are trying, even in these days of world conflict and war, to draw up a picture of planned society in the free India of the future.

Our immediate problem is to attack the appalling poverty and unemployment of India and to raise the standards of our people. That means vastly greater production which must be allied to juster and more equitable distribution, so that the increased wealth may spread out among the people. That means a rapid growth of industry, scientific agriculture and the social services, all coordinated together, under more or less state control, and directed towards the betterment of the people as a whole. The resources of India are vast and if wisely used should yield rich results in the near future.

We do not believe in a rigid autarchy, but we do want to make India self-sufficient in regard to her needs as far as this is possible. We want to develop international trade, importing articles which we cannot easily produce and exporting such articles as the rest of the world wants from us. We do not propose to submit to the economic imperialism of any other country or to impose our own on others. We believe that nations of the world can cooperate together in building a world economy which is advantageous for all and in this work we shall gladly co-operate. But this economy cannot be based on the individual profit motive, nor can it subsist within the framework of an imperialist system. It means a new world order, both politically and economically, and free nations cooperating together for their own as well as the larger good.

1. **Describe Nehru's approach to government in an independent India.**
2. **What is the "new world order" that Nehru proposes?**

PRIMARY SOURCE 20.3

Together (1941)

This poster, used to recruit troops for the British army during World War II, shows soldiers of various ethnicities from around the empire marching together.

1. **What message did the British government try to convey with this recruiting poster?**
2. **How does this poster contradict or support claims that authors of other documents made?**

PRIMARY SOURCE 20.4

Speech at the Bandung Asian-African Conference in Indonesia (1955), Sukarno

This excerpted speech comes from the Bandung Asian-African conference in 1955, which was a follow-up to an earlier conference of nonaligned countries, also held in Indonesia, in 1949. These conferences began a conversation among nationalist leaders across Asia and Africa about how to proceed with decolonization and what kinds of governments and goals would be possible. Though President Sukarno led Indonesia to independence before this address, he became head of an autocratic government just two years later.

We are living in a world of fear. The life of man today is corroded and made bitter by fear. Fear of the future, fear of the hydrogen bomb, fear of ideologies. Perhaps this fear is a greater danger than the danger itself, because it is fear which drives men to act foolishly, to act thoughtlessly, to act dangerously. . . . All of us, I am certain, are united by more important things than those which superficially divide us. We are united, for instance, by a common detestation of colonialism in whatever form it appears. We are united by a common detestation of racialism. And we are united by a common determination to preserve and stabilise peace in the world. . . . We are often told "Colonialism is dead." Let us not be deceived or even soothed by that. I say to you, colonialism is not yet dead. How can we say it is dead, so long as vast areas of Asia and Africa are unfree. And, I beg of you do not think of colonialism only in the classic form which we of Indonesia, and our brothers in different parts of Asia and Africa, knew. Colonialism has also its modern dress, in the form of economic control, intellectual control, actual physical control by a small but alien community within a nation. It is a skillful and determined enemy, and it appears in many guises. It does not give up its loot easily. Wherever, whenever and however it appears, colonialism is an evil thing, and one which must be eradicated from the earth. . . . Not so very long ago we argued that peace was necessary for us because an outbreak of fighting in our part of the world would imperil our precious independence, so recently won at such great cost. Today, the picture is more black. War would not only mean a threat to our independence, it may mean the end of civilisation and even of human life. There is a force loose in the world whose potentiality for evil no man truly knows. Even in practice and rehearsal for war the effects may well be building up into something of unknown horror. . . .

No task is more urgent than that of preserving peace. Without peace our independence means little. The rehabilitation and upbuilding of our countries will have little meaning. Our revolutions will not be allowed to run their course. . . .

What can we do? The peoples of Asia and Africa wield little physical power. Even their economic strength is dispersed and slight. We cannot indulge in power politics. Diplomacy for us is not a matter of the big stick. Our statesmen, by and large, are not backed up with serried ranks of jet bombers.

What can we do? We can do much! We can inject the voice of reason into world affairs. We can mobilise all the spiritual, all the moral, all the political strength of Asia and Africa on the side of peace. Yes, we! We, the peoples of Asia and Africa, 1,400,000,000 strong, far more than half the human population of the world, we can mobilise what I have called the **Moral Violence of Nations** in favour of peace. We can demonstrate to the minority of the world which lives on the other continents that we, the majority are for peace, not for war, and that whatever strength we have will always be thrown on to the side of peace.

1. **What does President Sukarno mean by colonialism's "modern dress"?**
2. **What path does President Sukarno suggest as a way forward for current and former colonies?**

PRIMARY SOURCE 20.5

On Negritude (1959), Léopold Sédar Senghor

Léopold Sédar Senghor served several terms in the French National Assembly as an elected representative from the French colony in Senegal. In this document, he presents a different, "third way," in which he advocates a specifically African form of socialism. His idea of "Negritude," or black civilization, offered a solution that distinguished black cultural forms from European ones; it has broad appeal in francophone Africa as well as in the Caribbean region. He later served as Senegal's first president for two decades.

In the respective programs of our former parties, all of us used to proclaim our attachment to socialism. This was a good thing, but it was not enough. Most of the time, we were satisfied with stereotyped formulas and vague aspirations, which we called scientific socialism—as if socialism did not mean a return to original sources. Above all, we need to make an effort to rethink the basic texts in the light of the Negro African realities. . . .

Can we integrate Negro African cultural values, especially religious values, into socialism? We must answer that question once and for all with an unequivocal "Yes.". . .

We are not Communists for a practical reason. The anxiety for human dignity, the need for freedom—man's freedom, the freedoms of collectivities—which animate Marx's thought and provide its revolutionary ferment—this anxiety and this need are unknown to Communism, whose major deviation is Stalinism. The "dictatorship of the proletariat," which was to be only temporary, becomes the dictatorship of the part and state by perpetuating itself. . . .

The paradox of socialistic construction in Communist countries—in the Soviet Union at least—is that it increasingly resembles capitalistic construction in the United States, the American way of life, with high salaries, refrigerators, washing machines, and television sets. And it has less art and freedom of thought. Nevertheless, we shall not be won over by a regime of liberal capitalism and free enterprise. We cannot close our eyes to segregation, although the government combats it; nor can we accept the elevation of material success to a way of life.

We stand for a middle course, for a democratic socialism which goes so far as to integrate spiritual values, a socialism which ties in with the old ethical current of the French socialists. . . . In so far as they are idealists, they fulfill the requirements of the Negro African soul, the requirements of men of all races and countries. . . .

A third revolution is taking place, as a reaction against capitalistic and Communistic materialism—one that will integrate moral, if not religious, values with the political and economic contributions of the two great revolutions. In this revolution, the colored peoples, including the Negro African, must play their part; they must bring their contribution to the construction of the new planetary civilization.

What Is Negritude?

Assimilation was a failure; we could assimilate mathematics or the French language, but we could never strip off our black skins or root out black souls. And so we set out on a fervent quest for the "holy grail": our collective soul. And we came upon it. . . .

Negritude is the *whole complex of civilized values—cultural, economic, social, and political—which characterize the black peoples*, or, more precisely, the Negro-African world. All these values are essentially informed by intuitive reason, because this sentient reason, the reason which comes to grips, expresses itself emotionally, through that self-surrender, that coalescence of subject and object; through myths, by which I mean the archetypal images of the collective soul; and, above all, through primordial rhythms, synchronized with those of the cosmos. In other words, the sense of communion, the gift of mythmaking, the gift of rhythm, such are the essential elements of Negritude, which you will find indelibly stamped on all the works and activities of the black man.

1. **What is the "middle course" that Senghor proposes?**
2. **How do you think Negritude could be a replacement for Marxism as it was practiced in the middle of the twentieth century?**

PRIMARY SOURCE 20.6

"On Revolutionary Medicine" (1960), Che Guevara

Guevara was an Argentinian doctor who became radicalized as he toured Latin America, eventually winding up in Cuba and becoming one of Fidel Castro's main advisors and a minister in the new revolutionary government. He left Cuba in 1965 to bring his ideology to Africa and Latin America, but was executed after his capture in Bolivia in 1967. In this document, Che, as he was known, presents his version of moving the world forward.

*

After graduation, due to special circumstances and perhaps also to my character, I began to travel throughout America, and I became acquainted with all of it. Except for Haiti and Santo Domingo, I have visited, to some extent, all the other Latin American countries. Because of the circumstances in which I traveled, first as a student and later as a doctor, I came into close contact with poverty, hunger and disease; with the inability to treat a child because of lack of money; with the stupefaction provoked by the continual hunger and punishment, to the point that a father can accept the loss of a son as an unimportant accident, as occurs often in the downtrodden classes of our American homeland. And I began to realize at that time that there were things that were almost as important to me as becoming famous for making a significant contribution to medical science: I wanted to help those people.

But I continued to be, as we all continue to be always, a child of my environment, and I wanted to help those people with my own personal efforts. I had already traveled a great deal—I was in Guatemala at the time . . . and I had begun to make some notes to guide the conduct of the revolutionary doctor. I began to investigate what was needed to be a revolutionary doctor. . . .

Then I realized a fundamental thing: For one to be a revolutionary doctor or to be a revolutionary at all, there must first be a revolution. Isolated individual endeavour, for all its purity of ideals, is of no use, and the desire to sacrifice an entire lifetime to the noblest of ideals serves no purpose if one works alone, solitarily, in some corner of America, fighting against adverse governments and social conditions which prevent progress. To create a revolution, one must have what there is in Cuba—the mobilization of a whole people, who learn by the use of arms and the exercise of militant unity to understand the value of arms and the value of unity.

And now we have come to the nucleus of the problem we have before us at this time. Today one finally has the right and even the duty to be, above all things, a revolutionary doctor, that is to say a man who utilizes the technical knowledge of his profession in the service of the revolution and the people. But now old questions reappear: How does one actually carry out a work of social welfare? How does one unite individual endeavour with the needs of society?

We are at the end of an era, and not only here in Cuba. No matter what is hoped or said to the contrary, the form of capitalism we have known, in which we were raised, and under which we have suffered, is being defeated all over the world. The monopolies are being overthrown; collective science is scoring new and important triumphs daily. In the Americas we have had the proud and devoted duty to be the vanguard of a movement of liberation, which began a long time ago on the other subjugated continents, Africa and Asia. Such a profound social change demands equally profound changes in the mental structure of the people.

Individualism, in the form of the individual action of a person alone in a social milieu, must disappear in Cuba. In the future individualism ought to be the efficient utilization of the whole individual for the absolute benefit of a collectivity. It is not enough that this idea is understood today, that you all comprehend the things I am saying and are ready to think a little about the present and the past and what the future ought to be. In order to change a way of thinking, it is necessary to undergo profound internal changes and to witness profound external changes, especially in the performance of our duties and obligations to society.

1. **Why did Che believe that revolution was the only way forward?**
2. **Compare this document with Primary Source 20.2. Both authors wanted their respective societies to improve and progress. How did they propose to affect these changes?**

PRIMARY SOURCE 20.7

Chinese Nationalism is better than Chinese Communism (1961), Tsiang Tingfu

In these excerpts from a speech by the Republic of China's (Taiwan's) ambassador to Canada, Tsiang Tingfu details some of the changes that his government made to the island of Taiwan after it relocated there in 1949 following its loss in the Chinese revolution. The Nationalist government of China clearly distinguished itself from Communist China (referred to here as the Mainland), and though the people were generally of the same Chinese

ethnicity as the Communists, each group moved towards a distinct form of government—with the belief that they would eventually reunite. That debate continues to this day.

*

My Government and people, situated for the time being on the Island of Taiwan, find ourselves on the very front line of the world-wide fight against international Communism. This fact has conditioned much of our life and work.

We belong to that category of people who are afflicted with overpopulation and, at the same time, economic underdevelopment. With us, the quick raising of the standard of living is of the utmost urgency. It would be untrue to say that the people in underdeveloped countries have no regard for principles and ideals. At the same time, it would be unrealistic to ignore the fact that the people in such countries desire most of all more and better food, clothing, housing, schooling, and medical care. For this reason, in the post-war period, my Government has given its first attention to economic development.

We have striven to show that the Chinese people can make economic progress faster under conditions of freedom than under Communism. I believe we have demonstrated this beyond any possible doubt. I further believe that this demonstration has validity not only for China but for the other countries of Asia as well.

In our programme of economic development, we have given priority to agriculture. . . . In the first place, we have carried out an agrarian reform assuring to the farmer, ownership of the land he cultivates, thus relieving him of the burden of land rent. We did this by restricting the area a landlord could own, and by arranging for the tenant to buy the land through annual payments over a period of ten years. For the sake of the many landlords who could not wait for payments spread over ten years, my Government denationalized a number of industries and paid the landlords in industrial stocks. Under this scheme, the farmers have been making their annual payments to the Government. What actually happened was that the land-owning class transferred its assets from the land to industries. . . . This reform has given considerable material relief to the farmers. It has also stimulated their interest in farming and heightened their morale. Today, Taiwan is a land of prosperous and contented farmers.

The second . . . activity pursued by my Government in . . . agriculture has been the extension of the benefits of modern science to the farming population. Before coming to the Island, the Government had already organized the Central Agricultural Research Institute. The scientists in that Institute had done considerable experimentation in the improvement of rice, wheat, and cotton; in the study of soil; in the insecticides and irrigation; and in the breeding of farm animals. . . .

We have been able to give to the farmers of Taiwan new varieties of rice which increase the yield by 11 to 13 percent. We have also brought to the Island better breeds of hogs, buffaloes, chickens, turkeys, and sheep. We have taught the farmers how to fight animal and plant diseases. We have analyzed the soil and taught the farmers the proper chemical fertilizers to use. We have helped the farmers to build better irrigation facilities. . . .

All underdeveloped countries cry for industrialization. We, on the Island of Taiwan, are not an exception. In this respect, we started almost from scratch because the Island of Taiwan during the fifty years of Japanese administration, from 1895 to 1945, had developed no industries.

Formerly, the Island imported all its cotton yarn and cloth from Japan. Today, in textiles, Taiwan is not only self-sufficient, but even has a surplus for export.

We have built on the Island an aluminum industry, utilizing raw materials imported from Southeast Asia. We import crude oil from the Persian Gulf and provide ourselves with all the finished petroleum products we need. We have built up a glass industry. We have taken up artificial fibres. We are self-sufficient in electrical appliances and even export some.

Let me pause at this point to call your attention to the differences between our economic development and that of the Mainland under Communism. Whereas they have collectivized the land, we have individualized land ownership. It is our firm belief that the farmer who cultivates his own land, on his own account, is the most efficient producer. In the second place, we have emphasized the development of light rather than heavy industries, and, for this reason, the economic development of the Island of Taiwan has immediately raised the standard of living. In the third place, we practise on the Island what you might call a mixed economy. Some of the industries are government owned, such as railways and electric power. Many fields are left to private industries. The present tendency is for the field of private enterprise to expand. This is, of course, the opposite of what the Communists are doing on the Mainland.

1. **What specific government achievements does Tsiang Tingfu point to in this speech?**
2. **Compare Tsiang Tingfu's speech with Primary Sources 20.1, 20.2, and 20.5. Why do these authors propose different courses of action to solve similar problems?**

Questions for Analysis

Interpretation

1. Why might Marxist thought, based on industrial Europe, pose a problem for the nationalist and revolutionary leaders represented in these documents?

Argumentation

2. Do you think that the programs and ideas put forward here were revolutionary? Why or why not?

Argumentation

3. In your view, and according to these documents, what role should government play in economic development?

Long Essay Question

Synthesis

Based on what you have read in the chapter and the documents above, evaluate the degree to which these Third World leaders successfully articulated workable solutions to the postwar problems that they encountered.

Before You Read This Chapter

GLOBAL STORYLINES

- Following the collapse of the three-world order, new global markets and communications networks integrate the world but also create deep inequalities.
- New technologies and vast population movements make global culture more homogeneous.
- Globalization, supranational organizations (like the World Bank, the European Union, and the United Nations), and religious fundamentalism erode the power of the nation-state.

CORE OBJECTIVES

- **IDENTIFY** the transnational forces that eroded the power of the nation-state in the last third of the twentieth century, and **EXPLAIN** how they did so.
- **DESCRIBE** the relationship between global migration, new technologies, and the spread of cultural influences during and after the Cold War.
- **DESCRIBE** how globalization and population changes affected the environment, and vice versa.
- **EVALUATE** the degree to which globalization changed societies, and **COMPARE** globalization after the end of the Cold War to earlier forms of globalization.

CHAPTER

21

Globalization

1970–2000

KEY TERMS

AIDS (Acquired Immunodeficiency Syndrome) p. 821
developing world p. 807
European Union (EU) p. 809
globalization p. 801
global warming p. 826
Nelson Mandela p. 806
supranational organizations p. 826
Tiananmen Square p. 830
truth commissions p. 828

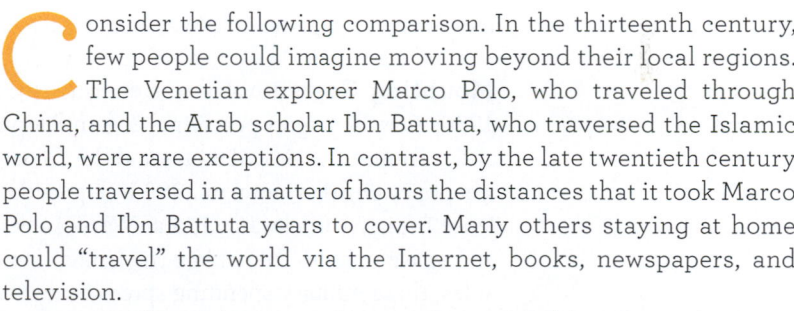

Consider the following comparison. In the thirteenth century, few people could imagine moving beyond their local regions. The Venetian explorer Marco Polo, who traveled through China, and the Arab scholar Ibn Battuta, who traversed the Islamic world, were rare exceptions. In contrast, by the late twentieth century people traversed in a matter of hours the distances that it took Marco Polo and Ibn Battuta years to cover. Many others staying at home could "travel" the world via the Internet, books, newspapers, and television.

But not all travelers moved about so comfortably. Many migrants—desperate to escape political chaos, persecution, or poverty—slipped across borders in the dark of night, traveled as human cargo inside containers, or fled their homelands on foot. Billions of others still had no access to the global age's technological wonders and economic opportunities. Thus, while **globalization** (the development of integrated worldwide cultural and economic structures) created possibilities for some, it also caused deeper inequalities.

The forces driving global integration—and inequality—were no longer the political empires of old. By the mid-twentieth century, the European empires had lost their sway. The Cold War and decolonization movements that had produced the three-world order no longer influenced world affairs. Power structures in the First World, under stress in the 1970s, did not crack. But those in the Second World did. Thus, the Cold War ended with the implosion of the Soviet bloc. The Third World also splintered, with some areas becoming highly advanced and others falling into deep poverty. To be sure, nation-states remained essential for establishing democratic institutions and protecting human rights, but supranational institutions—institutions that transcended nation-state borders, like the European Union and the International Monetary Fund (IMF)—often impinged on their autonomy. A new global order emerged with a unified marketplace and unhindered flows of capital, commerce, culture, and labor.

Removing Obstacles to Globalization

COMPARISON

IDENTIFY the transnational forces that eroded the power of the nation-state in the last third of the twentieth century, and **EXPLAIN** how they did so.

The collapse of the Soviet Union brought the Cold War to an end. At the same time, the capitalist First World gave up its last colonial possessions, and the remnants of white settler supremacy disintegrated. But as this occurred, the formerly colonized Third World's dream of a "third way" also vanished. As empires withdrew, they revealed a world integrated by markets for capital and labor, culture, and technology, rather than forced loyalties to imperial masters or rival superpowers.

ENDING THE COLD WAR

A world divided between two hostile factions limited the prospects for a global exchange of peoples, ideas, and resources. There was widespread exchange within the rival blocs, but for other countries the pressure from the Soviet Union and the United States to align with a superpower imposed limits to interaction, even with neighboring states. Pushing against the Cold War superpower framework, however, were strong nationalist aspirations and religious movements, which the Cold War order tried to control, or in some cases inflame, at great cost.

Mounting Costs Rivalry was enormously costly to the superpowers. The 1970s and 1980s saw the largest peacetime accumulation of arms in history. Despite myriad treaties and summits, the United States and the Soviet Union stockpiled nuclear and conventional weaponry. Furthermore, in 1983 U.S. president Ronald Reagan unveiled the Strategic Defense Initiative (nicknamed "Star Wars"), an elaborate and expensive plan to use satellites and space missiles to insulate the United States from incoming nuclear bombs. For both sides, these military spending sprees brought economic troubles.

Other pressures within and outside the United States and the Soviet Union also strained the Cold War order. The Soviet Union sent troops to prop up a puppet regime in Afghanistan, only to fall into a bloody war against insurgents financed and armed by the United States. The resulting stalemate undermined the image of the mighty Soviet armed forces, and mothers of Soviet soldiers protested their government's involvements abroad. In Europe and North America, the antinuclear movement rallied millions to the streets. Western industrialists worried about competition from Japan, which had been plowing money into rapid industrialization rather than arms. Political leaders also grappled with distressingly high unemployment rates. Thus, both sides shared a common crisis: fatigue from the Cold War, and an economic challenge from East Asia.

The Soviet Bloc Collapses In the end, the Soviet bloc collapsed (see Map 21.1). Even though planned economies employed the entire Soviet population, they failed to fill stores

NORTH SEA
DENMARK
BALTIC SEA
0 100 200 300 Miles
0 100 200 300 Kilometers
1989: Mass demonstrations, fall of the Berlin Wall
1990: Reunited with West Germany
1980 onward: Solidarity leads opposition
1981: Crackdown against Solidarity, driving it underground
1989: Solidarity wins 99 of the 100 seats in parliament that it is permitted to contest
Gdansk
POLAND
Warsaw
NETHERLANDS
EAST GERMANY
Berlin
BELGIUM
Leipzig
LUX.
WEST GERMANY
1989: Mass demonstrations
1990: Multiparty elections
1993: Czechoslovakia splits into Czech Republic and Slovak Republic
SOVIET UNION
Prague
CZECH REPUBLIC
CZECHOSLOVAKIA
SLOVAKIA
Bratislava
1989: Removal of barbed wire on border with Austria allows East German tourists to cross westward
1990: Multiparty elections
FRANCE
1989: National uprising against Ceausescu
1992: First multiparty general election
1996: First non-Communist government
SWITZERLAND
AUSTRIA
Budapest
HUNGARY
1990: Multiparty elections
SLOVENIA
ROMANIA
Timisoara
1990: Multiparty elections
1991–1992: War between Croats and Serbs
CROATIA
BOSNIA-HERZEGOVINA
Belgrade
Bucharest
1992: Fighting begins between Serbs and Bosnian Muslims
1995: Divided in two
YUGOSLAVIA
SERBIA
Danube R.
BLACK SEA
ITALY
MONTENEGRO
KOSOVO
BULGARIA
Sofia
1990: Multiparty elections
1991: Dissolved into warring states
MACEDONIA
Tirana
ALBANIA
1989: Demonstrations
1990: Multiparty elections
1989: Loses autonomy from Serbia
1998–1999: Fighting between Serbs and ethnic Albanians
2000: First free elections
GREECE
1990: Multiparty elections
2001: Fighting erupts between Macedonians and ethnic Albanians
TURKEY
1990: Demonstrations, civil war
1991: Multiparty elections
Civil unrest
MEDITERRANEAN SEA

MAP 21.1 | Collapse of the Communist Bloc in Europe

The Soviet Union's domination of eastern Europe ended precipitously in 1989. The political map of eastern and central Europe took on a different shape under European integration.

- What significant event in many communist countries signaled the collapse of communism?
- In what part of eastern and central Europe did the most political instability and conflict occur?
- According to your reading, why did the end of communist rule cause the reshuffling of political boundaries in the region?

Lech Walesa A Polish electrician from the Lenin Shipyard in the Baltic port city of Gdansk, Walesa spearheaded the formation of Solidarity, a mass independent trade union of workers who battled the communist regime that ruled in their name. He later was elected president of post-communist Poland.

with sufficient consumer goods. Socialist health care and benefits lagged behind those provided by the United States and western European states. Authoritarian political structures relied on deception and coercion rather than elections and civic activism. Although communists had promised to beat capitalism by building socialism on the way to achieving full communism, the communist paradise was nowhere on the horizon. The gap between socialism and capitalism was growing.

Events in Poland were one catalyst in socialism's undoing. In 1980, the newly appointed Polish pope, John Paul, the first non-Italian pope in over 450 years, supported mass strikes at the Lenin Shipyard in Gdansk, which led to the formation of the Soviet bloc's first independent trade union, Solidarity. As Communist Party members in Poland defected to its side, the union became a society-wide movement; it aimed not to reform socialism (as in Czechoslovakia in 1968; see Chapter 20) but to overcome it. A crackdown by the Polish military and police put most of Solidarity's leadership in prison and drove the movement underground, but Soviet intelligence officials secretly worried that Solidarity could not be easily eradicated.

The most consequential factor in the collapse of the Soviet superpower was the reform effort launched by Mikhail Gorbachev, who became general secretary of the Soviet Communist Party in 1985. Under this effort (known as *perestroika*, meaning "reconstruction"), Gorbachev permitted competitive elections for Communist Party posts, relaxed censorship, allowed civic associations, legalized small nonstate businesses, granted autonomy to state firms, and encouraged the republics to be responsible for their own affairs within the Soviet Union. These reforms were linked with dramatic arms-control initiatives to ease the superpower burden on the Soviet Union. Gorbachev then began withdrawing troops from Afghanistan and informed eastern European leaders that they could not count on Moscow's armed intervention to prop up their regimes.

Having set out to improve socialism, however, Gorbachev instead destabilized it. Civic groups called not for reform of the system, but for its liquidation. Eastern European states declared their intention to leave the Soviet orbit, and some of the union republics began to push for independence. In response, disgruntled factions within the Communist Party and the Soviet military tried to preserve the destabilized old order by staging a coup attempt in 1991. However, the former Communist Party boss of Moscow and elected president of the Russian republic, Boris Yeltsin, rallied the opposition and faced down the hard-liners. Under Yeltsin, Russia, like Ukraine and the other Soviet republics, became a refuge for discontented Soviet elites. Thereafter, those elites abandoned the cause of the Soviet Union and divided up state property among themselves. The Soviet Union broke apart into independent states (see Map 21.2). The Cold War, which began as a tense standoff between World War II allies, ended when the eastern bloc failed to keep up with economic and technological development of its rivals.

AFRICA AND THE END OF WHITE RULE

Although the aftermath of World War II saw the dismantling of most of Europe's empires, remnants of colonial rule remained in southern Africa (see Map 20.6 on p. 773). Here,

MAP 21.2 | The Breakup of the Soviet Union

The Soviet Union broke apart in 1991. Compare this map with Map 17.6 (see p. 663), which illustrates Russian expansion in the nineteenth century.

- Which parts of the old Russian Empire remained under Russian rule, and which territories established their own states?
- In what areas did large migrations accompany the breakup, and for what reasons?
- According to your reading, how did the breakup of the Soviet Union change Russia's status in Europe and Asia?

whites clung to centuries-old notions of their racial superiority over non-Europeans. Final decolonization meant that self-rule would return to all of Africa. The end of colonialism also set the stage for former colonies to find new trading and investment partners and to become more integrated with the wider world.

The Last Holdouts The last African territories under direct European control were the Portuguese colonies of southern and western Africa. However, by the mid-1970s efforts to suppress African nationalist movements had exhausted Portugal's resources. As African nationalist demands led to a hurried Portuguese withdrawal from Guinea-Bissau, Angola, and Mozambique, formal European colonialism in Africa came to an end.

But white rule still prevailed elsewhere in Africa. In Rhodesia, a white minority resisted international pressure to allow black rule. In the end, independent African states helped support a liberation guerrilla movement under Robert Mugabe. Surrounded, Rhodesian whites finally lost control in 1979. The new constitutional government renamed the country Zimbabwe, erasing from Africa's map the name of the long-deceased British expansionist Cecil Rhodes (see Chapter 17).

South Africa and Nelson Mandela The final outpost of white rule was South Africa, where the European minority was larger, richer, and more entrenched than elsewhere in the region. Yet, in the countryside and cities, defiance of white rule was growing. Africans lobbed rocks and crude bombs at tanks and organized mass strikes against the multinational-owned mines.

At the same time, pressures from abroad to end the racist apartheid system were mounting. The International Olympic Committee banned South African athletes starting in 1970. American students insisted that their universities divest themselves of companies with investments in South Africa. As international pressures grew, foreign governments—even that of the United States, once South Africa's staunchest ally—applied economic sanctions against South Africa. A swelling worldwide chorus demanded that **Nelson Mandela**, the imprisoned leader of the African National Congress (ANC), be freed. The white political elite eventually realized that it was better to negotiate new

The End of Apartheid *(Left)* Nelson Mandela, running for president in 1994 as the candidate of the African National Congress, here casts a ballot in the first all-races election in South Africa. This election ended apartheid and saw the African National Congress take control of the Republic of South Africa. *(Right)* After the overwhelming electoral triumph of Mandela, F. W. de Klerk, leader of the once-powerful Afrikaner-dominated National Party, shakes hands with his successor.

arrangements than to endure international condemnation and years of internal warfare against a majority population. Ensuing negotiations produced South Africa's first free, mass elections in 1994. These brought an overwhelming victory to the ANC, with Nelson Mandela elected as president.

Still, African leaders faced immense problems in building stable political communities. Although they set out to destroy the vestiges of colonial political structures and to build African-based public institutions, those leaders struggled to find a third way between the superpower blocs. Ethnic and religious rivalries, held in check during the colonial period, now blazed forth. Civil wars erupted in many countries—most violently in Nigeria, Sudan, and Zaire—and military leaders were drawn into politics. By the 1990s, the continent was aflame with civil strife. Armed conflicts that started with the Cold War endured well after it ended even though white rule had finally come to an end throughout the entire continent.

Unleashing Globalization

As obstacles to international integration began to dissolve, capital, commodities, people, and culture crossed borders with ever-greater freedom. Even though these movements had occurred throughout history, the global age changed their scale. At the same time, never had there been such unequal access to the fruits of these exchanges. Several factors contributed to increasing integration and to new power arrangements: international banking, expanded international trade, population migrations, and technical breakthroughs in communications.

COMPARISON

DESCRIBE the relationship between global migration, new technologies, and the spread of cultural influences during and after the Cold War.

FINANCE AND TRADE

The increased international flow of goods and capital was well under way in the 1970s, but the end of the Cold War removed many impediments to globalization. During the 1990s, even the strongest nation-states felt the effects of economic globalization.

Global Finance and Deregulated Markets Major transformations occurred in the world's financial system in the 1970s. America's budget and trade deficits prompted president Richard Nixon to take the dollar off the gold standard, an action that enabled the yen, the lira, the pound, the franc, and other national currencies to cut their ties to the American dollar. Now international financiers enjoyed greater freedom from national regulators and found fresh business opportunities.

The primary agents of the heightened global financial activity were banks. Based mainly in London, New York, and Tokyo, big banks attracted large amounts of capital for lucrative ventures around the world. Revenues from oil producers provided a large infusion of cash into the global economy in the 1970s. At the same time, banks joined forces to issue mammoth loans to developing countries.

No international financial organization was more influential than the International Monetary Fund (IMF), which came into existence after World War II with a view to raising capital from all of the participating states so as to be able to lend funds to states in need. During the 1980s it emerged as a central player, especially in response to debt crises in what came to be called the **developing world**, a term that emerged as the prospect of finding a third way between the superpower blocs began to fade; it referred to poor countries in the Third World and eastern bloc. Throughout the 1970s, European, Japanese, and North American banks had loaned money on very easy terms to cash-strapped Third World and eastern-bloc borrowers. But what was once good business soon turned sour. In 1982, a wave of defaults, in which governments and other borrowers found themselves unable to repay their loans, threatened to overrun Latin America in particular. Throughout the 1980s, international banks and the IMF kept heavily indebted customers solvent. The IMF offered short-term loans to governments on condition that recipients produce balanced budgets, compel civilian populations to give up subsidies on essential products, and cease to import far more than they exported. Latin Americans led the way in reorganizing their finances and thus pioneered the process of expanding domestic production while at the same time engaging in robust international trade. All across the world, tariffs and other barriers to foreign trade crumbled, state enterprises became private firms, and foreign banks and multinational companies took a great interest in investing in these newly reformed economies.

Effects of Integrated Networks New technologies and institutions enabled many more financial investors and traders to participate in the integrated networks of world finance. The Internet and online trading accelerated the movement of capital across borders. Rapid changes in financial and currency markets soon created problems, however. When the Mexican economy went into paralysis in 1994, the crisis was so extreme that not even the IMF could bail it out; the U.S. Treasury issued the largest international loan in history to pull Mexico out of its economic tailspin. Despite acting as the lender in that instance, the United States emerged in the new financial order as the world's largest borrower because it imported far more than it exported. Early in the new millennium, its net foreign debt soared past $2 trillion—a 700 percent increase since the early 1990s. Much of this debt was owed to China, which had a huge trade surplus with the United States.

Globalization increased commercial, as well as financial, interdependence. The total value of goods and services exchanged through world trade increased nearly tenfold between 1973 and 1998, and trade in Asia grew even faster. Where an American would once have worn American-made clothes (Levi's), driven an American car (a Ford), and watched an American television (made by Zenith), such was rarely the case by century's end. Increasingly, consumers bought foreign goods and services and sold a greater share of their own output abroad. This pattern had always been true of smaller regions like Central America and southern Africa. But in the 1980s it intensified as countries with cheap and skilled labor, like China, India, and Brazil, were able to undersell their competitors in world markets.

International trade also shifted the international division of labor. After World War II, Europeans and North Americans dominated manufacturing, while Third World countries supplied raw materials. But by the 1990s this was no longer the case. Brazil became a major airplane maker, South Korea exported millions of automobiles, and China emerged as the world's largest source of textiles, footwear, and electronics.

The most remarkable global shift involved East Asian industry and commerce. Manufactured goods, including high-technology products, now came from the eastern fringe of Afro-Eurasia as often as from its western fringe. Japan blazed the Asian trail: between 1965 and 1990 its share of world trade doubled to almost 10 percent. China, too, flexed its economic muscle. When Deng Xiaoping took power in 1978, China was already a growing economy. Under Deng, China started to become an economic powerhouse. For the next two decades, China chalked up astounding 10 percent annual growth rates, swelling its share of world GDP (Gross Domestic Product, the value of goods and services produced) from 5 percent to 12 percent.

For East Asia as a whole, its share of world exports doubled in the same period. Smaller countries using state support for economic development, like Singapore, Taiwan, South

Korea, and Hong Kong, became mini-powerhouses. By the early 1990s, these countries and Japan were also major investors abroad. As East Asia's share of world production quickly increased, the U.S. and European shares decreased.

Regional Trade Blocs and Growing Inequalities Industrialization of previously less developed countries, combined with lower trade barriers, increased the pressures of world competition on national economies. Some areas responded by establishing regional trade blocs in an effort to create larger markets for themselves and stay competitive in an ever more integrated world economy.

The most complete regional integration occurred in Europe, where states slashed trade barriers and harmonized their commercial policies toward the rest of the world. In 1993, the Maastricht Treaty established the **European Union (EU)** under its current name, and what had been conceived as a trading and financial bloc began to evolve into a political union as well, a supranational organization that encroached on the sovereignty of its member states. In 2002, a number of the European Union states deepened their economic interdependence by adopting a single currency, the euro. A few of them—most notably the United Kingdom—did not want to give up control of their own national currency. By 2012, the European Union had twenty-seven members, with seventeen members using the euro.

Although international trade then increased, it also became increasingly unequal. High-technology and high-value goods now occupied an ever-greater share of the manufacturing and exports of the world's richest countries. For "rich" countries as a whole, about half of total GDP reflected the production and distribution of such goods as computers, software, and pharmaceuticals, and services like insurance and banking, which, collectively, gave those countries a competitive advantage. Poor nations, by contrast, generally remained locked in the production of low-tech goods and the export of raw materials. Increasingly, technology and knowledge divided the world into affluent, technically sophisticated countries and poor, technically underdeveloped regions.

MIGRATION

Migration, a constant feature of world history, became more pronounced in the twentieth century (see Map 21.3). Although after 1970 fewer Europeans were on the move, many more Asians, Africans, and Latin Americans were, chasing jobs in the richer countries. By 2000, there were 120 million migrants scattered across 152 countries, up from 75 million in 1965.

Patterns of Migration Migratory flows often followed the contours of past colonial and political ties. Where North America and Europe had had colonies or dependencies, their political withdrawal left tracks for migrants to follow. Indians and Pakistanis moved to Britain; so did Jamaicans. Dominicans, Haitians, and Mexicans went to the United States. Algerians and Vietnamese moved to France. Where emerging rich societies cultivated close diplomatic ties, these relations opened migratory gates. This was true of Germany's relationship with Turkey, of Japan's with South Korea, and of Canada's with Hong Kong.

International migration was often an extension of regional and national migration from poorer, rural areas to urban centers. In Nigeria, for example, rural-urban migration intensified after 1970. In 1900, Nigeria's capital at the time, Lagos, had a population of 41,847. At the century's end, Lagos had more than 10 million people, with predictions that this number would double by 2025. The key to Lagos's boom in the 1970s was the existence of large oil reserves in the country and the high prices that

CANADA
UNITED STATES
MEXICO
BELIZE
GUATEMALA
NICARAGUA
CUBA
HAITI
COLOMBIA
BRAZIL
ARGENTINA
GREAT BRITAIN
SWITZ.
FRANCE
SPAIN
MOROCCO
TUNISIA
ALGERIA
NIGER
IVORY COAST
NIGERIA
ATLANTIC OCEAN
PACIFIC OCEAN
East Europeans 1918–1919
East Europeans 1918–1919
Russian Jews to USA 1980s and 1990s
European Jews to USA 1930s
Algerian colons to France 1962
West Indians to Britain
Spaniards to Mexico 1936
Jamaicans, Haitians, and Dominicans to USA 1990–
1950–
1960–
1960–1980
1980
1970–
1970
Foreign-born people as percentage of total population (latest available year)
Less than 1.5%
1.5%–2.9%
3.0%–7.5%
More than 7.5%
Data not available
Migration
0
1000
2000 Miles
0
1000
2000 Kilometers

MAP 21.3 | World Migration, 1918–1998

The world's population continued to grow and move around in the twentieth century.

- Looking at this map, identify the countries that had the greatest increase in foreign-born people as a percentage of total population.
- Then compare the areas of most rapid population growth during the nineteenth century with those parts of the world that, according to this map, had the highest percentage of foreign-born people in the twentieth century. What are the similarities and differences?
- During the twentieth century, which parts of the world were the sending areas, and which were the receiving territories? See also Map 18.1, p. 681.

Lagos, Nigeria During the twentieth century, Lagos was one of the fastest-growing and most crowded cities in Africa.

oil fetched in international markets. When the Organization of Petroleum Exporting Countries (OPEC) sent oil prices soaring, money poured into Nigeria. The government kept most of it in its largest city. That, in turn, spurred people to move to Lagos. This rural-urban migration increased Lagos's population by 14 percent per year in the 1970s and 1980s. No government—least of all a new, weakly supported one like Nigeria's—could cope with such a huge influx. Electricity supplies failed regularly in and around Lagos. There were never enough schools, teachers, or textbooks. But the city burst with the vitality of new arrivals, prompting one immigrant to exclaim: "It's a terrible place; I want to go there!"

One of the biggest changes in world migration patterns took place in the United States. Having all but closed its coastal borders on the Pacific in the late nineteenth century and on the Atlantic in the 1920s, the United States enacted a major immigration reform in 1965. By 2000, 27 million immigrants lived there, accounting for almost 10 percent of the population—double the share in 1970 and approaching levels not seen since the early twentieth century. The profile of migration to the United States also changed. In 1970, there were more Canadians or Germans than Mexicans living in the United States. Over the next thirty years, the Mexican influx rose tenfold and by 2000 accounted for almost one-third of immigrants in the United States, with the flow of legal and illegal immigrants from Mexico and Central America having an especially dramatic impact on the border states. The numbers migrating from Asia also surged, accounting for over 40 percent of all immigrants to the United States in the 1990s.

Temporary Migrants Some migrants moved for temporary sojourns. At least that was the original intent. Into the 1950s and 1960s, southern Europeans moved northward; but when Spain, Portugal, Greece, and Italy also became wealthy societies, not only did the exodus decline, but these countries became magnets for Middle Eastern, North African, and then, later, eastern European migrants. The economic downturn in Europe in the 1970s and resulting high unemployment, however, made integration difficult. Most migrants from Asia and Africa went initially to Europe in search of temporary jobs as "guest workers." With time, they and their families who followed them settled in their host countries, often living in dilapidated public housing projects, isolated from city centers and public services. The existence of welfare programs made them less likely to leave and return "home" than earlier generations of labor migrants.

In Japan, too, immigrants were not easily incorporated. Tokyo's policy in the 1970s resembled guest-worker programs. Discouraging permanent settlement and immigration, Japan encouraged mainly itinerant workers to move to the country, yet its expanding economy required increasing numbers of these temporary migrants. Indeed, Japan's deep reluctance to recruit large numbers of minorities, for fear of their settling down, led to dire labor shortages. After Japan, the economic tigers of Hong Kong, Taiwan, and Malaysia all became hosts for temporary migrants. Millions of guest workers moved there, and ultimately the migrants sank deeper roots, especially once their children entered school.

Resident Noncitizens and Refugees Arguments in Los Angeles over schools and health care for resident noncitizens became part of a global debate over the rights and protections afforded to migrants. In Argentina, up to 500,000 undocumented Peruvians, Bolivians, and Paraguayans also lived without rights as citizens. Even more staggering, between 3 and 8 million migrants moved from Mozambique, Zimbabwe, and Lesotho to South Africa. In some Middle Eastern countries, like Saudi Arabia and Kuwait, foreign-born workers constituted over 70 percent of the workforce. In general, migrants were only partially accommodated, while many were fully excluded from host societies. Thus, even though population movements flowed across political, kinship, and market networks, demographic reshuffling heightened national concerns about the ethnic makeup of political communities.

Forced migrations remained a major problem. In contrast to earlier centuries' forced migration of slaves from Africa, recent involuntary flows involved refugees fleeing civil war and torture. Many suffered for weeks, months, or years in refugee camps on the periphery of violence. The greatest concentration of refugees occurred in the world's poorest region—Africa. Africans were often caught up in ethnic and religious conflicts that generated vast refugee camps, where survival depended on the generosity of host governments and international contributions.

Whether migrants traveled in search of work or fled persecution, they posed a series of challenges for host countries. If migrants crossed borders easily, they often struggled to receive basic rights. Especially during economic downturns, discrimination often led to violent conflicts among recent immigrants, long-time residents (often themselves of immigrant origin), and the state's security forces. Conflicts erupted over religion and culture, notably in French efforts to prevent women from wearing Muslim headscarves in public and the English-only movement in the United States. Governments in immigrant-receiving countries everywhere grappled with the challenge of extending citizenship to newcomers and then respecting their desires to dress, worship, and celebrate traditions from their families' homelands.

GLOBAL CULTURE

Migrations and new technologies helped create a more global entertainment culture. In this domain, globalization is often equated with Americanization. Yet American entertainments themselves reflected artistic practices from across the globe, as one mass culture met another. On the global scale, there was less cultural diversity in 2000 than in 1300; but in terms of individuals' everyday experience, the potential for experiencing cultural diversity, if one could afford the technology to do so, increased.

Current Trends in World History

Urbanization as a Global Phenomenon: Transforming Bombay to Mumbai

The city has played a pivotal role in world history since it first emerged thousands of years ago along the Tigris and Euphrates rivers in Mesopotamia (modern-day Iraq). People have ever since flocked to cities for the social and economic advantages that these locations offered. By the end of the twentieth century, the proportion of people living in cities, usually defined as having populations over 5,000 or 10,000, exceeded 50 percent in the wealthiest countries and was approaching that proportion in the less developed countries.

Of the burgeoning cities in the developing world, one of the most dynamic is Mumbai in India. Acquired in the sixteenth century by the Portuguese, who then transferred its control to the East India Company, Bombay (as it was named at the time) developed as a port city for colonial commerce. It profited from the cotton trade, developed a vibrant textile industry, attracted migrants, and acquired a cosmopolitan image. India gained its independence from Britain in 1947, and in 1996 Bombay was renamed "Mumbai." Still, it epitomizes the modern face of the nation, and its increasingly heterogeneous population reflects the larger Indian melting pot.

Beginning in the 1980s, however, the nature of the city's relationship with the world economy started to change. The cotton textile industry, Bombay's economic backbone, went into a decline. Industrial employment fell sharply. Moreover, the share of informal household enterprises, small shops, petty subcontractors, and casual laborers rose, along with banking and insurance. Economic liberalization removed hurdles against foreign businesses and brought the city directly into the global economy.

Today Mumbai occupies a strategic place in transnational geography. This is evident in the increasing presence of financial institutions, trading organizations, insurance companies, telecommunications corporations, and information technology enterprises with worldwide operations. Even the city's vibrant film industry addresses a global, not just national, audience. Rather appropriately, Bombay cinema has been nicknamed "Bollywood." The city, however, still attracts a large number of poor migrants who live in slums or call the pavements their home. The gap between Bombay's rich and poor has grown alarmingly. Millions who eke out a miserable living stand in stark contrast to a tiny elite enriched by the global economy.

Globalization has also affected its residents' identity. In the 1990s, the political party then in power in Maharashtra was the Shiv Sena, a nativist regional party named after a seventeenth-century

New Media Technology was key in spreading entertainment. In the 1970s, for example, cassette tapes became the dominant medium for popular music, sidelining the long-playing record and the short-lived eight-track tape. Television was another globalizing force, as American producers bundled old dramas and situation comedies to stations worldwide. Brazilian soap operas began to appear in Spanish-language American TV markets in the 1980s, often inducing Mexican viewers to rush home from work to catch the latest episode. Latin American television shows and music were distributed in the United States in areas with large Spanish-speaking populations. Bombay also produced its fair share of programs for viewers of British television and today produces roughly twice as many films per year as Hollywood. (See **Current Trends in World History: Urbanization as a Global Phenomenon**.) In terms of box-office revenues, Hollywood remains the leading producer of films in the world, helped in no small measure by its ability to send movies across borders and also by the actors from around the world who star in its films.

Television's globalizing effects were especially evident in sports. Soccer (known as football outside the United States) became an international passion, with devoted national followings for national teams. Indeed, by the 1980s soccer was *the* world sport, with television ratings increasingly determining its schedule. Organizers of the 1986 World Cup in Mexico insisted that big soccer matches take place at midday so that games could be

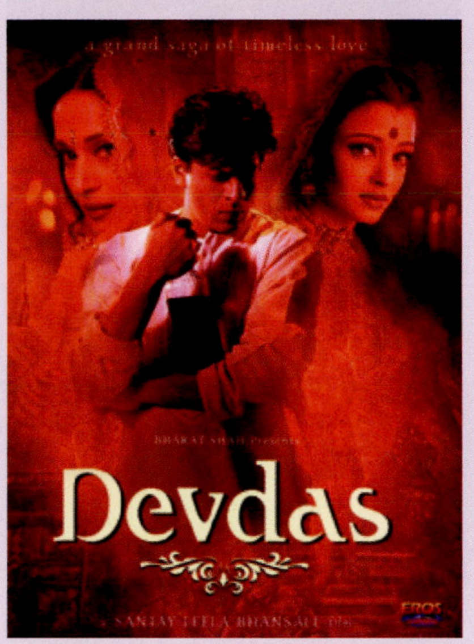

Bollywood Bombay cinema, or Bollywood, has an increasing global presence. This is the poster for *Devdas*, a three-hour romance that won awards in India and around the world.

Maratha chieftain who opposed the Mughal Empire. As the industrial economy and trade unions gave way to the service sector and unorganized labor, the Shiv Sena utilized the social and political fluidity produced by globalization to win support for its nativist ideology. Mumbai's cosmopolitan image went up in smoke in 1992–1993, when the Shiv Sena led pogroms against the city's Muslim residents. In response, a Muslim underworld don, according to police investigations, engineered a series of bomb blasts in March 1993. Since then the city has experienced episodes of violence, none more gruesome than the terrorist attacks on two luxury hotels, a crowded railway station, and a Jewish center in November 2006. Ironically, the terrorists chose to attack Mumbai because of its economic importance and reputation as a cosmopolitan city.

Mumbai today illustrates the uneven effects of globalization. The society is sharply divided, economic disparities are great, and the city's politics is a cauldron of conflicting identities. These are the local forms in which this vast and influential city experiences globalization.

QUESTIONS FOR ANALYSIS

- Contrast the discussion of migration to Mumbai here with that to other parts of the world, notably western Europe and Japan, in the body of the chapter.
- How does Mumbai fit into the larger theme of "Worlds Together, Worlds Apart"?

Explore Further

Suketu Mehta, *Maximum City: Bombay Lost and Found* (2005).

Gyan Prakash, *Mumbai Fables* (2010).

televised live at prime time in Europe, although teams had to play under the scorching sun. In many parts of the globe, major American sports also made particularly deep inroads as more foreigners participated in them and as television broadcast American games in other countries. The National Basketball Association (and the athletic footwear firm Nike) was particularly successful in international marketing; in the process, it made Michael Jordan the world's best-known athlete in the late twentieth century.

Cultural Exchanges Technology was not the only driving force of world cultures; migration and exchange were also important. For example, as people moved around they brought their own musical tastes and borrowed others. Reggae, born in the 1960s among Jamaica's Rastafarians, became a sensation in London and Toronto, where large West Indian communities had migrated. Reggae lyrics and realist imagery invoked a black countercultural spirit and a call for a return to African roots. Soon, Bob Marley and the Wailers, reggae's flagship band, played to audiences worldwide. In northeast Brazil, where African culture emerged from decades of disdain, Bob Marley became a folk hero. In Soweto, South Africa, populated by black workers, he was a symbol of resistance.

Reggae propelled a shift in black American music. In broadcasting reggae, DJs often merged sounds and chant lyrics over a beat, a "talkover" form that soon characterized rap music as well. This was a disruptive concept in the late 1970s, but within ten years rap

Baseball Goes International The 1980s and 1990s saw an influx of ballplayers from Latin America and quite a few from Asia as well. (*Left*) Boston Red Sox slugger David Ortiz hails from the Dominican Republic. (*Right*) Ichiro Suzuki from Japan has been a top player for the Seattle Mariners and the New York Yankees.

had become mainstream. Rap lyrics emulated reggae realism by focusing on black problems, but they also opened a new domain of controversies involving gang worldviews. On the world stage, Latino rappers stressed multicultural themes, often in "Spanglish." Asian rap stressed the genre as a vehicle for cross-cultural sharing and epitomized the ability of new cultural forms to bring peoples together.

Local Culture World cultures may have become more integrated and homogeneous, but they did not completely replace national and local cultures. Indeed, technology and migration often reinforced the appeal of "national" cultural icons, as national celebrities gained popularity among immigrant groups abroad. Inexpensive new technology introduced these stars to more and more people. In Egypt, the most popular singer of the Nasser years was Umm Kalthum, who became the favorite of Arab middle classes via radio. In 1975 she was given a state funeral, the likes of which had rarely been seen.

Nonetheless, as the market for world cultures grew increasingly competitive, performers increasingly employed a wider array of styles and also challenged biases and conventions. Among the breakthroughs that have occurred since the 1970s is the triumph of black performers (Bob Marley, Dorothy Masuka), black athletes (Pelé, Michael Jordan), and black writers (Toni Morrison, Chinua Achebe). Competition also shattered some sexual biases. Female performers such as Madonna became popular icons. So did gay performers, starting with the Village People, whose campy multicultural anthem "YMCA" created a place for a new generation of homosexual or bisexual artists. Of course, beyond Europe and North America, flirting with sexual conventions had its limits. In the Middle East, female video artists continued to wear veils—but they still swung their hips. Relatively homogeneous national cultures, often dominated by men representing the ethnic majority, gave way to a wider variety of entertainers and artists who broke loose from confining local cultures.

COMMUNICATIONS

Computer technology drove a revolution in global communications networks. In the late 1980s, while working in Switzerland, the British physicist Tim Berners-Lee devised a way to pool data stored on various computers. Whereas previous electronic links had existed only between major universities and research stations, Berners-Lee made data more accessible by creating the World Wide Web. With each use and each connection, and as people entered more data, however, the Web grew unmanageably crowded and difficult to navigate. The early 1990s saw the first commercial browsers used in navigating the so-called Internet. Suddenly people were communicating across global networks more easily than with neighbors and more inexpensively than with local phone calls.

The change created a new generation of wealth. CEOs of top companies like General Motors, Royal Dutch Shell, and Merck had less net worth than Michael Dell (hardware maker), Bill Gates (software maker), and Jeff Bezos (creator of Amazon.com). Shares of Internet firms, known as dot-coms, swept the world's stock markets. Money from these companies flowed globally as they established offices worldwide. Software and Internet technologies developed enormous economies of scale and thus became prone to monopolization as they took over smaller companies.

Bob Marley In the 1970s, young Europeans and North Americans began to listen to music from the Third World. Among the most popular was Jamaican-based reggae, and its most renowned artist, Bob Marley. Marley's music combined rock and roll with African rhythms and lyrics about freedom and redemption for the downtrodden of the world.

While the Internet revolution provided new means to share and sell information, it also reinforced hierarchies between haves and have-nots. Great swaths of the world's population living outside big cities, especially in low-income countries, had no access to the Internet. The have-nots were poor not just from lack of capital but from lack of access to knowledge and new media.

Characteristics of the New Global Order

While providing access to an unimaginable array of goods and services, globalization also deepened world inequalities. Families changed, and life spans increased. Education and good health determined one's status in society as never before. Populations expanded dramatically, requiring greater industrial and agricultural output from all parts of the world. While many parts of the world consumed more than ever before, others struggled with famine and the consequences of environmental change.

COMPARISON

EVALUATE the degree to which globalization changed societies, and **COMPARE** globalization after the end of the Cold War to earlier forms of globalization.

THE DEMOGRAPHY OF GLOBALIZATION

It took 160 years (1800–1960) for the world's population to increase from 1 billion to 3 billion; over the next forty years (1960–2000) it jumped from 3 billion to over 6 billion. Behind this steepening curve were two important developments: a decline in mortality, especially among children, and a rise in life expectancy.

Population growth was hardly equal worldwide (see Map 21.4 and **Analyzing Global Developments: Globalization**). In Europe, population growth peaked around 1900, and it moved upward only gradually from 400 million to 730 million during the twentieth century, with little growth after the 1970s. North America's population quadrupled over the same period, mainly because of immigration. The other population booms in the twentieth century occurred in Asia (400 percent), Africa (550 percent), and Latin America (700 percent).

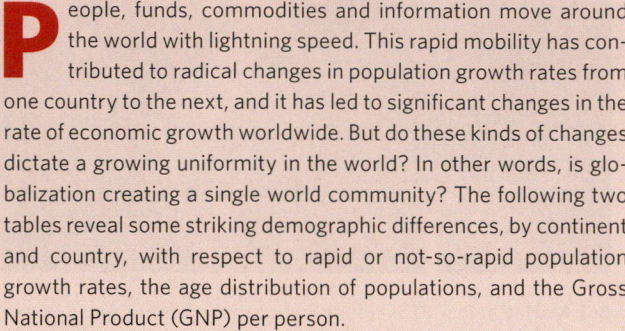

Analyzing Global Developments

Globalization: One World or Many?

People, funds, commodities and information move around the world with lightning speed. This rapid mobility has contributed to radical changes in population growth rates from one country to the next, and it has led to significant changes in the rate of economic growth worldwide. But do these kinds of changes dictate a growing uniformity in the world? In other words, is globalization creating a single world community? The following two tables reveal some striking demographic differences, by continent and country, with respect to rapid or not-so-rapid population growth rates, the age distribution of populations, and the Gross National Product (GNP) per person.

QUESTIONS FOR ANALYSIS

- Which of the continents has the fastest growing population? Why would this be the case?
- Although these tables do not provide data on the HIV/AIDS epidemic (see Map E.5 for that data), we know that Africa has been the most severely impacted continent. What impact is HIV/AIDS having on African population growth rates? Why do you think that its effects are so muted?
- According to these tables, Russia and Japan have negative population growth rates. What factors would account for these downward trends? What sorts of problems do you think that these countries are likely to encounter?
- Japan and Germany are the only countries that have smaller percentages of the populations under the age of fifteen than over the age of sixty-five. In contrast, the countries of sub-Saharan Africa have the largest proportion of their populations under age fifteen. What are likely causes for these developments in Japan, Russia, and sub-Saharan Africa? What problems are these countries likely to encounter as they move forward?
- Does this data suggest that the world is becoming more unified or integrated?

Table 1. Top 10 Most Populous Countries, 2012 and 2050

2012	POPULATION (MILLIONS)	2050	POPULATION (MILLIONS)
China	1,350	India	1,691
India	1,260	China	1,311
United States	314	United States	423
Indonesia	241	Nigeria	402
Brazil	194	Pakistan	314
Pakistan	180	Indonesia	309
Nigeria	170	Bangladesh	226
Bangladesh	153	Brazil	213
Russia	143	Democratic Republic of Congo	194
Japan	128	Ethiopia	166

Source: Population Reference Bureau, 2012: World Population Data Sheet, Washington, D.C., pp. 2, 6–9.

Table 2. World Population References for 2012 and Projection for 2050

CONTINENTS AND SELECTED COUNTRIES	POPULATION, 2012 (MILLIONS)	RATE OF NATURAL INCREASE (%)	PROJECTED POPULATION, 2050 (MILLIONS)	PERCENT OF POPULATION		GNP PER CAPITA (US $)
				UNDER AGE 15	OVER AGE 65	
World	7,058	+1.2	9,624	26	8	10,760
Africa	1,072	+2.5	2,339	41	3	2,630
Egypt	82.3	+2.0	135.6	32	4	5,760
Nigeria	170.1	+2.6	402.4	44	3	1,910
South Africa	51.1	+0.9	57.2	31	5	2,240
Democratic Republic of Congo	69.1	+2.8	194.2	46	3	320
The Americas	948	+1.0	1,212	25	9	23,870
United States	349	+0.5	471	20	13	47,310
Brazil	194.3	+1.0	213.4	24	7	11,000
Mexico	116.1	+1.5	143.9	29	6	14,400
Haiti	10.3	+1.8	14.2	36	4	1,180
Asia	4,260	+1.1	5,284	25	7	6,860
China	1,350.4	+0.5	1,310.7	16	9	7,640
India	1,259.7	+1.5	1,691.1	31	5	3,430
Japan	127.6	−0.2	119.8	13	24	34,610
Indonesia	241.0	+1.3	309.4	27	6	4,200
Europe	740	0.0	732	16	16	27,080
United Kingdom	63.2	0.4	79.6	18	17	35,840
France	63.6	0.4	78.4	19	17	34,750
Germany	81.8	−0.2	71.5	13	21	38,100
Russia	143.2	−0.1	127.8	15	13	19,240

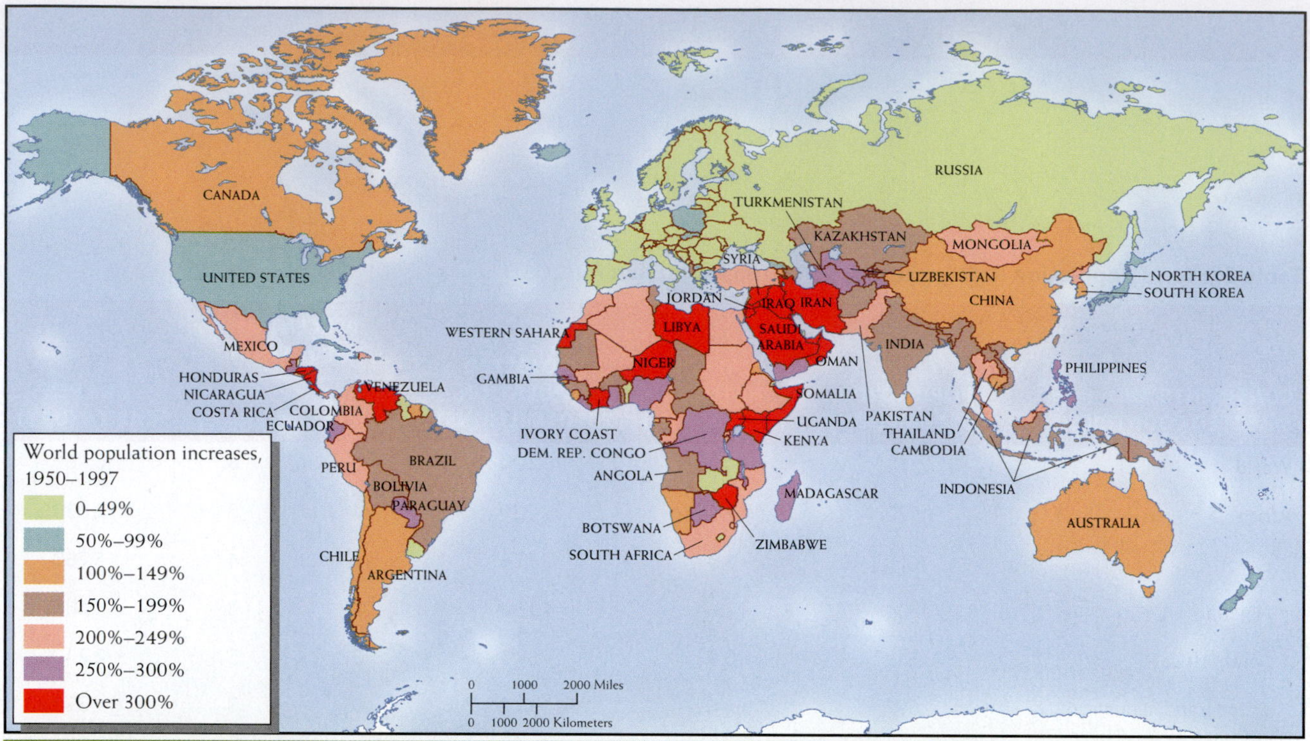

MAP 21.4 | World Population Increases, 1950–1997

The world's population more than doubled between 1950 and 1997, rising from approximately 2.5 billion to nearly 6 billion.

- Which countries had the largest population increases over these five decades?
- Why do you suppose these countries experienced such high population increases?
- According to your reading, why did western Europe and Russia have the lowest population increases?

China and India each passed the billion-person mark. Increases were greatest in cities. By the 1980s, the world's largest cities were Asian, African, and Latin American. Greater Tokyo-Yokohama had 30 million inhabitants, while Mexico City had 20 million, São Paulo 17 million, Cairo 16 million, Calcutta 15 million, and Jakarta 12 million.

Population growth slowed most dramatically in richer societies. For some, like Italy, the growth rate declined to zero, as the number of births no longer exceeded the number of deaths. More recently enriched societies like Korea, Taiwan, and Hong Kong also had fewer births. Societies that did not see their birthrates decline by the same rate (much of Africa, southern Asia, and impoverished parts of Latin America) had difficulty raising income levels. But even among poor nations, birthrates declined after the 1970s.

The most remarkable turnaround occurred in China, where the government instituted a "one-child family" policy in 1979 with rewards for compliance and penalties for transgression. The bias in favor of sons (long a feature of China's patrilineal system, which emphasized descent through the male line), together with the availability of ultrasound scanners, promoted the widespread—albeit illegal—practice of prenatal sex selection.

In general, however, declining family size resulted from choice. In rich countries, more women deferred having children as education, career prospects, and birth-control devices provided incentives and methods to postpone starting a family. In addition, love became a precondition to marriage and family formation in societies that had previously emphasized arranged marriages.

Families In many countries, the legal definition of families became more fluid in this period. Here again, the changes reflected women's choices and the relationship between love and marriage. First, couples chose to end their marriages at unprecedented rates. In Belgium and Britain late in the twentieth century, fewer than half of all marriages survived. China's divorce rate soared too. In Beijing, by century's end it approached 25 percent—double the 1990 rate. As of 2000, women initiated more than 70 percent of divorces.

As marriages became shorter-lived, new forms of child-rearing proliferated. Europeans, including the supposedly more traditional Italians and Greeks, abandoned nuclear family conventions. In those European countries where divorce remained difficult, more couples lived together without getting married. In the United States, out-of-wedlock childbirths constituted one-third of all births in the late 1990s, with only about half of American children living in households with both parents (compared with nearly three-quarters of children in the early 1970s).

Aging Longer life spans also affected families, as more infants survived childhood and lived to be old. The populations of industrialized nations "grayed" considerably as the median age increased and the percentage of the population over age sixty-five grew. In western Europe and Japan, graying rates were especially pronounced. Japan's birthrate plummeted, and the citizenry aged at such a rate that the country began to depopulate. From a population of 127 million in 2000, estimates forecast a decline to 105 million by 2050.

The aging population presented new challenges for families. For centuries, being a parent meant providing for children until they could be self-sufficient. Old age, the years of relatively unproductive labor, was brief. Communities and households absorbed the cost of caring for the elderly. Household savings became family bequests to future, not older, generations. But as populations aged, retirees needed their own and society's savings to survive. So public and private pension funds swelled to accumulate future pools of money for the retired. In Germany, over 30 percent of the government's social policy spending went into the state pension fund.

In Africa, where publicly supported pension funds were rare, the aged faced bleaker futures. Whereas in earlier times the elderly were respected founts of wisdom, colonial rule and the postcolonial world elevated the young—especially those with Western educations and lifestyles. Then, in the 1970s, as birthrates soared, the demand on family resources to care for infants and children rose at the very moment when society's resource base began to shrink. The elderly could no longer work, but neither could they rely on the household's support.

Health The spread of contagious diseases also reflected inequities in the globalized world. Although microbes have no respect for borders, the effects of public-health regulations, antibiotics, and vaccination campaigns reduced the spread of contagions. By the late twentieth century, not only did nutrition and healthy habits count (as they always had), but access to medicines did too.

What used to be universal afflictions in previous centuries now just affected certain peoples. Water treatment and proper sewerage, for example, had banished cholera from most urban centers by the mid-twentieth century. More recently, however, its deadly grip again reached across Asia and into the eastern Mediterranean, parts of Latin America and the Caribbean, and much of sub-Saharan Africa. Thus, diseases proliferated where urban squalor was most acute—in cities with the greatest post-1970s population growth.

In the 1970s, entirely new diseases began to devastate the world's population. Consider **AIDS (Acquired Immunodeficiency Syndrome)**, which in its first two decades killed 12 million people. First detected in 1981, AIDS was initially stigmatized as a "gay cancer" (it appeared primarily in homosexual men) and received little attention. But as it

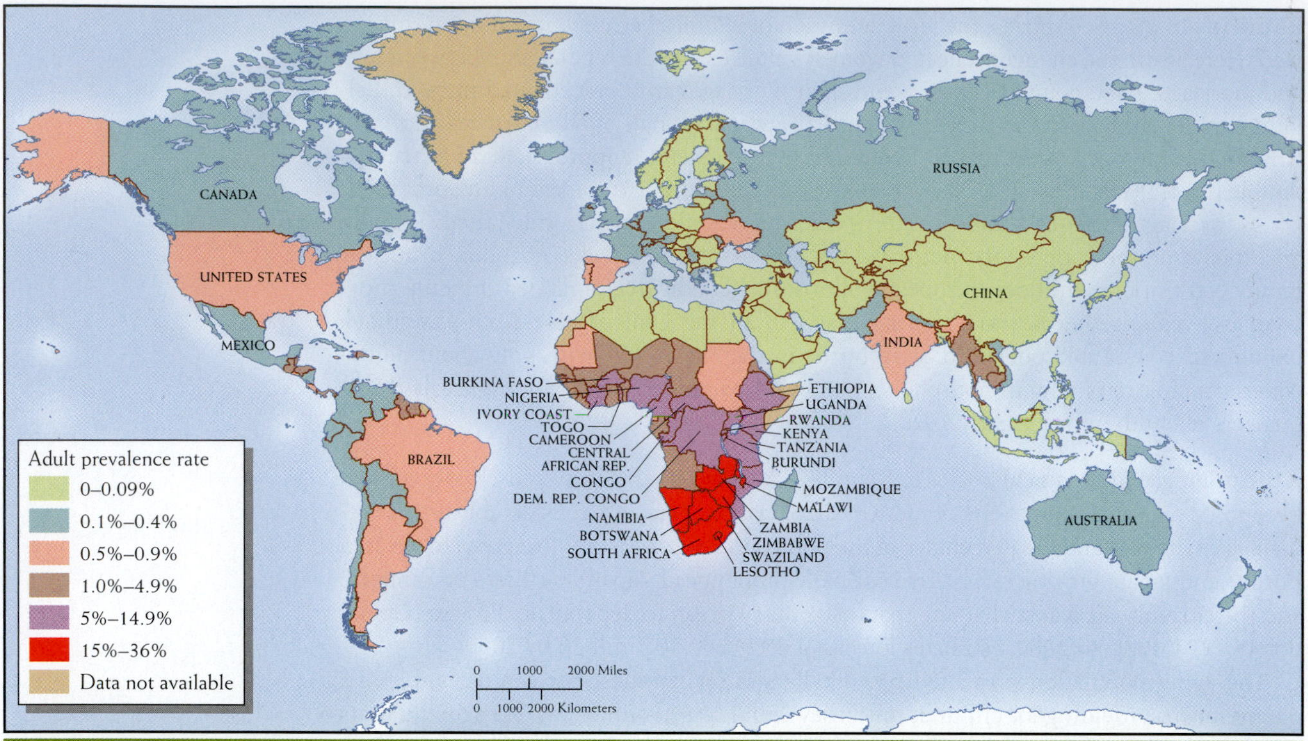

MAP 21.5 | HIV Infection across the World, 1999

HIV, which leads to AIDS, spread across the whole world, providing further evidence of global interconnectedness. The outbreak began in Africa.

- Where in Africa have the highest rates of HIV infection occurred?
- Which countries *outside* the African continent have had the highest rates of infection, and why is this so?
- Which countries have the lowest rates of HIV infection, and why is this so?

spread to heterosexuals and public awareness about it increased, a new campaign urged the practice of safe sex, control of blood supplies, and restrictions on sharing hypodermic needles. In Europe and North America, where the campaigns intensified and new drugs kept the virus under control, AIDS rates stabilized.

New treatments were very expensive, however, leaving the poor and disadvantaged still vulnerable to infection. By 2000, 33 million people had AIDS (the vast majority in poor countries) and even more were infected with HIV, the human immunodeficiency virus that causes AIDS (see Map 21.5). At least two-thirds of those with AIDS lived in Africa below the Sahara. In India, 7 million carried the virus; in China, the figure topped 1 million.

Education Access to education increasingly separated the haves from the have-nots. Moreover, because educational opportunities usually favored men, schooling shaped differences between males and females. In sub-Saharan Africa and in India, for example, literacy rates were, respectively, 63 and 64 percent for men and only 39 and 40 percent for women as of 2000. In the Arab world, the gap between men and women decreased somewhat by the end of the twentieth century. Yet low levels of literacy overall and the depressed levels for women continued to impede each region's efforts to combat poverty.

Gender bias also remained in rich societies. For decades, however, women and girls pressed for equal access to education, with some astounding results. In the United States, by the late 1980s, more than half of all college degrees went to women. Chinese women made even greater strides, although roadblocks persisted. Ironically, with China's recent market reforms women's access to basic education regressed, as families, particularly in rural areas, reverted to spending their limited resources on educating sons. Thus, in 2000, up to 70 percent of China's 140 million illiterates were female.

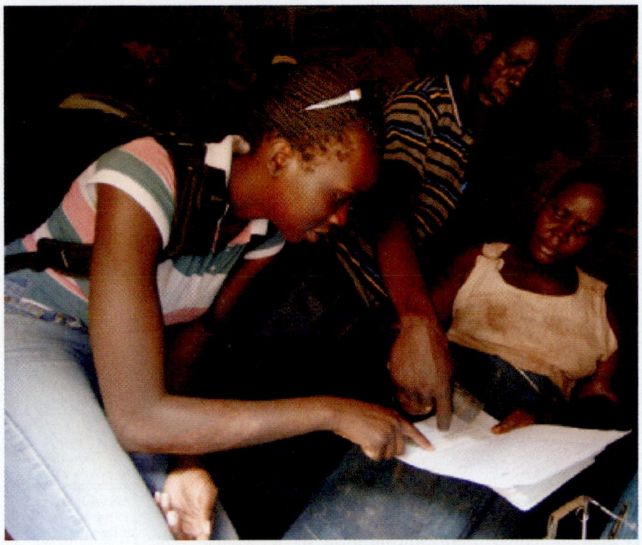

African Women and Education Though women's education lagged behind that of men in Africa, a number of women, like Stella Kenyi, pictured here, graduated from African high schools and attended universities at home or abroad. Kenyi taught business skills to men and women in Sudan after completing an undergraduate degree at Davidson College in North Carolina.

Women and Work Although more women held jobs outside the home, they lacked full equality at work. Limited by job discrimination and burdens of child-rearing, women's participation in the workforce reached a fairly stable level by the 1980s. The percentage of women at the top of the corporate pyramid was considerably smaller than their proportion in the labor force or their college graduation rates. Women worldwide had difficulties breaking through the "glass ceiling"—a seemingly invisible barrier to women's advancement. Consequently, while the difference between men's and women's incomes narrowed, a significant gap persisted.

Working outside the home led to problems inside the home. Who would take care of the children? Changing gender norms in rich countries sparked major migration streams. Jamaican and Filipino women, for example, migrated by the thousands in the 1970s and 1980s to Canada and Australia to work as nannies to raise money to send back home, where they had often left their own children. In South Africa and Brazil, local women served as domestic servants and nannies. They were doing the jobs that once belonged to middle- and upper-class homemakers, women who now wanted the same rights as men: to parent *and* to work.

The deeply ingrained inequality between men and women prompted calls for change. Feminist movements arose mainly in Europe and in North America in the 1960s and then became global in the 1970s. In 1975, the first truly international women's forum took place in Mexico City. But becoming global did not necessarily imply overturning local customs. What feminists called for was not the abolition of gender differences, but equal treatment—equal pay and equal opportunities for obtaining jobs and advancement. In general, then, in spite of rapid population growth, inequalities between and within societies remained in this period. The most glaring were between the rich and poor countries although well-to-do middle classes emerged everywhere in the world and tended to congregate in the big cities.

Agricultural Production The most immediate challenge facing many societies was how to feed their increasing populations. Yet, changing agrarian practices made a huge difference in increasing food production. Starting in the 1950s, the "green revolution," which relied on chemical fertilizers, herbicides, and pesticides, produced dramatically larger harvests. Then, in the 1970s, biologists began offering genetically engineered crops that multiplied yields at an even faster rate.

COMPARISON

DESCRIBE how globalization and population changes affected the environment, and vice versa.

But these breakthroughs were not evenly distributed. American farmers, the biggest innovators, were the greatest beneficiaries. For example, by century's end they produced approximately one-ninth of the world's wheat and two-fifths of its corn. From this output, American exports accounted for about one-third of the world's international wheat trade and four-fifths of all corn exports. The most dramatic transformation occurred in China. Beginning in the late 1970s, the Chinese government broke up some of the old collective farms and restored

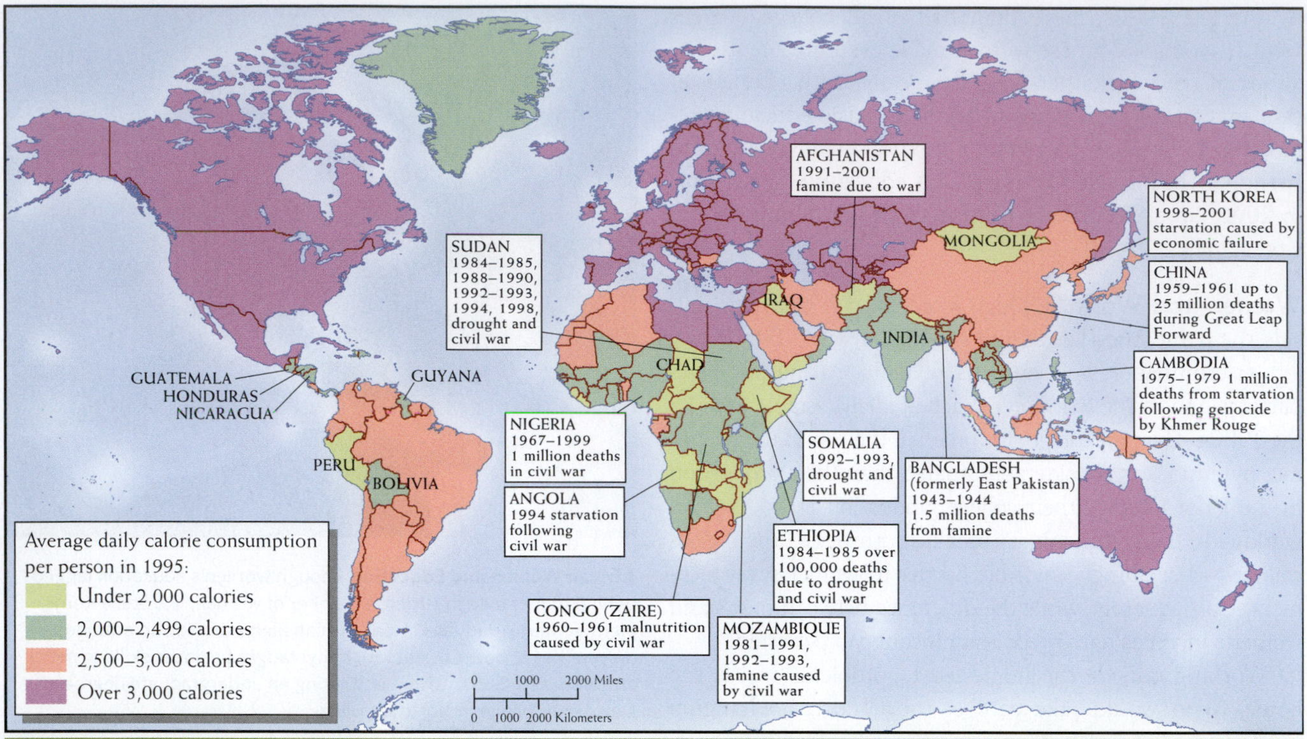

MAP 21.6 | Food Consumption and Famine since the 1940s

There is perhaps no better indicator of the division of the world into rich and poor, haves and have-nots, than this map on food consumption and famine.

- Which parts of the world have had the most difficulty in feeding their populations?
- What have been some of the causes of famine and malnourishment in these regions?
- How much have famine and malnourishment been due to human actions, and how much to climate and other matters over which human beings have little control?

the individual household as the basic economic unit in rural areas. Thereafter, agricultural output surged by roughly 9 percent per year and nearly doubled between 1978 and 1986.

While biology and chemistry allowed some farmers to get more out of their land, others simply opened up new lands to cultivation. The most notorious frontier expansion occurred in the Amazon River basin. Populations flocked to the Amazon frontier, largely from impoverished areas in northeastern Brazil. They cleared (by fire) cheap land, staked their claims, and, like nineteenth-century American homesteaders, tried to get ahead by cultivating crops and raising livestock. But the promise of bounty failed: the soils were poor and easily eroded, and land titles provided little security, especially once large speculators moved into the area. So the frontiersmen moved farther inland to repeat the cycle. By the 1980s, migrants to the Amazon River basin had burned away much of the jungle, contaminated the environment, reduced the stock of diverse plant and animal life, and fostered social conflict in the Brazilian hinterland.

Nor were "breadbasket" areas always able to feed exploding populations. This was especially true in Africa from the 1970s onward, when domestic food production could not keep pace with population growth (see Map 21.6). Food shortages increased in frequency and duration, wiping out large numbers of sub-Saharan peoples. The protruding ribs on African children became a clichéd image of the region.

Saving the Amazon The rise of an international environmental movement in the 1970s led to alliances with local indigenous and environmental leaders, especially in the Amazon. *(Left)* One of the most prominent advocates of the rights of indigenous people and the need to protect imperiled jungles was the British musician Sting. Here he is pictured alongside one of the Amazon's foremost Indian leaders, Bep Koroti Paiakan. *(Right)* Farmers and ranchers cut and burned the Amazon at a ferocious rate in pursuit of frontier lands. In these remote regions, it was hard for local authorities to enforce conservation laws.

What explained Africa's famines? As the Indian Nobel Prize–winning economist Amartya Sen observed, famines—and their increasing frequency—are not natural disasters; they are man-made. Food shortages in Africa stemmed largely from governments that ignored the rural sector and its politically unorganized farmers. Unable to persuade their governments to raise prices for their crops, the farmers lacked incentives to expand production. Food shortages were also by-products of global inequalities. At the urging of the IMF, African countries earmarked hefty chunks of their economies to agrarian exports to repay debts incurred in the 1970s. This left them without enough foodstuffs domestically, and thus they actually became food importers.

Natural Resources and the Environment The consumption of water, oil, and other natural resources became matters of international concern late in the twentieth century. So did pollution control and the disposal of waste products. Part of this internationalization reflected the recognition that individual nations could not solve environmental issues on their own. Air and water, after all, do not stop flowing at political boundaries.

Americans consumed a disproportionate share of the world's natural resources. By 2000, they were using water at a per capita rate three times the world's average. Indeed, extensive irrigation was crucial to California's agricultural sector, the most productive and profitable in the world. Gathering more water also allowed a desert metropolis like Los Angeles to grow.

In the United States and Canada, attempts to curb energy consumption saw little success, and the United States grew more dependent on imported oil. In the late 1990s, North American demand for fuel-guzzling sport utility vehicles intensified oil imports. Dependence on foreign sources locked oil importers into recurring clashes with oil exporters.

As Canadians saw their northern lakes fill up with acid rain (precipitation laced with sulfur, mainly from coal-fired plants), they urged their southern neighbor to curb emissions. Thus, reciprocal agreements between Canada and the United States took shape in the 1980s. Europeans, also beset by acid rain, likewise negotiated regional environmental treaties. But some polluters simply moved overseas to poorer and less powerful nations. As the West cleaned up its environment, the rest of the world paid the price.

Other problems crossed man-made borders as well. These included the greenhouse effect and **global warming** (release into the air of human-produced carbons that contribute to rising temperatures worldwide), ocean pollution, and declining biological diversity. International meetings in Rio de Janeiro and Kyoto in the 1990s urged restricting emission of gases that led to global warming, but a global accord proved impossible to achieve.

The response to environmental crises has been uneven at best. Where environmentalists acquired political power, they forced regulators to curb carbon emissions, a problem that grew with the rise in automobile traffic in cities like Tokyo, Mexico City, and Los Angeles. But controls on fossil-fuel emissions depended on power and wealth, for it was hard to impose restrictions in societies where high energy use seemed a necessity of economic life. Even the Japanese, pioneers of clean fuel as early as the 1960s, were polluters in other spheres long thereafter. With increasing controls at home, Japanese industrialists went abroad to unload hazardous waste. U.S. industrialists did the same, sending hazardous waste to Mexico. Argentina and Canada sent their nuclear waste not abroad, but to poor provinces desperate for jobs.

Even as some states enacted measures to protect the environment, environmental concerns did not observe boundary lines. At the end of the twentieth century, global guidelines for regulating the impact of human activities on the environment had eluded the world's leaders.

Citizenship in the Global World

Since the nineteenth century, nation-states were supposed to be key in defining the rights of citizens. But after the 1970s, people realized that international and supranational organizations often had more influence over their lives than did their own national governments, especially in the developing world. However, these organizations failed to stop the violence that erupted in many regions during this period. Religion also undermined the influence of nation-states, as religious groups often came into conflict with one another and with secular principles.

SUPRANATIONAL ORGANIZATIONS

New organizations with international responsibilities took shape after World War II for the purpose of facilitating global activities. These **supranational organizations** (organizations that transcend national boundaries) were intended to facilitate globalization and manage crisis situations; they impinged on the autonomy of all but the most powerful states.

Among the most prominent supranational organizations were the World Bank and the International Monetary Fund, which provided vital economic assistance to poorer nations. The World Bank, originally named the International Bank for Reconstruction and Development, was designed primarily to provide financial assistance for big development projects. In contrast, the IMF provided funds and technical assistance to countries whose economies were in trouble. A good example of the World Bank's agenda was the financial support that it gave to the government of Ghana in the 1960s for the Volta River project, which was intended to create an electrical grid for that country. Nonetheless, both the World Bank and the International Monetary Fund required that recipient governments implement far-reaching economic reforms, such as devaluation of the currency and the privatization of public sector companies; these reforms were often deeply unpopular and led to riots and charges that these international groups were agents of a new kind of imperialism.

Another set of supranational bodies, international nongovernmental organizations (NGOs), also stepped forward late in the twentieth century. Many championed human rights or highlighted environmental problems. Others, like the International Committee of the Red Cross, once dedicated to war relief, became more active in peacetime, sheltering the homeless or providing food for famine victims. What united NGOs was not so much their goals but the way they pursued them: autonomously, rather than through state power.

International NGOs reached a new level of influence in the 1970s because most nation-states at that time were still not democracies. Of the 121 countries in the world in 1980, only 37 were democracies, accounting for only 35 percent of the globe's population. People found it difficult to rely on authoritarians to uphold their rights as citizens. Indeed, despite adopting a Universal Declaration of Human Rights in 1948, the United Nations, (another international organization created after World War II and intended to provide a forum for settling international problems), was a latecomer to enforcing human rights provisions, largely because its own members were the self-same authoritarians.

NGOs, then, took the lead in trying to make the language of human rights stick. The brutality of military regimes in Latin America inspired the emerging network of international human rights organizations to take action. After the overthrow of Chile's Salvador Allende in 1973, political groups created by the Catholic Church protested the military junta's harsh repression. When the Argentine military began killing tens of thousands of innocent civilians in 1976 and news of their torture techniques leaked out, human rights movements again took action. Prominent among them was Amnesty International. Formed in 1961 to defend prisoners of conscience (detained for their beliefs, color, sex, ethnic origin, language, or religion), Amnesty International catalogued human rights violations worldwide. By 2000, an extensive network of associations was informing the public, lobbying governments, and pressuring U.N. member nations to live up to commitments to respect the rights of citizens.

VIOLENCE

International organizations and NGOs could play only a limited role in preserving peace and strengthening human rights. The end of the Cold War left entire regions in such turmoil that even the most effective humanitarian agencies could not prevent mass killings.

Consider the Balkans in the 1990s. In the territorial remains of Yugoslavia, groups of Serbs, Croats, Bosnians, ethnic Albanians, and others fought for control. Former neighbors, fueled by opportunistic leaders' rhetoric, no longer saw themselves as citizens of diverse political communities. Instead, demagogues trumpeted the superiority of ethnically defined states. Ethnic Serbians took up arms against their Croat neighbors, and vice versa. When international agencies moved in to try to bolster public authority, they failed as Yugoslavia's ethnic mosaic imploded into civil war.

Some of the most gruesome scenes of political violence occurred in Africa, where many nation-states struggled to uphold the rule of law for all citizens. Here, tension often erupted in conflict between ethnic groups. The failure of African agriculture to sustain growing populations, as well as unequal access to resources like education, made ethnic rivalries worse. Droughts, famine, and corruption ignited the rivalries into riots and killings—even into bitter civil war and the breakdown of centralized authority.

Events in Rwanda reflected Africa's horrifying experience with political violence. Friction grew between the majority Hutus (agrarian people, often very poor) and the minority Tutsis (herders, often with better education, wealthier, and chosen by the Belgians to rule over the Hutus) after the two peoples had intermarried and lived side by side for many generations. Some resentful Hutus blamed the Tutsis for all their woes. As tensions mounted, the United Nations dispatched peacekeeping troops. Moderate Hutus urged continued peaceful coexistence, only to be shouted down by government forces in command of radio

Rwandan Refugees Perhaps as many as 800,000 Tutsis were killed in 1994 as the Hutus turned against the local Tutsi population while Rwanda was being invaded by a Tutsi-led army from Uganda. Not surprisingly, the massacre led to an enormous refugee crisis.

stations and a mass propaganda machine. Although alerted to the impending problem, U.N. forces, fearing a clash and uncertain of their mandate, failed to prevent the violence.

The failure on the part of the international community, including the United States, which did not have troops on the ground and which had no clear policy toward Rwanda, gave the Hutu government a green light to wipe out opponents. In 100 days of carnage in 1994, Hutu militias massacred 800,000 Tutsis and moderate Hutus. This was not, as many proclaimed, the militarization of ancient ethnic rivalries, for many Hutus were butchered as they tried to defend Tutsi friends, relatives, and neighbors. Meanwhile, the ensuing refugee crisis destabilized neighboring countries. The Rwanda genocide sent riptides across eastern and central Africa, creating a whole new generation of conflicts.

Some societies, however, tried to put political violence behind them. In Argentina, El Salvador, Guatemala, and South Africa, the transition to democracy compelled elected rulers to establish inquiries into past rulers' human rights abuses. These **truth commissions** were vital for creating a new aura of legitimacy for democracies and for promising to uphold the rights of individuals. In South Africa, many blacks backed the new president, Nelson Mandela, but also demanded a reckoning with the punitive experience of the apartheid past. To avoid a backlash against the former white rulers, the South African leadership opted to record the past events rather than avenge them. The Rwandan catastrophe is the best example of the failure of international organizations to deal with a crisis, which eventually mushroomed into a genocide. Elsewhere, in famine areas and big development projects, the supranationals enjoyed more success.

RELIGIOUS FOUNDATIONS OF POLITICS

Secular concerns for human rights and international peace were not the only foundations for politics after the Cold War. In many regions, people wanted religion to define the moral fabric of political communities. Very often, religion provided a way to reimagine the nation-state, just as globalization was undermining national autonomy.

Hindu Nationalism In India, Hindu nationalism offered a communal identity for a country being rapidly transformed by globalization. In the 1980s, India freed market forces, privatized state firms, and withdrew from its role as welfare provider. Economic reforms under the ruling Congress Party sparked economic growth, thereby creating one of Asia's largest, best-educated, and most affluent middle class. But because these changes also widened the gap between rich and poor, lower classes and castes formed political parties to challenge the traditional elites. With established hierarchies and loyalties eroding, Hindu nationalists argued that religion could now fill the role once occupied by a secular state. Claiming that the ideology of *Hindutva* ("Hinduness") would bring the help that secular nationalism had failed to give, Hindu militants trumpeted the idea of India as a nation of Hindus (the majority), with minorities relegated to a lesser status. The chief beneficiary of the politics established by economic liberalization was a Hindu nationalist party, the Bhartiya Janata Party (BJP), or Indian People's Party. It was the political arm of an alliance of Hindu organizations devoted to establishing India as a Hindu state. By the late 1980s, a BJP coalition came to power and sought to transform the nation-state into a moral community, but without challenging the economic forces of globalization.

Islamic Conservatism In some cases, religion provided a way to resist seemingly American-dominated globalization. One of the most spirited challenges arose in the Islamic Middle East. Here, many people believed that modernizing and westernizing programs were leading their societies toward rampant materialism and unchecked individualism. Critics included traditional clerics and young western-educated elites whose job prospects seemed bleak and who felt that the promise of modernization had failed. Having criticized modernizing processes since the nineteenth century, Islamic conservatives flourished once more in the 1970s, as global markets and social tensions undermined secular leadership.

The most revolutionary Islamic movement arose in Iran, where clerics forced the shah, the country's ruler, from power in 1979. The revolt pitted a group of religious officials possessing only pamphlets, tracts, and tapes against the military arsenal and the vast intelligence apparatus of the Iranian state. Shah Mohammad Reza Pahlavi had enjoyed U.S. technical and military support since the Americans had helped place him on the throne in 1953. His bloated army and police force, as well as his brutally effective intelligence service, had crushed all challenges to his authority. The shah also had benefited from oil revenues, which soared after 1973. Yet the uneven distribution of income, the oppressive police state, and the royal family's ostentatious lifestyle fueled widespread discontent.

The most powerful critique came from the mullahs (Muslim scholars or religious teachers), who found in the Ayatollah Ruhollah Khomeini a courageous leader. Khomeini used his traditional Islamic education and his training in Muslim ethics to accuse the shah's government of gross violations of Islamic norms. He also identified the shah's ally, America, as the great Satan. With opposition mounting, the shah fled the country in 1979. In his wake, Khomeini established a theocratic state ruled by a council of Islamic clerics. Although some Iranians grumbled about aspects of this return to Islam, they prided themselves on having inspired a revolution based on principles other than those drawn from the West.

Religious Conservatism in the United States The search for religious foundations of politics in the global age reached beyond nonwestern societies. Indeed, in the United States, religion became a potent force after the 1970s as the membership and activism of conservative, fundamentalist Protestant churches eclipsed mainstream denominations. Insisting on a literal interpretation of the Bible, Protestant fundamentalists argued against secularizing trends in American society. This traditionalist crusade took up a broad range of cultural and political issues. Religious conservatives (predominantly evangelical Protestants, but also some Catholics and Orthodox Jews) attacked many of the social changes that had emerged from liberation movements of the 1960s. Shifting sexual and familial relations were sore points, but the religious conservatives especially targeted public leaders who, they felt, had abandoned the moral purpose of authority by legalizing abortion and supporting secular values.

ACCEPTANCE OF AND RESISTANCE TO DEMOCRACY

New sources of power and new social movements drastically changed politics in the global age. Increasingly, international organizations were decisive in defining the conditions of democratic citizenship. Perhaps most remarkable was how much democracy spread toward the end of the twentieth century. In South Africa, Russia, and Guatemala, elections now decided politicians' fate. In this sense, the world's societies embraced the idea that people had a right to choose their own representatives. Nevertheless, democracy did not triumph everywhere.

An important holdout was China. Mao died in 1976, and within a few years his successor, Deng Xiaoping, opened the nation's economy to market forces. But Deng and other Chinese Communist Party leaders resisted multiparty competition. Instead of capitalism and western-style democracy, they maintained that China should follow its own path to modernity. By the late 1980s, economic reforms had produced spectacular increases in production and rising standards of living for most of China's people. But the widening gap between rich and poor, together with increasing public awareness of corruption within the party and the government, triggered popular discontent. Worker strikes and slowdowns, peasant unrest, and student activism spread.

Tiananmen Square This white plaster and styrofoam statue, inspired in part by the Statue of Liberty and dubbed the Goddess of Democracy, was created by students in Beijing in the spring of 1989. It was brought to Tiananmen Square and unveiled at the end of May in an attempt to reinvigorate the democracy movement and the spirits of the protesters. For five days it captured worldwide attention, until it was toppled by a tank on June 4 and crushed as the Chinese People's Liberation Army cleared the square of its democracy advocates.

On April 22, 1989, some 100,000 people gathered in **Tiananmen Square** at the heart of Beijing in silent defiance of a government ban on assembling. The regime responded by declaring martial law. Two huge protest demonstrations followed, and residents erected barricades to defend the city against government troops. As the protest's momentum waned, a twenty-eight-foot icon, partly inspired by the Statue of Liberty, was unveiled at the square, capturing the imagination of the crowd and the attention of the cameras. But by then the government had assembled troops to crush the movement. In a night of terror that began at dusk on June 3, the People's Liberation Army turned their guns against the people.

In Mexico, democracy finally triumphed, as the single party that had dominated the country for seventy-one years fell after the election of Vicente Fox in 2000. Until that time, Mexican rulers had combined patronage and rigged elections to stay in office. By the 1980s, corruption and abuse permeated the system. The abuse of democratic rights fell hardest on poor communities, especially those with large numbers of indigenous people.

Mexico, South Africa, and China were powerful examples of how men and women in every corner of the earth yearned to choose their own leaders. In 1994, millions of previously disenfranchised South Africans lined up for hours to cast a vote for their new black African president, Nelson Mandela. In 2000, the Mexican electorate turned

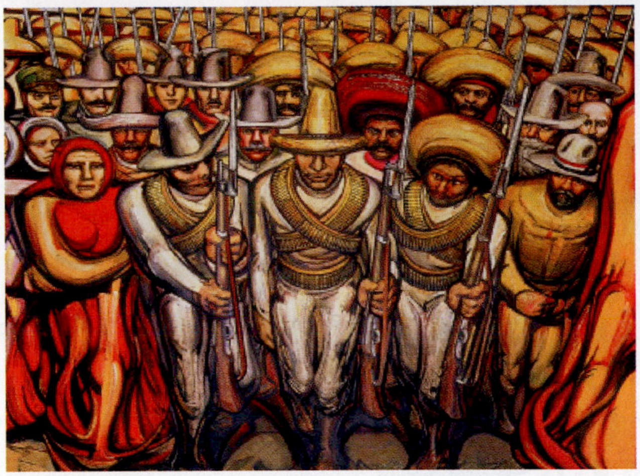

Protests in Mexico (*Left*) After generations of oppression and exclusion, peasants of Chiapas, in southern Mexico, called for democracy and respect for their right to land. When Mexican authorities refused to bend, peasants took up arms. While they knew that they posed no military threat to the Mexican army, the Zapatista rebels used the world media and international organizations to embarrass the national political establishment into allowing reforms. (*Right*) Among the great Mexican muralists of the twentieth century, David Alfaro Siqueiros most advocated class struggle. In this 1957 mural image, *The People in Arms*, Siqueiros portrays Mexican peasants as they pick up arms in 1910 to fight for a new order. Paintings such as these provided inspiration for movements such as the Chiapas rebellion.

out the ruling party, while in China the ruling Communist Party had to call in the army to prevent regime change and democratic reforms.

Conclusion

In the thirteenth century (as long before), a few travelers like Ibn Battuta and Marco Polo ventured over long distances to trade, to explore, and to convert souls; yet communications technology was rudimentary, making long-distance mobility and exchange expensive, rare, and perilous. The world was much more a series of communities set apart than a world bound together by culture, capital, and communication networks.

By the late twentieth century, that balance had changed. Food, entertainment, clothing, and even family life were becoming more similar worldwide. To be sure, some local differences remained. In 2000, local cultures lived on, and in some cases were revived, through challenges to the authority of nation-states. No longer did the nation-state or any single level of community life define collective identities. At the same time, worldwide purveyors of cultural and commercial resources offered local communities the same kinds of products, from aspirin to Nike shoes. Exchanges across local and national boundaries became easier. For the first time, many of the world's peoples felt they belonged to a global culture.

New technologies, new methods of production and investment, and the greater importance of personal health and education created new possibilities—and greater inequalities. Indeed, the gaps between haves and have-nots in 2000 were astonishing. For as humanity harnessed new technologies to accelerate exchanges across and within cultures, an ever-larger gulf separated those who participated in global networks from those on the margins. This inequality produced a range of different political and cultural forms after the collapse of the three-world order. Thus, as the world became more integrated, it also grew apart along ever-deeper lines.

After You Read This Chapter

Go to INQUIZITIVE to see what you've learned—and learn what you've missed—with personalized feedback along the way.

TRACING THE GLOBAL STORYLINES

FOCUS ON: *Globalization*

REMOVING OBSTACLES TO GLOBALIZATION

- Communism's fall and the end of the Cold War improve prospects for global exchange of peoples, ideas, and resources.
- Final decolonization in Angola, Mozambique, and Guinea-Bissau, and the end of apartheid in South Africa return self-rule throughout Africa.

UNLEASHING GLOBALIZATION

- Financial deregulation and the end of gold and silver standards allow money to move freely across borders but lead to a Third World debt crisis.
- Widespread migrations occur as people in Africa, Asia, and Latin America move to Europe and America, following the tracks of their former colonizers.
- Revolutions in culture and communications make cultural diversity more possible for those who can afford it.

THE NEW GLOBAL ORDER

- Globalization leads to dramatic population expansion, requiring greater agricultural and industrial output.
- Family structure changes, life spans increase, and more goods are available, yet inequalities deepen as education and good health determine social status as never before.
- As globalization erodes the power of the nation-state, greater violence occurs between and within states. Nongovernmental organizations (NGOs) and religion become resources for dealing with violence and inequality and for reimagining the nation-state.

CHRONOLOGY

THE AMERICAS
- U.S. announces Strategic Defense Initiative (SDI) 1983

EUROPE

SOVIET UNION

AFRICA

THE MIDDLE EAST
- Khomeini establishes theocratic state in Iran 1979

SOUTH ASIA

EAST ASIA
- Deng Xiaoping reforms China 1978–1992

1970

1980

THINKING ABOUT GLOBAL CONNECTIONS

- ***Thinking about* Worlds Together, Worlds Apart *and Globalization*** How did globalization shape patterns of inequality? After the Cold War standoff between superpower blocs, trade, migration, and communications reshaped the terms on which peoples interacted with one another around the world. Industry, agriculture, culture, and the arts all linked peoples and regions together in different ways. Consider differences in all these domains. What kinds of inequalities were most significant?

- ***Thinking about Changing Power Relationships and Globalization*** What kind of resistance movements did globalization generate, both within the core regions of the developed world and elsewhere? How did feminism, labor, and environmental reform movements resemble and differ from their predecessors? How did Hindu nationalism and religious conservatism differ from each other and from earlier nationalist and religious or pan movements?

- ***Thinking about Environmental Impacts and Globalization*** Explain the relationship between globalization, climate change, and the environment. The consumption of water, oil, and other natural resources became major national and international issues. How did the organization of agricultural and industrial production change, and what influence did those changes have on global warming, acid rain, and air pollution? Identify efforts to limit damage to the environment and evaluate their success.

STUDY QUESTIONS

1. Describe the new global order that replaced the so-called three-world order in the 1970s.
2. Analyze the role of the IMF in the **developing world**. On what terms did it provide assistance, who benefited, and what kind of sacrifices did it impose?
3. Explain the relationship between **supranational organizations** like the **European Union** and state sovereignty.
4. Explain the end of the Cold War. How, and to what degree, did U.S. policies contribute to the Soviet Union's demise?
5. Analyze how **globalization** transformed popular culture. To what extent does global popular culture reflect American culture and to what extent did it shape American culture?
6. Explain how **globalization** transformed world demography. What patterns emerged in terms of international migration?
7. Explain how environmentalists fought **global warming**. What kind of approach did they take? What kind of changes occurred, and how effective were they?
8. Explain trends in industrial production and consumption over the last several decades. Who produced the goods, and who consumed them?
9. Analyze both the spread of HIV/**AIDS** among geographic regions and socioeconomic groups around the world.

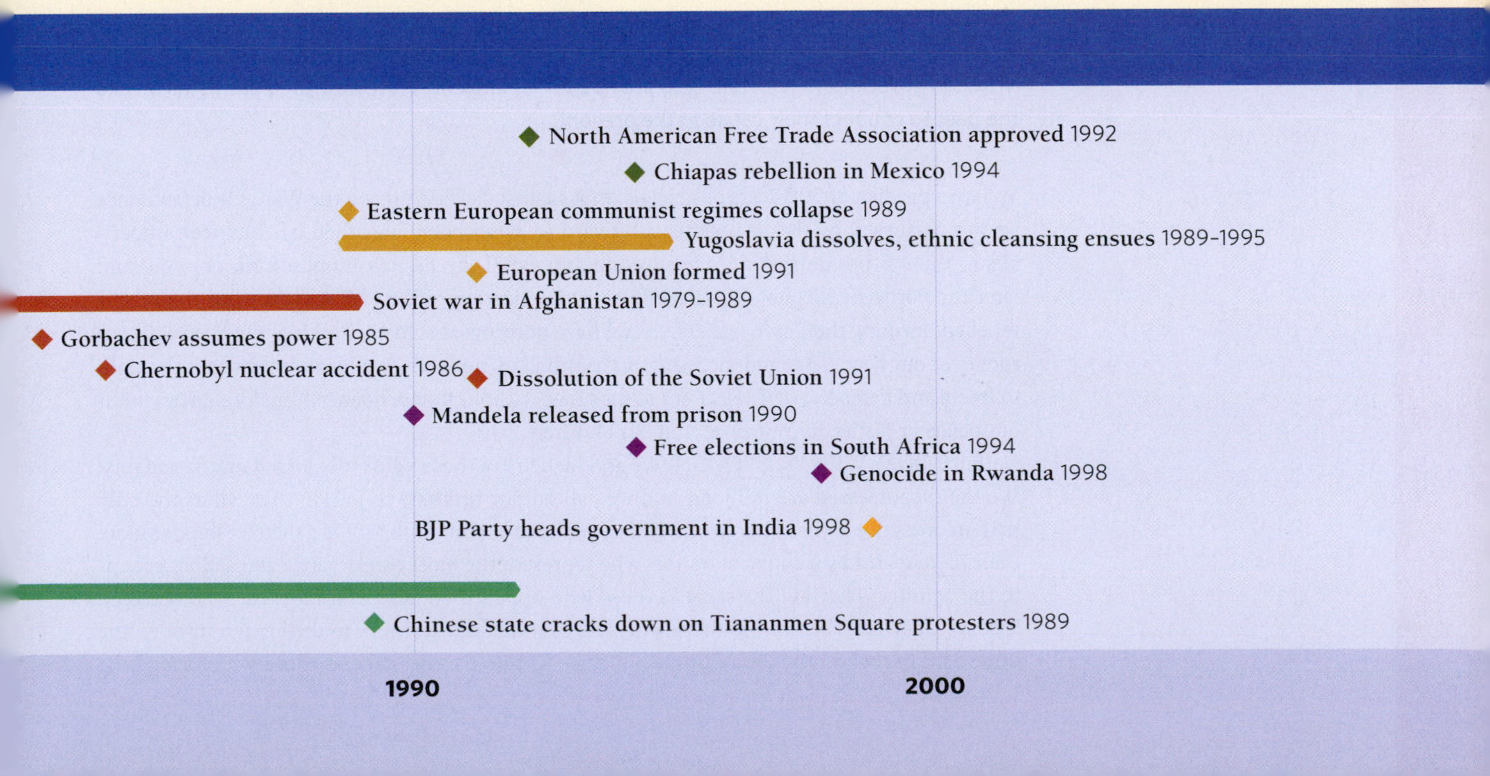

North American Free Trade Association approved 1992
Chiapas rebellion in Mexico 1994
Eastern European communist regimes collapse 1989
Yugoslavia dissolves, ethnic cleansing ensues 1989–1995
European Union formed 1991
Soviet war in Afghanistan 1979–1989
Gorbachev assumes power 1985
Chernobyl nuclear accident 1986
Dissolution of the Soviet Union 1991
Mandela released from prison 1990
Free elections in South Africa 1994
Genocide in Rwanda 1998
BJP Party heads government in India 1998
Chinese state cracks down on Tiananmen Square protesters 1989
1990
2000

Going to the Source

Evaluating Globalization

Globalization refers to the increasing interdependence of states and societies since the 1980s. The degree to which this has happened is quite impressive, but its full effects have yet to be seen. Even so, historians are often reluctant to comment on such recent events because interpreting them can change very easily with the passage of time.

Many advocates of economic growth argue that globalization creates more wealth and higher standards of living for all. Opponents question the sustainability of continuous economic expansion, especially as it has led to rising political and economic inequality, environmental degradation, and challenges to the rights of indigenous peoples. The benefits and the costs of globalization are especially evident in developing nations, whose standards of living have risen, but not equally for all people. The documents in this section all come from the relatively recent past. Even so, the question that has been apparent throughout this textbook remains: what happens as "worlds apart" *become* "worlds together"? How should historians evaluate these changes?

PRIMARY SOURCE 21.1

Declaration of War against the Mexican Government (1993), EZLN

On January 1, 1994, a group of mostly Amerindians living in a jungle region in Chiapas, Mexico, took up arms against the Mexican government, calling for a restoration of the principles of the Mexican Revolution and protesting the confiscation of their land. This declaration from the General Council of the Zapatista Army for National Liberation (EZLN) sought international support for their conflict with Mexican authorities as it charged the Mexican government with failing to provide for its citizens. Note how the Zapatistas invoke the past to connect their cause to the present.

We are a product of 500 years of struggle: first against slavery, during the War of Independence against Spain led by the insurgents; afterward to avoid being absorbed by American imperialism; then to promulgate our constitution and expel the French Empire from our soil; and later the Porfirista dictatorship denied us just application of the Reform laws, and the people rebelled, forming their own leaders; . . . we have nothing, absolutely nothing, not even a decent roof over our heads, no land, no work, no health care, no food, or education; without the right to freely and democratically elect our authorities; without independence from foreigners, without peace or justice for ourselves and our children.

But TODAY WE SAY, ENOUGH! We are the heirs of those who truly forged our nationality. We the dispossessed are millions, and we call on our brothers to join in this call as the only path in order not to die of hunger in the face of the insatiable ambition of a dictatorship for more than 70 years led by a clique of traitors who represent the most conservative and sellout groups in the country. They are the same as those who opposed Hidalgo and Morelos, who betrayed Vicente Guerrero, the same as those who sold over half our territory to the foreign invader, the same as those who brought a European prince to rule us, the same as those who formed the dictatorship of the Porfirista "scientists," the same as those who opposed the Oil Expropriation, the same as those who massacred the railroad workers in 1958 and the students in 1968, the same as those who today take everything from us, absolutely everything.

To prevent this, and as our last hope, after having tried everything to put into practice the legality based on our Magna Carta, we resort to it, to our Constitution, to apply Constitutional Article 39, which says: "National sovereignty resides essentially and originally in the people. All public power emanates from the people and is instituted for the people's benefit. The people have, at all times, the unalienable right to alter or modify the form of their government."

Therefore, according to our Constitution, we issue this statement to the Mexican federal army, the basic pillar of the Mexican dictatorship that we suffer. . . . In conformity with this Declaration of War, we ask the other branches of the Nation's government to meet to restore the legality and the stability of the Nation by deposing the dictator. . . .

PEOPLE OF MEXICO: We, upright and free men and women, are conscious that the war we declare is a last resort, but it is just. The dictators have been applying an undeclared genocidal war against our people for many years. Therefore we ask for your decided participation in support of this plan of the Mexican people in their struggle for work, land, housing, food, health care, education, independence, liberty, democracy, justice, and peace.

1. **Why do the EZLN believe that their cause is just? How do they make that case?**
2. **Why do you think the EZLN sought international support for their cause rather than just appealing to the Mexican government?**

PRIMARY SOURCE 21.2

"Democracy as a Universal Value" (1999), Amartya Sen

Amartya Sen, a Nobel Prize-winning economist who has largely focused his work on international development, describes here a connection between democracy and famine, or rather the lack of democracy and famine. His work primarily explores issues of political economy—the relationship between governments, their policy, and their economies. This selection focuses specifically on democracy, which theoretically is government that both represents the people who put it into power and is responsive to popular will. Note how he places India within a global context by talking about problems beyond regional boundaries.

[I]n the terrible history of famines in the world, no substantial famine has ever occurred in any independent and democratic country with a relatively free press. We cannot find exceptions to this rule, no matter where we look: the recent famines of Ethiopia, Somalia, or other dictatorial regimes; famines in the Soviet Union in the 1930s; China's 1958–61 famine with the failure of the Great Leap Forward; or earlier still, the famines in Ireland or India under alien rule. China, although it was in many ways doing much better economically than India, still managed (unlike India) to have a famine, indeed the largest recorded famine in world history: Nearly 30 million people died in the famine of 1958–61, while faulty governmental policies remained uncorrected for three full years. The policies went uncriticized because there were no opposition parties in parliament, no free press, and no multiparty elections. Indeed, it is precisely this lack of challenge that allowed the deeply defective policies to continue even though they were killing millions each year. . . .

Famines are often associated with what look like natural disasters, and commentators often settle for the simplicity of explaining famines by pointing to these events: the floods in China during the failed Great Leap Forward, the droughts in Ethiopia, or crop failures in North

Korea. Nevertheless, many countries with similar natural problems, or even worse ones, manage perfectly well, because a responsive government intervenes to help alleviate hunger. . . . Even the poorest democratic countries that have faced terrible droughts or floods or other natural disasters (such as India in 1973, or Zimbabwe and Botswana in the early 1980s) have been able to feed their people without experiencing a famine.

Famines are easy to prevent if there is a serious effort to do so, and a democratic government, facing elections and criticisms from opposition parties and independent newspapers, cannot help but make such an effort. Not surprisingly, while India continued to have famines under British rule right up to independence (the last famine, which I witnessed as a child, was in 1943, four years before independence), they disappeared suddenly with the establishment of a multiparty democracy and a free press. . . .

When things go fine and everything is routinely good, this instrumental role of democracy may not be particularly missed. It is when things get fouled up, for one reason or another, that the political incentives provided by democratic governance acquire great practical value.

1. **According to Sen, how do democracies prevent crises such as famines?**
2. **How have disasters such as famines become global issues?**

PRIMARY SOURCE 21.3

"Why Gender Matters" (2000), World Bank

In *Using Subsidies to Close Gender Gaps in Education*, a report by the World Bank, researchers found that better education, and especially better education for girls, improves economic development among the poor. The report suggests ways in which places such as Bangladesh and Pakistan have found ways to encourage education for girls.

Evaluations of recent initiatives that subsidize the costs of schooling indicate that demand-side interventions can increase girls' enrollments and close gender gaps in education. A school stipend program established in Bangladesh in 1982 subsidizes various school expenses for girls who enroll in secondary school. In the first program evaluation girls' enrollment rate in the pilot areas rose from 27 percent, similar to the national average, to 44 percent over five years, more than twice the national average. . . . After girls' tuition was eliminated nationwide in 1992 and the stipend program was expanded to all rural areas, girls' enrollment rate climbed to 48 percent at the national level. There have also been gains in the number of girls appearing for exams and in women's enrollments at intermediate colleges. . . . While boys' enrollment rates also rose during this period, they did not rise as quickly as girls'.

Two recent programs in Balochistan, Pakistan, illustrate the potential benefits of reducing costs and improving physical access. Before the projects there were questions about whether girls' low enrollments were due to cultural barriers that cause parents to hold their daughters out of school or to inadequate supply of appropriate schools. Program evaluations suggest that improved physical access, subsidized costs, and culturally appropriate design can sharply increase girls' enrollments.

The first program, in Quetta, the capital of Balochistan, uses a subsidy tied to girls' enrollment to support the creation of schools in poor urban neighborhoods by local NGOs. The schools admit boys as long as they make up less than half of total enrollments. In rural Balochistan the second program has been expanding the supply of local, single-sex primary schools for girls by encouraging parental involvement in establishing the schools and by subsidizing the recruitment of female teachers from the local community. The results: girls' enrollments rose 33 percent in Quetta and 22 percent in rural areas. Interestingly, both programs appear to have also expanded boys' enrollments, suggesting that increasing girls' educational opportunities may have spillover benefits for boys.

1. **According to the World Bank, what factors positively affect girls' enrollment in the countries described in this report?**
2. **How would educating girls lead to changes in social and economic life in Pakistan? How might this change affect other developing countries?**

PRIMARY SOURCE 21.4

Women and Labor in North America (2001)

This document describes the ways in which companies from wealthier countries use factories in the developing world to reduce labor costs. The author describes the human cost of these efforts to increase corporate profits, particularly to women and girls in the workforce. Sometimes policies such as the creation of free trade zones, currency devaluation, privatization, and outsourcing, which effectively encourage this transborder "exploitation," are called "neoliberal," in reference to earlier versions of liberalism.

*

The deepening of the economic crisis in Mexico, especially under the International Monetary Fund's pressure to devaluate the peso in 1976, 1982, and 1994, forced many women to work in both the formal and informal economy to survive and meet childbearing and household responsibilities. Maria Antonia Flores was forced to work two jobs after her husband abandoned the family, leaving her with three children to support. She had no choice but to leave her children home alone . . . Arrieta . . . because her job in an auto parts assembly *maquiladora* [factory] failed to bring in sufficient income. [To] compensate for the shortfall, she worked longer hours at her *maquila* job and "moonlighted" elsewhere: "We made chassis for cars and the headlights. I worked lots! I worked 12 hours more or less because they paid us so little that if you worked more, you got more money. I did this because the schools in Mexico don't provide everything. You have to buy the books, notebooks, *todos, todos* [everything]. And I had five kids. It's very expensive. I also . . . sold ceramics. I did many things to get more money for my kids."

In the three decades following its humble beginnings in the mid 1960s, the *maquila* sector swelled to more than 2,000 plants employing an estimated 776,000 people, over 10 percent of Mexico's labor force. In 1985, maquiladoras overtook tourism as the largest source of foreign exchange. . . .

[T]his author met some of Mexico's newest proletarians . . . indigenous women . . . workers. . . . Standing packed like cattle in the back of the trucks each morning the women headed for jobs sewing for name brand manufacturers like Guess?, VF Corporation (producing Lee brand clothing), Gap, Sun Apparel (producing brands such as Polo, Arizona, and Express), Cherokee, Ditto Apparel of California, Levi's, and others. The workers told the U.S. delegation members that their wages averaged U.S. $30–$50 a week for 12-hour work days, six days a week. Some workers reported having to do *veladas* [all-nighters] once or twice a week. Employees often stayed longer without pay if they did not finish high production goals.

Girls as young as 12 and 13 worked in the factories. Workers were searched when they left for lunch and again at the end of the day to check that they weren't stealing materials. Women were routinely given urine tests when hired and those found to be pregnant were promptly fired, in violation of Mexican labor law. Although the workers had organized an independent union several years earlier, Tehuacán's Human Right's Commission members told us it had collapsed after one of its leaders was assassinated. . . .

1. **What effect did Mexico's economic crisis have on low-wage workers in that country?**
2. **Explain the ways in which the contemporary global economy, as evidenced in this description, creates new kinds of inequalities.**

PRIMARY SOURCE 21.5

The Kimberley Declaration *(2002)*

The Kimberley Declaration was a statement by the Indigenous Peoples group at the International Indigenous Peoples Summit on Sustainable Development in August 2002 in Kimberley, South Africa. It argues for the rights of indigenous peoples across the world, especially for environmental, intellectual, and cultural heritage rights.

As peoples, we reaffirm our rights to self-determination and to own, control and manage our ancestral lands and territories, waters and other resources. . . .

We are the original peoples tied to the land by our umbilical cords and the dust of our ancestors. Our special places are sacred and demand the highest respect. Disturbing the remains of our families and elders is desecration of the greatest magnitude and constitutes a grave violation of our human rights. We call for the full and immediate repatriation of all Khoi-San human remains currently held in museums and other institutions throughout the world, as well as all the human remains of all other Indigenous Peoples. We maintain the rights to our sacred and ceremonial sites and ancestral remains, including access to burial, archaeological and historic sites. . . .

Our traditional knowledge systems must be respected, promoted and protected; our collective intellectual property rights must be guaranteed and ensured. Our traditional knowledge is not in the public domain; it is collective, cultural and intellectual property protected under our customary law. Unauthorized use and misappropriation of traditional knowledge is theft.

Economic globalization constitutes one of the main obstacles for the recognition of the rights of Indigenous Peoples. Transnational corporations and industrialized countries impose their global agenda on the negotiations and agreements of the United Nations system, the World Bank, the International Monetary Fund, the World Trade Organization and other bodies which reduce the rights enshrined in national constitutions and in international conventions and agreements. Unsustainable extraction, harvesting, production and consumption patterns lead to climate change, widespread pollution and environmental destruction, evicting us from our lands and creating immense levels of poverty and disease.

We are deeply concerned that the activities of multinational mining corporations on Indigenous lands have led to the loss and desecration of our lands, as exemplified here on Khoi-San territory. These activities have caused immense health problems, interfered with access to, and occupation of our sacred sites, destroyed and depleted Mother Earth, and undermined our cultures.

Indigenous Peoples, our lands and territories are not objects of tourism development. . . . We are responsible to defend our lands, territories and indigenous peoples against tourism exploitation by governments, development agencies, private enterprises, NGOs, and individuals.

Recognizing the vital role that pastoralism and hunting-gathering play in the livelihoods of many Indigenous Peoples, we urge governments to recognize, accept, support and invest in pastoralism and hunting-gathering as viable and sustainable economic systems. . . .

We are determined to ensure the equal participation of all Indigenous Peoples throughout the world in all aspects of planning for a sustainable future with the inclusion of women, men, elders and youth. Equal access to resources is required to achieve this participation.

We urge the United Nations to promote respect for the recognition, observance and enforcement of treaties, agreements and other constructive arrangements concluded between Indigenous Peoples and States, or their successors, according to their original spirit and intent, and to have States honor and respect such treaties, agreements and other constructive arrangements.

1. **According to this declaration, how has economic globalization affected indigenous rights?**
2. **Compare and analyze the demands in the Kimberley Declaration with those made by the EZLN in Primary Source 21.1.**

PRIMARY SOURCE 21.6

"The Case for Contamination" (2006), Kwame Anthony Appiah

This excerpt from an article written by Kwame Anthony Appiah describes a visit to Appiah's hometown in Ghana, which prompts him to reflect on the impact of globalization on developing nations and their cultures. Appiah is currently a professor at New York University.

I'm seated, with my mother, on a palace veranda, cooled by a breeze from the royal garden. Before us, on a dais, is an empty throne, its arms and legs embossed with polished brass, the back and seat covered in black-and-gold silk. In front of the steps to the dais, there are two columns of people, mostly men, facing one another, seated on carved wooden stools, the cloths they wear wrapped around their chests, leaving their shoulders bare. There is a quiet buzz of conversation. Outside in the garden, peacocks screech. At last, the blowing of a ram's horn announces the arrival of the king of Asante, its tones sounding his honorific, *kotokohene*, "porcupine chief." Everyone stands until the king has settled on the throne. Then, when we sit, a chorus sings songs in praise of him, which are interspersed with the playing of a flute. It is a Wednesday festival day in Kumasi, the town in Ghana where I grew up.

Unless you're one of a few million Ghanaians, this will probably seem a relatively unfamiliar world, perhaps even an exotic one. You might suppose that this Wednesday festival belongs quaintly to an African past. But before the king arrived, people were taking calls on cellphones, and among those passing the time in quiet conversation were a dozen men in suits, representatives of an insurance company. And the meetings in the office next to the veranda are about contemporary issues: H.I.V./AIDS, the educational needs of 21st-century children, the teaching of science and technology at the local university. When my turn comes to be formally presented, the king asks me about Princeton, where I teach. I ask him when he'll next be in the States. In a few weeks, he says cheerfully. He's got a meeting with the head of the World Bank. . . .

What are we to make of this? On Kumasi's Wednesday festival day, I've seen visitors from England and the United States wince at what they regard as the intrusion of modernity on timeless, traditional rituals—more evidence, they think, of a pressure in the modern world toward uniformity. They react like the assistant on the film set who's supposed to check that the extras in a sword-and-sandals movie aren't wearing wristwatches. And such purists are not alone. In the past couple of years, UNESCO's members have spent a great deal of time trying to hammer out a convention on the "protection and promotion" of cultural diversity. The drafters worried that "the processes of globalization . . . represent a challenge for cultural diversity, namely in view of risks of imbalances between rich and poor countries." The fear is that the values and images of Western mass culture, like some invasive weed, are threatening to choke out the world's native flora. . . .

Yes, globalization can produce homogeneity. But globalization is also a threat to homogeneity. You can see this as clearly in Kumasi as anywhere. One thing Kumasi isn't—simply because it's a city—is homogeneous. English, German, Chinese, Syrian, Lebanese, Burkinabe, Ivorian, Nigerian, Indian: I can find you families of each description. I can find you Asante people, whose ancestors have lived in this town for centuries, but also Hausa households that have been around for centuries, too. There are people there from every region of the country as well, speaking scores of languages. But if you travel just a little way outside Kumasi . . . you won't have difficulty finding villages that are fairly mono-cultural. . . . When people talk of the homogeneity produced by globalization, what they are talking about is this: Even here, the villagers will have radios (though the language will be local); you will be able to get a discussion going about Ronaldo, Mike Tyson or Tupac; and you will probably be able to find a bottle of Guinness or Coca-Cola (as well as of Star or Club, Ghana's own fine lagers). But has access to these things made the place more homogeneous or less? And what can you tell about people's souls from the fact that they drink Coca-Cola?

It's true that the enclaves of homogeneity you find these days—in Asante as in Pennsylvania—are less distinctive than they were a century ago, but mostly in good ways. More of them have access to effective medicines. More of them have access to clean drinking water, and more of them have schools. Where, as is still too common, they don't have these things, it's something not to celebrate but to deplore. And whatever loss of difference there has been, they are constantly inventing new forms of difference: new hairstyles, new slang, even, from time to time, new religions. No one could say that the world's villages are becoming anything like the same. . . .

But preserving culture—in the sense of such cultural artifacts—is different from preserving cultures. And the cultural preservationists often pursue the latter, trying to ensure that the Huli of Papua New Guinea (or even Sikhs in Toronto) maintain their "authentic" ways. What makes a cultural expression authentic, though? Are we to stop the importation of baseball caps into Vietnam so that the Zao will continue to wear their colorful red headdresses? Why not ask the Zao? Shouldn't the choice be theirs? . . .

Besides, trying to find some primordially authentic culture can be like peeling an onion. The textiles most people think of as traditional West African cloths are known as Java prints; they arrived in the 19th century with the Javanese batiks sold, and often milled, by the Dutch. The traditional garb of Herero women in Namibia derives from the attire of 19th-century German missionaries, though it is still unmistakably Herero, not least because the fabrics used have a distinctly un-Lutheran range of colors. And so with our kente cloth: the silk was always imported, traded by Europeans, produced in Asia. This tradition was once an innovation. Should we reject it for that reason as untraditional? How far back must one go? . . . Cultures are made of continuities and changes, and the identity of a society can survive through these changes. Societies without change aren't authentic; they're just dead. . . .

1. **Describe some of the positive effects that Appiah believes have come from globalization.**
2. **Why might critics of globalization be surprised by some of Appiah's views?**

PRIMARY SOURCE 21.7

Modern Beijing

This photograph of Beijing depicts the effects of the rapid growth of China's capital city, a result of China's integration into the global economy.

1. **Why do you think the air in this image is so gray, making it difficult to see?**
2. **Explain the connection between globalization and environmental degradation.**

Questions for Analysis

Causation
1. Describe the effects of globalization on women and the poor.

Argumentation
2. Why have the rights of indigenous peoples become a significant issue in an era of globalization?

Contextualization
3. How has the role of national government changed in the era of contemporary globalization?

Interpretation
4. In your view, does economic globalization encourage or exacerbate inequality? Explain your answer.

Long Essay Question

Synthesis

Based on what you have read in the chapter and the documents above, evaluate whether current globalization is a net positive force in world history or a net negative force. Do the benefits of globalization outweigh the costs?

THE TRUE ADMINISTRATION OF JUSTICE IS THE FIRMEST PILLAR OF GOO
porations
PEOPLE too"
?!
99:1
SPECULATE
THOSE ODDS
JOBS, JUSTICE, AND EDUCATION
JOBS
NOT
CUTS

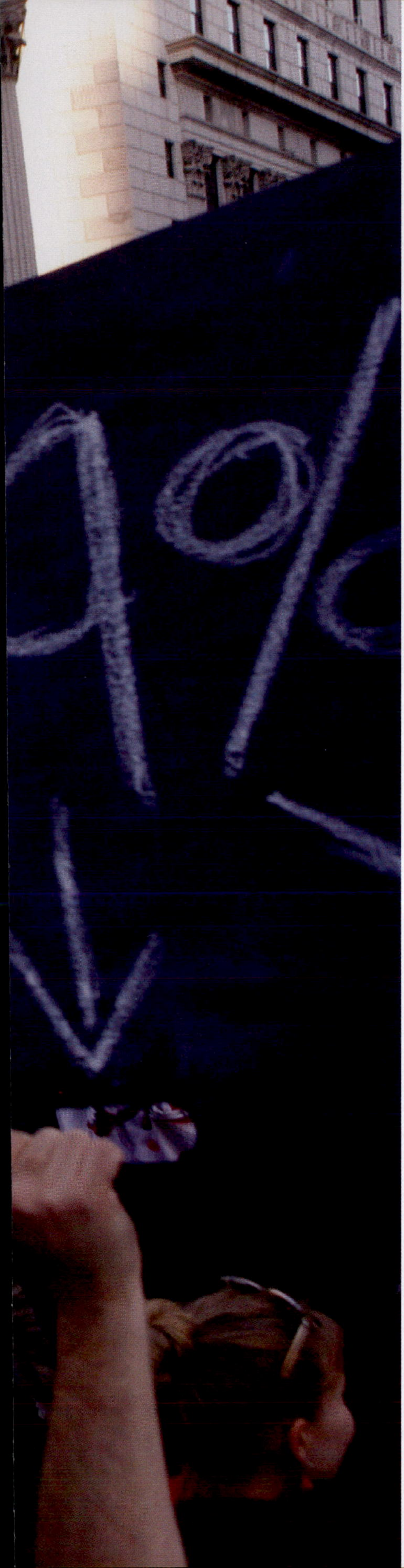

2001–The Present

On December 31, 1999, people worldwide celebrated the beginning of a new millennium. With the Cold War over, optimists hoped for an end to the history of ideological conflict that had bloodied the twentieth century. They looked forward to an era of peace and prosperity. But in the first decade of the new millennium, it became painfully clear that while the global economy and new technologies had brought the world together as never before, ideals that challenged the emerging world order dominated by the United States could still blow things apart. People across the world faced common challenges while also experiencing opportunities and challenges specific to their regions as they sought economic progress and true political independence.

Global Challenges

Less than two years into the twenty-first century, terrorist violence shattered the exuberance that had welcomed the new millennium. On September 11, 2001, nineteen hijackers commandeered four airplanes. The hijackers slammed two of the planes into the World Trade Center in

9/11 (*Right*) The North Tower already aflame, this photograph captures a second hijacked jet an instant before it crashes into the South Tower of New York's World Trade Center on September 11, 2001. (*Left*) Firefighters search for survivors in the smoldering ruins.

New York City and a third into the Pentagon building (home of the U.S. Department of Defense) in Washington, D.C. The fourth hijacked plane was diverted from its intended target—the White House or the Capitol—by the courageous actions of its passengers and crashed in a field in southwestern Pennsylvania. Television captured the event live for global viewers, recording the horrifying images of the Trade Center's twin towers engulfed in flames, then crumbling into a heap of ash and twisted metal. In the months and years that followed, countries grappled with a "war on terror," conflicts with militant Islamic groups, and a global economic crisis. The same globalizing forces that created new connections around the world also contributed to new challenges and conflicts.

WAR ON TERROR

The terrorist attack of 9/11 created outrage across the world. Anger focused on Osama bin Laden and al-Qaeda, the loosely organized militant network of Islamist groups that had organized the attack. The militants claimed that it was a response to the United States' imperialist policies in the Middle East. George W. Bush, who had become president after a close and disputed election the year before, gained broad public support for his tough talk about bringing terrorists to justice and for his insistence that the events of September 11 had introduced a divide between the "pre-9/11 world" and the "post-9/11" one. Domestically, Bush pushed for security measures to curb future terrorist violence and secure the American homeland.

Internationally, President Bush declared a "global war on terror." With the nearly unanimous backing of the American people, as well as strong support from many nations, Bush sent American forces to Afghanistan to hunt down bin Laden, destroy al-Qaeda training camps, and topple the Taliban government that had provided a haven for the terrorists. Expanding the battlefront in 2003, the Bush administration ordered an invasion of Iraq, falsely charging its brutal dictator, Saddam Hussein, with abetting the terrorist assault of 9/11 and producing weapons of mass destruction. As in Afghanistan, the initial offensive went well, but defeating the Iraqi army and finding Hussein proved easier than restoring order to the country.

Helped by a growing chorus of disapproval of the Iraq war, Barack Obama secured the American presidency in 2008. Following through on his campaign promise, President Obama announced plans to end the Iraq war and refocus attention on Afghanistan. The Democratic president ended the Iraq occupation in 2011 despite the fact that ethnic and religious tensions were still roiling the country, and announced that American troops would withdraw from Afghanistan in 2014. In 2011, U.S. forces finally succeeded in finding and killing Osama bin Laden, but terrorism remained a global concern.

ISLAMIC MILITANCY

In spite of the war on terror, Islamic militancy has gained a strong foothold in many parts of the world, and some radical Islamists were prepared to employ violence against secular governments in their regions as well as against western influences. Elections in Iraq under American occupation were won by sectarian and regionalist parties only partially committed to including other ethnic and religious groups in the government. In Afghanistan, American and NATO troops have weakened al-Qaeda, but the Taliban remains a significant force. In Pakistan, militant groups, long supported and used by the military in its proxy wars in Kashmir and Afghanistan, have grown, with some even turning against the regime itself in order to impose their radical agenda. Syria descended into a violent civil war, pitting the Assad regime against a variety of foes. Millions have been displaced and, as of summer 2014, at least 400,000 killed. Sunni militants, expelled from an alliance with al-Qaeda for excessive brutality, which they called Islamic State in Iraq and Syria (ISIS), took advantage of the United States withdrawal from Iraq and the civil war in Syria to dramatically increase the level of violence in the region. Unlike al-Qaeda, ISIS systematically targeted fellow Muslims, especially Shiites, and endeavored to control territory rather than promote global jihad. ISIS activities in Iraq necessitated increased military involvement of the United States and its allies in the region.

At the most general level, the appeal of radical Islam is connected to globalization. Confronting a world transformed and woven ever so tightly by economic, political, and cultural forces larger than the nation, the radical Islamists offer a return to the fundamental elements of the Muslim faith as a global alternative to what they consider as modern, Western, and un-Islamic influences.

Local conditions have conspired to lend traction to this global vision. In the Arab world, with the exception of oil-rich Persian Gulf states, poverty and economic insecurity are widespread. The long domination of the region by oppressive and dictatorial regimes has bred discontent that, in the absence of democratic institutions, finds an outlet in radical Islam. The continuing plight of Palestinians is a source of fury against Israel and its principal ally, the United States. Many in the Asian and African world see the recent actions of the United States and western powers through the memory of their previous colonial and imperial history. This is also true in Europe itself, where Muslim citizens see the exclusion and discrimination they endure as a continuation of the colonial past. Thus, in many ways, militant Islam has contributed to uncertainty in the global political environment in the twenty-first century.

CRISIS AND INEQUALITY IN THE GLOBAL ECONOMY

Beginning in 2007, the world economy fell into crisis. The problem began in the financial sector, the most globally interlinked of all. Seeking new sources of profits, investors from around the world poured their money into riskier and riskier investments—many of which were so complex that not even the regulators in charge of monitoring the financial sector could understand them.

One of the most enticing of these risky bets was real estate in the United States, where a frenzy of investment in the early 2000s created a "bubble" that drove real estate prices to

Global Financial Crisis When the major investment firm Lehman Brothers declared bankruptcy in September 2008, the world's increasingly integrated financial system teetered on the brink of collapse. Although massive government interventions kept the system afloat, they did not prevent severe downturns and sharply rising unemployment rates.

an unsustainable level. The bubble eventually burst, leading to a plunge in property values. This meant not only that banks and financial agencies were burdened with increasingly worthless assets but also that millions of homeowners could not afford to make their mortgage payments or sell their homes. Massive defaults on loans ripped through the world financial system. By the summer of 2008, there was a worldwide panic, and the banking system nearly collapsed. As it became more difficult to borrow money and consumers stopped spending, factories shut down and stores went bankrupt. Layoffs, higher taxes, and reduced consumption resulted in the contraction of developed economies and skyrocketing unemployment.

The financial crisis has brought signs of gathering discontent. In Europe, where, at last, economic and political integration within the EU had seemed to promise an end to conflict between states, the crisis created new tensions. In Greece, radical new parties arose to protest austerity measures or to take out frustrations on immigrants, and many blamed the richer nations, especially the Germans, for having profited from the creation of the eurozone at the expense of the poorer nations. For the first time in decades, vehement nationalist slogans came into wide circulation, and some commentators predicted that the common currency (the euro)—and perhaps even the European Union—in its current form would not last.

Even as economies emerged from the crisis, economic inequality among individuals and regions led to new challenges. The very same ongoing integration of the world economy that globalized the economic crisis also produced fresh wealth across the world. Brazil, Russia, China, India, Vietnam, Indonesia, and South Africa all became more prosperous than they were even just a decade before, leaving other states far behind economically. Capital, technology, and media brought the world together ever more closely. The movement of ideas and images across national borders accelerated. Social media like Facebook provided new lines of communication and connections, particularly among the young. New aspirations for employment, prosperity, consumption, and political expression appeared.

Occupy Wall Street Inspired by other stirrings around the world, this largely national movement was fueled by methods as novel as social media and as traditional as a sit-in. Here an Occupy Wall Street rally joins a labor union demonstration outside the New York County Courthouse in 2011.

However, the growth of prosperity and wealth around the world was highly unequal and accompanied by an unprecedented rise in the power and influence of corporations and financial institutions. Even as a global middle class came into being, inequality deepened. The "Occupy" movement that emerged in 2011, first in New York (as "Occupy Wall Street," then in other cities in the United States and several other countries, protested the growing gap between the rich and everyone else. Claiming to speak on behalf of the "99 percent" against the richest 1 percent, the Occupy activists, consisting largely of young people, railed against the banks and financial institutions that had benefited from government help during the economic crisis. Although the movement ran out of steam by the end of the year, it succeeded in inserting the growing inequality into political discussions.

GLOBAL WARMING

Global warming is just one of numerous environmental issues that have gained prominence in the new millennium. Leaders in Japan, Europe, and the United States acknowledge that humankind is contributing to, if not causing, the increase in temperatures and that climate change will bring catastrophic storms, severe droughts, famine, and flooding. In 2004, for example, an Indian Ocean earthquake, known as a tsunami, with its epicenter off the coasts of Indonesia, struck the west coast of Sumatra, Indonesia, bringing an estimated 168,000 deaths. In the United States, Hurricane Katrina in 2005 left much of New Orleans and the Mississippi Gulf Coast in ruins. Despite growing recognition that the planet needs healing, achieving a consensus on actions to address global warming has proved difficult.

The United States, the European Union, and Japan

While the global challenges of the twenty-first century touched virtually every corner of every region of the world, countries and regions experienced specific local changes, which were often related to globalizing forces. As we saw in the preceding section, the global political and economic crises of the early 2000s had a deep impact on the United States. Americans moved from supporting Bush to electing Barack Obama and tiring of the wars in Iraq and Afghanistan. The recession following the economic crisis resulted in soaring foreclosures, dwindling tax revenues, and millions thrown out of work. As the Obama administration sought to cope with the economic crisis, it encountered a conservative backlash. Europe and Japan also experienced internal divisions over social, economic, and political issues.

A CHANGING WESTERN EUROPE

Despite serious internal divisions, Europe's continuing integration was striking. By 2010, the European Union had widened its membership to twenty-seven countries, including ten nations that formerly had been part of the Soviet bloc. The process of EU unification did face some challenges and reversals. For example, as the European Union absorbed more and more of the territories that the Soviet Union had once controlled, the Russian president, Vladimir Putin, reacted by annexing Crimea in the Ukraine in 2014 and kept up constant pressure on eastern Ukraine, where many Russian-speaking and pro-Russian groups lived. In addition, voters in France and the Netherlands rejected the EU constitution. Still, viewed against the backdrop of twentieth-century total wars and genocides, it is remarkable that member states could bind themselves together in a union to which each relinquished significant degrees of sovereignty.

DEMOGRAPHIC ISSUES

One threat to future peace and prosperity in Europe—and the United States and Japan—is the interlocking set of issues posed by aging and immigration. Women in the European Union would have to bear 2 children on average to maintain its population of 500 million people, but women in the union now average only 1.5 offspring. Adding to demographic and labor pressures is the aging of the European population (see Chapter 21). With the percentage of elderly Europeans rising rapidly, sustaining the present workers-to-retirees ratio and paying for the region's burgeoning number of pensioners will require the European Union to attract and employ around 15 million immigrants annually.

That number has not been reached. European populations have been boosted by millions of immigrants, but sustainable economic growth has proven elusive. In prior generations, immigrants traveled from poor regions within Europe and farther afield to high-wage areas, and they left when work disappeared. After the oil crisis of the 1970s, however, the unemployed have stayed in Europe rather than returning "home," afraid of losing benefits and the right to return. A major part of immigration to Europe today consists of family reunifications, the arrival of dependents instead of workers, for whom there are no jobs. These immigrants, their children, and now grandchildren—many of them citizens—often live in impoverished circumstances; they face pervasive discrimination and periodic waves of xenophobic hostility directed especially against Muslims, who make up the majority of new arrivals. Islam now represents the fastest-growing religion in Europe, giving rise to anxiety over political disharmony based on ethnic and religious differences.

Europe is not alone in confronting the problems of an aging population and the integration of immigrants. As its baby-boom generation ages, the United States faces a similar imbalance between retirees and workers that endangers its Social Security system. Likewise, the flood of immigrants, particularly from Asia and Latin America, continues to shift the nation's ethnic composition. According to U.S. Census Bureau projections, in 2010 people of Latin American descent in the United States numbered nearly 48 million (about 15.5 percent of the population). The presence of so many Spanish-speakers troubles those who think the United States should remain an English-speaking country, and the degree to which immigrants should be required to assimilate remains a contentious issue. (For a global look at population growth and life expectancies, see Maps E.1 and E.2.)

In many respects, the dilemma of aging presses hardest of all today on Japan. Like Europeans and North Americans, the Japanese are marrying later and having fewer children. Japan's female population now averages barely 1.37 children, compared with nearly 3.7 in 1950. At the same time, Japanese life expectancy has reached eighty-five, the highest in the world, which further tilts the nation's age pyramid. In 1970 the elderly (those over age sixty-five) represented around 7 percent of the population; in 2005 it reached 20 percent, and is expected to hit 40 percent by 2050. Analysts surmise that Japan's population peaked at around 128 million and might decline to perhaps 90 million by 2050. Such a downturn bodes ill for Japan's dynamic economy, which is currently the world's third largest in terms of total GDP, China having moved into second place in 2012.

Like Europe and North America, Japan relies on immigrants to fill out its labor force. In the 1960s, the nation's booming economy experienced labor shortages, but neither the government nor major corporations chose to invite in foreign laborers. They preferred automation or recruitment of workers of Japanese descent from abroad. By the 1980s, however, deepening labor shortages and the yen's rising value led to an expanded dependence on immigrant workers. Recent estimates put the number of foreign nationals in Japan at nearly 2 million, or around 1.5 percent of the total population. Most of them hail from the Korean peninsula, the Philippines, Indochina, Brazil, and Iran, countries with a surplus of skilled workers.

ANTI-IMMIGRANT SENTIMENTS

In Europe, where unemployment rates remain higher than in Japan or North America, the political reaction against immigration has been sharpest. Far-right groups have demanded that immigration be halted or "foreigners" expelled. Support levels vary in each country, but across Europe the far right's electoral base appears to be around 15 percent; in some countries it is above 25 percent. The Freedom Party in Austria and the Northern

League and National Alliance in Italy regularly place cabinet representatives in coalition governments. Ultraright forces such as France's National Front, Denmark's People's Party, and the League of Polish Families sometimes pressure governing coalitions to slow EU integration and immigration, especially from Muslim countries.

In recent years, anti-immigrant sentiments in general and anti-Muslim ones in particular have risen in the wake of violent episodes. In Holland, the grisly murder of filmmaker Theo van Gogh by Mohammed Bouyeri in 2004 set off a national debate. Bouyeri claimed he was fulfilling his duty as a Muslim by killing van Gogh, who had made a film about the abuse of Muslim women. Following the assassination, many in Holland questioned the nation's traditional tolerance of diversity and expressed concern that Muslims were too alien in their values to ever fit in Dutch society. France confronted similar dilemmas after rioting rocked a series of poor neighborhoods in 2005, notably in Paris, protesting police brutality and the country's failure to offer equal opportunity to all. The riots also fed a nativist backlash that often blamed Muslims for the country's problems. Nicolas Sarkozy, France's interior minister at the time, spoke of power-scrubbing the "scum" from poor neighborhoods and ordered the deportation of immigrants convicted of rioting, while Jean-Marie Le Pen, leader of the far-right National Front, demanded that even naturalized citizens arrested as rioters be stripped of their citizenship.

Still more alarming to the Europeans' sense of well-being were several deadly terrorist attacks. A series of bombings of commuter trains in Madrid killed 191 people and wounded more than 2,000; in 2005, terrorists struck London's subways, leaving dozens dead and hundreds injured. In both cases, authorities pinned responsibility on al-Qaeda. But investigators also alleged that the operations were the work of Muslims who had resided in Spain or Britain for some time, which sparked doubts about the integration of all immigrants into European society. Those fears were exacerbated in May 2013 when a pair of British-born men who had converted to Islam ran down an off-duty soldier with a car, stabbed him, and hacked him to death with knives and a cleaver. Ever since the oil crisis of the 1970s, and especially since the economic crisis that began in 2007, all of the wealthiest countries in the world have struggled to compensate for aging populations with foreign migration and then dealt with xenophobic backlashes and conflict between entrenched, entitled citizens and unentitled immigrants.

China, India, and Russia

Fueling anti-immigrant fires in Europe, Japan, and North America is the increasing number of jobs being "outsourced" to China, India, and other countries. In the past, businesses had turned to immigrants to fill low-wage positions (and to keep all wages down). But at the end of the twentieth and the beginning of the twenty-first centuries, it has become more economical to relocate manufacturing to places where cheap labor is already available.

ECONOMIC GLOBALIZATION AND POLITICAL EFFECTS

In the new millennium, business mobility is not limited to low-skilled and low-wage jobs. Technological advances—particularly in computers and communication—have enabled all sorts of enterprises to operate from almost any point on the globe. No longer do educated workers have to leave India and China for employment in Europe or North America, because it is increasingly cost-effective for corporations to shift certain operations to those

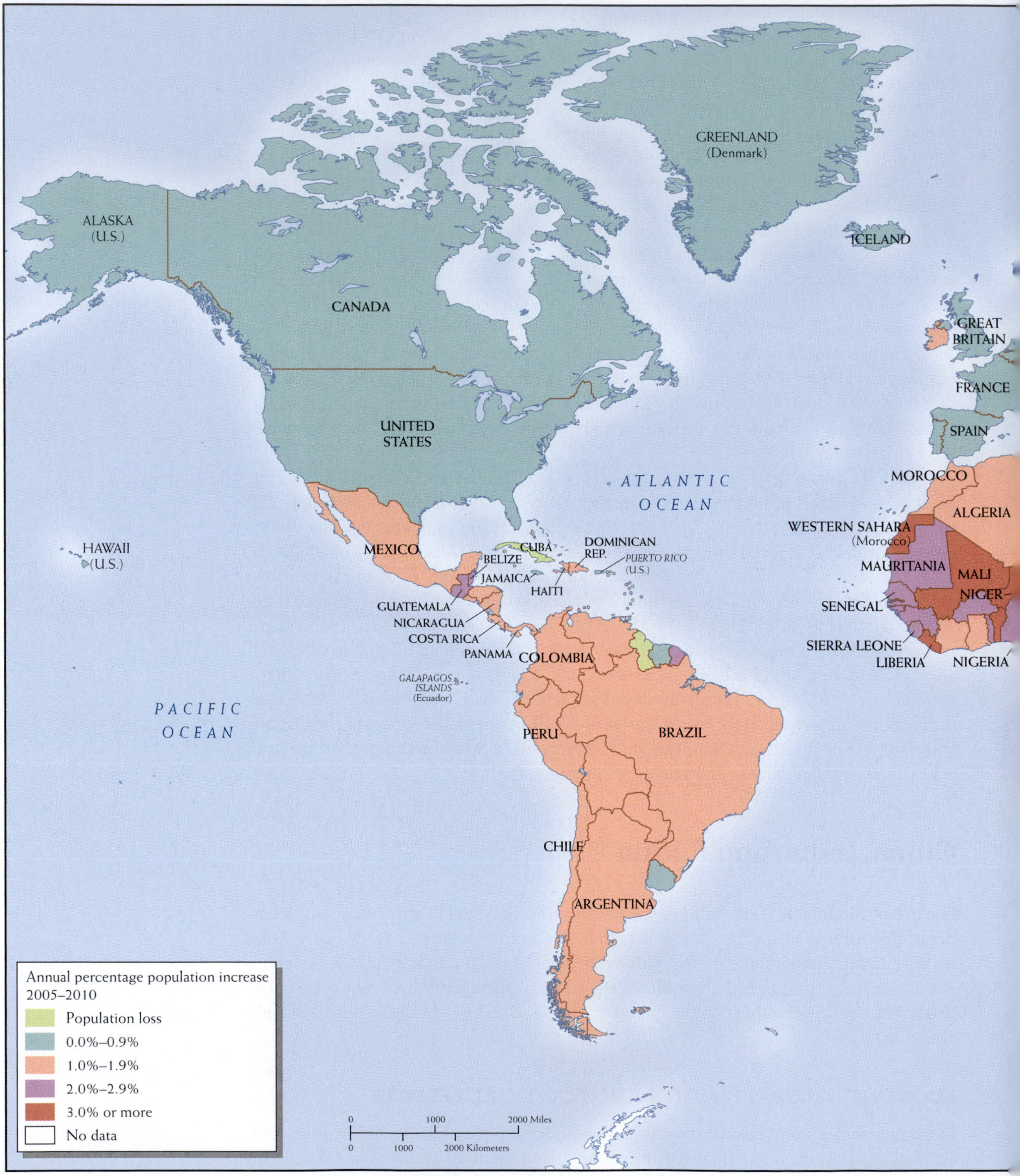
GREENLAND
(Denmark)
ICELAND
ALASKA
(U.S.)
CANADA
GREAT
BRITAIN
FRANCE
SPAIN
UNITED
STATES
ATLANTIC
OCEAN
MOROCCO
ALGERIA
WESTERN SAHARA
(Morocco)
HAWAII
(U.S.)
MEXICO
CUBA
BELIZE
DOMINICAN
REP.
PUERTO RICO
(U.S.)
JAMAICA
HAITI
MAURITANIA
MALI
NIGER
SENEGAL
GUATEMALA
NICARAGUA
COSTA RICA
PANAMA
COLOMBIA
SIERRA LEONE
LIBERIA
NIGERIA
GALAPAGOS
ISLANDS
(Ecuador)
PACIFIC
OCEAN
PERU
BRAZIL
CHILE
ARGENTINA
Annual percentage population increase
2005–2010
Population loss
0.0%–0.9%
1.0%–1.9%
2.0%–2.9%
3.0% or more
No data
0
1000
2000 Miles
0
1000
2000 Kilometers

MAP E.1 | Population Growth, 2005–2010

Strong demographic patterns at the beginning of the twenty-first century pose major problems for the industrialized societies of western Europe, North America, and Japan. As life expectancy increases and population growth slows, these regions' economies face labor shortages that have fueled immigration.

- According to this map and Map E.2, which regions of the world are prime candidates for sending migrants to the industrialized world?
- What cultural and political dilemmas does this phenomenon create?
- Which states within the industrialized world do you think have created the best environment for immigrant residents?

GREENLAND
(Denmark)
ICELAND
ALASKA
(U.S.)
CANADA
GREAT
BRITAIN
FRANCE
SPAIN
UNITED
STATES
ATLANTIC
OCEAN
MOROCCO
ALGERIA
WESTERN SAHARA
(Morocco)
HAWAII
(U.S.)
MEXICO
CUBA
DOMINICAN
REP.
PUERTO RICO
(U.S.)
BELIZE
JAMAICA
HAITI
MAURITANIA
MALI
NIGER
SENEGAL
GUATEMALA
NICARAGUA
COSTA RICA
PANAMA
COLOMBIA
SIERRA LEONE
LIBERIA
NIGERIA
GALAPAGOS
ISLANDS
(Ecuador)
PACIFIC
OCEAN
PERU
BRAZIL
CHILE
ARGENTINA
Life expectancies, 2008
Less than 50
50–59
60–69
70–79
Over 80
No data
0
1000
2000 Miles
0
1000
2000 Kilometers

MAP E.2 | Life Expectancies in Global Perspective, 2008

The increased attention to public health, medicine, nutrition, and education since as early as the nineteenth century has contributed to prolonging life expectancy around the world, as have the many scientific breakthroughs and technological advancements of the twentieth and twenty-first centuries.

- According to Map E.1 and this map, which regions experienced population increase but have lower life expectancy? Population decrease and high life expectancy? Explain.
- Which countries do not match the life expectancy trends of their geographical regions? Why?
- Looking at a world satellite map, do you note any correlations between a region's life expectancy and its physical environment? Why or why not?

Child Labor Girls in a Javanese village work in a factory transferring bundles of cotton yarn to bobbins to be used in handlooms.

countries. The playing field has been leveled in the globalized market economy, although countries with vast labor reserves such as China, India, and Russia still have a long way to go to achieve the per capita income levels enjoyed in the older capitalist societies like the United States, Europe, and Japan. Nonetheless, Russia, China, and India had healthy economic growth in the first years of the new century. With oil prices running high, Russia enjoyed windfall energy revenues that boosted budget and trade surpluses and expanded personal incomes.

At the same time that Russia's economy is opening to the world, however, its political system seems to be closing in on itself. In addressing the anarchy of the Yeltsin era (see Chapter 21), president Vladimir Putin presided over the repossession of television stations from billionaires and the reassignment of other private properties to the state (or to his colleagues from the former KGB). He also eliminated elections for regional executives and restricted nongovernmental organizations receiving foreign financing. In short, Russia's economy is now more firmly connected to the capitalist world, but its political system remains dominated by the executive branch. This situation has dashed hopes for the eventual consolidation of a real legislature and an independent judiciary that the Gorbachev-Yeltsin era seemed to promise.

The Chinese have followed a similar path, encouraging market economic reforms while quashing the possibilities for political liberalization. Their economic strategies seem to be successful. Over the last three decades, China's economy has grown at a breathtaking rate of over 9 percent annually, a spectacular ascent that shows few signs of slowing. Consumer goods made in China dominate so many markets that it is virtually impossible, as several newspaper reporters have found, to supply an American family's needs on a "China-free" diet. In 2012 China's economy became the second largest in the world, and projections—if current growth rates can be sustained—suggest that China will have the world's largest economy by midcentury.

In many ways, China's fortunes illustrate both the promises and the pitfalls of the economic reforms undertaken by many developing countries—what used to be called the Third World—in the era of globalization. On the one hand, despite the continued monopoly of political power by the Chinese Communist Party at home, the country has been fully integrated into the global capitalist economy. On the other hand, the reforms have caused political, social, and environmental problems that defy easy solutions.

The gap between rich and poor in China's more economically developed urban areas has widened at an alarming rate. Government statistics indicate that the richest 10 percent of households own 45 percent of private urban wealth, while the poorest tenth command less than 1.4 percent of the wealth in the cities.

At home and abroad, there are concerns about the environmental impact of China's economic development. China's homes and factories, for instance, use 40 percent more coal than those in the United States, and Chinese city dwellers suffer from some of the world's worst smog and least healthy air quality.

As its energy consumption and economy have soared, so has China's global standing. In the period after 1949, China was the eager junior partner to the Soviet Union, slavishly imitating the Stalinist developmental model until the Sino-Soviet split of the 1960s (see Chapter 20). Subsequently, Richard Nixon and Henry Kissinger's courting of Mao in 1972 opened up a global option for China that Mao's successors have exploited. China's shift in foreign policy orientation from an alliance with the Soviet Union to better relations with the United States has arguably been the most important geopolitical realignment in the contemporary world.

Moreover, China has become the number one trading partner with almost every country in Asia, displacing the United States. It has even become the top trading partner with Brazil as well as many countries in Africa. China has also replaced the United States as the largest customer for Saudi Arabian oil. China-India economic relations have strengthened, too. Although China faces numerous challenges, from environmental degradation to an aging population, it has regained the enormous global weight it held for centuries up to the eighteenth century. In fact, commentators have begun to speculate that China's authoritarian capitalism could be a model for other countries seeking rapid economic development without political liberalization.

INTERNAL DIVISIONS, EXTERNAL RIVALRIES

Internal divisions and external rivalries threaten to undo many benefits of economic globalization in India, China, and Russia. For example, in India a coalition led by the Bharatiya Janata Party (BJP), the Hindu nationalist party, embraced market liberalization after coming to power in 1998 and again in 2014. Over the five years that followed the triumph of the BJP, the government opened India to the global market economy with spectacular economic results. Growth rates topped 7 percent annually, and India's stock market boomed. India is now a favorite destination for the flow of international capital, particularly in the information technology sector.

At the same time that the BJP-led government promoted market reforms, it also championed *Hindutva* (Hinduness) as the bedrock of Indian identity. The dark side of that nationalism erupted in February 2002 after sixty Hindus perished in a fire that consumed a train compartment. A rumor immediately spread, authenticated by the BJP government in Gujarat, that Muslims and a "foreign hand" were responsible. For the next few months, Hindu mobs went on a rampage, burning Muslim homes and hacking the residents to death. Newspapers reported that government leaders and the police force assisted in this carnage or looked the other way as over 2,000 Muslims lost their lives.

The ongoing tension with neighboring Pakistan poses additional problems. Flexing its nationalist muscle, the Indian government exploded a nuclear device in 1998. Pakistan responded by exploding its own bombs, casting an ominous shadow over the two nations' unresolved conflict over Kashmir. In Kashmir, terrorist violence repeatedly disturbed the peace and brought the nuclear-armed neighbors close to a potentially devastating war. The tension between the two countries escalated in 2008 when a small band of terrorists from Pakistan carried out raids in Mumbai, slaughtering many civilians and security personnel before being subdued.

India and Pakistan appear to have taken a step away from that brink, in part because national elections in 2004

Hindu-Muslim Tensions In 2002, Gujarat was consumed by sectarian riots set off by a train fire in which fifty-nine Hindu pilgrims died. Although an Indian government investigation concluded that the fire was accidental, the incident sparked an orgy of violence by Hindu mobs against Muslims. Shown here is an angry right-wing Hindu party activist.

returned a coalition headed by the Congress Party to power in India. Its victory represented a setback to the Hindu nationalist effort to define India's identity in singular terms—at least for the time being.

Projecting recent trends into the future, many observers forecast a rearrangement of the world's economic order, with China and India especially moving to the fore during the twenty-first century. Yet China, India, and Russia, like other parts of the world, have not escaped from their pasts. These societies too struggle with widening internal divisions and potentially devastating external rivalries. (For a global look at hunger and disparities in income, see Maps E.3 and E.4.)

The Middle East, Africa, and Latin America

In the Middle East and Africa, it is hard to find signs of enduring peace or general prosperity, and although some countries in Latin America have enjoyed strong economic performances, others are among the poor nations of the world.

THE ARAB SPRING

The trigger for what became known as the Arab Spring occurred on December 17, 2010, with a seemingly futile act of a twenty-six-year-old Tunisian vegetable vendor and father of eight who set himself on fire outside a provincial office to protest constant police harassment. This singular act aroused the entire population of Tunisia against the ruling elite. Not only had the police confiscated Mohammed Bouazizi's vegetable stand, and not for the first time, but a policewoman had slapped him in the face. In explaining his decision to take his life, his sister exclaimed, "[I]n Sidi Bouzidi [where he resided] those with no connections and no money for bribes are humiliated and insulted and not allowed to live." As the story circulated through the country, large numbers poured out into the streets, demanding an end to the long-term dictatorship of Zine al-Abidine Ben Ali, who had taken over from Habib Bourguiba, Tunisia's president from independence in 1956 until 1978. The catchword of the protesters was "*dégage*," get out. With the army refusing to suppress the dissenters and the security police overwhelmed, Ben Ali took the only way open to him. He departed for Saudi Arabia on January 14, 2011.

Young Egyptian radicals watched events in Tunisia with growing interest. After all, if the Tunisians could get rid of their dictator, why not the Egyptians? On January 25, 2011, ironically a holiday to honor Egypt's police forces, by now an object of people's hatred, Egyptians of all backgrounds and ages assembled in Cairo's major plaza, Midan al-Tahrir, or Liberation Square, to let Egypt's president, Hosni Mubarak, know that he was no longer wanted. Their watchword, *irhal*, meaning "scram" in Arabic, expressed the protesters' contempt for him and his rule. On February 11, 2011, just three weeks after the first mass demonstration, Hosni Mubarak left office, turning the reins of power over to the Supreme Command of the Armed Forces.

The ouster of Ben Ali and Mubarak sent shock waves of excitement throughout the Arab world. Decades of pent-up rage could no longer be contained. An outpouring of protests occurred in all of the Arab world's major cities. The demands were consistent—the end of repression, the establishment of democratic institutions, and the ousting of rulers who had stayed in power too long and who did not represent the will of the people. The results were astonishing. Monarchs in Jordan and Morocco promised new constitutions. Bahraini Shiites successfully demanded a new constitution from their Sunni king, and Ali Saleh, ruler of Yemen since 1978, fled the country. Even Muammar Qaddafi, the Libyan strongman, in power since ousting King Idris in 1969, felt the sting of protest, though his ouster and eventual execution on October 20, 2011, in the city of Sirte, owed as much to NATO air power as it did to the rebel army that rose up to unseat him.

Although much of the world had misunderstood the causes of these uprisings, they were not hard to discern after the fact. In the first place, Arab populations, 60 percent of whom were under thirty years of age and had known no other rulers, resented the fact that the wave of democratic reforms that had swept through Russia, much of eastern and central Europe, and large parts of sub-Saharan Africa had passed them by. They saw no reason why they, too, should not have leaders who represented their wishes rather than rigged elections and fraudulent referendums that supported the wishes of the ruling elites. The young came to be known as the generation in waiting—waiting for jobs that never seemed to appear; waiting to have enough money to move out of their parents' homes; and waiting to get married and start families. The fact that Hafez al-Assad had passed power to his son, Bashar al-Assad in Syria, and Hosni Mubarak was grooming his son, Gamal, heightened the rage. Although the uprisings often took names that suggested peaceful protest—the Jasmine Revolution in Tunisia followed by the White Revolution in Egypt—in reality these outbursts reflected deep-seated and long-standing fury at rulers who were repressive, corrupt, and unresponsive to their people.

The dictatorships and monarchies had lost control over the media. The Qatari television station and newspaper, Al Jazeera, founded in 1995, became an open forum for all kinds of opinions. One of its most dramatic and widely quoted programs featured an intense discussion about whether the Arab populations did not have the right like those in the West to criticize their leaders. In addition, mobile phones, Facebook, Twitter, and other social media all helped dissenters communicate with one another and enabled groups to organize large assemblies outside the purview of the state.

The early results led euphoric protesters to believe that they could create new and more open societies. Dictators were ousted, free elections were held, and new constitutions were promised. But the progress was hard to sustain. In Tunisia, which thus far has accomplished more than the other states, a moderate Muslim Brotherhood party, al-Nahda, won control of parliament. Egypt, too, held elections that were won by the Muslim Brotherhood party, Justice and Development, but nullified by the courts. It also elected a Muslim Brotherhood president, Muhammad Morsi, who in an effort to be seen as a ruler of all the people resigned from the Brotherhood. Yet President Morsi failed to establish an inclusive government and was ousted by Egypt's military leader, General Abdel-Fattah el-Sisi, who was commander in chief of the Egyptian army and minister of defense in the Morsi government. On June 4, 2014, el-Sisi was elected president, promising to restore order to Egypt and imprisoning a large number of Muslim Brothers.

By far the most lethal outcome of the Arab Spring has occurred in Syria, where protesters, seeking the ouster of president Bashar al-Assad, have formed a free Syrian army, gained international recognition for their movement, and led protests that have resulted in violent confrontation with Assad's forces. To date, more than 400,000 Syrians have lost their lives in the conflict.

Although Bashar al-Assad remains in power and another Egyptian general rules Egypt, the forces unleashed by the Arab Spring are still at work. The ideals enunciated by the protesters—open societies, representative of the people, promoting economic progress—are still vibrant in the region.

GREENLAND
(Denmark)
ALASKA
(U.S.)
ICELAND
CANADA
GREAT
BRITAIN
FRANCE
UNITED
STATES
SPAIN
MOROCCO
ATLANTIC
OCEAN
BERMUDA
(Br.)
ALGERIA
WESTERN SAHARA
(Morocco)
HAWAII
(U.S.)
MEXICO
CUBA
DOMINICAN
REP.
PUERTO RICO
(U.S.)
BELIZE
JAMAICA
HAITI
MAURITANIA
MALI
NIGER
GUATEMALA
NICARAGUA
COSTA RICA
PANAMA
SENEGAL
SIERRA LEONE
LIBERIA
NIGERIA
COLOMBIA
GALAPAGOS
ISLANDS
(Ecuador)
PACIFIC
OCEAN
PERU
BRAZIL
CHILE
ARGENTINA
Hunger
<2.5%, extremely low
2.5%–4.0%, very low
5.0%–19.0%, moderately low
20.0%–34.0%, moderately high
>35.0%, very high
No data
0
1000
2000 Miles
0
1000
2000 Kilometers

MAP E.3 | Hunger Is a Global Problem

Despite much optimism, globalization has not yet shown the ability to meet the basic human needs of the entire world population.

- According to this map, in which regions is hunger very high?
- Comparing this map with Map E.4, identify at least twelve countries where hunger is very high *and* per capita income is low ($825 or less).
- What other characteristics do these regions share?

GREENLAND
(Denmark)
ALASKA
(U.S.)
ICELAND
CANADA
GREAT BRITAIN
FRANCE
SPAIN
UNITED STATES
ATLANTIC OCEAN
BERMUDA
(Br.)
MOROCCO
ALGERIA
BAHAMAS
WESTERN SAHARA
(Morocco)
HAWAII
(U.S.)
MEXICO
CUBA
DOMINICAN REP.
PUERTO RICO
(U.S.)
BELIZE
JAMAICA
HAITI
MAURITANIA
MALI
NIGER
SENEGAL
NIGERIA
GUATEMALA
NICARAGUA
COSTA RICA
PANAMA
COLOMBIA
SIERRA LEONE
LIBERIA
CÔTE D'IVOIRE
GHANA
BENIN
TOGO
GABON
GALAPAGOS ISLANDS
(Ecuador)
PACIFIC OCEAN
PERU
BRAZIL
CHILE
ARGENTINA
World income, 2007
$10,066 or more, high
$3,256–$10,065, upper middle
$826–$3,255, lower middle
$825 or less, low
No data
0
1000
2000 Miles
0
1000
2000 Kilometers

MAP E.4 | Rich and Poor Countries: The World by Income, 2007

Wealth and income derived from globalization have not been shared equally by the world population.

- Using this map, identify the regions with the highest per capita income and those with the lowest. What factors do you think account for this disparity?
- What historical antecedents helped to create this disparity?
- According to your reading, why have India and China, despite recent economic growth, failed to catch up with the United States, western European countries, and Japan in terms of per capita income?

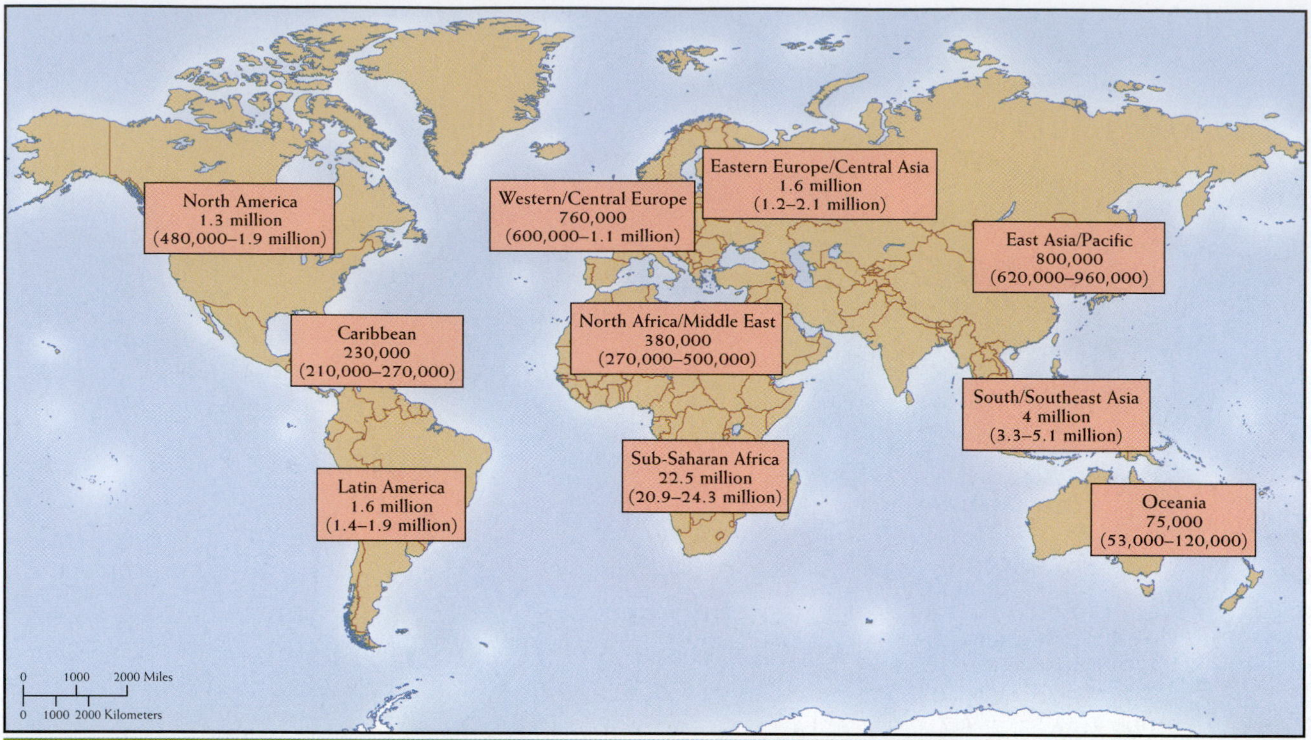

MAP E.5 | The Number of HIV-Positive People Worldwide, 2007

The spread of HIV threatens the development of human capital in the twenty-first century.

- According to this map, which region has the highest amount of HIV infection?
- Using Maps E.3 and E.4 as reference, what connections do you see between poverty and HIV prevalence?
- How does the spread of HIV compromise economic development in poorer regions of the world?

POVERTY, DISEASE, GENOCIDE

In much of the developing world, poverty, disease, and violence have persisted. The new millennium did not begin auspiciously for the peoples of Africa. The region remained the poorest in the world and suffered the uncontrolled and uncontrollable spread of HIV/AIDS. Of the thirty-eight sub-Saharan African countries surveyed in the most recent World Bank *Annual Development Report*, all but seven were low-income countries. The poorest of the poor (Burundi, the Republic of the Congo, and Liberia) reported per capita incomes of $150 or less. Botswana, which enjoyed the second-highest per capita income level at $6,120 (behind only mineral-rich Gabon), was so devastated by HIV/AIDS that life expectancy, once the highest in Africa at close to seventy years, had tumbled to fifty-one years in 2007 and was one of the lowest in the world. (For a global look at HIV incidence, see Map E.5.)

There are a few promising signs. Ghana embraced parliamentary and presidential elections. Civil strife ended in Mozambique and Angola. South Africa convened a Truth and Reconciliation Commission to put the trauma of apartheid behind it and to stay on the course of parliamentary democracy while addressing the gross income inequality between whites and blacks that was a legacy of the twentieth century.

But these have been exceptions to the rule in which political instability wrought misery and devastation. Many of Africa's countries (Liberia, Sierra Leone, Mali, the Ivory Coast, and the Central African Republic) were torn asunder because of ethnic

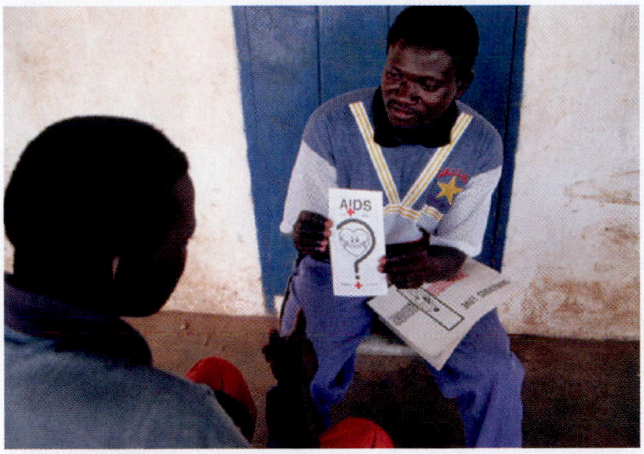

AIDS Awareness (*Left*) A Gambian health worker offers AIDS awareness literature. (*Right*) Due in part to the high cost of medicines, AIDS has taken a deadly toll on Africans, prompting this memorial in the Netherlands on December 1, 2009, which was designated World AIDS Day. The crosses represented the millions of Africans unable to gain access to AIDS medications.

and personal rivalries and required foreign interventions. Nigeria finally rid itself of unwanted military dictatorial control and moved to a civil, parliamentary system. But Nigeria's democratically elected presidents have barely been able to hold the country together. The peoples of the Niger Delta in the south continue to rebel and to demand a larger share of the oil wealth that its region produces, while in the impoverished northeast a Muslim group calling itself Boko Haram (meaning no Western learning) has carried out acts of shocking violence.

In 2003, just when Africa's longest-running civil war, pitting the animist and Christian southern Sudanese against the northern Muslim peoples, had seemingly been resolved only to flare up again, a new dispute broke out in western Sudan. In the region of Darfur, the state allowed local horse-riding, nomadic tribesmen to carry out ethnic-cleansing campaigns against settled agriculturalists. This has led to perhaps the worst case of displaced peoples in the early twenty-first century, with over 2 million refugees fleeing government terror and civil war to huddle in vast, miserable camps. As in Rwanda in the 1990s (see Chapter 21), genocide has once more visited Africa. But there is some hope. In the West African country of Liberia, after years of pitiless civil war, the rival groups agreed to put down their guns in 2004. In 2005, remarkable elections swept Ellen Johnson-Sirleaf into office to become Africa's first woman president.

Liberia's President Ellen Johnson-Sirleaf after her inauguration at the Capitol Building in Monrovia, on January 16, 2006. Johnson-Sirleaf is Africa's first elected woman president; she enjoys strong U.S. support and has vowed to fight graft and rebuild her country after years of war.

DEEPENING INEQUALITIES

Globalization has contributed to economic inequality in some of the poorest parts of the world. Compared with sub-Saharan Africa, Latin America's situation is not so bleak. Globalization has had profound effects on Latin America, but it has not created an entirely new age. Across the region, the divide between haves and have-nots has widened in what has historically been the world's most

São Paulo, Brazil An aerial view of one of São Paulo's biggest slums, Favela Morumbi; Favela Morumbi borders one of the city's richest neighborhoods, also called Morumbi.

unequal region. The very rich in Buenos Aires live like the very rich in Boston; magnates of Mexico City drive the same cars, eat the same food, read the same books, and vacation in the same spots as their social cousins from New York. They send their children to private schools in the United States and the United Kingdom to join a cosmopolitan elite. For Latin American elites, globalization has been a boon to their wealth and has facilitated integration into the international circulation of goods, ideas, and people. Many, in fact, identify less and less with a particular place in the world.

Some of the same features hold for the social bottom. Being disadvantaged and poor in southern Mexico looks a lot like being on the losing end in southern Africa: In both cases, poor people cling to tiny parcels of land, migrate long distances for seasonal jobs, and fight against insensitive authorities for their basic needs. Globalization has offered few opportunities to make it at home. Old factories have closed in Rosario, Argentina, when faced with competition from Japan; maize farmers in Mexico have to contend with imports from Iowa. In many cases, thanks to globalization, the main solution to the problem is to leave—to move to the city or across borders in search of opportunities elsewhere.

Latin Americans have responded to these challenges in many ways. One sweeping trend is for voters to elect left-wing governments. Most of these are not like the rebel firebrands of the 1960s. Instead, in Brazil, Chile, Argentina, and Uruguay, left-wing governments offer policies designed to soften the blows of globalization and meet basic needs for land, schools, and decent housing. Here the same pressures of globalization that contribute to leftist electoral triumphs limit what these fledgling governments can do. Elsewhere a more nationalist and populist brand of politics has emerged, one that decries globalization altogether, including widespread protests by the poor about the vast expenditure of funds to bring the World Football Cup to Brazil. Rather than softening its effects, Brazilian leaders promise to reverse them. In Venezuela, Ecuador, and Bolivia, presidents criticize imperialism and challenge American influence. Their message is that Latin America is better off being a world apart; being together, especially if it means cozying up to the United States, implies a future of subservience and impoverishment. But as many of these leaders also stifle criticism at home, being apart does not ensure empowerment and prosperity for all, either.

The appeal of antiglobalist politics is not limited to Latin America, or even to the underdeveloped world. In the most advanced industrial societies, as well as in rapidly rising nations like China and India, programs to check globalization or buffer people from its destabilizing effects have found receptive audiences. Still, opposition to deeper global integration continues to be greatest in the poorest parts of the world, where globalization's benefits are least apparent and its costs are often lethal.

Historians are better at interpreting the past than at forecasting the future, but what seems certain is that economic, cultural, political, and environmental developments will continue to encourage exchange and interaction, fostering the integration of peoples and cultures in the new millennium. But cultural and religious diversity, local political institutions and prerogatives, economic competition and environmental particularities will also persist. Yet, the dynamic tensions that both link our worlds together and keep our worlds apart will continue to be a decisive theme in world history.

Further Readings

CHAPTER 1: BECOMING HUMAN

Arsuaga, Juan Luis, *The Neanderthal's Necklace: In Search of the First Thinkers*, translated by Anthony Klatt (2002). A stimulating overview of prehistory that focuses on the Neanderthals and compares them with *Homo sapiens*.

Lawrence Barham and Peter Mitchell, *The First Africans: African Archaeology from the Earliest Toolmakers to Most Recent Foragers* (2008). New findings on the evolution of hominids in Africa.

Barker, Graeme, *Agricultural Revolution in Prehistory: Why Did Foragers Become Farmers?* (2006). The most recent, truly global, and up-to-date study of this momentous event in world history.

Bellwood, Peter, *First Farmers: The Origins of Agricultural Societies* (2005). A state-of-the-art global history of the origins of agriculture including recent archaeological, linguistic, and microbiological data.

Bogucki, Peter, *The Origins of Human Society* (1999). An authoritative overview of prehistory.

Cauvin, Jacques, *The Birth of the Gods and the Origins of Agriculture*, translated by Trevor Watkins from the original 1994 French publication (2000). An important work on the agricultural revolution of Southwest Asia and the evolution of symbolic thinking at this time.

Cavalli-Sforza, Luigi Luca, *Genes, Peoples, and Languages*, translated by Mark Selestad from the original 1996 French publication (2000). An expert's introduction to the use of gene research for revealing new information about the evolution of human beings in the distant past.

Childe, V. Gordon, *What Happened in History* (1964). A classic work by one of the pioneers in studying the early history and evolution of human beings. Though superseded in many respects, it is still an important place to start one's reading and a work of great power and emotion.

Clark, J. Desmond, and Steven A. Brandt (eds.), *From Hunters to Farmers: The Causes and Consequences of Food Production in Africa* (1984). Excellent essays on the agricultural revolution.

Coon, Carleton Stevens, *The Story of Man: From the First Human to Primitive Culture and Beyond*, 2nd ed. (1962). An important early work on the evolution of humans, emphasizing the distinctiveness of "races" around the world.

Cunliffe, Barry (ed.), *The Oxford Illustrated Prehistory of Europe* (1994). The definitive work on early European history.

Ehrenberg, Margaret, *Women in Prehistory* (1989). What was the role of women in hunting-and-gathering societies, and how greatly were women affected by the agricultural revolution? The author offers a number of stimulating generalizations.

Ehret, Christopher, *The Civilizations of Africa: A History to 1800* (2002). Although this is a general history of Africa, the author, a linguist and an expert on early African history, offers new information and new overviews of African peoples in very ancient times.

Fagan, Brian, *People of the Earth: An Introduction to World Prehistory* (1989). An authoritative overview of early history, widely used in classrooms.

Fage, J. D., and Roland Oliver (eds.), *The Cambridge History of Africa*, 8 vols. (1975–1984). A pioneering work of synthesis by two of the first and foremost scholars of the history of Africa. Volume 1 deals with African prehistory.

Frison, George C., *Survival by Hunting: Prehistoric Human Predators and Animal Prey* (2004). An archaeologist applies his knowledge of animal habitats, behavior, and hunting strategies to an examination of prehistoric hunting practices in the North American Great Plains and Rocky Mountains.

Gebauer, Anne Birgitte, and T. Douglas Price (eds.), *Transition to Agriculture in Prehistory* (1992). Excellent essays on the agricultural revolution, especially those written by the two editors.

Johnson, Donald, Lenora Johnson, and Blake Edgar, *Ancestors: In Search of Human Origins* (1999). A good overview of human evolution, with insightful essays on *Homo erectus* and *Homo sapiens*.

Jones, Steve, Robert Martin, and David Pilbeam (eds.), *The Cambridge Encyclopedia of Human Evolution* (1992). A superb guide to a wide range of subjects, crammed with up-to-date information on the most controversial and obscure topics of human evolution and early history.

Ki-Zerbo, J. (ed.), *Methodology and African Prehistory*, vol. 1 of the UNESCO General History of Africa (1981).

A general history of Africa, written for the most part by scholars of African descent.

Klein, Richard G., and Blake Edger, *The Dawn of Human Culture* (2002). A fine and reliable guide to the tangled history of human evolution.

Leakey, Richard, *The Origin of Humankind* (1994). A readable and exciting account of human evolution, written by the son of the pioneering archaeologists Louis and Mary Leakey, a scholar of equal stature to his parents.

Lewin, Roger, *The Origin of Modern Humans* (1993). Yet another good overview of human evolution, with useful chapters on early art and the use of symbols.

Loewe, Michael, and Edward Shaughnessy (eds.), *The Cambridge History of Ancient China: From the Origins of Civilization to 221 B.C.* (1999). A good review of the archaeology of ancient China.

Mellaart, James, *Çatal Höyük: A Neolithic Town in Anatolia* (1967). A detailed description of one of the first towns associated with the agricultural revolution in Southwest Asia.

Mithen, Steven, *The Prehistory of the Mind: The Cognitive Origins of Art and Science* (1996). A stimulating discussion of the impact of biological and cultural evolution on the cognitive structure of the human mind.

Olson, Steve, *Mapping Human History: Genes, Race, and Our Common Origins* (2003). Using the findings of genetics and attacking the racial thinking of an earlier generation of archaeologists, the author writes powerfully about the unity of all human beings.

Price, T. Douglas (ed.), *Europe's First Farmers* (2000). A discussion of the agricultural revolution in Europe.

Price, T. Douglas, and Anne Birgitte Gebauer (eds.), *Last Hunters—First Farmers: New Perspectives on the Prehistoric Transition to Agriculture* (1996). An exciting collection of essays by some of the leading scholars in the field studying the transition from hunting and gathering to settled agriculture.

Scarre, Chris (ed.), *The Human Past: World Prehistory and the Development of Human Societies* (2005). An encyclopedia and an overview rolled up into one mammoth volume, written by leading figures in the field of early human history.

Shaw, Thurstan, Paul Sinclair, Bassey Andah, and Alex Okpoko (eds.), *The Archaeology of Africa: Food, Metals, and Towns* (1993). Up-to-date research on the earliest history of human beings in Africa.

Smith, Bruce D., *The Emergence of Agriculture* (1995). How early humans domesticated wild animals and plants.

Stringer, Christopher, and Robin McKie, *African Exodus: The Origins of Modern Humanity* (1996). Detailed data on why Africa was the source of human origins and why *Homo sapiens* is a recent wanderer out of Africa.

Tattersall, Ian, *The Fossil Trail: How We Know What We Think We Know about Human Evolution* (1995). A passionately written book about early archaeological discoveries and the centrality of Africa in human evolution.

———, *The World from Beginnings to 4000 BCE* (2008). A brief up-to-date overview of humanity's early history by a leading authority.

———, *Masters of the Planet: The Search for Our Human Origins* (2012). The most recent survey of human evolution.

Van Oosterzee, Penny, *Dragon Bones: The Story of Peking Man* (2000). Describes how the late-nineteenth-century unearthing of sites in China containing fossils of animals used for medicinal purposes led to the discovery of the fossils of the Peking Man.

Weiss, Mark L., and Alan E. Mann, *Human Biology and Behavior: An Anthropological Perspective* (1996). The authors stress the contribution that biological research has made and continues to make to unravel the mystery of human evolution.

Wrangham, Richard, *Catching Fire: How Cooking Made Us Human* (2009). The author shows how fire made it possible for humans to have a more varied and richer diet but also one that provided energy for the one organ—the brain—that consumes the most energy.

CHAPTER 2: RIVERS, CITIES, AND FIRST STATES, 3500–2000 BCE

Adams, Robert McCormick, *The Evolution of Urban Society* (1966). A classic study of the social, political, and economic processes that led to the development of the first urban civilizations.

Algaze, Guillermo, *The Uruk World System: The Dynamics of Expansion of Early Mesopotamian Civilization* (1993). A compelling argument for the colonization of the Tigris and Euphrates valley by the proto-Sumerians at the end of the fourth millennium BCE.

Andrews, Carol, *Egyptian Mummies* (1998). An illustrated summary of Egyptian mummification and burial practices.

Bagley, Robert, *Ancient Sichuan: Treasures from a Lost Civilization* (2001). Describes the remarkable findings in Southwest China, particularly at Sanxingdui, which have challenged earlier accounts of the Shang dynasty's central role in the rise of early Chinese civilization.

Bar-Yosef, Ofar, and Anatoly Khazanov (eds.), *Pastoralism in the Levant: Archaeological Materials in Anthropological Perspectives* (1992). Classic study of the role of nomads in the development of societies in the Levant during the Neolithic period.

Bruhns, Karen Olsen, *Ancient South America* (1994). The best basic text on pre-Columbian South American cultures.

Butzer, Karl W., *Early Hydraulic Civilization in Egypt: A Study of Cultural Ecology* (1976). The best work on how the Egyptians dealt with the Nile floods and the influence that these arrangements had on the overall organization of society.

Cunliffe, Barry, *Europe Between the Oceans, 9000 BC–AD 1000* (2008). A very up-to-date and spectacularly illustrated account of early Europe.

Habu, Junko, *Ancient Jomon of Japan* (2004). Study of prehistoric Jomon hunter-gatherers on the Japanese archipelago that incorporates several different aspects of anthropological studies, including hunter-gatherer archaeology, settlement archaeology, and pottery analysis.

Jacobsen, Thorkild, *The Treasures of Darkness: A History of Mesopotamian Religion* (1976). Best introduction to the religious and philosophical thought of ancient Mesopotamia.

Kemp, Barry J., *Ancient Egypt: Anatomy of a Civilization* (1989). A synthetic overview of the culture of the pharaohs.

Kramer, Samuel Noah, *The Sumerians: Their History, Culture and Character* (1963). Classic study of the Sumerians and their culture by a pioneer in Sumerian studies.

Pollock, Susan, *Ancient Mesopotamia: The Eden That Never Was* (1999). An analysis of the social and economic development of Mesopotamia from the beginnings of settlement until the reign of Hammurapi.

Possehl, Gregory L., *Indus Age: The Beginnings* (1999). The second of four volumes analyzing the history of the Indus Valley civilization.

Postgate, J. N., *Early Mesopotamia: Society and Economy at the Dawn of History* (1992). A study of the economic and political development of the Sumerian civilization.

Preziosi, Donald, and L. A. Hitchcock, *Aegean Art and Architecture* (1999). One of the best general guides to the figurative and decorative art produced both by the Minoans and Mycenaeans and by related early societies in the region of the Aegean.

Ratnagar, Shereen, *Trading Encounters: From the Euphrates to the Indus in the Bronze Age*, 2nd ed. (2004). A comprehensive presentation of the evidence for the relationship between the Indus Valley and its western neighbors.

———, *Understanding Harappa: Civilization in the Greater Indus Valley* (2001). Harappan site archaeological data of the last century organized into a historical narrative comprehensible to the general audience.

Rice, Michael, *Egypt's Legacy: The Archetypes of Western Civilization, 3000–300 BC* (1997). The author argues for the decisive influence of Egyptian culture on the whole of the Mediterranean and its later historical development.

Roaf, Michael, *Cultural Atlas of Mesopotamia and the Ancient Near East* (1990). A comprehensive compendium of the historical and cultural development of the Mesopotamian civilization from the Neolithic background through the Persian Empire.

Shaw, Ian (ed.), *The Oxford History of Ancient Egypt* (2000). The most up-to-date and comprehensive account of the history of Egypt down to the Greek invasion.

Thorp, Robert, *The Chinese Neolithic: Trajectories to Early States* (2005). Uses the latest archaeological evidence to describe the development of early Bronze Age cultures in North and northwestern China from about 2000 BCE.

CHAPTER 3: NOMADS, TERRITORIAL STATES, AND MICROSOCIETIES, 2000–1200 BCE

Allan, Sarah, *The Shape of the Turtle: Myth, Art and Cosmos in Early China* (1991). Explains the roles of divination and sacrifice in artistic representations of the Shang cosmology.

Allen, James P., *Middle Egyptian: An Introduction to the Language and Culture of Hieroglyphs* (2000). An introduction to the system of writing and its use in Ancient Egypt.

Anthony, David W., *The Horse, the Wheel, and Language: How Bronze-Age Riders from the Eurasian Steppes Shaped the Modern World* (2007). A superb analysis of the origins and spread of the Indo-European peoples.

Arnold, Dieter, *Building in Ancient Egypt: Pharaonic Stone Masonry* (1996). Details the complex construction of monumental stone architecture in ancient Egypt.

Baines, John, and Jaromir Málek, *Atlas of Ancient Egypt* (1980). Useful compilation of information on ancient Egyptian society, religion, history, and geography.

Beal, Richard H., *The Organization of the Hittite Military* (1992). A detailed study based on textual sources of the world's first chariot-based army.

Bogucki, Peter, and Pam J. Crabtree (eds.), *Ancient Europe 8000 BC–AD 1000: Encyclopedia of the Barbarian World*, 2 vols. (2004). An indispensable handbook on the economic, social, artistic, and religious life in Europe during this period.

Bruhns, Karen Olsen, *Ancient South America* (1994). The best basic text on pre-Columbian South American cultures.

Bryant, Edwin, *The Quest for the Origins of Vedic Culture: The Indo-Aryan Migration Debate* (2001). Insight into the highly charged debate on who the Indo-European speakers were, where they originated, and where they migrated to.

Castleden, Rodney, *The Mycenaeans* (2005). One of the best current surveys of all aspects of the Mycenaean Greeks.

Chadwick, John, *The Decipherment of Linear B*, 2nd ed. (1968). Not only a retelling of the story of the decipherment of the Linear B script but also an introduction to the actual content and function of the tablets themselves.

Cline, E. H., *Sailing the Wine-Dark Sea: International Trade and the Late Bronze Age Aegean* (1994). An excellent account of the trade and contacts between the Aegean and other areas of the Mediterranean, Europe, and the Near East during the late Bronze Age.

Cunliffe, Barry, *Facing the Ocean: The Atlantic and Its Peoples, 8000 BC–AD 1500* (2001). An in-depth, highly useful treatment of western Europe during this period.

——— (ed.), *Prehistoric Europe: An Illustrated History* (1997). A state-of-the-art treatment of first farmers, agricultural developments, and material culture in prehistoric Europe.

Davis, W. V., and L. Schofield, *Egypt, the Aegean and the Levant: Interconnections in the Second Millennium BC* (1995). A discussion of the complex interactions in the eastern Mediterranean during the "international age."

Doumas, Christos, *Thera: Pompeii of the Ancient Aegean* (1983). A study of the tremendous volcanic eruption and explosion that destroyed the Minoan settlement on the island of Thera.

Drews, Robert, *Coming of the Greeks: Indo-European Conquests in the Aegean and the Near East* (1988). A good survey of the evidence for the "invasions" or "movements of peoples" that reconfigured the world of the eastern Mediterranean and Near East.

Finley, M. I., *The World of Odysseus*, 2nd rev. ed. (1977; reprint, 2002). The classic work that describes what might be recovered about the social values and behaviors of men and women in the period of the so-called Dark Ages of early Greek history.

Frankfort, Henri, *Ancient Egyptian Religion: An Interpretation* (1948; reprint, 2000). A classic study of Egyptian religion and culture during the pharaonic period.

Keightley, David N., *The Ancestral Landscape: Time, Space, and Community in Late Shang China, ca. 1200–1045 BC* (2000). Provides insights into the nature of royal kinship that undergirded the Shang court and its regional domains.

Kemp, Barry J., *Ancient Egypt: Anatomy of a Civilization* (2006). A definitive presentation of the history, culture, and religion of ancient Egypt.

Klein, Jacob, "The Marriage of Martu: The Urbanization of 'Barbaric' Nomads," in *Mutual Influences of Peoples and Cultures in the Ancient Near East*, ed. Meir Malul (1996).

Kristiansen, Kristian, *Europe before History* (1998). The finest recent survey of all the major developmental phases of European prehistory.

McIntosh, Jane, *Handbook to Life in Prehistoric Europe* (2006). Highlights the archaeological evidence that enables us to re-create the day-to-day life of different prehistoric communities in Europe.

Preziosi, Donald, and L. A. Hitchcock, *Aegean Art and Architecture* (1999). One of the best general guides to the figurative and decorative art produced both by the Minoans and Mycenaeans and by related early societies in the region of the Aegean.

Quirke, Stephen, *Ancient Egyptian Religion* (1992). A highly readable presentation of ancient Egyptian religion that summarizes the roles and attributions of the many Egyptian gods.

Robins, Gay, *The Art of Ancient Egypt* (1997). The most comprehensive survey to date of the art of pharaonic Egypt.

———, *Women in Ancient Egypt* (1993). An interesting survey of the place of women in Ancient Egyptian society.

Romer, John, *Ancient Lives: Daily Life in Egypt of the Pharaohs* (1990). A discussion of the economic and social lives of everyday ancient Egyptians.

Sandars, N. K., *The Sea Peoples: Warriors of the Ancient Mediterranean* (1985). A readable discussion of a very complex period of Levantine history.

Simpson, William Kelly (ed.), *The Literature of Ancient Egypt: An Anthology of Stories, Instructions, and Poetry* (1972). A compilation of the most important works of literature from Ancient Egypt.

Thorp, Robert L., *China in the Early Bronze Age: Shang Civilization* (2005). Reviews the archaeological discoveries near Anyang, site of two capitals of the Shang kings.

Warren, Peter, *The Aegean Civilizations: From Ancient Crete to Mycenae*, 2nd ed. (1989). An excellent textual and pictorial guide to all the basic aspects of the Minoan and Mycenaean societies.

Wilson, John A., *The Culture of Ancient Egypt* (1951). A classic study of the history and culture of pharaonic Egypt.

Yadin, Yigael, *The Art of Warfare in Biblical Lands in the Light of Archaeological Discovery* (1963). A well-illustrated presentation of the machinery of war in the second and first millennia BCE.

CHAPTER 4: FIRST EMPIRES AND COMMON CULTURES IN AFRO-EURASIA, 1250–325 BCE

Ahlström, Gosta W., *The History of Ancient Palestine from the Paleolithic Period to Alexander's Conquests* (1993). An excellent survey of the history of the region by a renowned expert, with good attention to the recent archaeological evidence.

Aubet, Maria Eugenia, *The Phoenicians and the West*, 2nd ed. (2001).

The basic survey of the Phoenician colonization of the western Mediterranean and Atlantic, with special attention to recent archaeological discoveries.

Behringer, Wolfgang, *A Cultural History of Climate*, Translated by Patrick Camiller (2010). A summary view of the place of climate in historical change, written by an expert in historical climatology.

Briant, Pierre, *From Cyrus to Alexander: A History of the Persian Empire*, trans. Peter T. Daniels (2002). A complex and comprehensive history of the Persian Empire by its finest modern scholar.

Bright, John, *A History of Israel*, 4th ed. (2000). An updated version of a classic and still very useful overview of the whole history of the Israelite people down to the end of the period covered in this chapter.

Cook, J. M., *The Persian Empire* (1983). An older but still useful, and highly readable, standard history of the Persian Empire.

Fagan, Brian, *The Long Summer: How Climate Changed Civilization* (2004). An accessible overview of the role of climate in historical change, written by one of the leading historians of ancient history and an individual who has brought together considerable evidence about climatic change and historical development.

Falkenhausen, Lothar von, *Chinese Society in the Age of Confucius (1000–250 BC): The Archaeological Evidence* (2006). A timely reassessment of early Chinese history that compares the literary texts on which it has traditionally been based to the new archaeological evidence.

Frye, Richard N., *The Heritage of Persia* (1963). This classic study of ancient Iran gives the political and literary history of the Persians and their successors.

Grayson, A. K., "Assyrian Civilization," in *Cambridge Ancient History*, vol. 3, pt. 2, pp. 194–228 (1992). The Assyrian and Babylonian empires and other states of the Near East, from the eighth to the sixth century BCE.

Hornung, Erik, *Akhenaten and the Religion of Light*, translated from the German by David Lorton (1999). An important, brief biography of Egypt's most controversial pharaoh.

———, *History of Ancient Egypt: An Introduction*, translated from the German by David Lorton (1999). An accessible overview of the history of ancient Egypt by a leading Egyptologist.

Isserlin, Benedikt J., *The Israelites* (1998). A very well-written and heavily illustrated history of all aspects of life in the regions of the Levant inhabited by the Israelites, equally good on the latest scholarship and the archaeological data.

Keay, John, *India: A History* (2010). A useful, readable overview of the sweep of Indian history.

Lancel, Serge, *Carthage: A History*, trans. Antonia Nevill (1997). By far the best single-volume history of the most important Phoenician colony in the Mediterranean (the first three chapters are especially relevant to materials covered in this chapter).

Lemche, Niels Peter, *Ancient Israel: A New History of Israelite Society* (1988). A quick, readable, and still up-to-date summary of the main phases and themes.

Lewis, Mark Edward, *Writing and Authority in Early China* (1999). A work that traces the changing uses of writing to command assent and obedience in early China.

Markoe, Glenn E., *Phoenicians* (2000). A thorough survey of the Phoenicians and their society as it first developed in the Levant and then expanded over the Mediterranean, with excellent illustrations of the diverse archaeological sites.

Matthews, Victor H., and Don C. Benjamin, *Social World of Ancient Israel, 1350–587 BCE* (1993). A thematic overview of the main occupational groups and social roles that characterized ancient Israelite society.

Oates, Joan, and David Oates, *Nimrud: An Assyrian Imperial City Revealed* (2001). A fine and highly readable summary of the state of our knowledge of the Assyrian Empire from the perspective of the early capital of Assurnasirpal II.

Oded, Bustenay, *Mass Deportations and Deportees in the Neo-Assyrian Empire* (1979). A detailed textual examination of the deportation strategy of the Assyrian kings. Good for in-depth research of the question.

Potts, D. T., *The Archaeology of Elam: Formation and Transformation of an Ancient Iranian State* (1999). The definitive study of the archaeology of western Iran from the Neolithic period through the Persian Empire.

Shaughnessy, Edward L., *Sources of Western Zhou History: Inscribed Bronze Vessels* (1992). Detailed work on the historiography and interpretation of the thousands of ritual bronze vessels discovered by China's archaeologists.

Stein, Burton, *A History of India*, 2nd ed., edited by David Arnold (2010). One of the standard general histories of India, brought up-to-date by a leading historian of the subcontinent.

Tanner, Harold M., *China: A History* (2009). A readable and up-to-date overview of the sweep of Chinese history.

Thapar, Romila, *From Lineage to State* (1984). The only book on early India that uses religious literature historically and analyzes major lineages to reveal the transition from tribal society to state institutions.

Tignor, Robert L., *Egypt: A Short History* (2010). A succinct treatment of the entire history of Egypt from the pharaohs to the present, with three chapters on the ancient period.

Tubb, Jonathan N., *Canaanites* (1998). The best recent survey, well illustrated, of one of the main ethnic groups dominating the culture of the Levant.

CHAPTER 5: WORLDS TURNED INSIDE OUT, 1000–350 BCE

Adams, William Y., *Nubia: Corridor to Africa* (1977). The authoritative historical overview of Nubia, the area of present-day Sudan just south of Egypt and a geographical connecting point between the Mediterranean and sub-Saharan Africa.

Armstrong, Karen, *Buddha* (2001). A readable and impressive account of the life of the Buddha.

Aubet, Maria Eugenia, *The Phoenicians and the West*, 2nd ed. (2001). The basic survey of the Phoenician colonization of the western Mediterranean and Atlantic, with special attention to recent archaeological discoveries.

Barker, Graeme, and Tom Rasmussen, *The Etruscans* (1998). The most up-to-date introduction to this important pre-Roman society in the Italian peninsula, with strong emphasis on broad social and material patterns of development as indicated by the archaeological evidence.

Bruhns, Karen Olsen, *Ancient South America* (1994). A very useful overview of recent debates and conclusions about pre-Columbian archaeology in South America, including both the Andes and the lowland and coastal regions.

Burkert, Walter, *Greek Religion*, trans. John Raffan (1985). The best one-volume introduction to early Greek religion, placing the Greeks in their larger Mediterranean and Near Eastern contexts.

Cartledge, Paul (ed.), *The Cambridge Illustrated History of Ancient Greece* (2002). An excellent history of the Greek city-states down to the time of Alexander the Great.

Chakravarti, Uma, *The Social Dimensions of Early Buddhism* (1987). A description of the life of Buddha drawn from early Buddhist texts.

Cho-yun, Hsu, *Ancient China in Transition* (1965). An account of the political, economic, social, and intellectual changes that occurred during the Warring States period.

Coarelli, Filippo (ed.), *Etruscan Cities* (1975). A brilliantly and lavishly illustrated guide to the material remains of the Etruscans: their cities, their magnificent tombs, and their architecture, painting, sculpture, and other art.

Coe, Michael, et al. (eds.), *The Olmec World: Ritual and Rulership* (1996). A collection of field-synthesizing articles with important illustrations, based on one of the most comprehensive exhibitions of Olmec art in the world.

Confucius, *The Analects (Lun Yü)*, trans. D. C. Lau (1979). An outstanding translation of the words of Confucius as recorded by his major disciples. Includes valuable historical material needed to provide the context for Confucius's teachings.

Falkenhausen, Lothar von, *Chinese Society in the Age of Confucius (100–250 BC)* (2006). The larger Chinese society under the influence of Confucian thought.

Finley, M. I., and H. W. Pleket, *The Olympic Games: The First Thousand Years* (2005). A fine description of the most famous of the Greek games; it explains how they exemplify the competitive spirit that marked many aspects of the Greek city-states.

Garlan, Yvon, *Slavery in Ancient Greece*, trans. Janet Lloyd (1988). A treatment of the emergence, development, and institutionalization of chattel slavery in the Greek city-states.

———, *War in the Ancient World: A Social History*, trans. Janet Lloyd (1976). A discussion of the emergence of the forms of warfare, including male citizens fighting in hoplite phalanxes and the development of siege warfare, that were typical of the Greek city-states.

Iliffe, John, *Africans: The History of a Continent*, 2nd ed. (2007). A first-rate scholarly survey of Africa from its beginnings, with a strong emphasis on demography.

Kagan, Donald, *The Peloponnesian War* (2004). A vivid description of the war that pitted the major Greek city-states, including Athens and Sparta, against each other over the latter half of the fifth century BCE.

Lancel, Serge, *Carthage: A History*, trans. Antonia Nevill (1997). By far the best single-volume history of the most important Phoenician colony in the Mediterranean.

Lewis, Mark Edward, *Sanctioned Violence in Early China* (1990). An analysis of the use of sanctioned violence as an element of statecraft from the Warring States period to the formation of the Qin and Han empires in the second half of the first millennium BCE.

———, *Writing and Authority in Early China* (1999). A revisionist account of the central role of writing and persuasion in models for the invention of a Chinese world empire.

Ling, Trevor, *The Buddha: Buddhist Civilization in India and Ceylon* (1972). An overview of Buddhism in India and Ceylon.

Lloyd, G. E. R., *Early Greek Science: Thales to Aristotle* (1970). An especially clear and concise introduction to the main developments and intellectuals that marked the emergence of critical secular thinking in the early Greek world.

Lloyd, G. E. R., and Nathan Sivin, *The Way and the Word: Science and Medicine in Early China and Greece* (2002). A comprehensive rethinking of the social and political settings in ancient China and city-state Greece that contributed to the different views of science and medicine that emerged in each place.

Mote, Frederick, *Intellectual Foundations of China* (1971). An early but still useful description of the seminal figures in China's early intellectual life.

Murray, Oswyn, *Early Greece*, 2nd ed. (1993). One of the best introductions to the emergence of the Greek city-states down to the end of the archaic age.

Osborne, Robin, *Archaic and Classical Greek Art* (1998). An outstanding book that clearly explains the main innovations in Greek art, setting them in their historical context.

———, *Greece in the Making, 1200–479 BC* (1999). The standard history of the whole early period of the Greek city-states characterized by an especially fine and judicious mix of archaeological data and literary sources.

Pallottino, Massimo, *The Etruscans*, rev. ed., trans. J. Cremona (1975). A fairly traditional but still classic survey of all aspects of Etruscan history, political and social institutions.

Redford, Donald B., *From Slave to Pharaoh: The Black Experience of Ancient Egypt* (2004). A description of Egypt's twenty-fifth dynasty, which was made up of Sudanese conquerors.

Schaberg, David, *A Patterned Past: Form and Thought in Early Chinese Historiography* (2002). A comprehensive study of the intellectual content of historical anecdotes by the followers of Confucius collected around the fourth century BCE.

Schaps, David, *The Invention of Coinage and the Monetization of Ancient Greece* (2004). A new analysis that offers a broad overview of the emergence of coined money in the Near East and the eastern Mediterranean and its effects on the spread of money-based markets.

Sharma, J. P., *Republics in Ancient India, c. 1500 B.C.–500 B.C.* (1968). Relying on information from early Buddhist texts, this book first revealed that South Asia had not only monarchies but also alternative polities.

Shaw, Thurston, *Nigeria: Its Archaeology and Early History* (1978). An important introduction to the early history of Nigeria by one of that country's leading archaeologists.

Shinnie, P. L., *Ancient Nubia* (1996). An excellent account of the history of the ancient Nubians, who, we are discovering, had great influence on Egypt and on the rest of tropical Africa.

Snodgrass, Anthony, *Archaic Greece: The Age of Experiment* (1981). A good introduction to the archaeological evidence of archaic Greece.

Taylor, Christopher, Richard Hare, and Jonathan Barnes, *Greek Philosophers* (1999). A fine, succinct, one-volume introduction to the major aspects of the three big thinkers who dominated the high period of classical Greek philosophy: Socrates, Plato, and Aristotle.

Torok, Laszlo, *Meroe: Six Studies on the Cultural Identity of an Ancient African State* (1995). A good collection of essays on the most recent work on Meroe.

The Kingdom of Kush: The Napatan and Meroitic Empires (1996). A fine book on these two important Nubian kingdoms.

CHAPTER 6: SHRINKING THE AFRO-EURASIAN WORLD, 350 BCE–250 CE

Bradley, Keith, *Slavery and Rebellion in the Roman World, 140 B.C.–70 B.C.* (1989). A description of the rise of large-scale plantation slavery in Sicily and Italy, and a detailed account of the three great slave wars.

Browning, Iain, *Palmyra* (1979). A narrative of the history of the important desert city that linked eastern and western trade routes.

Casson, Lionel, *The Periplus Maris Erythraei* (1989). An introduction to a typical ancient sailing manual, this one of the Red Sea and Indian Ocean.

———, *Ships and Seamanship in the Ancient World* (1995). The classic account of the ships and sailors that powered commerce and war on the high seas.

Colledge, Malcolm, *The Art of Palmyra* (1976). A well-illustrated introduction to the unusual art of Palmyra with its mixture of eastern and western elements.

Fowler, Barbara H., *The Hellenistic Aesthetic* (1989). How the artists in this new age saw and portrayed their world in new and different ways.

Green, Peter, *Alexander to Actium: The Historical Evolution of the Hellenistic Age* (1990). The best general guide to the whole period in all of its various aspects, and well illustrated.

Habicht, Christian, *Athens from Alexander to Antony*, trans. Deborah L. Schneider (1997). The authoritative account of what happened to the great city-state of Athens in this period.

Holt, Frank L., *Thundering Zeus: The Making of Hellenistic Bactria* (1999). A basic history of the most eastern of the kingdoms spawned by the conquests of Alexander the Great.

Hopkirk, Peter, *Foreign Devils on the Silk Road* (1984). A historiography of the explorations and researches on the central Asian Silk Road of the nineteenth and early twentieth centuries.

Juliano, Annette L., and Judith A. Lerner (eds.), *Nomads, Traders and Holy Men Along China's Silk Road* (2003). A description of the travelers along the Silk Road in human terms, focusing on warfare, markets, and religion.

Lane Fox, Robin, *Alexander the Great* (1973). Still the most readable and in many ways the sanest biography of the world conqueror.

Lewis, Naphtali, *Greeks in Ptolemaic Egypt* (1986). An account of the relationships between Greeks and Egyptians as seen through the lives of individual Greek settlers and colonists.

Liu, Xinru, *Ancient India and Ancient China* (1988). The first work to connect political and economic developments in India and China with the evolution and spread of Buddhism in the first half of the first millennium.

———, *The Silk Road in World History* (2010). A study of the history of the great trade and communications route that connected the different regions of Afro-Eurasia between the third century BCE and the thirteenth century CE.

Long, Antony A., *Hellenistic Philosophy: Stoics, Epicureans, Sceptics*, 2nd ed. (1986). One of the clearest guides to the main new trends in Greek philosophical thinking in the period.

Martin, Luther H., *Hellenistic Religions: An Introduction* (1987). An introduction to the principal new Hellenistic religions and cults that emerged in this period.

Mendels, Doron, *The Rise and Fall of Jewish Nationalism* (1992). A sophisticated account of the various phases of Jewish resistance in Judah to foreign domination.

Miller, James Innes, *The Spice Trade of the Roman Empire, 29 B.C. to A.D.* 641 (1969). A first-rate study of the spice trade in the Roman Empire.

Pomeroy, Sarah B., *Women in Hellenistic Egypt: From Alexander to Cleopatra* (1990). A highly readable investigation of women and family in the best-documented region of the Hellenistic world.

Ray, Himanshu P., *The Wind of Change: Buddhism and the Maritime Links of Early South Asia* (1994). Ray's study of Buddhism and maritime trade stretches from the Arabian Sea to the navigations between South Asia and Southeast Asia.

Rosenfield, John, *The Dynastic Art of the Kushans* (1967). Instead of focusing on the Gandharan Buddhist art itself, Rosenfield selects sculptures of Kushan royals and those representing nomadic populations in religious shrines to display the central Asian aspect of artworks of the period.

Rostovtzeff, Michael Ivanovich, *Caravan Cities*, trans. D. and T. Talbot Rice (1932). Though published more than seven decades ago, this small volume contains accurate descriptions of the ruins of many caravan cities in modern Jordan and Syria.

———, *The Social and Economic History of the Hellenistic World* (1941). A monumental achievement. One of the great works of history written in the twentieth century. An unsurpassed overview of all aspects of the politics and social and economic movements of the period. Despite its age, there is still nothing like it.

Schoff, Wilfred H. (ed. and trans.), *The Periplus of the Erythraean Sea* (1912). An invaluable tool for mapping the names and places from the Red Sea to Indian coastal areas during this period.

Shipley, Graham, *The Greek World after Alexander, 323–30 BC* (2000). A more up-to-date survey than Peter Green's work (above), with more emphasis on the historical detail in each period.

Tarn, W. W., *Greeks in Bactria and India* (1984). The most comprehensive coverage of Greek sources on Hellenistic states in Afghanistan and northwest India.

Thapar, Romila, *Ashoka and the Decline of the Mauryas* (1973). Using all available primary sources, including the edicts of Aśoka and Greek authors' accounts, Thapar gives the most authoritative analysis of the first and the most important empire in Indian history.

Vainker, Shelagh, *Chinese Silk: A Cultural History* (2004). A work that traces the cultural history of silk in China from its early origins to the twentieth century and considers its relationship to the other decorative arts. The author draws on the most recent archaeological evidence to emphasize the role of silk in Chinese history, trade, religion, and literature.

Wood, Francis, *The Silk Road: Two Thousand Years in the Heart of Asia* (2004). Illustrated with drawings, manuscripts, paintings, and artifacts to trace the Silk Road to its origins as far back as Alexander the Great, with an emphasis on its importance to cultural and religious movements.

Young, Gary K., *Rome's Eastern Trade: International Commerce and Imperial Policy, 31 BC–AD 305* (2001). This study examines the taxation and profits of eastern trade from the perspective of the Roman government.

CHAPTER 7: HAN DYNASTY CHINA AND IMPERIAL ROME, 300 BCE–300 CE

Bodde, Derk, *China's First Unifier: A Study of the Ch'in Dynasty as Seen in the Life of Li Ssu (280?–208 B.C.)* (1938). A classic account of the key Legalist adviser, Li Si, who formulated the Qin policy to enhance its autocratic power.

Bowman, Alan K., *Life and Letters on the Roman Frontier: Vindolanda and Its Peoples* (1994). An introduction to the exciting discovery of writing tablets at a Roman army base in northern Britain.

Bradley, Keith, *Slavery and Society at Rome* (1994). The best single overview of the major aspects of the slave system in the Roman Empire.

Chevallier, Raymond, *Roman Roads*, trans. N. H. Field (1976). A guide to the fundamentals of the construction, maintenance, administration, and mapping of Roman roads.

Coarelli, Fillipo (ed.), *Pompeii*, trans. Patricia Cockram (2006). A lavishly illustrated large volume that allows the reader to sense some of the wondrous wealth of the buried city of Pompeii.

Colledge, Malcolm A. R., *The Parthians* (1967). A bit dated but still a fundamental introduction to the Parthians, the major power on the eastern frontier of the Roman Empire.

Cornell, Tim, *The Beginnings of Rome: Italy and Rome from the Bronze Age to the Punic Wars, c. 2000 to 264 B.C.* (1995). The single best one-volume history of Rome through its early history to the first war with Carthage.

Cornell, Tim, and John Matthews, *Atlas of the Roman World* (1982). A history of the Roman world; much more than simply an atlas. It is provided not only with good maps and a gazetteer but also with marvelous color illustrations and a text that guides the reader through the basics of Roman history.

Csikszentmihalyi, Mark, *Readings in Han Chinese Thought* (2006). A volume presenting a representative selection of primary sources to illustrate the growth of ideas in early imperial times; a useful introduction to the key strains of thought during this crucial period.

Dixon, Suzanne, *The Roman Family* (1992). The best one-volume guide to the nature of the Roman family and family relations.

Garnsey, Peter, and Richard Saller, *The Roman Empire: Economy, Society, and Culture* (1987). A perceptive and critical introduction to three basic aspects of social life in the empire.

Giardina, Andrea (ed.), *The Romans*, trans. Lydia Cochrane (1993). Individual studies of important typical figures in Roman society, from the peasant and the bandit to the merchant and the soldier.

Goldsworthy, Adrian, *The Roman Army at War: 100 B.C.–A.D. 200* (1996). A summary history and analysis of the Roman army in action during the late Republic and early Empire.

Goodman, Martin, *The Roman World: 44 B.C.–A.D. 180* (1997). A newer basic history text covering the high Roman Empire.

Harris, William, *Ancient Literacy* (1989). A basic survey of what is known about communication in the form of writing and books in the Roman Empire.

Hopkins, Keith, *Death and Renewal: Sociological Studies in Roman History*, vol. 2 (1983). Innovative studies in Roman history, including one of the best on gladiators and another on death and funerals.

——, *A World Full of Gods: Pagans, Jews and Christians in the Roman Empire* (1999). A somewhat unusual but interesting and provocative look at the world of religions in the Roman Empire.

Juliano, Annette L., and Judith A. Lerner (eds.), *Nomads, Traders and Holy Men along China's Silk Road* (2003). A description of the travelers along the Silk Road in human terms, focusing on warfare, markets, and religion.

Kern, Martin, and Michael Hunter (eds.), *The Analects. A Western Han Text?* (2013): Challenges the assumption that the Confucian *Analects* was compiled before the Han Dynasty.

Kraus, Theodore, and Leonard von Matt, *Pompeii and Herculaneum: The Living Cities of the Dead*, trans. Robert E. Wolf (1975). A huge, lavishly illustrated compendium of all aspects of life in the buried cities of Pompeii and Herculaneum as preserved in the archaeological record.

Loewe, Michael, *The Government of the Qin and Han Empires: 221 BCE–220 CE* (2006). A useful overview of the government of the early empires of China. Topics include the structure of central government, provincial and local government, the armed forces, officials, government communications, the laws of the empire, and control of the people and the land.

Millar, Fergus, *The Crowd in the Late Republic* (1998). An innovative study of the democratic power of the citizens in the city of Rome itself.

——, *The Emperor in the Roman World, 31 B.C.–A.D. 337* (1992). Everything you might want to know about the Roman emperor, with special emphasis on his civil role as the administrator of an empire.

Potter, David, *Roman Empire at Bay: A.D. 180–395* (2004). A basic text covering the later Roman Empire, including the critical transition to a Christian state.

Potter, David S., and David J. Mattingly (eds.), *Life, Death, and Entertainment in the Roman Empire* (1999). A good introduction to basic aspects of Roman life in the empire, including the family, feeding the cities, religion, and popular entertainment.

Qian, Sima, *Records of the Grand Historian: Qin Dynasty*, trans. Burton Watson, 3rd ed. (1995). The classic work of Chinese history in a readable --NNGlation. The Han dynasty's Grand Historian describes the slow rise and meteoric fall of the Qin dynasty from the point of view of the succeeding dynasty, which Sima Qian witnessed or heard of during his lifetime.

Southern, Pat, *The Roman Army: A Social and Institutional History* (2006). A fundamental guide to all aspects of the Roman army.

Todd, Malcolm, *The Early Germans*, rev. ed. (2004). A basic survey of the peoples in central and western Europe at the time of the Roman Empire.

Vainker, Shelagh, *Chinese Silk: A Cultural History* (2004). A work that traces the cultural history of silk in China from its early origins to the twentieth century and considers its relationship to the other decorative arts. The author draws on the most recent archaeological evidence to emphasize the role of silk in Chinese history, trade, religion, and literature.

Wells, Peter S., *The Barbarians Speak: How the Conquered Peoples Shaped Roman Europe* (1999). The cultures of the peoples of central and northern Europe at the time of the Roman Empire and their impact on Roman culture.

Wood, Francis, *The Silk Road: Two Thousand Years in the Heart of Asia* (2004). A work illustrated with drawings, manuscripts, paintings, and artifacts to trace the Silk Road to its origins as far back as Alexander the Great. The author stresses the importance of the Silk Road to cultural and religious movements.

Woolf, Greg (ed.), *The Cambridge Illustrated History of the Roman World* (2005). A good guide to various aspects of Roman history, culture, and provincial life.

———, *Rome: An Empire's Story* (2012). An up-to-date narrative of the Roman Empire told according to major themes that are particularly relevant to world history.

CHAPTER 8: THE RISE OF UNIVERSAL RELIGIONS, 300–600 CE

Bowersock, G. W., Peter Brown, and Oleg Grabar (eds.), *Late Antiquity: A Guide to the Postclassical World* (1999). Essays and items for the entire period 150–750 CE. The volume covers the Roman, East Roman, Sasanian, and early Islamic worlds.

Brown, Peter, *The Rise of Western Christendom: Triumph and Diversity, A.D. 200–1000*, 2nd ed. (2003). The rise and spread of Christianity in Europe and Asia, with up-to-date bibliographies on all topics, maps, and time charts.

———, *The World of Late Antiquity: From Marcus Aurelius to Muhammad, AD 150–750* (1989). A social, religious, and cultural history of the late Roman and Sasanian empires, with illustrations and a time chart.

Bühler, G. (trans.), *The Laws of Manu* (1886). The classic translation of one of India's most important historical, legal, and religious texts.

Coe, Michael D., *The Maya*, 6th ed. (1999). A work by the world's most famous Mayanologist, with recent evidence, analyses, and illustrations.

Cowgill, George L., "The Central Mexican Highlands and the Rise of Teotihuacan to the Decline of Tula," in Richard Adams and Murdo Macleod (eds.), *The Cambridge History of the Native Peoples of the Americas*, vol. 2, *Mesoamerica*, Pt. 1 (2000). A thorough review of findings about urban states in central Mexico.

Fash, William L., *Scribes, Warriors and Kings: The City of Copan and the Ancient Maya* (2001). A fascinating and comprehensive study of one of the most elaborate of the Mayan city-kingdoms.

Fowden, Elizabeth Key, *The Barbarian Plain: Saint Sergius between Rome and Iran* (1999). The study of a major Christian shrine and its relations to Romans, Persians, and Arabs.

Fowden, Garth, *Empire to Commonwealth: The Consequences of Monotheism in Late Antiquity* (1993). A study of the relation between empire and world religions in western Asia.

Gombrich, Richard F., and Sheldon Pollack (eds.), *Clay Sanskrit Library* (2005–2006). All major works from the Gupta and post-Gupta periods, in both Sanskrit and English versions. During the Gupta period, classical Sanskrit literature reached its apex, with abundant drama, poetry, and folk stories.

Gordon, Charles, *The Age of Attila* (1960). The last century of the Roman Empire in western Europe, vividly illustrated from contemporary sources.

Harper, Prudence, *The Royal Hunter: The Art of the Sasanian Empire* (1978). The ideology of the Sasanian Empire as shown through excavated hoards of precious silverware.

Heather, Peter, *The Fall of the Roman Empire: A New History of Rome and the Barbarians* (2006). A military and political narrative based on up-to-date archaeological material.

Herrmann, Georgina, *Iranian Revival* (1977). The structure and horizons of the Sasanian Empire as revealed in its monuments.

Hillgarth, Jocelyn (ed.), *Christianity and Paganism, 350–750: The Conversion of Western Europe*, rev. ed. (1986). A collection of contemporary sources.

Holcombe, Charles, *In the Shadow of the Han: Literati Thought and Society at the Beginning of the Southern Dynasties* (1994). A clear and concise account of the evolution of thought in China after the fall of the Han dynasty in 220 CE. The book presents the rise of Buddhism and Daoism as popular religions as well as elite interests in classical learning in a time of political division and barbarian conquest in North and South China.

La Vaissière, Étienne de, *Sogdian Traders: A History*, trans. James Ward (2005). A summary of historical facts about the most important trading community and its commercial networks on the Silk Road, from the early centuries CE to its demise in the ninth century CE.

Little, Lester (ed.), *Plague and the End of Antiquity: The Pandemic of 541–750* (2008). A series of debates over the nature and impact of the first great pandemic attested in global history.

Liu, Xinru, and Lynda Norene Shaffer, *Connections across Eurasia: Transportation, Communication, and Cultural Exchanges on the Silk Roads* (2007). A survey of trade and religious activities on the Silk Road.

Maas, Michael, *Readings in Late Antiquity: A Source Book* (1999). Well-chosen extracts that illustrate the interrelation of Romans and non-Romans, and of Christians, Jews, and pagans.

Maas, Michael (ed.), *The Cambridge Companion to the Age of Justinian*

(2005). A survey of all aspects of the eastern Roman Empire in the sixth century CE.

Moffett, Samuel, *A History of Christianity in Asia*, vol. 1 (1993). Particularly valuable on Christians in China and India.

Munro-Hay, Stuart, *Aksum: An African Civilization of Late Antiquity* (1991). The origins of the Christian kingdom of Ethiopia.

Murdock, George P., *Africa: Its Peoples and Their History* (1959). A vital introduction to the peoples of Africa and their history.

Oliver, Roland, *The African Experience: From Olduvai Gorge to the Twenty-First Century* (1999). An important overview, written by one of the pioneering scholars of African history and one of the leading authorities on the Bantu migrations.

Pregadio, Fabrizio, *Great Clarity: Daoism and Alchemy in Early Medieval China* (2006). An examination of the religious aspects of Daoism. The book focuses on the relation of alchemy to the Daoist traditions of the third to sixth centuries CE and shows how alchemy was integrated into the elaborate body of doctrines and practices of Daoists at that time.

Tempels, Placide, *Bantu Philosophy* (1959). A highly influential effort to argue for the underlying cultural unity of all the Bantu peoples.

Vansina, Jan, *Paths in the Rainforests: Toward a History of Political Tradition in Equatorial Africa* (1990). The best work on Bantu history.

Walker, Joel, *The Legend of Mar Kardagh: Narrative and Christian Heroism in Late Antique Iraq* (2006). Christians and Zoroastrians in northern Iraq and in Iran.

Yarshater, Ehsan, *Encyclopedia Iranica* (1982–). A guide to all aspects of the Sasanian Empire and to religion and culture in the regions between Mesopotamia and central Asia.

Xuanzang, *Faxianzhuan Jiaoxhu*. Text excerpt translated by Xinru Liu.

Zürcher, E., *The Buddhist Conquest of China: The Spread and Adaptation of Buddhism in Early Medieval China*, 3rd ed. (2007). A reissue of the classic account of the assimilation of Buddhism in China during the medieval period, with particular focus on the religious and philosophical success of Buddhism among Chinese elites in South China.

CHAPTER 9: NEW EMPIRES AND COMMON CULTURES, 600–1000 CE

Ahmed, Leila, *Women and Gender in Islam* (1992). A superb overview of the relations between men and women throughout the history of Islam.

Aneirin, *Y Gododdin: Britain's Oldest Heroic Poem*, ed. and trans. A. O. H. Jarman (1988). A sixth-century Welsh text that describes the battle of the last Britons against the invading Anglo-Saxons.

Arberry, Arthur J., introduction to *The Koran Interpreted: A Translation*, trans. Arthur J. Arberry (1986). One of the most eloquent appreciations of this classical work of religion.

Augustine, *The City of God*, trans. H. Bettenson (1976). An excellent translation of Augustine's monumental work of history, philosophy, and religion.

Berkey, Jonathan P., *The Formation of Islam: Religion and Society in the Near East, 600–1800* (2005). A recent overview of the history of Islam before the modern era. It is particularly sensitive to the influence of external elements on the history of the Muslim peoples.

Bol, Peter, *This Culture of Ours: Intellectual Transitions in T'ang and Sung China* (1994). A study tracing the transformation of the shared culture of the Chinese learned elite from the seventh to the twelfth centuries.

Brown, Peter, *The Rise of Western Christendom: Triumph and Diversity, AD 200–1000*, 2nd ed. (2003). A description of the changes in Christianity in northern Europe and the emergence of the new cultures and political structures that coincided with this development.

Bulliet, Richard W., *Conversion to Islam in the Medieval Period: An Essay in Quantitative History* (1979). A study of the rate at which the populations overrun by Arab conquerors in the seventh century CE embraced the religion of their rulers.

Cook, Michael, *The Koran: A Very Short Introduction* (2000). A useful overview of Islam's holy book.

———, *Muhammad* (1983). A brief but careful life of the Prophet that takes full account of the prolific and often controversial preexisting scholarship.

Creswell, K. A. C., *A Short Account of Early Muslim Architecture, Revised and supplemented by James W. Allan* (1992). The definitive treatment of the subject, brought up to date.

Cross, S. H., and O. P. Sherbowitz-Westor, trans., *The Russian Primary Chronicle* (1953). A vivid record of the Viking settlement of Kiev, of the conversion of Kiev, and of the princes of Kiev in the tenth and eleventh centuries.

Donner, Fred M., *The Early Islamic Conquests* (1981). The best account of the Arab conquests in the Persian and Byzantine empires in the seventh century.

Duncan, John, *The Origins of the Chosŏn Dynasty* (2000). A historical account of the early Korean dynasties from 900 to 1400.

Elman, Benjamin, *Precocious China: Civil Examinations, 1400–1900* (2013). Summary of civil exams in China from medieval times.

Fage, J. D., *Ghana: A Historical Introduction* (1966). A brief but authoritative history of Ghana from earliest times to the twentieth century.

Fisher, Humphrey J., *Slavery in the History of Muslim Black Africa* (2001). A general history of the relations between North Africa and black Africa, focusing on one of the most important aspects of contact—the slave trade.

Graham-Campbell, James, *Cultural Atlas of the Viking World* (1994). A positioning of the Vikings against their wider background in both western and eastern Europe.

Hawting, G. R., *The First Dynasty of Islam: The Umayyad Caliphate, A.D. 661–750* (2000). The essential scholarly treatment of Islam's first dynasty.

Herrmann, Georgina, *Iranian Revival* (1977). The structure and horizons of the Sasanian Empire as revealed in its monuments.

Hillgarth, J. N. (ed.), *Christianity and Paganism, 350–750: The Conversion of Western Europe*, rev. ed. (1986). A collection of contemporary sources.

Hodges, Richard, and David Whitehouse, *Mohammed, Charlemagne, and the Origins of Europe* (1983). A spirited comparison of Islam and the rise of Europe.

Hodgson, Marshall G. S., *The Venture of Islam: Conscience and History in a World Civilization*, 3 vols. (1977). A magnificent history of the Islamic peoples. Its first volume, *The Classical Age of Islam*, is basic reading for anyone interested in the history of the Muslim world.

Holdsworth, May, *Women of the Tang Dynasty* (1999). An account of women's lives during the Tang dynasty.

Hourani, Albert, *History of the Arab Peoples* (2002). The best overview of Arab history.

Jones, Gwynn, *The Norse Atlantic Saga* (1986). The Viking discovery of America.

Kennedy, Hugh, *The Prophet and the Age of the Caliphate: The Islamic Near East from the Sixth to the Eleventh Century* (2004). A very good synthesis of the rise and spread of Islam.

Lee, Peter, et al. (eds.), *Sources of Korean Tradition*, vol. 1 (1996). A unique view of Korean history through the eyes and words of the participants or witnesses themselves, as provided in translations of official documents, letters, and policies.

Levtzion, Nehemia, *Ancient Ghana and Mali* (1980). The best introduction to the kingdoms of West Africa.

Levtzion, Nehemia, and Jay Spaulding, *Medieval West Africa: Views from Arab Scholars and Merchants* (2003). An indispensable source book on early West African history.

Lewis, Bernard, *The Middle East: Two Thousand Years of History from the Rise of Christianity to the Present Day* (1995). A stimulating introduction to an area that has seen the emergence of three of the great world religions.

——— (trans.), *Islam from the Prophet Muhammad to the Capture of Constantinople*, vol. 2, *Religion and Society* (1974). A fine collection of original sources that portray various aspects of classical Islamic society.

Lewis, David Levering, *God's Crucible: Islam and the Making of Europe, 570–1215* (2008). An exciting and well-written overview of the high period of Islamic power and cultural attainments.

Middleton, John, *The Swahili: The Social Landscape of a Mercantile Community* (2000). An exciting synthesis of the Swahili culture of East Africa.

Miyazaki, Ichisada, *China's Examination Hell* (1981). A study of China's examination system.

Nurse, Derek, and Thomas Spear, *The Swahili: Reconstructing the History and Language of an African Society, 800–1500* (1984). A work that explores the history of the Muslim peoples who lived along the coast of East Africa.

Peters, F. E., *Muhammad and the Origins of Islam* (1994). A work that explores the early history of Islam and highlights the critical role that Muhammad played in promoting a new religion and a powerful Arab identity.

Pourshariati, Parveneh, *Decline and Fall of the Sasanian Empire* (2008). Fundamental analysis of the end of the Sasanian Empire and the reasons for the success of the Arab/Muslim invasions.

Robinson, Chase F., *The Formation of the Islamic World, Sixth to Eleventh Centuries*, vol. 1 in *The New Cambridge History of Islam* (2010). An authoritative and up-to-date six-volume overview of the history of Islam from the sixth century to the present.

Schirokauer, Conrad, et al., *A Brief History of Japanese Civilization*, 2nd ed. (2005). A balanced account; chapters focus on developments in art, religion, literature, and thought as well as on Japan's economic, political, and social history in medieval times.

Smith, Julia, *Europe after Rome: A New Cultural History, 500–1000* (2005). A vivid analysis of society and culture in so-called Dark Age Europe.

Totman, Conrad, *History of Japan* (2004). A recent and readable summary of Japanese history from ancient to modern times.

Twitchett, Denis, *The Birth of the Chinese Meritocracy: Bureaucrats and Examinations in T'ang China* (1976). A description of the role of the written civil examinations that began during the Tang dynasty.

———, *Financial Administration under the T'ang Dynasty* (1970). A pioneering account—based on rare Dunhuang documents that survived from medieval times in Buddhist grottoes in central Asia—of the political and economic system undergirding the Chinese imperial state.

Whittow, Mark, *The Making of Byzantium, 600–1025* (1996). A study on the survival and revival of the eastern Roman Empire as a major power in eastern Europe and Southwest Asia.

Wood, Ian, *The Missionary Life: Saints and the Evangelization of Europe, 400–1050* (2001). The horizons of Christians on the frontiers of Europe.

CHAPTER 10: BECOMING "THE WORLD," 1000–1300 CE

Allsen, Thomas, *Commodity and Exchange in the Mongol Empire: A Cultural History of Islamic Textiles* (1997). A study that uses golden brocade, the textile most treasured by Mongol rulers, as a lens through which to analyze the vast commercial networks facilitated by the Mongol conquests and control.

———, *Culture and Conquest in Mongol Eurasia* (2001). A work that emphasizes the cultural and scientific exchanges that took place across Afro-Eurasia as a result of the Mongol conquest.

Bartlett, Robert, *The Making of Europe: Conquest, Colonization and Cultural Change, 950–1350* (1993). The modes of cultural, political, and demographic expansion of feudal Europe along its frontiers, especially in eastern Europe.

Bay, Edna G., *Wives of the Leopards: Gender, Politics, and Culture in the Kingdom of Dahomey* (1998). A work that stresses the role of women in an important West African society and dips into the early history of this area.

Beach, D. N., *Shona and Zimbabwe, 900–1850: An Outline of Shona History* (1980). A good place to start for exploring the history of Great Zimbabwe.

Brooks, George E., *Landlords and Strangers: Ecology, Society, and Trade in Western Africa, 1000–1630* (1993). A survey assembled from primary sources of early West African history that stresses transregional connections.

Buzurg ibn Shahriyar of Ramhormuz, *The Book of the Wonders of India: Mainland, Sea and Islands*, ed. and trans. G. S. P. Freeman-Greenville (1981). A collection of stories told by sailors, both true and fantastic; they help us imagine the lives of sailors of the era.

Chappell, Sally A. Kitt, *Cahokia: Mirror of the Cosmos* (2002). A thorough and vivid account of the "mound people"; it explores not just what we know of Cahokia but how we know it.

Christian, David, *A Short History of Russia, Central Asia, and Mongolia*, vol. 1, *Inner Eurasia from Prehistory to the Mongol Empire* (1998). Essential reading for students interested in interconnections across the Afro-Eurasian landmass.

Curtin, Philip, *Cross-Cultural Trade in World History* (1984). A groundbreaking book on intercultural trade with a primary focus on Africa, especially the cross-Saharan trade and Swahili coastal trade.

Dawson, Christopher, *Mission to Asia* (1980). Accounts of China and the Mongol Empire brought back by Catholic missionaries and diplomats after 1240.

Foltz, Richard C., *Religions of the Silk Road: Overland Trade and Cultural Exchange from Antiquity to the Fifteenth Century* (1999). A study of the populations and the cities of the Silk Road as transmitters of culture across long distances.

Franklin, Simon, and Jonathan Shepherd, *The Emergence of Rus: 750–1200* (1996). The formation of medieval Russia between the Baltic and Black seas.

Gibb, Hamilton A. R., *Saladin: Studies in Islamic History*, ed. Yusuf Ibish (1974). A sympathetic portrait of one of Islam's leading political and military figures.

Goitein, S. D., *Letters of Medieval Jewish Traders* (1973). The classic study of medieval Jewish trading communities based on the commercial papers deposited in the Cairo Geniza (a synagogue storeroom) during the tenth and eleventh centuries; it explores not only commercial activities but also the personal lives of the traders around the Indian Ocean basin.

———, *A Mediterranean Society: An Abridgment in One Volume*, rev. and ed. Jacob Lassner (1999). A portrait of the Jewish merchant community with ties across the Afro-Eurasian landmass, based largely on the documents from the Cairo Geniza (of which Goitein was the primary researcher and interpreter).

———, "New Light on the Beginnings of the Karim Merchant," *Journal of Social and Economic History of the Orient* 1 (1958). Goitein's description of Egyptian trade.

Goitein, S. D., and Mordechai A. Friedman, *India Traders of the Middle Ages: Documents from the Cairo Geniza* (2008). Collection of documents (translated into English) and authoritative essays that explore the eleventh- and twelfth-century trade conducted by several prominent Jewish families along the Mediterranean and Indian Ocean routes.

Harris, Joseph E., *The African Presence in Asia: Consequences of the East African Slave Trade* (1971). One of the few books that looks broadly at the impact of Africans and African slavery on the societies of Asia.

Hartwell, Robert, "Demographic, Political, and Social Transformations of China, 750–1550," *Harvard Journal of Asiatic Studies* 42 (1982): 365–442. A pioneering study of the demographic changes that overtook China during the Tang and Song dynasties, which are described in light of political reform movements and social changes in this crucial era.

Historical Relations across the Indian Ocean: Report and Papers of the Meeting of Experts Organized by UNESCO at Port Louis, Mauritius, from 15 to 19 July, 1974 (1980). Excellent essays on the connections of Africa with Asia across the Indian Ocean.

Hitti, Philip, *An Arab-Syrian Gentleman and Warrior in the Period of the Crusades: Memoirs of Usāmah ibn-Munqidh* (1929). The Crusaders seen through Muslim eyes.

Hodgson, Natasha, *Women, Crusading, and the Holy Land in Historical Narrative* (2007). A book dealing with the Crusades and focusing on the place of women in them.

Holt, P. M., *The Age of the Crusades: The Near East from the Eleventh Century to 1517* (1984). The Crusades period as seen from the eastern Mediterranean and through the lens of a leading British scholar of the area.

Hymes, Robert, and Conrad Schirokauer (eds.), *Ordering the World: Approaches to State and Society in Sung Dynasty China* (1993). A collection of essays that traces the intellectual, social, and political movements that shaped the Song state and its elites.

Ibn Battuta, *The Travels of Ibn Battuta*, trans. H. A. R. Gibb (2002). A readable translation of the classic book, originally published in 1929.

Ibn Fadlan, Ahmad, *Ibn Fadlan's Journey to Russia: A Tenth Century Traveler from Baghdad to the Volga River*, trans. with commentary by Richard Frye (2005). A coherent summary of the observations of an envoy who traveled from Baghdad to Russia.

Irwin, Robert, *The Middle East in the Middle Ages: The Early Mamluk Sultanate, 1250–1582* (1986). Egypt under Mamluk rule.

Jeppie, Shamil, and Souleymane Bachir Diagne (eds.), *The Meanings of Timbuktu* (2008). New materials on the ancient Muslim city of Timbuktu by scholars who have been preserving its manuscripts and writing about its historical importance.

Lancaster, Lewis, Kikun Suh, and Chaishin Yu (eds.), *Buddhism in Koryo: A Royal Religion* (1996). A description of Buddhism at its height in the Koryo period, when the religion made significant contributions to the development of Korean culture.

Levtzion, Nehemia, and Randall L. Pouwels (eds.), *The History of Islam in Africa* (2000). A useful general survey of the place of Islam in African history.

Lewis, Bernard (trans.), *Islam: From the Prophet Muhammad to the Capture of Constantinople* (1974), vol. 2, *Religion and Society*. A fine collection of original sources that portray various aspects of classical Islamic society.

Lopez, Robert S., *The Commercial Revolution of the Middle Ages, 950–1350* (1976). An account focusing on the development around the Mediterranean of commercial practices such as the use of currency, accounting, and credit.

Lyons, Malcolm C. and D. E. P. Jackson, *Saladin: The Politics of the Holy War*, Cambridge (1984: reprint, 2001). The fundamental revisionist work on one of the more important historical figures of the time.

Maalouf, Amin, *The Crusades through Muslim Eyes*, trans. Jon Rothschild (1984). The European Crusaders as seen by the Muslim world.

Marcus, Harold G., *A History of Ethiopia* (2002). An authoritative overview of the history of this great culture.

Mass, Jeffrey, *Yoritomo and the Founding of the First Bakufu: The Origins of Dual Government in Japan* (1999). A revisionist account of how the Kamakura military leader Minamoto Yoritomo established the "dual polity" of court and warrior government in Japan.

McDermott, Joseph, *A Social History of the Chinese Book: Books and Literati Culture in Late Imperial China* (2006). The history of the book in China since the Song dynasty, with comparisons to the book's role in other civilizations, particularly the European.

McIntosh, Roderik, *The Peoples of the Middle Niger: The Island of Gold* (1988). A historical survey of an area often omitted from other textbooks.

Moore, Jerry D., *Cultural Landscapes in the Ancient Andes: Archaeologies of Place* (2005). The most recent and up-to-date analysis of findings based on recent archaeological evidence, emphasizing the importance of local cultures and diversity in the Andes.

Niane, D. T. (ed.), *Africa from the Twelfth to the Sixteenth Century*, vol. 4 of *General History of Africa* (1984). The general UNESCO history of Africa's volume on four centuries of African history. This work features the scholarship of Africans.

Oliver, Roland (ed.), *From c. 1050 to c. 1600*, vol. 3 of *The Cambridge History of Africa*, ed. J. D. Fage and Roland Oliver (1977). Another general survey of African history. This volume draws heavily on the work of British scholars.

Peters, Edward, *The First Crusade* (1971). The Crusaders as seen through their own eyes.

Petry, Carl F. (ed.), *Islamic Egypt, 640–1517*, vol. 1 of *The Cambridge History of Egypt*, ed. M. W. Daly (1998). A solid overview of the history of Islamic Egypt up to the Ottoman conquest.

Polo, Marco, *The Travels of Marco Polo*, ed. Manuel Komroff (1926). A solid translation of Marco Polo's famous account.

Popovic, Alexandre, *The Revolt of African Slaves in Iraq in the 3rd/9th Century*, trans. Leon King (1999). The account of a massive revolt against their slave masters by African slaves taken to labor in Iraq's mines and fields.

Scott, Robert, *Gothic Enterprise: A Guide to Understanding the Medieval Cathedral* (2003). The meaning and social function of religious building in medieval cities in northern Europe.

Shaffer, Lynda Norene, *Maritime Southeast Asia to 1500* (1996). A history of the peoples of the southeast fringe of the Eastern Hemisphere, up to the time that they became connected to the global commercial networks of the world.

Shimada, Izumi, "Evolution of Andean Diversity: Regional Formations (500 BCE–CE 600)," in Frank Salomon and Stuart Schwartz (eds.), *South America*, vol. 3 of *The Cambridge History of the Native Peoples of the Americas* (1999), Pt. 1, pp. 350–517. A splendid overview that contrasts the varieties of lowland and highland cultures.

Steinberg, David Joel, et al., *In Search of Southeast Asia: A Modern History* (1987). An account of the emergence of the modern Southeast Asian polities of Cambodia, Burma, Thailand, and Indonesia.

Tyerman, Christopher, *God's War: A New History of the Crusades* (2006). The balance of religious and nonreligious motivations in the Crusades.

Waley, Daniel, *The Italian City-Republics*, 3rd ed. (1988). The structures and culture of the new cities of medieval Italy.

Watson, Andrew, *Agricultural Innovation in the Early Islamic World: The Diffusion of Crops and Farming Techniques, 700–1100* (1983). An impressive study of the spread of new crops throughout the Muslim world.

CHAPTER 11: CRISES AND RECOVERY IN AFRO-EURASIA, 1300–1500

Bois, Guy, *The Crisis of Feudalism: Economy and Society in Eastern Normandy, c. 1300–1550* (1984). A good case study of a French region that illustrates the turmoil in fourteenth-century Europe.

Brook, Timothy, *Praying for Power: Buddhism and the Formation of Gentry Society in Late Ming China* (1994). An analysis of the role of a significant religious force in the political and social developments of the Ming.

Dardess, John, *A Ming Society: T'ai-ho County, Kiangsi, Fourteenth to Seventeenth Centuries* (1996). A work that covers the different changes and developments of a single locality in China through the centuries.

Dols, Michael W., *The Black Death in the Middle East* (1977). One of the few scholarly works to examine the Black Death outside Europe.

Dreyer, Edward, *Early Ming China: A Political History, 1355–1435* (1982). A useful account of the early years of the Ming dynasty.

Finkel, Caroline, *Osman's Dream: The Story of the Ottoman Empire, 1300–1923* (2005). The most authoritative overview of Ottoman history.

Hale, John, *The Civilization of Europe in the Renaissance* (1994). A beautifully crafted account of the politics, economics, and culture of the Renaissance period in western Europe.

Hodgson, Marshall, *The Venture of Islam: Conscience and History in a World Civilization*, vol. 3 (1974). A good volume on the workings of the Ottoman state.

Itzkowitz, Norman, *Ottoman Empire and Islamic Tradition* (1972). Another good book on the Ottoman state.

Jackson, Peter, *The Delhi Sultanate* (1999). A meticulous, highly specialized, political and military history.

Jackson, Peter, and Lawrence Lockhart (eds.), *The Cambridge History of Iran*, vol. 6 (1986). A volume that deals with the Timurid and Safavid periods in Iran.

Jones, E. L., *The European Miracle* (1981). A provocative work on the economic and social recovery from the Black Death.

Kafadar, Cemal, *Between Two Worlds: The Construction of the Ottoman State* (1995). A thorough reconsideration of the origins of one of the world's great land empires.

Karamustafa, Ahmed, *God's Unruly Friends: Dervish Groups in the Islamic Later Middle Period, 1200–1550* (1994). A book that describes the unorthodox Islamic activities that were occurring in the Islamic world prior to and alongside the establishment of the Ottoman and Safavid empires.

Levathes, Louise, *When China Ruled the Seas: The Treasure Fleet of the Dragon Throne, 1405–33* (1994). A book that provides a lively account of the Zheng He expeditions.

Lowry, Heath W., *The Nature of the Early Ottoman State* (2003). New perspectives on the rise of the Ottomans to prominence.

McNeill, William, *Plagues and Peoples* (1976). A pathbreaking work with a highly useful chapter on the spread of the Black Death throughout the Afro-Eurasian landmass.

Morgan, David, *Medieval Persia, 1040–1797* (1988). Contains an informative discussion of the Safavid state.

Peirce, Leslie, *The Imperial Harem: Women and Sovereignty in the Ottoman Empire* (1993). A work that describes the powerful place that imperial women had in political affairs.

Pirenne, Henri, *Economic and Social History of Medieval Europe* (1937). A classic study of the economic and social recovery from the Black Death.

Reid, James J., *Tribalism and Society in Islamic Iran, 1500–1629* (1983). A useful account of how the Mongols and other nomadic steppe peoples influenced Iran in the era when the Safavids were establishing their authority.

Singman, Jeffrey L. (ed.), *Daily Life in Medieval Europe* (1999). An introductory description of the social and material world experienced by Europeans of different walks of life.

Tuchman, Barbara W., *A Distant Mirror: The Calamitous Fourteenth Century* (1978). A book that shows, in a vigorous way, how war, famine, and pestilence devastated Europeans in the fourteenth century.

Wittek, Paul, *The Rise of the Ottoman Empire* (1958). A work that contains vital insights on the emergence of the Ottoman state amid the political chaos in Anatolia.

CHAPTER 12: CONTACT, COMMERCE, AND COLONIZATION, 1450–1600

Axtell, James, *Beyond 1492: Encounters in Colonial North America* (1992). A wonderfully informed speculation about Indian reactions to Europeans.

Brady, Thomas A., et al. (eds.), *Handbook of European History 1400–1600: Late Middle Ages, Renaissance, and Reformation, Structures and Assertions* (1996). A good synthetic survey of recent literature and historiographical debates.

Brook, Timothy, *Vermeer's Hat: The Seventeenth Century and the Dawn of the Global World* (2008). An interesting look at the connections forged across the globe through the works of a well-known European artist.

Cass, Victoria, *Dangerous Women: Warriors, Grannies, and Geishas of the Ming* (1999). An original study of Chinese female archetypes in memoirs, miscellanies, short stories, and novels.

Chaudhuri, K. N., *Trade and Civilisation in the Indian Ocean: An Economic History from the Rise of Islam to 1750* (1985). An excellent, comprehensive work that deals with the Indian Ocean economy and the appearance of European merchants there from the sixteenth century onward.

Clendinnen, Inga, *Aztecs: An Interpretation* (1991). Brilliantly reconstructs the culture of Tenochtitlán in the years before its conquest.

Crosby, Alfred W., *The Columbian Exchange: Biological and Cultural Consequences of 1492* (1972). A provocative discussion of the ecological consequences that followed the European "discovery" of the Americas.

———, *Ecological Imperialism: The Biological Expansion of Europe, 900–1900* (1986). Another important work on the ecological consequences of European expansion.

Curtin, Philip, *Cross-Cultural Trade in World History* (1984). A work stressing the role of trade and commerce in establishing cross-cultural contacts.

Febvre, Lucien, *The Problem of Unbelief in the Sixteenth Century: The Religion of Rabelais* (1982). A tour de force of intellectual history by the man who moved the study of the Reformation away from great men to the broader question of religious revival and mentalities.

Flynn, Dennis, and Arturo Giráldez (eds.), *Metals and Monies in an Emerging Global Economy* (1997). Contains several articles relating to silver and the Asian trade.

Frank, Andre Gunder, *ReOrient: Global Economy in the Asian Age* (1998). A reassessment of the role of Asia in the economic development of the world from around 1400 onward.

Glahn, Richard von, *Fountain of Fortune: Money and Monetary Policy in China, 1000–1700* (1996). Includes an excellent analysis of the history of silver in Ming China.

Gruzinski, Serge, *The Conquest of Mexico* (1993). An important work on the conquest of Mexico.

Habib, Irfan, *The Agrarian System of Mughal India* (1963). One of the best studies on the subject.

Hall, Richard Seymour, *Empires of the Monsoon: A History of the Indian Ocean and Its Invaders* (1996). A very engaging journalistic account with fabulous details.

Hodgson, Marshall, *The Venture of Islam*, vols. 2 and 3 (1974). A magisterial work that includes the Indian subcontinent in its careful study of the political and cultural history of the whole Islamic world.

Hulme, Peter, *Colonial Encounters: Europe and the Native Caribbean, 1492–1797* (1986). Presents an interesting interpretation of the encounters of Europeans and Native Americans.

Lach, Donald F., *Asia in the Making of Europe*, 5 books in 3 vols. (1965–). Perhaps the single most comprehensive and innovative guide to the European voyages of discovery.

Lockhart, James, and Stuart Schwartz, *Early Latin America* (1983). One of the finest studies of European expansion in the late fifteenth century.

McCann, James, *Maize and Grace: Africa's Encounter with a New World Crop, 1500–2000* (2005).

Melville, Elinor G. K., *A Plague of Sheep: Environmental Consequences of the Conquest of Mexico* (1994). A history of the transformation of a valley in Mexico from the Aztec period to the era of Spanish rule.

Mignolo, Walter D., *The Darker Side of the Renaissance: Literacy, Territoriality, and Colonization* (1995). Uses literary theory and literary images to present provocative interpretations of the encounter of Europeans and Native Americans.

Pagden, Anthony, *European Encounters with the New World* (1993). A complex look at the deep and lasting imprint of the New World on its conquerors.

Parker, Geoffrey, *The Military Revolution: Military Innovation and the Rise of the West, 1500–1800* (1996). Traces the changes in technology and tactics in the early modern period and discusses the political significance of this "revolution."

Pelikan, Jaroslav, *Reformation of Church and Dogma (1300–1700)* (1988). An important overview of major religious controversies.

Phillips, William D., and Carla Rahn Phillips, *The World of Christopher Columbus* (1992). One of the finest studies of European expansion in the late fifteenth century.

Russell-Wood, A. J. R., *The Portuguese Empire, 1415–1808* (1992). An important survey of early Portuguese exploration.

CHAPTER 13: WORLDS ENTANGLED, 1600–1750

Alam, Muzaffar, *The Crisis of Empire in Mughal North India* (1993). Represents the best of the new scholarly interpretations on the subject.

Bay, Edna, *Wives of the Leopard: Gender, Politics, and Culture in the Kingdom of Dahomey* (1998). A useful treatment of gender issues in Dahomey.

Blackburn, Robin, *The Making of New World Slavery: From the Baroque to the Modern, 1492–1800* (1997). A good place to begin when studying African slavery and the Atlantic slave trade, it compares the early expansion of the plantation systems across the Atlantic and throughout the Americas.

Calloway, Colin G., *One Vast Winter Count: The Native American West before Lewis and Clark* (2003). A sweeping survey of North American Indian histories prior to the nineteenth century.

Crossley, Pamela, *A Translucent Mirror: History and Identity in Qing Imperial Ideology* (1999). The author deals with the formation of identities such as "Manchu" and "Chinese" during the Qing period.

Eltis, David and Richardson, David, *Atlas of the Transatlantic Slave Trade* (2010). This work contains the most up-to-date data on the Atlantic slave trade, the numbers transported, where the captives came from, and where they landed.

Flynn, Dennis O., and Arturo Giraldez (eds.), *Metals and Money in an Emerging World Economy* (1997). A collection of articles about the place of silver in the world economy.

Forsyth, James, *A History of the Peoples of Siberia: Russia's North Asian Colony 1581–1990* (1992). A narrative overview of a violent history reminiscent of the western expansion of the United States.

Glahn, Richard von, *Fountains of Fortune: Money and Monetary Policy in China, 1000–1700* (1996). A discussion of the place of silver in the Chinese economy.

Halperin, Charles J., *Russia and the Golden Horde: The Mongol Impact on Medieval Russian History* (1985). A book on the rise of Muscovy, forebear of the Russian Empire, from within the Mongol realm.

Hämäläinen, Pekka, *The Comanche Empire* (2008). A book that inverts the conventional history of empires in North America by arguing that the Comanches were the most successful expansionist power in the middle of the continent during the eighteenth century.

Hattox, Ralph S., *Coffee and Coffeehouses: The Origins of a Social Beverage in the Medieval Near East* (1985). This work shows how widespread and popular coffee consumption and coffeehouses were around the world.

Huang, Ray, *1587, A Year of No Significance: The Ming Dynasty in Decline* (1981). An insightful analysis of the problems confronting the late Ming.

Lensen, George, *The Russian Push Toward Japan: Russo-Japanese Relations 1697–1875* (1959). A discussion of why and how Japan established its first border with another state and how Russia pursued its ambitions in the Pacific.

Lockhart, James, *The Nahuas After the Conquest* (1992). A landmark study of the social reorganization of Mesoamerican societies under Spanish rule.

Lovejoy, Paul, *Transformations in Slavery: A History of Slavery in Africa* (1983). An excellent discussion of African slavery.

Nakane, Chie, and Shinzaburo Oishi (eds.), *Tokugawa Japan: The Social and Economic Antecedents of Modern Japan* (1990). First-rate essays on Japanese village society, urban life, literacy, and culture.

Pamuk, Sevket, *A Monetary History of the Ottoman Empire* (2000). A discussion of the place of silver in the Ottoman Empire.

Parker, Geoffrey (ed.), *The Thirty Years' War* (1997). The standard account of the conflict and its outcomes.

Perdue, Peter C., *China Marches West: The Qing Conquest of Central Asia* (2005). This volume chronicles the expansion of the Qing Empire to its northwest, drawing comparisons to other colonial empires and their legacies.

Platonov, S. F., *Ivan the Terrible* (1986). Covers the controversies over Russia's infamous tsar.

Rawski, Evelyn, *The Last Emperors: A Social History of Qing Imperial Institutions* (1998). This volume explores the mechanisms and processes through which the Qing court negotiated its Manchu identity.

Reid, Anthony, *Charting the Shape of Early Modern Southeast Asia* (1999). A collection of articles by a leading historian of Southeast Asia.

Spence, Jonathan, and John Wills (eds.), *From Ming to Ch'ing: Conquest, Region, and Continuity in Seventeenth-Century China* (1979). Covers the various aspects of a tumultuous period of dynastic transition.

Taylor, Alan, *American Colonies: The Settling of North America* (2001). Brings together British, French, and Spanish colonial histories and shows how the fortunes of each were entangled with one another and with those of diverse Native American peoples.

Thornton, John, *Africa and Africans in the Making of the Atlantic World, 1400–1800* (1998). A wonderful discussion of how African slaves played a large role in the formation of the Atlantic world.

Thornton, John K., *The Kongolese Saint Anthony: Dona Beatriz Kimpa*

Vita and the Antonian Movement, 1684–1706 (1998). An excellent monograph on religious movements in the Kongo.

Toby, Ronald P., *State and Diplomacy in Early Modern Japan: Asia in the Development of the Tokugawa Bakufu* (1984). The author shows that the Japanese, far from being isolated from the outside world, engaged in vigorous and successful diplomacy.

Vilar, Pierre, *A History of Gold and Money* (1991). An excellent study of the development of the early silver and gold economies.

CHAPTER 14: CULTURES OF SPLENDOR AND POWER, 1500–1780

Axtell, James, *The Invasion of America: The Contest of Cultures in Colonial North America* (1985). Discusses the strategies of Christian missionaries in converting the Indians, as well as the success of Indians in converting Europeans.

Babaie, Sussan, *Isfahan and Its Palaces: Statecraft, Shi'ism and the Architecture of Conviviality in Early Modern Iran* (2008). An overview of the city of Isfahan, as the capital of the Safavid state.

Barmé, Geremie R., *The Forbidden City* (2008). A concise introduction to the history of one of the most important physical emblems of Chinese imperial power.

Berlin, Ira, *Many Thousands Gone: The First Two Centuries of Slavery in North America* (1998). Surveys the development of African-American culture in colonial North America.

Brook, Timothy, *The Confusions of Pleasure: Commerce and Culture in Ming China* (1999). An insightful survey of Ming society.

Clunas, Craig, *Superfluous Things: Material Culture and Social Status in Early Modern China* (1991). A good account of the late Ming elite's growing passion for material things.

Collcutt, Martin, Marius Jansen, and Isao Kumakura, *A Cultural Atlas of Japan* (1988). A sweeping look at the many different forms of Japanese cultural expression over the centuries, including the flourishing urban culture of Edo.

Darnton, Robert, *The Business of the Enlightenment: A Publishing History of the Encyclopédie, 1775–1800* (1979). The classic study of Europe's first great compendium of knowledge.

Dash, Mike, *Tulipomania: The Story of the World's Most Coveted Flower and the Extraordinary Passions It Aroused* (1999). A global perspective on and lively account of the spread of the tulip around the world as a flower signifying both beauty and status.

Elman, Benjamin A., *On Their Own Terms: Science in China, 1550–1900* (2005). A study of the development of "native" Chinese science and how the process interacted with the introduction of western science to China over the course of three and a half centuries.

Eze, Emmanuel Chukwudi (ed.), *Race and the Enlightenment: A Reader* (1997). Readings examining the idea of race in the context of the Enlightenment.

Fleischer, Cornell, *Bureaucrat and Intellectual in the Ottoman Empire: The Historian Mustafa Ali (1540–1600)* (1986). Offers good insight into the world of culture and intellectual vitality in the Ottoman Empire.

Grafton, Anthony, April Shelford, and Nancy Siraisi, *New Worlds, Ancient Texts: The Power of Tradition and the Shock of Discovery* (1995). A concise discussion of the impact of the New World on European thought.

Gutiérrez, Ramón, *When Jesus Came, the Corn Mothers Went Away: Marriage, Sexuality, and Power in New Mexico, 1500–1846* (1991). A provocative dissection of the spiritual dimensions of European colonialism in the Americas.

Harley, J. B., and David Woodward (eds.), *The History of Cartography*, vol. 2, Book 2: *Cartography in the Traditional East and Southeast Asian Societies* (1994). An authoritative treatment of the subject.

Horton, Robin, *Patterns of Thought in Africa and the West: Essays on Magic, Religion, and Science* (1993). Reflections on African patterns of thought and attitudes toward nature, which can help us understand African-American religious beliefs and resistance movements.

Keene, Donald, *The Japanese Discovery of Europe: Honda Toshiaki and Other Discoverers, 1720–1798* (1952). A study of the ways Japan managed to incorporate knowledge from the outside world with the development of national traditions.

Ko, Dorothy, *Teachers of the Inner Chambers: Women and Culture in Seventeenth-Century China* (1994). Explores the lives of elite women in late Ming and early Qing China.

Lewis, Bernard, *Race and Color in Islam* (1979). Examines the Islamic attitude toward race and color.

Morgan, Philip D., *Slave Counterpoint: Black Culture in the Eighteenth-Century Chesapeake and Lowcountry* (1998). Describes the development of African-American culture in colonial North America.

Munck, Thomas, *The Enlightenment: A Comparative Social History, 1721–1794* (2000). A wonderful survey, with unusual examples from the periphery, especially from Scandinavia and the Habsburg Empire.

Necipoglu, Gulru, *Architecture, Ceremonial, and Power: The Topkapi Palace in the Fifteenth and Sixteenth Centuries* (1991). A magnificently illustrated book that shows the enormous artistic talent that the Ottoman rulers poured into their imperial structure.

Publishing and the Print Culture in Late Imperial China (Special Issue), *Late Imperial China*, vol. 17, no. 1

(June 1996). Contains a collection of important articles with a foreword by the French cultural historian Roger Chartier.

Qaisar, Ahsan Jan, *The Indian Response to European Technology, AD 1498–1707* (1998). A meticulous, scholarly work on this little-studied subject.

Rizvi, Athar Abbas, *The Wonder That Was India,* vol. 2, *A Survey of the History and Culture of the Indian Sub-continent from the Coming of the Muslims to the British Conquest, 1200–1700* (1987). A deeply learned work in intellectual history.

Smith, Bernard, *European Vision and the South Pacific* (1985). An excellent cultural history of Cook's voyages.

Smith, Richard J., *Chinese Maps: Images of "All under Heaven"* (1996). Provides a good introduction to the history of cartography in China.

Welch, Anthony, *Shah Abbas and the Arts of Isfahan* (1973). Describes the astonishing architectural and artistic renaissance of the city of Isfahan under the Safavid ruler Shah Abbas.

Whitfield, Peter, *The Image of the World: Twenty Centuries of World Maps* (1994). A good introduction to the history of cartography in different parts of the world.

Wilks, Ivor, *Forests of Gold: Essays on the Akan and the Kingdom of Asante* (Athens, OH, 1993). A study that focuses on the Asante's drive for wealth.

Zilfi, Madeline C., *The Politics of Piety: The Ottoman Ulema in the Post-Classical Age (1600–1800)* (1988). Explores the cultural flourishing that took place within the Islamic world in this period.

CHAPTER 15: REORDERING THE WORLD, 1750–1850

Allen, Robert C., *The British Industrial Revolution in Global Perspective* (2009). The most recent and authoritative study of the industrial revolution in Britain and its implications around the world.

Anderson, Fred, *Crucible of War: The Seven Years' War and the Fate of Empire in British North America, 1754–1766* (2000). The best synthesis of the "great war for empire" that set the stage for the American Revolution.

Bayly, C. A., *Indian Society and the Making of the British Empire* (1998). A useful work on the early history of the British conquest of India.

Blackburn, Robin, *The Overthrow of Colonial Slavery, 1776–1848* (1988). Places the abolition of the Atlantic slave trade and colonial slavery in a large historical context.

Cambridge History of Egypt: Modern Egypt from 1517 to the End of the Twentieth Century, vol. 2 (1998). Volume 2 contains authoritative essays on all aspects of modern Egyptian history, including the impact of the French invasion and the rule of Muhammad Ali.

Chaudhuri, K. N., *The Trading World of Asia and the East India Company, 1660–1760* (1978). An authoritative economic history of the East India Company's operations.

Crafts, N. F. R., *British Economic Growth during the Industrial Revolution* (1985). A pioneering study that emphasizes a long-term, more gradual process of adaptation to new institutional and social circumstances.

de Vries, Jan, *Industrious Revolution: Consumer Behavior and the Household Economy, 1650 to the Present* (2008). A book on the lead-up to the industrial revolution, written by the leading economic historian who coined the term "industrious revolution."

Diamond, Jared, and James A. Robinson (eds.), *Natural Experiments of History* (2010). This book consists of eight comparative studies drawn from history, archaeology, economics, economic history, geography, and political science, covering a spectrum of approaches, ranging from a nonquantitative narrative style to quantitative statistical analyses.

Doyle, William, *The Oxford History of the French Revolution* (1990). A highly detailed discussion of the course of events.

Drescher, Seymour, *Abolition: A History of Slavery and Anti-Slavery* (2009). A recent and authoritative overview of slavery and its opponents.

Elvin, Mark, *The Retreat of the Elephants: An Environmental History of China* (2004). A study of the different ways in which China's natural environment was shaped.

Fick, Carolyn E., *The Making of Haiti: The Saint Domingue Revolution from Below* (1990). Provides a detailed account of the factors that led to the great slave rebellion on the island of Haiti at the end of the eighteenth century.

Findley, Carter, *Bureaucratic Reform in the Ottoman Empire: The Sublime Porte, 1789–1922* (1980). A useful guide to Ottoman reform efforts in the nineteenth century.

Geggus, David (ed.), *The Impact of the Haitian Revolution in the Atlantic World* (2001). A lively effort to disentangle the effects of the Haitian Revolution from those of the French Revolution.

Hevia, James, *Cherishing Men from Afar: Qing Guest Ritual and the Macartney Embassy of 1793* (1995). Offers a definitive interpretation of the nature of Sino-British conflict in the Qing period.

Hobsbawm, Eric, *Nations and Nationalism since 1780* (1990). An important overview of the rise of the nation-state and nationalism around the world.

Howe, Daniel Walker, *What Hath God Wrought: The Transformation of America, 1815–1848* (2007). A

Pulitzer Prize–winning interpretation of how new technologies and new ideas reshaped the economy, society, culture, and politics of the United States in the first half of the nineteenth century.

Hunt, Lynn, *Politics, Culture and Class in the French Revolution* (1984). Examines the influence of sociocultural shifts as causes and consequences of the French Revolution, emphasizing the symbols and practice of politics invented during the revolution.

Inikori, Joseph, *Africans and the Industrial Revolution in England* (2002). Demonstrates the important role that Africa and Africans played in facilitating the industrial revolution.

Isset, Christopher Mills, *State, Peasant, and Merchant in Qing Manchuria, 1644–1862* (2007). A study of the relationships between the sociopolitical structures and peasant lives in a key region during the Qing.

James, C. L. R., *The Black Jacobins: Toussaint L'Ouverture and the San Domingo Revolution* (1938). A classic chronicle of the only successful slave revolt in history, it provides a critical portrait of their leader, Toussaint L'Ouverture.

Jones, E. L., *Growth Recurring* (1988). Discusses the controversy over why the industrial revolution took place in Europe, stressing the unique ecological setting that encouraged long-term investment.

Kinsbruner, Jay, *Independence in Spanish America* (1994). A fine study of the Latin American revolutions that argues that the struggle was as much a civil war as a fight for national independence.

Landers, Jane, *Atlantic Creoles in the Age of Revolutions* (2011).A collection of fascinating and unique portraits of Atlantic world creoles who managed to move freely and purposefully through French, Spanish, and English colonies, and through Indian territory, in the unstable century between 1750 and 1850.

Mokyr, Joel, *Enlightened Economy: An Economic History of Britain, 1700–1850* (2009). Perspectives on the evolution of the British economy in the era that produced the industrial revolution.

———, *The Lever of Riches* (1990). An important study of the causes of the industrial revolution that emphasizes the role of small technological and organizational breakthroughs.

Naquin, Susan, and Evelyn Rawski, *Chinese Society in the Eighteenth Century* (1987). A survey of mid-Qing society.

Neal, Larry, *The Rise of Financial Capitalism* (1990). An important study of the making of financial markets.

Nikitenko, Aleksandr, *Up from Serfdom: My Childhood and Youth in Russia, 1804–1824* (2001). One of the very few recorded life stories of a Russian serf.

Pomeranz, Kenneth, *The Great Divergence: Europe, China, and the Making of the Modern World Economy* (2000). Offers explanations of why Europe and not some other place in the world, like parts of China or India, forged ahead economically in the nineteenth century.

Rudé, George, *Europe in the Eighteenth Century* (1972). Emphasizes the rise of a new class, the bourgeoisie, against the old aristocracy, as a cause of the French Revolution.

Wakeman, Frederic, Jr., "The Canton Trade and the Opium War," in John K. Fairbank (ed.), *The Cambridge History of China*, vol. 10 (1978), pp. 163–212. The standard account of the episode.

Wong, R. Bin, *China Transformed: Historical Change and the Limits of European Experience* (2000). Draws attention to the relative autonomy of merchant capitalists in relation to dynastic states in Europe compared to China.

Wood, Gordon S., *Empire of Liberty: A History of the Early Republic, 1789–1815* (2009). An excellent synthesis of the history of the United States in the tumultuous years between the ratification of the Constitution and the War of 1812.

Wortman, Richard, *Scenarios of Power: Myth and Ceremony in Russian Monarchy*, 2 vols. (1995–2000). Examines how dynastic Russia confronted the challenges of the revolutionary epoch.

CHAPTER 16: ALTERNATIVE VISIONS OF THE NINETEENTH CENTURY

Anderson, David M., *Revealing Prophets: Prophets in Eastern African History* (1995). Good discussion of the prophets in eastern Africa.

Beecher, Jonathan, *The Utopian Vision of Charles Fourier* (1983). A fine biography of this important thinker.

Boyd, Jean, *The Caliph's Sister: Nana Asma'u, 1793–1865, Teacher, Poet, and Islamic Leader* (1988). A study of the most powerful female Muslim leader in the Fulani religious revolt.

Clancy-Smith, Julia, *Rebel and Saint: Muslim Notables, Populist Protest, Colonial Encounter (Algeria and Tunisia, 1800–1904)* (1994). Examines Islamic protest movements against western encroachments in North Africa.

Clogg, Richard, *A Concise History of Greece* (1997). A good introduction to the history of Greece in its European context.

Dalrymple, William, *The Last Mughal: The Fall of a Dynasty: Delhi, 1857* (2007). A deeply researched and riveting account of Delhi during the 1857 revolt.

Danziger, Raphael, *Abd al-Qadir: Resistance to the French and Internal Consolidation* (1977). Still the indispensable work on this important Algerian Muslim leader.

Dowd, Gregory E., *A Spirited Resistance: The North American Indian Struggle for Unity, 1745–1815* (1992). Emphasizes the importance of prophets like Tenskwatawa in the building of pan-Indian confederations in the era between the Seven Years' War and the War of 1812.

Guha, Ranajit, *Elementary Aspects of Peasant Insurgency in Colonial India* (1983). Not specifically on the Indian Rebellion of 1857 but includes it in its pioneering "subalternist" interpretation of South Asian history.

Hamilton, Carolyn (ed.), *The Mfecane Aftermath: Reconstructive Debates in Southern African History* (1995). Debates on Shaka's *Mfecane* movement and its impact on southern Africa.

Hiskett, Mervyn, *The Sword of Truth: The Life and Times of the Shehu Usman dan Fodio* (1994). An authoritative study of the Fulani revolt in northern Nigeria.

Johnson, Douglas H., *Nuer Prophets: A History of Prophecy from the Upper Nile in the Nineteenth and Twentieth Centuries* (1994). Deals with African prophetic and charismatic movements in eastern Africa.

Keddie, Nikki, *An Islamic Response to Imperialism: Political and Religious Writings of Sayyid Jamal ad-Din "al-Afghani" (1968)*. Definitive information on the Afghani's life and influence, coupled with a translation of one of his most important essays.

Michael, Franz, and Chung-li Chang, *The Taiping Rebellion: History and Documents*, 3 vols. (1966–1971). The basic source for the history of the Taiping.

Mukherjee, Rudrangshu, *Awadh in Revolt 1857–58* (1984). A careful case study of the Indian Rebellion.

Omer-Cooper, J. D., *The Zulu Aftermath: A Nineteenth-Century Revolution in Bantu Africa* (1966). A good place to start in studying Shaka's *Mfecane* movement, which greatly rearranged the political and ethnic makeup of southern Africa.

Ostler, Jeffrey, *The Plains Sioux and U.S. Colonialism from Lewis and Clark to Wounded Knee* (2004). Uses the lens of colonial theory to track relations between the Sioux and the United States, offering fresh insights about the Ghost Dance movement.

Peires, J. B. (ed.), *Before and After Shaka* (1981). Discusses elements in the debate over Shaka's *Mfecane* movement.

Pilbeam, Pamela, *French Socialists Before Marx: Workers, Women and the Social Question in France* (2001). Describes the development of a variety of socialist ideas in early nineteenth-century France.

Reed, Nelson, *The Caste War of Yucatan* (1964). A classic narrative of the Caste War of the Yucatan.

Restall, Matthew, *The Maya World* (1997). Describes in economic and social terms the origins of the Yucatan upheaval in southern Mexico.

Ruedy, John, *Modern Algeria: The Origins and Development of a Nation* (2005). Still the best overview of the modern political history of Algeria.

Rugeley, Terry, *Rebellion Now and Forever: Mayans, Hispanics, and Caste War Violence in Yucatán, 1800–1880* (2009). Explains the combination of economic and cultural pressures that drove the Mayans in the Yucatan to revolt in the Caste War.

Spence, Jonathan, *God's Chinese Son: The Taiping Heavenly Kingdom of Hong Xiuquan* (1996). A fascinating portrayal of the Taiping through the prism of its founder.

Wagner, Rudolf, *Reenacting the Heavenly Vision: The Role of Religion in the Taiping Rebellion* (1982). A brief but insightful analysis of the religious elements in the Taiping's doctrines.

White, Richard, *The Middle Ground: Indians, Empires, and Republics in the Great Lakes Region, 1650–1815* (1991). A pathbreaking exploration of intercultural relations in North America that offers a provocative interpretation of the visions of Tenskwatawa and the efforts of Tecumseh to resist the expansion of the United States.

CHAPTER 17: NATIONS AND EMPIRES, 1850–1914

Berry, Sara, *Cocoa, Custom and Socio-Economic Change in Western Nigeria* (1975), Innovative study based on interviews with local farmers that suggests that farmer enterprise and microeconomic theory better explain the spectacular growth in cocoa production than grand economic theory.

Cain, P. A., and A. G. Hopkins, *British Imperialism: Innovation and Expansion, 1688–1914* (1993). An excellent discussion of British imperialism, especially British expansion into Africa.

Cooper, Frederick, *Colonialism in Question: Theory, Knowledge, History* (2005). A collection of essays by one of the leading scholars of colonial studies.

Cronon, William, *Nature's Metropolis: Chicago and the Great West* (1991). Makes connections among territorial expansion, industrialization, and urban development.

Davis, John, *Conflict and Control: Law and Order in Nineteenth-Century Italy* (1988). A superb study of the north-south and other rifts after Italian political unification.

Frankel, S. Herbert, *Capital Investment in Africa: Its Course and Effects* (1938). A careful study based on a mass of detailed figures and statistics on the general economic development of states in sub-Saharan Africa.

Friesen, Gerald, *The Canadian Prairies* (1984). The most comprehensive account of Canadian westward expansion.

Gluck, Carol, *Japan's Modern Myths: Ideology in the Late Meiji Period* (1985). A study of how states fashion useful historical traditions to consolidate and legitimize their rule.

Headrick, Daniel R., *The Tools of Empire: Technology and European Imperialism in the Nineteenth Century*

(1981). A useful general study of the relationship between imperialism and technology.

Herbst, Jeffrey, *States and Power in Africa: Comparative Lessons in Authority and Control* (2000). An overview of the impact of colonial rule on contemporary African states.

Hill, Polly, *The Gold Coast Cocoa Farmer: A Preliminary Survey* (1965).

Hine, Robert V., and John Mack Faragher, *The American West: A New Interpretive History* (2000). Presents an excellent synthesis of the conquests by which the United States expanded from the Atlantic to the Pacific.

Hobsbawm, Eric J., *Nations and Nationalism since 1780: Programme, Myth, Reality* (1993). An insightful survey of the origins and development of nationalist thought throughout Europe.

Hochschild, Adam, *King Leopold's Ghost* (1998). A full-scale, eminently readable study of Europe's most egregiously destructive colonial regime in Africa.

Lee, Leo Ou-fan, and Andrew Nathan, "The Beginnings of Mass Culture: Journalism and Fiction in the Late Ch'ing and Beyond," in David Johnson, Andrew Nathan, and Evelyn Rawski (eds.), *Popular Culture in Late Imperial China* (1985), pp. 360–95. An important article on the emergence of a mass-media market in late-nineteenth- and early twentieth-century China.

Lieven, Dominic, *Empire: The Russian Empire and Its Rivals* (2000). A comparison of the British, Ottoman, Habsburg, and Russian empires.

Mackenzie, John M., *Propaganda and Empire* (1984). Contains a series of useful chapters showing the importance of the empire to Britain.

Mamdani, Mahmood, *Citizen and State: Contemporary Africa and the Legacy of Late Colonialism* (1996). A survey of the impact of European colonial powers on African political systems.

McClintock, Anne, *Imperial Leather: Race, Gender and Sexuality in the Colonial Contest* (1995). A study of the imperial relationship between Victorian Britain and South Africa from the point of view of cultural studies.

McNeil, William, *Europe's Steppe Frontier: 1500–1800* (1964). An excellent study of the definitive victory of Russia's agricultural empire over grazing nomads and independent frontier people.

Mitchell, B. R., *International Historical Statistics: Africa, Asia, and Oceania, 1750–2005* (2007). This comparative volume provides data from over two centuries for all principal areas of economic and social activity in both eastern and western Europe.

Montgomery, David, *The Fall of the House of Labor: The Workplace, the State, and American Labor Activism, 1865–1925* (1987). An excellent discussion of changes in work in the late nineteenth century.

Myers, Ramon, and Mark Peattie (eds.), *The Japanese Colonial Empire, 1895–1945* (1984). A collection of essays exploring different aspects of Japanese colonialism.

Needell, Jeffrey, *A Tropical Belle Epoque: Elite Culture and Society in Turn-of-the-century Rio de Janeiro* (1987). Shows the strength of the Brazilian elites at the turn of the century.

Pan, Lynn (ed.), *The Encyclopedia of Chinese Overseas* (1999). A comprehensive coverage of the history of the Chinese diaspora.

Porter, Bernard, *The Absent-Minded Imperialists: What the British Really Thought about Empire* (2004). A careful dissection of the ways in which empire changed the British—and did not.

Stengers, Jean, *Combien le Congo a-t-il coûté à la Belgique* (1957). A detailed financial accounting of how much Leopold put into the Congo and how much he took out, underscoring just how ruthlessly he exploited this possession.

Topik, Steven, *The Political Economy of the Brazilian State, 1889–1930* (1987). An excellent discussion of the Brazilian state, and especially of its elites.

Walker, Mack, *German Home Towns: Community, State, and the General State, 1648–1871* (1971; reprint, 1998). A brilliant, street-level analysis of the Holy Roman Empire (the First Reich) and the run-up to the German unification of 1871 (the Second Reich).

Wasserman, Mark, *Everyday Life and Politics in Nineteenth-Century Mexico* (2000). Wonderfully captures the way in which people coped with social and economic dislocation in late-nineteenth-century Mexico.

Weeks, Theodore R., *Nation and State in Late Imperial Russia: Nationalism and Russification on the Western Frontier, 1863–1914* (1996). A good discussion of the Russian Empire's responses to the concept of the nation-state.

White, Richard, *Railroaded: The Transcontinentals and the Making of Modern America* (2011). A searing exposé of the corruptions and a startling critique of the economic and environmental costs associated with the expansion of railroad lines across Canada, the United States, and Mexico.

Yung Wing, *My Life in China and America* (1909). The autobiography of the first Chinese graduate of an American university.

CHAPTER 18: AN UNSETTLED WORLD, 1890–1914

Bayly, C. A., *The Birth of the Modern World, 1780–1914: Global Connections and Comparisons* (2004). A general study of the key political, economic, social, and cultural features of the modern era in world history.

Bergère, Marie-Claire, *Sun Yat-sen* (1998). Originally published in

French in 1994, this is a judicious biography of the man generally known as the father of the modern Chinese nation.

Chatterjee, Partha, *The Nation and Its Fragments* (1993). One of the most important works on Indian nationalism by a leading scholar of "subaltern studies."

Conrad, Joseph, *Heart of Darkness* (1899). First published in a magazine in 1899, this novella contained a searing critique of King Leopold's oppressive and exploitative policies in the Congo and was part of a growing concern for the effects that European empires were having around the world, especially in Africa.

Esherick, Joseph, "How the Qing became China," in Joseph W. Esherick, Hasan Kayali, and Eric Van Young (eds.), *Empire to Nation: Historical Perspectives on the Making of the Modern World* (2006). A study of the processes through which the Qing Empire became the nation-state of China.

———, *The Origins of the Boxer Uprising* (1987). The definitive account of the episode.

Everdell, William R., *The First Moderns: Profiles in the Origins of Twentieth-Century Thought* (1997). A rich account of the many faces of modernism, focusing particularly on science and art.

Finnane, Antonia, *Changing Clothes in China: Fashion, History, Nation* (2008). An exploration of changing Chinese identities from the perspective of clothing.

Gay, Peter, *The Cultivation of Hatred* (1994). A provocative discussion of the violent passions of the immediate pre–Great War era.

Gilmartin, Christina, Gail Hershatter, Lisa Rofel, and Tyrene White (eds.), *Engendering China: Women, Culture, and the State* (1994). Analyzes politics and society in modern China from the perspective of gender.

Hochschild, Adam, *King Leopold's Ghost: A Story of Greed, Terror, and Heroism in Colonial Africa* (1998). A well-written account of the violent colonial history of the Belgian Congo under King Leopold in the late nineteenth century.

Katz, Friedrich, *The Life and Times of Pancho Villa* (1998). An exploration of the Mexican Revolution that shows how Villa's armies destroyed the forces of Díaz and his followers.

Keddie, Nikki, *An Islamic Response to Imperialism: Political and Religious Writings of Sayyid Jamal ad-Din "al-Afghani"* (1968). Definitive information on the Afghani's life and influence, coupled with a translation of one of his most important essays.

Kern, Stephen, *The Culture of Time and Space 1880–1918* (1986). A useful study of the enormous changes in the experience of time and space in the age of late industrialism in Europe and America.

Kuhn, Philip, *Chinese among Others: Emigration in Modern Times* (2008). An overview of the history of Chinese migration.

McKeown, Adam, *Melancholy Order: Asian Migration and the Globalization of Borders* (2008). An examination of global migration patterns since the mid-nineteenth century and how regulations designed to restrict Asian migration to other parts of the world led to the modern regime of migration control.

Meade, Teresa, *"Civilizing" Rio: Reform and Resistance in a Brazilian City, 1889–1930* (1997). A wonderful study of cultural and class conflict in Brazil.

Pick, Daniel, *Faces of Degeneration: A European Disorder, c. 1848–c. 1918* (1993). A study of Europe's fear of social and biological decline, particularly focusing on France and Italy.

Pretorius, Fransjohn (ed.), *Scorched Earth* (2001). A study of the Anglo-Boer War in terms of its environmental impacts.

Sarkar, Sumit, *The Swadeshi Movement in Bengal* (1973). A comprehensive study of an early militant movement against British rule.

Schorske, Carl E. *Fin-de-Siècle Vienna: Politics and Culture* (1980). The classic treatment of the birth of modern ideas and political movements in turn-of-the-century Austria.

Trachtenberg, Alan, *The Incorporation of America: Culture and Society in the Gilded Age* (1982). A provocative synthesis of changes in the American economy, society, and culture in the last decades of the nineteenth century.

Wang, David Der-wei, *Fin-de-Siècle Splendor: Repressed Modernities of Late Qing Fiction, 1849–1911* (1997). A fine work that attempts to locate the "modern" within the writings of the late Qing period.

Warren, Louis, *Buffalo Bill's America: William Cody and the Wild West Show* (2005). A superb portrait of William F. Cody, the person; of Buffalo Bill, the persona Cody (and others) created; and of the popular culture his Wild West shows brought to audiences in Europe and North America.

Warwick, Peter, *Black People and the South African War, 1899–1902* (1983). An important study that reminds readers of the crucial involvement of black South Africans in this bloody conflict.

Womack, John, Jr., *Zapata and the Mexican Revolution* (1968). A major work on the Mexican Revolution that discusses peasant struggles in the state of Morelos in great detail.

CHAPTER 19: OF MASSES AND VISIONS OF THE MODERN, 1910–1939

Bloxham, Donald, *The Great Game of Genocide: Imperialism, Nationalism, and the Destruction of the Ottoman Armenians* (2005). The definitive work on the Armenian genocide, set in a wide historical context.

Brown, Judith, *Gandhi: Prisoner of Hope* (1990). A biography of Gandhi as a political activist.

De Grazia, Victoria, and Ellen Furlough (eds.), *The Sex of Things: Gender and Consumption in Historical Perspective* (1996). Pathbreaking essays on how gender affects consumption.

Dumenil, Lynn, *The Modern Temper: America in the 1920s* (1995). A general discussion of American culture in the decade after World War I.

Fainsod, Merle, *Smolensk under Soviet Rule* (1989). The most accessible and sophisticated interpretation of the Stalin revolution in the village.

Friedman, Edward, *Backward toward Revolution: The Chinese Revolutionary Party* (1974). An insightful look at the failure of liberalism in early republican China through the prism of the short-lived Chinese Revolutionary Party.

Gelvin, James, *Divided Loyalties: Nationalism and Mass Politics in Syria at the Close of Empire* (1998). Offers important insights into the development of nationalism in the Arab world.

Horne, John (ed.), *A Companion to World War I* (2010). A collection of articles written by leading scholars of World War I; the most comprehensive and up-to-date work on this war.

———, *State, Society, and Mobilization during the First World War* (1997). Essays on what it took to wage total war among all the belligerents.

Johnson, G. Wesley, *The Emergence of Black Politics in Senegal* (1971). A useful examination of the stirrings of African nationalism in Senegal.

Kennedy, David M., *Freedom from Fear: The American People in Depression and War, 1929–1945* (1999). A wonderful narrative of turbulent years.

Kershaw, Ian, *Hitler*, 2 vols. (1998–2000). A masterpiece combining biography and context.

Kimble, David, *A Political History of Ghana* (1963). An excellent discussion of the beginnings of African nationalism in Ghana.

Kotkin, Stephen, *Magnetic Mountain: Stalinism as a Civilization* (1995). Recaptures the atmosphere of a time when everything seemed possible, even creating a new world.

LeMahieu, D. L., *A Culture for Democracy: Mass Communication and the Cultivated Mind in Britain between the Wars* (1988). One of the great works on mass culture.

Lyttelton, Adrian, *The Seizure of Power: Fascism in Italy, 1919–1929* (1961). Still the classic account.

Marchand, Roland, *Advertising the American Dream: Making Way for Modernity, 1920–1945* (1985). An excellent discussion of the force of mass production and mass consumption.

Mazower, Mark, *Dark Continent: Europe's Twentieth Century* (1999). A wide-ranging overview of Europe's tempestuous twentieth century.

McKeown, Adam, *Melancholy Order: Asian Migration and the Globalization of Border* (2008). A major study of the vast movement of peoples around the globe between the middle of the nineteenth and the twentieth centuries.

Morrow, John H., Jr., *The Great War: An Imperial History* (2004). Places World War I in the context of European imperialism.

Nottingham, John, and Carl Rosberg, *The Myth of "Mau Mau": Nationalism in Kenya* (1966). Dispels the myths in describing the roots of nationalism in Kenya.

Rosenberg, Clifford, *Policing Paris: The Origins of Modern Immigration Control Between the Wars* (2006). Explores the first systematic efforts to enforce distinctions of nationality and citizenship status in a major urban setting.

Taylor, Jay, *The Generalissimo: Chiang Kai-shek and the Struggle for Modern China* (2009). The first serious biographical study of Chiang Kai-shek in English, although its reliance on Chiang's own diary as a source does raise some questions of historical interpretation.

Thorp, Rosemary (ed.), *Latin America in the 1930s* (1984). An important collection of essays on Latin America's response to the shakeup of the interwar years.

Tsin, Michael, *Nation, Governance, and Modernity in China: Canton, 1900–1927* (1999). An analysis of the vision and social dynamics behind the Guomindang-led revolution of the 1920s.

Vianna, Hermano, *The Mystery of Samba* (1999). Discusses the history of samba, emphasizing its African heritage as well as its persistent popular content.

Wakeman, Frederic, Jr., *Policing Shanghai, 1927–1937* (1995). An excellent account of Guomindang rule in China's largest city during the Nanjing decade.

Winter, J. M., *The Experience of World War* (1988). A comprehensive presentation of the many sides of the twentieth century.

Young, Louise, *Japan's Total Empire: Manchuria and the Culture of Wartime Imperialism* (1998). An innovative case study of Japanese imperialism and mass culture with broad implications.

CHAPTER 20: THE THREE-WORLD ORDER, 1940–1975

Aburish, Said K., *Nasser: The Last Arab* (2004). An impressive look at Egypt's most powerful political leader in the 1950s and 1960s.

Anderson, Jon Lee, *Che Guevara: A Revolutionary Life* (1997). A sweeping study of the radicalization of Latin American nationalism.

Bayly, Christopher, and Tim Harper, *Forgotten Armies: Britain's Asian Empire and the War with Japan* (2004). A brilliant social and military history of the Second World War as fought and lived in South and Southeast Asia.

Chatterjee, Partha, *Nationalist Thought and the Colonial World: A Derivative Discourse?* (1986). An influential interpretation of the ideological and political nature of Indian nationalism and the struggle for a postcolonial nation-state.

Crampton, R. J., *Eastern Europe in the Twentieth Century and After*, 2nd ed. (1997). Comprehensive overview covering all Soviet-bloc countries.

Dikötter, Frank, *Mao's Great Famine: The History of China's Most Devastating Catastrophe, 1958–1962* (2010). A recent detailed account of one of the greatest man-made disasters in twentieth-century history.

Dower, John W., *Embracing Defeat: Japan in the Wake of World War II* (1999). A prize-winning study of the transformation of one of the war's vanquished.

Elkins, Caroline, *Imperial Reckoning: The Untold Story of Britain's Gulag in Kenya* (2005). Pulitzer Prize–winning study of the brutal war to suppress the nationalist uprising in Kenya in the 1950s that ultimately led to independence for that country.

Evans, Martin, *Algeria: France's Undeclared War* (2011). Gives the history of the Algerian nationalist movements and provides an overview of the Algerian war for independence.

Feshbach Murray, and Alfred Friendly Jr. (1992). *Ecocide in the USSR: Health and Nation under Siege*. A crucial study of ecological disasters in the Soviet Union.

Gao Yuan, *Born Red: A Chronicle of the Cultural Revolution* (1987). A gripping personal account of the Cultural Revolution by a former Red Guard.

Gordon, Andrew (ed.), *Postwar Japan as History* (1993). Essays covering a wide range of topics on postwar Japan.

Hargreaves, John D., *Decolonization in Africa* (1996). A good place to start when exploring the history of African decolonization.

Hasan, Mushirul (ed.), *India's Partition: Process, Strategy and Mobilization* (1993). A useful anthology of scholarly articles, short stories, and primary documents on the partition of India.

Iriye, Akira, *Power and Culture: The Japanese-American War, 1941–1945* (1981). A discussion that goes beyond the military confrontation in Asia.

Jackson, Kenneth T., *Crabgrass Frontier: The Suburbanization of the United States* (1985). An insightful and influential consideration of the movement of the American population from cities to suburbs.

Jalal, Ayesha, *The Sole Spokesman: Jinnah, the Muslim League and the Demand for Pakistan* (1985). A study of the high politics leading to the violent partition of British India.

Keep, John L. H., *Last of the Empires: A History of the Soviet Union 1945–1991* (1995). A detailed overview of the core of the "Second World."

Morris, Benny, *Righteous Victims: A History of the Zionist-Arab Conflict, 1881–1999* (2000). On the Arab-Israeli War of 1948.

Patterson, James T., *Grand Expectations: The United States, 1945–1974* (1996). Synthesizes the American experience in the postwar decades.

Patterson, Thomas, *Contesting Castro* (1994). The best study of the tension between the United States and Cuba. Culminating in the Cuban Revolution, it explores the deep American misunderstanding of Cuban national aspirations.

Roberts, Geoffrey, *Stalin's Wars: From World War to Cold War, 1939–1953* (2007). A reassessment of Stalin's wartime leadership that conveys the vast scale of what took place.

Saich, Tony, and Hans van de Ven (eds.), *New Perspectives on the Chinese Communist Revolution* (1995). A collection of essays reexamining different aspects of the Chinese communist movement.

Schram, Stuart, *The Thought of Mao Tse-tung* (1989). Standard work on the subject.

Tignor, Robert L., *W. Arthur Lewis and the Birth of Development Economics* (2006). An intellectual biography of the Nobel Prize–winning, West Indian–born economist, who proposed formulas to promote the economic development of less developed societies and then sought to implement them in Africa and the West Indies.

Wiener, Douglas R., *A Little Corner of Freedom: Russian Nature Protection from Stalin to Gorbachev* (2002). A groundbreaking book about Russian environmentalism.

Zubkova, Elena, *Russia after the War: Hopes, Illusions, and Disappointments, 1945–1957* (1998). Uses formerly secret archives to catalogue the devastation and difficult reconstruction of one of the war's victors.

CHAPTER 21: GLOBALIZATION, 1970–2000

Collier, Paul, *The Bottom Billion: Why the Poorest Countries Fail and What Can Be Done About It* (2007). Shows that despite the world's advancing prosperity, more than a billion people have been left behind in abject poverty.

Davis, Deborah (ed.), *The Consumer Revolution in Urban China* (2000). A look at the different aspects of the recent, profound social transformation of urban China.

Davis, Mike, *City of Quartz: Excavating the Future in Los Angeles* (1990). Offers provocative reflections on the recent history, current condition, and possible future of Los Angeles.

Dutton, Michael, *Streetlife China* (1999). A fascinating portrayal of the survival tactics of those inhabiting the margins of society in modern China.

Eichengreen, Barry, *Globalizing Capital: A History of the International Monetary System* (1996). An insightful analysis of how international capital markets changed in the period from 1945 to 1980.

Ferguson, Niall and Moritz Schularick, "'Chimerica' and the Global Asset Market Boom," *International Finance* 10, no. 3 (Winter 2007): 215–39. Coined the term "Chimerica" to designate a single, intertwined economic entity made up of a productive partner, China, and a consuming partner, the United States.

Gourevitch, Philip, *We Wish to Inform You That Tomorrow We Will Be Killed with Our Families: Stories from Rwanda* (1999). A volume that reveals the hatreds that culminated in the Rwanda genocide.

Guillermoprieto, Alma, *Looking for History: Dispatches from Latin America* (2001). A collection of articles by the most important journalist reporting on Latin American affairs.

Han Minzhu (ed.), *Cries for Democracy: Writings and Speeches from the 1989 Chinese Democracy Movement* (1990). A collection of documents from the events leading up to the incident in Tiananmen Square on June 4, 1989.

Herbst, Jeffrey, *States and Power in Africa: Comparative Lessons in Authority and Control* (2000). Explores the political dilemmas facing modern African polities.

Honig, Emily, and Gail Hershatter, *Personal Voices: Chinese Women in the 1980's* (1988). A record of Chinese women during a period of rapid social change.

Huang, Yasheng, *Capitalism with Chinese Characteristics: Entrepreneurship and the State* (2008). A sharp, unsentimental inside look at China's market economy and its future prospects.

Klitgaard, Robert, *Tropical Gangsters* (1990). On the intimate connections between corrupt native elites and international aid agencies.

Kotkin, Stephen, *Armageddon Averted: The Soviet Collapse, 1970–2000* (2001). Places the surprise fall of the Soviet Union in the context of the great shifts in the post–World War II order.

Mamdani, Mahmood, *When Victims Become Killers: Colonialism, Nativism, and the Genocide in Rwanda* (2001). Discusses the genocide in Rwanda in light of the legacy of colonialism.

Mehta, Suketu, *Maximum City: Bombay Lost and Found* (2005). Examines one of the great, and contradictory, cities in the era of globalization.

Mottahedeh, Roy, *The Mantle of the Prophet: Religion and Politics in Iran*, 2nd ed. (2008). Perhaps the best book on the 1979 Iranian Revolution and its aftermath.

Nathan, Andrew, and Perry Link, *The Tiananmen Papers* (2002). An inside look at the divisions within the Chinese elite in connection with the 1989 crackdown.

Portes, Alejandro, and Rubén G. Rumbaut, *Immigrant America*, 2nd ed. (1996). A good comparative study of how immigration has transformed the United States.

Prakash, Gyan, *Mumbai Fables* (2010). A spirited account of the rise of India's most modern city, a center of intellectual, commercial, and political vitality.

Prunier, Gerald, *Africa's World War: Congo, the Rwandan Genocide, and the Making of a Continental Catastrophe* (2009). A chilling discussion of the spillover effects of the Rwandan genocide on central, eastern, and southern Africa.

Reinhart, Carmen, and Kenneth Rogoff, *This Time Is Different: Eight Centuries of Financial Folly* (2009). Explains the latest financial crash using historical perspective.

Sen, Amartya, *Poverty and Famines: An Essay on Entitlement and Deprivation* (1982). A major study that reoriented the study of famines from a narrow concentration on food supply to broader questions of ownership, exchange, and democracy.

Van Der Wee, Hermann, *Prosperity and Upheaval: The World Economy, 1945–1980* (1986). Describes very well the transformation and problems of the world economy, particularly from the 1960s onward.

Westad, Odd Arne, *The Global Cold War: Third World Interventions and the Making of our Times* (2007). A genuinely global perspective on the cold war and its consequences.

Winn, Peter, *Americas: The Changing Face of Latin America and the Caribbean* (1992). A useful portrayal of Latin America since the 1970s.

Glossary

Abd al-Rahman III Islamic ruler in Spain who held a countercaliphate and reigned from 912 to 961 CE.

aborigines Original, native inhabitants of a region, as opposed to invaders, colonizers, or later peoples of mixed ancestry.

absolute monarchy Form of government where one body, usually the monarch, controls the right to tax, judge, make war, and coin money. The term *enlightened absolutists* was often used to refer to state monarchies in seventeenth- and eighteenth-century Europe.

acid rain Precipitation containing large amounts of sulfur, mainly from coal-fired plants.

adaptation Ability to alter behavior and to innovate, finding new ways of doing things.

African National Congress (ANC) Multiracial organization founded in 1912 in an effort to end racial discrimination in South Africa.

Afrikaners Descendants of the original Dutch settlers of South Africa; formerly referred to as Boers.

Agones Athletic contests in ancient Greece.

Ahmosis Egyptian ruler in the southern part of the country who ruled from 1550 to 1525 BCE; Ahmosis used Hyksos weaponry—horse chariots in particular—to defeat the Hyksos themselves.

Ahura Mazda Supreme God of the Persians believed to have created the world and all that is good and to have appointed earthly kings.

AIDS (Acquired Immunodeficiency Syndrome) Virus that compromises the ability of the infected person's immune system to ward off disease. First detected in 1981, AIDS was initially stigmatized as a "gay cancer," but as it spread to heterosexuals, public awareness about it increased. In its first two decades, AIDS killed 12 million people.

Akbarnamah Mughal intellectual Abulfazl's *Book of Akbar,* which attempted to reconcile the traditional Sufi interest in the inner life within the worldly context of a great empire.

Alaric II Visigothic king who issued a simplified code of innovative imperial law.

Alexander the Great (356–323 BCE) Leader who used novel tactics and new kinds of armed forces to conquer the Persian Empire, which extended from Egypt and the Mediterranean Sea to the interior of what is now Afghanistan and as far as the Indus River valley. Alexander's conquests broke down barriers between the Mediterranean world and Southwest Asia and transferred massive amounts of wealth and power to the Mediterranean, transforming it into a more unified world of economic and cultural exchange.

Alexandria Port city in Egypt named after Alexander the Great. Alexandria was a model city in the Hellenistic world. It was built up by a multiethnic population from around the Mediterranean world.

Al-Khwarizmi Scientist and mathematician who lived from 780 to 850 CE and is known for having modified Indian digits into Arabic numerals.

Allied powers Name given to the alliance between Britain, France, Russia, and Italy, who fought against Germany and Austria-Hungary (the Central powers) in World War I. In World War II the name was used for the alliance between Britain, France, and America, who fought against the Axis powers (Germany, Italy, and Japan).

allomothering System by which mothers relied on other women, including their own mothers, daughters, sisters, and friends, to help in the nurturing and protecting of children.

alluvium Area of land created by river deposits.

alphabet A new system of writing using relatively few letters (22) developed by the Phoenicians in the mid–second millennium BCE.

American Railway Union Workers' union that initiated the Pullman Strike of 1894, which led to violence and ended in the leaders' arrest.

Amnesty International Non-governmental organization formed to defend "prisoners of conscience"—those detained for their beliefs, race, sex, ethnic origin, language, or religion.

Amorites Name that Mesopotamian urbanites called the transhumant herders from the Arabian desert. Around 2300 BCE, the Amorites, along with the Elamites, were at the center of newly formed dynasties in southern Mesopotamia.

Amun Once insignificant Egyptian god elevated to higher status by Amenemhet (1991–1962 BCE). *Amun* means "hidden" in Ancient Egyptian; the name was meant to convey the god's omnipresence.

Analects Texts that included the teachings and cultural ideals of Confucius.

anarchism Belief that society should be a free association of its members, not subject to government, laws, or police.

Anatolia Now mainly the area known as modern Turkey; in the sixth millennium BCE, people from Anatolia, Greece, and the Levant took to boats and populated the Aegean. Their small villages endured almost unchanged for two millennia.

Angkor Wat Magnificent Khmer Vaishnavite temple that crowned the royal palace in Angkor. It had statues representing the Hindu pantheon of gods.

Anglo-Boer War (1899–1902) Anticolonial struggle in South Africa between the British and the Afrikaners over the gold-rich Transvaal. In response to the Afrikaners' guerrilla tactics and in order to contain the local population, the British instituted the first concentration camps. Ultimately, Britain won the conflict.

animal domestication Gradual process that occurred simultaneously with or just before the domestication of plants, depending on the region.

annals Historical records. Notable annals are the cuneiform inscriptions that record successful Assyrian military campaigns.

Anti-Federalists Critics of the U.S. Constitution who sought to defend the people against the power of the federal government and insisted on a bill of rights to protect individual liberties from government intrusion.

apartheid Racial segregation policy of the Afrikaner-dominated South African government. Legislated in 1948 by the Afrikaner National Party, it had existed in South Africa for many years.

Arab-Israeli War of 1948–1949 Conflict between Israeli and Arab armies that arose in the wake of a U.N. vote to partition Palestine into Arab and Jewish territories. The war shattered the legitimacy of Arab ruling elites.

Aramaic Dialect of a Semitic language spoken in Southwest Asia; it became the lingua franca of the Persian Empire.

Aristotle (384–322 BCE) Philosopher who studied under Plato but came to different conclusions about nature and politics. Aristotle believed in collecting observations about nature and discerning patterns to ascertain how things worked.

Aryans Nomadic charioteers who spoke Indo-European languages and entered South Asia in 1500 BCE. The early Aryan settlers were herders.

Asante state State located in present-day Ghana, founded by the Asantes at the end of the seventeenth century. It grew in power in the next century because of its access to gold and its involvement in the slave trade.

ascetic One who rejects material possessions and physical pleasures.

Asiatic Society Cultural organization founded by British Orientalists who supported native culture but still believed in colonial rule.

Aśoka Emperor of the Mauryan dynasty from 268 to 231 BCE; he was a great conqueror and unifier of India. He is said to have embraced Buddhism toward the end of his life.

Assur One of two cities on the upper reaches of the Tigris River that were the heart of Assyria proper (the other was Nineveh).

Aśvaghosa First known Sanskrit writer. He may have lived from 80 to 150 CE and may have composed a biography of the Buddha.

Ataturk, Mustafa Kemal (1881–1938) Ottoman army officer and military hero who helped forge the modern Turkish nation-state. He and his followers deposed the sultan, declared Turkey a republic, and constructed a European-like secular state, eliminating Islam's hold over civil and political affairs.

Atlantic system New system of trade and expansion that linked Europe, Africa, and the Americas. It emerged in the wake of European voyages across the Atlantic Ocean.

Atma Vedic term signifying the eternal self, represented by the trinity of deities.

Atman In the Upanishads, an eternal being who exists everywhere. The atman never perishes but is reborn or transmigrates into another life.

Attila Sole ruler of all Hunnish tribes from 433 to 453 CE. Harsh and much feared, he formed the first empire to oppose Rome in northern Europe.

Augustus Title meaning "Revered One," assumed in 27 BCE by the Roman ruler Octavian (63–14 BCE). This was one of many titles he assumed; others included *imperator*, *princeps*, and *Caesar*.

australopithecines Hominid species that appeared 3 million years ago and, unlike other animals, walked on two legs. Their brain capacity was a little less than one-third of a modern human's or about the size of the brain capacity of today's African apes. Although not humans, they carried the genetic and biological material out of which modern humans would later emerge.

Austro-Hungarian Empire Dual monarchy established by the Habsburg family in 1867; it collapsed at the end of World War I.

authoritarianism Centralized and dictatorial form of government, proclaimed by its adherents to be superior to parliamentary democracy and especially effective at mobilizing the masses. This idea was widely accepted in parts of the world during the 1930s.

Avesta Compilation of holy works transmitted orally by priests for millennia and eventually recorded in the sixth century BCE.

axial age Term often used to describe the pivotal period of the first millennium BCE when radical thinkers across the "second-generation societies" of connected Eurasia—including the Greek philosophers of the Mediterranean, Zoroaster in Southwest Asia, Buddha in South Asia, and Confucius and Master Lao in East Asia—offered dramatically new ideas that challenged their times.

Axis powers The three aggressor states in World War II: Germany, Japan, and Italy.

Aztec Empire Mesoamerican empire that originated with a league of three Mexica cities in 1430 and gradually expanded through the Central Valley of Mexico, uniting numerous small, independent states under a single monarch who ruled with the help of counselors, military leaders, and priests. By the late fifteenth century, the Aztec realm may have embraced 25 million people. In 1521, they were defeated by the conquistador Hernán Cortés.

baby boom Post–World War II upswing in U.S. birth rates; it reversed a century of decline.

bactrian camel Two-humped animal domesticated in central Asia around 2500 BCE. The bactrian camel was heartier than the one-humped dromedary and became the animal of choice for the harsh and varied climates typical of Silk Road trade.

Bactria A Hellenistic kingdom that broke away from the Seleucids around 200 BCE to establish a state in the Gandhara region modern Pakistan, which served as a bridge between South Asia and the Mediterranean Greek world.

Baghdad Capital of the Islamic Empire under the Abbasid dynasty, founded in 762 CE (in modern-day Iraq). In the medieval period, it was a center of administration, scholarship, and cultural growth for what came to be known as the Golden Age of Islamic science.

Baghdad Pact (1955) Middle Eastern military alliance between countries friendly with America who were also willing to align themselves with the western countries against the Soviet Union.

Balam Na Stone temple and place of pilgrimage for the Mayan people of Mexico's Yucatan peninsula.

Balfour Declaration Letter (November 2, 1917) by Lord Arthur J. Balfour, British foreign secretary, that promised a homeland for the Jews in Palestine.

Bamboo Annals Shang stories and foundation myths that were written on bamboo strips and later collected.

Bantu Language first spoken by people who lived in the southeastern area of modern Nigeria around 1000 CE.

Bantu migrations Waves of rapid population movement from West Africa into eastern and southern Africa during the first millennium CE that brought advanced agricultural practices to these regions and absorbed most of the preexisting hunting-and-gathering populations.

barbarian Derogatory term used to describe pastoral nomads, painting them as enemies of civilization; the term *barbarian* used to have a more neutral meaning than it does today.

barbarian invasions Violent migration of people in the late fourth and fifth centuries into Roman territory. These migrants had long been used as non-Roman soldiers.

basilicas Early church buildings, based on old royal audience halls.

Battle of Adwa (1896) Battle in which the Ethiopians defeated Italian colonial forces; it inspired many of Africa's later national leaders.

Battle of Wounded Knee (1890) Bloody massacre of Sioux Ghost Dancers by U.S. armed forces.

Bay of Pigs (1961) Unsuccessful invasion of Cuba by Cuban exiles supported by the U.S. government. The invaders intended to incite an insurrection in Cuba and overthrow the communist regime of Fidel Castro.

Bedouins Nomadic pastoralists in the deserts of the Middle East.

Beer Hall Putsch (1923) Nazi intrusion into a meeting of Bavarian leaders in a Munich beer hall; the Nazis were attempting to force support for their cause; Adolf Hitler was imprisoned for a year after the incident.

Beghards (1500s) Eccentric European group whose members claimed to be in a state of grace that allowed them to do as they pleased—from adultery, free love, and nudity to murder; also called Brethren of Free Speech.

bell beaker Ancient drinking vessel, an artifact from Europe, so named because its shape resembles an inverted bell.

Berenice of Egypt Egyptian "queen" who helped rule over the Kingdom of the Nile from 320 to 280 BCE.

Beringia Prehistoric thousand-mile-long land bridge that linked Siberia and North America (which had not been populated by hominids). About 18,000 years ago, *Homo sapiens* edged into this landmass.

Berlin Airlift (1948) Supply of vital necessities to West Berlin by air transport primarily under U.S. auspices. It was initiated in response to a land and water blockade of the city instituted by the Soviet Union in the hope that the Allies would be forced to abandon West Berlin.

Berlin Wall Wall built by the communists in Berlin in 1961 to prevent citizens of East Germany from fleeing to West Germany; torn down in 1989.

Bhakti Religious practice that grew out of Hinduism and emphasizes personal devotion to gods.

bhakti Hinduism Popular form of Hinduism that emerged in the seventh century. The religion stresses devotion (*bhakti*) to God and uses vernacular languages (not Sanskrit) spoken by the common people.

big men Leaders of the extended household communities that formed village settlements in African rain forests.

big whites French plantation owners in Saint-Domingue (present-day Haiti) who created one of the wealthiest slave societies.

Bilad al-Sudan Arabic for "the land of the blacks"; it consisted of the land lying south of the Sahara.

bilharzia Debilitating water-borne illness. It was widespread in Egypt, where it infected peasants who worked in the irrigation canals.

Bill of Rights First ten amendments to the U.S. Constitution; ratified in 1791.

bipedalism Walking on two legs, thereby freeing hands and arms to carry objects such as weapons and tools; one of several traits that distinguished hominids.

Black Death Great epidemic of the bubonic plague that ravaged Europe, East Asia, and North Africa in the fourteenth century, killing large numbers, including perhaps as many as one-third of the European population.

Black Jacobins Nickname for the rebels in Saint-Domingue, including Toussaint L'Ouverture, a former slave who led the slaves of this French colony in the world's largest and most successful slave insurrection.

Black Panthers Radical African American group in the 1960s and 1970s; they advocated black separatism and pan-Africanism.

black shirts Fascist troops of Mussolini's regime; the squads received money from Italian landowners to attack socialist leaders.

Black Tuesday (October 29, 1929) Historic day when the U.S. stock market crashed, plunging the United States and international trading systems into crisis and leading the world into the "Great Depression."

blitzkrieg "Lightning war"; type of warfare in which the Germans, during World War II, used coordinated aerial bombing campaigns along with tanks and infantrymen in motorized vehicles.

Bodhisattvas In Mahayana Buddhism, enlightened demigods who were ready to reach *nirvana* but delayed so that they might help others attain it.

Bolívar, Simón (1783–1830) Venezuelan leader who urged his followers to become "American," to overcome their local identities. He wanted the liberated countries to form a Latin American confederation, urging Peru and Bolivia to join Venezuela, Ecuador, and Colombia in the "Gran Colombia."

Bolsheviks Former members of the Russian Social Democratic Party who advocated the destruction of capitalist political and economic institutions and started the Russian Revolution. In 1918 the Bolsheviks changed their name to the Russian Communist Party.

Book of the Dead Ancient Egyptian funerary text that contains drawings and paintings as well as spells describing how to prepare the jewelry and amulets that were buried with a person in preparation for the afterlife.

bourgeoisie The middle class. In Europe, they sought to be recognized not by birth or title, but by capital and property.

Boxer Protocol Written agreement between the victors of the Boxer Uprising and the Qing Empire in 1901 that placed western troops in Beijing and required the regime to pay exorbitant damages for foreign life and property.

Boxer Uprising (1899–1900) Chinese peasant movement that opposed foreign influence, especially that of Christian missionaries; it was put down after the Boxers were defeated by an army composed mostly of Japanese, Russians, British, French, and Americans.

Brahma One of three major deities that form a trinity in Vedic religion. Brahma signifies birth. *See also* Vishnu *and* Siva.

Brahmans Vedic priests who performed rituals and communicated with the gods. Brahmans provided guidance on how to live in balance with the forces of nature as represented by the various deities. The codification of Vedic principles into codes of law took place at the hands of the Brahmans. They memorized Vedic works and compiled commentaries on them. They also developed their own set of rules and rituals, which developed into a full-scale theology. Originally memorized and passed on orally, these may have been written down sometime after the beginning of the Common Era. Brahmanism was reborn as Hinduism sometime during the first half of the first millennium CE.

British Commonwealth of Nations Union formed in 1926 that conferred "dominion status" on Britain's white settler colonies in Canada, Australia, and New Zealand.

British East India Company *See* East India Company.

bronze Alloy of copper and tin brought into Europe from Anatolia; used to make hard-edged weapons.

brown shirts Troops of German men who advanced the Nazi cause by holding street marches, mass rallies, and confrontations and by beating Jews and anyone who opposed the Nazis.

bubonic plague Acute infectious disease caused by a bacterium that is transmitted to humans by fleas from infected rats. It ravaged Europe and parts of Asia in the fourteenth century. Sometimes referred to as the "Black Death."

Buddha (Siddhartha Gautama; 563–483 BCE) Indian ascetic who founded Buddhism.

Buddhism Major South Asian religion that aims to end human suffering through the renunciation of desire. Buddhists believe that removing the illusion of a separate identity would lead to a state of contentment (*nirvana*). These beliefs challenged the traditional Brahmanic teachings of the time and provided the peoples of South Asia with an alternative to established traditions.

bullion Uncoined gold or silver.

Byzantium Modern term for the eastern Roman Empire (lasting from the fourth to the fifteenth century), centered at its "new Rome," Constantinople (founded by emperor Constantine in 324 on the site of a Greek city, Byzantium).

Cahokia Commercial center for regional and long-distance trade in North America. Its hinterlands produced staples for urban consumers. In return, its crafts were exported inland by porters and to North American markets in canoes. *See also* Mound people.

calaveras Allegorical skeleton drawings by the Mexican printmaker and artist José Guadalupe Posada. The works drew on popular themes of betrayal, death, and festivity.

caliphate Institution that arose as the successor to Muhammad's leadership and became both the political and religious head of the Islamic community. Although the caliphs exercised political authority over the Muslim community and were the head of the religious community, the *ummah,* they did not inherit Muhammad's prophetic powers and were not authorities in religious doctrine.

Calvin, Jean (1509–1564) A French theologian during the Protestant Reformation. Calvin developed a Christianity that emphasized moral regeneration through church teachings and laid out a doctrine of predestination.

Candomblé Yoruba-based religion in northern Brazil; it interwove African practices and beliefs with Christianity.

canton system System officially established by imperial decree in 1759 that required European traders to have Chinese guild merchants act as guarantors for their good behavior and payment of fees.

caravan cities Set of networks at long-distance trade locations where groups of merchants could assemble during their journeys. Several of these developed into full-fledged cities, especially in the deserts of Arabia.

caravans Companies of men who transported and traded goods along overland routes in North Africa and central Asia; large caravans consisted of 600–1,000 camels and as many as 400 men.

caravansarais Inns along major trade routes that accommodated large numbers of traders, their animals, and their wares.

caravel Sailing vessel suited for nosing in and out of estuaries and navigating in waters with unpredictable currents and winds.

carrack Ship used on open bodies of water, such as the Mediterranean.

Carthage City in what is modern-day Tunisia; emblematic of the trading aspirations and activities of merchants in the Mediterranean. Pottery and other archaeological remains demonstrate that trading contacts with Carthage were as far-flung as Italy, Greece, France, Iberia, and West Africa.

cartography Mapmaking.

caste system Hierarchical system of organizing people and distributing labor.

Caste War of Yucatan (1847–1901) Conflict between Mayan Indians and the Mexican state over Indian autonomy and legal equality, which resulted in the Mexican takeover of the Yucatan peninsula.

Castro, Fidel (1926–) Cuban communist leader whose forces overthrew Batista's corrupt regime in early January 1959. Castro became increasingly radical as he consolidated power, announcing a massive redistribution of land and the nationalization of foreign oil refineries; he declared himself a socialist and aligned himself with the Soviet Union in the wake of the 1961 CIA-backed Bay of Pigs invasion.

Çatal Hüyük Site in Anatolia discovered in 1958. It was a dense honeycomb of settlements filled with rooms whose walls were covered with paintings of wild bulls, hunters, and pregnant women. Çatal Hüyük symbolizes an early transition into urban dwelling and dates to the eighth millennium BCE.

cathedra Bishop's seat, or throne, in a church.

Catholic Church Unifying institution for Christians in western Europe after the collapse of the Roman Empire. Rome became the spiritual capital of western Europe and the bishops of Rome emerged as popes, the supreme head of the church, who possessed great moral authority.

Cato the Elder (234–149 BCE) Roman statesman, often seen as emblematic of the transition from a Greek to a Roman world. Cato the Elder wrote a manual for the new economy of slave plantation agriculture, invested in shipping and trading, learned Greek rhetoric, and added the genre of history to Latin literature.

caudillos South American local military chieftains.

cave drawings Images on cave walls. The subjects are most often large game, although a few are images of humans. Other elements are impressions made by hands dipped in paint and pressed on a wall or abstract symbols and shapes.

Celali revolts (1595–1610) Peasant and artisan uprisings against the Ottoman state.

Central powers Defined in World War I as Germany and Austria-Hungary.

Chan Chan City founded between 850 and 900 CE by the Moche people in what is now modern-day Peru. It had a core population of 30,000 inhabitants.

Chan Santa Cruz Separate Mayan community formed as part of a crusade for spiritual salvation and the complete cultural separation of the Mayan Indians; means "little holy cross."

Chandra Gupta II King who reigned in South Asia from 320 to 335 CE. He shared his name with Chandragupta, the founder of the Mauryan Empire.

Chandravamsha One of two main lineages (the lunar one) of Vedic society, each with its own creation myth, ancestors, language, and rituals. Each lineage included many clans. *See* Suryavamsha.

chapatis Flat, unleavened Indian bread.

chariots Horse-driven carriages brought by the pastoral nomadic warriors from the steppes that became the favored mode of transportation for an urban aristocratic warrior class and for other men of power in agriculture-based societies. Control of chariot forces was the foundation of the new balance of power across Afro-Eurasia during the second millennium BCE.

charismatic Person who uses personal strengths or virtues, often laced with a divine aura, to command followers.

Charlemagne Emperor of the West and heir to Rome from 764 to 814 CE.

chartered companies Firms that were awarded monopoly trading rights over vast areas by European monarchs (e.g., Virginia Company, Dutch East India Company).

Chartism (1834–1848) Mass democratic movement to pass the Peoples' Charter in Britain, granting male suffrage, secret ballot, equal electoral districts, and annual parliaments, and absolving the requirement of property ownership for members of the parliament.

chattel slavery Form of slavery that sold people as property, the rise of which coincided with the expansion of city-states. Chattel slavery was eschewed by the Spartans, who also rejected the innovation of coin money.

Chavín A people who lived in what is now northern Peru from 1400 to 200 BCE. They were united more by culture and faith than by a unified political system.

Chernobyl (1986) Site in the Soviet Union (in Ukraine) of the meltdown of a nuclear reactor.

Chiang Kai-shek (1887–1975) Leader of the Guomindang following Sun Yat-sen's death who mobilized the Chinese masses through the New Life movement. In 1949 he lost the Chinese Revolution to the communists and moved his regime to Taiwan.

Chimu Empire South America's first empire; it developed during the first century of the second millennium in the Moche Valley on the Pacific coast.

chinampas Floating gardens used by Aztecs in the 1300s and 1400s to grow crops.

China's Sorrow Name for the Yellow River, which, when it changed course or flooded, could cause mass death and waves of migration.

chinoiserie Chinese silks, teas, tableware, jewelry, and paper; popular among Europeans in the seventeenth and eighteenth centuries.

Christendom Entire portion of the world in which Christianity prevailed.

Christianity Religion that originated at the height of the Roman Empire and in a direct confrontation with Roman imperial authority: the trial of Yeshua ben Yosef (Joshua son of Joseph; we know him today by the Greek form of his name, Jesus). Jesus was condemned for sedition and crucified. His followers believed that he was resurrected and that his teachings were not that of a man, but a god who had walked among human beings. At first, the Roman Empire refused to recognize Christianity and persecuted its followers, but in the fourth century CE Christianity was officially recognized as the Roman state religion.

Church of England Established form of Christianity in England dating from the sixteenth century.

city Highly populated concentration of economic, religious, and political power. The first cities appeared in river basins, which could produce a surplus of agriculture. The abundance of food freed most city inhabitants from the need to produce their own food, which allowed them to work in specialized professions.

city-state Political organization based on the authority of a single, large city that controls outlying territories.

Civil Rights Act (1964) U.S. legislation that banned segregation in public facilities, outlawed racial discrimination in employment, and marked an important step in correcting legal inequality.

civil rights movement Powerful movement for equal rights and the end of racial segregation in the United States that began in the 1950s with court victories against school segregation and nonviolent boycotts.

civil service examinations The world's first written civil service examination system, instituted by the Tang dynasty to recruit officials and bureaucrats. Open to most males, the exams tested a candidate's literary skills and knowledge of the Confucian classics. They helped to unite the Chinese state by making knowledge of a specific language and Confucian classics the only route to power.

Civil War, American (1861–1865) Conflict between the northern and southern states of America; this struggle led to the abolition of slavery in the United States.

clan A social group comprising many households, claiming descent from a common ancestor.

clandestine presses Small printing operations that published banned texts in the early modern era, especially in Switzerland and the Netherlands.

Clovis people Early humans in America who used basic chipped blades and pointed spears in pursuing prey. They extended the hunting traditions they had learned in Afro-Eurasia, such as establishing campsites and moving with their herds. They were known as "Clovis people" because the arrowhead point that they used was first found by archaeologists at a site near Clovis, New Mexico.

Code of Manu Part of the handiwork of Brahman priests; a representative code of law that incorporated social sanctions and practices and provided guidance for living within the caste system.

codex Early form of book, with separate pages bound together; it replaced the scroll as the main medium for written texts. The codex emerged around 300 CE.

cognitive skills Skills such as thought, memory, problem-solving, and—ultimately—language. Hominids were able to use these skills and their hands to create new adaptations, like tools, which helped them obtain food and avoid predators.

Cohong Chinese merchant guild that traded with Europeans under the Qing dynasty.

coins Form of money that replaced goods, which previously had been bartered for services and other products. Originally used mainly to hire mercenary soldiers, coins became the commonplace method of payment linking buyers and producers throughout the Mediterranean.

cold war (1945–1990) Ideological conflict in which the Soviet Union and eastern Europe opposed the United States and western Europe.

colonies Regions under the political control of another country.

colons French settler population in Algeria.

colosseum Huge amphitheater completed by Titus and dedicated in 80 CE. Originally begun by Flavian, the structure is named after a colossal statue of Nero that formerly stood beside it.

Columbian exchange Movements between Afro-Eurasia and the Americas of previously unknown plants, animals, people, diseases, and products that followed in the wake of Columbus's voyages.

commanderies Provinces. Shi Huangdi (First August Emperor) divided China into commanderies (*jun*) to enable the Qin dynasty to rule the massive state effectively. The thirty-six commanderies were then subdivided into counties (*xian*).

Communist Manifesto Pamphlet published by Karl Marx and Friedrich Engels in 1848 at a time when political revolutions were sweeping Europe. It called on the workers of all nations to unite in overthrowing capitalism.

Compromise of 1867 Agreement between the Habsburgs and the peoples living in Hungarian parts of the empire that the Habsburg state would be officially known as the Austro-Hungarian Empire.

concession areas Territories, usually ports, where Chinese emperors allowed European merchants to trade and European people to settle.

Confucian ideals The ideals of honoring tradition, emphasizing the responsibility of the emperor, and respect for the lessons of history, promoted by Confucius, which the Han dynasty made the official doctrine of the empire by 50 BCE.

Confucianism Ethics, beliefs, and practices stipulated by the Chinese philosopher Kong Qiu, or Confucius, which served as a guide for Chinese society up to modern times.

Confucius (551–479 BCE) Influential teacher, thinker, and leader in China who developed a set of principles for ethical living. He believed that coercive laws and punishment would not be needed to maintain order in society if men following his ethics ruled. He taught his philosophy to anyone who was intelligent and willing to work, which allowed men to gain entry into the ruling class through education.

cong tube Ritual object crafted by the Liangzhu. A cong tube was made of jade and was used in divination practices.

Congo Independent State Large colonial state in Africa created by Leopold II, king of Belgium, during the 1880s, and ruled by him alone. After rumors of mass slaughter and enslavement, the Belgian parliament took the land and formed a Belgian colony.

Congress of Vienna (1814–1815) International conference to reorganize Europe after the downfall of Napoleon. European monarchies agreed to respect each other's borders and to cooperate in guarding against future revolutions and war.

conquistadors Spanish military leaders who led the conquest of the New World in the sixteenth century.

Constantine Roman emperor who converted to Christianity in 312 CE. In 313, he issued a proclamation that gave Christians new freedoms in the empire. He also founded Constantinople (at first called "New Rome").

Constantinople Capital city, formerly known as Byzantium, which was founded as the New Rome by Constantine the Great.

Constitutional Convention (1787) Meeting to formulate the Constitution of the United States of America.

Contra rebels Opponents of the Sandinistas in Nicaragua; they were armed and financed by the United States and other anticommunist countries (1980).

Conversion of Constantine A significant political and religious turning point in the Roman Empire. Before the decisive battle for Rome in 312 CE, Constantine supposedly had a dream in which he was told to place a sign with the opening letters of Christ's name on his soldiers' shields. Constantine won the ensuing battle; he soon issued a proclamation giving privileges to Christian bishops. The edict spread Christianity through the institutions and across the byways of the Roman Empire.

conversos Jewish and Muslim converts to Christianity in the Iberian Peninsula and the New World.

Coptic Form of Christianity practiced in Egypt. It was doctrinally different from Christianity elsewhere, and Coptic Christians had their own views of Christology, or the nature of Christ.

Corn Laws Laws that imposed tariffs on grain imported to Great Britain, intended to protect British farming interests. The Corn Laws were abolished in 1846 as part of a British movement in favor of free trade.

cosmology Branch of metaphysics devoted to understanding the order of the universe.

cosmopolitans A development referring to the inhabitants of the multiethnic cities that thrived in the Hellenistic world; literally meaning "citizens belonging to the whole world," as opposed to a particular city-state.

Council of Nicaea Church council convened in 325 CE by Constantine and presided over by him as well. At this council, a Christian creed was articulated and made into a formula that expressed the philosophical and technical elements of Christian belief.

Counter-Reformation Movement to counter the spread of the Reformation; initiated by the Catholic Church at the Council of Trent in 1545. The Catholic Church enacted reforms to attack clerical corruption and it placed a greater emphasis on individual spirituality. During this time, the Jesuits were founded to help revive the Catholic Church.

coup d'état Overthrow of established state by a group of conspirators, usually from the military.

creation narratives Narratives constructed by different cultures that draw on their belief systems and available evidence to explain the origins of the world and humanity.

creed Formal statement of faith or expression of a belief system. A Christian creed or "credo" was formulated by the Council of Nicaea in 325 CE.

creoles Persons of full-blooded European descent who were born in the Spanish American colonies.

Crimean War (1853–1856) War waged by Russia against Great Britain and France. Spurred by Russia's encroachment on Ottoman territories, the conflict revealed Russia's military weakness when Russian forces fell to British and French troops.

crossbow Innovative weapon used at the end of the Warring States period that allowed archers to shoot their enemies with accuracy, even from a distance.

Crusades Wave of attacks launched in the late eleventh century by western Europeans. The First Crusade began in 1095, when Pope Urban II appealed to the warrior nobility of France to free Jerusalem from Muslim rule. Four subsequent Crusades were fought over the next two centuries.

Cuban Missile Crisis (1962) Diplomatic standoff between the United States and the Soviet Union that was provoked by the Soviet Union's attempt to base nuclear missiles in Cuba; it brought the world close to a nuclear war.

cult Religious movement, often based on the worship of a particular god or goddess.

cultigen Organism that has diverged from its ancestors through domestication or cultivation.

cuneiform Wedge-shaped form of writing. As people combined rebus symbols with other visual marks that contained meaning, they became able to record and transmit messages over long distances by using abstract symbols or signs to denote concepts; such signs later came to represent syllables, which could be joined into words. By impressing these signs into wet clay with the cut end of a reed, scribes engaged in cuneiform.

Cyrus the Great Founder of the Persian Empire. This sixth-century ruler (559–529 BCE) conquered the Medes and unified the Iranian kingdoms.

Daimyo Ruling lords who commanded private armies in pre-Meiji Japan.

dan Fodio, Usman (1754–1817) Fulani Muslim cleric whose visions led him to challenge the Hausa ruling classes, whom he believed were insufficiently faithful to Islamic beliefs and practices. His ideas gained support among those who had suffered under the Hausa landlords. In 1804, his supporters and allies overthrew the Hausa in what is today northern Nigeria.

Daoism School of thought developed at the end of the Warring States period that focused on the importance of following the Dao, or the natural way of the cosmos. Daoism emphasized the need to accept the world as it was rather than trying to change it through politics or the government. Unlike Confucianism, Daoism scorned rigid rituals and social hierarchies.

Dar al-Islam Arabic for "the House of Islam"; it describes a sense of common identity.

Darius I (521–486 BCE) Leader who put the emerging unified Persian Empire onto solid footing after Cyrus's death.

Darwin, Charles (1809–1882) British scientist who became convinced that the species of organic life had evolved under the uniform pressure of natural laws, not by means of a special, one-time creation as described in the Bible.

D-Day (June 6, 1944) Day of the Allied invasion of Normandy under General Dwight Eisenhower to liberate western Europe from German occupation.

Dear Boy Nickname of an early human remain discovered in 1931 by a team of archaeologists named the Leakeys. They discovered an almost totally intact skull. Other objects discovered with Dear Boy demonstrated that by the time of Dear Boy, early humans had begun to fashion tools and to use them for butchering animals and possibly for hunting and killing smaller animals.

Decembrists Russian army officers who were influenced by events in revolutionary France and formed secret societies that espoused liberal governance. They were put down by Nicholas I in December 1825.

Declaration of Independence U.S. document stating the theory of government on which America was founded.

Declaration of the Rights of Man and Citizen (1789) French charter of liberties formulated by the National Assembly that marked the end of dynastic and aristocratic rule. The seventeen articles later became the preamble to the new constitution, which the assembly finished in 1791.

decolonization End of empire and emergence of new independent nation-states in Asia and Africa as a result of the defeat of Japan in World War II and weakened European influence after the war.

Delhi Sultanate (1206–1526) Turkish regime of northern India. The regime strengthened the cultural diversity and tolerance that were a hallmark of the Indian social order, which allowed it to bring about political integration without enforcing cultural homogeneity.

democracy The idea that people, through membership in a nation, should choose their own representatives and be governed by them.

Democritus Thinker in ancient Greece who lived from 470 to 360 BCE; he deduced the existence of the atom and postulated that there was such a thing as an indivisible particle.

demotic writing The second of two basic forms of ancient Egyptian writing. Demotic was a cursive script written with ink on papyrus, on pottery, or on other absorbent objects. It was the most common and practical form of writing in Egypt and was used for administrative record keeping and in private or pseudo-private forms like letters and works of literature. *See also* Hieroglyphs.

developing world Term applied to countries collectively called the Third World during the cold war and seeking to develop viable nation-states and prosperous economies.

Devshirme System of taking non-Muslim children in place of taxes in order to educate them in Ottoman Muslim ways and prepare them for service in the sultan's bureaucracy.

Dhamma Moral code espoused by Aśoka in the Kalinga edict, which was meant to apply to all—Buddhists, Brahmans, and Greeks alike.

***Dhimma* system** Ottoman law that permitted followers of religions other than Islam, such as Armenian Christians, Greek Orthodox Christians, and Jews, to choose their own religious leaders and to settle internal disputes within their religious communities as long as they accepted Islam's political dominion.

dhows Ships used by Arab seafarers; the dhow's large sails were rigged to maximize the capture of wind.

Dien Bien Phu (1954) Defining battle in the war between French colonialists and the Viet Minh that secured North Vietnam for Ho Chi Minh and his army and left the south to form its own government to be supported by France and the United States.

Din-I-llahi "House of worship" in which the Mughal emperor Akbar engaged in religious debate with Hindu, Muslim, Jain, Parsi, and Christian theologians.

Diogenes Greek philosopher who lived from 412 to 323 BCE and who espoused a doctrine of self-sufficiency and freedom from social laws and customs. He rejected cultural norms as out of tune with nature and therefore false.

Directory Temporary military committee that took over the affairs of the state of France in 1795 from the radicals and held control until the coup of Napoleon Bonaparte.

divination The interpretation of rituals used to communicate the wishes of gods or royal ancestors to foretell future events. Divination was used to legitimize royal authority and demand tribute.

Djoser Ancient Egyptian king who reigned from 2630 to 2611 BCE. He was the second king of the Third Dynasty and celebrated the Sed festival in his tomb complex at Saqqara.

domestication Bringing a wild animal or plant under human control.

Dominion in the British Commonwealth Canadian promise to keep up the country's fealty to the British crown, even after its independence in 1867. Later applied to Australia and New Zealand.

Dong Zhongshu Emperor Wu's chief minister, who advocated a more powerful view of Confucius by promoting texts that focused on Confucius as a man who possessed aspects of divinity.

double-outrigger canoes Vessels used by early Austronesians to cross the Taiwan Straits and colonize islands in the Pacific. These sturdy canoes could cover over 120 miles per day.

Duma Russian parliament.

Dutch learning Broad term for European teachings that were strictly regulated by the shoguns inside Japan.

dynastic cycle Political narrative in which influential families vied for supremacy. Upon gaining power, they legitimated their authority by claiming to be the heirs of previous grand dynasts and by preserving or revitalizing the ancestors' virtuous governing ways. This continuity conferred divine support.

dynasty Hereditary ruling family that passed control from one generation to the next.

Earth Summit (1992) Meeting in Rio de Janeiro between many of the world's governments in an effort to address international environmental problems.

East India Company (1600–1858) British charter company created to outperform Portuguese and Spanish traders in the Far East; in the eighteenth century the company became, in effect, the ruler of a large part of India.

Eastern Front Battlefront between Berlin and Moscow during World War I and World War II.

Edict of Nantes (1598) Edict issued by Henry IV to end the French Wars of Religion. The edict declared France a Catholic country but tolerated some Protestant worship.

Egyptian Middle Kingdom Period of Egyptian history lasting from about 2040 to 1640 BCE, characterized by a consolidation of power and building activity in Upper Egypt.

Eiffel Tower Steel monument completed in 1889 for the Paris Exposition. It was twice the height of any other building at the time.

eight-legged essay Highly structured essay form with eight parts, required on Chinese civil service examinations.

Ekklesia Church or early gathering committed to leaders chosen by God and fellow believers.

Ekpe Powerful slave trade institution that organized the supply and purchase of slaves inland from the Gulf of Guinea in West Africa.

Elamites A people with their capital in the upland valley of modern Fars who became a cohesive polity that incorporated transhumant people of the Zagros Mountains. A group of Elamites who migrated south and west into Mesopotamia helped conquer the Third Dynasty of Ur in 2400 BCE.

empire Group of states or different ethnic groups under a single sovereign power.

Enabling Act (1933) Emergency act passed by the Reichstag (German parliament) that helped transform Hitler from Germany's chancellor, or prime minister, into a dictator following the suspicious burning of the Reichstag building and a suspension of civil liberties.

enclosure A movement in which landowners took control of lands that traditionally had been common property serving local needs.

encomenderos Commanders of the labor services of the colonized peoples in Spanish America.

encomiendas Grants from European Spanish governors to control the labor services of colonized people.

Endeavor Ship of Captain James Cook, whose celebrated voyages to the South Pacific in the late eighteenth century supplied Europe with information about the plants, birds, landscapes, and people of this uncharted territory.

Engels, Friedrich (1820–1895) German social and political philosopher who collaborated with Karl Marx on many publications, including *The Communist Manifesto*.

English Navigation Act of 1651 Act stipulating that only English ships could carry goods between the mother country and its colonies.

English Peasants' Revolt (1381) Uprising of serfs and free farm workers that began as a protest against a tax levied to raise money for a war on France. The revolt was suppressed but led to the gradual emergence of a free peasantry as labor shortages made it impossible to keep peasants bound to the soil.

enlightened absolutists Seventeenth- and eighteenth-century monarchs who claimed to rule rationally and in the best interests of their subjects and who hired loyal bureaucrats to implement the knowledge of the new age.

Enlightenment Intellectual movement in eighteenth-century Europe stressing natural laws and reason as the basis of authority.

entrepôts Trading stations at the borders between communities, which made exchange possible among many different partners. Long-distance traders could also replenish their supplies at these stations.

Epicurus Greek philosopher who espoused emphasis on the self. He lived from 341 to 279 BCE and founded a school in Athens called The Garden. He stressed the importance of sensation, teaching that pleasurable sensations were good and painful sensations bad. Members of his school sought to find peace and relaxation by avoiding unpleasantness or suffering.

Estates-General French quasi-parliamentary body called in 1789 to deal with the financial problems that afflicted France. It had not met since 1614.

Etruscans A dominant people on the Italian peninsula until the fourth century BCE. The Etruscan states were part of the foundation of the Roman Empire.

eunuchs Loyal and well-paid men who were surgically castrated as youths and remained in service to the caliph or emperor. Both Abbasid and Tang rulers relied for protection on a cadre of eunuchs.

Eurasia The combined area of Europe and Asia.

European Union (EU) International body organized after World War II as an attempt at reconciliation between Germany and the rest of Europe. It initially aimed to forge closer industrial cooperation. Eventually, through various treaties, many European states relinquished some of their sovereignty, and the cooperation became a full-fledged union with a single currency, the euro, and with a somewhat less powerful common European parliament.

evolution Process by which the different species of the world—its plants and animals—make changes in response to their environment that enable them to survive and increase in numbers.

Exclusion Act of 1882 U.S. congressional act prohibiting nearly all immigration from China to the United States; fueled by animosity toward Chinese workers in the American West.

Ezo Present-day Hokkaido, Japan's fourth main island.

Fascism Mass political movement founded by Benito Mussolini that emphasized nationalism, militarism, and the omnipotence of the state.

Fascists Radical right-wing group of disaffected veterans that formed around Mussolini in 1919 and a few years later came to power in Rome.

Fatehpur Sikri Mughal emperor Akbar's temporary capital near Agra.

Fatimids Shiite dynasty that ruled parts of the Islamic Empire beginning in the tenth century CE. They were based in Egypt and founded the city of Cairo.

February Revolution (1917) The first of two uprisings of the Russian Revolution, which led to the end of the Romanov dynasty.

Federal Deposit Insurance Corporation (FDIC) Organization created in 1933 to guarantee all bank deposits up to $5,000 as part of the New Deal in the United States.

Federal Republic of Germany (1949–1990) Country formed of the areas occupied by the Allies after World War II. Also known as West Germany, this country experienced rapid demilitarization, democratization, and integration into the world economy.

Federal Reserve Act (1913) U.S. legislation that created a series of boards to monitor the supply and demand of the nation's money.

Federalists Supporters of the ratification of the U.S. Constitution, which was written to replace the Articles of Confederation.

feminist movements Movements that called for equal treatment for men and women—equal pay and equal opportunities for obtaining jobs and advancement. Feminism arose mainly in Europe and in North America in the 1960s and then became global in the 1970s.

Ferangi Arabic word meaning "Frank," which was used to describe Crusaders.

Fertile Crescent Site of the world's first agricultural revolution; an area in Southwest Asia, bounded by the Mediterranean Sea in the west and the Zagros Mountains in the east.

feudalism System instituted in medieval Europe after the collapse of the Carolingian Empire (814 CE) whereby each peasant was under the authority of a lord.

fiefdoms Medieval economic and political units.

First World Term invented during the cold war to refer to western Europe and North America (also known as the "free world" or the West); Japan later joined this group. Following the principles of liberal modernism, First World states sought to organize the world on the basis of capitalism and democracy.

Five Pillars of Islam The five tenets, or main aspects, of Islamic practice: testification or bearing witness that there is no God other than God (Allah, in Arabic) and that Muhammad is the messenger of God; praying five times a day; fasting from sunup to sundown every day during Ramadan (a month on the Islamic calendar); giving alms; and making a pilgrimage to Mecca.

Five-Year Plan Soviet effort launched under Stalin in 1928 to replace the market with a state-owned and state-managed economy, to promote rapid economic development over a five-year period of time and thereby "catch and overtake" the leading capitalist countries. The First Five-Year Plan was followed by the Second Five-Year Plan (1933–1937), and so on, until the collapse of the Soviet Union in 1991.

Flagellants European social group that came into existence during the bubonic plague in the fourteenth century; they believed that the plague was the wrath of God.

floating population Poor migrant workers in China who supplied labor under Emperor Wu.

Fluitschips Dutch shipping vessels that could carry heavy bulky cargo with relatively small crews.

flying cash Letters of exchange—early predecessors of paper cash instead of coins—first developed by guilds in the northwestern Shanxi. By the thirteenth century, paper money had eclipsed coins.

Fondûqs Complexes in caravan cities that included hostels, storage houses, offices, and temples.

Forbidden City Palace city of the Ming and Qing dynasties.

Force Publique Colonial army used to maintain order in the Belgian Congo; during the early stages of King Leopold's rule, it was responsible for bullying local communities.

Fourierism Form of utopian socialism based on the ideas of Charles Fourier (1772–1837). Fourier envisioned communes where work was made enjoyable and systems of production and distribution were run without merchants. His ideas appealed to the middle class, especially women, as a higher form of Christian communalism.

free labor Wage-paying rather than slave labor.

free markets Unregulated markets.

Free Officers Movement Secret organization of Egyptian junior military officers who came to power in a coup d'état in 1952, forced King Faruq to abdicate, and consolidated their own control through dissolving the parliament, banning opposing parties, and rewriting the constitution.

free trade Domestic and international trade unencumbered by tariff barriers, quotas, and fees.

Front de Libération Nationale (FLN) Algerian anticolonial, nationalist party that waged an eight-year war against French troops, beginning in 1854, that forced nearly all of the 1 million colonists to leave.

Fulani Muslim group in West Africa that carried out religious revolts at the end of the eighteenth and the beginning of the nineteenth centuries in an effort to return to the pure Islam of the past.

fur trade Trading of animal pelts (especially beaver skins) by Indians for European goods in North America.

Gandharan art Buddhist sculptures, particularly from the northern Kushan territory, that show a high degree of Greek and Roman influences.

Gandhi, Mohandhas Karamchand (Mahatma) (1869–1948) Indian leader who led a nonviolent struggle for India's independence from Britain.

garrisons Military bases inside cities; often used for political purposes, such as protecting rulers and putting down domestic revolts or enforcing colonial rule.

garrison towns Stations for soldiers originally established in strategic locations to protect territorial acquisition. Eventually, they became towns. Alexander the Great's garrison towns evolved into cities that served as centers from which Hellenistic culture was spread to his easternmost territories.

gauchos Argentine, Brazilian, and Uruguayan cowboys who wanted a decentralized federation, with autonomy for their provinces and respect for their way of life.

Gdansk shipyard Site of mass strikes in Poland that led in 1980 to the formation of the first independent trade union, Solidarity, in the communist bloc.

gendered relations A relatively recent development that implies roles emerged only with the appearance of modern humans and perhaps Neanderthals. When humans began to think imaginatively and in complex symbolic ways and give voice to their insights, perhaps around 150,000 years ago, gender categories began to crystallize.

genealogy History of the descent of a person or family from a distant ancestor.

Geneva Peace Conference (1954) International conference to restore peace in Korea and Indochina. The chief participants were the United States, the Soviet Union, Great Britain, France, the People's Republic of China, North Korea, South Korea, Vietnam, the Viet Minh party, Laos, and Cambodia. The conference resulted in the division of North and South Vietnam.

Genoa One of two Italian cities (the other was Venice) that linked Europe, Africa, and Asia as nodes of commerce in 1300. Genoese ships linked the Mediterranean to the coast of Flanders through consistent routes along the Atlantic coasts of Spain, Portugal, and France.

German Democratic Republic Nation founded from the Soviet zone of occupation of Germany after World War II; also known as East Germany.

German Social Democratic Party Founded in 1875, the most powerful socialist party in Europe before 1917.

Ghana The most celebrated medieval political kingdom in West Africa.

Ghost Dance American Indian ritual performed in the nineteenth century in the hope of restoring the world to precolonial conditions.

Gilgamesh Heroic narrative written in the Babylonian dialect of Semitic Akkadian. This story and others like it were meant to circulate and unify the kingdom.

Girondins Liberal revolutionary group that supported the creation of a constitutional monarchy during the early stages of the French Revolution.

global warming Release into the air of human-made carbons that contribute to rising temperatures worldwide.

globalization Development of integrated worldwide cultural and economic structures.

globalizing empires Empires, such as the Han and the Roman, that covered immense amounts of territory, included huge, diverse populations, exerted influence beyond their own borders, and worked to integrate conquered peoples.

Gold Coast Name that European mariners and merchants gave to that part of West Africa from which gold was exported. This area was conquered by the British in the nineteenth century and became a British colony; upon independence, it became Ghana.

Goths One of the groups of "barbarian" migrants into Roman territory in the fourth century CE.

government schools Schools founded by the Han dynasty to provide an adequate number of officials to fill positions in the administrative bureaucracy. The Imperial University had 30,000 members by the second century BCE.

Gracchus brothers Two tribunes, the brothers Tiberius and Gaius Gracchus, who in 133 and 123–21 BCE attempted to institute land reforms that would guarantee all of Rome's poor citizens a basic amount of land that would qualify them for army service. Both men were assassinated.

Grand Canal Created in 486 BCE, a thousand-mile-long connector between the Yellow and Yangzi rivers, linking the north and south, respectively.

grand unity Guiding political idea embraced by Qin rulers and ministers, with an eye toward joining the states of the Central Plain into one empire and centralizing administration.

"Greased cartridge" controversy Controversy spawned by the rumor that cow and pig fat had been used to grease the shotguns of the sepoys in the British army in India. Believing that this was a British attempt to defile their religion and speed their conversion to Christianity, the sepoys mutinied against the British officers.

Great Depression Worldwide depression following the U.S. stock market crash on October 29, 1929.

great divide The division between economically developed nations and less developed nations.

Great East Asia Co-Prosperity Sphere Term used by the Japanese during the 1930s and 1940s to refer to Hong Kong, Singapore, Malaya, Burma, and other states that they seized during their run for expansion.

Great Flood One of many traditional Mesopotamian stories that were transmitted orally from one generation to another before being recorded. The Sumerian King List refers to this crucial event in Sumerian memory and identity. The Great Flood narrative assigned responsibility for Uruk's demise to the gods.

Great Game Competition over areas such as Turkistan, Persia (present-day Iran), and Afghanistan. The British (in India) and the Russians believed that controlling these areas was crucial to preventing their enemies' expansion.

Great League of Peace and Power Iroquois Indian alliance that united previously warring communities.

Great Leap Forward (1958–1961) Plan devised by Mao Zedong to achieve rapid agricultural and industrial growth in China. The plan failed miserably and more than 20 million people died.

great plaza at Isfahan The center of Safavid power in the seventeenth century created by Shah Abbas (r. 1587–1629) to represent the unification of trade, government, and religion under one supreme political authority.

Great Proletarian Cultural Revolution (1966–1976) Mass mobilization of urban Chinese youth inaugurated by Mao Zedong in an attempt to reinvigorate the Chinese revolution and to prevent the development of a bureaucratized Soviet style of communism; with this movement, Mao turned against his longtime associates in the communist party.

Great Trek Afrikaner migration to the interior of Africa after the British abolished slavery in the empire in 1833.

Great War (August 1914–November 1918) A total war involving the armies of Britain, France, and Russia (the Allies) against those of Germany, Austria-Hungary, and the Ottoman Empire (the Central Powers). Italy joined the Allies in 1915, and the United States joined them in 1917, helping tip the balance in favor of the Allies, who also drew upon the populations and material of their colonial possessions. Also known as World War I.

Greek Orthodoxy Enduring form of Christianity that used the framework of the "Roman" state inherited from Constantine and Justinian to protect itself from Roman Catholicism and Muslim forces. The Greek Orthodox capital was Constantinople and its spiritual empire included the Russian peoples, Baltic Slavs, and peoples living in southwest Asia.

Greek philosophers "Wisdom-lovers" of the ancient Greek city-states, including Socrates, Plato, Aristotle, and others, who pondered such issues as self-knowledge, political engagement and withdrawal, and the order of the world.

Greenbacks Members of the American political party of the late nineteenth century that worked to advance the interest of farmers by promoting cheap money.

griots Counselors and other officials to the royal family in African kingships. They were also responsible for the preservation and transmission of oral histories and repositories of knowledge.

Group Areas Act (1950) Act that divided South Africa into separate racial and tribal areas and required Africans to live in their own separate communities, including the "homelands."

guerrillas Portuguese and Spanish peasant bands who resisted the revolutionary and expansionist efforts of Napoleon; after the French word *guerre*.

guest workers Migrants looking for temporary employment abroad.

Gulag Administrative name for the vast system of forced labor camps under the Soviet regime; it originated in a small monastery near the Arctic Circle and spread throughout the Soviet Union and to other Soviet-style socialist countries. Penal labor was required of both ordinary criminals (rapists, murderers, thieves) and those accused of political crimes (counterrevolution, anti-Soviet agitation).

Gulf War (1991) Armed conflict between Iraq and a coalition of thirty-two nations, including the United States, Britain, Egypt, France, and Saudi Arabia. It was started by Iraq's invasion of Kuwait, which it had long claimed, on August 2, 1990.

gunpowder Explosive powder. By 1040, the first gunpowder recipes were being written down. Over the next 200 years, Song entrepreneurs invented several incendiary devices and techniques for controlling explosions.

gunpowder empires Muslim empires of the Ottomans, Safavids, and

Mughals that used cannonry and gunpowder to advance their military causes.

Guomindang Nationalist Party of China, founded just before World War I by Sun Yat-sen and later led by Chiang Kai-shek.

Habsburg Empire Ruling house of Austria, which once ruled both Spain and central Europe but came to settle in lands along the Danube River; it played a prominent role in European affairs for many centuries. In 1867, the Habsburg Empire was reorganized into the Austro-Hungarian Dual Monarchy, and in 1918 it collapsed.

Hadith Sayings attributed to the Prophet Muhammad and his early converts. Used to guide the behavior of Muslim peoples.

Hagia Sophia Enormous and impressive church sponsored by Justinian and built starting in 532 CE. At the time, it was the largest church in the world.

Hajj Pilgrimage to Mecca; an obligation for Muslims.

Hammurapi's Code Legal code created by Hammurapi, the most famous of the Mesopotamian rulers, who reigned from 1792 to 1750 BCE. Hammurapi sought to create social order by centralizing state authority and creating a grand legal structure that embodied paternal justice. The code was quite stratified, dividing society into three classes: free men, dependent men, and slaves, each with distinct rights and responsibilities.

Han agrarian ideal Guiding principle for the free peasantry that made up the base of Han society. In this system, peasants were honored for their labors, while merchants were subjected to a range of controls, including regulations on luxury consumption, and were belittled for not engaging in physical labor.

Han Chinese Inhabitants of China proper who considered others to be outsiders. They felt that they were the only authentic Chinese.

Han Fei Chinese state minister who lived from 280 to 223 BCE; he was a proponent and follower of Xunzi.

Han military Like its Roman counterpart, a ruthless military machine that expanded the empire and created stable conditions that permitted the safe transit of goods by caravans. Emperor Wu heavily influenced the transformation of the military forces and reinstituted a policy that made military service compulsory.

Hangzhou City and former provincial seaport that became the political center of the Chinese people in their ongoing struggles with northern steppe nomads. It was also one of China's gateways to the rest of the world by way of the South China Sea.

Hannibal Great Roman general from Carthage whose campaigns in the third century BCE swept from Spain toward the Italian peninsula. He crossed the Pyrenees and the Alps mountain ranges with war elephants. He was unable, however, to defeat the Romans in 217 BCE.

Harappa One of two cities that, by 2500 BCE, began to take the place of villages throughout the Indus River valley (the other was Mohenjo Daro). Each covered an area of about 250 acres and probably housed 35,000 residents.

harem Secluded women's quarters in Muslim households.

Harlem Renaissance Cultural movement in the 1920s that was based in Harlem, a part of New York City with a large African American population. The movement gave voice to black novelists, poets, painters, and musicians, many of whom used their art to protest racism; also referred to as the "New Negro movement."

harnesses Tools made from wood, bone, bronze, and iron for steering and controlling chariot horses. Harnesses discovered by archaeologists reveal the evolution of headgear from simple mouth bits to full bridles with headpiece, mouthpiece, and reins.

Hatshepsut Leader known as ancient Egypt's most powerful woman ruler. Hatshepsut served as regent for her young son, Thutmosis III, whose reign began in 1479 BCE. She remained co-regent until her death.

Haussmannization Redevelopment and beautification of urban centers; named after the city planner who "modernized" mid-nineteenth-century Paris.

Hegira "Emigration" of Muhammad and his followers out of a hostile Mecca to Yathrib, a city that was later called Medina. The year in which this journey took place, 622 CE, is also year 1 of the Islamic calendar.

Heian period Period from 794 to 1185, during which began the pattern of regents ruling Japan in the name of the sacred emperor.

Hellenism Process by which the individuality of the cultures of the earlier Greek city-states gave way to a uniform culture that stressed the common identity of all who embraced Greek ways. This culture emphasized the common denominators of language, style, and politics to which anyone, anywhere in the Afro-Eurasian world, could have access.

hieroglyphs One of two basic forms of Egyptian writing that were used in conjunction throughout antiquity. Hieroglyphs are pictorial symbols; the term derives from a Greek word meaning "sacred carving"—they were employed exclusively in temple, royal, and divine contexts. *See also* Demotic writing.

Hijra Tradition of Islam, whereby one withdraws from one's community to create another, more holy, one. The practice is based on the Prophet Muhammad's withdrawal from the city of Mecca to Medina in 622 CE.

Hinayana (Lesser Vehicle) Buddhism Form of Buddhism that accepted the divinity of Buddha himself but not of demigods, or bodhisattvas.

Hinduism A refashioning of the ancient Brahmanic Vedic religion, bringing it in accord with rural life and agrarian values. It emerged as the dominant faith in Indian society in the third century CE. Believers became vegetarians and adopted rituals of self-sacrifice. Three major deities—Brahma, Vishnu, and Siva—formed a trinity representing the three phases of the universe (birth, existence, and destruction, respectively) and the three expressions of the eternal self, or *atma*.

Hindu revivalism Movement to reconfigure traditional Hinduism to be less diverse and more amenable to producing a narrowed version of Indian tradition.

Hiroshima Japanese port devastated by an atomic bomb on August 6, 1945.

Hitler, Adolf (1889–1945) German dictator and leader of the Nazi Party who seized power in Germany after its economic collapse in the Great Depression. Hitler and his Nazi regime started World War II in Europe and systematically murdered Jews and other non-Aryan groups in the name of racial purity.

Hittites The Hittites were a chariot warrior group of Anatolia, which spread east to northern Syria, though they eventually faced weaknesses in their own homeland. Their heyday was marked by the reign of the king Supiliulimua (1380 to 1345 BCE), who preserved the Hittites' influence on the balance of power in the region between Mesopotamia and the Nile.

Holocaust Deliberate racial extermination of the Jews by the Nazis that claimed around 6 million European Jews.

Holy Roman Empire Enormous realm that encompassed much of Europe and aspired to be the Christian successor state to the Roman Empire. In the time of the Habsburg dynasts, the empire was a loose confederation of principalities that obeyed an emperor elected by elite lower-level sovereigns. Despite its size, the empire never effectively centralized power; it was split into Austrian and Spanish factions when Charles V abdicated to his sons in 1556.

Holy Russia Name applied to Muscovy and then to the Russian Empire by Slavic Eastern Orthodox clerics who were appalled by the Muslim conquest in 1453 of Constantinople (the capital of Byzantium and of eastern Christianity) and who were hopeful that Russia would become the new protector of the faith.

home charges Fees India was forced to pay to Britain as its colonial master; these fees included interest on railroad loans, salaries to colonial officers, and the maintenance of imperial troops outside India.

hominids Humanlike beings who walked erect and preceded modern humans.

Homo A word used by scientists to differentiate between pre-human and "true human" species.

Homo caudatus "Tailed man," believed by some European Enlightenment thinkers to be an early species of humankind.

Homo erectus Species that emerged about 1.5 million years ago and had a large brain and walked truly upright. *Homo erectus* means "Standing man."

Homo habilis Scientific term for "Skillful man." Tool-making ability truly made *Homo habilis* the forerunners, though very distant, of modern humans.

Homo sapiens The first humans; they emerged in a small region of Africa about 200,000 years ago and migrated out of Africa about 100,000 years ago. They had bigger brains and greater dexterity than previous hominid species, whom they eventually eclipsed.

homogeneity Uniformity of the languages, customs, and religion of a particular people or place. It can also be demonstrated by a consistent calendar, set of laws, administrative practices, and rituals.

horses Animals used by full-scale nomadic communities to dominate the steppe lands in western Afro-Eurasia by the second millennium BCE. Horse-riding nomads moved their large herds across immense tracts of land within zones defined by rivers, mountains, and other natural geographical features. In the arid zones of central Eurasia, the nomadic economies made horses a crucial component of survival.

Huguenots French Protestants who endured severe persecution in the sixteenth and seventeenth centuries.

humanism The Renaissance aspiration to know more about the human experience beyond what the Christian scriptures offered by reaching back into ancient Greek and Roman texts.

Hundred Days' Reform (1898) Abortive modernizing reform program of the Qing government of China.

hunting and gathering Lifestyle in which food is acquired through hunting animals, fishing, and foraging for wild berries, nuts, fruit, and grains, rather than planting crops, vines, or trees. As late as 1500, as much as 15 percent of the world's population still lived by this method.

Hyksos A western Semitic-speaking people whose name means "Rulers of Foreign Lands"; they overthrew the unstable Thirteenth Dynasty in Egypt around 1640 BCE. The Hyksos had mastered the art of horse chariots, and with those chariots and their superior bronze axes and composite bows (made of wood, horn, and sinew), they were able to defeat the pharaoh's foot soldiers.

Ibn Sina Philosopher and physician who lived from 980 to 1037 CE. He was also schooled in the Quran, geometry, literature, and Indian and Euclidian mathematics.

ideology Dominant set of ideas of a widespread culture or movement.

Il Duce Term designating the fascist Italian leader Benito Mussolini.

Iliad Epic Greek poem about the Trojan War, composed several centuries after the events it describes. It was based on oral tales passed down for generations.

Il-khanate Mongol-founded dynasty in thirteenth-century Persia.

Imam Muslim religious leader and politico-religious descendant of Ali; believed by some to have a special relationship with Allah.

imperialism Acquisition of new territories by a state and the incorporation of these territories into a political system as subordinate colonies.

Imperial University University founded in 136 BCE by Emperor Wu, where important discoveries such as the rational diagnoses of the body's functions, the magnetic compass, and high-quality paper were developed; significant as a mechanism by which the Han state inculcated Confucian thought into the elite.

Imperium Latin word used to express Romans' power and command over their subjects. It is the basis of the English words *empire* and *imperialism*.

Inca Empire Empire of Quechua-speaking rulers in the Andean valley of Cuzco that encompassed a population of 4 to 6 million. The Incas lacked a clear inheritance system, causing an internal split that Pizarro's forces exploited in 1533.

Indian Institutes of Technology (IIT) Institutions originally designed as engineering schools to expand knowledge and to modernize India, which produced a whole generation of pioneering computer engineers, many of whom moved to the United States.

Indian National Congress Formed in 1885, a political party deeply committed to constitutional methods, industrialization, and cultural nationalism.

Indian National Muslim League Founded in 1906, an organization dedicated to advancing the political interests of Muslims in India.

Indo-Greek Fusion of Indian and Greek culture in the area under the control of the Bactrians, in the northwestern region of India, around 200 BCE.

Indu What we would today call India. Called "Indu" by Xuanzang, a Chinese Buddhist pilgrim who visited the area in the 630s and 640s CE.

indulgences Church-sponsored fund-raising mechanism that gave certification that one's sins had been forgiven in return for money.

industrial revolution Gradual accumulation and diffusion of old and new technical knowledge that led to major economic changes in Britain, northwestern Europe, and North America, catapulting these countries ahead of the rest of the world in manufacturing and agricultural output and standards of living.

industrious revolution Dramatic economic change in which households that had traditionally produced for themselves decided to work harder and longer hours in order to produce more for the market, which enabled them to increase their income and standard of living. Areas that underwent the industrious revolution shifted from peasant farming to specialized production for the market.

innovation Creation of a new method that allowed humans to make better adaptations to their environment such as the making of new tools.

Inquisition Tribunal of the Roman Catholic Church that enforced religious orthodoxy during the Protestant Reformation.

internal and external alchemy In Daoist ritual, use of trance and meditation or chemicals and drugs, respectively, to cause transformations in the self.

International Monetary Fund (IMF) Agency founded in 1944 to help restore financial order in Europe and the rest of the world, to revive international trade, and to support the financial concerns of Third World governments.

invisible hand As described in Adam Smith's *The Wealth of Nations*, the idea that the operations of a free market produce economic efficiency and economic benefits for all.

iron Malleable metal found in combined forms almost everywhere in the world; it became the most important and widely used metal in world history after the Bronze Age.

Iron Curtain Term popularized by Winston Churchill after World War II to refer to a rift, or an iron curtain, that divided western Europe, under American influence, from eastern Europe, under the domination of the Soviet Union.

irrigation Technological advance whereby water delivery systems and water sluices in floodplains or riverine areas were channeled or redirected and used to nourish soil.

Islam A religion that dates to 610 CE, when Muhammad believed God came to him in a vision. Islam ("submission"—in this case, to the will of God) requires its followers to act righteously, to submit themselves to the one and only true God, and to care for the less fortunate. Muhammad's most insistent message was the oneness of God, a belief that has remained central to the Islamic faith ever since.

Jacobins Radical French political group that came into existence during the French Revolution and executed the French king and sought to remake French culture.

Jacquerie (1358) French peasant revolt in defiance of feudal restrictions.

jade The most important precious substance in East Asia. Jade was associated with goodness, purity, luck, and virtue, and was carved into such items as ceremonial knives, blade handles, religious objects, and elaborate jewelry.

Jagat Seths Enormous trading and banking empire in eastern India.

Jainism Along with Buddhism, one of the two systems of thought developed in the seventh century BCE that set themselves up against Brahmanism. Its founder, Vardhamana Mahavira, taught that the universe obeys its own everlasting rules that no god or other supernatural being could affect. The purpose of life was to purify one's soul in order to attain a state of permanent bliss, which could be accomplished through self-denial and the avoidance of harming other creatures.

Janissaries Corps of infantry soldiers recruited as children from the Christian provinces of the Ottoman Empire and brought up with intense loyalty to the Ottoman state and its sultan. The Ottoman sultan used these forces to clip local autonomy and to serve as his personal bodyguards.

Jati Social groups as defined by Hinduism's caste system.

Jesuits Religious order founded by Ignatius Loyola to counter the inroads of the Protestant Reformation; the Jesuits, or the Society of Jesus, were active in politics, education, and missionary work.

Jihad Literally, "striving" or "struggle." This word also connotes military efforts or "striving in the way of God." It also came to mean spiritual struggles against temptation or inner demons, especially in Sufi, or mystical, usage.

Jih-pen Chinese for "Japan."

Jim Crow laws Laws that codified racial segregation and inequality in the southern part of the United States after the Civil War.

Jizya Special tax that non-Muslims were forced to pay to their Islamic rulers in return for which they were given security and property and granted cultural autonomy.

jong Large ocean-going vessels, built by Southeast Asians, which plied the regional trade routes from the fifteenth century to the early sixteenth century.

Judah The southern kingdom of David, which had been an Assyrian vassal until 612 BCE, when it became a vassal of Assyria's successor, Babylon, against whom the people of Judah rebelled, resulting in the destruction of Jerusalem in the sixth century BCE.

Julius Caesar Formidable Roman general who lived from 100 to 44 BCE. He was also a man of letters, a great orator, and a ruthless military man who boasted that his campaigns had led to the deaths of over a million people.

junks Trusty seafaring vessels used in the South China Seas after 1000 CE. These helped make shipping by sea less dangerous.

Justinian Roman or Byzantine emperor who ascended to the throne in 527 CE. In addition to his many building projects and military expeditions, he issued a new law code.

Kabuki Theater performance that combined song, dance, and skillful staging to dramatize conflicts between duty and passion in Tokogawa, Japan.

Kamikaze Japanese for "divine winds" or typhoons; such a storm saved Japan from a Mongol attack.

Kanun Highly detailed system of Ottoman administrative law that jurists developed to deal with matters not treated in the religious law of Islam.

Karim Loose confederation of shippers banding together to protect convoys.

karma Literally "fate" or "action," in Confucian thought; this is a universal principle of cause and effect.

Kassites Nomads who entered Mesopotamia from the eastern Zagros Mountains and the Iranian plateau as early as 2000 BCE. They gradually integrated into Babylonian society by officiating at temples. By 1745 BCE, they had asserted order over the region, and they controlled southern Mesopotamia for the next 350 years, creating one of the territorial states.

Keynesian Revolution Post-Depression economic ideas developed by the British economist John Maynard Keynes, wherein the state took a greater role in managing the economy, stimulating it by increasing the money supply and creating jobs.

KGB Soviet political police and spy agency, formed as the Cheka not long after the Bolshevik coup in October 1917. Grew to more than 750,000 operatives with military rank by the 1980s.

Khan Ruler who was acclaimed at an assembly of elites and supposedly descended from Chinngis Khan on the male line; those not descended from Chinggis continually faced challenges to their legitimacy.

Khanate Major political unit of the vast Mongol empire. There were four Khanates, including the Yuan Empire in China, forged by Chinggis Khan's grandson Kubilai.

Kharijites Radical sect from the early days of Islam. The Kharijites seceded from the "party of Ali" (who themselves came to be known as the Shiites) because of disagreements over succession to the role of the caliph. They were known for their strict militant piety.

Khmers A people who created the most powerful empire in Southwest Asia between the tenth and thirteenth centuries in what is modern-day Cambodia.

Khomeini, Ayatollah Ruhollah (1902–1989) Iranian religious leader who used his traditional Islamic education and his training in Muslim ethics to accuse the shah's government of gross violations of Islamic norms. He also identified the shah's ally, America, as the great Satan. The shah fled the country in 1979; in his wake, Khomeini established a theocratic state ruled by a council of Islamic clerics.

Khufu A pyramid, among those put up in the Fourth Dynasty in ancient Egypt (2575–2465 BCE), which is the largest stone structure in the world. It is in an area called Giza, just outside modern-day Cairo.

Khusro I Anoshirwan Sasanian emperor who reigned from 530 to 579 CE. He was a model ruler and was seen as the personification of justice.

Kiev City that became one of the greatest cities of Europe after the eleventh century. It was built to be a small-scale Constantinople on the Dnieper.

Kikuyu Kenya's largest ethnic group; organizers of a revolt against the British in the 1950s.

King, Martin Luther, Jr. (1929–1968) Civil rights leader who borrowed his most effective weapon—the commitment to nonviolent protest and the appeal to conscience—from Gandhi.

Kingdom of Awadh One of the most prized lands for annexation and the fertile, opulent, and traditional vestige of Mughal rule in India.

Kingdom of Jerusalem What Crusaders set out to liberate when they launched their attack.

Kizilbash Mystical, Turkish-speaking tribesmen who facilitated the Safavid rise to power.

Knossos Area in Crete where, during the second millennium BCE, a primary palace town existed.

Koine Greek Common form of Greek that became the international spoken and written language in the Hellenistic world. This was a simpler everyday form of the ancient Greek language.

Koprulu reforms Reforms named after two grand viziers who revitalized the Ottoman Empire in the seventeenth century through administrative and budget trimming as well as by rebuilding the military.

Korean War (1950–1953) Cold war conflict between Soviet-backed North Korea and U.S.- and UN-backed South Korea. The two sides seesawed back and forth over the same boundaries until 1953, when an armistice divided the country at roughly the same spot as at the start of the war. Nothing had been gained. Losses, however, included 33,000 Americans, at least 250,000 Chinese, and up to 3 million Koreans.

Koryo dynasty Leading dynasty of the northern-based Koryo kingdom in Korea. It is from this dynasty that the name "Korea" derives.

Kremlin Once synonymous with the Soviet government; refers to Moscow's walled city center.

Kshatriyas Originally the warrior caste in Vedic society, the dominant clan members and ruling caste who controlled the land.

Ku Klux Klan Racist organization that first emerged in the U.S. South after the Civil War and then gained national strength as a radically traditionalist movement during the 1920s.

Kubilai Khan (1215–1294) Mongol leader who seized southern China after 1260 and founded the Yuan dynasty.

kulak Originally a pejorative word used to designate better-off peasants, the term used in the late 1920s and early 1930s to refer to any peasant, rich or poor, perceived as an opponent of the Soviet regime. Russian for "fist."

Kumarajiva Renowned Buddhist scholar and missionary who lived from 344 to 413 CE. He was brought to China by Chinese regional forces from Kucha, modern-day Xinjiang.

Kushans Northern nomadic group that migrated into South Asia in 50 CE. They unified the tribes of the region and set up the Kushan dynasty. The Kushans' empire embraced a large and diverse territory and played a critical role in the formation of the Silk Roads.

Labour Party Founded in Britain in 1900, the party that represented workers and was based on socialist principles.

laissez-faire The concept that the economy works best when it is left alone—that is, when the state does not regulate or interfere with the workings of the market.

"Land under the Yoke of Ashur" Lands not in Assyria proper, but under its authority; they had to pay the Assyrian Empire exorbitant amounts of tribute.

language System of communication reflecting cognitive abilities. Natural language is generally defined as words arranged in particular sequences to convey meaning and is unique to modern humans.

language families Related tongues with a common ancestral origin; language families contain languages that diverged from one another but share grammatical features and root vocabularies. More than a hundred language families exist.

Laozi Also known as Master Lao; perhaps a contemporary of Confucius, and the person after whom Daoism is named. His thought was elaborated upon by generations of thinkers.

latifundia Broad estates that produced goods for big urban markets, including wheat, grapes, olives, cattle, and sheep.

League of Nations Organization founded after World War I to solve international disputes through arbitration; it was dissolved in 1946 and its assets were transferred to the United Nations.

Legalism Also called Statism, a system of thought about how to live an ordered life. It was developed by Master Xun, or Xunzi (310–237 BCE). It is based on the principle that people, being inherently inclined toward evil, require authoritarian control to regulate their behavior.

Lenin, Nikolai (1870–1924) Leader of the Bolshevik Revolution in Russia and the first leader of the Soviet Union.

Liangzhu Culture spanning centuries from the fourth to the third millennium BCE that represented the last new Stone Age culture in the Yangzi River delta. One of the Ten Thousand States, it was highly stratified and is known for its jade objects.

liberalism Political and social theory that advocates representative government, free trade, and freedom of speech and religion.

limited-liability joint-stock company Company that mobilized capital from a large number of investors, called shareholders, who were not to be held personally liable for financial losses incurred by the company.

Linear A and B Two linear scripts first discovered on Crete in 1900. On the island of Crete and on the mainland areas of Greece, documents of the palace-centered societies were written on clay tablets in these two scripts. Linear A script, apparently written in Minoan, has not yet been deciphered. Linear B was first deciphered in the early 1950s.

"Little Europes" Urban landscapes between 1100 and 1200 composed of castles, churches, and towns in what are today Poland, the Czech Republic, Hungary, and the Baltic States.

Liu Bang Chinese emperor from 206 to 195 BCE; after declaring himself the prince of his home area of Han, in 202 BCE, Liu declared himself the first Han emperor.

llamas Animals similar in utility and function to camels in Afro-Eurasia. Llamas could carry heavy loads for long distances.

Long March (1934–1935) Trek of over 10,000 kilometers by Mao Zedong and his communist followers to establish a new base of operations in northwestern China.

Longshan peoples Peoples who lived in small agricultural and riverine villages in East Asia at the end of the third millennium BCE. They set the stage for the Shang in terms of a centralized state, urban life, and a cohesive culture.

lord Privileged landowner who exercised authority over the people who lived on his land.

lost generation The 17 million former members of the Red Guard and other Chinese youth who were denied education from the late 1960s to the mid-1970s as part of the Chinese government's attempt to prevent political disruptions.

Louisiana Purchase (1803) American purchase of French territory from Napoleon, including much of the present-day United States between the Mississippi River and the Rocky Mountains.

Lucy Relatively intact skeleton of a young adult female australopithecine unearthed in the valley of the Awash River in 1974 by an archaeological team working at a site in present-day Hadar, Ethiopia. The researchers nicknamed the skeleton Lucy. She stood just over three feet tall and walked upright at least some of the time. Her skull contained a brain within the ape size range. Also, her jaw and teeth were humanlike. Lucy's skeleton was relatively complete and at the time was the oldest hominid skeleton ever discovered.

Luftwaffe German air force.

Luther, Martin (1483–1546) A German monk and theologian who sought to reform the Catholic Church; he believed in salvation through faith alone, the importance of reading Scripture, and the priesthood of all believers. His Ninety-five Theses, which enumerated the abuses by the Catholic Church as well his reforms, started the Protestant Reformation.

Maastricht Treaty (1991) Treaty that formed the European Union, a fully integrated trading and financial bloc with its own bureaucracy and elected representatives.

Ma'at Term used in ancient Egypt to refer to stability or order, the achievement of which was the primary task of Egypt's ruling kings, the pharaohs.

Maccabees Leaders of a riot in Jerusalem in 166 BCE; the riot was a response to a Roman edict outlawing the practice of Judaism.

Madhyamika (Middle Way) Buddhism Chinese branch of Mahayana Buddhism established by Kumarajiva (344–413 CE) that used irony and paradox to show that reason was limited.

madrassas Higher schools of Muslim education that taught law, the Quran, religious sciences, and the regular sciences.

Mahayana (Greater Vehicle) Buddhism School of Buddhist theology that believed that the Buddha was a deity, unlike previous groups that had considered him a wise human being.

Mahdi The "chosen one" in Islam whose appearance was supposed to foretell the end of the world and the final day of reckoning for all people.

maize Grains, the crops that the settled agrarian communities across the Americas cultivated, along with legumes (beans) and tubers (potatoes).

Maji-Maji Revolt (early 1900s) Swahili insurrection against German colonialists; inspired by the belief that those who were anointed with specially blessed water (*maji*) would be immune to bullets. It resulted in 200,000–300,000 African deaths.

Mali Empire West African empire, founded by the legendary king Sundiata in the early thirteenth century. It facilitated thriving commerce, with routes linking the Atlantic Ocean, the Sahara, and beyond.

Mamluks (Arabic for "owned" or "possessed") Military men who ruled Egypt as an independent regime from 1250 until the Ottoman conquest in 1517.

Manaus Opera House Opera house built in the interior of Brazil in a lucrative rubber-growing area at the turn of the twentieth century.

Manchukuo Japanese puppet state in Manchuria in the 1930s.

Manchus Descendants of the Jurchens who helped the Ming army recapture Beijing in 1644 after its seizure by the outlaw Li Zicheng. The Manchus numbered around 1 million but controlled a domain that included perhaps 250 million people. Their rule lasted more than 250 years and became known as the Qing dynasty.

mandate of heaven Ideology established by Zhou dynasts to communicate the moral transfer of power. Originally a pact between the Zhou people and their supreme god, it evolved in the first century BCE into Chinese political doctrine.

Mande A people who lived in the area between the bend in the Senegal River and the bend in the Niger River east to west and from the Senegal River and Bandama River north to south. Also known as the Mandinka. Their civilization emerged around 1100.

Mandela, Nelson (1918–2013) Leader of the African National Congress (ANC) who was imprisoned for more than two decades by the apartheid regime in South Africa for his political beliefs; worldwide protests led to his release in 1990. In 1994 Mandela won the presidency in South Africa's first free mass elections.

Manifest Destiny Belief that it was God's will for the American people to expand their territory and political processes across the North American continent.

manorialism System in which the manor (a lord's home, its associated industry, and surrounding fields) served as the basic unit of economic power; an alternative to feudalism (the hierarchical relationships of king, lords, and peasantry) for thinking about the nature of power in western Europe, 1000–1300.

Mao Zedong (1893–1976) Chinese communist leader who rose to power during the Long March (1934). In 1949, he defeated the Nationalists and established a communist regime in China. Although many of Mao's efforts to transform China, such as the industrialization program of 1958 (known as the Great Leap Forward) and the Cultural Revolution of 1966, failed and brought great suffering to the people, he did instill a new spirit of independence in China and a sense of purpose after many decades of political and economic failure.

maroon community Sanctuary for runaway slaves in the Americas.

Marshall Plan Economic aid package given by the United States to Europe after World War II in hopes of a rapid period of reconstruction and economic gain, thereby securing the countries that received the aid from a communist takeover.

martyrs People executed by the Roman authorities for persisting in their Christian beliefs and refusing to submit to pagan ritual or belief.

Marx, Karl (1818–1883) German philosopher and economist who created Marxism and believed that a revolution of the working classes would overthrow the capitalist order and create a classless society.

Marxism Form of scientific socialism created by Karl Marx and Friedrich Engels that was rooted in a materialist theory of history: what mattered in history were the production of material goods and the ways in which society was organized into classes of producers and exploiters.

mass consumption Increased purchasing power in the early twentieth-century prosperous and mainly middle-class societies, stemming from mass production.

mass culture Distinctive form of popular culture that arose in the wake of World War I. It reflected the tastes of the working and the middle classes, who now had more time and money to spend on entertainment, and relied on new technologies, especially film and radio, which could reach an entire nation's population and consolidate their sense of being a single state.

mass production System in which factories were set up to produce huge quantities of identical products, reflecting the early twentieth-century world's demands for greater volume, faster speed, reduced cost, and standardized output.

Mastaba Word meaning "bench" in Arabic; it refers to a huge flat structure identical to earlier royal tombs of ancient Egypt.

Mau-Mau Revolt (1952–1957) Uprising orchestrated by a Kenyan guerrilla movement; this conflict forced the British to grant independence to the black majority in Kenya.

Mauryan Empire Dynasty extended by the Mauryans from 321 to 184 BCE, from the Indus Valley to the northwest areas of South Asia, in a region previously controlled by Persia. It was the first large-scale empire in South Asia and was to become the model for future Indian empires.

Mawali Non-Arab "clients" to Arab tribes in the early Islamic Empire. Because tribal patronage was so much a part of the Arabian cultural system, non-Arabs who converted to Islam affiliated themselves with a tribe and became clients of that tribe.

Maxim gun European weaponry that was capable of firing many bullets per second; it was used against Africans in the conquest of the continent.

Mayans Civilization that ruled over large stretches of Mesoamerica; it was composed of a series of kingdoms, each built around ritual centers rather than cities. The Mayans engaged neighboring peoples in warfare and trade and expanded borders through tributary relationships. They were not defined by a great ruler or one capital city, but by their shared religious beliefs.

McCarthyism Campaign by Republican senator Joseph McCarthy in the late 1940s and early 1950s to uncover closet communists, particularly in the State Department and in Hollywood.

Meat Inspection Act (1906) Legislation that provided for government supervision of meat-packing operations; it was part of a broader "Progressive" reform movement dedicated to correcting the negative consequences of urbanization and industrialization in the United States.

Mecca Arabian city in which Muhammad was born. Mecca was a trading center and pilgrimage destination in the pre-Islamic and Islamic periods. Exiled in 622 CE because of resistance to his message, Muhammad returned to Mecca in 630 CE and claimed the city for Islam.

Medes Rivals of the Assyrians and the Persians. The Medes inhabited the area from the Zagros Mountains to the modern city of Tehran; known as expert horsemen and archers, they were eventually defeated by the Persians.

megaliths Literally, "great stone"; the word *megalith* is used when describing structures such as Stonehenge. These massive structures are the result of cooperative planning and work.

megarons Large buildings found in Troy (level II) that are the predecessors of the classic Greek temple.

Meiji Empire Empire created under the leadership of Mutsuhito, emperor of Japan from 1868 until 1912. During the Meiji period Japan became a world industrial and naval power.

Meiji Restoration Reign of the Meiji emperor, which was characterized by a new nationalist identity, economic advances, and political transformation.

Mencius Disciple of Confucius who lived from 372 to 289 BCE.

mercantilism Economic theory that drove European empire builders. In this economic system, the world had a fixed amount of wealth, which meant one country's wealth came at the expense of another's. Mercantilism assumed that colonies existed for the sole purpose of enriching the country that controlled the colony.

Mercosur Free-trade pact between the governments of Argentina, Brazil, Paraguay, and Uruguay.

meritocracy Rule by persons of talent.

Meroe Ancient kingdom in what is today Sudan. It flourished for nearly a thousand years, from the fifth century BCE to the fifth century CE.

mestizos Mixed-blood offspring of Spanish settlers and native Indians.

métis Mixed-blood offspring of French settlers and native Indians.

Mexican Revolution (1910) Conflict fueled by the unequal distribution of land and by disgruntled workers; it erupted when political elites split over the succession of General Porfirio Díaz after decades of his rule. The fight lasted over ten years and cost 1 million lives, but it resulted in a widespread reform and a new constitution.

***Mfecane* movement** African political revolts in the first half of the nineteenth century that were caused by the expansionist methods of King Shaka of the Zulu people.

microsocieties Small-scale communities that had little interaction with others. These communities were the norm for peoples living in the Americas and islanders in the Pacific and Aegean from 2000 to 1200 BCE.

migration Long-distance travel for the purpose of resettlement. In the case of early man, the need to move was usually a response to an environmental shift, such as climate change during the Ice Age.

millenarian Believer in the imminent coming of a just and ideal society.

millenarian movement Broad, popular upheaval calling for the restoration of a bygone moral age, often led by charismatic spiritual prophets.

Millets Minority religious communities of the Ottoman Empire.

minaret Slender tower within a mosque from which Muslims are called to prayer.

minbar Pulpit inside a mosque from which Muslim religious speakers broadcast their message to the faithful.

Minoans A people who built a large number of elaborate, independent palace centers on Crete, at Knossos, and elsewhere around 2000 BCE. Named after the legendary King Minos, said to have ruled Crete at the time, they sailed throughout the Mediterranean and by 1600 BCE had planted colonies on many Aegean islands, which in turn became trading and mining centers.

mission civilisatrice Term French colonizers used to refer to France's form of "rationalized" colonial rule, which attempted to bring "civilization" to the "uncivilized."

mitochondrial DNA Form of DNA found outside the nucleus of cells, where it serves as cells' microscopic power packs. Examining mitochondrial DNA enables researchers to measure the genetic variation among living objects, including human beings.

Moche A people who extended their power and increased their wealth at the height of the Chimu Empire over several valleys in what is now Peru.

Model T First automobile, manufactured by the Ford Motor Company of Henry Ford, to be priced reasonably enough to be sold to the masses.

Modernists A generation of exuberant young artists, writers, and scientists in the late nineteenth century who broke with older conventions and sought new ways of seeing and describing the world.

Mohism School of thought in ancient China, named after Mo Di, or Mozi, who lived from 479 to 438 BCE. It emphasized one's obligation to society as a whole, not just to one's immediate family or social circle.

monarchy Political system in which one individual holds supreme power and passes that power on to his or her next of kin.

monasticism Christian way of life that originated in Egypt and was practiced as early as 300 CE in the Mediterranean. The word itself contains the meaning of a person "living alone" without marriage or family.

monetization An economic shift from a barter-based economy to one dependent on coin.

Mongols Combination of nomadic forest and prairie peoples who lived by hunting and livestock herding and were expert horsemen. Beginning in 1206, the Mongols launched a series of conquests that brought far-flung parts of the world together under their rule. By incorporating conquered peoples and adapting some of their customs, the Mongols created a unified empire that stretched from the Pacific Ocean to the shores of the eastern Mediterranean and the southern steppes of Eurasia.

monotheism The belief in only one god.

Moors Term employed by Europeans in the medieval period to refer to Muslim occupants of North Africa, the western Sahara, and the Iberian Peninsula.

mosque Place of worship for the people of Islam.

Mound people Name for the people of Cahokia, since its landscape was dominated by earthen monuments in the shapes of mounds. The mounds were carefully maintained and were the loci from which Cahokians paid respect to spiritual forces. *See also* Cahokia.

Mu Chinese ruler (956–918 BCE) who put forth a formal bureaucratic system of governance, appointing officials, supervisors, and military captains to whom he was not related. He also instituted a formal legal code.

muckrakers Journalists who aimed to expose political and commercial corruption in late-nineteenth- and early twentieth-century America.

Muftis Experts on Muslim religious law.

Mughal Empire One of Islam's greatest regimes. Established in 1526, it was a vigorous, centralized state whose political authority encompassed most of modern-day India. During the sixteenth century, it had a population of between 100 and 150 million.

Muhammad (570–632 CE) Prophet and founder of the Islamic faith. Born in Mecca in Saudi Arabia and orphaned when young, Muhammad lived under the protection of his uncle. His career as a prophet began around 610 CE, with his first experience of spiritual revelation.

Muhammad Ali Ruler of Egypt between 1805 and 1848. He initiated a set of modernizing reforms that sought to make Egypt competitive with the great powers.

mullahs Religious leaders in Iran who in the 1970s led a movement opposing Shah Reza Pahlavi and denounced American materialism and secularism.

multinational corporations Corporations based in many different countries that have global investment, trading, and distribution goals.

Muscovy The principality of Moscow. Originally a mixture of Slavs, Finnish tribes, Turkic speakers, and many others, Muscovy used territorial expansion and commercial networks to consolidate a powerful state and expanded to become the Russian Empire, a huge realm that spanned parts of Europe, much of northern Asia, numerous North Pacific islands, and even—for a time—a corner of North America (Alaska).

Muslim Brotherhood Egyptian organization founded in 1938 by Hassan al-Banna. It attacked liberal democracy as a cover for middle-class, business, and landowning interests and fought for a return to a purified Islam.

Muslim League National Muslim party of India.

Mussolini, Benito (1883–1945) Italian dictator and founder of the fascist movement in Italy. During World War II, he allied Italy with Germany and Japan.

Muwahhidin Term meaning "unitarians"; these were followers of the Wahhabi movement that emerged in the Arabian Peninsula in the eighteenth century.

Mycenaeans Mainland competitors of the Minoans; they took over Crete around 1400 BCE. Migrating to Greece from central Europe, they brought their Indo-European language, horse chariots, and metalworking skills, which they used to dominate until 1200 BCE.

Nagasaki Second Japanese city to be hit by an atomic bomb near the end of World War II.

Napoleon Bonaparte (1769–1821) General who rose to power in a post-Revolutionary coup d'état, eventually proclaiming himself emperor of France. He placed security and order ahead of social reform and created a civil legal code. Napoleon expanded his empire through military action, but after his disastrous Russian campaign, the united European powers defeated Napoleon and forced him into exile. He escaped and reassumed command of his army but was later defeated at the Battle of Waterloo.

Napoleonic Code Legal code drafted by Napoleon in 1804; it distilled different legal traditions to create one uniform law. The code confirmed the abolition of feudal privileges of all kinds and set the conditions for exercising property rights.

National Assembly of France Governing body of France that succeeded the Estates-General in 1789 during the French Revolution. It was composed of, and defined by, the delegates of the Third Estate.

National Association for the Advancement of Colored People (NAACP) Founded in 1910, the U.S. civil rights organization dedicated to ending inequality and segregation for black Americans.

National Recovery Administration (NRA) New Deal agency created in 1933 to prepare codes of fair administration and to plan for public works. It was later declared unconstitutional.

nationalism The idea that members of a shared community called a "nation" should have sovereignty within the borders of their state.

nation-state Form of political organization that derived legitimacy from its inhabitants, often referred to as citizens, who in theory, if not always in practice, shared a common language, common culture, and common history.

native learning Japanese movement to promote nativist intellectual traditions and the celebration of Japanese texts.

native paramountcy British form of "rationalized" colonial rule, which attempted to bring "civilization" to the "uncivilized" by proclaiming that when the interests of European settlers in Africa clashed with those of the African population, the latter should take precedence.

natural rights Belief that emerged in eighteenth-century western Europe and North America that rights fundamental to human nature were discernible to reason and should be affirmed in human-made law.

natural selection Charles Darwin's theory that populations grew faster than the food supply, creating a "struggle for existence" among species. In later work he showed how the passing on of individual traits was also determined by what he called sexual selection—according to which the "best" mates are chosen for their strength, beauty, or talents. The outcome: the "fittest" survived to reproduce, while the less adaptable did not.

Nazis (National Socialist German Workers Party) German organization dedicated to winning workers over from socialism to nationalism; the first Nazi Party platform combined nationalism with anticapitalism and anti-Semitism.

Neanderthals Members of an early wave of hominids from Africa who settled in western Afro-Eurasia, in an area reaching from present-day Uzbekistan and Iraq to Spain, approximately 150,000 years ago.

needle compass Crucial instrument made available to navigators after 1000 CE that helped guide sailors on the high seas. It was a Chinese invention.

negritos Hunter-gatherer inhabitants of the East Asian coastal islands who migrated there around 28,000 BCE but by 2000 BCE had been replaced by new migrants.

Negritude Statement of the virtues of the black identity and the validation of African culture and the African past, even in a westernizing world. This idea was shaped by African and African American intellectuals like Senegal's first president, Léopold Sédar Senghor.

Nehemiah Jewish eunuch of the Persian court who was given permission to rebuild the fortification walls around the city of Jerusalem from 440 to 437 BCE.

Neo-Assyrian Empire Afro-Eurasian empire that dominated around 950 BCE. The Neo-Assyrians extended their control over resources and people beyond their own borders, and their empire lasted for three centuries.

Nestorian Christians Denomination of Christians whose beliefs about Christ differed from those of the official Byzantine church. Named after Nestorius, former bishop of Constantinople, they emphasized the human aspects of Jesus.

New Deal President Franklin Delano Roosevelt's package of government reforms that were enacted during the 1930s to provide jobs for the unemployed, social welfare programs for the poor, and security to the financial markets.

New Economic Policy Enacted decrees of the Bolsheviks between 1921 and 1927 that grudgingly sanctioned private trade and private property.

New Negro movement *See* Harlem Renaissance.

New World Term applied to the Americas that reflected the Europeans' view that anything previously unknown to them was "new," even if it had existed and supported societies long before European explorers arrived on its shores.

nirvana Literally, nonexistence; *nirvana* is the state of complete liberation from the concerns of worldly life, as in Buddhist thought.

Nō drama Masked theater favored by Japanese bureaucrats and regional lords during the Tokugawa period.

Noble Eightfold Path Buddhist concept of a way of life by which people may rid themselves of individual desire to achieve *nirvana*. The path consists of wisdom, ethical behavior, and mental discipline.

Nok culture Spectacular culture that arose in what is today Nigeria, in the sixth century BCE. Iron smelting occurred there around 600 BCE. Thus the Nok people made the transition from stone to iron materials.

nomads People who move across vast distances without settling permanently in a particular place. Often pastoralists, nomads and transhumant herders introduced new forms of chariot-based warfare that transformed the Afro-Eurasian world.

non-governmental organizations (NGOs) Term used to refer to private organizations like the Red Cross that play a large role in international affairs.

nonviolent resistance (satyagraha) Moral and political philosophy of resistance developed by Indian National Congress leader Mohandas Gandhi. Gandhi believed that if Indians pursued self-reliance and self-control in a nonviolent way, the British would eventually have to leave.

North American Free Trade Agreement (NAFTA) Treaty negotiated in the early 1990s to promote free trade between Canada, the United States, and Mexico.

North Atlantic Treaty Organization (NATO) International organization set up in1949 to provide for the defense of western European countries and the United States from the perceived Soviet threat.

Northern Wei dynasty Regime founded in 386 CE by the Tuoba, a people originally from Inner Mongolia, that lasted one and a half centuries. The rulers of this dynasty adopted many practices of the earlier Chinese Han regime. At the same time, they struggled to consolidate authority over their own nomadic people. Ultimately, several decades of intense internal conflict led to the dynasty's downfall.

northwest passage Long-sought marine passageway between the Atlantic and Pacific oceans.

Oceania Collective name for the lands of Australia and New Zealand and the islands of the southwest Pacific Ocean.

Odyssey Composed in the eighth century BCE, an epic tale of the journey of Odysseus, who traveled the Mediterranean back to his home in Ithaca after the siege of Troy.

oikos The word for "small family unit" in ancient Greece, similar to the familia in Rome. Its structure, with men as heads of household over women and children, embodied the fundamental power structure in Greek city-states.

oligarchy Clique of privileged rulers.

Olmecs A people who emerged around 1500 BCE and lived in Mesoamerica. The name means those who "lived in the land of the rubber." Olmec society was composed of decentralized villages. Its members spoke the same language and worshipped the same gods.

Open Door Policy Policy proposed by American Secretary of State John Hay that would give all foreign nations equal access to trade with China. As European imperial powers carved out spheres of trade in late-nineteenth-century China, American leaders worried that the United States would be excluded from trade with China. To prevent this, Hay proposed the Open Door Policy.

Opium War (1839–1842) War fought between the British and Qing China over British trade in opium; resulted in granting to the British the right to trade in five different ports and the ceding of Hong Kong to the British.

oracle bones Animal bones used by Shang diviners. Diviners applied intense heat to the shoulder bones of cattle or to turtle shells, which caused them to crack. The diviners would then interpret the cracks as signs from the ancestors regarding royal plans and actions.

Organization of Petroleum Exporting Countries (OPEC) International association established in 1960 to coordinate price and supply policies of oil-producing states.

orientalism Genre of literature and painting that portrayed the non-western peoples of North Africa and Asia as exotic, sensuous, and economically backward with respect to Europeans.

orientalists Western scholars who specialized in the study of the East.

Orrorin tugenensis Predecessor to hominids that first appeared 6 million years ago.

Ottoman Empire Rulers of Anatolia, the Arab world, and much of southern and eastern Europe in the early sixteenth century. They transformed themselves from nomadic warrior bands who roamed the borderlands between Islamic and Christian worlds in Anatolia into sovereigns of a vast, bureaucratic empire. The Ottomans embraced a Sunni view of Islam. They adapted traditional Byzantine governmental practices but tried new ways of integrating the diverse peoples of their empire.

Pacific War (1879–1883) War between Chile and the alliance of Bolivia and Peru.

pagani Pejorative word used by Christians to designate pagans.

palace Official residence of the ruler, his family, and his entourage. The palace was both a social institution and a set of buildings. It first appeared around 2500 BCE, about a millennium later than the Mesopotamian temple, and quickly joined the temple as a defining landmark of city life. Eventually, it became a source of power rivaling the temple, and palace and temple life often blurred, as did the boundary between the sacred and the secular.

Palace of Versailles The palace complex, eleven miles away from the French capital of Paris, built by Louis XIV in the 1670s and 1680s to house and entertain his leading clergymen and nobles, with the hopes of diverting them from plotting against him.

Palmyra Roman trading depot in modern-day Syria; part of a network of trading cities that connected various regions of Afro-Eurasia.

pan movements Groups that sought to link people across state boundaries in new communities based on ethnicity or, in some cases, religion (e.g., pan-Germanism, pan-Islamism, pan-Slavism).

Pansophia Ideal republic of inquisitive Christians united in the search for knowledge of nature as a means of loving God.

papacy The institution of the pope; the Catholic spiritual leader in Rome.

papal Of, relating to, or issued by a pope.

Parthians Horse-riding people who pushed southward around the middle of the second century BCE and wiped out the Greek kingdoms in Iran. They then extended their power all the way to the Mediterranean, where they ran up against the Roman Empire in Anatolia and Mesopotamia.

pastoral nomadic communities Groups of people that moved their domesticated animals from place to place to meet the animals' demanding grazing requirements. Around 3500 BCE, western Afro-Eurasia witnessed the growth and spread of pastoral nomadic communities.

pastoralism Herding and breeding of sheep and goats or other animals as a primary means of subsistence.

paterfamilias Latin for "Father of the family," which itself was the foundation of the Roman social order.

patria Latin, meaning "fatherland."

patrons In the Roman system of patronage, men and women of wealth and high social status who protected dependents or "clients" of a lower class.

Pax Mongolica Term that refers to the political and especially the commercial stability that the vast Mongol Empire provided for the travelers and merchants of Eurasia during the thirteenth and fourteenth centuries.

Pax Romana Latin for "Roman Peace"; refers to the period between 25 BCE and 235 CE during which conditions in the Roman Empire were settled and peaceful.

Pax Sinica Period of peace (149–87 BCE) during which agriculture, commerce, and industry flourished in East Asia under the rule of the Han.

Peace Preservation Act (1925) Act instituted in Japan that specified up to ten years' hard labor for any member of an organization advocating a basic change in the political system or the abolition of private property.

Pearl Harbor American naval base in Hawaii on which the Japanese launched a surprise attack on December 7, 1941, bringing the United States into World War II.

Peloponnesian War War fought between 431 and 404 BCE between two of Greece's most powerful city-states, Athens and Sparta.

Peninsular War (1808–1814) Conflict in which the Portuguese and Spanish populations, supported by the British, resisted the French invasion under Napoleon of the Iberian Peninsula.

Peninsulars Spaniards who, although born in Spain, resided in the Spanish colonial territories. They regarded themselves as superior to Spaniards born in the colonies (creoles).

Peoples' Charter Document calling for universal suffrage for adult males, the secret ballot, electoral districts, and annual parliamentary elections. It was signed by over 3 million British between 1839 and 1842.

periplus Book that reflected sailing knowledge; in such books captains would record landing spots and ports. The word *periplus* literally means "sailing around."

Persepolis Darius I's capital city in the highlands of Fars; a ceremonial center and expression of imperial identity as well as an important administrative hub.

Peterloo Massacre (1819) The killing of 11 and wounding of 460 following a peaceful demonstration for political reform by workers in Manchester, England.

Petra City in modern-day Jordan that was the Nabataean capital. It profited greatly by supplying provisions and water to travelers and traders. Many of its houses and shrines were cut into the rocky mountains. *Petra* means "rock."

phalanx Military formation used by Philip II of Macedonia, whereby heavily armored infantry were closely arrayed in battle formation.

Philip II of Macedonia Father of Alexander the Great, under whose rule Macedonia developed into a large ethnic and territorial state. After unifying Macedonia, Philip went on to conquer neighboring states.

philosophes Enlightenment thinkers who applied scientific reasoning to human interaction and society as opposed to nature.

philosophia Literally "love of wisdom"; this system of thought originally included speculation on the nature of the cosmos, the environment, and human existence. It eventually came to include thought about the nature of humans and life in society.

Phoenicians Known as the Canaanites in the Bible, an ethnic group in the Levant under Assyrian rule in the seventh century BCE; they provided ships and sailors for battles in the Mediterranean. The word *Phoenician* refers to the purple dye they manufactured and widely traded, along with other commercial goods and services, throughout the Mediterranean. While part of wider Mesopotamian culture, their major contribution was the alphabet, first introduced in the second millennium BCE, which made far-reaching communication possible.

phonemes Primary and distinctive sounds that are characteristic of human language.

piety Strong sense of religious duty and devoutness, often inspiring extraordinary actions.

plant domestication Process of growing plants, harvesting their seeds, and saving some of the seeds for planting in subsequent growing cycles, resulting in a steady food supply. This process occurred as far back as 5000 BCE, when plants began to naturally retain their seeds. Plant domestication was practiced first in the southern Levant and spread from there into the rest of Southwest Asia.

Plato (427–347 BCE) Disciple of the great philosopher Socrates; his works are the only record we have of Socrates's teaching. He was also the author of formative philosophical works on ethics and politics.

plebs In Rome, term that referred to the "common people." Their interests were protected by officials called tribunes.

Pochteca Archaic term for merchants of the Mexicos.

polities Politically organized communities or states.

polyglot communities Societies composed of diverse linguistic and ethnic groups.

popular culture Affordable and accessible forms of art and entertainment available to people at all levels of society.

popular sovereignty The idea that the power of the state resides in the people.

populists Members of a political movement that supported U.S. farmers in late-nineteenth-century America. The term is often used generically to refer to political groups who appeal to the majority of the population.

potassium-argon dating Major dating technique based on the changing chemical structure of objects over time, since over time potassium decays into argon. This method makes possible the dating of objects up to a million years old.

potato famine (1840s) Severe famine in Ireland that led to the rise of radical political movements and the migration of large numbers of Irish to the United States.

potter's wheel Fast wheel that enabled people to mass-produce vessels in many different shapes. This advance, invented at the city of Uruk, enabled potters to make significant technical breakthroughs.

pottery Vessels made of mud and later clay that were used for storing and transporting food. The development of pottery was a major breakthrough.

Prague Spring (1968) Program of liberalization under a new communist party in Czechoslovakia that strove to create a democratic and pluralist socialism.

predestinarian Belief of many sixteenth- and seventeenth-century Protestant groups that God had foreordained the lives of individuals, including their bad and good deeds.

primitivism Western art movement of the late-nineteenth and early twentieth centuries that drew upon the so-called primitive art forms of Africa, Oceania, and pre-Columbian America.

progressive reformers Members of the U.S. reform movement in the early twentieth century that aimed to eliminate political corruption, improve working conditions, and regulate the power of large industrial and financial enterprises.

proletarians Industrial wage workers.

prophets Charismatic freelance religious men of power who found themselves in opposition to the formal power of the kings, bureaucrats, and priests.

Prophet's Town Indian village that was burned down by American forces in the early nineteenth century.

Protestant Reformation Religious movement initiated by sixteenth-century monk Martin Luther, who openly criticized the corruption in the Catholic Church and voiced his belief that Christians could speak directly to God. His doctrines gained wide support, and those who followed this new view of the Christianity rejected the authority of the papacy and the Catholic clergy, broke away from the Catholic Church, and called themselves "Protestants."

Protestantism Division of Christianity that emerged in western Europe from the Protestant Reformation.

Proto-Indo-European The parent of all the languages in the Indo-European family, which includes, among many others, English, German, Norwegian, Portuguese, French, Russian, Persian, Hindi, and Bengali.

Pullman Strike (1894) American Railway Union strike in response to wage cuts and firings.

Punic Wars Three wars waged between the Romans and Carthage in the third and second centuries BCE that resulted in the defeat of the Carthaginian hegemony in the western Mediterranean and demonstrated the might of the Roman military (army and navy) and the beginnings of Rome's aggressive foreign imperialism.

puppet states Governments with little power in the international arena that follow the dictates of their more powerful neighbors or patrons.

Puritans Seventeenth-century reform group of the Church of England; also known as dissenters or nonconformists.

Qadiriyya Sufi order that facilitated the spread of Islam into West Africa.

Qadis Judges in the Ottoman Empire.

qanats Underground water channels, vital for irrigation, which were used in Persia. Little evaporation occurred when water was being moved through qanats.

Qing dynasty (1644–1911) Minority Manchu rule over China that incorporated new territories, experienced substantial population growth, and sustained significant economic growth.

Questions of King Milanda (Milindapunha) Name of a second-century BCE text espousing the teachings of Buddhism as set forth by Menander, a Yavana king. It featured a discussion between the king and a sophisticated Buddhist sage named Nagasena.

Quetzalcoatl Ancient deity and legendary ruler of Native American peoples living in Mexico.

Quran The scripture of the Islamic faith. Originally a verbal recitation, the Quran was eventually compiled into a book in the order in which we have it today. According to traditional Islamic interpretation, the Quran was revealed to Muhammad by the angel Gabriel over a period of twenty-three years.

radicals Widely used term in nineteenth-century Europe that referred to those individuals and political organizations that favored the total reconfiguration of Europe's old state system.

radiocarbon isotope C^{14} Isotope contained by all living things, which plants acquire directly from the atmosphere and animals acquire indirectly when they consume plants or other animals. When living things die, the C^{14} isotope they contain begins to decay into a stable nonradioactive element, C^{12}. The rate of decay is regular and measurable, making it possible to ascertain the date of fossils that leave organic remains for ages of up to 40,000 years.

raj British crown's administration of India following the end of the East India Company's rule after the Rebellion of 1857.

raja "King" in the Kshatriya period in South Asia; could also refer to the head of a family, but indicated the person who had control of land and resources in South Asian city-states.

Ramadan Ninth month of the Muslim year, during which all Muslims must fast during daylight hours.

Rape of Nanjing Attack against the Chinese in which the Japanese slaughtered at least 100,000 civilians and raped thousands of women between December 1937 and February 1938.

Rashtriya Swayamsevak Sangh (RSS) (1925) Campaign to organize Hindus as a militant, modern community in India; translated in English as "National Volunteer Organization."

Rebellion of 1857 Indian uprising against the East India Company to bring religious purification, an egalitarian society, and local and communal solidarity without the interference of British rule.

rebus Probably originating in Uruk, a representation that transfers meaning from the name of a thing to the sound of that name. For example, a picture of a bee can represent the sound "b." Such pictures opened the door to writing: a technology of symbols that uses marks to represent specific discrete sounds.

Reconquista Spanish reconquest of territories lost to the Islamic Empire, beginning with Toledo in 1061.

Red Guards Chinese students who were the shock troopers in the early phases of Mao's Cultural Revolution in 1966–1968.

Red Lanterns Female supporters of the Chinese Boxers who rebelled against foreign intrusions in China at the turn of the twentieth century. Most were teenage girls and unmarried women and dressed in red garments.

Red Turban movement Diverse religious movement in China during the fourteenth century that spread the belief that the world was drawing to an end as Mongol rule was collapsing.

Reds Bolsheviks.

Reich German empire composed of Denmark, Austria, and parts of western France.

Reichstag The German parliament.

Reign of Terror Campaign at the height of the French Revolution in the early 1790s that used violence, including systematic execution of opponents of the revolution, to purge France of its enemies and to extend the revolution beyond its borders; radicals executed as many as 40,000 persons who were judged enemies of the state.

Renaissance Term meaning "rebirth" that historians use to characterize the expanded cultural production of European nations between 1430 and 1550. Emphasized a break from the church-centered medieval world and a new concept of humankind as the center of the world.

republican government Government in which power and rulership rest with representatives of the people—not a king.

Res publica Literally "public thing"; this referred to the Roman republic, in which policy and rules of behavior were determined by the Senate and by popular assemblies of the citizens.

Restoration period (1815–1848) European movement after the defeat of Napoleon to restore Europe to its pre-French revolutionary status and to quash radical movements.

Rift Valley Area of northeastern Africa where some of the most important early human archaeological discoveries of fossils were found, especially one of an intact skull that is 1.8 million years old.

river basin Area drained by a river, including all its tributaries. River basins were rich in fertile soil, water for irrigation, and plant and animal life, which made them attractive for human habitation. Cultivators were able to produce surplus agriculture to support the first cities.

riverine Term denoting an area whose inhabitants depend on irrigation for their well-being and whose populations are settled near great rivers. Egypt was, in a sense, the most riverine of all these cultures, in that it had no hinterland of plains as did Mesopotamia and the Indus Valley. Away from the banks of the Nile, there is only largely uninhabitable desert.

Roman army Military force of the Roman Empire. The Romans devised a military draft that could draw from a huge population. In their encounter with Hannibal, they lost up to 80,000 men in three separate encounters and still won the war.

Roman Catholicism Branch of Christianity established by 1000 CE in western Europe and led by the Roman papacy. In contrast to ancient Greek Orthodoxy, western Catholics believed that their church was destined to expand everywhere, and they set about converting the pagan tribes of northern Europe. Western Catholics contemptuously called the eastern Romans "Greeks" and condemned them for their "Byzantine" cunning.

Roman law Roman legal system, under which disputes were brought to the public courts and decisions were made by judges and sometimes by large juries. Rome's legal system featured written law and institutions for settling legal disputes.

roving bandits Large bands of dispossessed and marginalized peasants who vented their anger at tax collectors in the waning years of the Ming dynasty.

Royal Road A 1,600-mile road from Sardis in Anatolia to Susa in Iran; used by messengers, traders, the army, and those taking tribute to the king.

Russification Programs to assimilate people of over 146 dialects into the Russian Empire.

S.S. (*Schutzstaffel*) Hitler's security police force.

Sack of Constantinople Rampage in 1204 by the Frankish armies on the capital city of Constantinople.

sacred kingships Institutions that marked the centralized politics of West Africa. The inhabitants of these kingships believed that their kings were descendants of the gods.

Sahel region Area of sub-Saharan Africa with wetter and more temperate locations, especially in the upland massifs and their foothills, villages, and towns.

St. Bartholomew's Day Massacre (1572) Roman Catholic massacre of French Protestants in Paris.

St. Patrick Former slave brought to Ireland from Britain who later became a missionary, or the "Apostle of Ireland." He died in 470 CE.

Salt March (1930) A 240-mile trek to the sea in India, led by Mohandas Gandhi, to gather salt for free, thus breaking the British colonial monopoly on salt.

Samurai Japanese warriors who made up the private armies of Japanese daimyos.

Sandinista coalition Left-leaning Nicaraguan coalition of the 1970s and 1980s.

Sanskrit cosmopolis A cultural synthesis based on Hindu spiritual beliefs and articulated in the Sanskrit language that served to unify South Asia in place of a centralized empire.

Santería African-based religion, blended with Christian influences, that was first practiced by slaves in Cuba.

Sargon the Great King of Akkad, a city-state near modern Baghdad. Reigning from 2334 to 2279 BCE, Sargon helped bring the competitive era of city-states to an end and sponsored monumental works of architecture, art, and literature.

Sasanian Empire Empire that succeeded the Parthians in the mid-220s CE in Inner Eurasia. The Sasanian Empire controlled the trade crossroads of Afro-Eurasia and possessed a strong armored cavalry, which made them a powerful rival to Rome. The Sasanians were also tolerant of Judaism and Christianity, which allowed Christians to flourish.

sati Hindu practice whereby a woman was burned to death on the pyre of her dead husband.

satrap Governor of a province in the Persian Empire. Each satrap was a relative or intimate associate of the king.

satyagraha *See* nonviolent resistance.

scientific method Method of inquiry based on experimentation in nature. Many of its principles were first laid out by the philosopher Sir Francis Bacon (1561–1626), who claimed that real science entailed the formulation of hypotheses that could be tested in carefully controlled experiments.

Scramble for Africa European rush to colonize parts of Africa at the end of the nineteenth century.

scribes Those who wield writing tools; from the very beginning they were at the top of the social ladder, under the major power brokers.

Scythian ethos Warrior ethos that embodied the extremes of aggressive mounted-horse culture, c. 1000 BCE. In part the Scythian ethos was the result of the constant struggle between settlers, hunter-gatherers, and nomads on the northern frontier of Europe.

Sea Peoples Migrants from north of the Mediterranean who invaded the cities of Egypt and the Levant in the second millennium BCE. Once settled along the coast of the Levant, they became known as the Philistines and considerably disrupted the settlements of the Canaanites.

SEATO (Southeast Asia Treaty Organization) Military alliance of pro-American, anticommunist states in Southeast Asia from 1954 to 1977.

Second World Term invented during the cold war to refer to the communist countries, as opposed to the West (or First World) and the former colonies (or Third World).

second-generation societies Societies that expanded old ideas and methods by incorporating new aspects of culture and grafting them onto, or using them in combination with, established norms.

Seleucus Nikator Successor of Alexander the Great who lived from 358 to 281 BCE. He controlled Mesopotamia, Syria, Persia, and parts of the Punjab.

Self-Strengthening movement In the latter half of the nineteenth century, a movement of reformist Chinese bureaucrats that attempted to adopt western elements of learning and technological skill while retaining their core Chinese culture.

Semu Term meaning "outsiders" or non-Chinese people—Mongols, Tanguts, Khitan, Jurchen, Muslims, Tibetans, Persians, Turks, Nestorians, Jews, and Armenians—who became a new ruling elite over a Han majority population in the late thirteenth century.

sepoys Hindu and Muslim recruits of the East India Company's military force.

serfs Peasants who farmed the land and paid fees to be protected and governed by lords under a system of rule called feudalism.

settled agriculture Application of human labor and tools to a fixed plot of land for more than one growing cycle. It entails the changeover from a hunting-and-gathering lifestyle to one based on agriculture, which requires staying in one place until the soil has been exhausted.

Seven Years' War (1756–1763) Worldwide war that ended when Prussia defeated Austria, establishing itself as a European power, and when Britain gained control of India and many of France's colonies through the Treaty of Paris.

sexual revolution Increased freedom in sexual behavior, resulting in part from the advances in contraception, notably the introduction of oral contraception in 1960, which allowed men and women to limit childbearing and to have sex with less fear of pregnancy.

shah Traditional title of Persian rulers.

shamans Certain humans whose powers supposedly enabled them to commune with the supernatural and to transform themselves wholly or partly into beasts.

shamisen Three-stringed instrument, often played by Japanese geisha.

Shandingdong Man A *Homo sapiens* whose fossil remains and relics can be dated to about 18,000 years ago. His physical characteristics were close to those of modern humans, and he had a similar brain size.

Shang state Dynasty in northeastern China that ruled from 1600 to 1045 BCE. Though not as well defined by borders as the territorial states in the southwest of Asia, it did have a ruling lineage. Four fundamental elements of the Shang state were a metal industry based on copper, pottery making, standardized architectural forms and walled towns, and divination using animal bones.

Shanghai School Late-nineteenth-century style of painting characterized by an emphasis on spontaneous brushwork, feeling, and the incorporation of western influences into classical Chinese pieces.

sharecropping System of farming in which tenant farmers rented land and gave over a share of their crops to the land's owners. Sometimes seen as a cheap way for the state to conduct agricultural affairs, sharecropping often resulted in the impoverishment and marginalization of the underclass.

sharia Literally, "the way"; now used to indicate the philosophy and rulings of Islamic law.

Sharpeville Massacre (1960) Massacre of sixty-nine black Africans when police fired upon a rally against the recently passed laws requiring non-white South Africans to carry identity papers.

Shawnees Native American tribe that inhabited the Ohio valley during the eighteenth century.

Shays's Rebellion (1786) Uprising of armed farmers that broke out when the Massachusetts state government refused to offer them economic relief.

Shi Huangdi *See* Zheng.

Shiism One of the two main branches of Islam, practiced in the Safavid Empire. Although always a minority sect in the Islamic world, Shiism contains several subsects, each of which has slightly different interpretations of theology and politics.

Shiites Group of supporters of Ali, Muhammad's cousin and son-in-law, who wanted him to be the first caliph and believed that members of the Prophet's family deserved to rule. The leaders of the Shiite community are known as "Imam," which means "leaders."

Shinto Japan's official religion; it promoted the state and the emperor's divinity. The term means "the way of the gods."

shoguns Japanese military commanders. From 1192 to 1333, the Kamakura shoguns served as military "protectors" of the ruler in the city of Heian.

Shotoku Prince in the early Japanese Yamoto state (574–622 CE) who is credited with having introduced Buddhism to Japan.

shudras Literally "small ones"; workers and slaves from outside the Vedic lineage.

Siddhartha Gautama Another name for the Buddha; the most prominent opponent of the Brahman way of life; he lived from 563 to 483 BCE.

Sikhism Islamic-inspired religion that calls on its followers to renounce the caste system and to treat all believers as equal before God.

Silicon Valley Valley between the California cities of San Francisco and San Jose, known for its innovative computer and high-technology industries.

silk Luxury textile that became a vastly popular export from China (via the Silk Roads) to the cities of the Roman world.

Silk Roads Trade routes linking China with central Asia and the Mediterranean; it extended over 5,000 miles, land and sea included, and was so named because of the quantities of silk that were traded along it. The Silk Roads were a major factor in the development of civilizations in China, Egypt, Persia, India, and even Europe.

Silla One of three independent Korean states that may have emerged as early as the third century BCE. These states lasted until 668 CE, when Silla took control over the entire peninsula.

Silver Islands Term used by European merchants in the sixteenth century to refer to Japan, because of its substantial trade in silver with China.

Sino-Japanese War (1894–1895) Conflict over the control of Korea in which China was forced to cede the province of Taiwan to Japan.

Sipahi Urdu for "soldier."

Siva The third of three Vedic deities, signifying destruction. *See also* Brahma *and* Vishnu.

slave plantations System whereby labor was used for the cultivation of crops wholly for the sake of producing surplus that was then used for profit; slave plantations were a crucial part of the growth of the Mediterranean economy.

small seal script Unified script that was used to the exclusion of other scripts under the Qin, with the aim of centralizing administration; its use led to a less complicated style of clerical writing than had been in use under the Han.

social contract The idea, drawn from the writings of British philosopher John Locke, that the law should bind both ruler and people.

Social Darwinism Belief that Charles Darwin's theory of evolution was applicable to humans and justified the right of the ruling classes or countries to dominate the weak.

social hierarchies Distinctions between the privileged and the less privileged.

Social Security Act (1935) New Deal act that instituted old-age pensions and insurance for the unemployed.

socialism Political ideology that calls for a classless society with collective ownership of all property.

Socrates (469–399 BCE) Philosopher in Athens who encouraged people to reflect on ethics and morality. He stressed the importance of honor and integrity as opposed to wealth and power. Plato was his student.

Sogdians A people who lived in central Asia's commercial centers and maintained the stability and accessibility of the Silk Roads. They were crucial to the interconnectedness of the Afro-Eurasian landmass.

Solidarity The communist bloc's first independent trade union, it was established in Poland at the Gdansk shipyard.

Song dynasty Chinese dynasty that took over the mandate of heaven for three centuries starting in 976 CE. It ruled an era of many economic and political successes, but it eventually lost northern China to nomadic tribes.

Song porcelain Type of porcelain perfected during the Song period that was light, durable, and quite beautiful.

South African War (1899–1902) Conflict between the British and Dutch colonists of South Africa which resulted in bringing two Afrikaner republics under the control of the British. Often called the Boer War.

Soviet bloc International alliance that included the east European countries of the Warsaw Pact as well as the Soviet Union but also came to include Cuba.

Spanish-American War (1898) War between the United States and Spain in Cuba, Puerto Rico, and the Philippines. It ended with a treaty in which the United States took over the Philippines, Guam, and Puerto Rico; Cuba won partial independence.

speciation The formation of different species.

specie Money in coin.

species Group of animals or plants possessing one or more distinctive characteristics.

spiritual ferment Process that occurred after 300 CE in which religion touched more areas of society and culture than before and touched them in different, more demanding ways.

Spring and Autumn period Period between the eighth and fifth centuries BCE, during which China was ruled by the feudal system. Considered an anarchic and turbulent time, there were 148 different tributary states in this period.

Stalin, Joseph (1879–1953) Leader of the communist party and the Soviet Union; sought to create "socialism in one country."

steel A metal more malleable and stronger than iron that became essential for industries like shipbuilding and railways.

stoicism Widespread philosophical movement initiated by Zeno (334–262 BCE). Zeno and his followers sought to understand the role of people in relation to the cosmos. For the Stoics, everything was grounded in nature. Being in love with nature and living a good life required being in control of one's passions and thus indifferent to pleasure or pain.

Strait of Malacca Seagoing gateway to Southeast and East Asia.

Strategic Defense Initiative ("Star Wars") Master plan, championed by U.S. president Ronald Reagan in the 1980s, that envisions the deployment of satellites and space missiles to protect the United States from incoming nuclear bombs.

stupa Dome monument marking the burial site of relics of the Buddha.

Suez Canal Channel built in 1869 across the Isthmus of Suez to connect the Mediterranean Sea with the Red Sea and to lower the costs of international trade.

Sufi brotherhoods Mystics within Islam who were responsible for the expansion of Islam into many regions of the world.

Sufism Emotional and mystical form of Islam that appealed to the common people.

sultan Islamic political leader. In the Ottoman Empire, the sultan combined a warrior ethos with an unwavering devotion to Islam.

Sumerian King List Text that recounts the making of political dynasties. Recorded around 2000 BCE, it organizes the reigns of kings by dynasty, one city at a time.

Sumerian pantheon The Sumerian gods, each of whom had a home in a particular floodplain city. In the Sumerian belief system, both gods and the natural forces they controlled had to be revered.

Sumerian temples Homes of the gods and symbols of Sumerian imperial identity. Sumerian temples also represented the gods' ability to hoard wealth at sites where people exchanged goods and services. In addition, temples distinguished the urban from the rural world.

Sun Yat-sen (1866–1925) Chinese revolutionary and founder of the Nationalist Party in China.

Sunnis Orthodox Muslims. The majority sect of Islam, Sunnis originally supported the succession of Abu Bakr over Ali and supported the rule of consensus rather than family lineage for the succession to the Islamic caliphate. *See also* Shiism.

superior man In the Confucian view, a person of perfected moral character, fit to be a leader.

superpowers Label applied to the United States and the Soviet Union after World War II because of their size, their possession of the atomic bomb, and the fact that each embodied a model of civilization (capitalism or communism) applicable to the whole world.

supranational organizations International organizations such as nongovernmental organizations (NGOs), the World Bank, and the International Monetary Fund (IMF).

survival of the fittest Charles Darwin's belief that as animal populations grew and resources became scarce, a struggle for existence arose, the outcome of which was that only the "fittest" survived.

Suryavamsha The second lineage of two (the solar) in Vedic society. *See* Chandravamsha.

Swadeshi movement Voluntary organizations in India that championed the creation of indigenous manufacturing enterprises and schools of nationalist thought, in order to gain autonomy from Britain.

syndicalism Organization of workplace associations that included unskilled labor.

tabula rasa Term used by John Locke to describe the human mind before it begins to acquire ideas from experience; Latin for "clean slate."

Taiping Heavenly Kingdom (Heavenly Kingdom of Great Peace) Religious sect established by the Chinese prophet Hong Xiuquan in the mid-nineteenth century. Hong Xiuquan believed that he was Jesus's younger brother. The group struggled to rid the world of evil and "restore" the heavenly kingdom, imagined as a just and egalitarian order.

Taiping Rebellion Rebellion by followers of Hong Xiuquan and the Taiping Heavenly Kingdom against the Qing government over the economic and social turmoil caused by the Opium War. Despite raising an army of 100,000 rebels, the rebellion was crushed.

Taj Mahal Royal palace of the Mughal Empire, built by Shah Jahan in the seventeenth century in homage to his wife, Mumtaz.

Tale of Genji Japanese work written by Lady Murasaki that gives vivid accounts of Heian court life; Japan's first novel (early eleventh century).

talking cures Psychological practice developed by Sigmund Freud whereby the symptoms of neurotic and traumatized patients would decrease after regular periods of thoughtful discussion.

Talmud Huge volumes of oral commentary on Jewish law eventually compiled in two versions, the Palestinian and the Babylonian, in the fifth and sixth centuries BCE.

Talmud of Jerusalem Codified written volumes of the traditions of Judaism; produced by the rabbis of Galilee around 400 CE.

Tang dynasty (608–907 CE) Regime that promoted a cosmopolitan culture, turning China into the hub of East Asia cultural integration, while expanding the borders of their empire. In order to govern such a diverse empire, the Tang established a political culture and civil service based on Confucian teachings. Candidates for the civil service were required to take examinations, the first of their kind in the world.

Tanzimat Reorganization period of the Ottoman Empire in the mid-nineteenth century; modernizing reforms affected the military, trade, foreign relations, and civilian life.

tappers Rubber workers in Brazil, mostly either Indian or mixed-blood people.

Tarascans Mesoamerican society of the 1400s; rivals to and sometimes subjects of the Aztecs.

Tatish Ruler of Chan Santa Cruz during the Mexican Caste War. The term means "father."

Tecumseh (1768–1813) Shawnee who circulated Tenskwatawa's message of Indian renaissance among Indian villages from the Great Lakes to the Gulf Coast. He preached the need for Indian unity, insisting that Indians resist any American attempts to get them to sell more land. In response, thousands of followers renounced their ties to colonial ways and prepared to combat the expansion of the United States.

Tekkes Schools that taught devotional strategies and the religious knowledge for students to enter Sufi orders and become masters of the brotherhood.

temple Building where believers worshipped their gods and goddesses and where some peoples believed the deities had earthly residence.

Tenskwatawa (1768–1834) Shawnee prophet who urged disciples to abstain from alcohol and return to traditional customs, reducing dependence on European trade goods and severing connections to Christian missionaries. His message spread to other tribes, raising the specter of a pan-Indian confederacy.

Teotihuacán City-state in a large, mountainous valley in present-day Mexico; the first major community to emerge after the Olmecs.

territorial state Political form that emerged in the riverine cities of Mesopotamia, which was overwhelmed by the displacement of nomadic peoples. These states were kingdoms organized around charismatic rulers who headed large households; each had a defined physical border.

Third Estate The French people minus the clergy and the aristocracy; this term was popularized in the late eighteenth century and used to exalt the power of the bourgeoisie during the French Revolution.

Third Reich The German state from 1933 to 1945 under Adolf Hitler.

Third World Nations of the world, mostly in Asia, Latin America, and Africa, that were not highly industrialized like First World nations or tied to the Soviet bloc (the Second World).

Thirty Years' War (1618–1648) Conflict begun between Protestants and Catholics in Germany that escalated into a general European war fought against the unity and power of the Holy Roman Empire.

Tiananmen Square Largest public square in the world and site of the pro-democracy movement in 1989 that resulted in the killing of as many as a thousand protesters by the Chinese army.

Tiers monde Term meaning "Third World," coined by French intellectuals to describe countries seeking a "third way" between Soviet communism and western capitalism.

Tiglath Pileser III Assyrian ruler from 745 to 728 BCE. This leader instituted reforms that changed the administrative and social structure of the empire to make it more efficient and introduced a standing army.

Tiwanaku Another name for Tihuanaco, the first great Andean polity, on the shores of Lake Titicaca.

Tlaxcalans Mesoamerican society of the 1400s; these people were enemies of the powerful Aztec Empire.

Tokugawa shogunate Hereditary military administration founded in 1603 that ruled Japan while keeping the emperor as a figurehead; it was toppled in 1868 by reformers who felt that Japan should adopt, not reject, Western influences.

Toltecs A Mesoamerican people who, by 1000 CE, had filled the political vacuum created by the decline of the city of Teotihuacán.

tomb culture Warlike group from northeast Asia who arrived by sea in the middle of the third century CE and imposed their military and social power on southern Japan. These conquerors are known today as the tomb culture because of their elevated necropolises near present-day Osaka.

Topkapi Palace Political headquarters of the Ottoman Empire, located in Istanbul.

total war All-out war involving civilian populations as well as military forces, often used in reference to World War II.

transhumant migrants Nomads who entered settled territories in the second millennium BCE and moved their herds seasonally when resources became scarce.

Trans-Siberian Railroad Railroad built over very difficult terrain between 1891 and 1903 and subsequently expanded; it created an overland bridge for troops, peasant settlers, and commodities to move between Europe and the Pacific.

Treaty of Brest-Litovsk (1918) Separate peace between imperial Germany and the new Bolshevik regime in Russia. The treaty acknowledged the German victory on the Eastern Front and withdrew Russia from the war.

Treaty of Nanjing (1842) Treaty between China and Britain following the Opium War; it called for indemnities, the opening of new ports, and the cession of Hong Kong to the British.

Treaty of Tordesillas (1494) Treaty in which the pope decreed that the non-European world would be divided into spheres of trade and missionary responsibility between Spain and Portugal.

trickle trade Method by which a good is passed from one village to another, as in the case of obsidian among farming villages; the practice began around 7000 BCE. Also called "down-the-line trade."

Tripartite Pact (1940) Pact that stated that Germany, Italy, and Japan would act together in all future military ventures.

Triple Entente Alliance developed before World War I that eventually included Britain, France, and Russia.

Troy Important site founded around 3000 BCE in Anatolia, to the far west. Troy is legendary as the site of the war that was launched by the Greeks (the Achaeans) and that was recounted by Homer in the *Iliad*.

Truman Doctrine (1947) Declaration promising U.S. economic and military intervention, whenever and wherever needed, for the sake of preventing communist expansion.

Truth and Reconciliation Commission Quasi-judicial body established after the overthrow of the apartheid system in South Africa and the election of Nelson Mandela as the country's first black president in 1994. The commission was to gather evidence about crimes committed during the apartheid years. Those who showed remorse for their actions could appeal for clemency. The South African leaders believed that an airing of the grievances from this period would promote racial harmony and reconciliation.

truth commissions Elected officials' inquiries into human rights abuses by previous regimes. In Argentina, El Salvador, Guatemala, and South Africa, these commissions were vital for creating a new aura of legitimacy for democracies and for promising to uphold the rights of individuals.

tsar/czar Russian word derived from the Latin *Caesar* to refer to the Russian ruler of Kiev, and eventually to all rulers in Russia.

Tula Toltec capital city; a commercial hub and political and ceremonial center.

Uitlanders British populations living in Afrikaner republics; they were denied voting rights and subject to other forms of discrimination in the late nineteenth century. The term means "outsiders."

ulama Arabic word that means "learned ones" or "scholars"; used for those who devoted themselves to knowledge of Islamic sciences.

Umayyads Family who founded the first dynasty in Islam. They established family rule and dynastic succession to the role of caliph. The first Umayyad caliph established Damascus as his capital and was named Mu'awiya ibn Abi Sufyan.

Umma Arabic word for "community"; used to refer to the "Islamic polity" or "Islamic community."

Universal Declaration of Human Rights (1948) U.N. declaration that laid out the rights to which all human beings are entitled.

universalizing religions Religions that appeal to diverse populations; are easily adaptable across various cultural and geographical areas; promote universal rules and principles to guide behavior that transcend place, time, and specific cultural practices; are proselytized by energetic and charismatic missionaries; foster a deep sense of community felt by their converts; and are supported by powerful empires.

universitas Term used from the end of the twelfth century to denote scholars who came together, first in Paris. The term is borrowed from the merchant communities, where it denoted the equivalent of the modern "union."

Untouchables Caste in the Indian system whose jobs, usually in the more unsanitary aspects of urban life, rendered them "ritually and spiritually" impure.

Upanishads Vedic wisdom literature collected in the first half of the first millennium BCE. It took the form of dialogues between disciples and a sage.

urban-rural divide Division between those living in cities and those living in rural areas. One of history's most durable worldwide distinctions, the urban-rural divide eventually encompassed the globe. Where cities arose, communities adopted lifestyles based on the mass production of goods and on specialized labor. Those living in the countryside remained close to nature, cultivating the land or tending livestock. They diversified their labor and exchanged their grains and animal products for necessities available in urban centers.

utopian socialism The most visionary of all Restoration-era movements. Utopian socialists like Charles Fourier dreamed of transforming states, workplaces, and human relations and proposed plans to do so.

Vaishyas Householders or lesser clan members in Vedic society who worked the land and tended livestock.

Vardhamana Mahavira Advocate of Jainism who lived from 540 to 468 BCE; he emphasized interpretation of the Upanishads to govern and guide daily life.

varna Caste system established by the Vedas in 600 BCE.

vassal states Subordinate states that had to pay tribute in luxury goods, raw materials, and manpower as part of a broad confederation of polities under the kings' protection.

Vedas Rhymes, hymns, and explanatory texts composed by Aryan priests; the Vedas became their most holy scripture and part of their religious rituals. They were initially passed down orally, in Sanskrit. Brahmans, priests of Vedic culture, incorporated the texts into ritual and society. The Vedas are considered the final authority of Hinduism.

Vedic people People who came from the steppes of Inner Asia around 1500 BCE and entered the fertile lowlands of the Indus River basin, gradually moving as far south as the Deccan plateau. They called themselves Aryan, which means "respected ones," and spoke Sanskrit, an Indo-European language.

veiling Practice of modest dress required of respectable women in the Assyrian Empire, introduced by Assyrian authorities in the thirteenth century BCE.

Venus figures Representations of the goddess of fertility drawn on the Chauvet Cave in southeastern France. Discovered in 1994, they are probably about 35,000 years old.

Versailles Conference (1919) Peace conference between the victors of World War I; resulted in the Treaty of Versailles, which forced Germany to pay reparations and to give up its colonies to the victors.

Viet Cong Vietnamese communist group committed to overthrowing the government of South Vietnam and reunifying North and South Vietnam.

Viet Minh Group founded in 1941 by Ho Chi Minh to oppose the Japanese occupation of Indochina; it later fought the French colonial forces for independence. Also known as the Vietnamese Independent League.

Vietnam War (1965–1975) Conflict that resulted from concern over the spread of communism in Southeast Asia. The United States intervened on the side of South Vietnam in its struggle against peasant-supported Viet Cong guerrilla forces, who wanted to reunite Vietnam under a communist regime. Faced with antiwar opposition at home and ferocious resistance from the Vietnamese, American troops withdrew in 1973; the puppet South Vietnamese government collapsed two years later.

Vikings A people from Scandinavia who replaced the Franks as the dominant warrior class in northern Europe in the ninth century CE. They used their superior ships to loot other seagoing peoples and sailed up the rivers of central Russia to establish a trade route that connected Scandinavia and the Baltic with Constantinople and Baghdad. The Vikings established settlements in Iceland and Greenland and, briefly, North America.

Vishnu The second of three Vedic deities, signifying existence. *See also* Brahma *and* Siva.

viziers Bureaucrats of the Ottoman Empire.

Vodun Mixed religion of African and Christian customs practiced by slaves and free blacks in the colony of Saint-Domingue.

Voting Rights Act (1965) Law that granted universal suffrage in the United States.

Wafd Nationalist party that came into existence during a rebellion in Egypt in 1919 and held power sporadically after Egypt was granted limited independence from Britain in 1922.

Wahhabism Early eighteenth-century reform movement organized by Muhammad Ibn abd al-Wahhab, who preached the absolute oneness of Allah and a return to the pure Islam of Muhammad.

Wang Mang Han minister who usurped the throne in 9 CE because he believed that the Han had lost the mandate of heaven. He ruled until 23 CE.

war ethos Strong social commitment to a continuous state of war. The Roman army constantly drafted men and engaged in annual spring military campaigns. Soldiers were taught to embrace a sense of honor that did not allow them to accept defeat and commended those who repeatedly threw themselves into battle.

War of 1812 Conflict between Britain and the United States arising from U.S. grievances over oppressive British maritime practices in the Napoleonic Wars.

War on Poverty President Lyndon Johnson's push for an increased range of social programs and increased spending on social security, health, education, and assistance for the disabled.

Warring States period Period extending from the fifth century to 221 BCE, when the regional warring states were unified by the Qin dynasty.

Warsaw Pact (1955–1991) Military alliance between the Soviet Union and other communist states that was established in response to the creation of the North American Treaty Organization (NATO) alliance.

Weimar Republic (1919–1933) Constitutional Republic of Germany that was subverted by Hitler soon after he became chancellor.

Western Front Military front that stretched from the English Channel through Belgium and France to the Alps during World War I.

White and Blue Niles The two main branches of the Nile, rising out of central Africa and Ethiopia. They come together at the present-day capital city of Sudan, Khartoum.

White Lotus Rebellion Series of uprisings in northern China (1790–1800s) inspired by mystical beliefs in folk Buddhism and, at times, the idea of restoring the Ming dynasty.

White Wolf Mysterious militia leader, depicted in popular myth as a Chinese Robin Hood whose mission was to rid the country of the injustices of Yuan Shikai's government in the early years of the Chinese Republic (1910s).

Whites "Counterrevolutionaries" of the Bolshevik Revolution (1918–1921) who fought the Bolsheviks (the "Reds"); included former supporters of the tsar, Social Democrats, and large independent peasant armies.

witnessing Dying for one's faith, or becoming a martyr.

Wokou Supposedly Japanese pirates, many of whom were actually Chinese subjects of the Ming dynasty.

Works Progress Administration (WPA) New Deal program instituted in 1935 that put nearly 3 million people to work building roads, bridges, airports, and post offices.

World Bank International agency established in 1944 to provide economic assistance to war-torn and poor countries. Its formal title is the International Bank for Reconstruction and Development.

World War I *See* Great War.

World War II (1939–1945) Worldwide war that began in September 1939 in Europe, and even earlier in Asia, and pitted Britain, the United States, and the Soviet Union (the Allies) against Nazi Germany, Japan, and Italy (the Axis).

Wu or **Wudi** Chinese leader known as the "Martial Emperor" because of his many military campaigns during the Han dynasty. He reigned from 141 to 87 BCE.

Wu Zhao Chinese empress who lived from 626 to 706 CE. She began as a concubine in the court of Li Shimin and became the mother of his son's child. She eventually gained power equal to that of the emperor, and named herself regent when she finagled a place for one of her own sons after their father's death.

Xiongnu The most powerful and intrusive of the nomadic peoples; originally pastoralists from the eastern part of the Asian steppe in what is modern-day Mongolia. They appeared along the frontier with China in the late Zhou dynasty and by the third century BCE had become the most powerful of all the pastoral communities in that area.

Xunzi Confucian moralist whose ideas were influential to Qin rulers. He lived from 310 to 237 BCE and believed that rational statecraft was more reliable than fickle human nature and that strict laws and severe punishments could create stability in society.

Yalta Accords Results of the meeting between President Roosevelt, Prime Minister Churchill, and Premier Stalin that occurred in the Crimea in 1945 to plan for the postwar order.

Yavana kings Sanskrit name for Greek rulers, derived from the Greek name for the area of western Asia Minor called Ionia, a term that then extended to anyone who spoke Greek or came from the Mediterranean.

yellow press Newspapers that sought a mass circulation by featuring sensationalist reporting.

Yellow Turbans One of several local Chinese religious movements that emerged across the empire, especially under Wang Mang's officials, who considered him a usurper. The Yellow Turbans, so called because of the yellow scarves they wore around their heads, were Daoist millenarians.

Yin City that became the capital of the Shang in 1350 BCE, ushering in a golden age.

Young Egypt Antiliberal, fascist group that gained a large following in Egypt during the 1930s.

Young Italy Nationalist organization made up of young students and intellectuals, devoted to the unification and renewal of the Italian state.

Yuan dynasty Dynasty established by the Mongols after the defeat of the Song. The Yuan dynasty was strong from 1280 to 1368; its capital was at Dadu, or modern-day Beijing.

Yuan Mongols Mongol rulers of China who were overthrown by the Ming dynasty in 1368.

Yuezhi A Turkic nomadic people who roamed on pastoral lands to the west of the Xiongnu territory of central Mongolia. They had friendly relationships with the farming societies in China, but the Yuezhi detested the Xiongnu and had frequent armed clashes with them.

Zaibatsu Large-scale, family-owned corporations in Japan consisting of factories, import-export businesses, and banks that dominated the Japanese economy until 1945.

Zamindars Archaic tax system of the Mughal Empire where decentralized lords collected tribute for the emperor.

Zapatistas Group of indigenous rebels that rose up against the Mexican government in 1994 and drew inspiration from an earlier Mexican rebel, Emiliano Zapata.

Zheng King during the Qin era who defeated what was left of the Warring States between 230 and 221 BCE. He assumed the mandate of heaven from the Zhou and declared himself Shi Huangdi ("First August Emperor"), to distinguish himself from other kings.

Zheng He (1371–1433) Ming naval leader who established tributary relations with Southeast Asia, Indian Ocean ports, the Persian Gulf, and the east coast of Africa.

Zhong Shang Administrative central complex of the Shang.

Zhongguo Term originating in the ancient period and subsequently used to emphasize the central cultural and geographical location of China in the world; means "Middle Kingdom."

ziggurat By the end of the third millennium BCE, the elevated platform base of a Sumerian temple had transformed into a stepped platform called a *ziggurat*.

Zionism Political movement advocating the reestablishment of a Jewish homeland in Palestine.

Zoroaster Sometimes known as Zarathustra, thought to have been a teacher around 1000 BCE in eastern Iran and credited with having solidified the region's religious beliefs into a unified system that moved away from animistic nomadic beliefs. The main source for his teachings is a compilation called the Avesta.

Zoroastrianism Religion based on the teachings of Zoroaster that became the dominant religion of the Persian Empire.

Zulus African tribe that, under Shaka, created a ruthless warrior state in southern Africa in the early 1800s.

Credits

CHAPTER 1

Photo Credits Pages 2–3: Erich Lessing/Art Resource; p. 6 & 7: Volker Steger/Science Source; p. 8: Robert Preston/Alamy; p. 11: John Reader/Photo Researchers; p. 12: Staffan Widstrand/Corbis; p. 13: Pascal Goetgheluck/Photo Researchers; p. 14: Lionel Bret/Photo Researchers; p. 21: Images of Africa Photobank/Alamy; p. 22: Erich Lessing/Art Resource; p. 27: Copyright © Christie's Images Ltd. All rights reserved; p. 31: Boltin Picture Library/Bridgeman Art Library; p. 34 (top): Bruce Smith, The Emergence of Agriculture (New York: Diane Publishing Company, 1998), p. 104; p. 34 (bottom): De Agostini Picture Library/M. Seemuller/Bridgeman Images; p. 43: Erich Lessing/Art Resource.

Text Credits Primary Source 1.1 (pps. 38–39): Ainslee T. Embree (ed.), from *Sources of Indian Tradition, Vol. 1, From the Beginning to 1800*, 2nd ed., pp. 18–19. Edited and revised by Ainslie T. Embree. Copyright © 1988 Columbia University Press. Reprinted with permission of the publisher. Primary Source 1.2 (pps. 39–40): Genesis 1:1-31. The Scripture quotations contained herein are from the *New Revised Standard Version Bible*, copyright © 1989, by the Division of Christian Education of the National Council of the Churches of Christ in the U.S.A., and are used by permission. All rights reserved. Primary Source 1.3 (p. 40): From *Sources of Chinese Tradition*, 2nd Edition, Volume 2, pp. 346–347. Edited by Wm. Theodore de Bary and Richard Lufrano. Copyright © 2000 Columbia University Press. Reprinted with permission of the publisher. Primary Source 1.4 (pps. 40–41): Adrian Recinos, *Popol Vuh: The Sacred Book of the Ancient Quiche Maya*, English version by Delia Goetz & Sylvanus G. Morley, from the translation of Adrian Recinos. Copyright © 1950 The University of Oklahoma Press. Reproduced with permission. All rights reserved. Primary Source 1.5 (pps. 42–43): "Yoruba Creation Narrative" as translated by P.J. Criss. Reprinted by permission of the Estate of P.J. Criss.

CHAPTER 2

Photo Credits Pages 46–47: The Trustees of the British Museum/Bridgeman Art Library; p. 48: Granger Collection; p. 55: University of Pennsylvania Museum of Archaeology and Anthropology; p. 62 (left): Gianni Dagli Orti/Corbis; p. 62 (right): Christine Osborne/Corbis; p. 63 (left): Scala/Art Resource; p. 63 (right): Sandro Vannini/Corbis; p. 66 & 67: © Eric & David Hosking/Corbis; p. 69: Diego Lezama Orezzoli/Corbis; p. 70: Wikimedia Commons; p. 72: Asian Art & Archaeology, Inc./Corbis; p. 73: HIP/Art Resource; p. 75: Adam Woolfitt/Corbis; p. 84 (left): Copyright Harappa Archaeological Research Project/Harappa.com, Courtesy Dept. of Archaeology and Museums, Govt. of Pakistan; p. 84 (right): Copyright Harappa Archaeological Research Project/Harappa.com, Courtesy Dept. of Archaeology and Museums, Govt. of Pakistan; p. 85: Boromeo/Art Resource.

Text Credits Primary Sources 2.1, 2.2 (pps. 80–82): J. A. Black, G. Cunningham, E. Fluckiger-Hawker, E. Robson, and G. Zólyomi, from *The Electronic Text Corpus of Sumerian Literature* (University of Oxford, 1998–2006), www-etcsl.orient.ox.ac.uk/. Primary Source 2.3 (p. 82–83): "Satire of the Trades" from *Ancient Egyptian Literature, Vol. 1, The Old and Middle Kingdoms*, edited by Miriam Lichtheim. Copyright © 1975 University of California Press. Reprinted with permission.

CHAPTER 3

Photo Credits Pages 86–87: Scala/Art Resource; p. 89 (top left): Art Resource; p. 89 (top right): Scala/Art Resource; p. 89 (bottom right): JTB Photo Communications/Alamy; p. 94: Roger Wood/Corbis; p. 97: Sandro Vannini/Corbis; p. 98: Eric Lessing/Art Resource; p. 99: Berlin Museum; p. 101: National Museum of India, New Delhi; p. 107: Yale University Art Gallery/Art Resource; p. 110: Albrecht G. Schaefer/Corbis; p. 112: Institute of Nautical Archaeology, Bodrum, Turkey; p. 114: Erich Lessing/Art Resource.

Text Credits Primary Source 3.4 (p. 121): "Treaty between Tudhaliya IV and Shaushga-muwa of Amurru" from *Hittite Diplomatic Texts*, 2nd Ed. by Gary Beckman. Copyright © 1999 The Society of Biblical Literature. Reprinted with the permission of the publisher. Primary Source 3.6 (pps. 122–123): Earnest Caldwell, "Social Change and Written law in Early Chinese Legal Thought," From *Law and History Review* 32(1), p. 15. Reprinted by permission of Cambridge University Press.

CHAPTER 4

Photo Credits Pages 124–125: Dagli Orti/Louvre/Bridgeman Art Library; p. 127 (left): (c) A. Paul Jenkin/Animals Animals; p. 127 (right): S. Muller/Peter Arnold, Inc.; P 130 & 131: Wikimedia Commons; p. 133: The Trustees of the British Museum; p. 134: British Museum/Bridgeman Art Library; p. 137: EmmePi Iran/Alamy; p. 138: Erich Lessing/Art Resource, NY; p. 140: Scala/Art Resource, NY; p. 143 (left): Dagli Orti/Art Archive; p. 143 (right): Dagli Orti/Art Archive; p. 147: British Museum; p. 149: Giraudon/Art Resource; p. 151: Asia Society, New York: Mr. and Mrs. John D. Rockefeller 3rd Collection 1979, 100a,b. Photograph by Lynton Gardiner; P: 158: Spurlock Museum; p. 159: Bridgeman Art Library.

Text Credits Primary Source 4.2 (pp. 157–158): Roland G. Kent, from *Old Persian: Grammar, Texts, Lexicon*, 2nd Revised Ed. pp. 131–32. Copyright © 1953 American Oriental Society. Reprinted with permission. Primary Source 4.4 (158–159): "The Great Declaration" by King Wu. From *The Chinese Classics in Five Volumes. Volume 3: The Shoo King*, James Legge (ed.).

CHAPTER 5

Photo Credits Pages 162–163 (left): National Library of China; p. 162–163(center): Scala/Art Resource, NY; p. 162–163(right): Erich Lessing/Art Resource, NY; p. 169: Wikimedia Commons; p. 171: Erich Lessing/Art Resource, NY; p. 173 (left): Paul Almasy/Corbis; p. 173 (right): Corbis; p. 175: Borromeo/Art Resource, NY; p. 176: National Library of China; p. 177: Scala/Art Resource, NY; p. 179: The Bridgeman Art Library; p. 180 (left):Erich Lessing/Art Resource, NY; p. 180 (right): HIP/Art Resource, NY; p. 181: Scala/Art Resource, NY; p. 185 (left): Gillett Griffin; p. 185 (right): Gillett Griffin; p. 190: Erich Lessing/Art Resource, NY.

Text Credits Primary Source 5.1 (194–195): K.D. Irani (ed. & trans.), "Yasna 33" From The Gathas: The Hymns of Zarathushtra (Mumbai: K.R. Cama Oriental Institute, 1999), pp. 47–50. Used by permission of K.D. Irani. Primary Source 5.2 (195–196): Confucius, from *The Analects of Confucius*, translated by Simon Leys. Copyright © 1997 by Pierre Ryckmans. Used by permission of W.W. Norton & Company, Inc. Primary Source 5.4 (197–198): Excerpt from *The Buddhist Tradition in India, China & Japan* (1972), by William Theodore de Bary. Published by Vintage Books, a division of Random House LLC. Used by permission of Alfred A. Knopf, an imprint of the Knopf Doubleday Publishing Group, a division of Random House LLC. All rights reserved. Primary Source 5.6 (pps. 199–200): Ezekiel 18:5-20. The Scripture quotations contained herein are from *the New Revised Standard Version Bible*, copyright © 1989, by the Division of Christian Education of the National Council of the Churches of Christ in the U.S.A., and are used by permission. All rights reserved.

CHAPTER 6

Photo Credits Pages 202–203: © The Cleveland Museum of Art; p. 205 (top): Erich Lessing/Art Resource, NY; p. 205 (bottom): Lauros/Giraudon/The Bridgeman Art Library; p. 209: Vanni/Art Resource, NY; p. 214 & 215: Wikimedia Commons; p. 216 (left): Brian A. Vikander/Corbis; p. 216 (right): The Bridgeman Art Library; p. 217 (top): Courtesy of Bill Welch, "What I Like About Ancient Coins" http://www.forumancientcoins.com/moonmoth/ancientcoins.html; p. 217 (right): Courtesy of Bill Welch, "What I Like About Ancient Coins" http://www.forumancientcoins.com/moonmoth/ancientcoins.html; p. 218: © The Cleveland Museum of Art; p. 220 (left): The Metropolitan Museum of Art. Gift of Muneichi Nitta, 2003 (2003.593.1) Image © The Metropolitan Museum of Art; p. 220 (right): Image copyright © The Metropolitan Museum of Art/Art Resource, NY; p. 225: The Art Archive/Palmyra Museum Syria/Dagli Orti; p. 226: NASA/JPL; p. 240: Image courtesy of David Schulz.

Text Credits Primary Source 6.2 (pps. 235–237): Asoka, "The Kalinga Edict," from *Inscriptions of Asoka*, translated by D.C. Sircar. Reprinted from the Publications Division of the Ministry of Information and Broadcasting of India, 1967.

CHAPTER 7

Photo Credits Pages 242–243: Erich Lessing/Art Resource, NY; p. 247: Snark/Art Resource; p. 248 (top): Louis Mazzatenta/National Geographic Image Collection; p. 248 (bottom): The Bridgeman Art Library; p. 249: British Museum/Art Resource, NY; p. 250: Model of House, Chinese. 1st century C.E., Eastern Han Dynasty (25-220 C.E.). Earthenware with unfired coloring, 52 x 33 1/2 x 27 inches (132.1 x 85.1 x 68.6 cm). The Nelson-Atkins Museum of Art, Kansas City, Missouri. Purchase: Nelson Trust, 33-521. Photograph by Jamison Miller; p. 251 (top left): Royal Ontario Museum/Corbis; p. 251 (bottom left): Asian Art & Archaeology, Inc./Corbis; p. 251 (right): Asian Art & Archaeology, Inc./Corbis; p. 260: Vanni/Art Resource, NY; p. 261: Atlantide Phototravel/Corbis; p. 262 (left): Roger Wood/Corbis; p. 262 (right): Scala/Art Resource; p. 263: HIP/ Art Resource, NY; p. 267: Erich Lessing/Art Resource, NY; p. 268 & 269:The Metropolitan Museum of Art/Art Resource; p. 278: Public Domain/Wikipedia Commons.

Text Credits Primary Source 7.1 (p. 272): Dong Zhongshu, "Responsibilities of Han Rulership" from *Sources of Chinese Tradition, Volume 1*, Edited by Wm. Theodore de Bary and Richard

Lufrano,. Copyright © 1999 Columbia University Press. Reprinted with permission of the publisher. Primary Source 7.3 (pps. 274–275): "Debate on Salt and Iron" from *Sources of Chinese Tradition, Volume 1*, Edited by Wm. Theodore de Bary and Richard Lufrano, Copyright © 1999 Columbia University Press. Reprinted with permission of the publisher. Primary Source 7.5 (pps. 276–277): Ban Zhao, from *Pan Chao: Foremost Woman Scholar of China*. Translated by Nancy Lee Swann (New York: Russell & Russell, 1932, 1968). Used by permission of the American Historical Association. Primary Source 7.6 (p. 277): Mary R. Lefkowitz & Maureen B. Fant, eds. *Women's Life in Greece and Rome: A Source Book in Translation. Third Edition*. pp. 50–51. © 1982, 1992, 2005 Mary F. Lefkowitz and Maureen B. Fant. Reprinted with permission of Johns Hopkins University Press.

CHAPTER 8

Photo Credits Pages 280–281: Charles & Josette Lenars/Corbis; p. 283: Scala/Art Resource; p. 286: Scala/Art Resource; p. 291: Corbis Images; p. 294: Julian Chichester/Bridgeman Art Library; p. 295 (left): Art Resource; p. 295 (right): Dean Conger/Corbis; p. 298: akg-images/Werner Forman; p. 301: Réunion de Musées Nationaux/Art Resource, NY; p. 302: National Palace Museum, Taipei, China; p. 306: Gianni Dagli Orti/Corbis; p. 307: Angelo Hornak/Corbis; p. 308: Werner Forman/Art Resource, NY.

Text Credits Primary Source 8.2 (p. 313): Excerpt from *Egeria: Diary of a Pilgrimage*, from the Ancient Christian Writers Series, translated and annotated by George E. Gingras, Ph. D. Copyright © 1970 by Rev. Johannes Quasten, Rev. Walter J. Burghardt, SJ and Thomas Comerford Lawler. The Newman Press-Paulist Press. Used with permission www.paulistpress.com. Primary Source 8.4 (pps. 314–315): A.C. Bhaktivedanta Swami Prabhupāda (trans.), from *Srimad Bhagavatam: Third Canto* (Bhaktivedanta Book Trust, 1974), p. 16. Quoted text courtesy of The Bhaktivedanta Book Trust International, Inc. www.Krishna.com. Used with permission.

CHAPTER 9

Photo Credits Pages 320–321: Patrick Ward/Corbis; p. 322: Suhaib Salem/Reuters/Corbis; p. 329 (left): Vanni Archive/Corbis; p. 329 (right): Patrick Ward/Corbis; p. 331 (left): Gavin Hellier/JAI/Corbis; p. 331 (right): Christine Osborne/Corbis; p. 336 (left): Werner Forman/Art Resource, NY; p. 336 (right): Kurt Scholz/SuperStock; p. 342: Julia Waterlow/Eye Ubiquitous/Corbis; p. 344 (left): CulturalEyes-AusGS/Alamy; p. 344 (right): Wikimedia Commons; p. 347: Giraudon/Bridgeman Art Library; p. 348 (left): Alamy; p. 348 (right): Alamy; p. 350: Werner Forman/Art Resource; p. 351: Alamy; p. 356: Granger Collection.

Text Credits Primary Source 9.1 (pps. 354–355): Marmaduke Pickthall (trans.), "Sura 4" from *Qur'an*: A Norton Critical Edition, edited by Jane Dammen McAuliffe. Copyright © 2014 by W.W. Norton & Company, Inc. Used by permission of W.W. Norton & Company, Inc. Primary Source 9.4 (pps. 356–357): Heying Jenny Zhan and Robert Bradshaw (trans.), "The Book of Analects for Women: Consort Song," from *Journal of Historical Sociology* 9(3), pp. 261–269. Copyright © 1996 Blackwell Publishers Ltd. Reprinted by permission of John Wiley & Sons, Inc. Primary Source 9.6 (p. 358): Yu Xuanji, from *An Anthology of Chinese Literature, Beginnings to 1911*, edited and translated by Stephen Owen. Copyright © 1996 by W.W. Norton & Company, Inc. Used by permission of W.W. Norton & Company, Inc.

CHAPTER 10

Photo Credits Pages 360–361: HIP/Art Resource, NY; p. 362: Granger Collection; p. 363: Nik Wheeler/Corbis; p. 365: Alamy; p. 371: Keren Su/Corbis; p. 375 (top): Granger Collection; p. 375 (bottom): Christophe Loviny/Corbis; p. 379: The Art Archive; p. 380 & 381: Snark/Art Resource; p. 384: Werner Forman/Art Resource, NY; p. 386 (top): Charles & Josette Lenars/Corbis; p. 386 (bottom): Otto Lang/Corbis; p. 389: akg-images; p. 400: Granger Collection.

Text Credits Primary Source 10.2 (p. 397): Guyuk Khan, from *Mission to Asia: Narratives and Letters of the Franciscan Missionairies in Mongolia and China in the Thirteenth and Fourteenth Centuries*, Christopher Dawson, ed. (New York: Harper & Row, 1966). Reprinted by permission of HarperCollins Publishers. Primary Source 10.3 (p. 398): *The Monks of Ḳûblâi Khân, Emperor of China, or, The history of the life and travels of Rabban Ṣâwmâ, envoy and plenipotentiary of the Mongol khans to the kings of Europe, and Markôs who as Mâr Yahbh-Allâhâ III became Patriarch of the Nestorian Church in Asia*. Edited and translated by E.A. Wallis Budge (London: Religious Tract Society, 1928). Reprinted by permission of the Lutterworth Press.

CHAPTER 11

Photo Credits Pages 402–403: Snark/Art Resource; p. 405: The Granger Collection, New York; p. 409: Wikimedia Commons; p. 413: Album/Art Resource; p. 414: Yann Arthus-Bertrand/Corbis; p. 415: Stapleton Collection, UK/Bridgeman Art Library International Ltd; p. 418 & 419: Giraudon/Art Resource, NY; p. 421: The Granger Collection; p. 423 (left): Scala/Art Resource; p. 423 (right): Scala/Art Resource; p. 425: The Granger Collection, New York; p. 426: Réunion de

Musées Nationaux/Art Resource, NY; p. 429: The Jan Adkins Studio; p. 437: Bridgeman Art Library; p. 438 (top): Library of the Topkapi Palace Museum folio 31b, photograph courtesy of Talat Halman; p. 438 (right): Granger Collection.

Text Credits Primary Source 11.1 (p. 434): Robertus de Avesbury, "The Flagellants in England" from *The Black Death*, Rosemary Horrox, trans./ed., pp. 153-154. Copyright © Rosemary Horrox 1994. Reprinted with permission of Manchester University Press. Primary Source 11.2 (p. 435): Ming Shi-Lu, from *Southeast Asia in the Ming Shi-lu: An Open Access Resource*, Geoff Wade (trans.). Reprinted with permission of NUS Press, Singapore. Primary Source 11.5 (pp. 437–438): Ahmet Karamustafa, "Dervish Groups in the Ottoman Empire 1450-1550" from *God's Unruly Friends: Dervish Groups in the Islamic Later Middle Period*, pp. 6–7 (Oneworld Publications, 2006). Copyright © 1994 by the University of Utah Press. Used by permission of the University of Utah Press.

CHAPTER 12

Photo Credits Pages 440–441: Wychwood Editions; p. 442: Réunion de Musées Nationaux/Art Resource, NY; p. 443: akg-images/Cameraphoto; p. 444: Biblioteca Estense, Modena, Italy/ Scala/Art Resource, NY; p. 445: Bildarchiv Preussischer Kulturbesitz/Art Resource, NY; p. 449: The Granger Collection, New York; p. 450 (left):Granger Collection; p. 450 (right): The Art Archive/Government Palace Tlaxcala Mexico/Mireille Vautier; p. 455 & 456: Francois Guenet/Art Resource; p. 456 (bottom): The Granger Collection, New York; p. 461: Bridgeman Art Library; p. 466: The Art Archive/Maritime Museum Kronborg Castle Denmark/ Gianni Dagli Orti; p. 473: Granger Collection; p. 475: Réunion de Musées Nationaux/Art Resource.

Text Credits Primary Source 12.1 (p. 470): T'ien-Tsê Chang, from *Sino-Portuguese Trade From 1514 to 1644: A Synthesis of Portuguese and Chinese Sources* (Leyden: E.J. Brill, 1934), pp. 51–52. Reprinted by permission of Brill Academic Publishers. Primary Source 12.5 (p. 473): Jacques Cartier, from *The Voyages of Jacques Cartier*, Ramsay Cook (ed.), Copyright © 1993 University of Toronto Press. Reprinted with permission.

CHAPTER 13

Photo Credits Pages 478–479: Réunion de Musées Nationaux/Art Resource; p. 480 & 481 (right): British Museum, London/E.T. Archives, London/SuperStock; p. 481 (left): Chester Beatty Library and Gallery of Oriental Art, Dublin/ Bridgeman; p. 486: The Granger Collection, NY; p. 487: MPI/Getty Images; p. 488: MPI/Getty Images; p. 493 (left): © 1989 North Wind Picture Archives; p. 493 (right): Private Collection/The Bridgeman Art Gallery; p. 494: The Newberry Library; p. 495: Mary Evans Picture Library/The Image Works; p. 497: The Art Archive/Museum der Stadt Wien/Dagli Orti; p. 499: © The Metropolitan Museum of Art/Art Resource, NY; p. 503: The Art Archive; p. 508: Anne S. K. Brown Military Collection, Brown University Library; p. 511: Chateau de Versailles, France/Bridgeman Art :library; p. 518: Getty Images.

Text Credits Primary Source 13.2 (p. 517): Thomas Phillips, from *Documents Illustrative of the History of the Slave Trade to America, Vol. 1, No. 409* (New York: Octagon, 1965). Reprinted by permission of the Carnegie Institution. Primary Source 13.5 (p. 519): Olaudah Equiano, from *The Interesting Narrative of the Life of Olaudah Equiano, or Gustavus Vassa, the African, Written by Himself,* A Norton Critical Edition, pp. 38–41. Copyright © 2001 by W.W. Norton & Company, Inc. Used by permission of W.W. Norton & Company, Inc.

CHAPTER 14

Photo Credits Pages 522–523: Scala/ Art Resource, NY; p. 526 (left): Topkapi Palace Museum, Istanbul; p. 526 (right): Victoria & Albert Museum, London/ Art Resource, NY; p. 528: By permission of the trustees of the Chester Beatty Library and Gallery of Oriental Art; p. 530 & 531: Werner Forman/ Art Resource; p. 532 (left): Underwood & Underwood/Corbis; p. 532 (right): Underwood & Underwood/Corbis; p. 534: The British Library, London/ The Bridgeman Art Library; p. 536: Image copyright © The Metropolitan Museum of Art / Art Resource, NY; p. 541 (top): Private Collection/The Bridgeman Art Library; p. 541 (bottom): Private Collection/The Bridgeman Art Library; p. 544 (left): Museo de America, Madrid; p. 544 (right): Museo de America, Madrid; p. 546 (left): E.T. Archives, London/Superstock; p. 546 (right): The Granger Collection, New York; p. 552: Public Domain/Wikipedia Commons.

Text Credits Primary Source 14.2 (p. 553): Excerpt from The Great Learning for Women (Onna Daigaku), *Sources of Japanese Tradition,* 2nd Ed., Volume 2. Edited by William Theodore de Bary, Carol Gluck, and Arthur L. Tiedemann. Copyright © 2006 Columbia University Press. Reprinted with permission of the publisher. Primary Source 14.3 (p. 554): Jean-Jacques Rousseau, from *Rousseau's Political Writings:* A Norton Critical Edition, edited by Alan Ritter and Julia Conaway Bondanella, translated by Julia Conaway Bondanella. Copyright © 1988 by W.W. Norton & Company, Inc. Used by permission of W.W. Norton & Company, Inc.

CHAPTER 15

Photo Credits Pages 558–559: Stefano Bianchetti/Corbis; p. 564: Collection of the New-York Historical Society; p. 566: Hulton Archive/Getty Images;

p. 569: North Wind Picture Archives; p. 570 & 571: The Granger Collection, NY; p. 575: Granger Collection; p. 577: The Granger Collection, New York; p. 584: Courtesy of the director, National Army Museum, London; p. 586 (left): The British Library, London/The Bridgeman Art Library; p. 586 (right): North Wind Picture Archives; p. 595: Bridgeman Art Library.

Text Credits Primary Source 15.2 (pp. 593–594): "The Haitian Declaration of Independence, January 1, 1804" from *Slave Revolution in the Caribbean, 1789-1804: A Brief History with Documents* (2006). Edited by Laurent Dubois & John D. Garrigus. Reprinted by permission of Palgrave Macmillan US.

CHAPTER 16

Photo Credits Pages 600–601: Harvard-Yenching Library, Harvard University; p. 604 & 605: Wikimedia Commons; p. 608 (left): The British Library, London; p. 608 (right): National Archives, Zimbabwe; p. 611: Granger Collection; p. 612: Corbis; p. 615: Granger Collection; p. 616: Alamy; p. 620 (left): The Granger Collection, New York; p. 620 (right): Granger Collection; p. 624: Getty Images.

Text Credits Primary Source 16.1 (pps. 630–631): From "Kitab Al-Farq: A Work on the Habe Kingdoms Attributed to 'Uthman Dan Fodio,'" *Bulletin of the School of Oriental and African Studies*, Volume 23, Issue 03, October 1960, pp. 558- 579. Copyright © 1960 School of Oriental and African Studies. Reprinted with the permission of Cambridge University Press. Primary Source 16.2 (pps. 631–632): From "Words of Tenskwatawa," in *Messages and Letters of William Henry* Harrision, Edited by Logan Esarey. (Indianapolis: Indiana Historical Commission, 1922). Reprinted by permission of the Indiana Historical Society Press. Primary Source 16.3 (p. 632): Karl Marx and Friedrich Engels, from "The Communist Manifesto," in *The Marx-Engels Reader*, 2nd ed., pp. 473–83, 490–91, 500. Edited by Robert C. Tucker. Primary Source 16.4 (p. 633): From "The Principles of the Heavenly Nature," in *Sources of Chinese Tradition*, 2nd Edition, Volume 2, pp. 229–30. Edited by Wm. Theodore de Bary and Richard Lufrano. Copyright © 2000 Columbia University Press. Reprinted with permission of the publisher.

CHAPTER 17

Photo Credits Pages 636–637: Tsuneo Tamba Collection, Yokohama/ Laurie Platt Winfrey, Inc.; p. 641 (left): Granger Collection; p. 641 (right): The Granger Collection, New York/The Granger Collection; p. 643: Time & Life Pictures/Getty Images; p. 649: Bettmann/Corbis; p. 650 (left): Illustrated London News/Mary Evans Picture Library; p. 650 (right): Nizamps Good Works Project - Famine Relief: Road Building, Aurangabad 1895-1902. from Judith Gutman, Through Indian Eyes, Private Collection; p. 653 (left): Hulton Getty/Liaison; p. 653 (right): Private Collection/The Bridgeman Art Library; p. 654 & 655: Roger-Viollet, Paris/The Bridgeman Art Library; p. 656: The Art Archive; p. 658: Erich Lessing/Art Resource, NY; p. 660: The Art Archive; p. 674: Encyclopedia of the Ottoman Empire, by Gabor Agoston and Bruce Alan Masters.

Text Credits Primary Source 17.3 (pps. 670–671): Hoang Cao Khai, "Letter from Hoang Cao Khai to Phan Đinh Phung" from *Patterns of Vietnamese Response to Foreign Intervention, 1858-1900*. Copyright © 1967 by Yale University Southeast Asian Studies. Reprinted with permission. Primary Source 17.4 (pps. 671–672): Bal Gangdadhar Tilak, "Address to the Indian National Congress, 1907" *Sources of Indian Tradition*, edited by William Theodore de Bary. Copyright © 1958 Columbia University Press. Reprinted with permission of the publisher.

CHAPTER 18

Photo Credits Pages 676–677: SuperStock; p. 679 (left): Hulton Archive/ Getty Images; p. 679 (right): LL/Roger Viollet/Getty Images; p. 685: ullstein bild/The Granger Collection; p. 687: SuperStock; p. 692 (left): akg-images; p. 692 (right): Hulton-Deutsch Collection/Corbis; p. 695: Wikipedia Commons/Public Domain; p. 696 (left): © National Gallery, London/ Art Resource, NY; p. 696 (right): Erich Lessing/Art Resource, NY; p. 697 (left): Erich Lessing/Art Resource, NY; p. 697 (right): Scala/Art Resource, NY; p. 701: Schalkwijk/Art Resource, NY; p. 704: Gianni Dagli Orti/The Art Archive at Art Resource, NY; p. 713: Granger Collection.

Text Credits Primary Source 18.2 (pps. 709–710): "Lecture on Teaching and Learning, Sayyid Jamal ai-din ai-Afghani, November 8, 1882," from *Modernist Islam, 1840-1940: A Sourcebook*. Copyright © 2002 Oxford University Press. Reprinted with permission. Primary Source 18.4 (711–712): Qui Jin, "An Address to Two Hundred Million Fellow Countrywomen." Reprinted with the permission of Simon & Schuster Publishing Group, a division of Simon & Schuster, Inc. from the Free Press edition of *Chinese Civilization: A Sourcebook*, 2nd Edition by Patricia Buckley Ebrey. Copyright © 1993 by Patricia Buckley Ebrey. Copyright © 1981 by The Free Press. All rights reserved. Primary Source 18.5 (pps. 712–713): Margot Badran & Miriam Cooke (eds.), "Industrialization and Women's Freedom in Egypt" from *Opening the Gates: An Anthology of Arab Feminist Writing*, 2nd edition. Copyright © 1990. Reprinted with permission of Indiana University Press.

CHAPTER 19

Photo Credits Pages 716–717: The Illustrated London News Picture Library; p. 719: The Imperial War Museum; p. 721: Hulton-Deutsch Collection/Corbis; p. 723 (left): Sovfoto/Eastfoto; p. 723 (right): SuperStock; p. 729: Granger; p. 728: ©SF Palm/Stageimage/The Image Works; p. 731: Marion Post Wolcott/Library Of Congress/Getty Images; p. 732: Private Collection/The Bridgeman Art Library International Ltd; p. 738: Genevieve Naylor/Corbis; p. 740 & 741: The Granger Collection, New York/The Granger Collection; p. 742 (left): The Illustrated London News Picture Library; p. 742 (right): Private Collection/ The Bridgeman Art Library; p. 752: Detroit Institute of Arts, USA/Gift of Edsel B. Ford/Bridgeman Art Library.

Text Credits Primary Source 19.1 (pps. 748–749): M. K. Gandhi, From *Hind Swaraj and Other Writings*, edited by Anthony J. Parel, pp. 26–91. Copyright © 1997 Anthony J. Parel. Reprinted by permission of Cambridge University Press. Primary Source 19.6 (pps. 753–754): Jomo Kenyatta, Excerpt from *Facing Mount Kenya* by Jomo Kenyatta, published by Vintage Books, a division of Random House LLC. Used by permission of Alfred A. Knopf, an imprint of the Knopf Doubleday Publishing Group, a division of Random House LLC. All rights reserved.

CHAPTER 20

Photo Credits Pages 756–757: F.D.R. Library; p. 759 (left): The Illustrated London News Picture Library; p. 759 (right): Sovfoto/Eastfoto; p. 763 (left): Official U.S. Air Force Photo/TRH Pictures; p. 763 (right): U.N. Photo 149446 by Yosuke Yamahata/TRH Pictures; p. 766: NATO Photo/ TRH Pictures; p. 768: Bettmann/Corbis; p. 776: © Hulton-Deutsch Collection/Corbis; p. 778 (left): AP Photo; p. 778 (right): State Historical Society of Wisconsin Visual Materials Archive; p. 780 & 781: Wikimedia Commons; p. 783 (left): Roger-Viollet/The Image Works; p. 783 (right): Li Zhensheng; p. 784: Itar-Tass/Sovfoto; p. 787: Hulton-Deutsch Collection/Corbis; p. 794: Public Domain/Wikimedia Commons.

Text Credits Primary Source 20.4 (pps. 794–795): "President Sukarno's Speech at the Opening of the Bandung Asian-African Conference in Indonesia, 1955," Reprinted by permission of The Ministry of Foreign Affairs, Republic of Indonesia. Primary Source 20.5 (795–796): Léopold Sédar Senghor, Excerpts from *African Socialism* (New York: American Society of African Culture, 1959), trans. Mercer Cook. Reprinted by permission of Moorland-Spingarn Research Center, Howard University, Washington, DC. Primary Source 20.6 (pps. 796–797): Ambassador Tingfu F. Tsiang, Speech to the Empire Club of Canada, 1961. Reprinted with permission.

CHAPTER 21

Photo Credits Pages 800–801: AP Photo/Anat Givon; p. 804: Robert Maass/Corbis; p. 806 (left): Peter Magubane/ TimePix; p. 806 (right): David and Peter Turnley/Corbis; p. 812: George Esiri/Reuters/Corbis; p. 814 & 815: Mary Evans/EROS INTERNATIONAL/Ronald Grant/Everett Collection; p. 816 (left): Getty Images; p. 816 (right): AFLO/Nippon News/Corbis; p. 817: Jeff Albertson/Corbis; p. 823: Vanessa Vick/Redux; p. 825 (left): © Susan I. Cunningham/Panos Pictures; p. 825 (right): Douglas Engle/Corbis; p. 828: Peter Turnley/Corbis; p. 830: Jeff Widener/AP/Wide World Photos; p. 832 (left): Clive Shirley/Panos Pictures; p. 832 (right): Schalkwijk/ Art Resource, NY, © Estate of David Alfaro Siqueiros/ Licensed by VAGA, New York, NY; p. 841: Getty Images.

Text Credits Primary Source 21.2 (pps. 835–836): Amartya Kumar Sen, "Democracy as a Universal Value." *Journal of Democracy* 10:3 (1999), 6-9. © 1999 National Endowment for Democracy and the Johns Hopkins University Press. Reprinted with permission of Johns Hopkins University Press. Primary Source 21.3 (pps. 836–837): The World Bank, From "Using subsidies to close gender gaps in education," World Bank. 2001. *World Development Report 2000-2001: Attacking Poverty*, p. 122, Box 7.2. © World Bank. https://openknowledge.worldbank.org/handle/10986/11856 License: Creative Commons Attribution license (CC BY 3.0). Primary Source 21.5 (pps. 838–839): "The Kimberly Declaration," International Indigenous Peoples Summit on Sustainable Development Khoi-San Territory Kimberley, South Africa, 20-23 August 2002. Primary Source 21.6 (pps. 839–840): "The Case for Contamination," by Kwame Appiah. *New York Times Magazine*, January 2006. © 2006 The New York Times. All rights reserved. Used by permission and protected by the Copyright Laws of the United States. The printing, copying, redistribution, or retransmission of the Material without express written permission is prohibited.

CHAPTER 22

Photo Credits Pages 842–843: AP Photo/Jason DeCrow; p. 844 (left): Matt McDermott/Corbis Sygma; p. 844 (right): AP Photo/Carmen Taylor; p. 846 (top): AP Photo; p. 846 (bottom): AP Photo/Jason DeCrow; p. 854: Dean Conger/Corbis; p. 855: Sebastian D'Souza/AFP/Getty Images; p. 863 (top left): Liba Taylor/Corbis; p. 863 (top right): Herman Wouters/Hollandse Hoogte/Redux; p. 863 (bottom): Jason Reed/Reuters/Landov; p. 864: AP/Wide World Photos.

INDEX

Italic page references indicate maps, illustrations, or chronology entries.